The Crosswinds
of Freedom

THE
AMERICAN EXPERIMENT·VOLUME III

The Crosswinds
of Freedom

By
JAMES
MacGREGOR
BURNS

VINTAGE BOOKS
A DIVISION OF RANDOM HOUSE, INC
NEW YORK

First Vintage Books Edition, April 1990

Library of Congress Cataloging-in-Publication Data
Burns, James MacGregor.
    The crosswinds of freedom/by James MacGregor Burns.
        p.   cm.—(The American experiment ; v. 3)
    Includes bibliographical references.
    ISBN 0-679-72819-8
    1. United States—History—1933-1945.   2. United
States—History—1945-   I. Title.   II. Series: Burns,
James MacGregor.
    American experiment (Vintage Books (Firm)) ; v. 3.
    E806.B94   1990
    973.917—dc20   89-40493
                                                    CIP

Manufactured in the United States of America
10 9 8 7 6 5 4 3 2 1

We know through painful experience that freedom is never voluntarily given by the oppressor. It must be demanded by the oppressed. Frankly, I have yet to engage in a direct-action campaign that was "well-timed" in the view of those who have not suffered unduly from the disease of segregation.

For years now I have heard the word "Wait!" It rings in the ear of every Negro with piercing familiarity. . . . We have waited for more than 340 years for our constitutional and God-given rights. The nations of Asia and Africa are moving with jetlike speed toward gaining political independence, but we still creep at horse-and-buggy pace toward gaining a cup of coffee. . . .

We will reach the goal of freedom in Birmingham and all over the nation, because the goal of America is freedom.

Martin Luther King, Jr.
Letter from Birmingham Jail
April 16, 1963

Contents

PART III · Liberation Struggles

PART IV · The Crosswinds of Freedom

PART V · The Rebirth of Freedom?

PART I

What Kind of Freedom?

CHAPTER 1

The Crisis of Leadership

S LOWLY gaining speed, the glistening Ford Trimotor bumped across the grassy Albany airfield and nosed up into lowering clouds. It was July 2, 1932. The day before, the Democrats, meeting in Chicago, had nominated Franklin D. Roosevelt for President of the United States. Roosevelt and his family had received the news in their Hyde Park mansion after long hours in front of the radio listening to the bombastic speeches charged with hatred for Hoover Republicans and all their works. At the moment of greatest suspense the Roosevelt forces had gone over the top.

As the plane turned west Roosevelt had a chance to glimpse the Hudson, the river of American politics. With his twinkling pince-nez, his cockily uptilted cigarette holder, his double-breasted suit stretched across his big torso, his cheery, mobile features, he radiated exuberant self-confidence and a beguiling self-esteem as he leafed through a pile of congratulatory telegrams. He had long planned this little stroke of innovative leadership— to accept the nomination in person instead of awaiting a pompous notification weeks later. He was the first presidential candidate to fly; perhaps it was a tonic to this vigorous man, crippled since 1921 by polio, to demonstrate his mobility at the climactic hour. In any event, he could have fun with the press.

"I may go out by submarine to escape being followed by you men," he had twitted the reporters. Or he might ride out on a bicycle built for five. "Papa could sit in front and steer and my four sons could sit behind."

Part of his family was flying with him—his wife, Eleanor, and sons Elliott and John—along with counselor Samuel Rosenman, secretaries "Missy" LeHand and Grace Tully, and two state troopers as bodyguards. The rest of the family and Louis Howe, his longtime political confidant and aide, awaited the plane in Chicago. Eleanor Roosevelt, pressed by reporters, was staying in the background. "One person in politics is sufficient for one family," she had said the night before, while instructing the butler to bring frankfurters for the gathering. "I'll do as I've always done, accompany my husband on his trips and help in any way I can."

The plane pounded on, following the route of the old Erie Canal—the

3

thin artery that had pumped people and goods into Buffalo and points west, and farm produce back to the East. Now an economic blight lay across the land. For a time Roosevelt watched the deceptively lush fields unfold below; then he turned to Rosenman. They had work to do—trimming and polishing the acceptance speech. Over the radio came reports of the restive delegates in Chicago. Some were starting home. The disgruntled men of Tammany, sore over Al Smith's defeat, were planning to be gone before Roosevelt arrived. Convention managers were trying to enliven the delegates with songs and celebrities. On the plane Roosevelt and Rosenman huddled over the speech. It had to galvanize the weary delegates, the whole weary nation.

As buffeting winds pushed the plane far behind schedule, the two men lopped more and more paragraphs off the draft. Roosevelt had no time for the crowds that gathered at the refueling stops in Buffalo and Cleveland. While John was quietly sick in the rear of the plane, his father passed pages of his draft to Elliott and Eleanor, chain-smoked, joked with his family, and slept. When the plane touched down hours later in Chicago, Roosevelt boasted, "I was a good sailor," as he greeted his oldest child, Anna, and sons James and Franklin.

The airport scene was chaotic. Crowds pressed in around the candidate, knocking off his hat and leaving his glasses askew. Campaign manager James Farley pushed through to Roosevelt. "Jim, old pal—put it right there—great work!" Louis Howe was his usual dour self. Climbing into the candidate's car with him, Howe dismissed the Roosevelt and Rosenman draft, which had been telephoned to him the night before. Rosenman, forewarned of Howe's attitude, made his way through the throng to the candidate's car, only to hear Howe saying, as he thrust his own draft into Roosevelt's hand, "I tell you it's all right, Franklin. It's much better than the speech you've got now—and you can read it while you're driving down to the convention hall, and get familiar with it."

"But, Louis," Rosenman heard his boss say, "you know I can't deliver a speech that I've never done any work on myself, and that I've never even read. . . ." When Howe persisted, Roosevelt agreed to look it over. As his car moved through big crowds to the stadium, he lifted his hat and shouted "hellos" left and right, pausing to glance at Howe's prose. Finding Howe's opening paragraphs not radically different from his own draft, he put them on top of it.

Waiting at the Chicago Stadium, amid ankle-deep litter and half-eaten hot dogs, amid posters of FDR and discarded placards of his bested foes, amid the smoke and stink of a people's conclave, were the delegates in all their variety and contrariety—Louisiana populists and Brooklyn pols,

California radicals and Mississippi racists, Pittsburgh laborites and Philadelphia lawyers, Boston businessmen and Texas oilmen. The crowd stirred, then erupted in pandemonium, as Roosevelt, resplendent in a blue suit with a red rose, made his way stiffly across the platform on a son's arm, steadied himself at the podium. He looked up at the roaring crowd.

He plunged at once into his theme—leadership, the bankrupt conservative leadership of the Republican party, the ascendant liberal leadership of the "Democracy." After a tribute to the "great indomitable, unquenchable, progressive soul of our Commander-in-Chief, Woodrow Wilson," he declared that he accepted the 1932 party platform "100 per cent."

"As we enter this new battle, let us keep always present with us some of the ideals of the Party: The fact that the Democratic Party by tradition and by the continuing logic of history, past and present, is the bearer of liberalism and of progress, and at the same time of safety to our institutions." The failure of the Republican leadership—he would not attack the Republican party but only the leadership, "day in and day out," he promised—might bring about "unreasoning radicalism."

Roosevelt was speaking in his full, resonant voice. "To meet by reaction that danger of radicalism is to invite disaster. Reaction is no barrier to the radical. It is a challenge, a provocation. The way to meet that danger is to offer a workable program of reconstruction, and the party to offer it is the party with clean hands.

"This, and this only, is a proper protection against blind reaction on the one hand and an improvised, hit-or-miss, irresponsible opportunism on the other."

The candidate then challenged members of both parties: "Here and now I invite those nominal Republicans who find that their conscience cannot be squared with the groping and the failure of their party leaders to join hands with us; here and now, in equal measure, I warn those nominal Democrats who squint at the future with their faces turned toward the past, and who feel no responsibility to the demands of the new time, that they are out of step with their Party." The people wanted a genuine choice, not a choice between two reactionary doctrines. "Ours must be a party of liberal thought, of planned action, of enlightened international outlook, and of the greatest good to the greatest number of our citizens."

Roosevelt then made a series of positive—and prophetic—promises to the Democracy's constituencies: protection for the consumer, self-financing public works for the jobless, safeguarding land and timberland for the farmer, repeal of the Prohibition amendment for the thirsty, jobs for labor, a pared-down government for businessmen. But Roosevelt repeatedly sounded a higher note, especially as he concluded.

"On the farms, in the large metropolitan areas, in the smaller cities and in the villages, millions of our citizens cherish the hope that their old standards of living and of thought have not gone forever. Those millions cannot and shall not hope in vain.

"I pledge you, I pledge myself, to a new deal for the American people. Let us all here assembled constitute ourselves prophets of a new order of competence and of courage.

"This is more than a political campaign; it is a call to arms. Give me your help, not to win votes alone, but to win in this crusade to restore America to its own people."

THE DIVIDED LEGACY

"He had come in an airplane, symbol of the new age, touching the imagination of the people," wrote a reporter. But his roots lay in a horse-and-buggy era that had transmuted relentlessly into the railroad epoch, and then into the age of the automobile. Both in his heritage and in his growth he could say with Walt Whitman that he embraced multitudes.

He was born January 30, 1882, in a mansion high on a bluff overlooking the Hudson. Breast-fed for a year by his mother, Sara, he grew up in a home of enveloping security and tranquillity. An only child, he lived among doting parents and nurses, affectionate governesses and tutors, in a house that was warm and spacious though by no means palatial. Outside lay the grounds peopled by gardeners, coachmen, stable boys, farmhands. North and south along the river towered the mansions of the truly wealthy. It was the world of Currier & Ives come to life—sleighing on country rides past farmhouses wreathed in snow, stopping with his father in barnyards filled with horses and dogs, swimming and fishing in the majestic river, digging out of snowstorms—most memorably the great blizzard of 1888.

Occasionally the long mournful whistle of a train passing below carried into the home, but it brought no hint of the hates and fears simmering in the nation's urban and industrial world in the 1880s—no hint of the wants and needs of immigrants pouring by the hundreds of thousands into the city a hundred miles to the south, of the desperate strikes that swept the nation's railroads, of the bone-deep misery of countless southern and western farmers and their wives, of the massacre of workers in Chicago's Haymarket Square. The Roosevelts traveled by rail but never left their protected environment of family carriages, private railroad cars, of ships where there were always, as Sara said, "people one knows." Places they visited teemed with cousins and aunts and friends of their own social class. Nor did young Franklin leave this social cocoon when he departed for

Groton, one of the most exclusive schools in the nation, and later for Harvard's "Gold Coast."

It was hardly a life to ignite political ambition or a passionate lust for power, if these result from early material or psychological blows to self-esteem, as Harold D. Lasswell and others have contended. It was easy to understand how Roosevelt's future friends and rivals strove to overcome a sense of insecurity and inferiority in childhood: Winston Churchill, virtually ignored by his socially ambitious mother and by a father slowly going insane from syphilis, cabined and bullied in the cruel and rigid world of Victorian boarding schools; Benito Mussolini, son of a half-socialist, half-anarchist father, a mean-spirited and fiery-tempered youth, expelled from school at the age of ten for stabbing and wounding another boy; Adolf Hitler, orphaned in his teens and cast out into vagrancy; Josef Dzhugash-vili, later Stalin, living in the leaky adobe hut of a peasant cobbler in Georgia, a land seared by ancient hatreds.

Yet more subtle and significant psychological forces were molding young Franklin's personality. The Roosevelt and Delano families had been established long enough on the banks of the Hudson to despise the vulgar parvenus who were pushing to power and riches in the boom times of the nineteenth century. But the Roosevelts themselves were parvenus compared with the Schuylers and Van Rensselaers who had been living along the river for a century or more. Sara Roosevelt's father had made his fortune by selling Turkish and Indian opium to Chinese addicts. The comfortably well-off Roosevelts could not ignore the far wealthier families around them; for the rest of his life FDR would show an almost obsessive interest in the homes and trappings of the ostentatious "nouveaux riches," such as the Vanderbilts' baronial mansion a few miles to the north.

Nor could young Franklin escape direct confrontations with the social elite. At Groton he was barred from the inner social and athletic circles; at Harvard he was not tapped by Porcellian, the most exclusive club. He was seared by these rejections far more than he admitted in his breezy, dutiful letters to his parents. Many, including Eleanor Roosevelt, later wondered whether Franklin's rejection by young patricians, most of whom would go into brokerages and banking, led him to "desert his class" and to identify with life's outcasts. Being a Porcellian rejectee hardly catapulted Franklin into the proletariat; yet these class and psychic privations had a part in shaping his later views.

Far more important were the times he lived in—the heyday of turn-of-the-century progressivism, a muckraking press, and Theodore Roosevelt's Square Deal. And always there was the role model, in the other major branch of the Roosevelt family, of "Uncle Ted" himself—the New York

City police commissioner, Assistant Secretary of the Navy, seemingly sin-single-handed conqueror of San Juan Hill, and, during Franklin's Harvard years, President of the United States. Even more, there was the President's niece Eleanor Roosevelt.

Much has been made of Eleanor Roosevelt's bleak childhood—of her unloving mother who died when she was eight; of her handsome, dashing, adored father who showered endearments on her but deserted her again and again and then for good, dying of drink when she was ten; of her life as an orphan, neglected by her grandmother, tyrannized by her governess, and frightened by her alcoholic uncles. By her early teens she was a timid, sensitive, awkward child, with a wistful shadowed face and a tall figure usually attired in a shapeless, overly short dress. But this was not the Eleanor Roosevelt whom Franklin courted and married. By her late teens she had become far more at ease and poised in her family relationships, and with her warm and sympathetic manner, her expressive face and soft yet alert eyes, and above all her lively intelligence and quick compassion she had won a host of friends of both sexes. Her metamorphosis was largely the product of caring teachers—especially of the extraordinary Marie Souvestre, headmistress of the school Eleanor attended in England, a sophisticated, sharing, and demanding daughter of the French Enlight-enment who drew Eleanor to good literature, foreign cultures and lan-guages, and social radicalism.

The two young Roosevelts who ardently plighted their troth in March 1905 felt very much in rapport, but there were deep potential divisions between them—and within each of them. In her early years Eleanor had developed a compassion for fellow sufferers—for all sufferers—that she was never to lose. She was haunted for months by the tormented face of a ragged man who had tried to snatch a purse from a woman sitting near her. Roosevelt in those years was still moved far more by a patrician concern for people, in the abstract, by noblesse oblige—or by what his mother preferred to call "honneur oblige." Eleanor showed her concern day after day by teaching children at her settlement house. When Franklin once accompanied her to a tenement where one of her charges lay ill, he came out exclaiming, "My God, I didn't know people lived like that!"

Franklin's ambition seemed to soar with the taste of office rather than in advance of it. Unexpectedly a run for the state senate opened up for him; once nominated, he plunged into the struggle with enormous dash and energy, and won. He entered the state senate as a vaguely progressive anti-Tammanyite; in office he led a fight against Tammany and moved so far to the left as to become virtually a "farm-labor" legislator. A Wilsonian in 1912, he gained the post of Assistant Secretary of the Navy without much effort—but once in the job he became the most vigorous and committed navy man since Teddy Roosevelt himself had held the job. Action— and skill in action—spurred further ambition.

While Eleanor had her own values, commitments, and purposes, she was so self-effacing as to seem to lack ambition. Life closed in around her after her marriage. She had not only a mother-in-law who refused to let her son go but a husband who saw a clear demarcation between his public career and her family role. "I listened to all his plans with a great deal of interest," she said later. "It never occurred to me that I had any part to play." Having six babies in ten years—one died at seven months—narrowed and deepened her personal life. Her public role became a pale reflection of her husband's—entertaining legislators in Albany, doing the rounds of government wives in Washington, helping with Red Cross and other war activities. Her husband was not always supportive. When to Washington's amusement she blundered into telling *The New York Times* that in her wartime food-saving effort she had found that "making ten servants help me do my saving has not only been possible, but highly profitable," he wrote her cuttingly, "All I can say is that your latest newspaper campaign is a corker and I am proud to be the husband of the Originator, Discoverer and Inventor of the New Household Economy for Millionaires!"

Most devastating of all to Eleanor's self-esteem was her husband's wartime romance with Lucy Mercer. "Franklin's love of another woman brought her to almost total despair," according to Joseph P. Lash, but "she emerged from the ordeal a different woman." She said years later, "I faced myself, my surroundings, my world, honestly for the first time. I really grew up that year." She insisted that he break off with Lucy—or with her. A chastened husband, aware that a divorce would be politically devastating, and probably also under motherly pressure, chose the former. He knew too that his wife could be a great political asset, especially since women at last had won the right to vote in national elections.

Invited to join his campaign train when he ran for Vice President in 1920, Eleanor Roosevelt got her fill of the most grueling kind of electioneering. The Democratic debacle sent Roosevelt back to private life and gave his wife some hope of liberation from politics. This was not to be. Struck down by polio, Roosevelt endured intense physical and psychological pain with outward stoicism—he was rarely heard to complain—while Eleanor sought to keep the family on an even keel, served as her husband's political stand-in, and tried desperately to maintain her own composure as the mother of five children ranging from five to fifteen years old.

Franklin and Eleanor Roosevelt emerged from their ordeal tempered and matured, but not fundamentally changed in their political attitudes.

Having twice been defeated—in 1920 and earlier, in 1914, when he had made a try for the U.S. Senate—Roosevelt would proceed slowly, regaining his political base as he sought to regain his ability to walk. He would continue to pursue political *office*—making necessary compromises to achieve it but proceeding boldly on policy once in power. Eleanor would continue to pursue political *goals*—peace, help to the poor, women's rights, clean government—by working in the organizations necessary to achieve them. She became increasingly active in the Women's Trade Union League, founded in 1903 by Jane Addams, in peace efforts, and in the tedious job of trying to rebuild the New York State Democratic party. Everyday politics still did not excite her; Franklin was the politician, she said later, and she the agitator. So she acted within the boundaries set by her husband, who saw competitive politics as essentially men's business even while he sought laws that would aid women.

These two legacies divided the couple, now both in their forties, as they moved back into public life during the twenties—as Roosevelt accepted his party's draft for governor in 1928, as he campaigned vigorously and won a narrow victory while Eleanor intensified her party and campaign work, as he sought to carry out his liberal promises often against recalcitrant Republican legislators, as he won a landslide reelection for governor in 1930. The closer he came to the presidential nomination fight, the more he seemed to compromise, from Eleanor's standpoint—on the League of Nations, on Prohibition, on Tammany, on states' rights. But Roosevelt had a far better sense of the electoral complexities. On the League issue in particular he was the target of front-page fulminations by publisher William Randolph Hearst, who, Roosevelt knew, could influence delegates to the 1932 Democratic convention as well as newspaper readers. He caved in to Hearst. Eleanor conspired with her husband's staff members and friends to stiffen his resolve. When an angry Wilsonian came in to berate him for a "shabby" statement on the League, he expressed regret and then asked his visitor if she would help make peace between Eleanor and him. "She hasn't spoken to me for three days!"

One hard political fact confronted Roosevelt—the disheveled, fragmented state of the Democratic party, whose convention a candidate could carry only by winning two-thirds of the delegate vote. The party wielded little political muscle as a national organization; during the mid-twenties the Democrats had not even had a national headquarters but rather lived off the largesse of millionaires like John J. Raskob and Bernard Baruch. Nationally the party was composed of ideological and regional shards, each of which seemed to be represented in the candidates who entered the nomination fight after Roosevelt took the lead—Al Smith for the urban

Democracy; House Speaker John Garner for the Southwest; demagogic Governor "Alfalfa Bill" Murray of Oklahoma for the rural West; Governor Albert Ritchie of Maryland for the old Jeffersonian, states' rights Democrats; Newton D. Baker for the Wilson internationalists; and a string of favorite sons.

Such a panoply of rivals both fortified and weakened Roosevelt—they fragmented his opposition but also threatened to slice off chunks of his own nationwide support. But he had many assets, as Arthur M. Schlesinger, Jr., summarized them: "a familiar name, a charming personality, demonstrated political popularity, an impressive executive record in Albany, a dramatic personal victory over illness, a wide and well-cultivated acquaintance across the country." With the devoted and expert help of Eleanor Roosevelt, Louis Howe, Jim Farley, Sam Rosenman, and a host of others, Roosevelt's bandwagon carried him to victory through a string of primaries, aside from a win by the ever-popular Smith in Massachusetts and by Garner in California. The Roosevelt forces arrived at the Chicago convention with a handsome majority of the delegates but tantalizingly short—by about 200 votes—of the necessary two-thirds.

Feverishly the governor's foes tried to head him off, clasping hands across ancient fissures in the party. The Roosevelt campaign effort almost blew up in Chicago when a group of FDR enthusiasts launched an attack against the two-thirds rule, thus giving the opposition a moral issue about "changing the rules of the game" and jeopardizing the support of Southerners who had long used the rule to protect racial and regional power. Roosevelt, who had originally planned to challenge the rule but had now lost control of the timing, retreated as gracefully as possible.

So he would have to attain the magic two-thirds, and he did, through the disarray of his opponents, the unflagging efforts of Farley and other FDR men on the convention floor and in the smoke-filled rooms, and—at a critical moment after the third ballot—the consummation of the candidate's patient courting of Texas's Garner and California senator William G. McAdoo and his genuflection before Hearst. Fearing that Baker might win if Roosevelt did not, the Californians and the Texans pooled their poker hands. The big card was the vice-presidential nomination for Garner. Once he agreed—reluctantly, because he had no great wish to quit the Speakership—the deal was made. To McAdoo was given the exquisite satisfaction of settling the convention score of 1924, when he had been denied the nomination by Al Smith.

"California came here to nominate a President of the United States," he shouted in the teeth of the howling and booing delegates. "She did not come to deadlock the Convention or to engage in another devastating contest like that of 1924." More hisses and groans. "California casts 44 votes for Franklin D. Roosevelt." Then bedlam.

"Good old McAdoo," Roosevelt exclaimed by his radio at Hyde Park. While Eleanor went to the kitchen to cook bacon and eggs, he began planning for the next morning's rendezvous with the waiting plane.

Out of the pandemonium in the Chicago Stadium a young novelist, John Dos Passos, walked down West Madison Street. Gradually the din of speeches faded from his ears. No one in the seedy crowd about him seemed to know of the "historic" event that had just taken place. He stepped down a flight of stairs into the darkness of the roadway under Michigan Avenue.

"This world too has its leisure class," he noted. "They lie in rows along the ledges above the roadway, huddled in grimed newspapers, gray sag-faced men in worn-out clothes, discards . . . men who have lost the power to want. Try to tell one of them that the *gre-eat* Franklin D. Roosevelt, Governor of the *gre-eat* state of New York, has been nominated by the *gre-eat* Democratic party as its candidate for President, and you'll get what the galleries at the convention gave Mr. McAdoo when they discovered that he had the votes of Texas and California in his pocket and was about to shovel them into the Roosevelt bandwagon, a prolonged and enthusiastic *Boooo.* Hoover or Roosevelt, it'll be the same cops."

*   *   *

The Democrats had their man. But who was he? Perhaps those who had sized him up best were the convention delegates and their leaders. Roosevelt was attractive, ambitious, electable, a reliable deal-maker; he was "available." But the press and the pundits were looking for a higher quality—leadership. In this they had found Roosevelt lacking. *The New Republic* had viewed him as utterly without the kind of "great intellectual force or supreme moral stamina" that underlay strong leadership. He hedged on everything, complained the Washington *Post.* Wishy-washy, said Henry Mencken. "Too easy to please"—not the dangerous enemy of anything, Walter Lippmann had said earlier in the year. "In boldness of political leadership," he was "certainly no Cleveland or Wilson," said *The Outlook.*

This criticism galled Roosevelt, but he could only respond privately. "Can't you see," he wrote to a Wilsonian outraged over his desertion of the League, "that loyalty to the ideals of Woodrow Wilson is just as strong in my heart as it is in yours—but have you ever stopped to consider that there is a difference between ideals and the methods of attaining them? Ideals do not change, but methods do change with every generation and world circumstance.

"Here is the difference between me and some of my fainthearted friends:

I am looking for the best modern vehicle to reach the goal of an ideal while they insist on a vehicle which was brand new and in good running order twelve years ago. Think this over! And for heaven's sake have a little faith." But his friends felt that *he* was being fainthearted. They knew, moreover, that on some issues he *was* consistent and committed—on big questions, such as the need for an activist government and a liberal Democratic party, and on specific issues, such as the vital role of electric power in his state and nation. He was not even consistent in his inconsistency.

Those who examined Roosevelt's inner circle for a clue to his fundamental and enduring beliefs were no less puzzled. By campaign time Roosevelt had collected around himself a group of "brain trusters" as diverse as they were talented. There were Columbia University political scientist Raymond Moley, a onetime city reformer who had since become most concerned about the "anarchy of concentrated economic power"; Adolf Berle, a child prodigy at Harvard who had continued to be so prodigious in law and economics that H. G. Wells once said of him that his worldview "seemed to contain all I had ever learnt and thought, but better arranged and closer to reality"; Rexford Tugwell, a Columbia economist who was both a romantic and a planner, an intellectual experimenter and a governmental centralizer. These men, united in their concern over the chaos, inefficiency, and cruelty of capitalist breakdown, were divided over monetary and other economic issues.

Also close to Roosevelt was another penetrating mind but of quite different cast—Felix Frankfurter of the Harvard Law School, an irrepressible pursuer of legal justice and good conversation, who abhorred utopian ideas for social reconstruction and called for economic decentralization and fair play through regulation of banking and securities. He was carrying the flag of his mentor, Justice Louis D. Brandeis, which was also the flag of many progressive—and powerful—Democrats and Republicans in Congress. Of quite different orientation were a number of self-styled "Jeffersonians" who preached states' rights, limited government, and above all economy and budget-balancing, and who with the help of Louis Howe could gain access to Roosevelt at critical moments. Others operated on the fringe: Cordell Hull, a courtly Tennessean and veteran politico whose suspicion of big business took the form mainly of a near-obsession against high tariffs; General Hugh Johnson, a colorful old army man even at the age of fifty, a Bernard Baruch protégé who believed both in budget-balancing *and* in central governmental direction of the economy; various monetary theorists; and Eleanor Roosevelt.

The candidate made no effort to impose intellectual unity on the core group—he had none to impose. But he did establish a clear line between "politics" and "policies." Farley, after being installed by Roosevelt in place of Raskob as Democratic national chairman, said to Moley, "I'm interested in getting him the votes—nothing else. Issues aren't my business. They're yours and his. You keep out of mine, and I'll keep out of yours." Roosevelt reposed such confidence in these diverse brains—they never made up a monolithic "trust"—that he left speech- and issue-planning under Moley's direction while he took off with three of his sons in a forty-foot yawl for a sail along the New England coast.

Roosevelt had several acute questions of campaign strategy to ponder as he sailed contentedly under sunny July skies, occasionally stopping at sleepy ports for political confabs. One was how to appeal to progressive Republicans. The inheritors of the cause of Theodore Roosevelt and Robert La Follette were still active in the GOP—and still frustrated. Rejecting Hoover, they had other alternatives besides Roosevelt: form a new progressive party, support Norman Thomas's Socialist party, or sit the election out. Some progressives, especially in the East, doubted Roosevelt's character and convictions. Why support a tweedledum Democrat? One progressive of impeccable credentials—George W. Norris of Nebraska—announced for Roosevelt early and staunchly, however, largely because of Roosevelt's consistent support of public electric power. Some progressives followed. A national progressive league for Roosevelt and Garner was formed under Norris. Hiram Johnson endorsed the Democratic candidate, as did Robert La Follette, Jr., despite his doubts about Roosevelt's commitment to social justice. Other progressives held back.

An easier question was whether Roosevelt should actively campaign at all. Some urged that he conduct a front-porch campaign, as presidential candidates had done in olden times. They felt that a campaign tour was unnecessary, that he might not be up to it physically. Garner, visiting Roosevelt at Hyde Park, advised that all the boss had to do was to stay alive until election day. Farley, passing on the mixed views of party leaders, favored an active campaign. Roosevelt took little urging. His Dutch was up, he told Farley. Soon he, Farley, and Howe were planning an election drive that became even more ambitious once the candidate got underway.

The toughest question of campaign strategy was whether the candidate should offer a coherent, challenging set of ideas or tailor his views to expedient campaign needs. Not only did Tugwell and other advisers want their boss to speak out; they wanted him to present a *program,* comprehensive, consistent, with focus and priorities. He was "weak on relations, on the conjunctural, the joining together of forces and processes, especially in the national economy," as Tugwell saw it. Roosevelt's scattered approach to policy gave force to acid comments by left-wing commentators,

Tugwell felt; he himself had boiled over in Chicago when he picked up a newspaper with a column by Heywood Broun calling Roosevelt "the cork-screw candidate of a convoluting convention."

Roosevelt continued to be disappointed and even hurt by the liberal intellectual critics. The intellectuals never allowed a politician the least leeway, he said to Tugwell; they were positively fearful of being caught in an approving mood. But what he was trying to do, Roosevelt continued, was to get elected, not simply arouse agitation and argument. Let Hoover be the ideologue—and be cramped by this. The Democrats, by staying more "flexible," could become the majority party. Leadership with such support might continue to win elections, perhaps for a generation.

By following a wobbly line somewhere between the middle and some-what left of middle Roosevelt made himself a difficult target for Hoover, but he also invited attacks from both right and left. The financier and industrialist Owen D. Young, after visiting Roosevelt at Hyde Park in midsummer, had the feeling that the governor "was avoiding real issues" with him and perhaps had met with him only for campaign cosmetics. A few days later Roosevelt reaped a whirlwind on the left. Sitting at lunch with Eleanor Roosevelt, Tugwell, and others, he took a call from Huey Long, whose angry voice carried to the others at the table. As Tugwell remembered the conversation, Long was furious because Roosevelt had seen that "stuffed shirt Owen Young" while the Kingfish sat down in Louisiana and never heard from anybody.

"God damn it, Frank, who d'you think got you nominated?"

"Well," said Roosevelt, "you had a lot to do with it."

"You sure as hell are forgettin' about it as fast as you can." Long complained that there was a "regular parade" of people like Young seeing the governor.

"Oh, I see a lot of people you don't read about. The newspaper boys only write up the ones their editors like."

If Roosevelt didn't stop listening to people like that, Long said, Roose-velt wouldn't carry the South. "You got to turn me loose."

"What d'you mean, turn you loose?" Roosevelt said. "You *are* loose."

"That Farley," said Long, "that's what I mean, and that Louis." They wouldn't give him any money. He wanted to work with Roosevelt directly. Was the governor coming South?

"No, I don't need to; your country there is safe enough."

"Don't fool yourself—it ain't safe at all. You've got to give these folks what they want. They want fat-back and greens. . . ." Long went on and on, shouting expletives and demands. When he finally hung up, Roosevelt sat ruminating for a few moments about how Long was leading people to

the promised land. "You know," he said, "that's the second most dangerous man in America." Pressed as to who was the *most* dangerous man, he
said, "Douglas MacArthur."

Ready to move left or right, or hover in the center, Roosevelt began his
speaking campaign in Columbus, Ohio, late in August with a denunciation
of Hoover's "Alice-in-Wonderland" economics, then presented his own
proposals for federal regulation of security exchanges, banks, and holding
companies. In Sea Girt, New Jersey, before a monster throng mobilized by
Boss Frank Hague of Jersey City, he called for repeal of Prohibition, as had
the Democratic platform, but coupled this with a sermon in favor of tem-
perance. In mid-September, in Topeka, he came out for the "planned use
of the land," lower taxes for farmers, federal credit for refinancing farm
mortgages, and the barest shadow of a voluntary domestic allotment plan
to manage farm surpluses, at the same time pulling back from the old
McNary-Haugen formula that he had indiscreetly endorsed in a book. In
Salt Lake City he took a quite different tack with a call for an integrated
federal transportation effort, including federal regulation and aid for the
floundering railroad industry.

Sharp disputes broke out among Roosevelt's advisers over these
speeches, with the result often a compromise. Thus the Topeka speech,
shaped by perhaps twenty-five minds, produced what Roosevelt wanted: "a
speech so broad in implications," according to Frank Freidel, "that it
would encompass all the aspirations of Western farmers no matter what
their prejudices, and at the same time so vague in its endorsement of
domestic allotment that it would not frighten conservative Easterners."

In the midst of this weaving and fencing Roosevelt gave a speech at the
Commonwealth Club in San Francisco that electrified progressives. It was
powerful in its parts: an invitation to "consider with me in the large, some
of the relationships of Government and economic life that go deeply into
our daily lives, our happiness, our future and our security"; a long review
of the rise of the centralized state and the struggle of the individual to
assert his rights; of the rise of the machine age and of the "financial Titans"
who had "pushed the railroads to the Pacific" ruthlessly and wastefully but
had built the railroads; of the decline of equality of opportunity under
capitalism; of the need for an "economic declaration of rights" to meet
deeply human needs. The speech was studded with acute insights, memorable phrases, and evocative ideas, well suited to his California audience
and especially to the venerable progressive Hiram Johnson.

But this notable address did not hang together. It began with the proposition that "America is new" and had "the great potentialities of youth"
but pages later concluded that "our industrial plant is built" and probably

overbuilt, "our last frontier has long since been reached," that the safety valve of the western frontier was gone, that "we are not able to invite the immigration from Europe to share our endless plenty." Hence the task was not expansion but the "soberer, less dramatic business of administering resources and plants already in hand," of "adjusting production to consumption," of "distributing wealth and products more equitably." The speech had been written by Berle and was delivered by the candidate with minimal change; Tugwell claimed Roosevelt never even saw it until he opened it on the lectern, and Moley disagreed with key parts of it.

The candidate's final string of speeches continued in this vein, rich in good ideas and specific proposals but often unconnected and even inconsistent. When he was presented with a speech draft endorsed by Hull calling for a general lowering of tariffs, and with another that called for gradual, bilateral "old-fashioned Yankee horse-trades," he left Moley speechless by instructing him to "weave the two together." Following a series of addresses calling for social justice, for action on unemployment and social welfare, he accused Hoover late in the campaign of reckless and extravagant spending, of burdening the people with taxes, of inflating the bureaucracy, of drastically unbalancing the budget. Herbert Hoover a spendthrift! Roosevelt made a flat promise to "reduce the cost of current Federal Government operations by 25 percent." By now critics were charging once again that no profound difference in policy separated the Democratic candidate from the Republican President.

Herbert Hoover saw profound differences. At first he had not taken his opponent's candidacy too seriously, telling his Secretary of State, Henry Stimson, that Roosevelt would be the easiest man to beat. But as the summer progressed and Roosevelt danced all around him on issues, Hoover's composure gave way; visitors found him shifting between dark pessimism and blazing anger at foes and deserters. In mid-September he told Stimson that while "he was gaining in the East he would lose everything west of the Alleghenies and would lose the election." Anger, indignation, pride, passion brought him out on the hustings in the fall. Painstakingly writing his own speeches, delivering them in a flat, hard monotone—Mencken said he could recite the Twenty-third Psalm and make it sound like a search warrant—Hoover tried to get a fix on this "chameleon on the Scotch plaid." As he drove down city streets he encountered boos and catcalls, signs reading "In Hoover we trusted; now we are busted"; the cold hostility of rows of onlookers.

There might have been a tragically ennobling aspect to the campaign, as the ideologue of the besieged order grimly defended his castle against the would-be usurper. But the campaign flattened out, despite frantic warnings by Hoover against fascist and socialist tendencies in the other camp, and demagogic attacks by Roosevelt on the "present Republican leadership" as the "Horsemen of Destruction, Delay, Deceit, Despair." If Hoover could not get a grip on Roosevelt, neither could Socialist Norman Thomas or the candidates of other minor parties. It was not 1896 or 1904 or 1912. In the gravest economic crisis they had ever known, the American people seemed bewildered and benumbed, lethargic amid the tempests of the politicians.

Polls—and especially the results of Maine's early state election—robbed the outcome of much suspense. Assembled on election night in Democratic party headquarters on the first floor of the Biltmore, Roosevelt's family and friends received favorable early returns and then reports of a near-sweep. Only Pennsylvania and five smaller states stayed with the President. Roosevelt won 22.8 million votes, Hoover 15.8 million, Norman Thomas 885,000, Communist William Z. Foster 103,000.

Louis Howe uncorked a bottle of sherry he had put away twenty years before in Albany. After receiving a gracious concession telegram from Hoover, the President-elect left for his Sixty-fifth Street house, to be met by his mother, who said, "I never thought particularly about my son being President, but if he's going to be President, I hope he'll be a good one!" Eleanor Roosevelt seemed in a less celebratory mood. She was happy for her husband, she told people, while to a close woman friend she confided that she had not wished to be First Lady. "If I wanted to be selfish, I could wish Franklin had not been elected." She had watched Mrs. Theodore Roosevelt and learned what it meant to be the wife of a President, and she did not like the prospect. It meant the end of her personal life.

She would have to work out her own salvation. She could not know yet that this might have to wait out the salvation of a nation.

THE "HUNDRED DAYS" OF ACTION

Four long months stretched ahead before the President-elect could take office, for the Constitution of 1787 had been drafted in a world of travel by carriage, sail, and horseback, not train, auto, and plane. During those four months lame-duck members of Congress would meet, debate and denounce, answer to no one, and go home.

Could human misery wait for constitutional processes? During the autumn the economy had fallen off even further—a result, Hoover convinced himself, of business fears of what the Democrats would do. As winter approached, business activity dropped to between a quarter and a third of "normalcy" and one worker out of five—perhaps one out of four—was jobless. The employed were hardly better off. Women lining slippers—one every forty-five seconds—in Manhattan sweatshops earned barely over one dollar for a nine-hour day. Girls sewing aprons for 2½ cents per apron could make 20 cents a day. "There is not a garbage-dump in Chicago which is not diligently haunted by the hungry," Edmund Wilson reported.

"Last summer in the hot weather when the smell was sickening and the flies were thick, there were a hundred people a day coming to one of the dumps, falling on the heap of refuse as soon as the truck had pulled out and digging in it with sticks and hands. They would devour all the pulp that was left on the old slices of watermelon and canteloupe till the rinds were as thin as paper; and they would take away and wash and cook discarded onions, turnips, potatoes, cabbage or carrots. Meat is a more difficult matter, but they salvage a good deal of that too. The best is the butcher's meat which has been frozen and hasn't spoiled. In the case of the other meat, there are usually bad parts that have to be cut out or they scald it and sprinkle it with soda to kill the rotten taste and the smell."

Poverty and despair lay deep over the farmlands as well. Farmers were burning corn in their stoves in places where coal cost four dollars a ton and corn sold for a third of that. Desperate men were brandishing hangman's nooses and shotguns to keep deputy sheriffs from foreclosing their mortgages and selling their acreage. Farmers bid in a neighbor's foreclosed farm for a dime, amid threats to serious bidders, and then turned the land back to the neighbor. But local action, they knew, was not enough. Farm leaders in Nebraska talked about marching tens of thousands of protesters to the state capitol and tearing it down if they were denied relief. Farm leaders in Washington warned of revolution in the countryside.

Who would take leadership during the interregnum? Not Congress. Weighted down by 158 members who had been given their walking papers in November, divided in party control, surly toward the President, unsure of the President-elect, the legislators fribbled and dawdled, squabbling over beer, deadlocking over relief, putting off action on farm mortgages and bank deposit legislation.

Not big business. Questioned by the Senate Finance Committee, noted businessmen admitted virtual intellectual bankruptcy. He had no solution, said one New York banker, "and I do not believe anybody else has." Myron C. Taylor of U.S. Steel and others saw only one possibility— retrenchment. Pleas to balance the budget sounded like a mindless litany in the hearing room. The business leadership of the nation had fallen from its highest level of influence, judged Walter Lippmann, to its lowest.

Nor would Roosevelt take leadership before he took office. He was still learning and listening while he cleaned up his gubernatorial affairs in New

York. Stopping off in Washington on trips to Warm Springs and back, he talked at length with congressional leaders, and found the Democrats as factionalized as ever. He tried to hold off pressure from the left. He received and listened attentively to a left-wing delegation planning a hunger march in Washington, but avoided taking a stand. "When I talk to him he says 'Fine! Fine! Fine!' " grumbled Huey Long. "But Joe Robinson"—Senate Majority Leader and the Kingfish's bête noire—"goes to see him the next day and again he says 'Fine! Fine! Fine!' Maybe he says 'Fine!' to everybody." Roosevelt did—to almost everybody—and visitors left with the feeling he agreed with them when he had meant simply that he understood them.

The one man with the constitutional authority and responsibility to lead was politically impotent as a lame duck. Herbert Hoover, however, was by no means eager to surrender leadership. When Britain asked the President for suspension of World War I debt payments to the United States and for a review of the whole debt situation, Hoover invited Roosevelt to discuss the matter with him. The President-elect was wary. He was no expert on the foreign debt question; he knew that Democratic congressional leaders were opposed to forsaking money that Europe "had hired," in Calvin Coolidge's words; and he wanted to maintain his own freedom of action. There followed a long and stately minuet of suspicious co-leaders, with little action.

The nation tried to size up its next President. "Your distant relative is an X in the equation," editor William Allen White wrote to Theodore Roosevelt, Jr. "He may develop his stubbornness into courage, his amiability into wisdom, his sense of superiority into statesmanship. Responsibility is a winepress that brings forth strange juices out of men." Wrote Lippmann earlier: "His good-will no one questions. He has proved that he has the gift of political sagacity. If only he will sail by the stars and not where the winds of opinion will take him, he will bring the ship into port."

The nation seemed to hunger for leadership—but what kind of leadership? Europe provided some models. In Germany, on January 30—Roosevelt's fifty-first birthday—a befuddled President von Hindenburg designated as Chancellor Adolf Hitler, who promptly dissolved the Reichstag, called an election, locked up opposition leaders, and terrorized the voters with an ersatz panic. Mussolini's Italy was shipping arms to Austrian fascists. In the Soviet Union, Josef Stalin was still mercilessly crushing his party opponents.

"The situation is critical, Franklin," Lippmann told the President-elect during a visit to Warm Springs. He reminded Roosevelt that Hitler had come to power over a paralyzed executive and deadlocked parliament. His host as usual was vague about specific plans. Two weeks later Lippmann wrote in his column that Congress should give the new President a free hand by refraining from debate and amendment for a year. Just at this time the nation was reminded of the explosive forces lying under the surface when Joseph Zangara, an unemployed bricklayer, took a shot at Roosevelt in Miami, missed him, and mortally wounded the mayor of Chicago, who was riding in an open car with the President-elect. "I do not hate Mr. Roosevelt personally," Zangara said, "I hate all Presidents . . . and I hate all officials and everybody who is rich."

About this time a very rich man, Henry Ford, was refusing the pleas of White House emissaries to help bail out two Michigan banks in which the automaker had millions of dollars of deposits. Let the crash come, Ford said. Soon the governor of Michigan proclaimed a bank holiday—and a ripple of fear spread through the nation. Once again Hoover sought to involve Roosevelt in an economic decision, urging him to assure the country that there would be no "tampering or inflation of the currency," that the budget would be balanced and government credit maintained. Roosevelt would not repudiate the "new deal" that he was slowly shaping. In a last desperate try, Hoover in two late-night phone calls on the eve of Inaugural Day asked Roosevelt whether he would endorse a White House executive order controlling bank withdrawals. The President-elect would not—the President must act on his own. As the White House clock struck midnight, Hoover said, "We are at the end of our string."

The government was paralyzed as the nation's financial structure seemed close to toppling. Ashen-faced bankers, sitting late in their offices totaling withdrawals, wondered whether their banks would pull through. On March 3 over $100 million in gold was withdrawn from the Treasury. Governor Herbert Lehman declared a banking holiday in New York. Illinois followed. As the Hoovers' bags were being packed in the White House, the fear that had been sweeping through the nation turned into panic.

A poem by Robert Sherwood appeared in the *Saturday Review of Literature:*

> Plodding feet
> Tramp—tramp
> The Grand Old Army's
> Breaking Camp.
> Blare of bugles
> Din—din
> The New Deal is moving in. . . .
> But where's the army of the unemployed?

> One would think they'd be overjoyed
> To join this pageant of renown—
> These festive rites. . . .

Washington, D.C., March 4, 1933. Perched on the icy branches of the gaunt trees overlooking the Capitol's east front, they waited for the ceremony to which they had no tickets: an old man in ancient, patched-up green tweeds; a pretty young redhead in a skimpy coat; an older woman in rags, her face lined with worry and pain; a college boy whose father was jobless. They watched the crowd below as rumors drifted through that Roosevelt had been shot, that the whole area was covered by army machine guns. The older woman prayed on her tree limb: "No more trouble, please, God. No more trouble."

They watched as dignitaries straggled down the Capitol steps: Herbert Hoover, morose and stony-faced; Chief Justice Charles Evans Hughes, his white beard fluttering a bit in the cold wind; Vice President Garner, shivering without an overcoat; finally Franklin D. Roosevelt, moving down the steps with agonizing slowness on the arm of his son James. They watched as the new President took the oath of office, his hand lying on the 300-year-old Roosevelt family Bible, open at Paul's First Epistle to the Corinthians: "though I have faith . . . and have not charity, I am nothing." And they watched as, still unsmiling, he gripped the rostrum firmly and looked out at the crowd.

"I am certain that my fellow Americans expect that on my induction into the Presidency I will address them with a candor and a decision which the present situation of our Nation impels." The cold wind riffled the pages of his text.

"This great nation will endure as it has endured, will revive and will prosper." The President's words rang out across the plaza. "So, first of all, let me assert my firm belief that the only thing we have to fear is fear itself—nameless, unreasoning, unjustified terror which paralyzes needed efforts to convert retreat into advance."

The great crowd stood in almost dead silence. Chin outthrust, face grave, Roosevelt went on: "In every dark hour of our national life a leadership of frankness and vigor has met with that understanding and support of the people themselves which is essential to victory."

The crowd began to respond as it caught the cadence of the phrases: "The money changers have fled from their high seats in the temple of our civilization. . . .

"This Nation asks for action, and action now. Our greatest primary task is to put people to work." The throng stirred to these words. The President gave the core of what would become the first New Deal programs. He touched on foreign policy only vaguely and briefly.

"In the field of world policy I would dedicate this Nation to the policy of the good neighbor—the neighbor who resolutely respects himself and, because he does so, respects the rights of others. . . ."

He hoped that the Constitution, with its normal balance of presidential and congressional power, would be adequate to the crisis. But if Congress did not respond to his proposals or act on its own, and if the national emergency continued, "I shall ask the Congress for the one remaining instrument to meet the crisis—broad Executive power to wage a war against the emergency, as great as the power that would be given to me if we were in fact invaded by a foreign foe." The American people wanted direct, vigorous action.

"They have asked for discipline and direction under leadership. They have made me the present instrument of their wishes. . . ."

As Roosevelt ended, he was still grim; but his face lighted up when the crowd seemed to come to life. The old man in the tree had broken into tears. "It was very, very solemn, and a little terrifying," Eleanor Roosevelt said later to reporters in the White House. "The crowds were so tremendous, and you felt that they would do anything—if only someone would tell them what to do."

Someone would. The new President had no sooner reviewed the inaugural parade and hosted a White House reception for a thousand guests than he swore in his cabinet en masse upstairs in the Oval Room. Washington had come alive with rumor and hope. Even while couples waltzed gaily at the inaugural balls, haggard men conferred hour after hour in the huge marble buildings along Pennsylvania Avenue. Republican holdovers and Democrats newly arrived in Washington sat side by side, telephoning anxious bankers, drawing up emergency orders, all the while feeling the financial pulse of the nation and world.

With the nation's finances paralyzed the new President gathered his lieutenants together for rapid action, but at his first cabinet meeting the day after the inaugural the group hardly looked like a team. After long and careful clearances with congressional and other leaders, Roosevelt had pieced together a kind of ministry of all the talents—or at least of all tastes and tendencies. Around him sat four old Wilson Jeffersonians, most notably Cordell Hull; two midwestern progressives and nominal Republicans, Secretary of Agriculture Henry Wallace and Interior Secretary Harold Ickes; and three New Yorkers, Jim Farley, the party and campaign expert, Frances Perkins, the first woman cabinet member ever appointed, and a real Republican, the new Treasury Secretary, William Woodin. Conspicuous by their absence was the party old guard; Roosevelt had not asked any of the three living Democratic presidential nominees to serve—not even his old running mate, James Cox—or any key member of the Wilson Administration save Carter Glass, who had declined the Treasury.

Later in the day Roosevelt conferred with a set of congressional leaders equally diverse in party and ideology. In a diary that he kept for two days and then gave up, Roosevelt gave the best account of the early meetings: "Conferences with Senator Glass, Hiram Johnson, Joe Robinson and Congressmen Steagall and Byrnes and Minority Leader Snell." All approved the President's calling a special session of Congress. "Secretary Woodin reported bankers' representatives much at sea as to what to do. Concluded that forty-eight different methods of handling banking situation impossible. Attorney General Cummings reported favorably on power to act under 1917 law, giving the President power to license, regulate, etc., export, hoarding, earmarking of gold or currency. Based on this opinion and on emergency decided on Proclamation declaring banking holiday." Then supper with Franklin Jr. and John before they returned to school, a talk with several reporters, a five-minute radio address for the American Legion, a late visit from Hull, and "Bed."

The next morning this leader, so ready for action, had an unnerving experience. Wheeled over by his valet to his office in the West Wing, he was left there alone in a big empty room. "There was nothing to be seen and nothing to be heard," as Tugwell was later to relate Roosevelt's account. "And for a few dreadful moments he hadn't a thought. He knew that the stimulus of human contact would break the spell; but where was everybody?" He felt physically helpless, paralyzed—but much worse, he wondered whether the national paralysis had struck to the center. "There must be buttons to push, but he couldn't see them. He pulled out a drawer or two; they had been cleaned out."

So he sat back in his chair and simply shouted. That shout brought his aides running. And with that shout there began what would go down in history as the "Hundred Days."

March 5—The President declared that an "extraordinary occasion" required Congress to convene on March 9.

March 6—The President proclaimed a bank holiday. This was an act of psychological leadership. The banks already *were* closed, by their own action or that of the states. Roosevelt played his role of crisis leader with such skill that his action in *keeping* the banks closed struck people with bracing effect. The far more daunting problem was reopening the banks in a way that would help them stay open, and here, in Frank Freidel's judgment, he had no clear idea. He relied on his own brain trusters, but even more on bankers and holdovers from the Hoover Administration—men who were cautious and conservative. The money-changers, chortled the left-wing press, were back in the temple.

March 10—The President asked Congress for authority to make "drastic economies" in government. "Too often in recent history," he said, "liberal governments have been wrecked on rocks of loose fiscal policy." National recovery depended on frugality. The address was straight out of the Chamber of Commerce—and Roosevelt's Pittsburgh campaign promises. Caught by surprise, lobbyists for veterans' groups wired their state and local bodies that benefits were in danger. The Democratic leadership in the House put down a revolt among the rank and file.

March 13—Beer! The President urged on Congress the legalization of the manufacture and sale of beer and light wines—the first step toward the repeal of the Volstead Act.

March 16—The President asked for a "new means to rescue agriculture"—an Agricultural Adjustment Act to hike farmers' buying power, slacken the pressure of farm mortgages, and raise the value of farm loans made by banks. It was none too soon. Angry farmers took matters into their own hands even as the bill was debated. Mobs of Iowans stopped eviction sales, manhandled bank agents and special deputies, fought with National Guard troops. In one town a "foreclosing judge" was dragged from his bench by masked men, mauled, half-strangled by a hangman's noose, forced to his knees, told to pray. When he entreated, "Oh Lord, I pray thee, do justice to all men," but still would not promise to drop the foreclosure proceeding, he was left half naked, smeared with dirt and grease.

March 21—The President proposed a bill close to his own heart—a Civilian Conservation Corps that would put tens of thousands of jobless young men to work in the nation's woodlands to protect the forests, fight floods and soil erosion—and in the process regenerate themselves and their skills. Like all big projects, he had told reporters earlier, "It is in a sense experimental, therefore we do not want to launch it on too big a scale until we know how practical it is." Congress legislated the plan before the end of the month. In the same message the President asked for a big program of federal emergency relief to feed and clothe millions of destitute Americans; Congress gave him this bill within two months.

March 29—The President urged on Congress the federal supervision of investment securities, because of the "obligation upon us to insist that every issue of new securities to be sold in interstate commerce shall be accompanied by full publicity and information." To the old doctrine of caveat emptor, he said, must be added the further doctrine: "Let the seller also beware." Roosevelt had no completed bill to offer—only the services of advisers who were already battling among themselves over the bill and were soon negotiating a tangle of policy concepts and specifics with members of Congress and their staffs. There was strong support on the Hill, however, especially on the part of Sam Rayburn of Texas and other old Wilsonians, and Congress passed in May a bill levying heavy penalties for failing to file full and honest information with the government.

April 5—By executive order the President prohibited "the hoarding of gold coin, gold bullion, and gold certificates" and directed all holders of gold to turn it over to a bank, in order to strengthen the nation's financial structure and "to give the Government that element of freedom of action" necessary as the "very basis of its monetary goal and objective."

April 10—The President "suggested" to Congress a project as close to his heart as the CCC, and for the same reason—it would nurture both people and the environment. This was for a Tennessee Valley Authority charged with the duty of planning for the "proper use, conservation and development of the natural resources of the Tennessee River drainage basin and its adjoining territory." In his broad vision the President saw the enterprise as transcending mere power development and encompassing flood control, soil conservation, reforestation, retirement of marginal lands, industrial distribution and diversification—"national planning for a complete river watershed." No one more eagerly welcomed this bill on Capitol Hill than George Norris, who with liberal allies in both parties had for more than a decade fought efforts to sell the government-built Muscle Shoals dam and power plant, which would now become part of a vast program of public development, ownership, and control.

During the interregnum the President-elect had led Norris and other congressional leaders on a tour of the valley. Pulling up at the dam at Muscle Shoals, Roosevelt watched the surging waters pour through the spillway—and go to waste. He had publicly promised that now these waters would be harnessed. He called Norris up from the car behind him. "This ought to be a happy day for you, George." It was, said Norris; "I can see my dreams coming true." He added half aloud as he walked back to his car: "Thank God for a President who can dream dreams!" With Norris looking on exultantly, Roosevelt signed the TVA bill in mid-May.

April 13—As foreclosures rose to a thousand a day, the President asked for legislation to protect home ownership as a guarantee of economic and social stability. The government would refinance mortgages of small owners, some of whom had lost their homes as far back as 1930. Congress passed this measure with enthusiasm.

May 4—The President urged emergency railroad legislation that would establish a coordinator of transportation to help or compel carriers to avoid duplication of service and waste and encourage financial reorganizations. Both houses passed bills within a month of Roosevelt's request.

May 17—The President sent a double recommendation to Congress—"for the machinery necessary for a great cooperative movement throughout all industry" for reemployment, a shorter working week, decent wages, and the prevention of "unfair competition and disastrous overproduction"; and for granting the President "full power to start a large program of direct employment" at a cost of about $3.3 billion. The resulting National Industrial Recovery Act was a legacy of World War I mobilization and the 1920s trade association movement, and the immediate product of brainstorming and horse-trading among an unusually large number of advisers and politicians in the legislature and the executive. Offering enticements to labor as well as capital, the bill was assailed from both right and left on Capitol Hill and barely survived the Senate gantlet. "History probably will record the National Industrial Recovery Act," said Roosevelt when he signed it on June 16, "as the most important and far-reaching legislation ever enacted by the American Congress."

So with that signing ended the Hundred Days—a policy explosion without precedent in American history—but of what enduring effect none could foresee.

"Discipline and Direction Under Leadership"?

At the center of the action sat Franklin Roosevelt, presiding, instructing, wheedling, persuading, enticing, pressuring, negotiating, manipulating, conceding, horse-trading, placating, mediating—leading and following, leading and misleading. People marveled how the President, his cigarette holder deployed more jauntily than ever, appeared to bounce and skip through the day, despite his inability to walk, as he punctuated solemn conferences with jests, long and somewhat imaginary stories, and great booming laughter. While still in bed in the morning, his large torso looming over legs that hardly ribbed the sheets, he spouted ideas, questions, instructions to his aides. Wheeled over to the west wing, he swung into his office chair for long hours of visitors, letters, telephone calls, emergency sessions.

Calvin Coolidge had allegedly disposed of visitors by a simple formula: "Don't talk back to 'em." Roosevelt used talk as a tool of influence, outtalking his advisers, outtalking department heads, even outtalking visiting senators.

The President soon proved himself an artist in government—in his fine

sense of timing, his adroit application of pressure, his face-to-face persua-
siveness, his craft in playing not only foes but friends off against one
another. Like a creative artist, Frances Perkins said, he would begin his
picture "without a clear idea of what he intends to paint or how it shall be
laid out upon the canvas, and then, as he paints, his plan evolves out of
the material he is painting." He could think and feel his way into political
situations with imagination, intuition, insight.

These traits dominated his policy thinking as well as his political calculating—and with less success. People close to Roosevelt were dismayed by his
casual and disorderly intellectual habits. To Adolf Berle his judgments of
people and ideas were "primarily instinctive and not rational," his learning
came not from books but from people. He read not books but newspapers,
perhaps half a dozen before breakfast—devoured them "like a combine
eating up grain," a friend noted. He was not so much a creator of ideas
as a broker of them. He did not assemble his ideas into a comprehensive
and ordered program, with priorities and interconnections. Just as he lived
each day for itself, as he liked to tell friends, so he appeared to flirt with
each idea as it came along.

Everything seemed to conspire to fortify these intellectual habits of the
new President—his eclectic education and reading, the ideologically divided party he led, the factionalized Congress he confronted, above all the
advisers he had chosen and who had chosen him. His chief brain truster
during 1933 was Ray Moley. Prickly and hard-driving, the former Columbia professor—now Assistant Secretary of State—shared some of his
boss's political shrewdness and opportunism, intuitive judgment, and
keenness in evaluating friend and foe. But Roosevelt also talked at length
with Berle about banking, railroad, and monetary problems, and Berle's
ideas for raising business to a higher level of efficiency and responsibility;
with Tugwell about conservation, agriculture, and industrial discipline,
and Tugwell's notions of democratic planning of the economy.

These brain trusters had their differences, but they seemed three of a
kind compared with Roosevelt's other advisers, formal and informal: his
old-time Hudson Valley friend and neighbor Henry Morgenthau, humanitarian by heritage and sensibility but cautiously conservative in economic
policy; budget director Lewis Douglas, absolutely dedicated to governmental penny-pinching and fiscal orthodoxy; Treasury Under Secretary
Dean Acheson, close to Douglas in his economics; Jesse Jones, Texas
business mogul who now ran the Reconstruction Finance Corporation.
Another broad influence on Roosevelt was the lively correspondence
and visitation with Felix Frankfurter, who discreetly spoke for Justice
Brandeis's bias against economic and governmental giantism even as the

Harvard Law School professor helped people Washington agencies with young activists who would make their own diverse marks in coming months.

Most remarkable of all was that one-woman brain trust, Eleanor Roosevelt—and all the more influential for not being viewed in that role. Through quick visits to her husband while he was still breakfasting in bed, little chits and memos, thick reports infiltrated into the executive offices, the visitors she invited to the White House, and her own influence on public opinion and Washington attitudes, she soon became a penetrating voice for the humanitarian liberal-left. Through a wide correspondence— she received 300,000 pieces of mail the first year—her press conferences and newspaper columns, her speeches and magazine articles, her widely advertised (and criticized) trips to CCC camps and coal mines, she began to build up a potentially powerful constituency of her own. Historian Mary Beard wrote admiringly of her ability to give "inspiration to the married, solace to the lovelorn, assistance to the homemaker, menus to the cook, and help to the educator, direction to the employer, caution to the warrior, and deeper awareness of its primordial force to the 'weaker sex.'" The First Lady also served as a model for other women in Washington government. Her close friend Frances Perkins, with her labor and urban concerns and constituencies, had special access to both Roosevelts, and women like Molly Dewson of the Democratic National Committee learned that they could be, all at the same time, competent, caring, and controversial.

Such was the flux and flow of advice to the President that no one really knew which advisers were influential or why or when. Who was having the President's ear at the moment provoked jealousies worthy of the royal courts of old. The President's mind seemed awesomely accessible—to the kitchen cabinet, to department heads like Ickes and Perkins, to experts coming through Washington. The President would be seen talking animatedly with men regarded by the orthodox—though not necessarily by history—as quacks.

Roosevelt was following no set course, left, right, or center. He was leading by guess and by God. He not only admitted to playing by ear but boasted of it. He was a football quarterback, he told reporters, calling a new play after he saw how the last one turned out. Snap judgments had to be made. But Washington wondered what lay back of the snap judgments—some ideology or philosophy?

Neither of these, but rather a loose collection of values—Roosevelt's warm humanitarianism, his belief that the needy must be helped, that government must step in when private institutions could not do the job, and that now—in 1933—this meant the federal government. The President also had a fine grasp of political and governmental nuts and bolts. But between the two levels of grand philosophy and policy specifics he would be experimental, eclectic, nonprogrammatic, nondoctrinaire. He would be a broker of ideas as well as of interests and individuals.

As a master broker Roosevelt presided over a grand concert of interests. Labor, farmers, businessmen, investors, unemployed youth, some of the poor—all got a slice of the first New Deal, at least on paper. FDR assumed the role of bipartisan leader, "president of all the people," virtually the national father. He happily cited a Nebraska congressman's definition of the New Deal as an effort "to cement our society, rich and poor, manual worker and brain worker, into a voluntary brotherhood of freemen, standing together, striving together, for the common good of all." Government, he told a convention of bankers, was "essentially the outward expression of the unity and the leadership of all groups." All this seemed a long cry from the "discipline and direction under leadership" he had promised in his inaugural address.

Congress, though more responsive to regional and special interests, quickened to the energy that radiated from the President. Even some Republicans fell over themselves to express support for the Democratic Roosevelt. In many respects the Chief Executive was Chief Legislator. Congress was by no means supine. Conservative Democratic senators like Carter Glass and Harry F. Byrd of Virginia usually opposed the President's bills. Congress as a whole, however, was more positive than even Roosevelt toward the New Deal. Many congressmen wanted more inflation than Roosevelt, ampler spending for people's needs, greater generosity to veterans and farmers, bigger public works, tougher policies toward Wall Street. The President skillfully brokered with the congressional left. For the conservative Democrats in the Senate he had growing hostility. Byrd opposed the AAA, FDR told Tugwell, because, as an apple grower, "he's afraid you'll force him to pay more than ten cents an hour for his apple pickers."

As master broker Roosevelt for a time could stay above the political and ideological battles raging around him. In the distribution of good things— whether government money or patronage jobs or social policy or his smile of approval—he could act as transactional leader within the existing system. He might give TVA to the left and economy to the right, but as a compromising broker rather than ideological leader he would not move decisively left or right. Social justice, he said, "ought not to consist of robbing Peter to pay Paul."

It all seemed to work beautifully for a time. Employment, prices, income all soared in the weeks after the Hundred Days. The industrial production index nearly doubled from March to July. Unemployment fell off from around 15 million at the time of Roosevelt's inaugural to about 11 million in October, a drop in the jobless rate from about 30 to about 22 percent.

Roosevelt's popularity floated high on this first gust of recovery. "If he burned down the capitol," said Will Rogers, "we would cheer and say, 'well, we at least got a fire started anyhow.'"

He won praise from Bertie McCormick's Republican Chicago *Tribune* and William Randolph Hearst's New York *American*. Daily, White House mailmen hauled in sacks of mail, most of it laudatory, some of it fulsome. An adviser found the President happily leafing through a sheaf of this mail. He was sorting letters he had received from British subjects addressing him as "Your Majesty" or "Lord Roosevelt" or in other monarchical terms. Why? He wanted to send them to King George V for his "amusement." History has not recorded that His Majesty was amused.

Psychology overwhelmed economics. In sad reality at least 10 million Americans remained jobless in 1933, and industrial production was still far below that of the prosperity years and even the first year of the depression. In October 3 million families—at least 12 million people—still depended on unemployment relief of about $23 a month, which covered food but left little or nothing for rent and utilities. But people *felt* better—and this was largely Roosevelt's doing. He exuded cheerfulness. He raised hopes and expectations. Above all, he *acted;* for several months he simply dominated the front pages of the nation's newspapers with his speeches, bill-signings, trips, executive orders, pronunciamentos.

His fireside chats carried his buoyant presence directly into home and hearth. "I want to talk for a few minutes with the people of the United States about banking," he said at the start of his first fireside chat in mid-March. "I want to tell you what has been done in the last few days, why it was done, and what the next steps are going to be." And he proceeded to do just that, in simple, human terms. Read later in cold print, the chats seemed a bit limp and pedestrian. Read by Roosevelt over the radio, they sounded warm, intimate, homely. Watching him deliver a fireside chat, Frances Perkins sensed that he could actually see the families listening at the other end. "His face would smile and light up as though he were actually sitting on the front porch or in the parlor with them." The President took care not to overuse this device, giving only four chats the first year, at two- or three-month intervals.

Nor did he overstrain the press conference as a way of reaching people. He held these twice a week, to the joy of the White House press corps, but the sessions were often more frustrating than rewarding to the reporters. Roosevelt was a master at withholding information. He spent much of the half hour jovially fencing and parrying with the reporters, or offering them tidbits, or lecturing them. Crowding around the President's gadget-covered desk, the correspondents pressed him hard, with mixed results. Roosevelt wanted to control the flow of information, to create his own sensations, to set his own timing. He was not the first or the last President to do all this; he was simply more effective than most.

*　　*　　*

Nothing epitomized the New Deal in action better than the National Recovery Act and Administration—epitomized Roosevelt's Concert of Interests, his role of broker, the psychological impact of the Hundred Days, the fundamental problems of the "broker state" at work. As boss of NRA, Roosevelt chose General Hugh Johnson, who was a mass of contradictions himself—outwardly a tough old cavalryman with a leathery face, squint eyes, and a rough bark of a voice, inwardly an amalgam of public commitment, touchy ego, maudlin sentimentality, business savvy, and as clamorous and picturesque as a sideshow barker. The general's first job was to persuade employers to draw up codes of fair competition, a task he attacked like a cavalry charge. Once approved by the President and given the force of law, the codes were designed to discourage wasteful, junglelike competition by setting more orderly pricing and marketing policies, and to benefit workers by establishing higher wages, shorter hours, better working conditions, and the end of child labor. As part of the deal, antitrust policies would be softened so that businessmen could cooperate in setting up the codes. Code signers could affix the "Blue Eagle" label to products and shopwindows.

With Johnson as bugler, the NRA galvanized the American people like a national call to arms. Suddenly the Blue Eagle was everywhere—on magazine covers, in the movies, on girls in chorus lines. (But not on Ford cars; Henry Ford perversely refused to sign the automobile code, then lived up to it anyway.) Rushing from city to city in an army plane, dishing out Boy Scout-style enthusiasm, biting criticism, and wisecracks at every stop, Johnson pressured and coaxed businessmen to endorse the codes, then gathered them in Washington for the signing and orating. As the very personification of recovery, the general staged a monster Blue Eagle parade on New York's Fifth Avenue. For hours he reviewed the parade of a quarter million persons, with another million and a half cheering from the sidewalks. Not since 1917 had Americans savored such a throbbing sense of marching unity.

As the months passed, though, the questions became more and more urgent: Unity for what? Marching to where? Under pressure for quick results, Johnson dealt with the business and labor leaders closest at hand, those who were most vocal, best organized, most skillful in dealing with bureaucrats and politicians. Inevitably he delegated crucial pricing and production decisions to the dominant interests, which often turned out to be the biggest corporations. The NRA was becoming a breeder of monopoly, charged Senator Gerald Nye. Who would speak for unorganized consumers? A Consumers' Advisory Board was set up but without adequate political muscle; its members, Tugwell said, were "spearheads without shafts."

Union labor, being organized, fared better under NRA. Section 7(a) of the act boldly proclaimed that employees "shall have the right to organize and bargain collectively through representatives of their own choosing, and shall be free from the interference, restraint, or coercion of employers" in choosing their representatives. No one seeking or holding a job "shall be required as a condition of employment to join any company union or to refrain from joining, organizing, or assisting a labor organization of his own choosing." Union leaders greeted this as labor's Magna Carta—comparable to Lincoln's Emancipation Proclamation, said John L. Lewis—and the message was clear: Organize. "THE PRESIDENT WANTS YOU TO JOIN A UNION," placards read. "Forget about injunctions, yellow dog contracts, black lists and the fear of dismissal." But there were complications. President William Green and the American Federation of Labor old guard wanted to organize workers into separate craft unions, even in huge auto plants, while Lewis and the rising young militants around him wanted to organize all the workers in a plant or company or industry into big, solid industrial unions.

Employers bridled at 7(a). Many set up company unions—or "employee representation plans"—which came to be run by company stooges. Labor responded with a rash of strikes during the summer of 1933; by September nearly 300,000 workers had walked out. The "concert of interests" seemed to be emitting discordant noises. "N.R.A. means National Run Around," read a sign hoisted on a picket line. The President set up special boards, trimmed NRA's power, eased Johnson out, and put in more domesticated chiefs, but to little avail; during 1934 the NRA eagle fluttered through heavy weather.

In the end the significance of the National Recovery Administration was not its impact on economic recovery, which was mixed, but its curbing of child labor, sweatshops, and unfair trade practices, its big boost to unionization and its modest protection to consumers. Why then was the NRA finally dismissed as a failure, even privately by Roosevelt himself? Largely because it failed in its highly touted supreme aim of bringing capital, labor, and other interests into a happy concert under the "Broker State," and by artificially raising prices and restricting production, it only marginally helped produce recovery.

If the Concert of Interests did not work, what would? Public works, the companion piece to the NRA, was launched with little of the drama of the Blue Eagle, under the leadership of one of the most committed and stout-hearted New Dealers, Secretary of the Interior Harold Ickes. Touchy and cantankerous, suspicious of friend and foe—and especially of government contractors—"Honest Harold" did not hesitate to use government snoopers to check on suspect PWA employees and their financial connections. Ickes was in no great hurry; his big projects needed careful planning and budgeting as well as laborious scrutiny by the secretary himself. When the public works program finally got underway it built gas and electric power plants, jails and hospitals, sewage and water systems, bridges, docks, and tunnels—and aircraft carriers, cruisers, destroyers, army and navy airplanes. But the $9 billion that PWA ultimately spent were not central to recovery during Roosevelt's first two years.

Much quicker to get underway was the federal relief program under a lanky young ex-director of private welfare programs named Harry Hopkins, who acted almost as fast as he talked. Appointed Federal Emergency Relief Administrator with a grant of half a billion dollars, Hopkins began authorizing millions of dollars in relief even while he was waiting in a hallway to be moved into his office. Since he could give money only to the state and local public relief agencies, which in turn administered relief programs, he could do little more than monitor the levels of compassion and competence with which programs were carried out. Behind his cynical, wisecracking façade Hopkins was deeply concerned with guarding the dignity, pride, and self-esteem of people on relief. Hence he was eager that the unemployed be given jobs and not merely handouts, but job programs cost more money. Late in 1933 Hopkins persuaded Roosevelt to launch a massive crash program to employ 4 million. In its brief existence, the Civil Works Administration undertook the building or rebuilding of vast numbers of roads, parks, schools, playgrounds, swimming pools, and other "light," short-term projects, in contrast to the PWA's "heavy" jobs.

It was this massive spending on work relief, supplemented by that of the PWA, the TVA, the CCC, the AAA, and other programs, that in 1933 and 1934 provided the central thrust of the early New Deal. It was not really planned that way; Roosevelt was responding not to grand ideology or to grand economics but to sheer human needs that he recognized and that Eleanor Roosevelt, Hopkins, Perkins, and the others brought to him. This was part of Roosevelt's political strength in the face of the bewildering problems of 1933 and 1934: the ability to follow ad hoc, expedient policies; to mediate between liberals and moderates, ideologues and politicians, spenders and economizers; to move so quickly and deftly from policy to policy, posture to posture, as to keep his adversaries guessing and off balance; and hence to avoid being cornered by left or right—all the while helping millions of people in need.

Was this oscillating middle way also the President's weakness? Instead of standing above the contending groups in society his administration often became part of the struggle, even sundered by it. By trying to do so many different—even competing—things, he did few that were adequate to the desperate needs. In trying to be both budget-balancer and provider, he satisfied neither the economizers nor those who believed that only a truly massive spending program would produce a massive recovery. By flirting with groups and movements stretched across the political spectrum he lost an opportunity to mobilize and lead forces arrayed from a "little left of center" to the far left. Perhaps the basic problem was one of intellectual grasp. "Roosevelt had a cogent overall interpretation of presidential leadership," in James Sargent's judgment, but the "disorder and ambiguity of his thought and expression" intruded when he "attempted to transfer his general thinking to specific proposals and actions." Thus, in December 1933 the President told a press conference that "somewhere" between Douglas's efforts to economize and "those who want to spend ten billion additional on public works, we will get somewhere. . . ."

In foreign policy, where Presidents usually have a freer hand, Roosevelt was equally vigorous, versatile, volatile—and opportunistic. At heart still an old Wilsonian, he had made enough concessions to Hearst and other nationalists to leave himself in an ambivalent position from the start of his administration. In choosing Cordell Hull for Secretary of State he was recognizing a man who had made no secret of his hope to crown his lifework for expanded trade and economic cooperation among nations. But in his domestic policies, with the backing of Moley, Tugwell, and others, the President was seeking a moderate rise in farm and industrial prices, which he did not want washed out by an inundation of cheap goods from abroad. Moreover, he had inherited a dubious bequest from Hoover: to take part in an International Monetary and Economic Conference set for London in the early summer, which might conflict with his early decision to go off the gold standard and his plan to free his monetary policy—especially his moderate "reflation" efforts—from entanglement with the international gold standard.

Roosevelt's approach to the London Conference reflected his crossed purposes and mixed counsel in foreign affairs. Despite his skepticism about the London gathering, he threw himself into the posture of world leader by receiving foreign representatives, including British Prime Minister Ramsay MacDonald, at the White House in April. Rosy pieties at these meetings raised hopes for the conference. Then the President sent to London a delegation headed by Hull but including also such protectionists as Senator Key Pittman of Nevada; the President had even tried to enlist the Senate's supreme isolationist, Hiram Johnson, who shrewdly declined. In London the American delegation wandered in a fog of confusion which was only intensified by Roosevelt's belated dispatch of Moley as "liaison" and ultimately, apparently, as possible fall guy. Suddenly there arrived a sharp message from Roosevelt in effect scolding the delegates for trifling with efforts for an artificial and temporary monetary stability and for ignoring fundamental ills. Confounded, the conference limped on for a few weeks and then quit, amid sharp recriminations and general hopelessness.

Roosevelt's torpedoing of the conference did not usher in wholly nationalist policies, however; he preferred to keep dual strategies in play. In the fall he set up a committee of low-tariff men to prepare a bill for the 1934 session of Congress. On their recommendation Roosevelt asked Congress for presidential authority to make commercial agreements with foreign nations under which rates could be revised 50 percent either way. The passage of this bill was a triumph for Hull's internationalism.

But what about Roosevelt's? In the fall of 1933 he was still pursuing the nationalist economic policies for which his London Conference "bombshell message" had freed him. One of these policies was to shore up domestic prices by buying gold—a device that had been sold the President by a monetary theorist. So for some weeks there occurred a most extraordinary episode in presidential history—the President of the United States meeting every morning with his new Acting Secretary of the Treasury, Henry Morgenthau, to set the price of gold. Since edging prices upward rather than any precise figure was the aim, Roosevelt could rather arbitrarily set the figure within a certain range. Once when he proposed to Morgenthau an increase to twenty-one cents, he twitted the solemn secretary by explaining, "It's a lucky number, because it's three times seven."

Also in the fall, however, Roosevelt brought off what in history might rank as potentially the most significantly internationalist act of all—recognition of the Soviet Union. This action followed lengthy haggling over terms, Washington holding out hopes for expanded trade and Moscow making vague promises to stop abetting revolutionary activity in the United States and to protect the right of free religious worship of Americans in Russia. Eleanor Roosevelt liked to tell of visiting a schoolroom where the Soviet Union had been blacked out—actually "whited out"—on a map of the world, leaving only a void. Roosevelt now had begun to fill that void.

* * *

To some inside the Roosevelt administration the New Deal by summer 1934 appeared in disarray, if not chaos. "Public works" was almost at a full stop, Berle observed, and NRA rapidly disintegrating. "We have an administration in very bad shape indeed." Key officials, especially on the right, were quitting the administration. Lewis Douglas left in August and Acheson was preparing to leave. Some projects failed or badly faltered: the gold purchase venture; an effort by Ickes to impose some order in the chaotic oil industry; an effort by the Federal Surplus Relief Corporation to provide food for the needy and to stabilize the commodity markets. The last two of these fell afoul of industry pressures and fragmentation. The President's abrupt cancellation of private carriers' airmail contracts on the grounds of collusion and the assumption by the Air Corps of the flying of the mails led to a series of plane crashes and pilot deaths in the February 1934 storms—a much-publicized disaster that might have brought down a less popular President.

The public as a whole had quite a different view of the administration. It saw a President who was doing his damnedest, quick to confront specific problems, brilliant at explaining his deeds and hopes, always positive, exuberant, seemingly on top of things. The public saw a leader.

For that public the ultimate test was economic recovery, and the flush of prosperity felt strong by fall 1934, compared to the miseries of March 1933. Could "bucks" be converted to ballots? A third of the senators and all the representatives were up for reelection. Roosevelt's tactic was to stand above the party battle, in line with his bipartisan posture of "leader of all the people." But he helped friendly candidates indirectly, and he posed the campaign issue by asking in a fireside chat, "Are you better off than you were last year? Are your debts less burdensome? Is your bank account more secure? Are your working conditions better? Is your faith in your own individual future more firmly grounded?"

The result was a resounding verdict for the President and his New Deal. Typically Presidents lost ground in midterm congressional elections, but in 1934 Democratic strength rose from 313 to 322 in the House and—incredibly—from 59 to 69 in the Senate. A clutch of highly conservative Republican senators was sacked. "Some of our friends think the majority top-heavy," Garner wrote the President, "but if properly handled, the House and Senate will be all right and I am sure you can arrange that."

Next month a late vote came in from Britain. "The courage, the power and the scale" of Roosevelt's effort, wrote Winston Churchill, "must enlist the ardent sympathy of every country, and his success could not fail to lift the whole world forward into the sunlight of an easier and more genial age." The British Conservative was seeking to place Roosevelt in the broadest sweep of history.

"Roosevelt is an explorer who has embarked on a voyage as uncertain as that of Columbus, and upon a quest which might conceivably be as important as the discovery of the New World."

CHAPTER 2

The Arc of Conflict

T HE winter of 1934 was the hardest time of all, the young factory worker said. At one point the family ate only potatoes and dog meat. "We sold everything we could except the piano. Mama wouldn't let that go. . . . All of us had taken our music lessons on it—especially my sister, the one who died when I was little. I guess that was the real reason Mama wouldn't let it go."

In Macon County, Georgia, the NRA meant to many blacks "Negro Removal Act" or "Negro Rarely Allowed," and to some whites "Negro Relief Act" or "No Roosevelt Again."

In a country town outside Boston a decorous bridge party ended up in merriment and high jinks, with the ladies scissoring off their partners' long neckties just below the knot. "I hope that wasn't your best tie, Charles," the hostess joked. Charles was an MIT graduate now ekeing out a living from a chicken farm. "My dear," he said with a tight smile, "it was my only one."

"Close to me four children moved up and down the row with nimble fingers" picking currants, a jobless writer related. "The parents scolded or cajoled as the hot day wore on and the kids whined or sulked under the monotonous work. Their ages ranged from six to twelve or thirteen." Two younger girls tended a baby on a blanket under a tree. "For one day's work of nearly ten hours the father collected for himself, his wife, and four children $2.44."

From Florida a Du Pont in-law and vice president indignantly wrote a friend: "A cook on my houseboat at Fort Myers quit because the government was paying him a dollar an hour as a painter."

An Indiana housewife wrote to the local newspaper about living on $1.50 a week. "Those in charge of relief have never known actual hunger and want. . . . Just what does our government expect us to do when our rent is due? When we need a doctor? . . . It is always the people with full stomachs who tell us poor people to keep happy."

J. P. Morgan's family often warned visitors not to mention Roosevelt's name to the old man—it might raise his blood pressure to dangerous heights. It was not safe to mention *any* Roosevelt. When someone had let fall the name of Theodore Roosevelt, Morgan had burst out, "God damn all Roosevelts!"

In Garden City, Kansas, the skies blackened as whirlwinds of black dust beat on the farmhouses. "The doors and windows were all shut tightly, yet those tiny particles seemed to seep through the very walls. It got into cupboards and clothes closets; our faces were as dirty as if we had rolled in the dirt; our hair was gray and stiff and we ground dirt between our teeth."

A community sing in a migratory labor camp in California hymned an old sharecropper's lament:

> Eleven Cent cotton and forty cent meat
> How in the world can a poor man eat?
> Flour up high, cotton down low,
> How in the world can you raise the dough?
> Clothes worn out, shoes run down,
> Old slouch hat with a hole in the crown. . . .

These were the voices of some Americans not during the Hoover depression but a year or two after Roosevelt's Hundred Days. Overall, the statistics looked good. New private and public construction put in place rose from $2.9 billion in 1933 to $3.7 billion in 1934 and $4.2 billion in 1935. Average weekly earnings of production workers went up from $16.65 in 1933 to $18.20 the next year and $19.91 the year after that. Unemployment fell in these same years from 12.8 million to 11.3 to 10.6. But these improvements looked almost pathetic compared with the 1929 figures—only 1.5 million jobless that year, weekly paychecks of almost $25 for factory workers, nearly $11 billion in construction. As usual, women did worse than men and improved their lot more slowly. Roosevelt's central goal and promise—recovery—had been only fractionally accomplished.

Yet the smell and feel of a strong recovery lasted for at least a year after the Hundred Days. Roosevelt's exuberance, experimentation, concern— above all, the sheer range and variety of his activism—symbolized a nation on the march, looking forward. And there had been so much change and progress in so many areas: NRA had begun to bring some order and equity to what had been pure jungle conflict; depositors' savings were safe; millions of the poor were receiving relief jobs or at least relief; magnificent projects like the Tennessee Valley Authority had been launched; the government was policing—or at least monitoring—Wall Street; farm income had been boosted and stabilized; new conservation programs were underway; the sight of the dispossessed family huddling outside its ancestral home while the slick-talking auctioneer sold it off was far less common across the great agricultural regions of the nation.

Yet millions of people were still in dire want—all the more so because promises from Washington and state capitals had sharpened their hopes and appetites. The President was now caught up in one of the most dynamic and compelling transformational situations that a free people can experience. Not only did the basic wants exist in harrowing abundance; they had been acknowledged and legitimated by the New Dealers to the point that now they had become publicly recognized needs. As political leaders made more promises, offered more assurances, aroused more hope, these needs were converted into popular expectations that were addressed back to the leaders—any leaders. And as leaders sought followers, as politicians competed for votes, popular expectations changed into feelings of entitlement and in turn into demands by followers on leaders. Who then would become the true leaders?

CLASS WAR IN AMERICA

"In the summer of 1933, a nice old gentleman wearing a silk hat fell off the end of a pier. He was unable to swim. A friend ran down the pier, dived overboard and pulled him out: but the silk hat floated off with the tide. After the old gentleman had been revived, he was effusive in his thanks. He praised his friend for saving his life. Today, three years later, the old gentleman is berating his friend because the silk hat was lost."

Roosevelt was a bit disingenuous in telling this story. Having watched the counterattack of leaders of finance on both Cousin Ted's and Woodrow Wilson's progressivism, he could hardly have been astonished that capitalists would turn against the New Deal. Still, he was genuinely perplexed as to why the right-wing counterattack came so quickly, and in such angry and often ugly form. As the master conductor of the concert of interests, had he not responded to business needs—in his stern call for economy, his refusal to support left-wing proposals such as the socialization of banking, his early insistence on self-liquidating public works, his initial coolness even to federal guarantee of bank deposits, his defiance of the American Legion on veterans' pensions? Had he not received praise from such diverse conservatives as Henry L. Stimson, Walter Lippmann, and Hamilton Fish, such conservative newspapers as *The Wall Street Journal* and the Hearst chain? Had not the NRA and other measures tried to be evenhanded between capital and labor?

Many on the right were not placated by these measures, and their fury rose in the months after the Hundred Days. In his speeches and posture, if not always in his policies, Roosevelt was challenging some of the fundamental values of the old American right—its definition of liberty as freedom from governmental regulation and control, its belief in individualism in contrast to the "collectivist" NRA and AAA, its attachment to laissez faire and limited government in contrast to the leviathan that Roosevelt seemed to be erecting, its championship of thrift in public spending, its reverence for the Constitution and the checks and balances designed to frustrate popular majorities seeking to control the presidency and Congress. Some of the more venerable spokesmen for American conservatism in the 1930s had sat in Yale and other classrooms when Spencerian Social Darwinism—above all, the belief that progress emerges out of competition and the struggle for survival—had been relayed by the likes of William Graham Sumner and other eminent teachers.

It was inevitable that these powerful men would come into conflict with the President unless he hewed to a conservative line—and Roosevelt the improviser and experimenter would hew to no ideology during the early New Deal. Rumblings on the right began to be heard by late 1933. An organized counterattack on the New Deal was developing strongly by mid-1934, at a time when protest on the left—aside from socialists and communists who had been against the Administration from the start as a matter of course—was still mixed and unfocused. And leadership of the right was taken initially not by conservative Republicans or big businessmen but by Democrats.

The most notable of these Democrats was the party's hero of the 1920s, Al Smith, who had now become the unhappiest warrior of them all. His desertion of the "collectivist" New Deal signaled a poignant effort of the old business leadership of the Bourbon Democracy, now aided by disaffected urbanites, to hold the Democratic party to its earlier "Jeffersonian" ways. John J. Raskob, a close friend of Smith's, had retired from active directorship of General Motors in 1928 to head up both the Democratic National Committee and the Smith campaign. After Smith's defeat Raskob and Jouett Shouse, a Kansas newspaper editor and politico, ran the party. Roosevelt's vanquishing of Smith at the 1932 Democratic convention left both Raskob and Shouse in political eclipse. By early 1934 a Du Pont vice president was corresponding with Raskob about Roosevelt's seeking to set labor against capital, buying votes from the poor, attacking corporate wealth, and other transgressions. Why not, Raskob asked the Du Pont man, set up an organization to combat the idea that businessmen were crooks and similar iniquitous notions?

From these seeds there rapidly grew a unique organization, the American Liberty League. Top men in General Motors, Du Pont, and other corporations took the lead with Raskob and Shouse in setting it up, sometimes meeting with Smith in his office at the Empire State Building. Most of the participants by now were Republicans, but the group secured as members of its board of directors not only Smith but the 1924 Democratic presidential nominee, John W. Davis. Heavily financed by Du Pont and other big corporations, the League by the end of summer 1934 was ready to go into action as the anti-New Deal voice of business.

Shouse first paid a courtesy call on the President in mid-August to assure him of the League's "absolutely non-partisan character." Roosevelt could not have been more agreeable. After hearing out Shouse's list of objectives—chiefly the protection of enterprise and of property—the President said airily, "I can subscribe to that one hundred per cent." He might use League people to help him prepare the next federal budget, he volunteered, and he even called in his press secretary in Shouse's presence and instructed him to announce the President's endorsement of the League when it went public.

As usual, Roosevelt bided his time. Late in August he told reporters amiably that Shouse had stopped by and had pulled out of his pocket a couple of "Commandments"—the need to protect property and to safeguard profits. What about other commandments? he had asked Shouse. The League said nothing about teaching respect for the rights of individuals against those who would exploit them, or the duty of government to find jobs for all those who wished to work. The President quoted a gentleman "with a rather ribald sense of humor" as saying that the League believed in two things—love God and then forget your neighbor.

Had Shouse asked him to join? a reporter asked. "I don't think he did," Roosevelt said with a grin. "Must have been an oversight."

With this press-conference baiting of the League, the war was on between Roosevelt and the right. Conservative pamphlets had the New Deal putting the nation on the brink of chaos, destroying states' rights, plunging the country into bankruptcy, leading the people into socialism, dictatorship, and tyranny. The New Deal was communist or fascist, or perhaps both. Roosevelt must have been puzzled by a question that has eluded historians for at least half a century: why such emotional intensity? Surely not because of economic deprivation; business was enjoying a moderate boom under the early New Deal. Surely not wholly because of loss of power; Roosevelt had given business leaders a voice and some influence in policy-making, albeit only as a junior partner.

Perhaps the most likely explanation is a psychological one. The vehemence of the right-wing counterattack can be seen as deriving chiefly from acute feelings of insecurity and lowered status in the business community. Roosevelt had robbed capitalists of something even more important than some of their money and their power. He had threatened their self-esteem. The men who had been the economic lords of creation now inhabited a world where political leaders were masters of headlines and recipients of deference, even adulation. Men who had claimed for themselves Righteousness and Civic Virtue, even during the Hoover depression years, now found themselves whipping boys for vote-cadging politicians—or even in the dock. Roosevelt, said a French observer, had exploded one of the most popular of American myths—he had dissociated the concept of wealth from the concept of virtue.

And Roosevelt's own psychology? His pride and self-esteem were also at stake. He was sensitive to criticism from the right, especially from people of his own class. He wrote a Harvard classmate, a Boston banker, that he had heard of some remarks the classmate had made, and "because of what I felt to be a very old and real friendship these remarks hurt." He wrote another friend bitterly about the "dinner-party conversations in some of the best houses in Newport." Doubtless he felt demeaned and deserted by the same types of people who had stood apart from him in his school and college years. It was often charged, Richard Hofstadter noted, that Roosevelt was betraying his class, "but if by his class one means the whole policy-making, power-wielding stratum, it would be just as true to say that his class betrayed him." And the President was still acting and sounding far more like a Groton gentleman than were many of his erstwhile schoolmates.

As psychology overrode economics on both sides, the business community's intensifying feelings of guilt, apprehension, and lowered self-esteem fueled a mounting hatred for Roosevelt that began to assume pathological dimensions. He was called, privately or publicly, the Pied Piper of Hyde Park, the High Priest of Repudiation, Franklin "Deficit" Roosevelt, a Little Napoleon, Roosevelt the Tyrant, a Svengali, and of course a communist. One card that was smirkingly passed around had the caption "Can you answer the $64 Question?":

> WHAT MAN SAID TO "THAT" WOMAN?
> "You kiss the negroes
> I'll kiss the Jews,
> We'll stay in the White House,
> As long as we choose."

Another card read:

THE PRESIDENT'S WIFE
IS SUING FOR DIVORCE BECAUSE
SHE IS NOT GETTING WHAT HE IS GIVING
THE OTHER PEOPLE

There developed a curious obsession with Roosevelt's physical disability; "that cripple in the White House" was also rumored to have cancer or syphilis. But the main charge was of insanity—like fervent ideologues everywhere, his foes felt that their chief enemy could not merely be wrong; he must be crazy.

On the farthest reaches of the right—a world away from responsible conservatism—lay the political scavengers of anti-Semitism, and "Rosenfeld" became a prime target. His "Jew Deal" was run by Frankfurter, Brandeis, Baruch, Morgenthau, Cohen, and other "legal kikes." A host of groups sprang up—white shirts, silver shirts, blue shirts—to purvey this line through speeches and pamphlets with such titles as *There Is a Jewish World Plot, The Jewish New Deal, Aryan Americanism,* and—inevitably—the fake *Protocols of the Learned Elders of Zion,* the final proof of the international Jewish plot to take over the world. All these groups—as well as the white-sheeted Ku Klux Klan—were united by hate and fear of liberalism, socialism, and communism and by the passionate belief that the New Deal embodied these heresies.

*   *   *

With the Liberty League as its political action committee, American capitalism by late 1934 had declared war on the New Deal. Even more, it had declared a kind of class war on militant unions and all the hostile elements it perceived on the underside of American life. In the charges and the whispers against Roosevelt, in the hatred of the upper class for the President as a "traitor to his class," capitalists largely initiated the very class war they imputed to Roosevelt and the left.

But where was the class enemy? The forces of labor, liberalism, and the left in 1933 and 1934 resembled more a guerrilla army living off the land than the solid ranks of the proletarian masses. For a half-century or more, labor and other groups—most dramatically the Knights of Labor in the 1880s—had made sporadic efforts to unite workers, skilled and unskilled, in a broad and durable radical movement. All had failed. A national organization mainly of craft unions, the American Federation of Labor, had come to dominate the labor field under the leadership of Samuel Gompers, apostle of business unionism. During the "business decade" of the 1920s the AFL had declined in membership and influence. During the "Hoover depression" the Federation had declined even further. No other national labor or left-wing organization yet challenged it. No political party had arisen to unite workers and farmers politically since Robert La Follette's short-lived Progressive party of 1924.

A rash of strikes had broken out across the nation with the first flush of prosperity in 1933. As union organizers exploited NRA's Section 7(a) and the slightly tighter labor market, workers flocked into the big AFL organizations—into Lewis's United Mine Workers, into Sidney Hillman's Amalgamated Clothing Workers, into David Dubinsky's International Ladies' Garment Workers' Union, into the United Textile Workers of America, and to a lesser degree into the hundreds of craft unions of carpenters, plumbers, electricians, bricklayers, and other skilled workers. And with more organization—and with more employers' counterattacks against organization—came more waves of walkouts during 1934. Some strikes failed in their objectives, some succeeded—but one in particular served to arouse the fears of upper and middle classes alike. This was the San Francisco general strike of late spring 1934.

In no other city were the workers historically more militant, the employers more anti-union, and the newspaper owners—Hearst, the Knowlands—more reactionary than in the city by the Golden Gate. Few workers had sharper grievances than the longshoremen over the way the shipping companies ran the daily shape-up. Men gathered in bleak hiring halls along the Embarcadero at six in the morning, hoping to catch the eye of the dispatcher for a day's work. This functionary could choose one man because he was a good worker, or was a cousin, or would slip him a five-spot, and send another man back into the street because he was "unreliable." Longshoremen despised this "slave mart," for even if chosen they remained slaves—slaves to the hook that inexorably plunged into the cargo hold and "must never hang," that is, must never dangle idly for even a few moments.

Enflamed by this issue, the San Francisco conflict followed the classic path of escalation in the spring of 1934. The International Longshoremen's Association demanded union recognition under the NRA; the shipping companies rejected the demand; the longshoremen struck on the Embarcadero; the companies hired strikebreakers, boarding them luxuriously on vessels; strikers hunted down scabs, kicking in their teeth or breaking their legs over a curb. Then the battle widened as the Teamsters and other unions struck in support of the longshoremen, the bosses unified their ranks through their Industrial Association of industrial, banking, railroad, and shipping interests, and more radical union leaders gained influence. Foremost of these was an intense, wiry immigrant from Australia named Harry Bridges, whose determination to win justice for labor and cynicism about ways and means had both been strengthened in the years he had spent as sailor and longshoreman.

Violence erupted when the employers sent trucks full of strikebreakers through picket lines; strikers let fly with bricks and spikes, police responded with billy sticks, tear gas, and bullets. San Francisco became a sprawling, shifting battlefield as thousands more strikers and sympathizers converged on the scene. Two men died on "Bloody Thursday"; scores, perhaps hundreds, were hurt. Now a general strike was imminent, as more and more unions fell into line.

The threat of a general strike—the nation had experienced perhaps two in its entire history—touched off widespread hysteria. The press warned of revolution and the Red Menace; rumors circulated about an imminent communist invasion of the Bay area; vigilantes smashed union offices; the mayor swore in several hundred deputy policemen; the governor called out the National Guard; Bridges and his men hung tough. Would the nation's armed forces also be necessary? Officials turned to the Commander-in-Chief. But Roosevelt was not at his White House GHQ. He was in fact cruising Pacific waters on the USS *Houston*. "Everybody demanded that I sail into San Francisco Bay," the President said later, "all flags flying and guns double shotted, and end the strike. They went completely off the handle."

One person who had not gone off the handle was Frances Perkins. Controlling in Washington much of the communications with the President, the Secretary of Labor and her aides played down the gravity of the crisis in messages to the cruiser. She then helped arrange for a series of arbitration efforts that produced settlements by the fall. In the give-and-take of the new agreements one item stood out: the ILA alone now had the power to name the dispatcher. Despite his communist connections and rhetoric, Harry Bridges emerged as a hero of waterfront labor. But Frances Perkins, resolute and discerning under the most intense pressures, was the true heroine of deescalation.

Class war had been raging in Minneapolis in the same weeks that violence swept San Francisco. The broad pattern was much the same: employers traditionally dead set against unionization and especially the union shop; workers suffering from unemployment and low wages in the city's great railroad, timber, iron ore, farm, and transportation industries, now battered by depression; probably the nation's most militant workers' leadership, headed by Ray Dunne. He had five brothers, all brought up as Roman Catholics, all unionists, several of them leftists of various hues. The escalation too followed the familiar pattern: organization of workers—in this case truck drivers—under the spur of 7(a); categorical rejection by employers of the closed shop because they could never bargain away the "workers' liberties"; elaborate preparations on both sides for a showdown; an incident; bloody skirmishes between police with clubs and pickets with baseball bats; a truce; new tension; then "Bloody Friday"—July 20, 1934— as police with shotguns killed two strikers and left scores of others with wounds in their backsides.

Both sides had sought this showdown, but it settled nothing. As tension mounted again Governor Floyd Olson, onetime Wobbly and longtime farm-labor progressive, called in the National Guard and with fine impartiality raided first the union headquarters and then the anti-union Citizens Alliance. Both sides turned to Roosevelt, but he would not intervene— publicly. Privately he put pressure on the employers through Jesse Jones, who used as leverage the RFC's power to give or withhold credit to Minneapolis's beleaguered banks and businesses. Attacked on their weakest flank, the employers finally agreed to representation elections for the workers and to other concessions. The agreement left the Dunne brothers with a notable victory and also in the same kind of theoretical quandary that confronted Harry Bridges at the end: How could the State—which in the Marxist view of capitalism must of necessity reflect the interests of the ruling classes—have come ultimately to the aid of the workers? And in this case through that embodiment of Texas wealth, enterprise, and individualism, Jesse Jones?

Where union organization was weak, however, business control of the State was far more naked. Such was the case with textile workers, especially in the South. Embittered over cruelly low wages and long hours, and over the body-racking stretch-out that tied machine tenders to heavier workloads, cotton workers struck in nine states from Maine to Georgia. Over 350,000 workers walked off the job or stayed home. "The 1934 general strike in the textile industry," according to Robert R. R. Brooks, "was unquestionably the greatest single industrial conflict in the history of American organized labor"—and it struck concomitant fear among employers. In mill towns across the South they fought back through sheriff's deputies, the National Guard, espionage, and terrorism, and the strikers suffered hundreds of casualties. In North Carolina, Roosevelt's old boss Josephus Daniels wrote him that in almost every instance "the troops might as well have been under the direction of the mill owners."

In the North, Rhode Island governor Theodore Green called in troops, in part because he saw the strike as virtually a communist revolt. Workers were shot down in Saylesville and Warren. The governor, nearly beside himself, called on the President to prevent communists and outlaws from "destroying cities" and marching on the statehouse. After checking with the FBI, the President took no such action. But on the other hand he gave the textile workers little help, and the big strike collapsed. Labor failed also in other big industries: steel, automobiles, tires.

Workers were facing once again a hard truth—unorganized, they were almost impotent economically and politically. This reality also confronted poorer Americans who lived on the land. Farmers who owned their own spreads in the Midwest and Northeast acted through the big farm associations like the Grange and the American Farm Bureau Federation. But sharecroppers in the South and farm workers in the West and elsewhere lacked organizational muscle. And they were suffering.

"Sharecropping, once the backbone of the South's agricultural empire, is rapidly giving way to an even more vicious system of labor extraction," Erskine Caldwell wrote in the mid-thirties. "The new style is driving the sharecropper away from the fertile land, away from schools for his children, away from contact with civilization. The sharecropper of yesterday is the wage worker of today, the man who peddles his brawn and muscle for twenty-five and thirty cents a day, and who is lucky if he works one day a week during the winter months, and still luckier if he can collect it in cash instead of in corn meal or old clothes."

The AAA had aroused the hopes and expectations of sharecroppers too, but little of Washington's money trickled down to them. Some whites and blacks, working together, formed the Southern Tenant Farmers' Union under local and outside—mainly Socialist party—leadership, only to be met with threats from farm owners, vigilantes with whips and loaded shotguns, sheriffs with arrest orders. An Arkansas preacher told a *New York Times* reporter: "It would have been better to have a few no-account, shiftless people killed at the start than to have all this fuss raised up." The federal government was attacked for stirring up "niggers" to think that they would be given forty acres. To some observers blacks were still in a condition of slavery—but so were many whites.

Even more wretched than the sharecroppers were the itinerant farm workers, who had no land or place to call their own and existed in a succession of shanties and hovels, many of them lacking running water, sanitation, or even window screens. Many of these farm workers were former sharecroppers who had made their way north or west to join Arkies from Arkansas and Okies from dust-ridden Oklahoma in a vast army of wanderers. They had been infected by New Deal hopes and promises, as had their brothers and sisters in the East. In the summer of 1933 tobacco workers in the Connecticut Valley rose in indignation over their meager wages, as did cranberry pickers in the bogs of Cape Cod and citrus fruit pickers in Florida. Next year onion diggers in southern Appalachia, farm and cannery workers in New Jersey, pecan shellers in the San Antonio area, and hosts of other farm workers struck over wages and other issues. This wave of protest culminated in the spacious farmlands of California's Imperial Valley.

The lettuce and fruit-and-vegetable workers of California not only ran the bloody gamut that had now become endemic—terrorism, vigilantes, false arrests, kidnappings, clubs, shotguns, invocation of the red menace, calling in of the troops. In California the whole union effort was savaged— organization meetings, peaceful travel by organizers, union headquarters themselves. Employer intransigence played directly into the hands of the militant union leaders, many of whom were communists. The strikes in the Imperial Valley, in Irving Bernstein's judgment, were less a labor dispute than a "proto-Fascist offensive" by the growers and shippers and business-dominated local officials. When the southern California branch of the American Civil Liberties Union, seeing a direct challenge to the constitutional rights of American citizens, conducted a "Good Will" tour of the valley, the group was surrounded by an angry mob in Brawley and sent back to Los Angeles.

*   *   *

America in 1934 was rife with upper-class hostility toward the poor. Was there to be class war? The vast majority of Americans in 1934, even those in deepest want, would have answered no. Most would have understood neither the question nor the very notion of class war. They thought in terms of their immediate boss or foreman, the bank that held their mortgage, the men who had hired them to dig potatoes or pick fruit, the minister they listened to on Sunday, their union leader if they had one. Most did not see themselves as belonging to a class. They simply knew where they stood in the distribution of food, shelter, and clothing.

Two sets of Americans, however, did understand the idea of class war, and in varying degrees expected it. American capitalists, speaking through the Liberty League, increasingly warned of the Red Menace at home and abroad, of agitators, Moscow-trained or homegrown, subverting republican institutions, of a climactic attack of a proletariat of some kind against individual liberty and free enterprise. In general, though, capitalist action was more telling than capitalist oratory. In their refusal to recognize unions of the workers' own choosing, their resistance to labor demands, their ready use of scabs, stool pigeons, police, sheriff's deputies, and ultimately the National Guard, employers—whether great industrialists in Detroit

and Pittsburgh or little operators of apple orchards—tended to foment the
very class feeling, if not the class consciousness, that they deplored.

If some capitalists practiced class conflict without preaching it, some
anticapitalists preached the class struggle without practicing it. Forced to
pitch their appeals to an enormous range of groups and situations—from
Manhattan garment workers to Pittsburgh steelworkers to southern tenant
farmers to Texas pecan pickers to California longshoremen—communists
and other left radicals adapted their tactics to local possibilities. Even so,
they were still banking on the doctrine that in the long run the bleak and
needful conditions of existence for millions of workers and farmers would
draw them inexorably into class attitudes and class politics.

But how long the long run? Even by their own doctrine, the prologue
to class war in America was not being written during the early New Deal.
That doctrine assumed not only the objective conditions for lower-class
solidarity but a sharpening consciousness of deprivation and need. Such
consciousness could not develop spontaneously but required a heightened
sense of conflict with social and economic elites. Such a sense of class
conflict required in turn, as Lenin had practiced and preached, the kind of
transcending and transforming leadership that could lift people out of
their parochial day-to-day concerns to a vision of a better future in a new
society. Radicals needed to persuade the working class that it had only two
alternatives—staying with the "capitalistic-liberal-bourgeois-neofascist coalition presently running America," as the jargon had it, or joining a
radical movement or party dedicated to overthrowing the system and all
its evils. There was no choice in between.

American socialists, fundamentally pluralist, rejected this harsh class
division. But some citizens endorsed it. During the early New Deal an
eighteen-year-old youth on relief wrote a poem called "Prayer of Bitter
Men":

> We are the men who ride the swaying freights,
> We are the men whom Life has beaten down,
> Leaving for Death nought but the final pain
> Of degradation. Men who stand in line
> An hour for a bowl of watered soup,
> Grudgingly given, savagely received.
> We are the Ishmaels, outcasts of the earth,
> Who shrink before the sordidness of Life
> And cringe before the filthiness of Death.
> Will there not come a great, a glittering Man,

A radiant leader with a heavier sword
To crush to earth the enemies who crush
Those who seek food and freedom on the roads?
We care not if Thy flag be white or red,
Come, ruthless Savior, messenger of God,
Lenin or Christ, we follow Thy bright sword.

"LENIN OR CHRIST"—OR A PATH BETWEEN?

Heightening the class consciousness of the masses, sharpening their sense of conflict with the capitalist elites, providing militant cadres to lead these great efforts—all this lay at the very heart of the Communist strategy in the United States. Under the eyes of Lenin himself, the Communist International in 1920 had proclaimed its aim "to fight by all available means, including armed struggle, for the overthrow of the international bourgeoisie." In 1928, four years after Lenin's death, the Sixth World Congress had called on communists everywhere to smash capitalism, if necessary by force. As always, Communist leaders in the United States danced to the international party tune.

On the eve of the 1930s the Communist party in the United States listed around ten thousand members, many of them in the needle and building trades or jobless, with relatively few in basic industries like steel. The membership included only a scattering of blacks, farmers, and working women. The communist movement was broader than the party. Communist foreign-language newspapers had a readership of perhaps 200,000, though the circulation of the English-language *Daily Worker* was only a small fraction of this number. Through trade union, "Women's Work," Negro, and other apparatuses party members penetrated many other organizations. The movement had hosts of sympathizers, including a sprinkling of the very rich.

The great depression should have been a boon to American communism. At last the mightiest industrial nation of them all appeared to be succumbing to the historical inevitability of boom and bust, working-class misery, and proletarian revolution. Party membership, indeed, almost doubled by the end of 1932. But then it shrank by more than three thousand during the next six months. What was wrong? Despite its much touted and feared internal discipline, the American Communist party was so rent with factionalism that Stalin himself dressed down its leaders in Moscow. Even more, the great mass of American workers, stirred though they might be by specific Communist charges and promises, were cool toward left-wing ideologies in general, communist dogma in particular, and an American Communist party that—as they correctly perceived—was always under the overt or covert control of the Kremlin. But these had long been obstacles for the Communists. How now to sharpen class consciousness under the continuing depression? The answer in the early New Deal years appeared to be to redouble the Communists' tactic of the "united front from below"—the strategy of co-opting other organizations not by deals with their leaders (the "united front from above") but by forging links with rank-and-file memberships and involving them in the communist movement. By the beginning of 1935 Communist leader Earl Browder—as aggressive in combat as he was bourgeois in appearance—could claim a mass following of over half a million, though signed-up members numbered around 30,000.

The Communists wooed peace lovers and anti-Nazis with the American League Against War and Fascism, young people with the American Youth Congress, artists and authors with the American Writers' Congress. But the main target was the working class—factory hands, farm laborers, semi-skilled and some skilled workers. Here the vaunted leadership skills of the Communists failed them. In the late 1920s, the party had tried to set up separate "red unions" to draw workers from established ones, but these failed miserably. They were quietly liquidated during 1934 and early 1935, while the leadership lamely called for organizing separately *and* at the same time infiltrating the merely "reformist" unions, working, for instance, "among the A.F. of L. workers wherever they are organized." This stratagem failed too, for penetrating and dominating the Federation was like invading and capturing a guerrilla army in a swampland; Communists did eventually manage to establish footholds in key industrial unions.

Determined never to be outflanked on the left, the American Communists could not ignore a competing force on their immediate right—the Socialist party. American socialists could look back to their days of glory—to the vibrant leadership of Eugene Debs, to the stunning election results of 1912, when hundreds of socialists were elected to state legislatures and city councils, to the 885,000 votes Norman Thomas won twenty years later. They could boast of able and experienced leadership, especially that of Thomas himself, the benign visionary and eloquent Presbyterian, product of both Princeton and East Harlem slums. "His humane and appealing version of Socialism," Arthur M. Schlesinger, Jr., noted, won "many disciples in the churches and on the campuses: where Debs had Americanized Socialism for the working class, Thomas Americanized it for the middle class."

But the socialists, like the communists and most other radical movements, were divided, and at a time when a united effort was most needed.

Seasoned but defanged older leaders jousted with young "Militants" whose clenched-fist salutes and socialist-left views appeared to some old-timers as smacking of communism. Young, college-educated socialists with middle-class backgrounds wanted to move more vigorously toward more radical goals than did the old guard, with its working-class and immigrant origins. Militants also fought with Militants. Socialist comrades battled over hard questions: how closely should they work with the labor movement, itself divided; should the party preach revolution or evolution, class war or class harmony; should socialists fight the New Deal or invade and reform it; how, specifically, could a radical, egalitarian socialist movement work with a conservative, craft-union-dominated AFL? Thomas, himself more sympathetic to the radical Militant wing, tried to hold the movement together.

As reaction and fascism mobilized in Europe against a divided left, Thomas also tried to make peace with the Communists, but too many hatreds, ancient and current, stood in the way. Early in 1934 New York Socialists and unionists called a mass meeting in Madison Square Garden to protest the murderous suppression of Austrian Social Democrats by the clerical-fascist Dollfuss regime. Determined to take over the meeting from the "social fascists," hundreds of communists broke into the Garden, drowned out David Dubinsky and other speakers, and tried to take over the podium. The meeting broke up in a melee of fistfights, bottle-throwing, and knifings. He was now convinced, Thomas wrote his fellow civil libertarian and friend Roger Baldwin, "that a united front with Communists is impossible." But both sides went back to speaking to each other. They had to. In the Archey Road, Finley Peter Dunne's philosophizing barkeep Mr. Dooley had observed, "when a man and a woman found they simply couldn't go on living together, they went on livin' together." The two movements were bound to each other, if only out of shared political frustration and a common capitalist enemy.

Both groups had failed to provide leadership to the great mass of industrial and farm workers. A new, far more dynamic leadership was already emerging out of the industrial grass roots of the nation. This leadership, bursting through the old confining structures of craft fiefdom and business unionism, moved American labor into the new era of corporate capitalism and shaped the labor movement for decades to come. It was leadership committed to a simple but bold idea—industrial unionism.

The American Federation of Labor embraced industrial unions, such as the Mine Workers, as well as craft unions, but its dominant ideas and institutions were still vintage Gompers—limited political action; ad hoc, day-to-day tactics; fear even of benevolent government; the granting of exclusive territories to the big national unions that comprised the AFL; organization of workers on the basis of occupations and skills rather than whole industries, such as auto or steel. Suddenly, in late 1933 and in 1934, the Federation had a bonanza on its hands—hundreds of thousands of less skilled workers, historically the hardest to awaken but now, in the heady climate of the New Deal, *eager* to join unions in their plants or industries. How to exploit this bonanza, which the Federation had not earned but which had sprung out of partial recovery, Roosevelt's inspirational leadership, NRA's Section 7(a), and heightened hopes and expectations?

The Federation's answer was to dump the unorganized into "federal unions"—big catchall bodies, weak and short-lived—until these workers could be parceled out to existing unions and their locals. But now, amid the organizing fever of 1934, something was different. Taking on a life of their own, the federal unions generated their own leaders, who began insisting that the AFL authorize them to form broad-based industrial unions. Youthful, defiant, impatient, as Irving Bernstein has described them, those leaders knew that only workers united industry by industry, plant by plant, could prevail against unified corporate elites. They were supported, rather surprisingly, by such publications as *Fortune* and the *Literary Digest,* such notables as Walter Lippmann and General Johnson.

But the decision would be made within the AFL, and the Federation was sorely divided. On one side of the issue sat the chiefs of the AFL's great national craft unions, men like John Frey of the Metal Trades, obsessively protective of his machinists' craft enclaves; William "Big Bill" Hutcheson, the big, burly, rough-spoken head of the Carpenters; Dan Tobin, the smooth, seasoned boss of the Teamsters. Hutcheson, an active Republican who had supported Hoover in 1932, and Tobin, an ally of Roosevelt's, personified the vaunted "nonpartisanship" of the Federation. In the dead center of the contestants sat William Green, cautious, deliberate, his rounded face and form seemingly smoothed out by years of conciliation and compromise.

On the left, preaching industrial unionism, were such leaders as George L. Berry, the veteran head of the pressmen, and two men who had emerged out of the tumultuous immigrant world of New York City, David Dubinsky of the International Ladies' Garment Workers' Union and Sidney Hillman of the Amalgamated Clothing Workers. No one doubted who was their chieftain—John L. Lewis. With his huge miner's torso, his shaggy eyebrows beneath a shock of hair, his face fixed in an almost perpetual scowl, his deep rumbling voice, he was a formidable figure both to mine owners and to his AFL rivals.

And so the argument raged at numberless council and committee meet-

ings between the November 1934 and October 1935 conventions of the
Federation. The craft unionists evoked ancient dogma about labor unity
and settled arrangements, raised the bogey of "dual unionism," and de-
precated mass-production workers as fair-weather members who would
join the new union for higher wages and then pull out. Lewis & Co. urged
that above all the Federation must take in the millions clamoring at its
gates and organize them in mighty locals that could challenge General
Motors and Ford and U.S. Steel. Neither side was monolithic; Green tried
conciliation, and men like Dubinsky sought to restrain Lewis from moving
too far ahead of his small group. In this fluid situation there was only one
constant: the old guard had the votes.

One short hard punch dramatized the final rupture. Hour after hour
delegates to the 1935 AFL convention in Atlantic City had debated a
minority report in favor of industrial unionism. Finally Lewis took the
floor. "The labor movement," he said, "is organized upon a principle that
the strong shall help the weak." Hence it was morally wrong for craft
unions that stood on their own feet "like mighty oaks"not to help weak
unions exposed to "the lightning and the gale." If they rejected the minority report, "high wassail" would prevail at the banquet tables of the mighty.
The convention voted it down. Two days later Lewis, trying to revive the
issue, ran into Hutcheson's parliamentary objection. "Small potatoes,"
Lewis shouted, and Hutcheson responded in kind. As Lewis moved back
to his seat he and Hutcheson had another exchange. Hearing the word
"bastard," Lewis sent Hutcheson to the floor with that one punch. He then
straightened his collar and tie, relit his cigar, and sauntered casually to the
podium.

"You shouldn't have done that, John," said President Green. "He called
me a foul name," said Lewis. "Oh," said Green, "I didn't know that."

Three weeks later Lewis, Hillman, Dubinsky, and others set up a Committee for Industrial Organization, with Lewis as chairman. Despite the
group's promises to work within the Federation, labor was now headed
toward civil war, as the craft unionists took an increasingly adamant stand,
and pressure from aroused grass-roots leaders pushed Lewis & Co. toward
a separate organization. Desperately Green tried to mediate. Not only had
he risen through an industrial union, the Miners, but he had written eloquently in favor of industrial unionism as concentrating the strength of
skilled and unskilled. Lewis played on this past in a letter to Green:

"Why not return to your father's house? You will be welcome. If you care
to dissociate yourself from your present position, the Committee for Industrial Organization will be happy to make you its Chairman in my stead."
"I am in my father's house," Green replied. "It is my firm purpose to

remain there." In more than thirty years in the labor movement, he added pointedly, "I have never aligned myself with any . . . dual movement."

* * *

Consciously or not, American communists, socialists, and trade unionists were acting in the spirit of the great working-class movements that had emerged during the industrial revolution. Millions of Americans, however, had grown up in another, more middle-class tradition that rivaled working-class ideology in its intellectual and moral power and its social impact. This was the social-reform movement within the three great Western religions, stemming from the emphasis on collective morality, philanthropy, and responsibility in Judaism; from reformism, abolitionism, and the missionary spirit—including missions to the urban poor—in the Protestant churches; from the heightened Roman Catholic concern with social justice.

This last was not least. As the miseries of the factory system became more acute and widespread during the nineteenth century, Catholics had turned back to the teachings of Thomas Aquinas of six hundred years before—especially his definition of a just order that balances social duties with individual rights—and to other thinkers and actors in the Thomist tradition. These ideas came to a dramatic focus in 1891 with Pope Leo XIII's encyclical *Rerum novarum,* or *On the Condition of the Working Class.* While broadly concerned with maintaining an ordered and equitable society under the tutelage of the Church, Leo's call for social action to relieve poverty was a trumpet blast for hundreds of young priests who every day, in their parishes, confronted the human wreckage left behind by the march of industry.

In the industrial city of Toronto at the end of the century existed an order, the Basilian Fathers, that was deeply stirred by the Catholic movement for social justice. To a school run by this order there came a twelve-year-old boy escorted by his parents, a seamstress and a church sexton. The boy's mother, it was said, on giving birth had murmured a prayer: "A girl—for the—convent," or if a boy, "please, God—a priest." Brought up by these pious parents, the boy did become a priest, after starring at school as scholar and athlete. Before his proud mother in the front pew he celebrated his first mass in the summer of 1916. His name was Charles E. Coughlin.

There seemed nothing remarkable about this young priest as he went about his parish duties during the next few years—except for two things. One was his persuasive, almost enticing voice, warm, resonant, portentous. The other was his willingness to use that newfangled device, the radio. He had hardly settled into his final parish in Royal Oak, twelve miles north of downtown Detroit, when he began building a new church, using up-to-date fund-raising devices, and arranging with a local radio station to offer sermons over the air in order to attract new parishioners. Soon that voice—adorned with a bit of an Irish brogue and charged with such "manly, heart-warming, confidential intimacy, such emotional and ingratiating charm," in Wallace Stegner's words, as to be one of the "great speaking voices of the twentieth century"—was attracting listeners by the thousands, then by the tens of thousands, and finally by the millions.

Success did not soon spoil Charles Coughlin—or at least cause him to forget who he was and where he was. He was a priest under the authority of a bishop to whom he gave unceasing and proper obeisance, receiving in turn the protection—against politicians, the public, even others in the hierarchy—that only a bishop could provide. And he was a priest in the Detroit area, a social wilderness even before the depression and an economic wasteland after it struck. Sickened by the poverty and desperation all around him—Detroit had the highest jobless rate of any major city by April 1930—the young priest struck directly at the foundation of the problem: unbridled capitalism. It was not worth saving, he charged; "in fact it is a detriment to civilization." Often he coupled these attacks with denunciations of communism, socialism, divorce, birth control, Prohibition.

Plenty of people were attacking capitalism by this time; Coughlin stood out for his audacity. He named names: Herbert Hoover, the Rothschilds, the Dillon-Reads, the "Four Horsemen of the Apocalypse"—Morgan, Mellon, Mills, and Meyer. He lambasted such Catholic heroes as Al Smith for "selling out" to Morgan and other capitalists, such Catholic dignitaries as William Cardinal O'Connell for his notorious "silence on social justice." By 1934 Coughlin was simply a phenomenon, with a steady weekly audience of at least ten million, scores of assistants to handle the million letters that might come in after a major speech, and a magnificent new church of his own next to a 150-foot stone tower in which he had his office.

One man the young priest revered, aside from his bishop—Franklin D. Roosevelt. He had had some contact with the New York governor before and during the 1932 campaign, and had even worked quietly for him at the convention; he could not openly endorse Roosevelt but made up for this with ferocious attacks on Hoover. After the Hundred Days, however, his adulation became public, and almost total. It was "Roosevelt or Ruin." The New Deal was "Christ's Deal." Coughlin wrote fulsome letters to the President, praising FDR as magnificent, fearless, a natural-born artist with the radio. He adjured his followers to support the President, to love him. Even more, he began to insinuate himself into the extended White House. He referred to the President as the "boss"; called staff members by their first names; offered free advice. On their part, friends of the Administration such as Joseph Kennedy and Frank Murphy held Coughlin's hand to keep him on board.

As Roosevelt's popularity waxed, so did Coughlin's. His mail, his audience, his unsolicited donations from listeners rose to new highs. Earlier Coughlin had demonstrated his power when CBS, the radio network over which he spoke, asked him to water down his fiery speeches. CBS retreated after Coughlin indignantly appealed to his listeners. When CBS later refused to renew his contract, the "Radio Priest" simply organized his own network. Thereafter he could overcome complaints from local radio stations by threatening to take his orations—and his audiences—elsewhere. And his audiences were broadening as he reached out beyond the desperately needful people of industrial Michigan to members of the lower-middle and middle-middle classes—to persons who had gained and were clinging to some bourgeois respectability, to skilled craft workers, even to farmers.

By 1934 Coughlin appeared unassailable, for his power lay in his own personal constituency—his audience. For him the power was the medium that linked him to his followers. But his followers had power over him too. His listeners were leading him even while he was leading them. As Coughlin lauded Roosevelt and denounced the "plutocrats," he aroused his listeners' hopes and hatreds to fever pitch. Soon the priest began to have policy differences with the President; Coughlin's central concern was with money and its control, which he wanted shifted from the bankers to the government, while Roosevelt had broader legislative concerns. But the widening gap was both political and psychological; Coughlin was now on a separate trajectory from the President's, and his deep-seated ideological differences with FDR were bound to mount under electoral pressures.

Late in 1934 Coughlin announced his plan to form a new association, the National Union for Social Justice, as "an articulate, organized lobby of the people." Thus he would mobilize his audience for action. There would be card files, membership lists, local meetings. But no one doubted the nature of the symbol and the instrument of the new organization. It was the microphone.

The microphone gave another commanding figure a strong grip on the imagination of the American people during the early 1930s. Huey Long was one of the first politicians to use radio, as far back as the mid-1920s, but the power of his visual impact—his rumpled hair, loosened collar, and violent gestures—did not carry through the medium, and his sharp, insistent voice contrasted with Coughlin's smooth and sonorous delivery. As he reached for a national audience in the early 1930s, however, Long learned to moderate his voice and switch easily back and forth between "Luziana corn pone" for home audiences and a clear and resonant style for the networks. By 1935 his political speeches over NBC were reaching huge audiences, exceeded only by those of Coughlin and Roosevelt.

What Long said, as much as how he said it, was arresting. Although his policy positions shifted somewhat over the years, his central, unvarying pitch was that Roosevelt, Morgan, and the rest had seized control of the nation's riches. The only solution was his Share Our Wealth plan. He offered "facts and figures." Two percent of the people owned 60 percent of the wealth, he contended. It was as though all Americans had been invited to a great barbecue. "God called: 'Come to my feast.'" But the big capitalists "stepped up and took enough for 120,000,000 people and left only enough for 5,000,000 for all the other 125,000,000 to eat. And so many millions must go hungry and without these good things God gave us unless we call on them to put some of it back."

How put it back? Long proposed that the government confiscate all inheritances of more than $1 million, take in income tax any and all money a person made over $1 million in a year, and heavily tax existing wealth. Then would come the sharing. The government would guarantee every needy family a minimum income of $2000–$3000 a year. Even better, each such family would be granted a basic "household estate" of $5000, "enough for a home, an automobile, a radio," and other goods. Government would also support stepped-up aid to farmers, pensions for the aged, education for the young, public works, shorter working hours. Long left many of the details vague and the complexities unaddressed, but he promised to call in "some great minds" to help him.

Such proposals created an uproar in the press, even in the New Deal atmosphere. All this was demagogic pandering at its worst, cried conservative editors. Long himself, as H. L. Mencken had perceived earlier, was "simply a backwoods demagogue of the oldest and most familiar model— impudent, blackguardly, and infinitely prehensile." It was easy for economists to punch holes in his economic program; at the very least, the available money, no matter how drastically squeezed out of the rich, would not have met the human needs he dramatized. Still, however simplistic the plan, it was not "an attempt to divert attention away from real problems; it did not focus resentment on irrelevant scapegoats or phony villains," Alan Brinkley concluded. "It pointed, instead, to an issue of genuine importance; for the concentration of wealth was, even if not in precisely the form Long described it, a fundamental dilemma of the American economy." It was also a fundamental moral dilemma of American democracy.

Long expected the uproar, he welcomed it, he thrived on it. He was a child of conflict, born in a state almost schizoid in its division between the Catholic, French Cajun, and mercantile cultures of southern Louisiana and the Protestant, lumber, oil, small-farm cultures upstate, born in the northern poor-white region that had been seared by populist and other challenges to the old white power structure. As a child he had embodied conflict, fighting—though not physically if he could help it—with his brothers and playmates, infuriating his teachers and other elders with his impudent questions, later harshly attacking anyone who stood in the way of his political ambition. His pugnacity and tireless campaigning paid off early. In 1918, at the age of twenty-five, he was elected the youngest member ever of the state's Railroad Commission. He then spent ten years stumping up and down the state, and in 1928 won the governorship.

He looked the part of the fighter as he castigated his enemies, his rubbery features tightening in righteous wrath, hair streaming down on his face, arms pumping, voice driving and piercing. His tactics as governor provoked his foes to fight back through investigations, the courts, an impeachment effort, appeals to Washington, but with little success. Long's power stemmed more and more from practical action. Out of his contempt for the old guard, the wide exposure to suffering people he had gained as a door-to-door salesman, and the snubs he was handed by the socially privileged of his adopted city of Shreveport came a lifelong concern for the poor that as governor he converted into tangible results. In a state crying for expanded public services, he and his allies immensely enlarged the Louisiana highway system, built bridges, improved public health services, provided schoolchildren with free textbooks, upgraded the school system in general and Louisiana State University very much in particular.

A "bad Huey" appeared to struggle with a "good Huey"—his ruthless power-seeking versus his concern for people, his challenge to the establishment that included an unconstitutional effort to tax advertising in large newspapers, his attack on privilege that left out solid measures such as child-labor laws, minimum-wage laws, old-age insurance. Still, by the early 1930s the "Kingfish," as he now liked to be called, had clamped so firm a grip on Louisiana politics that he could agitate on the national stage as a United States senator. This brought him into political collusion and then collision with Roosevelt.

The collusion was strictly practical. When the Roosevelt forces at the 1932 Democratic convention supported the seating of Long's delegation, the senator worked to keep Louisiana and other southern delegates in line for the New York governor. The two men had never liked each other. Long considered Roosevelt a political dilettante; after Montana senator Burton Wheeler, along with George Norris, had helped bring him around to the governor, Long told Wheeler, "I didn't like your son of a bitch," but would support him. Roosevelt, for his part, viewed the Louisiana senator as one more strident voice that could be kept in harmony by judicious combinations of evasion, flattery, and deals. But behind practicalities and personalities lay an ideological conflict that Roosevelt had not yet fully grasped. Long was determined to carry his populist and egalitarian ideas into the national arena, while the President was still engaged in brokerage. Meanwhile, the Kingfish would maintain his grip on his Louisiana base, using his own judicious combination of force, fraud, and favors.

The collision was not long in coming. The Hundred Days electrified the country but turned off Huey Long. He opposed the Economy Act, anti-inflation efforts, the Administration's rejection of the veterans' bonus payment, and above all the NRA. On a visit to Roosevelt, the Kingfish played the boor, keeping his straw hat on, or whipping it off to tap the President on the knee or elbow; but he could not puncture FDR's genial façade. "What the hell is the use of coming down to see this fellow," he muttered on leaving the White House, "I can't win any decision over him." About ready to break away from Long, the Administration cut off patronage and reopened a suspended probe of Louisiana shenanigans. Long compared Hoover to a hoot owl and Roosevelt to a scrootch owl.

"A hoot owl bangs into the roost and knocks the hen clean off, and catches her while she's falling. But a scrootch owl slips into the roost and scrootches up to the hen and talks softly to her. And the hen just falls in love with him, and the first thing you know, *there ain't no hen.*"

Long would evade the scrootch owl. Early in 1934 he announced over a radio network his plan for a new national organization, the Share Our Wealth Society, with the slogan "Every Man a King." It would fight for the egalitarian principles the Kingfish had long since proclaimed: heavy taxes on big fortunes and incomes, guaranteed family income, and the rest. Long was now adding a plan for local Share Our Wealth clubs that would blanket the nation. Popular reaction was quick, strong, and sustained. Tens of thousands of letters and applications poured into Long's offices during the succeeding months—so many that Long had to set up a work force that spilled out of his Senate office into extra rooms and even into the corridors. By the end of 1934 his Share Our Wealth movement boasted of having three million members—though observers then and later differed over the extent to which this was a solid following or a "glorified mailing list."

By this time Long had established a communications kingdom of his own, embracing his monthly newspaper, *American Progress;* his autobiography, *Every Man a King;* a huge mailing and "membership" list; and frequent recourse to the NBC radio network. This last was crucial. Ad-libbing freely, using his voice skillfully, attacking his foes unstintingly, quoting the Bible promiscuously, he built up by 1935 one of NBC's biggest audiences.

It was clear that the 1936 election campaign would be dominated by three masters of the radio. The age of electronic political communication was already underway.

THE POLITICS OF TUMULT

On the face of it, Roosevelt seemed to be riding high politically as he entered his midterm in January 1935. He and his party had won a convincing victory in the congressional elections two months before. Many of his New Deal programs were solidly in place. The great mass of people still loved him, many to the point of veneration.

The President, in fact, was headed into a time of troubles, and he may have known this, at least intuitively. While European affairs were relatively quiet for the moment, Hitler had consolidated his power and seemed more threatening and truculent than ever. Not to be outdone, Mussolini was threatening war in Ethiopia over territory on the border of Italian Somaliland. The murder of King Alexander of Yugoslavia by a Croatian terrorist in Marseilles had left people with revived memories of the assassination in Sarajevo twenty years earlier, and its dire consequences. In January the President, a supporter of the World Court, was handed a sharp reminder about the limits of his own power over foreign relations when the Senate vote for membership in the World Court failed of the required two-thirds.

But Roosevelt's main troubles lay at home. Politically he was little daunted by the resurgence of business opposition on the right, because the Liberty League and the rest gave him choice campaign targets. Far more threatening was the mobilization of popular forces behind Long, Coughlin, and the other voices of protest; and probably Roosevelt sensed that the expectations he had aroused in his first two years were rising to new heights and would now sweep back onto the Administration. It is doubtful, though, that the President yet felt intimidated by this prospect; he was an old hand, after all, at operating in the political center against both right and left.

Rather, his main problem during these cold winter weeks was intellectual. This leader who had showed himself such a master of experimentation, improvisation, and tactical maneuver now had to face hard strategic alternatives that embraced policy and program as well as politics. He had still made no final choice between conciliating or at least mollifying business and seriously reforming it, between ordering and rationalizing business in the spirit of the NRA and atomizing or regulating it in the spirit of Louis Brandeis, between balancing the budget and spending heavily to meet acute human needs. Go left or stay in the center? To move right was not an option for the New Deal.

Nor could the President fall back on concerted advice from his staff. Raymond Moley, frustrated by FDR's improvisations, was drifting back to private life; Tugwell saw the New Deal as incomplete; Berle feared that the Administration was disintegrating. Louis Howe, who had kept his boss close to the great constituencies of need that made up the foundation of the Democratic party, lay dying of emphysema during the early months of 1935; he slipped away in mid-April. Even before Howe's death, Eleanor Roosevelt felt that her husband was seeing a narrower range of advisers. Molly Dewson, on the firing line at Democratic party headquarters, was concerned about the President's faltering leadership. To worriers the First Lady gave the President's response: "Please say to everyone who tells you that the President is not giving leadership" that he was working closely with Congress, "but this is a democracy after all, and if he once started insisting on having his own way immediately, we should shortly find ourselves with a dictatorship. . . .

"The ups and downs in people's feelings, particularly on the liberal side, are an old, old story. The liberals always get discouraged when they do not see the measures they are interested in go through immediately. . . .

"Franklin says for Heaven's sake, all you Democratic leaders calm down and feel sure of ultimate success. It will do a lot in satisfying other people."

Western and southern farmers were especially impatient with FDR by 1935. For two years agricultural politics, policy, and administration had epitomized the character of the first New Deal: improvised, experimental, controversial but neither radical nor conservative, basically humane. The Agricultural Adjustment Act had been hammered out during early 1933 amid heavy pressures from farm interests and desperate farmers. These pressures had continued to affect its administration, and the fearsome drought of 1934 had intensified the desperation. Supporters of diverse policies—higher farm prices and inflation in general, the old McNary-Haugen scheme for stimulating farm sales abroad and stabilizing farm prices at home, refinancing of farm debts, raising farm prices by cutting down production—continued to fight for their particular road to agricultural salvation.

Roosevelt's farm effort embraced elements of these and other policies, but the heart of the Agricultural Adjustment Administration program lay in the Domestic Allotment plan. This meant "plowing every third row under" and slaughtering little pigs (so they would not become big hogs and inflate supply). Nothing could have been more shocking to a world with a half-billion or more hungry people, to a nation that measured progress by productivity, to millions of Americans long undernourished, and to the farmers themselves. In Georgia, a cotton planter carefully marked off twenty-five acres to be plowed up and told several tenants that someday soon he would tell them to go to it. A field investigator overheard the tenants' murmured conversation.

"You know," said one, "I ain't never pulled up no cotton stalks befo', and somehow I don't like the idea."

"I been feelin' sorter funeral-like all afternoon," said another. But a third had a happier thought.

"Let's swap work that day; you plow up mine, and I'll plow up yours."

Henry Wallace and his Agriculture Department appeared to face almost insuperable problems. They had to cope with a hundred or so zealots in the farm bloc in Congress who watched their every move. In the Senate they confronted some of the most powerful and prestigious lawmakers, many of them prima donnas. From the old, northern-based Grange on the right to the National Farmers' Holiday Association on the left they were lobbied by some of the most potent farm and commodity groups in the nation, including the well-entrenched American Farm Bureau Federation and the militant Tenant Farmers' Union. Processors, railroad and other transportation interests, farm equipment makers, rural banks, and others stood guard over their turfs. These groups were as quick to unite against a minor perceived threat as they were slow to unite behind a program for farmers as a whole.

Bolstered by Roosevelt's backing and popularity, funds from processing taxes, and inspirited leadership by talented federal administrators, the AAA promulgated its rules, set up its field staffs, issued its millions of checks, and pumped money into the nation's fiscal bloodstream. Yet the AAA paid a price. To get quick results it often had to make peace with legislators, state officials, county farm agents, with the whole panoply of state and regional interests and institutions. Some states had wanted the AAA to be administered through their own departments of agriculture. In Georgia—the President's "adopted state"—the right-wing populist governor, Eugene Talmadge, followed policies almost opposite to those of the New Deal.

Like an old wooden plow worn and splintered by rocky soil, the Agriculture Department, and especially the AAA, was itself cleft by the economic and political ground it worked in. Offices and bureaus dependent on client groups jousted with one another. Old department hands fought with young New Deal activists. Interests inside and outside the department competed for funds. Centralizers debated with Brandeisian decentralizers. Quick-action enthusiasts pleaded with due-process literalists. A major result of these internal conflicts was that the AAA did reasonably well the work that everyone wanted—getting money into the hands of "constituents"—but did not have the grass-roots clout to bring about fundamental change.

One of these conflicts seemed relatively unimportant in itself but triggered a major crisis in the department. Virtually all the New Dealers in Agriculture were intent on getting AAA money into the hands of tenant farmers and sharecroppers as well as planters and landlords. But some feared "unnecessarily" provoking local resistance, especially of dominant white groups in the South. The question of whether the 1934–35 cotton contract required the landlord to keep the same tenants or the same *number* of tenants brought matters to a head. Militant New Dealers feared that the latter interpretation would enable landlords to "hire and fire" tenants at will within their set number. When the AAA's general counsel, Jerome Frank, interpreted the contract to require the retention of tenants, AAA chief Chester Davis sacked him and several of his associates.

*   *   *

This much-publicized "purge" of February 1935 exposed Roosevelt's plight at midterm. His farm laws, improvisations, and experiments had opened a hornet's nest of controversial policies, programs, and personalities that were failing to bring a genuine new deal to hundreds of thousands of tenants, sharecroppers, and farm laborers. Along with the financial and psychological relief he had given millions of people, he had aroused consciousness of the need for change without bringing about fundamental or enduring transformation. Hence he confronted farm groups and constituencies more aroused and hopeful than ever. Poor farmers, however, still lacked the catalytic leadership that could jolt them into effective political action; the question by 1935 was whether they would turn to Franklin Roosevelt or some other leadership between "Lenin and Christ."

The power of leadership at this point was being demonstrated by a most unlikely man and a most unlikely group of dispossessed—the elderly poor and insecure. Dr. Francis Townsend hardly looked the part of the charismatic leader—he was old and ailing and plain and bespectacled, resembling a bit the farmer in Grant Wood's "American Gothic"; he had a monotonous speaking voice, he had little money left over from his medical practice, and now he was jobless. The people he mobilized appeared to be about the least combustible in the nation: elderly, largely nonpolitical, living on farms or in small towns or cities, heavily Protestant, retired on small incomes if any. Hardly materials for a political explosion, certainly, and yet Townsend and his elderly followers became a political phenomenon during Roosevelt's first term. The Townsend cause enrolled at least two million people in some seven thousand clubs across the nation. Reporters groped to understand the movement, but they had only to look at its causes.

Dr. Townsend was addressing a dire need—not only the financial poverty of so many of the elderly but their social and psychological predicament. Part of the human price of industrialization and urbanization, many of these men and women had lost their homes and their savings, or barely held on to them; they had left their children back on the old farm, or lost their jobs through a swift-changing technology. They had become isolated, in Talcott Parsons's view, from "kinship, occupational, and community ties" and hence were ripe for political agitation. They needed help, and Dr. Townsend had a plan, a most wonderful plan: give everyone over sixty federal pensions of $200 a month, with the delectable requirement that the money be spent within the month and thereby bolster the whole economy. A federal sales tax would pay for the scheme. It seemed like the economic equivalent of perpetual motion.

Then there was the doctor himself, who proved to be a master of hype. He liked to tell how he had looked out of his bathroom window one day in Long Beach, California, to see three haggard old women rummaging through garbage cans, how he had burst out into a string of epithets that he wanted God Himself to hear, how he said he would shout "until the whole country hears," and invented the movement on the spot. In fact, it was no sudden revelation. Townsend himself had come to the end of a long road—born in a log cabin in northern Illinois, he had led something of a Horatio Alger life without the Algerian reward. After picking up jobs as ranch hand, farm laborer, mine-mucker, and teacher in the West, he worked his way through medical college and then endured a hard life as a country doctor in South Dakota. Later, as a medical officer treating the Long Beach indigent during the depression, he had ample reason and time to ponder the plight of the elderly and to concoct his plan.

Not especially religious himself, Townsend invested his venture with a powerful evangelical appeal. He proclaimed that his movement would have as mighty an impact as Christianity. At their club meetings Townsendites sang hymns (including a "new" one, "Onward, Townsend soldiers / Marching as to war"), idolized the doctor as a Christ-like, God-given leader, and discussed how best to budget and spend the anticipated $200. Townsend and his top organizers installed ministers as key regional and state directors. Yet he kept the movement centralized, and he adroitly made it seem safe and respectable, as well as transformative, by such devices as labeling his proposed sales tax a "transaction tax."

By January 1935 the Townsend movement towered on the political horizon. The Townsend leadership was not above inflating the number of its clubs and members, and a credulous press often exaggerated the Townsendites' strength; *Time* overstated the number of clubs by at least fivefold. Stanley High, a minister and friend of the Administration, wrote in to the White House that the more he saw of the movement, the more its power impressed him. "It is doing for a certain class of people what—a few years ago—was done by the prohibition movement: giving them a sublimation outlet." And had not the drys actually altered the Constitution of the United States?

In what had long ago been part of the "old Northwest"—Wisconsin, Minnesota, and neighboring areas—other storm clouds were rising, where the hopes and expectations of progressives in all their colorations, independent, liberal, radical, socialistic, had glowed anew with the coming of the New Deal. In Wisconsin, "Fighting Bob" La Follette's dissimilar sons— the cool, thoughtful "young Senator Bob" and the often tempestuous and passionate "Governor Phil"—were united in carrying on their father's radical mission. They had also carried on the progressive tradition of political independence when, in 1934, they trounced both major parties at the Wisconsin polls. Roosevelt at a press conference had opportunistically expressed a preference for Bob La Follette over possible Democratic candidates for senator. What now would be the relationship between the rejuvenated Progressive party of Wisconsin and the New Deal? There was talk of party realignment—but of which party, in what direction? Much would turn on the future direction of FDR's currently faltering New Deal.

The La Follettes worked closely with Minnesota governor Floyd Olson, an even more radical leader. While Phil talked vaguely of a cooperative, nonsocialistic society, Olson on the hustings denounced liberalism, fascism, capitalism, communism with equal gusto. What was he *for?* As governor he had called for public power, insurance for the jobless, a state income tax, and of course mortgage relief. For the nation he preached the gospel of "collective ownership of the means of production and distribution," though he was no Marxist. If his proposals were somewhat fuzzy, the political power he wielded as head of his militant, well-organized Farmer-Labor party was clear and commanding. Olson too talked about a third party for 1936, headed perhaps by Bob La Follette. What about 1940? he was asked. Said Olson: "Maybe by then I won't be radical enough."

It was from the Far West, however, and especially California, that Roosevelt and the nation learned how tumultuous, arousing, colorful, and nutty the politics of protest could be. No one could remember a political leader like Upton Sinclair, winner of the Golden State's Democratic gubernatorial primary in 1934. A talkative, ebullient man then in his mid-fifties, Upton Sinclair had never stopped writing, protesting, and politicking since the kindling days of *The Jungle* and *The Brass Check,* his famous muckraking works. Indignant over the idle land, factories, and people he saw all about him in the early thirties, he concocted a plan that, he proclaimed categorically, would end poverty in California. And it was called just that: End Poverty in California. Under his plan the state would acquire farmland and factories, turn them over to the jobless to grow food and make their own clothes and furniture and shoes, and issue scrip that could be used for the exchange of produce and goods. Always the utopian, Sinclair dreamed of the establishment ultimately of networks of workers' and farmers' villages. It would be the Cooperative Commonwealth.

The killing of Upton Sinclair's dream was testament to the novelist's long avowal of unpopular causes, the ingenuity of California's power elites, and the Machiavellianism of Franklin Roosevelt.

Like other communitarian plans that had been advanced in America for over a century, EPIC was no real threat to corporate property or profit; nevertheless, the business interests of California—backed up by Republican party leaders, Hollywood moguls and movie stars, and a new type of hatchet job by professional public relations experts—portrayed the onetime muckraker as an atheistic, anarchist communist and a believer in free love, telepathy, and vegetarianism to boot. Fake photographs and newsreels showed California being invaded by bums and tramps seeking an end to their own poverty at the expense of the state's taxpayers. All this worked in the mercurial, personality-dominated political environment of the Golden State.

Sinclair had fairly beaten the old Wilsonian politico George Creel in the Democratic primary, but the usual White House endorsement of a Democratic candidate was not forthcoming. He appealed to Roosevelt and had no answer. He appealed to Eleanor Roosevelt, who ordinarily supported the EPIC type of local initiative. Instructed by her husband to "(1) Say nothing and (2) Do nothing," she wrote Sinclair a guarded reply. But FDR was not content to do nothing. He allowed Administration operatives to make a deal with the conservative Republican candidate, Frank Merriam, under which Merriam would proclaim, if he won, that his victory could not have happened without Democratic support and hence was no repudiation of the New Deal. And that was how the Democratic candidate was ditched, to the benefit of a Republican candidate who had come out for "Roosevelt's policies," the Townsend plan, and funny-money schemes.

Upton Sinclair the writer had the last word. Having authored *I, Governor of California and How I Ended Poverty* before his campaign, he now produced *I, Candidate for Governor: And How I Got Licked,* in which he told all. Soon he would be writing his Lanny Budd novels, which apotheosize FDR, the man who had deserted him.

* * *

In the half-century since the fateful year of 1935, historians of the New Deal have puzzled over Roosevelt's alleged "turn to the left." Did he indeed turn to the left—and what was the "left" to which he turned? Was it from the centrist, bipartisan essence of the "First" New Deal to the radical, populist thrust of the "Second"? Was it from government as regulator and atomizer of concentrated economic power to government as planner and coordinator of it? Was it from government as broker and unifier of major interests to government as a vehicle for more social justice and equality? Was the "Second" New Deal, in short, fundamentally more radical than the "First"? And if it was, why did FDR shift, and at the time that he did—the summer of 1935? Was it a result mainly of external forces, political and economic, working on him, or of intellectual and psychological influences working within him, or of some baffling combination of the two?

Surely a shift to the left seemed logical politically. The Democratic gains in the 1934 midterm elections had confirmed the popularity of FDR and his program. The 1934 ferment in farm and factory, the increasingly strident and persuasive voices of Long, Coughlin, and the others, the pressures from New Deal Democrats and liberal Republicans in Congress—all these appeared to set the stage for a White House call for action as the new year opened and a new Congress got underway. But that was not how the President behaved. He was obviously cool to a measure that would have seemed ideal for both policy and political reasons—New York Senator Robert Wagner's bill to guarantee labor's right to organize. His January State of the Union message, moderate in tone and policy recommendation, was hardly a foretaste of the stormy days to come, calling as it did for a "genuine period of good feeling, sustained by a sense of purposeful progress."

One piece in the puzzle is clear. The President's dismay over the defeat of the World Court and his intellectual uncertainty did not quickly pass, in contrast to earlier periods when he had been briefly down in the dumps. Activists who saw the President during the spring of 1935 remarked on his passivity and touchiness, almost as though he were suffering from a physical ailment. "I must say that the President seemed to me to be distinctly dispirited," Ickes noted in his diary late in February. ". . . He looked tired and he seemed to lack fighting vigor or the buoyancy that has always characterized him." Ickes doubted that he could put through even his moderate program.

Was Roosevelt at last stopped, immobilized? Instead of preparing to make a mighty strategic choice between programs, between left and center, between ideologies and strategies, at this point he was picking his way, step by step, amid great pressures, moving a bit right or left as he faced specific problems. This was Roosevelt the fox, not the lion. Balancing and brokering from day to day, he was both capable of dealing with events and vulnerable to them. And then, in the spring of 1935, there occurred a series of acts that altered the political climate. These were actions, not of Roosevelt himself or his friends, but of his adversaries.

At the end of April the United States Chamber of Commerce held its annual conference in Washington. Gone and apparently forgotten were the days when the Chamber, speaking for a cowering business community, had endorsed much of the New Deal and even given the President a rising ovation. Now the nation's business leaders—especially small businessmen who felt distanced from Washington—were ready to counterattack the New Deal. A delegate accused the Administration of trying to "Sovietize the country." The Chamber voted its opposition to much of the New Deal already in place. Thomas J. Watson privately apologized to the President for such unrestrained criticism, and Winthrop Aldrich of the Chase National Bank, Walter Gifford of American Telephone and Telegraph, Myron Taylor of U.S. Steel, and a few other "industrial statesmen" who were now less anti-New Deal than most smaller entrepreneurs paid a placatory visit to the White House, but the President had heard the message from the wards and precincts of conservatism.

Most of FDR's business foes could only protest, but there were other conservatives—conservatives with teeth. These were five men who made up a majority on the bench of the Supreme Court of the United States. Aside from one Wilson appointment, they were the legatees of Republican Presidents who had chosen safe and dependable men from the world where business, the bar, and politics converged. The minority of four were also legatees of one Democratic and several Republican Presidents—Chief Justice Hughes, appointed by Hoover; Brandeis (Wilson); Harlan F. Stone (Coolidge); and Benjamin N. Cardozo (Hoover).

No President can be sure that his judicial appointees fully share his political philosophy or will continue to share it. There was no compact old guard majority on the Court arrayed against a solid minority expressing the views of Wilsonian democracy and liberal Republicanism. Majorities and minorities recombined fluidly as individual cases were heard. But the ideology of the 1920s—indeed, of the nineteenth century—hung closely enough over the Court as to produce a virtual massacre of New Deal measures between January 1935 and the spring of 1936. Stricken down successively were the "hot oil" provisions of the NRA Act, the Railroad Pension Act, the NRA itself, the farm mortgage law, the Agricultural Adjustment Act, the Guffey Bituminous Coal Act, and the Municipal Bankruptcy Act.

One act that escaped the judicial guillotine caused Roosevelt as much worry as several that died under it. In January 1935 the High Court began hearing arguments on the power of the government to impair the obligation of contracts, public and private, a power Congress had claimed during the Hundred Days in nullifying the gold clauses in such contracts. A decision affirming the sanctity of contracts would put in jeopardy the power of Congress to control monetary policy and would bring dire practical consequences. The public debt would immediately jump by $10 billion, while the total debt—which FDR was still vainly hoping to reduce—would soar to almost $70 billion. Bondholders, demanding full gold value for their bonds of $1.69 for every dollar, would reap a bonanza.

Apprehensively, Roosevelt, Morgenthau, and their aides waited in the White House for the Court's verdict to come over the ticker. Then the good news: by a 5–4 vote the justices upheld the government. Undoubtedly the President's relief was deeply tinged with bitterness. For one thing, Chief Justice Hughes, in a tortured ruling for the Court, held that government bonds, in contrast to private obligations, were contractual obligations that Congress had unconstitutionally violated, but that the plaintiff had suffered only nominal damage and could not sue in the Court of Claims. More than ever the President must have reflected about the ungrateful capitalist and the lost top hat. His gold policy had been designed to stabilize the financial markets, to shore up capitalism—was this the response of the business community? Justice James C. McReynolds from the bench had accused the government of confiscation, repudiation, destroying the Constitution; and in court, during a twenty-minute extemporaneous harangue, he said, "This is Nero at his worst."

If any case had been designed to stir Roosevelt's deepest feelings against a certain type of capitalist—bondholders, coupon-clippers, the idle rich—it was the Gold Clause cases. Even in the eminence of the presidency he could recall the kind of men who, as youths, had excluded him from the inner circles of Groton and Harvard, the men who later had fought both his presidential heroes, TR and Wilson. Certainly as a power broker he could now see the judicial handwriting on the Supreme Court façade. "I shudder at the closeness of five to four decisions in these important matters," he wrote. Hence he was not surprised by the Supreme Court decision against the NRA on May 27, though he could hardly have expected the unanimous thumbs-down. But once again his class had betrayed him— was not the NRA, even with its dire problems, his best effort to harmonize and stabilize industry and business, to find a middle way between collectivism and unbridled competition?

*   *   *

The right-wing counterattack on the New Deal—through the Supreme Court, small business spokesmen, and a thousand lesser channels—served as a catalytic factor in the forces now pushing the President out of his drift and indecision. By now the President was feeling heavy pressure from the left as well. In mid-May, a week after the Court invalidated the Railroad Pension Act and appeared to question whether old-age pensions lay within the scope of federal commerce power in the Constitution, a group of liberal senators met with Roosevelt for a long talk. La Follette, Johnson, Norris, Wheeler, and Costigan, all of whom had been members of the National Progressive League for Roosevelt in 1932, were there, along with cabinet members Ickes and Wallace, and Felix Frankfurter, who had organized the meeting.

La Follette in particular was brutally frank: The President must reassert leadership. It was well that business spokesmen had attacked him, for now business had put its cards on the table. The best answer to Long and Coughlin was to press ahead on the legislative program. In the light of opposition within the Democratic party, La Follette reminded the President that Theodore Roosevelt had not hesitated to take open issue with members of his own party. FDR might have to do the same thing. Frankfurter brought a warning from Brandeis that it was the "eleventh hour." The President seemed to be in a fighting mood when the group left.

He was still in a fighting mood at the end of May after the Court's voiding of the NRA. To his press conference he delivered a one-and-a-half-hour monologue on the substance of the decision. First he quoted a series of poignant letters from small businessmen—a cigar maker, store owner, printer, "drug-store people"—asking in effect, the President said, "please save us." Smiling, speaking calmly and simply, pausing only to stab out a cigarette and fix a new one in his long ivory holder, Roosevelt dwelt on how the Framers had written the interstate commerce clause into the Constitution back in the "horse-and-buggy" age, how impossible it had become for forty-eight states to deal with nationwide economic needs, and how "we have been relegated to the horse-and-buggy definition of interstate commerce." Thus did the President of the United States put in his dissenting opinion to a holding of the Supreme Court of the United States.

Where next for the nation, asked the President—toward federal or toward state power over national economic and social problems? "Don't call it right or left; that is just first-year high-school language, just about. It is not right or left—it is a question for national decision."

What "national decision" for Roosevelt? Whatever his dislike of the cloudy terms, he was now tilted toward the cloudy liberal-labor-left. But would he go with the Moley-Tugwell-Berle strategy of coordinated national planning and control or with the strategy of decentralized administration, small institutions, and local initiatives urged by Frankfurter, Ben Cohen, and Tommy Corcoran?

The first gun in this struggle had already been fired. On what the New Dealers were already calling "Black Monday"—the day the High Court killed the NRA—Corcoran had started to leave the chamber after the session when a page tapped him on the shoulder and asked him to come to the robing room. There Corcoran found Brandeis holding his arms up to be derobed, looking "for a moment like a black-winged angel of destruction." The justice spoke sharply to his young friend:

"This is the end of this business of centralization, and I want you to go back and tell the President that we're not going to let this government centralize everything. It's come to an end. As for your young men, you call them together and tell them to get out of Washington—tell them to go home, back to the states. That is where they must do their work." Corcoran duly got word to the President—but "Tommy the Cork," as FDR called him, and many of his young colleagues never left Washington.

A message from Brandeis, direct or indirect, was never taken lightly in the Roosevelt White House. For years the justice had been bombarding the Administration with advice, sometimes directly to Roosevelt, usually indirectly through Frankfurter or other mutual friends. The Administration viewed the justice not merely as an adviser, or even as a justice, but as "Isaiah," a prophet of profound wisdom. He and Frankfurter, moreover, had served virtually as a New Deal scouting and recruiting agency, peopling not only the White House but the whole Administration with talented activists. Always implicit but unspoken in Brandeis's counsel was the fact that the justice not only could give advice—he could enforce it from the high bench. Now that threat had been made explicit.

By now Roosevelt was asserting leadership, and clearly toward the left, but he still faced a choice, among others, between the "Brandeisian" left and the "Tugwellian" left. Even though his friends and advisers, most of whom were hostile to bigness, redoubled their efforts after NRA's invalidation, the President still hankered for the kind of "collectivist" control over business that had been embodied in the NRA. But any White House insiders who expected a grand strategic decision from their boss did not know their man. He was not wont to choose between lofty philosophical principles. Rather he would exploit immediate opportunities by modernizing old ideas, applying the results of his own experiments, choosing eclectically among disparate policies, and responding to the pressures of interest groups, especially the rising power of industrial labor. He would find decision in day-to-day action, by throwing himself into new legislative battles.

Late in May began the "Second Hundred Days." Reverting to his old role of Chief Legislator, the President bluntly told congressional chieftains that certain bills *must* be passed. Congress, which had been dawdling, was suddenly spurred into action, with the progressives in each chamber now riding high. Laboring in the heat, without air conditioning, Congress responded to the presidential spur.

July 5, 1935—Having given the green light earlier to Senator Robert Wagner, the President signs Wagner's National Labor Relations Act—the augmented legacy of NRA's Section 7(a)—and declares that the high goal of the act is a better relationship between labor and management by "assuring the employees the right of collective bargaining" and providing "an orderly procedure for determining who is entitled to represent the employees." A five-person independent quasi-judicial body will administer the act.

August 14—FDR signs the Social Security Act. "Today a hope of many years' standing is in large part fulfilled," he says. After the "startling industrial changes" that in the past century have threatened the security of person and family, "this social security measure gives at least some protection to thirty million of our citizens who will reap direct benefits through unemployment compensation, through old-age pensions and through increased services for the protection of children and the prevention of ill health."

August 24—The President signs the Banking Act of 1935, which centers control of the money market in the Federal Reserve. This was largely the brainchild of Marriner Eccles at the Federal Reserve Board. The President had predicted to Eccles that "it will be a knock-down and drag-out fight to get it through," and he was right. Not only leading bankers but old Senator Glass, father of the Federal Reserve System in Wilson days, fought tenaciously against "political control" and won some modifying changes. After the President, at the signing, handed one of the pens to Glass, someone whispered, "He should have given him an eraser instead."

August 26—Roosevelt signs the Public Utility Holding Company Act. This measure, designed to curb the power of gigantic utility holding companies over their operating subsidiaries, had been urged by the President in January; when he renewed pressure for the bill, the utilities fought back with an intensive propaganda and lobbying campaign. They feared especially FDR's demand for a "death sentence," as it came to be called, for utility holding companies that could not show they served a sound economic purpose. Senator Wheeler and Congressman Sam Rayburn had carried the fight in Congress, and Senator Alben Barkley of Kentucky pushed through the final compromise version. This allowed a holding company to control more than one public utility system if potential additional systems could otherwise not survive economically. The utility chieftains—especially an unusually articulate spokesman named Wendell Willkie—remained utterly hostile to the measure.

August 31—The President signs the Revenue Act of 1935. In mid-May he had shocked the business community with a message to Congress contending that "great accumulations of wealth cannot be justified on the basis of personal and family security" and calling for taxes on "inherited economic power." Congress, after a sharp struggle in the country and on the Hill, enacted a measure increasing rates for estate and gift taxes, boosted the surtax rates for large incomes, imposed a graduated rate on corporation income, and placed a special tax on corporations' undistributed earnings.

These bills—the Big Five—were the essence of the Second Hundred Days. But the momentum of that year initiated or invigorated many other elements of the New Deal: rural electrification, youth programs, protection of natural resources, farm credit, above all the WPA and other spending programs for the needy—covering almost the whole of Roosevelt's concerns and amounting in effect to the Second New Deal. Probably the most important of these programs—certainly the most important in its direct impact on people's lives—was Harry Hopkins's Works Progress Administration, designed to replace the faltering federal-state-local direct relief efforts with a big national works program for jobless employables. Even while Congress passed the Second Hundred Days laws, Hopkins was gearing up his agency to spend the $5 billion appropriated for the first year. Within that year WPA rolls numbered almost 3.5 million people. Hopkins's was the most visible and controversial New Deal program; gangs of WPA workers repairing roads or bridges were often jeered at by passersby still lucky enough to have jobs and cars.

*   *   *

Studying Roosevelt's 1935 measures and actions, observers were still uncertain whether the President was at last opting for the Brandeis-Frankfurter anti-bigness stance. Was he moving strongly in a progressive, even radical direction toward economic equality and social justice?

The Brandeis school feared bigness both in business and in government—but to what extent was a strong and unified federal government needed to curb *private* concentrated power? Could decentralized governmental power compel diffused economic power? It seemed unlikely. Yet the progressive senators were hardly in a mood to substitute big public bureaucracies for big private ones, except for such huge programs as AAA and Social Security that clearly demanded massive government. The holding company bill, administered by a relatively small regulatory agency like the SEC, was a model for the decentralizers.

A big federal program or bureau, on the other hand, did not necessarily mean monolithic and centralized power. The NRA had provided for codemaking by private interests as well as by Hugh Johnson's diktats. The AAA provided for farmers' referendums. The Tennessee Valley Authority embraced extensive local decision making as well as regional. The 1935 "wealth tax" was in part an assault on big business. The decentralizers' rhetoric rarely took into account such subtleties or ambivalences. Senator Wheeler, according to Ronald Mulder, believed that a proper use of governmental power could decentralize both the economy and the government. "Excessive centralization in whatever form it may exist negated American ideals," Wheeler said. The Brandeis school may have won some symbolic victories in the Second Hundred Days, but the balance between bigness and smallness, between central and local control, did not fundamentally change.

Equality? The fierce reaction of Liberty Leaguers and other conservatives—including judges—to the "radicalism" and "Bolshevism" of the Second New Deal left FDR with a more liberal image than ever. To a considerable degree this was deserved. But the measures of the Second Hundred Days did not constitute a major shift toward economic equality and social justice. Because the President had an insurance model in mind for Social Security, this vital program was financed by payroll taxes that were as regressive as sales taxes. The payroll tax, according to Mark Leff, reaped as much each month in federal revenue as the controversial income tax increase under the 1935 wealth tax did in a whole year. In short, the Social Security Act sought social security, not income redistribution—though in the long run the first was hardly possible without the latter. Many of the other key 1935 bills, as well as lesser ones, had been watered down by congressional and business opposition.

The acid test for Roosevelt's liberalism—and that of all Presidents—was tax policy. Here again the President was left with a sharpened progressive image, and deservedly so, for his original bill had strong redistributionist elements. Yet these were much weakened in the legislative labyrinth. On close analysis, indeed, the Second New Deal appeared a creature less of ideological or policy consistency than of legislative and electoral necessity. Roosevelt had made no philosophically based or motivated grand strategic deployment to the left. He was more like the commander of a guerrilla army whose scattered columns, fighting blindly in the mountains through dense ravines and thickets, suddenly converge, half by plan and half by coincidence, and debouch into the plain below.

And if the Politician-in-Chief should ever forget the centrality of politics, there were those who would remind him. In particular there was one boisterous, pudgy-faced senator who by early 1935 was in open revolt against the White House. Huey Long attacked the Social Security bill for the payroll tax, the stinginess of its pensions for the aged, and other inadequacies. But the Kingfish's great moment came when FDR's tax message was read to the Senate. As the President's specific proposals were spelled out, Huey pranced around the chamber grinning broadly, rolling his eyes in mock amazement, pointing to himself, and letting it be known that the President was stealing his thunder.

A few days later, the Kingfish was at it again. He was glad that the President had joined him at last, he proclaimed. He had some questions for FDR, he said, and if the President answered them satisfactorily, he—the Kingfish—would retire from politics, his work done. Delightedly he quoted Will Rogers's comment:

"I would sure liked to have seen Huey's face when he was woke up in the middle of the night by the President, who said, 'Lay over, Huey, I want to get in bed with you.' "

APPEAL TO THE PEOPLE

"We have earned the hatred of entrenched greed. The very nature of the problem that we faced made it necessary to drive some people from power and strictly to regulate others." The "unscrupulous money-changers" stood indicted in the court of public opinion. They had admitted their failure and abdicated. "Abdicated! Yes, in 1933, but now with the passing of danger they forget their damaging admissions and withdraw their abdication."

It was the evening of January 3, 1936. From the rostrum of the House of Representatives, Franklin D. Roosevelt looked out at the crowded and boisterous chamber. This was his annual message on the state of the union, and it had started out as a state paper, as he described the growing world crisis. In October, Mussolini's forces had invaded Ethiopia, and two months later France and Britain had agreed to the conquest of Haile Selassie's hapless country. "Nations seeking expansion, seeking the rectification of injustices springing from former wars, or seeking outlets for trade, for population or even for their own peaceful contributions to the progress of civilization, fail to demonstrate that patience necessary to attain reasonable and legitimate objectives by peaceful negotiation or by an appeal to the finer instincts of world justice." But the President hurried on to what was obviously a campaign speech. Indeed, he had insisted on departing from precedent and speaking in the evening in order to reach millions of radio listeners in their homes.

"The rulers of the exchanges of mankind's goods" now "seek the restoration of their selfish power. They offer to lead us back round the same old corner into the same old dreary street." Lowering his voice confidentially, rocking back and forth behind the rostrum, FDR was drawing blood. Cheers and rebel yells burst from the Democrats, while the little band of Republicans looked on in bitter silence.

"They steal the livery of great national constitutional ideals to serve discredited special interests." They would "gang up" against the people's liberties. They would extend to government the principles many of them had instilled into their own affairs: "autocracy toward labor, toward stockholders, toward consumers, toward public sentiment." Any doubt that this was the campaign kickoff for 1936 evaporated when the President concluded by anticipating "a balance of the national budget" and seeing no need for new taxes.

But where were the battle lines? Like the Napoleonic general of the armies who surveys the terrain, sizes up the enemy, mobilizes and measures his own troops, and makes sense of it all, the President by attacking early sought to control the theater of combat. As he reconnoitered the political terrain, however, with his sharp eye for divisions on both sides he could see little but factionalism and confusion. The ideological left was divided as usual between communists and socialists, and both these movements were deeply cleft between moderate and militant elements. Father Coughlin was reorganizing his National Union for Social Justice while keeping some distance from rival organizations. The AFL and the new CIO were still busy at fratricide. Dr. Townsend had become increasingly hostile to FDR and was considering a third-party effort. As for the President's own party, Al Smith and the rest of the old guard were attacking the President at every opportunity and were now aided and abetted by young ideologues of fiscal orthodoxy such as Dean Acheson and Lewis Douglas and by a host of conservative Southerners.

One figure no longer dominated the politics of protest. Two months after his waggish response to FDR's tax bill on the Senate floor, Huey Long had conducted a final one-man filibuster in the upper chamber and returned home. He was flirting with the notion of seeking to deny Roosevelt a second term by uniting the followers of Townsend, Coughlin, Sinclair, and others against him, thus electing a Republican, who would make such a mess of things that a true believer in sharing the wealth—and who else but the Kingfish himself?—would win the presidency in 1940. And the results of a poll commissioned in spring 1935 by the Democratic National Committee indicated that this was no idle threat. As a third-party candidate, Long might receive three to four million votes, enough, James Farley feared, to give him "the balance of power in the 1936 election."

Early in September in the Louisiana state capitol, after sauntering around the House chamber telling jokes and barking out orders, Long had swept into one of the marble corridors, followed by his bodyguards. A slight bespectacled man stepped out from behind a pillar, brushed through the guards, and shot one bullet into Huey Long's stomach. The guards then shot down the assailant and poured bullets into his prone body. He was a young and brilliant Baton Rouge physician who hated Long and his dictatorship and was ready to die in an act of tyrannicide.

After a bungled operation the Kingfish died a day and a half later, murmuring, it was said, "God, don't let me die. I have so much to do." Quickly a Long lieutenant, Gerald L. K. Smith, stepped forth to convert the third-party movement into his personal political base. Driven out of Louisiana politics by the inheritors of Long's organization, Smith by early 1936 was seeking to build a nationwide coalition against the President.

Roosevelt was now building his own electoral coalition—far broader than the Democratic party. Indeed, there already existed a coalition of groups that New Deal laws and money had aided. The President had called the roll in his address to Congress—farmers reaping higher prices, homeowners enjoying lower interest rates, workers now able to join in unions of their own choosing, the aged cherishing the prospect of pensions, young people in the CCC, the jobless, investors now protected against speculators. Roosevelt already was instructing Farley and his own political aides to establish campaign organizations that would make direct appeals to such groups.

To the President's critics this was special-interest politics of the most sordid type. Perhaps they were unduly concerned. The critical presidential reelection campaigns in American history had turned not merely on group allegiances but on presidential qualities that far transcended narrow interest—qualities of trust, commitment, leadership, vision—as well as on widely felt popular benefit and improvement. Although Roosevelt's popularity as measured by polls had dropped, he still ranked high in public esteem. And he appeared to be fulfilling the supreme promise he had made in 1932—recovery. Unemployment was down by more than one-third from its height of at least 13 million and national income had increased almost two-thirds from the $40 billion level of 1933.

Yet the half-filled glass was also half empty. There were still over 9 million jobless in early 1936. Reemployment during the first term was a result less of careful planning than of direct spending to meet human needs, especially following the big work-relief and public works programs of 1935. Huge sections of the population, moreover, were beyond even the long reach of the New Deal. Millions of poor people on the land—tenants, sharecroppers, farm laborers, migrant workers—had hardly felt the impact of New Deal agricultural programs. Nor had millions of southern blacks, imprisoned in local racist cultures and discriminatory state economic and political structures, and the last to reap benefits from the New Deal because reactionary lawmakers in Washington stood guard over white privilege back home.

Nor had millions of women. Although the New Deal brought unprecedented numbers of women into the government bureaucracy, working women continued to face oppressive job and wage discrimination, and, in a tight labor market, they had little leverage and few options. Married women in particular suffered from the popular notion that unemployment could be reduced by simply denying them jobs. And women were practically excluded from the heavy construction projects at the core of the relief efforts of the PWA and other agencies.

The plight of poor farmers, blacks, and women, however, hardly seemed to preoccupy Roosevelt's conservative opposition. The President's heightened militancy quickly aroused an oratorical counteroffensive. Triumphantly the Liberty League presented Al Smith in Washington's Mayflower Hotel to a great throng that numbered Du Ponts, disaffected Democrats such as Raskob and Davis, and two thousand others. Decked out in white tie and tails, Al had never been more sulphurous. "It's all right with me if they want to disguise themselves as Norman Thomas, or Karl Marx, or Lenin, or any of the rest of that bunch," he shouted, "but what I won't stand for is allowing them to march under the banner of Jefferson, Jackson, or Cleveland." There could be only one capital, he warned, Washington or Moscow—"the clear, pure, fresh air of free America, or the foul breath of Communistic Russia." He warned further that come election day he might take a walk—and he did so.

If the key issue against the New Deal was to be its alleged secret Red sympathies, the leader of the opposition must be William Randolph Hearst. In the happy days of 1932, the publisher had helped tilt the nomination toward FDR. Now his papers addressed the President as "you and your fellow Communists" and ran little ditties like:

> A Red New Deal with a Soviet Seal
> Endorsed by a Moscow hand,
> The strange result of an alien cult
> In a liberty-loving land.

Almost comical was Hearst's détente with Smith, whom he had once excoriated. But for Roosevelt the message was clear: with the great bulk of the press against him, he must rely all the more on radio.

FDR's most menacing foes were still the conservatives with teeth—the conservative majority on the Supreme Court and the federal judges across the land who were tying up Administration programs with injunctions, occasionally adorned with anti-New Deal stump speeches from the bench. When in early 1936 the High Court had struck down the Agricultural Adjustment Act by a 6–3 vote—on the ground that the processing tax was not a genuine tax but a vehicle for regulating agriculture—Stone, dissenting, had called the decision a tortured construction of the Constitution and warned that the judiciary was "not the only agency of government that must be assumed to have the capacity to govern." His brethren little heeded his admonition, as the beheading of other New Deal measures followed. Then came the most lethal decision of all, a voiding of a New York measure setting a minimum wage for women. The High Court was now thwarting *state* power as well as national.

"There is grim irony," Stone wrote in his dissent, "in speaking of the freedom of contract of those who, because of their economic necessities, give their service for less than is needful to keep body and soul together." As for Roosevelt, he was no longer offering dissenting opinions. Indeed, he was curiously mute. Like the Tar Baby, he "ain't sayin' nothin'. "

* * *

By late spring both parties were mobilizing for battle. From the start Generalissimo Roosevelt directed operations from his own command post, bypassing Farley as needed. He dealt directly with Lewis and other labor leaders. He mollified businessmen by giving a long White House luncheon for business friends of Commerce Secretary Daniel C. Roper. He set up a new "nonpartisan" organization, with the imposing title of the Good Neighbor League, to appeal to religious, black, civic, and related groups across the nation. Above all he sought to attract support from women. With his backing Eleanor Roosevelt, Frances Perkins, and Molly Dewson organized election cadres of women across the nation. Once again the First Lady demonstrated her capacity to shift almost overnight from her posture of gracious serenity to that of a hardheaded machine politician—who nonetheless viewed campaigns as essentially vehicles for educating the public.

But Roosevelt would hold the spotlight. "There's one issue in this campaign," he told Moley in one of their last meetings, according to the former brain truster. "It's myself, and people must be either for me or against me."

In June the Republicans, torn between their heart and their head—between their feeling for their old stalwart, Herbert Hoover, and their practical need for a new face—chose Governor Alfred M. Landon of Kansas to head their ticket and Colonel Frank Knox, publisher of the Chicago *Daily News,* as his running mate. Both men were proud old Bull Moosers. Hoover, who had been castigating the New Deal in speeches around the country for years, hoped forlornly that one big speech at the convention might win him the nomination. A smashing speech it was, but the GOP rank and file knew that a ticket headed by Hoover would buy a journey to defeat. In Landon they found a decent, moderate man, with just the qualities of common sense, homely competence, and rocklike "soundness" that the party hoped to contrast with the nutty theorist in the White House, and yet with a progressive past and reputation. His square, guileless face, rimless glasses, and slightly graying hair made the Kansas governor look like a million other middle-aged, middle-class Americans.

The Democratic convention later in June was a one-man show—even though the man was not present until the end. FDR supervised the writing of an exuberantly New Deal platform, planned the schedule, and hand-picked the members of crucial delegations, such as California's. He also forced through the convention a vital change—substitution of a simple majority for the Democracy's historic two-thirds requirement for presidential nominations, a rule that had tied up countless conclaves and almost dished Roosevelt's hopes in 1932. The President had astutely asked Bennett Champ Clark, son of a victim of the requirement in 1912, to move the adoption of majority rule.

The convention came fully to life only when the President arrived at Philadelphia's Franklin Field stadium to accept the nomination. Before a wildly enthusiastic throng of 100,000, he accused the opposition of seeking to hide behind the flag and the Constitution. "Today," he said, "we stand committed to the proposition that freedom is no half-and-half affair. If the average citizen is guaranteed equal opportunity in the polling place, he must have equal opportunity in the market place." Then the climactic sentences:

"Better the occasional faults of a Government that lives in a spirit of charity than the consistent omissions of a Government frozen in the ice of its own indifference.

"There is a mysterious cycle in human events. To some generations much is given. Of other generations much is expected. *This* generation of Americans has a rendezvous with destiny. . . .

"I accept the commission you have tendered me. I join—" A roar burst across the stadium and drowned out the final words: "with you. I am enlisted for the duration of the war."

By midsummer both parties confronted a third force that suddenly seemed to be threatening. Both Coughlin and Townsend had been mustering their troops for action. They hated and feared Roosevelt, held the Republican old guard in utter contempt, and viewed each other with suspicion. The Kingfish was gone, but now two new leaders emerged. Gerald Smith proved to be not only a rousing tub-thumper but a coalition-builder. Befriending Townsend, he brought the doctor into contact with Coughlin and won the priest's support for an alliance. Since all three men were prima donnas, a compromise candidate was needed. Congressman William Lemke of North Dakota, a longtime agrarian radical whose seamed, leathery face and rustic clothes belied his years at Georgetown University and Yale Law School, would serve. Soon he was denouncing the President as the "bewildered Kerensky of a provisional government" and Landon as "the dying shadow of a past civilization." His hastily organized Union party boasted that it could command 25 million votes or more and at the least throw the election to Landon, thus paving the way to Huey Long's great goal for 1940.

It was clear also by midsummer that Roosevelt had little to fear from the parties of the old left, even as balance-of-power forces. The age-old failure of the broad American labor-liberal-left to unite seemed almost caricatured in the Socialists' internal divisions. At their convention in May they had renominated Norman Thomas but split over another issue; a large number of old-liners walked out and formed the Social Democratic Federation, leaving the Socialist party with a strong leftward tilt. Caught in the middle, Thomas saw some of his supporters move further to the left while others—including Hillman and Dubinsky—joined the New Deal camp.

American Communists also had their frustrations. Moscow's switch to a new popular front, antifascist strategy had left anti–New Deal zealots in an embarrassing position: after lambasting Roosevelt and his New Deal, now they must support him. Yet despite their deep distrust of the President, they much preferred him to Landon, whom they labeled a forerunner of fascism. While the Socialists shifted sharply to the left, Harvey Klehr noted, the Communists passed them headed to the right. Meantime the comrades unveiled their patriotic slogan "COMMUNISM IS TWENTIETH-CENTURY AMERICANISM."

The Republican campaigners were the first off the mark, and a good start it was, as Americans seemed to take to this outspoken Midwesterner with his sensible ideas and moderate positions. Buoyed by ample press support and good crowds, he attacked the New Deal at some of its weaker points and argued that he could meet the people's needs more effectively and cheaply. As the weeks passed, however, he ran into more and more difficulties—his own fatigue, his repetitiousness, growing boredom and lack of response in the crowds. Moreover, he had no target, as FDR was lying low.

Landon's nemesis was Herbert Hoover. Frozen out of the Landon campaign circle, thirsting for vindication, hating Roosevelt, the former President concluded that the candidate lacked fire and that he would provide it. Hoover's attacks on the New Deal were so virulent as to be self-defeating, but in the process he and other hard-liners drew Landon into their vortex. Soon the Kansan was leveling extreme charges against his adversary. Pressured from the Republican right and the center, Landon never found a solid, consistent theme. By October his campaign was slowly and inexorably sinking, buoyed only by falsely optimistic polls in the *Literary Digest.*

The campaign of the Union party proved an exercise in self-destruction, performed before an indifferent press and public. Landon's troubles with Hoover were as nothing compared to Lemke's with Coughlin. Virtually ignoring his party's candidate, the radio priest concentrated his fire on Roosevelt as "anti-God," anti-American, pro-Red. The New Deal was "a broken down Colossus," he shouted, "its left leg standing on ancient Capitalism and its right mired in the red mud of Communism." He carried his red-baiting of the Administration to such a point, with ominous undertones of anti-Semitism, that his bishop, his cardinal, and even the Vatican rebuked him. Undeterred, Coughlin boasted that he would throw Roosevelt out of his office just "as I was instrumental in removing Herbert Hoover," and cried, "If I don't deliver 9,000,000 votes for William Lemke, I'm through with radio forever." Smith and even Townsend also became vituperative, but they were cool to each other, and to Lemke. With too many leaders and too little money and organization, the Union party was in tatters by the middle of the fall.

By then Roosevelt was just starting his formal campaign. Always a master of timing, he stood aside until his foes had exhausted themselves and their audiences. His crowds seemed to get bigger and more enthusiastic as theirs dwindled during the autumn days. Spoken with power and passion but without stridency, his radio addresses were unusually effective, reaching widely across the electorate. He knew, too, when to leave well enough alone: he let friendly Catholic hierarchs answer Coughlin; he ignored pinpricks; when some of his campaign leaders almost panicked in the wake of a telling last-minute Republican attack on Social Security taxes and "name tags," the President kept his nerve. His final campaign trips through the Northeast could fairly be described as triumphal processions.

He brought his campaign to a stunning climax in Madison Square Garden before a crowd of enthusiasts who seemed to thirst for political blood:

"For nearly four years now you have had an Administration which instead of twirling its thumbs has rolled up its sleeves. And I can assure you that we will keep our sleeves rolled up.

"We had to struggle with the old enemies of peace—business and financial monopoly, speculation, reckless banking, class antagonism, sectionalism, war profiteering.

"*They* had begun to consider the Government of the United States as a mere appendage to their own affairs. And we know now that Government by *organized money* is just as dangerous as Government by *organized mob*.

"Never before in all our history have these forces been so united against one candidate as they stand today. They are unanimous in their hate for *me*—and I welcome their hatred.

"I should like to have it said of my first Administration"—Roosevelt's voice was rising—"that in it the forces of selfishness and of lust for power met their match.

"I should like to have it said—" A thunderclap of cheers and applause burst from the crowd.

"Wait a moment! I should like to have it said of my second Administration that in it these forces met their master." The crowd let out a great guttural roar.

"*Of course* we will continue to seek to improve working conditions for the workers of America. . . . *Of course* we will continue to work for cheaper electricity. . . . *Of course* we will continue our efforts in behalf of the farmers of America . . . for young men and women . . . for the crippled, for the blind, for the mothers. . . .

"For these things, too, and for a multitude of things like them, *we have only just begun to fight.*"

CHAPTER 3

The Crisis of Majority Rule

F OR more than one hundred years, ever since Jeffersonian times, presidential candidates of humane and liberal tendencies had been seeking to muster popular majorities strong and stout enough to sustain their work. Their success had been mixed at best. Lincoln and Wilson won office, but only with a minority of the popular vote against divided opposition. Theodore Roosevelt and Franklin Roosevelt won popular majorities only to encounter opposition inside the governmental or party system. Somehow conservative Republican leadership had been able to achieve "compact majorities," especially in the late nineteenth century and in the 1920s. Somehow liberal Democrats and progressive Republicans had been unable to create durable majority coalitions.

Suddenly, on Wednesday morning, November 4, 1936, the political landscape seemed altered and the old hope renewed. It was not merely a Roosevelt victory, the press proclaimed, but a tidal wave, an earthquake, a landslide, "the blizzard of '36." The President carried every state save Maine and Vermont, swept the electoral college by 523 to 8, won the popular vote by 27,748,000 to 16,680,000. Lemke's 892,000 votes amounted to less than 2 percent of the total. The outcome was historic: Roosevelt had won the largest presidential vote up to that time, the largest presidential plurality, the largest proportion of electoral votes since 1820; he had helped win the largest House majority since 1855, the largest Senate majority since 1869. The new House would have 331 Democrats and 89 Republicans, with 13 members of other parties; the Senate, 76 Democrats, 16 Republicans, and 4 "others." The Democratic hurricane swept through state legislatures and county courthouses across the nation. And the Democrats for the first time made deep inroads into the black vote.

So Franklin Roosevelt had his majority, a magnificent majority in electoral breadth and legislative depth. What would he do with it? Few doubted that he would have to face up to the one lingering majority of conservatives—that on the Supreme Court. Later on, some would propagate the myth that the President, intoxicated with his success, suddenly and recklessly pounced on the High Court. In fact, the battle was long in the making, for it reflected a conflict built deep into the heart of the constitutional system, popular attitudes, and the ambitions of leaders.

The Framers of the Constitution had been deeply ambivalent toward the idea and practice of majority rule. Believers in republican government, they had to accept the ultimate power of the people as expressed in electoral and legislative majorities. But as devout believers too in minority rights, they wished to curb the power of popular majorities, composed perhaps of debt-ridden farmers, to invade property rights. For them Shays's rebellion early in 1787 had been the great warning bell in the night. At Philadelphia the founders shaped a constitution that would thwart sudden and passionate expressions of the popular will. A majority would need to win the House of Representatives, the presidency, and the Senate before it could work its will—and its will might be cooled off in the process as surely as cold milk could chill hot tea. And if all this failed, there would be the courts, which would exercise some major, though not wholly defined, restraints on legislative and executive policy.

Not all the founding fathers favored such curbs on popular rule. Thomas Jefferson, who was absent from the Philadelphia convention but always present in the Framers' thoughts, not only backed legislative majority rule but talked grandly about popular rule and the right of the people to revolt every generation or so. To be sure, Jefferson, as a libertarian and democrat, set as a "sacred principle that if the will of the Majority is in all cases to prevail, that will, to be rightful, must be reasonable"—it must not violate the minority's "equal rights." But he had confidence that a majority of free Americans would never trample on the liberties of fellow Americans as guaranteed in bills of rights.

While FDR spurned grandiose constitutional theory, he had a good working knowledge of the Framers' checks and balances as vehicles for frustrating popular impulses and thwarting social change. He had learned even more from historical narratives, as a politician delving into the past in order to defend his positions of the present. But most of all he learned from people—from Jefferson and Jackson and their difficulties with the Federalist-Whig court of John Marshall, from Lincoln, from the judicial erosion of black rights during Reconstruction, and above all from Cousin Ted's blasts against reactionary judges.

Roosevelt had long recognized that the High Court was no chaste and lofty sanctum protected by vestal virgins of the law against political contamination, but rather an institution drenched in politics at least since the days of Marshall. Even more, he tended to look at the Court in personal rather than institutional terms. To him Hughes was not an Olympian jurist but a former politico, presidential candidate, and stalwart Republican.

McReynolds was not a fine Wilsonian philosopher but a fanatical reactionary; Roosevelt would not have been surprised to learn of a letter from McReynolds to his brother in which he described the President as lacking "brains to understand what he is doing," as "bad through and through," and controlled by the radicals around him. Even Brandeis—the "Isaiah" whom FDR admired—had labored indefatigably for Roosevelt's own goals and had advised New Deal officials closely, though usually indirectly, on policy measures—and then had turned suddenly against the Administration in demolishing the NRA. "Where was Ben Cardozo?" Roosevelt said on hearing of the 9–0 verdict against the NRA. "And what about old Isaiah?"

Hence it was not surprising that the President, forced by polarizing political pressures to rise above interest-group brokerage and bolstered by his big 1936 majority vote, now would confront minority power entrenched in the Supreme Court of the United States.

COURT-PACKING: THE SWITCH IN TIME

The New Deal and the Old Court had almost collided in February 1935 in the Gold Clause cases. If the Court had decided against the Administration, Roosevelt had planned to defy the Court because to "stand idly by" and permit the decision to take effect would "imperil the economic and political security of this nation." The decision if enforced, he intended to proclaim, would result in unconscionable profits to investors, bankruptcy for railroads and corporations, default by state and local governments, intensified mortgage foreclosures, a hike in the national debt—in short, would plunge the nation into an economic crisis.

After the narrow 5–4 decision in his favor, a relieved President wrote jauntily to Joseph P. Kennedy, chairman of the Securities and Exchange Commission: "How fortunate it is that his Exchanges will never know how close they came to being closed up by a stroke of the pen of one 'J.P.K.' " FDR seemed a bit crestfallen, however, that he had not been able to deliver the "marvelous radio address" he planned. It was the justices who gave the speeches. Hughes scolded the President in the majority opinion, while the archreactionary McReynolds in his extemporaneous dissent lamented that "Shame and humiliation are upon us now."

But the gold cases had been only a respite, as the Court returned to its massacre of 1935. After "Black Monday"—the NRA along with two other anti-Administration decisions—the President began seriously and systematically to consider what could be done about the Court. During the next two years he devoted, on a reasonable estimate, several hundred hours of thought and reading and discussion to the problem. He would have had to do this even if he had preferred not to, for the press was agitating the issue and members of Congress were proposing scores of measures to curb the Court. Labor had been stung by the voiding in *Carter* of the Guffey Coal Act, which provided for a wages-and-hours code and collective bargaining for mineworkers, and it was now fearful of a similar fate for the Wagner and Social Security acts; its spokesmen attacked the Court for putting property rights above human rights and called for some kind of remedy. And after every anti-Administration decision the White House received a spate of letters from the general public.

"President Andrew Jackson, our greatest Democrat, defied the Supreme Court," a Mississippi editor wired FDR. "Hope you will do the same." From Los Angeles came a complaint about "that body of nine old has-beens, half-deaf, half-blind, full-of-palsy men." To see that they were behind the times, "all you have to do is to look at Charles Hughes' whiskers." Demanded a Chicago businessman, "Are you aware that the people at large are getting damned tired of the United States Supreme Court, and that, if left to a popular vote, it would be kicked out?"

The President was aware; more than once he told intimates that there would be "marching" farmers and workers throughout the land if the Court tried to throw out the New Deal. When the Administration quietly lofted trial balloons intimating court reform, the public appeared unperturbed. But what to do? Roosevelt and Attorney General Homer S. Cummings examined a variety of proposals and found virtually insuperable objections to all of them.

A constitutional amendment? Almost anything could be done on paper through formal change of the Constitution. One day at lunch with his ambassador to Italy, Breckinridge Long, the President talked rather freely about possibilities. Long noted in his diary: "The amendments are not yet in specific or concrete form but might be broached under three headings: first, to define Inter-State Commerce with authority to Congress to legislate on the subject; second, to define certain phases of Inter-State Commerce; and third, taking a page from Lloyd George, to give authority to the Congress to pass over the veto of the Supreme Court legislation which the Court held unconstitutional." The President was recalling the historic effort of a British Prime Minister (in fact Asquith, not Lloyd George) to overcome opposition in the House of Lords by threatening to create several hundred peers.

The President considered various permutations and combinations of these and other options but two problems dominated the discussions. The Supreme Court itself would interpret to its own advantage a constitutional amendment, unless it was drastic and explicit, but such an amendment probably would not pass. And could *any* amendment pass? The President often mentioned the power of a few state legislatures, heavily influenced by corporation money—$15 to $20 million, he estimated—to block an amendment. At best this route would take years.

Congressional action? There were precedents for the national legislature's increasing or reducing the size of the Court, limiting the scope of the Court's review power, determining judicial structure and processes, setting terms for retirement. Senator Norris asked Congress now to have the courage to pass legislation requiring a unanimous decision by the High Court to strike down an act of Congress. Others urged that Congress simply enlarge the Court by another two or three members, but Cummings in particular feared there would be considerable prejudice against "packing the Court," as he described it. Compulsory retirement at seventy? This might appear to be a personal attack on the older justices, including Brandeis, and could easily be voided by the Court as an unconstitutional intrusion into its own domain.

Do nothing? Let nature take its course? Older justices—especially Willis Van Devanter—had stuck it out through Roosevelt's first term; surely they would quit or die if FDR won reelection. The President, however, was not at all sure that the Supreme Court would follow the election returns, especially since he felt that certain conservatives on the Court were personally hostile to him. He could imagine old Van Devanter gleefully putting off his retirement month after month just to spite the President. He could not leave the crucial matter of timing in the opposition's hands.

And so the pondering and analyzing went on during most of 1935 and 1936, amid great secrecy. Like Brer Fox watching Brer Rabbit become entangled with the Tar Baby, he lay low—and the Court did become more involved in a potential constitutional crisis with its devastating 1936 invalidations of the AAA and other measures. But the President would not even make the Court an explicit campaign issue. The Democratic platform offered only a vague plan on the matter, and Roosevelt said nothing explicitly about it in his campaign speeches. Implicitly he raised the issue every time he proclaimed that his New Deal would go forward if he received the mandate of the people.

That mandate came in full force on November 3, 1936, and now the President had to act quickly on the momentum of his victory, before the Court could strike down more New Deal laws. Day after day he pored over alternatives with Cummings, who used a secret White House entrance to evade the press. The amendment route was rejected, as the President and the Attorney General leaned toward two separate proposals—appointment of new justices and compulsory retirement at seventy. But each of these seemed weak and unattractive in itself.

A suggestion came in from the famed constitutionalist at Princeton, Edward S. Corwin, the most influential of several academic specialists with whom Cummings had been consulting. Why not combine the two approaches with an act of Congress authorizing the President, "whenever a majority of the Justices" are "seventy or more years old, to nominate enough new justices of less than that age to make a majority"?

About this time Cummings struck a bonanza in the departmental archives—a recommendation from an earlier Attorney General that when any federal judge (except Supreme Court members) "fails to avail himself of the privilege of retiring now granted by law" (at age seventy, after having served ten years, upon full pay), the President could with the consent of the Senate appoint another judge. That Attorney General had been none other than James McReynolds, who had served in the Wilson Administration. With glee Cummings and Roosevelt pounced on this find. Why not apply it to the Supreme Court? Linking the notion of retirement to that of new appointments especially attracted the President, with his relish for tactical combinations.

It was with this recommendation in mind that the President stood before Chief Justice Charles Evans Hughes on January 20, 1937, to take for the second time the inaugural oath of office. When Hughes read the oath with slow and rising emphasis as he came to the words "promise to support the Constitution," the President wanted, he would recall, to cry out, "Yes, but it's the Constitution as *I* understand it, flexible enough to meet any new problem of democracy." Then FDR turned to address the inaugural crowd. It was not a sunny picture he painted but a picture of tasks still undone, promises unfulfilled, human needs unmet:

"I see millions of families trying to live on incomes so meager that the pall of family disaster hangs over them day by day. . . .

"I see millions denied education, recreation, and the opportunity to better their lot and the lot of their children . . . millions lacking the means to buy the products of farm and factory. . . .

"I see one-third of a nation ill-housed, ill-clad, ill-nourished.

"It is not in despair that I paint you that picture. I paint it for you in hope—because the Nation, seeing and understanding the injustice in it, proposes to paint it out."

All this demanded political leadership, he concluded; and he promised to supply it.

*　　*　　*

On February 5, 1937, Roosevelt revealed his Court plan to an extraordinary joint session of cabinet members and congressional leaders. They heard him with mixed emotions, some like Ickes with delight, others like Garner with doubts, still others with the deepest misgivings. Under the President's plan, for every Supreme Court justice who failed to quit the bench within six months after reaching seventy, the President would be empowered to appoint a new justice, up to a total of six. The President did not solicit much comment; quickly he wheeled off to meet a waiting group of newspapermen.

Bursts of laughter swept the press conference as the President went over his plan. Roosevelt presided like an impresario, occasionally throwing his head back and joining in the laughter. He was savoring his triumph. His plan, he expected, would bring quick resignations, protect his big measures of the Second Hundred Days—and dish the conservative opposition on and off the Court. He would extract the conservatives' teeth. Demanding absolute secrecy until the message was released, he took special pleasure from the surprise he had achieved.

Surprise—and shock. Riding back to the Capitol, the congressional leaders sat in stunned silence. Suddenly Hatton Sumners of Texas, chairman of the House Judiciary Committee, turned to the others. "Boys," he said, "here's where I cash in." At the Capitol legislators stood about in little knots, variously elated and indignant after reading the message. In the Supreme Court the attorney at bar paused a moment, sensing a sudden change in mood, after a page slipped through the draperies behind the dais and handed a message to each justice. Hughes shifted restlessly in his chair. Van Devanter looked grim; others sat with their judicial mien unruffled.

The proposal set off a fire storm in the press. "This is the beginning of pure personal government," wrote columnist Dorothy Thompson. "Do you want it? Do you like it?" Her home paper, the New York *Herald Tribune*, compared Roosevelt to Louis XIV—*"L'état, c'est moi."* If the plan passed, Henry Mencken predicted, "the court will become as ductile as a gob of chewing gum, changing shape from day to day and even from hour to hour as this or that wizard edges his way to the President's ear." Herbert Hoover took to the air: if a troop of "President's judges" could be sent into the halls of justice to capture political power, he said, that "is not judicial process. That is force." The nation faced a grave crisis, opined the Protestant Episcopal Bishop of New York. "These proposals would be a death blow to our constitutional democracy."

But it was on the Hill—most immediately in the Senate—that the issue would be decided. "What a grand fight it is going to be!" Roosevelt had written a friend. Instead of a straight fight between Democrats and Republicans or between liberals and conservatives, however, the battle degenerated into guerrilla warfare. Progressives like Burt Wheeler and Hiram Johnson opposed the bill, as did important Democrats like Joseph O'Mahoney of Wyoming, Tom Connally of Texas, Bennett Clark of Missouri. La Follette and some other progressives spoke up strongly for the measure. A host of conservative or moderate Democrats from both North and South opposed the bill, as did the small band of Republicans, but the latter decided to step back and let the Democrats split over the measure. Among some southern lawmakers a deep racial fear stirred; seeing sinister motives in the Court plan, Josiah W. Bailey of North Carolina said the President was determined "to get the Negro vote and I do not have to tell you what *this* means."

As the factional lines firmed up, about a third of the Senate was flatly opposed to the bill, another third favored it, leaving the rest with the crucial votes. Even some of the President's supporters, however, had serious misgivings. Democratic loyalist chieftains like Majority Leader Joe Robinson were angered by the President's secrecy in preparing the bill, by his refusal to work with his congressional leaders. They were also put off by FDR's disingenuousness in presenting the Court plan not in the name of liberalism and constitutional reform but on the ground that the justices were behind in their work, and thus as a measure to produce greater efficiency and expedition in the courts.

Within a few weeks Roosevelt recognized this error. Abruptly shifting tactics, he decided to wage his campaign squarely on the basic issue of bringing the Court in line with the people. At a Democratic victory dinner early in March he seemed to be in the best of humor, but his voice was stern and commanding. He had given warning during the campaign, he observed, that "we had only just begun to fight. Did some people really believe we did not mean it? Well—I meant it, and you meant it." Once again he spoke of "one-third of this Nation" as "ill-nourished, ill-clad, ill-housed."

The President's switch came too late. Already another master politician was organizing his own opposition and preparing the means of puncturing the President's weakest argument.

That master politician was Charles Evans Hughes. Incensed by the "Court-packing" measure, eager in particular to rebut the President's charge of inefficiency, the Chief Justice chafed under the Court's historic self-denial of an overt political role. Roosevelt's charge relating to the internal operations of the Court gave him just the opportunity he needed to intervene in the struggle. But how to be politically effective without appearing to be political? Brandeis, also indignant over the Court proposal, at this point suggested to Wheeler that the Montana senator ask Hughes to rebut the charge of inefficiency. Hughes not only was willing to do so but wished to make a personal appearance before the Senate Judiciary Committee, until Brandeis dissuaded him on the grounds that a letter would be enough.

It was. Hughes's clear and convincing rebuttal of the inefficiency charge marked a turning point in the Court battle. Ironically the Chief Justice, that devotee of protocol, neglected to clear his letter with most of the justices, leaving a good deal of ill feeling on the part of Stone in particular. But no matter; Hughes's colleagues were not likely to complain publicly and never did. After all, the Chief was warding off presidential invasion of their turf.

Far more momentous developments were now underway in the Court. Early in April, Roosevelt had still been optimistic about the Court bill's prospects. Warned of the opposition's determination both on the Hill and in the High Court, the President replied, "We'll smoke 'em out. If delay helps them, we must press for an early vote." But support was draining away, and then on April 12 came Hughes's coup. In a packed, tense courtroom the Chief Justice read the long-anticipated holding of the Court on the Wagner Act. It was a vote to sustain the measure. In the 5–4 decision, Justice Owen J. Roberts was the swing man, voting with the pro-Wagner majority. He had heralded his shift earlier by reversing his vote of 1936 against state minimum-wage laws.

Why was Roberts switching? Frankfurter believed he knew why. "And now," he wrote "Dear Frank," the President, "with the shift by Roberts, even a blind man ought to see that the Court is in politics, and understand how the Constitution is 'judicially' construed. It is a deep object lesson—a lurid demonstration—of the relation of men to the 'meaning' of the Constitution." Roberts's behavior, the Harvard law professor added, had come on top of the Hughes letter. "*That* was a characteristic Hughes performance"—part and parcel of his "pretended withdrawal from considerations of policy," even while he was shaping them. Later Frankfurter regretted that he had imputed political considerations to Roberts, but careful analysis has made clear that Roberts began switching shortly after Roosevelt received his mandate the previous November.

Hughes also appeared to be shifting away from some of his anti-New Deal positions, but like most politician-judges he had been flexible enough in those positions to make the jump plausible. In any event, his new stance was more important politically than judicially. He had consolidated a majority of the Court behind him; he had taken the heart out of the President's argument about the Court's inefficiency; he had upheld a measure dear to labor, whose interest in reform seemed to slacken after the Wagner law was upheld. And he had done all this without undue sacrifice of the Court's dignity. The politician-judge had bested the politician-President.

Roosevelt was all bravado. "I have been chortling all morning," he told reporters after the Court switch. "I have been having a perfectly grand time." He compared the *Herald Tribune*'s enthusiastic hailing of the Wagner Act decision with its approval two years before of a famous "brief" by Liberty League lawyers "invalidating" that act.

"Well, I have been having more fun," he went on, amid guffaws from reporters. "And I haven't read the Washington Post, and I haven't got the Chicago Tribune yet. Or the Boston Herald. . . ."

Still, the President must have sensed the change in the situation. He might have declared victory and quit the battle, but his personal prestige was now so involved that he carried on the fight. Prospects dipped even further when Van Devanter announced his intention to resign. More bad luck as well as a personal loss followed when Robinson, who had been carrying the burden of the exhausting Court fight, fell dead in his hotel room, a copy of the *Congressional Record* in his hand. When Robinson's heart was ruptured, ruptured as well were the bonds of fellow senators' personal loyalty to him—bonds on which the Majority Leader, who hoped to take Van Devanter's place, had depended to win the Court fight and thus renew FDR's obligation to him. A week later Vice President Garner came in to see the President.

"How did you find the court situation, Jack?" FDR asked.

"Do you want it with the bark on or off, Cap'n?"

"The rough way," Roosevelt said.

"All right. You are beat. You haven't got the votes."

*   *   *

Almost lost in the final smoke of battle was Roosevelt's victory on the Wagner Act. The High Court's switch could not have upheld a more vital New Deal measure. Like its predecessor, Section 7(a) of the NRA, the Wagner Act had helped stimulate workers' self-organization in the nation's industrial heartland, and had hence brought about a major redistribution of power. To be sure, the impact of the measure on unionization was limited by employers' legal and physical obstruction, but the opposition of the bosses made it all the more central and valuable to the workers. On the floor of the Senate, Robert Wagner denounced the "organized and calculated and cold-blooded sit-down" against the law, which had come "not from the common people, but from a few great vested interests." Make men free, "and they will be able to negotiate without fighting."

Men and women were already making themselves free. During 1936 and early 1937 tens of thousands of workers took matters into their own hands in the big auto, steel, rubber, and other mass-production industries of the nation. While Lewis and other CIO leaders were busy separating themselves from the AFL and deciding on a grand strategy for organizing big industry, rank-and-file leaders were using a most marvelous weapon—the sit-down. Employed during the mid-thirties by coal miners throughout Europe and by textile workers in India, the sit-down was a ready instrument of spontaneous, militant action. In the United States during 1937, 400,000 workers conducted almost 400 sit-down strikes in more than a dozen industries, and in the process transformed—for a time at least—the industrial world they lived in.

It was a simple but daring device. Workers merely sat down amid their assembly lines—perhaps on the auto cushions they were supposed to install. If it was a "quickie" sit-down, workers would resume work after a few minutes, having sent their message to management. If it lasted days or weeks, workers' friends and family sent in food and blankets. No need to set up picket lines; no need to worry about scabs. Management would hesitate to drive the strikers out for fear of bloodshed and damage to machinery. And sitting down in their own workplaces gave people an intoxicating sense of power. Some of them sang:

> When they tie the can to a union man,
>   Sit down! Sit down!
> When they give him the sack they'll take him back,
>   Sit down! Sit down!
> When the speed-up comes, just twiddle your thumbs,
>   Sit down! Sit down!
> When the boss won't talk don't take a walk,
>   Sit down! Sit down!

But the very potency of the weapon brought risks. It required shop-floor leadership of rare coolness, steadfastness, and judgment as well as militancy. A long sit-down required a measure of community support, and it demanded solidarity among and between Irish and Polish and Italians, whites out of Appalachia, blacks from the South. Above all, the sit-down was a direct and flagrant attack on the property rights of owners, a challenge to conventional middle-class attitudes, and a temptation to police, prosecutors, and judges who could use anti-trespass and other laws against it.

Originally John Lewis & Co. had planned to concentrate first on Big Steel, on the theory that "as steel goes, so goes" unionization and much else. During early 1936, however, "quickie" shutdowns swept through the huge tire plants of Akron, and major sit-downs swept through the automobile industry during the following year. Encouraged by FDR's big win over the GOP, and under some guidance from Lewis, workers concentrated on Fisher and other plants that supplied bodies and parts to General Motors plants.

Sometimes strikes broke out over an incident, as when an active unionist was fired for jumping over a conveyor line in his hurry to get to a toilet three hundred yards away. But there was a broader logic in auto workers taking the lead, and against GM. Auto workers were already famous for their youthfulness and bravado. Their shop-floor militancy easily shifted into tumultuous, old-fashioned syndicalism, tending toward confrontation and violence. The structure of work in the auto industry encouraged militance: skilled workers such as welders and metal polishers who stuck together in small groups, partly to protect their jobs; a dense system of shop stewards who stayed close to their men; and considerable direct dealing between stewards and foremen.

So General Motors was the target—and some target! By 1937 GM was the world's biggest manufacturing corporation in number of employees, sales, and profits. It was not "big but colossal," *Fortune* enthused, "the hugest technological organism of our technological age," the "world's most complicated and most profitable manufacturing enterprise." Its Chevrolet, Pontiac, Oldsmobile, Buick, and Cadillac–La Salle divisions, along with its Yellow taxi and related operations, claimed 45 percent of the American market. Considered by some the best-managed corporation in the country, under the leadership of Alfred P. Sloan, Jr., William Knudsen, and big Du Pont stockholders, GM had achieved a fine balance between centralized policy-making and decentralized operations. GM was tough on its executives, its suppliers, and its union employees. All this contrasted with the auto workers: undisciplined, factionalized, poorly coordinated, infested with spies for GM. It was David versus Goliath, and of course David had to win.

"The most critical labor conflict of the nineteen thirties," as Walter Galenson called it, erupted in Flint as 1937 dawned, and swept through Toledo, Detroit, and other cities. Flint set the pace. Organized in squads of fifteen under a captain, the sit-ins there carried on strike duties, conducted health and safety inspections, played cards and checkers, attended classes in labor history, did KP, ate meals brought in from outside, and settled down at night among their products, sometimes in cushy Fisher bodies. General Motors seemed muscle-bound. A friendly judge in Flint who ordered the strikers out of a Fisher plant was exposed as all too friendly—he owned several thousand shares of GM stock. When GM cut off food and heat, strikers drove off encroaching police with a barrage of pop bottles and brickbats.

This violence projected Governor Frank Murphy into the struggle. Murphy was a far cry from the compliant Republican politicos who so often had aided big corporations in their labor struggles. Proud of his Irish heritage, devout in his Roman Catholicism, gentle in manner, he was also a stalwart civil libertarian, a committed liberal Democrat, and so ambitious as to talk of becoming the first Catholic President of the United States. Murphy called out the National Guard, not to attack the strikers but to curb violence on both sides. He also tried to mediate the dispute; when this failed, negotiations shifted to Washington, where the newly reinaugurated President and Frances Perkins pressured Sloan and Lewis for settlement. Tension mounted as the auto workers occupied another huge GM plant, a judge unencumbered by GM stock issued a new injunction, and Murphy warned Lewis that the authorities would have to carry out the court order.

While the strikers sweated it out, Lewis loudly stuck to his demand for exclusive representation of his auto workers, Sloan refused for a time even to meet with the CIO leader, Murphy kept his troops at the ready but refused to send them in, and he and Lewis had a dramatic face-off in Michigan. Throughout, Roosevelt and Perkins sought to bring the two sides together and head off a violent showdown. At last, one cold fact prevailed: the strikers had cut GM's auto production to a driblet. Quite suddenly, GM capitulated, granting recognition to the auto workers as bargaining agent for "those employees of the Corporation who are members of the Union," and pledging not to bargain with any other union for six months. Soon strikers were leaving the plants singing "Solidarity Forever." They knew that *they* had won the battle. Soon Chrysler—but not Ford—followed GM.

As GM goes, so goes steel—at least Big Steel. Eager to crack U.S. Steel, inheritor of Carnegie's policy of low wages and Frick's anti-unionism, Lewis had established the Steel Workers Organizing Committee, CIO, under his longtime protégé and lieutenant Philip Murray. A warm and compassionate man who, as Murray Kempton wrote, touched "the love and not the fears of men," Murray had a steely determination easily aroused to anger when his fundamental faith in unionism and industrial democracy was challenged. Working closely with ethnic and black leaders, claiming Roosevelt's blessing with the message "The President Wants *You* to Join the Union" (he didn't know whether they were referring to him or to President Lewis, FDR told reporters archly), Murray exploited above all the presence of a multitude of company unions throughout U.S. Steel. He would turn these "kept unions" on their heads by co-opting rebels in restless company unions and converting them into rank-and-file leaders under his own direction.

By January 1937 the SWOC claimed over 100,000 members, U.S. Steel was witnessing sit-down strikes spreading through other mass-production industries, and its chief, Myron Taylor, was reassessing his company's whole labor strategy. His chance encounter with Lewis in Washington's Mayflower Hotel led to a series of secret negotiations in the capital and an agreement that startled the nation. In what has been called the most important single document in the history of the American labor movement, the corporation agreed to bargain with SWOC (though only for the workers it represented), gave a 10 percent wage boost across the board, and granted the forty-hour week with time and a half for overtime. A million Carnegie and Frick workers, someone observed, might have stirred in their early graves.

Little Steel was a far different story. Led by the redoubtable Tom Girdler of Republic Steel, the heads of the smaller, independent companies not only were fiercely determined to resist unionization but had a strategy of resistance—the "Mohawk Valley formula." Brand the union leaders as extremists, the formula prescribed. Mobilize the community by threatening to shut down the plant. Build up an anti-union armed force of police, vigilantes, and special deputies. Set up a puppet association of "loyal" employees to stage a conspicuous back-to-work movement. Have a citizens' committee demand reopening of the plant. Resume operations to any extent possible, announce that the plant is in full operation, and denounce the remaining dissidents as thwarters of the sacred right to work.

Given such a strategy of resistance, and given a militant union flushed with victories over Big Steel, clashes and riots were inevitable. They culminated in South Chicago on Memorial Day 1937, when marchers seeking to mass-picket Republic Steel confronted police marshaled two blocks from the gate. Someone threw a tree limb at the police, a cop fired his revolver into the air, some in the crowd threw rocks—and then the police fired point-blank into the massed men, women, and children, killing ten and wounding at least eighty. Three policemen were hospitalized. By the summer of 1937 Bethlehem, Republic, and other Little Steel companies were still holding out against the SWOC. The Mohawk Valley formula was working.

CONGRESS-PURGING: THE BROKEN SPELL

Behind the great waves of unionization in auto and steel were not only pent-up demands and militant leaders but a vast expansion of production in the mid-thirties. As in the past, mass industrialization buoyed mass organization, as though capitalism and unionism American style required each other. As sales of passenger cars almost doubled from 1933 and 1934 to 1936 and 1937, the number of auto production workers rose by about a half from 1933 to 1937. Iron and steel output doubled in the same period, employment there also rising by about a half. But what rose in the great waves would drop in the troughs. In midsummer 1937 tremors of recession began spreading through the economy. The stock market slid and then a jarring series of sell orders tumbled prices to new lows.

Suddenly it seemed like 1929 all over again. People talked of "Black Tuesday"—October 19, 1937—when prices cascaded, in Henry Morgenthau's words, "amid an hysteria resembling a mob in a theater fire." And for a time the Roosevelt Administration reacted much in the manner of the Hoover government eight years before. The crash looked to Berle "like 1903—a rich man's panic." Her statisticians expected an early business upturn, Secretary Perkins reported. The President, suspecting that big business was trying to drive the market down to hurt the Administration, was cautiously hopeful. He did not yet realize that it was his own sharp cutback in federal spending that, far more than any business action, had precipitated the slump. A flurry of White House meetings resulted in little action. Then began a series of sickening drops that continued through the fall and winter as the "Roosevelt recession" deepened, with unemployment, which had been cut from 12.8 million in 1933 to 7.7 million in 1937, rising to 10.4 million in 1938.

"Everything will work out all right if we just sit tight and keep quiet," the President had told his cabinet three weeks before Black Tuesday. He asked Commerce Secretary Roper to stop "giving out so many Hooverish statements." But sitting tight worked no better for FDR than it had for Hoover. His cabinet members brought him more bad news. "We are headed right into another depression," Morgenthau told him. "The question is, Mr. President—what are we going to do about it?"

The President did not know what to do about it. Berle found him "ill, tired and obviously confused." Morgenthau found him worried about fascism abroad and the possibility that it would come to America in the form of big businessmen organizing to put their own man into the White House.

And at a cabinet meeting early in November, FDR betrayed his irritation and anxiety.

"Of course, I am glad to hear from the various members of the Cabinet their sad story of how bad business conditions are," Roosevelt began cuttingly, as Morgenthau recalled in his diary. "Last night when I went to bed, alongside of my bed was the darnedest letter you ever saw from Henry." The President's anger was rising.

"I am sick and tired of being told by the Cabinet, by Henry and by everybody else for the last two weeks what's the matter with the country and nobody suggests what I should do."

Morgenthau spoke up. "You can do something about public utilities. You can do something about the railroads. You could do something about housing. Above all, you must do something to reassure business."

"You want me to turn on the old record."

What business wanted to know, the secretary said, was "Are we headed toward state Socialism or are we going to continue on a capitalistic basis?"

"I have told them that again and again."

"All right, Mr. President, tell them for the fifteenth time. That's what they want to know."

Wallace, for his part, thought the President should do something about labor, while Farley urged him to tell the country that he was going to reduce the cost of government.

"All right, Jim; I will turn on the old record."

More desperately than ever the President reached out for advice, but the advice he received was still sharply conflicting. Morgenthau used the slump to urge the President almost daily to retrench even further and balance the budget. But while he and Farley wanted to conciliate business, Ickes, Perkins, and sometimes Wallace sought an expansion of New Deal social programs. Staff people were even more divided. Many in the Treasury backed Morgenthau, but throughout the Administration economists of Keynesian persuasion were pointing to the recession as evidence that the Administration had spent too little, not too much. The most powerful advocates of spending were Marriner Eccles at the Federal Reserve and Harry Hopkins, but Hopkins was ill during the critical days. A brilliant assortment of economists and lawyers scattered through the government—Herman Oliphant in Treasury, Mordecai Ezekiel in Agriculture, Lauchlin Currie under Eccles, Leon Henderson under Hopkins—fought their daily battles with memos and mimeograph machines.

The opposition was busy too. Early in December the National Association of Manufacturers, meeting at the Waldorf-Astoria Hotel in New York, adopted resolutions that to New Dealers indicated big business had learned nothing and forgotten nothing. Manufacturing was "shackled by restrictive legislation, burdened with excessive taxes, continually in doubt as to the nature and permanency of government policies, crippled by labor difficulties and handicapped by inability to secure funds from investors." When factories prospered, America prospered. The recommendations were no fresher than the plaints: Reduce taxes on business. Stop laws that reduced incentive to invest funds. Repeal laws that incited labor controversies. Produce more wealth rather than redistribute it. Above all, bolster "business confidence."

It was a dismal December, with Roosevelt still beset and uncertain, little clusters of New Dealers meeting secretly for feverish discussion, and the recession worsening. Differences over solutions remained acute in both cabinet and staffs. The old conflict between central planners and trustbusters broke out again. Keynesians pressed for much larger spending, but they were divided over proposals for modest pump priming, heavy compensatory spending, and an attack on "secular stagnation" that would call for massive controls, planning, and long-run spending. Morgenthau stuck to his budget-balancing pitch like a man obsessed. Some advisers wanted a comprehensive approach; others would concentrate on rejuvenating specific industries, such as railroads and housing.

Amidst it all the President fretted and pondered. Never had people seen him reach out so far for advice and counsel. During early 1938 businessmen streamed into the White House on the President's invitation to press their ideas on him. The Administration sponsored in Washington a conference of small businessmen that became so turbulent that police had to be called. The Business Advisory Council, through its spokesman, Averell Harriman, asked the President to provide leadership around which they could rally. A hundred thousand Detroiters turned out for a relief demonstration; three thousand youth delegates convened in Washington to demand a "youth act" that would provide part-time jobs.

"There is in Chicago," Grace Abbott wrote Molly Dewson at the Democratic National Committee, "and in a very large part of the country, more suffering than there was in 1933 when the President came into office. It is a common sight to see children salvaging food from garbage cans."

Bitterly Roosevelt attacked his critics who came up with no constructive proposals of their own. At a press conference with editors of trade papers he complained of people whose advice was in the form of "Yes, but—." "They will say, 'Oh, yes, we are in favor of flood control, but we do not like this way of doing it.' Or, 'We do not like this party doing it, or this President doing it.' " They were all for this or that but not if it cost money.

It was a set of conditions, not a theoretical breakthrough, that finally moved the President out of his faineancy. In March the stock market's halting decline suddenly turned into a panicky drop; unemployment and relief rolls were still growing. The economic decline since September had become the sharpest the nation had ever known. And a critical set of congressional elections would be coming in November. On a train trip back from Georgia in the spring Roosevelt looked out the window at the nondescript men and women who—five years after his inauguration—were still waiting for him along the track to wave and smile. He turned to an aide. *"They* understand what we're trying to do." He knew that now he must act for them.

Once FDR decided, there was no looking back. In mid-April 1938 he asked Congress for a three-billion-dollar spending bill. Over a billion dollars would go to the WPA; smaller sums would go to the CCC, the National Youth Administration, and the Farm Security Administration. He did not forsake the Brandeisians; a bit later he agreed with congressional leaders on a full-scale investigation of concentrated economic power through what would become the Temporary National Economic Committee. An anguished Morgenthau threatened to resign when he saw his last chance at budget-balancing go glimmering. His boss was tough, warning him that he would go down through history as having quit under fire. Morgenthau stayed, reflecting that the ties that bound him and the President together transcended even this issue.

In his message to Congress the President stressed that the situation called for an act of collective will by the nation's leadership, under the "discipline of democracy." In his fireside chat he repeated this point. "Our capacity is limited only by our ability to work together. What is needed is the will." Obviously the President had summoned that will, after being almost immobilized by the shock of the steep and sudden slump. Once again he might mobilize the will of the people. But could he summon the political leadership and followership of the nation?

* * *

The answer lay in a tangle of leadership elements—the President's own morale and determination, the attitudes of key members of Congress who were both his followers and yet leaders in their own right—and in the nation's voters, who would exert their own leadership in the elections of 1938 and 1940. The answer lay also in the linkages between President and people—most notably in the organized interests of the nation and in the political parties. And by the summer of 1938 all these elements lay in a state of discord and disarray.

Angered by opposition in Congress, embittered by the savage attacks of business leaders, frustrated by the intractability of the economic situation, Roosevelt was more determined than ever to protect the New Deal from conservative counterattacks and if possible to extend it. While he was as willing as ever to horse-trade with Congress, he was now taking the most militant and radical stance of his entire public career; more than ever before, he would use the stratagems of the fox but only to augment the power of the lion. Repeatedly during 1937 and early 1938 he tried to rally his forces in Congress and country.

Roosevelt's inept handling of the Court bill, and above all his defeat on the issue, had made him seem vulnerable within a few months of his great mandate of 1936. While many members of Congress had sympathized with FDR's objectives, in the light of the reactionary Supreme Court decisions of 1935 and 1936, they had been appalled by his methods. Above all, in this sixth year of the New Deal, and after sixteen months of the Court fight and other grueling conflicts, they were tired of "must bills," tired of crises, tired of being called "rubber-stamp yes-men," tired of bustling, pushing young zealots from the White House. Their attitudes could be summed up in the anguished phone call of one congressman to the White House in April 1938: "For God's sake, don't send us any more controversial legislation!" An index to the congressional mind of 1937-38 was the fate of the President's bill to reorganize the executive branch.

On the face of it, no measure could have seemed less controversial than the reorganization bill. For years Presidents from both parties, with the help of business and other management experts, had been trying to make the executive establishment more responsible, accountable, effective, and efficient, mainly through strengthening the President's executive controls. But FDR was unlucky—or maladroit—enough to bring in the reorganization bill about the same time as the Court proposal. Tainted by this association, the bill languished in 1937.

Next year the storm broke out in full fury. In this time of Hitler, Stalin, and Mussolini, opponents dubbed the proposal the "dictator bill." Still, White House forces were holding their own when an unlucky adjournment over the weekend enabled Father Coughlin, Frank Gannett's National Committee to Uphold Constitutional Government, Hearst's newspapers, and even President Green of the AFL to mobilize opposition against the bill. A blizzard of telegrams—300,000 by some counts—hit Congress on Monday morning. Congressmen ran for cover.

The President issued an extraordinary statement:

"I have no inclination to be a dictator.

"I have none of the qualifications which would make me a successful dictator.

"I have too much historical background and too much knowledge of existing dictatorships to make me desire any form of dictatorship for a democracy like the United States of America."

Rarely had Roosevelt been forced so much on the defensive. And it was not enough. Despite his willingness also to accept some weakening changes in the measure, the House recommitted the bill by a 204–196 vote. Six Progressives, two Farmer-Laborites, and 108 Democrats voted against the Administration.

The journey of wages-and-hours legislation through legislative obstacles was, like the course of the reorganization bill, a clear reflection of the congressional mind. By the mid-thirties the United States was far behind other industrialized nations in wages-and-hours standards. NRA codes, during their brief existence, had sought to set decent wages for a shorter workweek. The wages-and-hours bill the Administration had brought into Congress in 1937 after the death of the NRA was ground to pieces between the labor-liberal bloc and the southern bloc. The main obstacle was the House Rules Committee, in which two conservative southern Democrats held the balance of power, Howard W. Smith of Virginia and Edward E. Cox of Georgia. When the bill was held over to the 1938 session, once again the Rules Committee balked. A discharge petition was necessary to pry the bill out of Smith's and Cox's hands.

Afraid that too few representatives would sign the petition, the Administration resorted to a typical Rooseveltian stratagem. Senator Claude Pepper, a staunch FDR supporter, was involved in a slam-bang race for renomination in Florida. The White House had reason to believe that he would win big. Since Pepper was an open and stalwart backer of the wage-hour bill, White House tacticians—and especially the Tactician-in-Chief—calculated that if the Florida congressman could be induced to speak vigorously for it, his win would be interpreted as a southern endorsement of the bill. As an inducement to Pepper, the White House turned a $10,000 fund over to his campaign. The stratagem worked. After Pepper's decisive victory so many representatives crowded around to sign the petition in the well of the House that proceedings were delayed. Liberated from Rules, the bill passed the House by a heavy vote. Senators threatened to filibuster it to death, but after further compromises the bill finally became law in June.

"That's that," said Roosevelt as he signed the measure. It was a sigh of relief over the outcome, of disappointment over the weakening compromises—and perhaps of dismay over the hurdles in the legislative process. Part of the problem lay with the President himself, for the White House had failed to establish close relationships with rank-and-file Democrats in the lower chamber. When Pittsburgh Democratic boss David Lawrence wanted to bring in three new Democratic congressmen to meet the President early in 1937, FDR put him off, finally allotted three minutes, and then postponed even that appointment. "There is a group of aggressive progressive Democrats who have stuck by you through thick and thin," Representative Kent Keller wrote the President the next year, ". . . and I do not believe that you have ever called in a single one of this group" to consult about policy.

As Washington returned more and more to "politics as usual" in 1937 and 1938 after the glory days of the early New Deal, organized interest groups appeared to play a more dominant role. For some bills, indeed, the imprimatur of pressure-group leaders was now as important as the sponsorship of the White House. Low-paid workers had had insufficient political strength to smooth passage of the wage-hour bill, while the leadership of the AFL retained much of its old hostility toward minimum-wage laws. The reorganization bill had had tough going because there was only thin, generalized public support for a streamlined executive branch. For spending programs, however, Congress gave many millions more to FDR than he had requested in his message of April 1938. Farm programs were continued without undue political controversy or delay. Earlier programs had helped create a huge constituency of the needy expecting and demanding such programs.

Organized and organizing workers and farmers had helped build the New Deal, which in its turn had invigorated the labor and farm movements and organizations. Thereupon the groups ran ahead of the New Deal, pressing for recognition and rewards that the Roosevelt Administration would not or could not grant. John L. Lewis's Committee for Industrial Organization, more hostile than ever to the AFL, was one of the most militant of these groups. Once dependent on Roosevelt's political and psychological patronage, and on legislation such as the Wagner Act, the CIO was becoming more independent of the Administration and willing to put pressure on it. And Lewis, angry over "broken promises," was infuriated by FDR's statement during the sit-down strikes: "A plague on both your houses."

With his pug face wearing its customary scowl, the CIO leader wanted a payoff for his help to FDR in 1936. It was not forthcoming, as Roosevelt played his own brand of group politics. But Lewis could play his too. The transformation of the original CIO into the Congress of Industrial Organizations late in 1938, with Lewis as president and Murray and Hillman as vice presidents, signified not only a wider separation from the AFL but the determination of the CIO to follow its own economic and political course—with or without Roosevelt's patronage.

Crucial in the mix of leadership factors was FDR's own popularity. The President in 1938 was losing public favor, as measured by polls, not only among upper-income voters but even more among middle- and lower-income groups. In fact, the decline was not as steep as it seemed, and even at the lowest point of his popularity in 1938 he commanded the support of a bare majority of the people. But in the flush days of the early New Deal he had given the *impression* of much greater popularity. Public attitudes were also highly ambivalent. The vast majority—even of executives and professional people—approved of him personally, or at least "liked his personality," as the *Fortune* pollsters phrased it. Newspaper reports squared with the poll results. Support was much lower for his "methods," his advisers and associates, and some of his policies. Opinion, as the polls registered it, was significantly, but not sharply, skewed by income; of five major economic groups—blacks, poor, lower-middle, upper-middle, and high-income—all but the first two opposed the President's methods. Running through the opposition was a streak of fear of FDR's power and his use of it.

*   *   *

A determined and even vengeful President, a New Deal still not fully dealt, a Congress moving toward all-out resistance to the Administration, group interests fired with both hope and disillusion, congressional elections nearing in the fall of 1938—the tangle of leadership elements had become a gridlock of political forces. How unlock it? At some point in the spring of 1938 the President came to a drastic decision—it was high time for a party showdown, time for a purge of anti-New Deal Democrats in Congress. That Roosevelt could come to this decision was the true measure of both the intensity of his feeling and the urgency of his situation. He did not enjoy personal confrontations. He would rather manipulate his adversaries, or maneuver around them, than attack head-on.

That Roosevelt would seek a solution within the Democratic party was another measure of his concern. If the Democracy appeared to be a part of the problem rather than a solution to it, the President had to share the blame for this. For some years he had variously used, not used, and abused the Democracy as it served his electoral interests—by taking little leadership in developing grass-roots organizations, by flirting with laborite third parties in New York and a few other states and with the La Follette Progressives in Wisconsin, by building up and exploiting his personal leadership and *personalismo* rather than shaping and utilizing collective party leadership. In suddenly assuming active generalship of the party, moreover, the President was invading political turf far better defended than he may have realized.

Doubtless he had observed the experience of the GOP. In many ways—and often unnoticed by the national press—the conservatives who dominated the Republican party had been trying "soft purges" of GOP liberals, just as New Dealers had been considering ways and means of overcoming conservatives in the Democracy. Right-wing Democrats and Republicans had toyed with the idea of coalition, just as New Deal Democrats and liberal Republicans had done. FDR's purge effort was not new—but it was bigger, more intensive, more dramatic.

It was more visible and open, because the President wanted it that way. Firing the opening salvo in a fireside chat in June 1938, he lashed out at "Copperheads"—reviving the term for pro-peace Democrats of the Civil War—who in the great fight for liberalism wanted "peace at any price," and he defined the issue in 1938 as between liberals who saw that new conditions called for new remedies and conservatives who believed that individual initiative and private philanthropy would solve the nation's problems. As President of the United States, he said disingenuously, he was not himself taking part in primaries or asking people to vote Democratic. But—

"As the head of the Democratic party . . . charged with the responsibility of the definitely liberal declaration of principles set forth in the 1936 Democratic platform," he had every right to speak out in clear instances when liberal and conservative Democrats were opposing each other.

The drive for party realignment, James Patterson noted later, was at last underway. But the President was not mainly thinking in grand strategic terms. That was not his interest at the moment. He simply wanted to rid Congress of men who were obstructing the New Deal. And he would invade southern and other states and meet his foes on their own political ground.

The conflict that followed in the Democratic party had all the intensity of fratricidal strife, along with a few touches of comic opera. A host of Democratic politicians had to calculate whether to stick with the President or break with him or somehow hide, whether to work with Republicans in an ad hoc coalition or rely on their own party, how to take some credit for the more popular elements of the New Deal without being labeled yes-men for the White House.

Roosevelt too had to calculate just how he would grant recognition or withhold it and what kinds of blessings he would bestow. The President was put to the test in Kentucky, where he was strongly backing his loyal Senate Majority Leader, Alben Barkley, over the ebullient governor of the state, A. B. "Happy" Chandler. Greeting the presidential train, Happy deftly slid into the presidential limousine to take his bows too, while Barkley smoldered and Roosevelt maintained his usual sang-froid. As the "purge train" continued on its way, the President gave his apostolic benediction to good friends like Congressmen Lyndon Johnson and Maury Maverick in Texas, delicately criticized Senator "Cotton Ed" Smith of South Carolina for allegedly saying that a family could live on fifty cents a day, and later, in Maryland, stumped for two days against the urbane Senator Millard Tydings.

The hardest confrontation for Roosevelt came in Georgia, his "adopted state," where the venerable Senator Walter George was fighting off a challenge from Lawrence Camp, a young attorney hand-picked by the Administration. While George sat impassively on the platform a few feet away, the President addressed a throng of 50,000 persons at Barnesville:

"Let me make it clear," he said, that the senator "is, and I hope always will be, my personal friend. He is beyond question, beyond any possible question, a gentleman and a scholar." But a candidate had to answer two questions, FDR went on. "First, has the record of the candidate shown, while differing perhaps in details, a constant active fighting attitude in favor of the broad objectives of the party and of the Government as they are constituted today; and secondly, does the candidate really, in his heart, deep down in his heart, believe in those objectives?" George, he asserted, could not answer yes.

"Mr. President," said the senator when Roosevelt finished, "I want you to know that I accept the challenge."

"Let's always be friends," Roosevelt replied smilingly.

The purge had provoked the nation's press. Editors and columnists condemned Roosevelt's "meddling" in "local" elections. Cartoonists pictured him as a donkey rider, a pants kicker, a big-game hunter. A White House cabal was sounding the death knell of representative government, former brain truster Raymond Moley wrote in *Newsweek.* Liberals criticized the President for conducting the purge in an improvised, unplanned way. Feeling was most intense within the Democracy. Some party leaders evaded the issue: Farley was in Alaska part of the time, and Garner, increasingly turned off by the New Deal, would not meet the President in Texas. Southern conservatives were the most bitter; to them the purge was an assault on the southern way of life as well as on their own power in the party. The southern people, said Senator Glass, "may wake up too late to find that the negrophiles who are running the Democratic Party now will soon precipitate another Reconstruction period for us."

With their votes southern whites gave their verdict: the South would remain unreconstructed. George, Smith, and Tydings, FDR's chief targets, all won decisively. Maverick and other FDR supporters—though not Lyndon Johnson—lost in Texas. While Barkley beat Chandler in Kentucky, several anti-New Dealers or semi-New Dealers won in northern states. FDR had one small but pleasing consolation prize. His friends in New York had used both American Labor party support and Democratic bosses to replace John O'Connor, FDR's foe on the Rules Committee, with James H. Fay, a war veteran with impeccable Irish antecedents. Still, the purge had been a "bust," as Farley had predicted. Said the President glumly, "It takes a long, long time to bring the past up to the present."

But the nadir of FDR's fortunes was yet to come. In the fall congressional elections the Republicans almost doubled their strength in the House and added eight senators to their small band in the upper chamber. While the liberal bloc in the House was halved, the Republicans lost not a single seat. Some promising Republicans with fresh appeal won in statewide elections as well: Leverett Saltonstall in Massachusetts, Robert A. Taft in Ohio, John Bricker in Ohio, Harold Stassen in Minnesota, while the young Tom Dewey almost overcame the redoubtable Herbert Lehman for governor of New York. A trio of progressive governors failed of reelection: Frank Murphy in Michigan, Philip La Follette in Wisconsin, Elmer Benson in Minnesota.

The President sought to play down the results. In the time-honored way of Presidents explaining midterm election setbacks, he contended that the trouble lay in local scandals and squabbles, labor strikes, poor candidates. And after all, his party still held big majorities in the House and Senate. But one fact could not be blinked: Franklin D. Roosevelt had suffered his first major electoral defeat in eighteen years.

*   *   *

FDR would willingly defy conservatives but not constituents. If it was a mark of his courage that he would press his fight for liberalism following his Court-packing and other legislative defeats and the "Roosevelt recession," it was a mark of his caution that he took a much more moderate posture after the congressional and state election returns of 1938. He told the new Congress in January 1939 that "having passed the period of internal conflict in the launching of our program of social reform," he and they must now "preserve our reforms." Not that he would surrender the New Deal ship. He warned the Democracy, in a Jackson Day dinner speech, against being the "Democratic Tweedledum" to a "Republican Tweedledee." And he made a spate of major appointments guaranteed to raise conservative hackles: Hopkins to follow Roper as Secretary of Commerce, the now unemployed Frank Murphy to take Cummings's place as Attorney General, Frankfurter to replace Cardozo in Holmes's old seat on the Supreme Court, William O. Douglas to succeed Brandeis on the high bench.

But if Roosevelt would not retreat, he would not advance. He reverted once again to his old economic orthodoxy, refusing to equalize old-age benefits between rich and poor states by raising the federal contribution to Social Security. "Not one nickel more," he said. "Not one solitary nickel. Once you get off the 50-50 matching basis the sky's the limit." He refused to support Wagner's proposed national health program embracing medical insurance and funds for child and maternity care, public health services, and hospital construction. He complained to Morgenthau, according to the secretary, that he was "sick and tired of having a lot of long-haired people around here who want a billion dollars for schools, a billion dollars for public health."

The President now seemed almost rueful about his public image. "You undergraduates who see me for the first time," he told a delighted student audience at Chapel Hill, "have read . . . that I am, at the very least, an ogre—a consorter with Communists, a destroyer of the rich, a breaker of our ancient traditions." They had heard, he went on amid laughter, that he had invented the economic royalist, was about to plunge the nation into both war and bankruptcy, and "breakfasted every morning on a dish of 'grilled millionaire.'

"Actually I am an exceedingly mild mannered person—a practitioner of peace, both domestic and foreign, a believer in the capitalistic system, and for my breakfast a devotee of scrambled eggs."

Even if the President had wished to expand the New Deal, Congress would have stopped him. The election results had bolstered southern committee chairmen as the power elite on Capitol Hill. They not only held the balance of power between Republicans and New Deal Democrats but used the ancient weapons of congressional attack on presidential leadership. The House Committee on Un-American Activities, chaired by Texan Martin Dies, renewed its jabs at Ickes, Hopkins, Perkins, and other officials for their "softness on communists." Another committee under Howard W. Smith exposed reds and irregularities in the National Labor Relations Board. A conservative coalition of southern Democrats attacked the President's crucial appointing power, both by enforcing "senatorial courtesy" against top appointments and by restricting the political activities of lower-echelon federal employees. Even more, Congress slashed funds for some New Deal agencies, and especially for administrative functions that in the long run might critically influence the impact of programs—planning, research, economic analysis, information, staffing.

The New Deal lived on, however, in substance and style—and no one personified it more arrestingly than Eleanor Roosevelt. It was in these waning days of the domestic New Deal that she moved to the fore as a leader extraordinarily sensitive to needs her husband's program had not fully met. It was not surprising that she would work for women's rights, or concern herself with dire problems of housing, health, and poverty in field and factory, or devote an enormous amount of time to the plight of the nation's young people, several million of whom lacked jobs.

But the First Lady advanced as well into the nation's most sensitive political and social battlefield—the needs and rights of black Americans. She established close working relationships with black leaders like Mary McLeod Bethune and Walter White while her husband remained cautious. She strongly supported an antilynching bill, in contrast to her husband, who deplored the horrifying lynchings in the South but dared not recommend legislation for fear of alienating southern congressional leaders who could kill or mutilate his other measures.

Eleanor Roosevelt not only had to cope with her husband's caution, with aides close to Roosevelt who fretted over the pressure that black leaders put on their boss, with attacks on her in Congress, but had to walk a delicate line between respect for her husband's political situation and her own right to speak and act for herself. Even more, she had to cope with herself—with her own class and cultural origins, with the influence on her of a great-aunt who had had slaves as personal servants, and with her own tendency to use words like "darky" and "pickaninny." She learned as she led, and led as she learned.

Her symbolic role came to a magnificent climax in the spring of 1939 when the Daughters of the American Revolution refused to permit Marian Anderson to sing in Constitution Hall. The First Lady promptly resigned her membership in the DAR and set about, with the enthusiastic help of Ickes and the permission of the President, to help make arrangements for the contralto to sing in front of the Lincoln Memorial. Seventy-five thousand people mustered at the base of the memorial and along the Mall, a setting that Ickes called "unique, majestic, and impressive." Marian Anderson began her performance with "America," a paean to liberty. She ended it with "Nobody Knows the Trouble I've Seen," an ode to justice and a reminder of inequality.

DEADLOCK AT THE CENTER

Why did you lose? *The Nation* had asked the three progressive governors who failed of reelection in 1938, and the answers were revealing. They saw their defeats as part of a national reaction against the New Deal. People believed that government somehow "had muffed the ball," said La Follette, that it "had tried to do the right thing, but that in spite of all our relief spending, pump-priming, and social legislation we were back where we started from—in the midst of depression." Benson of Minnesota and Murphy of Michigan also saw the Roosevelt recession—though they did not call it that—as the underlying problem, especially in the farm areas of their states. La Follette quoted an agricultural economist on the big Republican gains among farmers: "I guess you can't beat the price of cheese."

Some New Dealers decided by the late thirties that the Administration had not only mismanaged the economy but mismanaged the New Deal itself. FDR's lieutenants came in for a full share of blame. The peppery, cantankerous Ickes caused endless friction as he fought with all comers—Johnson, Morgenthau, Perkins, Hopkins, and especially Wallace. Other rivalries heating up in the Administration were fair game for Washington reporters. The President frowned on these conflicts, but his administrative methods seemed to encourage them; he even appeared to enjoy pitting bureaucrat against bureaucrat. He delegated power so loosely that agency chiefs found themselves entangled in crisscrossed lines of authority. That New Deal programs were uncoordinated and improvised also made for friction. And the President was often an enigmatic boss.

"You are a wonderful person but you are one of the most difficult men to work with that I have ever known," Ickes blurted out to FDR one day, according to his diary.

"Because I get too hard at times?" Roosevelt asked.

"No, you never get too hard but you won't talk frankly even with people who are loyal to you and of whose loyalty you are fully convinced. You keep your cards close up against your belly."

Some have found method in FDR's administrative madness. His technique of fuzzy delegation, according to Arthur Schlesinger, Jr., "often provided a testing of initiative, competence and imagination which produced far better results than by playing safe by the book." By flouting the administrative rule of "making a mesh of things," even at the risk of making a mess of them, the President avoided hardened arteries of structure and control. And as usual he was willing to take on the burden of salving the aches and lacerations that resulted from the administrative infighting.

Yet Roosevelt himself had serious qualms about this way of running things. Since his years in the Navy Department he had maintained a strong interest in executive leadership, planning, and management. He set up an Executive Council of cabinet officers in 1933 and later a National Emergency Council of wider membership; these dwindled into mere clearinghouses of information. By 1936 the President was so troubled by the organizational confusion and policy disorder of the New Deal that he was surprised the Republicans did not make it a crucial issue in the campaign. Realizing that "the President needs help," he established the Committee on Administrative Management, which developed many of the proposals that made up his ill-fated reorganization proposal of 1937. One of the committee's few recommendations that survived the legislative gantlet was its proposal that the President be given six assistants with "a passion for anonymity."

If the President wanted better management, why did he tolerate and even encourage tangled lines of organization, duplication of effort, and administrative cross-purposes in the executive branch? Partly because he had no choice. He utterly lacked the personnel, machinery, and power for centralized supervision and management. For six years the President's staff consisted of a press aide, an executive assistant, a bevy of devoted secretaries, one or two speech writers, a legal counsel, and a handful of advisers from outside the White House. To hold the scattered strings of administrative control in his own hands, to get his instructions carried out, to keep subordinates from ganging up on him, even to find out what was going on in the lower echelons, he had his lieutenants come to him, be dependent on him, confide in him, let him pass out rewards and penalties. Hence the Chief Executive became also Chief Disorganizer and Chief Manipulator.

Even more, the disarray of presidential management and planning was part of the peculiar American system of checks and balances in the structure of the federal government and indeed in the whole federal-state-local pyramid of government. There was nothing FDR could do about this; the Framers of the Constitution had bequeathed it all, and the essential structure had not altered in a century and a half. Roosevelt had to work with all the blockages, slowdowns, veto traps, and compromises built into a system deliberately fashioned to thwart rapid governmental response to popular majorities and to thwart consistent and continuous follow-through on policy and program.

The crucial test for Roosevelt was his capacity to wring from the system as much of a New Deal program as was possible, and he met this test magnificently. Day after day, he patiently, cunningly, even cynically, pulled strings, played on men's ambitions, exploited their vanities, applied soothing syrup—inspired them, manipulated them, raised them up, put them off, and eased them away when they were no longer useful to him.

He did all this so well, indeed, that he may never have recognized how much the system eroded the substance and impact of his New Deal programs. Even more, he never truly confronted the system that in the end would defeat him. All his personal politicking, coaxing, and manipulating could not pack the Supreme Court or purge Congress or reorganize the executive branch, but he was successful enough in his daily maneuvering and dealing to achieve at least half-victories on many policies. Indeed, these partial victories may have helped the President to misconceive the constitutional system of delay and deadlock that he faced. In calling for Court reform he had described President, Congress, and judiciary as three workhorses proceeding in harness, and he had rebuked the Supreme Court for not doing its part on the team. But the Framers had not set up the federal government to be a team—quite the opposite.

The problem was that the President faced more than groups of legislators and judges and bureaucrats who happened to differ with him. He confronted men and women who were leaders of institutions that had different constitutional foundations, traditions, career patterns, political constituencies, and ideological or policy outlooks than the President's. Hence to attack individuals in these institutions was not only to trigger opposition from their friends and followers but to activate the full powers of the institutions themselves. To challenge a congressional committee chairman like Senator George meant taking on the seniority system and all that went with it. To seek to add members to the Supreme Court was to challenge the whole judicial system. To curb the independence of an agency like the Army Corps of Engineers or the Federal Reserve Board was to activate a host of client interests backing such agencies. Inevitably New Deal programs were morselized in the ensuing clashes.

In olden times a President in this predicament might have used his leadership of the governmental and party team to put through party programs over opposition in Congress, state governments, and even the judiciary. This choice was not open to FDR by the late 1930s, for he had not been a strong party leader and his party was not unified philosophically or organizationally. The Democratic party by the mid-nineteenth century had lost much of its egalitarian spirit of Jeffersonian days and had become an alliance of northern commercial and southern agrarian interests and a vehicle of compromise over slavery. For a century, beginning with Martin

Van Buren and continuing through FDR, the party had honored a largely unspoken bargain: Northerners would be granted the presidential nomination, Southerners would maintain balance-of-power control in Congress And this bargain embraced an even less spoken one: northern Democrats would not threaten white hegemony in the South in a quest for black votes. Woodrow Wilson, of southern background, had scrupulously lived up to this bargain, as had FDR less scrupulously in expressing sympathy for the plight of blacks but shunning civil rights legislation.

The Democracy was weakened and compromised in other ways as well. The adoption of the primary system and the other middle-class, "good government," and antiparty reforms in the early years of this century had robbed the party leadership of its most potent tool—control over nominations. Many city and other local elections had become nonpartisan, at least in form, and party patronage had been curbed. Since 1933 Jim Farley had provided skillful leadership in Washington, but the party as an organization was withering at the grass roots. It had become too spindly in most rural and small-town areas, too muscle-bound in many urban, "boss-ridden" precincts, and too conservative and conventional in general to recruit the millions of workers, youths, elderly persons, women, and others who were now turning to their own organizations. The Democracy, which had originally gathered strength as a mass movement under "radical" leadership, had lost its power to mobilize the masses.

Nor was FDR the man to recruit and mobilize the tired and tattered battalions left in the party. Few Presidents had ignored or bypassed their party organizations more than he had. During the emergency year of 1933 he had played down his role of party leader even to the extent of shunning Jefferson Day celebrations. We are thinking, he said piously the next year, "about Government, and not merely about party." That same year he backed Bob La Follette and other Progressive candidates over Democratic party nominees but cold-shouldered the "left-wing" Upton Sinclair, the Democratic gubernatorial nominee in California. In 1936 he leaned heavily on Farley and the national Democracy but bypassed the party in setting up a separate election group of laborites and the "nonpartisan" Good Neighbor League. Both these groups worked for Roosevelt in particular but not for Democratic party candidates in general.

Then, in 1938, the "nonpartisan" leader who had brought the Democratic party great victories but also neglected and bypassed it, suddenly, with lizardlike rapidity, dubbed himself "head of the Democratic party," held himself responsible for carrying out the party program, and began purging the party of its unfaithful. Roosevelt watchers were bewildered: what strategy was FDR following now? During his first year or two, during the emergency days, it had been a strategy of bipartisanship, as Roosevelt tried to unite both parties behind the NRA and other programs. Then he had switched to a conventional party strategy of uniting the Democracy by devoting much time and political capital to mediating between northern liberals and southern conservatives, at the risk of alienating labor, urban, and left-wing leaders. This approach helped him win his nationwide victory in 1936, but then, with his Court-packing and other ventures he had moved left in search of a different political base. The difference between an electoral victory for Roosevelt and his party in 1936 and a collective victory for his liberal program became clear as his personal coalition collapsed in 1937 and 1938 in the face of counterattacks by southern conservatives and desertions by some northern progressives and laborites.

*   *   *

The Grand Strategist appeared to be more a Grand Experimenter. But Roosevelt had the fine quality of learning from his victories and defeats. He had learned from the purge something about the outer limits of his power to reshape the Democratic party in the South. His defeats at the hands of George et al. and his inability even to gain a toehold in such bastions as Senator Glass's Virginia had suggested that a quick and improvised personal campaign was not enough; only a carefully planned, comprehensive, and long-run effort had any chance of overcoming such redoubts. At the same time his success in ousting O'Connor in Manhattan indicated that there might be more possibilities in the North than the President had realized.

What were those possibilities? The most arresting had for some years been a dream of a number of Democrats—including at times of Roosevelt himself. This was to convert the Democratic party into the clearly liberal-left party of the nation. "We'll have eight years in Washington," Tugwell remembered his boss saying to some liberal friends in 1932. "By that time there may not be a Democratic party, but there will be a Progressive one." Wallace and Ickes and other Administration leaders tended to agree. But just what did FDR intend? To make a dramatic appeal to third-party leaders and members to join the Democratic party? Or to desert his own party, set up a new progressive party as Theodore Roosevelt had done in 1912, and lead liberal Democrats into it? Or simply to try to oust southern conservatives from the Democracy and hope that progressives would join a clearly liberalized Democratic party?

The purge had proved that the last option would not transform the Democracy; even after FDR's honest effort to purge southern conservatives, progressives did not flock to the Democratic party banner, perhaps because the effort had failed. The option of a new party was out. Unlike Theodore Roosevelt, the President was not a party-breaker. Besides, FDR was in office, while Cousin Theodore had been out of it and wanting back in. What about seeking to liberalize the Democratic party? To a considerable extent the President had already done this, in party program and policy. But it was notable that such Democratic leaders as Al Smith had not deserted the party—they had merely deserted Roosevelt. Nor were southern Democrats quitting. Even after FDR showed them the door and tried to push them through it, they refused to leave their father's mansion—partly because it was their father's mansion.

So eight years after making that electrifying statement to Tugwell, Roosevelt was no nearer to creating a cleanly progressive party. The reason may have been clear to him as a practical matter if not in theory. He was not dealing with a two-party system in which liberal and conservative crossovers would be easy—conservative Democrats hungering to switch over to a right-wing GOP, or liberal Republicans panting to join the Democracy. He was coping with a four-party system in which right-wing Democrats enjoyed their power in Congress and were wary of joining a Republican party that contained hosts of liberals, while liberal Republicans enjoyed their considerable power over presidential nominations and were not eager to join a party of southern Negro-oppressors and northern city bosses.

The four-party system, then, stretched across a spectrum in which Roosevelt Democrats stood on the moderate left, Hughes and Landon Republicans were near the center, George and Tydings and Byrd Democrats stood to the right of center, and congressional Republican leaders held well to the right of them. These four parties were not merely party wings or collections of like-minded voters. They were built into government. Presidential Democrats held the office, with a boost from the electoral college, which favored Democratic contenders from the big urban states. The presidential Republican party tended to dominate presidential nominating conventions. Over on the conservative side of the spectrum the two congressional parties were happy to stay in their places, partly because each had a virtual stranglehold on certain party policies and partly because, sitting cheek by jowl ideologically, they had their own conservative coalition.

Reshaping the Democracy into a liberal party that could compete with a reshaped conservative Republican party was a forbidding prospect for FDR, in short, because the parties had already been realigned into a durable four-party system. Hence it was not surprising that FDR gave up this particular battle, at least for the time being. He had good reasons to do so. His own political stock was low after the purge struggle; he faced the likelihood of losing more and more influence as he neared the end of his second and presumably last term; heightening tension abroad was beginning to affect domestic politics and might bring its own realignment of political forces. It is doubtful that the President conceptualized the problem systematically; but certainly he had a feeling in his gut that he had tried to liberalize American politics and failed.

So he would return to the "politics of *personalismo*"—the politics of personal leadership, of putting together ad hoc coalitions in Congress and the country as opportunity dictated, of gaining short-run advances on a few fronts instead of making a policy or program breakthrough on a big front. Once again he would become Tactician-in-Chief, the transactional leader of the Broker State. But there was a price to pay for Roosevelt and his Administration: continued administrative cross-purposes, policy disarray, short-run planning, and political expediency, counterbalanced to some degree by advantages of flexibility and adaptability in the face of increasingly visible signs of new troubles abroad.

The price for much of the nation was more severe. In mobilizing his great majority of 1936, Roosevelt had raised hopes that he was realizing an ambition that had mesmerized the American left for more than a century—that a mighty coalition of liberal reformers, egalitarian leftists, women and black liberationists, urban radicals, socialist reconstructionists, and their allies could build and maintain a solid majority left of center, win political power, and enact into law their version of the ideology of liberty, equality, and fraternity. In their time—especially in the 1920s—conservative Republicans had exploited their own "compact majority"; surely the 1930s would be the time of a united liberal-labor-left.

It was not to be. The reasons were manifold: deep divisions within the popular majority; the powerful resistances of the political system to broad popular control, as the Framers had intended; Roosevelt's proclivity for short-run, "practical," ad hoc ventures and measures; the necessarily experimental and tentative nature of much of the New Deal. But perhaps the profoundest obstacle to a united and effective left majority was far less visible and yet all the more powerful, gripping the minds of leaders and followers alike. This was the set of "inarticulate major premises" informing the action and inaction of American liberalism and the American left during the days of the New Deal.

THE FISSION OF IDEAS

The idea that still gripped the American mind in the 1930s, as it had in the previous century and the century before that, was liberty—the "most precious trait," John Dewey called it, the "very seal of individuality." But the idea of liberty—or freedom—was still more a source of ambivalence than of coherence in the American consciousness. Just as the idea had been used both to defend and to attack first slavery and then capitalist power in the nineteenth century, so it was used both to defend and to attack the New Deal in the twentieth. "Negative" liberty as the precious right of Americans to be protected against interference by government and other outside intruders, "positive" liberty as the right to use government for the protection and expansion of individual rights—this crucial distinction now defined the struggle over the meaning of freedom.

The idea of freedom crowned the great Enlightenment and revolutionary trinity of liberty, equality, and fraternity, and these words could well have been inscribed on the banner of 1930s liberalism in America and of the New Deal. But to lengthen the arc along which New Deal liberal ideas were arrayed was merely to broaden the ambiguity. No one saw the incoherence of liberalism more keenly than its leading explicator in America, John Dewey. The nineteenth-century liberals who had been the dedicated and effective foes of absolutism, he wrote in 1935, had themselves become intellectual absolutists. Their doctrine had become frozen. "Since the ends of liberalism are liberty and the opportunity of individuals to secure full realization of their potentialities," and since "organized social planning" alone could secure these objectives, he urged, liberalism must for the sake of its ends reverse its means.

Had the famous "pragmatist" given up his faith in hardheaded experimentation, in testing ideas by their concrete results, only to embrace a new doctrine? Not fundamentally. But this former denizen of Hull-House, who had shared Jane Addams's concern over how the other ninetenths lived and had named a daughter for her, now saw the relation of knowing and acting in a more urgent context. Ideas and theory, he wrote in *The Journal of Philosophy* in 1935, must be "taken as methods of action tested and continuously revised by the consequences they produce in actual social conditions." That was the old Dewey. But the "experimental method is not just messing around nor doing a little of this and a little of that in the hope that things will improve." This was the Dewey who feared that the New Deal was doing exactly that. Just as the experimental method in science had to be controlled by "comprehensive ideas, projected in possibilities to be realized by action," so that method in society had to be directed by a "coherent body of ideas." This was the newest Dewey.

A coherent body of ideas, however, was precisely what the New Deal lacked after six years and more in office. The reasons go far to explain the intellectual incongruities of the New Deal.

The heritage of progressive thought was fragmented. The heritage lived on in old Bull Moosers and old Wilsonians who were still divided over whether trusts should be destroyed or controlled, pitted the New Freedom as represented by Brandeis against the kind of national power and responsibility urged by Herbert Croly, weighed the competing virtues of legal opportunity versus equal social and economic opportunity, and debated the extent to which government should aid women and blacks and poor farmers as well as more organized groups. The national government—how big and powerful it should be, how it should be used—was still the hard question that cut through the ranks of old progressives. Interviewing a sample of elderly survivors, historian Otis Graham found them deeply divided over the New Deal, with perhaps a 60-40 split against it. Among women progressives, Ida Tarbell opposed the New Deal, while Lillian Wald and Mary Wooley, president of Mount Holyoke, "followed their progressivism straight into the arms of the New Deal."

Durable continuities did of course link the old progressivism to the New Deal: a concern for large numbers of poor Americans, opposition to concentrated economic power, some commitment to equal opportunity to achieve social justice. These views left a heavy mark on much of the New Deal's economic legislation—especially on securities and other regulation and on the NRA and the AAA. "There is much evidence of a direct reform bloodline," Graham concluded. "Yet to anyone conversant with much progressive thought at the more popular levels—a good example would be Winston Churchill's novels *Coniston* (1906) and *Mister Crewe's Career* (1908), which faithfully represent the progressive ethos—or to anyone unable to dismiss the progressive credentials of F.D.R.-haters like James R. Garfield, Bainbridge Colby, or James A. Reed, or the slightly less angry William Allen White, the case for progressive-New Deal similarity bogs down in crippling qualifications."

If the thin bloodline from progressivism to the New Deal left the latter with even less intellectual coherence than the former, New Deal thought did not undergo the dialectical competition with opposing sets of doctrines that might have given it force and focus. Certainly the Socialists offered little intellectual opposition, though Norman Thomas eloquently and passionately continued to pose moral issues about capitalism in general and southern peonage in particular. Defections on the left and right appeared to leave the party weaker but no less factionalized and its doctrine in some disarray.

American socialism still suffered from its historic handicap: by "swallowing up both peasantry and proletariat into the 'petit-bourgeois' scheme," as Louis Hartz wrote later, the nation "prevented socialism from challenging its Liberal Reform in any effective way." The Socialists were still unable to gain a national hearing for the questions they rightfully wished to pose for Roosevelt: If socialist ventures like TVA worked, why would not *more* socialism? If the New Deal had carried out the 1932 Socialist platform, as some charged, why did it do so "only on a stretcher"? Was the New Deal really state capitalism and a prelude to fascism?

American communists were even less equipped to serve the classic left opposition role of forcing the governing elite to harden its intellectual defenses and unify its doctrine, for the communists were no longer in opposition, at least publicly. It was still the era of the Popular Front, and the Communist party in the United States had prospered, by 1938 almost tripling its 1934 enrollment of 26,000. This expansion brought into the party a greater diversity of members and attitudes, and Moscow doubtless tolerated more day-to-day, freewheeling discussion of doctrine and tactics. But ultimate control of both strategy and ideology remained in the hands of the Comintern. Neither rank-and-file talkfests nor Stalin's party line had an appreciable influence on New Deal thought during this period of softened antagonism.

So it fell quite logically to the conservative opposition, not the left competition, to establish a dialectical relationship with Roosevelt doctrine. The American right wing, however, appeared to be in as much intellectual disarray as the competing isms. The eighteenth- and nineteenth-century conservatism—the old "Toryism" that prized authority, hierarchy, order, continuity, stability, and the bonds of moral obligation to class and country, and feared egalitarianism, liberty in the form of license, crass commercialism, and excessive individualism—had only partially given way to new doctrinal trends on the right. But the newer conservatism had also divided into a variety of doctrines as it encountered the pluralism of American life. Even aside from the far-right groups bordering on neofascism, Clinton Rossiter identified "ultra-conservatives" such as Hearst editors, author Freda Utley, and columnist Westbrook Pegler; "middle-of-the-road conservatives" like the still vocal Herbert Hoover; and "liberal conservatives" like Walter Lippmann. Each group had its centers of thought and action: the old conservatives, in different guises, in both southern agrarian and northern Roman Catholic circles; the "bourgeois" conservatives in small-business, small-town cultures; and the moderates in the larger corporate and publishing hierarchies. Out of this congeries of conservative groupings and doctrines it was still impossible for either conservative leaders or their liberal adversaries to discern a consistent, comprehensive philosophy that would keep New Dealers on their intellectual toes.

The incoherence of doctrine was exacerbated by the ambiguity of concept that dominated everyday discourse in press, pulpit, and pub. *Liberty?* Not only the old dichotomy between "freedom from" and "freedom to" muddied discussion but more explicit and operational questions: Whose liberty? Liberty to do what or be free from what? What kind of liberty—Bill of Rights liberties or more recent freedoms, economic, social, psychological, sexual? Freedom under what conditions—depression, affluence, war? *Equality?* Of *opportunity* or of *condition?* What kind of opportunity—economic, educational, medical-access, athletic, artistic? And to start when—at the fetal stage, at birth, in preschool years, during what stage of school and in what kind of school? If equality of condition—financial, sexual, legal, political? *Individualism?* Independence from the government, separateness from the mass, a large sphere of privacy, removal of all improper and artificial restraints? Or *individuality*—self-development and self-realization? The crisis in American culture, Dewey said, could be solved by the recovery of a "composed, effective and creative individuality," or by a new individualism through democratic socialism—a fine sentiment that also reflected the ambiguity of concepts.

* * *

Political ideas during the late 1930s took almost kaleidoscopic patterns, but to consider only what Americans thought would be to consider only one dimension. Equally important was how they thought, and how the channels or structures of thought impinged on decision-making. How people thought concerned the relation among ideas and between ideas and action, the impact of ideas on policy-making, and always the linkage between thought and power.

John Dewey had strong views about how people thought and should think, views made more urgent by the dramatic need in the 1930s for fresh ideas. He preached the need for "freed intelligence," meaning by intelligence the "conversion of past experience into knowledge and projection of that knowledge in ideas and purposes that anticipate what may come to be in the future and that indicate how to realize what is desired." This rather common-sense notion, however, did not appear to impress the left. In a *Nation* article titled "The Pathos of Liberalism," Reinhold Niebuhr, a forty-three-year-old theologian at Union Theological Seminary, argued that freed intelligence alone was no safe instrument of social change. This simply betrayed a basic weakness in the liberal approach to politics, said Niebuhr. Dewey's concept failed to take into account "the perennial and inevitable character of the subordination of reason to interest in the social struggle"; the idea of "freed intelligence" presumed a degree of rational freedom from particular interests and perspectives that was, in Niebuhr's view, "incompatible with the very constitution of human nature." For Niebuhr, all life was an expression of power.

It was a curious indictment of Dewey, who so closely linked his ideas of intelligence and thoughtful experimentation to specific and effective action. But Niebuhr's emphasis on power was also a scarcely veiled attack on the kind of pragmatism with which Dewey was identified. This was not the kind of philosophic pragmatism, or even "pragmatic idealism," in Bernard Bailyn's term, that had its roots in the ideas of Peirce and James. It was not the brand of pragmatism that emphasized the interrelationship between clearly defined ends and specific means—emphasized the need of shaping ends to practical necessities and means to high purposes. It was a far narrower pragmatism that elevated eclectic experimentation, expediency, political opportunism, self-justifying technique, and automatic compromise to the level of the principled if not the virtuous.

If compelling and explicit ideas were necessary to the effective use of power in the American democracy, pragmatism of this sort could not do the job. Lacking were the intermediate ends and operational means that linked higher purposes—the broadening of liberty, the expansion of equality of opportunity—to the day-to-day actions of government that affected people's relief checks, WPA jobs, savings, taxes, recreation, roads, parks, homes. In the United States, Tocqueville had observed, "ideas are all either extremely minute and clear or extremely general and vague; what lies between is a void." A century later the "Tocquevillian void" still bifurcated ideas. It was not that the New Deal had no ideology but that its ideology in its central linkages was so soft and shapeless, such a rickety edifice of related and unrelated ends and means. Through the Tocquevillian void philosophy and power could not hear each other. And the less effective and efficient these programs were, the more the necessary expansion of the New Deal became compromised and politically precarious.

This central problem for the New Dealers was immensely enhanced by the nature of the political system in which they operated. Political opinions and pressures were channeled to Washington through thousands of avenues and agencies. Several hundred members of Congress kept close to their towns and precincts. Local unions, chambers of commerce, bar associations, medical societies, organized relief recipients, and other interest and protest groups had lines of influence running into Capitol Hill, the White House, and bureaucracies. Pressures on Washington were also generated in state and local governments.

If the United States had possessed a strong, essentially two-party system like the British, with the majority party responsible for governing and the minority party for opposing, effective opinion would have been channeled into some coherence. A multi-party system, with peasants, proletariat, and bourgeoisie broadly represented in agrarian, left, and center-right parties, again would have provided some channeling. But the Democratic and Republican parties embraced such wide, variegated, and overlapping groups as to render neither party clearly reflective of an ideological grouping or strongly supportive of government or opposition.

In the absence of broadly organized, programmatic, membership-rooted parties, channels of public opinion and political influence tended to center in political offices and their incumbents, from village fence viewer to President. Personal factions, interlocking with interest and other groups, clustered around these offices like bees around their hives. The fairly rigid structure of American governmental offices, mostly ordained by the Constitution or by state charters, gave a large measure of stability and continuity to the pattern of influence, as reflected in the four-party system.

The implications of this four-party structure for Roosevelt's governance and doctrine were formidable. He was clearly the leader of the presidential Democratic party, just as men like George and Byrd and Howard Smith and (increasingly) John Garner led the congressional Democrats, Alf Landon briefly in 1936 led the presidential Republicans, and a group of little-known ranking members of key House and Senate committees led the congressional Republicans. Since his party less and less commanded a majority in Congress during the late 1930s, the President had to broker and bargain with the leadership of the three other parties. Thus his position was not wholly unlike that of a French premier of his day, constantly seeking to build coalitions under the Third Republic.

The consequences for Roosevelt politically were mixed. On the one hand, he was enormously constrained by coalition politics that constantly eroded comprehensive programs and their funding, by institutional rigidities such as the seniority system in Congress, by the absence of a powerful majority party that could sustain him in Congress and country. On the other hand, the very fragmentation of the system, the inchoate nature of opposing doctrines and leadership groups, gave him, as a master of political footwork, marvelous opportunities to push his controversial policies through the formidable but scattered opposition. But there were always limits as to how far he could carry the "policy ball," always the question of whether it might be plucked out of his hands, as in the Court fight.

*   *   *

Within a quarter century of the congressional counterattack on the Roosevelt program, some historians were judging the New Deal as harshly as critics on the left had done during the 1930s. Roosevelt's New Deal, said

Jacob Cohen, had developed no new philosophy of reform, "relying on a patched up merger of Teddy Roosevelt's New Nationalism and Wilson's New Freedom." The New Deal marked the last act of the old order, not the first act of the new. The New Deal, Barton Bernstein concluded, could have achieved more—"in redistributing income, in reshaping power relations, in restructuring the economy, and in extending meaningful representation and participation in the polity." Even many of Roosevelt's more humane reforms, Bernstein wrote, had been "generally faltering and shallow, of more value to the middle classes, of less value to organized workers," and even less to "marginal men." "The story of many New Deal agencies was a sad story," Paul Conkin concluded, "the ever recurring story of what might have been."

Revisionists pointed to the critical transition days of early March 1933 as a time when Roosevelt, dealing with terrified bankers pleading for federal action, could have socialized or nationalized the banks. Still others held that, at the very least, the President and Congress could have created a national central banking system that would have given Washington comprehensive control of the banks without "expropriating" them. Such a move would have accorded with century-old attitudes in the Democratic party and would not have alarmed moderates. The conventional view had been that Roosevelt, providing strong leadership, coolly steered crisis banking policy between shoals left and right. This too was challenged by revisionist historians who demonstrated that the President during those critical days delegated banking policy to a group of conservative holdovers from the Hoover White House who, with almost equally conservative Roosevelt men, were intent on preserving the existing banking system, not fundamentally changing it.

These revisionist historians, of whatever color, were defying members of their own historical establishment who contended that even to discuss questions of "what might have been" or of "what did not happen in history" was to be ahistorical and hence unprofessional. Nevertheless the revisionists were quite right to submit at least preliminary judgments. Historians of all varieties constantly make judgments, in the topics they choose, in the facts that they select and the facts that they ignore, in allotting praise and blame, even when they do not explicitly analyze alternatives. The issue is not whether historians discuss what might have been but how well, by what criteria, they discuss it.

The most valid and crucial criterion of what leaders have done or not done is their success or failure in meeting *their* own standards—that is, fulfilling their own goals, realizing their own values—not necessarily the standards or goals or values of the historian writing in a later era with different values. Historians may apply their own standards, but this is a very different enterprise. Some historians have criticized FDR for failing to "socialize" not merely the banking system but the whole economy. But Roosevelt was no socialist, almost all his advisers were not socialists, his party never adopted a socialist program, and the electorate, judging from the Socialist party's lack of popular appeal, had little yearning for socialism. That the New Deal included one or two socialist experiments such as TVA—and indeed brought that one off with great éclat—is no proof that the New Dealers or the American people had broader socialist aims.

Even less did the New Deal aspire under the influence of Brandeis and his circle to a systematic decentralization of economic power, on the ideological ground that "smallness is beautiful." Nor did it wish to "restructure" the economy in any other systematic way—it wished only to subsidize it, stimulate it, make it more productive of jobs and higher wages. Neither did it propose to reshape power relations in any fundamental sense. It sought simply to bring labor, the unemployed, youths, and to a degree blacks into a wider and fairer balance of power.

Even judged by its own values and goals, however, the record of the New Deal was mixed. Roosevelt's supreme immediate aim, defined by personal and party promises, was recovery; he achieved partial recovery by the mid-thirties, lost ground in the "Roosevelt Recession," and regained partial recovery after passage of his big spending bill of 1938. He wanted to make government more humane and caring, and he achieved this for millions of the poor, by placing a floor under them, but other millions were no better off, no more secure than before. Though his tax and other proposals were intended substantially to redistribute income, they succeeded merely to a moderate degree. He wanted to make government more responsive to citizens previously underrepresented, and particularly the millions of the poor, and he helped his party rid itself of the two-thirds rule, but he had little success in either liberalizing the Court or softening the grip of conservative committee chairmen on legislation.

Why such mixed results, by his own standards, on the part of a President who combined compassion and political skill to an extraordinary degree, had the aid of scores of the most talented men and women, enjoyed enormous support in Congress and among the people for at least four years, and had the depression crisis to give his Administration force and momentum?

Was it a personal failure? Roosevelt, it is said, simply did not have the gut commitment to his values and goals that would have enabled him to fight his way through to complete victory. But the President's struggles day in and day out, his ceaseless efforts to patch together ad hoc coalitions to put his measures through, his willingness to brook the opposition of the most formidable adversaries, his fervent and repeated appeals to the people, his tireless maneuvering and manipulating and horse-trading, his feverish experimenting in search of solutions, belie this notion.

Was it an institutional failure? The New Dealers, it is said, were trying to put twentieth-century programs and policies through an eighteenth-century governmental system; inexorably the delays and the checks and the vetoes made impossible integrated and comprehensive and massive programs of recovery and reform. Rather the system either fostered slowdown and compromise or invited highly personal presidential intervention that could mass political influence at a particular point for a brief time and put something through but not launch and sustain a big and comprehensive effort. That this was a major obstacle to New Deal success, as proposed in earlier pages of this volume, has been widely accepted by political scientists and political practitioners, most notably by the Politician-in-Chief himself, Franklin D. Roosevelt.

Or was it primarily an intellectual failure? The President's reliance on his political machinery had at length failed him, Adolf Berle noted late in 1937, and he predicted that unless FDR was ready to be not a political organizer but an intellectual leader, he would be fighting a rearguard action for the next three years. Such an intellectual failure could have stemmed from the incoherence of public opinion, the disarray of the "public philosophy," the New Dealers' meager or faulty theorizing. Neither of the first two of these factors—neither the fragmented and ephemeral reflection of popular attitudes nor the divided and amorphous carryover of powerful ideas from the past—provided the New Dealers with adequate sets of guides and limits to governmental action. The New Deal would have to fashion an ideology of its own, and such an ideology must consist of more than Roosevelt's magnificent enunciations of broad ends, more than the New Dealers' versatile and eclectic employment of "practical" political and governmental means. It would need to include the political strategies and operational codes necessary to link ends and means. Such linkages doubtless would have to include ideas for long-term party and governmental reorganizations and modernizations far more sweeping than Roosevelt's limited and mainly abortive efforts at governmental reform.

Was there any way out for Roosevelt? Was there any idea or combination of ideas that could have generated a strategy adequate to meet New Deal goals of economic recovery and political modernization, consistent with the President's basic values, satisfying public opinion, carrying on at least part of the progressive political heritage, and avoiding the institutional veto traps and slowdowns? There was—the twin idea of massive spending and other fiscal strategies combined with national and regional planning.

To some of the young New Deal economists, heavy deficit spending appeared to be the ideal solution to continued economic stagnation. On the whole, Congress liked to spend, especially on public works back home. The Court would not threaten the federal government's spending power; Justice Stone at a social affair whispered into Frances Perkins's ear, "My dear, the taxing power is sufficient for everything you want and need." The publication of John Maynard Keynes's *The General Theory of Employment, Interest, and Money* in 1936 equipped the economists with the necessary technical theory and data. Above all, spending offered the President a middle way between doctrinaire economizing and doctrinaire socialism.

Roosevelt would never have read a book as dense as *The General Theory,* but he had something much better—Keynes himself. During the early months of the New Deal the Cambridge economist wrote Roosevelt and his advisers long and warm letters about economic policy. But in May 1934, when the President and the economist met in the White House, both were disappointed by their exchange. "He left a whole rigamarole of figures," Roosevelt wrote Perkins. "He must be a mathematician rather than a political economist." The President was no economist, Keynes remarked to friends.

Why did not the President seize on such an enticing solution, especially during the "Roosevelt Recession"? In part because his advisers were divided, as were friendly members of Congress; some were more intent on raising taxes, controlling prices, or undertaking short-run "pump priming" until business could man the pumps. But the main reason was intellectual. Roosevelt was unable as a thinker to seize the opportunity that Keynesian economics gave him. At heart he was as addicted to balancing the budget—someday—as he was to squirreling away bits of string and hanging on to old suits. Keynes called for such massive spending, such dramatic budget-unbalancing, as to stagger even Roosevelt's imagination. It was a middle way, to be sure, but it called for such radical and unorthodox pursuit of this middle way as to give it the flavor of extremism.

A Keynesian solution, moreover, called for an unprecedented degree of planning, not only in the fiscal areas of spending, taxing, investment, price policy, and the like, but in physical planning of public works, housing, transportation, urban rehabilitation, and much else. It seemed to be an auspicious time for comprehensive planning, which was increasingly the vogue in business, education, and even religion.

Roosevelt was a planner, but more of the nuts-and-bolts variety. During his second term he established the National Resources Planning Board and other planning entities, but these units, partly because of hostility in Congress, lacked political muscle and adequate funds. The failure of the President's reorganization bill had left the executive branch as Balkanized as ever, hardly the vehicle for unifying the Administration and its programs. The Soviets with their five-year plans gave the whole business a slightly sinister cast, and pundits such as Walter Lippmann attacked the proposal as bureaucratic, collectivist, and authoritarian. The outcome was unfortunate. Favoring regional as well as national planning, the President wanted to extend comprehensive programs like the TVA to other valleys, including the Missouri. These proposals died in the legislative labyrinth.

"We are at one of those uncommon junctures of human affairs," Keynes had said in the 1930s, "when we can be saved by the solution of intellectual problems and in no other way." Fiscal strategy and comprehensive planning were largely intellectual problems, embracing the whole realm of thought from minute plans to supreme values.

*   *   *

To what extent, then, had Roosevelt realized his own value of equality as he neared the end of his second term? Fifty years later, historians were still in disagreement. A Soviet historian came to the New Deal's defense. "There is no reason why radical historians," wrote Nikolai Sivachev, a Soviet specialist on the New Deal, "should not admit that Roosevelt's services to the monopolies does not exclude the possibility of the New Deal's bringing about a significant change in the structure of American capitalism, that the New Deal reforms bear the stamp of the struggle of the working class and of all democratic Americans for social progress." Facing the structured inequality in American society, Roosevelt did not become a transforming leader, but the image of a compassionate, beleaguered President fighting to tame capitalism and to deal out a new hand, even if from an old deck of cards, would be fixed in the national memory for decades to come.

On the other great value—liberty—Roosevelt's reputation would rest more securely. Despite all the charges that big government would crush Bill of Rights liberties, these continued intact. Indeed, Roosevelt was now beginning to articulate his belief that political and religious liberties were symbiotic with social and economic freedom. Even more, he was symbolizing and inspiring self-expression and creativity among artists and writers across the nation. If, as Alfred Kazin wrote at the time, the New Deal was "weakest in philosophy," the President was also, in H. G. Wells's words, "a ganglion for reception, expression, transmission, combination, and realization"—and hence a leader who helped bring about at the grass roots an explosion of artistic creativity in his time.

THE PEOPLE'S ART

The floor of the House of Representatives, June 15, 1938. Amid howls of laughter, members of the House are watching the antics of Congressman Dewey Short, Republican from the Missouri Ozarks. Florid of face, squat of figure, the onetime preacher has joined the debate over a bill to set up a permanent federal agency to aid the arts. He will resign from the House, the "Sage of the Ozarks" declaims, if he can help run the division dealing with the dance. He burlesques a tap dance in the aisle, amid more merriment, then rises to his toes to mimic ballet dancers. Art should not be subsidized, he says, for the only good art comes from suffering artists. Nobody can "feel comfortable or enjoy listening to the strains of Mendelssohn with the seat of his pants out." More hilarity. The Snopeses of Capitol Hill then help kill the measure, 195–35.

This forensic lynching bee against the arts measure was part of the massive counterattack launched by the Republican–southern Democratic coalition against the New Deal from 1937 to 1939. The cultural projects of the Roosevelt Administration were especially enticing targets. The right-wing coalition used two old congressional weapons—investigation and financial veto. Witnesses before the House Committee on Un-American Activities testified that art and theater and writers' projects were infested with communists, that the leadership was communist or communist-influenced, that in New York City the Workers' Alliance, a relief recipients' union, ran the theater project and the Communist party ran the union. The editor of the conservative *National Republic,* in his testimony, denounced art "smeared upon the walls" by reds on relief. The headlines were gratifying to the right wing, despite occasional embarrassments, such as when the name of one Christopher Marlowe surfaced during testimony and a committeeman demanded to know, "Is he a Communist?" A year later a southern Democratic and Republican coalition controlling a House appropriations subcommittee crippled the arts, writers', and music projects and in effect killed the federal theater program.

The assault on New Deal cultural programs marked the beginning of the end of one of the most humane, imaginative, generous, and daring efforts of the federal government to meet the dire needs and enlarge the opportunities of the nation's artists. For a man who had no great personal interest in the arts, Roosevelt had devoted an extraordinary amount of time to developing, nurturing, financing, and protecting the cultural programs, which in turn required an enormous amount of placating and conciliating the strong-minded persons involved. He did this in part because of his heritage of patrician patronage of the arts, but far more because he knew that the nation's artists were among the most vulnerable in a depression.

Eleanor Roosevelt supported the cultural programs at key junctures, put "federal" art in the White House, and spoke up against censorship of art, telling a group of museum directors in December 1933 that it was "unbelievable that a great nation" could fail to use "its creative talents to the fullest." Aiding and abetting the effort were tough-minded administrators—Ickes, Morgenthau, Hopkins, and many less known—who early on glimpsed the need for a qualitative as well as a quantitative liberalism. But the true heroes of the effort were the unsung or less sung leaders of the national and local programs, along with the artists, actors, musicians, and writers who, working for a pittance, responded by producing a cornucopia of cultural productions, notable always for quantity but often too for quality.

The New Deal art program had got off to an early start because the federal government owned thousands of post offices and other buildings whose walls were temptingly empty. Roosevelt had been in office hardly two months when muralist George Biddle, one of the Philadelphia Biddles and a Groton and Harvard schoolmate of Roosevelt, wrote FDR about the grand achievements of muralists of the Mexican revolution. Young American artists were eager to capture the "Roosevelt-guided social revolution" on the public walls of the nation. The President directed him to the Treasury, central custodian of federal buildings. With tentative support from such leading muralists as Thomas Hart Benton, Edward Laning, Reginald Marsh, and Henry Varnum Poor, Biddle plunged into the field of federal subsidy of the arts, amid fears that it was a briar patch.

A briar patch it was—not only of bureaucratic rivalries, but of ancient conflict between traditionalists and the avant-garde, between artists of competing schools. Biddle and his colleagues were soon dealing with problems that had always bedeviled subsidized art, whether sponsored by state, church, or private patrons. Any relationship between free-spirited artists and institutions dealing with art involved an "awkward embrace" that the honeyed words of politicians and bureaucrats could not ease. To what degree should established artists be favored over the mainly needy ones? To what extent should the "feds" yield to local control or even institutionalize it? How much artistic freedom should be allowed for projects subsidized by the taxpayers? To what degree should artists be supervised—for example, the time they were putting into their work? Who should decide what art should be not only subsidized but chosen for exhibit? What are the criteria for excellence in art?

These problems rolled in on the public works art directors in the form not merely of in-basket paper but of raging conflicts in the field. In San Francisco, newspaper editors were given a "pre-vue" of new murals in the Coit Tower created under the public works art program, only to discover a miner in one panel reading a well-known local communist weekly, in another panel a hammer and sickle and a call that the "Workers of the World Unite," and—worst blow of all—renditions of many left-wing front pages but no representation of the establishment San Francisco *Chronicle*. During the ensuing flap the city park commission locked the big doors to the tower, the local Artists' and Writers' Union picketed the closed edifice, and the tower opened again after several months, with only one "subversive" item—a Soviet emblem—missing.

In Washington, the artist Rockwell Kent had his own little joke. Illustrating the expansion of the postal service in a mural for the capital's Post Office Building, he portrayed Alaskan Eskimos dispatching a letter in one panel and black Puerto Rican women receiving it in a second. All very patriotic—except that on close scrutiny the message was found to be a call for freedom for both dependencies. After much amusement over Kent's joke, the Treasury paid the artist off and blanked out the message. When Paul Cadmus portrayed sailors frolicking with "curvaceous damsels of obviously insecure reputation" in his "The Fleet's In," an admiral denounced it, the Navy asked that it be withdrawn from a forthcoming exhibition at the Corcoran Gallery, and it was.

These and other imbroglios hardly dampened cultural productivity. During the first few months of the public works program artists turned out well over 10,000 pieces of art and craft—over 3,000 oils, almost 3,000 watercolors, numerous prints, etchings, woodcuts, poster panels, and a lesser number of carvings, decorative maps, pottery, tapestries, mosaics. But even these figures were dwarfed by the productivity of artists working under the Federal Art Project of the Works Progress Administration, which behind the strong leadership of Harry Hopkins and the Project's chief, Holger Cahill, got underway with heavy funding in 1935. The Art Project was designedly a relief effort, part of the overall WPA cultural program embracing artists, writers, musicians, actors, and others. But by enabling artists to do their own work, even at $20 or $30 a week, it produced an explosion of "people's art" without parallel in American history. If the output of the public works projects could be numbered by the thousands, that of the FAP could be by the tens or hundreds of thousands—over 100,000 easel works (oil, watercolor, tempera, pastel), 17,000 pieces of sculpture, an estimated 240,000 copies of over 10,000 original designs in varied print media.

Enormous quantity—but quality? The level of work under the FAP was so varied as to defy generalization. Such artists, later to be famous, as Willem de Kooning, Anton Refregier, Chaim Gross, and Peter Hurd would credit the program with helping them in their careers. But the aim was to include as many artists as possible, good or bad, and to bring the people's art to the people, in regional and local centers across the nation. The FAP not only promoted art exhibits and gallery tours on a vast scale but stressed art as a learning experience for the masses by sponsoring educational programs under hundreds of teachers in settlement houses, hospitals, clubs, parks, and even—especially for children—zoos. A disciple of John Dewey, Cahill believed that art was a matter less of the rare masterpiece than of vitalizing "democracy in the arts" through community participation.

The more the FAP reached out to the wider public, however, the more controversial and hence political it became. The conflicts that had plagued the public works program bedeviled the FAP even more. Cutbacks in the program in response to Roosevelt's post-election economizing produced anger and resentment in art centers. New York artists, the most militant in the nation, marched in December 1936 to WPA headquarters on East Sixty-ninth Street, occupied the offices of New York City FAP chief Audrey McMahon, and stayed on despite threats of being blacklisted. The artists locked arms to confront the police, who dragged them out amid the thud of nightsticks, shrieks of pain, and the wounding of a dozen artists and policemen. As total WPA rolls were cut by one million from the pre-election high of two and a half million, artists and other recipients could have bitterly recalled the words of FDR's Madison Square Garden speech: "For all these things"—including useful work for the needy unemployed—"we have only just begun to fight." Both FDR's retrenchment and the protest of the artists helped trigger the congressional counterattack of 1937 and 1938.

One reason the art program aroused such controversy was its sheer visibility on the public walls and in the new and old art centers of the nation. Even more visible—and vulnerable—was the Federal Theatre Project. The FTP shared many of the ecstasies and the burdens of the other cultural programs—wide outreach to needy theater people, enormous output, some brilliant productions, support from the Roosevelts, especially Eleanor, along with parsimony in funding, bureaucratic tangles, censorship, red-baiting, and cutbacks. But the Federal Theatre, like the figure over a Broadway marquee, was always larger than life—in its leadership, its daring, its visibility, and its downfall.

Its head was the most striking of all the persons who ran WPA cultural projects, Hallie Flanagan. Creator of an experimental theater first at Grinnell College and then at Vassar, she had participated at Harvard in George Pierce Baker's noted theatrical laboratory, the 47 Workshop, and studied European and Russian theater abroad before establishing her own reputation for experiment. Broadway impresarios were still underestimating the daring and determination of this small, mild-mannered woman when Hopkins recruited her, but he did not. Soon she was making the hard decisions: dealing with the tough stage unions, giving preference in hiring to skilled professionals, choosing the most controversial plays for production and at the same time dreaming of creating a great and enduring national theater out of the relief project. She collected a remarkable staff and set of associates: Eddie Dowling, national director of vaudeville; Elmer Rice, head of the New York City project, and his assistant Philip Barber; Charles Coburn, director for New England; Jasper Deeter, director for Pennsylvania.

"We live in a changing world," Flanagan told her associates when they first met at her headquarters in the old McLean mansion on Dupont Circle; "man is whispering through space, soaring to the stars, flinging miles of steel and glass into the air. Shall the theatre continue to huddle in the confines of a painted box set? The movies, in their kaleidoscopic speed and juxtaposition of external objects and internal emotions, are seeking to find visible and audible expression for the tempo and psychology of our time. The stage too must experiment—with ideas, with psychological relationship of men and women, with speech and rhythm forms, with dance and movement, with color and light—or it must and should become a museum product." The theater, she added, must not ignore problems of wealth and poverty, peace and war, the role of government—or the changing social order would ignore the theater.

Flanagan followed up this rhetoric with arresting productions. In spring 1936 the Federal Theatre put on the New York premiere of *Murder in the Cathedral*, T. S. Eliot's verse drama about Thomas à Becket. The play, which had been turned down by the Theatre Guild, left audience members, including Eleanor Roosevelt, deeply moved. An especially innovative production was *Macbeth*, set in a castle in Haiti during Napoleonic times, produced by John Houseman, directed by Orson Welles, and staged in Harlem with black actors. On opening night the Negro Elks' eighty-piece brass band marched past the Lafayette Theatre in their scarlet-and-gold uniforms, while thousands lined up for tickets. The show got enthusiastic reviews from Burns Mantle of the New York *Daily News* and other critics. Everyone knew, a black woman watching the show for the fifth time told a London reporter, that "this Mr. Shakespeare had always intended his plays to be acted by Negroes."

But by far the boldest venture of the Theatre Project was the "Living Newspaper." Conceived by Flanagan and sponsored by the Newspaper Guild, the Living Newspaper Unit operated like a city room with editors and reporters. "Great ingenuity was displayed," Edmond Gagey observed, "in devising new technical methods or devices—employment of a loud-speaker for the voice of the Living Newspaper or of an old tenement house; frequent use of scrim, projection, and moving pictures; action on different levels of ramps with imaginative use of spotlight and blackout; playing of scenes in silhouette; clever stage business and properties to illustrate abstract points."

No issue, no matter how thorny, seemed to daunt Flanagan & Co. The White House in effect killed the first Living Newspaper, *Ethiopia,* on the ground that it involved the impersonation of foreign leaders, Haile Selassie and Mussolini. Despite frantic appeals by Flanagan through Eleanor Roosevelt and the angry resignation of Elmer Rice, the show reached the boards only for the press. But other productions were equally provocative. *Triple-A Plowed Under* dramatized the farm problem in a series of sharp vignettes: mortgages foreclosed, farms auctioned off, crops dumped, all amid ravaging drought. Attacks on the greed of middlemen and words of Earl Browder interspersed with those of Jefferson and Al Smith did not win favor from the right—especially when it was not Browder who was booed. *Injunction Granted,* originally designed as a balanced picture of labor's treatment in the courts, turned out on opening night to be a strong dose of militant unionism. Even Flanagan was upset by its leftward tilt, but the play went on, with a few modifications. *Power,* an attack on the utilities and a call for public ownership, was a piece of calculated propaganda; the Living Newspaper staff, Brooks Atkinson wrote, had "come out impartially against the electric light and power industry, and for the TVA." Perhaps the most powerful of the plays, *One-Third of a Nation,* was the most brilliant, the most professional, and the best received by the critics. With its set showing a four-story tenement full of rickety stairs, beat-up furniture, dirt and disarray, *One-Third of a Nation* was a pointed reminder of New Deal promises made and still unfulfilled. *It Can't Happen Here,* a dramatization of Sinclair Lewis's novel showing how fascism could, was seen by hundreds of thousands in New York and a score of other cities.

The FTP offered much more than these electrifying productions. It embraced regional efforts, most notably in Chicago and Los Angeles, and a host of state amateur theater groups—eighteen in North Carolina alone. At its height it involved not only great actors and directors but a peak work force of about ten thousand stagehands and electricians and cue girls as well as actors and playwrights. Flanagan recognized that modern dance could express vital ideas and encouraged Helen Tamiris to develop an independent dance unit that had a brief but stormy and creative life until it was merged again with the Theatre Project.

But the FTP never shed its image of being centered in New York City, radical, and iconoclastic. Hence it was all the more vulnerable to the budget-cutters in Washington, and to both the red-baiters in Congress and the communists themselves who attacked it from the left. The FTP was the first of the cultural programs to be killed on Capitol Hill. Said the chastened but indomitable Flanagan, "The theatre, when it's good, is always dangerous."

It was acutely ironic that the theater and other New Deal cultural programs should have been shut down because of their "radicalism," for they were at the heart of the revival of cultural nationalism in the 1930s. That decade, in Charles Alexander's look back four decades later, brought a "remarkable celebration in American thought and culture of the goodness and glory of the nation and its people." This was true "as much in architecture, where modernists linked adaptable, utilitarian design to the task of social reconstruction, as it was in music, where composers were often willing to exploit native folk and popular resources, or in the literary or visual arts, where the social and artistic values of realism prevailed." Coming home from European or spiritual exile, intellectuals and artists not only rediscovered the American present; "as the decade progressed they more and more explored the national past, seeking enduring values, precedents for action, even meaningful legends with which to fashion the most elaborate version thus far of a usable past."

*   *   *

Throughout the decade public arts programs existed side by side with private ventures. The public was not always clear as to what was "socialistic" and what was "commercial." Thus it was the FTP that put on the musical drama *The Cradle Will Rock,* but it was the International Ladies' Garment Workers' Union that produced the equally pro-union and anti-capitalist *Pins and Needles.* The federal art programs covered public buildings with murals and paintings, but independent and established artists like Reginald Marsh, John Steuart Curry, and Grant Wood were painting on their own. Rather than crushing private or commercial ventures, the federal cultural programs appeared to stimulate them. On occasion, feds fought one another. WPA officials in Washington, fearful about the approaching Federal Theatre production of *The Cradle Will Rock* during the bitter struggle between labor and Little Steel, put off the presentation at the last moment. After vain protests and appeals, author Marc Blitzstein and director Orson Welles led the opening-night audience from the Maxine Elliott Theatre twenty blocks to the old Venice Theatre, where actors and stagehands improvised a performance that would be talked about—and reenacted—decades later.

The Federal Writers' Project was a prime example of the easy coexistence of public and private cultural enterprise. When the FWP came under the usual attack on Capitol Hill, forty-four publishers wrote a joint letter to the investigating subcommittee asserting that the work of the writers was a "genuine, valuable and objective contribution to the understanding of American life" and not a vehicle of propaganda. While the publishers unduly played down the left bias in enclaves of the project, prestigious houses such as Random House and Houghton Mifflin had enough confidence in the FWP to undertake cooperative publishing with it. Certainly the FWP needed every friend it could mobilize, as it suffered along with the other cultural projects from the usual congressional barrages about reds, waste, administrative incompetence.

The Federal Writers' Project shared much else with its sister programs in the arts—a gifted leadership, though often erratic in the case of the writers' program, the unswerving support of Eleanor Roosevelt and the cautious backing of her husband, the inadequacy of funds in view of the need, and the image of being a New York project despite the existence of strong state programs, fourteen of which were headed by women. It could boast of the usual huge output: around 6,500 writers in four years produced several hundred publications on a wide diversity of subjects, with the help of thousands of volunteer consultants, most of them college teachers, who helped prepare FWP manuscripts. And the quality of the output, as in the other projects, varied wildly. It was at worst pure hack stuff and at best enduring work, such as the two thousand slave narratives based on interviews with former slaves and collated in seventeen volumes.

The showcase of the Writers' Project was its American Guide Series. Rising almost spontaneously from under the noses of the WPA planners, the idea was to employ writers, editors, historians, researchers, art critics, archaeologists, map draftsmen, geologists, and other professionals to prepare local, state, and regional "Baedekers." But some hoped that these would be more than Baedekers—that they would dig into the roots of American history and culture and hence would become, as Alfred Kazin later put it, part of an "extraordinary national self-scrutiny."

The series was most impressive for its sheer size and range—as though it wished to manifest the size and range of the nation it covered. By 1942 the collection consisted of 276 volumes and 701 pamphlets; even so, the FWP had still not published any of the regional guides originally planned.

Once again the quality was grossly uneven, but at its best the series presented known and unknown writers at their most creative and imaginative. For the Massachusetts guide Conrad Aiken anonymously described the "wonderful ghostliness" of old Deerfield as "the perfect and beautiful statement of the tragic and creative moment when one civilization is destroyed by another." He also paid tribute to the "profound individualism" of which Massachusetts had been such a prodigal and brilliant source—only to provoke the wrath of leftists who argued that the good in America had stemmed from popular, collective action. The guide calmly published both views, "each in effect arguing against the other."

Not all the difficulties of the Massachusetts guide were settled so easily. The day after the first copy off the Houghton Mifflin press was presented to the governor, the Boston *Traveler* headlined "Sacco Vanzetti Permeate New WPA Guide." It seemed that the guide described the Boston Tea Party in nine lines and the Sacco-Vanzetti case in forty-one. Other "revelations"—and headlines—followed about the guide's handling of the Boston police strike, the great 1912 strike of textile workers, child labor, and other skeletons in the Bay State closet. The governor denounced the book, declared that the writers should go back to where they came from if they didn't like America, and collaborated with the state librarian in an effort to strike from the guide references to organized labor, welfare legislation, and Labor Day. In Washington, Harry Hopkins laughed off the affair, and in Boston the guide sold like hotcakes.

Other state guides came under literary attack for poor style or for history that was only guidebook-deep. But their critics missed the essential point of the guides and of the whole Writers' Project—to mobilize hundreds of writers who in turn could dig into the heart and mind, the very bone and sinew, of the nation. They wrote mainly about people—famous and infamous, heroic and villainous, remembered and forgotten. "It is doubtful," wrote Robert Cantwell in *The New Republic,* "if there has ever been assembled anywhere such a portrait, so laboriously and carefully documented, of such a fanciful, impulsive, childlike, absent-minded, capricious and ingenious people."

So the guides abounded in people, presented often in exquisite and loving detail, like the jobless man whose opening words to the FWP interviewer were: "I admit it, I'm a hog. In other words human. I enjoy women and a pair of doughnuts like anybody else. Say tomorrow I wake up I'm covered in communism, say I can go and get what I want by asking—I want six wives. You maybe want twenty-four suits. . . ." Or like John D. Rockefeller golfing in Florida, wearing a straw hat tied with a shawl-like handkerchief under his chin as he bicycled "from stroke to stroke, followed by two valets, one with milk and crackers, the other with a blanket to be spread on the ground when he wishes to rest."

And so it was possible for Alfred Kazin to write that the enormous and remarkable body of writing of the Depression era, for all its shapelessness, offered the fullest expression of the national consciousness. It was the "story of a vast new literature in itself, some of it fanatical or callow, some of it not writing at all, much of it laboriously solid and curious and humble, whose subject was the American scene and whose drive was always the need, born of the depression and the international crisis, to chart America and to possess it." And because much of this literature dealt with the 1930s, inevitably much of it dealt with economic hope and despair.

*   *   *

"Jus' let me get out to California," says Grandpa Joad. "Gonna get me a whole big bunch of grapes off a bush, or whatever, an' I'm gonna squash 'em on my face an' let 'em run offen my chin." Getting to California—the Joads have been thinking of this for months. The real Joads were the half-million refugees created when the great dust storms swept through the Plains and border states, reducing almost 100 million acres to dust. For a time the uprooted became wanderers, traveling like sleepwalkers, but most were headed west in rattletrap cars and trucks, in a grim reenactment of the American dream. Headed west to California, the last paradise, where the land was rich and jobs were for the asking. But their hopes were blighted—as Ma Joad had expected, the promises had been "too nice, kinda."

John Steinbeck had made this trek too. In 1939 he published the novel that documented the Okie experience, *The Grapes of Wrath*. In California his family, the Joads, encounter the people in paradise: farm owners who offer jobs to migrants at starvation wages—take it or leave—and sheriffs who move them like cattle from miserable camp to worse camp and Californians who hiss "Okie" at them no matter what state they hail from. The Joads' meager savings evaporate; they find no place to rest; they are abused, tricked, exploited. The family falls apart—the grandparents die, a son-in-law deserts, a baby is stillborn, a son avenges a preacher by attacking a strikebreaker. In the end a tremendous rain descends, like a second Flood, and this ironic rain, whose absence had denied the Joads life in Oklahoma, now forces them to take cowering refuge in a barn. They must leave behind their truck, their belongings. They have nothing left.

Steinbeck's book set off a fire storm of controversy and made the thirty-seven-year-old novelist famous. Inevitably attacked as a Communist propagandist, Steinbeck in fact had made one of the principal themes of an earlier novel, *In Dubious Battle,* the darker side of Communist activists—their fanaticism, their subordination of the strikers' needs to the party's political goals, their provocativeness, and hence the "dubiousness" of the battle. Far from advocating communism, *The Grapes of Wrath* offered no coherent program whatever but rather a mystic union of Emerson's transcendentalism, Whitman's mass democracy, and Jefferson's agrarian populism. It beckoned readers back to the time when men and the land were one, when greed yielded to selflessness, "for the quality of owning freezes you forever into 'I,' and cuts you off forever from the 'we.' " A federal migrant camp offers a glimpse of utopia, where the life-principles are cooperation and sharing, and where the Joads have a few weeks to learn to "feel like people again."

But Steinbeck speaks best through his characters. Ma Joad, indomitable defender of the family unit against all comers: "Use' ta be the fambly was fust. It ain't so now. It's anybody. Worse off we get, the more we got to do." Jim Casy, a preacher who accompanies the Joads to California and has given up conventional Christianity for the faith that "all men got one big soul ever'-body's a part of." Young Tom Joad, who takes on Casy's burden when the preacher is murdered for leading a migrant workers' strike, assaults the murderer, and must flee. But, he tells his mother, "I'll be ever'where—wherever you look. Wherever they's a fight so hungry people can eat, I'll be there. . . . An' when our folks eat the stuff they raise an' live in the houses they build—why, I'll be there."

Woody Guthrie was there too, a real-life Okie who rode the freights through the South and Southwest during the dust bowl years, playing and singing to anyone who would listen. Growing up in a disintegrating home, in his teens he was an "alley rat" living among old cowboys and onetime outlaws and plain down-and-outers, listening to their yarns about the glory days of the West. When the dust storms hit in the spring of 1935, Woody was still only a twenty-three-year-old soda jerk in Pampa, Texas, but then he began to travel. "This dusty old dust is a-getting my home / and I've got to be drifting along. . . ."

On the road, thrown among the dust-blown, Guthrie's alley-rat "I" was transmuted into an impassioned "we." He "had never considered himself part of any group before," according to Joe Klein. "But here he was, an Okie, and these were his people." And as more and more he saw what was happening to them, his music took on a new bite. "I never did make up many songs about the cow trails or the moon skipping through the sky, but at first it was funny songs of what all's wrong, and how it turned out good or bad. Then I got a little braver and made up songs telling what I thought was wrong and how to make it right, songs that said what everybody in that country was thinking." Guthrie gathered a repertoire of old tunes—ballads, hymns, country blues—from hoboes and migrants and fitted his own lyrics to them. "The way I figure, there are two kinds of singing and two kinds of songs," he said. "Living songs and dying songs." He would sing both. Drawing from the Wobblies' old *Little Red Songbook,* his lyrics became more pointed in pathos and politics:

> We got out to the West Coast broke,
> So dad gum hungry I thought I'd croak,
> And I bummed up a spud or two,
> And my wife fixed up a 'tater stew.
> We poured the kids full of it.
> Mighty thin stew, though: you could read
>   a magazine right through it.
> Always have figured that if it had been just
>   a little bit thinner
> some of these here politicians could have
>   seen through it.

Two thousand miles to the east, the trouble with Studs Lonigan is that he cannot speak his true feelings, deep and powerful feelings of revolt against Chicago's drab Irish middle class, with its petty aspirations and empty values and spiritual poverty. Studs is crushed between a latent conscience desperate to emerge, which enables him to grasp vaguely that something is wrong with his world, and his lack of knowledge, either of himself or of society, that would make his rebellion effective. Robbed of any model for revolt, Studs falls back on the hackneyed American rebel of dime novels and juvenile fantasies, on the model of the tough guy as boxer, outlaw, hoodlum, soldier, or teen gang leader. Shadowboxing before a mirror, cursing his sister, drinking himself into a stupor, strutting among his adolescent admirers, Lonigan must constantly affirm to himself that he is indeed "real stuff." But by adopting the pose and vocabulary of the tough guy, he can neither fully tolerate nor articulate genuine emotions and impulses.

In the park with Lucy, the fifteen-year-old Studs has a feeling "that seemed to flow through him like nice warm water," but he feels "goofy and fruity about having it, and felt that he hadn't better let anyone know he had thoughts like that. . . . If some of the kids knew what he was doing and thinking, they'd laugh their ears off." How can he express his feeling to Lucy? "He couldn't even say a damn thing about how it all made him want to feel strong and good, and made him want to do things and be big and brave for her." So when he parts from her in frustration he feels "more and more of a hell of a Goddam goof." After this moment of feeble perception the shutters close once again, and Studs spends the rest of his life caught between growing apprehension of early death and pathetic nostalgia for lost chances. He dies in 1931 at the age of thirty, of heart failure.

The man who created Studs Lonigan, James T. Farrell, himself was raised in an Irish middle-class home in Studs's Chicago neighborhood. The author believed that only his critical instinct and his intellectual curiosity had saved him from Studs's fate. He was lucky enough to have had good teachers, who encouraged him in his writing and wide reading, strengthened his self-confidence, and opened the shutters wide for the literary and intellectual worlds that lay beyond. Studs never had such teachers, such leaders, who could have responded to his wants and needs, protected and bolstered his self-esteem, taught him some skills, and encouraged him to self-fulfillment. In leaving Studs as a youth of suppressed conscience unable to rise to moral consciousness and hence unequipped to move on to political or some other collective action, Farrell personified the masses of Americans imprisoned in enclaves of self-doubt, self-hate, and self-destruction.

The fictional Studs Lonigan of Chicago would never have met the fictional Bigger Thomas of Chicago, except perhaps during the real-life race riot of 1919, which began when a black youth at a segregated beach stepped into "white waters" and ended with the deaths of twenty-two blacks and fourteen whites. Studs and his gang were there. "The streets were like avenues of the dead. They only caught a ten-year-old Negro boy. They took his clothes off, and burned them. They burned his tail with lighted matches, made him step on lighted matches, urinated on him, sent him off running naked with a couple of slaps in the face." Bigger Thomas might have been there, momentarily freed from his cage. He lives with his mother, brother, and sister in a squalid one-room apartment in Chicago's black belt. Unlike the Joads, the Thomases do not even begin as a prideful family; they taunt and nag and torment one another. Bigger is locked in a cage of unemployment, ignorance, petty criminality, fearful hatred of whites and even blacks. He knows that the moment he becomes fully conscious of what his life means, he will kill himself or someone else. In the apartment he encounters a rat, also trapped, and explodes. "Bigger took a shoe and pounded the rat's head, crushing it, cursing hysterically: 'You sonofabitch!' "

Later Bigger does kill two persons—a young white woman without meaning to, his girlfriend Bessie meaning to. His criminality liberates him: "He had murdered and had created a new life for himself. It was something that was all his own, and it was the first time in his life he had had anything that others could not take from him." Filled with elation, he is transformed from a victim of his environment into an existential actor: "Never had he had the chance to live out the consequences of his actions; never had his will been so free as in this night and day of fear and murder and flight." When Boris Max, his communist lawyer, a kindly white whom Bigger trusts, offers the judge an impassioned plea that Bigger's crimes are the result of circumstances, that "we must deal here with a dislocation of life involving millions of people," Bigger resists this view of him. Max's argument robs him of his freedom, his individuality. And so when Bigger, in his cell—his final cage—hours away from execution and longing more than ever to talk with Max, insists passionately upon his responsibility, Max's eyes fill with terror as he gropes for his hat "like a blind man," uncomprehending that for Bigger:

"What I killed for, I *am*! . . . What I killed for must've been good! . . . I didn't know I was really alive in this world until I felt things hard enough to kill for 'em."

The creator of *Native Son*'s Bigger Thomas, Richard Wright, had grown up in the South and then in Chicago, "ringed by walls," as he later put it. "Tension would set in at the mere mention of whites," he remembered. "It was as though I was continuously reacting to the threat of some natural force whose hostile behavior could not be predicted," as though he had been the "victim of a thousand lynchings." But, unlike Studs and Bigger, he found a way out—reading. Resorting to a ruse to borrow books from a whites-only library, he began with Mencken's *A Book of Prefaces.* It startled him. "What was this?" he wondered. "Yes, this man was fighting, fighting with words." Then perhaps he too could use words as weapons. But he could not wholly break out of his own cage. By the late 1930s, Daniel Aaron speculated, Wright was leading a double intellectual life: the black Marxist who sought to bring "scattered but kindred peoples into a whole" and the private man, the novelist who idealized the isolated, existential individual.

Many of the authors and artists of the 1930s were trying to bring scattered but kindred peoples together, striving to release them from their separate cages and to raise them to an individual and collective consciousness they had never known, hoping to complete the task of psychological and political mobilization that the New Dealers had started but not finished. It was altogether fitting that one of their most articulate creations was a man who never said a word, never even appeared in a book or on a stage. By 1935 the Group, an experiment in collective theater, had scored some striking successes by importing the Stanislavsky method, which taught actors to inhabit their characters, and by insisting that "the blood and bones of a living stage must be the blood and bones of the actuality around us." In January 1935, amid many doubts, the Group put on *Waiting for Lefty* by a rather untried playwright, Clifford Odets.

A somewhat simplistic play, like all agitprop, about a taxi strike, *Waiting for Lefty* dramatized a drivers' meeting, with the entire theater serving as a union hall and the audience as union members. As the tension and oratory mounted, the first-night audience took on the call for "STRIKE!" with such fervor that the actors stood frozen on the stage, gaping at the cheering, stamping mass. "STRIKE! STRIKE!" But strike for what? Against what? The audience did not seem to know or care. Liberated, it felt unencumbered by the need to act or even choose. How had Odets achieved this magic that night after night brought suburban matrons and Wall Street tycoons to stamp their feet and shake their fists?

In part by never producing Lefty. For Lefty was dead.

PART II

Strategies of
Freedom

CHAPTER 4

Freedom Under Siege

I N April 1939 the "winds of war" were swiftly enveloping Europe. With decisive help from Hitler and Mussolini, General Francisco Franco had just clamped his grip on all of Spain. The Nazis had completed their occupation of Czechoslovakia and were now turning to the conquest of Poland. Mussolini had sent troops into helpless little Albania as a springboard against Yugoslavia and Greece. Franklin D. Roosevelt, like the other leaders of Western democracies, had stood by impotent while the aggressors moved from attack to attack. But if Roosevelt could not act, he could at least talk. On April 14, 1939, he sent an appeal personally to Adolf Hitler, Chancellor of the German Reich. A similar message went to Premier Benito Mussolini.

"You realize, I am sure," the President began, "that throughout the world hundreds of millions of human beings are living today in constant fear of a new war or even a series of wars." Three nations in Europe, one in Africa, and vast territory of another in the Far East—he did not identify these nations—had had their independence crushed or had been occupied. Then Roosevelt came to the point.

"You have repeatedly asserted that you and the German people have no desire for war. If this is true there need be no war. . . ." Could Roosevelt, as "a friendly intermediary," have a frank statement as to the Führer's intentions—a statement that he could pass on to other nations?

"Are you willing to give assurance that your armed forces will not attack or invade the territory or possessions of the following independent nations: Finland, Estonia, Latvia, Lithuania, Sweden, Norway, Denmark, The Netherlands, Belgium, Great Britain and Ireland, France, Portugal, Spain, Switzerland, Liechtenstein, Luxemburg, Poland, Hungary, Rumania, Yugoslavia, Russia, Bulgaria, Greece, Turkey, Iraq, the Arabias, Syria, Palestine, Egypt and Iran." If the President received such assurance, which would have to cover the next ten years at least, the United States "would be prepared to take part in discussions looking toward the most practical manner of opening up avenues of international trade to the end that every Nation of the earth may be enabled to buy and sell on equal terms in the world market as well as to possess assurance of obtaining the materials and products of peaceful economic life."

In Hitler's Chancellery and Mussolini's Palazzo Venezia, men stared at this message with amusement and incredulity. Hermann Göring said that Roosevelt must be "suffering from an incipient mental disease," and Mussolini thought the message a result of the illness that had crippled him. At first disdaining to respond to so "contemptible a creature" as the "present President of the United States," Hitler then saw a superb opportunity to dish this hypocritical moralist of the West. First he demanded—and received—from the nations Roosevelt listed assurances that they did not feel threatened by Germany. When little Latvia sent an obscure reply, the German minister in Riga was instructed to inform Latvia that unless a clear negative was received, its leaders would be considered accomplices of Roosevelt; Latvia quickly complied. Next Hitler summoned his puppet Reichstag to meet in the Kroll Opera House for a direct response to Roosevelt. Sitting through the two-hour harangue, CBS correspondent William Shirer judged it probably the most brilliant he had heard Hitler give, for "sheer eloquence, craftiness, irony, sarcasm and hypocrisy."

While Göring in the President's chair grimaced and snickered, Hitler ticked off the "threatened" nations one by one and announced their negative responses. Ireland had more to fear from English aggression than German. The deputies roared when the Führer assured Roosevelt that he did not plan an attack on the United States either. He castigated the President for talking about conferences when the United States had not joined "the greatest conference of all time," the League of Nations. Roosevelt, he said, had spoken of the general fear of war, but Germany had had nothing to do with the "fourteen wars" that had been waged since 1919, or with the twenty-six "violent interventions" since that year, of which the United States had committed six. Germany respected the Monroe Doctrine and did not interfere in Central or South America; why should the United States meddle in Europe? Roosevelt talked about disarmament—but Germany had for all time learned her lesson since appearing unarmed at the Versailles conference table and being "subjected to even greater degradations than can ever have been inflicted on the chieftains of Sioux tribes." Mocking laughter swept through the old opera house as the Führer scored his points.

Then Hitler came to his peroration:

"Mr. Roosevelt! I fully understand that the vastness of your nation and the immense wealth of your country allow you to feel responsible for the history of the whole world and for the history of all nations. I, sir, am placed in a much more modest and smaller sphere. . . ." He had sought only to serve the German people.

"I have conquered chaos in Germany, re-established order and enormously increased production in all branches of our national economy." Boasting of finding useful work for "the whole of 7,000,000 unemployed," doubtless as a contrast with Roosevelt's partial success at recovery, he went on: "Not only have I reunited the German people politically, but I have also re-armed them" and destroyed "sheet by sheet" the Versailles treaty containing the "vilest oppression" in history. "I have brought back to the Reich provinces stolen from us in 1919; I have led back to their native country millions of Germans who were torn away from us and were in misery; I have re-established the historic unity of German living space and, Mr. Roosevelt, I have endeavored to attain all this without spilling blood. . . .

"You, Mr. Roosevelt, have a much easier task in comparison. You became President of the United States in 1933 when I became Chancellor of the Reich." Roosevelt headed "one of the largest and wealthiest States in the world." His own world, the Führer concluded, was much smaller but "more precious than anything else," for it comprised his own people.

This masterpiece of defense and demagoguery, which the Nazis arranged to be fully publicized in the United States and elsewhere, was greeted by Roosevelt's enemies at home as a deserved put-down for his naïve and provocative meddling. "Hitler had all the better of the argument," said the isolationist Senator Hiram Johnson. "Roosevelt put his chin out and got a resounding whack." While neither the President nor Hull had been optimistic about the outcome, in his first widely publicized encounter with Hitler, Roosevelt had come off a clear second best.

But Hitler's speech was far more than a collection of debater's points, far more than a tissue of lies about Hitler's pacific policies; ominously—by two omissions—it presaged the future. The first was Hitler's crafty skimming over Poland in his list of nations he was not threatening. The other was the absence of his usual diatribe against Russia. Like most observers, Roosevelt was hardly aware of the omission. Within four months, on the signing of the Nazi-Soviet pact, he would understand. He would also understand that, as the leader of a constitutional democracy, he was challenged not by Hitler alone but by Stalin as well—by two dictators who could move with speed, decision, and power, unrestrained by the peoples they led.

Once upon a time Hitler had been more friendly. "I have sympathy with President Roosevelt," the Führer had said in mid-1933, "because he marches straight to his objective over Congress, over lobbies, over stub-born bureaucracies." Hitler was describing the FDR of the Hundred Days; he could hardly have been more wrong about the real Roosevelt, who rather than marching straight to his goals, almost invariably skirmished, sidestepped, retreated, feinted, parried, danced and pirouetted as he picked his way through the minefields toward his goal of security and survival.

THE ZIGZAG ROAD TO WAR

In heritage and upbringing Franklin Roosevelt was internationalist to the bone. Some of his forebears had been world travelers who traded and invested in Asian and South American enterprises. First taken to Europe at the age of three, during the 1890s he stayed almost every year in France, England, and Germany for a few months. During these years, European governesses at Hyde Park tutored him in French and German, which he would retain workably if not fluently for the rest of his life. Weekly the *Illustrated London News* brought news and pictures of the top-hatted states-men in London and the other capitals, of the glamorous social doings in the cosmopolitan worlds of spas and fox hunts and society balls.

The years at Groton and Harvard broadened young Roosevelt's world-view. He debated international issues—naval expansion, or the Boer War, or Hawaiian or Philippine self-rule—with his fellows; he gloried in the Cuban exploits of Cousin Ted, who brought his robust activism to Groton, where he spoke to the boys; he fully supported the Square Deal President's foreign policy, whether pacific or belligerent. Lodged in the Wilson Ad-ministration in the spring of 1913, less than a year and a half before war broke out in Europe, he was at times more the Wilsonian internationalist than Wilson himself. Later in the 1920s the onetime big-navy man, still an internationalist, not only supported the five-power Washington Treaty for naval reduction but berated Coolidge for wishing to rebuild the Navy on "an enormous scale."

During the late 1920s, however, FDR's internationalism waned—in part a political response to the defeat he and Cox had suffered in 1920 on the League of Nations issue, partly an acquiescence in the decade's reaction against the idealism and utopianism of Wilsonian days, but altogether a reflection of FDR's rising presidential ambitions. His switch on the League issue was only the most evident example of his general shift to a more nationalist position.

Still, the electorate had long been accustomed to candidates' opportun-ism as they faced the ordeal of running for President. The test of Roosevelt's basic beliefs would come when he exercised the considerable powers of the presidency. The Hundred Days proved his drive and sense of direction in domestic policy. Could he lead in foreign policy making too? His recognition of the Soviet Union demonstrated some boldness, at least, and his intervention in the London economic conference was at least a decisive act, whatever its nationalist impact.

But the mid-1930s were a tough time for any kind of internationalist leadership as Americans retreated to their psychological storm cellars in the face of trouble abroad. Since public-opinion polling was still in its infancy, and other indicators were partial and impressionistic, we do not have wholly reliable guides to opinion during the mid-1930s, but one poll result in February 1937 was so emphatic as not to be doubted. Asked if another war like World War I came in Europe, "should America take part again?" 95 percent of the sample answered "No!" The next month the same percentage favored "doing everything possible to keep us out of foreign wars," as against doing "everything possible to prevent war between foreign countries, even if it means threatening to fight countries which start wars."

Behind this emphatic affirmation of isolationism lay a fluid, negative, uninformed public opinion that provided an unstable foundation for a consistent and coherent foreign policy. In this broth lay hard lumps of isolationist feeling, composed largely of millions of Americans in the more rural, insular areas of the nation and other millions of Americans of German, Irish, and Italian descent hostile to Britain, and still more millions of persons who were prisoners of ancient fears and shibboleths—that wily foreign diplomats always played Uncle Sam for a sucker, that the nation had never lost a war or won a peace conference, that salvation lay in keeping free of permanent alliances, just as George Washington had urged.

Besides needing to gauge the currents of public opinion and public ignorance, the President had to assess political forces in other lands. The thrust of the Nazi ideology, the balance of power in the French Chamber of Deputies, the foreign policy attitudes of British labor, the paranoia and lethal struggles within the Kremlin, the fortunes of Chinese warlords, nationalistic strivings in southern Asia, were all elements in the equation of world power. Reading long letters from his ambassadors, lunching with foreign envoys, quizzing his unofficial agents who had just seen Göring or Mussolini or a Chinese or Japanese diplomat, leafing through thick State Department studies, Roosevelt had to make judgments from day to day on mighty imponderables imperfectly understood. No wonder that he moved warily on the darkling terrain of foreign policy.

"In the present European situation I feel very much as if I were groping for a door in a blank wall," he wrote a friend early in 1934. "The situation may get better and enable us to give some leadership."

Leadership? That was precisely what FDR's critics, both interventionists and isolationists, felt he was not providing during the years when action by an American President might make the difference. Others were providing their own kind of leadership—the isolationist bloc in the Senate headed by men like William Borah and Burton Wheeler; out in the country, the increasingly rabid "America Firsters" glued to the radio for the sermons of Father Coughlin, who could be depended on to berate the red devils, foreign and domestic; pacifists led by such prestigious figures as Norman Thomas; belligerently isolationist press lords such as Hearst and McCormick. But the President had to deal with problems of ways and means they could hardly imagine or did not care to. In Washington he confronted a Congress deeply divided over the mechanics of neutrality but leaning sharply toward isolationism; a Democratic party leadership internationalist by heritage but fragmented in region and ethnicity; and even a divided set of advisers ranging from the internationalists in the State Department like Hull, William Phillips, and Sumner Welles to moderate unilateralists like Moley and Ickes, and an economic nationalist, George N. Peek, a "foreign trade adviser" until the implacable Hull forced him out.

The President's responsibility transcended all these partial views and interests. Somehow he had to speak for the American people as a whole, to take a "reasonable" and representative stance in foreign relations however erratic or mystifying at times, to avoid the "veto traps" set for him on the Hill and even in his own Administration, and above all to win national—presidential and congressional—elections. And he had to do all this amid intellectual confusion. He and his adversaries at home had a common goal—national security. But whether this goal could be achieved through collective efforts with allies abroad or by the unilateral efforts of a Fortress America was a biting issue.

Each side was fragmented in turn by internal quarrels. Even the terms of discourse were clouded; some "isolationists" did not wish at all to isolate the nation from certain parts of the world, notably the Far East; some "internationalists" had little interest in certain parts of the world, notably the Far East. As to Latin America, almost all sides backed the Monroe Doctrine in some form. Isolationists were selectively unilateralist, wary of international commitments. "They did not oppose all American activity abroad," according to Wayne S. Cole, "but they wanted to leave Americans free to determine for themselves when, where, how, and whether the United States should involve itself abroad. They did not want to be bound by prior commitments in alliances or international organizations."

If in heritage Roosevelt was an internationalist, at heart he was an interventionist, as instinctively activist in redressing problems abroad as in helping people at home. Moreover, he was worried about the weaknesses of democratic leadership, as in the French parliamentary system; addressing the Woodrow Wilson Foundation, he asserted roundly that "the blame for the danger to world peace lies not in the world population but in the political leaders of that population." Yet his own leadership during these critical months responded far more to the isolationist pressures in the electorate than to his activist, worldly instincts. Whatever his deeper feelings—and these were obscure to biographers even decades later—he strengthened the isolationist cause by virtually joining it. Any President during this period, given the confused state of public opinion and political combat, would have had to pick his way cautiously through the foreign policy maze of the mid-thirties. But Roosevelt appeared to mirror the general confusion and division rather than to transcend it.

The Senate investigation of the munitions industry, an egregious case in point, was one of the best planned, most spectacular, most effective antiwar efforts during the thirties. In the white marble caucus room of the Senate Office Building, flanking the stern young chairman, Gerald P. Nye, Republican populist from North Dakota, sat other stalwarts of American isolationism, including Republican Arthur H. Vandenberg of Michigan and Democrat Bennett Champ Clark of Missouri. The mission of the committee was beyond reproach: to expose the evil machinations of arms makers in fomenting strife and to "take the profits out of war." The villains in the drama were delectably evil: Du Ponts, Morgan partners, and other bloodsucking "merchants of death" who day after day confessed their sins. The heroine was an ethereal figure called Peace. Crowded into the big room was the chorus, muttering with indignation as the sordid story unfolded. Intensively covered and dramatized by the press, the committee dominated headlines for months.

Roosevelt was no innocent bystander. He had publicly urged the Senate to appoint such a committee; he gave the committee full access to executive papers that disclosed the skulduggery of bankers and diplomats; he endorsed Nye's drastic proposals to curb arms makers' profits. Hull was deeply disturbed by the Administration's cooperativeness with the committee. The President—and the Secretary of State too, he admitted to himself—were marking time, unwilling to stand against the isolationist wave until it abated. Indeed, Hull himself had offered to supply information to the investigators.

The President's volatile stand on neutrality legislation was an even more significant sign of his—and his nation's—uncertainty over the effective response to international aggression. Probably at no other time in his presidency did FDR confront such a tangle of perplexities, both moral and operational, as in the struggle over neutrality.

The key issue was not neutrality in itself—almost all Americans favored it, or said they did—but how much discretion the President should have in cutting off arms and other supplies to nations at war. Paradoxically the Supreme Court was recognizing at this time, in the Curtiss-Wright case, the "very delicate, plenary and exclusive power" of the President "as the sole organ of the Federal government in the field of international relations." So it was not formal authority that the Chief of State lacked, but a leadership strategy to cope with his adversaries at home and abroad. He had had great luck with the mandatory 1935 act that required him to ban arms both to Italy and to Ethiopia, thus potentially hurting Italy, with its need for modern arms, far more than Ethiopia. For months thereafter his foreign policy consisted essentially of juggling as he faced the isolationist opposition in the Senate with its special weapon of the filibuster, his own advisers with their varied counsels, the often irresolute democracies, the all too resolute pacifist and isolationist groups at home, unpredictable "enemy" nations abroad, and the shifting fortunes of diplomacy and war. So uncertain was the President over fundamental strategy that during an early phase of congressional debate over neutrality measures he changed his mind on important issues, according to Robert Dallek's analysis, no less than four times within a short period. And his luck ran out in Spain, where the mandatory law—and the vociferous feelings of many Catholic leaders—made it impossible for him to help the beleaguered Republican armies, increasingly dominated by communists, against Franco's attacks.

No other American could have juggled more skillfully than did Roosevelt, but juggling was not enough. Some urged him to apply the magic touch of the first and second Hundred Days, but the President had run out of magic, especially following the domestic political setbacks early in his second term. Since no one abroad appeared able to supply effective leadership, he told reporters in midsummer 1937, people were looking for someone outside Europe "to come forward with a hat and a rabbit in it." Well, the President went on, "I haven't got a hat and I haven't got a rabbit in it."

Others called on the President to educate the public on the gravity of the situation abroad and the measures necessary to deal with it. But the best way to educate is to exert strong leadership in speech and action on foreign policy—something Roosevelt had found virtually impossible during his first term, and prospects for leadership appeared little improved in the first year of his second term. Early in October 1937, in a major speech in Chicago, he proclaimed that the "peace-loving nations must make a concerted effort in opposition to those violations of treaties and those ignorings of humane instincts which today are creating a state of international anarchy and instability from which there is no escape through mere isolation or neutrality," and he called for a quarantine of lawbreaking nations similar to quarantine against the spread of disease. Although the President was vague about the kind of quarantine, the need for collective action, and other specifics, his speech set off an uproar. The AFL resolved against involvement in foreign wars. Isolationist congressmen threatened FDR with impeachment. And few in the Democratic party or even in his Administration backed up the President, except for ardent interventionists.

"It's a terrible thing," he said later to Sam Rosenman, "to look over your shoulder when you are trying to lead—and to find no one there." The President quickly pulled back—too quickly, according to some critics, for he appeared to have harbored undue expectations about the public response, then to have been disappointed by the mixed reaction, and then to have overreacted to that reaction.

And so Roosevelt marched forward two paces, retreated one, and sidestepped, meantime indulging in moral rhetoric and vague threats that unduly raised his followers' expectations while markedly inflaming his isolationist opposition. It was not Roosevelt but Hitler who "marched straight to his objective" over political opposition at home and his divided adversaries in Europe. The Führer's power, even within Germany, was by no means absolute; he too had to overcome foot-dragging and resistance in the state bureaucracy, in the Army, and in the party; sometimes he too had to pause or even retreat. But he found that audacious and aggressive acts abroad expanded his power base, while reducing his foes to sputtering indignation and rhetorical protest.

March 7, 1936—Hitler thrust his troops into the Rhineland, against the advice of some of his generals. France hesitated, Britain equivocated, the League declared Germany guilty of breaching the Versailles treaty. No one acted. Though deeply disturbed, Roosevelt did nothing and said nothing. Later Hitler admitted that if the French had marched into the Rhineland, he and his troops would have had to withdraw "with our tails between our legs."

November 6, 1937—Hitler with Mussolini and the Japanese leaders proclaimed the Rome-Berlin-Tokyo Anti-Comintern Pact. The Japanese smashed deeper into China. The democracies remained united in rhetoric, divided over action.

March 12, 1938—German troops and tanks swept across the Austrian border to be greeted by cheering crowds. Roosevelt was privately concerned, publicly silent.

September 12, 1938—Before a frenzied crowd at Nuremberg, Hitler demanded "justice" for Sudeten Germans in Czechoslovakia. Roosevelt appealed to all parties for peace, avoided replying to a plea from President Eduard Beneš of Czechoslovakia that he urge Britain and France not to desert Prague, and declined to permit Chamberlain to broadcast a message directly to the American people. Mobilizing his troops and threatening war, bullying his adversaries through diplomatic notes and face to face, Hitler pressured Chamberlain, the French, and even the Czechs into granting him the Sudeten districts and the fortifications that lay within them. Suddenly the old city of Munich, site of the decisive conference, became a symbol of appeasement. While the President could not say with Winston Churchill, "We have sustained a total, unmitigated defeat," he was now profoundly pessimistic about the chances for peace in Europe.

The Ides of March 1939—Skillfully wielding diplomacy, threat, and subversion, Hitler seized the rump of Bohemia and put Moravia under Nazi "protection." Hungary, snatching at the bone tossed by the Führer, gobbled up Ruthenia. "Never in my life," FDR wrote a friend, "have I seen things moving in the world with more cross currents or with greater velocity." In early April, Mussolini invaded Albania, and a week later the President sent the appeal to which the Führer replied so mockingly before the jeering Reichstag deputies.

The President now redoubled his efforts to obtain repeal of the arms embargo from the Senate. Repeal was the best way to deter Hitler, he argued, and to safeguard national security in the event of war. The Senate isolationists were more stubborn than ever. Roosevelt tried to encourage Chairman Pittman of the Senate Foreign Relations Committee to push repeal through by agreeing to boost the price for domestic silver; having been properly bribed, Pittman still could not deliver a solid majority from his committee. At a meeting in the President's study in mid-July 1939, Senate leaders sat, drinks in hand, while FDR pressed his case. Finally Borah spoke up.

"There's not going to be any war this year," he said. "All this hysteria is manufactured and artificial."

"I wish the Senator would come down to my office and read the cables," Hull said. Borah waved him quiet.

"I have sources of information in Europe that I regard as more reliable than those of the State Department." Hull almost burst into tears; Roosevelt was silent; then Vice President Garner polled the senators on repeal. Then he turned to the President. "Well, Captain," he said, "we may as well face the facts. You haven't got the votes; and that's all there is to it."

Roosevelt could not be so unruffled. He warned House leaders that Germany and Italy had at least a fifty-fifty chance of winning a war, after which they would threaten Latin America. Soon, he predicted, we would find ourselves surrounded by hostile states in this hemisphere. Further, the Japanese, who "always like to play with the big boys," would probably go into a hard-and-fast alliance with the Germans and Italians. If the United States resisted this threat, the three Axis states would be tempted "to try another quick war with us."

The President was not so prescient, however, about the likely effect on Hitler of a repeal of the arms embargo. To the Führer this would have been but a pinprick among the momentous events in the making in Europe. Stalin, after having been excluded from the Western decision to sacrifice Czechoslovakia, suspected that Munich was a Western plot to divert Hitler to the east. He could play that game too; he might divert Hitler to the west and let the fascists and capitalists fight it out. Cautious feelers between Moscow and Berlin about enlarging trade led to political discussions, then to the decision that the fierce ideological war between the two countries could be suspended for the sake of *Realpolitik*. Stalin dropped Foreign Minister Maxim Litvinov, the apostle of collective security with the West, in favor of Vyacheslav Molotov, a hard-liner.

Years later, at Yalta, Stalin would tell Churchill that decisive action by the Allies would have headed off Moscow's turn to Berlin. But the Allies did not act; they diddled, fearful of the price that Stalin might exact for collaboration. Then came the last two scenes of the prewar drama:

August 23, 1939—In the Kremlin, Molotov and German Foreign Minister Joachim von Ribbentrop sealed the Nazi-Soviet nonaggression pact. During the evening festivities that followed, Stalin drank to Hitler's health, saying, "I know how much the German nation loves its Führer." The new era in German-Russian relations was repeatedly and royally toasted. On hearing the catastrophic news Roosevelt sent Hitler a last despairing plea for peace. Hitler replied with action, not words.

September 1, 1939—Germany fell on Poland from the west; Russia invaded from the east over two weeks later. Britain and France indicated that they would live up to their treaty obligations to Poland.

September 3, 1939—Britain and France declared war on Germany. In New York, amid crushed communist and left-wing illusions about the Popular Front, the English poet W. H. Auden wrote:

I sit in one of the dives
On Fifty-Second Street
Uncertain and afraid
As the clever hopes expire
Of a low dishonest decade:
Waves of anger and fear
Circulate over the bright
And darkened lands of the earth,
Obsessing our private lives;
The unmentionable odour of death
Offends the September night.

In London, Ambassador Joseph Kennedy cried out, his voice choking: "It's the end of the world . . . the end of everything."

* * *

For Franklin Roosevelt, the coming of war in Europe was not the end of everything but the opening of new opportunities. At last Americans had to stop speculating about the possibility of war in Europe and start facing the reality of it. Congress did so by decisively repealing the arms embargo and authorizing "cash and carry" exports to warring powers—but only after the Administration conducted a massive propaganda effort on and off the Hill, and with the provision that American merchant ships must not enter combat zones. The noninterventionists, dreading the prospect of Americans being hornswoggled into a second world war, conducted their own campaign. Spearheaded by Colonel Charles A. Lindbergh, Father Coughlin, and Borah & Co., a national radio campaign clogged congressional offices with a deluge of mail—a million letters, telegrams, and postcards, it was estimated. Roosevelt once again promised that he would be guided by "one single hard-headed thought—keeping America out of this war."

By the time Congress passed the measure, at the end of October 1939, German and Soviet troops had overrun Poland and divided the spoils of war. There followed a curious and dispiriting period for the President. It was so quiet on the western front that people began to talk about the "Phony War." One front was not quiet. Late in the fall Stalin's troops and planes attacked Finland to bolster the northern defenses of the Soviet Union. Angry at "this dreadful rape of Finland," the President could find no way to help Helsinki, in part because he feared taking action that would push the Soviets closer to Berlin and farther from London and Paris. After a heroic three-month resistance Finland yielded territory and made other concessions.

Most irksome of all was Washington's relationship with London itself. For some years Roosevelt and Chamberlain had had an icy contempt for each other—the Prime Minister viewing FDR as something of a dilettante overly given to personal diplomacy and overly fearful of his own electorate, Roosevelt seeing the British leader as rigid toward his American friends and conciliatory to his Nazi enemies. That each government had long suspected the other was seeking to advance its economic interests at the expense of its ally incidentally provided ammunition in each country to leftists who contended that both bourgeois governments were far more interested in protecting capitalism than in thwarting fascism.

For London "cash and carry" turned out to be a considerable disappointment; by taking American ships off the seas it helped the German blockade. To tighten their blockade of Germany the British searched American ships and violated American "neutrality zones," arousing folk memories of historic encounters with Britain on the high seas. The President told his friend Winston Churchill, who had become First Lord of the Admiralty at war's outbreak, "I would not be frank unless I told you that there has been much public criticism here."

By early spring of 1940 the President was caught in a strategic stalemate abroad and a political bind at home. He had based his policy of "all aid short of war" so conspicuously on the supreme goal of keeping the nation out of war that any move on his part to help the allies beyond "cash and carry" brought down the wrath of isolationists. At home he faced a presidential election amid rising pressure from Administration Democrats— and from within himself—to be a candidate. But he could defy with no more impunity the tradition barring a third term than he could defy the almost hysterical popular fear of being sucked into another European war. "The country as a whole does not yet have any deep sense of world crisis," he had written at the start of the year. Only a great crisis could resolve his strategic and political impasse. It came on April 9, 1940.

At dawn German infantry struck across the naked Danish border. Soon Hitler's troops were disgorging from destroyers, barges, and troopships along the Norwegian coast. "Today we can have no illusions," Roosevelt warned a few days later in a Pan American Day address. Nor, it soon developed, could there be any illusions about Britain's capacity even to protect neighboring countries on the North Sea. The Nazis had laid their plans with thoroughness and imagination; the British response was improvised, ill planned, and inadequate. Amid bitter criticism Chamberlain prepared to resign; Churchill would shortly take his place. Then, on May 10, Hitler struck again.

At dawn a sheet of German fire and steel swept across the Dutch and Belgian frontiers. As siren-screaming dive bombers roared down through the spring air and parachutists seized airfields, 120 divisions of German assault troops poised for battle. And somewhere behind this stupendous power was the demoniac genius Hitler, proclaiming that the battle would "decide the destiny of the German people for a thousand years." A half-million Allied troops moved up behind the Belgian troops. Then, advancing with shocking speed, German tanks and motorized troops cut around the Allied flanks in great encircling sweeps and converted Belgium into a vast trap for the defenders. Within five days German tanks burst through the ill-defended Ardennes hills and began their lightning dash across northern France.

"The scene has darkened swiftly," Churchill cabled Roosevelt on May 15. "The small countries are simply smashed up, one by one, like matchwood." He knew that Mussolini would hurry in to share the loot. "We expect to be attacked here ourselves." The next few days brought news of disaster after disaster. Pouring through the Ardennes gap, German armor curved west toward the Channel, pinning masses of French and British troops against the sea. Soon Roosevelt was receiving desperate appeals for military aid from British and French leaders to prevent what Churchill called a "Nazified Europe." As France neared collapse, Premier Paul Reynaud in a last, desperate appeal asked Roosevelt to intervene with force, or at least the threat of force. Otherwise France would "go under like a drowning man."

Never in his whole political career did Roosevelt face a harsher test of his leadership under crisis conditions than in those spring days of 1940. He took the British and French warnings with the utmost seriousness, including the threat that the French fleet probably, and the British fleet possibly, would fall into Hitler's hands if the two allies went under. But at home he still faced a Congress more skittish than ever about sending modern arms from America's arsenal across the Atlantic; when David I. Walsh, chairman of the Senate Naval Affairs Committee, discovered that twenty new motor torpedo boats were to be sent to Britain, the Massachusetts senator went into a towering rage and threatened to force legislation prohibiting the sale of *anything*. To be sure, public opinion surged toward support of the democracies after Britain evacuated its troops from Dunkirk, but it was still afflicted by the fateful reservation—all aid *short of war*. About two-thirds of those polled favored aid, but nearly two-thirds considered it more important for America to stay out of war than to aid Britain at the risk of war. And the isolationists were still in full cry, though there were some defections in the ranks after the fall of France.

All this—and a presidential election campaign ahead. Somehow during these feverish days the President had time and energy to follow the fights over state delegations to the Democratic convention, to enjoy victories scored by Roosevelt slates in Texas, California, and elsewhere, to watch the spirited preconvention Republican race among Senators Robert Taft and Arthur Vandenberg, young Tom Dewey, and a political newcomer, utility tycoon Wendell Willkie. The anti-third-term bugaboo was still the unmeasurable factor in FDR's own candidacy. He was so closemouthed about his plans that correspondents and cartoonists pictured him as the Sphinx.

But at the very least FDR would take no step that committed him to run—or not run—for President. His success on this score was marked. Even more, he took certain measures that would help him if he did decide to run. One was to assume a bipartisan stance. Another, a piece of pure Machiavellianism, was to enlarge the field of candidates and thereby diffuse the potential opposition within the Democracy. Unlike a dictator, who clings to his leadership position by excluding and perhaps killing rivals, the President welcomed them and even put a large bee in their bonnet, when none might have existed, by playing up their presidential qualifications. Hull, Hopkins, and others far less known received the "treatment." Experienced enough to know they were receiving it, these men nevertheless could not leave the White House without hopes a tiny bit enhanced.

During the "hundred days" from mid-June to mid-October—one of the epochal turning points of world history—Americans were engulfed in a turbulent flow of events:

June 10—Italy declared war on France. "The hand that held the dagger has struck it into the back of its neighbor," declared the President in a Charlottesville speech.

June 17—The French government, now headed by Marshal Henri Philippe Pétain, asked Germany for armistice terms.

June 20—FDR consternated the GOP by appointing two Republicans to his cabinet—the former Secretary of State Henry L. Stimson as the new Secretary of War and Chicago publisher Frank Knox as Navy Secretary.

June 28—The Republicans convened in Philadelphia to choose a candidate for President. In a four-way race, Vandenberg was far behind at the starting gate, Dewey began strongly and then faded, Willkie started weakly and gained steadily in the next five ballots, and he and Taft made it a two-man race before Willkie, amid wild enthusiasm and chanting galleries, swept to a majority.

July 3—The British destroyed or immobilized major units of the French fleet anchored at Oran, Algeria.

July 7—Pressed as to his plans by Farley on the eve of the Democratic convention, Roosevelt said that he did not want to run but, "Jim, if nominated and elected, I could not in these times refuse to take the inaugural oath, even if I knew I would be dead within thirty days." Next day, Farley left for the convention determined that FDR would not receive an unopposed draft.

July 16—Barkley read to the Democrats assembled in Chicago a message from FDR asserting that he had absolutely no desire to run again for President and that delegates were free to vote for whomever they wished. During the stunned silence that followed, a single thunderous voice burst out of the loudspeakers, braying "WE WANT ROOSEVELT!" As a potbellied little man in the basement pressed his lips to the microphone and repeated his call, delegates and spectators took up the cry. "ROOSEVELT, ROOSEVELT, ROOSEVELT." The results of the first and only ballot the next day: Farley 72, Garner 61, Tydings 9, Hull 5, FDR 946. Roosevelt's choice of the progressive Henry Wallace for Vice President so upset the party leadership that Eleanor Roosevelt and others were recruited to placate the delegates.

August 8—German bombers opened a massive offensive against the British industrial heartland. During the sixteen-week Battle of Britain the defenders destroyed 1,700 German aircraft, while the Royal Air Force lost 915 fighters.

September 3—As the Battle of Britain roared toward a climax and after weeks of negotiation, Roosevelt and Churchill concluded the "destroyer deal." Informed by Churchill in midsummer that "the whole fate of the war" might be decided by the dispatch of fifty or sixty old destroyers and that "in the long history of the world, this is a thing to do now," Roosevelt had held off for fear of congressional reaction. It was only after the pro-British, Manhattan-based Century Group and others urged an exchange of destroyers for British concession of key possessions in the Western Hemisphere, and on the understanding that Willkie would not oppose the deal, that the President agreed to the swap by executive order. His "horse trade," under which the United States received ninety-nine-year leases on naval and air bases from Newfoundland to British Guiana, was well received by Congress and public.

October 12—Chastened by British resistance in his hopes for a cross-Channel invasion of England, Hitler finally called off the project. His thoughts turned east.

October 16—Following congressional passage of the Selective Service Act in mid-September, Roosevelt took symbolic as well as actual leadership of the muster, speaking movingly to the nation about its significance and presiding magisterially at the first drawing from the goldfish bowl.

The President had worried about pressing for the draft in the middle of a reelection campaign. After taking a moderately interventionist line early in his campaign, to the approbation of eastern internationalists like Walter Lippmann, Henry Luce, and Dorothy Thompson, Willkie suddenly switched toward isolationism when he found his early strength dwindling. His new position lost him Lippmann's and Thompson's backing but brought him into "a temporary alliance with people for whom he had contempt," according to a biographer, "including such isolationist stalwarts" as Hamilton Fish, Lindbergh, and McCormick. It also helped win him an endorsement from John L. Lewis, who had turned bitterly against FDR. Willkie's new line appeared to boost him in the presidential polls.

While Ickes and other activists agonized, the President stuck to the appearance of nonpartisanship until late in October. Then he attacked. Few commanders have sized up the terrain more shrewdly, rallied their restless battalions more boldly, and struck at the enemy's weak points more tellingly than did FDR during the two-week blitz that he unleashed on October 23. From his declaration that night to a roaring crowd in Philadelphia that "I am an old campaigner and I love a good fight," to his attack not on Willkie but on the congressional Republicans symbolized by "Ma-a-a-rtin, Ba-a-a-rton, and Fish," to his rash promise in Boston to the "mothers and fathers of America" that "your boys are not going to be sent into any foreign wars," he stayed on the offensive.

With Lewis, antiwar socialists, and the communists attacking the Administration in a strange partnership, the President noted that there was something "very ominous in this combination that has been forming within the Republican Party between the extreme reactionary and the extreme radical elements of this country." On election night the President was so worried by the apparent closeness of the contest that he untypically took the early returns alone. But his victory was decisive: 449 electoral votes to 82 for Willkie, and a popular-vote margin of five million. FDR won every city, save one, with a population over 400,000. Labor had stuck with him—including Lewis's mine workers. Willkie picked up five million more votes than Landon had four years before.

"I'm happy I've won, but sorry Wendell lost," Roosevelt told his son James. The two men quickly buried their campaign hatchets. When Willkie visited the White House after the election, the two men were overheard swapping campaign anecdotes amid great bursts of laughter.

THE WAR OF TWO WORLDS

In front of a bristling artillery piece at the Rheinmetall-Borsig Works of Berlin, Adolf Hitler poured out his wrath on the capitalists of the world, their kept press and political parties. The stakes, he told the assembled workers, were far greater than the fate of one nation. "Two worlds are in conflict, two philosophies of life . . . Gold versus labor." One of these worlds would crack up.

Three weeks later, in a fireside chat on the eve of 1941, Roosevelt accepted the gage of battle. Citing Hitler's remark about "two opposing worlds," the President said, "In other words, the Axis not only admits but *proclaims* that there can be no ultimate peace between their philosophy of government and our philosophy of government." The "Nazi masters of Germany have made it clear that they intend not only to dominate all life and thought in their own country, but also to enslave the whole of Europe, and then to use the resources of Europe to dominate the rest of the world."

Wearing his pince-nez and his usual bow tie, the President was sitting in front of a plain desk covered with microphones labeled NBC, CBS, MBS. Around him in the little room crowded a small and mixed company: his mother, Sara, Cordell Hull and other cabinet members, and Clark Gable and his wife, Carole Lombard.

The American appeasers, the President went on, "tell you that the Axis powers are going to win anyway; that all this bloodshed in the world could be saved; that the United States might just as well throw its influence into the scale of a dictated peace, and get the best out of it that we can.

"They call it a 'negotiated peace.' Nonsense! Is it a negotiated peace if a gang of outlaws surrounds your community and on threat of extermination makes you pay tribute to save your own skins?" After these bellicose words the President once again renewed his pledge to keep out of war.

"Thinking in terms of today and tomorrow, I make the direct statement to the American people that there is far less chance of the United States getting into war, if we do all we can now to support the nations defending themselves against attack by the Axis than if we acquiesce in their defeat, submit tamely to an Axis victory, and wait our turn to be the object of attack in another war later on." Admittedly, he said, there was risk in any course. But his "sole purpose" was to keep war away from the United States. His listeners could "nail any talk about sending armies to Europe as deliberate untruth." America, he proclaimed in the grand climax of his talk, "must be the great arsenal of democracy."

Roosevelt's talk, by far his most militant response to Hitler's challenge, sent a thrill of hope across the anti-Nazi world—to Londoners who on that very night were reeling from a stupendous firebombing by the Nazis, to Frenchmen and Dutchmen crouching by their radios, to impatient interventionists at home listening to Roosevelt's strong, resonant voice by their own firesides. His speech aroused isolationists to a new pitch. More than ever they were convinced that Roosevelt was now plotting to bring the nation into a shooting war.

They did not know their man. It was not Roosevelt's style or strategy to fashion a grand political and military strategy that in turn would produce a clear-cut decision. Rather, he kept his eye constantly cocked on public opinion, especially as reflected in Congress. It was never clear when he crossed the momentous threshold from viewing "all aid short of war" as a way of keeping out of war to seeing it as a way of winning an inevitable war. More likely he approached the threshold warily, evaded it, skirted around it, and then found himself past it, without having ever decisively stepped over it. Intellectually, he had no secret plan to involve the United States in the war; strategically, he was not a plotter.

But the isolationists in a fundamental sense were more justified in their suspicions than perhaps even they wholly recognized. For the crucial question in these epochal days was not what Roosevelt was secretly thinking. It was what he was publicly doing, whether or not even he realized the full implications of all he was doing. And what he was doing was inextricably linked with its impact on public opinion and Congress and cabinet at home, on the arousal of expectations in London and fears in Berlin and Tokyo, on the forging of a closer alliance between Germany and Japan. And what Roosevelt and Churchill did, how Hitler reacted to it, how Congress and public responded, unleashed further events that ineluctably brought the United States into the war. Thus it can be said in retrospect that the several months beginning with Roosevelt's reelection in early November—another "hundred days," as it turned out—marked the start of the country's intervention in World War II. It was, not in mind but in effect, the Administration's declaration of war.

That declaration began with the American voters' decision, by a clear-cut majority, to endorse the more strongly interventionist of the two major-party candidates. Hitler could read election returns. Now he began to take seriously the likelihood of American entrance into the war, even while he underestimated the American military-industrial potential. As a global strategist he saw the interrelationships of national power. If the Russian threat against Germany were removed, he told his generals, "we could wage war on Britain indefinitely. If Russia collapsed, Japan would be greatly relieved; this in turn would mean increased danger to the U.S.A."

By tying down the United States in the Pacific, the Japanese would draw the Americans away from Europe, making Britain more vulnerable.

Churchill too could read election returns—and his own shipping losses. Early in December he wrote Roosevelt that those losses had been over 400,000 tons in the five weeks ending November 3. "The enemy commands the ports all around the northern and western coasts of France. He is increasingly basing his submarines, flying-boats, and combat planes on these ports." In his letter—"one of the most important I ever wrote"—he laid out his urgent requests: American aid in keeping the supply routes open to Britain, which would help ensure continued British resistance and would not, Churchill said, provoke Hitler into fighting the United States; Roosevelt's "good offices" to induce Eire to cooperate on such matters; and above all dollars to help Britain pay for massive supplies of planes, ships, tanks, and other arms.

"I believe you will agree," Churchill concluded, "that it would be wrong in principle and mutually disadvantageous in effect if at the height of this struggle Great Britain were to be divested of all saleable assets, so that after the victory was won with our blood, civilization saved, and the time gained for the United States to be fully armed against all eventualities, we should stand stripped to the bone."

Carrying Churchill's letter, a seaplane splashed down next to the cruiser *Tuscaloosa* off Antigua, where the President was vacationing in the bright Caribbean sun. He read the letter with a poker face and seemed unmoved, but Hopkins sensed during the next few days "that he was refueling, the way he so often does when he seems to be resting and carefree. . . . Then, one evening, he suddenly came out with it—the whole program." The whole program was Lend-Lease—the simple but drastic idea that the United States could send Britain munitions without charge and be repaid, not in dollars, but in kind, after the war was over. The President could not doubt Britain's financial urgency; word came from Washington that London evidently had less than $2 billion available to pay for $5 billion in orders.

Back home, in press conferences, speeches, his eve-of-1941 fireside chat, and in his inaugural address, the President used the momentum of his election victory to press for massively increased aid to Britain. He wanted to "get rid of the silly, foolish old dollar sign," he told reporters, and offered an example. "Suppose my neighbor's home catches fire, and I have a length of garden hose four or five hundred feet away. If he can take my garden hose and connect it up with his hydrant, I may help him to put out his fire." Afterward he would ask for no money from his neighbor—only to have his garden hose back. Few challenged Roosevelt's analogy, save for

Senator Robert A. Taft, who said that lending war equipment was like lending chewing gum—you wouldn't want it back.

Isolationists pounced on the bill as soon as it was introduced into Congress in mid-January. The great debate got off to an acrimonious start when Wheeler called the bill "the New Deal's triple A foreign policy; it will plow under every fourth American boy." Telling the press they could quote him, Roosevelt labeled this remark "the most untruthful, as the most dastardly, unpatriotic thing that has ever been said." Wheeler, Hamilton Fish, and others pictured the bill as an act of war. It was a bill for the "destruction of the American Republic," thundered the Chicago *Tribune;* a bill designed to scuttle American democracy, cried Father Coughlin. Lindbergh urged in congressional hearings that America should concentrate on building up her air power and retire behind continental defenses; he predicted German victory in Europe but denied he favored it. Claiming he was barred from testifying, the blatantly anti-Semitic Gerald L. K. Smith threatened to bring in a petition with two million signatures against the bill. Almost drowned out in the furor were the words of thoughtful critics of the bill such as the historian Charles A. Beard, who warned that the measure would engage the government "officially in the conflicts of Europe and Asia."

The passage early in March 1941 of Lend-Lease by overwhelming majorities—60–31 in the Senate and 317–71 in the House—had just the effect that interventionists wanted and isolationists feared: deeper entanglement of the United States in the war. The stakes were higher now: Roosevelt's in having supplies reach England, Churchill's in receiving them, Hitler's in halting them. All the stakes were raised after the Führer's unstoppable armies invaded Yugoslavia and Greece in April. As the spring days lengthened, the Nazi threat to North Atlantic shipping grew sharply, as did pressure on Roosevelt from Stimson, Knox, and other interventionists to convoy ships through the submarine-infested waters. But Roosevelt feared that convoying would move him too far ahead of public opinion. He would only patrol—but his naval and air patrols, he confided to his war cabinet, would notify British convoys of the whereabouts of Nazi raiders.

Slowly—all too slowly for his impatient advisers—the President involved his navy and his nation in the Battle of the Atlantic. He did everything save convert his "undeclared naval war" into a declared one: he took over the defense of Greenland from Denmark; authorized British ships to be repaired in American shipyards and British pilots to be trained on American airfields; transferred ten Coast Guard cutters to the Royal Navy; sent his patrol ships farther north and east; proclaimed an "unlimited national emergency." His destroyers became ever bolder in tracking U-boats and reporting their locations. Roosevelt half feared, half hoped for some incident in the brumous mists of the North Atlantic. But it had to be a major incident that would unite the country, not a minor incident that might merely inflame the debate at home. When the American freighter *Robin Moor* was sunk in the South Atlantic by a U-boat in June, the President found it an inadequate excuse to start convoying.

By late spring 1941 Roosevelt was impaled on the horns of his own strategic dilemma. He had so insisted that aid was a means of avoiding rather than preparing for war that he cloaked his aggressive Atlantic patrolling in secrecy. Hitler could ignore small provocations; Roosevelt dared not try a large one, such as armed convoying, which would divide Congress and the electorate. So he had become hostage to Hitler's strategy; as long as the Führer refrained from responding to an action of FDR's as *casus belli*, the President was imprisoned in his policy of aid short of war.

Only another momentous event now could free the President from his dilemma. Germany's massive invasion of Russia in June 1941 transformed the global struggle but it only served to worsen FDR's predicament. For Hitler, now that he was fighting on two fronts, was all the more intent on keeping the United States out of the European war, and hence all the more intent on edging Japan toward a more belligerent posture in the Pacific. More than ever on the global chessboard, Roosevelt seemed to be a pawn edging ahead one or two steps, or a knight moving obliquely—and certainly not a queen radiating power across the board or a king offered as the supreme prize of battle.

*   *   *

If the President felt constrained in the Atlantic, he felt positively frustrated in the Pacific. On becoming President he had inherited an enmity between his own country and Japan that he had found no opportunity to overcome. In the fall of 1931, a year and a half before he entered the White House, Japanese officers of the Kwantung Army had used a manufactured incident to attack and then take over Manchuria, which Tokyo thereupon recognized as Manchukuo. Soon Hoover's Secretary of State, Henry Stimson, had promulgated the "Stimson Doctrine," which held that the United States would not acknowledge agreements impairing the sovereignty of the Republic of China. Later Japan denounced the Washington Naval Treaty of 1922, quit the League of Nations, promulgated the "new order" as a substitute for the "antiquated" Open Door policy, and stepped up its aggressive activities in North China. Stimson, now FDR's Secretary of War, pressed the President to take a firmer stand in the Pacific. Whenever the Administration appeared to be making concessions to Japan at the expense

of China, moreover, protests and lamentations arrived from the beleaguered President Chiang Kai-shek in Chungking.

It was no simple matter, the President was discovering, to be aggressive
in the Atlantic and pacific in the Pacific. Around the globe the fronts were
linked in numberless ways: Tokyo would benefit from the success of Hitler's drive east into Russia; Hitler hoped for Japanese action against
Russia; Britain's interests in Asia were imperiled; Vichy's authority over
Indochina was vulnerable; the Dutch had a presence in the East Indies; and
these all were further linked with the interests of secondary powers. The
President had to calculate how these fears and ambitions were cantilevered
by the complex and ever-shifting strains and thrusts of military power and
strategy. One blow could upset the swaying, quivering mobile of global
balances, but what kind of blow and with what effect?

And always the President had to act amid the murk of secret plans and
obscure rivalries. "The Japs are having a real drag-down and knock-out
fight among themselves," he wrote Ickes early in July 1941, "and have
been for the past week—trying to decide which way they are going to
jump—attack Russia, attack the South Seas (thus throwing in their lot
definitely with Germany) or whether they will sit on the fence and be more
friendly with us. No one knows what the decision will be." The Japanese
leaders had no less difficulty divining the Administration's intentions.
Through myopic eyes the inscrutable Orient and the incomprehensible
Occident viewed each other.

Events were no less cloudy in the Atlantic. The five months of diplomatic
activity, military planning, and incidents from the early summer of 1941
to the end of November were among the most critical and complex in the
history of American foreign relations. Not only were the events themselves
significant, but how they were perceived or misperceived by the other side
closely affected the course of events.

In mid-August, Roosevelt and Churchill met secretly at Argentia Bay off
Newfoundland. It was less a time of close military planning than an opportunity for the two leaders to size each other up face to face, discuss postwar
problems and opportunities, and issue an eloquent Wilsonian Atlantic
Charter of war aims. To Hitler it was a meeting of warmongers plotting
the "final destruction of the Nazi tyranny"—a phrase in the sixth article of
the Charter.

Only three weeks after the Argentia rendezvous, the American destroyer
Greer encountered a U-boat southeast of Iceland, tracked it for several
hours, all the while reporting its location to a nearby British bomber, and
later became itself engaged in an indecisive battle of depth charges and
torpedoes with the German submarine, which assumed its adversary was

British. Six weeks later the American destroyer *Kearny* sped four hundred miles to the aid of a stricken convoy, joined in depth-bombing the attacking wolf pack, and was hit by a torpedo that killed eleven American seamen and put the *Kearny* out of action.

Roosevelt grossly exaggerated the provocativeness of the German actions and minimized that of the American in his public reaction to the incidents. Following the *Kearny* episode he said in a major address, "Very simply and very bluntly—we are pledged to pull our own oar in the destruction of Hitlerism." Berlin boiled with indignation. For once the master falsifier had been outfalsified. From Hitler's headquarters on the Russian front came a statement that "the United States has attacked Germany." But Hitler would not yet escalate incidents into war.

Things were somewhat quieter—but potentially even more explosive—on the opposite side of the globe.

Each of the big powers in the Pacific played from poker hands that changed month to month as the shifting circumstances of war dealt out the cards. The problem was not so much lack of communication as too much of it. As factions tussled for influence in each capital—diplomats against soldiers, politicians against bureaucrats, old diplomatic hands against new—the official and unofficial channels were a source as much of confusion as of clarity. Amid the day-to-day chatter and bustle the leaders lost perspective on the towering conditions and events, hopes and expectations, that were holding the Pacific theater in their grip.

The most crucial of these forces was the increasing determination of the Japanese to hold and extend their presence in China. This was a matter not simply of global strategy but of national pride and ideology. The Japanese could not forget the American exclusion of Orientals and other racist discriminations; they could not ignore America's use of the Monroe Doctrine to buttress its political and economic power in Latin America; they could not ignore Washington's imperial and colonial ventures in the Pacific. The jingoists of Tokyo were demanding that Japan pursue its old nationalist and imperialist ambitions. Japan was heavily dependent on external sources, including the United States, for economic and military materials, and Washington was withholding high-octane gasoline and scrap iron; warriors and diplomats in Tokyo were therefore determined to extend their grip to Indochina and to the economic lifelines in the South Seas.

Half a world away Churchill had a clear set of priorities, or at least hopes. His greatest hope was that the United States would declare war on Germany, but he saw this as unrealistic in view of Hitler's spurning the gage of battle in the Atlantic. The next great hope in his global wish list was for a war between Japan and the United States, which Britain would join "within the hour," but Washington would take the lead in protecting both American and British interests in the Pacific. His mortal fear was that events would leave Britain facing Japan alone and thus locked into the kind of two-front war that all the contestants sought to avert. Hence the Prime Minister devoted much time in 1941 to helping stiffen Washington's posture toward Tokyo.

And Roosevelt? He too had his priorities, but his wish list was the shortest and simplest of them all. He hoped above all not to be involved in a shooting war in the Pacific when the real enemy was Adolf Hitler. He too feared a two-front war. He recognized, of course, that understandings between the two Axis countries would sooner or later turn a war against Japan into a war with Germany, but much depended on what was sooner and what was later. Hence Roosevelt's essential stratagem, through all the diplomatic windings and twistings of fall 1941, was to play for time—to drag out negotiations, to be conciliatory at one point and tough at another, all the while coping with pressures from London and Chungking to be more resolute. And he needed time for rearmament.

But time, more than Roosevelt realized, was an even greater imperative for the Japanese; they were as insistent on speed as Roosevelt on delay. Tokyo diplomats and militarists alike recognized that the only chance for Japan in a total war was a smashing victory over its adversaries, the establishment of a huge and impregnable defense bastion, and the rapid military and economic consolidation of conquests in China and to the south. Otherwise the immense economic and military power of the United States and Britain would prevail in two or three years. For some months during 1941 the military leaders of Japan allowed the diplomats to pursue their negotiations in case Japan could achieve its goals through parleys rather than war. Early in September they set a deadline—if there was no agreement by mid-October, Japan would prepare itself for battle against the United States, Britain, and Holland. This was the most momentous decision in the tortuous road to war in the East.

For there was no agreement. The more the Japanese and American leaders understood each other, the more they understood how much they disagreed. Tokyo was bent on expansion to the west and south, Washington on stopping it. Both sides were the victims of miscalculation, false hopes, unreal expectations—Tokyo that it could win a lasting victory through a quick stroke, Washington that the Japanese would strike south toward the possessions of beleaguered Britain, France, and Holland, possibly toward the Philippines, but certainly not at Oahu. That island, Army Chief of Staff George C. Marshall had assured Roosevelt in May 1941, was "the strongest fortress in the world."

*   *   *

In the White House during the evening of December 6, a young naval aide carried up to the President's study a locked pouch containing communications from Tokyo to the Japanese embassy in Washington. For over a year these messages had been decoded by American cryptanalysts. The President was seated at his desk; Hopkins paced slowly back and forth. Both men carefully read through the messages. The young aide later recalled their reactions:

"This means war," Roosevelt said.

Since war would undoubtedly come at the convenience of the Japanese, Hopkins observed, it was too bad that the United States could not strike the first blow and prevent a surprise.

"No, we can't do that," the President said. "We are a democracy and a peaceful people." Then he added, raising his voice a bit, "But we have a good record."

That same evening Japanese carriers northwest of Oahu were turning to starboard and speeding south with relentless accuracy, amid mounting seas, toward Pearl Harbor.

*   *   *

Thundering down over the green fields of Oahu, the attacking aviators could hardly believe how calm and orderly everything seemed—Pearl Harbor and Honolulu bathed in the bright morning sunlight, the orderly rows of barracks and aircraft, the white highway wriggling through the hills, and the great battlewagons anchored two by two along the mooring quays. Their commander, Fuchida Mitsuo, remembered the mightiest fleets he had seen assembled in German and French harbors, but, he said later, he had never seen warships anchored so closely together. In the next 140 minutes 181 Japanese fighters, dive bombers, and torpedo planes ranged up and down Oahu almost at will, leaving four battleships sunk or sinking, four others mauled, 150 aircraft destroyed, barracks and airfields ravaged, more than 2,300 soldiers and sailors killed. The Japanese lost around thirty planes before turning back to their carriers.

It was a brilliant stroke, planned with imagination and painstaking care, executed with audacity, and backed up with a superbly equipped and trained naval force. The Japanese had some luck—their flattops had been undetected—but they had bad luck too, for of the carriers they expected to find at Pearl that day, one was being repaired in Puget Sound and two were off on sea missions. The Japanese gained, however, from the poor military intelligence and the lazy security and communications arrangements of the American command. Above all, they benefited from the Americans' faulty ideas—especially the idea that the "Japs" would never—never—attack the powerful fortress on Oahu. Despite later accusations, Washington did not "plan it that way"; the Japanese did that. Not a conspiracy theory but a complacency theory explains the surprise at Pearl Harbor—pervasive complacency in Washington and at every other level over Hawaii's state of readiness, over Tokyo's alleged military weakness, and over the degree of American knowledge of Japanese intentions and capabilities.

In Washington, Navy Secretary Knox exclaimed "My God!" when the flash came in: AIR RAID ON PEARL HARBOR. THIS IS NO DRILL. "This can't be true! This must mean the Philippines." Knox telephoned the President, who was sitting at his desk talking with Hopkins. There must be some mistake, Hopkins said. Roosevelt disagreed; it was just the kind of unexpected thing, he said, that the Japanese would do. Soon the horrifying details were coming in.

In Tokyo hundreds of loudspeakers blared out the news in the streets. Some older people moved off to the Palace gates to pray for victory. The Emperor toned down an imperial rescript, adding his personal regret that the Empire was at war. In a radio address Prime Minister Tojo warned of a long war for the future of Japan and East Asia. There followed a recorded martial song:

> Across the sea, corpses in the water;
> Across the mountain, corpses in the field.
> I shall die only for the Emperor,
> I shall never look back.

At Chequers, Winston Churchill had a moment of pure joy. So he had won after all. Yes, after Dunkirk, the fall of France, the fear of invasion, the U-boat struggle in the Atlantic, after seventeen months of Britain's lonely fight—the war was won. England would live; the Commonwealth and the Empire would live. The war would last long, but all the rest would be merely the proper application of overwhelming force. People had said that the Americans were soft, he reflected—divided, talkative, affluent, fearful of shedding blood. But he knew better—he had studied the Civil War, fought out to the last desperate inch.

In Berlin, just returned from the Russian front, where the Red Army was vigorously counterattacking, Adolf Hitler had little hesitation in fulfilling his obligation to his Pacific ally, even though Tokyo had not given him advance word of Pearl Harbor. He and Ribbentrop had orally promised Japan that Germany would fight the United States if Japan did. But this promise was not the main reason for Hitler's decision. The Führer felt that the Americans had already declared war on *him* by attacking his ships—a feeling confirmed when Roosevelt in a fireside chat two days after Pearl Harbor declared flatly that "Germany and Italy, regardless of any formal declaration of war, consider themselves at war with the United States at this moment just as much as they consider themselves at war with Britain or Russia." Both Hitler and Roosevelt recognized the inevitably wide involvement of nations locked in a global war. Even so, there was a manic quality to Hitler's decision to war on the United States. Audacity and bravado had worked for him in the past; they would work again. He loathed Roosevelt personally with almost hysterical intensity. This manic quality explains in part the only real mystery in Hitler's behavior after Pearl Harbor—his failure to press Japan harder to attack Russia, as a quid pro quo. Perhaps, though, Hitler recognized reality here. The Japanese would never take on the colossus to the north as long as they were so engaged in operations to the south.

And engaged they were in the weeks after Pearl Harbor. Some hours after Pearl Harbor—long enough to be fully alerted—Douglas MacArthur's air and naval forces were devastated in the Philippines. If confusion was the story of Pearl, befuddlement and indecision marked MacArthur and his commanders on Luzon. So dense was the fog of battle that a half century later historians were still trying to pierce it. Washington had contributed to complacency by sending out a handful of heavy bombers as a deterrent to Tokyo; these and most of MacArthur's other aircraft were smashed on the field. Once again the Japanese bombers and fighters left virtually unscathed.

After immobilizing American bases on Luzon and crippling British sea power in the Pacific by sinking the *Repulse* and the *Prince of Wales,* the Japanese carried out their audacious and carefully planned strategy of expanding their island empire through Malaya, Burma, the Dutch East Indies, and the western Pacific islands. To the amazement of the Allied defenders, within an incredibly few weeks after Pearl Harbor the empire threatened Midway and Hawaii to the east, Australia to the south, and even India to the west.

*   *   *

The bombs and torpedoes that shattered the towering battlewagons at Pearl Harbor and MacArthur's forces on Luzon on Sunday, December 7,

1941, had shattered also some of the towering illusions of the day: that the Japanese would back down if American and British deterrence was powerful enough; that the enemy would not really fight because he was undertrained and ill equipped and even—in the case of Japanese aviators—too nearsighted to fly planes; that if the Japanese did go to war, they would attack British or Dutch possessions and not American; or if they did have the nerve to take on the United States they would attack the Philippines and perhaps Guam but never Pearl Harbor. Shattered also was Roosevelt's notion that he could pursue undisturbed his strategy of aggressiveness in the Atlantic and caution in the Pacific. Now he faced the two-front war that he had tried so hard to avoid; and for months he would have to fight on the wrong—the far western—front.

Britain's enemies boxed the compass: Nazi sea power to the west and north and east, German land power to the south in France, Italian naval forces in the Mediterranean, the Japanese by land and by sea in Asia and the Pacific. Both Germany and Japan now confronted adversaries on several fronts. Only Russia now faced just one foe—but one was enough. The million or more German troops grinding their way eastward into the Russian heartland comprised at this time land power without parallel in history.

Both the Allies and the Axis were forced to conduct coordinated strategies, since concentration on one front inevitably robbed others. Hence each coalition strove for unity. But each nation had also separate interests, hardly papered over by the much-publicized conferences and consultations. Some American leaders, with eyes to public opinion as reflected in Congress, were tempted to turn westward against the Japanese, especially after the loss of Luzon and the agonizing siege of Corregidor. British leaders, scourged by memories of the bloodbaths of World War I, feared launching a premature invasion of France that could lead to another stalemate. The Russians had one central interest outside their borders—a massive Anglo-American cross-Channel attack to lighten the awful German pressure on the Soviet Union. And each nation had some separate leverage. The Americans could shift their forces between the two oceans, the British could build up attacking power along the whole periphery, the Russians could warn of impending collapse or even loft hardly veiled threats of another deal with Hitler.

These global coalitions and conflicts weighed heavily on Roosevelt and Churchill when the Prime Minister late in December arrived at the White House for a long Christmas visit. Churchill had the delicate double objective of concentrating the Anglo-American effort in Europe rather than the Pacific, yet avoiding a commitment of the European effort to a cross-

Channel attack. Soon he presented his case to Roosevelt and the Joint Chiefs of Staff for an Allied invasion of northwestern Africa, designed to hook up with British troops renewing their drive west along the North African coast into Tunisia.

The Prime Minister promptly ran head-on into the sturdy opposition of General Marshall. The quintessential professional soldier, the Chief of Staff had been raised in the American military tradition, symbolized by Ulysses S. Grant, of massing central and coordinated forces for assaults straight into the enemy heartland. Marshall feared not only dispersion of effort in Africa but even more that success in the Mediterranean, with all its enticing openings for future moves, would pull men and munitions away from the central effort in Western Europe. With Roosevelt not committed in either direction, except to the primacy of Europe in general, the African issue was left unresolved. This made the outcome more dependent on events—that is, on the actions of lesser leaders.

The top leaders found it easier to agree, with their allies, on the ends for which the vast conflict would be fought. In jointly composing a "Declaration of United Nations" Roosevelt and Churchill could accord on almost all items except freedom for India. Far stickier, in view of the need to gain the adherence of the atheistic Russian leaders, was the President's insistence on "religious freedom" as a goal. Only after Roosevelt had convinced envoy Maxim Litvinov, plucked out of obscurity by Stalin as a gesture to his allies, that religious freedom included the right to have no religion at all, and only after Litvinov won the permission of a dubious Number One in Moscow, could a proud President and Prime Minister issue the declaration. Signed by twenty-six nations—an array much like the group that both Roosevelt and Hitler had appealed to in 1939—the central provision made it the purpose of the Allies "to defend life, liberty, independence, and religious freedom, and to preserve human rights and justice in their own lands as well as in other lands."

Victory seemed far away in the following weeks of early 1942, however, as the Japanese extended their grip on the western and southwestern Pacific and the Nazis continued to hammer Russia. For months the Allies knew nothing save defeat. But before the end of 1942 they had fought three crucial battles that if lost would have meant a very different war and a far longer struggle.

The first of these critical battles was a series of engagements in the southwestern Pacific that continued through most of 1942.

While still consolidating their hold on the Philippines and routing a fleet of American, British, and Dutch warships in the Java Sea, the Japanese began a 2,000-mile advance through eastern New Guinea and further southeast through the Solomon Islands. Early in May a large Japanese fleet, covered by three carriers, sped west through the Coral Sea to seize Port Moresby, a key Australian base on the narrow eastern neck of New Guinea. Alerted to Japanese plans by cryptanalytic intercepts, an American fleet, protected by the carriers *Yorktown* and *Lexington,* moved to the attack. In the first sea battle in history fought only by carrier planes, the American fleet under the command of Rear Admiral Frank Jack Fletcher sank one Japanese carrier and damaged other warships, while losing the *Lexington*. This indecisive engagement was enough to stem Tokyo's southern advance.

A thousand miles to the east the Japanese land advance had come to a halt at Guadalcanal, an island at the southeastern end of the Solomons. Now the Americans turned to counterattack. The Navy surprised the lightly defended island with an amphibious landing early in August, only to be surprised in turn by a Japanese night attack that devastated the blundering American support fleet in one of the most mortifying defeats the American Navy had ever suffered. For a time virtually cut off from base, the Marines on Guadalcanal captured an almost completed airfield— promptly renamed Henderson Field—and held off fierce Japanese coun- terattacks. On the seas around Guadalcanal, violent naval and air battles erupted as both sides sought to control access to the island. For the Marines Guadalcanal became a "green hell," a hot and stinking island full of thorn-studded vines, mosquitoes, malaria, dysentery, "loathsome crawl- ing things," and rain and humidity that turned food and supplies into mold and rot. But in this hell Americans proved that on the ground as well as on the sea and in the air, they could fight on equal terms and win against a brave and tenacious foe.

The second of these decisive battles, Midway, was a reverse replay of Pearl Harbor. The American carriers absent from Pearl Harbor that day now had their chance to redress the naval balance in the Pacific; the Japanese now had their chance to smash the flattops that had eluded them. If the Americans wanted revenge, so did the Japanese, and for a very special reason. In mid-April, American bombers had suddenly appeared out of nowhere over Tokyo. These were Colonel James Doolittle's army bombers that almost unbelievably had been flown off the carrier *Hornet* by B-25 pilots who had never even practiced this feat. The bombing had little physical but an enormous psychological effect on the Japanese, and espe- cially on the high command, which now resolved on a hazardous sea attack on Midway thousands of miles to the east, an attack that would both avenge this insult and thwart a repeat performance.

Midway also reversed Pearl Harbor in giving the Americans the advantage of surprise and luck. As Tokyo's plans developed and a great force of carriers and battleships sortied east toward Midway late in May, cryptologists and radio traffic analysts in naval intelligence had tracked enemy plans and movements. Feinting to the north in a failed effort to draw away Admiral Chester Nimitz's fleet units, Admiral Yamamoto's main force of carriers headed straight east. The Americans were ready for them. Wave after wave of torpedo planes and high-flying bombers descended on the attacking warships, only to be devastated by skilled Japanese gunners and Zero pilots. One torpedo squadron lost ten of its fourteen planes and another was totally destroyed—without either squadron scoring a hit. Then American dive bombers arrived by a stroke of luck just as the flight decks of Yamamoto's carriers were cluttered with planes preparing for the next attack. In a few minutes three Japanese carriers were infernos of fire and explosions. Dive bombers sank a fourth carrier later in the day. The *Yorktown* was set afire in a counterstroke and was finished off the next day by a Japanese submarine. Yamamoto ordered a retirement. The Japanese had now lost the initiative in the mid-Pacific.

The third turn-of-the-tide battle was already on the planning tables. While war during spring 1942 raged in the Pacific, Washington and London had continued to struggle over their "Hitler first" strategy—when and where to strike in Europe. As Allied fortunes of war sank around the world, with Japanese victories in the Pacific, Red Army reverses on the long Russian front, the capture of Tobruk in Libya by German general Erwin Rommel, and staggering shipping losses in the Atlantic, Roosevelt felt the pressure of public opinion for more aggressive prosecution of the war, but centered in the Pacific, which was already serving as the biggest suction pump of all. Setbacks along the immense Japanese periphery from the Aleutians to Burma drew men and munitions to the Pacific theater. With no front opened in Europe to match those in the Pacific, Roosevelt and his chiefs of staff sought desperately to bring their power to bear across the Atlantic.

But where? The British still resisted an early cross-Channel attack. The Russians still pressed for an assault in force. Roosevelt still sought major action *somewhere*. Stimson and Marshall still fought "dispersion." General Dwight Eisenhower, who was assuming an ever larger role as a war planner, spoke his superiors' views as well when he noted that a cross-Channel attack would be "one hell of a job" but was better than "sitting on our fannies giving out stuff in driblets all over the world." Back and forth swayed the battle over strategy between American and British planners; some joked that it was the biggest fight going. But soon it was summer of 1942, too late to take advantage of good invasion weather in the Channel.

The major assault on the Continent was put off to 1943, as much by delay and default as by decision, in favor of an attack in North Africa for the fall of 1942.

However modest the North African plan appeared compared to a massive continental assault, it was bizarre and daring enough in itself. The United States' attack would be launched initially not against its mortal enemy, Germany, but against its oldest ally, France—albeit a France run by Nazi hirelings in Vichy. Its success might turn more on political than on military factors. It was long opposed by the very generals and admirals who would have to carry it out. And no wonder—the plan called for moving tens of thousands of troops across thousands of miles of Atlantic waters infested by U-boats, landing them on difficult North African beaches, deploying them to cope with French forces under Vichy command, to link up with British and other Allied troops pushing west and catch Rommel's forces in a vise, and to do all this with untried sailors and soldiers. There was always the fear too that Hitler's friend Franco might close the Straits of Gibraltar and thus cut the invasion lifeline or even allow the Führer to thrust his own divisions through Spain and into Africa.

Mirabile dictu, the military plan worked. In the early hours of November 8, 1942, troops scrambled ashore at a dozen target points along the shoulder of northwestern Africa from south of Casablanca to east of Algiers. Luck was with them: the Atlantic surf was unusually calm; the U-boats had been successfully feinted off; French troops put up only scattered resistance. There lay ahead a long struggle, during which American troops were bloodied, before Allied forces could corner the Germans in Tunisia. But the unseasoned American soldiers and sailors in North Africa, as in the Pacific, showed that they could meet the enemy, take their losses, persist, and ultimately win through.

Oddly, Roosevelt's luck rose with the military landings, which had to be somewhat improvised, and fell with the political operation, on which he and Churchill had lavished much effort and thought. The initial attack appeared to outrage alike the Vichy French, the non-Vichy French, and the anti-Vichy French. When an "arrangement" was finally struck with the local Vichyites then in apparent command, Roosevelt was roundly berated for the sordid deal with the French admiral Jean Darlan. But the President said he would "walk with the Devil" until he had crossed the bridge. And he could proclaim high ideals. Disembarking troops were issued a letter from their Commander-in-Chief: "Upon the outcome depends the freedom of your lives: the freedom of the lives of those you love." BBC London broadcast his words in French to the French: "My friends . . . I salute again and reiterate my faith in Liberty, Equality, and Fraternity."

The Production of War

The war would be won, Churchill had exulted after hearing the news of Pearl Harbor—all the rest would be merely the "proper application of overwhelming force." He was right. Once the Allies had won the initiative in the desperate battles of 1942, especially at Midway and Stalingrad, they never relinquished it for long, despite many defeats and setbacks. In every major engagement on the western front there was always more, much delayed at times, sometimes inferior in quality, but always more—more men, and from the overflowing war plants more munitions, more supplies, more planes and tanks and landing craft. Although for a time every theater felt starved, the Allies could plan their major attacks months in advance, achieve enormous buildups, and feed in mountains of backup supplies as the troops moved forward.

The troops themselves were in many ways production workers. Usually they did not advance in splendid array as in a pageant, or fight with bayonets and pistols in Hollywood fashion. Typically soldiers wormed ahead on their bellies as they encountered strong points, manhandled their light weapons into place, poured in fire and explosives, and moved on; or if the enemy defenses held, they called up reinforcements, asked for bigger tools such as tanks, waited, summoned artillery, heavy mortars, planes, unleashed a holocaust of metal and fire, waited. . . . The press glorified "tough, elite troops" serving as the "cutting edge of war." More likely at the end of the long supply lines was a thin, almost invisible line of men with grimy hands and hairy faces, in shapeless work clothes, cursing and bitching as they fed the machines of war.

There was always more, mainly because Americans by 1943 were creating the biggest war-production boom in history. It was slow to take off while the idea of business as usual persisted. Many businessmen, enjoying their best profits since 1929, were slow to convert; many workers were quick to strike; and Washington's efforts to mobilize and coordinate were often weak and inept. FDR's much-publicized goals for 1942 of 60,000 planes and 45,000 tanks were not met. For months after Pearl Harbor, the automobile industry continued to produce passenger cars. But the military defeats of early 1942 helped produce a sense of crisis that brought all the producers together in a stupendous united effort. Typewriter factories turned out machine guns, toaster plants made gun mounts, pot and pan makers assembled and loaded flares. In Minnesota a tombstone manufacturer put his grinders to work facing the edges of steel plates for welding.

Americans were doing what they had always done best—making things—and the results were as astounding as Carnegie's and Ford's feats of old. Airplane output jumped from 2,100 in 1939 to 48,000 in 1942 and 96,000 in 1944. From mid-1940 to mid-1945 Americans made more than 100,000 tanks, 370,000 artillery pieces, 87,000 warships, almost 2.5 million trucks, nearly 5 million tons of aircraft bombs, about 44 billion rounds of small-arms ammunition. In 1943 steelworkers produced 12 tons for every American soldier. Production of locomotives quintupled, of aluminum quadrupled, of industrial chemicals tripled. The United States alone furnished in 1944 60 percent of the Allied combat munitions, which helped to guarantee a three-to-one edge in arms over the Axis.

Once again, as in the days of the Yankee entrepreneurs, technology paced production. America's production superiority still rested on its unrivaled stock of special-purpose machine tools. The precision of these tools promised that when all the parts were brought together, as in the case of the 2 million parts needed to make one of Ford's B-24 bombers, they would fit exquisitely. Specific technological advances, such as welding rather than riveting, radically hastened production, especially of ships. A heavy dependence on subcontracting brought a few small firms back into some of the prominence they had enjoyed during America's industrial growth—along with the multitude of tinkerers they sheltered.

But enormous production did no good, as shipbuilders kept reminding Americans, unless it got to the fronts. Frightful shipping losses and enormously heightened global demands required a production miracle. Such it appeared to be. Americans produced over 53 million tons of shipping during the war. Improved methods of prefabrication and precision assembly cut the average time for constructing a 10,500-ton Liberty ship from 200 days in 1941 to 40 in 1942.

At Yard Two, Richmond Shipyards, California, in November 1942, long-necked cranes towered above crews swarming over the shipways, lifting and gently setting down 100-ton prefabricated sections of Hull 440. Work continued through the night. By the end of Day One the hull was shaped, three bulkheads and the entire engine assembly installed, and 18,000 feet of welding complete. On Day Two the rest of the bulkheads, the sheer strakes, fantail, freshwater tanks, and midship deckhouses were in place. The upper deck was finished. On Day Three the six-story "whirly" cranes lifted all of the superstructure—deckhouses, masts, windlass—onto the ship and the big rudder and antiaircraft guns were added. Day Four was devoted to finishing up welding and riveting and electrical wiring. By the end of that day Hull 440 was complete, outfitted with life belts, coat hangers, and signs in the toilets reading "Water Unfit for Drinking." Then Hull 440, now named *Robert E. Peary,* its flags flying and coat of gray paint scarcely dry, proudly slid down the ways—and stayed afloat.

Shipbuilders, like sailors and soldiers, enjoyed telling their own Paul Bunyan stories. One yarn was about the woman who, according to the singer Gracie Fields, was invited to christen a new ship. She was brought to an empty launching way and handed a bottle of champagne.

"But where is the ship?" the bewildered guest asked.

"You just start swinging the bottle, lady," a worker replied. "We'll have the ship there."

*   *   *

For some Americans it was the best of times, for some the worst, and for some it was both. On the face of things, never had so many Americans had it so good. At last jobs were abundant; full employment was achieved just a decade after the New Deal got underway. The labor force grew 36 percent during the war years, while the average workweek lengthened from 37.7 hours to 46.6. Wages soared. Average hourly pay in manufacturing rose from 73 cents in 1941 to $1.02 in 1945; average weekly wages almost doubled.

The rising tide of prosperity lifted all income groups, but some rose much more than others. Most notably, the poorer persons did best relatively. From 1941 to 1945 family incomes of the lowest fifth grew 68 percent and of the second-lowest fifth 59 percent, while family incomes of the top fifth rose 20 percent. At last Americans were seeing the poorest of their fellow citizens lifted out of the bleakest poverty—a goal sought futilely by progressives, socialists, New Dealers, and some capitalists, a goal rarely achieved by liberal democracies or by self-proclaimed egalitarian revolutionary or totalitarian regimes. But by a bitter irony it was a goal now achieved almost incidentally as part of a very different but transcending goal—winning a war.

For a time Americans—especially the poor—spent as they had never spent before. Consumer spending as a whole rose from $66 billion in 1939 to $104 billion in 1944. As durable goods like washing machines and refrigerators became more scarce, however, spending shifted from goods that might have provided poor people with an improved quality of life to more transient satisfactions. Racetrack attendance rose by two million a year, while the amount bet skyrocketed. Movie theaters were often open around the clock to accommodate three shifts, and nightclubs boomed. So did jewelry and cosmetics—except those with ingredients that were needed for munitions. To a degree, however, rising incomes lifted all consumer spending, save for scarce or rationed items. Book sales rose 20 percent a year as cheap paperbacks came into their own. Pocket Books, whose sales had been in the hundreds of thousands before the war, sold 40 million copies in 1943. Comic books, catering to servicemen as well as children, became a billion-dollar business. Tourism, however, stagnated because of gasoline rationing, though Miami had some success with its advertisements that weary war workers could "Rest Faster Here."

If in a material way some of the poor had never had it so good, more fundamentally they hardly escaped their poverty of health, speech, education, and aspiration, or their vulnerability. Many of them had to move from rural areas in order to find the big-paying jobs. They were part of one of the biggest migrations in American history, as some 15 million of the civilian population left their home counties and poured into Detroit–Willow Run, Mobile County, Los Angeles, San Diego, by the hundreds of thousands. They were the new Okies—Okies with jobs but little else. Schools were sometimes so crowded that countless children did not attend at all. Inadequate child care and lack of extended families among migrants left young children to their own devices while their mothers worked the graveyard shift. A Los Angeles social worker counted forty-five babies locked in cars in a single parking lot near war plants. Housing was so scarce in Bath, Maine, that fifty families stuck out an intensely cold winter in trailers banked with snow. In Beaumont, Texas, people were nauseated by the stench of an out-of-control garbage dump near the shipyards.

Whatever their income group, the best-organized did best. From the very start of the defense effort businessmen moved into Washington to run the industrial mobilization agencies. Shortly after Pearl Harbor the President created the War Production Board under Donald Nelson, who would be the "final authority" on production issues. Nelson, formerly chief purchasing agent for Sears, Roebuck, was an unpretentious, agreeable man who preferred persuasion over wielding the big stick but lacked FDR's sense of timing and relish for control. "On this job . . . we must have down here men who understand and can deal with industry's intricate structure and operation," Nelson said. Naturally such men had to come chiefly from industry itself. Businessmen were moving up in the New Deal Administration, *Business Week* exulted, "replacing New Dealers as they go."

Many executives in government, including three-fourths of those in WPB, were dollar-a-year men who continued to draw their corporate salaries, an arrangement that angered Harry S Truman, chairman of the Senate's Special Committee to Investigate the Defense Program. Unimpressed by Nelson's contention that dollar-a-year men could not afford to give up their corporation salaries for lower federal pay, Truman wrote: "The com-

mittee does not like to have procurement matters entrusted to men who
have given such hostages to fortune." But even Truman conceded that if
necessary the executives should be hired. "We want to win the war."

For business, voluntary cooperation was patriotic, and also good for
both its image and its profits. Industry received lush incentives to maximize
production. Contracts were made on a cost-plus basis; the government
undertook to pay all costs plus a fixed fee, or guaranteed profit, and
thereby freed the contractor of risk. "Of course it contributes to waste,"
said the president of Bell Aviation. "For maximum economy, go flat price.
If you want maximum output, you have to go fixed fee." The government
also subsidized or made low-interest loans for expanding production facilities—which would be made available to companies at fire-sale prices when
the war ended. Not surprisingly, net corporate profits rose from $6.4
billion in 1940 to $10.8 billion in 1944. In five years corporate assets
almost doubled to nearly $100 billion. Said Secretary of War Stimson: in
a capitalistic society at war, "you have to let business make money out of
the process or business won't work."

Big business certainly. For many small enterprises, the war years
brought anxiety and disappointment. The Administration lacked a firm
policy on using small business, which in turn had few friends among
military procurement officers; these tended to favor large corporations
with whom they had established contacts. The Truman Committee took up
the cause of small business and two agencies were created: the Small War
Plants Division within WPB and the separate Small War Plants Corporation. Nevertheless small firms received only a tiny percentage of army
contracts, and half a million small enterprises went out of business from
1941 to 1943. At the top of the pyramid two-thirds of all wartime contracts
went to a hundred firms, with ten corporations receiving almost one-third
of the business.

Organized workers also made out relatively well. Union membership,
fueled by the huge job expansion, rose from under nine million in 1940
to almost fifteen in 1945. The AFL claimed seven million members, the
CIO six million. Five weeks after Pearl Harbor the President established
the National War Labor Board, composed of four public members, four
from industry, and four representatives of labor. Much stronger than its
predecessor agency, the Defense Mediation Board, the NWLB could take
over a labor dispute on its own authority and impose settlement rather
than merely recommend it. The board boldly took on the problem of
closed shop versus open. Under a statesmanlike formula, "maintenance of
voluntarily established membership," workers were given a fifteen-day

grace period during which they could quit their union and still keep their jobs. After that they had to pay union dues for the life of the contract.

The Labor Board epitomized the three-way partnership among government, industry, and labor that was supposed to preside over economic mobilization. Labor had demanded an equal partnership—after all, it provided the sinews of production—but soon felt relegated to a junior status. In return for a no-strike pledge that some national union leaders made after Pearl Harbor, labor expected more than token representation in the industry-dominated mobilization agencies. But labor "advisory committees" were appointed and ignored. When Walter Reuther, an astute young vice president of the auto workers, early on proposed an ambitious plan to convert the auto industry's excess capacity to the production of 500 aircraft a day under the supervision of a government-industry-labor board, the idea was dismissed as "socialism."

CIO president Philip Murray had joined in the no-strike pledge, but later he began to lose control of the rank and file, who he said were showing an "attitude of rebellion." Grass-roots leaders, unfettered by "partnership" promises, responded to the grievances of men and women working perhaps eleven hours a day, living in shacks and trailers, driving or busing for hours to and from work. Wages for some had risen 15 percent under a 1942 "Little Steel" formula, but this was barely enough to compensate for inflation, and prices continued to rise during 1942 and 1943—another 8 percent, the government admitted, another 28 percent, labor claimed. As in the past, the tight labor market put extra leverage in the hands of union organizers and strike provokers. The result was 3,700 work stoppages in 1943, even more in 1944. Ford alone experienced 773 wildcat strikes between 1941 and 1945.

The most conspicuous nonpartner was John L. Lewis, more militant and truculent than ever. True to his 1940 pledge, Lewis had resigned as CIO president after FDR's reelection. As head still of the United Mine Workers he kept his base in the pits, but in the early war years he was an isolated figure nationally. The miners too, after early wage boosts, suffered with frozen wage rates and rising prices. "When the mine workers' children cry for food," Lewis thundered, "they cannot be satisfied with a 'Little Steel Formula.'" Pledged to support the war effort, Lewis was reluctant to strike, but his oratory inspired militant rank-and-file miners who moved ahead of him. In January 1943 they staged unauthorized walkouts, with the demand that Lewis immediately negotiate a $2-a-day pay boost. Emboldened by the miners' demands even as he put them back to work, Lewis negotiated fruitlessly with the mine owners for six weeks, boycotted the

NWLB when it took over the case, and resisted both presidential appeals and presidential threats, including one to draft men up to the age of sixty-five (Lewis was sixty-three).

"Speaking for the soldiers, John Lewis," trumpeted the service journal *Stars and Stripes,* "damn your coal black soul." Earl Browder, at this point militarized as well as communized, denounced Lewis's "insurrection against the war." The conflict drifted on into the fall, the miners remaining adamant and Lewis maintaining a public image of inflexibility while in fact making compromise after compromise. FDR joked that he would gladly resign *his* presidency if only Lewis would commit suicide. The agreement finally signed in November 1943 brought the miners $2 more a week rather than $2 a day, but Lewis had demonstrated that he and his union were willing to arouse the public's wrath if necessary to make the Little Steel formula bend a bit.

The least organized Americans, of course, were women and blacks. The increase in income for these groups, as for the poor in general, was in contrast to their actual well-being. Although firms were reluctant to hire women until the pool of male workers was depleted, by 1943 women made up a big part of the work force in such war industries as steel (18.5 percent), aircraft (39), communications equipment (51), small-arms ammunition (47), and rubber products (38). Women operated drill presses, milling machines, cranes, turret lathes. They burred and painted and doped, riveted and welded and loaded. They drove buses and taxis, served as police officers and football coaches. Ford put a team of manicurists to work filing precision instruments. By August 1944 over 18 million women had jobs, nearly twice as many as in early 1941.

But even in wartime, when "equal pay for equal work" was proclaimed, women in manufacturing earned $34.50 weekly in 1944, while men made $57.50. Many unions admitted women, if only because they feared that employers would otherwise use them to undercut union wage scales, but some unions, including the Teamsters, admitted women only "for the duration," as though they were industrially dispensable when the war ended. That was the myth of Rosie the Riveter. Though Rosie had been happy as a housewife, she went to work for patriotic reasons. She enjoyed her war work but would eagerly return to housework after the duration, when men would return to reclaim their jobs.

Like white women, black men had to wait for jobs until the manpower shortage became acute, and that wait could be "mighty slow." As of September 1941 more than half the jobs created by federal defense contracts were as a matter of company policy closed to blacks, but by 1944 Negro workers made up 7.5 percent of employment in war production. The wage differential between whites and blacks closed somewhat—from worse than a ratio of one to two in 1940 to that of $2,000 to $2,600 in 1944. Sometimes unions were more discriminatory than employers. Blacks had their own "unions" in the NAACP, its membership expanding explosively with the enrollment of black servicemen, and in the newly founded Congress of Racial Equality, which used sit-ins in its strategy of nonviolent direct action. In the human pressure cookers of the big industrial centers, race riots exploded in Detroit and Los Angeles in June 1943, both touched off by white servicemen stationed nearby.

And to be both black *and* female? In September 1942 only fifty black women worked in war plants, and even two years later only 13.4 percent of employed Negro women worked in manufacturing of any sort. More than half provided domestic and personal services. In a St. Louis electric company 64 percent of the employees were white women, 24 percent black men, and 12 percent white men, but the company hired not a single black woman despite a government order to do so. Black women were typically the sweepers, janitors, and material handlers; one in a Baltimore arsenal lifted fifty-five-pound boxes of TNT all day long for $18 a week.

And so the production of war drew on the vast industrial energies of Americans, lifting some out of money poverty but not out of social poverty, reflecting both the power of the organized and the vulnerability of the unorganized but leaving class relationships essentially unchanged. Except in one respect—there was a new instant underclass created by anti-Japanese racism on the West Coast, popular fears of a "Jap invasion," army overzealousness, and timid politicians in Washington and Sacramento. This consisted of almost the entire West Coast population of 120,000 Japanese-Americans now living behind barbed wire in concentration camps.

They had been routed out of their homes some weeks after Pearl Harbor, tagged like checked parcels, and dispatched to assembly centers—hastily converted racetracks, fairgrounds, stockyards—where they might be housed in stables, searched at will, and ringed by guards and searchlights. After a few months they were loaded onto trains and shipped, with blinds drawn, to camps in the deserts of Arizona and California, the barren flatlands of Utah, the swampy lowlands of Arkansas—ten camps in all. Families lived in cramped tar-paper barracks, ate in mess halls, used communal showers and toilets. They cleared sagebrush, dug irrigation canals, produced vegetables and poultry. They were the new money-poor, earning $8 to $16 a month.

"When I first entered our room, I became sick to my stomach," Stanley Shimabukuro wrote from the Santa Anita assembly camp. "There were seven beds in the room and no furnishings nor any partitions to separate the males and the females of the family." The food was terrible. "I feel so sorry for granduncle and grandauntie." Two weeks later he found a ray of hope. His parents, he wrote, were showing signs of a new faith in "what I'd like to call a Brotherhood of Mankind" as against the persecution of yellow men by whites. In another camp a child asked, "When can we go back to America?"

No protesting voice of consequence was raised as Americans watched their friends and neighbors lose their most precious possession, liberty. Few wondered why Japanese were penned up but not Germans or Italians. No party of consequence opposed the "relocation," as it was called. The normal checks and balances of politics were suspended, as were the normal checks and balances of the Constitution. Congress later ratified the act and the Supreme Court much later validated it. The relocation deeply disturbed Morgenthau and Ickes, but the cabinet registered no opposition. Walter Lippmann, so zealous of individual liberties back in New Deal days, urged strong measures on the ground that the Pacific Coast was officially a combat zone. Senator Taft challenged the legislation, but his objection was to the wording and form of the bill, not to the relocation itself. Attorney General Francis Biddle at first strongly opposed evacuation, then washed his hands of the matter.

*   *   *

"Politics is out," Roosevelt told reporters in March 1942. In assuming nonpartisanship the Commander-in-Chief had suspended some of the traditional political processes. There was now no loyal opposition to confront the White House and propose major alternatives—only individual critics shooting from all directions. But politics in democratic America could never be adjourned, war or no war. The only question was what form politics would assume.

It would take an electoral form in any event, since the 1942 congressional and state elections lay ahead. Well aware of Woodrow Wilson's setback in 1918, the President adopted a hands-off policy. "When a country is at war," he told reporters, "we want Congressmen, regardless of party—get that—to back up the Government of the United States." But the Politician-in-Chief could no more abstain from politicking than a toper from a drink. He tried without success to produce a strong Democratic challenger to Thomas Dewey's gubernatorial quest in New York. He was no more successful in seeking to unite Democrats and liberal Republicans against his old Dutchess County neighbor and antagonist Hamilton Fish. He publicly endorsed the independent reelection campaign of Senator George Norris, sending him a note—"If this be treason, let every citizen of Nebraska hear about it"—but failed in his effort to keep a Democrat out of the race.

With a low turnout on election day, Republicans gained a surprising 44 seats in the House and 9 in the Senate. Wilson had called for a Democratic Congress in 1918, a commentator noted, and had lost seats in both House and Senate; FDR had not called for anything and had lost twice as many. Republican gubernatorial candidates Dewey in New York, Earl Warren in California, Harold Stassen in Minnesota, John Bricker in Ohio, all won. The independent Norris lost. When Congress convened in 1943, southern and border-state Democrats held 120 of the 222 Democratic seats in the House and 29 of 57 in the Senate. With conservative Republicans they could form a majority. The anti-Roosevelt conservative coalition was alive and well again.

The new Congress set about gutting whatever was vulnerable in the remaining New Deal. The legislators in 1942 had already refused to allocate funds for the firstborn of the New Deal agencies, the Civilian Conservation Corps, and even ardent New Dealers had to grant with FDR that the WPA now deserved an "honorable discharge." But the same could not so easily be said of the National Resources Planning Board, the Farm Security Administration, or the Rural Electrification Administration, which Congress axed, gutted, or starved in 1943. In that year Congress rejected the Wagner-Murray-Dingell bill to expand Social Security coverage, even though Roosevelt had gone out of his way to take any New Deal label off it. And the Smith-Connally bill, giving the government wide powers to end work stoppages, was passed over his veto. John L. Lewis had got his comeuppance.

Having now doffed the garb of "Dr. New Deal," as he put it, and donned that of "Dr. Win-the-War," Roosevelt could accept the counterattack on New Deal measures with some equanimity. But the attack on his domestic war program was something else. On the critical issue of financing the war, he believed he could not afford to surrender. Congress in 1942 had passed tax legislation that raised $7 billion in additional revenue, boosted corporation taxes and the excess-profits tax, and brought millions of Americans onto the tax rolls for the first time. By mid-1943, however, the government was spending nearly $7 billion a month on the war, the national debt had risen since 1939 from $40.4 billion to $136.7 billion, and consumers would be left with more than $40 billion that available goods and services could not soak up. A flood of debt and inflation threatened the war economy.

To dam this flood Treasury Secretary Morgenthau in October 1943 called for $10.5 billion in new revenue, over half to come from personal income taxes and the rest from corporate, excise, and gift and estate taxes.

The House Ways and Means Committee threw out the Administration proposals and drafted a bill of its own that would raise just $2 billion in new taxes. This bill the full House and Senate passed after their conferees had merrily ratified the tax concessions the two chambers had granted business. It was "really a vicious piece of legislation," Rosenman said, riddled with special-interest provisions.

His boss agreed. In a biting veto message FDR called the congressional measure "a tax relief bill providing relief not for the needy but for the greedy." He would not be content with this "small piece of crust." Now it was Majority Leader Barkley's turn to become indignant. He had advised the President against a veto, he brooded; now here was this sarcastic message. In high dudgeon Barkley stood before the Senate to denounce the President's "relief for the greedy" crack as a "calculated and deliberate assault upon the legislative integrity of every Member of Congress." The stage was now set for a political charade. Barkley indicated he would resign as Majority Leader. FDR wrote him a placatory letter hoping that he wouldn't, and that the Senate Democrats would reelect him if he did. Barkley resigned anyway, the Senate Democrats met and reelected him— all amid exploding flashbulbs and torrents of excited newspaper talk.

The flap was over in a few days, with Barkley back in his post as the Administration workhorse. But a residue of bitterness remained. And a fiscal crisis in the making, for Congress by heavy majorities passed its tax bill, the first time in history a revenue bill had become law over a presidential veto. For all practical purposes, Roosevelt now felt, the nation had a Republican Congress.

*   *   *

The penning up of over 100,000 fellow Americans, the wartime restrictions on almost everyone's individual liberty, the continued subordination of women and blacks, the contrast between the material well-being of tens of millions of Americans and the deep and ceaseless sorrow of those who had lost fathers, brothers, and sons (and the first few mothers, sisters, and daughters), the impoverished lives of even high-flying, big-spending war workers—all this should have sharpened questions about the fundamental meaning of the war. Yes, avenging Pearl Harbor—yes, beating Hitler—yes, winning, winning—but beyond that, what? Four months after Pearl Harbor half the respondents in a survey admitted that they had "no clear idea of what the war was all about." A year after Pearl Harbor fully one-third still had no "clear idea." The vast majority had no notion—or only the foggiest—of the Atlantic Charter or of the freedoms the nation was defending.

Still, the concentration on winning the war, under the leadership of Dr.

Win-the-War, had a profound psychological impact on people. They felt included, involved, integrated with their fellow citizens. Even in remote areas people could tend Victory gardens, take part in civil defense, collect rubber or scrap metal or paper, turn in cans of fat, serve on rationing boards. Six hundred thousand people manned observation posts against enemy planes that never came. One such sentinel at the gates was a Connecticut woman of eighty-six years, three-quarters blind but with 20/20 hearing and sense of duty. For many this feeling of participating and sharing helped make up for the shabbiness of their wartime living and the emptiness of their war lives. At least for a time—the longer the war continued, Richard Polenberg concluded, the more people turned to "private and personal concerns."

Even participation and sharing were not enough—what was the war *for*? During World War I, George Creel's Committee on Public Information, with its wide powers of propaganda and censorship, had aroused such intense opposition that Roosevelt shied away from any similar agency. He created first the Office of Facts and Figures, under poet and Librarian of Congress Archibald MacLeish, and later the Office of War Information, which absorbed OFF and was directed by Elmer Davis, a journalist much respected for his terse and factual radio reporting. Charged with both putting out information and facilitating understanding of the war, Davis soon encountered the traditional opposition of the military to full dissemination of war news.

More surprising was OWI's internal division over how to explain the meaning of the war. The "writers" followed MacLeish's belief that Americans should begin at once to try to grasp what they were fighting for and hence that OWI should dramatize issues in a way that would "excite and encourage discussion." The "advertisers" contended that OWI should "state the truth in terms that will be understood by all levels of intelligence." The advertisers gained such ascendancy within OWI that many writers resigned in the spring of 1943, one of them leaving behind a mock poster displaying a Coke bottle wrapped in an American flag with the legend: "Step right up and get your four delicious freedoms."

Such government-sponsored shows as *This Is War!* explained the fighting to "all levels of intelligence" by trivializing it. Broadcast into 20 million homes, *This Is War!* began with *"Music: ominous"*—"What we say tonight has to do with blood and with love and with anger, and also with a big job in the making. Laughter can wait. Soft music can have the evening off. . . . There's a war on." OWI encouraged radio stations to broadcast one-minute plugs of the war. At least there was some down-to-earth humor. On Jack Benny's "Victory Parade" his partner, Mary Livingston, told of her uncle who had shed twenty-three pounds by eating nothing but soup. "Nothing but soup?" exclaimed Benny, the straight man. "S-a-a-y, he musta had a lot of will-power!" Then Livingston's punch line: "No, my Aunt gave his teeth to the Rubber-drive."

Hollywood was quick to get into uniform. Producers met the demands of the OWI advertisers and the public by playing up martial themes, casting servicemen as romantic leads, and replacing gangsters as public enemies with Nips and Huns. The Japanese, usually played by Chinese-Americans or Korean-Americans—except for Peter Lorre, a German who could also do Nazis—were portrayed as treacherous, sly, cruel, and prone to saying things like "The Rising Sun never sets, so her spies never sleep." The GIs were average Joes, modest, stoic, loyal to the sweet girl they'd left behind. They explained the war in simple terms: "It doesn't matter where a man dies, so long as he dies for freedom." At its peak Hollywood was packing war themes into a third of its films, from *God Is My Co-Pilot* to *We've Never Been Licked* to *Four Jills in a Jeep.* But filmmakers lost interest in war themes about the same time audiences did. In July 1943, *Variety* headlined: "STUDIOS SHELVE WAR STORIES AS THEY SHOW 40% BOX OFFICE DECLINE."

Tin Pan Alley chimed in with "We'll Knock the Japs Right Into the Laps of the Nazis," "You're a Sap, Mister Jap," "To Be Specific, It's Our Pacific," "Over Here," "Stalin Wasn't Stallin'." None of these measured up to World War I's "Over There." The most popular tune of the war—dolefully sung by men on sunny atolls and by their wives and sweethearts back home—was Irving Berlin's "White Christmas," crooned by Bing Crosby.

Even more pervasive than the sentimentalizing and trivializing of the war was its commercialization. "Fertilizer can win the war." Prune juice was good for "America behind the guns." A maker of bedroom furniture advertised that "America's greatest fortress is the American home." Mineral water helped "keep America fit in war time." A manufacturer of air conditioning claimed that a Japanese ship was torpedoed because part of a periscope had been produced in an air-conditioned factory. The makers of Coca-Cola, seeking to keep their sugar allotment, persuaded the government to make Coke an essential war product. A bomber pilot coming across an ad headed "Who's Afraid of the Big Focke-Wulf?" scrawled across it *"I* am" and mailed it to the manufacturer.

But few soldiers objected to the commercialization, especially when the ads spoke of home. If the GIs had an ideology, that was it. They wanted to win the war so they could go home. Meanwhile they made ersatz homes of their bivouacs. "The American soldier is a born housewife," Ernie Pyle wrote from the front. "They wish to hell they were someplace else," Bill Mauldin wrote. "They wish to hell the mud was dry and they wish to hell their coffee was hot. They want to go home. But they stay in their wet holes and fight, and then climb out and crawl through minefields and fight some more." They fought to go home.

"What would you say you were fighting for?" John Hersey asked a group of Marines on Guadalcanal. "Today, here in this valley, what are you fighting for?" The men fell silent, they looked distracted. Finally one of them spoke: "Jesus, what I'd give for a piece of blueberry pie." Soldiers talked less about returning to democracy, historian John Blum observed, than about creature comforts and affluence after the war. They talked about hot baths, flush toilets, a nice little roadster, a mother's cooking, a blonde on each arm, a bottle of Scotch, a cabin on five acres, running their own filling station, fresh eggs.

Some would never come home. A new war photograph repelled soldiers and civilians alike. It showed a gray sea lapping at three men, armed, helmeted, booted, swelling into their fatigues, face down, sinking into the sand, dead. Was it an epigraph to the Japanese martial song about "across the sea, corpses in the water" when an American soldier-poet wrote of

> . . . the slow, incessant waves
> curving and falling, the white foam lifting
> the white sand drifting
> over your face, your outflung hand . . .
> you have come a long way, a world away, to sleep . . .

THE RAINBOW COALITION EMBATTLED

For Roosevelt and Churchill 1943 was a year of conferring and planning, as they presided over an almost nonstop series of traveling strategy meetings. The President met with Churchill at Casablanca in January 1943, as well as with the feuding French generals Henri Giraud and Charles de Gaulle; with British Foreign Secretary Anthony Eden in Washington in March; with Churchill and the Combined Chiefs of Staff in Washington in May. Late in August he met with the Prime Minister and their military and diplomatic staffs in Quebec, and these meetings continued in Washington the next month. Then these sessions broadened into a series of global climaxes: Roosevelt, Churchill, Chiang Kai-shek, and military staffs in Cairo in late November; Roosevelt, Churchill, and Stalin in Teheran at the end of November; Roosevelt and Churchill in Cairo in early December.

It was in these conferences that crucial war and postwar strategy was hammered out. It was also where a fundamental rigidity in Big Three relationships became more and more evident.

For Roosevelt, getting there was half the fun. When he left the White House on an early January 1943 evening with Hopkins and a small party, boarded the presidential train at a secret siding near the Bureau of Engraving and Printing, and started a slow train trip to Miami, he was gay, relaxed, and full of anticipation. He was soon to see Churchill, a new continent, combat troops. He would travel by plane for the first time since his flight to the Democratic convention eleven years before. He would be the first President to fly, the first to leave the United States during wartime, and the first since Lincoln to visit an active theater of war. After taxiing out of Miami harbor on a Pan American Clipper the President missed nothing as he flew over the Citadel in Haiti, scanned the jungles of Dutch Guiana, glimpsed the Amazon, then slept during the long overnight trip to British Gambia, where he drove through the old slaving port of Bathurst and was appalled by the ragged, glum-looking natives and reports of disease and high mortality rates. Thence he flew over the snowcapped Atlas Mountains and into Casablanca.

The President encountered few surprises at Casablanca. Churchill and his big staff, having laid their conference plans with exquisite care, were as resistant as ever to an early cross-Channel attack in force. Like an old roué viewing a beach beauty, Churchill could not resist casting a lascivious eye on the eastern Mediterranean, with all its delicious curves and tempting cleavages. In the plenitude of deep harbors and wide landing beaches he saw ways to strengthen his lifelines to and from the Dominions and colonies, keep Hitler off balance, and find entrances to Southern and Eastern Europe that might offset the potential expansion of Soviet power. And FDR's military advisers, intent on winning the present war, were just as adamant as ever against drawing troops and weapons into the eastern Mediterranean suction pump, even while their own enormous pump in the Pacific sucked vast amounts of supplies away from Europe and General Henry "Hap" Arnold's bombers consumed enormous resources in Britain for their ever-intensifying assaults on the Continent.

Roosevelt was still in the middle. Long eager to launch a major offensive, he wanted to thrust across the Channel but also at the underbelly if possible. The British approach had always had some appeal for him, since it kept major options open, allowed for quick and perhaps easy victories, kept American troops active and moving, might knock Italy out of the war, and provided Stalin with at least the semblance of a second front. By the close of the long and often heated Casablanca talks the Anglo-Americans were broadly agreed on priorities for 1943: overcome the U-boat menace in the Atlantic; send all possible aid to Russia but not at prohibitive cost; center Mediterranean operations on the capture of Sicily; carry on the bomber offensive and the buildup for the cross-Channel invasion; counterattack Japan and support China.

What about the real second front—when and where and how big? The specter at Casablanca was Josef Stalin, who had been invited but declined because of his war burdens. He wanted one thing and one thing only out of Casablanca—absolute and foolproof assurance that the invasion of France would be launched in early 1943, as promised. And this was precisely the assurance he did not receive in the weeks following the conference. On the contrary, after the Wehrmacht poured tens of thousands of troops through Italy into Africa, broke through the Kasserine Pass in Tunisia, and took many Americans prisoner, Churchill warned Stalin that these reverses would delay clearing the Axis out of Africa. Confirmed in his suspicion of the fecklessness or worse of the whole Mediterranean effort, Stalin responded in cold anger:

"At the height of fighting against the Hitler troops, in February and March, the Anglo-Saxon offensive in North Africa, far from having been stepped up, has been called off." Meantime Germany had moved thirty-six divisions—six armored—to the eastern front. "I must give a most emphatic warning, in the interest of our common cause, of the grave danger with which further delay in opening a second front in France is fraught."

"Grave danger." What did Stalin mean? That the Soviet front might collapse? That Stalin might go it alone, militarily and diplomatically? That he might even make a deal with Hitler? The last seemed out of the question, but so had the Nazi-Soviet pact appeared before August 1939. Stalin nursed the gravest suspicions about his allies. For him the delay in the second front was not merely a question of strategy; hundreds of thousands of Russians would perish as a result. Were his "allies" hoping that Russians and Germans would exhaust themselves in mortal combat, leaving the Anglo-Americans supreme on the Continent? Was that why they had been so deceitful about the second front? The dictator's suspicions were dark. Were they trying to help Russia just enough to keep the Soviets in the war, but not so much as to help them win it?

It was evident by mid-1943 that Roosevelt and Churchill must meet with Stalin before the delay in opening a second front brought the anti-Nazi coalition to collapse. But no conference could take place until the Allies could agree on the cross-Channel attack. In meeting after meeting the military leaders thrashed out their differences, postponing the second front until sometime in 1944. The successful invasion of Sicily in midsummer and Mussolini's resignation helped Roosevelt at the Quebec talks to gain British agreement to an invasion of northwestern France in May 1944, even while Churchill and indeed Roosevelt still cast lingering glances at the eastern Mediterranean. In September, Stalin agreed to a Big Three meeting, provided it was near Soviet borders, in Iran. Soon the President was happily preparing for another long trip, during which he would meet not only Stalin for the first time but Chiang Kai-shek.

This time the Commander-in-Chief and his Joint Chiefs crossed the Atlantic on a battleship, the *Iowa*, 58,000 tons, almost a fifth of a mile long, 210,000 horsepower, 157 guns including nine sixteen-inchers. After a calm trip—aside from an errant torpedo from an escorting destroyer that almost hit the dreadnought—the *Iowa* put into Oran, on the old Barbary Coast. With Eisenhower, the President toured the recent battle area and flew along the Nile into Cairo. There he met Madame Chiang, who had charmed the President in a tête-à-tête in Washington, and the Generalissimo. The President beheld a small man in a neat khaki uniform, with a serene unwrinkled face below a clean-shaven pate. Roosevelt had to summon up all his tact in the meetings that followed, for MacArthur's and Nimitz's successes in the Pacific were rendering a China strategy obsolete. Chiang and the Madame left with rosy promises about China's postwar role but only vague pledges of an amphibious operation in the Bay of Bengal.

Then on to Teheran—and Stalin. Once again the President watched eagerly as his plane flew over storied Sinai and Jerusalem, the Dead Sea, the green valleys of the Tigris and the Euphrates, and into Teheran. Soon he met Stalin, a short compact man dressed in a tightly buttoned, mustard-colored uniform with large gold epaulets. "Seems very confident, very sure of himself, moves slowly—altogether quite impressive, I'd say," the President observed later.

At his first formal meeting with the President and Prime Minister, Stalin disdained oratory and came straight to the point—his point. The Nazis could be smashed only by a direct assault through France, not by an attack through Italy or the Balkans. Roosevelt restated his commitment to an early cross-Channel attack, but he also appeared to be flirting with the Balkans as well. Churchill too made the cross-Channel pledge, but he similarly dallied with Allied possibilities in Italy and points east. Once again it seemed that little had changed, with Stalin demanding an early second front, Churchill resisting it, and Roosevelt, as Churchill would later complain, drifting to and fro. But at least the three men could thrash things out face to face.

And so the hard, blunt talk went on for three days, Stalin doodling, smoking a pipe, scratching words on gridded pieces of paper; Churchill glowering behind his glasses, gesticulating with his cigar, lofting into flights of oratory; Roosevelt fitting cigarette after cigarette into his long holder, listening, calculating, interposing, placating. At some point on the third day the balance swung slowly but inexorably against Churchill and an attack at the periphery. Cross-Channel, combined with a landing in southern France, was confirmed for May 1944. Churchill, celebrating the start of his seventieth year that day, gave in with good grace, partly because the Combined Chiefs of Staff had agreed on attack plans, partly because Stalin had privately warned him face to face about the impact in Moscow of further delay.

That evening, at Roosevelt's birthday party for Churchill, the President properly saluted George VI, the Prime Minister toasted Roosevelt as the defender of democracy and Stalin as Stalin the Great, the Marshal saluted the Russian people and American production—especially of 10,000 planes a month. In a last word, at two in the morning, the President spoke of the coalition as a rainbow of "many varying colors," blending into "one glorious whole." At Teheran, "the varying ideals of our nations" could "come together in a harmonious whole."

*   *   *

A brilliant ceremony had symbolized the hard-won agreement at Teheran. Between rows of towering British and Soviet soldiers Churchill presented Stalin with the Sword of Stalingrad, forged by British craftsmen and given by King George to the "steel-hearted citizens of Stalingrad." Stalin kissed the gleaming blade, then showed the weapon to Roosevelt, who drew the long blade from the scabbard and held it aloft. The soldiers and civilians of Stalingrad had stood off the Nazis, then counterattacked and encircled them. Now it was time for the Allies to marshal their forces for the attack across the Channel.

By June 1944 the coastal areas of southern England were one vast staging area. Rows of new Mustang fighters perched wing to wing on small airfields behind the coast. Along pleasant English lanes stood ungainly amphibious vehicles, stacks of bombs, tires, wheels, reels of cable. Landing ships built on Lake Michigan and floated down the Mississippi were packed beam to beam in the ports. Long ugly LSTs (landing ships with tanks) constructed in California, their front ends gaping wide, were ready to disgorge tanks, trucks, bulldozers. Far inland lay the reserve production of war, for use in France: hundreds of new locomotives, thousands of freight and tanker cars, tens of thousands of trucks. Nothing could stop this massed power—except bad weather. Eisenhower postponed the attack once in the face of high winds and heavy clouds; two days later, with the forecast still dubious, he said calmly, "O.K., let's go."

Roosevelt and his commanders waited in suspense as the mightiest amphibious assault the world had ever known moved across the Channel, toward Normandy; paratroopers floated down in the dark over the pastures of the Cotentin Peninsula; warships poured shells and rockets into beach targets; bombers and fighters filled the dawn skies. Yet rarely has a great battle been decided so much in advance as the invasion of France— decided not so much by tactics as by strategy. The long delay in mounting the second front had made possible this stupendous buildup, had forced the Russians to engage the bulk of Nazi land forces, had enabled the Allies to mount a whole separate invasion of southern France. The invaders had almost total command of the sea and the air; the vaunted Luftwaffe had been reduced to fewer than 120 fighters in the defense area, and only two Allied destroyers and a number of smaller vessels were lost in the attack.

The invaders had outfoxed the defenders as well as outgunned them. The Allies' remarkable decoder, Ultra, provided Eisenhower with virtually the enemy's whole order of battle. The German radar that survived shelling was foiled by devices simulating a different landing. The Führer was so certain that the first landings were a feint that he delayed the dispatch of two Panzer divisions. General Rommel, commanding the defenders, was not even at the front; he had left the day before the invasion to visit Hitler at Berchtesgaden. But it was sheer Allied power that made the overwhelming difference: a million and a half Americans, another million British and Canadians, tens of thousands of Norwegians, Danes, Frenchmen, Belgians, Czechs, Poles, and others; 900 warships, including twenty-six battleships and heavy cruisers, 163 air bases directly supporting the offensive—and 124,000 hospital beds ready for the wounded.

Not that everything on D-Day went according to plan. Off Utah beach landing craft were swamped in the heavy seas, while other craft were swept by a strong current past their assigned beaches. Strong enemy defenses, surviving heavy bombardment, poured a withering fire on the invaders. For hours masses of men and equipment jammed the beaches. Radios and other equipment failed to function. But the Allies' superior power allowed for this sort of thing; some spearheads would be blunted, but others would break through. By nightfall on D-Day, although none of the Allied landings had reached the designated target lines, almost continuous thickets of ships were disgorging war power along miles and miles of coast. That evening an enormously relieved President led his fellow Americans in prayer for "our sons, pride of our Nation," and for the people at home who must wait out their long travail and the inevitable sorrow.

During the next few weeks, while the Allies deepened their bridgehead, bested the Germans in stiff fighting, and joined with troops moving up from almost unopposed landings in southern France, American commanders in the Pacific continued to give Eisenhower and his lieutenants some lessons in the tactics of combined sea, air, and land power. To be sure, the imperatives of war differed there. Strategy in Europe called for mass, focus, unity of purpose, singleness of command—under Eisenhower. Strategy in the Pacific was prone to dispersion, opportunism, competing arms and commands—under an admiral and two generals. In the great arc stretching ten thousand miles from the Aleutians south and west and then north into Southeast Asia, Nimitz continued to command the northern and central Pacific, MacArthur the southwestern Pacific, and Joseph W. Stilwell the China-Burma-India theater.

At times hostility within the Allied camp almost rivaled the feeling against the enemy. Stilwell was furious at Chiang, whom he privately called "Peanut," for his unwillingness to come to grips with the enemy and the widespread corruption in his government and army. MacArthur was still incensed by the Navy's plans for a straight thrust through the central Pacific. Such a direct attack, he instructed the Joint Chiefs, would degenerate into a spate of separate seaborne attacks against powerful island defenses that could fend off carrier-based planes, and—he did not add—would leave him underemployed. Attacks from *his* theater, on the other hand, would be launched from bases closest to the targets and could choose the most lightly defended enemy positions for destruction.

Evidently MacArthur did not realize that not only he but Nimitz too was perfecting the fine art of island-hopping. In November 1943 Nimitz's naval, air, and ground forces began their long campaign west across the Pacific by capturing Tarawa and Makin in the Gilbert Islands. Three months later they seized Kwajalein and Eniwetok in the Marshalls. Four months after that they assaulted Saipan and then Guam in the Marianas. Challenged on their own territory, a big Japanese naval force—nine carriers, eighteen battleships and cruisers, 430 carrier-based aircraft—struck from the west with orders to annihilate the invaders. But it was the Americans who did the annihilating, in what became known as the "Great Marianas Turkey Shoot." In two days the Japanese lost three flattops, including their flagship, and 400 aircraft, and a month later the Tojo government fell.

MacArthur was not to be outdone, by either the Japanese or the American Navy. During early 1944 his sea, air, and land forces occupied the Admiralty Islands and landed in Dutch New Guinea. In October, MacArthur redeemed his promise—"I shall return"—when his forces invaded

Leyte in the central Philippines. Again the Japanese fleet sortied out to battle, this time losing four carriers and eleven battleships and cruisers. By the end of 1944 Japanese sea power had been virtually destroyed, as the Allies closed in on their home islands from east and south.

*   *   *

During the rise and fall of the fortunes of war Roosevelt could not ignore the requirements of political leadership both at home and abroad. He had two primary tasks: to persuade Americans of the need for and importance of coalition with Russia, and to counter Hitler's global ideological appeal.

The first task proved surprisingly easy, largely because American press and public opinion had swung strongly on their own initiative to the cause of the beleaguered Soviets. Popular support for treating Russia "as a full partner" rose sharply after Pearl Harbor. *Time,* which had featured "Man of the Year" Stalin as a bad guy in January 1940, presented him as a good guy on its front cover three years later. The Chicago *Tribune* was now calling communists not satanic but merely "cockeyed." Stalin was "killing the men who would kill Americans," opined the New York *Herald Tribune.* Wendell Willkie and other eminent personalities led the demand for a second front. Quentin Reynolds defended Stalin's purges as having eliminated Russia's fifth column.

It seemed to take an old communist to resist the new appeal. " 'Don't say a word against Stalin or he won't accept our tanks!' " Max Eastman wrote in *Reader's Digest,* "seems to be the attitude of some of those who are now giving away the national treasure so avidly."

Roosevelt was more concerned with that master propagandist, Hitler. As a longtime promoter of the idea of freedom the President could hardly ignore the fact that the Führer was increasingly exploiting that very same symbol in his appeals to friend and foe. Having once narrowly defined freedom as essentially *Lebensraum* for good Germans, now Hitler was shifting its meaning to freedom for the masses to enjoy national and personal security and the good things of life. Freedom in America and Britain he derided as license for the plutocrats within democracies to exploit the people. A Nazi school for propagandists taught that Americans preached liberty and equality but had surrendered to lobbyists and the kept press. Roosevelt in turn repeatedly assailed Hitler's freedom as license for the Nazis to dominate and enslave the human race.

But what about freedom in America? The President tried to make the term relevant to real human problems and social conditions. "The essence of our struggle today is that man shall be free," he had said a month after Pearl Harbor. "There can be no real freedom for the common man without enlightened social policies." His Four Freedoms included freedom from want. He spelled out for Congress an economic bill of rights in January 1941; three years later he presented this "second Bill of Rights" in sharper detail: the right to good jobs and to adequate food and clothing and recreation; the right of every family to a decent home and adequate medical care; the right to adequate protection from the economic fears of old age and sickness and accident and unemployment; the right to a good education.

"For unless there is security here at home there cannot be lasting peace in the world."

These words, in January 1944, could have applied as well to FDR's electoral security, for they presented in essence his domestic program. Once again he would have to run for reelection. But this time, unlike 1940, he was not about to play political games; in July he simply notified the Democratic party that he was available. His handling of vice-presidential ambitions in 1944, however, was much like his crafty management of presidential rivals four years earlier. Vice President Henry Wallace was willing to go on, but he was unpopular with party professionals and conservatives. FDR gave Wallace a personal letter of support but on various other occasions threw enticements in the paths of James F. Byrnes, Hull, Barkley, Rayburn, Supreme Court Justice William O. Douglas, and several others. In the end he let the party leaders make the choice—Senator Harry Truman of Missouri, a stalwart New Dealer who had also demonstrated his independence, especially in his leadership of the war investigation committee.

It was the Republicans who seemed at first to face a donnybrook among a host of strong potential candidacies—until they began to fall like tenpins. Willkie was drubbed so badly in the Wisconsin primary, winning not a single delegate, that he immediately dropped out. MacArthur, who had privately expressed interest, issued a Sherman-like statement when one of his more ardent conservative boosters ineptly released a letter from the general hinting darkly of "the sinister drama of our present chaos and confusion" and of a New Deal "monarchy." Taft deferred to his fellow Ohioan, Governor John Bricker. "And then there was one"—Tom Dewey of New York, a young veteran in Republican politics who now drove straight down the open road to the GOP nomination. Eternally plagued by his image—the only man who could strut sitting down, the groom on the wedding cake, the Boy Orator of the Platitude—Dewey had shown his drive and professional skill in winning the New York governorship, a political prize monopolized for two decades by the Democrats.

Dewey's main problem, it soon developed, was a paucity of issues. He could deplore Roosevelt's handling of the war, but the summer of 1944 was a season of triumphs in Europe and the Pacific. He could condemn the Roosevelt Administration's economic policies, but the war economy was prospering. He could denounce Roosevelt's postwar plans, but only at the risk of antagonizing large sections of the nation's leadership who were calling for bipartisan support for a bipartisan foreign policy. It was most infuriating of all that his adversary piously adhered to his role of Commander-in-Chief and refused to campaign—or when he campaigned, did so in the form of war inspection trips. Like half a dozen challengers before him, Dewey was finding FDR an elusive and tantalizing foe.

While Dewey sought some opening, others went for the jugular. A whispering campaign about Roosevelt's health had him dying of everything from cancer to syphilis—if he was not dead already. Rumors were floated that he had left his terrier Fala behind in the Aleutians and had sent a destroyer to retrieve it. A story was told that when Truman's name had come up for the vice presidency FDR had said, "Clear it with Sidney." Now Roosevelt was "clearing everything" with Hillman, and labor's Political Action Committee was scheming to bring out a huge working-class vote. Billboards read: "SIDNEY HILLMAN AND BROWDER'S COMMUNISTS HAVE REGISTERED. HAVE YOU?"

Now Roosevelt saw *his* opening and struck. At a Teamsters union dinner in Washington late in September he spoke mournfully, with a mock-serious expression, about the opposition:

"These Republican leaders have not been content with attacks—on me, or my wife, or on my sons. No, not content with that, they now include my little dog, Fala. Well, of course, *I* don't resent attacks, and my family doesn't resent attacks, but"—a pause, and then quickly—"Fala *does* resent them." The room burst into cheers and laughter.

Infuriated by Roosevelt's ridicule, and with his own campaign still faltering, Dewey told an Oklahoma audience that he would have to depart from the high road in order to "keep the record straight." The issue of communism that he had earlier left to others he now took up with a prosecutor's fury. FDR, he said, was indeed "indispensable"—indispensable "to Sidney Hillman and the Political Action Committee, he's indispensable to Earl Browder, the ex-convict and pardoned leader of the Communist Party." The whole Democratic party, he charged, had been taken over by Browder and Hillman. Allowed to look at the draft of one of her husband's speeches, Mrs. Dewey said sharply, "Bricker could have written it." In this speech Dewey charged that Roosevelt had pardoned Browder in time to organize support for his campaign.

This challenge Roosevelt could not dismiss with jokes. It came at a time when American opinion toward Russia appeared to be cooling. It was one thing for Americans to have sympathized with a beleaguered Soviet Union and to have asked, "If Russia falls, who next?" It was quite different to be asking when the Red Army was marching west, "If Russia wins, what next?" Once again the old-time foes of Soviet communism were becoming more vocal—the Hearst papers, the conservative leadership of the AFL, Roman Catholic bishops. Thoughtful commentators including Walter Lippmann and Reinhold Niebuhr were apprehensive—though Lippmann was so repelled by Dewey's late-campaign tactics as to decide to vote, glumly, for FDR.

The President dealt with the health rumors, which immensely annoyed him, by taking long campaign trips in an open car, sometimes in a pouring rain. He answered charges of the Administration's military incompetence by pointing to the glorious victories of Eisenhower, MacArthur, and Nimitz. He dealt with the charge of communist influence largely by evading it. "I can't talk about my opponent the way I would like to sometimes," he said at the end of the campaign, "because I try to think that I am a Christian." Later that day, in Boston, he rebutted the charge.

Polls predicted such a close result that Roosevelt's victory by 432 electoral votes to Dewey's 99 came as a surprise. Even so, the race had been something of a close-run thing. Roosevelt's popular-vote margin of 3.6 million was the smallest since 1916—and this at the very height of the nation's military successes, at the peak of war prosperity, and after a poor Republican campaign. Perhaps the figures reflected a deep current—warweariness, and a trend toward "privatization." It had been a bitter, unedifying contest at a time when a world-transforming conflict was reaching its climax and posing momentous postwar questions. Said the President, going to bed after Dewey's concession, "I still think he is a son of a bitch."

*   *   *

Three months after his reelection, and two weeks after his fourth-term inauguration at the south portico of the White House, Franklin Roosevelt in his plane *Sacred Cow* touched down on the icy runway of the Soviet airport of Saki in the Crimea. Joined by Prime Minister Churchill, the President rode slowly in his jeep before a guard of honor, while the Prime Minister plodded alongside. The Soviet soldiers stood frozen to attention, their commander holding his sword in front of him like a great icicle. Shortly Roosevelt was speeding in a limousine, with his daughter Anna at his side, to Yalta, ninety miles away. He scanned everything with lively interest—the endless lines of guards, some of them young women with tommy guns; the gutted buildings and burned-out tanks; and later the snow-covered mountains through which the caravan threaded its way to the coast of the Black Sea. Soon the President was installed in Livadia Palace, a fifty-room summer place of the czars overlooking gardens filled with cypress, cedar, and yew.

Yalta. Neither Roosevelt nor Churchill could have expected that this would become the most famous—the most notorious—of wartime conferences, for the crucial decisions had been made at Casablanca and Quebec and Teheran and a host of other meetings, and Yalta essentially confirmed as well as updated and applied some of the earlier plans. Churchill would have been astonished at Yalta's later reputation as a sellout to the Russians by naïve Anglo-Americans; he had never held illusions about the Soviets. Roosevelt would have been perplexed—or perhaps amused—by reports of the "sick man at Yalta"; he found the energy to get through an enormous amount of business and indeed to conduct a whole separate set of negotiations with Stalin, chiefly over the Far East.

The three men met as victors. By February 1945 the conquest of Germany was clearly in sight. Red Army troops had invested Budapest, captured Warsaw, and overrun East Prussia, and were within forty miles of Berlin. On the western front the Allies had been delayed for weeks by a surprise German counterattack in the Ardennes forest leading to the bloody Battle of the Bulge, but Eisenhower's forces had retaken the lost ground and were beginning an offensive that would carry them across the Rhine. In the Philippines, MacArthur's troops were closing in on Manila; in the Pacific, Nimitz's amphibious forces were laying plans for assaults on Okinawa and Iwo Jima, stepping-stones to the home islands. Assembled with the three leaders at Yalta were some of the men who had planned the political and military offensives: Marshall, Admiral William Leahy, Hopkins, and the ambassador to the Soviet Union, W. Averell Harriman; Molotov, his deputy Andrei Vishinsky, and the ambassador to the United States, Andrei Gromyko; Eden and a big retinue of seasoned Britons.

The Yalta Conference dealt with a wide range of issues, including postwar arrangements for regions like the Baltic and the Balkans and for the division of Germany. But for Roosevelt three issues were preeminent—and in each case he held weak cards.

The knottiest of these was Poland. The Big Three had long agreed that the war-racked nation would be picked up like a carpetbag and set down a few hundred kilometers to the west, satisfying Russia's appetite for real estate, penalizing Germany's, and taming Warsaw's. But who would run postwar Poland? For some time Moscow had been dealing with the "Lublin Poles," a coalition dominated by Polish communists, while London and Washington dealt with the "London Poles," the Polish government-in-exile in the British capital. Roosevelt was under no illusions about Soviet plans for Poland. As the conference met, the Red Army was completing Poland's liberation—or rather, its occupation. The question was how much representation for noncommunist Polish elements could be extracted from a Kremlin that viewed liberals and conservatives as bourgeois exploiters if not fascists, and was absolutely determined both to create a buffer state against future invasions from the west and to consolidate Soviet control of Eastern Europe.

Roosevelt, reminding Stalin of the "six or seven million" Polish-Americans who opposed recognizing the Lublin group because it represented only a small portion of the Polish people, urged a government of national unity. Churchill backed the President. But Stalin was adamant. "During the last thirty years our German enemy" had passed through Poland twice, he said. And he admonished Churchill for proposing that a Polish government be established at Yalta, when no Poles were present. "I am called a dictator and not a democrat," he said, "but I have enough democratic feeling to refuse to create a Polish government without the Poles being consulted." During the next three days Roosevelt and Churchill, step by step, drew formal concessions from the Russians for a more inclusive government, free and unfettered elections, and participation by the London Poles. But it was probable that Washington and London would have little actual influence over the holding and policing of elections.

The President was nearing the end of his leverage with Stalin. And a cardinal reason for that was Roosevelt's supreme military goal at Yalta— the participation of Russia in the war against Japan. The President and his military chiefs had long agreed that Soviet action on the Asiatic mainland was imperative to avoid unacceptable American losses. Nor was there any question that Russia would intervene; this had long been agreed upon, and it was to Moscow's interest anyway. The question was when and how and with what power the Red Army would intervene. Would it hold back while the Allied forces assaulted the bulk of the Japanese troops in the home islands and on the mainland—and then move in for the spoils? Or would the Russians take their share of the burden from the start?

Was history playing a grotesque trick? For three long years Stalin had urged—demanded—pleaded for a second front in France and the Anglo-Americans had taken their time about it, or so it seemed to the Kremlin, finally crossing the Channel when it suited their own interests. Now it was Roosevelt who was asking for a second front and Stalin who could take his time. Stalin made the most of his bargaining position by gaining confirmation of a host of political concessions: return of southern Sakhalin to Russia; cession of the Kurile Islands to the Soviet Union; preservation of the Moscow-controlled regime in Outer Mongolia; internationalization of the port of Dairen; recognition of Moscow's "pre-eminent interests" in Manchuria. On some issues the President asked for postponement so he could consult the absent Chiang. In return Stalin promised in writing that he would enter the war against Japan two or three months after the surrender of Germany.

For any misgivings Roosevelt had about certain compromises at Yalta he had a great consolation—but one that also served to narrow his leverage. This was agreement on the shape of the United Nations, his third supreme goal at Yalta. Here the President was acting not only out of his own hopes and convictions but for a large body of liberal and internationalist feeling in the United States expressed by such diverse notables as Henry Wallace and Wendell Willkie (before the latter's death in the fall of 1944). There was no question that a UN would be established; the question was its power and structure. Roosevelt found Churchill cooperative though skeptical, Stalin grudgingly responsive but insistent on the principle of great-power unanimity. Stalin and Molotov were still pushing their outlandish idea that the Soviet Union should have sixteen votes in the proposed assembly, one for each of its sixteen component republics. When Molotov suddenly cut down the request to two extra votes, and the British—doubtless with an eye on their own dominions—appeared to go along with this compromise, Roosevelt felt he had to agree.

Some in Roosevelt's delegation thought he had compromised too much, but the President believed that an effective United Nations organization could rectify the failings of Yalta and earlier conferences. He was so eager for its establishment that he risked being a hostage to its success. "Mr. President," Leahy said at one point, "this is so elastic that the Russians can stretch it all the way from Yalta to Washington without even technically breaking it."

"I know, Bill—I know it. But it's the best I can do." The two men were discussing the Polish settlement, but the exchange could have related to any of the major Yalta compromises. Holding only weak hands in the great poker game of Yalta, Roosevelt believed he had won the foundations of future peace. It was with hope and even exultation that he and his party left Yalta for the long journey home.

Above all, he left with confidence that, whatever the problems ahead, he could resolve them through his personal intervention—whether it was dealing with Stalin over Poland, or with Chiang over Far Eastern settlements, or even with Churchill or de Gaulle over imperialism in India or colonialism in Indochina. But Roosevelt did not know, for neither his doctor nor anyone else had ever told him, that his heart had been failing for several years. On his return from Yalta people in the White House—especially the correspondents—noted more than ever before how gray and scrawny he appeared, even vacant of face with his jaw drooping and mouth falling open—but then how he would suddenly come to life, tell a joke, his laughter booming out above theirs. He appeared to compartmentalize his health and malaise as he did the rest of his life, alternating intervals of intense activity like Yalta with long periods of rest away from Washington.

He looked forward to his trip to San Francisco for the founding meeting of the United Nations in April, and to a voyage to England later in the spring with the First Lady. What a grand reception he would receive from the British! But first he would report to Congress, and then he would journey to Warm Springs at the end of March for an old soldier's R&R—rest and recreation.

CHAPTER 5

Cold War: The Fearful Giants

A FTER buffeting heavy seas off the Chesapeake capes, the cruiser *Quincy* glided into Newport News on February 27, 1945, bringing the Commander-in-Chief back from Yalta. Two days later Roosevelt was wheeled into the well of the House of Representatives and seated in a red plush chair in front of a small table. Apologizing for speaking while sitting—"it makes it a lot easier for me not to have to carry about ten pounds of steel around on the bottom of my legs"—he reported optimistically on Yalta but warned that whether it was entirely fruitful or not lay in the hands of "you here in the halls of the American Congress."

Those looking down from the packed galleries—Eleanor Roosevelt, visiting royalty and dignitaries—watched the President with concern. It was uncharacteristic of him to refer to his disability. Slightly stooped over the table, he spoke in a flat tone, slurring his words and stumbling a bit over his text. The resonant voice of old had lost its timbre; it was the voice of an invalid. Friend and foe noted his gaunt face and trembling hand. Yet his flagging voice rose to a note of desperate urgency at the climax of his address.

"Twenty-five years ago, American fighting men looked to the statesmen of the world to finish the work of peace for which they fought and suffered. We failed—we failed them then. We cannot fail them again, and expect the world to survive again." Yalta "ought to spell the end of the system of unilateral action, the exclusive alliances, the spheres of influence, the balances of power, and all the other expedients that have been tried for centuries—and have always failed." He called once again for a universal organization of peace-loving nations.

Almost the whole of his fourth term apparently lay before the President—plenty of time to organize the new United Nations, finish off Hitler, throw the full weight of Allied power against Japan, and strengthen his working partnership with Stalin. In fact only eight short weeks remained to Roosevelt, and in half that time relations with Moscow turned sour.

Again Poland was the main engine of conflict, just as it had been in 1939 and before. Within the loose framework of the Yalta agreement, Stalin was absolutely determined to install reliable communists as rulers of Poland. He was already operating on a bald sphere-of-interest basis: the Anglo-Americans were to have a free hand in Greece and points west, and the Russians in Poland and the Balkans. Churchill cabled Roosevelt: "Poland has lost her frontier. Is she now to lose her freedom?" He might have to reveal in Parliament, Churchill added, a British-American "divergence" unless the Allies confronted the "utter breakdown of what was settled at Yalta."

The crisis in the "Rainbow Coalition" became even more acute when Stalin suspected that Anglo-American talks with the defeated Germans in Italy were the first step toward a negotiated separate peace—a violation of the Big Three pledge to require an unconditional surrender to all three Allies jointly. Angry messages flew back and forth between Moscow and the Western capitals. Stalin, once again facing the old bogey of German troops being released in the West to fight in the East, accused the West of not merely a "misunderstanding but something worse." Roosevelt cabled Stalin that he bitterly resented Stalin's "informers" for their "vile misrepresentations of my actions or those of my trusted subordinates." The President perhaps was even more upset when he learned that not Molotov but only Ambassador Gromyko would head the Soviet delegation to the San Francisco UN organizing conference. If this reflected Stalin's downgrading of the UN, it was a serious blow to Roosevelt's high hopes for postwar unity.

Still, Roosevelt's spirits seemed to brighten by April, when events reached one of the great climacterics of history. The whole German defense structure was crumbling west of the Rhine. The Red Army was across the Oder and grinding its way westward against last-ditch resistance. After a bloody struggle, a huge amphibious task force that in February had launched a massive invasion of Iwo Jima was mopping up the tiny island. On April 1 Nimitz's men invaded Okinawa and made rapid progress during the first days ashore, while the invasion fleet stood guard offshore and beat off hundreds of suicide attacks by Japanese aircraft.

Relations with Stalin seemed to ease a bit in early April. On the afternoon of April 11 the President dictated the draft of a speech for Jefferson Day: ". . . Today we are faced with the preeminent fact that, if civilization is to survive, we must cultivate the science of human relationships—the ability of all peoples, of all kinds, to live together and work together, in the same world at peace. . . .

"The work, my friends, is peace. More than an end of this war—an end to the beginnings of all wars. Yes, an end, forever, to this impractical, unrealistic settlement of the differences between governments by the mass killing of peoples. . . .

"The only limit to our realization of tomorrow will be our doubts of today. Let us move forward with strong and active faith."

The Death and Life of Franklin D. Roosevelt

Franklin Roosevelt died April 12, 1945, at his second home in Warm Springs, Georgia, among greening trees and flowering dogwood and wild violets. He died in the company of women he held dear—his secretary Grace Tully, his cousins Margaret Suckley and Laura Delano, and his friend Lucy Mercer Rutherfurd. Eleanor Roosevelt, notified at the White House, arrived in time to accompany her husband's body on the funeral train that next day rolled slowly north through Georgia and the Carolinas into Virginia. Glimpsing the weeping faces and solemn crowds at the little depots and crossroads, she remembered:

> A lonesome train on a lonesome track,
> Seven coaches painted black. . . .
> A slow train, a quiet train,
> Carrying Lincoln home again. . . .

Following the obsequies in Washington, the funeral train once again headed north, now pulling seventeen cars filled with officials and politicians. The train passed through New Jersey and Manhattan and up the east bank of the Hudson. At Garrison, across from West Point, men removed their hats just as men had done when Lincoln's funeral car passed eighty years ago that spring. At the little siding at Hyde Park cannon sounded twenty-one times as the coffin was moved from the train to a horse-drawn caisson. Behind the bier another horse, hooded and with stirrups reversed, led the little procession as it toiled up the steep slope to the rose garden on the bluff above. There stood Eleanor Roosevelt, Anna, and one son who could be freed from war duty, along with President Harry Truman and his cabinet, and a phalanx of six hundred West Point cadets.

The aged rector prayed as servicemen lowered the body into the grave. Cadets fired three volleys. A bugler played taps. The soldier was home.

*   *   *

The death of any President leaves Americans in shock and grief. The passing of Roosevelt left them also empty and disoriented. Millions of Americans in their teens and twenties had never really known another

President. For them Roosevelt *was* the presidency. And for many he would continue to be. More than any President since Jefferson, FDR dominated his times; more than any President since Lincoln, his ideals and policies would influence the presidencies to come.

The man people most vividly remembered in their mourning was the FDR who had electrified the nation on entering the White House hardly more than a dozen years before. That Roosevelt had touched their hearts and minds and bodies with a reassuring immediacy; the enduring effects of FDR's leadership in peace and war remained to be tested. The New Deal laws and programs had virtually transformed major aspects of American life—economic security, agriculture, labor relations, banking, welfare, conservation, and much else. FDR had bequeathed the powers and structure of the modern presidency, its penetrating impact on people's lives, an expanded and rejuvenated federal government. He had mobilized millions of new voters and partially realigned the balance of parties. And as William Leuchtenburg later made clear, he would cast his shadow over future presidencies by setting the agenda of policy, establishing the standards for measuring presidential leadership, leaving a federal government filled with his people and his ideas.

Roosevelt's greatest service to mankind, Isaiah Berlin wrote from a British perspective, was proving it possible "to be politically effective and yet benevolent and human"; that "the promotion of social justice and individual liberty" did not necessarily mean the end of effective government; that "individual liberty—a loose texture of society"—could be reconciled with "the indispensable minimum of organizing and authority."

It was harder to assess the man than the presidency. "Great men have two lives," Adolf Berle said in a tribute to his old boss, "one which occurs while they work on this earth; a second which begins at the day of their death and continues as long as their ideas and conceptions remain powerful." But the more Roosevelt's "second life"—his heritage of ideas and decisions, examples and innovations—was examined, the more fragmented it appeared to be. For not only did Roosevelt conduct multiple and sometimes clashing policies at any one time, he shifted from plan to plan, from program to program, with such nonchalance as to leave his friends perplexed and his adversaries aiming at a moving target.

He started off as a crisis manager who simultaneously economized in order to balance the budget, pushed through a socialistic venture in the Tennessee Valley, tightened and expanded the regulation of banking and agriculture, and sought to concert the interests of workers and industrialists under the NRA. Soon he gave up on economizing, began to spend lavishly on emergency relief projects and later on the WPA, built and restored bridges, dams, roads, and other public services while diverting funds to construct aircraft carriers, went in for major relief expenditures as he approached the 1936 election, reverted to economizing after it, then turned back to heavier spending in the recession years of 1938 and 1939. Meantime FDR experimented with such imaginative ventures as the Civilian Conservation Corps, the National Youth Administration, rural electrification, soil conservation, housing subsidies.

He held mixed views about private and public centralization. The New Deal monopoly policies, economist Ellis Hawley concluded, were a study in "economic confusion," as Washington shifted from government-sponsored cartelization under the NRA, marketing agreements, and coal policy to trustbusting rhetoric and antimonopoly measures such as the Wheeler-Rayburn utility holding company act. New Deal economic planning, according to Hawley, came in a "disjointed, almost haphazard manner, in response to specific pressures, problems, and needs, and without benefit of any preconceived plan or integrating theory." Herbert Stein summarized the first four years as "fiscal drift." That term and the next left an ambiguous heritage to later administrations.

Juggling economic policies from day to day amid his own Tocquevillian void, Roosevelt did not always exhibit grace under pressure. During the economic crisis in spring 1938 he had angry meetings with Morgenthau, whom the President evidently felt he could safely rebuke as an old friend and neighbor. The Treasury Secretary for his part grumbled in his extensive diary about Roosevelt's "helterskelter" planning and his lost sense of proportion. A year later, with unemployment still ranging up toward 10 million, the President and the Secretary were still wrangling, Morgenthau was still talking about resignation, Eleanor Roosevelt was still talking him out of it. When Morgenthau asked for an appointment to present a statement on taxation—two hours, he thought, would be needed—his boss asked him instead to leave it so that he could "read it a little bit at a time at my bedside."

Seeking some intellectual order in the disarray of Roosevelt's economic programs, historians identified a first and second New Deal, but there were in fact several New Deals as the President groped for the key to full recovery. Historians discerned a third New Deal late in Roosevelt's second term that emanated from his effort to find institutional solutions to faltering economic strategies. Thwarted in his efforts to build an executive-legislative-judicial team, he sought to improve presidential planning by creating the National Resources Planning Board under a Delano uncle, establishing more presidential control over "independent" regulatory commissions, enlarging the White House policy staff, proposing the

"Seven TVA's bill" that would establish regional planning authorities in the Missouri and other great riverbeds. Most of these efforts failed in the face of bureaucratic inertia and congressional fears of "fascist type" concentration of power that would destroy state and local authority.

It would remain for World War II to supply Washington with the authority, the planning and enforcement tools, and the purposefulness that earlier New Deal efforts had lacked. Massive doses of "war Keynesianism" and military manpower drafts finally enabled the "fourth New Deal" to realize its supreme aim of ending unemployment. In the mushrooming of federal agencies and personnel, the huge military planning agencies, the centralization of authority, the subordination of courts and Congress, the New Deal found the firm linkage of ends and means that had eluded it during Roosevelt's first two terms. The irony of war prosperity was inescapable.

The domestic New Deal ended up as a lavish policy feast, which later Presidents and Congresses could use as precedents and learning experiences, especially in the realms of economic reform and social welfare. The New Deal recruited a brilliant corps of innovators, planners, and dreamers who invigorated later administrations, Republican as well as Democratic, for decades. The tragedy of the domestic New Deal was that it failed to fashion an effective economic strategy and stick with it. Conceivably a rigorous and sustained budget-balancing effort from the start would have encouraged, as in past economic cycles, a sharp recovery of investor confidence, but Roosevelt for reasons both humanitarian and political soon rejected this harsh policy. Conceivably the NRA could have been reorganized after its voiding by the High Court and converted into a comprehensive venture in industrial rationalization and economic planning, but the President gave up on it. He favored somewhat redistributionist tax policies, but not to the extent where they might have served as a decisive step toward a more egalitarian society. He played with antimonopoly policies, regionalization, encouragement of local initiatives without ever surrendering his strong reliance on national action. Above all he failed to carry through the one strategy that was politically the most feasible and economically the soundest for a depressed economy—broad fiscal planning encompassing monetary, investment, pricing, interest rate, public works, and welfare policies, a strategy based not on occasional "pump priming" but on the heavy and continuous deficit spending that later fueled the war economy.

If the New Deal domestic heritage was mixed at best, the image of the head New Dealer remained clear and vibrant in the people's memory—that of a cheerful, buoyant, warmhearted man absolutely committed to his goals of economic recovery and social justice, a very political man who could strike deals and manipulate men and win elections, an orator who could touch people's hearts as they sat by a fireside, a man who always seemed in motion despite the polio-wasted legs of which, at least in public, he never complained and never explained. He had his bad days when he was negative and critical and even spiteful but he always bounced back, causing Morgenthau or Ickes or some other complainer to put his resignation statement back into his pocket and hearken anew to his boss's uncertain trumpet.

A dozen years later Holmes's perception could be both affirmed and extended—a first-class temperament and second-class intellect, yes, but also, throughout the presidential years, superb intelligence and rarely failing insight.

*   *   *

As a war leader too, Roosevelt was a deeply divided man—divided between the Soldier of the Faith, the principled leader, the man of ideals, crusading for a spacious and coherent vision, and the man of *Realpolitik*, Machiavelli's Prince, the leader intent on narrow, manageable, short-run goals, careful always to protect and husband his power in a world of shifting moods and capricious fortune. This dualism not only cleft Roosevelt but divided his advisers within themselves and from one another. And it reflected central dichotomies within the American people, who vacillated between the evangelical moods of idealism, sentimentalism, and utopianism and traditions of national self-protection, prudence, and power politics.

Roosevelt demonstrated his purposeful, principled, steady, and coherent leadership most strikingly as Commander-in-Chief and war propagandist. He brilliantly articulated the ideals of freedom for which the nation fought and he provided ample and steadfast support to the men and women who were fighting for those ideals. For a leader who had intervened almost promiscuously in the decisions of his domestic agencies he was remarkably self-restrained in dealing with his generals and admirals. Even when he might have exploited some incident for his own political gain—as in the case of General George Patton's slapping two soldiers in Sicily—he was silent. For a highly political man, he left selection of his generals to the top command; even Stimson acknowledged his "scrupulous abstention from personal and political pressure." He overturned few sentences after courts-martial.

As an old navy man the Commander-in-Chief offered numerous suggestions and queries to the armed services, but he largely left them alone. Only when it came to political matters did he exert close authority. He insisted on the principle of unconditional surrender, arousing misgivings among some in the Pentagon even though it flowed directly out of the American military tradition. Roosevelt recognized the political significance of the doctrine, which had been fully vetted in the State Department, for maintaining unity among the Rainbow Coalition, discouraging divisive surrender offers by the enemy, and setting things straight for postwar peacekeeping efforts. Robert Dallek concluded that Roosevelt was the "principal architect" of the basic strategic decisions that brought the early defeat of the Axis.

Roosevelt the Prince, the global politician, the Machiavellian leader, lived uneasily with Roosevelt the Soldier of the Faith. FDR dealt not only with Churchill behind Stalin's back but with Stalin behind Churchill's. He misled the American people on his aggressive posture in the Atlantic. He failed to communicate to Polish leaders—or to the American people—the full gravity of Soviet intransigence about their western borders. He did not share atomic secrets with his Russian ally. Remembering talks with Roosevelt during wartime, de Gaulle was to write of FDR's "light touches," made "so skillfully that it was difficult to contradict this artist, this seducer, in any categorical way." In numberless other political decisions—or in military decisions involving politics—Roosevelt manipulated, dissimulated, horse-traded, always on the grounds that this was the prudent or practical or realistic way to act.

He appeared to combine the most striking qualities of his two great presidential mentors—the martial vigor of Theodore Roosevelt and the idealism of Woodrow Wilson. But just as both those qualities were evident in both those men, FDR appeared to embrace principle and *Realpolitik* almost indiscriminately. Part of his strength lay in this; it was hard to know what Roosevelt one was dealing with. William James had spoken of the "once-born," those who easily fitted into the ideology of their time, and of those "divided selves" who went through a second birth, seizing on a second ideology. Raised in a stable and secure home, comfortable in his self-identity despite some injuries to his self-esteem, Roosevelt in many respects was the classic once-born leader. But he shifted so widely in his priorities of political leadership during his long career that he appeared at least thrice-born—not only as Dr. New Deal and Dr. Win-the-War but ultimately as Dr. Win-the-Peace.

Both Roosevelt's idealism and his *Realpolitik* were effective; the problem lay in the linkage between the two. He often failed to work out the intermediary ends and means necessary to accomplish his purposes. Thus he could proclaim unconditional surrender but practice some kind of deal with Darlan and later the Italians. The more he preached his lofty ends and practiced his limited means, the more he widened the gap between popular expectations and actual possibilities. Not only did this derangement of ends and means lead to crushed hopes and disillusion at home; it would help sow the seeds of cold war later. The Kremlin contrasted Roosevelt's coalition rhetoric with his Britain-first strategy and falsely suspected a bourgeois conspiracy to destroy Soviet communism. Indians and Chinese contrasted his anticolonial words with his military concessions to colonial powers, and falsely inferred that he was an imperialist at heart and a hypocrite to boot.

Like most of the more effective Presidents, Roosevelt made his White House years a magnificent learning experience for himself and those around him. Like the great teaching Presidents in the early years of the republic—notably Washington, Jefferson, Jackson—he educated the American people in the uses of government to achieve great national purposes. Like the other world leaders of his time, he aroused people's hopes, converted them into expectations and entitlements, and then responded to the demands that his followers—now become leaders—put on *him.* Like the stronger Presidents of the past century—notably Lincoln, Theodore Roosevelt, Wilson—he moved broadly to the left of the political spectrum in which he operated. But if his commitment to liberty and equality—to freedom—was realized most fully and paradoxically in the war years, he ended up in this posture as the result not of a steady evolution but rather of a series of jumps from role to role, as in the case of Dr. New Deal shifting suddenly to Dr. Win-the-War.

This capacity to compartmentalize his presidency and even his personality over time, and at any one time, gave him political advantages. It also helped explain the greatest moral failure of his presidency—a failure even greater and far more disastrous than his authorization of relocation camps for Japanese-Americans. This was his inaction in the face of the Holocaust. For years Roosevelt, like other Western leaders, had denounced Nazi persecution of the Jews. During the months after Pearl Harbor, reports began to reach the White House that something unspeakably more horrible was taking place—the "final solution of the Jewish question": calculated, mechanized, bureaucratized murder on a colossal scale. Reports came too of people by the hundreds and thousands buried or burned alive, of infants swung by the heels and dashed against walls, of boxcars groaning with their loads of sick, freezing, starving, suffocating, dying "passengers."

The totality of this holocaust was matched by the near-totality of failure on the part of everything that was supposed to stand guard against barbarism—press, church, public opinion, government itself. Newspapers became so inured to the reports, or found them so "beyond belief," that an authentic account of the murder of tens of thousands of Jews might be put on an inside page next to marriage announcements. Leaders of the Christian churches within the United States and outside were almost silent. The public, misled by atrocity stories about the Germans during World War I, wondered if it was being bamboozled again. State Department officials, irresponsibly slow to react to anguished pleas and demands for help, appeared to reflect the moral lethargy and the endemic anti-Semitism among the public and Congress.

The President was not wholly passive. Persuaded by Morgenthau and others that Hull's people were hopelessly inadequate to the situation, he established the War Refugee Board under his direct supervision. He authorized hostage deals and other specific operations that saved a number of Jews. He periodically denounced the slaughter in the strongest terms. But between his word and his deed lay a void. Urged to disrupt the shipment of human cargo by bombing the rail lines to the extermination factory of Auschwitz in Poland, he reverted to his role of Dr. Win-the-War, contending that all resources must be directed to the military destruction of Nazism and that such diversions would postpone that day. Yet even as that day approached, even as American bombers overflew the rail lines, overflew Auschwitz itself, European Jewry fell as steadily to its destruction as sand through an hourglass, until only three million, then only two million, then only one million, and finally only a handful of Jews remained alive, and these physically and psychologically devastated. On this ultimate crime against humanity the President never displayed—never sought to display—the consistent and compelling moral leadership that would break through bureaucratic callousness, legislative resistance, popular ignorance and apathy.

So Franklin Roosevelt left a highly divided legacy to a people themselves classically devoted on the one hand to lofty global ideals and on the other to narrow isolationist self-protection, with weak linkage between. But he left also a living legacy—living on in the unquenchable memories of his own leadership, living on also in the persons to whom he immediately passed on the legacy. One was his Vice President, a practical politician. The other was his wife, an impractical politician. They would become both allies and antagonists, politically and symbolically, in the nation's postwar leadership. Isaiah Berlin spoke of Eleanor Roosevelt's "greatness of character and goodness of heart." She possessed much more than this, including some of the militance and tenacity of her Uncle Theodore—but character and goodness of heart would not be the least of the qualities she would bring to the struggle for peace.

THE LONG TELEGRAM

So swiftly did the cold war envelop the Rainbow Coalition during 1945 that for decades historians would search for the sources of this early and acrimonious falling-out between Moscow and Washington. Two comrades-in-arms, who had come together from opposite sides of the globe to beat down the most murderous and monstrous threat the modern world had known, appeared suddenly to turn on each other in a new war of words and weapons. The turnabout seemed to defy conventional explanation. These two great nations had no common land borders to fight over, no heritage of ancient rivalries, no dire economic conflict, no clashing territorial ambitions. For a century before 1917 their main contact had been a mutually satisfactory real estate deal over Alaska.

American visitors to the Soviet Union noted how the two countries appeared to resemble each other: huge continental nations with comparable populations, both boasting revolutions to celebrate and world-famous leaders—Lincoln and Wilson, Lenin and Trotsky—to glorify or denigrate. Visitors from the American Midwest felt at home when they observed the immense, gently undulating plains, the seasons suddenly changing from the deep snow of winter to the bottomless mud of spring to blinding summer light and drought, the "deep, mournful, yet mellifluous and muted bellowing" of the huge steam locomotives as they rumbled across the flat plain. Russians, when you got to know them, seemed a lot like Americans—friendly, talkative, boastful, fascinated by new cars, machines, household gadgets.

Most of these appearances were deceptive. Russian history, society, psychology, culture were profoundly different from the American. The flat plains that for Americans were havens of peace and isolation—at least since the dispersion of the Indians—were for Russians avenues of attack from neighboring countries. The vast majority of Soviet citizens were peasants—religious, fatalistic, isolated in their remote and scattered villages, tending to suspicion toward outsiders. The Russian temperament, far more than the American, appeared to be at odds with itself—a popular craving for authority, leadership, and collective controls clashing with a tendency to be "independent to the point of anarchy," in Edward Crankshaw's words, "and expansive to the point of incoherence." Although both peoples apotheosized common values in their sacred documents—freedom, justice, equality, human rights—American children in their families and schools and churches had been taught to abhor communism, Soviet children to abhor capitalism and the fascism it allegedly spawned. Each side not only hated the other's ideology but feared it. The "reds" were seeking to arouse the world proletariat against the democratic—the American—way of life; the American warmongers sought to encircle and crush the Russian Revolution—had they not tried to stifle it in its cradle in 1919?

A quarter century after the Russian Revolution, each nation grotesquely misperceived the other's "plot" for "world domination." United States propagandists and press quoted Marxist predictions of inevitable war, not bothering to point out that Lenin had preached the inevitability of war among the capitalistic nations rather than between communism and capitalism. Soviet propagandists seized on the more extreme statements of American leaders—notably that of a then obscure American senator named Harry S Truman, who had said during the frightful summer days of 1941, as the Nazis were rolling across the Russian plains, "If we see that Germany is winning we ought to help Russia and if Russia is winning we ought to help Germany and that way let them kill as many as possible," though he added that he did not want to see Hitler victorious under any circumstances.

Many on each side misperceived the other side's *wish* for world communism or world capitalism to become the global way of life as an elaborately blueprinted *plot* for world conquest. These fears persisted throughout World War II, certainly among Americans and probably among Soviet citizens as they were continually reminded of the West's "perfidious" failure to mount the cross-Channel invasion. Even during the euphoria of wartime collaboration, polls showed that many Americans were not counting on the Russians to "cooperate" after the war.

Was any reality perceivable through the mists of ideology? Patterns of behavior were discernible to those who looked for them, but the patterns were mixed. The Bolsheviks had waged ideological warfare against the West ever since winning power, but the trumpet calls were rarely more than bombast. In Finland and Poland and elsewhere, Moscow had shown a ferocious determination to exert control over border countries, but its aim seemed far more to prevent these nations from serving as stepping-stones for invading armies than to make them bases for Red Army moves against Western Europe or Japan. The Kremlin subsidized Communist parties around the world, but invariably subordinated those parties' interests to its own state interests when they collided. And the West had some knowledge of Stalin's massive party purges, in which thousands of old comrades perished, and of his "de-kulakization" and forced collectivization campaigns, in which millions of peasants were executed or sent to Siberian labor camps or died of starvation—but these were "internal matters."

For its part, the West had waged an abortive hot war and then a long cold war against the Soviet Union. The United States had a monopoly on nuclear arms for years following World War II, while the Soviets were still militarily depleted and economically devastated, but Washington did not use the ultimate weapon. State and Defense Department officials adopted a series of carefully considered position papers, culminating in 1950 with NSC-68, which pictured the Soviet Union as "animated by a new fanatic faith, antithetical to our own," and as seeking to "impose its absolute authority over the rest of the world," but Washington did not back up this dire assessment with military action. Above all, the Americans and British had followed their own national interests in the timing of the second front, as postwar revelations of Lord Beaverbrook and others made clear, and had left Moscow feeling deceived and millions of Russians without the sons, fathers, and brothers who had taken the brunt of the Nazi onslaught, but the Kremlin realists could not have doubted that, had the situation been reversed, they would have done exactly the same.

The cold war, in short, had started early and had never ended, not even during the war. The conflict was far too deeply rooted to be quickly or easily eliminated, but it could be managed or overridden by strong and purposeful leadership. That was the kind of leadership Roosevelt and Churchill had supplied throughout most of the shooting war, in collaboration with Stalin. During both 1942, the year of shocking defeats, and the planning year of 1943 the two Western leaders and their staffs had hammered out the shape of final victory in tandem with the Russians. After five years of doubt and agony men had mastered events, at least for the moment. Now with Hitler gone as a unifying force, could Harry Truman and his Administration offer the same kind of leadership after the war? The issue was not long in doubt.

*   *   *

Harry Truman would never forget his meeting with Eleanor Roosevelt after he was suddenly summoned from the Capitol to her study on April 12, 1945. "Harry," she had said quietly, "the President is dead." Speechless for a moment, he had asked her if there was anything he could do. "Is there anything *we* can do for *you?*" she had replied. "For you are the one in trouble now." The widowed First Lady knew well the toll exacted by the presidency. Within a few months the new President was lamenting that being Chief Executive was like "riding a tiger," as he desperately sought to keep on top of events before they got on top of him.

Rarely had a new President appeared so poorly prepared for the job. The Missourian had never visited Europe since shipping back from his

World War I service as an artilleryman in France. A decent, hardworking New Deal senator, Truman had been chosen as FDR's running mate largely because, of all the hopefuls, he would "hurt the President least." Roosevelt barely knew him, and made little effort to see him or keep him informed—even about the A-bomb—during the months after their November victory. The last of the Vice President's few messages to the President concerned a patronage matter. Politically Truman traded on his plain manners, blunt speech, and I'm-from-Missouri skepticism toward Senate windbags and Washington pundits. Behind the heavy spectacles and homespun features, however, lay a tangle of incongruities—a jaunty self-confidence along with feelings of inadequacy; a calm and sometimes stubborn resoluteness along with sudden flaring rages when he was crossed; a rustic morality that still accommodated itself easily to the unsavory Pendergast machine. He was a high school graduate moving in a world of college-educated men, but he took pride in his wide reading in American history.

Along with these ambivalences the new President inherited FDR's divided legacy of principled, idealistic leadership and short-run *Realpolitik* manipulation. The organizational meeting of the United Nations, opening two weeks after Truman took the oath of office, symbolized both the high ideals and the political pragmatics of the new President and of the nations' representatives who assembled there. In a brief, simple address piped in by direct wire, Truman urged the delegates to "rise above personal interests" and "provide the machinery, which will make future peace, not only possible, but certain." But Poland's seat at the conference lay empty, for Washington and Moscow were still at odds over the composition of the new Warsaw leadership. Also roiling the San Francisco assembly was Stalin's insistence that one power could not only veto a move to use force but veto even discussion of the question. Happily, Harry Hopkins, in his last major mission to Moscow—he would be dead of hemochromatosis in nine months—persuaded Stalin to withdraw Moscow's position on the veto. But even Hopkins could make little progress on Poland.

Overwhelmed by events, irked by the old Roosevelt hands in his cabinet who he felt shared little of FDR's greatness, immersed in paperwork as he tried feverishly to brief himself on the hard decisions facing him, Commander-in-Chief Harry Truman at least had the satisfaction of presiding over the last battles of the European war, as Allied spearheads stabbed into Germany from east and west. Late in April, American and Soviet soldiers met and clasped hands at Torgau, on the Elbe, while British forces were taking Bremen. Within a few days all ended for the Axis in a leaders' *Götterdämmerung,* as Mussolini and his mistress were shot to death by Italian partisans in a town on Lake Como, Dr. and Frau Goebbels killed their six young children and themselves, and Hitler and his bride of thirty-six hours committed suicide in their bunker as the Russians closed in. The German command—what was left of it—unconditionally surrendered on May 7, 1945.

Japan now fought on alone. American forces completed the conquest of Okinawa late in June, in what historians optimistically called the "last battle," but losses on this Ryukyu island were so staggering—over 11,000 GIs, marines, and sailors dead, over 33,000 wounded—combined with those earlier on Iwo Jima, as to boost Allied estimates of the human cost of invading the home islands. From the Potsdam Conference in Berlin late in July, the Big Three issued an unconditional surrender ultimatum to Tokyo.

This conference was a most remarkable affair. It was the first and only wartime summit meeting attended by Truman, and the last for Winston Churchill, who during the proceedings was replaced by Labour's Clement Attlee as Prime Minister. At times the conferees appeared more like future adversaries than victorious allies, as the Anglo-Americans tussled with the Russians over the future of Germany, reparations, and—more and more bitterly—Poland. Asserting that Poland must never again be able to "open the gates to Germany," Stalin was adamant that the "London Poles" have no more than token representation in the communist-dominated government. Most remarkable of all was the virtually unmentioned fact hanging over the conference, the fact of American development of the atomic bomb—fleetingly mentioned by the Americans because they thought they had kept the secret from the Russians, unmentioned by Stalin because he knew the "secret" but did not want Truman to know that he knew it.

Of all the legacies Truman received from Roosevelt, the A-bomb was at once the most constricting and most liberating, the most utopian and most deadly. Truman was "restricted politically, psychologically, and institutionally from critically reassessing" Roosevelt's legacy of the bomb, in Barton Bernstein's judgment. The bomb that had been developed as a military weapon in response to fears that the Germans would have it first was now—after a successful test in the Alamogordo desert of New Mexico—ready for use against Orientals.

Months before Stimson informed Truman of the "most terrible weapon ever known in human history," however, the Secretary of War had been contemplating its future political uses as well. The atomic bomb would give the United States "a royal straight flush and we mustn't be a fool about the way we play it." This kind of talk pleased the poker-playing President. The "cards" were in American hands, Truman claimed, and he meant "to play them as American cards." On the other hand, some scientists and Administration officials hoped the bomb might be a weapon for world peace or at the very least might gain the "liberalization of Soviet society" as a precondition for postwar cooperation. But would Stalin join in the poker game or even higher pursuits? Truman was disappointed at the Potsdam Conference when he mentioned the mighty weapon in vague terms to Stalin and the dictator showed only casual interest.

Typically, American planners were thinking more in short-run military terms than in geopolitical. All available forces were now concentrated in the western Pacific. American bombers, stepping up their attacks from ever nearer bases, incinerated hundreds of thousands of Japanese civilians in Tokyo and other cities. While Japanese diplomats felt out Soviet officials on a deal with Russia, the Anglo-Americans approached their momentous decision about using the atomic weapon, with Moscow unconsulted. The American leaders were divided, some arguing that the dreadful weapon was not needed at all, others that a demonstration would be enough, still others that the time-honored American strategy of heavy direct military assault would work again. Whatever his private doubts, Truman took the line that it was a purely military decision, that he did not want to disrupt the enormously costly atomic effort underway, and that a "one-two" punch would knock Japan out of the war, averting hundreds of thousands of American casualties and possibly millions of Japanese. As no one could authoritatively predict how strongly the Japanese would fight on their own soil, the simple, short-range, "practical" strategy of using all available weapons overcame any concerns about long-range consequences.

The Japanese climax surpassed even the German. So powerful was the will to resist that even after two bombs obliterated much of Hiroshima and Nagasaki and after Soviet troops smashed into Manchuria, Japanese civilian and military leaders argued for days whether to capitulate. Assured that the throne would be protected even under the terms of unconditional surrender, the civilian leaders won out after narrowly averting a palace revolt by officers determined to fight to the finish. On September 2, 1945, MacArthur presided over the Japanese capitulation in Tokyo harbor on the steel decks of the battleship *Missouri*.

* * *

Long before the hot war ended against Japan, the cold war between the Soviets and the Anglo-Americans was becoming more and more frigid. If the main reason for unleashing the atomic holocaust on Japan was short-run military, the Americans were not unhappy that they could demonstrate the A-bomb to the Russians. The Russians, however, appeared not to be intimidated by the awesome new weapon—partly because they had not been surprised by it. At Potsdam, just after Truman had told Stalin vaguely about the big bomb, Stalin had passed the "news" on to Molotov. "Let them," his Foreign Minister had said, adding, "We'll have to . . . speed things up." Did he mean speed up work on their own bomb—or prepare for war against Japan?

In the atmosphere of rising hostility, the Soviet invasion of Manchuria, launched even earlier than the Yalta agreement had called for, won few plaudits in Washington. The Russians simply wanted to be in on the kill—and the booty. Still, some American officials were hopeful and even conciliatory. On his trip home from Potsdam, Truman had told the officers of the *Augusta* that "Stalin was an SOB but of course he thinks I'm one, too." Stalin was like Boss Pendergast, Truman told a friend later, a man who would size up a question quickly and stand by his agreements. He even mused that Stalin "had a politburo on his hands like the 80th Congress."

Even more hopeful and conciliatory, for a time, was Truman's Secretary of State, James F. Byrnes. An old Senate hand, briefly a Supreme Court justice and then wartime economic czar, "Jimmie" believed that friendliness, old-time horse-trading, lengthy talk, and perhaps a spot of bourbon could thaw out any adversary, even a communist. When Japan surrendered, Byrnes looked forward to the first meeting of the Council of Foreign Ministers that had been set up to carry forward Allied collaboration. That conference, in London shortly after V-J Day, Byrnes found frustrating and a bit baffling. Preach though he might about the need for "free elections" and representative government in Poland and the Balkans, he could make no dent in the adamantine resolve of Moscow to control its spheres of interest.

As for the bomb, at a cocktail party, Molotov suddenly raised his glass and said, "Here's to the atom bomb—we've got it!" At this point another Russian took Molotov by the shoulder and led him from the room. Byrnes stood there perplexed. Was Molotov bluffing? Had he had one glass too many of vodka? Was the whole thing staged? Or—God forbid—did the Russians "have it"?

* * *

"I'm dreaming of a white Christmas," the soldiers had sung on barren atolls and in sweltering jungles, and by the end of 1945, millions of men and women had returned from the wars to their white and green Christmases at home. The joyous family reunions were hardly marred by thoughts of war; the world was at peace. Few could have believed that the next five years could be as crucial and traumatic, if less lethal, a period in world history as the previous five, that those years indeed would end in another hot war.

Nor could the men in Washington so imagine. By the end of 1945 the leaders who had inherited FDR's dual legacy were themselves even more ambivalent about the best posture toward Russia. Some saw Moscow pursuing traditional "state" interests—protecting her borders, establishing control in her own spheres of interest, pursuing old-fashioned bargaining and balance-of-power politics. Others saw "imperial Bolshevism" embarked on global conquest. This ambivalence both fostered and reflected a dualism among the American people, who were divided between a conciliatory and a get-tough policy toward Moscow. Most Americans favored holding on to the "secret" of the bomb, according to polls in late 1945, but most would also turn the United Nations into "a kind of world government" with the power to restrict the use of the atomic weapon.

Few Americans considered that the Kremlin also might be divided, in part because they perceived Soviet rule as far more monolithic than any Western regime. Yet Stalin too had to heed hard-liners like Andrei Zhdanov, who preached ideological war and revolution to communists abroad, yet also give ear to the many officials and diplomats who had worked with the Anglo-Americans during the war and favored collaboration. Number One blew hot and cold; he certainly had his own reservations about using communist centers abroad, "leaving them in the lurch whenever they slipped out of his grasp," the Yugoslav leader Milovan Djilas noted; but he was not slow to meddle abroad when he saw a Soviet advantage. The Russians talked tough but hardly seemed to be preparing for a war—they labeled 1946 the "Year of Cement." And somewhere in the background lay the Russian people, taught to hate and fear the imperialists but holding wartime memories of Anglo-American collaboration against the Hitlerites—and broken promises about an early second front.

After Stalin spoke in the Bolshoi Theater early in February 1946 on the eve of a Soviet "election," American perplexity about the Russians mounted. Despite praise of the Big Three's "anti-Fascist coalition" during the war, and a heavy emphasis on Soviet reconstruction through another Five-Year Plan, the speech was ambiguous enough in its foreign policy implications to arouse a new debate in Washington. Was Stalin talking conciliation, isolationism, or remilitarization? Supreme Court Justice William O. Douglas privately said it was a "Declaration of World War III." The State Department queried its most seasoned Russian expert in Moscow, George Kennan, who responded with an 8,000-word telegram.

Clattering in through State's tickers, the "long telegram," as it came to be called, had a quick and lasting impact. Kennan described Soviet official

policy as based on the premises that Russia lived amid antagonistic capitalistic encirclement, that capitalist nations inevitably generated wars among
themselves, that to escape from their inner conflicts capitalist nations
intervened against socialist governments. Hence Moscow's official policy
was to strengthen the Soviet state by any means possible, advance Soviet
power abroad wherever feasible, weaken Western ties to colonial peoples,
take part in the United Nations only in order to protect and advance its own
interests. Russia's unofficial or "subterranean" policies were even more
baleful: to "undermine general and strategic potential of major Western
powers" by a host of subversive measures, to destroy individual governments that might stand in the Soviet path (even Switzerland), to do "everything possible" to "set major Western powers against each other."

"In summary," Kennan telegraphed, "we have here a political force
committed fanatically to the belief that with U.S. there can be no permanent modus vivendi, that it is desirable and necessary that the internal
harmony of our state be disrupted, our traditional way of life be destroyed,
the international authority of our state be broken, if Soviet power is to be
secure."

Kennan's telegram brought the thrill of vindication to Washington hard-
liners and, coming from a diplomat in the field, impressed waverers. The
ideas were not all that novel; it was Kennan's dramatic and apocalyptic
presentation of them that galvanized Washington officialdom. Above all,
it was Kennan's imputing of vast skill and incredible efficiency to a regime
that had so often seemed incompetent. Not only did the Kremlin have
"complete power of disposition over energies of one of the world's greatest peoples and resources of the world's richest national territory," cabled
Kennan breathlessly, but it had "an elaborate and far-flung apparatus for
exertion of its influence in other countries, an apparatus of amazing flexibility and versatility, managed by people whose experience and skill in
underground methods are presumably without parallel in history."

If this secret telegram sharpened Administration fears of Soviet power,
the most famous Anglo-American in the world helped harden attitudes
toward the Russians among a far wider public. Winston Churchill, introduced by President Truman, told a Missouri college audience that from
"Stettin in the Baltic to Trieste in the Adriatic, an iron curtain has descended across the continent." Communists and fifth columnists constituted a "growing challenge and peril to Christian civilization." Wanting
not war but only the fruits of war, the Russians admired nothing so much
as strength. Hence Americans and British must form a permanent military
alliance, centered on their combined military forces and atomic monopoly.
The speech caused such a storm that American officials, including the

President, discreetly but distinctly distanced themselves from the former Prime Minister. But these subtleties eluded the men in the Kremlin. Denouncing the Anglo-American in a *Pravda* interview for plotting against the Soviet Union's right to exist, Stalin called Churchill a Hitlerite racial theorist, stoked memories of the 1918 intervention in Russia, and castigated his wartime ally for his "call to war with the Soviet Union."

*   *   *

For almost a year after Kennan's cable and Churchill's speech the spiral of hostility slowly mounted. The Kremlin tightened its grip on Poland and the Balkans, save for Yugoslavia, while the Americans extended their guard over Greece and Turkey. Meetings of Foreign Ministers erupted in quarrels over "free elections" in Stalin's buffer states, the disposition of Germany, and reparations. Zhdanov demanded a crackdown on the "putrid and baneful" influence of bourgeois culture in the Soviet Union, and the American public, still divided and uncertain, became more and more drawn into the spiral. But the spiraling slowed at times. The Foreign Ministers finally agreed on a host of postwar treaty settlements; the Administration urged control of atomic energy through an international agency, though one dominated by Washington; Stalin withdrew his troops from Iran after a sharp confrontation in which Washington tried out, within the framework of the United Nations, its strategy of "get tougher"; Truman, despite deepening suspicion and fear of the Soviet Union, did not yet openly support Churchill's hard line.

Then, late in 1946, the spiral of confrontation began to quicken. A number of forces converged. As Moscow appeared to become more intransigent, perceptions and misperceptions of Soviet behavior narrowed and hardened among Truman lieutenants who had to deal daily with the Russians. Navy Secretary James Forrestal, former head of the investment firm of Dillon, Read, not only worried about the dangers of communism but inundated his colleagues with hundreds of copies of anti-Soviet reports and warnings—most notably, Kennan's long telegram. Slowly Forrestal's worry was becoming an obsession. Dean Acheson, after finding his natural niche in the State Department, took increasing leadership there even as he held decreasing hopes of dealing with the Russians.

Kennan's telegram became more and more influential—especially after it was offered to the public in a *Foreign Affairs* article by "X"—even as Kennan worried more and more about overreaction to it. A clear omen was seen in the fate of Secretary of State Byrnes, whose efforts at conciliation with the Soviets had fared less well than his give-and-take with senators. After Truman became increasingly critical of Byrnes's soft approach to

Moscow, the secretary took a harder line, but by now he and his boss were drifting apart.

Increasingly the President, so lacking in broad executive experience or in FDR's ability to manipulate and stay on top of his advisers, was becoming a prisoner of his staff. An even more important cause of the President's hardening, however, was clearly political. In the congressional elections of November 1946 the Republicans ran a skillful negative campaign. Their slogan "Had enough?" promiscuously fused grievances over inflation, strikes, price controls, meat shortages—and fears of communism at home and abroad. The Republicans swept the Senate and House for the first time in sixteen years. The Chicago *Tribune* called it "the greatest victory for the Republic since Appomattox." Harry Truman had lost his first election as President.

Now controlled by Republicans, the House Un-American Activities Committee early in 1947 planned a dramatic effort to "expose and ferret out the communists and communist sympathizers in the federal government." The election had brought into Congress the "Class of '46," which included such anticommunist militants as Richard Nixon of California, William Jenner of Indiana, and Joseph McCarthy of Wisconsin. Truman, responding to the political currents, tried to play their game and beat them to the punch. Proclaiming that the presence in the government service of "any" disloyal or subversive person constituted a "threat to our democratic processes," he created a Federal Employee Loyalty Program that, operating through scores of loyalty boards at lower levels, was empowered to sack employees for "membership in, affiliation with, or sympathetic association with any foreign or domestic organization" that might be designated by the Attorney General as "totalitarian, fascist, communist, or subversive." The Attorney General's "little list" was compiled without giving a hearing to named organizations or specifying the nature of the threat they posed.

Worse was to come. Employees under investigation were granted a hearing and the right to appeal, but the burden of proof was on them. They had in effect to prove their loyalty. They need not know the accusations; the specification of charges, according to Truman's executive order, was "to be as complete as security provisions make possible." Nor could they hope to confront their accusers, for in almost all cases the FBI, intent upon protecting its informants, withheld the sources of derogatory information. Loyalty boards quizzed employees as to their views of coexistence, peace, civil liberties, and other horrendous things advocated by the Communist party. Said a top loyalty boss, "The man who fears that his thinking will be curbed by a check of loyalty may be thinking things that tend to be disloyal to his country."

To those who cried out that the program threatened the most basic and old-fashioned American value—individual liberty—the Administration retorted that communism threatened liberty even more. Moreover, it contended, the Democrats must clean house or the Republicans in their zeal would burn the whole house down. If the White House thought that its loyalty boards could outshine the real "red hunters," however, it had underestimated the congressional lust to investigate. In the fall of 1947 HUAC opened a star-spangled extravaganza on communism in Hollywood. The dapper character actor Adolphe Menjou testified that anyone "attending any meeting at which Paul Robeson appears, and applauds, can be considered a Communist." Gary Cooper, whose appearance evoked sighs from the audience, said of communism, "From what I hear, I don't like it because it isn't on the level." Friendly witnesses had a glorious time trading in rumor and speculation.

The mood changed when the Hollywood Ten—a group of screenwriters, producers, and directors—contended that HUAC had no right to ask them about Communist party membership. Much shouting and gaveling-down ensued, all before an avid press. The Ten, who had expected their appeal to the First Amendment to be upheld in the courts, were fined and jailed for contempt and blacklisted by the studios. A purge by terrified Hollywood and radio executives followed. Some 350 Hollywood actors, writers, and directors and perhaps 1,500 television and radio employees lost their jobs in the next few years. Some ex-communists, on the other hand, came before the committee to expiate their sins—to name names, denounce former comrades, provide delectable details of disloyal activities. Some admitted their own sins but refused to name others; some named names reluctantly; some named them eagerly; and a few took up ex-communism as a livelihood, testifying at trials, writing books, touring the lecture circuit, acting as "expert consultants."

Most of the government people targeted by HUAC were small game until, one day in 1948, a pudgy, rumpled, troubled man appeared before HUAC, a man who had consorted with tramps and prostitutes as well as communists, a self-confessed thief and perjurer. His name was Whittaker Chambers. He had come to name several government officials. One name leapt out, a Harvard Law School graduate, protégé of Felix Frankfurter, clerk for Justice Holmes, rising young State Department hand, adviser at Yalta, presider at the UN organizing meeting, now head of the Carnegie Endowment. His name was Alger Hiss.

Two days after Chambers named Hiss as a communist, Hiss testified that he was not. So persuasive was Hiss, so boyish of face and earnest and attractive of demeanor, that he received congratulations from spectators and even handshakes from HUAC members. One Republican committee-man moaned, "We've been had! We're ruined." But another member thought differently. Richard Nixon kept the case alive, arranged a Hiss-Chambers confrontation, pursued loopholes and inconsistencies in Hiss's testimony. When the young New Dealer sued Chambers for libel, Cham-bers produced the "pumpkin papers"—microfilms of classified State De-partment material he had hidden in a hollowed-out pumpkin on his farm—as evidence that Hiss had been not only a Communist party member in the 1930s but a spy for the Soviet Union. Four days later, Hiss was indicted for perjury.

As the Republicans continued to exploit the communism issue, Presi-dent Truman tried to defuse this atomic bomb of domestic politics. The menace of communism was not foreign agents, he told a Chicago audience, but the areas of American society in which the promise of democracy remained unfulfilled. He dismissed one HUAC hearing as a "red herring." But Truman could not bottle up the genie of suspicion he had helped release. The spiral of fear intensified among Americans as the spiral of hostility intensified between Washington and Moscow.

*   *   *

A sudden sharp crisis early in 1947 spun the Administration toward a sphere-of-interest commitment in the eastern Mediterranean that almost equaled the Soviet Union's in Eastern Europe. Warned by the British that they could no longer shore up Athens with economic and military aid, informed by advisers that the crisis-laden Greek government was near the breaking point, Truman responded largely to the communist threat. Mos-cow expected Greece to fall into its hands soon like a "ripe plum," said an Administration adviser. Then "the whole Near East and part of North Africa" was "certain to pass under Soviet influence." The domino theory was gaining adherents. In fact, although communists in neighboring Bal-kan countries were stirring up what trouble they could in the ancient "cradle of democracy," Stalin himself was observing his sphere-of-interest deal with Churchill. If the domino was falling, it was falling of its own weight.

In mid-March, Truman asked Congress for $400 million for Greek and Turkish aid. "It must be the policy of the United States," he told a joint session of Congress, "to support free peoples who are resisting attempted subjugation by armed minorities or by outside pressures." This urgent call to economic and military arms, soon named the Truman Doctrine, was followed three months later by a momentous proposal to shore up the European economy, still stricken by the effects of total war. General Marshall, now Secretary of State, from the steps of Memorial Church in Harvard Yard portrayed to "you gentlemen" of the graduating class—and to T. S. Eliot, another honorary degree recipient that day—a Europe near "breakdown," requiring "substantial additional help." Marshall announced that the United States would do everything possible to "assist in the return of normal economic health in the world, without which there can be no political stability and no assured peace." American policy, he said, was directed "not against any country or doctrine but against hunger, poverty, desperation, and chaos." Such an effort could not be piecemeal, however—all nations must join, pool their needs, and present Washington with a single combined request.

At once the new plan—the Marshall Plan—was swept into the spiral of East-West hostility. It quickly became evident that Congress, now dominated by Senator Taft and other economizers and budget balancers, would respond far more enthusiastically to an "anticommunist" measure than to a welfare program for Europeans. But the more the plan was sold as anticommunist, the more Russian suspicions of it were inflamed. Invited to take part, Moscow at first seemed tempted, sending a delegation to Paris for consultations with other Europeans, then coldly declined, rightly suspecting that many of the inviters hoped that this particular guest would not sup at the table. Over the following weeks, while Congress debated the plan and the billions of dollars requested, Stalin immensely helped its passage by establishing the Cominform—the "Communist Information Bureau"—to replace the old Comintern, and by clamping harsh controls on Czechoslovakia just as debate over Marshall Plan funding came to a head. Then it was Washington's turn to react, as Truman called for a renewed draft, worked out collective security arrangements with Western Europe, and declared his intention to set up an independent West German state.

The cold war appeared on the verge of turning red hot, as the spiral of fear and hatred reached its apogee. In part the hatred was the logical manifestation of Great Power conflict over ideology and interest. But even more it was a reflex of perceptions. Washington underestimated Moscow's absolute determination to control its bordering states and grossly exaggerated Soviet designs outside its sphere. Moscow exaggerated Truman's disposition to use atomic weapons and underestimated his genuine concern over the European economy and his absolute determination to unify Western Europe, including the West Germans, behind an anticommunist strategy. And behind the misperception lay age-old psychological tendencies, among which Ralph K. White included diabolical enemy images and moral self-images, overconfidence and worst-case thinking.

*   *   *

The growing anticommunist militancy that buoyed the Administration ran into political volleys from all directions—from Taft unilateralists, old-fashioned isolationists, pro-Soviet radicals, and a handful of pundits and publicists who viewed themselves as "realistic" as the most hard-nosed Truman hand. Among the latter stood Walter Lippmann, who differed so sharply with George Kennan that he devoted fourteen successive columns to refuting the "X" article—and to lambasting the Truman Doctrine, which Kennan's long telegram had helped inspire. The Truman strategy was too grandiose, Lippmann contended, too indiscriminately global, too unrealistic in view of the nation's limited resources, and based on false premises—especially the perception of Moscow as pursuing ideological and messianic goals rather than traditional sphere-of-interest and balance-of-power statecraft.

The Truman Administration could dismiss hostile pundits as not having the votes, unilateralists as mere go-it-aloners, isolationists as head-in-the-sand ostriches. But as 1947 gave way to the election year of 1948, the political leaders in Washington could not dismiss one man who was neither isolationist nor unilateralist and might have some critical votes. This was Henry Wallace, behind whom loomed at times the evocative figure of Eleanor Roosevelt. While Truman had switched back and forth between Roosevelt's dual foreign policy tracks of Wilsonian idealism and conventional power politics, Wallace stayed squarely on the former path. He was still serving as Secretary of Commerce, the post FDR had chosen for him after easing him out of the vice-presidency. During 1946, as Truman's advisers and Soviet provocations drew the President into an ever stronger cold war posture, Wallace's friends—old-line pacifists, anti-anticommunists, liberals and radicals of all stripes, scientists heartsick over Hiroshima—fortified Wallace's own determination to break with the White House.

The messy rupture began with a Madison Square Garden speech before the National Citizens Political Action Committee. Hissed whenever he said anything derogatory about Russia, Wallace called for a "real peace treaty" between the United States and the Soviets, amid such provocative remarks as "We should recognize that we have no more business in the *political* affairs of Eastern Europe than Russia has in the *political* affairs of Latin America, Western Europe and the United States." Wallace added—correctly—that the President had gone over the speech, and had said it represented Administration policy.

A Washington tempest followed. Byrnes threatened to resign. Vandenberg said that the Republicans could "only cooperate with one Secretary of State at a time." Truman explained lamely that there had been a misunderstanding—he had only approved Wallace's right to give the speech, not its contents. In a long face-to-face meeting Wallace told Truman that the people feared that American policy was leading to war, adding pointedly, "You, yourself, as Harry Truman really believed in my speech." But Harry Truman the President made clear that he must keep unity in his cabinet and present a united front abroad. The President revealed his true feelings the next day in a memorandum about Wallace:

"He is a pacifist one hundred per cent. He wants us to disband our armed forces, give Russia our atomic secrets and trust a bunch of adventurers in the Kremlin Politburo. I do not understand a 'dreamer' like that. . . . The Reds, phonies and the 'parlor pinks' seem to be banded together and are becoming a national danger.

"I am afraid," he added, "that they are a sabotage front for Uncle Joe Stalin." These remarks were a measure of Truman's tendency to strike out at his adversaries in crude personal terms and of the completeness of his break with the anti–cold war forces.

Eleanor Roosevelt followed the rupture with rising concern. She had worked with Wallace during the New Deal and respected his idealism and commitment; she had counseled Truman on how to get along with both Churchill and Stalin. In the United Nations she was experiencing firsthand Soviet suspicion and stubbornness. As Truman and Wallace spun away from each other, she was left isolated in the void between them. She believed Wallace was unwise to make speeches in Europe criticizing Administration policy; she was disturbed by the go-it-alone aspects of the Truman Doctrine and by the President's failure to offer relief and rehabilitation in cooperation with the UN. While lauding Wallace's commitment to world understanding, she also approved of the Marshall Plan and admired its author. As the Wallace forces moved toward establishing a third party, however, Eleanor Roosevelt knew where she would stand. She had always believed in working within the Democratic party.

*   *   *

Political leaders on all sides had long expected 1948 to be a "showdown year." At long last the Republicans could battle someone other than Franklin Roosevelt. The Democrats could no longer depend on the electoral magician in the White House. The Wallace movement, soon to be converted into the Progressive party, expected at least to hold a critical balance of power. Within each party too, rival leaderships hoped to establish their factional dominance. Conservative Republicans headed by Senator Taft planned to wrest their party away from men of the Willkie, Stimson, and Dewey stamp. The presidential Republicans, headed by aggressive young activists like Harold Stassen, Henry Cabot Lodge, Jr., and Dewey himself, labored to deny party leadership to the isolationists and to set the GOP on a steady course of moderation in domestic policy and of internationalism abroad. On the Democratic side, hawks and doves, as they would come to be called, fought for the soul of the Democracy, as did states' righters against the Truman forces backing the social welfare and reformist programs of his Fair Deal.

In the center of the Democratic battlefield stood Harry Truman. Not for decades—certainly not since William Howard Taft had been beset by La Follette Progressives and Teddy Roosevelt Square Dealers in 1912—had a President seemed so isolated and deserted as Truman when he announced his candidacy early in March 1948. The Henry Wallace Progressives threatened to carve deeply into the "peace vote." A number of labor leaders, personally furious with Truman after he had cold-shouldered them during a rash of postwar strikes, threatened to sit the election out. Americans for Democratic Action, a liberal, anticommunist group founded by Eleanor Roosevelt and a host of academics, politicos, and assorted old New Dealers, was sticking with the Democracy, but some of its leaders were working to draft the popular General Eisenhower as the Democratic standard-bearer. The Republicans appeared likely to renominate Dewey, who had his own lines into labor, liberal, and black enclaves.

Through it all Truman appeared his usual feisty self. He not only aroused antagonism—he seemed to solicit it. In the face of conservative opposition to his Fair Deal economic measures he inflamed southern Democrats even further with his sweeping civil rights message of February 1948. Based on the recommendations of a special presidential commission chaired by Charles E. Wilson, head of General Electric, the message called for a permanent federal commission on civil rights, a permanent fair employment practices commission, the outlawing of segregation in schools and transportation and other public facilities, and a federal antilynching law. Truman's central strategy, however, was to stand on his Fair Deal extension of the New Deal—housing, welfare, labor and consumer protection, farm subsidies.

Soon Truman was besieged on three fronts. The GOP duly nominated Dewey on a moderately liberal and internationalist platform, a band of solid Southerners bolted the Democratic convention and later nominated

Governor Strom Thurmond of South Carolina for President on the States' Rights or "Dixiecrat" ticket, and a Progressive convention nominated Wallace. Truman's whole instinct was to fight back, like the French general who cried, "My left flank is in ruins, my right flank is retreating, my center is caving in. Good! I shall attack." By midsummer the voters were being treated to a four-cornered race reminiscent of 1912, as Truman crisscrossed the country in an exhausting "whistlestop" campaign by train, Wallace made his rustic, low-key appearances before hyperbolic crowds, Thurmond sought enough electoral votes to throw the presidential race into the House of Representatives, and Dewey tried to appear presidential in order to become presidential.

For a time, fortune scarcely favored the bold. At the Democratic convention Young Turks headed by Hubert Humphrey, the thirty-seven-year-old mayor of Minneapolis, had pushed through a strengthened civil rights plank that threatened to alienate even more of the southern Democracy. Zigzagging across the country, the Truman campaign repeatedly ran out of money, requiring frenzied appeals to fat cats, usually to oil barons with ready cash. Toward the end of the campaign the election forecasts, including roundups by *The New York Times* and other periodicals, had Truman so far behind Dewey as to arouse despair in the President's entourage. Shown a poll of "fifty political experts," all of whom predicted a big Dewey win, Truman blinked, grinned, and said, "Oh, well, those damn fellows; they're always wrong anyway. Forget it, boys, and let's get on with the job."

In the end, fortune did favor the bold. The Dixiecrat bolt backfired, as most southern Democrats stuck with Truman while northern blacks credited his timely civil rights position. Two or three million Republicans stayed home out of overconfidence, or so Dewey later complained. Wallace's strength steadily ebbed as liberals and laborites feared to waste their ballots on a third-party ticket. They also suspected extensive communist influence over the campaign, and rightly so. Warned of this influence, Wallace was unwilling even to investigate, for fear that he would be guilty of the very red-baiting that he had warned Americans against. He felt far more pressed from the right. Bold enough to stay overnight in the homes of southern blacks, he would remember his campaign through the South as "one long succession of tomatoes and eggs." The author of *The Century of the Common Man* later remarked that the "common man can be very, very barbarous."

Dewey, seeking to soften memories of his blatant linking of the Democrats with communism in 1944, took the high road, lost his fighting edge, and embraced bipartisanship in foreign policy to the degree that he could not exploit Truman's chief vulnerabilities. The President skillfully employed FDR's tactic of attacking the congressional rather than the presidential Republicans. He called Congress into special session, challenged the Republicans to pass the legislation demanded in their party platform, and hung the congressional failure to do so around Dewey's neck.

Truman's close but decisive victory was so unexpected as to be sensational. It quickly became the pride of historians prone to demonstrate the power of individual leadership against historical forces. People saw "a brave man," in Richard Kirkendall's words, "fighting almost alone against great odds," and bringing off the greatest upset in American history. But Truman finally won by not fighting alone. With the help of Stalin's aggressive blockade of land traffic between Berlin and West Germany, he played on the anticommunism latent in millions of Americans. He received Eleanor Roosevelt's benediction and exploited the momentum and mythology of the Roosevelt heritage. He depended heavily on the Democratic party, which produced a set of congressional victories as significant as the presidential. He remobilized the economic voting groups of farmers, workers, and urban consumers bequeathed by Roosevelt.

The gutsy little man from Missouri had ridden these forces, even guided them, rather than being overwhelmed by them. Americans, recovering from their election-night shock, took this underdog—this winning underdog—to their bosom.

THE SPIRAL OF FEAR

For the political leadership of the nation 1948 had indeed been a showdown. For Dewey, whose popular vote fell short of his 1944 total, it would be the end of the presidential road. Thurmond's States' Rights party, winning 1,169,000 popular votes and 38 electoral votes, fell far short of its electoral hopes in the South. The Wallace Progressives, garnering even fewer popular votes than the Dixiecrats and no electoral votes, learned once again the bias of American traditions and elections against third parties. Congressional Republican leaders, set up as a perfect target by the Democrats, lost their House and Senate majorities. And renowned political prophets suffered the derision of the winners and the wrath of the losers who castigated them for their sloppy polling techniques.

For the longer run, however, the 1948 election was less dramatic. In the lexicon of political scientists, it was a "maintaining election," reflecting persisting party loyalties and stable group attachments. The excitement of a four-cornered battle had not brought out a big vote. In many respects the 1948 election was a fifth presidential victory for FDR and the New Deal. For most Americans, voting Democratic had become a habit.

Yet in a far more momentous way 1948 was a different kind of maintaining election—an election that sustained the Truman Administration in its Fair Deal posture but above all in its anticommunism. It seemed likely that Truman's loyalty program and his increasingly hard line toward Moscow had blunted Republican charges of "soft on communism" and helped turn Dewey against the weapon he had used in 1944. Even more, the election ratified the sphere-of-interest strategy on which the Truman Doctrine and the Marshall Plan and other Administration foreign policies were grounded. The Administration's unofficial protectorate over Greece and Turkey, its insistence on holding West Berlin through a resourceful airsupply program—along with its reluctance to interfere in the Soviet sphere—suggested that the war-torn world of the early 1940s was settling down into some kind of Great Power stability based on mutual containment.

Maintaining that stability, however, would call for the most exacting statecraft on all sides; it would call for clear perceptions of nations' interests, dependable estimates of the military potential and intentions of rival powers, sophisticated political intelligence about the interplay of national interests within and among rival blocs, realistic estimates of strategic possibilities and impossibilities, skillful national leadership and tenacious diplomacy. The historic balances of power of past centuries had depended on the statecraft of military and political leaders possessing such Bismarckian qualities. But the sphere-of-interest, balance-of-power way of stabilizing international relationships—especially difficult for democracies to manage—was always hostage to one powerful force: change. Alterations in the actual military and economic power of rival and friendly nations, combined with misperceptions of popular attitudes and the intentions of leaders, all in a context of fear and hostility, could—and often did—bring the trembling mobiles of the balance of power crashing down.

The years 1948 and 1949 bristled with events full of potential for arousing fear and hostility, misperceptions and miscalculations, among the Great Powers. The mysterious, awesome might of the atomic weapon was proving a source more of fear than of security among nations. Evidence of atomic espionage by Soviet spies struck fear in American hearts that the Russians would steal the "secret" of the bomb. The Soviets, knowing that Washington would never permit international controls that would give Moscow that secret, worked feverishly on their own bomb. Despite scientists' advice that Moscow would not be slow to develop an atomic weapon, many Administration officials confidently assumed that they would continue to hold this trump card. Then in September 1949 came the dread news: winds blowing high over North America were carrying radiation from a Soviet atomic test. A few months later Truman announced that the United States would begin to develop the hydrogen bomb—potentially many times more destructive than the A-bomb.

Germany was another crisis point. The standoff following the Soviet blockade and the Western airlift left heightened fears and hostility on each side, in turn drawing the divided Germans into the East-West spheres of interest. This balance-of-power tendency might have stabilized the situation, save that a divided Berlin remained a tempting and vulnerable island in eastern Germany. Officials on each side, moreover, now feared that the adversary would seek to draw all of Germany into its own embrace. Step by fearful step, the two camps lost the opportunity, limited in any event, to shape a unified and disarmed Germany.

But the most profound change—perhaps the most significant transformation of the mid-twentieth century—was threatening the balance of power on the other side of the globe. The civil war in China had accelerated, despite patient efforts by General Marshall to mediate the conflict. By the end of 1947 Mao Tse-tung's communist armies had won control of Manchuria and by the end of 1948 most of northern China; during 1949 it became clear that soon they would drive Chiang Kai-shek's Nationalist forces off the Chinese mainland. Chiang's withdrawal to Taiwan created one more outpost—a counterpart to Berlin—that could be protected against invasion only by Western power. And it left fear and anger among Americans who cherished their country's historic involvement and sympathy with China—most recently with Chiang and Madame Chiang's Republican China, which they imagined could be guided toward Western-style democracy.

It was not in Germany or China, however, or in some atomic confrontation, but in the little-known land of the Koreans that statecraft failed and the balance of power began a wild oscillation.

Although this remote land, protruding into the Sea of Japan out of the great haunch of Manchuria, had for centuries been a jousting ground for rival powers, it had been viewed during the postwar years of tension as one of the less likely theaters of hot war. Divided along an "administrative dividing line"—the 38th parallel—after World War II, Korea fell into the hands of militant communists in the north headed by Kim Il Sung in Pyongyang and militant anticommunists in the south headed by Syngman Rhee in Seoul. The two regimes, each hoping to take over the whole country, glared covetously at each other's lands across the parallel.

In January 1950, Dean Acheson, Marshall's successor as Secretary of State, described to Washington journalists an American defense perimeter that ran from the Aleutians to the Ryukyus to the Philippines but excluded

Korea, though the secretary added that if such other areas were invaded the people attacked must resist with the help if necessary "of the entire civilized world under the charter of the United Nations." American occupation troops pulled out of South Korea, leaving light weapons and ammunition but no aircraft, tanks, or heavy naval craft. Washington's idea was that Rhee would be able to defend but not attack. Moscow, Peking, and Pyongyang looked on with interest.

The war that erupted after North Korean troops drove through the parallel on June 25, 1950, was in part an old-fashioned campaign of movement and maneuver. Within two days President Truman, without waiting for Congress to act, ordered United States air and naval forces to Korea and authorized the dispatch of a regimental combat team within a week. The North Koreans quickly captured Seoul and drove south down the peninsula, seizing Pohang on the southeastern coast by early September and cornering their foe at the foot of the peninsula. On September 15, American forces under General MacArthur struck back with a brilliantly conceived and executed landing at Inchon, on the coast west of Seoul. Within eleven days the counterattackers had captured Seoul, and by late October they had taken Pyongyang, a hundred miles to the north. Intoxicated by his success at Inchon, by hopes of a glorious triumph over communism, and by visions of his return home to a hero's welcome, MacArthur drove his troops still further north, toward the Manchurian border.

The world looked on aghast—World War II was not yet five years over in the Pacific and Americans were once again fighting Asians. How could this "most unnecessary of wars" have started?

The misperceptions that dominated the Korean War rivaled the blunders that had led to hostilities in earlier centuries when both intelligence and communication among nations were still primitive. Its origins were parochial. Kim feared that Rhee would wipe out communists in the south and then turn north; Rhee feared that Pyongyang would seek to "unify" the country by mobilizing those same southern communists. According to Khrushchev's later account, Kim, during a trip to Moscow, sought Stalin's permission to strike south and topple Rhee. Somewhat reluctantly Stalin assented, doubtless calculating on a large gain at small risk. Even so, Stalin ordered all Soviet advisers out of North Korea so that Moscow would not be compromised in the venture. He also had Kim clear the decision with Mao, or perhaps did so himself when Mao visited Moscow. Both the Russian and the Chinese dictator expected that the Americans would not intervene, at least not in time to stop Kim's conquest of the south. But Truman, under attack himself for "losing China," was not going to "lose" more real estate. The fall of South Korea would gravely menace Japan.

The Americans and South Koreans counterattacked far more quickly and effectively than the communist leaders had expected. But now it was the Americans' turn for miscalculation.

Truman, assuming wrongly that Moscow had instigated the invasion and that Korea was the first step in the communist march to world conquest, had hopes of rolling back communist power and unifying Korea. Now, with the North Korean forces reeling backwards, he could win a relatively cheap victory. But it would not be cheap. After MacArthur's forces neared the Yalu River and launched a general assault to win the war, the Chinese counterattacked in heavy force. Soon it was MacArthur's army, divided and immobilized in the mountain passes, suffering bitterly in the winter snow and ice, bleeding heavily from close Chinese pursuit, that stumbled back to positions on the other side of the 38th parallel. There the two sides sparred with each other for years, suffering further heavy casualties, until an armistice was signed in July 1953, a few months after the death of Stalin.

Both sides had failed to assess correctly the other's strategic capability. Both sides were militarily unprepared for the battle they would undertake. Each had underestimated the other's willingness to fight and then had exaggerated the other's fighting as part of a long-planned strategy of global conquest. Each assumed that the "other" Korea was the enemy's puppet. Originally Korea had not been part of either side's master plan, but the outbreak of the Korean War, resulting from miscalculations and misperceptions, made Korea part of a crisis plan.

Then, too, the Korean War had a dire and unexpected impact on the relationship of Moscow and Peking. It was, Adam Ulam concluded, one of the biggest blunders of postwar Soviet foreign policy. "On the surface it appeared as a master stroke to make Peking the lightning rod for America's wrath and frustration while the Soviet Union remained a sympathetic by-stander. In fact, those two years when the Chinese had to assume the burden of the fighting marked their psychological emancipation and speeded up the process of equalization between the two states" that had begun with negotiations between Mao and Stalin in Moscow. The increasing tension between Peking and Moscow heartened Western leaders, but it was a further destabilizing factor in the quivering balance of power around the globe.

Perhaps the Korean War's major effect in the United States was on the mass public's fears and hostility. Anticommunists now cried out that their warnings had been justified, that the North Korean attack proved Russia to be bent on world conquest, that the Chinese attack across the Yalu confirmed that Peking was bent on Asian conquest. It was in this context that anticommunist feeling was reaching a new pitch among Americans.

*　　*　　*

After his election "in his own right," President Truman carried on his anticommunist campaign, holding that his "responsible" efforts might moderate or head off the "irresponsible" red hunters. In July 1948 his Justice Department won the indictment of twelve Communist party leaders, including Eugene Dennis and Gus Hall, for violating the 1940 Smith Act, which made it a crime "to teach and advocate the overthrow of the United States government by force and violence." The trial dragged on through most of 1949. The prosecution based its case largely on the testimony of ex-communists and on readings from "Marxist-Leninist" classics, with former *Daily Worker* managing editor Louis Budenz explaining that however innocent the language of the classics might appear, it had an altogether different and sinister meaning to trained communists. The twelve sought but failed to put "the Government . . . on trial." The judge's charge to the jury that there was "sufficient danger of a substantial evil" eliminated the "clear and present" test of the First Amendment from the jury's deliberations. Conviction duly followed.

Administration actions of this sort, however, appeared not to quench popular fears of the reds at home and abroad but to stoke them. Those fears flamed higher after the Chinese intervention across the Yalu and Harry Truman's sacking of MacArthur for publicly advocating, against Administration policy, that the war be carried to communist China. Korea was now closely linked with "Red China." A militant "China Lobby," embracing such notables as Clare Boothe Luce, David Dubinsky of the International Ladies' Garment Workers' Union, and James Farley, and such publications as the Hearst newspapers and the Luce magazines, kept up a drumfire: Who lost China? Senator Taft charged that "the proper kind of sincere aid to the Nationalist Government a few years ago could have stopped communism in China," but a "pro-Communist group in the State Department" had promoted "at every opportunity the Communist cause in China."

At the center of the China Lobby's target stood Dean Acheson. This sternest of cold warriors was described in the Senate as having "whined" and "whimpered" as he "slobbered over the shoes of his Muscovite masters." Acheson was vulnerable. Though lacking a political base of his own, he made no attempt to modify his bristling Groton–Yale–Eastern Establishment demeanor. Acheson showed his class manners and his moral code when he told reporters that he would never "turn my back" on Alger Hiss, but this only goaded his foes to a new fury.

"I look at that fellow, I watch his smart-aleck manner and his British clothes and that New Dealism," cried Senator Hugh Butler of Nebraska, "and I want to shout, Get out, Get out. You stand for everything that has been wrong with the United States for years."

During the late forties the war on "reds in America" had lacked a single dominant leader—or perhaps it had suffered from too many leaders vying for headlines and photographs. Then there emerged a figure that only a movement of the fearful and the paranoid could have brought to the fore. Decades later it was difficult for historians to fathom just why an obscure junior senator from Wisconsin named Joseph R. McCarthy suddenly became the notorious spokesman and symbol of American anticommunism at home. "Tail-gunner Joe," as he was somewhat derisively called, had won some note in 1946 by shooting down a famous senator and heir to a great Wisconsin dynasty, Robert M. La Follette, Jr. In Washington he soon won a small reputation for abusing Senate procedures, harassing witnesses, and using "the multiple untruth," as Richard Rovere later termed it. He employed these tactics indiscriminately against advocates of public housing, communists, fellow senators.

McCarthy had been casting about for some exploitable cause when the GOP sent him out on a routine barnstorming trip in February 1950. At Wheeling, West Virginia, he offered to an audience of Republican women the usual grab bag of parings from newspaper columns, Senate testimony, and anticommunist talks—this time a two-week-old Nixon speech, which he plagiarized. After the tired old cracks at traitors and fellow travelers and striped-pants diplomats in the State Department, McCarthy tried his version of the Big Lie. "While I cannot take the time to name all the men in the State Department who have been named as active members of the Communist Party and members of a spy ring," he said, "I have here in my hand a list of 205—a list of names that were made known to the Secretary of State as being members of the Communist Party and who nevertheless are still working and shaping policy in the State Department."

This was pretty stale talk, and the Wheeling speech itself received little press attention. But as McCarthy continued his tour and spewed out charges and numbers, he gathered more and more headlines. It was still not clear why. His Wheeling "list" had come from a 1946 letter—which he did not "hold in his hand"—to Congress from Secretary Byrnes. The letter reported on a preliminary screening, made no mention of Communist party membership, contained no names; and McCarthy had no idea how many of them were still in State. But something about this man increasingly riveted press attention—his sullen, jowly, dark-shaven features, his menacing voice, the recklessness with which he offered specific figures instead of hazy accusations.

Indeed, he had the audacity to renew his charges on the Senate floor. Fishing papers out of his briefcase, he embarked on an eight-hour, case-by-case analysis of what were now "81 loyalty risks." His speech was a master-piece of distortion of a two-year-old House of Representatives report drawn from unsifted State Department files that were in turn based, in many cases, on rumor and hearsay. McCarthy promoted a suspect in the House report from an "active fellow traveler" to an "active Communist," converted a man "inclined towards Communism" into simply a "Commu-nist," transformed a "friend of someone believed to be a Communist" into a "close pal of a known Communist." Even Senator Taft called it a "per-fectly reckless performance."

Questioned by a Senate investigating committee under the chairman-ship of Maryland Democrat Millard Tydings, McCarthy twisted and parried and obfuscated. Pressed for names, he threw out those of culprits with abandon and sometimes, it seemed, at random. After a four-month investi-gation the committee concluded that McCarthy had perpetrated a "fraud and a hoax" on the Senate.

But for many Republicans the Wisconsin senator was now changing from an embarrassment to an artillery piece in a wider war. Any Republi-can could use this freewheeling red hunter against the Democrats without taking responsibility for him. And conservative, isolationist Republicans could use him against moderate, internationalist ones. Soon Taft, despite private doubts, was encouraging McCarthy to "keep talking and if one case doesn't work out, he should proceed with another one." Moderate Repub-licans were prepared neither to embrace McCarthy nor to join his Demo-cratic foes. Rather they sought a middle ground that proved to be unstable. After seven moderates, headed by Margaret Chase Smith of Maine, issued a "Declaration of Conscience" that scored both Truman and the exploiters of fear, five of the seven backed away as they felt the political heat.

That heat was rising as the elections of 1950 and 1952 neared. McCarthy received hundreds of invitations to speak for his party's candidates, more than all other senators combined. He appeared in fifteen states, most notably in Illinois, where he backed Everett Dirksen, and in Maryland, where he opposed Tydings. In the 1950 elections Democrats kept control of both houses, but the result was seen as a stunning triumph for McCarthy, who brandished the scalps of at least five anti-McCarthy sena-tors, including Tydings. Later election analysis deflated McCarthy's role, but it was the perception that counted. To oppose the Wisconsin senator, it appeared, was to commit political suicide. A reporter noted in 1951: "The ghost of Senator Tydings hangs over the Senate."

His 1950 crusade elevated McCarthy to the high priesthood of Republican right-wing extremism. McCarthyism, said the rising young conservative William F. Buckley, Jr., "is a movement around which men of good will and stern morality can close ranks." The trick of McCarthy's success was becoming clear too. He appeared to have an almost instinctive skill for manipulating the press during an age of fear. He dexterously handled the wire services, which supplied most of the country's newspapers and radio stations with national news. He knew how to make headlines and catch deadlines; he knew that wild charges were played big while denials were buried among the want ads; he knew that the wilder the charge, the bigger the headline.

Covering McCarthy was a "shattering experience," remembered George Reedy of the United Press. "We had to take what McCarthy said at face value. Joe couldn't find a Communist in Red Square—he didn't know Karl Marx from Groucho—but he was a United States Senator." He was also both a reflector and an exploiter of the age of fear.

* * *

It was in this atmosphere of hostility and fear that Americans entered the election year of 1952. Already the sides were lining up but more so within the parties than between them. Senator Taft, cherishing his growing image of "Mr. Republican," had already made clear his aim to win the nomination that twice had eluded him. Harry Truman, beset by the triple charges of "K1-C2" (Korea, corruption, and Communism), was not expected to run again—unless some Dixiecrat or populist Democrat threatened to make off with the nomination. McCarthy continued to play his own game. And to the consternation of Taft Republicans, the hated "Eastern Establishment," after losing twice with Dewey, was preparing to foist another "New Deal Republican" onto the Grand Old Party.

That Establishment was busy recruiting its man. Dwight Eisenhower's wartime reputation and popularity, projected through his soldierly bearing and infectious smile, made him the favorite of both Democrats and Republicans for their presidential candidate. A stint as president of Columbia University, glamorized by the New York press, followed by his appointment as Supreme Allied Commander in Europe, had kept the general in the center of the public eye. By late 1951 Dewey, Senator Henry Cabot Lodge of Massachusetts, and a dozen other northeastern senators and governors were forming an Eisenhower organization and dispatching missionaries to NATO headquarters in Paris to draft their man.

Their man was proving curiously undraftable. Appealing to his ambition was useless. He had pretty well hit his peak in history, he liked to tell visitors, when he accepted the German surrender in 1945. "Now why should I want to get into a completely foreign field and try to top that?" The old soldier, now in his sixty-second year, also had the typical distaste of the American military man for the seamy side of politics. But he also had a sense of duty, even of indispensability, and it was on these vulnerabilities that the recruiters played while the "isolationist" Taft threatened to win the nomination, the Korean War festered, and China appeared more and more "lost." Ike wanted the expression of duty to take tangible form, however—nomination and even election by acclamation. As Taft proceeded to line up delegates early in 1952, it became clear that the convention would not draft the general. Playing on his combative instincts, the missionaries won his grudging agreement to come home and fight for his nomination.

By late spring, when he returned home, Ike was ready for a fight, but not for the one that awaited him. Somewhat familiar with the ideological warfare between the old guard and young moderates within the GOP, he still had not realized the intensity of that conflict. It was not merely isolationists versus internationalists, or eastern and western "coastal" Republicans against midwestern Republicanism. The GOP was virtually two parties, each with its own ideology, traditions, and policies, its own leadership, electoral following, institutional foundations in federal and state governments. These two parties, one entrenched in Congress and state legislatures, the other in the federal and state executive branches, ordinarily kept their distance, but they could not escape collision in the campaign for delegates to the GOP national convention.

The Taft and Eisenhower forces came into sharpest conflict in Texas, where anti-Truman Democrats, anti-Taft Republicans, and just plain "I Like Ike" voters sought to wrest convention votes away from the old-guard regulars. Fierce battles erupted in precinct caucuses when the regulars, many of them accustomed to holding these meetings in their front parlors, found "one-day Republicans" crowding in to vote for Ike. Some precinct bosses ousted the intruders, who then held rump caucuses out on the lawn; other "hosts" were shoved out of their own homes and had to hold their own rump meetings outside. The upshot, after the Taft-controlled state convention met, was a ferocious fight over two competing delegate slates to the national convention.

This kind of fight over delegates' credentials was nothing new; indeed, Taft could remember a similar battle between his father and Theodore Roosevelt in 1912. Whether a party should represent the old dependables who stuck with it in good times and bad, for power or profit or principle, or the independents and volunteers and irregulars who "raided" the party either from opportunism or from idealism was one of the oldest political questions, in both theory and practice. What was new was the skill of the public relations men around Eisenhower in elevating the matter to a transcending moral issue. Soon his forces were embarked not on a messy old credentials dispute but on a crusade for moral purity. THOU SHALT NOT STEAL, proclaimed Dewey, Lodge & Co. Ike forces waved signs: ROB WITH BOB and GRAFT WITH TAFT. Eisenhower joined with his followers in denouncing the "Texas steal." Taft offered to compromise, but how could the Ike crusaders compromise on a moral issue?

It was one of the more spurious "moral" issues in American history, but it was nonetheless effective. The Eisenhower forces won the credentials fight at the national convention in Chicago and then, with their strength augmented, held full command. There was hell to pay. Thrusting a limp, quivering finger toward the New York delegation, Taft stalwart Everett Dirksen, senator from Illinois, from the convention podium charged Dewey with taking "us down the path to defeat." He cried, "Don't take us down that road again!" Conservatives and moderates blasted one another on the convention floor. But Ike had the votes. Despite a prompt and friendly visit from the nominee, Taft left Chicago a deeply embittered man. His presidential road, like Dewey's in 1948, had come to an end. But he could not understand why. He had taken the traditional path toward the White House. He was "Mr. Republican." He asked a reporter, "Why do they hate me so?"

Could the two Republican parties remarry, at least for the campaign? It was a matter for negotiation. After demanding assurances from the nominee that he would exclude Dewey as Secretary of State from an Eisenhower cabinet and give the Taft forces equal representation, Taft was more conciliatory at a breakfast meeting on New York's Morningside Heights. Eisenhower, after barely looking at it, approved a statement making "liberty against creeping socialization" the central campaign issue, promising to "battle communism throughout the world and in the United States," and playing down the foreign policy differences between the two men.

Democrats would have viewed Ike's "surrender at Morningside Heights" with pleasure, except that they were plagued by their own divisions. Truman still planned not to run, but only if he could bequeath the office to an acceptable—i.e., pro-Administration—nominee. This ruled out an engaging young senator from Tennessee, Estes Kefauver, whose chairmanship of a committee investigating crime in politics had supplied Republicans with ammunition against White House "cronies." Southern

Democrats, still angry over the President's civil rights program, were planning once again to break out of the party tent in one direction or another. Truman's eye lingered on Adlai E. Stevenson, whose high-toned, good-humored governorship of Illinois was drawing national attention. But Stevenson was a curious political animal—he *liked* being governor and had little hankering for the White House. Offered the nomination by Truman, he declined. Pressed to run by hosts of Democrats ranging from Chicago bosses to Manhattan intellectuals, he repeatedly stated that he was not a candidate. To be sure, he did not issue a "Sherman," and some expert decoders of the Delphic utterances of politicians made much of his having said, not that he "would not" accept the nomination, but that he "could not." Others believed he had closed the door.

The vast majority of the delegates hardly knew Stevenson when this slight, balding, vibrant man welcomed them to Chicago in words of polished elegance and wit that many present would never forget. Here on the prairies of Illinois, he said, "we can see a long way in all directions." Here were no barriers to ideas and aspirations, no shackles on the mind or spirit, no iron conformity. Here the only Democratic governors chosen in a century had been John Peter Altgeld, a Protestant, Edward F. Dunne, a Catholic, and Henry Horner, a Jew. And "that, my friends, is the American story, written by the Democratic Party, here on the prairies of Illinois."

The delegates sat hushed, spellbound, as Stevenson turned to the Republicans. For almost a week "pompous phrases marched over this landscape in search of an idea, and the only idea they found was that the two great decades of progress in peace, victory in war, and bold leadership in this anxious hour were the misbegotten spawn of socialism, bungling, corruption," and the rest. "They captured, tied and dragged that ragged idea in here and furiously beat it to death. . . ." After all the denunciations of Washington he was surprised that his mail was delivered on time. "But we Democrats were not the only victims here. First they slaughtered each other, and then they went after us." This speech brought howls of laughter and wild applause, and helped produce Stevenson's nomination a few days later—one of the few genuine presidential drafts in American history.

With both nominees chosen, the election outcome turned on each candidate's capacity to unite and mobilize his party. Eisenhower's was the more formidable task. Placating Taft and the congressional Republicans was one thing; bringing around McCarthy and the McCarthyites was something else. Holding his nose, the general made the necessary concessions. In Indiana he shared a platform with Senator William Jenner, who had called Eisenhower's revered boss George Marshall a "front man for traitors" and a "living lie." In Wisconsin, under pressure from midwestern politicians and from McCarthy himself, he deleted from his speech a tribute to Marshall's "profoundest patriotism" in "the service of America."

But the harshest test of Eisenhower's effort to follow the high road while exploiting the low came with the revelation that running mate Richard Nixon, whom he had named in an effort to appease both Taft and the McCarthyites, possessed a "secret fund" fattened by businessmen. Although there was nothing illegal about the fund and the money had been used for legitimate campaign expenses, Nixon's charges of Democratic corruption exposed him to fierce counterattack. First the general allowed him to twist in the wind while Republican politicians and editors—most of them from the Eastern Establishment—urged the vice-presidential candidate to quit the ticket. Then he waited until Nixon delivered a maudlin television talk about his wife and his daughters and his dog, Checkers. Only after several hundred thousand or more telegrams and letters deluged the Republican party with expressions of support did he embrace Nixon as "my boy." The "boy" would never forgive Eisenhower for making him undergo this ordeal.

With biting humor Stevenson dug at these open sores in the GOP, quipping after the Eisenhower-Taft summit conference that Taft had lost the nomination but won the nominee, that the general was worried about Stevenson's funny bone but he was worried about the general's backbone. He liked poking fun at the war between the "two Republican" parties. But the Democratic candidate had his own two parties to deal with. With some Southerners ready to bolt again, the Democrats had adopted a platform exquisitely ambiguous on the key issue of federal fair employment legislation. They had chosen as Stevenson's running mate Senator John Sparkman of Alabama, whose record on civil rights was such that fifty black delegates had walked out of the convention. Stevenson was caught in the middle of this issue, while Eisenhower, inheriting much of Taft's symbolic and personal support in the South, took a conservative position on civil rights but a strong stand for ownership of the oil tidelands by the states. With the prestigious Senator Richard Russell applying steady pressure from the right, and black and white civil rights liberals from the left, Stevenson hoped that he could at least sweep the South in time-honored Democratic style.

But the South was no longer for the Democratic taking. Eisenhower proved to be the great unifier, just as his recruiters had hoped, and campaigned extensively in the South. Then, when he made the electrifying statement that he would "go to Korea"—after Stevenson had considered and rejected the idea as inappropriate for himself—election-watchers knew that the fight was over. The general swept the northern industrial states and carried Virginia, Florida, Texas, and Tennessee—but not the states of the "solid South" that had bolted the Democracy in 1948. Election analysis demonstrated that his winning margin was far more a tribute to his personal popularity than a victory for the GOP. Almost half the poor did not vote, but among the poor who did turn out, most voted for Ike.

"Someone asked me, as I came in, down on the street, how I felt," Stevenson told his weeping followers on election night. He was reminded of a story about Lincoln after an unsuccessful election. "He said he felt like a little boy who had stubbed his toe in the dark. He said that he was too old to cry, but it hurt too much to laugh."

The Price of Suspicion

The Senate Caucus Room, April 22, 1954. Bathed in brilliant television lights, senators, counsel, witnesses, bodyguards huddle around a small, coffin-shaped table, surrounded in turn by several score reporters. Men who are famous—and others who will be—are there: Joe McCarthy, smiling and frowning and giggling, his face heavier and stubblier than ever, the center of exploding flashbulbs; his aide, a smooth-faced young attorney named Roy Cohn; Joseph Welch, a little-known, old-fashioned-looking Boston attorney; Robert Kennedy, the twenty-nine-year-old minority counsel. Jammed into the room are four hundred spectators, including such Washington celebrities as Alice Roosevelt Longworth and "hostess with the mostest" Perle Mesta.

For weeks the eyes of the nation would be focused on this Senate cockpit. The formal issues seemed almost trivial, considering all the fuss: Did McCarthy and others put improper pressure on the Army in order to win preferential treatment for Private David Schine, Cohn's good friend; did Army officials use improper methods to deflect earlier McCarthy probes? The stakes in fact were much bigger. "They ranged from the integrity of the Armed Forces to the moral responsibilities of federal workers," in David Oshinsky's words, "from the separation of powers to the future of Senator McCarthy," pitting President against Congress, Republican against Republican, senator against senator.

The subcommittee chairman rapped an ashtray, the television lights brightened, the subcommittee's special counsel opened his mouth to speak, then:

"A point of order, Mr. Chairman. May I raise a point of order?"

Once again McCarthy was moving audaciously, outrageously, stealing the scene from all the others, putting himself at the center of the affair—and there he would remain day after day, exposing himself to millions of avid television watchers for 187 televised hours.

"Point of order, Mr. Chairman, point of order." The phrase engraved itself on the memory of a nation.

Fifteen months after Dwight Eisenhower had taken the oath of office the shadow of Joseph McCarthy lay across his Administration. At the moment the Wisconsin senator's target was the Army. It appeared, though, that he was attacking not only the usual suspects—Communists, fellow travelers, intellectuals, Democrats—but the very foundations of the republic: the armed forces, the Senate, the White House, even the churches. Earlier his man J. B. Matthews had charged in *The American Mercury* that the "largest single group supporting the Communist apparatus in the United States is composed of Protestant clergymen."

It was not as though the President had ignored the matter; it had been a source of attention, irritation, anger. But he had tried to defuse McCarthy rather than confront him. Ike's 1952 running mate, after all, had savaged Stevenson as an appeaser who "got his Ph.D. from Dean Acheson's College of Cowardly Communist Containment." In his Checkers speech, Nixon had attributed his slush-fund woes to those who had opposed him "in the dark days of the Hiss case." Later Nixon had charged that Stevenson "has not only testified for Alger Hiss, but he has never made a forthright statement deploring the damage that Hiss and others like him did to America because of the politics and comfort they received from the Truman Administration and its predecessors." To McCarthy these were weasel words. He had shown Nixon the real stuff, castigating Stevenson as the candidate of the *Daily Worker* and supporter of "the suicidal Kremlin-shaped policies of this nation."

The President raged at McCarthy privately but would not openly take him on. "I just will not—I *refuse*—to get into the gutter with that guy," he said to intimates. Moreover, he did not want to jeopardize his right-wing support in the Senate. A Republican White House, he hoped, would reassure and tame the Wisconsin "trouble-maker."

Such hopes were dashed within a month of Eisenhower's inaugural on January 20, 1953. Using as his vehicle the previously sleepy Permanent Subcommittee on Investigations, stacking it with loyal Republicans and dominating it as chairman, McCarthy went off on a rampage against the State Department, charging sabotage in State's Voice of America program, discovering communism in the Overseas Libraries Division, taking up cudgels against Eisenhower's friend Charles Bohlen, FDR's translator at Yalta. When the new President proposed Bohlen for ambassador to the

Soviet Union—a cold war nomination, considering Bohlen's record—McCarthy was infuriated. Bohlen was "at Roosevelt's left hand at Teheran and Yalta," he said. Dirksen orated: "I reject Yalta, so I reject Yalta men." After the "Yalta man" was confirmed Taft told the President, "No more Bohlens."

* * *

It was a severe burden on Eisenhower and the nation he now led that this legacy of the past rested so heavily on his Administration. Not since Herbert Hoover, at least, had a new President been better prepared to be Chief of State and chief foreign policy-maker. He had helped shape some of the nation's key policies abroad, such as its military and economic linkages with Western Europe. He had been trained from his West Point days to be a leader—to take charge, to plan ahead, to unite diverse men in common effort, to be consistent and persistent, to be "fair but firm." More and more distanced from Truman and the Democracy during the 1952 campaign, he was eager to launch new initiatives toward world peace and national security.

He had a typical piece of "Ike luck" when Joseph Stalin died only six weeks after he took office. Stalin had appeared increasingly paranoid during his last years; now he was succeeded by a collective leadership that seemed more moderate. Eisenhower's own collective leadership was bolstered by Republican majorities in House and Senate. Taft's election as Majority Leader in the upper chamber gave promise of a continuing collaboration between the President and the legislative leader who had fought him for the nomination and then fought for him in the election campaign.

To throw off the burdens of the recent past—the spiral of fear, the freezing of attitudes, the rigidification of policy—Eisenhower needed a Secretary of State who could devise and carry out fresh initiatives. His selection of John Foster Dulles seemed irreproachable, indeed almost inevitable. Grandson of a Republican Secretary of State under Harrison and nephew of a Democratic Secretary of State under Wilson, member himself of the American delegation to the Versailles peace conference of 1919, Dulles embodied the American foreign policy tradition. He was the one eastern internationalist whom Taft had approved for the job. To be sure, many found Dulles a windbag, a bore, and a prig. But the President could overlook such qualities in a man who seemed able to unite the two Republican parties and to make a fresh start in foreign policy.

The fresh start was slow in coming. Dulles seemed to maintain the worst of the Truman-Acheson cold war posture rather than shifting it. Like Acheson, he "approached relations with the Soviet Union as a zero-sum game," according to Gaddis Smith. "A gain in power for the United States was good. A gain for the Soviet Union was bad. An outcome of any issue that was advantageous to both sides was hard to imagine." The President could—and occasionally did—rein in his secretary. But Dulles was everlastingly at it, day after day, in speech after speech, junket after junket.

His rhetoric far surpassed his chief's. Eisenhower in his inaugural address warned that because "forces of good and evil are massed and armed and opposed as rarely before in history," it was all the more urgent to seek peace, especially since "science seems ready to confer upon us, as its final gift, the power to erase human life from this planet." Dulles in this same month of January 1953 declaimed that Soviet communism viewed people as "nothing more than somewhat superior animals," and that as long as communism held such conceptions, there could not be "any permanent reconciliation." He saw an "irreconcilable conflict." In the following months Dulles did more than negotiate with the hard-liners in Congress and in the country—he often represented them in Administration councils. Time and again he threatened to lay a blighting hand on the President's hopes and initiatives.

Thus Dulles's calls for liberation of Moscow's satellites and for "massive retaliation," which evoked countervailing fear and hostility in the Kremlin, went far beyond the President's vague calls for freedom for the captive peoples. At a time when Eisenhower was seeking to lower tension between the two sides in Korea and stabilize the front, Dulles was siding with Rhee's demands for reunification (under him) after a massive new "preemptive" strike to the north. At a time when Eisenhower was seeking to strengthen Western European unity and even help shape a "United States of Europe," his Secretary of State was threatening that the United States might go it alone. At a time when his chief was denouncing "book burning" in a speech at Dartmouth College (though he backed off a bit later), Dulles was still pressing for the clearing out of suspect volumes in overseas libraries. At a time when the President sought some stabilization of relations between Peking and Chiang's new government on Taiwan, Dulles favored "unleashing" the Nationalists for some kind of offensive on the mainland.

It was not that Dulles vetoed or openly sabotaged the President's plans and policies—in general, Eisenhower stayed on top of his Administration. Rather the Secretary of State frustrated that part of Eisenhower that wished to mobilize the forces for peace in the world and amplified that part of Ike that was a cold warrior. It was the old story of the "pragmatist" feeling his way, exploring opportunities, trying out initiatives, all the time that his true believer of a Secretary of State was scaring the adversaries—and even more the allies—half to death.

The tumultuous Middle East offered Eisenhower ample opportunity for "pragmatic" action. When Iran's Prime Minister, Muhammad Mossadegh, appeared soft on communism—he had accepted financial support from Moscow and political support from the Communist party in Iran—Eisenhower authorized a CIA-financed coup that drove Mossadegh out of office in 1953 and put Shah Muhammad Reza Pahlevi on his path to the throne. While the Administration was eager to help United States oil interests, Eisenhower's central motive was the "Soviet threat"; Eden reported to Churchill after a talk with the President that he "seemed obsessed by the fear of a Communist Iran." When the pro-Western government of Lebanon appeared likely to collapse in 1958 amid Christian and Moslem rioting, Eisenhower sent Marines into the country. In both cases the President had responded to what he perceived as a Soviet threat expressed directly or through "puppets"; in both cases he and his advisers miscalculated, for the real threat was militant Middle Eastern nationalism.

Still, Eisenhower's main accomplishment in his early years as President was what he did *not* do. After visiting along the Korean front lines, viewing the misery of the soldiers and sizing up the formidability of the mountainous terrain, he did not order an attack to the north. When the Chinese communists began to bombard the islands of Quemoy and Matsu off their coast late in the summer of 1954, the President rejected the advice of Air Force and Navy chiefs that the United States, together with Chiang, carry out bombing raids—including atomic bombing—on the mainland. Repeatedly, when the French were facing defeats in Indochina at the hands of the communist-led Vietminh, he resisted urgings of Vice President Nixon, of the chairman of the Joint Chiefs of Staff, and—off and on—of his Secretary of State to intervene with conventional and even atomic arms. "Five times in one year," observed his biographer Stephen Ambrose, "the experts advised the President to launch an atomic strike against China. Five times he said no."

Eisenhower's ability to say no to new departures in domestic policy as well as to adventurism abroad, his endless search for compromise and consensus, his acceptance of Establishment values led contemporary observers to describe his Administration derisively as the "bland leading the bland." By the 1980s historians were treating him more favorably, as fresh data revealed what political scientist Fred I. Greenstein termed his "hidden hand" legislative and political tactics, his effort to give a New Look—more atomic firepower, expanded Air Force, less cost for conventional arms—to his foreign policy, his concept of leadership as raising followers above their individualistic, short-term goals to embrace long-run moral goals. His main failing—lack of strong, consistent policy direction stemming from inability to link broad ends to explicit and specific means—reflected central ambiguities in this man of war who was also a man of peace.

Above all, in his presidency, a man of peace. For Eisenhower had to live with the horror of atomic war as few others did. On a June evening in 1955, as he was leaving the Oval Office, an aide hurried toward him to blurt out the fearful words—the enemy had attacked the United States—fifty-three of the biggest cities had been devastated—vast numbers were fleeing—there were uncounted dead—fallout had spread over the country. Casualty estimates were stupefying—up to 60 or even 100 million.

It was a mock exercise, of course—part of Operation Alert, an effort to simulate a real atomic attack. The President had instructed that he not be told in advance when the exercise would be mounted. If he "survived," he and his cabinet would be evacuated to a secret site in the Carolina mountains.

*   *   *

To build peace, time for Dwight Eisenhower ran short. Twelve weeks before he took office a hydrogen device as large as a two-story house, weighing some sixty-five tons, and almost a thousand times more powerful than the Hiroshima bomb, had obliterated a Pacific island a mile wide. Twelve weeks after taking office the President told a meeting of the American Society of Newspaper Editors that in exchange for certain Soviet concessions, including agreement on a "free and united Germany" and the "full independence of the East European nations," he was ready to sign an arms limitation agreement and to accept international control of atomic energy under a "practical system of inspection under the United Nations." He warned of a life of perpetual fear, of enormous financial costs. Struck even as he spoke by an intestinal attack that brought sweat, chills, and dizziness, he clung to the rostrum and went on:

"This world in arms is not spending money alone. It is spending the sweat of its laborers, the genius of its scientists, the hopes of its children." The cost of one heavy bomber equaled that of two fully equipped hospitals. A single fighter plane cost a half-million bushels of wheat. "This is not a way of life at all"—"it is humanity hanging from a cross of iron."

Late in August 1953 Moscow announced that it had tested an H-bomb. Before the United Nations in December the President proposed that the United States and the Soviet Union contribute part of their nuclear stockpiles to an international atomic energy agency. To this "Atoms for Peace" proposal the 3,500 delegates responded with a prolonged ovation, but the Russians, fearing it would enable the Americans to get ahead of them, answered with long stalling tactics. On March 1, 1954, the United States exploded a nuclear device on Namu Island in the Bikini atoll. The stupendous fireball lighted the skies for a hundred miles around; the wave of radiation sickened Marshallese on the islands and Japanese on an unlucky fishing boat, the *Lucky Dragon*. By now the H-bomb was becoming central to Western strategy; Britain and France would have the bomb before the decade was over.

The oratory continued while the atomic arsenals expanded. At a Geneva summit in the summer of 1955 the Soviets urged that the manufacture and use of atomic weapons be prohibited and that the armed forces of China, Russia, and the United States be limited to a million and a half men each. Eisenhower proposed that each nation give the other a "complete blueprint" of its military establishments and that each permit the other free photographic reconnaissance over its lands. The Russians rejected this "Open Skies" proposal as a bald espionage plot. A year later Adlai Stevenson, once again nominated by the Democrats, suggested suspension of nuclear tests; a year after that, in August 1957, the reelected President asked for a two-year suspension.

Eisenhower's initiatives were not working, nor were Moscow's. Fear continued to dominate diplomacy. And so did politics: Nixon had called Stevenson's proposal for a halt to nuclear tests "not only naïve but dangerous to our national security."

But the President could still display his greatest skill—not going to war. During the early 1950s both the Soviets and the Western powers became increasingly involved in the Middle East, largely because each side feared penetration of the area by the other. In part to neutralize a Soviet arms sale to Egypt, Dulles—at a time when the President was still recovering from a serious heart attack—first offered to help Egypt finance the building of the Aswan Dam, President Gamal Abdel Nasser's top economic priority, and then withdrew the offer. Both steps were taken in light of American strategic needs rather than the Egyptian people's needs. After Nasser nationalized the Suez Canal, Britain, France, and Israel, each for its own reasons, plotted—the term is not too strong—to retake the Suez. The Israelis drove into the Sinai while British and French forces attacked Egypt. A fully recovered and furious Eisenhower threw every ounce of his influence for a solid week into bringing the invasion to a halt. The President not only did not go to war—he stopped a war.

During this time came another and sterner test of Dulles declamation versus Eisenhower deescalation. Although "liberation of captive peoples" had been quietly dropped as an operational practicality during Eisenhower's first year in office, Administration propagandists kept alive hopes and expectations at home and abroad. In October 1956, after Poland was swept by rioting, a new leader, Wladyslaw Gomulka, warned Moscow defiantly that the Polish people would defend themselves against any effort to push them "off the road of democratization." Inspired by the Poles, Hungarians took to the streets against their Soviet-dominated government. Massive Soviet intervention followed against Hungarian "freedom fighters" hurling homemade Molotov cocktails at Russian tanks. Eisenhower's main concern was to give Moscow no reason to think that the United States would support the freedom fighters; he feared that Moscow might even start a third world war to maintain its hold on Eastern Europe.

"Liberation was a sham," wrote Stephen Ambrose. "Eisenhower had always known it. The Hungarians had yet to learn it."

Many on the Republican right shared such bitterness. Not least of these was Joe McCarthy, but in 1956 the Wisconsin senator could no longer threaten the President. The Army hearings had turned into a disaster for McCarthy, who revealed himself to the public as an inquisitorial bully. Near the end, after McCarthy had gratuitously pounced on a young, vulnerable lawyer, Welch said that he had not dreamed the senator could be so reckless and cruel "as to do an injury to that lad." When McCarthy, glowering and storming, resumed the attack, Welch told him to stop. "You have done enough. Have you no sense of decency, sir, at long last? Have you left no sense of decency?" The audience burst into applause. McCarthy was bewildered. Grim, sweating, he kept asking, "What did I do? What did I do?" Six months later the Senate formally "condemned" him for abusive conduct toward his fellow senators. In three years he was dead of alcoholism.

McCarthy left human wreckage behind him—men humiliated and browbeaten, their reputations tarnished. Among the diminished was Dwight Eisenhower. He had dealt with McCarthy in his own way, by indirection, by persuading others to attack him, by pronouncements that conspicuously failed to mention the senator by name, by blowing off steam to intimates, by various other "hidden hand" manipulations. He had damaged his foe, but he had never struck at his jugular. "Eisenhower's only significant contribution to McCarthy's downfall," according to a sympathetic biographer, "was the purely negative act of denying him access to executive records and personnel. Eisenhower's cautious, hesitant approach—or nonapproach—to the McCarthy issue did the President's reputation no good, and much harm."

McCarthy also left a legacy of unreasoning fear. Part of that legacy materialized weeks after the Army hearings ended, when Congress passed the Communist Control Act, in effect outlawing the Communist party, which was already moribund. The vote was overwhelming in each house. The author of the bill was Hubert H. Humphrey, Minnesota Democrat.

* * *

It was the communists in Russia, not in America, who posed the true challenge, and the challenge was not purely military. In October 1957 the Soviets launched Sputnik—"traveling companion"—the world's first man-made satellite. Sputnik II followed, carrying a dog and instruments. The feat was a "distinct surprise," Eisenhower admitted. The popular reaction at home astonished him even more. Americans were chagrined, astounded. The Russians were supposed to be far behind on such matters, to be backward in general. Americans indulged in an orgy of self-examination and scapegoating. Seizing on education as the source of the trouble, the authorities instituted crash programs in science and languages.

American scientists were already racing to loft their own Sputnik. After vast publicity a Vanguard rocket lifted off before television cameras. It rose for two seconds, attained an altitude of four feet, caught fire, crumpled down, and blew up. The world jeered. It was a hard time for Eisenhower. A committee headed by H. Rowan Gaither, Jr., had just given him a secret and frightening report that American military defenses were inadequate against the Russians, that Moscow had a huge nuclear arsenal, that its intercontinental ballistic missile would soon be operational, that the Soviet GNP was growing faster than the American, and more. The Gaither committee of experts was so frightened that three members urged an immediate preventive war. For the first time in its history, Eisenhower told Dulles, the United States was "scared."

Still, the President would not overreact. He knew—though he could not say so without compromising the source of his information—that the United States had great strategic superiority. But for how long? The Soviet challenge stirred him to one last effort, in the closing years of his Administration, toward détente with Moscow. And he now found himself dealing with a man in the Kremlin with whom it seemed possible to try such a venture. This was Nikita Khrushchev, who had emerged as the Soviet leader during the post-Stalin years.

Western leaders found Khrushchev almost a welcome relief from the grim gray men who had succeeded Stalin—and a striking contrast to the silent, implacable, paranoid Stalin. Short, broad, bald, no matter how well dressed he looked to Americans like an unmade bed. His earthiness, suspiciousness, rough speech revealed the "worker and peasant" origins of which he was proud; his shrewdness in Kremlin infighting, sense of timing, grasp of when to speak out with biting candor and when to be silent and patient reflected his long immersion in party affairs and foreign policy. At a showdown Plenum of the Central Committee, Khrushchev and his co-horts chastised Foreign Minister Molotov to his face for Stalinist, even "imperialist," interference in Tito's Yugoslavia, patronizing and arrogant intrusion into Polish affairs, blundering in approaches to Mao Tse-tung. There had probably never been another communist gathering, according to David Dallin, "at which so much unvarnished truth was spoken about Soviet behavior abroad." But the outcome had been carefully prepared: a solid vote against Molotov, followed by his "admission" of errors and his inevitable downfall.

Six months later, in February 1956, Khrushchev astounded the Twen-tieth Party Congress with a blistering attack on Stalinism—on its old as-sumptions that capitalist wars and violent revolutions were inevitable, that "peaceful coexistence" among nations with differing social systems was impossible. Amid perhaps uneasy cheers from the delegates, he castigated Stalin for his personality cult and dictatorial ways, for underestimating the American resolve to defend Korea, for his "lack of faith in the Chinese comrades," for his "shameful role" in Yugoslavia, and—jumping back more than fifteen years—for relying on his pact with Hitler and not prepar-ing for the Nazi attack. While Khrushchev and his allies made clear that the United States was still the great adversary, the speech signaled major departures in Soviet policy: a shift from bipolar confrontation to more conventional rules of multilateral diplomacy and pluralistic accommoda-tion; an acceptance of existing territorial arrangements in Europe; political rapprochement toward uncommitted neutrals and toward nationalist, even bourgeois, regimes; widening of the "socialist camp" to embrace indepen-dent communist states like China. And it was now clear that Khrushchev was cock of the walk.

Accepting an invitation from Eisenhower, the Soviet dictator in Septem-ber 1959 treated the United States with a visit. Khrushchev made the most of his twelve days, visiting the Eisenhowers in Washington and Camp David, appearing at the United Nations, seeing the sights in Hollywood and the Iowa heartland and industrial plants, all the while wisecracking, praising, arguing, criticizing, and complaining. His loudest complaint was that he and his party had not been allowed to visit Disneyland.

"Why not?" the dictator had asked as he reported to a Hollywood luncheon. "Is it by any chance because you now have rocket-launching pads there?" It was for his own safety, he had been told. "What is it? Has cholera or plague broken out there that I might catch?" His audience guffawed. "Or has Disneyland been seized by bandits who might destroy me?"

Khrushchev's visit survived such contretemps, however, and culminated in what came to be known as the "Spirit of Camp David." Though Khrushchev disappointed the President by appearing not at all impressed by the abundant American homes, highways, and cars that the President had arranged for him to see by helicopter—too crowded, expensive, and wasteful, the dictator said—he pleased his host by appearing more conciliatory about Berlin and agreeing tentatively to a summit meeting in Paris in August 1960.

A summit in Paris in the last year of his administration—the President now looked forward to this as the culmination of his efforts for peace. Could he will the means to this great end? As a man of peace he devoutly wished for détente with the Russians; as an old soldier he had to know what the Russians were up to, both as a military precaution and also as a means of keeping hard-liners and Pentagon spendthrifts at bay by assuring them that the Russians were not ready to go to war.

A remarkable new intelligence machine was serving this purpose—the U-2, capable of flying so high above the Soviet Union as to escape missile fire, but low enough to photograph military installations and preparations. It was this plane that assured Eisenhower of the Soviets' relative strategic weakness. Faced both by eager CIA demands for frequent flights and by warnings as to the potential Soviet reaction, the President monitored and limited the U-2 missions over Soviet territory. As the summit conference neared he cut the flights more sharply to avoid provoking Moscow. Finally he allowed one last foray by May 1. For fourteen days Russia was covered by clouds. On May 1 the weather cleared, and Francis Gary Powers took off from his U-2 base in Turkey for Bodö, Norway.

He never made it. The President was informed next day that the plane was missing and must be down inside Russia. Since the craft was equipped for self-destruct of both plane and pilot, Powers was surely dead. Eisenhower did nothing, on the assumption that Moscow would do nothing, at least publicly, in order not to jeopardize the summit. Eisenhower approved a statement that a weather plane had been lost. Next day the Kremlin published a photograph of a wrecked plane, calling it the spy plane—but it was not a U-2. Why? Khrushchev was luring the White House into a trap. The longer Eisenhower stuck to his story about a "weather plane," the more discredited he would be when the truth came out.

Then Khrushchev sprang his trap. He had "parts of the plane" and also "the pilot, who is quite alive and kicking." Hardly able to believe the news, the President now faced a terrible dilemma. He could admit that the Administration had lied but argue that Soviet secrecy had made overflights necessary. This might wreck the summit. Or he could say that the flight had been unauthorized. But as an old army man he could not confess that his outfit was out of his control; as President he could not legitimize charges that he had lost command of his Administration. Soon the Administration was caught in such a tangle of falsehoods, with the Kremlin joyfully exploiting every misstatement, as to leave Washington embarrassed, angry, and fearful of the implications for the summit.

"This was a sad and perplexed capital tonight," James Reston reported in *The New York Times,* "caught in a swirl of charges of clumsy administration, bad judgment and bad faith." The President was so upset that he talked briefly of resigning. He could hardly doubt the price to be paid: Khrushchev would not sit down at the summit with a President whose spy had invaded the Russian homeland—and on May Day, the worldwide communist holiday.

In retrospect, the incident was a microcosm of the ills—the fears, suspicions, misperceptions, and miscalculations—that had afflicted Soviet-American relationships for years. Just as the Kremlin had underestimated Washington's reaction to the invasion of South Korea, so Moscow underrated American fears of Soviet aggression—fears that in turn led to provocative spying. And typically men in the Kremlin viewed the whole affair not as a series of blunders but as a plot by the Pentagon or the CIA—perhaps by the President himself—to produce an incident that would abort the summit. The Americans repeated all their old errors: putting undue faith in intelligence technology, keeping "secret" the U-2 flights long after Moscow and other capitals—indeed, all but the American people—knew of them; allowing intelligence agencies too much influence over policy; evoking the worst of Soviet fears about intrusion onto their turf. Eisenhower and Khrushchev each underestimated the vulnerability of the other to hard-liners; hence each brought out the worst in the other.

It was one of the saddest moments in postwar history, for each of the leaders, in his better half, genuinely wished for détente. Eisenhower came off the worse. He went on to Paris, but the "summit was over before it started, all the hopes for détente and disarmament gone with it," in Ambrose's bleak words. He had only a few months left to see his Vice President, Nixon, defeated, a brash young Democrat elected, and no further progress toward détente. At least he could advise the nation. In his Farewell Address he pointed to the "conjunction of an immense military establishment and a large arms industry" and warned Americans that "we must guard against the acquisition of unwarranted influence, whether sought or unsought, by the military-industrial complex." The price of such acquisition could be the loss of freedom.

His great solace was that he had "kept the peace." People, he said later, asked how it had happened. "By God, it didn't just happen, I'll tell you that!" But he told a friend not long before his death in March 1969 that he had longed to bring world peace but "I was able only to contribute to a stalemate." Could anyone else have done better? Ike had the wry satisfaction of living through two Democratic presidencies for which the U-2 affair was a dress rehearsal—a minor flap compared to the real crises and stalemates of Cuba and Vietnam.

CHAPTER 6

The Imperium of Freedom

TOWARD the end of the 1950s the Soviet Union had about 3.6 million persons under arms, the United States about 2.5 million. Each nation maintained stupendous nuclear arsenals capable of devastating the other. With its more than 500 long-range B-52s, almost 1,800 medium-range bombers, twenty-three aircraft carriers, and three Polaris submarines, the United States was far ahead in the capability for continental attack or massive retaliation, while Soviet troops, tanks, land-based aircraft, and medium-range ballistic missiles confronted the European allies. British and other friendly forces bolstered the power of the West. Amid a remarkable variety of nuclear weapons—from recoilless riflelike Davy Crocketts for close-up infantry support to eight-inch howitzers to ballistic missiles—the Strategic Air Command wielded the most usable military might, for its "bombers could burst through the pervious screen that protected our opponent."

The nation's relative economic power was even more marked than its military. National economic productivity had grown strongly during the 1950s, as had the gross national product. Americans produced almost half the world's generation of electricity and large shares of its steel, copper, and coal. The nation's exports and imports dwarfed those of all other countries. In 1955 a congressional report had shown the United States leading the Soviet Union in virtually every dimension of economic power. "For the United States," economic historian David F. Noble summed it up, "the postwar decades were an expansive time, fertile ground for technological achievement and enchantment." Assured by their leaders—in this era before Sputnik—of their unrivaled military, economic, and industrial might, "infused with the pride, confidence, and triumphant optimism of victory, relatively unscarred by the actual horrors of war, and with the ruins of failed empires at their feet, Americans embarked upon their own ambiguous fling at empire."

An empire? Americans hardly thought in such grandiose terms. Yet their influence reached to the Caribbean, to Alaska and Hawaii, both of which became states in 1959, to old and to newly reconquered bases in the

Pacific, to their military protectorate Taiwan. Military, economic, diplomatic ties intertwined American power with Latin American nations through the Inter-American Treaty of Reciprocal Assistance of 1947, with European and Middle Eastern nations through the North Atlantic Treaty of 1949, with Australia, New Zealand, Pakistan, Thailand, and other nations through the Southeast Asia Collective Defense Treaty of 1954, with Japan and South Korea through mutual defense treaties. Dulles spent much of his time rushing from capital to capital repairing and refurbishing these ties. On the vast chessboard of Atlantic and Pacific power few doubted which nation held queen, castles, and knights.

European allies viewed American military and technological prowess with awe and fear. The Yanks' advanced aircraft, their H-bombs and capacity to deliver them, their magnificent flattops, along with their fancy big automobiles, refrigerators, computers, and other gadgetry, were the talk of European capitals. But foreigners feared that Americans with their awesome military power were like children playing with dangerous toys. European pundits wrote scorchingly of American pretensions of leading the "free world," of American soldiers and other visitors who scattered their dollars, Cokes, slang words, and bastard children across the Continent. French intellectuals attacked the new barbarism, while nourishing the consoling thought that Europe could serve, in Max Lerner's words, "the role of a cultural Greece to the American Rome—a Greece which, while conquered, takes the conqueror captive." Still, in the aftermath of the Marshall Plan most people in countries benefiting by the Plan admired America's "free elections" and other democratic institutions, saw the "real issue" as "communism and dictatorship versus democracy and freedom," and had faith in the Plan itself as aiding European economic recovery.

The Kremlin responded to Western militancy with its own provocations and interventions, threats and bluster, combined with occasional essays at détente. Behind its actions lay deep fears—of an increasingly independent and hostile China, a turbulent and unpredictable Middle East, unrest in its satellites that might lead to outbreaks of Titoism, a resurgent Germany. Above all Moscow feared renewal of the old threat of Western—now "capitalist"—encirclement. The view from Moscow was of American power stretching from the Aleutians through Korea and Japan to the Philippines, from Southeast Asia to Turkey and Greece up through Europe to Scandinavia. Acutely aware of his strategic nuclear inferiority, Khrushchev resorted even to bluff to conceal it—most notably when he flew the same squadron of his Bison bombers in circles around a reviewing stand at a 1955 Aviation Day ceremony.

Yet even uneasier and more mistrustful than the Russians in the late

1950s were most Americans. If a leader as levelheaded as Eisenhower could have been "obsessed" by fear of a communist Iran on the borders of the Soviet Union, it was hardly strange that many Americans, saturated from school days by talk of Soviet power and Bolshevik evil, should match fear with fear, anger with anger. Thus Khrushchev's paper-fort deception with his Bisons triggered in Washington a sharp "bomber gap" scare that in turn produced a quick boost in B-52 bomber-building. Visiting the United States, Europeans who viewed themselves as occupying the nuclear front lines were amused to find Americans huddling—intellectually if not physically—in bomb shelters. Americans during the 1950s found themselves feared in their image around the globe but fearful themselves of the future.

Not that most Americans worried about their survival as a nation. Having appointed themselves guardians of liberty, however, they feared for the survival of freedom in the Western world. As in the past, they were far more effective in saluting freedom than in defining it. But definition was crucial. FDR's Four Freedoms—of speech and religion, from fear and want—were only a starting point. What *kind* of freedom—individual, civil, economic, religious, ethnic? Freedom *for* whom—minorities, blacks, women, artists, intellectuals, censors of textbooks, extremists, pornographers, noncitizens? Freedom *when*—after World War II, after the cold war? Freedom *from* whom? The reds abroad? The "commies" at home? The "feds"? Corporation chiefs? Foremen? Deans? Religious zealots? Group and community pressures? It would become clear in the 1950s and 1960s that threats to these freedoms emanated from far more complex and numerous sources than the Politburos of Moscow and Peking.

THE TECHNOLOGY OF FREEDOM

The most striking aspect of freedom in America in the 1950s was its grounding in the nation's technological might and economic abundance. During the half century past, Americans had proved their capacity to outproduce their rivals in automobiles, domestic appliances, and a host of other manufactures; during the 1940s they had astonished the world with their feats in building ships and weapons. By the early 1950s Americans could—and did—boast that their per capita income of approximately $1,500 was roughly double that of the British and the Swedes, more than four times that of the Russians. With 7 percent of the world population, the United States had over 40 percent of the world's income.

Would freedom flower in America during the fifties amid such plenty?

The prospects were highly mixed. Historically freedom had flourished not where life was nasty, brutish, and short but in expanding economies that fostered equality of opportunity, more sharing, vertical and horizontal mobility. Still horrified by revelations about Nazi mass slaughter, shocked by new revelations about the monstrous "crimes of the Stalin era," many Americans valued their own liberties all the more. Yet the 1950s, at the height of cold war anxieties, turned out to be a decade of intolerance of other Americans' ideas. Individualism in the economic marketplace was not matched by individual liberty in the political and intellectual marketplace.

Advocates of the free market were happy with their economic freedoms during the Age of Eisenhower, however, and even more with their economic successes. "We have entered a period of accelerating bigness in all aspects of American life," proclaimed Eric Johnston confidently in 1957. "We have big business, big labor, big farming and big government." The former head of the United States Chamber of Commerce even mused whether this was the start of an age of "socialized capitalism." Certainly American business, if not "socializing," was consolidating, bureaucratizing, innovating, and proliferating at home and overseas. Over 4,000 mergers and acquisitions of manufacturing and mining concerns occurred during the 1950s—a dramatic number though almost 3,000 fewer than in the 1920s. Large firms took over smaller ones less to run risks than to minimize them; despite Joseph Schumpeter's warning of the "perennial gale of creative destruction," the survival rate of large firms during the decade was almost 100 percent. Elaborate systems of recruitment, personnel, information, and leadership training expanded in the big corporations, with the help of complex office machines and business school graduates.

The power of the American economy, however, lay far less in bigness and organization than in technological and scientific advances stemming from a century of experimentation and invention and later propelled by the imperative demands of two world wars and the cold war. And just as nineteenth-century army ordnance needs had promoted such important innovations as interchangeable parts, so world war needs fueled such varied practical achievements as penicillin, jet propulsion, and radar. Massive federal spending for invention and development carried on through the cold war years; by the late 1950s Washington was financing nearly 60 percent of the nation's total research and development budget. In one major respect, however, twentieth-century technology was more than simply a wider and more varied activity than that of the nineteenth. In Nathan Rosenberg's words, "an increasing proportion of technological changes" were now "dependent upon prior advances in systematized knowledge." Innovators were more dependent than in Edison's day on scientific disciplines such as physics and chemistry.

Some of the postwar advances in specific fields were spectacular. In October 1947, Captain Charles E. Yeager burst through the invisible barrier that had seemed to fix a limit to the speed of flight by flying the experimental rocket-powered X-1 faster than the speed of sound. In September 1948, an air force Sabre set a world speed record for jet fighters at 670 miles an hour; five years after that a Super Sabre became the first jet to cross the sound barrier, hitting 755, and in 1957 a Voodoo jet topped 1,200. The nuclear submarine *Nautilus* was reported to have used 8.3 pounds of uranium fuel to travel 60,000 miles. After the inglorious "Kaputnik" of the first Vanguard, the American space program made steady progress. And by 1960 the X-15 rocket plane was flying almost twice as fast as the Voodoo.

More down-to-earth, but crucial to a wider technology, were advances in the sector in which Yankee tinkerers had pioneered a century earlier with their milling and grinding machines. This was the machine tool industry. Severely depressed after its World War II expansion—300,000 machine tools were dumped onto the market after the war—the industry burgeoned during the cold war. Aircraft manufacture, a voracious consumer of machine tools, also became increasingly interlinked with the electronics industry, which was now producing its own miracles. Though eventually developing its own huge domestic market, for years electronics reflected wartime need for miniaturization of electrical circuits in proximity fuses for bombs, gunfire control mechanisms, radar and sonar. As late as the mid-1960s the federal government was still providing two-thirds of the "R&D" costs of the electrical equipment industry, which included such giants as General Electric and American Telephone and Telegraph.

Earthiest of all—and perhaps most important of all for its worldwide implications—was innovation in farming. Improved harvesters and other machines, combined with better fertilizers and sprays and new plant strains, produced higher output per acre, a vast increase in production, and a steep decrease in the total work hours in the United States devoted to agriculture. By 1960 8 percent of the labor force was occupied with farming, compared with 63 percent a century before. Hybrid corn, a systematic crossing of selected inbred lines, resulted in an increase in the average yield of corn per acre from 23 bushels in 1933 to 62 bushels in the mid-1960s. Thus hybrid corn research paid off handsomely, returning, it was estimated, seven times its cost by the mid-1950s. The lion's share of the boost in farm yield came from—and profited—huge family farms, commercial farms, and other components of "agribusiness" that controlled the production and marketing of key foods and fibers through vertical integration, while millions of small farmers and migrant farm workers clung to a precarious livelihood.

Out of the "Enormous Laboratory," as Max Lerner called it, poured not only new machines and gadgets but the makings of wholly new or immensely enlarged industries—television, antibiotics, electronics, jet aircraft, rocketry. But the actual laboratories that produced this cornucopia of hardware were also the scenes of quiet encounters in one of the oldest intellectual conflicts in America—between the ideal of pure science and the practices of applied science.

Many Americans still venerated the ideal of committed, disinterested science, of free, undirected research, of idle speculation and inspired hunch, of lack of pressure for immediate "practical" results, of a clear separation from the cash nexus—all the more because they could claim only one American in the past century who was comparable to such luminaries of European science as Darwin, Mendel, and Faraday. This was Josiah Willard Gibbs, the Yale mathematician whose work in thermodynamics, vector analysis, and statistical mechanics had belatedly won him an international reputation and whose laws of chemical energetics had enormous impact on processes as varied as the refining of oil, the synthesizing of rubber, and the separation of metals from their ores.

Of scientific eminences the postwar United States had its share—Isador Isaac Rabi and J. Robert Oppenheimer in physics, Hermann Joseph Muller in genetics, George Gaylord Simpson in evolutionary biology, Harlow Shapley in astrophysics, and scores of others. Yet most of these scientists largely depended on the theoretical work of Europeans. Most notably, it was the transformation of theoretical physics undertaken by Einstein, Heisenberg, and others in Germany that had laid the groundwork for atomic fission. Now, as the United States basked in its world economic supremacy, had the time and occasion come for Americans to make great theoretical contributions to pure science?

A century before, Karl Marx had warned that science could not for long be autonomous, that it was a social activity, that the nature of the demand for science was even more important than the quality of its supply. In America, science had to pay the piper. Giant corporations were eager to put vast sums of money into research, but of a special kind, really research *and development.* While the firms varied in their toleration of free research, sooner or later they expected a payoff in new inventions, patents, profits. The R&D departments emphasized team research, committee decisions, pooled facilities, narrowly focused investigation. There was little encouragement of idle curiosity, messing around, just looking out the window. "The underlying principle, rarely formulated precisely but ever present," a study concluded, "has been that originality can be organized; that, provided more people can be equipped with technical knowledge and brought together in larger groups, more new ideas must emerge; that mass production will produce originality just as it can produce sausages." Military needs created even heavier demands for scientific group-think and the organization man.

Politicians and scientists alike attacked the restrictions on Soviet science, but Americans could hardly be complacent. Aside from confronting seductive commercial and military demands on R&D, scientists had to contend with a popular double impulse to worship them and to fear them—the worship leading to unduly high popular expectations followed by disappointments, the fear leading to suspicion of their unorthodoxy and associations, as witness the classification of Robert Oppenheimer as a "security risk." Pleased by statements such as that of Harvard's president, James Conant—subsidies should go to persons, not projects—some scientists sought to protect their freedom of inquiry and communication by remaining in the universities. But scholars in the groves of academe were not free from political and press attacks, outside pressures for directed research, the temptations to undertake team projects and group authorship, the enticements of big corporate and military money.

Perhaps the major obstacle to "free science," however, was the empirical tradition in American scientific thought. The heroes of American popular science were the Thomas Edisons who disdained formal abstract knowledge or theorizing and preferred to tinker "by guess and by God" in their labs. It was this feet-on-the-ground compulsion that had channeled American genius into technology and engineering. If the nation were now to make as well a truly substantial contribution to scientific progress, greater freedom to reflect and to brood, freer play for the creative imagination, were crucial.

Possibly some of the applied scientists, ensconced in their big laboratories and snug in their teams, recalled the lot of Professor Gibbs. He had worked at Yale almost alone and undisturbed. He had no team. He had few close friends and few students. He had no wife or children. He had no pay from Yale for a decade or so, until Johns Hopkins in 1880 offered him a professorship with salary, at $3,000 a year. Only then did Yale put him on its payroll, at $2,000, "with prospects of an early increase."

*   *   *

One controversial application of "science" related to the men and women who in turn related to machines. Initially called "scientific management," it was first popularized by Frederick W. Taylor. After brilliant inventions of automatic grinding, forging, and tool-feeding mechanisms, Taylor had moved on at the turn of the century to time-and-motion studies designed to fit workers more closely to the imperatives of the machines and thereby increase industrial efficiency. The production process was functionalized and standardized by dividing it into measurable and controllable units of time and motion. Under Taylor's leadership the idea was picked up by a host of large corporations, including American Locomotive, Brighton Mills, Yale and Towne Lock. Machines, however, proved more easily manageable than men. Most workers preferred to follow their own motivations, rhythms, craft routines, group standards. A strike of molders in 1911 at the huge Watertown arsenal near Boston led to a government investigation and later a ban on Taylorism in government arsenals. A young assistant secretary, Franklin D. Roosevelt, imposed the ban in navy yards.

Turning away from Taylorism as a system of managerial dictation— Taylor himself declared each worker must become "one of a train of gearwheels"—some "industrial scientists" tried to civilize the production process by "human engineering" or "human relations." Psychologists and other social scientists were enlisted in this cause. Often benign in intent while manipulative in technique, "humanizing" turned out to be an effort to motivate workers through their own psychological processes rather than through managerial controls. Advocates of the method said that it promoted better communication, involved workers in at least minor decisions, enhanced "group feeling" and a sense of teamwork, fostered "leadership" as opposed to "control." During and after World War II, the idea of human relations in industry flourished.

Still the workers resisted. When Henry Ford II said that solving "the problem of human relations" would immensely speed up "progress toward lower costs," men and women on the line could wonder whether their welfare or lower costs and higher profits were the goal. Union heads spoke sarcastically of foremen receiving training in the art of convincing workers "that they really are deeply beloved by the boss," of employers "trooping to the special classes at Harvard" to learn that while the bosses were in business for a fast buck, workers reported to the plant each morning "for love, affection, and small friendly attentions."

A thirty-seven-year-old worker, interviewed at home, described what real life was like "on the line." His job was to spot-weld the front cowling onto an automobile underbody.

"I take a jig off the bench, put it in place and weld the parts together." The jig was all made up in advance. "Takes me one minute and fifty-two seconds for each job. I walk along the line as it moves. Then I snap the jig off, walk back down the line, throw it on the bench, grab another just in time to start on the next car."

He did this eight hours a day, with a breather in the morning and afternoon and a half-hour for lunch. "Sometimes the line breaks down. When it does we all yell 'Whoopee!' "

He hated his work. "I like a job where you feel like you're accomplishing something and doing it right." But everything was laid out for him. "The big thing is that steady push of the conveyor—a gigantic machine which I can't control." He had ideas for improvements but no one asked him. "You go by the bible."

Why not quit? "I'll tell you honest. I'm scared to leave." He was getting good pay, was on the pension plan, the lighting and ventilation were good, he could use the plant hospital. "Sorta trapped—you get what I mean?"

So how did he cope? By sharing the "misery" with his partner. "We gripe about the job 90 percent of the time." By walking out with the others when something intolerable happened—like when a guy was "bounced" because he was slow on the line. By snapping at his family when he got home, his wife added. The people who ran the plant, the worker said finally, were "pretty good guys themselves." But "you're just a number to them. They number the stock and they number you." He was just so much horsepower. "You're just a cog in the wheel."

His wife often wished he'd get another job. "He comes home at night, plops down in a chair and just sits. . . ."

If workers were not happy with their machines, applied scientists could invent a new machine that had less need of workers. This was automation. Mushrooming during the 1950s, the automatic equipment industry reached annual sales of over $6 billion by the end of the decade. World War II needs had hastened the development of electrical servomechanisms that operated on the principle of input-output flow and feedback in a continuously self-correcting control loop. Stimulated by such advances, the industry took off after the war and was soon integrating digital computers, sophisticated programming techniques, and vast data and memory banks into elaborate remote-control systems, including the automation of whole factories. By 1951 a Ford engine plant was feeding castings, already produced in an automated foundry, into precision broachers that machined the top and bottom of a cylinder block in thirteen seconds. Exclaimed an observer, "It just goes 'whoosh' and it is done."

"Automation is a magical key of creation," proclaimed the National

Association of Manufacturers. "Guided by electronics, powered by atomic energy, geared to the smooth, effortless workings of automation, the magic carpet of our free economy heads for distant and undreamed of horizons." Others were less euphoric but argued that automation would shrink the number of boring and degrading repetitive tasks, raise educable workers to higher levels of skill and pay, lessen worker fatigue, depression, and unrest.

Still others were not at all enchanted by the "whoosh." Union leaders stood *en garde*. The problem was not whether unions were for or against automation, said James B. Carey, president of the International Union of Electrical Workers. "The problem is whether or not the American people and our free society will be subjected to vast dislocations during the coming ten to twenty years, when the automatic operation of many industrial and clerical processes will be introduced." *Fortune* had published a photograph of the "old production line"—a vast room full of workers individually tending their machines—followed by drawings of the proposed "automatic factory." Not a worker was to be seen in the drawings—not even the ornery old "parts inspector." A photoelectric scanning device would do his job.

At a congressional hearing late in 1955 President Walter Reuther of the Automobile Workers roundly denounced the NAM's portrayal of automation as part of industrialization's "Second American Revolution." Had the NAM forgotten the misery that accompanied the first? Reuther asked. Displaced workers would not give up family ties, local roots, and neighborhood belongingness to go off to new jobs, even if they could find them and were young enough to take them. "Will automation mean the creation of whole new communities in some areas, while others are turned into ghost towns? How can we increase the market for goods and services sufficiently, and quickly enough, to match greatly accelerated increases in productivity?" Industry replied that displaced workers could find better jobs under automation, indeed that automation would create a bigger pie and "everybody's slice will be larger."

While the argument waxed, so did automation. Ford helped lead the way, with its partially automated cylinder-block line and automated production of crankshafts and small parts. As the number of workers "on the line" increased and the number doing more skilled "bench work" on parts and subassemblies dropped, auto worker militancy fell. It had been the more skilled workers, such as metal trimmers and torch welders, with their comradeship and critical production role, who had sparked the great strikes and demonstrations. "Automated" workers appeared to be psychologically atomized.

*   *   *

It was this wider impact of automation and of the tendencies that accompanied it—toward bigness, bureaucratization, even bondage—that concerned a wide array of social observers. Deep concern over such tendencies was almost as old as the trends themselves. From the rampaging machine wreckers at the dawn of the industrial revolution to the latest walkout in protest against automation, human beings had feared the machine as a threat to their status, income, security, and pride. Marx had seen that productive forces rising from technological-social change both reinforced the social order and undermined it. A century before Ford's automation William Morris fought to preserve handicrafts against the ravaging advance of the machine.

The Englishman Samuel Butler wrote in his 1872 anti-utopian novel, *Erewhon,* that man is supposed to be the master and the machine the servant, but "the servant glides by imperceptible approaches into the master," and now man is overly dependent on his "servant," and his very soul is becoming a machine-made thing. Man is in bondage; he can only "hope that the machines will use us kindly."

By the 1950s there was less concern over the economic and industrial effects of automation and other technological developments than over the psychological and social. Sociologists feared that the obsessive focus on production, combined with the fragmentation of workers' lives into numbing pressure on the job and emptiness outside it, in the long run would impair both efficiency and the health of the whole culture. Daniel Bell noted Freud's observation that work was the chief means of binding an individual to reality. "What will happen, then, when not only the worker but work itself is displaced by the machine?" Many social scientists were influenced by the work of Lewis Mumford, who in *Technics and Civilization* and other writings had graphically pictured the machine as part of a system of power, superfluous production as "purposeless materialism," and technology as increasingly the master of man. Two technologies existed side by side, Mumford wrote in the wake of the 1950s, "one authoritarian, the other democratic, the first system-centered, immensely powerful, but inherently unstable, the other man-centered, relatively weak, but resourceful and durable." It was time for human interventions in behalf of human alternatives.

The human use of human beings—this was the particular concern of Norbert Wiener, who published a book with this title at the start of the 1950s. A professor of mathematics at MIT and author of *Cybernetics,* which examined the dynamic role and implications of feedback in purposeful machines and animals, Wiener shared with a wide public his fears that "thinking machines" would render the human brain obsolete, especially in an era of mammoth war technology.

But what precisely was the impact of the machine, especially automation—and what could be done about it? During the 1950s the social scientists' diagnosis was twofold: alienation and *anomie*. Definitions of these phenomena varied widely, and hence diagnosis and prescriptions did as well. Alienation—from work, from family and community, from self? The standard answer was: all of the above. Specialization, compartmentalization, and routine left workers with little sense of accomplishment, fulfillment, or creativity on the job, and this emptiness carried over into life outside the workplace. But was the essential problem—both on the job and off it—the kind of powerlessness that Marx had analyzed, or the kind of "meaninglessness" that Karl Mannheim had seen as robbing persons of the capacity to make decisions, or the kind of normlessness that Emile Durkheim long since had analyzed in studies of *anomie*, or the sense of isolation and self-estrangement that was becoming the focus of social psychologists in the 1950s? Great disputes arose about these questions, with the social analysts themselves divided by discipline, specialization, and ideology.

The diagnosis of *anomie* aroused the sharpest concern, for it applied to a person's whole life. Defined broadly as the collapse of social norms that regulate social attitudes, expectations, and behavior, a condition of *anomie* could have a variety of effects: a normlessness marked by the feeling that "anything goes"; a hunger for direction and authority that might lead to a turning toward autocratic leaders; a craving for reassurance from peers and superiors; a proclivity to manipulate others in a culture lacking standards of more benign human interaction; even a tendency to rely on what Robert K. Merton called mysticism—"the workings of Fortune, Chance, Luck." But *anomie* remained a somewhat amorphous concept, overly extended, as Melvin Seeman complained, to a variety of social conditions and psychic states such as personal disorganization and cultural breakdown.

Inescapably the cardinal question arose—by what standard, what principle, what central value was the impact of technology being measured? Social observers were remarkably agreed: the test was freedom in all its dimensions and in all its equivalents such as liberty, liberation, individuality. Virtually every idea and program was advanced and defended by reference to this overriding value. "In the present situation of material and intellectual culture," wrote Herbert Marcuse, a philosopher of the émigré Frankfurt school, "the problem of values is, in the last analysis, identical with the problem of freedom." That one idea covered all that is "good, right and admirable" in the world. "Freedom—and this is the profound result of Kant's analysis—is the only 'fact' that 'is' only in its creation; it cannot be verified except by being exercised."

Marcuse had his own very definite idea, however, as to what freedom was or should be. Freedom was liberation from an increasingly impersonal, bureaucratic, oppressive technology, from the long and oppressive hours of work that drained people of their humanity, from the restrictions on human spontaneity, creativity, erotic fulfillment, and sensuous joy—restrictions of a Freudian as well as Calvinistic origin. The pursuit of happiness was the quest for freedom; indeed, freedom *was* happiness, in the fullest dimensions of both these noble concepts.

But other acolytes of Freedom saw different dimensions. They were not only like blind men feeling different parts of the elephant; each was loudly touting his part of the elephant as the whole elephant. For over two centuries Americans had debated and squabbled and even warred over the definition of freedom. During the 1950s the quarrel turned into a cacophony.

THE LANGUAGE OF FREEDOM

"We are children of freedom," Dean Acheson had proclaimed. All agreed, though not all knew what he meant. During the 1950s American leaders proclaimed freedom throughout the world and for all the world. Conflict and confusion over the principles and practices of freedom did not deter the ideologues of freedom from prescribing it for all. Even before Pearl Harbor, Henry Luce, editor-in-chief of *Time* and *Life* and *Fortune,* had urged the British to follow "America as the dynamic center of ever-widening spheres of enterprises, America . . . as the Good Samaritan, really believing that it is more blessed to give than to receive, and America as the powerhouse of the ideals of Justice and Freedom." Though Luce had some second thoughts, at the end of the 1950s he struck the same note: "The founding purpose of the United States was to make men free, and to enable them to be free and to preach the gospel of freedom to themselves and to all men."

Not only pundits but philosophers sounded this theme. Sidney Hook spoke for many of his fellow intellectuals when he urged on them the duty to publicize the "elementary truth" that what divided the world was "the issue of political freedom versus despotism." Politicians long before had climbed aboard the Freedom bandwagon with alacrity. If Roosevelt's Four Freedoms appeared a bit tattered and weather-beaten by now, many Americans remembered that his so-called "Economic Bill of Rights" had spelled out those freedoms in a most specific way, that Truman had sought to implement them, and that even Eisenhower was paying more than lip service to them.

To celebrate Freedom was to celebrate America, and vice versa. When Luce proclaimed in 1941 the belief—shared, he said, by "most men living"—that "the 20th Century must be to a significant degree an American Century," he laid out the peculiarly American ideals and institutions that must be shared with others—"our Bill of Rights, our Declaration of Independence, our Constitution, our magnificent industrial products, our technical skills." The reaction was not wholly favorable. Reinhold Niebuhr found an "egotistic corruption" in the very title, a critic dubbed Luce the Cecil Rhodes of journalism, and Henry Wallace countered Luce with a proclamation of the century of the common man. Was this the new American imperialism? Luce later talked less about the American Century but still pushed the doctrine.

Embarrassments occasionally marred this glowing portrait of Freedom versus Autocracy. Leading American intellectuals became furious over "party liners' control" of a 1949 Cultural and Scientific Conference for World Peace at New York's Waldorf-Astoria Hotel. Sidney Hook himself had been denied the rostrum to offer a paper disputing the Marxist doctrine of "class truth." In reply such European and American luminaries as André Malraux, John Dos Passos, Ignazio Silone, Tennessee Williams, Arthur Koestler, and Hook met in Berlin in June 1950 to inaugurate the Congress for Cultural Freedom. Supporting messages arrived from Eleanor Roosevelt and Niebuhr. After properly flaying totalitarian thought control, a number of participants proclaimed that the West must take its stand on communism—it was "either-or." Condemning those who preferred "neither-nor," the Congress set up a nucleus of internationally known writers who would have no truck with "neutrality" in the struggle for freedom. It would later develop that the activities of the Congress in the 1950s and 1960s were subsidized in part by the CIA, which disbursed funds through fake foundations.

Still, the American intellectuals did not need Washington gold to stiffen their resolve. Their views sprang from the very core of their belief in individual liberty and human rights. And they gained immeasurably both in their self-confidence and in their influence from their conviction that while the other side was ideological, their own position was not. They contended that after the passions of the New Deal era, the struggle with Hitlerism, and the polemics of the cold war, Americans were spurning ideology as the "opium of the intellectuals," in Raymond Aron's words, or coming to the "end of ideology," in Daniel Bell's. "Looking back from the standpoint of a newly-achieved moderation," wrote sociologist Edward Shils, "Western intellectuals view the ideological politics of Asia and Africa, and particularly nationalism and tribalism, as a sort of measles which afflicts a people in its childhood, but to which adults are practically immune."

Picturing ideology as a form of childhood measles was a curious indulgence on the part of intellectuals who themselves were acting as ideologists by any neutral definition of the term. If an ideology consists of a comprehensive set of goals or values, reflecting the mobilized attitudes of a large section of the public, expressed through institutions such as the press and the state, and legitimized by appropriate political, economic, and other establishments, then postwar Americans indeed possessed an ideology that was brilliantly expressed by its pundits and philosophers. It was an ideology of hazy, undefined ends and richly differentiated means—moderate and incremental policy-making machinery, a politics of bargaining and accommodation, a polity rich in voluntary associations and pluralistic groupings, all leading to a mixed economy and a stable, balanced, consensual society.

Ultimately this kind of society reflected a political ideology of consensus and compromise. Men of ideas such as Hook, Bell, Schlesinger, and Daniel Boorstin often differed on specific issues and reforms, but they struck historian Richard Pells as tending "to elevate existing American customs and institutions to a set of normative ideals." If they were more interested in analyzing society than in reforming it, however, their "retreat from ideology" did allow them to focus on current economic and political realities, Pells granted. "At the same time, their high regard for pragmatism and stability, together with their dread of fanaticism and upheaval, were reasonable and humane reactions to the catastrophic experiences of the twentieth century."

*   *   *

It was not that the social critics had wholly deserted their old vocation of judging their own culture. Even though their ideas had reflected the ideals of the European Enlightenment—but without passion, as Shils suggested—those ideas continued to arouse disputes within the still compelling trinity of liberty, equality, and fraternity. Amid the relative affluence of the 1950s critics now appeared less troubled by the lack of real equality of opportunity for the less privileged, far more concerned about the meaning of freedom for the middle classes and the threat to that freedom from solidarity of a smothering suburban kind. Most of the critics deplored the vast disparities in income and welfare among Americans—who could not?—but many of them now focused on psychological and cultural trends within the middle class rather than economic and social deprivations within the working class and the poor. Even the anxiety over automation amounted to a worry over psychological deprivation rather than over bread-and-butter issues of take-home pay.

And looking out over the social and physical landscape surrounding the cities, critics felt they had plenty to worry about. Huge eight-lane highways were grinding their way through the working-class sectors into the greener areas beyond, bringing in their wake concrete cloverleafs, shopping malls, towering apartment houses, and—much further out—suburban ranch houses complete with swimming pools, manicured greens, picture windows, and outdoor barbecue pits. These were the baronies of the new middle classes, "from the managerial employees and the 'idea men' in the talent professions at the top," Max Lerner wrote, "to the file clerks and sales girls at the bottom: a formless cluster of groups, torn from the land and from productive property, with nothing to sell except their skills, their personality, their eagerness to be secure, their subservience and silence."

The new middle classes, bursting with achievers and achievers-to-be, with postwar "baby-boomers," with creative skills, with ladders of upward mobility, were the source of enormous energy and talent in the America of the 1950s, and a source too of social and political equilibrium. But critics, even aside from the intellectual disdain for picture windows and barbecue pits, worried about more than dreary suburbs and empty lives. They fretted over psyches. A central fear carried over from earlier work by Erich Fromm, a German philosopher and psychoanalyst who had emigrated to the United States after Hitler's seizure of power. In 1941 Fromm published *Escape from Freedom*, which held that, upon the lifting of feudal ties and hierarchy, Protestantism had produced fearful and alienated persons, that industrialization had forced on such persons competitive, insecure lives that left them fearful of economic crises, loss of jobs, and imperialistic wars, and that the outcome was a tendency to submit to authoritarian leaders who offered them feelings of involvement, security, and power. This was the road to fascism. While Fromm feared these tendencies in all strata, he and his followers saw the middle classes—especially the lower middle classes—as most vulnerable to the appeal of fascism.

Other social critics eschewed such apocalyptic visions but they had major concerns of their own. In 1950 David Riesman, a University of Chicago social theorist still in his thirties, gained almost instant attention with *The Lonely Crowd*, a study of the "other-directed" personality that had replaced the "inner-directed" product of the Protestant ethic, which earlier had superseded the "tradition-directed" member of a hierarchical society held in the family embrace of clan, caste, and castle. In the affluent, leisure-minded postwar era, Riesman's other-directed man, anti-individualistic, group-centered, and conformist, put social solidarity and harmony over his own individuality and was ready to market his personality rather than his skill or creativity. *The Lonely Crowd* was studded with memorable phrases and insights: the oversteered child—from Bringing Up Children to Bringing Up Father—from craft skill to manipulative skill—from the bank account to the expense account—heavy harmony and lonely success—the automat versus the glad hand—captains of industry and captains of consumption.

In this book and in *Individualism Reconsidered*, a collection of essays, Riesman explored the implications of the new conformity for freedom. The pressure of the group on most individuals was so profound, he contended, that they doubted both their ability and their right to stand on their own. How then to protect the freedom of the individual, especially for the solitary man? Only by an appeal to resources within the person, to a heightened self-consciousness, an awareness of potentials and inadequacies, the will to exercise a freedom to make choices in a realm somewhere between anarchy and conformity. Ultimately Riesman sought to find a balance between individuality and comradeship.

Another social critic, William H. Whyte, Jr., wrote even more urgently about the influence of the scientific managers, the recruitment bias toward team players and mediocrity, the corporate demand for togetherness, adjustment, compromise, and conformity. A Princeton graduate and long-time *Fortune* editor, Whyte followed the spoor of his Organization Men in multiversities and suburbia and their flowering in the hierarchies of corporation boards, law factories, hospitals, banks, the military, education, and organized religion. The old-fashioned boss wanted only a man's sweat, he wrote, the modern boss his soul. "Group-think," company loyalty, committee decision-making were the order of the day.

Whyte's central concern was over the personal freedoms of individuals, their liberation from the group, the office, the organization. His solution, like Riesman's, was to appeal to the individual to be an individual, to broaden freedom within the group or organization. Nonconformists, however, must recognize the genuine needs of the organization even as they explored crevices, escape mechanisms, room at the bottom. Was this enough? Even Whyte seemed unsure.

Hailed as the latest in social criticism, the work of both Riesman and Whyte had old-fashioned assumptions and goals. Their appeal to the individual to win liberation from group, community, and office was hardly more than a sophisticated modernization of the eighteenth- and nineteenth-century search for liberty from church and state. Such Bill of Rights liberties were fundamental but were they enough? What was freedom *for?* Released from their social or other bonds, how could human beings define and achieve more positive freedoms—even those as simple and fundamental as FDR's Four Freedoms? Riesman and Whyte and their colleagues grappled with this kind of question too, but at best they could foresee some kind of murky balance between autonomy and togetherness. Hence they appeared to leave humankind in an existential predicament.

Herbert Marcuse did not share such intellectual inhibitions. Borrowing heavily from Hegel as well as Marx, he explored the interiors of freedom and proposed a dialectical consciousness able to perceive an alternative to any given reality and to use reason to judge between true and false needs. To think dialectically was freedom itself, the vital creative act. Marcuse wanted theory geared to human needs; he wanted the productive system to serve the needs of the entire society; he wanted people to test all the possibilities of erotic and intellectual fulfillment; he wanted them to convert their bodies into instruments of pleasure. But the means of reaching this utopia he left fuzzy.

And so the acolytes of Freedom argued and agonized over its meaning in a modern age. If intellectual progress seemed slow—if the very terms were misty, if the content of Freedom was so comprehensive as to seem all-inclusive, if the priorities among types of freedom lacked precision, if the ways of expanding freedom ranged from the overly utilitarian to the foolishly utopian—if all this was true, at least the theorists and practitioners of Freedom were bumping up against its wider and deeper dimensions, organizational, industrial, psychological, cultural, and sexual.

*   *   *

At the very heart of the American idea of freedom were still the noble "First Freedoms" of thought and speech, press and religion. And of these freedoms none was more vigorously pressed and expressed in the fifties than the right of newspapers and other media to offer information and opinion without interference by public authority or hostile group. Even as the press proclaimed and practiced freedom, however, the media faced threats to their liberties far less from outside foes than from internal tendencies toward consolidation and conformity.

Automation continued to transform the production of newspapers as it did other industries. Mergenthaler's Blue Streak Comet bypassed the venerable Linotype keyboard by using teletype tape for matrix assembly. Harris-Intertype's Monarch speeded up slug-casting by tape that performed over ten operations per second. Old-time newshawks, weaned on their Linotype, looked on in amazement as tape-triggered brass matrices streamed into the assembly, "making a clinking rhythm like that of a poker player at Las Vegas riffling silver dollars," *Editor & Publisher* reported, "and quicker than you could say 'aces back-to-back,' column-width slugs lined up at the rate of fourteen per minute." Technology continued apace. By the late 1950s Interstate's Fotosetter, arraying characters by photography on acetate film for the printing plate, was offering a variety of type sizes. Even the larger dailies were now using the wire services' teletypesetters that transmitted tape ready for the composing machines.

Enormously expensive, the new machines called for heavy investments that in turn encouraged newspaper consolidations. William Randolph Hearst's death at the start of the decade and the succession of his five sons as heads of Hearst Consolidated Publications were a reminder that consolidation was one of the oldest habits in the newspaper game, even under the aegis of flamboyant tycoons like the erratic crusader and art collector of San Simeon. By 1960 hundreds of newspapers were organized in "groups," a term the trade preferred to "chains." The new Hearst—but far more reserved in manner and provocativeness—was Samuel I. Newhouse, who controlled the Portland *Oregonian,* the St. Louis *Globe-Democrat,* and over a dozen other major papers and magazines. Newhouse astutely combined mergers and cost-cutting techniques. The extent to which consolidation led to conformity—or on the other hand provided papers with the financial capacity *not* to conform—remained a simmering issue in the newspaper world.

What was not in dispute, however, was that newspapers had become big business—and were assuming the views that went with it. The great majority of newspapers—and an even larger proportion of total newspaper circulation—had been Republican for so long that people took the one-party press almost for granted; some analysts concluded that many readers simply discounted the conservative bias of editors and columnists. More insidious and hence more influential was the press's tendency toward conformity. By using a term like red, Marxist, socialist, or reactionary, Max Lerner wrote, the newspapers "cast it outside the pale of discussion. By a black magic they place a taboo on it." Equally insidiously, many newspapers played it safe, featuring comics, crossword puzzles, and games and dramatizing sensations of crime and sex at the same time that their editorial pages were monuments of insipidity.

In the decade of the growing cold war the most marked effect of press conformity was to rally around the cold war. A *Protestant* magazine article charged that the press and radio "first lay down a terrific barrage against the Red Menace. Headlines without a shred of substance shriek of atom bombs, or plots to overthrow our government, of espionage, of high treason, and of other blood-curdling crimes." This was the prelude to labeling *all* opposition as "red." A longtime press-watcher, Curtis MacDougall of Northwestern University's journalism school, noted that when an Associated Press correspondent found no war fever in Moscow, his dispatch was buried in inside pages; if he had reported the opposite, it would have been headlined. Polls indicated that the percentage of Americans who viewed a third world war as inevitable rose steadily from 32 percent in late 1945 to 73 percent in early 1948. Many Americans, influenced both by official and press hysteria and demagoguery at home and by events abroad, obviously did see a red menace.

Later it seemed apparent that most journalists were not biased in their reporting but rather, emerging as they did from the same class and cultural environment, shared cold war assumptions that dominated their perception of events. These assumptions made it more tempting for journalists not only to report happenings but to take part in them. The austere Walter Lippmann had a notable role in conceiving and shaping as well as reporting and analyzing the Marshall Plan. Some reporters complained of being "used" by government, others boasted of it, but in fact officials and reporters were each using the other, for their own purposes. This intertwining of government and press became so close during the 1950s that Douglass Cater, a journalist himself, described the press as the fourth branch of government, full of journalistic brokers and middlemen, compartmentalized much like the government itself, trading information with publicity-seeking politicians, and exerting an influence on government that astonished visitors from abroad—especially British journalists, who generally maintained a certain deference toward the cabinet government in London.

It was not an era for journalistic innovation. Would-be enterprisers in publishing could hardly forget the sad story of the newspaper *PM,* which had risen in the early forties and then fallen despite the brilliant editorship of Ralph Ingersoll, heavy advances by Marshall Field III and other investors, and reporting by a stable of top-flight writers. FDR himself had welcomed the new paper, in part because its refusal to take advertising, Roosevelt wrote Ingersoll, "appeals to me as a new and promising formula for freedom of the press." Strident, opinionated, ranging in its collective views from left liberal to liberal left, *PM* had to abandon its policy of not running advertising and then was itself abandoned by Field. The Chicago publisher had other problems. He had started the Chicago *Sun* in 1941, purchased the Chicago *Times* six years later, combined the two—and found that McCormick's *Tribune* had a lock on newsstands, the best comics, and Associated Press membership.

A brilliant innovation of the 1920s, however, was more prosperous—and more controversial—than ever thirty years later. *Time* magazine's circulation soared during the 1950s from 1.65 million to 2.54 million at decade's end. *Life,* launched by Time Inc. in 1936, with its circulation base up to 5.6 million by the mid-fifties, belonged to the elite family of mass-circulation magazines: *Reader's Digest* (10.4 million), which had begun to take advertising; *The Saturday Evening Post* (4.8 million); *Look* (4.1 million biweekly); *Collier's* (3.8 million biweekly); *Woman's Home Companion* (4.1 million monthly). It was estimated that advertisers had put well over a billion dollars into *Life* during its first twenty years. By 1960 the total assets of Time Inc., which now included several magazines and a variety of other enterprises, had risen to $230 million, almost a tenfold increase in twenty years.

Preacher and sermonizer, innovator and enterpriser, moralizer and manipulator, Henry Luce ran his empire with a sometimes imperious, sometimes gentle hand. He delegated considerable authority to his subordinates, but the compelling suggestions, pithy comments, and measured exhortations that streamed from his office, along with his custom of directly editing each magazine for a week or two while the managing editor stood aside, brought his forceful presence into every editorial department. Luce made no secret of his own political views—he was for God, country, the GOP, free enterprise, and Yale, not necessarily in that order. All the editorial convictions of Time Inc., Luce wrote his editors in a paper titled "The Practice of Freedom," could be summarized in one word, Freedom, by which Luce meant the Bill of Rights, representative government, and competitive free enterprise.

Luce played high politics in the Republican party, throwing his own and sometimes his magazines' weight behind favored candidates such as Wendell Willkie. But like many an American President, he saw far less power looking out of his office than others saw looking in. Many of his best writers and editors were New or Fair Dealers. Most could easily find jobs elsewhere. And to the "top performers," as John Kobler wrote, "Luce developed a strong, deep, possessive attachment." He would brook considerable independence before he would let go a man like Theodore White, who came to differ with him sharply over China policy, but in the end, of course, it was never Luce who went. *Life* itself seemed indestructible until it was challenged by a medium that was bringing pictures—up-to-the-minute moving pictures—into the nation's living rooms.

Television was only beginning to come into its own by 1950, but one thing was already clear—the new medium would be a commercial proposition. Just as a small group of teachers, parents, and others had tried to salvage radio for educational purposes and failed, so in the 1950s a comparable group strove to hold a number of channels for higher intellectual levels and standards of taste. Indeed, in that decade television achieved a kind of "Golden Age" as artists and intellectuals experimented with innovative forms of entertainment, featured Edward R. Murrow's *See It Now* on CBS and NBC's *Today Show,* and premiered Laurence Olivier's feature film *Richard III* before it hit the movie-house circuit.

But even the most optimistic innovators in television could not ignore the millions of "little black boxes" that by the mid-fifties sat in most American homes—radio sets that were also chambers of horrors to the critics. The listener could turn the knob from station to station and hear the same programming—endless popular music dispensed by jabbering disc jockeys and punctuated by a profusion of commercials along with a few news snippets. By 1960, with over 500 commercial television stations, TV appeared to be headed in the same direction that radio had taken. The reformers could not overcome the combined power of advertisers and broadcasters, who resisted invasion of their immensely profitable turf by invoking both the spirit of free enterprise and the sanctity of free speech.

* * *

A pervasive complacency, a burgeoning middle class, suburban togetherness, automated workers, widespread *anomie* and escapism, media pitched to the lowest common denominator, trivialization of thought—all these in different ways helped produce a politics of blandness, conformity, and consensus during the 1950s. To be sure, President Eisenhower had begun his Administration in 1953 with constructive purposes, buttressed by Republican majorities in House and Senate. On the domestic front he had created a new department, Health, Education, and Welfare, established the Air Force Academy, replaced mandatory farm price supports with flexible supports based on "modernized parity," won a housing act that somewhat expanded public housing and eased the burden of home mortgages, and signed legislation establishing a thirteen-year construction program for a 41,000-mile interstate system of highways. On foreign policy he sought to carry on a bipartisan approach, working with leaders of the Democratic minority like Senator Walter George of Georgia, just as Truman had collaborated with Republican senator Arthur Vandenberg.

Bipartisanship in foreign policy, however, was largely a façade behind which the two parties fought each other and—even more—factions within the parties fought one another. Democrats were as usual splintered into almost as many fragments as there were Democratic leaders, but they broadly fell into a Truman-Acheson-Harriman camp calling for hard-line policies toward the Soviets, and a circle that included Eleanor Roosevelt, Tennessee senator Estes Kefauver, and Connecticut governor Chester Bowles, supporting various forms of détente, with Adlai Stevenson seeking to bridge the gap. The Republicans had their own sharp differences— especially between backers of such ideas as massive retaliation and Dulles's brinkmanship and old-time isolationists like Taft and his followers.

Bipartisanship was a skimpy blanket hauled out at every point of military crisis or foreign policy quandary so that it could cloak differences and present a national posture of harmony and unity. "Politics must stop at the water's edge," the politicians and pundits would cry out. This was nothing new. In 1948 bipartisanship had been used to thwart the posing of fundamental alternatives to cold war assumptions. Writing a quarter century later, Robert A. Divine found it "a tragedy that the containment policy did not receive the careful analysis and debate it merited. Wallace's attack on Truman's policy suffered from emotional charges and flabby rhetoric, but beneath the shrill oratory there were important objections to the 'get tough with Russia' policy that deserved thoughtful consideration rather than contemptuous dismissal as Communist propaganda." It was estimated that less than 1 percent of the nation's newspapers supported Wallace's views in 1948, and many gave him short shrift even in their news columns. Neither Dewey in 1948 nor Eisenhower in 1952 challenged the cold war assumptions of the Truman Administration. The argument was over means, not ends, over cold war tactics, not strategy.

Cold war assumptions continued to grip the American mind during the fifties. A soothing bipartisanship discouraged clear, focused debate and shrouded fundamental choices in a cocoon of bland harmony. The most visible impact of consensus was on the election of 1956. Along with Eisenhower's personal popularity and the rally-'round-the-President impact of the Budapest revolt against Moscow and the Suez crisis, that consensus helped produce Stevenson's staggering 1956 loss to Eisenhower. The President carried both the electoral college and the popular vote by an even bigger margin than in 1952. His challenger won only Missouri and six southern states. Shifting back and forth between bipartisan agreement and opposition on details but always following cold war assumptions, Stevenson simply could not come to grips with the amiable figure in the Oval Office. The Democratic party—especially the Democratic leaders in Congress—had not built up a credible, consistent, comprehensive foreign policy program resting on premises different from cold war encirclement and containment of Russia.

Part of the trouble was that Americans, unlike the British, had no loyal but militant opposition with an institutional base. The Democratic party as such was too fragmented to provide a coherent alternative program to a strategy of containment, which after all it had bequeathed to the Eisenhower Republicans in 1952. Following the 1956 debacle the Democrats sought to remedy this situation by establishing the Democratic Advisory Committee (later Council). In joining it Stevenson called for "strong, searching, and constructive opposition." The DAC's advisory committees on policy included perhaps the most remarkable collection of political and policy brains of the era: William Benton, Bowles, Senators Kefauver and Herbert Lehman, political scientist Hans Morgenthau, Michigan governor G. Mennen Williams on foreign policy; economists John Kenneth Galbraith, Marriner Eccles, Walter Heller, Leon Keyserling, Isador Lubin, and historian Arthur Schlesinger, Jr., on domestic policy; labor leaders James B. Carey, Sidney Hillman, David J. McDonald, Walter Reuther on industrial policy. The DAC issued brilliant position papers but in doing so revealed anew the policy splits within the Democracy—especially the deep divisions between the presidential Democrats and the congressional Democrats. The Democratic leaders of the House and Senate casually boycotted the Council.

The most conspicuous victim of cold war consensus was the twice-defeated Stevenson. A man of such sparkling wit and elegant charm that he made even the most sophisticated "madly for Adlai," a scintillating speaker who eschewed bombast and banality, a politician with a high sense of responsibility and probity, he was unable to break out of the intellectual cocoon of containment and put forward a comprehensive alternative strategy. Instead he called for specific changes—an end to the draft and a ban on H-bomb testing—but both of these lay in the field of military expertise where the voters preferred to trust the general in the White House. Stevenson's campaign faults—endless reworking of speeches, immoderate moderation, excessive cautiousness—were not simply personal failings. They were the flaws of a candidate whose party, fellow leaders, and personal philosophy left him in a consensual void in which he desperately cast about for some winning stance and failed to find it.

Could the Democrats have found another leader who could have united the party behind a strategy of détente? It was unlikely, given the divisions in the party. But there was one leader who transcended the divisions, who maintained good personal relations with Truman, Harriman, Stevenson, and the congressional leaders even as she campaigned for peace. This was Eleanor Roosevelt. During these years she threw herself into the war against war and poverty, the campaign for civil rights and social welfare. She proved herself once again a consummate politician, as in the 1956 campaign when her appearance for Stevenson at the Democratic convention proved crucial in stemming a last-minute push by Harry Truman for Harriman. Though she was seventy years old by the mid-1950s, it was not really her age that prevented her from becoming the acknowledged leader of the Democratic party, perhaps even its candidate. The explanation was simpler. She was a woman.

Still, the political failures of the 1950s had much deeper sources than the Democrats' incapacity to offer a united front behind an alternative foreign policy. They lay in the cold war consensus that in turn stemmed from the spiral of fear and hate that continued to dominate Soviet-American relations. This spiral thwarted the steady, day-to-day diplomacy, the thoughtful and imaginative planning, the flexible but purposeful policies necessary to deal with Khrushchev. In the absence of such determined statecraft, problems festered, tempers rose, crises broke out, Americans rallied behind the President, Congress delegated him gobs of power. Brinkmanship was the inevitable result of drift and indecision. It was not Eisenhower's fault that the crises of Hungary and Suez erupted at the height of the 1956 campaign. It was simply his luck.

DILEMMAS OF FREEDOM

If the Democrats would not challenge cold war assumptions, who would? Not the media as a whole in the climate of the fifties, nor the churches, nor the educators. In Western society the task of political criticism and social dissent, if all other leaders or groups failed, lay with the intelligentsia. Freed of close dependency on institutions, the intellectual, in Richard Hofstadter's words, "examines, ponders, wonders, theorizes, criticizes, imagines," rather than seeking to manipulate or accommodate. During the 1950s American foreign policy was the target of the most searching criticism by four men—a journalist, a diplomat, a professor, and a theologian— who in the view of some were reminiscent of the great thinkers of the eighteenth-century constitutional founding era in the breadth and depth of their intellectual power.

If Walter Lippmann, George Kennan, Hans Morgenthau, and Reinhold Niebuhr could even be compared with the men of 1787, it was in part because they, like the Framers, had lived and reflected in a time of almost ceaseless ferment and conflict. Reaching adulthood early in the century, they had witnessed all its traumas—World War I and its aftermath, the great depression, the rise of Nazism, World War II, the slave-labor camps and death factories, the incinerated cities and the atom bomb and hydrogen bomb, the cold war. They had known evil in much the way that J. Robert Oppenheimer could say to President Truman: "In some sort of crude sense, which no vulgarity, no humor, no overstatement can quite extinguish, the physicists have known sin; and this is a knowledge which they cannot lose."

Lippmann, oldest of the four, was still in his early sixties when Eisenhower first ran for office. Although he backed the general over Stevenson in 1952, the noted columnist was as unsparing of Republican foreign policy as he had been of Democratic. Just as he had attacked Truman's NATO policy as the work of "zealous cold warriors" who sought to bribe and bully nations into an anti-Soviet alliance, now he questioned the Southeast Asia Treaty Organization, incidentally noting that it included only one Southeast Asian nation. Just as he had confronted Acheson in a blazing argument over the Truman Doctrine and later called for his resignation, now he lectured Dulles face to face—and was lectured back.

Lippmann could consistently criticize Democrats and Republicans because he consistently thought in terms of fixed assumptions: that foreign policy must act always for a carefully defined national interest, that world peace depended on a balancing of national interests, that great nations must wield their power circumspectly amid a network of secondary as well as primary powers, that prudent diplomacy called for professional foreign-policy-makers insulated against the wilder passions and selfish interests of the masses, that apocalyptic visions and abstract "solutions" must be rejected in favor of "practical" arrangements such as old-fashioned spheres of interest and regional neutralization. These ideas were broad and flexible enough to allow for a variety of applications and even contradictions; his support for a global equilibrium of power with the Soviets, for example, appeared to clash with his calls for withdrawals from Berlin and from Taiwan and Southeast Asia.

The traumas of the age of Korea and McCarthyism had indeed left Lippmann so pessimistic about the paralysis and indecision of democracies that his faith in popular rule fell even lower than it had been in the years when he was writing *Public Opinion* and *The Phantom Public.* The people, he argued in what he hoped would be his culminating masterwork, *The Public Philosophy,* had "acquired power they are incapable of exercising, and the governments they elect have lost powers which they must recover if they are to govern." He called for the restoration of "government strong enough to govern, strong enough to resist the encroachment of the assemblies and of mass opinions, and strong enough to guarantee private liberty against the pressure of the masses." Jumping on this sentence, Archibald MacLeish, former Librarian of Congress, now a Harvard professor, and always a poet, accused Lippmann of narrowing freedom to fit within the rational, ordered society in which the columnist appeared to believe. He accused Lippmann flatly of being opposed to real freedom and democracy. Lippmann indignantly responded that he *did* believe in freedom—his kind of freedom.

While Lippmann was seeking a "public philosophy" as the intellectual foundation for the kind of polity and policies he favored, George Kennan was coping with the aftermath of the "X" article that Lippmann had attacked so tellingly. Kennan's harsh portrait of Soviet power and motivation became so rigid a dogma in Administration councils as to leave the diplomat penitent and fearful. He continued to write and speak against the "legalistic-moralistic" approach to world affairs—and especially its application to Russia—that he felt had crippled Roosevelt's dealing with wartime problems and possibilities. Kennan continued to preach "realism," but under Acheson's State Department leadership it was increasingly evident that once you founded your foreign policy strategy on "realism," you were on treacherous ground. It could lead to endless ambiguities and self-contradictions, as it did even with Kennan. And tougher and more "realistic" realists could make a dogma out of what Kennan, at least, had seen as a policy of prudence. By 1950 Kennan was so disturbed by the Administration's cold war extremism as to greet with relief an invitation from Oppenheimer, now head of the Institute for Advanced Study at Princeton, to continue his historical studies there.

In the quiet of the Institute, Kennan hoped to think through his own premises and experiences. He had maintained his friendship with Lippmann despite their differences over containment and over specific policies, and those very differences between two men who prided themselves on their "realism" illustrated the pitfalls of the concept. When it came to military alliances, German policy, disengagement in Europe, summitry, and indeed the whole strategy toward Russia especially after Stalin, what was realistic? Who admitted to being *un*realistic? The concept had no intrinsic meaning. The problem was especially acute for Kennan because behind the cool façade of the diplomat and the detachment of the historian lay a deeply humane, sensitive, and indeed moral person who had seen the errors of "realists" in power, viewed diplomacy as the vocation of skilled men of the highest probity and responsibility, and insisted that a nation must seek to live up to its own moral standards even while rejecting the will-o'-the-wisp of global utopianism. And the more Kennan pondered in the groves of academe, the more he questioned the whole philosophy of cold war containment.

What seemed to be lacking in both Kennan and Lippmann was an overriding philosophy of international relations and a coherent strategic concept that could stand the test of repeated shocks like Korea and Berlin,

Hungary and Suez, as well as the endless currents of change. And no one seemed readier to supply this need than Hans J. Morgenthau, a professor of international relations at the University of Chicago. A veritable child of conflict, Morgenthau had grown up in a Bavarian city seared by race hatred even in the early 1920s; when, as a young *Gymnasium* student at the top of his class, he was chosen to give the annual Founder's Day address, the deposed duke of the region sat in the front row during the speech holding his nose in an obviously anti-Semitic gesture. Morgenthau left Germany as the Nazis moved toward power and later settled in Madrid to teach diplomacy, only to be overwhelmed by the Spanish Civil War; he made his way to Paris during the Popular Front days and then to Brooklyn College, only to be vilified there by young ideologues who were put off by the émigré's sober and scholarly approach to some of the passionate questions of the day.

Later, at Chicago, Morgenthau produced a series of volumes—*Scientific Man vs. Power Politics, Politics Among Nations, In Defense of the National Interest*—that marked him as a formidable strategist of international politics. Morgenthau began with the premise that power politics, "rooted in the lust for power which is common to all men," was inseparable from all social life. There was no escape from it: "whenever we act with reference to our fellowmen, we must sin and we must still sin when we refuse to act." Power was the central, almost the exclusive, foundation of national interest and criterion of foreign policy. Such power, essentially military, must of course be prudently managed, but managed also quickly and decisively, which required strong executive leadership. The executive branch, however, took little initiative in foreign policy, Morgenthau lamented to the Senate Foreign Relations Committee in 1959, because it feared Congress, and Congress feared public opinion. Yet public opinion, he went on in much the same vein as Lippmann, should be not the cause but the result of "dynamic executive and congressional leadership." Public-opinion polls measured the impact of past leadership, not the potential of the new. They must not be the yardstick of foreign policy.

"The history of America," Morgenthau instructed Senators J. William Fulbright, Mike Mansfield, and Wayne Morse among others, "is the story of the enthusiastic responses of the American people to dynamic leadership on behalf of foreign policies which can be shown to have a positive bearing upon the national interest."

Critics were not slow to challenge Morgenthau's realism. If the national interest was the foundation of foreign policy, they said, the power underlying it must be clear and measurable, which meant military power—but even this power had often been miscalculated by both its wielders and its targets. The professor himself, the critics added unkindly, had miscalculated the national interest—for example, in his expectation that the Soviets would risk or even start a ground war in Europe once they acquired nuclear power. There were, moreover, other tangible and intangible bases of power—economic, psychological, ideological—that had to be included in assessing the might of nations. Yet if these were included, the "national interest" became such a tangle of multiple, shifting, and dynamic forces as to defy measurement and analysis. Hence to be for the national interest or for realism was no more clarifying than to be for wisdom or common sense or statecraft. Who wasn't?

Realism, in short, was a necessary but inadequate component of a strategy of international relations. It was a preoccupation with means—the marshaling of power—in a series of world crises that called for a sense of proportion and perspective, a wider comprehension of ends, a philosophy of world politics, even a theology of the human condition. If this was the call, it appeared to have been answered in the 1950s by a theologian-philosopher-politician who had for twenty years been leaving church pulpits and college campuses dazzled by his stabbing oratory and pungent sermonizing. This was Reinhold Niebuhr.

Schooled at Elmhurst College in Illinois and at Yale Divinity School, he had held an evangelical pulpit in Detroit until 1928, when he joined the Union Theological Seminary in New York, much to the dismay of the established theologians there who deplored his lack of a doctorate, his bumptious midwestern manner, and his outspoken radicalism. His years in Detroit had left Niebuhr filled with fierce indignation over the industrial and human wasteland he had witnessed outside his own middle-class parish.

Detroit made Niebuhr a socialist; then for the next thirty years he followed a zigzag route through a series of doctrines and causes as he tried to come to grips with the depression, the New Deal, and the cold war. What kept him from intellectual faddism was his philosophical ambivalence—his tendency to embrace different doctrines at the same time in a kind of continuous internal dialectic; even while proclaiming a thesis he nurtured the seeds of its antithesis. Thus in Detroit he proclaimed the Social Gospel of Walter Rauschenbusch even while he exhibited, in his passion for new ideas and his instinct for irony and political practicality, many of the intellectual traits of the pragmatism of James and Dewey. His Detroit experience and the onset of the depression now moved him toward Marxist ideas, but it was Niebuhr's own brand of Marxism, shot through with concern over the havoc of capitalism, fear of rising fascism, an ornery repugnance for communist dogma and messianism, and a hatred for Soviet bureaucracy and oppression. During the late 1930s, after holding the New Deal in some distaste for its opportunism and its "whirligig" of reform, he deserted Norman Thomas and the socialists to vote for Roosevelt. This shift too was marked by ambivalence: Niebuhr, who turned to FDR in part because of the President's resistance to Nazism, had earlier attacked him for expanding the Navy.

By the 1940s Niebuhr could best be described as a liberal realist who was faithful to his earlier Social Gospel compassion in seeking to push the Roosevelt and Truman Administrations further to the left, in the process taking active leadership in Americans for Democratic Action and other liberal groups. At the same time he took a militant stand against Soviet expansionism and left-wing dogmatics. The old tensions and ambivalences remained. During the war he had hoped that "the companionship in a common purpose" with Russia would persuade the Soviets "to disavow political forms and fanaticisms which outrage standards of freedom established in the Western world." This was the kind of "liberal illusion" that Niebuhr at other times denounced. He inveighed against American pride and self-righteousness but he also educated a rising generation of politicians in "realistic," hard-nosed politics—in the notion, according to Richard W. Fox, that "moral men had to play hardball."

By the 1950s Niebuhr had reached the height of his fame. "He was the father of us all," George Kennan said of him. The ADA in a formal resolution named him its "spiritual father." The theologian's words excited so many agnostics, backsliders, and heretics that someone proposed a new group, "atheists for Niebuhr." How to account for this extraordinary influence? The answer lay less in Niebuhr's own ideological "whirligig" over the years than in the power of his theology of human nature. Whatever his current credal passion, it was informed by his biblical awareness of original sin, but sin now armed by technology with new destructive power, his rejection of Jeffersonian "illusions" for a Dostoevskian recognition of human evil, his sensitivity to human alienation, anxiety, and the "dizziness of freedom," his constant reminders of pride, aggressiveness, sinfulness. Always sin—sin as the "narcosis of the soul."

Audiences would never forget the sight of this man behind pulpit or rostrum, his bald pate gleaming as he pitched his hawklike face forward, his words tumbling out as his whole body seemed to weave and thrust, while his listeners tried frantically to scribble down his dazzling epigrams and polemical outbursts. His written words also had a stunning impact; for Harvey Cox his first reading of *Moral Man and Immoral Society,* gulped down in one sitting, was an intense revelation that made him "an instant Niebuhrian." But when the sermons and books were digested, the question remained whether Niebuhr had done much more than clothe liberal realism in a powerful theological frame without resolving the ultimate in his paradoxes—the tension between liberal compassion, hopes and dreams, and hardheaded realism. Was Niebuhr simply one more example of the great Tocquevillian failure in American intellectuals—the failure to connect practical expedient politics informed by human possibility and limitation to lofty but explicit goals that might challenge the best in humankind?

No more than Morgenthau or the others did Niebuhr take on the toughest intellectual task of all: to explore the dimensions of liberty, the structure of freedom, the ambivalences of equality—and the tension among these values—and to link these with the strengths and weaknesses of American institutions, politics, and leadership. What was desperately needed in postwar America was analysis of the intervening linkages between ends and means, but this would have called for an analysis of political parties and electoral processes and public opinion and governmental structures—analysis hardly conducive to evangelical sermonizing and radical rhetoric. It was this failure that—granted the empirical richness and political wisdom of Lippmann and Kennan, Morgenthau and Niebuhr—set them a rung below the intellectual leadership of the 1780s. The Framers had crafted a constitution that superbly fixed their goals of individual liberty to concrete governmental institutions and electoral processes—so superbly that leadership in the 1950s still had to operate through their centuries-old system in seeking to reach twentieth-century goals.

*   *   *

Nor did these four political analysts—in even sharper contrast with the Framers in their time—hold much sway over foreign, even European, opinion. Kennan, a visiting professor at Oxford in 1957–58, lectured for the BBC on "Russia, the Atom and the West." The stoutly anticommunist newspaper *Le Figaro* ran Lippmann columns. Lippmann indeed had a fan in General de Gaulle, who found *Le Crépuscule des démocraties*—the French edition of *The Public Philosophy*—full of "rare perceptions," mainly because the two men shared strong doubts about the equation of democracy with parliamentarism and the "usurpation of popular sovereignty by professional politicians," in de Gaulle's words. But in general the ideas of the four were hardly exportable, conditioned as those ideas were by America's geopolitical worldview.

Other things American, however, were most exportable. Europeans found their continent awash in American advertising and consumer goods. Turn the corner near Beethoven Strasse in Amsterdam or push your way through Piccadilly Circus or parade down the Champs-Élysées and you could hardly escape the ads for Kent cigarettes or Coca-Cola or Ford cars. Or escape the products themselves in the shops—Maxwell House coffee and Sea & Ski suntan lotion and Heinz tomato ketchup and Revlon lipstick. American cars seemed to be conquering European streets and mores, crowding highways, requiring car parks, changing suburban and recreation patterns.

Americans were exporting their corporations along with their goods. In the late fifties some two hundred American companies a year were settling in Belgium, Holland, and France, and about the same number in Britain. These enterprises employed tens of thousands of Americans and Europeans. Businessmen and politicians denounced the invaders for paying higher wages and salaries and for "disruption of orderly marketing." American loans, or American management practices, or American competition would make Britain—or France or Italy or Belgium—the "49th State." The Yankee traders, moreover, were taking back European art and other treasures. A London antique shop featured in its window a bristling sign: "Americans are not served."

Other Europeans fought back in ways known to old cultures. Despite much advertising, some American products simply could not make a go of it: Campbell soups had trouble competing in the home of famous *potages;* the British did not take to motherly Betty Crocker and her cake mixes; General Mills tried to market Cheerios but Londoners stuck with their cornflakes and their kippers. Europeans attacked American economic and cultural "imperialism": the Marshall Plan as a "dollar noose," American loans as the work of a "shabby moneylender," American managers as crass and unknowing, American GIs as "overpaid, oversexed, and over here." For some Americans the height of indignity was a report by a *Russian,* the Soviet writer Ilya Ehrenburg, after a trip to the States that Americans suffered from "spiritual standardization"—"the same houses, the same furniture, the same crockery."

No place on the globe, critics complained, escaped "Coca-colonization." Arthur Koestler noted: "The motorbus which carries the traveller at 5 A.M. from Bangkok airport to the center of the capital of Thailand has a loudspeaker through which American crooners purr at him, and makes him wonder whether his journey was really necessary. The Arabian desert is ploughed by Cadillacs, and the exhibition of Eskimo handicrafts at the airport of Anchorage, Alaska, bears the same hallmark of the Late Woolworth Period as the idols of Krishna, made of plastic, which are worshipped in Indian homes."

How could the "other" America be presented abroad—the good America, the America of books and music, of the Bill of Rights and representative government, especially at a time when the Kremlin was reputed to be spending half a billion dollars a year on propaganda? This was the job of the United States Information Agency, the successor to a series of agencies going back to the wartime propaganda units. By the end of the decade the USIA was running a wide range of information and cultural activities—books, films, lectures, radio programs, exhibits, student and teaching exchanges—through 200 posts in over 80 countries. No agency was more vulnerable politically both at home and abroad; while young European radicals were assaulting overseas libraries from the outside, McCarthy's men were doing so from the inside. Some overseas librarians hid books by Tom Paine and other radicals; a few timid souls actually burned books—only about a dozen, but enough to touch burning memories of the Nazis. "For the free world outside the U.S.," wrote a Canadian journalist, "McCarthyism is not just a spectacle. It is a tragedy."

McCarthy's assault on the Bill of Rights symbolized the USIA's broader problem. Which America, what kind of America, should it seek to present abroad—America in all its variety, its freedoms and oppressions, its high culture and its barbarism, its noble principles and its often egregious practices? "France was a land, England was a people," Scott Fitzgerald had written, "but America, having still about it that quality of an idea, was harder to utter." America was liberty, individual rights, Freedom—these were the foundation stones. But then there was that spectacle of the long-tolerated McCarthy. . . .

By the 1950s private philanthropic foundations were deeply involved in international affairs, especially in the Third World. The Ford Foundation devoted over $50 million—about a third of its total spending—to international programs from 1951 through 1954. While much of this effort abroad was for practical economic development programs, it also had a strong ideological cast. For years Ford helped finance the Congress for Cultural Freedom, which Ford officials defined as an effort "to combat tyranny and to advance freedom in Europe and Asia." The tyranny was Marxism, Soviet style, and the freedom was the Bill of Rights, American style, but the implications of extending civil liberties to poverty-stricken peoples rather than helping them achieve social and economic freedoms were left largely unexplored.

*　　*　　*

The men and women who had the most influence, however unwittingly, on European perceptions of the United States were American writers and artists. The late 1940s and the 1950s brought an Indian summer of the sparkling literary era that had stretched from World War I through the 1930s. Still shining or at least flickering in the afterglow of that era were the giants of the 1920s. Sinclair Lewis died at the start of the fifties but only after publishing a final volume of social criticism, *Kingsblood Royal*, an attack on racial prejudice. Although the best work of Robert Frost was behind him, he was still the most widely read serious poet in America. Ernest Hemingway published *Across the River and into the Trees* in 1950 and *The Old Man and the Sea* two years later, followed by the award of a Pulitzer Prize and, in 1954, the Nobel Prize in literature. William Faulkner, who had won the Nobel five years earlier, published *Requiem for a Nun* in 1951 and *A Fable* in 1954, and he completed his trilogy about the Snopes clan with *The Town* and *The Mansion* during the late fifties. Soon after the end of the decade, the pens of Hemingway, Faulkner, and Frost would be stayed for good.

Crowding onto the literary scene were younger writers who brought a springtime of creativity even while the Indian summer waned. Between 1947 and 1955 playwright Arthur Miller gave to the stage *All My Sons, Death of a Salesman, The Crucible, A View from the Bridge.* Ralph Ellison wrote a single stunning novel, *The Invisible Man;* J. D. Salinger published *The Catcher in the Rye* and *Franny and Zooey;* Saul Bellow contributed *The Adventures of Augie March* and *Henderson the Rain King;* playwright Tennessee Williams, after his brilliant *The Glass Menagerie* and *A Streetcar Named Desire,* wrote *The Rose Tattoo, Camino Real, Cat on a Hot Tin Roof.* These five men were in their late thirties or early forties; even younger was Norman Mailer, who had brought out *The Naked and the Dead,* a war novel, at the age of twenty-five and wrote two significant works, *Barbary Shore* and *The Deer Park,* in the 1950s.

Of all the tests of great literature, two are most clearly measurable—longevity and universality. The permanence of the notable work of the Indian summer could not be tested for another century, but the universality of the older generation of writers had striking demonstration during the 1950s.

France had been the supreme testing ground abroad for American writers, in part because French critics viewed themselves as the ultimate tribunal of international letters. The literati of Paris had been peculiarly generous to American novelists, some of whom they had known during the novelists' self-imposed exiles in France in the twenties. Lewis's *Babbitt* had sold 80,000 copies in France within a few months of publication; at least thirteen of his other works were translated into French by the end of the thirties. During that decade, the "greatest literary development in France," in the judgment of Jean-Paul Sartre, was the discovery of Faulkner, Dos Passos, Caldwell, and one or two other writers; at once, he added, "for thousands of young intellectuals, the American novel took its place, together with jazz and the movies, among the best of the importations from the United States." Even André Gide, the grand old man of French letters, said that "no contemporary literature" excited his interest more than that of young America.

And of these "young" Americans, no one excited the French more than Hemingway. His subjects fascinated them—bloody prizefighters, hired killers, disemboweled matadors, crippled soldiers, hunters of wild animals, deep-sea fishermen, as André Maurois summed them up. They liked his style even more—the simplicity of word and deed, the flat unemotional perceptions, the code of courage and personal honor, the clean, hard writing style, the celebration of *nada*—nothingness. It was a style that was said to have influenced Camus. By 1952 *For Whom the Bell Tolls* had sold over 160,000 copies in a French-language edition.

In the long run, the reputation of Faulkner in France surpassed even Hemingway's. The literati liked the sense of tragic pessimism in the Mississippian, his metaphysical approach to time, his "magical, fantastic, and tragic" universe, as one reviewer wrote, inhabited by "a strange music, an unforgettable rhythm of incantation." If Hemingway influenced Camus, Faulkner, according to Sartre, inspired Simone de Beauvoir's technique of substituting a more subtle order of time for the usual chronology. Some French critics viewed Faulkner as America's best—even the world's best—novelist, much to the discomfiture of Hemingway, who at least had the consolation of vastly outselling Faulkner in France. Americans were wrong to treat Faulkner as a regionalist, Paris critics asserted; he was rather a "universal writer" in the fullest sense.

It was not only Faulkner and Hemingway that France celebrated, and it was not only France that celebrated American writers. Across the Continent there appeared a hunger for Steinbeck, Dos Passos, Fitzgerald, and others, and for Westerns and detective stories as well. A German writer told many years later of how he had cadged books from American GIs during the occupation and built his literary education on crates of Armed Services Editions, "courtesy of the American taxpayer."

Why this transatlantic appeal of American writers? Italian novelist Cesare Pavese, who translated earlier American classics as well as Faulkner and Hemingway, said he had found "a thoughtful and barbaric America, happy and quarrelsome, dissolute and fruitful, heavy with all the world's past, but also young and innocent." Was this all there was to it—Europeans in one of their recurring "discoveries" of a simple, innocent, youthful America, refreshing to jaded continental sensibilities? Were either the established or the rising American writers of the 1950s telling them anything about the heart and mind and soul of America? What ultimately did this big, bustling country stand for?

Hemingway did not answer this question—he had no intention to. He dwelt on men's—it was almost always men's—individual fear and bravery, desire and frustration, struggle and death. Like Robert Jordan in *For Whom the Bell Tolls,* he had no political beliefs except a furious antifascism and an all-embracing individualism. "You believe in Life, Liberty and the Pursuit of Happiness," Robert is told by "himself," but himself wants these good things for individuals, not nations. Hemingway's *The Old Man and the Sea* superbly portrayed a man's struggle against a personal adversary and a fated defeat by an inexorable environment, but had nothing to say about collective effort and frustration.

With his closeness to the land, his love of community and region, his feeling for the "presentness of the past," his old-fashioned sense of religious morality, William Faulkner appeared far more likely than Hemingway to plumb the mind and heart of the country. He was very much in the American literary tradition—indeed, two traditions, as Hyatt Waggoner suggested: the romantic symbolism of Hawthorne and Melville, the naturalism of Howells, Twain, and Dreiser. The people of Yoknapatawpha County—their greed and cunning, their moral and physical vulgarity, and the struggles of some to break the chains of fate and rise to some kind of human stature—were lifted in his charged prose to the level of universality and tragedy that the French critics so praised. But Faulkner, like Hemingway, was far more concerned with private values and personal afflictions than with public substantive values like political and economic freedom. When he did call for individual rights and liberty in his books and public addresses, they were largely *his* kind of rights and liberty—a sphere of private space, artistic independence that no government could be allowed to invade. The broader picture of "what the country stood for" that emerged from his writings was murky, even muddled.

A marvelous line from Faulkner's *Absalom, Absalom,* noted by Malcolm Cowley, summed up the eloquence and the despair of modern human existence: "moving from a terror in which you cannot believe, toward a safety in which you have no faith." This was the folly and impotence of America but by no means its essence.

Robert Frost even more than Faulkner defined freedom in his sayings

and writings as personal liberty against the state, whether New Deal bureaucracy or the compulsory public school. And his freedom too, on closer
inspection, turned out to be the crucial but self-serving independence of
the man of letters. "We prate of freedom," he said. "All I would keep for
myself is the freedom of my material—the condition of body and mind now
and then to summons aptly from the vast chaos of all I have lived through."
And he wrote:

> Keep off each other and keep each other off.
> You see the beauty of my proposal is
> It needn't wait on general revolution.
> I bid you to a one-man revolution—
> The only revolution that is coming.

Many of Frost's finest poems celebrated the independent, self-reliant,
skeptical country man, who could say with the poet, "The freedom I'd like
to give is the freedom I'd like to have." But this was a negative freedom
largely irrelevant to the human needs of millions of industrialized, urban-
ized, automated Americans. There was one thing Frost could not do,
Granville Hicks had written earlier. He "cannot give us the sense of belonging in the industrial, scientific, Freudian world in which we find ourselves." The poet never did, never wanted to.

What writer, then, did manage to present the essence of the American
experiment in the realm of ideas and values? Surely not Norman Mailer,
who in the 1950s was still preoccupied with self-promotion, self-definition,
self-resolution, with orgasm as true love, ideology as illusion, the hipster
as the "wise primitive." Surely not Tennessee Williams, who epitomized
the decade's concern with personal trauma and private values, or J. D.
Salinger's adolescents in constant rebellion against the "phony bastards"
around them, or Saul Bellow's characters—unforgettable but largely
preoccupied with their own psyches.

The writer who came closest to dramatizing the great public issues and
values was a playwright. Manhattan-born Arthur Miller, the son of a garment manufacturer afflicted by the depression, rebelled against commercial values and middle-class hypocrisy much as his fellow writers did. But
he used his characters to dramatize social as well as personal needs and
failures. The "right dramatic form," he wrote in 1956, "is the everlastingly
sought balance between order and the need of our souls for freedom; the
relatedness between our vaguest longings, our inner questions, and private lives and the life of the generality of men which is our society and our
world." His great plays—notably *Death of a Salesman* and *The Crucible*—were

in part direct responses to the threat to people's hopes and dreams from a business civilization that degraded them and the threat to personal liberty from McCarthyism. Predictably Miller was attacked from the right; more significantly, he was criticized from the left for not being radical enough, for not being clear whether it was Willy Loman who was at fault or the society that produced him, for not tying his plays more explicitly to current issues.

Miller easily survived his critics. But even though his plays were produced in Europe, he had only a limited impact abroad. The ambiguities in his dramas—the ambivalences in Miller reflecting those in the larger culture—were enough to blur his powerful portrait of America's yearnings toward both liberty and order, freedom and security, individualism and solidarity. The portrait was not clear to all Americans either. Miller himself wryly mentioned the man who came out of a performance of *Death of a Salesman* exclaiming, "I always said that New England territory was no damned good."

If American writers were unsure of what their nation stood for, it was not surprising that Europeans were equally puzzled. European intellectuals had long labeled the country's commitment to freedom as either self-indulgence bordering on anarchy or a boorish egalitarianism bending toward class leveling. "I am held to be a master of irony," George Bernard Shaw had gibed. "But not even I would have had the idea of erecting a Statue of Liberty in New York." On the other hand, Europeans had to and did admire the American commitment to some notion of freedom in two wars and the cold war. If Europeans, with their long exposure to Americans, were left uncertain, what could be expected of the Soviets, with their very different, very ideological conception of freedom?

A remarkable meeting in San Francisco in September 1959 between Nikita Khrushchev and nine American labor leaders headed by Walter Reuther helped answer this question. For two hours the two sides went at it, Khrushchev reddening, pounding the table, shouting out his arguments, the union men roaring back in a cacophony of indignant voices. More and more the argument narrowed down to the question of freedom—for workers in East Germany, for Hungarian "freedom fighters," for West Germans, for Americans. Khrushchev was soon on his feet. Suddenly, according to the official record, he gave a burlesque demonstration of the dance he had witnessed during the Hollywood rehearsal of the forthcoming film *Can-Can.* He turned his back to the table, bent downward, flipped his coat up, and gave an imitation of the cancan.

"This is a dance in which girls pull up their skirts," the Premier fulminated. "This is what you call freedom—freedom for the girls to show their backsides. To us it is pornography. The culture of people who want pornography. It's capitalism that makes the girls that way."

The meeting sputtered toward its end.

"We are interested in how best to advance the interest of workers under freedom," Reuther said.

"You have your point of view; we have ours," Khrushchev replied. "They are irreconcilable."

CHAPTER 7

The Free and the Unfree

O NLY a tiny portion of the people of the world had ever taken part in the global controversy over the nature of freedom. Yet, whether this lofty idea was defined in its core as individual civil and political liberty or as the broadest social and economic opportunity and equality, whether—in FDR's terms—freedom was not only of speech and worship but also from want and fear, the meaning of freedom had enormous potential implications for the billions of people who were as remote from the controversy as if they lived on another planet.

The vast majority of these persons lived in peasant huts or city shanties. They subsisted on 2,000 calories a day or even less, barely enough to supply the energy needed for bodily survival. In the cities they lived perforce on a day-to-day, even hour-to hour economy, as they scrounged for enough money or food to carry them through the day. In the country they lived seasonally, planting their single crops on postage-stamp plots, but were often at the mercy of landlords, moneylenders, drought, and flood. In time of dire need they might resort to begging, pilfering, to sending their children out to beg or toil. At best they might live four or five or six to a shack, often in curtained-off tiers of straw mats.

The most eloquent world leader could not reach these people. They had no magazines, newspapers, or books—and could not read them if they had, for the great majority were illiterate. They might possess a radio, if they had electricity and if the national regime wanted a direct line to them; more likely they could attend a community radio or perhaps a film. Many blocks away, or across the valley somewhere, there might be a school—perhaps a two-room hutch for the hundreds of children in the area. Few attended—there were better uses for them. In southern India twelve-year-old untouchables bobbed up and down in lime pits stamping hides with their bare feet; elsewhere in Asia children might be sent out in time of famine to pick the undigested oats from horse droppings.

Around the globe, wherever the sun was hottest typically the poverty was direst. Its burning rays brought light and energy but also drought and flood to southern Asia, to tropical and Saharan Africa, to Brazil and her neighbors to the west. The overhead sun traced the global hunger belt. In the late 1950s "developed" countries outside the communist bloc had less than one-fifth of the world's population but over three-fifths of the world's gross national product. The communist bloc including Asia claimed a third of the global population and a fifth of the GNP. That left the rest of the world—a billion and a third people—with the rest of the GNP, less than 15 percent. More starkly, about half the world's population of almost three billion had a GNP per head of $100 or less by the end of the fifties.

There was nothing new about this abject poverty; much of humankind had always been in dire want. It was the sheer number of people now inhabiting the earth, and therefore the sheer scope of privation, that was new. World population had climbed from less than 1.2 billion in 1850 to around 1.6 billion in 1900 and then surged to 2.4 billion by 1950. There was virtually no chance of slowing down the population increase in the next half century because it was propelled by almost inexorable forces: the nineteenth- and twentieth-century revolutions in personal and public hygiene, medicine, agriculture, industrial productivity. On the contrary, experts in demography fully anticipated a further population spurt during the late twentieth century.

It was not simply a matter of numbers, however, but of the revolution in attitudes created by people having longer life spans, working more productively, living and toiling in denser clusters. These attitudes were focused and steeled by two powerful intertwined tendencies. One was the heating up of fierce nationalist feelings and rivalries that swept Asia and Africa during the late nineteenth and early twentieth centuries. A sense of common fate "united peoples divided by older social barriers of ethnicity, class, rank, culture, religion," in Peter Worsley's words. "People drew together, and were *forced* together." They united against their colonial masters; what they united for was not so clear. The other development was world war, accompanied by multitudinous smaller wars. Economically stimulated by the colonial powers' ravenous exploitation of their natural resources, Third World peoples were also psychologically charged when the British and Americans appeared vulnerable to Third World nationalism. And vulnerable as well to other races: at Singapore, Pearl Harbor, and elsewhere, Oriental power—at least for a few electrifying months—seemed able to take the measure of the white master.

"O masters, lords and rulers in all lands, / How will the Future reckon with this Man?" poet Edwin Markham had asked at the turn of the century after gazing at a reproduction of Millet's *The Man with the Hoe.* How answer his brute question "when whirlwinds of rebellion shake the world"? When would the "dumb Terror" cry out? For the most part he did not. The man with the hoe stayed chained to his plot, his cottage, his village, his tribe, imprisoned in a structure of poverty embracing every aspect of his existence: his poor nourishment, ill health, ignorance, illiteracy, lack of motivation, opportunity, hope. Studies of Indian villages portrayed communities whose hierarchy of castes and classes appeared utterly impervious to external influence or internal disruption.

Others revolted. They rose against their colonial masters or the local colonial surrogates or their own national or tribal despots. Some rebels, following the paths of the great liberal European leaders they had studied in their school textbooks, chose the course of party competition, voteseeking, parliamentary maneuver, cabinet leadership. Others turned to Marxist doctrines and Leninist tactics, focusing hatred against colonists, landlords, plantation owners, moneylenders, storekeepers—against all "capitalists." The result had been a variety of communist and socialist regimes, some of them collaborating with the master models in Moscow and later Peking, others following their own nationalist versions of Marxism.

The path that rising peoples followed was not chosen by the collective voice or vote of the people acting en masse. Nor on the other hand did one leader or a tiny set of leaders at the top make the decision. It came of shifting combinations of national leaders, grass-roots activists, and followers, varying from nation to nation, region to region. But at least one broad pattern could be discerned in this complex process. While "arousing the masses," leaders inspired subleaders who tended to challenge and overtake the original leaders and then remove or even execute them. Thus revolutions devoured their own children. As leaders responded to wants and turned them into socially legitimated needs, people were not content for long; after food in their bellies and security in their homes they wanted higher things—self-esteem and self-fulfillment. Seeking votes, politicians offered people hope and found the collective hope they aroused turning into expectations that soon became entitlements that soon became demands. And once the followers put demands on their leaders and the leaders followed the followers, the followers were the true leaders.

Other poverty-stricken people found a quite different way out—migration. For some this meant moving from the countryside into the burgeoning cities—or into the shacks that clustered in the city but were not part of it. For others, whether early immigrants such as the Irish or later ones like the Chinese, it meant voyages of several thousand miles across the high seas to new lives and new leaders, new freedoms and new frustrations.

It so happened that during the 1960s, when demands for economic and social as well as political and constitutional freedoms were echoing throughout the Third World, Americans came under the leadership of two

Presidents who—more than any of their predecessors for at least a century—had lived among migrant peoples who had come to the United States seeking liberty of thought and expression and equality of opportunity. John Kennedy had grown up among the descendants of the Irish who had fled from British oppression, and in his city constituencies he had seen people imprisoned in urban poverty that matched the rural deprivations of the old country. As a young schoolteacher, Lyndon Johnson had entered the lives of children descended from some of the several million Mexicans who had remained in the Southwest following the Mexican-American war or who had later crossed the border to find jobs. Could not these two Presidents take the lead in teaching the American people—and themselves—how to understand the cries for freedom rising from the Third World, and how to respond to them?

THE BOSTON IRISH

In the late 1840s the trickle of Irish immigrants into Boston had suddenly turned into a flood. In less than a decade over 120,000 Hibernians crossed over the gangplank and, full of wild hopes and apprehensions, descended into the tumult of the dock. The central cause of this sudden spurt could hardly have appeared more remote to the Brahmin world of Beacon Hill—yet it would profoundly alter that world. It was a fungus in Irish fields that left potato stalks slimy and stinking and the spuds underground small and mushy. The blight devastated Ireland's single main crop. More than half a million Irish people died of starvation and related illnesses in the famine, it was estimated, while hundreds of thousands of others in fury and desperation sought escape to England, Canada, and America.

It was not the first time that the Irish had wondered if God's curse lay on their country. For centuries they had known oppression from the alien regime across the Irish Sea. Repeated rebellions had brought bloody reprisals and massacres. The Irish "always went forth to battle and they always fell," a poet lamented. The English government had planted thousands of Presbyterian Scots in northern Ireland—a move that would divide the country for at least four centuries. Irish Catholics were denied the right to vote, to serve on juries, to teach school, to enter a university, to marry a Protestant, to own much land, to join the bar, to work for the government. Slowly, grudgingly, London made concessions, but it was all too late. By the early nineteenth century the Irish had turned inward, to their land, their family, their superstitions, their villages, their grievances, and above all their religion.

It was a colonized people who made their way across the Atlantic, only to meet—in Boston, at least—new colonial masters. Here again were Protestant overlords who dominated intellectual and cultural life, occupied the economic and political power centers, controlled the major press organs, dominated the election process. Most of the Irish exchanged their hovels in County Kerry for tenements off filthy alleys, their farm labor for pick-and-shovel jobs on roads or canals, or drudgery in Protestant kitchens or factories. But they did not exchange their church, their one dependable institution. The Irish in Boston continued to hunker down together, to cling to their songs and wakes and taverns, their sly ways of frustrating their oppressors.

But something was different in America. It was a nation that appeared to prize its constitutional processes and Bill of Rights, a people that affirmed—even if they often failed to practice—the supreme principles of liberty and equality. And it was a land of bursting economic opportunity, however uneven. In many respects Boston, compared with the bustling cities to the south and west, was already experiencing an economic decline, but the city was a job cornucopia compared to the old country.

The Boston Irish found three ladders out of privation. Sports was the handiest—literally handy for a man quick with his fists. Hero to Boston Irishmen was John L. Sullivan, who discovered his prowess at the age of nineteen by knocking his foe into the orchestra pit with his first blow. Sullivan took on all comers, promising $25 to anyone who could knock him out. In 1882 he vanquished the national heavyweight champion, Paddy Ryan; seven years later he fought Jack Kilrain for seventy-five rounds with bare knuckles; three years after that he lost the championship to Gentleman Jim Corbett and with it a purse of $45,000. So prestigious were Irish boxers that some aspiring pugilists without a drop of Irish blood took Hibernian names.

For more ambitious Boston Irish, the main ladder was political. In the United States, Irishmen's votes counted just as much as any others, sometimes more if counted by the right people. By the 1870s the Boston Irish were electing city aldermen and state legislators, then mayors and congressmen. Outdoing the Protestants in dispensing patronage, soon they were making their friends and supporters policemen, inspectors, firemen, and the like. With their ready tongues, their quick wit, their concern for families living in their ward or precinct if not for people en masse, their flair for building personal followings, their vaunted "human touch," and with their numbers, the Irish soon captured Boston, except for brief periods of reform protest. Newcomers from other countries had many of these qualities too, but the Irish (or many of them) enjoyed one inestimable advantage—they were the only "new" immigrants to arrive speaking English.

Belatedly it was the economic ladder that carried some Boston Irish to the top. Much has been made of the job discrimination the Irish faced—the signs reading "None need apply but Americans," the white-collar promotions reserved for Protestants, the shunting off of talented young Irishmen into domestic and service jobs. Less has been made of the handicaps that many of the Irish brought to job-seeking and advancement: illiteracy, inability to speak English well, lack of vocational skills and of a feel for the rhythms of the city. Despite all this, sizable numbers of the Boston Irish went into business and finance and thrived. This was partly because they had entrepreneurial skills that could not be denied, partly because the better-assimilated second and third generations suffered fewer handicaps and found a variety of channels in a nationally expanding economy, partly because the most stiff-necked State Street banker would deal even with Irishmen as long as he could make a dollar.

The social environment was changing too. The "No Irish" notices came down, the Boston *Transcript* finally stopped running "Protestant only" job ads, and more and more non-Catholics voted for Catholics running for office—but of course not yet for the presidency. The changing image of the Irish was reflected in *Puck,* a journal of "mirth and fun" published in New York but widely circulated in Boston. In the 1880s *Puck* caricatured Bridget in the kitchen and Paddy in his shanty swarming with pigs, chickens, and children. "In front of these leaking, tumbledown shacks sits the Hibernian male, clay pipe sticking from a large, baboon-like mouth in an underslung jaw," in John Appel's description of the caricature. Paddy was "eternally hostile to Great Britain; prepared to send his and Bridget's hard-earned dollars to support lazy relatives or harebrained, landlord-murdering, dynamite-happy compatriots in the Emerald Isle or the United States." Later the cartoonists featured the second generation of financially successful contractors and their upward-striving wives, and still later *Puck*'s savage thrusts at the Irish and other immigrants died away, as did the journal itself.

Still, the transition into politics, business, and the professions was never easy. Economically the Irish could follow the path of Social Darwinism or of a Horatio Alger hero, but still be excluded from the Protestant old-boy network of corporate decision-makers. Educationally they could send their children to Protestant schools, knowing that their sons might be accepted on the football field or baseball diamond but not in a fraternity or in a dormitory clique. Socially they could meet members of their own class at Boston events, but not enter the Somerset Club. Politically they operated under the umbrella of the Democratic party, but the Democracy served them as a patronage machine rather than as a political and programmatic movement. Ideologically they shared the welfare liberalism of progressive-minded Protestants, but they recoiled from their social liberalism, feminist (and, earlier, abolitionist) leanings, intellectual eclecticism and tolerance, and Bill of Rights absolutism, which clashed with Catholic moral and social conservatism.

The Irish could be, in short, wholly "American" in their behavior—ambitious, cosmopolitan, active in the party of their choice, contributors to charity, hostile to radical causes and groups, paying obeisance to the higher American values, sharing in the nation's love of heroes in the political and sports arenas. But "structurally" they were not integrated into the American system. They stood a bit apart, somewhat quizzical, sardonic, critical of many of the modernist and secular trends in American life.

*   *   *

Probably no family in Boston embodied the Irish Catholic heritage and ambivalences more fatefully, or seized on the new land's opportunities more eagerly, than the Kennedys. The generations followed the classic sequence. During the famine Patrick Kennedy, a County Wexford tenant farmer, walked—so it is said—from his cottage to the packet ship that took him to Boston. There he worked as a barrel maker, married Bridget Murphy, fathered four children, and died of the cholera in his early thirties. His son Patrick Joseph attended a parochial and then a public school, worked as a dockhand, saved his money, bought a tavern in Haymarket Square, and then branched out into both politics and finance, building his own Democratic party organization and helping to establish an East Boston bank. He won the hand of Mary Hickey, at the time a bit above his station. Their firstborn, Joseph Patrick, attended parochial school through the lower grades, then Boston Latin, then Harvard. In 1914, when he was in his mid-twenties, he married Rose Elizabeth Fitzgerald. Rose was the bright and beauteous daughter of Boston mayor John ("Honey Fitz") Fitzgerald, who had been born in a tenement near the Old North Church of parents from County Wexford.

The Kennedy-Fitzgerald clans, packed with Murphys and Hickeys and Connellys as well, were claimed by an admiring Bostonian to be "Irish as Paddy's pig." Yet the second generation of that clan—PJ's and Honey Fitz's generation—had begun to veer from the shanty Irish stereotype. With his jokes about the auld sod, all too frequent warbling of "Sweet Adeline," fondness for jigs and wakes, Honey Fitz was the very caricature of the merry little Irishman, but he penetrated Protestant society through his athletic feats at Boston Latin and after, and he even enrolled in Harvard Medical School, dropping out after his father's early death. Not only did PJ see his son into Harvard but this "typical Irish boss" ended up an affluent banker and liquor wholesaler living in a fine colonial mansion.

Honey Fitz and PJ moved toward success without apparent trauma, in part because they accepted the rules of the social game—equal, but separate. This was precisely what Joe Kennedy would not accept. He must be not separate but included, not equal but at the top. And this he never fully achieved. With strong initial boosts from his father and father-in-law he went on to a highly remunerative career in Boston banking, in films, liquor, stock speculation, and real estate. But riches never brought him acceptance from men whom he often despised anyway. While Groucho Marx remarked that he would not join the kind of club that would let him in, Kennedy *would* join it—but the club would not let him in. Still, despite his own womanizing, he could take enormous solace in his loyal wife and rapidly growing family of nine children—especially in his firstborn and namesake, Joe Jr. And he could send his four sons to Harvard.

John Kennedy grew up half Irish, half Harvard, conventionally Catholic in religious matters, secular and skeptical in intellectual. He dealt with such dualities by compartmentalizing his life and perhaps even his thoughts. He dutifully followed his mother's admonitions about attending mass, but he ignored theology and spurned religiosity. He was properly pious and decorous when occasion demanded it, but at Choate school he headed a "mucker's club" that rebelled against the headmaster and his rules. He became a bread-and-butter Democrat who shunned the orthodox liberalism of Americans for Democratic Action and the American Civil Liberties Union. His detachment from traditional American Catholicism, wrote his friend Arthur Schlesinger, was part of his detachment from middle-class parochialism, the business ethos, ritualistic liberalism.

Rather early in his life there began to develop a public John Kennedy and a private Jack. The fierce competitor in football, sailing, swimming, and roughhousing concealed the youth who was racked and often immobilized by a series of illnesses. The son of Boston actually grew up mainly in New York, Cape Cod, and Palm Beach. The image of the clean-cut all-American youth was shrouded in obsessive womanizing that started remarkably early in his life and lasted until the end of it. He wrote grandly of courage and leadership in politics but usually practiced caution and shrewdness. He took the orthodox anticommunist posture in public while in private he more and more favored flexibility toward the Soviet Union. He demonstrated independence in his behavior and his career choices, even while he was closely dependent at critical junctures on his father's money, connections, and advice.

He was not even committed to a political career until his brother Joe was killed piloting a bomber over the English Channel in 1944. A constituency opened up too, when James Michael Curley, who represented everything the Kennedys now detested in Boston politics—pugnacious demagoguery, silver-tongued blarney, flamboyant appeals to the shanty Irish, corruption—relinquished his 11th Congressional District seat in 1946 to run for mayor. Since the 11th was as heavily Democratic as it was Catholic, the big fight would come in the party primary. Almost a dozen hopefuls, including one woman, jumped into the race.

Soon this old working-class district was treated to the spectacle of a gaunt, hollow-eyed twenty-nine-year-old, still yellow from South Pacific Atabrine, handshaking his way through Maverick Square, the Italian North End, tenements, and factories. The young Kennedy did not take to this glad-handing easily; shy and slow with the sweet talk, he developed his own style of direct, informal, pithy speech. More decisive in such a free-for-all, however, was father Joe's quiet mobilization of media attention, subway and billboard advertising, and tens of thousands of reprints of a *Reader's Digest* abridgment of an account by John Hersey of Kennedy's steady leadership after the loss of his PT boat in the South Pacific. The primary outcome—a clear lead by Kennedy over his nearest rival—was sobering as well as gratifying: after all the months of hoopla and beating of the bushes by all the candidates, fewer than a third of the registered voters bothered to vote.

His congressional race taught the ambitious young politician a lesson in American politics that was wholly congenial to a Kennedy—it was all against all in a big game of King of the Rock. You gather your friends and family around you, raise money, organize a personal following, ignore the party organization except when you can exploit it, keep flailing about in one big donnybrook—and the devil take the hindmost. Anything goes, almost; when the Kennedy people feared that one Joseph Russo might win a plurality (and hence victory) with just the Italian vote, they dug up another Joseph Russo to split his vote.

In the House of Representatives, Kennedy did not find that political lesson any less useful. Party leadership and organization were weak; the House Democrats were fragmented into a host of shifting factions; despite advice from his elders that in the House you must "go along to get along," you really did best by endlessly wheeling and dealing in a system of free political enterprise.

But life in the House, partly for these reasons, was boring as well; he "felt like a worm there," Kennedy later complained. Soon he was setting his sights on statewide office, whether senator or governor he did not much care; either could be a stepping-stone to still higher office. It became clear that in 1952 the congressman could have a clear shot—that is, without major opposition in a primary—at Henry Cabot Lodge for Lodge's seat in the Senate. It was a sobering prospect. Grandson of Woodrow Wilson's nemesis, Lodge had inherited much of the old senator's Irish and isolationist support. After roundly defeating Jim Curley for the Senate seat in 1936 he had resigned for combat service, then returned and beaten the "unbeatable" incumbent, David I. Walsh. Having won new prestige from having helped draft Eisenhower for the Republican presidential nomination, Lodge was now the unbeatable one.

The contest that followed was one of the most significant of the postwar years—not because of the contestants, notable though they were; not because of the money spent, which was probably no greater than in many other Senate races; but because Kennedy's campaign epitomized a "new politics," involving massive use of the media, variety of focus on candidate image and *personalismo,* extraordinary exploitation of family money and friends, and attacks on the foe from both the right flank and the left with little regard to program or ideology.

In the fall of 1952 tens of thousands of Massachusetts women, responding to personalized invitations, turned out to meet mother and son, share some refreshment, and enjoy a political gathering with hardly a hint of sordid politics in the air. While John Kennedy's father financed these affairs, his mother and sisters made them a spectacular success. No other candidates were invited, of course. Jack was running solo. He ran his campaign out of his own city and town headquarters and kept his distance from Democrats competing for other offices who might be a drag on his own campaign; many a party hand working for the whole ticket looked forlornly out of a second-floor cubbyhole to see the glittering Kennedy storefront headquarters across the way. Only Kennedy literature was available there.

How to attack Lodge, who held the strategic middle ground as the "centrist," moderate Republican candidate? Kennedy, with a crucial assist from his father, enfiladed that centrism from opposite sides of the political spectrum. He targeted conservative Republicans still angry over Eisenhower's "theft" of the Republican nomination. Joe Kennedy served as the contact with anti-Eisenhower publishers; his exquisitely well-timed promise of a half-million-dollar loan to the publisher of the noisily right-wing Boston *Post* greased the way for the publisher's abrupt switch from Lodge to Kennedy. Over on the liberal side of the spectrum Jack Kennedy played up bread-and-butter issues, his promise to do MORE for Massachusetts, his past and future helpfulness to labor, consumers, and other clients of the Democracy. On Joe McCarthy—a friend of his father's—and on McCarthyism the candidate remained absolutely mum.

Courage and caution paid off. Kennedy beat Lodge by a margin of 70,000 in a total vote of over 2.6 million. In January 1953 he took his seat in the upper chamber. The new president of the Senate was Richard M. Nixon. The new Minority Leader of the Senate Democrats was Lyndon B. Johnson.

THE SOUTHERN POOR

When the "famine Irish" shipped into American ports during the late 1840s they found themselves among the descendants of great waves of earlier immigrants—of the seventeenth- and eighteenth-century colonials, of Huguenot French and a diversity of Germans, and of large numbers of Protestant Scotch-Irish, many of whom had settled in Pennsylvania and Virginia and then fanned out to the borderlands. Like the Irish Catholics, many of these migrants had come in search of free religion and speech, free education and enterprise, freedom from class distinction and compulsory military service. The famine Irish encountered one other type of "immigrant," however—black men and women who had been kidnapped or traded out of Africa and smuggled into southern ports. A few blacks had made their way to northern cities, where they often fought with the Irish over the economic scraps, but most ended up on the cotton and tobacco and rice plantations of the South.

At the dawn of the twentieth century large numbers of the northern Irish, but only a small fraction of rural blacks, had won economic and political freedoms. Emancipated slaves had emerged from the Civil War and Reconstruction with somewhat broadened constitutional rights and liberties, only to have their advances virtually nullified later in the century by Jim Crow laws that robbed them of their newly won right to vote and systematically separated them from whites in schools, workplaces, and public facilities. By the 1950s southern rural blacks, ravaged further by the great depression, by pervasive segregation and discrimination, and by the mechanical cotton picker and other technological changes, comprised the poorest of the poor. Macon County, Alabama, an 82 percent black cotton-growing land that included Tuskegee, illustrated the situation at its worst. Of several hundred tenant dwellings surveyed in the 1930s, more than half had open privies, almost that proportion had no sewage disposal whatever, eighty-one had no water on the place.

There was a cruel poverty of aspiration as well. Whether the nation enjoyed prosperity or depression, conditions for the southern poor hardly improved over the years. FDR called the South "the nation's No. 1 economic problem" and channeled funds into the area, but the structure of poverty remained unchanged. By 1960 seven out of ten of the nation's black families earning under $3,000 a year lived in the South, as compared to four out of ten white families. Clearly a multitude of whites also suffered poverty in the South, but like the Boston Irish they could take educational, entrepreneurial, and employment paths to personal freedom. Southern blacks could not—and far worse, their children could not. An 1896 Supreme Court decision that most blacks had not even heard of, *Plessy* v. *Ferguson,* had set the precedent for "separate but equal" schools that had remained separate but grossly unequal. Black schoolchildren were still systematically shunted out of the mainstream of opportunity.

Southern blacks were immobilized in their own caste, in their own class structure. At the bottom of the pyramid were blacks still effectively or even literally in peonage. Growing out of wage agreements following emancipation, serving as a crude path from bondage to "freedom," enforced by the whip and the chain gang, peonage had served as a means of labor control through keeping blacks constantly in debt. Nonpayment left blacks in the toils of the law and hence, in many cases, of the boss man. Isolated cases of peonage were still being reported in the 1950s. Two Alabama farmers were imprisoned in 1954 for paying blacks' jail fines by working them in the fields; one of the blacks who was bailed out had later been beaten to death when he tried to flee.

A step above peonage were the sharecroppers, tenant farmers, wandering job-seekers, a kind of rural proletariat locked into its own mores, illiteracy, and low motivation. A black middle class embraced farm owners, artisans, steady workers, elementary and perhaps high school graduates, churchgoers. At the top were a few hundred thousand established business people, lawyers and ministers and teachers and other professionals, even plantation owners. They had "made it" through sheer pluck and a bit of luck.

But no black, high or low, peon or professional, could escape shattering blows to self-esteem. Carl Rowan, a Tennessee-born black journalist, returned to the South in 1951 to report on race relations there. Soon his stories in the Minneapolis *Morning Tribune* and later his book *South of Freedom* were pricking the conscience of the nation. They were old stories to southern blacks: the little white girl pointing to the well-dressed Rowan and crying, "Momma, Momma, look at the pretty nigger!"—the black Charleston schools operating on double shifts—"colored" waiting to board a bus until all the whites had entered—one black doctor in Georgia for over 7,500 blacks—Harvey's Bar B-Q Stand in Rowan's hometown, owned by a black and segregated—the man whose grandson was lynched a few days before the actual culprit was found—blacks who could go anywhere as long as they wore a white coat and black bow tie—blacks who could go anywhere if they were or pretended to be African diplomats, and not Americans—and everywhere (including Washington, D.C.) segregated hotels, restaurants, waiting rooms, schools, laundries, and movie theaters.

How escape caste and class? Some blacks conducted desperate little rebellions of their own, almost invariably to be crushed. Some quietly hunkered down in their own protective storm cellars of home or community. Some acculturated, imitating white ways, but color was still the impassable barrier to "uppity niggers." Many fled to the North or other parts of the South. During the 1950s the Southeast registered a net loss of almost 1.5 million blacks. Between 1940 and 1960 the percentage of the nation's blacks living in the Southeast fell from 61 to 45, with the black farm population dropping by about two-thirds.

Blacks were tempted north in much the same ways European immigrants had been tempted west, by glowing reports of jobs, schools, "freedom," but often they found that they had merely exchanged their rural ghettos for urban ones. Migratory workers, black and white, followed the crops north, moving as the crops ripened—citrus fruit and tomatoes and potatoes in Florida, corn and snap beans in the Carolinas, berries and fruits in Virginia and Maryland, then the table vegetables of New Jersey and New York and, late in the fall, the potatoes of Maine. Encountering working and living conditions like those of the California Okies, many East Coast migrants returned home bitterly disillusioned about freedom north of "south of freedom."

Even more remarkable was the migration of southern blacks within the South. Hundreds of thousands living in rural areas moved into southern cities; hundreds of thousands living in the "core" or "solid" South moved to the "rim" states, especially Florida, Louisiana, and Virginia. Some never made it, returning home or ending up as migratory labor within the South. But for countless blacks the move from country to city, from heartland to "rim," brought better jobs, schools, and living conditions. A few even won white-collar positions, though most black women became household or service workers, and the number of them employed in private households increased during the 1950s.

On the surface, early in the 1950s the economic and political system of the Deep South seemed little changed. Underneath, a vast social transformation was underway, including the emergence of young black activists and a dramatic rise in the number of black children, more of whom now were getting some schooling. But whether blacks would break out of their social and psychological bonds depended on a liberating leadership that still lacked power at either the national or the community level.

*   *   *

Many rural whites in the South were poverty-stricken too, in their lack of good education, housing, nutrition, medical care, but they did not share these conditions with the blacks; the two races were often more sharply segregated in low-income areas than in middle-class. Entrenched white poverty extended to Appalachia, which included northern sections of Alabama, Georgia, North Carolina, and Tennessee as well as all of West Virginia and parts of five more northern states. Southern Appalachia in particular presented the familiar pathology of poverty—"low income, high unemployment, lack of urbanization, low educational achievement, and a low level of living," as one report summarized it. Typically poor Appalachian whites lacked even the "niggers" to look down on, but in coal-mining towns where the companies had recruited blacks from the South, the races lived, prayed, and schooled separately. A white coal miner related that after he had worked agreeably with a "colored boy" for some weeks and then quit merely to take a better job, his former boss looked him up and told him, "Jackson, if you will come back to work for me I'll fire every damn Nigger on the job."

It was a land of magnificent mountain ranges and wretched little "hollers," of abundant natural resources and human deprivation, of fierce family feuds and touching personal loyalties. In eastern Kentucky lay Harlan County, "bloody Harlan," ravaged in the 1930s by strikes, lockouts, and the killing of striking coal miners and scabs. But beginning in Appalachia, reaching across most of Tennessee, and extending into adjacent states stretched a vast experiment in the taming of nature and the betterment of human lives. This was the Tennessee Valley Authority. One of the New Deal's most daring and enlightened ventures, the TVA by 1960 had grown into a huge complex of thirty dams mainly on the Tennessee and Cumberland rivers, flood-control projects, electric power generating plants, river-traffic expansion, fertilizer production, forestry protection and technology, malaria control, recreational development. The Authority's significance lay in the way these activities interlinked and impinged upon people's lives and enterprises. In an area of the country dominated by the caprices of nature and the limited vision of leaders, here was a project that connected commerce with flood prevention, promotion of traffic with water control, river-taming with cheap electricity, parks with regional development, altogether a supreme effort at rational planning. In a benign transformation of the people's environment—at least until the advent of nuclear power—a new inland world was created, of lakes gleaming like diamond pendants along the once turbulent Tennessee and Cumberland rivers, of sailing and fishing, swimming and camping, hiking and animal watching.

Far to the west, past the Mississippi River and Louisiana and eastern Texas, lay that part of the South that appeared the least southern of all. The hill country of central Texas sat in the south-center of the plains that stretched down the middle of Texas west of the Balcones Escarpment. The hill country, west of Austin and northwest of San Antonio, was grassy, giving way to brush, thin-soiled, dry, windy, and subject to drought—a poor land barely supporting poor people. To the hill country settlers had come throughout the last century, to raise cattle and cotton. By the end of the century the hill country was in a long decline, as cattle ate away the grass that shielded the soil even as cotton drained the soil itself. Here Lyndon B. Johnson was born in the summer of 1908; this land shaped him as a Southerner and politician.

Within a few years Lyndon was showing qualities that would mark him for the rest of his life; he was bossy, competitive, restless, and ornery. For a time he and his father, Sam Ealy, and mother, Rebekah Baines, and four siblings lived in a warm family circle. He adored his mother and admired his father, a Democratic state representative of populist principles. And Lyndon heard much about his idealistic grandfather who had been an unsuccessful populist candidate for the Texas legislature. But by the time Lyndon was in his teens, gangling, big-eared, thin-faced, he was rebelling against Sam, who had fallen on hard times in a down cycle of the boom-and-bust economy of central Texas. Now the family lived in relative poverty and—Lyndon suspected—was the butt of ridicule for having lived high on the hog and fallen so low.

The solution for young Johnson was escape. He fled to the company of older men and women in the neighborhood; journeyed south and worked eleven hours a day in a huge cotton gin, boiling hot and thick with lint and dust; made his way west to California, where he clerked in a cousin's law office; returned home and worked with a road gang; and finally went off to college, to Southwest Texas State Teachers College at San Marcos. Some of LBJ's enduring traits were shaped at San Marcos, as he played up to the college president and faculty, bossed the younger students, manipulated school elections, organized the underrepresented students against an elite group of star athletes—a strange mixture of bootlicker and bully, in the eyes of critical schoolmates. He took a year off to make some money by teaching in the "Mexican school" in Cotulla, a town of crumbling shanties situated on a desolate plain fifty miles from the Rio Grande.

Almost everywhere young Johnson went he saw poverty—at home in his own family, among the cotton gin workers, at college, where some of the students were poorer than he. He found abject poverty in Cotulla, where there was no school lunch hour because the pupils had no lunch, and no playground except a debris-littered vacant lot. Undaunted, LBJ threw himself into the job, inspiring and disciplining the students, motivating the teachers, galvanizing much of the town. Promoted to principal at the very start, he demonstrated an insatiable need for respect and deference, but he exhibited as well a big heart. Discovering that the school janitor could not speak English, he spent hours before and after class time tutoring him—he also insisted that the school be spanking clean.

Graduated from San Marcos in 1930, Johnson carried his competitiveness and his compassion, his raw ambition and his populist instincts, into a series of jobs—public-speaking teacher in Houston, Texas state director of the National Youth Administration, aide to a Texas congressman, candidate for Congress. If LBJ's political character was foreshadowed in college, his political career was portended in his first campaign for the House. When the incumbent representative died in 1937 and the governor called a special "sudden death" election (that is, no runoff), Johnson heard that the widow of the deceased was thinking of running. To head her off he announced at once—before the body was cold, as some Texans saw it—and she stayed out. There followed a wild melee as LBJ, twenty-eight years old and one of the most obscure of the contenders, scoured the district for votes, scrounged the countryside for money, and wrapped himself around with FDR's coattails. His gargantuan energy, along with one of the biggest war chests Texas had seen for a House race, brought him a convincing win over eight rivals.

In Washington and Texas politics the young congressman showed a flair for combining political savvy, feverish energy, and corporation money. When the Roosevelt White House suddenly needed funds in 1940 to help beleaguered Democratic candidates for Congress, Johnson raised tens of thousands of dollars. Increasingly, as he planned to run for the first Senate seat available, he was drawn toward the world of the Texas rich—into the "endless chains of inter- and intra-city, family and club, formal and informal relationships which characterize the Texas monied establishment," in Neal Peirce's words. This world had several dimensions.

Jesse Jones, banker, publisher of the Houston *Chronicle,* financial backer of the Democratic party, FDR's head of the Reconstruction Finance Corporation and Secretary of Commerce, typified the old dominion of agriculture and lumber and banking and real estate. Intertwined with this business dominion was the "old" establishment of oil based on the huge fields of southern Texas—notably Spindletop—and controlled by such big eastern corporations as Standard Oil, Gulf, and Sun. The drilling of the sensational five-billion-barrel East Texas fields in the early 1930s—the "poor man's pool"—had enriched hundreds of wildcatters who promptly became the *nouveaux riches*—the *très très riches*—of Texas. Bitter quarrels often erupted within and among these groups but in crucial ways they stood together: they were *Texans,* proud and independent; they were almost casual gamblers, whether in oil or in stocks, on crops or on cards; they stood united against both "Wall Street capitalism" and western egalitarian populism; and no business group in the country had a better grasp of the politics of economics and the economics of politics.

The young congressman had an uncanny ability to draw political money from older businessmen, in part because he knew how to defer to them, flatter them, *listen* to them. And he needed big money when a Senate seat opened up in 1941—again because the incumbent had died. Embarking on a huge statewide campaign requiring a big and costly personal organization, once again running on FDR's coattails, he raised tens of thousands of dollars from both Texas contractors and Washington New Dealers—only to be ignominiously defeated by Governor "Pappy" ("Pass the Biscuits") O'Daniel and his hillbilly band that included two of Pappy's sons, fiddler Patty Boy and banjo-playing Mickey Wickey. When a second Senate seat opened in 1948, Johnson waged another campaign of furious energy and big campaign contributions, but with a difference. This time he distanced himself from the memory of FDR and even from Truman; and this time he won—but with a margin of fewer than 100 votes out of 900,000 cast, leaving him with an imperishable nickname in Texas, "Landslide Lyndon."

*　　*　　*

The Senate that Lyndon Johnson entered in January 1949 was already peopled by famous men—the reserved and formidable Richard Russell of Georgia, FDR's 1938 purge target Walter George, the racist Mississippian James Eastland, the liberal Republican Wayne Morse of Oregon, the Senate president and United States Vice President, Alben Barkley. Johnson's own "Class of 1948" glittered with younger talent: Estes Kefauver, Huey's son Russell Long, civil rights leader Hubert Humphrey of Minnesota, the dean of the liberal Democrats, Paul Douglas of Illinois. But three years later, as Doris Kearns noted, it was none of the above who was elected Democratic party whip, but rather the little-known newcomer from Texas.

Two years later, Johnson was chosen Minority Leader, and two years after that, when the Democrats regained control of the upper chamber, he became the Senate Majority Leader.

How could this "youngster" rise so fast in what looked like a gerontocracy? In part because he deferred to the gerontocrats—men like Russell who stood guard over Senate rules and customs. Once again LBJ showed his capacity to adjust to his environment—and then dominate it. From his old roles of Texas populist and flag waver for FDR and the New Deal he shifted easily into the transactional leadership of a parliamentary coalition broker. The Senate and he seemed made for each other, as he quickly mastered its procedures, nosed out its corridors and cloakrooms of power, calculated the influence of parties, blocs, and individual senators.

The Senate mastered him as well. It softened the sharp edges of his personality, dampened down the fire of his populist ideology, and forced him to operate within its own channels. As Democratic leader, Johnson was perched at the center of a four-way clustering of Senate power. On his farther left were the liberal Democrats, mainly from the North and led by such senators as Humphrey and Douglas. To his immediate left sat the moderate Republicans headed by politicos close to the Eisenhower White House and by East and West Coast Republicans. Just to the right sat a cluster of conservative Democrats, mainly Southerners like Russell and Eastland, entrenched in powerful committees such as Finance and Judiciary. And to the farther right were the congressional Republicans, headed by Everett Dirksen of Illinois and largely responsive to the conservative business interests of the nation's hinterland. LBJ's talents lay in keeping his distance from each of these groups even while he traded with all of them.

His talents were put to the test by the harshest challenge the Senate had faced since the 1937 Court fight or even the League of Nations struggle. Johnson's wheeling and dealing, his coalition making and unmaking, his geeing and hawing, worked reasonably well as long as he was trading with the White House and among the Senate parties over bread-and-butter legislation. He brokered between Eisenhower's modest proposals for housing, farm, defense, and education and programs opposed or supported by congressional factions. There were limits: Republicans would not retreat on the anti-union Taft-Hartley Act, which LBJ had defended; Democrats fought off major erosion of New Deal and Fair Deal legislation. But these were mainly "quantitative" measures on which the Majority Leader could skillfully cut deals involving the size of appropriations and the extent of regulations.

The storm that gathered during the 1950s was not over such quantifiable matters, however, but over a transcending moral and ideological issue. This was freedom for southern and other Negroes. For many decades major civil rights legislation had been the great "undoable" for the United States Senate. The old, southern-dominated Democracy had lived off racism politically. FDR hated discrimination, whether in the South or the North, but feared to throw an explosive issue into Congress that would shatter his North-South Democratic coalition; as World War II approached he set up a Fair Employment Practices Committee under pressure from militant blacks, but he only weakly defended it against its enemies. Year after year, Truman's broad civil rights proposals to Congress were killed in committee or on the floor. "Negroes could protest, presidents could recommend, party platforms could endorse, the House of Representatives could act," James Sundquist noted, "but no civil rights bill could become law without a change in the Senate rule requiring a two-thirds majority to end debate." And the filibuster rule itself could be protected by a filibuster. In the House the Rules Committee, controlling the traffic flow of bills, was almost equally lethal, and in both chambers southern committee gerontocrats shielded by the seniority rule stood in phalanxes against civil rights spear carriers.

A grim interplay of personality, politics, and place, the civil rights battle by the mid-1950s was so convoluted as both to demand and to defy untangling. The two cardinal issues were black voting rights in the South and desegregation of schools and other public facilities. With notable exceptions northern presidential Democrats favored both a voting rights bill and school desegregation; presidential "waterside" Republicans, including the Eisenhower Administration, supported vote legislation but backed a school bill only to the degree that they feared that northern Democratic appeals to black voters might swing the next election; congressional Democrats would accept a weak voting bill but indignantly opposed a school bill; and congressional Republicans put either or both issues at the bottom of their priority lists. With racial tension mounting in the South, the government of the United States seemed mired in deadlock over civil rights.

Suddenly the third horse in the American *troika* came galloping to the rescue when the Supreme Court—supposedly the "nonpolitical" branch—in the Brown case on May 17, 1954, held racially segregated public schools in violation of the Fourteenth Amendment. The decision burst on the front pages of the nation's newspapers like a bombshell, but Court-watchers were not so surprised. Roosevelt appointees, including Hugo Black, William O. Douglas, and Felix Frankfurter, still held a majority on the High Court; gifted black and white attorneys for the NAACP and other civil rights organizations had been pressing the courts for redress; and the Supreme Court in 1950 had struck down state laws failing to satisfy blacks' Fourteenth Amendment rights in higher or professional education. Still, the Brown decision was breathtaking—in its extension of these rights to hundreds of thousands of children in elementary schools and in its frank reversal of the pro-segregation Plessy decision of 1896 and its endorsement by all nine justices, headed by Eisenhower appointee Earl Warren.

But even the Supreme Court, acting decisively in the policy void left by anti-civil rights congressional leadership and presidential nonleadership, could not shake the Senate bastion. How would the justices' decision be enforced, especially since the Warren Court had left open the implementation formula? Against the gathering civil rights forces North and South the southern Democratic senators fought to defend the right to filibuster—which for them was a fight for the "southern way of life." Johnson, eternally balancing interests, institutions, and ideologies, struggled to find some common ground. "I knew that if I failed to produce on this one," he said later, "my leadership would be broken into a hundred pieces."

The upshot was the Civil Rights Act of 1957, which emerged from the legislative obstacle race as a weak voting rights bill, stripped of its provisions enforcing school desegregation. Liberal Democrats found some consolation in the hope that once southern blacks gained the right to vote with the help of the new measure, they could use their newfound power to gain more goals. Others, including many blacks, contended that Negroes could win freedom and equality only by pressing ahead on all fronts—desegregation, fair employment, housing, welfare, as well as voting—in a manner that allowed these changes to be mutually reinforcing. This strategic issue was never put to the test because the voting measure of 1957 produced very little voting. Two years later fewer than two hundred blacks were registered to vote in Alabama's Dallas County, only a total of five blacks in three other Alabama counties. For countless blacks and others, "liberal democracy," American style, did not appear to be working even for the most elementary of rights, the right to vote.

*   *   *

Nor did "liberal democracy" now have the luxury of time. Even as Eisenhower signed the 1957 bill in mid-September, tension was rising over the barring of blacks from Little Rock high schools by order of the governor. In two weeks the President reluctantly sent a thousand federal paratroopers to the Arkansas capital to force integration against the will of the state government and the mob. The blacks there were making school integration, not voting rights, the issue. As the mobilized civil rights forces pursued direct action and as massive resistance and rioting by whites broke out elsewhere in the lower South, it was more and more evident that Congress must once again face the issues of voting rights and schools.

A long guerrilla battle broke out in the Capitol contrapuntally to the struggle in the South. Once again the filibuster rule stood firm in the Senate; indeed, this kind of obstruction reached a new high when a moderate civil rights bill ran into a filibuster in the Senate Judiciary *Committee*, which was found to have no cloture rule. With Eisenhower offering little support because, he said, he had "very little faith in the ability of statutory law to change the human heart, or to eliminate prejudice," the 1957 voting rights bill was somewhat strengthened in 1960 but enforcement of school desegregation was killed.

Johnson was still the Negotiator-in-Chief, bargaining with the White House and helping build coalitions for or against specific sections of the civil rights bill. But now the political environment was changing as the 1960 presidential election neared. And Lyndon Johnson, determined to seek the presidency, confronted a rival who as a senator was no great shakes but was vigorously building a national constituency. This was John F. Kennedy.

The two men had more in common than either might wish to admit. Each had had a nurturing mother and a demanding father who had fired up his ambition and helped satisfy it. Each had represented a poverty-stricken congressional district that he had won after furious battles with a bevy of fellow Democrats. Both had been bored in the House of Representatives. Each was highly ambitious, politically cautious, rhetorically bold. Both had had serious health problems. Navy veterans, they were part of the postwar generation of tough-minded, "pragmatic" politicians. But the differences between them were more profound. JFK had observed poverty; LBJ had lived in it. Kennedy could depend on his father to supply political money; Johnson had to turn to businessmen outside his family. The Massachusetts senator had an inbred cosmopolitan style that the Majority Leader disdained and envied. The biggest contrast, though, lay in their constituencies—Johnson's in the Senate, in the congressional parties he traded with, and in the South; Kennedy's in the larger, urban, ethnic states that held the big, balance-of-power chunks of the electoral college.

On civil rights Kennedy had hardly shown a profile in courage. He had favored sending the 1957 measure to that graveyard of civil rights legislation, the Judiciary Committee, to the outrage of black leaders and northern liberals, and to the delight of southern senators including Eastland, who promptly stated his support for Kennedy for President. Later he lined up with the liberals in voting for the desegregation part of a 1960 bill, although—or perhaps because—it had little chance of passing. His civil rights stand, as his loyal aide Theodore Sorensen later lamented, was still "shaped primarily by political expediency instead of basic human principles."

The shape of "political expediency" had changed by 1960. While Johnson as an established national leader thought he could campaign for the presidency from the Senate, Kennedy knew that he must convert his magazine-cover fame into grass-roots voting support in the key presidential primaries, every one of which posed critical challenges for him. He had to placate ADA liberals turned off by his compromises on McCarthy and civil rights, veteran party leaders like Harry Truman who flatly opposed him, southern conservatives against him for both religious and ideological reasons, Stevenson loyalists who wanted their man to have the opportunity to run against someone besides Ike.

The Kennedy people believed they could deal with such traditional political pressures, but three other "issues" bristled: the candidate's religion, his youth, and his father. The Kennedy office made intensive studies of the "Catholic element" in voting, put out analyses suggesting the *advantages* of a Catholic running for office, and were immensely relieved when Protestant West Virginia, stimulated by heavy campaign spending, gave Kennedy a clear win over Humphrey in its primary. Kennedy rebutted the youth issue with talk about a "new generation of leadership." His father and his father's money he handled with humor. To a 1958 Gridiron Club dinner, he read a telegram from his "generous daddy": "Dear Jack—Don't buy a single vote more than is necessary—I'll be damned if I'm going to pay for a landslide." The remorseless correspondents replied with a song at the next year's Gridiron to the tune of "All of Me":

> All of us
> Why not take all of us
> Fabulous
> You can't live without us
> My son Jack
> Heads the procession
> Groomed for succession. . . .

Brilliantly supported by a small campaign group headed by the versatile Sorensen, amply financed by his father, intensively covered by television that projected his image to millions of new tube watchers, and assisted by Kennedy enthusiasts who traveled hundreds of miles to "help Jack," Kennedy picked his way adroitly through the political minefields and lined up enough Democratic convention delegates weeks in advance to bring him victory on the first ballot in Los Angeles.

Trounced on the convention floor, Johnson now had to contemplate the humiliation of being passed over for running mate. He wanted to be Vice President, both to position himself as JFK's successor someday and because he believed that he could convert any job—even Throttlebottom's—into a power base. Kennedy's first-ballot victory was followed by a wild day in which the candidate and his brother Robert lost control of the process of picking a running mate—a process that LBJ would have handled with brutal skill. The struggle over the vice-presidential choice was so complex and murky that historians were still differing in their accounts decades later, but this much seemed clear: in the maneuvering before the convention, Kennedy had long and seriously considered LBJ, but the names of Humphrey, Missouri Senator Stuart Symington, Governors G. Mennen Williams of Michigan and Orville Freeman of Minnesota, and others had also been put forward; in a typical politicians' confrontation, the nominee halfheartedly offered his beaten rival the nomination and LBJ halfheartedly declined, in part because "Mr. Sam" Rayburn opposed acceptance; labor and liberal leaders implored the Kennedy people to reject Johnson; hours of confusion passed as pro- and anti-Johnson people pressured Kennedy, and LBJ's friends pressured him to run and not to run; Bobby offered to try to persuade LBJ not to accept and Jack wished him good luck; Bobby's missions ran into an increasingly indignant Johnson and retinue; and JFK suddenly put an end to the whole business by telling Johnson he not only wanted him but would fight for him. That was what Johnson, burning with indignation at "that little shit-ass" Bobby, wanted to hear.

One vice-presidential nomination was far from enough, however, to assuage the various wounds left by the Los Angeles convention. Even before it ended, the party seemed to crack: Russell had quit the convention early because he feared the "evil threat" to "our Southland" of the pro-civil rights party platform, while Eleanor Roosevelt quietly departed out of disappointment that her close friend and ally Adlai Stevenson had neither made much effort for the nomination nor been accorded the support she felt was due him. Harry Truman hadn't put in an appearance; nine days before the convention opened, he had blasted Kennedy at a televised press conference and condemned the convention as a "prearranged affair." Protestant spokesmen were hostile; some leading Catholics feared that a Kennedy campaign would simply exacerbate ancient hostilities.

Of all the specific fence-mending he had to do, the most crucial to Kennedy was a reconciliation with Eleanor Roosevelt, the conscience of the party and the channel to alienated Stevensonians and ADA liberals who could have critical influence in California and New York. So skillfully did Kennedy handle a showdown meeting with the former First Lady in Hyde Park—like Napoleon and Alexander's meeting on their "raft at Tilsit," he called it—that she warmed to him and soon became one of his most enthusiastic campaigners.

Some of his fences mended, Kennedy plunged into his campaign. Awaiting him was Richard M. Nixon, who had won Ike's glum support, easily fought off an inept challenge by Governor Nelson Rockefeller of New York, and been nominated by acclamation.

The battle that followed left glowing images on the nation's memory: Nixon's lightning trips to all fifty states, including Hawaii and Alaska, as he had rashly promised—Kennedy's audacious mission to Texas, where he assured a gathering of the Houston Ministerial Association, chaired by Norman Vincent Peale, that he believed in "an America where the separation of church and state is absolute"—the first of four televised debates, with Nixon holding his own on substance but losing on the television screen—Kennedy's compassionate and astute telephone call to Mrs. Martin Luther King, Jr., after her husband was jailed in Georgia—and the huge crowds, swollen by the debates, and fronted by long lines of "jumpers" bobbing up and down in waves as the candidates passed. Then the long tense election evening, as Kennedy took an early lead, only to watch it slowly erode and leave him with the narrowest of victories.

THE INVISIBLE LATINS

"To those peoples in the huts and villages of half the globe struggling to break the bonds of mass misery, we pledge our best efforts to help them help themselves, for whatever period is required—not because the Communists may be doing it, not because we seek their votes, but because it is right." John F. Kennedy looked out at the sea of faces in the Capitol Plaza reflecting the cold January sun. "If a free society cannot help the many who are poor, it cannot save the few who are rich." The new President's voice was strong and confident.

"To our sister republics south of our border, we offer a special pledge—to convert our good words into good deeds—in a new alliance for progress—to assist free men and free governments in casting off the chains of poverty. But this peaceful revolution of hope cannot become the prey of hostile powers. Let all our neighbors know that we shall join with them to oppose aggression or subversion anywhere in the Americas. And let every other power know that this hemisphere intends to remain the master of its own house."

So finely honed were the bracing inaugural words, so masterfully delivered, so euphorically received, that many missed the deep ambivalences and dichotomies interwoven throughout:

Man "holds in his mortal hands the power to abolish all forms of human poverty and all forms of human life." Americans still had their old "revolutionary beliefs." *But:* "Let the word go forth from this time and place, to friend and foe alike, that the torch has been passed to a new generation of Americans—born in this century, tempered by war, disciplined by a hard and bitter peace, proud of our ancient heritage—and unwilling to witness or permit the slow undoing of those human rights . . . to which we are committed today at home and around the world."

Let every nation know that "we shall pay any price, bear any burden, meet any hardship, support any friend, oppose any foe to assure the survival and the success of liberty."

Kennedy decried the cost of arms, the "steady spread of the deadly atom" and urged that "both sides begin anew the quest for peace." *But:* "We dare not tempt them with weakness. For only when our arms are sufficient beyond doubt can we be certain beyond doubt that they will never be employed."

"Let us never fear to negotiate." *But:* "Let us never negotiate out of fear."

"Now the trumpet summons us again—not as a call to bear arms, though arms we need—not as a call to battle, though embattled we are—but a call to bear the burden of a long twilight struggle . . . against the common enemies of man: tyranny, poverty, disease and war itself." *But:* "In the long history of the world, only a few generations have been granted the role of defending freedom in its hour of maximum danger. I do not shrink from this responsibility—I welcome it."

The whole inaugural address, like many before and since, was a "celebration of freedom," in Kennedy's words—of liberty, the ranks of the free, of revolutionary rights, of a free society, of free men and free governments, of the freedom of humankind. But far more than the other addresses, Kennedy's reflected the nation's uncertainty and confusion over the meaning of freedom.

Did Kennedy's ambivalences reflect, in his own character and ideology, polarities that had originated in his earlier divided self? Or were they merely the familiar hedging of the American politician? Probably both, but the sheer breadth of his inaugural dichotomies suggested more that they were deep-seated. In the end, however, the new President's words would be tested in action. Within two months of his inaugural Kennedy spoke to the Latin American diplomatic corps in the East Room of the White House in the language of hope:

"I have called on all people of the hemisphere to join in a new Alliance for Progress—*Alianza para Progreso*—a vast cooperative effort, unparalleled in magnitude and nobility of purpose, to satisfy the basic needs of the American people for homes, work and land, health and schools—*techo, trabajo y terra, salud y escuela.*" He laid out a program for economic development through national planning, regional marketing, commodity stabilization, hemispheric cooperation in education and research. "Let us once again transform the American continent into a vast crucible of revolutionary ideas and efforts—a tribute to the power of the creative energies of free men and women—an example to all the world that liberty and progress walk hand in hand."

*   *   *

Enchanted by this eloquent, dynamic young President, inspired by both his rhetoric and his recommendations, the diplomats in the East Room that day burst into applause. "We have not heard such words since Franklin Roosevelt," the Venezuelan ambassador remarked to Kennedy aide Arthur Schlesinger. But mixed with the new hope of the Latin Americans was their collective memory of their earlier relationship with the "colossus of the North."

It was only a half century since imperial American interventions in Central America and the Caribbean, hardly more than thirty years since Calvin Coolidge had sent troops into Nicaragua to help check the insurrectionist leader Augusto Sandino. To be sure, President Hoover and Secretary of State Stimson had talked a less interventionist line in the early 1930s, and FDR and Hull's Good Neighbor policy, with its emphasis on the lowering of trade barriers and nonintervention, had come as a powerful breath of fresh air to Latin Americans. Even under FDR, however, Washington remained deeply involved in the internal affairs of nations such as Cuba, and the Good Neighbor idea itself had been more a fine helping of rhetoric about freedom and the equal rights of all the American nations than a vehicle of economic or social reform. The main continuities of Washington's interventionist policy toward Latin America over the decades had been unpredictability and volatility. For most Americans, Latin America was the great "invisible" land that burst onto the national consciousness only when some crisis—a revolution, a natural catastrophe, a phenomenon like Juan and Evita Perón of Argentina—for a brief time seized the headlines.

The diplomats facing Kennedy in the East Room represented a region with some of the most entrenched poverty on the globe. The Latin American per capita income was not only low—$325 a year—but seemed static. Over two-thirds of the Latins lived in dire want. This figure both reflected and concealed the enormous disparity of income: 2 percent of the people owned three-quarters of all arable land and about one-half of all personal wealth. Twenty-four million Mexicans, out of a population of 35 million, lived in homes without electric lights; 30 million urban Latins lacked city-controlled drinking water; the average Peruvian subsisted on 1,900 calories a day, enough for bare survival.

But even these figures hardly told the story. While the Latins had scored some notable economic achievements, their poor lived in a Gordian knot of poverty, the thongs of which pulled ever tighter in its crushing embrace. Against limited resources the population was expanding faster than any other in the world. Only half of children under eighteen—only a quarter in rural areas—attended school. Half of the whole Latin population was illiterate. Life expectancy ranged from 33 years in Haiti to 39 in Brazil to 57 in Argentina—as against 67 years in the United States. Investigating the human condition behind such figures, an anthropologist found a "culture of poverty" in the very heart of great cities like San Juan and Mexico City—a poverty of "segregation and discrimination, fear, suspicion or apathy" thwarting involvement of the poor in the wider society; a poverty that drained hope, expectation, motivation, morale, opportunity; a "family" poverty comprised of the "absence of childhood" as a long, protected stage in the life cycle, "early initiation into sex, free unions of consensual marriage," frequent abandonment of wives and children, "a trend toward female- or mother-centered families," individual feelings of helplessness, dependence, and inferiority. These were the truly mute, invisible Latins; these were the unfree.

The bewildering diversity of Latin American peoples, nationalisms, cultures, and subcultures had produced a variety of American diplomatic and military responses over the decades. After the earlier times of hostility and intervention Washington's relations with Mexico had come to a happy plateau. Two fine ambassadors, Coolidge's and Hoover's Dwight Morrow and FDR's Josephus Daniels, helped to defuse and finally settle through skillful diplomacy and political compromise the long-simmering issue of Mexican expropriation of the oil properties of United States companies. Mexico, under its own able leadership, appeared to help teach Americans how to live with avowed revolutionaries next door.

The rest of Latin America made up a patchwork of old-style *caudillo* regimes, such as Generalissimo Rafael Trujillo's in the Dominican Republic, François Duvalier's in Haiti, and Somoza's in Nicaragua; of conservative, more or less democratic regimes, as in Ecuador, Chile, Panama, and Peru; of newly established liberal regimes, as in Brazil, Colombia, and Venezuela; and of revolutionary regimes in Bolivia and most notably Cuba. The "postrevolutionary" regimes of Mexico and Uruguay had demonstrated that Latin American nations could pass through upheavals and achieve "politically durable and relatively prosperous regimes" without undue guidance from the "motherland" of American nations born in revolution—the United States of America. Latin Americans had long been familiar with Washington orators who declaimed about glorious revolutions in history and in theory—United States style, of course—and attacked contemporary revolutions in process.

* * *

If the United States had given birth to the very model of the successful "democratic" revolution, Cuba was the father of revolutionary failure. The slave revolts that began in the sixteenth century and rose to horrifying proportions in the nineteenth, the revolt of *vegueros*—planters—against the tobacco monopolists early in the eighteenth century, and the ten-year war against Spanish rule ending in 1878, were put down with slaughter and torture. The rebellion against Spain, during which the Spanish commander ordered that any doctor, schoolteacher, or lawyer captured with the rebels should be instantly shot, took 200,000 lives and left a land seared with hatred. Cubans finally won their independence at the end of the century only to fall under the writ of the North Americans who had helped them gain it.

From the days of Theodore Roosevelt, who wanted to teach the "cheating, mañana lot" to behave properly, Cuba stood as a classic example of United States intervention in Latin America. Washington tolerated and supported corrupt and brutal dictators in Havana as long as American economic and security interests—especially its huge base at Guantánamo—were protected. By the 1950s "American companies controlled 40 percent of the island's sugar lands, 80 percent of its public utilities, 90 percent of the mines and cattle ranches, and, in combination with Shell, substantially all the oil business." Although part of the rationale for heavy Yankee investment—equal to one-third of Cuba's gross national product— was that it would raise the people's living standards, hundreds of thousands of cane-cutters, tobacco-field laborers, and other peasants lived in the usual poverty. The Cuban labor forces also included 100,000 or more sugar-mill workers, who formed the core of the island nation's labor movements, as well as several hundred thousand jobless people, some of whom found seasonal work in the fields for a few meager months.

For a time after Fidel Castro and a small army of guerrillas, following initial blundering attacks, through sheer tenacity and fanatical determination drove the malodorous Batista regime out of power, Washington and Havana maintained a semblance of harmony; Castro even visited the United States and conducted virtually a sidewalk campaign tour. Relations hardened when Castro seized American-owned oil refineries and other properties and Congress cut the quota on Cuban sugar. By the time he left office a hesitant Eisenhower, prodded by Vice President Nixon, was organizing a CIA-backed invasion of Cuba by exiles. This stratagem had worked in Guatemala six years before—why not in Cuba?

John Kennedy had once called Fidel Castro "part of the legacy of Bolívar," part of that "earlier revolution which won its war against Spain but left largely untouched the indigenous feudal order." By the fall of 1960, however, Castro had turned to the Kremlin for support and Kennedy was locked in a bitter campaign struggle with Nixon, who had proposed to the annual American Legion convention that the "cancer" of Castroism be eliminated through a "quarantine." The Democratic nominee was not to be outdone. Nixon, who for security reasons could not reveal the "Cuba project," was enraged when he read a *New York Times* headline: "Kennedy Asks Aid for Cuban Rebels to Defeat Castro, Urges Support of Exiles and 'Fighters for Freedom.' " The Vice President used his fourth television debate with Kennedy to call his foe's proposals "the most dangerously irresponsible recommendations," all the while knowing that it was more than a White House recommendation—it was White House policy.

It was against this background of escalating, vote-huckstering anti-Castroism that the new President inaugurated his bold Alliance for Progress. He was now imprisoned by his own campaign rhetoric and promises, by the invasion plans already underway, by CIA support for those plans. Faced with a situation calling either for direct military action, as against Mexico in olden times, or for self-restraint and diplomacy, the new President was politically and intellectually able to do neither. Rather he clung to the "middle way" of an invasion by refugees shielded by a deployment of United States air and sea power that must—on this Kennedy insisted—remain invisible. The success of the venture depended finally on the hope, founded on the Guatemalan experience, that once the rebels had landed, support for Castro among the Cuban military and population would collapse. Kennedy's staff shared a tendency toward group-think that discouraged dissent from this notion.

The invasion that got underway in mid-April 1961 became a world-class example of military misadventure. Almost everything that could go wrong did go wrong: bad communications, faulty intelligence, unexpected reefs, poor coordination of arms, inadequate numbers and equipment. The real failure, however, was not operational but psychological and political. Even if the invaders had landed in force and moved inland, they would have failed. For the effect of the invasion on the Cuban people was just the opposite of Washington's hopes. Mobilized not merely by the fast-moving, well-prepared Castro but by fierce nationalistic instincts, the "invisible" Cubans emerged to support the dictator's smashing counterattacks.

Humiliated by failure, heartsore over the hundreds of rebels killed or taken prisoner, Kennedy rose to one of his finest hours in taking personal responsibility for the fiasco. "There's an old saying that victory has a hundred fathers and defeat is an orphan," he told the press. "I am the responsible officer of the government." Privately, he was furious at the CIA, the military, and above all himself. "All my life I've known better than to depend on the experts," he said to Sorensen. "How could I have been so stupid, to let them go ahead?"

*   *   *

Vienna, June 1961. After dazzling Charles de Gaulle and the crowds in Paris with the young President's vitality and humor and the First Lady's dark beauty and Oleg Cassini gowns, the presidential couple flew on to Vienna for a much-heralded summit conference. Greeting them warmly, Khrushchev insisted that he wanted to "shake her hand first." But once the talks began, the mood turned cold and heavy and not even a glittering dinner in the Schönbrunn Palace could dispel it. . . .

Kennedy's thrust against Castroism had plunged Latin Americans more deeply into the global cold war. Once upon a time Washington had been able to isolate Latin politics from European rivalries, coldly informing London and Paris and Berlin that the North Americans would deal with their neighbors to the south under the Monroe Doctrine, which was conveniently adapted to Washington's needs of all seasons. But during the cold war Latin America became part of the great trembling mobile of global politics, and the Bay of Pigs fiasco sent a tremor through the quivering balances.

The Bay of Pigs intersected with another Kremlin sortie over Berlin. Kennedy had hoped that Berlin could be left in its impasse while he dealt with Castro but Khrushchev was not so obliging. In Vienna he presented Kennedy with a demand that if the two Germanys could not agree on a means of reunification in six months, then each should sign a separate peace treaty with the World War II victors. At this point, as a new European crisis loomed, both Moscow and Washington were caught in the spiral of fear. While boasting about his big missile force Khrushchev knew that he was far behind the Americans. Despite his campaign charges of a huge "missile gap," Kennedy now knew that the United States was far ahead on missiles but he feared that the Soviets were rapidly filling the gap.

The summer tension of 1961 rose to a fever pitch as the Kremlin stuck to its "deadline diplomacy" and Americans glimpsed the possibility of nuclear war. Kennedy and his Defense Secretary, Robert McNamara, somberly discussed the nation's capacity to absorb a Soviet nuclear attack and then launch a devastating strike against the Russians. At the height of the war fever the President gave the most frightening speech Americans had heard from the White House since Pearl Harbor. Seated at a desk surrounded by the panoply of his office, speaking with a cold militancy, he called for a big expansion in armed manpower, a boost in nonnuclear arms, and an emergency civil defense program. A kind of midsummer madness swept the nation as Americans rushed to build bomb shelters and to debate whether it was morally justified to slam the shelter door shut against desperate intruders—or even shoot them down.

"I don't know when I've been happier," Harry Truman wrote the President, "than when I listened to your great speech." But Eleanor Roosevelt worried in a newspaper column that civilian defense measures would induce a war psychosis, and later she urged on him a demilitarized Central Europe and a tenacious give-and-take for arms reduction regardless of whatever charges of "appeasement" it might bring. Khrushchev suddenly transformed the whole Berlin issue by allowing the East Germans to stem the flow of desperate refugees to the West. Soon Berlin was split by the Wall.

The spiral of fear mounted in late 1961 and early 1962 as Moscow and Washington spurred the arms race. Then the Kremlin came to a decision that would startle the world, for it amounted to nuclear adventurism. This was to emplace missiles in friendly Cuba. At first it was hard for the Administration to believe that Moscow was deploying missiles capable of bearing nuclear warheads on a vulnerable island some 6,000 miles from Russia. But Khrushchev had his reasons. In the wake of the Bay of Pigs, Cuba offered him a delicious opportunity to protect a friend—and a position of strength in the Caribbean—against further "imperialist" onslaughts. The Chairman, moreover, had to negotiate with his own hardliners, especially in the military. But the Kremlin acted also out of fear bordering on paranoia. If Russia was far behind on intercontinental missiles and could not catch up for years, what better way to close this real missile gap than by deploying Soviet medium-range or intermediate-range ballistic missiles only a few hundred miles from cities and military installations in the southern United States?

The operation must be secret, of course, until the Russians had emplaced enough missiles to scare off or defeat an early United States response. But the sharp photographic eyes of the high-flying U-2s quickly spotted launching sites under construction in Cuba for MRBMs and IRBMs. This time, instead of rushing to action, the President convened a loose assembly of cabinet members, security advisers, and others under the informal leadership of his brother Robert, the Attorney General. Day after day as new intelligence flowed in, members of this "ExCom" analyzed and debated alternative courses of action. While some shifted ground and no firm lines developed, the group split roughly between "hawks" like Dean Acheson and most of the military participants and "doves" such as Stevenson, George Ball, Sorensen, and Robert Kennedy himself. The President occasionally took part, but he listened far more than he talked. More than anyone else, he had to calculate the political element, for Republicans in Congress would leap on another Bay of Pigs, another "surrender." And the Commander-in-Chief alone would make the final decision. At an off-the-record session with several hundred newspaper editors during the crisis, he quoted the bullfighter's lament:

> Bullfight critics ranked in rows
> Crowd the enormous Plaza full;
> But only one is there who knows—
> And he's the man who fights the bull.

As the ExCom debated, Soviet freighters capable of bearing missiles were headed toward Cuba, nearing the quarantine line Kennedy had drawn around the island. Time was running out. Some in the group wanted an air strike on Cuba, even an invasion, but a very different resolution was taking shape. Messages were running between Moscow and Washington through formal and informal channels, and each side was taking care to leave fallback positions and "escape hatches" open to the other. It became clear that Khrushchev would agree to pull out his missiles if Kennedy made a hard promise not to invade Cuba and a soft—that is, orally communicated—promise later to pull American missiles out of Turkey. To be sure, the Administration had planned to remove those outdated Jupiter missiles anyway, but this mattered not to Khrushchev. He had a deal he could present to his own hard-liners. The freighters slowed, paused, and turned back.

The nation had waited, poised breathlessly on the brink, while the quiet debate and diplomacy had gone ahead. Now, after days of fear and even terror, people around the globe breathed a huge sigh of relief. The President met a storm of applause that was like balm to the wounds still aching from the Bay of Pigs. It had been a "close-run thing" that depended on an unusual degree of flexibility in both the Kremlin and the White House. Both leaders had had the desire and the authority to face down their hawks. The President learned from the crisis, Robert Kennedy said later, not to "humiliate" Khrushchev "or push him over the brink." It later became known, indeed, that Kennedy was prepared to offer Moscow an outright exchange of Turkish and Cuban missile withdrawal if Khrushchev had remained adamant.

In the post-crisis euphoria, however, hard facts were ignored. There had been some intelligence lapses as well as triumphs. Early diplomatic opportunities had not been exploited. At one or two points the war hawks, American and Russian, had almost carried the day. Khrushchev's standing in the Politburo was undermined by his combination of adventurism and withdrawal. In any event, it was clear that his retreat from Cuba resulted far less from diplomatic statesmanship than from his recognition that the Russians were immensely outgunned in intercontinental nuclear arms. This would not long be the case. For the relentless arms race carried on.

THE REVOLUTIONARY ASIANS

"To those new states whom we welcome to the ranks of the free," John Kennedy had proclaimed in his inaugural address, "we pledge our word that one form of colonial control shall not have passed away merely to be replaced by a far more iron tyranny. We shall not always expect to find them supporting our view. But we shall always hope to find them strongly supporting their own freedom—and to remember that, in the past, those who foolishly sought power by riding the back of the tiger ended up inside." A few words later he called for that "peaceful revolution of hope" which would help "free men and free governments" cast off the chains of poverty.

Within a few months of inauguration, Kennedy was plunged into both an intellectual and a military struggle over the meaning and application of those evocative terms, Freedom and Revolution. In Moscow, Nikita Khrushchev had no doubts about these ideas and their relationship. If Khrushchev sensed in Vienna that the young President had never seriously read "Lenin or any of the Soviet theoretical writers," which doubtless was the case, Khrushchev could not have known that Kennedy had read few of the Western theorists either. "Kennedy wanted to maintain the status quo

in the world," the Soviet First Secretary would recall, including the "inviol-
ability of borders *plus the enforced preservation of a country's internal social and
political system.*" More than ever Khrushchev saw his own opportunity to
appeal to the potentially revolutionary masses of the world.

Fidel Castro was quick to advance his own Marxist-Leninist concept of
revolution. Washington's baleful hostility to him after the missile crisis—
its continued efforts to bring down his regime, to sabotage electric power
plants and other targets, and even to assassinate him—combined with his
own increasing ideological militancy, helped to push the Cuban revolutionaries deeper into their embrace with the Soviet Union. But Castro continued to have his differences with the Kremlin, and not least of these was
his rejection of sacrosanct Marxist-Leninist doctrine that revolution must
grow out of the urban proletariat; Cuba had a paucity of urban proletari-
ans. Régis Debray, a young Frenchman teaching in Havana, wrote, with the
help of Castro and others, *Revolution in the Revolution?*, which turned upside
down traditional Leninist dogma that revolutionary mass consciousness
aroused by militant party leadership must precede revolutionary action.
Military action must come first to produce that consciousness, argued
Debray. And Castro's close friend Ché Guevara prepared to crusade
through Africa and Latin America preaching the need for revolutionary
guerrilla action. Still, while communism looked monolithic to many in
Washington, doctrinal disputes and personal rivalries sharply divided
communist parties and leaders the world over.

More than ever Kennedy staked his Latin American hopes on the Alliance for Progress. Conceived in large part as a response to Castroism,
guided by meetings of Latin representatives, buttressed by investment
money from the developed countries, the Alliance was Kennedy's kind of
revolution. Two years after the euphoric White House kickoff, however,
the Alliance was making slow progress in overcoming poverty in Latin
America. The effort in Washington suffered in part from the usual bureaucratic delays, competing interests, and inadequate funding, in part from
lack of political leadership strong enough to prevent diversion of effort
away from the imperatives of the antipoverty struggle and toward the
demands of the nation's corporations and military. But the transcending
problem was that Washington was attempting to work through existing
Latin governmental structures and political processes, and with capitalist
enterprises and assumptions, such as the protection of private property,
that were inadequate to the aims of the Alliance.

The Bay of Pigs had been, for this vigorous young President, a bitter
lesson in the confines and cunning of history—in the momentum of events,
the tangle of conflicting forces, the power of bureaucracies, the volatility

of mass opinion. In the end he had settled for the middle way between no invasion and an all-out one—and the middle way had turned out to be perhaps the worst way of all. In the missile crisis he had finally settled on a mid-course between an air strike on Soviet installations and Stevenson's proposal for yielding Guantánamo as well as Turkish and Italian missile bases in return for missile withdrawal from Cuba. This time the middle course had worked, but largely because the Soviets did not wish to gamble further on war when they still lagged behind the United States in nuclear arms.

* * *

From Western traders and missionaries Asian leaders had been hearing for almost two centuries about the republic that had rebelled against its English masters. Even in the 1780s American revolutionary scenes were portrayed on Chinese porcelain and wallpaper. Japanese in Nagasaki heard that "a military official named Washington, and a civil official named Franklin," had stood up in an assembly and cried, "We must not lose this heaven-given opportunity" to sever relations with the English forever. After the revolution, rulers and subjects lived alike, Nagasaki heard, with similar homes and food; even when officials were clothed with authority and the masses regarded them "with respectful fear," it was only for a fixed term of years.

Later, despite America's imperial ventures, the Chinese still seemed to have a special regard for the white people almost halfway across the world. Sun Yat-sen, "father of the Chinese Republic," noted how Westerners had extolled liberty and had even said, "Give me liberty or give me death," though he added that "liberty develops as the power of the people develops." Chiang Kai-shek studied the implications of the French and American revolutions for Chinese nationalism and anticolonialism. The young, poverty-stricken Mao Tse-tung, after reading about the American struggles for independence in a borrowed book, remarked to a friend about the "eight long, bitter years" of the fighting under Washington. During World War II, Mao praised FDR and Henry Wallace as worthy heirs of Jefferson and Lincoln. But the American war of independence was never really his kind of uprising. A revolution was not a dinner party or painting a picture or doing embroidery, he wrote sternly, but "an act of violence by which one class overthrows another."

Southern and southeastern Asians as well as Chinese could hardly ignore the lustrous example of a developing young nation that had thrown off the shackles of its own mother country. But Americans could ignore *them;* in a 1942 poll 60 percent of Americans could not locate either China or India on a map. This was after Pearl Harbor, an event that swiveled American eyes westward and would forever alter United States relations with Asian peoples.

Roosevelt and Churchill's Atlantic Charter of August 1941 had apparently proclaimed the self-determination of all peoples, but Churchill told Parliament that the Charter applied only to those under the Nazi yoke. FDR was in a quandary. Mohandas Gandhi, leading the nationalist forces in India, repeatedly appealed to the President for support, while the Prime Minister remained adamantly opposed to granting India its independence until after the war. As the Japanese advanced through Burma toward India following Pearl Harbor, Roosevelt had pressed Churchill for a compromise acceptable to Gandhi and Nehru, and Vice President Wallace spoke publicly of America's duty to oppose imperialism in all forms. Encouraged by Washington's stand, Gandhi and Nehru were all the more disappointed and angry when FDR repeatedly backed off from a showdown with Churchill.

"Dear Friend," Gandhi wrote Roosevelt on July 1, 1942. He told of his and his country's many connections with the United States, of how he had profited from the writings of Thoreau and Emerson, how he cherished his personal friendships in Britain. Then the thrust to the heart: "I venture to think that the Allied declaration that the Allies are fighting to make the world safe for freedom of the individual and for democracy sounds hollow, so long as India and, for that matter, Africa are exploited by Great Britain, and America has the Negro problem in her own home." Chiang Kai-shek too urged the President to help "restore to India her complete freedom."

Despite pressure from Eleanor Roosevelt and Administration officials, the President put first his military partnership with Churchill, and the imprisonment of Gandhi, Nehru, and other nationalist leaders in August 1942 ended hopes for a compromise. Roosevelt blew hot and cold over India throughout the war. Only a few weeks before his death he complained to an adviser that Churchill failed to understand that 1.1 billion "brown people" resented rule by a "handful of whites"—and "1,100,000,-000 potential enemies are dangerous."

The struggles of the billion "brown people" gripped the conscience of American leaders following the war. Indian leaders—most notably Nehru himself—asked why a "revolutionary country" like the United States gave so little help to Indians in their struggle for freedom. The United States, in the eyes of many Asians, was tainted by its merely passive opposition to the efforts of the colonial powers to hang on to their possessions in Asia—especially in India and Indochina.

Onto this uneasy scene in southern Asia in 1952 came the sturdy figure of Eleanor Roosevelt, fresh from her work on the United Nations Human Rights Commission. She had her own special recollections of the Indian struggle—not only of FDR's deference to Churchill but of a curious telegram of condolence from Gandhi on her husband's death that included "congratulations" that the President had been "spared humiliating spectacle of being party to peace which threatens to be prelude to war bloodier still if possible." Eleanor Roosevelt's journey to the old colonized nations of the Middle East and southern Asia became a kind of triumphal procession. In India she suffered endless entertainments, paid homage to Gandhi at the spot where he had been assassinated, visited famous caves, worked an old spinning wheel in the spirit of the Mahatma, dealt amiably with aroused students, met with as many women and women's groups as possible, and was upset only when she was denied a ride on an elephant.

By the 1960s Americans had come to know much more about this Asian 1.1 billion—now approaching 2 billion—especially about India, which had a population greater than Latin America and Africa combined. They knew something of the intractable poverty that held village people imprisoned generation after generation, the staggering health problems, the literacy rate that ranged from 15 to 35 percent across the continent, the tens of thousands living their lives out on the streets of Calcutta and Bombay. What the American people did not know fully was the potential for protest and violence among the hundreds of millions whom the colonial powers had made dangerous. Gauging this potential was a task for leadership. As a senator John Kennedy had won attention for his anticolonial speeches. As a congressman he had toured Indochina and India, even interviewing a rather distant Nehru. Now, as President, he viewed India as the "key area" of Asia.

The new Administration, recognizing that India's first need was stepped-up economic aid, quickly won from Congress a massive increase in funds for Indian development. Even half a billion dollars, spread over a period of years, amounted to only pitifully few dimes for every Indian and could have no more than a marginal influence on the vast subcontinent's economy. More important were the psychology and politics of the new approach to India. Perceiving that no government is touchier than one that has just achieved independence, the Kennedy White House put far less emphasis on policies that had antagonized New Delhi in the past, such as "buy American" requirements encased in foreign aid provisions. It was now accepted that tax money exacted from Americans, including capitalists, would flow into India's "public sector"—i.e., socialist enterprises. American politicians who abhorred planning had to accept the Indian determination to fit foreign aid into a series of five-year plans. And

Kennedy adroitly recognized India's need for self-esteem when he sent to New Delhi John Kenneth Galbraith, perhaps the ablest—certainly the drollest—of a string of prestigious envoys assigned to the Indian capital.

Still, Indian policy under Kennedy continued to be heavily influenced by the cold war strategy that under both Truman and Eisenhower had tilted economic aid toward Western Europe, as a counterweight to Soviet power, and hence given aid to developing countries a low priority. While Moscow had its doubts about the Indian brand of socialism, the Kremlin had been only too happy during the 1950s to exploit Washington's heavy-handedness toward New Delhi. The Kennedy Administration indeed inherited a set of Indian attitudes that would have given any cold warrior pause. Public-opinion polls in India during the late 1950s, even accepting a fairly large margin of error, indicated that Russia enjoyed more prestige and popularity than the United States.

How could this be? It seemed incredible to American pundits and politicians that the Soviet Union, which they viewed as a boorish, aggressive nation, could have made such inroads among the Indian masses. Certainly the reason in part lay in Soviet anticolonialism and its acceptance of India's revolution. The situation changed abruptly in the fall of 1962, however, when Chinese and Indian troops fought obscure battles over disputed frontier areas. When Khrushchev informed New Delhi that Moscow would not intercede in behalf of India, Nehru turned to Kennedy for assistance. Putting aside his long irritation over New Delhi's nonalignment policies and its preachings against the cold war, Kennedy responded quickly, graciously, and—within several constraints—practically, with light armaments.

Close working relationships between Nehru and Galbraith, and Galbraith's successor, Chester Bowles, took some of the kinks out of the grim interplay of ideology and strategy. And a different kind of sojourner in India leavened the two nations' relationship. During a visit to Washington late in 1961 Nehru had appeared cool and aloof even during informal talks in the White House, perhaps because of disappointment over Kennedy's first year of militant foreign policy-making. The President later told Schlesinger that it was the "worst head-of-state visit" he had had. But the one time Nehru appeared his old self, the President noted, was in animated talk with Jacqueline Kennedy. When the Indian Prime Minister invited the First Lady to India, she and the President had accepted with alacrity.

The trip was a total success. The Prime Minister was most gracious, the First Lady most captivating—and she went on to Pakistan to maintain Washington's evenhandedness toward the rival nations. Her journey to southern Asia was the capsheaf of one of the notable foreign policy successes of the Kennedy Administration—winning the friendship of the Indian people and most of its leaders. And Jacqueline Kennedy got to ride an elephant.

*　　*　　*

John Kennedy could get along with Nehru and other Indian leaders, for they spoke the same language. This was true literally—Nehru and others spoke the King's English better than most Americans. It was true intellectually too, for the President could talk Indian revolutionary language. He could understand something of the nature and needs of India's revolution—really a struggle for independence against the English not wholly unlike the American experience almost two centuries earlier, save for the nonviolent tactics of the insurrection and the bloody civil strife that erupted between Moslem and Hindu in the wake of partition. In Southeast Asia, however, the Kennedy White House had to deal with revolutionary ideas and leaders of a very different sort.

For centuries Southeast Asia had been the tinderbox of Asia. After countless wars, civil and uncivil, and bloodily suppressed uprisings, this land of great mountain ranges and long valleys, of thin upland soil and lush deltas, of ancient hatreds and polyglot cultures, had come in the main under harsh colonial rule. By the 1930s and 1940s intellectuals, peasants, and workers were listening to Marxist revolutionary voices as well as to revolutionaries American style. Perhaps more than others in Asia, Indochinese peoples took heart from the Japanese blows against white prestige, even as they suffered under Japanese occupation. Freedom—early liberation from Tokyo's iron hand, final liberation from colonial rule—was the rallying cry for Burmese, Siamese, Indonesians, the peoples of Indochina. But what kind of freedom? A rising leader in Indochina, Ho Chi Minh, later asserted his agreement with the American Declaration of Independence and its evocation of equality as well as liberty, by opening his own declaration of independence with the words of Jefferson.

Probably no Western leader had a more abiding concern for the future of Indochina than Franklin Roosevelt. Impelled in part by Wilsonian idealism and even more by a bitter scorn for French colonial oppression and cruelties, especially in Vietnam, FDR made clear to his wartime partners—Churchill, Stalin, and Chiang—that he would veto any return of French troops to Indochina after the war. The danger of setting off Churchill's explosive temper, however, was so contrary to Roosevelt's feline approach that he preferred to put his case to Anthony Eden, who liked to describe back in London FDR's "cheerful fecklessness" about such matters. Feckless Roosevelt was not; but he subordinated long-run political planning to immediate military needs, just as he subordinated Asian strategy to European. Roosevelt until his death stuck to his principled opposition to French reoccupation but his month-to-month dealings with allies on the matter were ambiguous enough to enable Truman to accept the French return to Indochina without appearing to challenge his predecessor's anticolonialism.

From his House and Senate vantage points John Kennedy watched while the Truman White House and the Acheson State Department pumped hundreds of millions of dollars into the French effort allegedly to defend the principles of freedom in Indochina; while the Eisenhower White House in 1954 stood twice at the edge of war in northern Vietnam as Dulles, Nixon, and military leaders urged American air strikes to rescue the beleaguered French troops in Dien Bien Phu; while the Geneva Accords of the same year, which the United States did not sign but had pledged halfheartedly to support, provided for armistices in Laos, Vietnam, and Cambodia and partitioned Vietnam at the 17th parallel until a nationwide election could be held in 1956 under the supervision of an international commission; while Washington backed the Ngo Dinh Diem regime in the south despite its increasing corruption and incompetence; while Diem put off promised reforms and, with quiet American acquiescence, the unification election, lost support in the country, and tried to cope with communist National Liberation Front insurgents—known pejoratively as Vietcong—in the south.

And now John Kennedy as President confronted this tangle of complexities. He was convinced that he could certainly do better in Indochina than had the dispirited Eisenhower Administration, but the new President's problem lay not only in the quagmire that was forming in Vietnam, or in the readiness of American war hawks and McCarthyites to pounce on any sign of Administration willingness to "lose Indochina" as the Truman Administration had "lost China." Part of the problem lay in Kennedy's head—in the major articulate premises he brought into the White House, in the deep division within him over fundamental strategy, in his "pragmatic solutions" of taking small, "practical" steps in order to avoid or postpone a decisive intellectual and strategic commitment.

On Capitol Hill, Kennedy had echoed the conventional wisdom: that the United States must help thwart "the onrushing tide of Communism from engulfing all Asia," that Vietnam was a "proving ground for democracy in Asia" and a test of "American responsibility and determination," that—the domino theory—"our security may be lost piece by piece, country by country." And he dared not run the risk—at least before the election of

1964—of appearing soft on the Indochina issue. Still resonating to the Bay of Pigs failure and feeling vulnerable on a compromise settlement in Laos he had agreed to, he told Galbraith, "There are limits to the number of defeats I can defend in one twelve-month period."

On the other hand, Kennedy was a seasoned and sophisticated politician who loved to prick banalities and challenge shibboleths. Believing more in the "confusion theory" of history than the "conspiracy theory," he did not conjure up terrifying images of the Soviet Politburo sitting at the center of a web of world power and masterminding grand strategies for the military conquest of the West; indeed, tension between Moscow and Peking in these very years was refuting the theory of monistic communist power. As for the threat from Republican and other war hawks, he knew that at times presidential politicians must take risks in order to pursue responsible policies. And after all, who had won fame for a book called *Profiles in Courage*?

Kennedy's response to his own intellectual dilemma was reflected in the diversity of advisers he consulted. On Vietnam policy, Secretary of State Dean Rusk, Defense Secretary McNamara, National Security Adviser McGeorge Bundy, Walt W. Rostow, and most of the military leaders were generally hawkish, at least initially; George Ball of the State Department, Chester Bowles, Averell Harriman, and Galbraith were decidedly dovish. Some of Kennedy's advisers shared his view that the United States must recognize and even aid the revolutionary forces that were rising out of the peasant villages of Asia; others shared his view that the Indochinese revolutions were not good revolutions of the American or even the French variety, but malevolent revolutions of Marxist inspiration and Leninist strategy.

The result was a tendency on Kennedy's part to take the middle ground between strategies and advisers on the day-to-day problems that inexorably surfaced. Thus between those who argued for a heavy military commitment in Vietnam and those for a minimal one, he initially sent to Vietnam 400 soldiers from the Special Forces and 100 additional military advisers; and at the same time authorized secret warfare against North Vietnam by South Vietnamese trained and directed by the CIA and the Special Forces. He evaded a negotiated settlement but also spoke of the danger of escalation. He devoutly wished to win the allegiance of the peasants of Indochina but his Special Forces used tactics of defoliation, flesh-burning napalm, and forced penning of farmers in "strategic hamlets" that gained countless recruits for the communist adversary. He wanted Diem toppled but feared to take overt steps; his signal to Vietnamese generals that the United States would not "thwart a change of government" spurred a coup, but he was sickened by Diem's brutal assassination. Each of the middle-of-the-road steps in fact pulled the Administration deeper into the Vietnam morass— but without the debate and decision, both comprehensive and focused, that at the least might have prepared the American people for the perils ahead.

As he entered his third summer in the White House, John Kennedy's progress in defining the dimensions and prospects of popular aspirations for freedom in the Third World was lagging far behind the benign rhetoric of 1960 and 1961. He and most of his advisers had assumed that peoples like the Cubans and the Vietnamese aspired at least as strongly to Western-style liberal constitutional procedures and Bill of Rights protections as they did to national independence and to revolutionary concepts of social and political equality. Chester Bowles, a key drafter of Roosevelt's "Economic Bill of Rights" during the war and ambassador to India under Truman, had as Under Secretary of State in the Kennedy Administration a firsthand view of the White House "realists" who had made error after error in dealing with Third World nations. Exiled back to New Delhi in 1963 as a fuzzy-minded idealist, Bowles went off with the dismal conclusion that the Kennedy Administration had fallen far short of his hopes. He had found "almost no intellectual leadership that has seriously challenged the conventional wisdom or ventured beyond the limited and now inadequate concepts of the New Deal."

Even sterner challenges to Kennedy's and Johnson's intellectual leadership lay ahead, at the hands of some of their fellow Americans.

PART III

Liberation Struggles

CHAPTER 8

Striding Toward Freedom

<hr>

D URING the kindling times of the 1960s hitherto little-known persons— blacks, women, college students, southern preachers—took moral and political leadership of the nation in boldly claiming their civil rights. For a few brief shining years, neighborhood people challenged authority, aroused the consciousness of followers as to their true needs, and spurred the conscience of their fellow Americans. Day after day, for weeks at a time, the national media—especially television and the picture magazines— brought into tens of millions of homes images of helmeted troops with upraised clubs, snarling police dogs lunging at protesters, black persons kneeling in prayer for their persecutors as well as for themselves. The black protesters—and the student and women activists who would follow—for a decade would stir the conscience of the nation.

This assumption of leadership by the poor and the persecuted stood in sharp contrast to the nation's policy making during previous decades. Franklin Roosevelt had come into office with little mandate from the people for programs except to "do something, anything" about the depression. New Deal policies were responses far less to local or regional initiatives than to proposals of Washington politicians and intellectuals who in turn drew from a bank of ideas built by liberal and left leaders of the progressive and Wilson eras. Truman's initiatives such as the Truman Doctrine and the Marshall Plan were responses to urgent appeals from abroad and to war experience, in an atmosphere of rising cold war hostility, and they led and shaped, rather than followed, public opinion. The Supreme Court's school desegregation decision in 1954 was a result more of the justices' collective conscience and practical wisdom than of nascent popular pressure; indeed, that decision in *Brown* would doubtless have failed of passage if it had been offered to the American electorate in the form of a national referendum.

A renowned political economist, Joseph Schumpeter, wrote in the early 1940s that the people do not rule in democracies. The democratic method, he said, was "that institutional arrangement for arriving at political decisions in which individuals acquire the power to decide by means of a competitive struggle for the people's vote." People did not autonomously take initiatives, organize themselves, and direct policy. This was a provoking contradiction to the great American faith in Lincoln's "government of the people, by the people, for the people."

Schumpeter's observation was in fact only a half-truth. Historians could point to countless examples of spontaneous leadership by community or group activists in labor conflicts, populist upheavals, revolutionary situations. On a national scale Gandhi was showing, even as Schumpeter wrote, that a leader's deep involvement with his followers could give them, in Erik Erikson's words, a sense of participation that would raise them to power.

But that was India. Had Americans become so manipulated from above, so enervated politically—had the national and state and even city governments become so distant and the presidency so powerful and all-encompassing—that people in their neighborhoods and communities could no longer take their futures into their own hands? Had the vaunted old frontier spirit, the populist rebelliousness, the famous community "get up and go" disappeared from American life? If collective action was necessary, how broad—reaching out to which groups and movements and regions and parties and national leaderships—must that collective action be? Or would heroic individual action be enough to get results?

The protesters of the 1960s responded with actions as well as words.

Onward, Christian Soldiers

Dusk had fallen on December 1, 1955, when Rosa Parks, a tailor's assistant, finished her long day's work in a large department store in Montgomery, the capital of Alabama and the first capital of the Confederacy. While heading for the bus stop across Court Square, which had once been a center of slave auctions, she observed the dangling Christmas lights and a bright banner reading "Peace on Earth, Goodwill to Men." After paying her bus fare she settled down in a row between the "whites only" section and the rear seats, according to the custom that blacks could sit in the middle section if the back was filled.

When a white man boarded the bus, the driver ordered Rosa Parks and three other black passengers to the rear so that the man could sit. The three other blacks stood up; Parks did not budge. Then the threats, the summoning of the police, the arrest, the quick conviction, incarceration. Through it all Rosa Parks felt little fear. She had had enough.

"The time had just come when I had been pushed as far as I could stand to be pushed," she said later. "I had decided that I would have to know once and for all what rights I had as a human being and a citizen." Besides, her feet hurt.

The time had come . . . Rosa Parks's was a heroic act of defiance, an individual act of leadership. But it was not wholly spontaneous, nor did she act alone. Long active in the civil rights effort, she had taken part in an integration workshop in Tennessee at the Highlander Folk School, an important training center for southern community activists and labor organizers. There Parks "found out for the first time in my adult life that this could be a unified society." There she had gained strength "to persevere in my work for freedom." Later she had served for years as a leader in the Montgomery and Alabama NAACP. Her bus arrest was by no means her first brush with authority; indeed, a decade earlier this same driver had ejected her for refusing to enter through the back door.

Rosa Parks's support group quickly mobilized. E. D. Nixon, long a militant leader of the local NAACP and the regional Brotherhood of Sleeping Car Porters, rushed to the jail to bail her out. Nixon had been waiting for just such a test case to challenge the constitutionality of the bus segregation law. Three Montgomery women had been arrested for similar "crimes" in the past year, but the city, in order to avoid just such a challenge, had not pursued the charge. With Rosa Parks the city blundered, and from Nixon's point of view, she was the ideal victim—no one commanded more respect in the black community.

Word of Rosa Parks's arrest sped through black Montgomery. The Women's Political Council, a civil rights group of black professional women, had been talking for months about a bus boycott. This was the time. Soon members were handing out leaflets and conferring with Nixon, who agreed to lead the effort. When he arrived home that evening he took a sheet of paper and drew a rough sketch of the city, measuring distances with a slide rule. He found that people could walk to work from anywhere in Montgomery if they wanted to. He said to his wife, "We can beat this thing."

Nixon realized, though, that the boycott could not succeed without the united support of the black ministers, the most influential black leaders in Montgomery as elsewhere. He called them one by one, starting with Ralph Abernathy, the passionate young pastor of the Baptist church Parks attended, a man with an earthy sense of humor and a "gift of laughing people into positive action." Abernathy was enthusiastic. Third on the list was twenty-six-year-old Martin Luther King, Jr., minister of the Dexter Street Baptist Church, hardly more than a stone's throw from the gleaming white state office buildings surrounding the Capitol.

King had grown up in Atlanta, Georgia, a hundred fifty miles to the northeast, the son of a prosperous minister of one of the largest Baptist congregations in the nation. "Daddy" King had long been indignant over segregation; he had led efforts against discrimination as early as the 1930s, including a voting rights march to city hall. Though he ruled his home "like a fierce Old Testament patriarch" and often whipped his kids, Martin Jr. called him "a real father to me." Martin, the second child and first son, showed extraordinary gifts. He seemed to excel at everything—schoolwork, sports (especially wrestling), dancing, debate, oratory. From age six he soloed hymns at church services and conventions, and by his early teens his voice had matured into a rich, deep baritone that awed his listeners in song or speech.

Pricked by the thorns of segregation but steadied by his mother's counsel to believe he was "somebody," young King resolved to improve the lives of black people. At first he rebelled against Daddy King's demand that he follow in his ministerial footsteps, but he changed his mind and served as assistant pastor in his father's church. Later he graduated from Atlanta's Morehouse College, attended Crozer Seminary in Pennsylvania, and earned his doctorate at Boston University. During these years King read Niebuhr, whose paradoxes fascinated him; Marx, whose materialism alienated him; and especially Walter Rauschenbusch, whose belief in a Christian commonwealth *on earth,* loving, spiritual, sharing, stirred his imagination. The young theologian searched for ways in which these ideas and those of the great Western philosophers, from Plato and Aristotle to Mill and Locke, could be converted to effective methods of social change. Hired to take over the Montgomery church, he moved there with his wife, Coretta Scott King, a gifted singer who had given up a musical career to marry him.

In the eyes of Montgomery blacks, King was no zealot. His church was a respectable one, with a largely middle-class congregation, and though he had gained a reputation for being a social activist, he had just turned down a chance to head the local NAACP. But King's brothers and sisters throughout Montgomery were already leading the way. Nixon had set up a meeting of black ministers and community leaders at King's church. Women's Political Council activists and ministers then spread word of the bus boycott to Montgomery's 50,000 blacks over the weekend, especially at church services. Monday morning thousands were driven to work in black cabs with specially cut rates, or rode mules or horses, or walked. Barely a dozen blacks rode buses. The Montgomery Improvement Association was formed to coordinate efforts, but it was left to a mass meeting to decide whether the boycott would continue. And King, who had, to his surprise and despite his reluctance, been drafted to head the MIA, would address it.

So fast were events moving that King had only twenty minutes to prepare what he believed would be the most decisive speech of his life—one that must not only fire up his audience but blend militance with moderation. Almost paralyzed by feelings of anxiety and inadequacy, he prayed; he had time only to sketch a mental outline and tore off to the church. He found it overflowing. As the meeting opened the powerful refrains of "Onward, Christian Soldiers" swelled through the church and outside, where three or four thousand people stood patiently in the cold night listening to the meeting through loudspeakers. After prayers and scripture readings, King walked to the pulpit.

He gazed out at the audience, at the people crowded onto the floor and the balcony, at the television cameras. Speaking without notes, he told, simply but passionately, the story of Rosa Parks and others who had been mistreated on the buses. He exhorted the boycotters to use persuasion, not coercion, and ended: "If you will protest courageously, and yet with dignity and Christian love, when the history books are written in future generations, the historians will have to pause and say, 'There lived a great people—a black people—who injected new meaning and dignity into the veins of civilization.' This is our challenge and our overwhelming responsibility." His electrifying words brought waves of applause, which rose again when Rosa Parks was presented. Abernathy read the boycott demands, to more wild cheering. This was, King wrote later, the first great meeting of the freedom movement.

The city responded by forbidding black taxis to lower their fares. Undaunted, the boycott organizers set up an efficient car-pool system modeled on a similar Baton Rouge action two years before. A small army of ministers, businesspeople, teachers, laborers, and others, driving cars and dusty pickups and shiny new church-owned station wagons, collected passengers at forty-eight dispatch stations to carry them to work. Hymns wafted out of car windows as the "rolling churches" crisscrossed the city with what arch-segregationists at a White Citizens' Council meeting glumly admitted was "military precision." Some blacks preferred to walk. Mother Pollard vowed to King that she would walk until it was over.

"But aren't your feet tired?" King asked her.

"Yes," she said, "my feet is tired, but my soul is rested."

As mass meetings were rotated among churches, ministers took turns giving rousing talks to maintain militance. But it was a carefully controlled militance. King had been fascinated by nonviolent doctrines ever since reading Thoreau's essay on civil disobedience at Morehouse and then studying Gandhi's *Autobiography* at Crozer, but it was all intellectual until Rosa Parks made it come alive for him. Tutored also by the pacific reflections of Rauschenbusch and the advice in person of Bayard Rustin and others, King now got a quick education in the practice of *satyagraha,* or truth force. With his fellow ministers King toured the church meetings, turning them into schools of "Christianity in action," nonviolent resistance, and direct-action techniques.

Victory came, slow and hard. City officials, fighting every inch of the way, sought to divide the boycott leaders from one another, concocted a bogus settlement, and prosecuted King and hundreds of others. Moments arose during the year-long boycott when black commitment to tactical nonviolence was sorely tested by bombings of homes and churches. But the boycott was still going strong when on a climactic day in November 1956 the city won an injunction to shut down the car pools, the boycott's circulatory system, while the U.S. Supreme Court upheld a prior ruling of the federal court in Montgomery that the city and state bus laws were unconstitutional.

Four days before Christmas 8,000 souls voted to end the boycott, the largest and longest protest by black people in the nation's history to that date. Soon the desegregated buses were moving smoothly despite sporadic acts of violence. Martin Luther King, Jr., emerged from the ordeal the most prominent black leader since Booker T. Washington, a man of quite different ideological cast. The freedom movement appeared to have taken off.

*   *   *

But where to? How far? In what way? The Montgomery boycott did not trigger a wave of protest actions throughout the South. In that same year of 1955, when Rosa Parks would not budge, Emmett Till, a fourteen-year-old Chicago black visiting relatives in Mississippi, was dragged from their home for having "whistled" at a white woman. He was beaten, his testicles cut off, and his body dumped into the Tallahatchie River with a cotton-gin fan chained around his neck. North and South, people recoiled with horror, but the atrocity had little more impact; the confessed killers were of course acquitted. In 1957 Eisenhower's dispatch of paratroopers to Little Rock produced sensational headlines, but it was followed by resolutions in state legislatures pitting state sovereignty against federal court decisions, and by school absenteeism and occasional rioting—and precious little school integration in most southern states.

Black leaders were neither daunted nor dumbfounded by the frustration of the civil rights movement. But now northern observers were at last seeing more clearly what blacks were up against—a system of discrimination and segregation entrenched in an array of mutually reinforcing ideological, social, political, and legal barriers.

There still was, of course—there always had been—the "Other South": the South of racial tolerance and Christian brotherhood. Noted newspapermen embodied this heritage: Harry S. Ashmore of the *Arkansas Gazette,* Hodding Carter of the *Delta Democrat-Times* in Mississippi, Ralph McGill of the Atlanta *Constitution,* Buford Boone of the Tuscaloosa *News.* Harry Golden, publisher of the *Carolina Israelite,* won chuckles even from his enemies when he described himself as a member of three minorities—"I'm a Jew, a Yankee, and a radical"—and when he proposed the Golden Vertical Negro Plan, which would integrate the races in the schools by providing desks without seats, in the same way that blacks and whites shopped standing up side by side in city drugstores and supermarkets. But these were lonely voices. The notion of black inferiority was built into the minds of most of even the better-educated Southerners. Writing on the Other South of the nineteenth century, Carl Degler noted that with the coming of the twentieth "the great period of Southern dissent on a widespread and organized basis came to an end." When Buford Boone attacked white violence in a talk to whites in western Alabama in 1957, from the audience came shouts of "Kill him!" and "Hang him!"

The white dogma of Negro inferiority took form in the southern mind as a mishmash of stereotypes and shibboleths: "Mongrelization"—white men must protect the purity of blue-eyed, golden-haired southern girls—Negro blood had destroyed Rome—the "curse of Ham" in Genesis defined the black race—blacks were superior only in sports and entertainment—the "good colored" were quiet and law-abiding—Negroes preferred their own segregated schools. Some of these shibboleths combined with anti-Semitism; thus activist Negroes were mere pawns of the Jews. And as the fear of communism swept the country during the 1950s, southern demagogues linked civil rights leaders to Moscow.

White children in the South picked up these stereotypes in their homes or churches or in play with other kids. Some of their most insidious notions were reinforced by grammar and high school texts. These abounded with tales of the happy relationships between masters and slaves, of slaves who after Emancipation remained with their masters because they knew who their friends were. Slavery, the children read, was the earliest form of Social Security. The Klan was a law-enforcement agency. There were the inevitable portraits of blacks as happy dancers and singers, with their "bright rows of white teeth," of the lazy black, the carefree childlike black.

But in these schoolbooks recent-day blacks and their history remained misty and shrouded. Typically there was no mention of *Brown,* of black leaders, or of the civil rights struggle.

An array of southern organizations reflected and relayed these ideas. The most active and conspicuous, with a large membership of "respectable" whites, were the Citizens' Councils that erupted across the South in the wake of *Brown.* First membership cardholder and Confederacy-wide head of the Association of Citizens' Councils of America was Robert "Tut" Patterson, a onetime football player for Ole Miss. Patterson drafted a long-range platform for the Councils' official newspaper, advocating the "recognition of racial differences as fact," the migration of blacks and whites seeking integration to states sanctioning it, laws ensuring the "future racial integrity" of black and white communities, "strict enforcement of state voter qualification laws," separate public schools for the black and white races. Other groups ranged from prestigious organizations for the protection of states' rights and grass-roots independence to disreputable "white brotherhoods" and the like, and the abominable Klan.

These groups were part and parcel of a political system that built ideas, interests, institutions, and leaders into a fortress of racism and inequality. A tragic paradox lay across the South. Ordinarily southern state governments were politically so unrepresentative, and organizationally so slack, that progressive action to meet human needs—even if only white needs—was weak and faltering. Governors' powers were limited; legislatures were dominated by reactionary rural cliques; the one-party system of Democrats inflated the politics of personality and demagoguery and thwarted a rationally competitive politics of intelligent policy choices.

By the end of the 1940s the most astute analyst of southern politics, the Texan V. O. Key, Jr., could conclude that politics was the South's greatest problem. "The South's heritage from crises of the past," Key wrote, "its problems of adjustment of racial relations on a scale unparalleled in any western nation, its poverty associated with an agrarian economy which in places is almost feudal in character, the long habituation of many of its people to nonparticipation in political life"—all these put the South's political system under an enormous burden. Those who loved the South, he concluded, "are left with the cold, hard fact that the South as a whole has developed no system or practice of political organization and leadership" able to carry that burden.

Once *Brown* and other events challenged southern racism, however, southern leaders sprang into united action to obstruct progress and protect white privilege, drowsy legislatures churned out legislation, governors rushed to the school doors, registrars redoubled their vigilance against black invasion of the polls. White Citizens' Councils, "employing the powerful weapons of economic reprisal, political pressure, psychological and emotional terror, and social ostracism," coordinated the efforts of hitherto slack state officials. Within four years of *Brown*, state legislatures passed 196 segregation laws—measures for placement or assignment of pupils, grants for private education, repeal of compulsory school attendance, even provisions for the possible abolition of public schools. The country, said Harry Ashmore, had not seen such a mass of restrictive legislation since the days of the Know-Nothings.

* * *

Such was the suddenly restocked and rearmed fortress that civil rights leaders confronted in the late 1950s. Their weapons seemed puny, measured by ordinary criteria of political warfare. Southern blacks typically could not vote, could not run for office, lacked extra cash for politics, often could not even protest. But they had their own secret weapon of enormous potential power—their sense of outrage welling up from years of oppression, their moral fervor rising out of their belief in America's promise of liberty and equality for all. And they had their political and moral arm—their churches.

Through every twist and turn of the southern civil rights movement during the late 1950s and 1960s, the black church—Baptist churches mainly, but also Methodist—would be its driving force and institutional base, at once spiritual, moral, cultural, political, organizational. Nat Turner was only one of the Baptist preachers who had led slave revolts, and black churches North and South played vital roles in the abolitionist movement. After Reconstruction, however, the combative spirit of many southern churches leaked away as they accommodated to Jim Crow; many black ministers gained influence and prestige as brokers between white elites and black folk. Still, as E. Franklin Frazier wrote, with the "elimination of Negroes from the political life of the American community," the Negro church became the only arena in which blacks could "assert themselves" and in which the "thirst for power could be satisfied."

The old marks of the resistance to slavery were still evident as the black church grew stronger: charismatic leaders insulated from white society; a large, tightly organized congregation; a communications network; an independent financial base; relatively safe meeting places for planning tactics and generating commitment; and most critically, the "common church culture," grounded in a rich heritage of empowering prayers and spirituals that could be directly channeled to political goals. Ever since slavery the male preacher had been the accepted community leader, closely attuned to the needs and aspirations of his black followers. Oratorical mesmerists like King had ready opportunity to reshape the cultural content of black religion into a weapon of protest by reinterpreting biblical stories or portraying Moses and Jesus as revolutionaries. The dynamic relationship between the charismatic clergy and the common church culture fashioned a mighty engine of grass-roots social power.

Who would direct this power? This question was largely settled in 1957, when the Southern Christian Leadership Conference took form, in Aldon Morris's words, "to unite community leaders by bringing them directly into leadership positions while simultaneously organizing the black masses." Indeed, the mass base of the church was "built into" the SCLC structure. The SCLC nurtured extraordinary second-cadre leaders, both in its Atlanta headquarters and in the affiliates—Fred Shuttlesworth, Hosea Williams, James Revel, Andrew Young, Ralph Abernathy. The focus of authority and the center of attention was young King, who showed a "rare talent for attracting and using the skills and ideas of brilliant aides and administrators"—he was compared to FDR on this score—and provided a degree of tough organizational power.

SCLC moved into the political vacuum after the Montgomery boycott, but as it solidified itself organizationally and financially, it floundered in charting a strategy for the budding movement. It mounted a southern-wide voter registration campaign but with little success. The momentum of the freedom movement slowed to a crawl.

Angry and frustrated, black activists passionately debated new tactics and strategies. With SCLC divided over ways and means, other black organizations challenged the movement leadership. In 1942 James Farmer and others had founded the Congress of Racial Equality, which had pioneered the use of nonviolent direct action to integrate Chicago restaurants. Five years later CORE had joined the Fellowship of Reconciliation in a freedom ride through the upper South. But by 1960 CORE too was frustrated and uncertain. Then a handful of college students and a lone black woman took leadership.

Late Monday afternoon on February 1, 1960, four well-dressed young men, first-year students at the mainly black North Carolina A&T College in Greensboro, bought some school supplies at Woolworth's, then sat down and ordered coffee and doughnuts. "I'm sorry," the waitress said, "we don't serve you here." "Why not?" the students asked. The waitress called the manager, who tried to reason with them, while a cop paced back and forth swinging his club but uncertain what to do. The students held their seats until the store, now crowded with onlookers, closed for the day. The move had been carefully planned as a team effort. Though they were much influenced by Gandhi, a protester said later, what had precipitated the action was the "courage each of us instilled within each other." Growing numbers of students joined them at the lunch counter every day that week; soon virtually all of the area's college students, as well as students from Greensboro's black high school and hundreds of others, were sitting in, picketing, or boycotting segregated eating places.

By wire service and student grapevine, news of the sudden protest flashed across North Carolina and the rest of the nation. It was "like a fever." The next week students staged lunch-counter sit-ins in Winston-Salem, Durham, and other communities. By February's end protests had erupted in over thirty cities in seven states and by April had swept through the entire South. Again and again young men and women stayed resolute and nonviolent when ketchup and other food were flung at them, lighted cigarettes were jabbed into them, white toughs set on them with little police interference. As the actions grew larger and better organized and moved deeper into the South, white violence increased along with black arrests. Would this movement peter out? Black leaders again debated strategy.

One woman had her own answer. When black activist Ella Baker first heard about the sit-ins she called her contacts at southern colleges. "What are you all going to do?" she asked in her deep resonant voice. "It is time to move." Then in her mid-fifties, Baker had acquired a grass-roots wisdom in her three decades of organizing. She remembered hearing, as a young child in a small North Carolina town, her ninety-year-old grandmother tell stories about slave revolts. The grandmother, flogged for refusing to marry the man chosen by the owner, had instead married a rebellious slave preacher. Valedictorian of her class at Raleigh's Shaw University, Baker moved to Harlem just before the depression. During the 1930s she traveled the country setting up black consumer co-ops, then began a long association with the NAACP, organizing chapters through the South. She had an extraordinary ability to give people, especially young people, a deeper understanding of social change.

But Ella Baker was a woman, and even though she had become executive director of SCLC, she had never felt accepted by King and his lieutenants. They did not take seriously her bold ideas for improving SCLC and its voting rights campaign. Growing more and more critical of its centralized, charismatic leadership, she resigned in the summer of 1960.

Baker saw that the new student movement would not last without a structure to coordinate local groups. Borrowing funds from SCLC, she organized a southern-wide conference of student activists from over fifty colleges and high schools at Shaw University during Easter weekend. King

spoke to two hundred fervent activists, but Baker fought an effort by SCLC
to capture the students as its youth wing. Like most of the students, she
believed they needed an autonomous organization "with the right to direct
their own affairs and even make their own mistakes"; and she hoped they
would be more militant in their nonviolence than SCLC. The young activists thoroughly agreed. After setting up a loosely structured Student
Nonviolent Coordinating Committee, with delegates from every southern
state, they committed themselves to nonviolence as the "foundation of our
purpose, the presupposition of our belief, and the manner of our action."

And so SNCC—"Snick," as people called it—was born. Inspired by Ella
Baker, SNCC came to embody a brand of leadership that would clash with
the leadership model of SCLC. Students tended to agree with her view that
the centrality of one or a few charismatic leaders able to attract big crowds,
big media, and big money was dangerous, for the charismatic leader got
to the point of believing "that he *is* the movement." They liked her idea
of "group-centered leadership"—the idea that the movement needed people willing and able to develop leadership among other people and not
operate as leaders above the crowd. They believed with her that black
people in the South would have to rely on themselves and not on outside
leaders. Above all, they agreed that SNCC must, in its organization and
methods, prefigure the values of the redemptive society they sought to
build, and that since they all shared both a hostility to authority and the
risk of death, "we are all leaders." This seeming anti-leadership ethos was
actually an affirmation of an alternative kind of leadership—decentralized,
participatory, comradely.

*   *   *

But still the fortress of racism stood. By the end of 1960 hundreds of
eating places had been opened to all, while tens of thousands of lunch
counters, schools, terminals, drinking fountains, toilets, buses, lodging
places remained barred to blacks. Increasingly, leaders in SCLC if not
SNCC evaluated the advantages and dangers of turning to the federal
government for help.

Turning to the white man's government out of desperation was nothing
new for southern blacks. In the 1860s the government fought a war first
for the Union and then, increasingly, to abolish slavery, but war and reconstruction ended with blacks merely in a new form of servitude. The national Republican party, with its Lincoln tradition, and later the New Deal,
with its social welfare concerns, handed out various favors to blacks, but
it was the coming of a war fought for democracy and freedom and against
Nazi racism that brought blacks such tangible benefits as jobs and welfare

programs. Later, neither Truman Democrats nor Eisenhower Republicans appeared willing or able to deliver on their parties' commitments to the men and women "freed" almost a century earlier.

By the 1960s "turning to the feds" raised in sharpest form the central political and even philosophical question facing blacks: to what extent should they rely on the white majority in the nation as a whole to respond to black needs and aspirations? Should they risk once again being forgotten, sold out, double-crossed? To the contention that Theodore Roosevelt's Square Deal, FDR's New Deal, and Truman's Fair Deal gave economic help or at least a measure of social and psychic support to blacks, came the response that that help was at best incidental to helping needy whites and at worst "mere crumbs." But the argument remained that action by blacks alone, though vitally necessary, was tragically inadequate, given the power of the southern white fortress. No one made this point with such overwhelming intellectual authority, philosophical imagination, and analytical skill as a Swedish scholar who had so immersed himself in the American racial dilemma as to become a citizen in thought if not in law. His name was Gunnar Myrdal.

In his 1,000-page study, *An American Dilemma,* sponsored by the Carnegie Corporation and published in 1942, Myrdal drew a portrait of black-white relationships in America in all their rich and evil complexity and explored the paradoxes that made up the dilemma: the continuing power of the American ideals of liberty and equality even as they existed side by side with gross racism and injustice and structures of inequality; the tragedy as well as the opportunity of the white majority—mostly "good people," wanting to be "rational and just," pleading to their consciences that they meant well even when things went wrong. Equally arresting—and even more relevant in 1962, when Myrdal brought out a twentieth anniversary edition—was his argument, powerfully supported by both historical data and sociological theory, that blacks must use *all* possible weapons in their effort to conquer the fortress of racism, and that these weapons most decidedly should include the moral passion, the credal ideals, the institutional machinery, and the collective leadership available among the American people as a whole. The civil rights movement must, in short, fight not only in the streets and at the lunch counters but in Washington and the state capitols.

For southern black leaders, turning to Washington looked more promising as the long Eisenhower Administration ground to an end in January 1961. They had been pleased by John Kennedy's call to Coretta King after her husband's jailing, by the nominee's acceptance of the strong party platform shaped by liberal Democrats, by the campaigner's fine promises about civil rights. But they were disappointed by JFK's selection of John-son as running mate, and even more by his early presidential actions and inactions. As a student of revolution, King was appalled by the Bay of Pigs. It reflected, he thought, a failure by Kennedy and the nation to "under-stand the meaning of the revolution taking place in the world," which resulted in the loss of any "real moral voice to speak to the conscience of humanity." When King met with the President for the first time in the White House, in spring 1961, his moralizing tone put JFK off—moral sentiment generally tended to make Kennedy uncomfortable—but King, for his part, was even more put off by the President's plan to delay legisla-tive action on civil rights.

For the acid test of Kennedy's leadership, as black leaders saw it, was his willingness to push, lever, bargain—move in some way, any way—a strong civil rights bill through Congress. But for Kennedy, southern power in Congress was a racist command post. With their chairmanships of key congressional committees, their mastery of the fine art of parliamentary delay, their formidable weapon-in-reserve of the Senate filibuster, the Southerners held a barricade not only against civil rights measures but against his whole legislative program. He argued, as Presidents had before him, that his economic and social measures—minimum-wage boosts, hous-ing and education programs, and the like—would benefit blacks even more than whites. The President, moreover, had an alternative strategy. He insisted to King that the people he had put in charge of civil rights policy—notably his brother Robert as Attorney General—and the executive actions he could take in certain spheres against discrimination enabled him to strengthen civil rights with simple strokes of the pen. And blacks had long heard this kind of talk too.

If this first White House meeting between Kennedy and King brought something of a standoff, it also reflected in both of them the kinds of moral dilemmas Myrdal had described. King, an old negotiator himself, could hardly ignore the President's need to conciliate Congress. Even "Daddy" King had been a compromiser in his own way; the son could remember his father's saying, after the call to Coretta, that he was switching from Nixon to Kennedy despite JFK's Catholicism: "But I'll take a Catholic or the Devil himself if he'll wipe the tears from my daughter-in-law's eyes." And Kennedy had to respect King's position. The President was caught at this point, Arthur Schlesinger wrote later, in a "terrible ambivalence about civil rights." He was certain that his executive strategy was the only possible one, but he recognized the injustice of the delay—and liberal Republicans were only too happy to remind him of this publicly. Still, with the southern fortress intact, he was determined to hold off on sending a major civil rights program to the Hill.

So once more blacks were being told: "Wait."

MARCHING AS TO WAR

Some would not wait. Early in May 1961 thirteen activists, about half of them white, boarded two buses in Washington, D.C., and headed south. As the Supreme Court had just outlawed segregated bus terminals, James Farmer and other CORE leaders now hoped that "putting the movement on wheels," and refusing to bail out of jail, would rivet the nation's attention and force Washington to carry out the law. The thirteen bus riders planned to traverse every Deep South state and end in New Orleans. They eluded violence until Rock Hill, South Carolina, where seminary student and SNCC organizer John Lewis, along with a white former navy commander now turned pacifist, Albert Bigelow, were set upon by white toughs as they entered the waiting rooms.

The doughty thirteen bused on through Georgia and across the border into Alabama. There, in Anniston, a roaring mob with iron bars attacked one of the Greyhound buses, smashed windows and slashed tires, and forced it to a stop outside of town. A fire bomb was thrown into the bus, which erupted in a blazing inferno. Gasping and choking, the protesters barely escaped before the bus exploded. When the second bus pulled into Anniston an hour later, whites charged in, beat up the freedom riders, and made blacks sit apart from whites as the bus drove on to Birmingham.

There a bigger mob awaited the riders. "As we entered the white waiting room and approached the lunch counter," veteran CORE activist Jim Peck related, he and a black youth "were grabbed bodily and pushed toward the alleyway." The whites attacked with fists and pipes. When Peck regained consciousness, blood was flowing down his face. "I tried to stop the flow with a handkerchief but it soon became soaked." "Everybody who got off the bus was clubbed, kicked or beaten," wrote an FBI informant in the Klan. "When people looked up, I couldn't see their faces for blood." He observed several FBI men making movies of the beatings. No Klansman was arrested.

Across the South, blacks were watching transfixed. From Nashville SNCC students made their way toward Birmingham despite fears of death that they did not hide from one another. Arrested at the Birmingham bus terminal, held for a day in "protective custody" and then "deported" a hundred miles to the Tennessee border, they made their way back, only to be bloodied by the mob.

The Kennedy brothers followed these happenings with dismay. Violence was a dire threat to their strategy of compromise and delay. Preparing at this juncture for his meeting with Khrushchev, the President said abruptly to an aide about the riders, "Tell them to call it off! Stop them!" Said the aide, "I don't think anybody's going to stop them right now." He was right.

Birmingham was more than a bloodletting; it posed a crisis of strategy for both the Kennedy Administration and the civil rights movement. In Washington the Attorney General, coping with the crisis on an hour-to-hour basis, urged Alabama governor John Patterson to give the riders safe passage across the state, helped arrange bus transportation to Montgomery for the beleaguered activists, conferred with black leaders, and after repeated rebuffs from Patterson and others, dispatched five hundred marshals under Byron White's command to the Alabama capital. The Kennedy effort to avoid bloodshed was clearly not working. But neither was Martin Luther King's, as he watched civil rights activists encounter the kind of violence he abhorred. Still, when a mass meeting was quickly called at Ralph Abernathy's church in Montgomery, King flew in to speak in support of the freedom riders.

Even a Baptist church was no sanctuary. As King conferred in the church basement with Farmer, Abernathy, and others, a mob gathered outside. King and Robert Kennedy talked by phone: King wanted the Attorney General to protect the church and the riders; Kennedy urged King to stop the freedom rides to allow a cooling-off period. When King relayed this message to the group, Farmer said, "Please tell the Attorney General that we have been cooling off for 350 years." Upstairs at the mass meeting people emboldened themselves with spirited singing while rocks smashed through the stained-glass windows, showering people in the pews with glass. The mob appeared about to break down the doors when U.S. marshals dispersed them with tear gas.

Early next morning, after nightlong negotiations among Robert Kennedy, the local National Guard general, and black leaders, the beleaguered churchgoers were driven home in army trucks. A few days later two busloads of freedom riders, escorted by National Guardsmen and highway patrolmen, drove to Jackson, Mississippi. People in Jackson gaped as National Guardsmen led the protesters into the bus station and local police first opened doors for them, then arrested them. The riders served almost two months in grim state pens, where defiant singing of freedom songs helped pull them through. During the summer hundreds of SNCC activists descended on the Jackson bus station and promptly joined their brothers and sisters in jail. They later agreed that prison had served as their training ground, steeling their commitment to a necessary but unpredictable struggle.

Even as the mob's stones smashed through the windows of Abernathy's church in Montgomery, conflict of a different sort had divided some of the black leaders conferring in the church basement. King was acting less as a leader than as a mediator who dealt on the phone with Robert Kennedy and other authorities. Farmer and Abernathy and an embattled student leader, Diane Nash, put steady pressure on King against compromise or cooling off. Later, when the young riders left for Jackson and King refused to accompany them because he was on probation, a young protester said, "We're all on probation. That doesn't stop us. We're in a war." But King had to deal with the Kennedys. The night that Abernathy and the other freedom riders arrived in Jackson and were promptly arrested, King telephoned the Attorney General. Kennedy wanted to get the protesters out of jail; King said they would stay in.

"It's a matter of conscience and morality," the young pastor told the young Attorney General over the phone. "They must use their lives and their bodies to right a wrong."

"Their staying in jail," Kennedy replied, would not have "the slightest effect" on him.

"Perhaps it would help if students came down here by the hundreds," King said, "by the hundreds of thousands."

Kennedy bristled. "Do as you wish," he said, "but don't make statements that sound like a threat. That's not the way to deal with us."

There was an awkward pause. Then King tried again.

"It's difficult to understand the position of oppressed people. Ours is a way out—creative, moral and nonviolent. It is not tied to black supremacy or Communism but to the plight of the oppressed. It can save the soul of America. You must understand that we've made no gains without pressure and I hope that pressure will always be moral, legal and peaceful."

"But the problem won't be settled in Jackson, Mississippi," Kennedy said, "but by strong federal action."

He was hopeful, King said, "but I am different than my father. I feel the need of being free now!"

If the people in jail didn't want to stay, Kennedy said, "we can get them out."

"They'll stay."

*　*　*

The dispute among black leaders about strategy carried over into the next great phase of the movement, in Albany, the hub of rural southwestern Georgia. Once again taking the lead, SNCC organizers moved into the city in the fall of 1961, forged a coalition of local college students and older residents, and launched waves of nonviolent protests to integrate the bus station and other public places. Soon hundreds of blacks were languishing in jail, sometimes dozens in cells designed for six. When the campaign sagged, local leaders—over the objections of some SNCC leaders who wished to keep this a local people's movement—implored King to "just speak for us one night." King had not planned to become involved in Albany, but he went; once there he had not planned to stay, but his arrival and speeches incited a huge and emotional response, a march downtown headed by King, and his arrest along with that of many others. Both his incarceration and his subsequent bail-out sparked fervent demonstrations.

Spiritually the "Albany Movement" was a triumph, as an unprecedented expression of black cultural power. It was the "singing movement," as protesters of all ages poured out their souls in freedom songs melded with old slave spirituals. Singing was the language of protest—especially for the illiterate—the vital tool to build solidarity, sustain morale, instill courage, and deepen commitment. "We Shall Overcome," led by an Albany State student activist, Bernice Reagon, became the movement's anthem, sung at the end of every big meeting—all standing, crossing arms and holding hands, gently swaying back and forth, singing so powerfully that, SNCC's Charles Sherrod remembered, "nobody knew what kept the top of the church on its four walls."

If the final test for blacks was political impact, however, Albany was a disaster. The city's astute police chief, Laurie Pritchett, systematically and "nonviolently" herded protesters into city and nearby county jails, determined to avoid incidents that could cause an explosion of national outrage. King, in and out of jail, was caught between compromisers in the movement, who accepted poor deals with the city, and militants, who deemed King too conciliatory, too passive, but also too interfering in their local efforts. At one point, enraged by the kicking of a pregnant woman while she was taking food to protesters in a jail thirty-five miles from the city, Albany blacks went on a rampage, flinging bottles and stones at the Albany police. King, grieving over this violation of nonviolence, canceled a scheduled march and, in the spirit of Gandhi, declared a day of penance. But "Pritchett's jails," wrote historian Carl Brauer, "had proven to be stronger than the endurance of Albany's black people."

It was becoming dramatically clear that progress in civil rights depended less on the first-cadre white political leadership in Washington, important though that was, than on the second-cadre black leadership in Atlanta and Montgomery, and even more on the third-cadre leadership of students, older black women, and white protesters from the North. Then, in the fall of 1962, a single black student showed that one man could make a crucial difference.

Inspired by JFK's inaugural address, James Meredith the next day had applied for admission to the whites-only University of Mississippi at Oxford. "Nobody handpicked me," he said later; he felt a "Divine Responsibility" to break white supremacy, starting with Ole Miss. He would not evade the issue through a "sneak registration" in Jackson. Governor Ross Barnett of Mississippi was equally adamant. He himself would go to jail, he said at one point, before he would let "that boy," backed by the "Communist" NAACP, get into Ole Miss. After Barnett's endless stalling in the face of a federal circuit court's order to the university to admit, Justice Hugo Black handed down an enforcing order from the Supreme Court, while Barnett roared defiance and white hatred mounted in Oxford.

The episodes that followed burned into the nation's memory: the President dispatching federal marshals to the Oxford area—rednecks and Citizens' Council militants advancing into the area by the truckload—the President's telephone appeal to Barnett to carry out the court orders—the governor's public defiance even while he privately discussed deals with the Kennedys—the President federalizing the Mississippi National Guard—the marshals moving onto the campus, five hundred strong—the gathering crowd becoming increasingly hostile, while Meredith waited in a dormitory—the mob surging into the line of marshals behind a barrage of rocks and bottles and, soon, bullets, while the marshals tried to protect themselves by firing canisters of tear gas—the beleaguered marshals' request that the Army be sent and then the agonizingly slow arrival of the troops—the two bystanders killed, the scores of marshals wounded, the hundreds of rioters taken into custody—finally, the registration of the indomitable Meredith at daybreak, on a campus reeking of smoke and hatred.

During the ten days leading to this night of violence, Robert Kennedy had been in repeated telephone contact with Barnett. Each had done his share of feinting, bluffing, dealing. They agreed on a "sneak registration" (which Barnett shortly repudiated); Kennedy for a time pulled back a federal convoy, to avert violence and save the governor from political "embarrassment." He had also instructed the marshals in their remarkable self-restraint. The Kennedys operated amid intense pressures, ranging from Third World reactions to those of southern Democrats on the Hill, while Barnett had more leeway. Both sides wished above all to avoid violence; both got it. The Oxford crisis shocked the Kennedys. With all the good communications and give-and-take, how could it end in bloodshed?

"We lacked," an aide said, "a sense of Southern history"—a sense of the power of rooted ideology and historic extremism. At Oxford, Arthur Schlesinger wrote later, the Kennedys began to understand "how profoundly the republic had been trapped by its history." The Kennedys were trapped too by their own history, above all by the notion that the give-and-take of brokerage politics would work amid the polarized politics of reaction and revolution. Hence it was not surprising that, when Robert Kennedy and his associates conducted a review of their handling of the situation, they appeared mainly concerned about their operational failures, as though they could outmaneuver history through tactical methods rather than through a transformation of their own moral attitudes and political strategy.

*   *   *

Black leaders had even more reason than the White House to reassess the lessons of Ole Miss and the earlier struggles. For them registering one man at the university was only a start; they viewed the Kennedy's efforts as, at worst, manipulation of blacks as pawns, mere tokenism at best. Even moderates like King felt depressed after Oxford. The Kennedy Administration was better on civil rights than its predecessors, he granted, but it was helping to constrict a movement that should be "breaking out into the open plains of progress." A "sweeping revolutionary force," he said, was being "pressed into a narrow tunnel."

But even if only a tunnel, a tunnel to where? Black leaders disagreed not only over means—nonviolent direct action appealing to the liberal conscience against more conventional pressure on the federal government—but also over goals. Should across-the-board civil rights policies be the top priority, or was it better to concentrate on voting rights as the crucial first step to all other rights? A conflict simmered inside SNCC between advocates of more civil disobedience against desegregation and those who held that racism would not be overcome until blacks had political power, which meant vote power. The direct-actionists suspected that the voting registration strategy was merely a White House device to enlarge the black constituency for the next election.

King and the SCLC leadership, after a two-day strategy review, decided to put desegregation first. Direct action in department stores and lunch counters, they calculated, could bring concrete results and at the same time focus intensified pressure on the White House. For their next target they chose Birmingham.

Birmingham. For blacks, this city, the industrial center of the South, was the American Johannesburg, the most segregated metropolis in the country, the self-styled "magic city" that was really the "tragic city." The white power structure consisted of three mutually reinforcing elements: the business and industrial elites who ran the Birmingham economy; the political elites who maintained the racial status quo, ranging from Governor George C. Wallace in Montgomery to the "magic city's" Commissioner of Public Safety, Eugene "Bull" Connor; and the Ku Klux Klan and other racist groups that abounded in the city and its outskirts. To challenge this structure SCLC had in Birmingham one of its strongest affiliates, headed by one of its most militant leaders, Fred Shuttlesworth. SCLC's strategy was to throw its resources into mass demonstrations and store boycotts, with the hope of splitting the business elite from the political leaders. SCLC saw the campaign as a drama, progressing act by act until it reached the crisis, followed by the denouement when white power would be forced to yield.

By March 1963, SCLC people were moving into the streets. After a few skirmishes Connor won a state court injunction barring King and his companions from leading more protests. He would violate the order, King asserted at a spirited mass meeting, even though the movement had run out of funds and he was needed to raise bail money. On Good Friday the jeans-clad King and Abernathy and fifty others marched downtown in a glare of publicity. When the two walked up to the burly Connor and knelt in prayer, police grabbed them by the back of their shirts, threw them into paddy wagons, then seized the others. King was held incommunicado in a dark cell with no mattress or blanket until, at Coretta King's request, John Kennedy interceded and conditions improved.

Soon the prisoner was busy scribbling on scraps of paper and in the margins of a newspaper. He was responding to a letter in that newspaper by white Alabama clergy condemning his tactics and timing. In biting sentences King laid down his creed: "We know through painful experience that freedom is never voluntarily given by the oppressor; it must be demanded by the oppressed. . . . We have waited for more than 340 years for our constitutional and God-given rights. The nations of Asia and Africa are moving with jetlike speed toward gaining political independence, but we still creep at horse-and-buggy pace toward gaining a cup of coffee at a lunch counter. . . . I have almost reached the regrettable conclusion that the Negro's great stumbling block in his stride toward freedom is not the White Citizens' Councilor or the Ku Klux Klanner, but the white moderate, who is more devoted to 'order' than to justice. . . . If our white brothers dismiss as 'rabble-rousers' and 'outside agitators' those of us who employ nonviolent direct action and if they refuse to support our nonviolent efforts, millions of Negroes will, out of frustration and despair, seek solace and security in black-nationalist ideologies—a development that would inevitably lead to a frightening racial nightmare." This became the "Letter from Birmingham Jail," the most cogent and moving justification of civil disobedience since Thoreau's essay.

Marching to Birmingham's city hall, wave after wave of men and women were mauled by police dogs, hurled against walls and pavements by fire hoses that shot out water with cannonlike force, jammed into jails that soon were overflowing. But when King and Abernathy were released, the crusade began to flag. As a last resort to revive media attention, black leaders dispatched battalions of children—some as young as six—who marched with songs and shouts of "We want freedom," endured dogs and fire hoses, and rode off in school buses to jail cheering and singing. With the passing days the police became rougher, as young blacks on the sidelines hurled the usual street missiles.

Black activists fought the battle of the media along with the battle in the streets. They had long experienced not only the conservative bias of many southern newspapers but also the tendency of the southern media to play down or even ignore demonstrations taking place in front of their own offices. "We don't want to fan the flames," an editor explained. But the activists needed to break through middle-class white apathy. Thus it was all the more crucial to arouse the national media, which reached not only a mass audience but to some degree brought the news of southern conflict into southern homes.

Just as SCLC leaders hoped, Bull Connor's police dogs and fire hoses galvanized the nation's conscience, including the leaders' in Washington. Fearing a violent uprising, the White House sent in mediators. This interposition, combined with efforts of local white moderates to negotiate a compromise, touched off a raging dispute among the black leadership. When King agreed to a temporary halt in the protests, Shuttlesworth, who had been hospitalized with a severe fire-hose injury, rounded on the pastor. He shouted that President Kennedy "doesn't live down here, and I live down here. . . . Tell him King can't call it off."

King pleaded for unity. "I'll be damned if you'll have it like this," Shuttlesworth cried. "You're mister big, but you're going to be mister S-H-I-T." Then he walked out.

Yet both the blacks' militance and their moderation were working. The business leaders, threatened by the paralyzing boycott and damning publicity, agreed to desegregation demands, though city officials remained intransigent. The vaunted white power structure was not so shatterproof after all. Still, the blacks' victory was a mixed one, with continuing divisions among their leadership, recriminations from George Wallace and others of the white old guard, a Ku Klux Klan rally in a local park, the bombing of the home of King's brother, and more rioting. Bull Connor had clearly lost, however, as the electrifying drama of Birmingham, conveyed by extraordinary television coverage, projected his snarling, biting police dogs to the nation and the world.

* * *

Birmingham projected into the White House. The President told a group of civil rights liberals that a newspaper picture that morning of a police dog attacking a black woman had made him "sick." John Kennedy was going through his own crisis of conscience during the spring of 1963. At the start of the year he had decided once again not to seek major civil rights legislation, for the usual reasons—it would not pass, it would alienate southern Democratic leaders, it would hurt the rest of his program. He had begun to move from this position by the end of February, when he submitted proposals to strengthen desegregation programs and to buttress voting rights, and told Congress flatly that racial discrimination was not only economically costly: "Above all, it is wrong." Black leaders were disappointed by the slimness of the program, however, and even more by the President's failure to push even these proposals. He himself believed the Administration was "sincere," King said, but he floated what he called the "cynical view" that it wanted the votes of both sides and was "paralyzed by the conflicting needs of each." The Administration did indeed seemed paralyzed on civil rights legislation.

But events—and those who made them—were in the saddle. The SCLC's "street leaders" and their jailings by Bull Connor brought tempers North and South to a fever heat. In New York, Robert Kennedy met with a group of blacks gathered by the novelist James Baldwin, including the singers Lena Horne and Harry Belafonte, the brilliant social psychologist Kenneth B. Clark, and Jerome Smith, a freedom rider who held a CORE record for beatings and jailings. Smith drew Kennedy's attention at the start by saying he was "nauseated" at being in the same room with him, that he was not sure how long he would stay nonviolent, that he would "Never! Never! Never!" fight for his country. The artists joined in with their own castigations. The Attorney General vainly tried to turn the subject to Clark's facts and figures, but "none of us wanted to hear figures and percentages and all that stuff" in the light of Birmingham, Lena Horne said.

"It was all emotion, hysteria—they stood up and orated—they cursed—some of them wept and left the room," Kennedy told Arthur Schlesinger despairingly. In three hours of confrontation neither side believed it had communicated with the other. And yet the blacks in their outrage had. Kennedy "resented the experience," Schlesinger wrote later, "but it pierced him all the same. His tormentors made no sense; but in a way they made all sense."

The tormentors of the centrists, the activists on both sides, were still in the saddle. Armed with a federal district court ruling, young blacks planned to renew their effort to register at the University of Alabama at Tuscaloosa. Alabama governor Wallace, having sworn at his inaugural that he would "draw the line in the dust" and stand and fight for "Segregation now! Segregation tomorrow! Segregation forever!" and having resolved that he would never again be "out-nigguhed" following an earlier electoral defeat, prepared to defy the feds publicly while dealing with them privately. John and Robert Kennedy, still haunted by Meredith and Oxford, were ready to let Wallace have his day in the sun if he would then let the blacks register. So after further posturing and fire-breathing, Wallace positioned himself for the best television shots at the registration building door and read his proclamation denouncing the feds, while Assistant Attorney General Nicholas Katzenbach confronted him. Then both retired; the blacks proceeded to their dormitories and later quietly registered. No one blocked the door.

The day was June 11, 1963. That evening, after anxious hours, the President addressed the nation on radio and television. The nation faced a moral crisis, he said.

"The Negro baby born in America today, regardless of the section of the Nation in which he is born, has about one-half as much chance of completing a high school as a white baby born in the same place on the same day, one-third as much chance of completing college, one-third as much chance of becoming a professional man, twice as much chance of becoming unemployed. . . .

"The heart of the question is whether all Americans are to be afforded equal rights and equal opportunities, whether we are going to treat our fellow Americans as we want to be treated. . . .

"We preach freedom around the world, and we mean it, and we cherish our freedom here at home, but are we to say to the world, and much more importantly, to each other that this is a land of the free except for the Negroes; that we have no second-class citizens except Negroes . . . ?"

Eight days later the President asked Congress for measures to ban the segregation of public facilities, give the Attorney General authority to initiate proceedings against the segregation of schools, expand educational and training programs, grant a permanent statutory basis for his Committee on Equal Employment Opportunity. While Kennedy renewed the voting rights recommendations he had urged in February, the heart of the June 1963 proposals lay in their antisegregation provisions. Still divided themselves over whether desegregation or voting rights was the better strategy, black leaders were disappointed that the President did not ask for more—but grimly determined that he would at least get what he asked.

As the engines of delay and deadlock were wheeled into action on the Hill, the Council on United Civil Rights Leadership, a coalition of the "Big Six"—the NAACP's Roy Wilkins, Whitney Young of the Urban League, Martin Luther King, James Farmer of CORE, SNCC executive secretary James Forman (rotating with SNCC's chair, John Lewis), and Dorothy Height of the National Council of Negro Women—debated how to put pressure on Congress. At an earlier leadership meeting, it was recalled, the revered labor leader A. Philip Randolph had proposed that the Big Six organize a massive march on Washington; after all, Randolph's mere threat to invade the capital back in 1941 had pushed FDR into banning discrimination in war industries. The leaders seized on a "march for jobs and freedom" that would unify all factions of the movement.

They conferred with the President, who was cool to the idea, fearing that it would give members of Congress an easy way out by charging intimidation. It was, he suggested, ill-timed.

"It may seem ill-timed," King said. "Frankly, I have never engaged in any direct action movement which did not seem ill-timed." The leaders resolved to go ahead.

*   *   *

August 28, 1963, the Mall, Washington, D.C. A quarter of a million people, black and white together, gathered in the summer heat at the Washington Monument and then surged forth to the Lincoln Memorial. They had come on buses and trains, many from the Deep South. Large contingents represented white religious faiths and, despite lack of backing by the AFL-CIO, many labor unions. Haunting freedom songs—"We Shall Overcome" sung by Joan Baez, "Oh, Freedom!" by Odetta—blended with speeches by the civil rights leadership. SNCC's John Lewis pierced the uplifting mood by denouncing the inadequacy of conventional liberalism and Kennedy's legislative program to complete "the unfinished revolution of 1776."

Around midafternoon Martin Luther King stood beneath the brooding face of Abraham Lincoln. Inspired by the sea of upturned black and white faces, he left his carefully crafted text and in rippling cadences and rich colors, he painted his vibrant dream of racial justice. Repeatedly invoking his phrase, "I have a *dream,*" responding to the people in rhythm with him, he implored that freedom ring from the hilltops of New Hampshire, the mountains of New York and Pennsylvania, and even more, from Georgia's Stone Mountain. "Let freedom ring from Lookout Mountain of Tennessee. Let freedom ring from every hill and mole hill of Mississippi. From every mountain top, let freedom ring.

"When we let freedom ring, when we let it ring from every village and every hamlet, from every state and from every city, we will be able to speed up that day when all of God's children, black men and white men, Jews and Gentiles, Protestants and Catholics, will be able to join hands and sing in the words of the old Negro spiritual, 'Free at last! Free at last! Thank God almighty, we are free at last!' "

A euphoric group of blacks, save for Coretta King, who to her distress was left to repair to her hotel room, met with the President following the rally. Having first opposed the march and then cooperated with it—to the point, some militants charged, of cooptation—Kennedy now shared in the moment of relief and triumph. He was "bubbling over with the success of the event," Wilkins recalled. But out on the Mall some blacks remained skeptical and even cynical. Listening to King, young activist Anne Moody had told herself that back in Mississippi they had never had time to sleep, much less dream. An angry black man had shouted: "Fuck that dream, Martin. Now, goddamit, NOW!"

It was a luminous moment in a season of death and despair. The very evening of Kennedy's June television address, NAACP leader Medgar Evers had been shot down as he returned to his home in Mississippi; later the President consoled the Evers family in the White House. By the end of the summer nearly 14,000 persons had been arrested in seventy-five cities in the South alone. Two weeks after the March, on a Sunday morning, a dynamite bomb exploded in Birmingham's Sixteenth Street Baptist Church, a center of the spring crusade, killing four black girls as they were donning their choir robes.

During some of the tense days of school and university integration a few Americans North and South had dreamt their own special dream—that the President of the United States would walk hand in hand with two small black children toward a schoolhouse door, or that John F. Kennedy rather than a subordinate federal official would stand up to a southern governor at a university registration place. Even if the Secret Service had approved this risky act, JFK would never have favored such a melodramatic gesture. But in the increasingly polarized atmosphere of fall 1963 he was willing to venture into politically hostile land. This was Texas, some of whose cities harbored not only extreme racists but fanatical rightists, anti-Castro Cubans, Puerto Rican nationalists, black militants, violent leftists. Dallas, a center of Texas politics and finance, was also a center of hatred. There Lyndon B. Johnson himself had been beset by a hostile crowd during the 1960 campaign; there Adlai Stevenson had been spat upon earlier this very fall. Stevenson had been shown handbills screaming WANTED FOR TREASON under a photograph of Kennedy.

The President would journey to Texas not to confront Southerners over civil rights but to seek common ground. So in San Antonio he would visit the new Aero-Space Medical Health Center and greet crowds of Mexican-Americans. In Houston he would talk to Latin American citizens about the Alliance for Progress. In Fort Worth he would discuss his defense program, which not coincidentally had brought huge contracts to General Dynamics and other corporations located in Texas. In Dallas at the Trade Mart he intended to describe the Administration's pro-business policies to Texas business leaders. In all these places he would seek to recognize his congressional and other supporters, placate rival factions in the Texas Democracy, raise money for his own reelection campaign. Told by a southern friend that he was about to enter a hornet's nest, Kennedy said drily, "Well, that'll add interest."

And so San Antonio, Houston, Fort Worth, in lovely weather before exuberant crowds. Then Dallas, the cavalcade, the open presidential limousine, the sharp turn left where the Texas School Book Depository overlooked Dealey Plaza, the unerring bullets . . .

The searing, the exalting events of the twentieth century had left millions of Americans with memories of just where they had been, what they had been doing, when they heard the news—of Lindbergh's arrival in Paris, of Roosevelt's bank holiday, of Pearl Harbor, of Hiroshima or the war's end. But nothing so riveted the memory as the horrifying news from Dallas. (This author was teaching a class in American government in a basement room of the First Congregational Church of Williamstown, Massachusetts, when a student came to the door with an early report of Kennedy's wounding; the class continued in a half-daze, then broke up in shocked incredulity when someone burst in with the wrenching second report.) The earlier unforgettable events had been understandable, they had made some sense. Kennedy's death seemed inexplicable, senseless. Daniel Patrick Moynihan said to an interviewer: "You know the French author Camus—he said the world was absurd. A Christian couldn't think that, but the utter senselessness, the meaninglessness . . . We all of us know down here that politics is a tough game. And I don't think there's any point in being Irish if you don't know that the world is going to break your heart eventually. . . . Mary McGrory said to me that we'll never laugh again. And I said, 'Heavens. We'll laugh again. It's just that we'll never be young again.' " Searching for meaning, people looked for a conspiracy, villains, motives.

Investigations, official findings on the assassination, did not satisfy most Americans, nor did the passage of time put the event into a comfortable perspective. But John Kennedy, a fatalist who had lost a brother and a sister in aircraft tragedies, might have seen Dallas only as the ultimate proof of his favorite adage: "Life is unfair." So was death.

*   *   *

John Kennedy had planned on almost three thousand days in office; he was given a third of that. Lincoln and McKinley had enjoyed at least full first terms and the satisfaction of reelections. It was the brutal cutting off of a young leader of a young administration that appalled people. After earlier mishaps, he had been coming into the fullness not only of his presidential power but of personal fulfillment. He had told a friend some months before his presidential campaign that while some people had their liberalism "made" by their late twenties, "I didn't. I was caught in cross currents and eddies. It was only later that I got into the stream of things."

Still caught in these crosscurrents, the President for a year or two seemed to be four persons: a rhetorical radical delivering the ringing speeches Theodore Sorensen and others prepared for him; the policy liberal carefully husbanding his power and weighing the balance of interests and attitudes; the fiscal conservative, always intent, like FDR, on balancing the budget and, like FDR, always failing; and the institutional conservative who accepted the constraints around him and planned on vitalizing the torpid governmental system by jolts of New Frontier electricity. These four Kennedys could not coexist for long and they did not; toward the end the eloquent leader was moving the policy liberal toward stronger positions and toward Keynesian economics, although not toward any assault on the institutional chains and checks.

Watching Kennedy during his early presidential months, pundits and politicians noted his calculating approach to politics and policy, his personal self-control and self-containment. Civil rights posed the great test of these qualities. For two years he and his brother Robert had analyzed the mounting struggle in the South by the same standards as they had conventional and quantifiable problems like taxation or Social Security. Just as the policies and priorities could be weighed and balanced off against one another, so the prescriptions could be measured out in droplets—for southern blacks, voter education and registration programs, case-by-case litigation, step-by-step policy making.

The passion in the black movement, in contrast, was beyond calculation.

By Kennedy's third year in office that passion could not be contained. When Birmingham and other flash points threatened to burst into flames, King warned the Administration that it was at a "historic crossroad" and now it must face "its moral commitment and with it, its political fortunes." Kennedy the rhetorical radical must come across. Within a few weeks Kennedy recognized the "moral crisis" that could not be met by repression or tokenism. Still, the leadership had come from the bottom, from Rosa Parks and all her counterparts across the South who had acted while others preached. They created the events that in turn moved the Administration. The White House had mainly reacted.

These leaders had given Kennedy, indeed the whole nation, a lesson in freedom. For Kennedy freedom had meant Bill of Rights liberties, constitutional procedures, liberal tolerance. For blacks freedom meant also self-expression, self-respect, dignity, status, power. They had their own language of freedom—they talked about freedom rides, freedom songs, freedom schools, the freedom movement. They were following Ella Baker's cardinal principle: *You must let the oppressed themselves define their own freedom.* In the end it was not his Irish-American heritage but civil rights principles backed up by black pressure that moved John Kennedy toward an expanded concept of freedom.

An eager lover of life and fun and paradox, a man of rationality and restraint and realism, he had only an amused contempt for the theatrical gesture, the sentimental idealist, the quixotic hero. This made the cause of his death—the smashing, blinding bullets arching out of nowhere—all the more incomprehensible, all the more unbearable to those who had known and loved him.

WE SHALL OVERCOME

Lyndon B. Johnson lost no time in taking the oath of office, grasping firmly the reins of power, and making passage of the civil rights bill his top legislative priority. "We have talked long enough in this country about equal rights," he told Congress in a brief address five days after the assassination. "We have talked for one hundred years or more. It is time now to write the next chapter, and to write it in the books of law." This was the kind of talk black leaders wanted to hear—and had not expected to hear from the Johnson they had known.

But it was Congress that passed the laws, and Congress on civil rights continued to provide a masterly example of American government in inaction. The civil rights bill was still in the hands of the House Rules Committee, chaired by Judge Howard W. Smith, the venerable Virginian who had led the counterattack against FDR's New Deal in the late 1930s. At a critical moment during the combat over the 1957 civil rights bill he had delayed consideration by discovering that he must return home to inspect a barn that had burned, upon which Speaker Rayburn quipped that although he knew Howard Smith would do anything to block a civil rights bill, "I never knew he would resort to arson." Finally opening proceedings before the Rules Committee in January 1964, he proved that he had not exhausted his parliamentary bag of tricks when he scheduled day after day of hearings on what he called this "nefarious bill." At last voted out of the Rules Committee, the measure had then to run the House gantlet of days of debate on complex provisions and amendments. Smith threw male members of the House into confusion by moving to add the word "sex" to the list of forbidden discriminations—race, creed, color, and national origin. Designed more to kill the bill than to promote equal rights for women, his amendment prevailed after vigorous lobbying by the National Women's Party.

By early 1964, however, parliamentary maneuvers alone could not stop a measure whose time had come. When the bill passed the House 290–130, the four-party split was once again evident as 86 Democrats from the states of the old Confederacy voted against the bill and 138 Republicans supported it, while "aye" votes by 11 representatives from the "outer rim" states of the South indicated some erosion in southern congressional opposition to civil rights. Republican support for the measure reflected both the historic allegiance of presidential Republicans to the party of Lincoln and their hopes and fears about the forthcoming presidential election; it was also a response after his death to John Kennedy's assiduous courting of Republican votes for his civil rights bill.

And then the Senate. The four-party split on civil rights broadly prevailed in the upper chamber too, but backers of the measure faced there the single most venerable and formidable weapon of delay in the congressional arsenal—the filibuster. Southern senators, proclaiming that they were prepared for "a battle to the last ditch—to the death," made clear that they would filibuster the bill at every possible point in the tortuous Senate process. Civil rights Democrats under the leadership of majority whip Hubert H. Humphrey and civil rights Republicans led by Thomas H. Kuchel of California teamed up to try to muster the two-thirds vote necessary to invoke cloture and end debate. Civil rights advocates were apprehensive. Their adversaries included such skilled obstructionists as Richard Russell, John Stennis, and Strom Thurmond; Thurmond had established the filibuster record in the Senate with an uninterrupted twenty-four-hour speech against the 1957 civil rights bill.

Feeling in the nation mounted as the Southerners conducted their talka-thons. A Coordinating Committee for Fundamental American Freedoms, Inc., headed by the arch-reactionary publisher of the Manchester *Union Leader* in New Hampshire, William Loeb, Jr., but largely financed by Missis-sippians, charged that the bill was a "billion dollar blackjack." A formida-ble leadership network united the civil rights coalition—the President of the United States, congressional leaders, labor spokesmen, a "leadership conference" busily lobbying on behalf of the fourscore organizations it embraced. Crucial to the effort were the organizing and lobbying efforts of religious bodies. "We have seen cardinals, bishops, elders, stated clerks, common preachers, priests, and rabbis come to Washington to press for passage of the bill," Senator Russell complained. "They have sought to make its passage a great moral issue."

Week after week the Senate debate droned on—through eighty-two working days, 6,300 pages of the *Congressional Record,* ten million words. Throughout Johnson stood steadfast for the bill, rejecting major changes, prodding and advising Humphrey, twisting people's arms, wheeling and dealing. Pivotal in the Senate was one man, Everett Dirksen of Illinois, long a leader of the congressional Republicans on the Hill. The President drew Humphrey aside at a White House breakfast for legislative leaders.

"The bill can't pass unless you get Ev Dirksen," LBJ said. "You and I are going to get Ev. It's going to take time. We're going to get him. You make up your mind now that you've got to spend time with Ev Dirksen. You've got to let him have a piece of the action. He's got to look good all the time. Don't let these bomb throwers, now, talk you out of seeing Dirksen. You get in there to see Dirksen. You drink with Dirksen! You talk with Dirksen! You listen to Dirksen!"

Humphrey did—and so did Johnson. Having measured the man during their years together in the Senate, the President, said a White House aide, "never let him alone for thirty minutes." Dirksen was heavily cross-pres-sured by attitudes among his Illinois constituents, including a mounting number of blacks, by his friendships with both Kennedy and Johnson, by public-opinion polls favorable to civil rights, by his conservative Republi-can cronies and his Democratic allies in the South who warned him that backing the measure would "kill off" Republican hopes for victory in November, and above all, perhaps, by his own moral concern over the struggle. In the end he not only switched; he became a Senate crusader for civil rights.

Finally, with the civil rights lobbyists working day and night while the filibusterers did likewise, a cloture petition was filed. Dirksen's led the names on the petition. Soon the Senate voted cloture 71–29—the first time it ever did so on a civil rights bill. Passage of the bill followed. Only one Democrat outside the South—Robert C. Byrd of West Virginia—and only four non-southern Republicans voted against. One of them was Barry Goldwater of Arizona.

President Johnson signed the Civil Rights Act of 1964 on July 2 in the East Room of the White House, where John F. Kennedy had lain in state seven months earlier. The new law, LBJ told the nation, was designed neither to punish nor to divide, but "to promote a more abiding commitment to freedom." Later he handed out seventy-two pens to the backers of the act clustered around him. The leaders were happy and self-satisfied. The battle had been a long and hard one. One hundred years before, Yankee troops were smashing through the South with victories that marked the turning point of the Civil War. A century was a long time, but the system finally had produced.

Yet the power of the President, of the Justice Department, of congressional majorities, of the Supreme Court, had not been enough. It was the civil rights street people who had pushed and prodded that system into action. Whether or not they received pens that night, they had been the real leaders.

*   *   *

The civil rights measure that Lyndon Johnson signed in July 1964 outlawed discrimination in public accommodations, authorized the Attorney General to initiate suits to desegregate public facilities including schools, barred discrimination in employment on the basis of race, color, religion, sex, or national origin. It gave a little more protection to voting rights—mainly by banning denial of registration because of trivial errors in filling out forms—but it largely bypassed the issue of the denial to blacks of the right to register and vote. Many still believed that blacks must secure their rights by gaining voting power in the political system—power that they could use to fight *all* the ills that beset them, power they could exercise through city councils and state governments as well as in Washington, power that could be brought to bear on the sheriffs, school boards, state troopers, mayors, city police, who were so often the bane of their lives. And what could be more appropriate in a democracy—more citizenlike, more unthreatening—than to seek the right to vote?

Two years before LBJ signed the 1964 act, a tired but strong-willed woman with a warm smile and great shining eyes had walked into a meeting at her church in Ruleville, a Mississippi Delta town not far from where Emmett Till had been bludgeoned to death. "Until then I'd never heard of no mass meeting and I didn't know that a Negro could register and vote," Fannie Lou Hamer recalled. James Forman and other SNCC activists ran the meeting. "When they asked for those to raise their hands who'd go down to the courthouse the next day, I raised mine. Had it up high as I could get it. I guess if I'd had any sense I'd a-been a little scared, but what was the point of being scared. The only thing they could do to me was kill me and it seemed like they'd been trying to do that a little bit at a time ever since I could remember."

Forty-four years old, Hamer was the youngest of twenty children of sharecropper parents. She had picked cotton all her life, for the past eighteen years with her husband on a nearby plantation. She had always known poverty and injustice; when her parents were getting a little ahead a white farmer had poisoned their mules. For a long time she had wanted to help her kind. "Just listenin' at 'em, I could just see myself votin' people outa office that I know was wrong and didn't do nothin' to help the poor."

With seventeen others Hamer rode on a bus chartered by SNCC to the county seat of Indianola, birthplace of the White Citizens' Councils, where the registrar "brought a big old book out there, and he gave me the sixteenth section of the Constitution of Mississippi, and that was dealing with de facto laws, and I didn't know nothin' about no de facto laws." She "flunked out" along with the others. Driving home, they were all arrested because the bus was "too yellow." The plantation owner kicked Hamer off the land, and the house where she stayed in town was shot up by vigilantes. It was one hell of a winter. "Pap couldn't get a job nowhere 'cause everybody knew he was my husband." But they made it through. Soon Hamer joined SNCC as an organizer.

SNCC had been struggling since 1961 to register black voters in the closed society of Mississippi. Although blacks made up almost half the population, local intimidation, along with the state literacy test and poll tax, held them down to 5 percent of the registered voters. The old debate in the southern black movement between those who advocated civil disobedience in resistance to segregation and those who argued that blacks must first pursue political power now intensified. At an August 1961 SNCC conference at Highlander, Ella Baker had mediated the issue with a proposal to have two wings in SNCC, one for direct action and one for voter registration. As it turned out, no action was riskier, more militant, even potentially more revolutionary than organizing blacks to vote in Mississippi, whose reputation for terrorism had made it the most dreaded state on SNCC's target list and virtually off limits to SCLC.

Mississippi more than lived up to its reputation. When Bob Moses, the driving force behind the SNCC voting campaign, had moved to the small southern Mississippi city of McComb in July 1961 to set up the first of a string of registration "schools," he and his cohorts were routinely arrested and beaten—more than once in a place called Liberty. Herbert Lee, a local farmer and father of nine, was gunned down by a state legislator who was never prosecuted; after a protest march Moses and others were jailed for two months. Routed for the moment, they left McComb, recruited people from the grass roots, and fanned out into several other counties in the flat Delta country. Risk and repression became a way of life. Diane Nash, now married to James Bevel and pregnant, was jailed after teaching nonviolence to young people; refusing bail, she declared that "since my child will be a black child, born in Mississippi, whether I am in jail or not he will be born in prison."

Fannie Lou Hamer was in the thick of the struggle. She and others were locked up for trying to use a whites-only café. The next moments burned into her memory: the shrieks from blows in other cells—the cop yelling at her, "You, bitch, you, we gon' make you wish you was dead"—the two black prisoners forced to beat her with a long blackjack—screaming into the mattress so the sound would not come out—the injuries that never left her. It was while she was in jail that Medgar Evers was killed. But the black leaders persisted in Mississippi, turning increasingly to electoral tactics as 1964 approached. Black and white activists canvassed the state, persuading over 80,000 black people to cast symbolic "freedom ballots" in churches, in stores, and on the street.

Early in 1964, SNCC began a campaign to sign up voters for the Mississippi Freedom Democratic Party, which sought to challenge the lily-white Democrats for accreditation as the Mississippi delegation at the Democratic national convention to be held in Atlantic City in August. Black leaders launched a large project to import hundreds of white college students to help in a climactic registration campaign. Three activists—two white and one black—were arrested for speeding, turned over to the Klan, beaten, mutilated, and shot to death (for which crimes seven whites were later convicted in a federal court). Still the students flocked in by the hundreds, living with black families in ramshackle "freedom houses," teaching the three R's and black history and the meaning of democracy in "freedom schools," escorting to the courthouse blacks who dared try to register. After modest gains the registration crusade waned as plans focused on gaining seats at the Democratic national convention. Party conclaves in each county, some threatened by hostile whites, chose delegates to the five congressional district conventions, which in turn sent delegates to the state convention in Jackson.

Some of the delegates came to Jackson straight out of tar-paper shacks, wearing borrowed suits, with no memory of political involvement, but catching on, participant Sally Belfrage reported, "with some extraordinary inner sense to how the process worked, down to its smallest nuance and finagle." The eight hundred grass-roots representatives, mostly black and poor and including many women, chose sixty-eight delegates to journey to Atlantic City. At last blacks could challenge white power inside one of its power centers. Or could they?

*   *   *

The Boardwalk, Atlantic City, late August 1964. Balloons and bunting adorned the façades of the convention hotels; the very ocean air smelled like "popcorn and seaweed"; the severe features of LBJ frowned from countless posters. Across the water a huge billboard, proclaiming "In Your Heart You Know He's Right," reminded Democrats that Barry Goldwater, the champion of the Republican right wing, had been nominated by the GOP six weeks before. Crowding the boardwalk in their Sunday best were hundreds of southern blacks, who had journeyed with the MFDP delegates to the resort town. Delegates and their backers had two tasks: to lobby vigorously for the seating of their "freedom delegation" in place of the official "lily-whites" and to sustain an around-the-clock vigil on the boardwalk.

Fannie Lou Hamer stole the show by picturing graphically before television cameras her gripping tale of being beaten in jail, that "woesome time for us when we was arrested in Winona." All they had wanted to do, she said, was "to register, to become first-class citizens, and if the Freedom Democratic Party is not seated now, I question America. Is this America the land of the free and the home of the brave?"

With the President watching with a hawk's eye from Washington, his aides, instructed to gain any kind of compromise that would avert an uproar on TV, had planned to offer the MFDP no votes but the privilege of the floor, along with a new rule that would open Democratic parties in the South to blacks in the future. So electrifying was the testimony of Hamer and others, expertly stage-managed by the redoubtable civil rights lawyer Joseph Rauh, that this compromise collapsed in the face of the public response and Freedom Party militance.

The Johnson people now offered the MFDP a slightly better deal—two at-large votes as well as the promised nondiscrimination rule for the future. A formidable array of civil rights notables—King, Bayard Rustin, Wilkins, Humphrey, Rauh, and even Walter Reuther, who flew to Atlantic City at the behest of the White House—were willing to go along with this, but despite intense pressure an overwhelming majority of the MFDP delegates dug in their heels. Two token seats, handpicked by the whites? "We didn't come all this way for no two seats!" Hamer proclaimed. And what good was a nondiscrimination rule without a guarantee of black voting rights? So that deal too collapsed. MFDP delegates in protest occupied the empty seats of the lily-white delegation, which had walked out in their own protest against Johnson's brokerage.

In the evening the boardwalk vigil broke into song amid cries of "Freedom Now!" But it was not freedom now; this battle was lost. The little army that had tried to inject moral passion and commitment into pragmatic electoral politics returned to its southern battlefield, dejected, disillusioned, but by no means defeatist. Its troops had learned once again that to deal on equal terms with the "big boys" they had to wield power on their own. But power meant votes—and they were still seeking to put their hands on the ballots that were their passports to freedom and democracy.

*   *   *

When Lyndon Johnson trounced Barry Goldwater in November 1964, taking 43.1 million popular votes to Goldwater's 27.2 million and all but 52 of the 538 electoral votes, the reasons were manifold: the nation's post-assassination tribute to John Kennedy, LBJ's vigorous coalition building, rising prosperity, the Arizonan's inept handling of moderates in his own party, the President's reassurances about nuclear war. Black votes for LBJ in the "Solid South" were not a reason. Despite their hard struggles, most blacks could not vote for the President even if they wished to do so. Only 23 percent of Alabama's blacks were registered to vote in 1964, only 6.7 percent of Mississippi's. Against a certified Southerner, or at least Southwesterner, Goldwater carried the belt of southern states from South Carolina through Louisiana. The Democracy, even with a Texan heading the ticket, was still losing its old white bulwark in the Solid South without gaining a new electoral base there. But after the big November win complacent leadership of the Democratic party lost little sleep over the problem.

So once again it fell to the most physically vulnerable, the most politically impotent people in the United States to act in this moral crisis of American freedom. In January 1965, SCLC launched a crucial voting rights campaign in Selma, Alabama, a city with one of the most egregious registration barriers. Fresh from the pinnacle of world acclaim for winning the Nobel Peace Prize, King led a march toward the county courthouse in Selma, where after kneeling in prayer he and Abernathy and hundreds of others were jailed. Within a week over three thousand more had been arrested. In the nearby town of Marion, after state troopers set upon black people during a peaceful march, young Jimmie Lee Jackson was shot down as he tried to protect his mother and grandfather, both badly beaten. When Jackson died a few days later, SCLC's James Bevel and local black leaders resolved to march from Selma to the state capitol in Montgomery, though Governor Wallace had banned such action and King was in Atlanta.

On a Sunday early in March six hundred people strode out of Brown Chapel, crossed over the Alabama River, and ran straight into a solid phalanx of helmeted and gas-masked state troopers, who with little warning lunged at them with clubs and whips, cracking heads and lobbing tear-gas grenades. Troopers and the sheriff's posse pursued them back to the church, using whips and cattle prods, hurling one youth through a stained-glass window that depicted Jesus. When King, who was keeping in close touch with federal authorities, told the Selma marchers to "put on their walking shoes" and this time personally led them across the bridge to face the troopers—only to turn the long column around abruptly and lead them back into town, as if by prearrangement—SNCC leaders denounced him for the apparent deal. But King was still trying to draw the line between militance and violence.

By now protests sounded across the country, as pictures of mounted horsemen flailing and clubbing fleeing blacks in the initial fracas appeared on television screens and front pages, and SCLC flashed telegrams to hundreds of northern clergy urging them to join King in two days to pick up the march. President Johnson was aroused to the finest words and most important domestic action of his presidency. Calling for a strong voting bill with provisions for federal registrars and the banning of literacy tests, he told a joint session of Congress, his big frame hunched over the podium, that at times history and fate met in a single moment in a single place "to shape a turning point in man's unending search for freedom." So it had been at Lexington and Concord and at Appomattox, and so "it was last week in Selma." Congress applauded and began the long process of passing the measure.

The Selma activists would not wait or let up. A few hundred marchers once again set off for Montgomery, now guarded by ten times as many troops deployed by the President. For five days these "mudcaked pilgrims" trekked through the heat and drenching rain, through dense swamps, past half-collapsed shacks, rickety Baptist churches, a dilapidated black school at a place called Trickem. Along the way, or encamped at night, they sang.

We shall overcome,
We shall overcome,
We shall overcome some day.
Oh, deep in my heart

I do believe,
We shall walk in peace some day.

Or the more militant:

Onward, Christian soldiers, marching as to war,
With the cross of Jesus going on before!
Christ, the royal Master, leads against the foe;
Forward into battle see His banners go!

At the end, after the marchers surged into Montgomery while Wallace peered out from his office, Martin Luther King stood near the bronze star marking the site where Confederate President Jefferson Davis had been inaugurated.

"*How* long?" he asked. "*Not* long," he answered, repeating the litany again and again as more voices joined the stirring rhythm.

"*How* long?" he concluded. "*Not* long, because mine eyes have seen the glory of the coming of the Lord; tramping out the vintage where the grapes of wrath are stored . . .

"*His truth is marching on!*"

*   *   *

Euphoria could never last very long in the struggle for civil rights. One of King's rapt listeners that day was Viola Liuzzo, a white volunteer from Detroit who was helping to ferry the marchers back to Selma. She was shot to death by four Klansmen—one of them an FBI informer—as she was driving on a desolate highway in the swamps of Lowndes County. When LBJ was finally able to sign a strong voting rights bill early in August 1965, he could proudly declaim, "They came in darkness and they came in chains. And today we strike away the last major shackles of those fierce and ancient bonds." But shackles remained. And even as the President spoke, the civil rights movement was changing, dividing, turning more to the black ghettos in the North.

SNCC was beset by growing pains as well as battle fatigue. An influx of white organizers after "Freedom Summer" intensified black-white friction. Conflict mounted between the more group-oriented leaders, represented by Ella Baker and Bob Moses, who were trying to carry on the original SNCC spirit and lifestyle, and the "hard-liners," led by James Forman and Cleveland Sellers, who wanted a more disciplined, centralized, and politically effective organization. And a very different kind of leadership was arising outside of SNCC, in the cities of the North.

The black leaders in the South were waging their struggles for a constituency that was eroding. During the 1960s the South lost nearly one-eighth of its black population. In another of America's massive migrations, almost a million and a half blacks "left the South for the already over-crowded ghettos and marginal neighborhoods of the urban North" be-tween 1960 and 1970. By 1960 blacks numbered over half of Washington's population, over a quarter of the people of Philadelphia, Detroit, Cleve-land, and St. Louis, almost a quarter of Chicago and Houston. The ghetto populations of Brooklyn, Queens, and Manhattan were around 95 percent black. It cost "roughly a thousand dollars" in lost wages to be black, it was estimated; the economic cost to the nation of discrimination was over ten billion a year.

It took a child of the ghetto to translate these figures into human terms. In a stunning portrait of the Harlem he had known for forty years—the Harlem where his family had "moved from house to house, and from neighborhood to neighborhood, within the walls of the ghetto," in a des-perate effort to flee its creeping blight—Kenneth Clark etched the sociol-ogy and pathology of the black poor. *Dark Ghetto* was his "anguished cry" about the life and plight of these urban prisoners. Clark captured the physical ugliness of Harlem, the dead-end jobs, dilapidated housing, street kids killed by cars in their only playground, broken families, absent fathers, insensitive social workers, rampant venereal disease, drug addicts vomit-ing in the Tombs, the gang leaders and dope peddlers. He captured the bitter, angry talk of the streets too: "The flag here in America is for white men" who will "lynch you" and "fry you"—"The only thing you can do is to kill us"—"I'm not a man, none of us are men!"—"Why in the hell—now this is more or less a colored neighborhood—why do they have so many white cops?"—"So we're out on the sidewalk, right on the sidewalk; we might feel like dancing, or one might want to play something on his horn. Right away here comes a cop."

There was nothing new in all this; what was new was the sheer number and size of the ghettos by the 1960s, along with hardening intractability of the conditions. Bad nourishment, education, motivation, housing, poor speech habits, combined with few hopes, low expectations, no jobs—all these fortified one another and produced the prison that millions of blacks could not escape.

Also new was the rise of black leaders attuned to the pathology and politics of the city. One of these was Malcolm X. Son of a Baptist minister who had organized for Marcus Garvey's Universal Negro Improvement Association, Malcolm Little had worked as a shoeshine boy and in a dining car, then made his way as a hustler, drug dealer, and pimp. Jailed for robbery, he wrote to Elijah Muhammad, leader of the Nation of Islam, or

Black Muslims. On his release he converted to the sect and took the name Malcolm X.

A tall, thin, copper-colored man, charming and witty offstage but polemical in the podium or pulpit, he soon won followers with his blistering attacks on the Kennedys, on King, on integration and intermarriage, on the white people as devils. He broke with Muhammad in March 1964 and in a hurricane of activity set up his own Muslim group, founded the Organization of Afro-American Unity, and made two long journeys to the Middle East and Africa, during which he converted to orthodox Islam and communed with African revolutionary leaders.

He shaped a grand strategy—to ground the struggle of Afro-Americans firmly in the global majority of people of color, to gain moral and material help from Third World countries, to raise the "civil rights struggle" to the level of "human rights"—and as a beginning to put American racism on trial before the United Nations. Less and less was Malcolm a separatist as the years passed, or even a pure and simple black nationalist. Nor was he a Marxist, though he identified with African-style socialism. While he castigated civil rights leaders like King for their caution and compromise, he wanted to cooperate with the freedom movement. But he disdained the "masochism" of nonviolence and justified not only armed self-defense but "tit for tat" revenge against the Klan and other white terrorists. Ultimately he believed that freedom would come "either by ballots or by bullets," but he also called for freedom *"by any means necessary."*

While equally radical, Stokely Carmichael was of a different cut from Malcolm. He had made his way out of the New York ghetto to the select Bronx High School of Science and then to Howard University, from which he moved into the Mississippi freedom struggle. Concluding that blacks could not rely on white allies and must create their own power base independent of the Democratic party, Carmichael mobilized local citizens, notably ministers and older women, to form the Lowndes County Freedom Organization. Its symbol was a black panther, which when pressured "moves back until it is cornered," explained a local leader, "then it comes out fighting for life or death." In May 1966, Carmichael was elected chair of SNCC, while the former freedom rider Ruby Doris Smith Robinson replaced Forman as executive secretary, at a pivotal meeting that decided that white SNCC members should henceforth organize only white communities.

One month later, James Meredith was wounded by a shotgun blast while on a one-man "march against fear" from Memphis to Jackson. Black leaders gathered in Memphis to discuss taking up Meredith's fallen banner.

Carmichael, supported by armed members of the paramilitary Deacons for Defense, demanded that the march be confined to blacks, that the Deacons be authorized to provide armed protection for marchers, and that the trek be used to "highlight the need for independent, black political units." The NAACP's Roy Wilkins and Whitney Young of the Urban League angrily packed their bags and returned to New York. King, Carmichael, and Floyd McKissick, representing CORE, hammered out a compromise. But as the Meredith march wound slowly through the Delta bitter disagreements persisted.

Carmichael was arrested in Greenwood and greeted upon his release by a huge night rally. "This is the twenty-seventh time I have been arrested," he shouted, "and I ain't going to jail no more." The crowd cheered him on. "The only way we gonna stop them white men from whuppin' us is to take over. We been saying freedom for six years and we ain't got nothin'. What we gonna start saying now is *Black Power!*" Calls for "Black Power!" rose again and again from the crowd. The cry, which starkly encapsulated SNCC's new political vision, electrified black youth even as it ignited a storm of criticism from older leaders and liberal allies. On the march the nightly rallies turned into contests over which chant—"Black Power" or "Freedom Now"—could drown out the other.

King had met with Carmichael and other SNCC leaders to try to break the deepening impasse. King said he understood the new slogan's magnetic appeal to young blacks who, after he and others had lifted their expectations, now felt betrayed because their elders had not delivered. But the slogan would be self-defeating, he insisted; while the concept of black power was sound, the image it conjured up would alarm the media. Every other ethnic group had created its own power base, Carmichael replied—why not black people?

"That is just the point," King answered. "No one has ever heard the Jews publicly chant a slogan of Jewish power, but they have power." The same was true of the Irish and Italians. "Neither group has used a slogan of Irish or Italian power, but they have worked hard to achieve it. This is exactly what we must do." They must build racial pride and through a program, not merely a slogan, "refute the notion that black is evil and ugly."

"Martin, I deliberately decided to raise this issue on the march in order to give it a national forum," Carmichael admitted, "and force you to take a stand for Black Power."

King laughed, "I have been used before. One more time won't hurt."

Neither side swayed the other, but out of respect for their veteran leader, the SNCC and CORE chiefs agreed to defer using either slogan until the expedition was over. Later King disavowed the "Black Power" slogan, but he never repudiated Carmichael or SNCC; he still hoped for a united black movement.

This was not to be. Pressures were building up, now in the North, that would drive black leadership further apart. The assassination of Malcolm X in February 1965 led to fears of a "holy war" between his followers and those loyal to Elijah Muhammad. SNCC was already shifting its center of gravity to the North. Brilliantly focusing the pent-up anger of urban blacks, Carmichael became the leading popularizer of Black Power and an international media star. The ambiguity, complexity, and poetry of Black Power gave it mystique: its democratic aspirations for black self-determination; its critique of integration as a one-way street; its irresistible insistence, in the spirit of Malcolm X, on racial pride and the beauty of blackness; and for some, inspired by Algerian psychiatrist and revolutionary Frantz Fanon, the glorification of violence as a psychic need and an end in itself.

King was moving left too, but not this fast. He remained the apostle of nonviolence, but he was edging closer to SNCC's belief in long-term community organizing, toward grass-roots, class-based interracial alliances of the poor. Always a philosopher of social change, he was thinking more of a "reconstruction of the entire society, a revolution of values." The old-line black organizations were moving too, but more slowly. At its 1966 convention the NAACP sharply questioned "Black Power" as a slogan just after the CORE convention had endorsed it. Blacks were losing one of their mightiest weapons—unity.

It was the old story of younger, more radical leaders pushing to the fore on the billows of revolution as the tidal wave of change surged toward distant shores. But this tidal wave was about to be transformed by forces boiling up from the back yards and front stoops of city blacks—and from age-old but resharpened conflicts at the opposite ends of the globe.

CHAPTER 9

The World Turned Upside Down

I n the "100 days of 1965," stretching from June to late October of that
year, Congress passed and the President signed the Medicare bill, long
heatedly fought by the American Medical Association; the epochal Voting
Rights bill; Omnibus Housing, which mandated stepped-up rent supplements to low-income families; a measure to create a new Department of
Housing and Urban Development; another measure to establish the National Foundation for the Arts and the Humanities; a major broadening of
the immigration laws; the Water Quality bill, requiring states to set and
enforce water quality standards for all interstate waters within their borders; and the Clean Air Act of 1965, which supplemented and strengthened the Clean Air Act of 1963, targeting now automobile exhaust, following three years of controversy touched off by Rachel Carson's *Silent Spring*.
Earlier in the year the first large-scale program of aid to elementary and
secondary schools had been enacted, and fueled with a grant of $1.3
billion.

In the midst of this flood of legislation stood Lyndon Johnson, still using
the techniques of personal persuasion he had honed in the Senate, techniques now backed up by a formidable array of White House resources.
With a shrewd eye for the strengths and vulnerabilities, appetites and
sensitivities of his targets, the President spent hundreds of hours on the
telephone or face to face, bullying and pleading, bidding and dealing,
placating and mediating, all in the currency, now hard and now soft, of
presidential-congressional exchange. If the Kennedys had gloried in using
the arts of "blarney, bludgeon, and boodle," LBJ inflated all these, Texas
style.

It was by no means a one-man show. Working closely with the White
House in the Senate were Hubert Humphrey, still ebullient even as Vice
President, and Mike Mansfield, the dour Majority Leader. In the House,
where John McCormack was Speaker and the well-liked Carl Albert of
Oklahoma was Majority Leader, a band of liberal Democrats, headed by
the astute and resolute Missourian Richard Bolling, helped marshal the

huge Democratic majority that Johnson had helped bring into the lower chamber in the 1964 election.

These were the creative months of the Great Society that Johnson sought to build. The currents of history converged in a fashion that the labor-liberal-left forces in America had rarely known: the program that John F. Kennedy had advanced with his glowing rhetoric; the homage the nation wished to pay to the martyred young President; Barry Goldwater's conservative campaign, which catalyzed and united a new Democratic party coalition; the Congress and its committees liberalized; and a new President determined to show that a Texan and a Southerner could fight for a progressive program, that a politician stigmatized for his wheeling and dealing on Capitol Hill could become a great President in the tradition of FDR.

These should have been the memorable, the glory times of the Great Society, when programs were introduced that would transform the lives of countless Americans for decades to come—but glory times they were not. For the attention of Americans was increasingly distracted by events nine thousand miles away, and LBJ seemed as crippled in dealing with this growing crisis as he had been creative in leading his domestic program through Congress.

For Johnson was now swaying under the full burden of the divided legacy of Kennedy's foreign policy—the pacific legacy of the Peace Corps, the resolution of the missile crisis, the test ban treaty, the hard legacy of confrontation in Europe and escalation in Vietnam. The Peace Corps, established by Kennedy within six weeks of his inauguration, had become a special link with his successor. It was a reminder to LBJ of the hopes and ideals of his days in the National Youth Administration; he liked its chief, Sargent Shriver, whom he made head of his Job Corps; and the work of the volunteers—helping people grow better crops and dig better wells and build better habitations—was the kind of thing that appealed to the new President's belief in benign progress, in gritty, hands-on social change without trauma. Attacked on the right as "global do-goodism" and on the left for being merely a disguised form of American cultural imperialism and indeed as an opiate to calm the potentially revolutionary masses, the Peace Corps, with its thousands of volunteers in developing countries around the world, was nevertheless an exquisitely appropriate living memorial to John Kennedy.

But Kennedy had left another living heritage—thousands of American troops in Vietnam. The onetime "military advisers" had escalated to a force of some 16,000 personnel by the time of JFK's death. They were now conducting "combat support" missions and they were now dying in action—77 had in 1963. Lyndon Johnson inherited Kennedy's war—and the divisions within the Administration over its conduct. He would continue the creeping escalation.

PEOPLE OF THIS GENERATION

At the start the peace movement appeared innocuous, even quixotic. It was indeed hard to find a start. Ever since Hiroshima, of course, antiwar activists had been protesting the bomb. Radical pacifists, many of them Quakers, had agitated especially against civil defense drills, but the scourge of McCarthyism had thinned their ranks. Scientists, including some who had worked on the bomb, became so alarmed about the dangers of radioactive fallout that they sought to educate their colleagues and the public; some even hoped to "bridge the gap between East and West" and unite the world scientific community as a step toward peace. Made credible by such technical expertise, the issue of atmospheric testing galvanized a movement to stop nuclear tests, just when the orbiting of Sputnik heightened America's fear of Soviet technological progress.

At the cutting edge of the peace movement in the mid-fifties was the Committee for Nonviolent Action, which sponsored a number of daring and imaginative projects. In 1958, Earle and Barbara Reynolds and their family, piloting the good ship *Phoenix* built in Hiroshima, penetrated the vast Pacific area that the Atomic Energy Commission had blocked off for H-bomb tests that summer. Arrested and detained at the navy base on Kwajalein atoll, Barbara Reynolds and her son witnessed in the night a dirty orange light, like a "gigantic flash bulb," illuminating the dark clouds.

Later that year, after CNVA protested the construction of a missile base near Cheyenne, Wyoming, five men and women were imprisoned for blocking trucks. The next year, when the militants launched Omaha Action, a campaign of community education and civil disobedience to halt the building of missile silos, one of those arrested for climbing over a fence was A. J. Muste, the seventy-four-year-old ringleader and chair of CNVA, longtime radical pacifist, labor leader, strike organizer, incorrigible civil disobedient. After CNVA settled in New London, Connecticut, where missile-firing Polaris submarines were built, peace guerrillas paddled out to board the subs or block their launching. They were repulsed.

Tired of being yelled at to "tell it to the Russians," a group of Americans and Europeans walked through the Iron Curtain into East Germany and Poland, made their way to Moscow's Red Square, held a vigil, and passed out leaflets urging disarmament. "I went to jail because I refused to serve in the U.S. Army," Bradford Lyttle told a crowd in Minsk. "I have protested against American rockets aimed at your cities and families. There are Soviet rockets aimed at my city and my family. Are you demonstrating against that?"

CNVA carried on two more years of peace walks, test site invasions, campus rallies, marches. Women Strike for Peace organized a simultaneous protest by 50,000 women in a few dozen cities. To complement the direct action of CNVA with more conventional political activity, peace activists and "nuclear pacifists"—among them Nobel Prize-winning chemist Linus Pauling and noted journalist Norman Cousins—had in 1957 formed the National Committee for a Sane Nuclear Policy. SANE quickly grew into a major national organization and, like CNVA, broadened its goal to general disarmament. But it underwent a purge of alleged communist members and many radical pacifists resigned in protest.

Then, when Washington and Moscow in August 1963 agreed on a limited test ban treaty, some activists for a time assumed that the government was serious about negotiating a halt to the arms race, that a thaw in the cold war might even be at hand. After all the bold and quixotic actions— was it in part because of them?—a little chunk of peace had been won but the peace movement seemed defused. New allies were soon to arrive, however, from ranks of young Americans who saw themselves as among the most powerless people in America.

*   *   *

Sixty members of a little-known student group, Students for a Democratic Society, convened in June 1962 at the United Auto Workers' FDR Camp on the southern shore of Lake Huron, forty miles north of Detroit. This was not the usual student beer bust—these men and women were deadly serious. Under a different name SDS had served for decades as the student wing of the democratic-socialist League for Industrial Democracy, but since 1960 it had been asserting more independence, symbolized by its change of name. SDS field secretary Tom Hayden, a journalism student at the University of Michigan and editor of the campus paper, had worked with SNCC on voter registration in Georgia and had suffered the usual beatings and jailings. Hayden and SDS president Al Haber hoped that radical students could link up with the black student activists. But much as they admired SNCC's spirit and political style, their aims were broader.

The conferees broke off into small study groups to revise the rough draft of a manifesto mainly written by Hayden, who had been analyzing the ideas of myriad thinkers. The students then focused on what they called the "bones," essential matters worth an hour's debate, as against "widgets," of medium importance, and "gizmos," worth only ten minutes. The pieces were then sewn back together into a patchwork quilt that emerged as a stinging moral critique of American society and a compelling vision of a regenerated democracy.

"We are people of this generation," the Port Huron Statement began, "bred in at least modest comfort, housed now in universities, looking uncomfortably to the world we inherit." They did not spare their teachers—"their curriculums change more slowly than the living events of the world; their skills and silence are purchased by investors in the arms race; passion is called unscholastic." Indeed, they spared virtually nothing and no one—the brokers of politics, militarism, the economic system, the universities, passive students.

The manifesto proclaimed in fresh and forceful prose a radicalism that exalted aspirations for personal empowerment, wholeness, and authenticity; transformed what might seem personal needs and troubles into legitimate political concerns; and brought to light the hidden linkages in the web of issues that plagued the nation and the world. From the heart of the message issued its call for a new kind of democracy:

"We would replace power rooted in possession, privilege, or circumstance by power and uniqueness rooted in love, reflectiveness, reason, and creativity. As a *social system* we seek the establishment of a democracy of individual participation, governed by two central aims: that the individual share in those social decisions determining the quality and direction of his life, that society be organized to encourage independence in men and provide the media for their common participation." Politics should bring people out of isolation into community. All major institutions—political, economic, cultural, educational—had to be fully democratized. Thus the students, historian Wini Breines noted, "sought to create both a community within the movement and structural transformation in the larger society." They were eager to serve as transforming leaders who would rise above the shabby brokerage of institutional life. But even the most ardent, as they left Port Huron after five days of nonstop debate, could hardly know that they had helped set the stage for the surge of grass-roots democratic activity and New Left militance in the 1960s.

It was not by historical accident that the SDS appeared at this time. Its members and the New Left in general were catalyzed by the southern freedom movement and in particular by SNCC, some of whose values and organizing style SDS imitated and refined, as well as by the ban-the-bomb movement and efforts to restore civil liberties in the wake of McCarthyism. At a deeper level, the New Left was a direct response to the cool conformist culture of the 1950s with its ethic of acquisitiveness, its model of the unquestioning "organization man," its "Catch-22" insanities that seemed to apply more to the cold war than to World War II. Caught in the yawning chasms between American ideals of self-fulfillment and the felt experience of bureaucratic manipulation and personal emptiness, between the possibilities for freedom and creativity offered by technology and the harsh realities of spiritual poverty, middle-class youth was "growing up absurd," the title of Paul Goodman's book. Our abundant society, Goodman wrote, "has no Honor. It has no Community."

Unable to make sense of their world, angered by what they saw as almost universal hypocrisy, many young people acted out their semi-conscious critique of the "system" through deviant behavior of one kind or another: as rebels without causes, as followers of the Beat subculture of nonconformity, as spiritual dropouts. Beat figures like Allen Ginsberg and Jack Kerouac were role models for many of the rebels, and the existentialisms of Sartre and Camus their chosen philosophy.

If the passionate and sardonic Goodman was the chief interpreter of youthful cultural alienation, the equally committed and iconoclastic C. Wright Mills, a Texas-bred Columbia University sociologist, was centrally involved in translating it into overt political expression and commitment. Criticized for imputing too much power to the interlocking "power elite" of corporate, military, and political leaders, and for other nonconforming social science, Mills feared that in both superpowers "we now witness the rise of the cheerful robot, the technological idiot, the crackpot realist," all of them embodying the common ethos of "rationality without reason." His solution was less programmatic than a matter of transforming consciousness: to make reason into an instrument for restless and rebellious social criticism, for penetrating society's invisible controlling assumptions and interlocking power systems; to convince intellectuals, especially the young intelligentsia, of their moral responsibility to tackle the real problems of the era; and to lead the academy, and then all of society, out of conformity and apathy and into informed engagement. His words and spirit had shone through every page of the Port Huron Statement, adopted three months after his death from a heart attack at forty-five.

* * *

High noon, Berkeley, October 1, 1964. Two deans and the campus police chief advanced on a young man sitting at a table in Sproul Hall Plaza at the University of California's 27,000-student campus across the bay from San Francisco. The table displayed literature on the Congress of Racial Equality and a collection jar, violating a campus ban on advocacy and fund-raising. When CORE organizer Jack Weinberg refused to take down the table the security people put him under arrest, but a large crowd gathered around him shouting, "Take all of us!" A police car arrived, the cops hustled Weinberg into it, only to find a sea of students surging around them and then sitting down. Mario Savio, a philosophy major just in from the Mississippi Freedom Summer, jumped on top of the police car—a perfect soapbox—and after politely removing his shoes demanded Weinberg's release and an end to the ban on free speech.

For thirty-two hours the students held the police car hostage—with Weinberg still in it—while student reinforcements lined up to revel in the delights of free speech. Bettina Aptheker, who as a teenager had marched against the bomb and Jim Crow and had picketed her local Woolworth's in Brooklyn in support of the southern sit-ins, "got inspired," as she said later. After fending off nervousness she climbed up to face the television lights and cameras that pierced the darkness. "There was this tremendous glare of light" and "roar from the crowd" that seemed to come out of nowhere. She remembered one of her favorite quotations from black leader Frederick Douglass and yelled at the crowd, "Power concedes nothing without a demand." The next evening Savio announced an armistice with university administrators. The students freed the police car and later paid for its badly dented roof. A brief calm settled over the campus.

Unexpected though it was, the police-car sit-in was a spark struck off from long-growing friction between students and authorities, and a spark that ignited afresh the fires of campus rebellion. A "free speech" movement had been kindling at least since May 1960, when Berkeley students had tried to attend hearings of the House Un-American Activities Committee in San Francisco; repeatedly refused admission, they staged a sit-in, only to be washed out of the rotunda and down the steps of city hall by fire hoses. Dozens were arrested. Savio and others involved in the police-car sit-in had been suspended by the university after earlier protests. Then, when the university abruptly extended its ban on political activity to a small strip of pavement that had been a haven for political talk and recruiting, activists lashed back that October noon. They were being treated like southern blacks, they protested—their own civil rights were being violated. The university authorities were thrown off guard by the readiness and vehemence of their young adversaries.

In the heady days after the armistice an unusually broad coalition of student groups, ranging from Goldwaterites and Young Republicans to socialists and Maoists, formed the Free Speech Movement. Because of lingering McCarthyism and relentless red-baiting, "we had to convince people that we were small 'd' democrats in addition to whatever else we were," Savio said later. "We were hung up about democracy." They sought to make FSM a model of participatory democracy. Students chose representatives to a large executive committee, which in turn elected delegates to a small steering committee that carried out the larger body's policies and tactics from day to day. The steering committee tried to act by the Quaker method of consensus and the FSM ethic of openness. Aptheker, Savio, and others spent many long nights churning out leaflets with detailed accounts of the day's happenings; these were printed by dawn and handed out, 20,000 daily, by 8 A.M. The FSM, however, lacked a key dimension of democracy—there were few women in leadership positions.

The university itself served as one of FSM's best organizers. When the movement seemed to be losing steam, Berkeley's chancellor rejuvenated it by bringing new charges against Savio and another leader. Aroused once again, a thousand students took over Sproul Hall, administration headquarters. After a night electrified by Joan Baez's singing "We Shall Overcome," and nourished by peanut butter sandwiches, Charlie Chaplin films, and "Free University" classes, the students were beset by hundreds of police who rooted them out floor by floor. Eight hundred were arrested, the biggest campus civil disobedience in the country's history.

In response, graduate students organized a strike so widely supported that it shut down the university. Scores of professors emerged from their studies to back the movement. In a remarkable faculty decision the Academic Senate voted overwhelmingly to back the FSM demands. After the vote, Aptheker recalled, "we students parted ranks, forming an aisle through which the faculty seemed to formally march in a new kind of academic procession." It was only then, ten weeks after the police-car sit-in, that the regents rescinded the ban on campus free speech.

The Berkeley rebellion, scrupulously nonviolent, the first major white student movement since the 1930s and the first to employ mass direct action on campus, involved much more than traditional political freedoms. Many students felt alienated by the intellectual assembly line of a huge, impersonal "multiversity" harnessed to the needs of large corporations and the Pentagon. Berkeley political theorists Sheldon Wolin and John Schaar observed that the students were "ill-housed, and ill-clad, and ill-nourished not in the material sense, but in the intellectual and spiritual senses." Students contended that they were being bent, folded, spindled, and mutilated by faceless bureaucrats; they were fighting to gain more control over their lives. They saw the university's intellectual repression as of a piece with its contribution to basic social ills, from automation to the nuclear arms race, and they hoped that by forcing the institution to live up to its original scholarly ideals, they could take a big step toward reshaping the entire society.

Clark Kerr, president of the University of California, did not feel like a faceless bureaucrat, pawn of the power elite, or a master of power. He felt more like a punching bag. "The university president in the United States," he wrote in 1963, "is expected to be a friend of the students, a colleague of the faculty, a good fellow with the alumni, a sound administrator with the trustees, a good speaker with the public, an astute bargainer with the foundations and the federal agencies, a politician with the state legislature, a friend of industry, labor, and agriculture, a persuasive diplomat with donors, a champion of education generally, a supporter of the professions (particularly law and medicine), a spokesman to the press, a scholar in his own right, a public servant at the state and national levels, a devotee of opera and football equally, a decent human being, a good husband and father, an active member of a church." Kerr played most of these roles with skill and versatility.

Yet there was something gravely lacking in all this, and the students sensed it. In trying to deal with what historian Frederick Rudolph called the "delicate balance of interests," in searching ever for consensus, in settling for day-to-day "practical steps" of management and persuasion, Kerr and a host of other university heads evaded the crucial tasks of clarifying educational goals, setting priorities, being controversial, leading rather than mediating and bargaining. Students saw themselves as the least of a president's concerns. They were now making the multiversity a political battleground.

*　　*　　*

While a few of the FSM leaders like Savio had been tutored in civil rights protest in Mississippi, most of the campus dissidents were so immersed in their own battles against the multiversity that for a time they paid little attention to struggles hundreds of miles away in the South or nine thousand miles away in Southeast Asia. The Port Huron Statement had referred to the "Southern struggle against racial bigotry" and Vietnam, American imperialism, and the bomb only as items in a much wider set of problems. Southern black leaders were also so preoccupied with endless crisis and confrontation that they had little time either for the "rich rebels" in northern universities or for peasants far across the Pacific. As the civil rights struggle moved North during the 1960s, widening the arc of black concerns, and as the war in Vietnam escalated, blacks and students were drawn together in the vortex of a new conflict. But the civil rights battle in the North still remained to be fought out.

In mid-August 1965, just a few days after LBJ signed the Voting Rights Act, the Watts section of Los Angeles burst into violence. It seemed a curious location for a "race riot"—not a place of dark and towering tenements, but a ghetto, in the Los Angeles style, of bungalows and ranch houses, intermixed with trash-filled alleys, boarded-up stores, bars and pool halls, drunks and drug peddlers. It was 98 percent black. Starting with a routine arrest of a black youth suspected of drunken driving, the violence whirled out through the streets on the wings of rumor. Day after day, in torrid heat, blacks looted and torched stores, pelted cops and passing cars, randomly attacked whites, hurled Molotov cocktails, ambushed firemen and policemen.

Once again neighborhood people—in this case street people—were taking the lead, but this was a leadership of nihilism. In their fury blacks set scores of major fires, tried to burn a local community hospital, and torched the shops of other blacks despite signs on storefronts pleading ownership by a "Black Brother" or "Soul Brother." The rioters were "burning their city now, as the insane sometimes mutilate themselves," wrote a reporter for the Los Angeles *Times,* himself black.

Martin Luther King flew to Los Angeles and walked the debris-strewn streets of Watts among smoldering ruins of shops and houses, imploring the locals to turn away from violence, which had brought ten thousand National Guard troops into the area. King provoked argument, skepticism, even heckling. Some youngsters told him, "We won."

"How can you say you won," King demanded, "when thirty-four Negroes are dead, your community is destroyed, and whites are using the riots as an excuse for inaction?"

"We won," a jobless young man responded, "because we made the whole world pay attention to us."

Increasingly blacks were turning to the ideas King had fought—to separation from whites rather than integration, to street riots rather than nonviolence, to the religion of the Nation of Islam rather than Christianity. Elijah Muhammad, suspected by some of having instigated the murder of Malcolm X, continued to lead the Nation, with its Muslim schools, businesses, and publications, including *Muhammad Speaks,* the Muslim weekly newspaper. In 1962 the paper had printed Muhammad's "Muslim Program," in which he had trumpeted that since blacks could not get along with whites "in peace and equality, after giving them 400 years of our sweat and blood and receiving in return some of the worst treatment human beings have ever experienced, we believe our contributions to this land and the suffering forced upon us by white America, justifies our demand for complete separation in a state or territory of our own." He demanded separate schools and a ban on "intermarriage or race mixing."

Such an ideology called for political separatism as well. This was the strategy of Black Power. Born in the anger of the Meredith march through

Mississippi, this potent idea was carried North by Stokely Carmichael and other militants and debated at a National Conference on Black Power attended by a thousand delegates in Newark in midsummer 1967. In the spirit of Malcolm X's black nationalist program, the aim now was to organize a separate black "third force," which was either to gain control of one or both major parties or to strike out on its own. The most extreme expression of political separatism was the Black Panther party, founded by Huey P. Newton and Bobby George Seale a year and a half after Malcolm's death. His party, Panther chairman Seale said, "realizes that the white power structure's real power is its military force." So blacks had to organize themselves "and put a shotgun in every black man's home."

The force of black desperation and anger was now both vitalizing and fragmenting the black leadership. The once liberal-left NAACP now stood on the right of an array of black groups. King's SCLC was shifting a bit to the left, and SNCC even more so, as it dropped much of its white membership. Also on the left stood CORE, but it still sought to work through the machinery of the two big parties. On the far left, separated from the rest by their cult of violence, stood the Panthers. "The thrust of Black Power into national politics sounded the death knell of civil-rights alliances," according to historian Thomas L. Blair. "It brought the black masses into what Frederick Douglass called the 'awful roar of struggle.' It revealed basic differences over ideology, methods, tactics, and strategy" among black groups as well as conflicts over power and status within the Democratic-liberal-labor-left civil rights coalition.

Yet at the heart of the new black politics was a powerful political consciousness rooted in an old and expanding black culture. More blacks were turning, for reasons ideological and spiritual, to their origins in Africa, to their way stations in the Caribbean. They looked up to their own heroes and celebrities, to their own artists, writers, musicians, dancers, their own actors on and off Broadway and in the ghetto, their own black history and myths. They read such journals as *Black Theatre, Black Scholar, Black Poetry, Black Enterprise. Negro Digest* changed its name to *Black World,* as blacks drove the very word "Negro," and all it connoted, out of their vocabulary and their conscious lives. There was black dress, food, slang, jazz, hairstyles, and black jive and rapping, and above all black soul, which encompassed all of these things and more. Black religion embraced Christianity, Islam, and varieties thereof, including fundamentalism, evangelicalism, Catholicism, belief in the Kawaida value system or in a Christian black nationalism that proclaimed Jesus as the Black Messiah. Many of these beliefs were in flux; black Roman Catholics, for example, tripled in number over the three postwar decades.

*   *   *

Thus Black Power had its own rich culture, history, literature, religion, style, values. But it lacked a coherent political strategy, and the issue of strategy more and more arrayed black against black. Even while he led the Meredith march through the Mississippi heat, King could hear young blacks behind him bitterly criticizing nonviolence. "If one of these damn white Mississippi crackers touches me," he heard a young voice say, "I'm gonna knock the hell out of him." They should sing, someone said, "We Shall Overrun," not "Overcome."

The issue of strategy came to a head in a new and bitter battlefield: Chicago. After his successes in the South, King decided to make the "City of the Big Shoulders" his first major northern target, not only to force Mayor Richard Daley to end racism in hiring and housing but to prove that nonviolence could work in northern ghettos. To show his commitment he settled in a shabby, urine-stenched tenement in one of Chicago's worst slums. During the long planning and mobilizing process Black Power militants booed King on the streets. Though hurt and angry, he reflected that he and the other leaders had preached freedom and promised freedom but had been "unable to deliver on our promises." Few could question King's militance in Chicago. After affixing a set of demands to the metal door of City Hall, in Martin Luther style except for the adhesive tape, King readied his forces for nonviolent sit-ins, camp-ins, boycotts.

It was too late. The street people moved first. In the 100-degree heat youths turned on water hydrants and reveled in the cold jets, but when they were accosted by the police, violence erupted, turning that night and the next day into open war between hundreds of police and thousands of blacks. In vain King and his associates toured the war-swept area preaching nonviolence. By the time several thousand National Guardsmen started patrolling the area, two persons had been killed, 56 injured, almost 300 jailed. King grimly proceeded with his demonstrations. Day after day blacks marched through white areas of Chicago. They were met with epithets, Confederate flags, rocks, bottles, bricks.

"I've never seen anything like it," King said. In all the demonstrations down South he had "never seen—even in Mississippi and Alabama—mobs as hostile and as hate-filled as I've seen in Chicago." Somewhat intimidated, and under heavy pressure from Chicago's Catholic hierarchy, Daley met with King and other black leaders to patch together an agreement on housing, mainly consisting of promises. Some blacks praised King for forcing the mayor to the bargaining table. Others called it a sellout.

So the black leaders continued to divide and argue over political ways and means. In all the diversity of attitudes and style, however, there could be discerned a remarkable agreement over the highest values and ultimate ends. Just as blacks from left to right apotheosized liberty and equality, so did both black nationalists and Muslims. Elijah Muhammad's 1962 manifesto proclaimed at the very start, "We want freedom," as did the Black Panther party program six years later. Blacks invariably backed egalitarian ideas as well. Inevitably interpretations of such values differed. Thus the Muslims declared they wanted "full and complete freedom" and spelled this out, while the Panthers defined their freedom as "power to determine the destiny of our black community." Whether this kind of agreement on overarching values, camouflaging disagreement over specific policies and tactics, could serve as a basis of political unity remained as dubious in the black community as it always had in the white.

A storm was rising in the mid-sixties, however, that would bring blacks into stronger harmony. As LBJ's escalation in Indochina proceeded apace, blacks were drawn more and more into the Vietnam resistance, out of motives ranging from compassion for people of color in Indochina to distaste for "whitey's war" fought so disproportionately by black men. As King became increasingly outspoken against the war, the White House distanced itself from him and the black movement. This hurt, because time and again King still needed Administration help. But he could not resist this higher call. "We must combine the *fervor* of the civil rights movement with the peace movement," he said in February 1967, in his first talk entirely devoted to Vietnam. "We must demonstrate, teach and preach, until *the very foundations of our nation are shaken.*"

ROLLING THUNDER

He had known from the start, Lyndon Johnson told Doris Kearns the year after he left the White House, that he would be crucified either way he moved.

"If I left the woman I really loved—the Great Society—in order to get involved with that bitch of a war on the other side of the world, then I would lose everything at home. All my programs. All my hopes to feed the hungry and shelter the homeless. All my dreams to provide education and medical care to the browns and the blacks and the lame and the poor. But if I left that war and let the Communists take over South Vietnam, then I would be seen as a coward and my nation would be seen as an appeaser and we would both find it impossible to accomplish anything for anybody anywhere on the entire globe."

LBJ elaborated. "Oh, I could see it coming all right. History provided too many cases where the sound of the bugle put an immediate end to the hopes and dreams of the best reformers." The Spanish-American War had drowned the populist spirit—World War I, Wilson's New Freedom—World War II, the New Deal. It could happen again. The conservatives always loved a war. "Oh, they'd use it to say they were against my programs, not because they were against the poor—why, they were as generous and charitable as the best of Americans—but because the war had to come first. First, we had to beat those Godless Communists and then we could worry about the homeless Americans. And the generals. Oh, they'd love the war, too." That was why he had been so suspicious of the military.

"Yet everything I knew about history told me that if I got out of Vietnam and let Ho Chi Minh run through the streets of Saigon, then I'd be doing exactly what Chamberlain did in World War II. I'd be giving a big fat reward for aggression. And I knew that if we let Communist aggression succeed in taking over South Vietnam, there would follow in this country an endless national debate—a mean and destructive debate—that would shatter my Presidency, kill my administration, and damage our democracy." Truman and Acheson had lost their effectiveness when the communists took over in China. The "loss" of China helped cause the rise of McCarthy. But compared to what might have happened in Vietnam, all that was "chickenshit."

The former President had lost none of his bombast, sarcasm, Texas high coloring, his capacity to oversimplify history. But wholly authentic in this discourse was the self-portrait of a leader who had been deeply divided about his choices as he had perceived them. As usual, he had dealt with his options by personalizing them. He remembered just what he had felt and whom he had feared in those years: Bobby Kennedy would be out front telling everyone that Lyndon Johnson had betrayed John Kennedy's commitment to South Vietnam. LBJ would be called a coward, an unmanly man, a man without a spine. He had nightmares, he said, about people running toward him shouting "Coward! Traitor! Weakling!" But he feared World War III even more.

Always the image of Roosevelt loomed before him as exemplar and guide—FDR, who had led the nation so skillfully against Hitlerism despite the doubters and the defeatists. World War II had shown that the defense of little nations like Czechoslovakia was necessary to the security of big nations; that the democracies must unite in the face of aggression; that nations must live up to their promises and commitments. LBJ knew of Hans Morgenthau's warning against treating Vietnam in European terms—but had not Roosevelt's and Truman's way of standing up to aggression worked against Japan? Against North Korea?

So Johnson had reasoned. It seemed historically fitting, in retrospect, that he had dealt with his first Vietnam "crisis" much as Roosevelt had exploited Nazi "aggression" in the North Atlantic. Just as FDR had converted provocative acts on both sides into a simple act of Nazi hostility, just as he had grossly oversimplified murky actions in the misty waters south of Greenland, so Johnson seized on equally minor, two-sided, and confused encounters between an American destroyer and North Vietnamese patrol boats in the Gulf of Tonkin in August 1964 to step up the war. After ordering reprisal air strikes against North Vietnam, LBJ asked congressional approval for a resolution—drafted in the White House several months before the Tonkin Gulf incident—that would empower the President as Commander-in-Chief to take all necessary measures to repel any armed attack against forces of the United States. After brief hearings at which the Administration failed to provide Congress with vital information about the Gulf of Tonkin encounters, disingenuously suggesting that the attack on the destroyer had been unprovoked, the House gave Johnson his mandate by a vote of 414–0, the Senate by 88–2. Only the outspoken former Republican Wayne Morse of Oregon and Democrat Ernest Gruening of Alaska voted against the White House.

The escalation continued. National Liberation Front forces attacked a U.S. base at Pleiku in February 1965, killing eight Americans. Johnson ordered air strikes and sent in the first official American troops—no longer "advisers." The sequence became tedious: land battles, more troops mobilized on both sides, lulls in the struggle marked by calls for negotiation, more battles.

Later, when Johnson talked to Kearns and others about his nightmares, about awaking and prowling the White House and visiting the situation room to scrutinize the latest battle reports, some said that the President had become unhinged. But if this was the case, the whole White House had been a little mad, for the President had acted not alone but on the advice of such presumably sober and experienced advisers as Secretary of State Dean Rusk, Defense Secretary Robert McNamara, McGeorge Bundy, Walt Rostow, and many others who were largely holdovers from the JFK White House. Some said that LBJ had become a fanatical anticommunist in the face of Hanoi's resistance. But the President was no fanatic. He often spoke loudly while wielding a relatively small stick, limiting attacks in both intensity and duration, holding back the military all-outers, spending hours selecting bombing targets that would not provoke Chinese or Soviet retaliation. He constantly pleaded that he was seeking not to crush communism in Russia or China or North Vietnam—merely to preserve South Vietnam as a bastion of present, or future, freedom. Indeed he staked his most eager hopes on his numerous economic aid and social reform programs in Vietnam—a kind of Indochinese Great Society. He would bring to the Vietnamese democracy American style, honest elections, Bill of Rights liberties. Like his predecessor, he failed to see that the Vietnamese wanted freedom as *they* defined it—and the first freedom was liberation from imperial or neocolonial control.

His motivation was far less psychological or ideological than political and conceptual. The Gulf of Tonkin brush occurred hardly two weeks after the nomination of Barry Goldwater, and the Republicans were already making clear that they would campaign against the party that had lost Poland and China and was now about to lose Indochina. Even after his November triumph, Johnson feared that other rivals lay in wait for him, not only in the GOP but in both the hawk and dove wings of the Democratic party. Yet the conceptual factor was perhaps more influential, certainly more insidious. Every small escalation seemed so sensible, so practical, so moderate. Each little step was based on careful analysis, ample intelligence, elaborate quantification. Like good pragmatists, like eminently reasonable men, the leaders experimented with a variety of strategies and tactics. When none worked—and none ever did—they tried something else.

Moreover, they were not wholly distracted by Southeast Asia—not at first anyway. They were guarding Atlantic ramparts against communism as well. Early in 1963, Kennedy had dispatched Vice President Johnson to the Dominican Republic for the inauguration of Juan Bosch, a litterateur and leftist, noncommunist politician, as President. Photographs depicted LBJ and Bosch in a warm Latin *abrazo.* After the generals overthrew Bosch six months later, civilian and army supporters of the deposed President struck back in April 1965. Johnson promptly dispatched the Marines, ostensibly to save lives but mainly because of some scattered indications that communists were among the pro-Bosch forces. Within three weeks 22,000 American troops were patrolling the small nation—the first major overt military intervention in a Latin nation in forty years. The Administration never produced convincing evidence of significant communist involvement, but once again Washington was captive to the phantom threat of unified global communism. God forbid that there be another Cuba in the Caribbean!

*   *   *

The Americans used the latest, most sophisticated intelligence technology in Indochina, but their analysis of political information was faulty. Otherwise they might have grasped that the communists too lacked global unity; that the communist world too was torn by geopolitical differences, national rivalries, factional quarrels, leadership rivalries; that Hanoi faced many of the same types of problems with friends and foes that Washington did—faithless allies, coalition weaknesses, great powers ultimately devoted to their own national interests and perhaps willing in a pinch to "lose" Vietnam or some other small communist ally.

As usual, big powers had plenty of advice for small allies. Mao Tse-tung urged the Vietnamese communists to follow the strategy of protracted conflict he had developed and tested against the Japanese and the Chinese Nationalists. Lin Piao wrote an important article humbly analyzing mistakes made during the Chinese Revolution but obviously reproaching Hanoi for being intent on escalating and not knowing when to pull back. The Vietnamese hardly took this advice with fraternal grace. They had long memories of Chinese aggression over the centuries, of Chinese arrogance toward lesser peoples, of the Chinese "sellout" of their Vietnamese comrades at Geneva in 1954, when Vietnam was partitioned at the 17th parallel. Did Peking wish to keep Vietnam divided and impotent so that the Chinese could dominate Indochina?

Nor did the Hanoi regime have any more comradely love for the Russians. Moscow too had been a party to the Geneva Accords; at a critical moment Molotov, surrounded by Mendès-France, Chou En-lai, and Eden, had hammered down with the finality of a blacksmith's blows the agreement that provided for partition. Hanoi rightly suspected that the Russians saw Vietnam as a pawn in great power rivalry, were far more concerned about their relationship with China, and above all feared that escalation in Southeast Asia would lead to World War III. Hanoi no doubt suspected all this—what it did not fully grasp was the extent to which Lyndon Johnson too feared that escalation might trigger a nuclear war.

What Hanoi did know by 1965 was that Hanoi must go it alone. The North Vietnamese could extract help from Moscow and Peking by expertly playing one off against the other, but the extent of military and logistical aid finally turned on shifting great power relationships as well as Hanoi's needs. The North Vietnamese people had to survive under merciless American bombing while Hanoi mounted its own land infiltration and attacks to the south. During 1966 the Pentagon's Rolling Thunder saturated North Vietnamese military centers, supply depots, and infiltration tracks with 136,000 tons of bombs. Mammoth B-52s, each carrying almost thirty tons of explosives, left the countryside scarred and towns and villages destroyed. McNamara privately admitted that North Vietnamese civilian casualties were running up to one thousand a month.

Rolling Thunder was ill named, for it implied an Administration steadfastness that did not exist. The Joint Chiefs were urging a stepped-up, unrestricted air war; others contended that bombing could not succeed against a government and people like the North Vietnamese. Here too Johnson took the "practical" middle path, adopting a stop-and-go escalation. This not only hardened popular anger and resistance in North Vietnam without shocking it into defeatism but enabled Hanoi, with its small and widely dispersed factories, to establish alternative transportation routes and place workers underground. Tens of thousands of men, women, and children worked and even lived in an estimated 30,000 miles of tunnels.

Under the holocaust of bombs Hanoi was still able to dispatch troops and supplies to the south. Even the official United States estimates acknowledged that perhaps 90,000 men infiltrated south in 1967, almost three times the number that had done so two years earlier. As usual the airmen boasted of bombing with surgical precision and as usual they exaggerated—it was hard to identify the infiltration routes and even harder to hit them. North Vietnamese engineers and laborers quickly filled in craters and improvised pontoon bridges, while drivers camouflaged their trucks with palm fronds and traveled at night, their headlights turned off, by following white markers along the roads. Americans marveled at the "ant labor" that could put back into operation in several days a key pass leading to the Ho Chi Minh Trail.

In the south the Americans massed military technology on the ground as awesome as the B-52s in the air. In what their general, William Westmoreland, called the "most sophisticated war in history," they tried to apply the latest weapons to old-fashioned guerrilla warfare. "To locate an ever elusive enemy," in George Herring's summary, "the military used small, portable radar units and 'people sniffers' which picked up the odor of human urine. IBM 1430 computers were programmed to predict likely times and places of enemy attacks. Herbicides were used on a wide scale and with devastating ecological consequences to deprive the Vietcong of natural cover. C-123 'RANCHHAND' crews, with the sardonic motto 'Only You Can Prevent Forests,' sprayed more than 100 million pounds of chemicals such as Agent Orange over millions of acres of forests, destroying an estimated one-half of South Vietnam's timberlands and leaving human costs yet to be determined. C-47 transports were converted into awesome gunships (called 'Puff the Magic Dragon') that could fire 18,000 rounds a minute."

But it was still the human factor that made the difference. "I have no army, I have no finances, I have no education system," Ho Chi Minh had said. "I have only my *hatred*"—a hatred, Frances FitzGerald wrote later, that was the "key to the vast, secret torrents of energy that lay buried within the Vietnamese people." But it was more than hatred. It was the determi-

nation of a rigorously propagandized and disciplined people led by ideologues. It was pride in their defeat of the French and now their standing
up against the Americans. It was hope in their future of national independence—a hope that had stirred Americans two centuries before. It was
faith in their kind of freedom.

Washington, D.C., Holy Saturday, April 17, 1965. A warm cloudless day in
the nation's capital, one of those dreamlike spring days that made the city
of cherry blossoms appear like a fairy-tale picture book of democracy.
While military officials in the big government buildings toiled during the
weekend over escalation plans for Vietnam, tens of thousands of war
protesters were flocking into town on buses and trains and on foot. After
picketing the White House the petitioners moved on to the Washington
Monument, where they heard peace songs by Joan Baez and Judy Collins
and speeches by Bob Moses, Staughton Lynd, I. F. Stone, and Senator
Gruening. Paul Potter, head of SDS, which had organized the march,
closed it with a passionate and prophetic call to his listeners to build a
broad social movement that "will, if necessary, respond to the Administration war effort with massive civil disobedience all over the country," and
beyond that, to try to change the whole "system" that had produced the
war.

One by one Lyndon Johnson was also losing the support of men who had
backed him. Martin Luther King, wondering when America would learn to
understand the nationalistic spirit awakened within the colored people of
the world, including the Vietnamese, broke with the Administration during
the summer of 1965 on the issue. Walter Lippmann, discovering that the
President had been planning to escalate the war even while telling the
columnist that the war "had to be won on the non-military side," and
feeling the Administration's cool breath to boot, never set foot in Johnson's White House after the spring of 1965. Other notables also broke with
the White House and the response was the same—excommunication.

But it was the protesters in the streets—especially the young—who were
still leading the way. In the wake of the April march, SDS campus chapters,
coffers, and protests burgeoned, with excited coverage by the media. Others had not waited for SDS to lead the swelling movement. In an earlier
striking display of the 1960s phenomenon of leadership welling up from
below, University of Michigan students and faculty in March had organized
an all-night teach-in that drew thousands—an idea quickly copied at scores
of other campuses, where antiwar professors debated State Department
"truth teams" before large audiences. In late July 1965, just after LBJ
announced a doubling of draft calls, CNVA troops marched on the New
York induction center, carrying signs reading: "The President has de-

clared war—we haven't." On the twentieth anniversary of Hiroshima and Nagasaki an "Assembly of Unrepresented People" gathered in Washington for workshops and direct action that would connect black voting rights with Vietnam, creating a "peace *and* freedom" movement; a few hundred were arrested as they tried to invade the Capitol nonviolently with a "Declaration for Peace." The Assembly gave birth to the first national antiwar coalition, the National Coordinating Committee to End the War in Vietnam, composed of thirty-three organizations.

It was across the country that the thunder rolled. In Oakland, protesters sat down in front of army trains carrying soldiers bound for Vietnam. An eighty-two-year-old woman, a refugee from Nazi Germany, followed the example of Vietnamese Buddhist monks and nuns and set herself afire on a Detroit street. In New York, pacifist David Miller lighted a flame to his draft card before cameras at the induction center, the first public defiance of a new law which had made draft card destruction punishable by five years in prison. In the fall of 1965 the National Coordinating Committee sponsored international days of protest, with thousands taking to the streets in cities across the country and as far-flung as Tokyo. A thirty-two-year-old Quaker from Baltimore also sat down—within view of McNamara's window at the Pentagon—poured kerosene over his body, and died in a small inferno. A young Catholic Worker activist immolated himself in front of the United Nations, after having witnessed a draft-card burning during which hecklers yelled, "Burn yourselves, not your cards!"

As protests erupted across the country, attracting ever-greater numbers of people and intense television coverage, antiwar activists hotly debated age-old questions of strategy and organization: Should they maintain their bias against centralization or recognize the frequent need for leadership? Should they concentrate on the single issue of the Vietnam War or reach out to the varied concerns of other groups, especially blacks and students? Should they admit, or at least work with, communists, or steer clear of them as dangerous allies? The last issue was especially complex not only because liberal groups like the ADA and old-line labor unions in general opposed inclusion of "Stalinists" but because the communists were as usual divided into orthodox CPers, Maoists, Trotskyites, young communists, and other factions, who fought among themselves.

Cutting across these questions and groups was a conflict that pervaded the whole antiwar movement, a conflict, partly of generations, of classes, of tactics, a conflict of the Old Left, of the industrial trade unions, the nonrevolutionary socialists, the League for Industrial Democracy, of ADA "liberal reformism," of political writers like Max Lerner and John P. Roche and novelists like Saul Bellow and Ralph Ellison, arrayed against the New

Left, with its own dogmas, against SDS and other militant organizations, against numerous academic Marxists, writer Norman Mailer and poet Robert Lowell, *The Nation* and the *New York Review of Books,* radical chic, "resistance and reconstruction." Intellectuals pitched ferociously into the fray—some critics said because of guilt over their having legitimated confrontation by the young. Susan Sontag described America as a "criminal, sinister country—swollen with priggishness, numbed by affluence, bemused by the monstrous conceit that it has the mandate to dispose of the destiny of the world, *of life itself,* in terms of its own interests and jargon."

"These alienated intellectuals," exclaimed John Roche, now an LBJ aide, to Jimmy Breslin. "Mainly the New York artsy-crafty set. They're in the *Partisan Review* and the *New York Review* and publications like that. The West Side jackal bins, I call them. They intend to launch a revolution from Riverside Drive." He named names—Irving Howe, Alfred Kazin, Dr. Benjamin Spock, Mailer . . .

Anti-Vietnam protest reached a new peak in April 1967, when at least a quarter million people gathered at the sprawling Sheep Meadow in Central Park and marched to the United Nations to hear King, Spock, Carmichael, and other notables speak passionately against the war. Though dizzied by the size of the New York rally, SDS leaders and some of their older associates were becoming convinced that protest was not enough—they must move on to resistance. Once again the rank-and-file activists took the lead: a three-day takeover of the University of Chicago administration building—Harvard SDS activists surrounding McNamara's car and heatedly interrogating him—"We Won't Go" statements and signings of students on dozens of campuses—an intense but nonviolent effort to obstruct Dow Chemical recruiting at the University of Wisconsin, triggering a ferocious assault by riot-clad police—and in late October 1967, a march on the very center of the "military-industrial complex," the Pentagon, that huge, squat, World War II rampart across the Potomac from Washington.

The battle of the Pentagon was carefully planned as a rally for beginners, a "be-in" for hippies, an act of militant civil disobedience for the already committed, and as a "creative synthesis" of "Gandhi and guerrilla." First an array of "witches, warlocks, holymen, seers, prophets, mystics, saints, sorcerers, shamans, troubadours, minstrels, bards, roadmen, and madmen," led by the Diggers, a West Coast group of artists-organizers and "anarchists of the deed," and by a rock band called the Fugs, invoked every bit of their magic to levitate the Pentagon and exorcise its demonic spirits. Unaccountably the Pentagon did not levitate. After an SDS vanguard and others broke through a cordon of MPs and National Guardsmen and seized high ground in the plaza before the building, several thousand more protesters pressed their way up against solid rows of rigid young soldiers carrying bayoneted M-14s. Through bullhorns and face to face the protesters conducted a teach-in to win over the troops.

"Join us!" they shouted, and then more gently, "You are our brothers." They pleaded with the soldiers, sang to them, placed flowers in their upraised gun barrels. The rigid lines hardly wavered, nor did their confronters. As night fell and cold set in, protesters built campfires from posters and debris and shared their marijuana joints. When someone yelled "Burn a draft card! Keep warm!" hundreds of little flames flickered in the darkness—the ultimate "burn-in." When the television cameras were gone, a flying wedge of troops broke them up with clubs and rifle butts. The next day the remaining protesters, singing "This Land Is Your Land," quietly offered themselves for jail.

*   *   *

By this time, late 1967, the number of American troops in Vietnam was approaching a half million. Facing resistance in Vietnam and at home as strong as ever, Johnson struggled with his own ambivalence. He burned under the protesters' caricature of him as a wild Texan aching to fire his six-shooters come high noon. Even in the White House he could hear the protesters, out on Pennsylvania Avenue, chanting, "Hey, hey, LBJ, how many kids have you killed today?" More and more the war heightened the war within himself. He hated to escalate, while step by step he escalated. Close associates—George Ball, Bill Moyers, and more recently McNamara—had broken away from him largely because of Vietnam. To the Chiefs of Staff, especially anxious for even fewer restrictions on bombing, he grumbled, "Bomb, bomb, bomb, that's all you know." He would not provoke Peking or Moscow. "I'm not going to spit in China's face," he said. On the other hand, "We can't hunker down like a jackass in a hailstorm." LBJ was no longer exhibiting the kind of Rooseveltian leadership that he prized.

It was now Hanoi, not Washington, that was preparing for a major escalation. Even more than Johnson, the communist leaders recognized an intensifying deadlock in the south. They detected worrisome signs. The party cadres seemed to be losing some of their revolutionary zeal after years of war. They were ignoring the doctrine "from the masses, to the masses," losing touch with the villages, appearing even "passive and pessimistic." It was time for bold revolutionary action, for the shock of violence. Hanoi carefully planned devastating attacks at over a hundred cities and towns, aimed at reinvigorating the military cadres, carrying the war for the first time from the countryside into urban areas, arousing the revolutionary potential among the South Vietnamese masses, and throwing both the Americans and the Saigon regime off balance. The attack would be launched at the start of Tet, the lunar new year holiday that by long custom had been observed with a cease-fire.

The Tet offensive burst out in South Vietnam like an eruption of electrical storms. From the tip of the delta to the northern border the communists struck at five of the six major cities and most of the provincial capitals. Their most publicized feat was an invasion of the fortresslike United States embassy in Saigon, their most dramatic victory the temporary capture of Hué. No quarter was shown: the attackers executed hundreds of soldiers and civilians in Hué; the chief of South Vietnam's national police shot a bound captive out of hand on the streets of Saigon in full view of cameramen. Taken by surprise, American and South Vietnamese forces rallied strongly enough to recapture all the lost centers, usually after savage combat.

Blood-soaked bodies lying on the embassy lawn—the corpses of American dead piled on a personnel carrier—a Saigon official murdering a frightened and helpless captive—these pictures shocked the American public all the more after a series of optimistic statements by the commanding general in Vietnam, William Westmoreland. A serious military setback to Hanoi was converted by the press coverage into proof that the Administration had been lying about progress in Vietnam. Even the avuncular Walter Cronkite, who had flown to Vietnam for a firsthand look at Tet, was said to have demanded, "What the hell is going on? I thought we were winning the war!" "It seems now more certain than ever that the bloody experience of Vietnam is to end in a stalemate," the CBS newscaster told his huge audience in a special report when he returned to New York.

In vain LBJ insisted that once "the American people know the facts," the communists would not "achieve a psychological victory." This was what they had achieved. The public after a decade of Vietnam had had enough "facts." It wanted the truth.

And the truth was that the United States could win this war only at a price it would not pay. The Administration even now did not fully recognize this; intense debates broke out in the White House, the State Department, and the Pentagon in response to the generals' request for another 206,000 men—which would have required mobilization of the reserves—to launch a post-Tet counterattack. Even the Pentagon was at war with itself. Civilian advisers to McNamara's successor, the noted Washington lawyer Clark Clifford, warned that further escalation would send shock waves through the nation. But the military pressed for more. Clifford, who himself had turned against the war, convened for Johnson's benefit a meeting of the so-called Wise Men, pillars of the national security establishment like Dean Acheson, John McCloy, McGeorge Bundy, Cyrus Vance.

It was a moment of truth for men brought up in a world when, time and again, American power had made the crucial difference in Europe, in the Pacific, in Korea. Now they told LBJ, like the gentlemen they were but in blunt language, that the war policy was bankrupt, the cost, political and financial, was too high. The key point, Vance said later, was that division in the country "was growing with such acuteness" as to threaten to "tear the United States apart." Said LBJ: "The establishment bastards have bailed out."

Politics was already dividing the nation—this was election year 1968. Vietnam dominated the scene as the presidential primaries got underway. "The President is confronted with the resistance, open or passive, of the whole military generation, their teachers, their friends, their families," Walter Lippmann wrote. Public approval of Johnson's handling of the war dropped to an all-time low of 26 percent after Tet—hard reading for a President who followed polls as closely as his blood pressure. Sensing LBJ's weakness, Senator Eugene McCarthy entered the New Hampshire primary. A product, along with Humphrey and a dozen other national leaders, of Minnesota's potent Democratic-Farmer-Labor school of doctrinal politics, McCarthy was committed to ending the Vietnam war. When he gained a remarkable 42 percent of the New Hampshire Democratic vote, he lost to the President but captured the nation's headlines. For LBJ it was a political Tet—he had mobilized the most electoral power but lost the psychological battle.

No leader was more confounded by the New Hampshire surprise than Robert Kennedy, Senator from New York since 1964. Tet had shocked him into making his most passionate speech against the war; it had also made McCarthy formidable. Yet a Gallup poll showed that 70 percent of the American people wanted to continue the bombing. All save Johnson assumed that LBJ would run again; no major party in the twentieth century had repudiated its man in the White House. Now, after New Hampshire, McCarthy might have LBJ on the run. For weeks Kennedy and his old political friends had agonized over the New York senator's running. They divided over it too: Ted Kennedy and Ted Sorensen opposed the idea, while others saw no alternative. Robert Kennedy, as competitive as ever, could not allow this rival to preempt the Vietnam issue or indeed the whole anti-Johnson movement. In mid-March, Kennedy announced for the presidency in the caucus room of the old Senate office building, where John Kennedy had thrown his hat into the ring eight years earlier.

During this month the White House had been undergoing its own agonizing over Vietnam. On March 31, Johnson took to the airwaves to announce a unilateral halt of all United States air and naval bombardment of most of the populated areas of the north. He called on Hanoi to join in negotiations. Then, as his listeners stared speechless at their television screens, the President said at the end of his talk, "I shall not seek, and I will not accept, the nomination of my party for another term as your President." He had had enough, he told Doris Kearns later. He was being stampeded from all directions—"rioting blacks, demonstrating students, marching welfare mothers, squawking professors, and hysterical reporters." Then the thing he had feared most—Bobby Kennedy back in the fray, embodying the Kennedy heritage.

April was the cruelest month. Martin Luther King's dream came to an end, for him, on the balcony of the black-owned Lorraine Motel in Memphis, where he had been championing a strike by garbagemen. One shot from a sniper's rifle flew across the motel's courtyard, cut King's spinal column, and crumpled him to the floor. Within hours blacks in cities and towns across the nation exploded in wrath and frustration against this ultimate racial crime. Over 2,000 fires were set, over 2,000 people arrested, over 20,000 injured. The nation's capital suffered the worst devastation, with ten deaths and over 700 fires. A white man was dragged from his car and stabbed to death. William Manchester noted the bitter irony: the death of the greatest prophet of nonviolence touched off the worst outburst of arson, looting, and crime in the nation's history.

Clearly the war issue had catalyzed black revolt and student unrest, not superseded them. The three issues collided and coalesced at Columbia University in the same tempestuous month of April. A few hundred student activists, after demonstrating against the university's ties with a Pentagon think tank for war research, left the campus and descended into the hilly Harlem park—a buffer zone between the old university and the teeming ghetto below—where Columbia was building a gymnasium with a bottom level that would offer a "separate-but-equal" facility for Harlem. After tearing down a fence and denouncing "Gym Crow," the students headed back to the campus, occupied the main undergraduate building, and "imprisoned" an acting dean. When black students who had joined the takeover asked the whites to leave so that the blacks could "go all the way," the white activists surged toward the administration building, Low Library, heaved a board through a window, and made themselves at home in the suite of President Grayson Kirk.

For several days the strike gathered momentum, as the blacks renamed their captive building Malcolm X Hall, the whites experimented with techniques of participatory democracy and communal living, and three more buildings were occupied. An arm's-length alliance between black and white students kept the forces of law at bay while the administration negotiated with the occupiers through the faculty. The stickler was amnesty. Several tense days of deadlock followed—then a thousand cops smashed through the barricades and arrested 700, leaving 150 injured. A new strike ended classes for the year. In the end the gym was abandoned, so the children of Harlem lost; students never won amnesty; Kirk retired from the university.

"Oh, God. When is this violence going to stop?" Robert Kennedy had cried out when he was told that King had been shot. His cry could as well have resounded in Europe, as 1968 became the "year of the barricades," with eruptions of protest and reprisal in a long arc from art colleges in Britain to huge labor walkouts and street violence in France to university turbulence in Madrid to students marching in Belgrade and chanting "Free art, free theater" in Warsaw. By late June Kennedy was campaigning in the style his brother Jack had made famous. But people were sensing in him a compassion and desperate concern beyond anything Kennedys had before exhibited on the hustings. His blue eyes, Jack Newfield had noticed earlier, "were now sad rather than cold, haunted rather than hostile." He spoke for the poor, the underclass that establishment and students alike had bypassed. The poor "are hidden in our society," he would say. "No one sees them any more." But he did.

Liberals backing McCarthy were furious with him as a Johnny-come-lately and as a Kennedy. McCarthy himself, waging a campaign of issues, warned against presidential power and the Kennedy type of "personalization of the presidency" at the expense of the kind of leadership that "must exist in every man and every woman." Such adversaries Kennedy could at least see and even respect. Out there somewhere were the haters and the killers. Early in June, on a Tuesday evening in Los Angeles, after hearing the California primary returns that gave him a clear win over McCarthy and a realistic chance for the presidency, and after giving a brief talk for the poor and against violence, he left the hotel ballroom by a "safer" route through the kitchen for his own appointment in Samarra.

In a very real sense, David Broder wrote later, the Democratic party never recovered in 1968 from the shock of Robert Kennedy's assassination. Certainly the suspense was gone, for Hubert Humphrey, inheriting the established labor-liberal leadership in the Democracy, was bound to win the convention endorsement in Mayor Daley's Chicago. Others did keenly look forward to the convention—most notably the Youth International Party or "Yippies," which aimed at shaping the youth culture into a revolutionary fighting force, using sensational media events instead of grass-roots organizing. They would nominate for President a live pig named "Pigasus." While the Yippies helped turn the convention into the theater of the absurd, with others they made it a theater of conflict. Bathed in the eerie glare of TV lights, protesters and police fought it out in the heart of the city. In the convention hall Senator Abraham Ribicoff, in a dramatic nominating speech for Senator George McGovern, told Mayor Daley and the other delegates, "With George McGovern, we wouldn't have Gestapo tactics on the streets of Chicago," turning the mayor purple with rage.

When Richard Nixon completed the first leg of his comeback from the bitter defeats of the 1960 presidential election and the 1962 California gubernatorial race by easily winning the Republican nomination over New York governor Nelson Rockefeller, the stage seemed set for a climactic and even historic collision between warring philosophies, programs, and politicians. No one provoked Democrats as readily as Nixon, who intended to keep the focus on Democratic failures rather than Republican proposals. President Johnson's anointment of Humphrey, however grudging, put the burden of defending the Democratic party record on the Vice President, however much he might want to strike out on his own. George Wallace's entrance into the race challenged both parties but especially the Administration's civil rights record. Eager to meet this challenge, black leaders stepped up their voter registration efforts. In a year already filled with tumult and bloodshed some observers anticipated a "real Donnybrook."

The campaign did indeed get underway amid suspense and excitement, as Humphrey sought to reach out to the peace forces without antagonizing the still powerful and still proud President in the White House, as Nixon tried to go on the attack without reviving memories of the red-baiting "Tricky Dick" of the 1940s and 1950s, and as Wallace made a direct populist pitch to segregationists, fundamentalists, and blue-collar labor in their own vernacular. Wallace enlivened matters by choosing as his running mate on the American Independent ticket retired general Curtis E. LeMay, former chief of the Strategic Air Command, who presented a caricature of the bomb-wielding militarist and appeared, in Marshall Frady's words, as "politically graceful as an irate buffalo on a waxed waltz floor."

These political pyrotechnics were deceptive. The campaign became largely a battle of personalities rather than policies, mainly because Humphrey and Nixon hewed so closely to a centrist, consensual position on the issue of Vietnam that most voters saw little difference in their positions—

and those voters who did see a distinction did not agree on which candidate was more hawk or more dove. Nixon was a "master of ambiguity" on Vietnam, a scholarly study concluded, and Humphrey "alternated between protestations of loyalty to current policy, and hints that he really disagreed with it." Wallace, charging that there was not a "dime's worth of difference" between the Tweedledum and Tweedledee candidates, appealed directly to the "forgotten Americans" and their sense of political alienation, powerlessness, estrangement from government, loss of freedom—and to their chauvinism, racism, and hatred of war resisters in the colleges.

"I'm going to ask my Attorney General," he said in his standard speech, "to seek an indictment against every professor in this country who calls for a communist victory"—voice rising—"and see if I can't put them under a good jail somewhere." Loud cheers. "I'm sick and tired of seeing these few college students raise money, blood, and clothes for the communists and fly the Vietcong flag; they ought to be dragged by the hair of their heads and stuck under a good jail also."

In the end the election contest settled into the electoral pattern of the preceding two decades. After assiduously courting the southern vote, Wallace carried five states of the old Solid South and Nixon five of the southern "rim states"; Humphrey won only Texas. Since southern states had been voting Republican or independent for President off and on for several decades, this was a predictable outcome in light of the Democrats' civil rights posture. Winning 9.9 million votes nationally against Nixon's 31.8 million and Humphrey's 31.3 million, Wallace ran the strongest race against major-party candidates since La Follette in 1924. Humphrey, holding the labor vote against Wallace, carried the old Democratic party bastions of the industrial Northeast.

In splitting their vote almost evenly between Nixon and Humphrey, voters gave little guidance to leaders on Vietnam, for the major-party candidates had given little guidance to them. Well could reporter David Broder sum up the central paradox of the 1968 election: "a year of almost unprecedented violence and turmoil, a year of wild political oscillations and extremes, produced a terribly conventional result." But the election had one decisive outcome. Richard M. Nixon was the next President of the United States.

INTO THE QUICKSAND

On January 19, 1969, the day before the inauguration of Richard Nixon as President, ten thousand "militant—but for the most part genial" demonstrators, led by four active-duty GIs, marched on the Capitol in opposition to the continuing war. The next day, armed only with banners, chanting protesters organized by the National Mobilization Committee conducted a peaceful incursion into the inaugural ceremony and the parade to the White House. But as the presidential motorcade crawled down Pennsylvania Avenue, a shower of projectiles—sticks, stones, bottles, smoke bombs—landed on the limousines of the new regime. The Mobe publicly condemned this violent action by an SDS faction—the first such disruption of an inaugural.

The world did not pay much attention. Its eyes were on the new President, who had come back from the defeats of 1960 and 1962 to inch his way up to the top of the greasy pole. It was the new Nixon, certified so by publicists and politicians. The old President-watcher Walter Lippmann, in choosing him over Humphrey, had discerned a "new Nixon, a maturer and mellower man who is no longer clawing his way to the top." Theodore White would say, in his best-seller on the 1968 election, that the "Nixon of 1968 was so different from the Nixon of 1960 that the whole personality required re-exploration." A happy Nixon on election night had promised to "bridge the generation gap" and "bring the American people together." His inaugural address was conciliatory too.

But was there indeed a new Nixon? The first test was bound to be Vietnam. Nixon had promised—and the country expected—more decisive action to end the war in Indochina without dishonor. But how? On what terms? Leaders of both parties had long broadly agreed on the strategy of "Vietnamization"—of phasing out American troops while South Vietnam took control of its own military defense. Johnson's strategy had been gradual escalation, extensive though selective bombing, and promises to Saigon of support for the South Vietnam regime along with assurances to Hanoi that he would not challenge its legitimacy in the north. Nixon too favored help to Saigon along with a phased pullout, but twenty years later, after studying the available records and the myriad memoirs, historians were not clear whether Nixon and his adviser Henry Kissinger planned on keeping South Vietnam viable no matter what—the old policy—or on pulling out of South Vietnam no matter what. And that would be a crucial distinction.

"We will not make the same old mistakes," Kissinger said in 1969. "We will make our own." But the American people would not tolerate many more mistakes in Vietnam.

From the start Vietnam brought out Nixon's basic dualism. He would step up negotiation with Hanoi and speed up withdrawal of American troops. Maintaining continuity with previous Presidents, he would "seek the opportunity," as he said in an address to the nation in mid-May 1969, "for the South Vietnamese people to determine their own political future without outside interference." If the war had to go on, it was "a war for peace." If that phrase reminded some less of Woodrow Wilson than of George Orwell ("War Is Peace"), the new President still was eager to end the bloodletting in Vietnam. "I'm not going to end up like LBJ," he said, "holed up in the White House, afraid to show my face on the street. I'm going to stop that war. Fast."

But his other means of stopping the war—"fast"—was to enhance it. He could not forget his days in the White House under Eisenhower when Ike had won a favorable settlement in Korea, as Nixon saw it, by threatening China with massive escalation, even the use of nuclear weapons. Surely a jolting threat would succeed against another obdurate enemy in Asia.

"I call it the Madman Theory, Bob," Chief of Staff H. R. Haldeman reported his boss's telling him during the 1968 campaign. "I want the North Vietnamese to believe I've reached the point where I might do *anything* to stop the war. We'll just slip the word to them that, 'for God's sake, you know Nixon is obsessed about Communism. We can't restrain him when he's angry—and he has his hand on the nuclear button'—and Ho Chi Minh himself will be in Paris in two days begging for peace."

Certainly Ho was not begging for peace at the moment. Late in February his forces launched a new offensive that inflicted heavy losses on American troops, now approaching their peak level of 543,400. Within a few weeks the President expanded the bombing in Laos, sending in B-52s for the first time, and began a secret air war in Cambodia; for over a year the bombing orders were burned after each sortie. By intensifying the war outside Vietnam, Nixon and Kissinger were showing Hanoi and Moscow that they would break the restraints LBJ had imposed. Sensing that the war would not soon end, the antiwar and black movements during Nixon's first hundred days escalated in size and militance as dramatically as the secret enlargement of the war. More and more students were taking part in protests, which often brought a rash of strikes and building takeovers, amid considerable property destruction and violence.

And now a strange thing happened to the Nixon White House. It fell into the same Vietnam pattern as had the previous Administration it had so condemned—the same heavy military actions interspersed with clandestine negotiations, the same expansion and contraction of the war as the prospects of a settlement waxed and waned, the same effort to strengthen the South Vietnamese forces, the same caution about unduly provoking Moscow or Peking.

The White House did not understand that the Vietnam War, despite all the escalation, refused to fit the pattern of Western wars—authoritative decisions by the political and military leaders at the top, the marshaling of disciplined armies on the field, the mobilization of patriotic support at home. To an extraordinary degree the course of events in Vietnam turned on the motivation, morale, and self-discipline of third cadres, whether regulars or guerrillas, in the field, and on the protesting activists in the streets and neighborhoods of America. The outcome of all wars of historic importance is determined to a degree by the skill and resoluteness of foot soldiers on the political battlefield as well as the military. The crucial role of these factors in Vietnam was enormously enhanced by the fact that not two opposing armies but five had thrown their weight into the shifting balance of forces: Hanoi's regulars in the south, the NLF, Saigon's troops, American GIs, and the army of protesters back home. These military and political cadres formed a grid of countervailing forces that dominated Nixon's White House even more than Johnson's.

Of the staying power of the communists there could be little doubt, after almost a decade of their battling the American invader following their earlier rout of the French. Despite extensive indoctrination by Hanoi in its version of Marxism, the regulars and the guerrillas were motivated far more by sheer hate—of all invaders, Chinese, Japanese, French, or American, of imperialists and exploiters who had controlled their country, cruel landlords, greedy police, and village officials who acted as puppets of the alien rulers—and by hope of freedom as they defined it. "Only by revolutionary violence can the masses defeat aggressive imperialism and its lackeys and overthrow the reactionary administration to take power," their leader General Vo Nguyen Giap had written in 1964. Violent revolution was their means of achieving power; whether this means of achieving freedom might ultimately corrode that noble end was a question postponed. At times recruitment and morale sank, especially among the guerrillas, but their ideology of hate and hope and their refusal, unlike their enemy, to be distracted by the "illusion of peace" always brought them back to one transcending goal, victory.

With Nixon's critical decision to push "Vietnamization" of the war in order to assure American families that their fathers, sons, and brothers, husbands and boyfriends, would soon be returning, the staying power of Saigon's troops became of central importance to the White House during 1969. Most Americans in Saigon, forgetting that their own politicians had pioneered in the arts of bribery and boodle, had little but contempt for the corrupt, divided Saigon government with its brief king-of-the-rock regimes. They often lost patience with the South Vietnamese troops they sought to instruct in the techniques of mechanized war. Still, the fifth government after Diem was stabilized under Nguyen Van Thieu, and after intensive efforts by Saigon and Washington to beef up and modernize the South Vietnamese armed forces, these numbered about a million strong by the end of 1969, with ample weapons and supplies at their disposal. Everything then depended on the working out by Saigon and Washington of long-range plans for an orderly and successful execution of Vietnamization, but the necessary control and consistency were lacking in both capitals. Given the weaknesses at the top, the South Vietnamese troops showed more staying power than might have been expected.

So did the American troops in Vietnam, but their situation was quite different. Fighting nine thousand miles from home, holding only the vaguest notions of what they were fighting for or against, facing day after day appalling mud, heat, dust, downpours, and an elusive enemy who attacked with grenades, mines, ambushes, night infiltrations, and other guerrilla tactics, the GIs held up relatively well until Nixon's troop pullback policy left the remaining Vietnam force even less aware of the purpose of the war and even more eager to get out fast. As morale and discipline fell, a whole drug culture developed. Ugly racial hatreds surfaced. "Fragging"—men killing their own officers—rose to unprecedented heights. Americans at home were shocked to learn, eighteen months after it happened, that in March 1968 GIs had gunned down at least 450 helpless South Vietnamese civilians—children, women, old men—at My Lai. The great number of GIs dug in and held on, but by 1969 they were a declining part of the grid of countervailing forces.

The most dynamic force in this grid was busy mobilizing, recruiting, and deploying not in Indochina but in the United States, as antiwar protesters stepped up their demonstrations across the country. Far more ominous for the Administration, protest was now flaring in and around the armed services. More and more soldiers were going AWOL to avoid being sentenced to Vietnam; a few found temporary sanctuary in churches and movement dwellings. Service people were now joining peace marches as "GI coffeehouses" in Vietnam, elsewhere abroad, and back home helped to galvanize discontent at military bases. Draft resistance and evasion were widening. During the Vietnam era it was estimated that more than half a million men were draft offenders; of these over 200,000 were actually accused of draft offenses, 25,000 were indicted, almost 9,000 were convicted, and 4,000 were sentenced to prison, serving an average of eighteen months. Nearly half of the half million draft offenders had failed even to register for the draft; of these only a few were prosecuted. Some 40,000 presumed draft offenders and military deserters fled to Canada and other countries.

Protest took spectacular forms, as activists vied for headlines. In July

1969, five women, calling themselves Women Against Daddy Warbucks, darted into Manhattan draft board offices, stole dozens of draft files, and tore the "1" and the "A" from typewriters to exorcise the 1-A denoting draft eligibles. Two days later they surfaced at Rockefeller Center to toss the confettied draft records into the teeth of the multinational corporations concentrated there. This climaxed a dozen nonviolent raids on draft boards and on Dow Chemical that had started two years earlier when Jesuit priest Philip Berrigan and two others poured their own blood (mixed with duck blood) on draft files in Baltimore as their way of combining Gandhi and guerrilla, thus pushing nonviolent direct action to its outer limit. Some months later the Catonsville Nine—Berrigan, his brother Daniel, also a Jesuit priest, and seven other radical Catholics—made a bonfire of draft files with homemade "napalm," declaring, "We believe some property has no right to exist." These activists, carefully avoiding harm to persons, calmly accepted the consequences, often jail.

In a relentless spiral, militant protest edged toward outright armed struggle, as New Left activists lost patience with nonviolence. Many SDSers felt frustrated with their failure to build a more radical movement, except at a few places like Stanford. With the infiltration of SDS by the Progressive Labor party, a self-styled Marxist-Leninist-Maoist cadre, SDS meetings became scenes of ideological forensics. Bitter quarrels and shouting matches erupted over the correct line—"vanguarditis," Carl Oglesby called it—in recruiting and organizing. To counter the growing appeal of PL's organizational vigor and anti-imperialist political dogma, the National Office won adoption of a proposal to forge a "Revolutionary Youth Movement" of the working class. Marxism became, wrote Jim Miller, "a weapon in an internal power struggle."

This sectarian extremism culminated at the SDS convention in Chicago in June 1969. The National Office contingent handed delegates a long-winded RYM treatise entitled "You Don't Need a Weatherman to Know Which Way the Wind Blows"—a line from Bob Dylan—and setting forth what Kirkpatrick Sale described as "a peculiar mix of New Left attitudes clothed in Old Left arguments, the instincts of the sixties ground through a mill of the thirties, the liberating heritage of SDS dressed up in leaden boots from the past." The assembly soon degenerated into mindless name-calling and slogan-shouting, enlivened by a few fistfights in the back. RYM leader Bernardine Dohrn, a brilliant young attorney who had worked with the National Lawyers Guild, led a walkout of a majority opposed to PL. When she returned later to the rump session with her forces and declared that all PL members were expelled from SDS, the RYM faction, several hundred strong, marched out into the Chicago night. Over the summer

RYM in turn split into two parts, one of which became "Weatherman," pledged to urban guerrilla warfare in support of Third World revolution.

And so SDS died as a national entity. The "organized New Left disintegrated into warring factions over precisely the question of how to transcend the limits of student radicalism," Richard Flacks, a leader of SDS in the early days, concluded. "The era of *campus* confrontation and *student* revolutionism has ended not because it failed, but because it reached the limit of its possibilities."

*   *   *

Divided as they were, the protesters could hardly grasp their growing impact on the White House. Nixon was still groping for some kind of middle way even while the student-led demonstrations single-mindedly focused on ending the war, and even while Hanoi's spokesmen made clear their absolute determination to win it. The White House was caught in a vise largely of its own making. It was trying to fend off protest at home, conduct air and ground attacks against North Vietnam, and "Vietnamize" the war even while the Saigon regime feared the departure of the Americans. In early summer 1969 the President decided to "go for broke" to end the war, according to his memoirs, "either by negotiated agreement or by an increased use of force."

It must have been the first time in history that a war leader adjusted his war-and-peace scenario to the academic calendar. "Once the summer was over," Nixon remembered, and the colleges as well as Congress returned from vacation in September, "a massive new antiwar tide would sweep the country during the fall and winter." He decided to set November 1, 1969—the first anniversary of a bombing halt that LBJ had desperately gambled on during the final days of the 1968 election—as the deadline for an ultimatum to North Vietnam. He instructed Kissinger to draw up an operation—"Duck Hook" it was called—to force Hanoi to its knees. Soon the national security aide and his staff were working up such alternatives as massive carpet bombing of Hanoi and other cities, mining Haiphong harbor and inland waterways, bombing dikes on the Red River delta, even using tactical nuclear weapons to cut off supply routes from Russia and China. But Nixon had been right about the protesters. Four blocks from the White House another team of planners was hard at work organizing a huge Moratorium, a day of nationwide protest against the war.

The peace forces got there first. On October 15, another thunderous wave of protest rolled across the nation. Students, workers, homemakers, politicians, executives broke from their routines to join marches, rallies, vigils, teach-ins, doorbell ringings, and readings of the rolls of war dead.

Few campuses were untouched. At Whittier College, Nixon's alma mater in California's Orange County, the college president's wife lit a "flame of life" to burn until the war ended. Women in Los Alamos, New Mexico, birthplace of the atomic bomb, blocked a bridge leading to war plants. At the county courthouse in Lexington, Kentucky, a large crowd listened quietly to the names of the state's war dead; a woman walked up to the microphone and uttered a single name. "This is my son," she said. "He was killed last week."

Caught between Hanoi's steadfast pursuit of victory and the protesters' demand for peace, Nixon suddenly switched from his intended ultimatum to a speech in defense of Vietnamization. Delaying his address for two days so that it would not adversely affect a Republican candidate in a New Jersey state election, the President contended that a quick pullout from Vietnam would produce a bloodbath and a loss of confidence in American leadership at home and abroad. Vietnamization would mean peace with honor. He had seen in San Francisco, he said, demonstrators with signs reading: "Lose in Vietnam, bring the boys home." Well, he would not allow a "vocal minority" to prevail over "the great silent majority." It was Nixon at his most ambidextrous:

"Let us be united for peace. Let us also be united against defeat. Because let us understand: North Vietnam cannot defeat or humiliate the United States. Only Americans can do that."

The protesters would have none of it. They saw Vietnamization as Nixon's "invisibility" stratagem to turn over the ground war to Saigon while he further expanded the air war, which was less accessible to the media. By reducing troops, draft calls, costs, and caskets returning from combat, he would make a pretense of winding down the war while in fact it would become more destructive than ever. In November the Moratorium and the Mobe's successor coalition, the New Mobe, in uneasy alliance, led the most ambitious demonstration yet, blanketing the nation but concentrated in Washington. In long, dark robes tens of thousands of protesters walked silently in a "March Against Death" from Arlington National Cemetery to Capitol Hill. Each wearing a cardboard placard with the name of an American soldier killed or a Vietnamese village destroyed, they shouted out the names as they passed the White House. The next day eleven coffins bearing the placards headed a vast procession from the Capitol to the Washington Monument. Over half a million people gathered there in the cold, setting a new turnout record.

By January 1970, the end of his first year in the White House, Nixon's Vietnam policy was still wavering between attack and withdrawal. Given time—much time—he might have stayed atop his swaying tightrope indefinitely. But the dynamics of war were not so easily balanced abroad and brokered at home. In March 1970, Prince Norodom Sihanouk, Cambodia's Chief of State, who had been walking his own tightrope in dealing with Hanoi, Peking, Washington, and Saigon and with ambitious subordinates in his capital at Phnom Penh, was deposed while on a trip to Europe. Whether or not Washington had any hand in the overthrow—and Kissinger hotly denied it—the new President, Lon Nol, was friendly to the Americans.

The coup upset a delicate balance. Hanoi's forces had been taking advantage of long-established "sanctuaries" in Cambodia that protected their vital supply lines to the south, and Washington had been blasting these strong points. South Vietnamese certainly, and Americans probably, had been infiltrating across the South Vietnam border into Cambodia, for various reasons and with various covers. All parties concealed—or at least denied—their involvement. Now facing an unfriendly government in Phnom Penh, Hanoi's forces in the sanctuary areas attacked farther west into Cambodia in order to avoid entrapment by U.S. and Saigon forces and strengthen their hand for future operations.

Whether this episode remained merely one more of the age-old shifts of power in the murky politics of Indochina depended on how the rival capitals responded. Commander-in-Chief Nixon was already poised for action. Hanoi's "aggression" struck at all his vulnerabilities—his feeling that he had been playing the good guy in not escalating the war, his awareness that the fall election campaigns would be starting soon and the Administration had little to boast about, his fear of "losing" Cambodia, and above all his concern that Hanoi was strengthening its capacity to disrupt Vietnamization. Bypassing his Secretaries of State and Defense, who had expressed qualms about the idea, but with the solid support of Kissinger and some of the military, the President late in April resolved on a joint "incursion" by Americans and South Vietnamese against Hanoi's sanctuaries.

"If, when the chips are down," he said in announcing the invasion, "the world's most powerful nation, the United States of America, acts like a pitiful, helpless giant, the forces of totalitarianism and anarchy will threaten free nations and free institutions throughout the world." Like so many of Washington's much-touted operations in Vietnam, the Cambodia incursion gained mixed results at best. GIs and South Vietnamese forces captured large stocks of supplies and cleared a few square miles of jungle, but once again the elusive North Vietnamese troops and their headquarters personnel escaped the net.

Back home the reaction of the antiwar forces was not mixed. Furious students protested on several hundred campuses, some of which were closed for months. Student outrage boiled over following press reports that Nixon during a visit to the Pentagon had said of other protesters, "You see these bums, you know, blowing up the campuses." At some universities students attacked or sacked ROTC buildings. After a weekend of turmoil at Kent State University in Ohio, during which the ROTC building was gutted, edgy National Guardsmen, ordered to disperse even peaceful assemblies, suddenly turned and fired on a crowd of demonstrating students. They killed two women and two men, two of them bystanders. Less noticed by a stunned nation was the even more arbitrary killing of two black students by police at Jackson State College in Mississippi. The Vietnam bloodbath had overflowed into the groves of academe.

Militarily, Cambodia left the war little changed. Washington pulled its troops back by the end of June; Hanoi, its timetable somewhat disrupted by the operation, restocked its supply depots and reestablished its sanctuaries. There followed a year of fight-talk-fight on both sides. Hanoi could not mount a decisive attack, nor could the Americans. Protests continued, fueled by a rising number of Vietnam veterans, some of whom at Christmastime 1971 occupied the Statue of Liberty as a war protest and hung the American flag upside down from Liberty's crown. The Administration appeared physically as well as politically under siege, as demonstrators ringed the White House.

* * *

In his cell in the grim, fortresslike Latuna prison near El Paso, Texas, where he was doing two years for draft resistance, Randy Kehler opened his *New York Times* on a Sunday in mid-June 1971. Splashed across the front page was the first installment of the Pentagon's own secret history of the Vietnam War, ordered by Defense Secretary McNamara in 1967 to uncover what had gone wrong. The forty-seven volumes of memos, cables, reports, and analysis documenting a pattern of governmental deception and confusion might never have seen the light of day without Kehler. For a few weeks publication of the Pentagon Papers in the *Times* and the Washington *Post* once again fired up the debate over Vietnam.

The man who leaked the secret history was forty-year-old Daniel Ellsberg. For years he had seemed the model young careerist on the rise. After a stint as a Marine infantry commander, he had spent years as a national security bureaucrat, a specialist in crisis decision making and nuclear command and control, a Pentagon functionary involved intimately in the early escalation of the Vietnam War, a "pacification" officer in South Vietnam, and an author of the Pentagon history. He returned from Vietnam opposed to the war effort—at first not because it was wrong or immoral but because of its dishonesty, corruption, and futility. For two years he crusaded in the corridors of power, lobbying high officials like McNamara and Walt Rostow and advising presidential candidates in 1968, especially Robert Kennedy. Nothing seemed to work.

Gradually Ellsberg fell in with people who had been remote from his world—a nonviolent activist from India who said that "for me, the concept of enemy doesn't exist"; war resisters who defied the popular image of them as "guilt-ridden, fanatic extremists"; a Quaker activist, about to be locked up for refusing induction; and Kehler, who said he looked forward to joining David Harris and other friends in jail and had no remorse or fear, because he knew, he told a war resisters' conference, that "lots of people around the world like you will carry on." Later Ellsberg thought: these were "our best, our very best, and we're sending them to prison, more important, we're in a world where they feel they just had to go to prison."

It was Kehler who provided the spark. Now Ellsberg knew that he would have to join the war resisters even if it meant jail. With the help of his children he xeroxed his top-secret volumes of the Pentagon report, and after fruitless efforts to involve prominent Senate doves, he turned the history over to *The New York Times.* When the Pentagon Papers appeared a month later the Justice Department won injunctions against further publication in the *Times* and the *Post,* a "prior restraint" on press freedom that was overturned by the Supreme Court.

With his mind on reelection in 1972, Nixon saw the Pentagon Papers flap as an opportunity to create another Alger Hiss, who had served his earlier ambitions so well. By painting Ellsberg as the symbol of the extreme left, the Administration could tar with the same brush both the New Left and antiwar Democrats. As a political functionary named Charles Colson reported to the White House, moreover, the Pentagon Papers were "a tailor-made issue for causing deep and lasting divisions within the Democratic ranks." The Democratic party hardly needed GOP help on divisiveness. Already carrying their heritage of disunity, they were busy seeking to recruit blacks, students, war resisters, and women, all of whom had plenty of divisions of their own.

SONGS OF THE SIXTIES

When they'd finally all arrived they were, they sang, half a million strong—probably an exaggeration by a hundred thousand or so, but the Woodstock festival appeared so grandiose, in scope of music, attendance, media coverage, and social significance, that hyperbole seemed the only way to communicate its bigness. Attendance reached twice the anticipated 50,000 per day before dusk the first evening—and the organizers were forced to declare the concert free to all who had made the trek that August 1969 weekend to Max Yasgur's farm in upstate New York. A participant called it "three days of mud, drugs, and music." And how it rained, defiantly, on the greatest assemblage of rock 'n' roll and folk talent of the decade: Richie Havens; Joan Baez; Arlo Guthrie; Joe Cocker; Crosby, Stills, Nash, and Young; Santana; the Jefferson Airplane; Sly and the Family Stone; Jimi Hendrix; and the Who.

For three days music blasted from the amplifiers scattered around the eighty acres of natural bowl. But the music was secondary. Though Woodstock came "as a logical consequence of all the be-ins, love-ins, pop festivals, and tribal convocations that preceded it," wrote Bruce Cook, it was more than all of these, giving "to an entire generation not so much a sense of who they are, but (much more important) who they would like to be. . . . The first Eucharistic Congress of a new rock religion." And *Life* wrote: "Woodstock was less a music festival than a total experience, a phenomenon, a happening, high adventure, a near disaster and, in a small way, a struggle for survival."

The roots of rock 'n' roll—so named by a white Cleveland disc jockey who wanted to avoid the racial stigma carried by rhythm and blues—lie embedded in the early years of blues and country music. Before the 1950s whites had recorded "white music" while blacks recorded "black," and though their listeners crossed color lines, musically and thematically country and rhythm and blues remained equal but separate.

In the mid-1950s, when white groups began recording black songs, rhythm and blues gained hold and rock took off. "To make R & B acceptable," wrote composer and performer Frank Zappa, "the big shots of the record industry hired a bunch of little men with cigars and green visors, to synthesize and imitate the work of the Negroes. The visor men cranked out phony white rock." But whatever the commercially imposed limitations of the music, it was an infusion of energy into popular culture. Rock 'n' roll fans drove the new songs to the top of the charts. Opposition from the black artists whose works were being pilfered, from a Congress responding to industry pressure, and from the AM radio stations who recognized the exploitation for what it was, were all insufficient to halt the infestation of "phony white rock."

The music called "black" had faced all the usual objections from the conventional, but rock 'n' roll encountered a new and unique brand of opposition. Many adults found rock loud, often incomprehensible, and intolerably sexual. "If we cannot stem the tide of rock 'n' roll," warned a

Columbia University professor, "with its waves of rhythmic narcosis and of future waves of vicarious craze, we are preparing our own downfall in the midst of pandemic funeral dances." Boston Catholic leaders demanded the banning of rock. The San Antonio city council banished it from municipal swimming pool jukeboxes because it "attracted undesirable elements given to practicing their spastic gyrations in abbreviated bathing suits." Parents shuddered at such insinuating lyrics as "I need it / When the moon is bright / I need it / When you hold me tight / I need it / In the middle of the night" and their blood curdled when Little Richard yowled, "Wop-bop-a-loo-bop / A-wop-bam-boom!"

But that was part of the idea—the more adults deplored rock, the more it meant to the young. Rock burst in on a generation that, Nik Cohn noted, felt it had no music of its own, no clothes or clubs, no tribal identity. "Everything had to be shared with adults." The music began to generate its own social significance, at first vaguely and immaturely, but nevertheless giving a "divided people a sense that they may have something in common."

*　　*　　*

"The culturally alienated went in for cool jazz, and folk music was the vehicle for the politically active minority," wrote Jeff Greenfield. Folk had its origins in depression-era, vagabond protest music, but it was only infrequently available on commercial releases, and usually heard by the already converted until the voices and vibrancy of Joan Baez; the Kingston Trio; Peter, Paul and Mary; Phil Ochs; Pete Seeger; and, above all, Bob Dylan introduced a larger, if still selective, audience to the true music of protest and disaffection.

Dylan was "discovered" in a Greenwich Village club in 1961, where, upon entering, he had been asked for proof of age. His roots were middle-class, middle-American, but his voice was coarse, his music was of the road, his style was that of "the hungry, restless, freedom-loving friend and comrade of the oppressed." He rambled into New York from Minnesota with dreams of emulating Woody Guthrie—"the greatest holiest godliest one in the world." After his "discovery" he made his first album, playing alone with a harmonica and an acoustic guitar. The record cost Columbia Records just $402 to produce.

Dylan was not the popularizer of his greatest hit, "Blowing in the Wind." He performed the song on tour and the mimeographed magazine *Broadside* published the lyrics, but not until the popular folk trio Peter, Paul and Mary heard and recorded it did it sell a million copies.

How many roads must a man walk down
    before you call him a man?
How many seas must a white dove sail
    before she sleeps in the sand?
How many times must the cannonballs fly
    before they're forever banned?
The answer, my friend, is blowing in the wind,
    the answer is blowing in the wind.

That recording single-handedly "established topical song as the most important development of the folk revival," and Dylan as its premier artist.

Though he was never to dominate the music industry as the Beatles would, Dylan earned a commitment from his fans perhaps even deeper than the loyalty the Beatles enjoyed. Yet his followers' expectations of him as the "musical great white hope of the Left" proved a burden. When, on the last night of the 1965 Newport Folk Festival, Dylan stepped onto the stage carrying an electric guitar and launched into a rocking version of "Maggie's Farm," the audience for a moment sat in stunned silence, then heckled him off the stage with shrill cries of "Play folk music! . . . Sell out! . . . This is a folk festival!"

If Dylan's folk fans felt betrayed by his electrification, he saw it as evolution and synthesis. *Village Voice* critic Jack Newfield commented, "If Whitman were alive today, he too would be playing an electric guitar." Dylan had succeeded in bringing the feeling of folk—modern, protest folk—to the masses of rock. Proof of his success came in one month of 1965, when no fewer than forty-eight Dylan originals were recorded and released to a rapturous public.

*   *   *

They were four scruffy lads from the run-down port city of Liverpool playing seedy clubs in Britain and Germany until a shrewd manager repackaged them as waggish, cuddly moptops. The Beatles' first success was sudden and phenomenal. In the annus mirabilis of 1963, their music became "one of the most persistent noises heard over England since the air-raid sirens were dismantled." They sold more than two and a half million records that year, performed for royalty on the same bill with Maurice Chevalier and Marlene Dietrich, and needed squads of bobbies to protect them from screeching, scratching, fainting Beatlemaniacs.

The Beatles commenced their personal conquest of the United States when, on February 7, 1964, ten thousand teenagers gave them a hysterical welcome at Kennedy Airport in New York. Airport officials were incredulous—they had seen nothing like it, "not even for kings and queens!" 73 million people watched the Beatles perform on Ed Sullivan's television show. They played at Carnegie Hall in New York, and one fifteen-year-old fan from New Hampshire who was there with 6,000 others described the essential Beatlemaniacal delusion: "You really do believe they can see you, just you alone, when they're up on the stage. That's why you scream, so they'll notice you. I always felt John could see me. It was like a dream. Just me and John together and no one else."

With such albums as *Revolver, Sgt. Pepper's Lonely Hearts Club Band, The Beatles,* and *Abbey Road,* the Beatles revolutionized rock and opened it to new possibilities. They spearheaded a British invasion that, as Ellen Willis noted, proved "that the mainstream of mass culture could produce folk music—that is, antiestablishment music." Most antiestablishment and jolting to American sensibilities were Mick Jagger's Rolling Stones, with their "twentieth century working-class songs." As Jerry Hopkins put it, the "Beatles asked teenaged American females for their hands; the Stones asked for their pants." Their music harked back to rock's gritty, jarring, erotic origins in the blues, and in appearance the Stones cultivated ugliness and overt sexuality. They exuded contempt—and earned millions.

Groups inspired by the Beatles, such as the Beach Boys, and duos, such as Simon and Garfunkel, carried a sound even President Reagan would, years later, admit appreciating. But still newer sounds—more moody, less accessible, more personal—emerged from San Francisco bands, and they shifted the center of avant-garde rock from Britain to California.

Late in 1965 two benefit concerts were held in San Francisco, the first featuring the music of the Jefferson Airplane, with Allen Ginsberg leading three thousand in the chanting of mantras, and the second in the Fillmore Auditorium with the Grateful Dead. On the heels of these successes and at the urging of author Ken Kesey, came the seminal San Francisco "Trips Festival," "a three-day mixed-media attempt to recreate an LSD experience without the LSD." The Festival marked the beginning of the Haight-Ashbury era with its psychedelia, mind-bending drugs, sandalwood, body painting, tribal Love-Ins and Human Be-Ins.

San Francisco also produced Janis Joplin's Big Brother and the Holding Company, and Country Joe and the Fish (originally called Country Mao and the Fish, after a saying of the Chairman's, "Every fish in the sea is a potential convert"). The Dead challenged their audiences to fly on LSD, Joplin seduced hers, and Country Joe sang "1-2-3 What are we fightin' for / Don't ask me—I don't give a damn / Next stop is Vietnam / And it's

5–6–7 / Open up the pearly gates / Well, there ain't no time to wonder why / Whoopee! / We're all gonna die."

*　　*　　*

Country Joe sang his "Fixin' to Die Rag" at Woodstock, but that "first Eucharistic Congress" illustrated the tensions between the rock and counterculture and the New Left and antiwar movement. "Rock and Roll, Rock culture, hip, pop, and youth culture," wrote radical Tom Smucker, "all spring out of middle-class reality, and spring out of capitalism, and all spring out of affluence." While rock took overtly political forms and served up songs of social significance, typically it described freedom as the road to individual happiness, to personal self-fulfillment—a road that often had the contours of hedonism. Asked what was her "philosophy of life," Janis Joplin replied, "Getting stoned, staying happy, and having a good time." The point of drug use, wrote Todd Gitlin, was "to open a new space, an *inner* space, so that we could *space out,* live for the sheer exultant point of living." Though the counterculture assumed that its hedonism was intrinsically anticapitalist, it reflected the established culture's materialism, with, as William L. O'Neill noted, motorcycles, stereos, and electric guitars taking the place of big cars and ranch houses. Entrepreneurs trafficked in countercultural commodities, pushing strobe lights, Nehru jackets, surplus army clothes, incense, beads and bangles, posters, drugs, and, of course, records. By 1968 records were selling at a rate of nearly a billion dollars a year, and *Forbes* was counseling "Dad" not to dismiss rock as noise: "Try to dig it . . . it's the sound of money."

The counterculture's political vision was of a utopia from which politics was excluded, a pastoral Arcadia whose currency was amour. "All you need is love," sang the Beatles. "Love is all you need." The Jefferson Airplane urged, "Hey people now / Smile on your brother / Let me see you get together / Love one another right now." SUPERZAP THEM ALL WITH THE LOVE, exhorted a sign in a Los Angeles commune. The counterculture was out to save America with a "cultural and spiritual revolution which the young themselves will lead," but its approach to political action was antipolitical: the young were not to engage the established society but to disengage themselves from it, to drop out, to do their own thing. Social change was to be the outcome of individual self-realization. "We want the world and we want it now!" Jim Morrison snarled, but his vehicle of revolution was what he called "sexual politics." At a Doors concert, he said, "The sex starts with me, then moves out to include the charmed circle of musicians on stage," and then the audience. The audience went home, interacted "with the rest of reality, then I get it all back by interacting with that reality, so the whole sex thing works out to be one big ball of fire." "The idea of leadership is a false god," said Beatle John Lennon. "Following is not what it's all about, but leaving messages of 'This is what's happening to us. Hey, what's happening to you?' " The Vietnam war was over, he sang, when you wanted it to be.

This was a sea, Andrew Kopkind noted, in which political radicals found it difficult to swim. Though much of the New Left was "hippyized"— borrowing clothes, long hair, language, sexual and drug practices from the rock culture—that culture, in radical eyes, had evolved too little from its origins as an immature teen rebellion against "adults." Gitlin, an SDS leader, worried that love should feel ashamed "when it was founded on privilege."

Tom Smucker of the Movement for a Democratic Society wondered whether it was politically correct even to participate at Woodstock. When he heard that Abbie Hoffman had wrested from the weekend's promoters space for a "Movement City," he decided to go as a "test to see if the Movement could relate to something hip." But how best to approach the hippies? Various suggestions were made, including: "Point out to people that what they were doing isn't real. Bread and Circuses, Co-optation, The Plastic Straitjacket, that it was happening under Capitalism and therefore phony." The MDS set up its booth in Movement City with a small printing press and heaps of literature. But in the City they were far from the center of action—where the "plain old campers" were—and soon they themselves abandoned the booth. "Leaflets blowing through a field, a printing press in the rain that was never used" were the "symbol of all our political activity." Radicals failed to understand, he concluded, that Woodstock was not a political event but "another Rock and Roll adventure," another example of "how you survive in affluent middle-class adolescence, and beyond. You take the good things, which are lying here or there, and turn them into something you can dig or turn yourself into someone who can dig them. You ignore the rest.

"We didn't build the city, that's for sure."

Perhaps better even than Woodstock, an earlier incident at a Berkeley student strike illustrated the decade's troubled connection between music and politics. To the audience an organizer shouted, "Let's sing 'Solidarity Forever.' " But no one seemed to know the words of that epic anthem of working-class revolt and there was an uncomfortable silence, until someone in the back started harmonizing the words of the Beatles' "Yellow Submarine." These innocuous if familiar lyrics were immediately and enthusiastically taken up by the thousands assembled.

CHAPTER 10

Liberty, Equality, Sisterhood

EARLY in November 1962, as the glowing colors along the Hudson were turning to autumn sere, Eleanor Roosevelt died in her cottage in the hills above the river. Until the final weeks of pain and confinement she had carried on her private responsibilities, keeping in touch with her five off-spring and myriad grandchildren and in-laws and ex-laws, serving hot dogs to youngsters from a school for troubled children, trudging through shops for the right presents at Christmastime, helping a black poet find a publisher, faithfully attending church, where she paid pew rent and put two dollars into the plate on Sunday mornings. Occasionally she faced small moral dilemmas. Offered $35,000 to do a margarine commercial, she struggled with her conscience overnight and in the morning decided she would do it. "For that amount of money," she said, "I can save 6,000 lives"—through CARE packages.

She labored under her more public responsibilities as well, lecturing at Brandeis, pressuring John Kennedy about more appointments for women, publicizing the lot of migratory workers, writing her column—now taken by about forty newspapers after all the controversies. She remained as conventional about personal behavior as she was progressive about social responsibility; thus she was visibly annoyed when a granddaughter failed to return from a party by midnight. Her energy and prestige remained so high in her late seventies that Kennedy recruited her to chair his Commission on the Status of Women; from this position she peppered him and others in authority with letters of warm encouragement or gentle reproach on women's issues and much else.

The long trajectory of Eleanor Roosevelt's public life had spanned six decades of women's evolving needs and interests. Opposed in her early years even to woman suffrage, she had expanded her own consciousness as she moved through the world of women's clubs, the League of Women Voters, reform groups seeking to protect working women, the Democratic party anterooms to which women were relegated, barred from the chambers of power. By the 1960s she had seen it all: the pervasive discrimination against women in education and employment, the crucial role they could play in grass-roots politics, their inability often to perpetuate and institutionalize their gains, their need to establish a base in the political parties—especially her party, of course—rather than wasting their energies on third-party forays. Originally opposed to the Equal Rights Amendment for fear it would jeopardize hard-won legal protection for women, she was open-minded enough later to reverse her position. And she learned that a President's widow could be voted America's "Most Admired Woman" sixteen years after her husband's death and still crave the warmth of intimate human love.

Always a social reformer rather than a militant feminist, she died on the eve of a profound transformation in the consciousness, behavior, and status of American women. The people she had worked with—Frances Perkins, Molly Dewson, the much-admired black leader Mary McLeod Bethune—had been primarily concerned with women's pay, living conditions, education for jobs, relegation to the lowest rung of the opportunity ladder. This deep-biting economic inequality was thoroughly documented in the report of the commission transmitted to President Kennedy on the first anniversary of Eleanor Roosevelt's death and two weeks before Kennedy's assassination. Most of the economic problems facing women were centuries old; in the 1960s progress was still coming by inches. While blacks and students and antiwar protesters were seizing the headlines, women on the whole appeared inactive except to the degree they were involved in black and antiwar movements led largely by men.

Women lacked the kind of event—economic collapse, Pearl Harbor, Vietnam—that was needed to electrify the people and jolt the government out of its semi-paralysis. Their crisis was still an invisible one—a crisis of frustration and desperation. It was a "problem that has no name."

*   *   *

Diary of four hours in the life of Marion Hudson, wife of Henry, mother of two, maker of a home of seven rooms, university student, part-time employee.

5.30   Henry wakes up to go to work. "Trucking" by Marvin Gay can be heard all over the house at full volume. I'm awake.
5.35   Henry turns down the radio just a little.
5.40   Bathroom light is on. Kitchen light is on. Hallway light is on. (Why can't he turn off these lights when he's finished in a particular room!)
6.00   Monique and Tracey are awake. (Who isn't after the troops have just been called out—meaning Henry.)
6.05   Gave Monique a bottle and changed her diaper.

6.06 Told Tracey he could not have a peanut butter and jelly sandwich at this *ghastly* hour. (Didn't say ghastly.)

6.15 Henry is off to the post office.

6.16 Get up to cut off the lights.

6.17 Settle down for some *sleep.*

6.30 Tracey is up—walking around in the house—scares me half to death.

6.31 Tracey starts pounding me on my back to wake up. He didn't make it to the bathroom. His pajamas are wet.

6.32 I tell Tracey I am going to beat him half to death if he doesn't change those pajamas.

6.33 Tracey gets in my bed.

6.40 We both finally doze off.

6.41 Tracey is awake again. He wants some Bosco.

6.42 I threaten him with a severe beating.

7.00 Thoroughly exhausted from scolding Tracey, I get up and make him some delicious Bosco. (Actually I feel like dumping the whole glass on top of him.)

7.05 It's no use. I can't get back to sleep. Tell Tracey to go upstairs and play with his trucks. Nothing else to do but daydream and think of what I have to do and wear.

7.25 Tracey wants a piece of pie.

7.30 I get up and turn on Tracey's TV so he can watch *Little Rascals.*

8.00 Monique wants to get out of her crib. I let her yell till 8:30.

8.30 I'm up and ready. The wheels begin to move into motion.

8.45 Wash Monique and Tracey. Get them dressed. Fuss with Tracey about what shoes he is going to wear. He wants to wear his cowboy boots instead of the black ones.

9.00 Feed them breakfast. Eggs, Spam and toast. Turn on *Sesame Street.* Tracey doesn't want his eggs. More confrontation.

9.05 Pack the kids tote bag to take over to Grandma's. Tell Tracey he cannot take his new trucks. "Yes, I have to go to school today." Clean off kitchen table and stove after Henry and myself.

9.10 Get dressed. Make up Tracey's and Monique's beds. Go into my room and make up the bed.

9.20 Pack my schoolbooks and coat. Gather Monique's and Tracey's coats and hats.

9.25 Start towards door. Run to freezer—take something out for dinner.

9.30 Monique just messed in her pants. Back to the bedroom.

Change her. Put her coat back on. Meanwhile Tracey is holler-
ing—he wants to go.

9.40   Get in car—head for Grandma's. . . .

BREAKING THROUGH THE SILKEN CURTAIN

During the "conformist fifties" Betty Friedan, a young Smith College
alumna, had been writing and editing articles with titles like "Millionaire's
Wife" and "I Was Afraid to Have a Baby" for popular magazines like
Cosmopolitan and *Mademoiselle.* She had also been reading works by the
psychologist Abraham Maslow, who contended that educated women
reached their highest self-realization not through husband and children
but through themselves, through their recognition of their own needs and
capacities, through "self-actualization." She had been reading surveys by
Dr. Alfred Kinsey which indicated that as American women advanced in
education and jobs, as they made "progress to equal participation in the
rights, education, work, and decisions of American society," they enjoyed
higher degrees of sexual fulfillment. In 1963 Friedan achieved her own
self-actualization with a book, *The Feminine Mystique,* that struck thousands
of American women like a thunderclap.

With unflinching certitude Friedan's book traced the web of myths and
illusions that bound middle-class women to the one-dimensional role of
housewife and mother—and the social forces that created and bolstered
them. After World War II, she contended, educators, social scientists, the
mass media, corporate advertising, and Freudian theories of female sexuality treated as "scientific religion" had together instilled in talented
women the belief that their only sources of fulfillment were sex, home, and
family. The well-educated and affluent suburban housewives she interviewed lived lives of quiet desperation, feeling inadequate, anxious, and
depressed in existences ruled by the feminine mystique. The core of the
modern woman's problem, she concluded, was not sex but identity. Just
as the Victorian culture barred women from gratifying their sexual needs,
"our culture does not permit women to accept or gratify their basic need
to grow and fulfill their potentialities as human beings."

Though Friedan demonstrated that "the problem that has no name" was
social and structural, not personal, her remedy was the reverse: that
women exercise individual will and choice, that they find their identity by
making their own life plans for meaningful work outside the home. She
tacitly assumed that, at least for white middle-class women, *institutions* did
not have to change substantially. Friedan ended her book with no call to

collective action, no appeal to politics. But politics would not leave her alone.

Her start as a political activist was triggered by that act "conceived out of wedlock"—Chairman Howard Smith's failed effort to kill the Civil Rights Act of 1964 by adding "sex" to the title outlawing discrimination in employment. The word "sex" stayed and the measure was enacted, but the Equal Employment Opportunity Commission, evidently considering its addition a fluke and lacking effective enforcement powers, took little or no action on thousands of complaints filed by women. At a June 1966 conference in Washington of state commissions on the status of women—bodies spawned by Kennedy's original commission that were now a "seething underground of women"—activist women urged passage of a resolution that the EEOC carry out the ban against sexual discrimination in employment. Stunned when the proposal could not even reach the floor—at a conference entitled "Targets for Action"—the activists turned to Friedan, who was attending the conclave to get material for her next book. She had already been urged by women in the underground—especially in the press, government, and unions—to start a movement modeled on the blacks' successful effort.

Now the moment had arrived. During the final plenary session two dozen women from government, state commissions, and unions hastily gathered to lay plans. Friedan would later wonder whether the cabinet members and other high officials "who talked down to us at lunch knew that those two front tables, so rudely, agitatedly whispering to one another and passing around notes written on paper napkins, were under their very noses organizing NOW, the National Organization for Women, the first and major structure of the modern women's movement."

* * *

When it was formally established in October 1966, NOW had about three hundred charter members, a few of whom were men. The delegates elected Friedan president. Despite the leadership role of Aileen Hernandez, a black and a disaffected EEOC commissioner, who later would succeed Friedan as president, NOW activists were mainly white middle-class professionals in their mid-twenties to mid-forties.

"We, men and women," NOW's statement of purpose began, ". . . believe that the time has come for a new movement toward true equality for all women in America, and toward a fully equal partnership of the sexes, as part of the worldwide revolution of human rights now taking place within and beyond our national borders." NOW would "break through the silken curtain of prejudice and discrimination against women in government, industry, the professions, the churches, the political parties, the judiciary, the labor unions, in education, science, medicine, law, religion and every other field of importance in American society." NOW would "not accept the traditional assumption that a woman has to choose between marriage and motherhood, on the one hand, and serious participation in industry or the professions on the other." The document set forth a formidable agenda of reform.

NOW began as a hierarchically structured body that made up for its lack of a mass base by expert use of the media. Her celebrity status, organizational skill, and boundless energy put Friedan in a central leadership role; she served as president until 1970. From the start, Friedan recounted, NOW members were reluctant "to hand over their individual autonomy and decision-making power to any body of leaders." They hoped that the local and individual participation built into the structure would encourage leadership among women at the grass roots. But a balance between hierarchy and autonomy was hard to attain. Even while they encouraged local initiative, national leaders usually ran the show and took the limelight, leading to conflicts between local chapters and the central body that were typically expressed in terms of feminist ideals. Elitist leadership, local activists said, was a value of the male world. The higher circles saw themselves as pressure-group activists, not mere servants of the locals' needs.

Inevitably NOW sharpened a set of issues that had divided women for generations, between such reformers as members of the League of Women Voters who believed in pressing women's issues one by one through lobbying and other interest-group tactics, and "transformers" in the old National Women's Party who campaigned for the total equality of women through militant political action. This conflict had erupted during the Kennedy Administration in a dispute between women leaders centered in the Women's Bureau and the President's Commission on the Status of Women under Eleanor Roosevelt, on the one hand, and feminists from the Women's Party now allied with movement activists, on the other. The former favored "specific bills for specific ills," which would be upheld by the courts under the Fourteenth Amendment, while the latter sought such fundamental changes as the Equal Rights Amendment to give broad constitutional support to equality. Both sides talked grandly of liberty and equality but defined these values differently: the reformers fought for the removal of injustices especially in the workplace, while feminists in the Women's Party tradition "placed special emphasis on personal freedom and accomplishment," on liberating the whole woman.

Early on, when NOW drew up a Bill of Rights for Women, labor delegates threatened to pull out because their unions opposed ERA, fearing it might nullify laws protecting working women. Then a group of members walked out in protest against NOW's support of reproductive freedom and repeal of abortion laws—probably the first time that "control of one's body" had been formally articulated as a woman's right. The dissidents formed the Women's Equity Action League (WEAL), which concentrated on fighting discrimination in education and employment and later joined hands with NOW on these issues and ERA.

Such differences hardly slowed NOW's momentum. Dividing up into myriad task forces on such issues as discrimination in employment and education, NOW activists showed their mettle in changing government policy, though the battle for enforcement often took years. NOW helped win from the Johnson White House an executive order barring sexual discrimination in federal contracts, including those with academic institutions. As the self-appointed watchdog of the EEOC, NOW successfully filed suit against the agency's upholding of sex-segregated want ads— "Help Wanted: Male" and "Help Wanted: Female." Activists dumped piles of newspapers at EEOC offices and followed with a national day of picketing. NOW ranged through the business world too, gaining a historic settlement with AT&T, which even the EEOC had singled out as the largest oppressor of women workers, and compelling the airlines to end the involuntary retirement of flight attendants when they married or turned thirty-two.

NOW was especially effective on Capitol Hill. Its representatives lobbied hard for the 1972 act that strengthened the EEOC's enforcement powers and expanded its jurisdiction. Its greatest success followed, as it spearheaded congressional passage of the Equal Rights Amendment in 1972— the prize winner of the bumper crop of women's rights legislation pushed through the 92nd Congress. The Equal Credit Opportunity Act of 1974, prohibiting credit discrimination on the basis of sex or marital status, was the fruit of intensive lobbying efforts by a coalition of women's groups, including NOW, WEAL, and the National Women's Political Caucus (NWPC). Leaders in these efforts were Friedan, New York congresswomen Bella Abzug and Shirley Chisholm, and Gloria Steinem, a founding editor of the new mass-circulation feminist magazine, *Ms.*

Working with black women was a quite different proposition. Probably the most oppressed large group in America, black women had the unique experience of being stigmatized both for their sex and for their color. During the 1940s, they made more gains in occupational status, education, and income than in the previous three decades. While still far behind in absolute terms, they surpassed not only white women but black men in relative gains. But though black women might earn more than before in better jobs, they still found the doors of real opportunity sealed shut against them. Their economic improvement quickened hopes and expectations that their cultural and political environment crushed. No wonder that, according to a Louis Harris poll for Virginia Slims, 62 percent of black women in 1972 favored efforts to strengthen women's status in society, compared with only 45 percent of white women. The different situations of black and white women caused many black women leaders to keep their distance from such white-dominated organizations as NOW and even to refer to the "white" women's liberation movement.

The more NOW expanded, the more it came to embrace women of differing interests and loyalties, such as trade unionists, blacks, professionals, housewives. A dramatic display of unity was needed, and a fine occasion was at hand—the fiftieth anniversary of the winning of female suffrage. Sensing that something grander than the usual demonstration was in order, Friedan conceived of a "Women's Strike for Equality" as a way to channel the energy of the burgeoning movement toward concrete political goals; it would show women, the media, the government "how powerful we were." When she proposed the idea during her farewell speech as head of NOW in March 1970, some delegates cheered, but others groaned, wondering how ridiculous they might appear if most American women did not strike. Hernandez and other leaders feared squandering resources on a crazy plan that was likely to fail.

Undaunted, Friedan and hundreds of NOW activists pulled out all the stops to bring together a wide national coalition of women's groups, including many younger and more militant participants, working out differences along the way. As a down payment toward equality the strike called for abortion on demand, twenty-four-hour child-care services, and equal opportunity in jobs and schooling. To enable women to participate in the strike privately in their homes and offices if they did not want to take to the streets, planners presented the strike as an opportunity "to do your own thing."

Locking arms with Judge Dorothy Kenyon, an eighty-two-year-old suffrage veteran, and with a young radical in blue jeans, Friedan on August 26, 1970, led a huge march of women—and some men—down Fifth Avenue. Defying police orders to stay on the sidewalks, they spilled into the street, holding banners high and calling out, "Come join us, sisters," to women waving from curbs and office windows. Women marched for equality in every other large city that day and in many smaller ones. It was the first nationwide mobilization *of* women *for* women since the direct action by suffragists, and the first time the movement was covered seriously by the media. Suddenly famous, NOW found its membership swelling. Most of the new recruits were homemakers and clerical workers rather than professional women.

"This is not a bedroom war," Friedan proclaimed that evening at a rally next to the New York Public Library, where she had written her pathbreaking book. "This is a political movement."

*　　*　　*

Friedan was not speaking for all women, not even all embattled women. Marion Hudson's *was* a bedroom war—a kitchen war—a war over children. Whether she realized it or not, Marion Hudson was a guerrilla in her own home, embattled with husband and children, mired in her "rat race" of an existence. She shared this kind of life with millions of other housewives—mothers—workers. Some liked it. Others accepted it because it was the way things were supposed to be—they read in *Life* about the "Busy Wife's Achievements" as "home manager, mother, hostess, and useful civic worker." Still others felt, as one "homemaker" told Friedan, that "by noon I'm ready for a padded cell."

During the sixties countless wives began rebelling against the "Busy Wife's" life, in part because the flammable writings of Friedan and others were coming into their homes via radio, television, and the popular press. Exposed to feminist arguments during the day, "trapped housewives" were now intellectually armed to confront their husbands at six. "By the time my husband walked in the door all hell would break loose," a woman said. "He was responsible for all the evils of the world and especially responsible for keeping me trapped."

Freed of the trap, what then? Some women became active in NOW or other women's political organizations. Some struck out for careers of their own, despite the impediments and difficulties. Some returned to college or university. Some did all these things. But numerous women—especially younger women, many of them veterans of the black freedom movement or the New Left—were not content with the means and ends of NOW. Political action, progress in education, even successful careers often appeared to them like tokenism. And because they insisted on going to what they called the "heart of the problem," they helped create a fundamental dualism in the women's movement between what came to be called the younger and older branches.

The heart of the problem, as the younger branch saw it, was the subjugation of women in personal relationships with men and in their domestic roles. What they scornfully called "careerism" was no solution, for it did not challenge the domestic division of labor and was open to only a minority. They demanded not equality of sex roles—which they likened to the Jim Crow doctrine of "separate but equal"—but their elimination. Theirs was a search for identity, self-expression, self-fulfillment.

They were emerging from the womb of conflict. Just as the nineteenth-century women's rights movement had grown out of the participation of black and white women in the crusade to abolish slavery—and the awareness of their second-class status in that movement—so the younger branch of the new feminist movement originated in the southern freedom struggle of the 1960s. That women passionately engaged in social activism would precipitate a revolt centering on ostensibly personal matters appeared ironic only to those who could not see that to these women the personal was the political, that women's inequality in the public world was on a continuum with inequality in private life.

That conservatives and "male chauvinists" would seek to put them down, protesting women expected. That their fellow rebels and radicals treated them almost as badly as the establishment did make them indignant. At a SNCC retreat late in 1964, Casey Hayden, an activist in both SDS and SNCC, and Mary King drafted a position paper protesting that assumptions of male superiority were "as widespread and deep rooted and every much as crippling to the woman as the assumptions of white supremacy are to the Negro." Why was it, they asked, that competent and experienced women in SNCC were almost automatically relegated to the "female" kinds of jobs—typing, desk work, filing, cooking, and the like—and rarely elevated to the "executive" kind? Stokely Carmichael's rebuttal to Hayden and King: "The only position for women in SNCC is prone." Though it might have been made in jest, the remark "generated feminist echoes throughout the country."

A year later, after little progress, Hayden and King took a tougher stance at an SDS "rethinking conference." SDS women were now beginning to organize and meet separately and to exclude men. They reacted eagerly to Hayden and King's strictures on the peace and freedom movements' own "sex-caste system." Three activists protested that they were "still the movement secretaries and the shit-workers," preparing the mailings and serving the food. Even more, they were "the free movement 'chicks'—free to screw any man who demanded it, or if we chose not to—free to be called hung-up, middle class and up-tight."

As women continued to be barred from decision-making, their anger and determination deepened. At the June 1967 SDS convention in Ann Arbor, the "Women's Liberation Workshop" offered a bold resolution not open to debate, declaring that women were "in a colonial relationship to men" and had to fight for their independence. The resolution demanded that "our brothers recognize that they must deal with their own problems of male chauvinism in their personal, social, and political relationships," and it insisted on full participation, especially in leadership roles. The resolution passed, despite a "constant hubbub" of catcalls and invective— the first time the New Left took a public stand against sexism.

THE LIBERATION OF WOMEN

Having begun to win a battle they had never wanted to fight, younger-branch activists were ready to organize on their own. The spark that ignited independent action was struck off in Chicago in September 1967 at the National Conference for a New Politics, an abortive effort to forge a militant alliance of blacks and whites. When in a condescending manner the NCNP leadership blocked Shulamith Firestone and other women from reading a radical resolution drafted by the women's caucus, on the ground that women's oppression was insignificant compared with racism, they had had enough. Firestone, Jo Freeman, and others formed the first autonomous women's liberation group in Chicago. Later that fall Firestone and Pamela Allen started New York Radical Women, which shortly organized a counter-demonstration to a Washington antiwar protest led by a coalition of mainstream women's peace groups. With a torchlight parade at Arlington Cemetery symbolizing "The Burial of Traditional Womanhood," Radical Women argued that "we cannot hope to move toward a better world or even a more democratic society at home until we begin to solve our own problems." Women left for home fired up to form their own collectives.

Why did these younger-branch feminist leaders not join NOW, which had formed in response to women's plight in the home as well as on the job? The activist women on all sides shared common values of liberty, equality, and sisterhood but they had major differences. NOW was relatively centralized in organization, hierarchical in power arrangements, focused on political organization and action, oriented toward Washington and state capitals. The women now springing into action were concerned less with policy goals than with self-consciousness, self-realization, self-identity; they wanted to reach the Marion Hudsons. Opposed to formal leadership, structure, and elitism, they urged networking and decentralization down to the smallest local gatherings. NOW abounded with stars; the new groups were hostile to celebrities and skeptical of "expert authority." NOW included men and worked with them. Many of the younger branch not only were critical of men for all the usual reasons but viewed them as the class enemy.

Such considerations prompted Firestone and Ellen Willis in early 1969 to establish Redstockings, which proclaimed that relationships between men and women were a conflict-ridden class relationship and could be resolved only by collective political action. About the same time radical dissidents in the New York NOW chapter tried to change the chapter bylaws to abolish hierarchy. When the chapter majority voted down a proposal by its flamboyant president, Ti-Grace Atkinson, either to abolish offices or to spread them around, she resigned in protest, telling the press that the division lay between "those who want women to have the opportunity to be oppressors, too, and those who want to destroy oppression itself."

Atkinson and other NOW insurgents joined former members of Radical Women to form a new group called the Feminists, whose founding principle was equal participation. To prevent the quick and the vocal from dominating meetings they set up an ingenious Lot and Disc system: all tasks were assigned by lot, and all members were given the same number of discs, one of which had to be spent for each utterance. Legend in the women's movement has it that at the first meeting the members used up their discs in fifteen minutes, and at the next meeting they hoarded them and said little. In other ways too the Feminists were different. They ruled that no more than one-third of their members could be living with men. They discouraged "star making" by choosing their media spokespersons by lot. Despite—or because of—this gallant effort to structure participatory democracy, and perhaps also because of its moral absolutism, the organization withered and died.

Radical feminist groups were now sprouting at an astounding rate, and were depleting New Left ranks, as word spread through networks. Starting them up had never been so easy or exciting, an organizer recalled. Binding together the radical feminists was a shared view of their plight as women. Leading off from French philosopher Simone de Beauvoir's insight that the world treats man as subject, woman as object, as Other, radical feminists were coming to see themselves as constituting an oppressed class, even a caste. The male-female division was the "primary class system" underlying all other class distinctions. Proclaimed the Redstockings Manifesto:

"Male supremacy is the oldest, most basic form of domination. All other forms of exploitation and oppression (racism, capitalism, imperialism, etc.) are extensions of male supremacy: men dominate women, a few men dominate the rest. All power structures throughout history have been male-dominated and male-oriented."

While male and female are biological, Kate Millett contended, gender, masculine or feminine, is cultural and thus learned; anatomy is *not* destiny. Women—and men—would be truly liberated when they could free themselves from "the tyranny of sexual-social category and conformity to sexual stereotype," as well as from racial caste and economic class. The goal of expunging oppressive sex roles was the touchstone of radical feminism. Many agreed that this required the abolition of marriage and the traditional family, but some went further to demand an end to heterosexuality. In her book *The Dialectic of Sex,* Firestone called for a full-fledged feminist revolution, made possible by technological advances, enabling women to seize control of reproduction and make childbearing and child-raising the responsibility of society rather than solely of individual women.

The heart of liberation was the consciousness-raising group. For radical feminists the CR group was at once a recruitment device, a process for shaping politics and ideology, and a microcosm of an egalitarian community that prefigured a feminist society. The participants, usually a group of from six to twenty, met in a safe, nurturing atmosphere to share their most intimate feelings and questions. Some groups followed a four-stage process: opening up, sharing, analyzing, abstracting—the last meaning to fit a resultant understanding "into an overview of our potential as human beings and the reality of our society, i.e., of developing an ideology." Some groups concentrated on sharing experiences: what it was like for a woman to sit passively in a car while a man walked around it to open the door—to fake an orgasm to protect both her own pride and her partner's—to try to maintain a dignified silence in the street when men hooted or stared at her—to wait on a husband who would not lift a hand in the kitchen.

Mainly these "rap groups" shared questions. Why should a woman spend so much time and money to "go unnatural" in order to attract a man? Should women be willing to sacrifice more than men do for the sake of marriage or companionship? How could they persuade the men they lived with to share housekeeping chores? In the warmth and intimacy of the rap sessions they talked about loving men and other women and the meaning of mutuality, about sexual violence in the bedroom and rape in marriage.

Raising consciousness was a first step to political action. Late in 1968 about two hundred women descended on the Atlantic City boardwalk to protest the Miss America Pageant as "patently degrading to women," according to a key organizer, "in propagating the Mindless Sex Object Image." The pageant had always been a lily-white, racist contest with never a black finalist; the winner toured Vietnam, "entertaining the troops as a Murder mascot"; the whole million-dollar affair was a "commercial shill-game" to sell the sponsors' products. Where else, the protesters demanded, could one find such a perfect combination of false American values—racism, militarism, capitalism, all packaged in the " 'ideal' symbol," a woman? The feminists picketed and performed guerrilla theater, auctioned off a dummy Miss America, crowned a live sheep as their winner, and tossed dishcloths, steno pads, women's magazines, girdles, bras, high heels, and "other instruments of torture to women" into a Freedom Trash Can.

* * *

As liberation groups and activities proliferated, a radicalization occurred typical of social movements, to the point of self-parody. On Halloween 1968 a coven from WITCH, the Women's International Terrorist Conspiracy from Hell, surfaced on Wall Street "to pit their ancient magic against the evil powers of the Financial District—the center of the Imperialistic Phallic Society." After plastering WITCH stickers onto the George Washington statue, the masked, wand-wielding witches danced around the big banks, chanting curses, and invaded the Stock Exchange to hex men of finance. The money changers stood in awe but unhexed. Soon the witches' covens and their offspring broadened out, casting their spells at bridal fairs, AT&T, the United Fruit Company, a marriage license bureau. Among the most imaginative was the nonviolent storming of a Boston radio station by women angered over an announcement that "chicks" were wanted as typists; the station manager was handed an offering of eight baby chicks.

Stunts and self-parody were tempting for their appeal to the media, which "discovered" feminism in the "grand press blitz" of 1970. Though often portrayed mockingly or trivialized as a fad, radical feminism found its coverage soar in major newspapers and magazines as well as on TV. And the feminists used Big Media's devouring appetite to score points against it. Organizers of the first Miss America protest made a decision that became movement policy—to speak only to female reporters. They were not "so naive as to think that women journalists would automatically give us more sympathetic coverage," Robin Morgan explained, but they wanted to make "a political statement consistent with our beliefs."

If the media influenced the women's movement to be bolder and more theatrical, the movement affected the media as well. Refusing to talk to male reporters helped generate more meaningful assignments for female journalists, freeing them from the "ghetto" of the woman's page. At *Newsweek*, after months of agitation and a complaint to the EEOC, female employees reached an accord with management to accelerate the hiring and promotion of women. Some radicals engaged in militant direct action, notably an eleven-hour sit-in at the *Ladies' Home Journal* to try to liberate it. They won the right to produce a special supplement on feminism. Employees seized and barricaded the avant-garde Grove Press to protest discrimination, the firing of women for organizing a union, and the publishing of erotica they felt degraded women—and were charged with resisting arrest when they demanded female cops.

More venturesome still for activists was to put out their own publications. The first feminist newspaper, *off our backs,* published in Washington, was followed by an effusion of journals and magazines—over one hundred by 1971. Notable were *Women: A Journal of Liberation, Quest, Signs,* and the glossy popular magazine *Ms.,* which reached a circulation of half a million. Closely linked to the alternative periodicals were feminist collectives that churned out everything from literary and political anthologies to nonsexist, nonracist children's books.

The younger branch became a great teaching movement. To learn more about what de Beauvoir called the "second sex," and to instruct young women in how to reclaim their past, feminist scholars initiated women's studies courses and programs on hundreds of campuses. Radical feminists who felt demeaned or mistreated by the male medical establishment, particularly with respect to birth control and pregnancy, organized self-help classes to enable women to know and care for their bodies and to conduct self-examinations. A group of Boston women taught a course on women's health that resulted in a collectively written handbook, *Our Bodies, Ourselves.* First printed by the New England Free Press in 1973, it became the most widely read of all feminist publications, translated into eleven languages and growing thicker with each edition—the bible of the women's health movement. Alternative clinics for women sprang up, specializing in pregnancy and abortion, along with a resurgence of natural childbirth, home birth, and midwifery.

The determination to control their own bodies helped empower especially the younger branch during the 1970s. Abortion, often self-induced, had been a common though risky practice for centuries; it did not become generally illegal in the United States until the medical elite campaigned against it after the Civil War. During the 1960s coalitions of professional men and women in some states gained modification of anti-abortion laws that permitted abortion by a physician under certain conditions but still left the decision to the doctor, usually male. Then the rising feminist movement turned the debate upside down, proclaiming that abortion was a woman's basic right, that the decision was hers alone, and that abortion laws must be repealed, not reformed.

"When we talk about women's rights," said one activist, "we can get all the rights in the world—the right to vote, the right to go to school—and none of them means a doggone thing if we don't own the flesh we stand in, if we can't control what happens to us, if the whole course of our lives can be changed by somebody else that can get us pregnant by accident, or by deceit, or by force."

Although initially even some feminists did not consider it a feminist issue, NOW leaders and others formed in 1969 the National Abortion Rights Action League, which along with other "pro-choice" groups mobilized for legislative and judicial changes. Radical feminists, who demanded not only abortion on demand but an end to coerced sterilization of poor, largely nonwhite women, joined with moderates to organize abortion teach-ins and testify at legislative hearings; characteristically, NOW activists gave legal testimony while radicals talked graphically about their own abortions and sometimes disrupted the formal proceeding with speechmaking and guerrilla theater.

These pressures, combined with other developments—the passage of liberalization laws in some states during the 1960s, rising concern for pregnant women's physical and psychological safety, and concern over population growth symbolized by the co-chairing of Planned Parenthood–World Population by ex-Presidents Truman and Eisenhower in 1965—helped produce the biggest pro-abortion rights victory of all from the all-male Supreme Court of the United States. In 1973, following extensive litigation, the Court in *Roe* v. *Wade* ruled that restrictions on abortion during the first trimester violated the constitutional right to privacy; abortion could be regulated in the second trimester only for the protection of a woman's well-being, and must be permitted even in the final three months if her health and survival should be at stake. Though *Roe* did not grant women an unconditional right to abortion, it came close enough since most abortions took place in the first trimester.

But even as feminists rejoiced, a passionate movement erupted against abortion, with *Roe* as the hate object. Led by conservative women, fundamentalist preachers, Catholic clergy, and leaders of the New Right, the "right-to-lifers" succeeded in persuading national, state, and local governments to whittle down the practical promise of *Roe*—in particular, to bar public funding of abortions, which mainly affected poor women. Anti-abortion women activists organized their own demonstrations and street protests. This fierce counterattack made abortion *the* social issue of the 1970s. The struggle was less about the right of the fetus, the sociologist Kristin Luker concluded, than about the role of women and *"the place and meaning of motherhood."* Many women, especially those deeply religious and of low-income backgrounds, perceived the feminist vision of self-empowerment as a serious threat.

A woman's control of her body encountered its most shocking and horrifying violation in the assault called rape. Wrote Andra Medea and Kathleen Thompson: "Rape is all the hatred, contempt, and oppression of women in this society concentrated in one act." Feminist thinkers like Susan Griffin and Susan Brownmiller developed broad analyses of rape that placed it on a continuum of male aggression and power rather than seeing it as a deviation or the result of uncontrolled "passion." Brownmiller examined the "masculine ideology of rape" that made it the ultimate expression of male domination and possession of women.

With reported rapes having doubled in half a decade, in part because women were gaining the boldness to report them, feminists undertook to educate the public and aid the victims. Early in 1971, the New York Radical Feminists organized the first rape "speak-outs," in which survivors talked openly about their ordeals, in the process "making rape a *speakable* crime, not a matter of shame." Soon women across the country were setting up hundreds of rape crisis centers offering emergency support services, especially phone "hot lines" womanned around the clock to counsel sisters in need. Feminists in NOW and other groups set up local and national task forces to lobby for such reforms as prohibiting court testimony about a victim's sexual history, for laws against marital rape, and for the creation of a national center for the prevention and control of rape.

As usual the younger branch took the lead in organizing creative direct action, from women's "anti-rape squads" that patrolled streets and pursued suspects to candlelit "take back the night" marches, born in Italy and Germany, that protested all violence against women. The growing public enlightenment about rape encouraged more and more women to break their silence about violence in the home, resulting in the formation of crisis centers and shelters for battered wives and children. Later in the decade many radicals zeroed in on purveyors of pornography, accusing them of dehumanizing women and promoting a cultural temper of hostility toward them. This led to vigorous debate within the women's movement pitting the evils of pornography against the evils of censorship and what could seem like a conservative moralist attack on sexual liberty.

* * *

During these days of intensive consciousness-raising, debate, and confrontation, two groups were watching and participating in the progress of the movement but not without reservations, at one in their mutual isolation but not always agreeing. These were lesbians and black women.

"What is a lesbian? A lesbian is the rage of all women condensed to the point of explosion. She is the woman who, often beginning at an extremely early age, acts in accordance with her inner compulsion to be a more complete and freer human being than her society . . . cares to allow her. These needs and actions, over a period of years, bring her into painful conflict with people, situations, the accepted ways of thinking, feeling and behaving, until she is in a state of continual war with everything around her, and usually with herself." So began a bold manifesto—"The Woman Identified Woman"—struck off by the Radicalesbians.

The issue of lesbianism in the women's movement steamed up as a vital, much-publicized controversy in both branches. Though a minority, lesbians from the start had made vital contributions to NOW as well as to radical groups—"carried the women's movement on their backs," said Millett—but by and large they had kept their sexual identity hidden. A police raid on a gay bar in New York's Greenwich Village in June 1969 and the violent resistance by gay men led to an upwelling of "gay pride" and helped to inspire male homosexuals and lesbians to conquer their fears and "come out." Lesbians, demanding the elimination of heterosexual dominance and homosexual stigmas, moved far beyond older groups like Daughters of Bilitis and the Mattachine Society, which had focused on civil rights and personal adjustment.

Lesbians felt doubly oppressed on the basis of their sexuality, "doubly outcast." They also believed that they met the feminist movement's own criteria for defining the liberated woman—"economic independence, sexual self-determination, that is, control over their own bodies and lifestyles." Thus it was fair and fitting that they be at the forefront of feminism, its "natural leaders." But many "straight" feminists in both branches feared the "lavender menace," as Betty Friedan called it, on the ground that their enemies would pounce on this Achilles' heel, equating feminism with lesbianism.

The issue was fought out in meeting after meeting over several years. At the second Congress to Unite Women in 1970 the lights suddenly went out on the first night; when they came back on moments later, women in lavender T-shirts paraded in front, claimed the microphone, and denounced the feminist movement for its heterosexism. Pro-lesbian resolutions passed at workshops over the weekend. The tide seemed to be turning when the president of New York NOW, to Friedan's consternation, encouraged the wearing of lavender armbands on a Manhattan march. The 1971 national NOW convention unequivocally resolved in support of lesbians' right to define their own sexuality and lifestyle and acknowledged "the oppression of lesbians as a legitimate concern of feminism."

By now lesbian activism had a momentum of its own. Some lesbian leaders had higher aspirations than for mere acceptance. They wanted the movement to adopt "lesbian-feminism" as its political creed, defined by their journal *The Furies* as a "critique of the institution and ideology of heterosexuality as a primary cornerstone of male supremacy." They called for complete separation from men and even from heterosexual feminists who were not "woman-identified." Feminists on the other side charged them with "vanguardism" and dogmatic moralism. Still, most feminists continued to work together across the sexual divide. The great promise of lesbian-feminism—its compelling vision of an autonomous women's culture flowering in many hues—lived on in such profound contributions to sisterhood as the poetry of Adrienne Rich, Audre Lorde, Judy Grahn, or the women's music of Meg Christian, Margie Adam, Kris Williamson, Holly Near. "Free spaces"—coffeehouses, music festivals, cultural happenings—proliferated, places where self-defining women could explore their commonalities as well as their differences.

This was not the world of black women, most of whom were poor or jobless or underemployed. Black feminist leaders were determined to make feminism a movement for all women and to establish themselves as a visible presence in its midst. With an equal stake in women's liberation and black freedom, they were central figures at the confluence of the two movements. Both to forge links between the movements and to "organize around those things which affect us most," black feminists formed their own groups, the most prominent being the National Black Feminist Organization, founded in 1973 by a diverse assemblage.

"We were married. We were on welfare. We were lesbians. We were students. We were hungry. We were well fed. We were single. We were old. We were young. Most of us were feminists. We were beautiful black women." So the NBFO members identified themselves. The statement of purpose proclaimed that the "distorted male-dominated media image of the Women's Liberation Movement has clouded the vital and revolutionary importance of this movement to Third World women."

On a smaller scale were groups like the Combahee River Collective in Boston, named after an 1863 guerrilla action in South Carolina, led by Harriet Tubman, that freed hundreds of slaves; they were "committed to working on those struggles in which race, sex and class are simultaneous factors in oppression," struggles against forced sterilization, rape, and domestic violence and for abortion and child care. Such concerns, they argued, united all women.

Other women of color, especially Latinas, overcame cultural barriers and divided loyalties to take part in the feminist movement. Chicana and Puerto Rican women formed autonomous organizations such as the Comisión Femenil Mexicana Nacional in the Southwest, the Mexican-American Women's Association, and the National Conference of Puerto Rican Women. Chicana activists were the backbone of the United Farm Workers' strikes and boycotts.

The trend in the feminist movement toward harnessing its breadth and diversity through coalition building culminated at the 1977 National Women's Conference in Houston. Established and financed by legislation pushed by Bella Abzug, who chaired the International Women's Year Commission that coordinated it, the conference met to propose measures to achieve full equality, which had been discussed earlier in public meetings involving over 100,000 women. The Houston delegates ranged from progressive church women, trade unionists, and community activists across a wide spectrum to the hard core of conservative "antis," sporting yellow "Majority" ribbons and seeking in vain to block resolutions in support of ERA and abortion rights. With middle-class whites *under*represented, it may have been one of the most all-embracing political conventions in American history.

It did not lack in theater. At the start of the proceedings, a multiracial team of relay runners carried into the convention center a flaming torch from Seneca Falls, New York, site of the first women's convention in 1848. During heated debate over a National Plan of Action a woman rose in the rear of the hall and said dramatically, "My name is Susan B. Anthony"; at the end of her remarks the grandniece of the revered leader joined others in chanting, "Failure Is Impossible!"—the elder Anthony's final public words. The climax of the gathering was the near-unanimous passage of a minority women's resolution, drafted by a joint caucus of blacks, Latinas, Asians, Pacific Islanders, and Native Americans, that called for recognition and alleviation of their "double discrimination." Among many conservatives who stood up to vote for it were two white Mississippians, a man and a woman who reached across the seated disapproving members of their delegation to grasp each other's hand. The coliseum swayed with "We Shall Overcome."

Aside from such peak moments, the movement as it matured came to feel less like a nurturing family, a "room of its own," and more like what it really was—a massive and complex coalition of women with much in common but many differences. Women of color who were vitally attuned to the "simultaneity of oppressions" felt the strongest need for linking issues and took the lead in building bridges of interdependence. The progress that had been made toward sisterhood did not blind feminist delegates to the big obstacles to unity that remained—above all, the many women they had not yet reached, represented by the "antis" at Houston. "Change means growth, and growth can be painful," said the black lesbian feminist Audre Lorde. Her remark summed up the intellectual and political struggles of the whole decade.

THE PERSONAL IS POLITICAL

How did "the movement" get started? How fully did it reach its goals? Years later veterans of the women's movement, like old campaigners re-fighting the battles of yore, were still debating how a movement that appeared to have lost most of its fire and focus after winning the vote in 1920 suddenly flamed up into a force that transformed the ideas and behavior of both women and men, at least in the upper and middle classes. Historians were already examining the origins of the movement, its linkages with the black and student revolts, its durability, the "real change" it produced in terms of its own aspirations, and the historians were discarding almost as many explanations as they found useful.

The movement emerged from volcanic economic and social changes in the years following World War II, according to one theory. The percentage of women in the total civilian work force rose from 28 in 1947 to 37 in 1968, bringing a huge increase of women who were exposed to both the temptations and the frustrations of the job mart and who shared with one another financial and occupational concerns. At the same time women's *relative* deprivation mounted as their share of "both quantitative and qualitative occupational rewards," in Jo Freeman's analysis, dwindled. This seeming paradox produced a volatile mixture—aroused hopes and crushed expectations.

Other explanations were that World War II had served as the catalyst of increased employment among women, producing a change in self-image as well as expectations that were rudely shattered after the war, as men took back the better jobs; and/or that social and class forces involved in urbanization and suburbanization, and the relatively greater deprivation of middle-class women, fostered a desire for reform; and/or that psychologically, the more women operated in the male sphere, the more they had to assert their identity as female. Having earlier possessed a self-identity, a fixed societal position, or at least a nurturing leadership role in the family, many women now operated in a twilight zone between low-paid jobs and family responsibilities. Wanting a life outside the home, yet feeling guilty about their husbands' unmet needs, they were driven by guilt and emptiness to smother their children with care, to treat them as though they "were hot-house plants psychologically." This "Rage of Women," as a *Look* article called it, was that identity crisis dramatized by Friedan as "the problem that has no name."

To be trapped between domestic demands and the need for "something more" was an old story for many American women, but powerful intellectual and ideological forces were sweeping the West during the 1960s. These were years of turbulence in Europe as well as the United States. Simone de Beauvoir, the novelist Doris Lessing, and others across the Atlantic had challenged the dominant image of woman's subordinate position. In the United States the black and student revolts lifted the banners of liberty and equality even as they fought with others and among themselves about the meaning and application of these values.

In proclaiming liberty, equality, and sisterhood, women too broke up into rival ideological camps. Feminists of the NOW camp typically held that women were equal to men but had been kept subordinate to them, that the goal was integration on an equal basis, through political action. Women's liberationists of the younger branch protested that they were treated as sex objects or as mere property, that they must act through psychological or social "woman power." Liberal feminists defined liberty as the absence of legal constraints on women and equality as equal opportunity to attain their goals. Marxist feminists saw themselves as victims of the capitalist system, liberty as protection against the coercion of economic necessity, and equality as the equal satisfaction of material needs. All this was aside from "sexual conservatives" who saw men and women as inherently unequal in abilities and held that unequals should be treated unequally.

Sisterhood was powerful enough to keep these differing values from tearing the women's movement apart. Indeed, conflicts over goals doubtless sharpened the impact of consciousness-raising. Borrowing from blacks' examples of standing up in meetings and testifying about their treatment by "the Man," borrowing even from Mao's way of criticism of oneself and others, "Speak pain to recall pain," consciousness-raising intensified as women in small groups spoke to one another about any and all of their "personal problems," including husbands, housework, making office coffee, shopping, curtailed ambitions, child care, male bosses, sexual relationships. The heart of these meetings was the probing by women of themselves and others about problems as *they* defined them.

The genius of these meetings lay in a leadership that was as potent as it was inconspicuous. It was a leadership of women by women, as experiences were exchanged, feelings evoked, attitudes articulated. Women exchanged leadership positions as the "rapping" moved from problem to problem. The effect was much in accord with the teachings of psychologists like Maslow whom Friedan and others had read—the raising of persons to higher levels of self-awareness, self-identity, self-protection, self-expression, and ultimately to creative self-fulfillment. The rap groups discussed the writings of leading thinkers in the women's movement too, and as they did so it became more and more evident that their personal problems were in many respects political problems, involving millions of women, widespread customs and attitudes, laws and judicial findings, governmental institutions and power.

At first cool to these "bitch sessions" as providing young women with a crutch that would divert them from political action, NOW came to see them as means of enlarging the mass base of the organization and at the same time meeting women's needs. NOW expanded from 14 chapters in 1967 to around 700 seven years later, while membership rose from 1,000 to perhaps 40,000. Yet NOW did not appear to grow proportionately in electoral strength, despite its emphasis on practical political action. Part of the problem was that its organizational structure failed to keep pace with the growth in membership.

But the main problem was the anti-leadership and anti-organization ideology and ethic in the women's movement. These tendencies existed in NOW to some degree but were offset by vigorous leadership at the top. The movement's younger branch was determined, on the other hand, as both the means and the end of social change, to replace the "masculine" principle of hierarchy with the ideology and practice of collective sisterhood. Less ambivalent than the New Left or NOW, radical feminists rejected hierarchical leadership altogether. This was partly a reaction to the seeming hypocrisy of movement groups that kicked hierarchy out the front door only to sneak it in through the back. But it was the result even more of the feminist notion that power meant "possession of the self" rather than manipulation of other people—hence women had to shun leadership of and by others in order to cultivate the strength to lead their own lives.

"Because so many of our struggles necessarily had to be carried on in isolation, in one-to-one relationships with men," an activist of the younger branch observed later, "it was imperative for women, as individuals, to gain the confidence to act autonomously, to lead *oneself*. So the moral distaste for leadership *by others* became an intensely practical tactic, completely appropriate to the tasks to be performed."

The absence of recognized leadership, however, did not prevent the rise of leaders who were more skillful verbally and in other ways. Describing what she called the "tyranny of structurelessness," Freeman—known in the movement by her nom de guerre, Joreen—noted that every group had a structure and that covert structures generated covert elites. Lack of formal structure thus became a way of masking power, which then became "capricious." Groups could not hold de facto leaders accountable; indeed, the covert elite's existence could hardly be conceded. The unhappy consequence was difficulty in charting a clear direction for individual groups and the whole movement, leading in turn to diminished effectiveness. Sharing these concerns as the "euphoric period of consciousness-raising" ebbed, a number of activists began to put a higher priority first on lobbying and other pressure-group tactics and later on party and electoral action to uproot sexism.

This shift fostered more emphasis on political leadership, while "structurelessness" tended ironically to exacerbate the celebrity syndrome. One of radical feminism's loudest grievances was the male "star system" of the New Left, but the women had their own celebrities. And when the movement shunned the idea of official leaders or spokespersons, the media appointed their own whether or not they were truly representative. Not only did the grass-roots collectives, then, have little control over feminist stars, but resentments festered and eventually erupted in open denunciations of the stars as "elitist"—which pushed them even further away, sometimes to the movement's outer edges. Celebrity Kate Millett, whose *Sexual Politics* was a best-seller, said that she was made to feel a traitor to the whole movement.

"All the while," Millett wrote, "the movement is sending double signals: you absolutely must preach at our panel, star at our conference—implying, fink if you don't . . . and at the same time laying down a wonderfully uptight line about elitism." Millett had been anointed as a star by *Time* magazine, which put her on its cover in August 1970. When a few months later she publicly declared her bisexuality at a feminist conference, *Time* dethroned her, ruling that she had lost her credibility as the movement's "high priestess."

*	*	*

If the personal was the political, to what degree must the women's movement turn to political action? And what kind of political action? Women's differences on these questions deepened. Some women adamantly opposed a party and electoral strategy because it meant entering a male-dominated world and seeking to influence male-made and male-controlled institutions. They argued for individual and group face-to-face persuasion and confrontation in universities, corporations, law offices,

hospitals, government agencies—and in the streets. The great potential of
the women's movement, they contended, was not primarily in its electoral
power but rather in its *moral* power—its capacity to appeal to the conscience of the American people on issues of simple decency, justice, equality. And that appeal had to be dramatic, passionate, militant, uncompro-
mising, as black leaders had demonstrated in the previous decade.

Beware of a party and electoral strategy for two further reasons, these
women argued. To be effective in parties and elections required endless
compromises on moral principles as issues and policies were bargained out
amid many contending groups. And even if women helped win elections,
they would have to try to carry out their policies in a fragmented governmental system that required still further bargaining and sacrifice of principle. In the end women would become just one more pressure group and
lobbying organization, their moral appeal muted.

This view tended to dominate thinking among the younger branch.
While women were not neatly divided on the basis of competing strategies,
most feminists in the older branch came to believe that party participation
and electioneering were vitally necessary.

The older-branch leaders were confident they commanded the intellectual and political organization and strength necessary for a major electoral
and lobbying effort. The National Women's Political Caucus under Abzug
and Chisholm, now claiming hundreds of participating state and local
units, laid groundwork. With NOW and other allies, it threw its weight into
the internal struggles of groups with which the women's movement intended to work in electoral politics.

Organized labor was a prime target. Across the nation working women
had been fighting a long battle to persuade male-dominated trade unions
to pay more attention to their grievances about sexism and job discrimination and the paucity of women among the top leadership. With crucial help
from NOW, women trade unionists convinced the AFL-CIO finally to
abandon its opposition to ERA. Women also launched their own unions.
Probably the greatest gains were made by groups like "9 to 5," which
began to organize women office workers in Boston in 1973.

Professional women organized too, especially in academia, through autonomous caucuses and associations. Notable for their militance, caucuses
within scholarly organizations like the American Political Science Association raised hell at annual conventions on a host of problems plaguing
women scholars. Nowhere did feminists mount a more daring assault on
tradition than in churches and synagogues, as women fought for the ordi-
nation of female clergy, the degendering of sacred texts and even of God,

and the creation of a nonpatriarchal feminist theology. The National Coalition of American Nuns protested domination by priests "no matter what their hierarchical status."

Still, the acid test of institutional power, in the American governmental system, was electing a President and winning majorities in Congress. The older branch was far better prepared for the 1972 elections than it had been for 1968—in part because of the rules adopted after the 1968 Democratic convention for broader representation of women in the party's governing councils. These rules changes and a concentrated drive by NWPC paid off: women made up 40 percent of the delegates attending the 1972 convention compared with 13 percent four years earlier.

Thoroughly coached by the NWPC in the complex and often bizarre and ferocious processes of delegate selection, platform drafting, and credentials battles, women at the 1972 convention in Miami had a major role in convention decisions—above all in the nomination of George McGovern. Women had the heady experience of taking part in the inner strategy councils, helping to choose the running mate, and seeing one of their number, Jean Westwood, selected as the new chairperson of the Democratic National Committee. For their part, blacks doubled their percentage of delegates at the convention over 1968.

Sharing in the exercise of power, Democratic women encountered its disappointments as well. One of these was McGovern's sacrifice of a number of women delegates, whose seating he had promised to support, to the exigencies of convention politics. Representatives Shirley Chisholm and Abzug and other women's rights leaders complained that they were deserted on key platform planks, especially abortion rights. Women had a minor role in McGovern's choice of Senator Thomas Eagleton as his running mate, but virtually none in the selection of Sargent Shriver as Eagleton's replacement following a press flap over revelations that Eagleton years before had been hospitalized a few times for psychiatric disorders.

A more surprising and severe failure for the women's movement lay ahead. ERA had passed both houses of Congress early in 1972 with such heavy majorities, and with such enthusiastic support from Nixon as well as the Democratic candidates, that women expected the proposed constitutional amendment to gain swift passage through the required thirty-eight state legislatures. Within a year, thirty states had ratified ERA. But then its progress began to stall, under the pressure of a powerful "STOP ERA" coalition directed by a resourceful right-wing leader, Phyllis Schlafly, and composed of diverse antifeminist, radical right-wing, and business groups and of an unlikely alliance of Protestant fundamentalists, Orthodox Jews, and Catholics. State legislatures started to repeal their ratifications of the amendment, as STOP ERA played upon the fears of millions of American women and men who felt threatened by the women's movement or who believed that it had gone far enough. ERA, its opponents charged, would lead to the drafting of women and the denial to mothers of the custody of their children, to single-sex toilets and homosexual marriages. They linked the amendment to "forced busing, forced mixing, forced housing," as one ERA foe wrote to her senator. "Now forced women! No thank you!"

Its political setbacks were doubly unfortunate for the women's movement, for they tended to obscure the astonishing transformation in everyday attitudes and behavior that both the older and the younger branch had helped bring about. At least within the middle- and upper-income classes, sexual stereotyping of women in businesses, college faculties, hospitals, on athletic fields and military installations had markedly lessened. Equally notable were changes in speech, dress, deportment, parenting, housekeeping. Gentlemen who had grown up in an earlier school had to learn to refrain from opening doors for women and offering to carry their packages and walking between them and the curb, from referring to young women as "girls" or older women as "ladies"—even from standing up when a woman approached their restaurant table.

In this sense the personal was not so much the political as the psychological, the attitudinal, and the behavioral. Few of these changes had been caused or even affected by laws, nor were they sustained by them. The changes had emerged from women's aching needs for recognition, identity, self-assertion, self-fulfillment. They were enforced by no cops or prosecuting attorneys but by a kind of instinctive conspiracy among women to shame or cast down or freeze out the incautious or insensitive husband, teacher, store clerk, coach, bureaucrat. They had sprung not from a few protest meetings or public defiances but rather from thousands and thousands of tiny confrontations, inside and outside the home, as women looked up from their reading or returned from their rap session to conduct their own face-to-face insurrections.

At last women were bringing to bear on their own lives the values that men had been preaching for decades, for centuries. In this respect their activism was ideological, reflecting the values of liberty, equality, and sisterhood. But to define these values and their linkages, to array them in a hierarchy of priorities, to make the crucial connection between these values and the everyday lives and aspirations of women—and to envision the political strategies and organizations necessary to operationalize these values—this was a task of intellectual leadership. It was the availability of such leadership to the women's movement at every level that made the most critical difference in the complex forces leading to the transformation of women's lives.

For many women it was difficult to move from "personal" politics into the public arena. Women who were most experienced in movement politics and organization often had the most difficulty in the transition, because party and electoral politics had their own organizational imperatives, sacred turfs, lines of influence, points of access, rules, and taboos. Women's organizations had not been built as electoral machines; they were not easily convertible. Some women, on the other hand, feared that feminists would be *too* successful in invading big political institutions—they feared the kind of co-optation that would blunt their organizations' image and thrust, compromise their specific goals, and yet not have any lasting reform impact on the broader political system.

* * *

Election year 1972. For many leaders in the older branch of women activists and in the black and peace movements who had staked their political futures on working within the two-party system, 1972 beckoned as a test of this strategy. For many in the younger branch, and for many of their "agin the system" counterparts in the other movements, 1972 loomed as one more series of concessions and "sellouts" by left-liberal forces to a major party and its candidate, who would abandon the left if they won and blame the left if they lost. For historians then and later, 1972 was the culmination of one of the most turbulent decades in American history, from the nationwide mobilization of black protesters early in the 1960s to the fiery protests of student, anti-Vietnam, and women's forces later in the decade; from the first involvement of "advisers" in Indochina to the massive intervention of the late 1960s; from the assassination of John Kennedy in 1963 to the killing of Martin Luther King and Robert Kennedy five years later to the near-murder and political disabling of George Wallace in May 1972 after his impressive showings in several northern Democratic primaries.

If the 1972 presidential election outcome was a fair test of the strategy of older-branch leaders committed to the Democratic party, they failed. Nixon and his Vice President, Spiro T. Agnew, after a generally negative campaign interspersed with calls for "Peace with Honor," swept the nation, aside from Massachusetts and the District of Columbia. The Republicans won the largest popular vote margin in history, 47.2 to 29.2 million. And at last, with Wallace out of the game, Nixon carried the whole of the Solid South, which even Ike had failed to do. Older-branch leaders took solace in the high participation rate of women—especially blue-collar women, liberal and young women—in the campaign and their increased voting turnout, and in the continuing Democratic majorities in Congress despite the Nixon sweep. But it was small comfort after such high hopes.

If 1972 was a litmus test for women's political leadership and activism, it was even more so for the two other great movements of the 1960s. Blacks had developed such strength politically in numbers and organization by 1972 as to protect most of their gains; they could chalk 1972 defeats off as temporary setbacks. The anti-Vietnam activists suffered the worst defeat. The campaign was fought out largely on terms that they had set—Vietnam, arms reduction, the draft—and Nixon would have appeared to have won a mandate against them had he not pirouetted around both or all sides of the peace issue during the campaign.

So 1972 was a setback, but there would be other elections. To some women in both branches a more important long-run question was the quality of the established leadership and of the next generation of leaders, male or female. The 1960s—the fateful decade—had produced a burst of political talent: John Kennedy, who by 1963 was positioning himself to provide strong détente and civil rights leadership; Lyndon Johnson, who brought thirty years of New Deal, Fair Deal, and New Frontier promises to culmination; Martin Luther King, who taught blacks and whites how to be both militant and nonviolent; Robert Kennedy, probably the only leader of his generation who had the potential to have firmly united the black, peace, and women's movements with the Democratic party. Three of these leaders were killed; the other was politically disabled. Who would—who could—take their place?

With McGovern and Shriver decisively defeated and Humphrey and Muskie vanquished four years earlier, no potential successor was visible among the Democratic party leaders of either gender. Both the party and its allied movements, however, were rich in second-cadre leaders in Washington, the state capitals, and the myriad movement headquarters. Many of these men and women were talented speakers, negotiators, legislators, administrators, spokespersons for their causes. Was there a Martin Luther King among them? The more one studied King's life, the more one was impressed not simply by his obvious political skills but even more by his intellectual qualities. His life was a reminder that transforming leadership is a product of formal learning molded and burnished by combat and controversy. In theological school King had steeped himself in the writings of Gandhi and social theorist and activist Walter Rauschenbusch, of Niebuhr and R. H. Tawney, of Marx and Hegel. Hence he was able then and later to define and sort out his values, shape ways and means to achieve those values, and devise day-to-day political strategies and street tactics necessary to achieve the changes he sought. And he was a focus of conflict—in the black movement and organizations, with other black leaders such as Malcolm X, with white critics ranging from J. Edgar Hoover to benign but hostile editors and fellow ministers.

Much of the force of the 1960s movements lay in their intellectual strengths—in the kind of prolonged debate and analysis that went into the Port Huron Statement, the remarkable teaching of women by women that backed up their philosophy and strategy, the street seminars and walking debates of King and his co-leaders. For many, movement life had been a special form of higher education. But street skills and intellectual leadership were not enough. Also indispensable for effectiveness in American politics was individual and organizational persistence, sheer staying power—both as an expression of confidence and determination and as a warning to political friend and foe that you will be around for a long time and must be reckoned with. A century earlier the business leaders of the North, by moving into the top councils of the Republican party, and by staying with the GOP through thick and thin, had dominated the federal government for decades. In the 1930s the liberal-labor-left forces of the nation, by moving into the top councils of the Democratic party, and by staying with the Democracy through depression and war and cold war, through election triumphs and defeats, had put their stamp on federal and state policy-making. The insurrectionists of the 1960s left an array of groups and organizations devotedly carrying on their causes. But they neither maintained their influence in the Democratic party nor created a party of their own—they had not achieved staying power.

Paradoxically, even as the strength of the left was waning after its relative high point early in 1972, conservative movements were rising that within a decade would accomplish essentially what the left had not—would find their unifying and transforming leader, who in turn would seize control of a major political party after initial setbacks, would lead that party to victory, and then would firmly seize the reins of office and power.

All this lay in the future. At the moment—election night, November 7, 1972—Richard Nixon, strangely morose and withdrawn after his big win, contemplated four more years in the White House.

PART **IV**

The Crosswinds
of Freedom

CHAPTER 11

Prime Time: Peking and Moscow

F OUR years after he became President, a quarter century after he entered
politics, Richard Nixon the private man remained a figure of mystery
in the public mind. Some of the most gifted interpreters of American
politics and politicians could not seem to get a handle on him. Of all the
Presidents since 1789, Kenneth S. Davis wrote in the *Encyclopedia of American Biography* following the first term, Nixon was "probably the most baffling to contemporaries who sought truly to know and understand him as
mind, character, personality, and to relate this knowledge to major acts of
his public career." Most American Presidents have had complex personas;
save for a few war heroes, less complicated men are unable to "embrace
multitudes" and win their embrace. But Nixon was not merely complex,
he was opaque; not merely ambivalent as a policy maker but pulverized as
a personality.

He was a preacher of harmony who viewed his critics with a cold implacable hatred, a mildly pacifist Quaker who had favored dropping atomic
bombs—only three small ones, to be sure—to rescue the French at Dien
Bien Phu, a mediator between moderate and conservative factions of the
Republican party who seemed equally at home in either wing, a fierce
nationalist and practitioner of *Realpolitik* who held the idealistic, internationalist Wilson in veneration, a man of seething resentments and black
Irish hatreds who liked to appear with Billy Graham in politico-spiritual
assemblies dripping with cheerfulness and piety, an advocate of "guts" and
determination who swore that he was not a quitter but who finally quit, a
man who evaded personal confrontations but relished crises. Many political leaders are torn between conventional and "rational" alternatives,
between left and right alternatives, or between principled and practical
strategies of leadership. Nixon was so eviscerated by multiple lines of
tension and cleavage as to leave him a shredded man.

"Let's see—What'll I wear today?," Herblock, the Washington *Post*'s
political cartoonist, had Vice President Nixon saying upon rising and facing a choice of apparel labeled "Dead-End Gang," "All-American Boy,"
"Look, Folks, I'm a Statesman," and "Political Pitchman."

Challenged by this complexity, students of personality sought to un-cover the sources of Nixon's political character. James David Barber, analyzing types of presidential character, labeled Nixon "active-negative" —ambitious, power-seeking, devious, aggressive, hyperactive—as against "active-positive" (FDR, Truman, JFK), "passive-positive" (Taft, Harding), or "passive-negative" (Coolidge, possibly Ike). There was much interest in Nixon's early years: life with an often angry, financially insecure father, the death of two brothers, a beloved mother's prolonged absences. Psycho-historian Bruce Mazlish noted his fears of being unloved, of being consid-ered weak or timid. At the deepest level, Mazlish wrote, Nixon was a political actor whose role-taking substituted for "an insecurely held self." Psychiatrists diagnosed him—from afar—as orally and/or anally fixated, as a "compulsive obsessive," as driven by the need for power. An astute biographer, Garry Wills, emphasized more the impression Nixon gave of being adrift, of lacking a sense of place, of coming across as "the least 'authentic' man alive."

The President's domestic policy-making during his first term was no help to the search for the "real Nixon." Right-wing Republicans and con-servative southern Democrats had for decades listened to Nixon sound the tocsin against federal regulation and spending, and were hoping that his Administration would roll back four decades of liberal Democratic and moderate Republican reform; they were quickly disillusioned. Myriad pro-grams were extended—environmental protection, occupational safety and health, urban mass transit, farm price supports—and even expanded. The Clean Air Act of 1970, establishing comprehensive air pollution programs that sharply curbed carbon monoxide and hydrocarbon emissions in 1975 cars, appeared to be precisely the kind of legislation Nixon had long denounced for stifling free enterprise. On other matters, such as some of his judicial nominations, a series of crime and drug control acts, and his (unsustained) veto of a major water pollution control bill, he gave some satisfaction to the right. On still other issues such as civil rights—and especially women's rights—the Administration's record was mixed.

Eventually the President's domestic program dissolved into a jumble of disparate policies. Halfway through his term, in his January 1971 State of the Union address, he suddenly asked Congress for a "New American Revolution," which, after the hyperbole was extracted, still looked some-what radical: welfare reform, health insurance reform, major governmental reorganization, revenue sharing, "full prosperity in peacetime." Such proposals cloaked for a time the reality that Nixon was essentially bored by domestic policy-making—especially environmental—compared with foreign policy.

Without a firm hand from above, disputes broke out between liberal and conservative advisers—notably between Assistant for Urban Affairs Daniel Patrick Moynihan and economic specialist Arthur F. Burns. Burns, the former chief of Eisenhower's economic advisers, was perturbed by Nixon's quick policy decisions—it had taken only two minutes, he said, to persuade the President to go ahead with revenue sharing. During a long series of intra-Administration battles over welfare reform, Burns complained to friends that when he told presidential aide John Ehrlichman that Moynihan's guaranteed income plan was not in accord with the President's philosophy, Ehrlichman had asked, laughingly, "Don't you realize that the president doesn't have a philosophy?"

In foreign policy it was going to be different. After the disarray of LBJ's final years in office, the new Administration would propound a strategy of foreign and military policy-making—a strategy of Administration teamwork, careful setting of priorities, linkage among foreign policy initiatives—aimed at continuity, coordination, consistency. "If our policy is to embody a coherent vision of the world and a rational conception of America's interests," according to this plan, "our specific actions must be the products of rational and deliberate choice," as compared with the "series of piecemeal tactical decisions forced by the pressures of events" of the past.

The team that Nixon assembled for this "new strategy for peace" hardly appeared equal to this awesome task. His Secretary of State, William P. Rogers, was a respected lawyer who had had only a marginal relationship to foreign policy-making. A loyal friend of Nixon's from the early years, he had served as Attorney General under Eisenhower. Rogers and Nixon had drifted apart during their years in New York in the 1960s—in part, Rogers's friends believed, because of the former Attorney General's success as a big-league lawyer and on the Manhattan social circuit. The new President chose him as a skillful negotiator, not as a strategist or shaper of foreign policy; Nixon hoped to be his own Secretary of State. For Secretary of Defense he turned to Melvin Laird, a longtime congressman out of the Wisconsin heartland, an expert on military appropriations, and a shrewd middleman among Washington's power brokers. Neither secretary was well prepared to master his huge bureaucracy packed with talented specialists protecting their turfs and slowed by endless processes of clearance, consultation, and collective judgment.

Nor were they equipped to deal with the White House—with Nixon's consuming concern with foreign relations, his penchant for secrecy, his contempt for the "permanent" bureaucrats held over from previous Administrations. Even less could they cope with the youngish, rather innocuous-looking academic whom their boss had chosen as his Assistant for National Security Affairs. If they knew of Henry Kissinger, it was as a refugee from Germany who had served in army intelligence in Europe during the war, risen quickly through his wits in the academic community, gained access to the defense and foreign policy establishments while teaching at Harvard, acted as a foreign policy adviser to Nelson Rockefeller, developed close connections with leaders in both parties and all factions, and maneuvered himself into positions that made him a readily available candidate for national security aide to Nixon—or perhaps to Humphrey or even to Robert Kennedy if either had been elected.

Looking out on the Washington jungle through his heavy, old-fashioned spectacles, Kissinger thoroughly agreed with his new boss's plans for more consistent, coordinated, rational foreign policy-making. He too believed in teamwork, but there had to be a captain and a quarterback. Kissinger was ready to take charge of the team, not only to defend the United States against its foreign foes but to accomplish the even more difficult task of defending the President's and his own powers against domestic enemies— radical agitators, carping congressmen, overly inquisitive journalists, stubborn feds in State and Defense, White House rivals, the President's inner inner circle, the President himself.

Finding China

Few American leaders of national standing had rivaled Richard Nixon in denouncing communism in general and the Chinese communists in particular. He had climbed the first rung of the political ladder by stigmatizing his congressional opponent, the rather idealistic New Deal Democrat Jerry Voorhis, as communist-supported. He had clawed his way up the second rung, in a 1950 contest filled with red-baiting on both sides, by tarring his rival for the Senate, Helen Gahagan Douglas, as a consistent follower of "the Communist Party line." He made enormous political capital out of the Alger Hiss case. He became a favorite of the China Lobby that guarded the Taiwan ramparts in Washington and again and again during the 1950s castigated Truman and Acheson and other Democrats for "losing China." He warned of a monolithic, global communist conspiracy.

"Now, what do the Chinese Communists want?" he demanded during his election battle with John Kennedy in 1960. "They don't want just Quemoy and Matsu. They don't want just Formosa. They want the world."

Later in the sixties Nixon seemed to be changing his line on "Red China." In a 1967 essay for a foreign affairs journal, he wrote that, "taking the long view, we simply cannot afford to leave China forever outside the family of nations, there to nurture its fantasies, cherish its hates and threaten its neighbors." The essay was ambivalent enough to suggest a new Nixon, China sector. But on closer reading one found the old Nixon labeling China as the "epicenter of world revolution," referring to the "poison from the Thoughts of Mao," decrying Peking's "imperial ambitions" in Asia, and making clear that it was China that must change. And his approach, he carefully added, did "not mean, as many would simplistically have it, rushing to grant recognition to Peking, to admit it to the United Nations and to ply it with offers of trade—all of which would serve to confirm its rulers in their present course." The article was ambivalent enough to support wrath against Peking or rapprochement with it.

Yet he had a curiosity about China. He kept turning toward it, like a soldier of fortune to an old battle zone. He even tried to visit mainland China in 1965, when he was a private citizen, but LBJ's State Department denied him permission. Even before the end of his first presidential year, however, Nixon began an exchange of signals with the Chinese leadership. Each side had good reason for seeking rapprochement. Indeed Nixon had several: to play Moscow off against Peking, to take some striking initiative in a period when his foreign policy seemed moribund, to weaken Chinese ties to Hanoi, to draw this vast nation with its exploding population more into the world community, and above all to win reelection in 1972 by end-running the Democrats on the peace issue.

Peking had one towering reason for rapprochement with the American superpower: Russia. After veering apart earlier on ideological and geopolitical issues the two communist powers now were at each other's throats. A series of clashes broke out between Soviet and Chinese border guards during the spring of 1969 along the Amur River and on the Kazakhstan-Sinkiang border 3,000 miles to the west. Moscow was shifting into eastern Siberia a dozen infantry divisions, late-model Soviet aircraft, and even, it was rumored, nuclear-equipped missiles. In 1968 Moscow had demonstrated its own border phobia by its invasion of Czechoslovakia. Would China be next? There were reports that the Soviets were readying an attack. Peking desperately needed a nuclear ally, and there was only one available: the capitalist barbarians across the Pacific. It was time for triangular diplomacy.

In his increasingly mixed feelings toward China, Nixon was continuing an old American tradition of "a curious ambivalence in our China policy," as the historian John K. Fairbank called it, a gap between attitude and reality. For a century and a half Americans had gone to Cathay in a state of high-mindedness, intent on bringing proper religion, education, trade, and freedom to the Orientals. The reality they found was of an old culture fixed in its ways, stratified in its classes, oblivious of its innumerable poor, established in its religion. It was hard to exert much influence, benign or not, on this ancient people. So the Americans tended to talk of moral uplift but to act opportunistically. Thus they deplored the hold of opium on the masses while Yankee traders bought the drug in Turkey and sold it in Canton. For decades hardly more than junior partners to the British, they inveighed against imperialism and colonialism but accepted extraterritoriality and most-favored-nation treatment. Missionaries preached the Gospel—"When we step in here we bridge over in a second twelve hundred years of history," a booster of Protestant Christianity told the young army officer Joseph Stilwell in 1911—without much effect on the natives. When the Japanese invaded Manchuria in 1931, Washington replied with Stimson's righteous but ineffectual nonrecognition doctrine; during World War II the United States sent aid—including Stilwell—to China but kept eastern Asia at the bottom of its military priority list; and after the war provided aid to Chiang Kai-shek insufficient to dam the revolutionary forces of Mao, even if Chiang had used it effectively.

Ultimately the contradictory attitudes among Americans and Chinese produced conflicting memories. "The American memory," wrote Dennis Bloodworth, "was one to inspire a daydream of fond reminiscence—of selfless Protestant missionaries striving to save the heathen soul of nineteenth-century China; of a morally upright Washington that had stood aside when greedy European colonialists plundered the Celestial Empire, endowing it instead with the Open Door policy; of a generous administration that had lavished military aid and moral counsel on the Chinese during the war against Japan; and of a culture that had given them the precious message of democracy and the American way of life." The Chinese memory, observed Bloodworth, "had been scarred by all the love bites."

It was these crosswinds of history, memories, and attitudes, East and West, through which Richard Nixon would have to find his way. "When the moment comes to jump—leapfrog over the position immediately ahead," was Nixon's style as described by his speech writer William Safire. The President's leaping was more like the knight's on a chessboard—forward and to the side, after a cautious assessment of the new position. To influence Hanoi and counter Moscow he would use Peking. To reach Peking he would use Henry Kissinger.

* * *

The national security aide hardly appeared a promising player on the Chinese chessboard. An admirer of the nineteenth-century diplomats

Castlereagh and Metternich and a student of the post-Napoleonic "conference system" of powerful and independent Foreign Ministers managing an intricate balance of power, Kissinger had as little knowledge as his chief of Asian politics. Twenty years of distance from the Chinese leadership, he now discovered, had left Washington ignorant even of how to approach Peking. Its eastern Asia expertise decimated by the red hunts following the fall of China to the communists, the State Department had by now regained a pool of China hands. But here another difficulty arose. The President suspected the State Department of invariably leaking, so he viewed absolute secrecy as essential, while Professor Kissinger was contemptuous of the academic orientation of the experts at State. The department, for its part, was institutionally dubious about the "loose cannon" personal diplomacy of Presidents. Above all, Nixon did not wish to share with Secretary Rogers the glory of being the modern Marco Polo who had rediscovered China. He even wanted to omit any initial trip to China by an emissary because it would "take the glow off his own journey"—or so Kissinger supposed.

The approach to Peking, Kissinger wrote later, began like "an intricate minuet between us and the Chinese so delicately arranged that both sides could always maintain that they were not in contact, so stylized that neither side needed to bear the onus of an initiative." This was a Metternichian view; the rapprochement might rather be likened to one of those arranged marriages in the East, requiring much clandestine family negotiation through obscure channels and myriad brokers, carefully timed overtures and withdrawals, conjuring up of rival swains as a way of applying genteel pressure, and the final production of the blushing bride and her dowry.

Once the elaborately contrived invitation to Kissinger from Peking was received, Nixon and Kissinger plotted to keep this initial trip a secret not only from enemies like Russia but from rivals like the State Department. An elaborate cover was contrived for Kissinger, under which he would ostensibly tour Asian capitals but in fact would fly unobserved into China from friendly Pakistan. When the President finally broke the news to the Secretary of State—after Kissinger was well on his way—Nixon deceived Rogers, telling him that Kissinger's trip was in response to a last-minute invitation received while his aide was in Pakistan.

All this maneuvering hardly diminished Kissinger's excitement as he and three NSC colleagues flew from Islamabad to Peking early in July 1971. As Kissinger's plane crossed the snowcapped Himalayas, "thrusting toward the heavens in the roseate glow of a rising sun," and then flew for hours over arid deserts dotted by oases, he reflected that he was about to begin an extraordinary adventure that would make time stand still while he penetrated the mysteries of this almost unknown nation of 800 million people. Nor was he disappointed by the kaleidoscope of events: meeting the welcoming party in their Mao uniforms at a military airport on the outskirts of Peking—driving through wide, clean streets with little traffic save bicycles—settling down in guesthouses connected by tiny bridges around the former imperial fishing lake—driving to the Forbidden City, whose huge grounds had been closed off to the public—touring its superbly proportioned halls and gardens, stone carvings, and bronze lions—holding sessions in the Great Hall of the People, which struck Kissinger as a cross between Mussolini neoclassicism and communist baroque.

Most of all, Kissinger was impressed by the chief negotiator for the Chinese, Premier Chou En-lai. More than any leader save Mao, Chou incarnated the revolution. The product of a middle-class family in Kiangsu province, Chou in his twenties had studied in France and Germany. A veteran of the Long March, Premier of the People's Republic for over twenty years, he was a political survivor of the civil war, the war with Japan, the cold war, the Korean War, the Cultural Revolution, and the break with Moscow. Yet it was no embittered or fanatical zealot whom Kissinger faced but an urbane, knowledgeable statesman who appeared equally accomplished in history, philosophy, geopolitics, and humorous repartee.

The presidential aide found Chou a formidable adversary. And an informed one. Chou threw him off stride by quoting from a recent Nixon speech of which Kissinger knew nothing. Chou forcefully laid out Peking's position: that Taiwan was part of China; that China supported the North Vietnamese; that not only Russia and the United States but India and Japan were overly aggressive toward China; that China had no wish to be a superpower. Kissinger, compelled by the secrecy factor to work quickly and charged above all with producing an invitation to the President from Peking, made no serious effort to extract concessions from Chou or to offer any. He left Peking with the assurance of an invitation to Nixon. Three days later Chou flew to Hanoi to reassure the North Vietnamese that an American pullout from South Vietnam was China's main objective.

A euphoric Nixon preempted the networks to tell the world of Kissinger's just completed trip and his own forthcoming one. He reassured Russia that his search for "a new relationship with the People's Republic of China" was not directed against any other nation, and Taiwan that it would not "be at the expense of our old friends"—deceiving neither nation.

The White House began feverish preparations for the presidential visit. Kissinger was dispatched again to China to plan specific arrangements. Dismayed by the amount of publicity that the security aide was reaping from the China initiative, Nixon and Haldeman were determined that the presidential trip be bathed in television coverage. Network people received ample travel accommodations, at the expense of newspaper reporters. Long tormented far more by the print press than by the electronic, Nixon found the trip to China, Kissinger noted, "a great opportunity to get even." The Chinese fell in with the spirit of full television coverage, doubtless with more interest in its ratings in Moscow than in how it played in Washington.

His trip to China surpassed even Nixon's hopes. Air Force One arrived in Peking at 11:30 A.M. on February 21, 1972, which happened to be excellent television time—10:30 P.M.—in Washington and New York. Television cameras followed him as he and Mrs. Nixon descended the ramp and he extended his hand ostentatiously to the waiting Chou En-lai, while a Chinese band struck up "The Star-Spangled Banner." The handshake was symbolic—many years earlier, at the Geneva Conference on Indochina, John Foster Dulles, in one of his more boorish moments, had refused to shake hands with Chou. This injury, which the Chinese had never forgotten, Nixon now rectified. But he insisted on doing so alone; on the plane a burly aide blocked the aisle so that neither Kissinger nor anyone else could interrupt Nixon's solo performance before the cameras.

The drive into Peking was less successful from a public relations standpoint, since the Chinese masses appeared merely to be going about their business, unaware of the barbarians in their midst. But marvelous photograph opportunities opened up in the days following, as the presidential party toured the Forbidden City, the Ming Tombs, the Summer Palace, watched table tennis and gymnastics in the Sports Palace, attended a revolutionary ballet, and made the obligatory tour of the Great Wall, where Nixon proclaimed to the waiting press, "This is a great wall."

The President was elated early in the meetings when Chou sent word that Mao Tse-tung would see him. Taking Kissinger with him but not Rogers, who was excluded from the most important meetings, the President and his aide were driven to the Imperial City and ushered into a modest house. There they found Mao sitting in a medium-sized, book-lined study. Though ailing and infirm, the Chairman could not have been more affable. He joked to Nixon that "our common old friend," Chiang, did not approve of this meeting. To the President's suggestion that his writings had "changed the world," Mao replied modestly that he had been able to change only "a few places in the vicinity of Peking." He implied that he preferred to deal with predictable conservatives rather than wobbling liberals, and even added smilingly that "I voted for you during your last election." He skirted policy issues, preferring to discuss questions of "philosophy" and leaving specifics to his Premier. But it was clear that he looked on the Russians, not the Americans, as the real adversary.

Nixon was as willing to delegate the hard, hour-to-hour bargaining to Kissinger as Mao was to turn it over to Chou. The negotiators did not face momentous strategic decisions. The harsh facts of Soviet intimidation, Chinese and American commitments in Indochina, Chinese-American conflict over Taiwan, had already determined strategy. The problem rather was to reduce a complex balance of power to a formula that could be presented as a joint statement by Peking and Washington without unduly straining the alliances of either with third parties. The Americans were playing a three-dimensional game that required skill and patience. If they leaned too far toward Moscow, China might try to repair its old friendship with the Soviet Union; if too far toward Peking, the Russians might even try, Kissinger feared, a "preemptive attack on China." Vietnam and Taiwan had to fit into this broader framework.

The Shanghai Communiqué, issued at the end of the trip, spoke of the belief in freedom the two nations shared—the Americans in "individual freedom," the Chinese in "freedom and liberation." But then, using a formula worked out in earlier meetings, the communiqué listed the differences between the two countries. Taiwan was still the main issue. The Chinese reiterated that the island was wholly their internal affair. The Americans adroitly acknowledged and agreed "that all Chinese on either side of the Taiwan Strait maintain there is but one China and that Taiwan is a part of China." Hoping for a peaceful settlement of the question by the Chinese themselves, the United States "affirms the ultimate objective of the withdrawal of all U.S. forces and military installations from Taiwan. In the meantime, it will progressively reduce its forces and military installations on Taiwan as the tension in the area diminishes."

The presidential party flew back to Washington and a hero's welcome. Senators and congressmen from both parties, headed by Vice President Agnew, greeted Nixon at Andrews Air Force base and voiced strong support the next day at a conference. The Republican right did not seem unduly disturbed. Governor Ronald Reagan of California joked that the China initiative had been a wonderful television "pilot" and should be made into a series. A few newspapers wondered whether the future of Taiwan had been bartered away in exchange for a presidential visit, a dramatic initiative, and breaking the taboo of noncommunication between East and West. But in general the press was not critical. Indeed, when a reporter in Shanghai pressed Kissinger about the American commitment to Taiwan, Kissinger had said that he would "appreciate it" if the press would stop asking about it "in these circumstances," and the reporters desisted.

The voyagers were not modest about their success, or about its historic importance. It had been "the week that changed the world," as the President put it in a farewell banquet toast in China. Nixon's mere announcement of his forthcoming trip to Peking had "transformed the structure of international politics" overnight, Kissinger maintained years later. Certainly they had much to brag about. They had penetrated and demystified the inscrutable Orient, put Moscow on the defensive, and expanded trade and "people-to-people exchanges." They displayed extraordinary skill and patience not only in negotiating with their erstwhile enemies in Peking but in fending off their adversaries in State and Defense, in Congress, in the old China Lobby. Moreover, they had been blessed with that priceless gift for diplomats negotiating on a confused and darkling plain—luck. China's leadership had been undergoing a massive internal convulsion that still had not ended when Kissinger first arrived. Washington's political intelligence on China was so poor that the voyagers knew little of the intensity of the conflict between the anti-Soviet, moderate faction represented by Chou and the hard-line "anti-imperialists" led by Lin Piao and supported by the military. This left them in blissful ignorance of a conflict whose merest spasm could have upset all their plans.

Still, the test of their success lay in Moscow as well as in Peking. They were above all playing triangular diplomacy. Soon after returning the summiteers redoubled planning for another historic meeting.

*   *   *

At the end of March 1972, only four weeks after the return of the exuberant voyagers from China, three divisions of North Vietnamese infantry, backed by two hundred tanks and new recoilless artillery, smashed south across the Demilitarized Zone. There ensued one of the most bizarre series of events in the Vietnam War. While General Creighton Abrams's forces to the south had long anticipated such an attack, they took days to discern just what was happening. Although the United States had long been pulling out its troops by the thousands, Hanoi converted the attack into a major offensive after the breakthrough. Although strategic air and sea power could have little immediate impact on a land offensive, Nixon resumed intensive bombing of Haiphong and Hanoi—the first since 1968—and mined Haiphong harbor and other North Vietnamese ports. Although the White House at this point was desperately eager for a Moscow summit, mainly in order to persuade Moscow to persuade Hanoi to accept a settlement, American aircraft sought to interdict Soviet ships bringing military supplies to Hanoi, which risked provoking a major incident. Although such an event did occur when American bombs hit four Soviet merchant ships in Haiphong harbor, the Kremlin merely protested and continued with plans to welcome the Americans in Moscow.

All these incongruities could be explained by one circumstance—the desire of two nuclear superpowers to parley within the triangle of great-power rivalry, giving only secondary consideration to tertiary powers. But the incongruities challenged the popular shibboleth that Moscow or Peking headed up a massive, global, coordinated communist movement. For neither government had decisive influence over a North Vietnamese leadership that gloried in its own autonomy.

Washington's rapprochement with Moscow took much the same form as the opening to Peking. Once again the President dispatched Kissinger to "advance" the trip. Once again he sidetracked his Secretary of State—this time by repairing to Camp David, ostensibly with Kissinger, and then informing Rogers that his security aide had flown to Moscow on receiving a sudden invitation from Brezhnev. And once again the President blew hot and cold about the prospective summit. He was eager to be the first President since FDR to visit the U.S.S.R., the very first to go to Moscow—a trip that Ike had missed after the U-2 debacle. But he feared a debacle of his own making, if Moscow saw the parley as a means of strengthening its hand in Vietnam and weakening the American, or if on the other hand the Kremlin suddenly called off the whole summit. For Moscow was becoming huffy. When Kissinger invited Soviet ambassador Anatoly Dobrynin, with whom he had a close working relationship, to view Chinese-made films of Kissinger's Peking visits, this interlude of triangular diplomacy with a vengeance ended in a sharp exchange between the two over the American buildup in Southeast Asia.

But the Kremlin did not call off the summit, nor did the White House. The Soviet Union wanted to throw its weight against Chinese influence, to hold tight its corner of the triangle, to persuade Washington to put its full effort behind West German ratification of postwar treaties with Russia and Poland, to discuss arms control, to make deals for grain and other Soviet needs. Nixon's aims were simpler but no less compelling: to persuade Moscow to press Hanoi for an acceptable settlement; to emerge from a second summit as the supreme peacemaker; above all to dish the Democrats on the peace issue and win big in November.

Late in May 1972, Air Force One, bearing the President and Mrs. Nixon and the usual big presidential party, soared off into the skies over Washington, this time heading east. The mood, in Kissinger's memory, was optimistic, even jubilant, unspoiled by undue humility. "This has to be one of the great diplomatic coups of all times!" the President recalled Kissinger saying. "Three weeks ago everyone predicted it would be called off, and today we're on our way."

President Nikolai Podgorny, Premier Aleksei Kosygin, Foreign Minister Andrei Gromyko, and a conspicuously small crowd greeted the Americans at Moscow's Vnukovo Airport. As party boss, Brezhnev was not required to be there and chose not to be. The presidential motorcade raced to the Kremlin through emptied streets. Soon the Nixons were installed in opulent quarters inside the Kremlin's Grand Palace, and shortly after that the President was closeted with Brezhnev.

He faced a large, active man with heavy swept-back hair over bushy eyebrows and powerful features. Brezhnev's rapidly alternating friendliness and pugnacity reminded the President of Irish labor bosses back home, or even Chicago's Mayor Daley. Wasting little time on formalities, the General Secretary launched into vigorous complaints about Vietnam. This over, he became almost convivial as he proposed a close personal relationship between them and spoke of the memory of Franklin Roosevelt cherished by the Soviet people, and he warmed up even more when Nixon said that in his experience disputes among subordinates were usually overcome by agreement among the top leaders.

"If we leave all the decisions to the bureaucrats," Nixon ventured, "we will never achieve any progress." Brezhnev laughed heartily at this common complaint of leaders. Kissinger was not present at this initial meeting.

"They would simply bury us in paper!" the General Secretary said, slapping his hand on the table.

The parley that followed underwent the zigs and zags, the starts and stops, that had always characterized Soviet-American negotiations. The crucial business was nuclear arms negotiations. Kissinger conducted the hard bargaining. He and the President had kept control of the American side by excluding from a direct role in the summit talks not only Rogers but the SALT experts in Helsinki, who had been negotiating on arms for many months. Hour after hour, jotting down on yellow pads endless combinations and permutations of arms calculations, Kissinger hammered out compromises with his Kremlin counterparts, under the watchful eye of the President. And this was the greatest incongruity: here inside the Kremlin, the historic citadel of Russian authority, ringed by military might in and around the capital, in a nation bristling with nuclear arms, this magically transported White House, with its President and aides, secretaries and secretaries to secretaries, communications and transportation experts, security men and chauffeurs, was closeted with the Soviet power elite commanding those nuclear arms from a cluster of ancient buildings around them.

Communication was easy with the help of a gifted Soviet interpreter, but the language was arcane: throw weights and first strikes, hard targets and soft, silos and delivery vehicles, ABMs (antiballistic missiles), ICBMs (intercontinental ballistic missiles), and MIRVs (multiple independent reentry vehicles). These bland and bureaucratic terms, as Bernard Weisberger noted, "hid the appalling realities of the subject and made seemingly rational discussion possible." The two nuclear powers had continued to operate on the premise that their goal was not to win a nuclear exchange but to forestall one by making clear that if one side launched a first strike, the other would, with its surviving weapons, inflict an unbearable counterstrike. Thus neither side could hope for victory. But each side had to guard against the possibility that reckless leaders in the other camp might nevertheless be tempted to take out its weapons or to encase theirs in hardened silos and other devices, or to turn science fiction into reality by developing technology that could destroy or turn away incoming missiles. Thousands and thousands of nuclear weapons had been piled up in each nation to guard against the unthinkable—a situation in which one's own side had no nuclear weapons left and the other had at least one.

The key outcome of the Moscow summit was a strategic arms limitation treaty limiting the deployment of antiballistic missile systems to two for each country—one to protect the capital and one to protect an ICBM complex—and an "Interim Agreement" freezing for the next five years the number of ICBMs and submarine-launched missiles each side could possess. There were collateral agreements and understandings: a grain deal for the Soviets, who were facing a potentially catastrophic crop failure, implicit promises by Moscow that it would not intervene in Vietnam against the United States, and a set of "Basic Principles" piously promising that each nation would try to avoid military confrontations, would respect the norm of equality, would not seek unilateral advantage at the expense of the other, all this in the spirit of "reciprocity, mutual accommodation and mutual benefit."

In its detail, it was a small step. The Interim Agreement called for no reduction in offensive weapons systems, but simply established a cap on the number of missile launchers each country could build until a permanent agreement could be negotiated. No constraint was placed on the number of independently targeted warheads that could be placed on each missile. But symbolically it was a big step. After years of frustration the nuclear powers had proved that they could negotiate limits on offensive weaponry. "A First Step," *The New York Times* headlined, "but a Major

Stride." Once again the presidential party returned to a hero's welcome, with SALT treaty ratification assured—the ABM agreement was soon ratified by an 88–2 vote—and the President's reelection prospects further enhanced. Soon the White House promotion team was dramatizing his personal triumph in Moscow.

PEACE WITHOUT PEACE

On the evening of November 7, 1972, Richard M. Nixon stood at the pinnacle of world prestige and domestic power. Even the scattered first returns showed that he was winning a sweeping victory over George McGovern. With Eisenhower, he was only the second Republican in the century to win two presidential elections. Both his mixed batch of liberal-conservative domestic policies and his bomb-and-pull-out Vietnam tactics appeared to be handsomely vindicated in the election returns. He was concluding a year of achievement—the summits in Peking and Moscow, the SALT agreement, the apparent winding down of American involvement in Indochina. Only a week or so earlier Henry Kissinger had told the press, "We believe that peace is at hand."

But the President did not appear triumphant, or even happy, that night. He had a spell of melancholy, perhaps foreboding. Was it due to some revelations about campaign excesses that had come to light, and the possibility of far more serious disclosures? Or his failure to carry in a Republican Congress? Or the empty feeling that this would be his last campaign, that the conflict and crisis on which he thrived appeared to be over? Or merely the pain of having the cap on a top front tooth snap off while he was listening to the early returns? The next morning, looking cold and remote, he strode into a specially summoned meeting of the White House staff, thanked them perfunctorily, and turned the meeting over to Haldeman, who without ado ordered all staff members to submit their resignations immediately.

The most likely explanation for Nixon's malaise was Vietnam. Following North Vietnam's massive "Eastertide" attack across the DMZ in March and Washington's retaliatory bombing and blockade, Hanoi had continued its heavy offensive for weeks. The President had sporadically taken personal command of the air war, chafing when the weather was poor. "Let's get that weather cleared up," he exclaimed to Haldeman and John Mitchell one afternoon in April. "The bastards have never been bombed like they're going to be bombed this time." It wasn't just the weather. "The Air Force isn't worth a—I mean, they won't fly." In May the bombing reached its highest level of the war; the next month American planes dropped over 100,000 tons of bombs on North Vietnam. Even so the war was grinding down to a stalemate again. Thieu remained in power; the South Vietnamese Army was still largely intact; Hanoi had lost 100,000 men in the attack, perhaps four times Saigon's losses. On the other hand, tens of thousands of North Vietnamese troops were now ensconced in defensive positions well below the DMZ.

It was this last fact that now produced the single most crucial development in the latter stages of the Vietnam War—a development so carefully concealed from the American public, so muffled in diplomatic bargaining, so obscured in double-talk, that its full nature and import would not be clear for years. This was the signaling by Nixon and Kissinger to Hanoi through Moscow and other channels that the American troop withdrawal would continue even though Hanoi's troops stayed in place in South Vietnam, that Washington would not exact a troop withdrawal from Hanoi to match its own steady pullout of the ground forces that for years had been the principal support of the Saigon regime. This signal was wrapped in a shroud of self-protective premises and claims: that the South Vietnamese Army was now fortified enough by American arms and training to hold its own, that the North Vietnamese forces would wither away in the south as a result of their isolation from their bases across the DMZ, that the Americans could always return with heavy bombing and even with troops if Hanoi conducted further attacks.

The most remarkable aspect of Washington's yielding to Hanoi was that Nixon and Kissinger did not deceive themselves—they knew exactly what they were doing. They were at the very least taking an enormous gamble with the future of South Vietnam as an independent nation, at the worst laying the groundwork for a peace bound to collapse—a peace without honor. For few American leaders had warned more often than Nixon that communism was innately aggressive, that Hanoi was insatiably expansionist, that the communist enemy could be stopped only by counterforce, that to yield militarily to communists was to encourage them, not to desist, but to grab more. Kissinger could hardly have been unaware of the teachings of Vietnam's foremost military strategist, Vo Nguyen Giap—that revolutionary forces must know how to be patient but also when to strike. Indeed, Giap had called only a few months earlier for heavy attacks by combined regular and guerrilla forces.

One man who understood the situation with crystal clarity was President Nguyen Van Thieu in Saigon. When Nixon sent Kissinger's deputy Alexander Haig to Saigon early in October to urge the South Vietnam regime to go along with negotiations with Hanoi, Thieu had argued, protested, stormed, and finally broken into tears. The President's reaction to Haig's report of this episode, as reflected in Nixon's memoirs years later, revealed once again the disingenuous cynicism of his attitude toward what the South Vietnamese later would call Nixon's sellout.

"I sympathized with Thieu's position," the President wrote. "Almost the entire North Vietnamese Army—an estimated 120,000 troops that had poured across the DMZ during the spring invasion—were still in South Vietnam, and he was naturally skeptical of any plan that would lead to an American withdrawal without requiring a corresponding North Vietnamese withdrawal. I shared his view that the Communists' motives were entirely cynical. I knew, as he did, that they would observe the agreement only so long and so far as South Vietnam's strength and America's readiness to retaliate forced them to do so. But I felt that if we could negotiate an agreement on our terms, those conditions could be met." He sent Thieu a personal reassurance that he would agree to nothing without talking "personally with you well beforehand." Thieu did not want talk— he wanted a guarantee that his ally would not keep withdrawing its troops while his enemy's troops stayed in place.

Throughout the late summer and early fall of 1972, as the President became increasingly involved in campaign chores, Kissinger had been meeting secretly in Paris in a desperate effort to work out an agreement with Hanoi's negotiator, the redoubtable Le Duc Tho. Although eager to stop the bombing and to get on with their war with the Saigon regime now that their troops were in place, the North Vietnamese were in no great hurry; their intent now was to win the war with as few losses as possible. Kissinger, however, was under heavy time pressures: he wanted to demonstrate progress in the negotiations to help his chief ward off McGovern's expected peace offensive, to soften public demands that the remaining American troops continue to be pulled out on schedule, and above all to reach an agreement with both Hanoi and Saigon before Congress convened in January and began to slash appropriations for the war in Vietnam. The negotiators spent hundreds of hours on the fine-print questions involving a cease-fire, the return by Hanoi of American prisoners of war, the timing of the withdrawal of the remaining American forces—by August 1972 the last United States ground combat troops had been withdrawn— following the cease-fire, and some kind of tripartite commission that would supervise elections and otherwise help implement the agreement.

There was an Alice-in-Wonderland quality to these discussions: most of the key provisions of the draft agreement, aside from the return of POWs, would be made irrelevant by the transcending legitimation of Hanoi's presence in force south of the DMZ. And elaborate plans for electoral commissions and the like were preposterous given the deadly hatred that

was bound to remain between North and South Vietnamese and the repeated failures of communists and noncommunists in other lands to agree
on electoral arrangements, or even on what an election meant.

In mid-October, as the election campaign back home pounded to the
finish, Kissinger wrapped up the final details of an elaborate agreement
with Le Duc Tho. Tired but euphoric, he flew back to Washington with
what he viewed as "the finest compromise available." He basked in the
thought that McGovern had just put forward a peace program that "asked
much less of Hanoi than Hanoi had already conceded to us." When he and
Haig reported to Nixon in the President's "hideaway" suite across from the
White House in the old-time State Department building, Nixon was so
pleased that he ordered steak and wine to celebrate the breakthrough.

The last crucial step lay ahead—pressing Saigon into a settlement without risk of "sellout" accusations before election day. Reviewing the terms
as he flew to Saigon, Kissinger felt optimistic. The proposed cease-fire in
place would leave Thieu's government in control of 90 percent of the
population, Kissinger calculated, and the other provisions were beneficial.
To be sure, he had not gained Hanoi's agreement to withdraw its forces
from the south, but he comforted himself with the thought that if a clause
forbidding infiltration was honored, attrition would ease the threat to
Saigon.

Arriving in Saigon in this mood on October 19, Kissinger confidently
explained the details of the agreement to Thieu and his entourage. He was
unprepared for Thieu's response—total skepticism about the agreement,
total consternation at the prospect of being deserted by his American ally.
Kissinger argued, promised, threatened. All in vain. After five days of
fruitless exchanges he urged Nixon to bypass Saigon and sign with Hanoi.
This the President would not do. With election day just ahead, he did not
want to rouse Republican hawks or in any way jeopardize his expected
victory; moreover, he had misgivings about "losing" South Vietnam.
While furious with Thieu's intransigence, he decided that the only hope
now was for Kissinger to renegotiate better terms with Le Duc Tho.

Returning to Paris two weeks after the November election, Kissinger
found himself in a vise between North Vietnam scenting victory and South
Vietnam fighting for its existence. Hanoi, after making "maximum"
concessions in October, was hardly disposed to reopen the agreement in
any event and was given little incentive to do so. Kissinger's secret discussions with Le Duc Tho made little progress, as Tho responded to new
American demands in kind, by heightening his own demands, retracting
concessions, stalling. The White House, meanwhile, pursued carrot-and-
stick tactics with Saigon, sending more military hardware to South Viet-

nam—in the process making the little country the fourth-largest air power in the world—and assuring Thieu that if Hanoi violated the agreement the United States would immediately retaliate, while threatening to make peace without him if he refused to go along. At the same time only a stick was waved at Hanoi—another massive dose of bombing—if it did not make further concessions.

It was not an edifying moment in the White House. Kissinger, pursuing the negotiations in the now frigid atmosphere of Paris, found Nixon mercurial in mood and tactics, alternately bellicose and conciliatory, often withdrawn and sullen, fundamentally ambivalent in his posture toward the rival camps. Kissinger suspected that he was still fair game for White House rivals gunning for his seat—or at least maneuvering to oust him from it. Nixon for his part was concerned about Kissinger's emotional state—he was, Nixon noted in his diary in mid-December, "up and down"—under the pressures besetting him, especially after his aide hinted at resigning.

By early December, with the Paris talks deadlocked and Saigon still adamant, Nixon was moving toward a massive "retaliation" strike against North Vietnam. On December 13, the negotiations broke off and Kissinger returned to Washington disillusioned, exhausted, and angry. Gritting his teeth and clenching his fists, as Nixon later remembered, he called Hanoi's negotiators "just a bunch of shits. Tawdry, filthy shits." They made the Russians look good, he went on, "compared to the way the Russians make the Chinese look good" when it came to decent negotiating. It was time, Kissinger said, to resume bombing.

Ready for his last roll of the dice, the President ordered bombing in the north as well as the south and the reseeding of mines in Haiphong harbor. Still dubious about the zeal of the Air Force, he told the head of the Joint Chiefs of Staff, an admiral, "I don't want any more of this crap about the fact that we couldn't hit this target or that one. This is your chance to use military power effectively to win the war, and if you don't, I'll consider you responsible."

While Americans were celebrating the long Christmas holiday at home, American bombers ranged over the populous corridor between Hanoi and Haiphong, dropping more than 36,000 tons of bombs in the most intensive attack of the war. While Americans paid tribute to the Prince of Peace, B-52s killed at least 1,600 civilians.

At home the press exploded in indignation. Caught unprepared as a result of the White House penchant for secrecy, filled with hope after Kissinger's comment two months before that peace was at hand, repeatedly assured that Nixon was winding down American involvement, the

public saw the horrendous scenario being enacted again. Nixon was denounced as a madman "waging war by tantrum." Republican senator
George Aiken spoke of this "sorry Christmas present" for the American
people. Newspapers blazoned headlines: "Terror from the Skies," "New
Madness in Vietnam," "Beyond All Reason," "The Rain of Death Continues." Pope Paul VI told a Vatican audience that the bombing of "blessed"
Vietnam was causing him daily grief.

The bombing ended when Hanoi agreed to return to the bargaining
table, but the agreement Kissinger and Tho patched together in Paris
differed little from the October draft. The bombing had not obtained the
concessions that Nixon and Kissinger needed to gain Saigon's consent to
an agreement. Nor had this fierce Christmastide demonstration of Washington's willingness to "retaliate" persuaded Thieu. But now Nixon simply
imposed the agreement on him, with yet another promise that if Saigon
went along, the United States would "respond with full force" to North
Vietnamese violations. After stalling for a few days Thieu admitted that at
last he had no choice, saying resignedly, "I have done all that I can for my
country." On January 27, 1973, the agreement was signed in Paris by the
United States and the two rivals—and also by the Vietcong's Provisional
Revolutionary Government, which occupied "leopard spots" in the south.

*   *   *

President Nixon had hoped that the nation would be at peace in Southeast Asia when he began his second term, on January 20. But Thieu's
stalling tactics allowed him to talk only about the settlement soon to come.
Still, he could take satisfaction in the triumphs of his foreign policy and
look to the future. "We have the chance today," he told the inaugural
crowd, "to do more than ever before in our history to make life better in
America—to ensure better education, better health, better housing, better
transportation, a cleaner environment—to restore respect for law, to make
our communities more livable—and to ensure the God-given right of every
American to full and equal opportunity."

Even in this hour of triumph he could not ignore the pinpricks. He had
heard that some members of Eugene Ormandy's orchestra had asked to
be excused from performing in the inaugural concert at the Kennedy
Center and had to be ordered to come, but he was pleased that Ormandy
had wanted him to appear on the platform "just to show those left-wing
sons of bitches." He noted in his diary, "What a man he is." Then, on his
ride to the Capitol, demonstrators yelled "f-u-c-k" in the distance, and on
the way back the dissidents threw eggs at his cavalcade. The inaugural balls
went off well but they were so huge and packed he wondered whether his

would be the last of such affairs. Still he felt that he and his wife, Pat, had mixed well with the crowds, which was important because, he wrote in his diary, he needed to demonstrate his "affability." The White House staff just hadn't been able to get this across. "On the other hand, you can't overplay it."

With Vietnam evidently settled, he looked forward to more successes overseas. Planning was already underway for the next summit—a visit by Brezhnev to the United States. The President eagerly anticipated showing America to the Soviet leader—showing not only the White House and the monuments in Washington but, even more, southern California with its splendid freeways and homes. Once again Kissinger journeyed to Moscow to plan what would become known as Summit II. His "advancing" went well, aside from an ominous moment alone with Brezhnev in the General Secretary's hunting stand ninety miles northeast of Moscow, when Brezhnev suddenly started in on China. His brother had worked there, he said, and had found the Chinese treacherous and arrogant. Now China was building a nuclear arsenal—something would have to be done. To this rather crude gambit Kissinger was noncommittal. The next day Ambassador Dobrynin took Kissinger aside to confirm that Brezhnev had been wholly serious in his comments on China.

In style, Brezhnev's June visit surpassed Nixon's fondest hopes. The party boss was all exuberance and joviality in Washington and at Camp David as he worked the crowd on ceremonial occasions and enthusiastically accepted Nixon's gift of a Lincoln Continental donated by the Ford Motor Company. After a trip across the country with the President in Air Force One he appeared to be gratifyingly impressed, during a short helicopter ride to San Clemente, by the streams of cars on the roads below and the number of private houses. Some of the beachfront houses were owned by wealthy people, Nixon explained, but most of the others belonged to people who worked in factories and offices. Insisting on staying at San Clemente rather than on a nearby Marine base, the burly Russian agreeably settled in amidst the very feminine decor of Tricia Nixon's bedroom.

In substance Summit II could not match the pathbreaking achievements of the Moscow summit thirteen months earlier. The key product—mostly symbolic but a measure of some détente progress over the past year or two—was a joint "Agreement on the Prevention of Nuclear War." The agreement provided that the two powers would "act in such a manner as to prevent the development of situations capable of causing a dangerous exacerbation of their relations, as to avoid military confrontations, and as to exclude the outbreak of nuclear war between them and between either of the Parties and other countries"; that each would "refrain from the threat or use of force against the other Party, against the allies of the other Party and against other countries"; that if relations between them and other countries, or among other countries, appeared to involve the risk of nuclear war, the two parties would "immediately enter into urgent consultations with each other and make every effort to avert this risk."

It was a noble declaration—but how seriously made? Nixon suspected that Brezhnev wanted it out of fear that Washington might soon conclude a military agreement with China. Kissinger described it at the time as a "landmark" step toward the prevention of nuclear war, but his memoirs present it as a "bland set of principles that had been systematically stripped of all implications harmful to our interests." From their long agitation for its drafting and their public celebration of it, the Soviets appeared to take the declaration far more seriously. Both sides knew, however, that the success of the agreement depended on a "real life" test, which would depend in turn on each side's ability to see the agreement as a constraint upon its own options and not merely the other side's. And a test of all this came with alarming swiftness in that cockpit of violence, the Middle East.

A curious episode in San Clemente had foreshadowed it. After a convivial dinner filled with warm toasts and Brezhnev bear hugs, the Soviet leader retired early because of jet lag. The President was in his pajamas later in the evening when a Secret Service agent knocked on the door. It was a message from Kissinger: the Russians wanted to talk, immediately—Kissinger did not know why. Shortly Nixon and Kissinger were confronting Brezhnev, Gromyko, and Dobrynin in a stiff and emotional exchange over a Soviet proposal that the two nations agree then and there on a Middle East settlement calling for an Israeli withdrawal to the 1967 borders in return for an end to the state of belligerency. These were the standard Arab terms. Nixon replied coolly that he could not prejudice Israel's rights. Brezhnev warned in effect that if the two sides could not agree on this, war would break out again in the Middle East.

This summit confrontation occurred, Kissinger was to complain later, only a day after the signing of the agreement on the prevention of nuclear war. But he should not have been surprised by Brezhnev's thrust, however untimely, for the subject had come up in Kissinger's advance meeting in the Soviet Union, and indeed the Middle East had been a source of Soviet-American tension since the Six-Day War in 1967. That war, during which the U.S. Sixth Fleet had been put on alert and two aircraft carriers moved east from Crete, had left the Israelis victoriously occupying Syria's Golan Heights, Egypt's Sinai Peninsula and Gaza Strip, and Jordan's territory adjoining Israel west of the Jordan River. Ever since, Moscow and Washington had been pouring arms into the seething region, while the Arab nations sought some means of regaining the lands they had lost.

Early in October 1973, less than four months after Summit II, Egyptian and Syrian troops drove into the Sinai and the Golan Heights while Israel's guard was down during Yom Kippur. In the course of two weeks of fierce combat, as Israeli forces were pushed back but then gained the offensive, Moscow and Washington alternated in urging a cease-fire in place, depending on whose ally held the upper hand. Finally achieved, it collapsed when Israel, taking advantage of some earlier veiled encouragement by Kissinger and of a real or alleged violation of the truce by Egypt, completed its isolation of the Egyptian Third Army on the east side of the Suez Canal. Both Moscow and Cairo importuned Washington to force Israel to stop its advance. Brezhnev proposed a joint Soviet-American effort to restore the cease-fire, adding that failing joint action, Moscow would "be faced with the necessity urgently to consider the question of taking appropriate steps unilaterally." The word "unilaterally" leaped out of the message. This Washington would not tolerate.

There followed what Elizabeth Drew later called "Strangelove Day." Kissinger did not inform Nixon of Brezhnev's message, but rather convened an enlarged National Security Council meeting, which decided to issue a general military alert. The Strategic Air Command and other nuclear forces were alerted, along with field commands in Europe. Carriers moved toward the eastern Mediterranean. The next day the alert was claxoned on morning television news shows and blared in newspaper headlines. A message to Brezhnev warned that Washington would "in no event" accept unilateral action. A crisis reminiscent of the Cuban missile confrontation seemed in the making until the White House took one simple step that deflated the situation—it persuaded Israel to accept a cease-fire.

Washington was intent on diminishing Moscow's influence in the Middle East. Even a joint Russian-American peace effort, the White House feared, would advance Soviet interests there. According to Raymond Garthoff's careful analysis of the crisis, Kissinger also sought to demonstrate an American capacity to face down Moscow. The "Soviets subsided," Kissinger wrote later, "as soon as we showed our teeth." Four months after the lofty declarations of Summit II and after aggressive gestures by both Moscow and Washington, the Bear and the Eagle were once again following the law of the jungle.

* * *

By 1973 summitry was taking on a life of its own. Just as Summit II had little effect on the Middle East crisis, so the summits in general appeared to proceed on their own lofty plane, with only glancing impact on the *Realpolitik* of international rivalry. Thus Summit I had taken place notwithstanding North Vietnam's onslaught through the DMZ and the massive American bombing, and despite Hanoi's indignation at its perfidious ally. Day after day at the summits men solemnly discussed arms reduction deals without exerting any significant influence in the end on the ability of each nation to obliterate the other many times over. The Russians tried at the summits to turn the Americans against the Chinese without avail, for the Americans were having their own summits with the Chinese. Suspecting that mighty decisions were afoot, NATO and other allies were restive over summitry "plots," but they had little to fear. Washington would not forsake its crucial Western alliances for any deals at the summit. Indeed, the White House planned some kind of "Year of Europe" in 1973, but this initiative collapsed.

Though summitry went on—a third Soviet-American meeting was planned for June 1974 in Moscow—it was approaching a dead end. In part this was a result of a resurgence of hawks among both Democrats and Republicans who, sensing the President's vulnerabilities and incensed by what they saw as dangerous concessions at the summits, launched counterattacks against the whole strategy of détente. By Summit III press and public feeling appeared to be turning against summitry for several reasons: the dashed expectations following earlier meetings, especially Summit II; rising American resentment over Soviet mistreatment of Jews; Moscow's "meddling" in the Middle East, climaxed by its aid to Israel's foes. The Soviets had their own set of grievances, particularly the failure of Congress to grant them equal tariff treatment or to make large credits available. Doubts about détente were growing in the Kremlin. Inevitably Nixon's last summit in 1974, just before his fall (discussed in the next chapter) produced only limited agreements.

Gerald R. Ford, appointed to the vice-presidency by Nixon after Spiro Agnew's resignation and ascending to the presidency after Nixon's own resignation, made a valiant effort to restore the spirit of détente at his first summit, in Vladivostok in late November 1974. With the aging Brezhnev he reached agreement limiting each superpower to 2,400 strategic weapon systems, which could comprise a combination of heavy bombers, intercontinental ballistic missiles, submarine-launched ballistic missiles, and air-launched ballistic missiles. Eight months later Ford and leaders of the Soviet Union and thirty-three other nations signed in Helsinki a pathbreaking set of agreements designed to protect human rights and permit freer travel by each nation's citizens. But relations with Moscow were cooling as anti-Soviet feeling intensified at home, exacerbated by the Kremlin's expulsions of dissidents, most notably of the writer Aleksandr I. Solzhenitsyn. Ford's Secretary of Defense, James R. Schlesinger, became such an open critic of détente that the President fired him, leaving Schlesinger more pestiferous than ever outside the tent.

The harrowing collapse of South Vietnam in the spring of 1975 transcended all these events. Hanoi's drive to victory unrolled slowly but implacably against a foe that was gradually disintegrating under an appalling burden of political corruption, economic chaos, and military incompetence and demoralization. For two years the North Vietnamese built up their troop strength and logistical support in the south, including even an oil pipeline from the north. Then they struck with overwhelming speed and power. American radio and television brought the denouement home: the triumphant march of Hanoi's forces toward Saigon—the spreading panic in the capital—scores of American helicopters like great vultures rising and descending over the city—thousands of Vietnamese surging to the takeoff points, crying out to be saved—a marine clubbing them as they sought frantically to board the helicopters—the men and women and children left behind, now frantically seeking escape routes to the ocean and soon to risk their lives in small boats on the high seas.

One American would long be haunted by his own special memory—of an aged farmer who somehow made his way onto an evacuation plane still pulling his bullock on a rope. Soon after takeoff the terrified animal, rampaging on the aircraft, forced his way through a half-open exit, dragging his master with him. Moments later the American saw the farmer still holding the rope tied to his bullock as they both floated in space, then plunged to the red earth below.

FOREIGN POLICY: THE FALTERING EXPERIMENTS

While the Vietnam War was heading toward its *Götterdämmerung,* Americans were readying to celebrate the two hundredth anniversary of the era when their revolutionary ancestors conducted the long struggle for freedom from Britain. The fireworks, the patriotic speeches, the costumed parades, were a buoyant reminder of the Declaration that had freed the colonies to shape their own destiny as an independent nation. The lofty brigantines, frigates, and other men-of-war, stretching along the Hudson River with their ballooning sails and bright pennants, commemorated the beginning of an era when the small country with limited arms but consummate diplomacy held off the British and French and Spanish and secured a new republic.

In the two centuries since those days Americans had in effect conducted a series of experiments in foreign and military policy. In the endless *bouleversement* of international affairs the young nation almost went to war against its old French ally, fought a second war against Britain that ended ingloriously, ousted or exterminated Indians, conducted a risky invasion into Mexico's heartland, and then settled down to a long peace interrupted only by its own civil holocaust in the early 1860s. A period of internal expansion and warfare against Native Americans was punctuated by chauvinistic outbursts against Cubans and Canadians and Mexicans following some real or contrived incident. During the last third of the nineteenth century Americans established their Pacific dominion—Alaska, Hawaii, the Philippines, numerous islets—and intervened in Latin America during the 1890s to protect their commercial and political interests. It was said that the British built their empire in a fit of absentmindedness; this was almost as true of the Yankees.

During these years Washington alternated between spasms of expansionist activity and longer periods of absorption in domestic problems; then the first years of the twentieth century inexorably drew the nation into global demands and crises. Theodore Roosevelt, sword in one hand and dove in the other, could no more resist international challenges and enticements than he could domestic. Woodrow Wilson moved from "too proud to fight" to making the world "safe for Democracy" almost in a twinkling of the eye. Three Republican Presidents in the 1920s experimented with repudiation of the League of Nations, deep reductions in arms, intervention in Central America, and tariff boosting.

If American foreign policy making had appeared kaleidoscopic during the first third of the twentieth century, after 1932 it flashed across the public scene like images from a stepped-up movie projector. In a period of eight years FDR moved from policies of economic nationalism to semi-isolationism, to neutrality, to aid to the democracies, to all aid short of war, to military intervention in the North Atlantic. Eager at first to reduce American commitments abroad, Harry Truman was drawn into the intensifying cold war, into crises in Berlin, Greece, the Middle East, and Korea, ultimately almost into a war with China. Hoping to bring some order and stability to foreign relations, Eisenhower ran into a dangerous conflict over the Suez Canal, a desperate revolt in Hungary, crises in the Formosa Strait and Berlin, and a loss of credibility in the U-2 incident. Caught between clashing personal instincts toward détente and deterrence, and pulled politically between hawks and doves among Democrats and among the voters, Kennedy first stood by containment in Berlin and Cuba and then moved toward détente. Pledged to pursue peace in his 1964 contest with the bellicose Goldwater, LBJ sank steadily into the Vietnam quicksand even as he strove desperately for an "honorable" way out. Famous and infamous as a communist-fighter, Nixon opened relations with the communist power that a generation earlier had sent American troops reeling back toward the 38th parallel.

That Washington's foreign policy making was unstable, unpredictable, and volatile had long been a source of perplexity to allies and of suspicion to adversaries. British envoys would report back to London that they had enjoyed their stay in the American capital but could not find the government. Sophisticated Britons in Washington learned to maintain close contacts with Congress, the opposition party, and the media as they sought to divine the next actions of Presidents and Secretaries of State. Soviet Foreign Ministers and ambassadors were not so tolerant. Trying to make sense of the Washington kaleidoscope, they saw not merely inconstancy but duplicity and worse. If, as Andrei Gromyko complained, "a new leadership arrives and crosses out all that has been achieved before," the reason must be, in the eyes of *Pravda,* the machinations of militaristic and capitalistic forces within the "ruling circles of the United States."

Pravda was succumbing to paranoia. In fact, the direct source of the instability of American foreign policy lay far more in complexity and clutter than in conspiracy—in popular attitudes, party fragmentation, and governmental separation of powers. Students of public opinion had long noted that attitudes toward foreign policy among Americans lacked factual substance and intellectual depth, were not anchored to a "set of explicit value and means calculations," and took the form of shifting moods. Instead of a two-party system arraying popular attitudes behind a governing party and an opposition, the country had had a four-party politics that reflected and perpetuated the diversity and volatility of opinion, leading to "nonpartisan" policies responsive to everybody and nobody. The constitutional provision requiring two-thirds of the Senate to approve treaties, the congressional distribution of foreign policy making among a host of Senate and House committees, the wide breaches between White House and Capitol Hill were neither confusion nor conspiracy but rather applications of the checks and balances planned with exquisite artistry by the framers of the Constitution.

Even so, was a foreign policy of spasm and swerve inevitable? Did "underlying circumstances" doom the United States forever to short-run, ad hoc, volatile policy making in international affairs? Were tiny faltering steps, confusing and contradictory policies, vacillating half measures inevitable? A young Harvard scholar thought not. The past decade and a half, he wrote as Eisenhower's presidency came to an end, had been a period of stagnation and decline. "Fifteen years more of a deterioration of our position in the world such as we have experienced since World War II would find us reduced to Fortress America in a world in which we had become largely irrelevant." Americans must now choose between drift and decision.

The solution, Henry Kissinger had contended, lay not in altering institutions but in summoning to leadership men who could replace routine with purpose, substitute individual creativity for group mediocrity, elevate purpose and principle over "pragmatism" and opportunism, risk new departures at the expense of rote and routine. Above all, the German-born political scientist inveighed against sensible, expedient policies. "In a revolutionary period, it is precisely the 'practical' man who is most apt to become a prisoner of events. For what seems most natural to him is most in need of being overcome." The standing operating procedure would clash with the needs of creativity.

As if by a flying carpet, this scholar had been transported to a global decision center that could make innovative leadership possible, and eventually to a success and celebrity of which he could hardly have dreamed. "Only in America," as Americans liked to say—but it was by competence and conniving, not a feat of legerdemain, that the critic rose from political science to political power. All had begun well as Kissinger and Nixon rejected the old policies of alternating between acquiescence and confrontation, between compromise and containment, and proclaimed a new era of coherent, purposeful foreign policy making based on balancing interests with power.

Disillusionment came slowly for both. The President found that he had appointed as security aide a brilliant conceptualizer and articulate advocate who, however, appeared to seek the Washington spotlight as though it were the aide and not the President who would have to stand responsible for foreign policy at the next election. Kissinger found that he was working under—and to a degree taking lessons from—an expert manipulator who disliked the process of face-to-face, give-and-take negotiating, who often appeared psychologically insecure to the point of literally kicking out in his anger and then withdrawing to privacy and solitude, who employed secrecy and deception almost as a matter of course, who rejected "teamwork" in favor of a decision-making process that again and again excluded the participation of the Secretary of State and even of White House aides.

Both men were wily tacticians, resourceful crisis managers, brilliant opportunists. Both believed that leaders should *lead*—should press for decision and action despite foot-dragging bureaucrats and recalcitrant legislators, play enemies and even allies off against one another without apology, use almost any means to reach what they considered to be elevated goals. They were twentieth-century Machiavellians who maneuvered, manipulated, and mystified their adversaries and often their allies. In the end, however, whatever the various successes and failures of their foreign policy, Kissinger fell far short of the working principles he had set forth in his Harvard study.

Perhaps the most important of these principles was to be expected of a scholarly rationalist who had immersed himself in the leisurely and well-considered diplomacy of the nineteenth-century aristocrats. This was the idea of basing foreign policy tactics on a philosophy of international politics that could serve as a guide to the flood of day-to-day decision making. But often missing in his strategy in practice was the crucial linkage between the overall goal and the everyday means—a framework consisting of explicit concepts, clear choices among priorities, interrelated guidelines—without which statecraft puffs up into rhetoric or crumbles into bits of eclectic, unrelated twitches, jerks, and spasms. This was most evident in White House Soviet policy, which proclaimed lofty principles of cooperation and dealt also with prosaic problems such as grain, but failed to fashion the linkage between these that would make for long-run, stable, reasonably predictable dealings with Moscow, her enemies, and her allies, notably North Vietnam.

Another bête noire of Kissinger the scholar was the tendency of American foreign policy makers to seek out a "middle way," bipartisan agreement, popular consensus. This tendency, he warned, made for weak policy by committees, the fragmentation of consensus into a series of ad hoc decisions, the conversion of substantive issues into administrative or even technical ones, and ultimate resolution of a problem by morselization and "coordination" rather than through clear decision and action. But such was the fate of the Kissinger operation.

Such, in particular, was the fate of the policy toward Vietnam. Essentially, Nixon and Kissinger followed a middle way between an all-out military confrontation with Hanoi and a full-scale and early withdrawal from South Vietnam. Within the broad, bipartisan middle way there were violent fluctuations of policy as Nixon stepped up heavy bombing at the same time he was methodically pulling out ground forces.

Were there alternative strategies in Vietnam? At least three. One was to plan and undertake, with the full knowledge of the Saigon regime, a carefully planned, orderly withdrawal of all American power in South Vietnam, with full rearguard protection from GIs and aircraft, in a manner that would enable escapees to find safety in other lands and at least avoid the terrible later ordeals of the "boat people." Or Washington might have stepped up the bombing of North Vietnam so massively as to compel Hanoi to pull its troops north of the DMZ—an alternative that, however irrational, fitted Nixon's willingness to pose as a "madman" who could scare his foes into compromise. There was also the "Korea" or "heartland" alternative—establishing and maintaining a shrunken South Vietnam in the Saigon and delta regions, backed up by ready American sea, air, and ground power over a long period.

During Kissinger's rule the NSC offices in the White House were a place less of calm consideration of alternative strategies than of continual tension, sudden crises, flaring anger, confrontations, shouting matches, group resignations. Doubtless this state of affairs was due in part to Kissinger himself, with his endless manipulations and bullying ways. But it was due also to erratic presidential direction, because, as Kissinger later reflected, "there was no true Nixon." Several qualities fought for supremacy in the same man: he was "idealistic, thoughtful, generous," along with "vindictive, petty, emotional," "reflective, philosophical, stoical," along with "impetuous, impulsive, and erratic." Adlai Stevenson quipped during the 1960 campaign that no man since Lon Chaney had shown so many faces to the American public. Whether or not the President foiled his enemies, certainly he perplexed his associates. Anyone entering the Oval Office or Nixon's hideaway study might find a master of calm analysis or a prisoner of deep insecurities and dark passions.

*   *   *

The Nixon-Kissinger White House was an extreme version of the problems of other presidencies—the paper-thin bipartisanship, the absence of clear guidelines linking broad but explicit goals to everyday policy making, the atmosphere of recurrent tension and desperate crisis management. These problems stemmed from the fundamental and persistent failing in American foreign policy making—the lack of steadfast, coherent, "followthrough" decision and action—in short, of a *strategy* of international relations. A quarter century after Kissinger published his critique of ad hoc, volatile, zigzag foreign policy making, another young scholar could have made the same biting criticism of him, only with more urgency.

This failure encompassed a number of tendencies: the revival of a presidency imperial in scope and power and heavily personal in image and operation; the refusal of Presidents, especially in crisis times, to include in the decision process America's allies, congressional leaders, or even key cabinet officials; presidential exploitation of popular protest over an issue or incident, raising public expectations that whip back on the White House; and the traditional gulfs between Congress and the President, and between the houses of Congress, that produce the stalemates and slow-downs that in turn trigger spasms of action.

Many of these tendencies were not new. For decades Presidents had bypassed the Senate treaty-ratification hurdle by making executive agreements on crucial matters with nations around the globe. At least since the Civil War, Presidents had been using their war powers to the hilt and extending their inherent or emergency powers to almost every conceivable domestic crisis as well. Indeed, the kind of congressional-presidential friction that tempted Presidents to go it alone had begun almost as soon as the two branches of government were established in lower Manhattan in the spring of 1789. As for secret presidential adventurism, the researches of Abraham Sofaer have supported his surmise that, in Arthur Schlesinger's summary, "early presidents deliberately selected venturesome agents, deliberately kept their missions secret, deliberately gave them vague instructions, deliberately failed either to approve or to disapprove their constitutionally questionable plans and deliberately denied Congress and the public the information to determine whether aggressive acts were authorized." White House agents operating secretly in Iran in the 1980s were nothing new.

What was novel and portentous was the convergence of these tendencies, immensely magnified by the media. Kennedy's domination of press and electronic news during the missile crisis, Johnson's obsessive monitoring of the media, Nixon's access to television during both his foreign and his domestic struggles, demonstrated White House power to exploit television; but the media were willing accomplices. Presidents found it much easier to command the airwaves for direct appeal to the people than to consult congressional or even Administration leaders to shape a collective decision that might have future public support and staying power.

The power of the media to present foreign policy in quick, intense, staccato images put enormous emphasis on the appearance of national power as well as its reality. Once upon a time Winston Churchill had built his reputation partly on his ability to proclaim defeat. After Pearl Harbor, Roosevelt told the American people that the Japanese attack had "caused severe damage to American naval and military forces" and that it would not only be a long war but a hard war. Later, General Stilwell, despite PR hopes to cover up defeat in Burma, refreshingly said, "I claim we got a hell of a beating." After the missile crisis, on the other hand, Kennedy said that while Soviet missiles in Cuba would not have significantly changed the military balance of power, it would have appeared to change the political balance of power and "appearances contributed to reality," Johnson had deep psychological fears of appearing "soft." Nixon, commanding stupendous nuclear power, feared that the United States might appear "like a pitiful, helpless giant." The perception of power, John Lewis Gaddis concluded, "had become as important as power itself." The actuality of a nation's military power had a certain continuity and measurability, while the appearance of power could change overnight, thus intensifying the uncertainty, unpredictability, and volatility of Washington's role abroad.

In earlier days the United States had conducted successful experiments in foreign policy—or at least had occasionally persisted with a foreign policy strategy long enough to test whether it would be successful or not. Lend-Lease during World War II and its transmutation into the Marshall Plan after the war loomed as a strikingly effective, comprehensive, and long-run collective effort with other nations. More typically since 1932 Washington had tried short, staccato essays at economic isolation, political unilateralism, aid to allies, full partnership with allies including Russia, deterrence, containment, détente, triangular diplomacy with Russia and China, human rights.

Something important, however, was missing from this list. The transcending experiment Americans had not tried was a sustained, committed political-economic-ideological strategy of comprehensive détente as a road to world peace.

CHAPTER 12

Vice and Virtue

V IETNAM had left deep and tormenting scars across the body politic. It was not like the century's earlier wars that had ended with most Americans feeling victorious and the wars' original opponents at least acquiescent. After World War II those who had rallied against Nazism knew they had helped put down a monstrous and dangerous tyranny. After Korea, those who had supported the final settlement were satisfied to have restored the regional balance of power first upset by North Koreans attacking south and then by Americans attacking too far north.

After Vietnam, *all* felt defeated—the hawks who had pressed for a "victory," the doves who had wanted out, the veterans who returned to a sullen, ungrateful republic, the allies who had been enlisted in a hopeless cause, the Saigon leaders who felt deceived and betrayed, the anticommunist South Vietnamese who faced an anguished choice of fleeing to parts unknown or living under communist rule. Vietnam had displayed the ultimate strategic failure and moral bankruptcy of the "middle way," of "bipartisan" foreign policy making, day-to-day, step-by-step escalation and de-escalation. An undeclared war for ill-defined goals had ended with Americans frustrated, embittered, and divided.

"It was the guerrilla war to end all guerrilla wars until it somehow became simply a war to be ended," wrote Max Frankel in *The New York Times* a few days after Nixon announced the cease-fire of January 1973. "It was the proxy war to contain international Communism until it somehow became the central embarrassment to an era of Communist-capitalist détente. It was devised by a generation that wanted no more Munichs, meaning betrayals by appeasement, and it spawned a generation that wants no more salvations by intervention, no more Vietnams." Few could have guessed that the war would come to an even more tragic end two and a half years later, or that already it had helped to trigger the chain of events that would bring about the collapse of the Nixon presidency long before hostilities ended.

* * *

On Sunday morning, September 8, 1974—thirty days after he took of-fice—President Ford granted a "full, free, and absolute pardon unto Rich-ard Nixon" for all federal offenses "he has committed or may have commit-ted" or had helped commit as President. At once a fire storm of outraged telephone calls and telegrams broke upon the White House. Press and television editorialists thundered. But no one could do anything; the presi-dential power to pardon Presidents—or anyone else—was absolute and irreversible. Appearing on national television with the pardon in front of him, Ford stated that the former President would be excessively penalized in undergoing a protracted trial, "our people would again be polarized in their opinions," and the "credibility of our free institutions of government would again be challenged at home and abroad." He then signed the document in full view of the cameras.

Some Americans believed that nothing would prove the credibility of free institutions more dramatically, or set a better example for dictator-ships abroad, than the willingness to put a President on trial. Many simply suspected a Ford-Nixon deal. It was rumored that aides in the Ford White House knew of a call from Nixon to the new President: if Ford refused to grant him a full pardon, Nixon would announce publicly that Ford had promised the pardon in exchange for the presidency. Ford boldly ap-peared before the House Judiciary Subcommittee on Criminal Justice to declare, "There was no deal, period"; but the investigative reporting of Seymour M. Hersh suggested that Ford did have an outright arrangement with the man who had made him Vice President and then President. An-other possibility was that such carefully protected multi-channel negotia-tions were conducted between the two through intermediaries that the parleys aroused hopes that melded into expectations that led to under-standings that emerged as clear promises of a pardon, all conducted with the winks and nods, whispers and silences, gestures and mumbles that constitute the language of brokering politicians. Or perhaps Ford acted, as he claimed, in behalf of what he considered "the greatest good of all the people of the United States whose servant I am."

In a very different fashion, nevertheless, Nixon went on trial anyway. Ford's demonstration of presidential power and the debate over its cause and justice, the trials of high Watergate figures in the following months, the voluminous memoirs of Watergate heroes and villains in the following years, and Nixon's disbarment from practicing law in New York State had the more important effect of putting not merely Nixon but his whole Administration on trial, and even more, of exposing the most extraordi-nary and pervasive abuse of power in high places. There emerged a fright-ening portrait of an Administration conducting a political war of attempted extermination against its political enemies at home even while it was waging a military struggle in Southeast Asia. Viewing street demonstrators and student protesters not as legitimate political opponents but as threats to national security and subverters of the national interest, the White House developed a siege mentality.

This was not the first time an Administration had hunkered down into a psychology of besiegement; the previous Administration had exhibited similar signs and strains. But ultimately there was a difference between Lyndon Johnson and Richard Nixon. Until the end LBJ's instinct had been to move out to people, to consult Republicans like Dirksen, to include critics like George Ball. It was better, he liked to tell intimates, to have such people "inside the tent pissing out than outside the tent pissing in." And in the end Johnson was willing to quit voluntarily. Nixon's instinct was for exclusion—to suspect anybody and everybody, ignore them, fire them, exile them. And in the end he in effect was forced out of office.

But before that end the Nixon White House had abused power with awesome ingenuity. They had set up an extensive "enemies list" that ranged from political opponents like Jane Fonda, Shirley Chisholm, and Edmund Muskie to the heads of eastern universities and foundations, along with media figures, actors, even athletes, and included a mistake or two—non-enemy Professor Hans Morgenthau made the list because he was confused with enemy Robert Morgenthau, U.S. Attorney in New York City. They conducted a private investigation of Senator Edward Kennedy's 1969 automobile accident at Chappaquiddick in which a woman drowned. They tapped their foes and one another with wild abandon. They tried to subvert the IRS, the CIA, the FBI for political purposes. Though the so-called Huston Plan, which outlined a sinister program of surveillance of American citizens and proposed the use of "surreptitious entry"— burglary—for intelligence-gathering, was blocked by a nervous J. Edgar Hoover, it revealed the illegal lengths to which the Administration was willing to go in its war against political enemies. Parts of the plan were later implemented, and it was the inspiration of the "Plumbers" unit that burglarized the office of Daniel Ellsberg's California psychiatrist and of the team that broke into the Democratic National Committee offices in Washington's Watergate complex.

Not only the political war plans but the planners told much about the Nixon White House. Some of the inmates were of the order of Charles Colson, who liked to call himself a "flag-waving, kick-'em-in-the-nuts, anti-press, anti-liberal Nixon fanatic" and "the chief ass-kicker around the White House." Others were younger men like White House counsel John Dean, attractive, clean-cut, affable, flexible—ever so flexible. And willing—

ever so willing. When Nixon asserted to Dean on September 15, 1972, that the White House had not used the FBI or the Justice Department against its enemies, but that "things are going to change now. And they are either going to do it right or go," Dean exclaimed, "What an exciting prospect!"

The more that Watergate unfolded in the trials and memoirs of participants, in the brilliant reporting of Washington *Post* correspondents and of Hersh and J. Anthony Lukas and others, the more it appeared to be a morality tale, complete with villains and saints, winners and sinners, and a Greek chorus of Washington boosters and critics.

WATERGATE: A MORALITY TALE

The Polo Lounge, the Beverly Hills Hotel, Los Angeles, June 17, 1972. Jeb Stuart Magruder, deputy director of the Committee to Reelect the President—called CRP by its friends, CREEP by its foes—was breakfasting with aides when the phone call came from Washington. It was G. Gordon Liddy, insisting that Magruder drive ten miles to a "secure phone." "I haven't got time," Magruder replied impatiently. "What's so important?" Liddy said, "Our security chief was arrested in the Democratic headquarters in the Watergate last night." Magruder: *"What?"*

Magruder knew what. If the men who had tried to plant listening devices in the Democratic National Committee could, through CRP security chief James McCord, be linked to Liddy, counsel to CRP, they could be linked to himself, to his boss, CRP director John Mitchell, and therefore to *his* boss, the President of the United States. Magruder and his assistants hurried to Mitchell's suite in the hotel. They had only one thought at this point, Magruder remembered later: How could they get McCord out of jail? Some way must be found. "After all, *we* were the government; until very recently John Mitchell had been Attorney General of the United States." The break-in was not just hard-nosed politics; it was a crime that could destroy them all. With White House power behind them, it seemed inconceivable that they could not fix the problem. The decision for a cover-up was immediate and automatic; no one suggested anything else.

For Jeb Stuart Magruder, like many others caught in the Watergate web, this was a moment of truth, a point of passage. Magruder was no hard-boiled, cynical politico who had fought his way up from the precincts. A Staten Island high school and Williams College graduate, he had worked for IBM and other big corporations, run two small cosmetics companies in Chicago, managed southern California for Nixon in 1968 and accepted with alacrity a White House post as deputy director of communications the next year. Considered the perfect PR man, he was to go through much of the same anguish, the same passage from arrogance to humiliation, in the following nightmarish months of exposure as others in the White House, but he later related his experience more reflectively and revealingly than his colleagues.

During the "siege" days of 1970, Magruder recalled, the White House existed in "a state of permanent crisis." Now, after the Watergate break-in, the spacious mansion turned into a Hobbesian world of all against all, a Shakespearean stage of suspicious, frightened men shaken from their pinnacle and clawing for survival. To cover up the burglary White House chiefs and operatives destroyed their own documents, pried open and emptied the safes of others, pressured the CIA to pressure the FBI to limit its investigation. They arranged hush money for the burglars, though, as John Dean noted, "no one wanted to handle this dirty work. Everyone avoided the problem like leprosy." The White House "thought Mitchell should 'take care of' the payments because he had approved the Liddy plan" to burglarize the DNC, while the former Attorney General blamed the White House for sending him Liddy and pressing him for intelligence. Finally a "fund-raiser" was found in the President's personal attorney, Herbert Kalmbach, who over the next two months gathered $220,000 in $100 bills—soon to be known as CREEP calling cards. Now the frightened men in the White House began to jettison not only records but themselves and one another. Kalmbach quit while under FBI investigation.

In October 1972, Washington *Post* reporters Bob Woodward and Carl Bernstein, after months of patient sleuthing and with the guidance of a well-informed source—"Deep Throat"—whose identity only Woodward knew, tied the Watergate break-in to "a massive campaign of political spying and sabotage conducted on behalf of President Nixon's re-election and directed by" White House and CRP officials. During the January 1973 trial of the burglars, Judge John J. Sirica, dissatisfied with the efforts of Attorney General Richard Kleindienst's prosecutors, questioned defense witnesses from the bench. Late in March, McCord, whom "the government" had failed to spring and who feared a severe sentence if he refused to cooperate, charged that others besides the burglars had been involved and that perjury had been committed at the trial. The President was following every move.

* * *

The Oval Office, February 28, 1973. John Dean was once again reporting to the President. The two discussed ways to obstruct the select committee the Senate had established under Democrat Sam Ervin of North Carolina and Dean assured Nixon that despite the setbacks, the cover-up was still viable:

> DEAN: We have come a long road on this thing now. I had thought it was an impossible task to hold together until after the election until things started falling out, but we have made it this far and I am convinced we are going to make it the whole road and put this thing in the funny pages of the history books rather than anything serious because actually—
> NIXON: It will be somewhat serious but the main thing, of course, is also the isolation of the President.
> DEAN: Absolutely! Totally true!

But by March 13, the scenario Dean presented to the President was less optimistic:

> DEAN: There is a certain domino situation here. If some things start going, a lot of other things are going to start going, and there can be a lot of problems if everything starts falling. So there are dangers, Mr. President. . . . There is a reason for not everyone going up and testifying.

And on March 21, against Nixon's enthusiasm for continued hush-money payments—"You could get a million dollars. You could get it in cash. I know where it could be gotten"—Dean warned:

> DEAN: I think that there is no doubt about the seriousness of the problem we've got. We have a cancer within, close to the Presidency, that is growing. It is growing daily. It's compounded, growing geometrically now, because it compounds itself. . . . Basically, it is because (1) we are being blackmailed; (2) People are going to start perjuring themselves very quickly that have not had to perjure themselves to protect other people in the line. And there is no assurance—
> NIXON: That that won't bust?
> DEAN: That that won't bust.

Dean by this time was wondering who "would have to fall on his sword for the President." Himself? "Yes, I thought. Then, no. There had to be another way." But if he refused to fall, he might be pushed. Dean's other way was to beat his co-conspirators in the White House to the federal prosecutors and the Ervin committee and cut a deal.

* * *

Senate caucus room, hearings before the Watergate Committee, testimony of John Dean, June 25–29, 1973. Ponderously, inexorably, the two rival branches of the federal government were wheeling up their artillery against the abuse of presidential power. The judicial branch had demonstrated its power in Judge Sirica's court; there was talk of impeachment in the House, though it had yet to initiate such proceedings; the Senate select committee hearings had opened on May 17.

The counter-tactic Dean, and fellow Nixon aides John Ehrlichman and H. R. Haldeman, in consultation with the President, had devised had the White House taking "a public posture of full cooperation," as Dean recalled, while privately trying to "restrain the investigation and make it as difficult as possible to get information and witnesses." But with White House and CRP officials—Magruder and Dean himself among them—now jumping ship, the dark and criminal underside of the Nixon White House was being exposed to the Ervin committee and the full glare of television lights. On June 25, Dean began his testimony:

DEAN: To one who was in the White House and became somewhat familiar with its interworkings, the Watergate matter was an inevitable outgrowth of a climate of excessive concern over the political impact of demonstrators, excessive concern over leaks, an insatiable appetite for political intelligence, all coupled with a do-it-yourself White House staff, regardless of the law.

Dean's reading of his 245-page opening statement took up the entire first day of his testimony. The next day, Georgia Democrat Herman Talmadge questioned him:

TALMADGE: Mr. Dean, you realize, of course, that you have made very strong charges against the President of the United States that involves him in criminal offenses, do you not?
DEAN: Yes sir, I do.

But Dean kept his finger coolly pointed at the President. Later that day, Joseph Montoya, Democrat of New Mexico, questioned him:

MONTOYA: Now, on April 17, 1973, the President said this: "I condemn any attempts to cover up in this case, no matter who is involved." Do you believe he was telling the truth on that date?
DEAN: No, Sir.

MONTOYA: Will you state why?

DEAN: Well, because by that time, he knew the full implications of the case and Mr. Haldeman and Mr. Ehrlichman were certainly still on the staff and there was considerable resistance to their departure from the staff.

And on July 28, Tennessee Republican Howard Baker asked Dean the question he asked almost every witness—the question of the summer:

BAKER: What did the President know and when did he know it, about the cover-up?

DEAN: I would have to start back from personal knowledge, and that would be when I had a meeting on Sept. 15 [1972] when we discussed what was very clear to me in terms of cover-up. We discussed in terms of delaying lawsuits, compliments to me on my efforts to that point. Discussed timing and trials, because we didn't want them to occur before the election.

As the White House launched a massive counterattack—it was the word, it argued, of a self-acknowledged leader of the cover-up fighting and bargaining to save his skin against that of the President of the United States— John Dean's credibility became a chief topic of discussion. During the former counsel's testimony, a man just outside the caucus room assembled an impromptu jury of twelve fellow spectators to pass judgment on Dean's veracity and, implicitly, on Nixon's guilt. The vote was unanimous in Dean's favor. Two other spectators called out, "Make it fourteen."

Day after day that summer, the Ervin committee elicited the damning testimony: that the "enemies list" was designed for the harassment of its targets through the IRS and other means; that an attempt was made to forge State Department cables in order to implicate President Kennedy in the assassination of Vietnamese President Diem; that Nixon had tape-recorded his conversations in the White House and his hideaway office in the Executive Office Building; that Ehrlichman deemed the burglary of Daniel Ellsberg's psychiatrist as within the constitutional powers of the President.

More charges and revelations emerged from the committee and other investigations: that the President had taken fraudulent income-tax deductions; that he had used sizable government funds to improve his estates in Key Biscayne, Florida, and at San Clemente, California; that the financier and manufacturer Howard Hughes had made large secret donations of cash, supposedly for campaign purposes but apparently spent on private expenses by Nixon, his family, and his friends. The plea-bargained resignation in October 1973 of Spiro Agnew—charged with federal income-tax evasion for payoffs from construction company executives he had accepted while governor of Maryland and even as vice president—added to the portrait of a pervasive corruption surpassing even Grant's and Harding's Administrations.

Inch by inch Nixon fell back, fighting all the way, making public explanations that were soon proven false or declared "inoperative" by the White House itself, throwing his closest associates out of his careening sleigh as the wolves relentlessly closed in. Shortly before the Ervin committee began its hearings he shoved Haldeman and Ehrlichman out of the White House with garlands of praise and replaced Kleindienst as Attorney General with Elliot L. Richardson, who chose his old Harvard law professor, Archibald Cox, as special prosecutor. The struggle now was over presidential tapes that were believed relevant to the investigation. When Nixon balked at releasing the tapes either to Cox or to the Ervin committee, both subpoenaed him for this crucial evidence. Ordered by Judge Sirica to turn the tapes over to the court, the President proposed a compromise arrangement so egregiously self-protective that Cox turned it down.

Then the "Saturday Night Massacre"—Nixon commanded Richardson and then Deputy Attorney General William D. Ruckelshaus to sack Cox for defying a presidential order to give up his pursuit of the tapes through the courts. Both refused—Richardson resigned, Ruckelshaus was dismissed. Solicitor General Robert H. Bork, of the Yale law faculty, was hurriedly driven to the White House and designated Acting Attorney General, and promptly fired Cox. The outburst of public outrage once again drove Nixon back on the defensive. He agreed to hand the tapes over to Sirica, then reversed his "abolition" of the special prosecutor's office and chose for Cox's replacement a man whom Nixon expected to be more pliable, a conservative Texas Democrat, corporate lawyer, and reputed law-and-order man named Leon Jaworski. Nixon aroused more public suspicion when he handed over to Sirica a crucial tape with an eighteen-minute gap, which the court's panel of experts found had been caused by repeated, probably deliberate erasures.

Leon Jaworski did indeed turn out to be a law-and-order man. When the President, citing the doctrine of executive privilege, refused to turn over to him additional tapes involving conversations with his aides, Jaworski argued first before Judge Sirica, who upheld him, and then, when Nixon took the case to the Court of Appeals, went to the Supreme Court for "immediate settlement." On July 24, 1974, the Court rendered its decision in *United States of America* v. *Richard Nixon, President of the United States.* Chief Justice Warren E. Burger, after reading a brief tribute to his recently deceased predecessor, Earl Warren, summarized the Court's unanimous finding. The President's claim to executive privilege, the opinion held, "to withhold evidence that is demonstrably relevant in a criminal trial would cut deeply into the guarantee of due process of law and gravely impair the basic function of the courts." The privilege could not "prevail over the fundamental demands of due process of law in the fair administration of justice." When the news reached Nixon at San Clemente, according to Anthony Lukas, "the President exploded, cursing the man he had named chief justice," and reserving a few choice expletives for Harry A. Blackmun and Lewis F. Powell, Jr., his other appointees. At first Nixon seriously considered challenging the Court, but he feared adding to the likely impeachment charges, and the Court's unanimity made it impossible to claim that the decision was insufficiently definitive. In all the months of slow Chinese torture that Nixon suffered, it was probably the news from the High Bench that gave him the most sudden, piercing pain.

*　　*　　*

The Judiciary Committee, Room 2141, Rayburn House Office Building, 7:45 p.m., July 24, 1974. Over a hundred reporters looked on and about 40 million Americans watched on television as Chairman Peter Rodino rapped his gavel on the table. Solemnly he reminded the members of their responsibilities. "Make no mistake about it. This is a turning point, whatever we decide. Our judgment is not concerned with an individual but with a system of constitutional government. It has been the history and the good fortune of the United States, ever since the Founding Fathers, that each generation of citizens and their officials have been, within tolerable limits, faithful custodians of the Constitution and the rule of law." But the minds of his fellow committee members were very much on one individual—the President of the United States. There had been doubts that this unwieldy committee of thirty-eight members, many of them highly partisan, and polarized between "Democratic Firebrands" and "Republican Diehards," could handle the tough, risky task of impeachment.

Impeachment! During much of 1973 few even in the media had dared mention the word; it smacked of the impeachment and trial 105 years earlier of Andrew Johnson, an episode ill regarded in most recent histories. For months the committee and its big staff had been sorting through White House tapes and other records that the President, dragging his feet at every stage, had turned over to the committee or the courts. Day by day the specter of impeachment became more real. The Republican minority on the committee were an especially anguished lot. Many were personally as well as politically loyal to Nixon, who had done them many favors, including trips into their districts to give their campaigns the White House blessing. This was the case with Hamilton Fish, Jr., who to boot was the fourth consecutive Hamilton Fish to serve as a Republican member of Congress. His father, famed as a target of FDR's jibes at "Martin, Barton, and Fish," was still active, at eighty-five, in backing Nixon and demanding whether there could be "fair and impartial justice among the left-winged Democrats on the House Judiciary Committee who received large campaign contributions from organized labor."

But the younger Fish was slowly moving toward impeachment after the Saturday Night Massacre, which had socked him "right in the gut," and after reading tape transcripts. Some Republicans were outraged by the unending stream of revelations; others held out for "our President," while Rodino sought to "mass" the committee in order to stave off accusations of blind partisanship. The committee rose to the occasion, with some noble utterances during its deliberations.

Barbara Jordan, Texas Democrat, woman, black: "Earlier today we heard the beginning of the Preamble to the Constitution of the United States. 'We, the people . . .' It is a very eloquent beginning. But when that document was completed on the seventeenth of September in 1787 I was not included in that, 'We, the people.' I felt somehow for many years that George Washington and Alexander Hamilton just left me out by mistake. But through the process of amendment, interpretation, and court decision I have finally been included in 'We, the people.' Today, I am an inquisitor. My faith in the Constitution is whole, it is complete, it is total. I am not going to sit here and be an idle spectator to the diminution, the subversion, the destruction of the Constitution."

M. Caldwell Butler, Virginia Republican: "For years we Republicans have campaigned against corruption and misconduct. . . . But Watergate is our shame. Those things have happened in our house and it is our responsibility to do what we can to clear it up." He announced that he was inclining toward impeachment. "But there will be no joy in it for me."

On July 27, 1974, the committee voted 27–11 to recommend impeachment on the ground that the President had "engaged personally and through his subordinates and agents, in a course of conduct or plan designed to delay, impede, and obstruct the investigation" of the Watergate burglary. Two days later the committee voted, 28–10, an article charging that Nixon's conduct had violated the constitutional rights of citizens and impaired the proper administration of justice. The votes reflected a precarious coalition of committee Democrats and Republicans; the majority of Republicans still stood by their President.

But on August 5, Richard Nixon, in obedience to the Supreme Court decision, released the transcripts of three conversations which showed beyond any doubt that six days after the Watergate break-in—on June 23, 1972—he was at the center of the conspiracy to cover up that crime, obstructing justice by plotting to block the FBI investigation. "I was sick. I was shocked," a middle-level White House official told a journalist. "He had *lied* to me, to all of us. I think my first thought, before that sank in, was of those Republicans on the Judiciary Committee . . . those men who had risked their careers to defend him."

Now one of those men—Charles Wiggins—said, "I have reached the painful conclusion that the President of the United States should resign." If he did not, "I am prepared to conclude that the magnificent career of public service of Richard Nixon must be terminated involuntarily."

*   *   *

The White House, August 7–9, 1974. In the final days the two Nixons—the shrewd, confident calculator and the narcissist hovering between dreams of omnipotence and feelings of insecurity—emerged in the Watergate crucible. Even now he was a cold head counter, yet he appeared to be swinging erratically between holding out to the bitter end and throwing it all up. Senators Barry Goldwater and Hugh Scott and House Minority Leader John J. Rhodes arrived at the White House on August 7 to brief the President on the situation in Congress. After some small talk:

SCOTT: We've asked Barry to be our spokesman.

NIXON: Go ahead, Barry.

GOLDWATER: Mr. President, this isn't pleasant, but you want to know the situation and it isn't good.

NIXON: Pretty bad, huh? . . . How many would you say would be with me—a half dozen?

GOLDWATER: More than that, maybe sixteen to eighteen. . . . We've discussed the thing a lot and just about all of the guys have spoken up and there aren't many who would support you if it comes to that. I took kind of a nose count today, and I couldn't find more than four very firm votes, and those would be from older Southerners. Some are very worried about what's been going on, and are undecided, and I'm one of them.

NIXON: John, I know how you feel, what you've said, I respect it, but what's your estimate?

RHODES: About the same, Mr. President.

NIXON: Well, that's about the way I thought it was. I've got a very difficult decision to make, but I want you to know I'm going to make it for the best interests of the country. . . . I'm not interested in pensions. I'm not interested in pardons or amnesty. I'm going to make this decision for the best interests of the country.

SCOTT: Mr. President, we are all very saddened, but we have to tell you the facts.

NIXON: Never mind. There'll be no tears. I haven't cried since Eisenhower died. My family has been fine. I'm going to be all right. . . . Do I have any other options?

There were no options. After a bit more small talk his visitors left. The next night the President addressed the nation on television. He was calm, restrained. "As we look to the future, the first essential is to begin healing the wounds of this Nation, to put the bitterness and divisions of the recent past behind us and to rediscover those shared ideals that lie at the heart of our strength and unity as a great and as a free people." There was no admission of guilt, no word about the lies he had told or the laws he had broken or the trust he had violated; he would say only that "some of my judgments were wrong"—but he announced his resignation, effective the next day, August 9, at noon.

In the last hours the President vacillated between mourning and brief bouts of euphoria, between weeping and laughter. In his departing speech to cabinet and staff on the morning of August 9, he talked about the White House—"this house has a great heart"—and about his father, "a streetcar motorman first"—and about his mother—"my mother was a saint." Then an admonition from this man whose great hatreds had contributed to his fall: ". . . always remember, others may hate you, but those who hate you don't win unless you hate them, and then you destroy yourself."

Finally the scene, etched on the memory of America, of Nixon and his wife and daughters, their eyes brimming, walking out to the waiting helicopter. There in the door he turned to the crowd, and waved, a contorted smile on his face. From Andrews Air Force Base he and Mrs. Nixon flew west on the *Spirit of '76* to their home in San Clemente. Somewhere over central Missouri the presidency of Richard Nixon came to its end.

* * *

What did the President know? When did he know it? And when would the American people know what and when the President knew? These continued to be the critical questions facing Americans during most of the months of Watergate. The stunning answer came on August 5, 1974, when Nixon released the three damning tapes of June 23, 1972. At last the "smoking gun" lay before the people.

Knowing what had happened evoked the more compelling and intractable questions: Why? How could it have happened? Was Watergate due to one man, Richard Nixon, and his flaws of character? If so, why had he been joined in criminal and immoral acts by another thirty or forty men, not all of whom were close to him? Was Watergate, then, a product of the political institutions in which these men operated—of the "imperial presidency," a hostile and biased media, the whole political and constitutional system? But what had shaped these institutions—psychological forces within the political elite, a corruption of the American national character, economic and social tendencies inherent in an individualistic, dog-eat-dog culture?

Nixon's apologists defended him as a victim rather than a villain—as the legatee of dishonorable precedents set by previous Presidents, as the butt of a vindictive press, as simply acquiescing, in son-in-law David Eisenhower's words, "in the non-prosecution of aides who covered up a little operation into the opposition's political headquarters," a long-established practice "that no one took that seriously." John Kenneth Galbraith had predicted at the time of Nixon's resignation that someone would also advance the argument that "there's a little bit of Richard Nixon in all of us." Galbraith added, "I say the hell there is!"

A more persuasive explanation of Watergate put the whole episode in a political and institutional context. The "swelling of the presidency," wrote presidential scholar Thomas E. Cronin, had produced around the President a coterie of dozens of assistants, hundreds of presidential advisers, and "thousands of members of an institutional amalgam called the Executive Office of the President." This presidential establishment had become a "powerful inner sanctum of government, isolated from traditional, constitutional checks and balances." George E. Reedy, former press secretary to LBJ, saw beneath the President "a mass of intrigue, posturing, strutting, cringing, and pious 'commitment' to irrelevant windbaggery"—a "perfect setting for the conspiracy of mediocrity." John Dean remembered the "blind ambition" that had infected him and others in the White House.

Jeb Magruder wrote that the President's mounting insecurities and passions over Vietnam and the antiwar protests led to Watergate, for Presidents set the tone of their Administrations. But, Magruder continued, it was not enough to blame the atmosphere Nixon created. "No one forced me or the others to break the law," he said. "We could have objected to what was happening or resigned in protest. Instead, we convinced ourselves that wrong was right, and plunged ahead."

It was the sting of the media that drove Nixon to dangerous and desperate retaliatory tactics, some of his supporters contended. In fact, each side—all sides—exaggerated the extent to which the media supported their adversaries and, even more, the actual influence wielded by the media. The Watergate "battle of public opinion" was more like a vast guerrilla war in which a variety of political and media generals and colonels fought for advantage in the murk. Nixon repeatedly used television to reach the viewers over the heads of the press, but his credibility was suspect. Investigative reporters burrowed away, looking for fame as well as facts. Polls were used to influence public opinion as well as to test it. A polling organization friendly to the White House asked its sample: "Which action do you yourself feel is the more morally reprehensible— which is worse—the drowning of Mary Jo Kopechne at Chappaquiddick or the bugging of the Democratic National Committee?"

The nature of the public-opinion battle, moreover, changed during the two-year struggle. People tended to react to the early revelations as Democrats and Republicans, or as Nixon admirers and haters. The press, too, tended to divide along lines of party or presidential preference in 1972, when about seven of every ten newspapers endorsed Nixon and about one out of every twenty McGovern. At first the pro-Nixon newspapers tended to play down or ignore the Watergate burglary; then they faltered and shifted in the face of the avalanche of evidence of wrongdoing. All in all, two close students of Watergate public opinion concluded, grass-roots political attitudes had less an active than a reactive role in Watergate; they were not so much a powerful, cohesive force pressing for a certain action as simply a melting away of Nixon's old constituency, especially after the smoking-gun revelation, and he was left without his "base."

In the end it was not in the "tribunal" of public opinion that the issue was settled but in the more formal tribunals of the American political and constitutional system. If Nixon hoped he could save himself eventually as he had done with his "Checkers" appeal in 1952, he was underestimating the legislative branch. A Congress that for months had been stupefied and almost immobilized by shocking revelations roused itself to concerted action, voting in committee to impeach. Even so, the system might well not have worked except for investigative reporters who refused to quit, a remarkable series of blunders by Nixon, stretching from his original taping of the White House to his failure to destroy the tapes, and other "chance" or aberrant developments. In some respects the constitutional system thwarted rather than impeded action. The separation of powers and checks and balances, political scientist Larry Berman concluded, had not stopped "the espionage, the plumbers, the dirty tricks, the cover-up, the secret bombing of Cambodia, all the culmination of presidential imperialism." It was the capacity of key persons—journalists, legislators, judges, even men in the White House circle—to rise in

the face of doubt and suspicion and to defy the royal court itself that
made all the difference by 1974.

Ultimately, Watergate became a test of moral leadership—a test that the
White House dramatically failed to meet. There was no sense of embarrassment or shame, Magruder said later, "as we planned the cover-up. If
anything, there was a certain self-righteousness to our deliberations. We
had persuaded ourselves that what we had done, although technically
illegal, was not wrong or even unusual." Their foes were making a mountain out of a molehill. "We were not covering up a burglary, we were
safeguarding world peace." Besides, hadn't previous presidencies—especially the JFK White House—prepared the way for "hardball politics"?
Kennedy men had stolen the election of 1960 from their boss, some in the
White House still believed. They recalled the old story that members of
Kennedy's White House loved to tell about the JFK staff man who was
complaining of the misdeeds of the "rascals" in the enemy camp. When
another staff man remarked mildly that there were rascals in their own
camp as well, the first man said, "Ah, but they are *our* rascals!"

It fell to men like Archibald Cox and Elliot Richardson to exercise moral
leadership in the crucible, but a desperate President could always find a
complaisant man to carry out his orders. It was hard to accept the truth
that the President was a liar, Elizabeth Drew reflected as she read through
the smoking-gun tapes. It seemed impossible that a President was "capable
of looking at us in utter sincerity from the other side of the television
camera and telling us multiple, explicit, barefaced lies." She felt torn
between the "idea that people must be able to have some confidence in
their leaders and the idea that in this day of image manipulation a certain
skepticism may serve them well." Here was a fundamental question about
moral leadership in the American democracy. Perhaps a *New Yorker* cartoon of the time hinted at the nature of the problem, if not the answer.
It showed one man telling another man in a bar: "Look, Nixon's no
dope; if the people really wanted moral leadership, he'd give them moral
leadership."

CRIME AND PUNISHMENT

After Judge Sirica sentenced Jeb Magruder to a term of ten months to
four years in prison, the former White House aide had ample time to
analyze "why Watergate." He blamed excessive power in the White House,
Nixon's "instinct to overreact in political combat," and the lawbreaking by
White House staff "out of a combination of ambition, loyalty, and partisan
passion." Analyzing his own wrongdoing, he ascribed it in some degree to

the failure of his college professors to teach morality. Thus at Williams, political scientist Frederick L. Schuman had advocated a "tough power-politics approach to international diplomacy," chaplain William Sloane Coffin was too rigid and confrontational a moralist, and James MacGregor Burns, while ideological, did not teach enough morality in his politics courses. He reflected with some bitterness that Coffin had defended draft-card burning and other illegal activities, in turn provoking illegality in the White House, even though "two wrongs do not make a right."

Other Watergate wrongdoers also could reflect on the fortunes of political war. More than a score went to jail. Convicted of conspiracy, perjury, and obstruction of justice, Haldeman served eighteen months in prison; later he became vice president of a real estate development firm in Los Angeles. Ehrlichman, convicted of the same three crimes, emerged from eighteen months in jail fifty-seven, bearded, affable, and ready to embark on a career of writing about his Washington days. John Mitchell, convicted of conspiracy, obstruction of justice, and lying under oath, served nineteen months before being paroled, only to go through more years of ill health, disbarment, and separation from his wife, Martha, who later died of cancer. Charles Colson and Jeb Magruder, after serving seven months, turned successfully to Christian ministerial activities. G. Gordon Liddy, convicted both of the break-in and of conspiring to raid the office of Daniel Ellsberg's psychiatrist, served the longest Watergate prison sentence—fifty-two months—because he refused to talk, even under subpoena; he later became a celebrity lecturer and security consultant. A dozen other Watergaters served brief sentences, then turned to business, law, writing, and lecturing. All the key Watergate participants save Mitchell wrote works of fiction or fact about the episode; many of these were best-sellers.

And the chief co-conspirator? Ten years after the break-in, Richard Nixon had published his own best-selling memoir, moved from California to Manhattan to the New Jersey hinterland, continued to receive federal pensions and free office space and clerical help like all former Presidents, and earned over $3 million from his writings. He was lionized at home and abroad, defended his actions in television interviews, wrote on foreign policy and foreign leaders, advised President Reagan, and was attacked by Haldeman and others for further distorting the record. Nixon told a CBS interviewer that he "never" thought about Watergate. "I'm not going to spend my time just looking back and wringing my hands about something I can't do anything about."

Nixon's slow and careful reentry into public life only intensified the anger of those who believed he had deserved a conviction rather than a pardon. Here was the old-boy network in spades, now deciding the leadership of the nation. Here was the pinnacle of pardons, the Everest of exculpation, something for the book. It was the same old story—the big guys take care of themselves while the little guys get it in the neck.

Nixon's white-collar crimes happened to coincide with a dramatic rise in public consciousness of lawbreaking by persons in corporations, government, and other organizations. The FBI in the 1970s found that the frequency of such crimes as bribery, kickbacks, payoffs, and embezzlement was growing at an alarming rate. The costs of white-collar crime in goods and services, the Bureau estimated, eventually caused about a 15 percent markup for consumers. The FBI was now assigning over a fifth of its agents to the investigation of such crimes.

The moral ambiguity of the Nixon pardon was matched by confusion over the very nature of white-collar crime. Some Americans believed that, however heinous Nixon's misdeeds were, the pardon was justified because no other punishment could compare with the humiliation and mortification an American President must endure in quitting office in the face of looming impeachment. And so with white-collar people. A bank teller, an insurance clerk, a postal employee, a politician living in a tight-knit community and known to everyone, some Americans believed, faced far more embarrassment on conviction than thieves working some distance from their communities.

Many investigators of white-collar crime had little patience with such popular distinctions. In a social economy undergoing rapid organizational and technological changes during the 1960s and 1970s, they faced trying problems in even defining, measuring, and understanding white-collar crime before tackling the questions of deterrence and punishment. Two seasoned investigators virtually threw up their hands over the task of definition, finally settling for "an intuitively satisfying understanding" encompassing a broad range of offenses. A widely accepted working definition was "illegal acts committed by nonphysical means and by concealment or guile, to obtain money" and other personal or business advantages. Even so, differences over definition were so wide that estimates of the incidence of white-collar crime also varied widely. If the FBI was finding an alarming growth, was this because the Bureau was broadening its definition of white-collar crime, or because its expanded white-collar unit was uncovering more offenses, or because there really was an increase in white-collar crime?

Even more daunting was the assignment of responsibility, which in turn involved the imposing of penalties for crimes committed. Since the vast majority of these misdeeds occurred in organizations, who should be held responsible—the leaders, the subleaders, the rank and file, the whole organization? The President, all or part of the presidential staff, the whole presidency, indeed the whole executive branch? A corporation's top executives, its middle managers, the local managers perhaps "just following orders," the whole corporation, the capitalist system?

Responsibility might, on the other hand, be so widely diffused in a corporation that individual liability would be impossible to determine, or it might be hidden in its interstices. Or it might be both expedited by electronic technology and cloaked within it. With business operations increasingly computerized and computers serving as "vaults" for corporate assets, computer-related crime—difficult to detect when perpetrated skillfully, with higher per-incident losses than other white-collar crimes—became a "universal and uniform threat."

Most of the problems centered in large corporations. This was not new; two hundred years ago the Lord Chancellor of England had asked, "Did you ever expect a corporation to have a conscience, when it has no soul to be damned, and no body to be kicked?" and he was rumored to have added in a stage whisper, "By God, it ought to have both." Corporations also posed some of the most dramatic issues of responsibility. Thus in the 1970s the Ford Motor Company built Pintos with the metal fuel tank located behind the rear axle. Although a safety device would have cost only eleven dollars per car, Ford did not remedy the situation, despite a rash of rear-end collisions causing fiery deaths and injuries. After three young women were burned to death, an Indiana jury in 1980 acquitted Ford of reckless homicide charges. The Firestone Tire and Rubber Company, the first American firm to supply steel-belted radial tires in large quantities to automakers, acknowledged a large number of accidents associated with the tires. In 1978, pressed by the "feds," Firestone agreed to recall over seven million radial tires. Although many asbestos manufacturers knew of the danger of asbestosis and pneumoconiosis among their workers, few companies moved to rectify the situation.

Given the murky distribution of power in large corporations, to whom should punishment be meted out for misdeeds? And how large should the penalties be? Judges and juries faced dilemmas. If they levied moderate fines on executives—who in any event were usually protected against such liability so long as they had acted in "good faith"—these costs could be absorbed by the corporation and community in various ways and hence could not serve as much of a deterrent. If the court whacked the corporation with a huge fine, perhaps in the millions, the burden might fall on the innocent—the great majority of stockholders, the white-collar employees who might be denied a pay raise, and even the workers who might lose jobs if the fine was large enough to force the firm to scale down its operations or even submit to bankruptcy. An individual misdeed thus might be converted into a community crisis.

*   *   *

Most Americans were far more concerned about "street crime" than about white-collar crime, except when the latter had a physical impact, such as corporations leaving former employees gasping for breath on a hospital bed or customers incinerated in gasoline explosions. The estimated number of all offenses—street and white-collar—known to police almost quadrupled between 1960 and 1983, from 3.4 million to 12.1 million. Even when adjusted for a population increase from 179.3 million in 1960 to 234 million in 1983, the rise was still startling—from 1,887 per 100,000 persons to 5,159. Violent crimes such as murder, forcible rape, robbery, and aggravated assault quadrupled, while property crimes such as burglary, larceny-theft, and motor vehicle theft tripled. Thus there was a marked increase in crimes of an especially ugly and devastating nature.

An alarmed public watched the rising crime rate—and experienced it. In the early 1980s Americans, regardless of race, sex, education, income, size of city, or party membership, responded "more" to the Gallup poll question "Is there more crime in this area than there was a year ago, or less?" People felt less safe at home at night, more fearful of walking alone at night within a mile of their homes, widely concerned that their property might be vandalized, their home burglarized, that they might be robbed in the street and injured in the process.

The polling returns showed some anomalies. The fear was disproportionate to the actual numbers of victims. In 1982 fewer than one half of 1 percent of the national sample had been injured by a burglar at home, but nearly a third allowed that they worried at least a "good amount" about its happening. At the same time, 51 percent of the sample answered "too much" to the question "Do you think television news gives too much attention to stories about crime, not enough attention, or what?" while 29 percent answered "about right" and 18 percent "not enough."

The intensity of the national debate over the "cause and cure of crime" rose even faster than the crime rate. The centerpiece of the debate was the issue of poverty and crime. Since some supporters of LBJ's "War on Poverty" had touted it as a fundamental solution to the problem of crime arising from material poverty, it was easy for critics of that war, including anti-Great Society Republicans and the ideological right as well as skeptical scholars, to point out that crime had risen along with affluence. "Liberals first denied that crime *was* rising," James Q. Wilson wrote. "Then, when the facts became undeniable, they blamed it on social programs that, through lack of funds and will, had not yet produced *enough* gains and on police departments that, out of prejudice or ignorance, were brutal and unresponsive. It was not made clear, of course, just why more affluence would reduce crime when some affluence had seemingly increased it, or why criminals would be more fearful of gentle cops than of tough ones."

Others preferred to probe the "root causes" of crime. As a result of the "baby boom" following World War II, it was noted, the segment of the population from fifteen to twenty-four years old grew by over a million persons a year during the 1960s. This was said to be a highly crime-prone group that may have caused roughly half of the crime rise. Still others found the source of crime, especially white-collar crime, in the structure of economic and political power within American corporate capitalism. Still others contended that a growing underclass of the poor and alienated had been left in the slums; that the superabundance of expensive consumer goods for the middle classes, including costly cameras, color televisions, and the like, had boosted both the opportunity and the temptation of crime; that drugs in the 1960s and thereafter, like alcohol in the 1920s, had created an addictive subculture dependent on crime; that the root of the problem was not poverty in the measurable monetary sense but a culture of ignorance, apathy, degradation, mental and physical illness, low motivation, and damaged self-esteem that had little connection with rising affluence. Most likely the "root cause" lay in the reinforcing interaction of all or most of these factors.

There was little debate over the impact of rising crime on the criminal justice system. The number of criminal cases filed in all federal district courts rose from 28,000 in 1960 to almost 36,000 in 1983, in federal appeals courts from 623 to 4,790. Criminal trials completed soared from 3,500 to over 6,600 between the same years. These criminal cases in the federal courts had to compete for personnel and funds with an almost fivefold jump in federal civil filings, and all these with an explosion of criminal and civil cases in state and local courts. This enormously stepped-up caseload fell on a system of criminal justice with often ancient features—sheriffs and police, bailiffs and bail vendors, parole and probation officers, arraignments, charges, hearings, trials, postponements, continuances, depositions, grand and petit juries, sentences, appeals, revocations, clemency and pardons—a system that had hardly changed in essential form from the days of Dickens's *Bleak House.* It was as if a great mass of cars, buses, and trucks had suddenly overwhelmed an ancient network of roads, ferries, canals, horse trails, and tollhouses.

Months and years of delay was only the first of a series of stinging indictments brought against the whole criminal justice system. Plea bargaining had become so extensive, it was charged, that the court proceeding had often become but a charade in which pleas were recorded before a judge, satisfying the demands of justice while mocking them. Drawn disproportionately from the lower-middle and middle classes, juries often were not competent to rule on street crime. The failings of the system, wrote a Harvard law professor and former prosecutor, were not "isolable, incidental features of a generally sound process" but characteristic and intrinsic features. The "revolution in criminal procedure" that people liked to talk about, he said, was more a matter of just spinning wheels.

*   *   *

As Americans neared the bicentennial of the establishment of the federal judiciary in 1789, the intellectual disarray of the national deliberation over the state of the criminal justice system overshadowed the institutional disorder of the system itself. Lacking were close analyses of the relationship of immediate expedient means, short-run ends, and ultimate goals of criminal justice; careful ordering of policy priorities linked to fundamental values such as liberty and equality; a consideration, both imaginative and empirical, of the wider psychological, legal, and political ramifications of the social pathology of the culture of poverty; a capacity intellectually to transcend expediency and everyday coping in dealing with problems rising under the criminal justice system. Perhaps the most poignant, if not most serious, reflection of this intellectual disarray was a hardly concealed retreat from theory in favor of specific policies aimed at particular problems. Policy analysis probed not the root cause of a problem but what policy measures and tools might produce "at reasonable cost a desired alteration"—typically a reduction in specified forms of crime. There was one great advantage to "incapacitation" (incarceration) as a crime control strategy, James Wilson wrote—"it does not require us to make any assumptions about human nature."

In the wake of Watergate, the mushrooming of street crime, and horrendous insults by corporations and by government to people's health and their natural environment, there still was no grand debate over American values and the principles and workings of the criminal justice system. Gone were the days when French and American revolutionists had fought to protect the legal rights of individuals, regardless of social rank or class, against the establishment thinkers seeking to defend the ancient prerogatives of state and church. Gone even were the times, fifty years back, when "legal realists," often of New Deal persuasion, had jousted with sacrosanct legal principles that, embodied in judicial findings, could be applied "dispassionately" to current problems. Aside from a few intellectual ventures—notably the critical legal studies movement at Harvard and a handful of other law schools—the debate of the 1980s took the typically American form Tocqueville had noted a century and a half before: grandiose rhetoric about vague but compelling principles like "equal justice under law" and numerous small devices for tinkering with the system, with no firm analytical linkage between values, ordered priorities, and specific measures.

The clouds of rhetoric obscuring the ideological battle did not, however, fully cloak the trench warfare over specific principles and policies. In general, conservatives favored deterrence theories and practices, notably incarceration; in general, liberals supported reformation ideas and measures, notably rehabilitation. These conflicting principles affected choices made and policies pursued across the vast range of the criminal justice system—availability of public defenders, sentencing, parole and probation, indeed the whole gamut of Fourth, Fifth, and Sixth Amendment liberties. In the absence of intellectual clarity, however, these issues were typically settled on the basis of the short run, the expedient, the "practical," of the "facts" of each case rather than an overarching intellectual framework. Thus, plea bargaining was used by prosecutors and defense attorneys alike as a means to obtain quick, acceptable settlements. Rarely did the question arise as to the greater stakes involved. "If the punishment imposed is usually a 'normal price' for the crime and the defendant's benefit from his bargain is less than he hoped," Lloyd Weinreb observed, "nevertheless he is institutionally encouraged to believe that he is trading some of his freedom in order not to be deprived of more." And the easy trading of freedom—freedom from confinement—hardly accorded with this supreme American value.

By and large during the 1970s the hardheaded men, the practical people, the "tough-minded" pragmatists were in charge of the American criminal justice system. They were not stick-in-the-muds—they called for many a reform to energize the system: more police, more judges, more and bigger jails, capital punishment, "flat-time sentencing," severer sentences, various reorganizations of the court and penal systems. Their ultimate recourse in practicality was something no one loved in principle—the jail. For incarceration evaded all the tough intellectual issues and put the lawbreaker in a controlled situation.

But the inmates had their practicality too. "The warden might control his subordinates," a student of criminal justice noted, "but together they did not completely control the prison. An inmate subculture with a clearly defined power structure and differentiated roles exercised considerable power of its own. A trade-off between staff and inmates developed: the inmates accepted the general routine of prison life ('did time'), and in return the staff overlooked systematic violations of prison rules (contraband money, bootleg alcohol and drugs, pervasive homosexuality, including gang rapes, and random violence). Prison violence was frighteningly routine." On their own turf, someone gibed, the inmates were conducting their own form of plea bargaining.

Practical, hardheaded men were in charge at upstate New York's huge Attica prison in 1971: a warden who had worked his way up from the rank of prison guard and won a reputation as a disciplinarian; a seasoned corrections commissioner who would negotiate with inmates up to a point; a worldly governor, Nelson Rockefeller, who preferred to leave "local" crises in the hands of experienced professionals at the scene. Violence had swept New York prisons in recent months and these men knew that Attica, overcrowded with 2,200 inmates, was seething with unrest; they seemed less aware of subtler forces, such as the reaction of Attica's militant blacks to the killing of their hero, George Jackson, during an alleged breakout effort at San Quentin prison in California. A sudden fracas at Attica opened the floodgates of hatred between the inmates, most of them black, and the all-white guard unit. Hundreds of inmates, sweeping through cellblocks, beat up some of the guards, seized forty hostages, set fire to the chapel and the school. Shortly they formed a governing body and issued a set of demands.

During four taut and anguished days the inmates and the local authorities negotiated, while Rockefeller stuck to his Albany office and a group of observers, including the journalist Tom Wicker and the civil rights attorney William Kunstler, served as go-betweens. They could not break the deadlock. Suddenly, after inmates replied "Negative – negative!" to what amounted to an ultimatum from the authorities, state police and prison guards armed with rifles and shotguns moved in behind clouds of tear gas. Nine minutes later forty-three persons, including ten hostages, lay dead or dying. Cornered, cowed, stripped naked, surviving inmates were crowded back through tunnels to their cells.

A few months later, in a poetry workshop for Attica inmates, Clarence Phillips wrote:

> What makes a man free?
> Brass keys, a new court
> Decision, a paper signed
> By the old jail keeper? . . .
> What makes a man free?
> Unchained mind-power and

Control of self — Freedom now!
Freedom now! Freedom now!

CARTER: THE ARC OF MORALITY

The man who succeeded Gerald Ford on January 20, 1977, had swept
onto the American political scene like a gust of fresh air during the presidential primaries of the previous winter. A proud "outsider," an ex-gover-
nor from Georgia, Jimmy Carter had bested nationally known Democratic
pros like Henry M. Jackson, Sargent Shriver, and Morris Udall in the
preconvention battles. Then he had narrowly defeated President Ford—
the first time a White House incumbent had been beaten since Hoover in
1932—with an assist from the Watergate albatross hanging over the GOP.

By inauguration day Carter had acquired a lustrous media image. After
years of mendacity and mediocrity in government, now appeared this man
of religious conviction and high ethical standards. After years of drift and
deadlock in government, a leader of proved competence—competence at
running a business and a state, a submarine and a tractor, and those tough
primary campaigns, a demanding, clearheaded man—seemed to have
stepped forward. Even his appearance—his bluff, open face creased by a
wide smile, his hair style that looked both stylish and rustic, his quick,
buoyant ways—set him off from the gray, sedate men in high office.

To be sure, there was an air of mystery behind the sunny façade. For a
man with relatively brief political experience he showed an astonishing
flair for capturing nationwide media attention. As an upward striver who,
in the judgment of political scientist Betty Glad, had "proved to be a good,
but not extraordinary, governor," he seemed to be aiming a bit prema-
turely for the top job. A proud and self-confessed "idealist" speaking out
in round biblical terms, he said also that he was an "idealist without
illusions"—which, as in the case of John Kennedy, appeared to leave him
plenty of leeway. He had a knack of seeming both above politics and very
canny in political maneuver and combat. He appeared religious but not
pious, compassionate but not sentimental, moral but not moralistic.

If some in the media were put off by his southern Baptist ways—his joyful
hymn singing and hand holding in church, his appeals for more love and
compassion, his southern accent that seemed to grow thicker the nearer
he was to home—many Americans were happy that he was from the Deep
South, the first President to have roots in that region for over a century.
Surely he would bring fresh regional and cultural perspectives to bear on
big government in Washington. People looked to him to transcend the
racial conflicts that had wounded blacks, the South, and the nation. And

"Solid Southerners" were pleased that at last there was a President who spoke without an accent.

And now, on inaugural day, he demonstrated afresh his human touch and media appeal when he bounded out of his limousine on the way to the White House and walked down Pennsylvania Avenue hand in hand with the new First Lady and daughter Amy. In office he promptly pardoned Vietnam draft violators—a happy contrast with Ford's full pardon of Richard Nixon. When Carter fulfilled a campaign promise to keep close to the people by conducting a presidential "town meeting" in a small Massachusetts community, he brought the government home from its Washington remoteness, and incidentally offered a harvest of photo opportunities.

Carter's deepest concern was for human rights. This commitment had quickened in his own recent immersion in the struggle for civil rights in the South. He had been slow to enlist in that struggle, he freely admitted, but by the end of his governorship, "I had gained the trust and political support of some of the great civil rights leaders in my region of the country. To me, the political and social transformation of the Southland was a powerful demonstration of how moral principles should and could be applied effectively to the legal structure of our society." He well knew the view that Presidents had to choose between Wilsonian idealism and Niebuhrian realism, or between morality and power, but he rejected the dichotomy. "The demonstration of American idealism" was a practical and realistic "foundation for the exertion of American power and influence."

Carter was publicly pledged to the campaign for human rights. "Ours was the first nation to dedicate itself clearly to basic moral and philosophical principles," he had said in accepting his nomination for President. In his inaugural address he proclaimed that people around the world "are craving, and now demanding, their place in the sun—not just for the benefit of their own physical condition, but for basic human rights." His Secretary of State, Cyrus Vance, and his national security aide, Zbigniew Brzezinski—both members of the eastern foreign policy establishment—stood with him in his dedication to a "principled yet pragmatic defense of basic human rights," as Vance summarized it.

How apply this noble principle? The President could draw from a broad array of human rights—the heritage of civil and political liberties, such as freedom of thought, religion, speech, and press, forged over the centuries; the right to participate in government, a right much broadened in the Western world during the nineteenth century; personal protection rights against arbitrary arrest and imprisonment, inhuman treatment or punishment, degradation or torture, denial of a proper trial; or a battery of newfound freedoms, such as rights to food, shelter, health care, education.

Many of these rights were embodied in the United Nations charter, the Universal Declaration of Human Rights that in 1948 virtually all nations had approved at least in broad terms, and in the Helsinki agreements.

A week after Carter's inauguration the State Department warned Moscow that any effort to silence the noted physicist and dissident Andrei D. Sakharov would be a violation of "accepted international standards in the field of human rights." Dobrynin promptly telephoned Secretary Vance to protest interference in Soviet internal affairs. Undeterred, the Administration appeared to launch a campaign, expressing concern over the arrests of dissidents Aleksandr Ginzburg, Anatoly Shcharansky, and Yury Orlov, receiving a dissident in exile at the White House, planning substantial boosts in funding for Radio Free Europe and Radio Liberty and in broadcasts to Russia by the Voice of America. In mid-March 1977 the President, in an address to the United Nations General Assembly, once again stated his intention to press for human rights globally.

At the same time Carter was determined to pursue SALT II negotiations, despite warnings that the two efforts would collide. Vance, who had been urging quiet diplomacy as opposed to public pressure on human rights, journeyed to Moscow in late March hoping at least to pick up on negotiations as Ford and Kissinger had left them in Vladivostok, and if possible to move ahead with a much more ambitious and comprehensive plan of the President's. The Soviets, who had responded to the campaign for the dissidents with more arrests, were in no mood to bargain. After cataloguing alleged human rights violations in the United States and attacking the new SALT proposals as harmful to Soviet security, Brezhnev sent Vance home empty-handed.

Nothing more clearly reflected the fundamental ambiguity and the later shift in the Carter foreign relations approach than its rapidly evolving human rights policy. What began as Vance's ambivalent "principled yet pragmatic" posture became increasingly an attack on specific human rights violations that the Kremlin on its side chose to interpret as an onslaught against Soviet society. The American " 'defense of freedom,' " said *Pravda*, was part of the "very same designs to undermine the socialist system that our people have been compelled to counter in one or another form ever since 1917." When Carter contended that he was upholding an aspiration rather than attacking any nation, the Russians tended to suspect Brzezinski's motives rather than the President's moralisms. The human rights files in the Carter presidential library make clear what happened: the President's early utopian tributes to human rights encouraged Soviet, Polish, and other dissidents and their American supporters to put more pressure on the Administration, especially through sympathizers like the national security aide. At the same time that Moscow was condemning American human rights violations at home, black leaders were complaining to the White House that the Administration was retreating on its promises to minorities.

*   *   *

Nearer home Carter applied his foreign policy of "reason and morality" with considerable success during his first year in the White House. He and his wife had a long-standing interest in Latin America, had traveled there, and knew some Spanish. He saw in Latin America, according to Gaddis Smith, a "special opportunity to apply the philosophy of repentance and reform—admitting past mistakes, making the region a showcase for the human-rights policy." Of past mistakes there had been plenty—years of intervention, occupation, and domination. FDR's Good Neighbor policy had brought little surcease. The CIA-managed coup in Guatemala in 1954, John Kennedy's abortive invasion of Cuba, LBJ's intervention in the Dominican Republic, the efforts of the Nixon Administration and the CIA to undermine the duly elected leftist President of Chile, Salvador Allende, and their contribution to his eventual overthrow and death—all these and more still rankled in the memories of Latin American leaders, liberal and radical alike.

No act of Yankee imperialism was more bitterly recalled than the imposition on the Republic of Panama in 1903 by the United States and its Panamanian "puppets" of a treaty defining a strip of land ten miles wide connecting the two oceans while cutting Panama in two and giving the northern colossus near-sovereignty in perpetuity over the canal and the surrounding area. Following a bloody fracas between Panamanians and troops of the United States in 1964, negotiations had been dragging along under Johnson, Nixon, and Ford pointing toward the renegotiation of the 1903 treaty. Carter decided to move quickly. He was well aware of the virulent opposition to a settlement by nationalists in both countries. "We bought it, we paid for it, it's ours and we're going to keep it," had been one of Ronald Reagan's favorite punch lines in the 1976 presidential primaries. Backed up by Defense Secretary Harold Brown's view that the canal could best be kept in operation by "a cooperative effort with a friendly Panama" rather than by an "American garrison amid hostile surroundings," Carter and Vance negotiated with Panama two treaties, one repealing the 1903 treaty and providing for mixed Panamanian–United States operation of the canal until December 31, 1999, the second agreement defining the rights of the United States to defend the canal following Panama's assumption of control on that date.

The White House then threw itself into the battle for Senate ratification, using the time-honored tools of exhortation, bargaining, and arm twisting. The opposition counterattacked with its traditional devices of delay and diversion. Only a mighty effort to mobilize every scrap of his influence enabled the President in the spring of 1978 to win acceptance of the treaties, and then by only the thinnest of margins and at considerable loss of political capital. So virulent was the opposition that, as Carter glumly noted in his memoirs, a number of senators "plus one President" were defeated for reelection in part because of their support of the treaties.

As usual the Middle East confronted Washington with the most intractable problems of all. How defend Israel's security without antagonizing the Arab states? How persuade the Israelis to be more conciliatory toward the Arabs? How find a humane solution to the plight of the Palestinians, whether inhabitants of the occupied Gaza Strip and West Bank or holders of a precarious Israeli citizenship? How strengthen friendly Arab states militarily enough to steel their resistance to Soviet power but not embolden them also to threaten Israel? Carter approached these problems not only with the traditional top-priority commitment of Washington to Israel based on domestic political and national security considerations, but also with a deep moral concern. He believed "that the Jews who had survived the Holocaust deserved their own nation," and that this homeland for the Jews was "compatible with the teachings of the Bible, hence ordained by God."

For sixteen months Carter and Vance conducted an intensive, often desperate search for peace in the Middle East. It was their good fortune that Egypt was ruled by the remarkably farsighted President Anwar el-Sadat, with whom Carter established cordial personal relations, and that Israel came to be headed by a tough negotiator, Menachem Begin, who had enough standing with Israeli hard-liners to risk agreement with the Egyptians. In his own efforts in Washington and in the Middle East, Carter proved himself a resourceful and indefatigable mediator. Often his hopes flagged, particularly after Israeli troops invaded Lebanon in March 1978 in retaliation for a terrorist assault that cost the lives of thirty-five Israelis, all but two of them civilians. To maintain credibility with the Arabs he supported a UN condemnation of the invasion and demand that Israel withdraw its forces. The reaction of American Jews was so sharp, Carter wrote later, that "we had to postpone two major Democratic fund-raising banquets in New York and Los Angeles because so many party members had cancelled their reservations to attend."

Caught between implacable forces, Carter resolved in July 1978 that it "would be best, win or lose, to go all out" to obtain a peace agreement.

He persuaded Sadat and Begin to attend together a September meeting at Camp David. For thirteen days the President and his aides conducted with the two leaders a kind of footpath diplomacy between the cabins. The upshot was Sadat and Begin's agreement to two sets of guidelines: a framework for an Egyptian-Israeli peace providing that the Sinai would be turned over to Egypt by stages while protecting certain Israeli interests there; and a separate framework for "Peace in the Middle East," providing for a five-year period during which a self-governing authority under Egypt, Israel, and, it was hoped, Jordan, would replace the existing Israeli military government in the West Bank and Gaza, while the three nations negotiated the final status of the territories.

At perhaps the high point of his presidency Carter declared to a joint session of Congress, with Begin and Sadat present: "Today we are privileged to see the chance for one of the sometimes rare, bright moments in human history." But nothing important ever came easy for Jimmy Carter. When Begin and Sadat were unable to agree on final peace arrangements before the planned deadline of mid-December 1978, the President decided as "an act of desperation" to fly to Cairo and Jerusalem for personal diplomacy. Once again he demonstrated his flair for mediation, gaining agreement from both sides on the remaining thorny issues, with the aid of inducements and guarantees from the United States. Amid much pomp and circumstance, Sadat and Begin signed the final agreement on the White House lawn late in March 1979.

Wrote Carter in his diary, "I resolved to do everything possible to get out of the negotiating business!"

*　　*　　*

Over all these efforts abroad there fell—at least in American eyes—the shadow of the Kremlin. No matter how much the White House denounced violations of human rights outside the Kremlin's orbit the issue always came back to Soviet repression of dissidents. A major disturbance could not erupt in a newly emerging African nation without suspicion in the White House that Moscow plotters were afoot. The Administration began its peacekeeping effort in the Middle East in cooperation with the Soviet Union, only to turn away from it out of fear that Moscow was interested less in peace than in extending its own influence in the region. The more Washington pursued its rapprochement with Peking, the more it encountered hostility in Moscow. The Administration suspected that the Russians were bolstering their military strength in Cuba. Even the Panama settlement, which seemed far outside the Soviet sphere of influence, was almost fatally jeopardized by those Americans who feared that the strategically vital canal would under Panamanian control prove vulnerable to Soviet political or military threat.

The view from Moscow was clouded by its perception of an ever more threatening America. Washington was seeking to exclude Soviet influence in the Middle East—a strategic area in Russia's own back yard. The Americans were trying not only to make friends with the Chinese but to arm them against the Soviet Union, and thereby encircle it. Washington was trying to block the Soviet Union, as the mother communist nation, from exercising its right and duty to help both stabilize and strengthen "national liberation" movements in the fledgling nations. Above all was the matter of arms—the Soviet Union was on the verge of achieving some kind of nuclear parity with the United States, at which point the Carter Administration undertook a big new arms program that could result only in a spiraling arms race.

Both sets of perceptions were misconceptions. Washington was more interested in restoring triangular diplomacy with China than in exacerbating the Sino-Soviet rupture. The Russians were more interested in stability in the Middle East than in military advantage. Each side saw itself as defensive, peace-loving, cooperative, the other as offensive, aggressive, destructive. Looking at Moscow, Washington remembered the brutal invasion of Hungary in 1956, the shipping of missiles to Cuba in 1962, the suppression of Czechoslovakia in 1968. Looking at Washington, Moscow recalled the attack north of the 38th parallel into North Korea in 1950, the occupation of the Dominican Republic in 1965, the bombing of North Vietnam and invasion of Cambodia in the 1960s and 1970s.

Mutual suspicion and hostility of the two superpowers touched every part of the globe—even the smallest and weakest nations. The tiny Yemens were a prime example. South Yemen, with its major naval facilities at Aden, the former British port, accepted aid from Moscow and gave it access to the port. North Yemen, fearful of the Yemenis to the south, wanted American military aid. When the Soviets began to give heavy aid to Ethiopia in support of its dispute with Somalia, Brzezinski saw a new Soviet threat to the Middle East. The canny North Yemenis, seeing their chance to pay off the southerners and gain more aid from Washington, sent alarmist reports of a looming invasion from the south. Alert to this mortal peril, Washington sent American arms and advisers to North Yemen and dispatched the carrier *Constellation* to the Arabian Sea "to demonstrate our concern for the security of the Arabian Peninsula." In the end several Arab states mediated the scrap between the Yemenis—and North Yemen made an arms deal with the Russians twice the size of the American deal. The fight between the Yemenis, scholars later concluded, had not been plotted by Moscow.

"The United States," according to historian Gaddis Smith, "was responding, not to a reality, but to imaginary possibilities based on the assumption
of a sinister Soviet grand design."

Nor was Washington plotting in most of these situations. It was a classic
case of confusion rather than conspiracy. At the center of the confusion
was the President himself. He continued to be convinced, during his first
year in office, that he could crusade against human rights violations in
Russia and at the same time effectively pursue détente with Moscow. During his second year he was still talking détente and SALT II but emphasizing also the need to strengthen United States forces in Europe to meet the
"excessive Soviet buildup" there. By mid-1978, Carter's ambivalence was
so serious that Vance formally requested a review of relations with the
Soviets, noting "two differing views" of the relationship. The emphasis,
Vance said, had been on balancing cooperation against competition; was
the emphasis now merely on competition? When Carter at Annapolis in
June reaffirmed détente but now spoke a language of confrontation, the
press complained about "two different speeches," the "ambiguous message," and general "bafflement." Moscow, however, viewed the speech
solely as a challenge.

Carter was now enveloped in a widening division, especially between
Vance and Brzezinski. The Secretary of State, who had built his reputation
largely on high-level negotiations during the 1960s, spurned ideology in
favor of détente through persistent—and if necessary severe—diplomacy.
The national security adviser, son of a prewar Polish diplomat, had taken
a hard line toward Moscow since the 1950s. In 1962, during the Cuban
missile crisis, from his Columbia University post he had telegraphed the
Kennedy White House a warning against "any further delay in bombing
missile sites." Under Carter the two men repeatedly disagreed over policy
toward the Soviet Union—most notably the extent to which the "China
card" should be played against Moscow. And they insistently denied the
disagreement—until it came time for their memoirs. Vance remembered
the national security adviser as afflicted with "visceral anti-Sovietism."
Brzezinski evaluated the Secretary of State "as a member of both the legal
profession and the once-dominant Wasp elite," operating according to
"values and rules" that were of "declining relevance" to both American
and global politics.

The President saw the two men as balancing each other's strengths and
weaknesses, but instead of moving steadily between them, he followed a
zigzag path. His aim was still a summit meeting with the Russians for a
climactic effort to achieve a second SALT agreement. During 1978, however, playing the "China card" in a manner tantamount to playing with

fire, he allowed Brzezinski to journey to China, where the security adviser urged the not unwilling Chinese to step up their diplomatic and political moves against Moscow. The morbidly distrustful Russians suspected that the Yankees might sell "defensive weapons" to the Chinese.

The summit was further delayed while Carter amid intense publicity received and entertained Deng Xiaoping at the White House at the end of January 1979, only a few weeks after Washington broke formal diplomatic relations with Taiwan and established full relations with China. Carter and Deng got along famously, signing agreements for scientific and technological cooperation. The Chinese leader even confided to the President his tentative plans to make a punitive strike into Vietnam because of Hanoi's hostility to Peking. Carter tried weakly to discourage this, but the Chinese attacked within three weeks of Deng's visit to Washington.

On the eve of flying off in June 1979 for the summit the President announced his decision to develop the MX missile. By the time he and Brezhnev met in Vienna, much of the will in both camps for comprehensive peacemaking had slackened. Brezhnev, old and ailing, seemed to have lost his energy and grasp of issues. The two men signed a package of agreements, elaborately and cautiously negotiated over a period of many months, providing for limitations in land-based missiles, submarine-based MIRVed missiles, bombers equipped with multiple missiles, and other arms. SALT II was still a respectable step forward—if the step could be taken. Following the Soviet occupation of Afghanistan shortly after New Year's 1980, however, the President asked the Senate to defer action. This delay, and Reagan's condemnation of the treaty during the 1980 campaign, killed SALT II's chances—the most profound disappointment of his presidency, Carter said later.

*   *   *

Historians will long debate the causes of the malaise that afflicted Jimmy Carter's presidency about the time he began the last third of his term. Was it largely a personal failure of leadership on the part of Carter and his inner circle at a crucial point in his Administration? Or was the loss of momentum and direction during 1979 more the result of factors that plague every President—intractable foreign and domestic problems, a divided party, a fragmented Congress, a hostile press, limited political resources? Or was it a matter of sheer bad luck—a series of unpredictable events that overwhelmed the Administration?

In his disarmingly frank way, Carter himself admitted a failure of personal leadership. In midsummer of 1979, he removed his government to Camp David and summoned over a hundred Americans—political, business, labor, academic, and religious leaders—for long consultations, and then emerged to declare in an eagerly anticipated television speech that the nation was caught in a crisis of confidence, a condition of paralysis and stagnation, to which his detached, managerial style of leadership had contributed and at the center of which was the energy crisis, whose solution could "rekindle our sense of unity, our confidence in the future." At a specially convened cabinet meeting two days after the speech, he stated, according to a participant, "My government is not leading the country. The people have lost confidence in me, in the Congress, in themselves, and in this nation." A week before his 1980 election defeat he graded himself on CBS's *60 Minutes,* giving his presidency a B or a C plus on foreign policy, C on overall domestic policy, A on energy, C on the economy, and "maybe a B" on leadership. For a President, B and C are failing grades.

Carter's shifts toward the middle ground in domestic policy and confrontation in Soviet relations, along with his loss of popularity at home, had opened up a leadership vacuum that was bound to attract a liberal-left Democrat of the stripe of Robert Kennedy, Eugene McCarthy, George McGovern, or indeed the 1976-style Jimmy Carter. Would Edward Kennedy run? Since his brother Robert's assassination, Democratic party leaders and rank-and-file enthusiasts had been trying to recruit him, but the young senator had proved to be a master at saying no. Now, thoroughly disappointed by Carter, he decided to take on the toughest of political assignments, unseating a President of one's own party. At first Kennedy appeared unable to define his alternative program coherently, and when he took a fling at the dethroned Shah of Iran and the "umpteen billions of dollars that he's stolen from Iran," the media treated this as a campaign gaffe to be derided rather than a policy issue to be debated.

Carter's early handling of the seizure in November 1979 of the American embassy in Teheran and sixty-three American hostages produced the usual rally-'round-the-President surge in public opinion. Kennedy failed to gain momentum after running far behind the President in the Iowa caucuses. Later the senator picked up strong support in urban areas when he spoke firmly for détente abroad and anti-inflation controls at home, but he never headed his adversary. Some of the President's men argued that Kennedy's run hurt Carter in the fall contest with Ronald Reagan, but Democrats showed their usual capacity for reuniting before the final battle. In retrospect it appeared that Carter had defeated himself, largely by appearing to have faltered as a strong leader, a sitting duck for Reagan's charges of inadequacy and indecision.

Hamilton Jordan, Carter's aide and confidant, wrote after the 1980 defeat that he had "found many forces at play today that make the art of governing very difficult"—an "active and aggressive press," the fragmentation of political power, congressional resistance, special-interest groups, and the like. Conditions, in effect, made governing impossible. Leading students of the Carter presidency instead fixed the blame on the President himself. "Carter lacked any sense of political strategy," wrote political scientist Erwin C. Hargrove, "and thereby the majority of citizens came to believe that he was not in control of the events which most concerned them." If Carter was bedeviled by weak party support, congressional factionalism, bureaucratic power groups—and by the "iron triangles" interlocking these resistance forces—the question arises: to what degree did he seek to curb or even master these by leading and refashioning his divided party, for example, or by improving his poor congressional liaison office? He devoted little time to rebuilding either the party or the liaison office.

The "bad luck" theory of Carter's decline holds that he was simply engulfed by forces over which he had no control—the energy crisis, soaring gasoline prices, steep inflation, high interest rates, Kennedy's challenge, and above all the continuing hostage crisis and the brutal Soviet intervention in Afghanistan. As great leaders have demonstrated, however, setbacks can be—or can be made to be—spurs to action.

Perhaps Carter's greatest failure stemmed from his moralism in foreign policy combined with his flair for media showmanship. His reaction to the hostage seizure in Iran and to the Afghanistan intervention was not to put the crises in perspective and restrain public opinion but to dramatize the issues and further inflame the public. This politically expedient course, reflecting also Carter's moral judgment, brought the heady feeling in the short run of being the true spokesman and leader of the people, but it had severe longer-run effects. In helping to arouse the public, and then responding to that aroused public, Carter raised hopes and expectations inordinately. But Iran held on to the hostages and the Russians remained in Afghanistan. Nothing is more dangerous for a leader than a widening gap between expectations and realization.

This gap paralleled and exacerbated another one—between Carter's idealistic, uplifting foreign policy pronouncements and day-to-day specific policies. Preachments were not converted into explicit guidelines. A *strategic* approach was lacking. When initiatives had to be taken and tough choices made, the Administration lacked a hierarchy of priorities that could fill the gap between its global activism and the routine application of foreign policies. Carter alternated between born-again moralizing and engineering specifics. In this respect he shared one of the oldest intellectual weaknesses of American liberal activism.

GUN AND BIBLE

At the 1978 Harvard commencement a gaunt and towering figure out of the Russian past denounced not the evils of Soviet communism, as many in the audience had expected, but the American culture in which he had taken refuge. Aleksandr Solzhenitsyn delivered a powerful attack on the ideas and symbols most Americans held sacred—liberty, liberal democracy, even the pursuit of happiness. "Destructive and irresponsible freedom," he said, had produced an "abyss of human decadence"—violence, crime, pornography, "TV stupor," and "intolerable music." Solzhenitsyn had long been sounding the tocsin against freedom Western style. Civil liberty, he had said almost a decade before, had left the West "crawling on hands and knees," its will paralyzed, after it had supped "more than its fill of every kind of freedom." Indeed, to regard freedom "as the object of our existence" was nonsense.

If the Harvard audience responded to most of Solzhenitsyn's stinging attack with a measure of composure, it was perhaps in part because the university was by tradition a forum of protest. Graduate student Meldon E. Levine, delivering the English Oration in 1969, at the height of the student protest, in that same Harvard Yard, had challenged his audience of alumni, faculty, and parents to live up to their own standards of equality and justice, courage and trust. The students were "affirming the values which you have instilled in us," he said, "AND WE HAVE TAKEN YOU SERIOUSLY." And almost two centuries before, President Samuel Langdon of Harvard had lamented, "Have we not, especially in our Seaports, gone much too far into the pride and luxuries of life?" Was it not a fact that "profaneness, intemperance, unchastity, the love of pleasure, fraud, avarice, and other vices, are increasing among us from year to year?"

For more than three centuries, indeed, Americans had worried about other Americans' loss of virtue. Over the years, the definition of virtue— and of vice—had taken many forms. During the twenty years or so following President Langdon's protest of 1775 the most widely accepted idea of virtue was the subordination of private interests to the public good, demonstrated by direct, day-to-day participation in civic affairs. What were these private interests to be suppressed? Certainly the blasphemy and drinking and carnality and pleasure seeking that Langdon complained of, but even more the commercial avarice and frenzied moneymaking that promoted those vices and ultimately corrupted the republic. Vice and virtue were locked in a never-ending struggle for the soul of America.

The framers of the Constitution had enjoyed few illusions as to how that struggle might turn out, for their political and military battles in the 1770s and 1780s and their study of political philosophy had left them pessimistic about the nature of man, in contrast to its potential under the right circumstances. They had limited faith in the capacity of their fellow Americans to exhibit the classical virtues of self-discipline, courage, fortitude, and disinterested public service, even less faith in the power of Calvinism's austere morality to control appetites and passions, and only a faint hope that a benevolent tendency within human nature to sociability and community, as articulated by the Scottish philosophers, would prevail under the raw conditions of American life. Unwilling to pin their hopes on human virtue, they had fashioned rules and institutions—most notably the Constitution—that at the very least would channel and tame the forces of passion and cushion the play of individual and group interest.

Two centuries later, Americans were more divided than ever as to the cause and cure of vice and the nature and nurture of virtue. Ostensibly these matters were left to the deliberations and preachments of churchmen, but they too were divided in numberless ways, even within their own denominations. Families, schools, the military, the workplace, the tavern added to the variety of ethical codes. And beyond all this, American men and women professed moralities that they did not follow in practice. In the mid-1950s Max Lerner found that the moral code prescribed that "a man must be temperate in drink, prudent in avoiding games of chance, continent in sex, and governed by the values of religion and honor." A woman must be chaste and modest. But this formal code had been replaced by "an operative code which says that men and women may drink heavily provided they can 'carry' their liquor and not become alcoholics; that they may gamble provided they pay their gambling debts, don't cheat, or let their families starve; that a girl may have premarital sexual relations provided she is discreet enough not to get talked about or smart enough to marry her man in the end; that husband or wife may carry flirtations even into extramarital adventures, provided it is done furtively and does not jeopardize the family; or (if they are serious love affairs) provided that they end in a divorce and a remarriage."

Even as the moral code was cloaking "real sex" during the 1950s, unsentimental biologists were ripping aside the shields between sexual pretension and practice. In 1953, Dr. Alfred Kinsey and his colleagues published *Sexual Behavior in the Human Female* a few years after their similar study of the human male. In a huge sample of respondents, over 90 percent of the males and over 60 percent of the females had, by their own account, practiced masturbation; about half the men and over a quarter of the women reported having had some homosexual experience; 8 percent of

the males and about half that percentage of females admitted some experience with bestiality. Tens of millions of Americans, in short, were sexually
"perverse," according to the moral code. The Kinsey studies recorded the
assertion of 71 percent of the men and 50 percent of the women that they
had practiced premarital intercourse in their teens; indicated that adultery
and illegitimacy were far more common and widespread than commonly
supposed; reported that many boys of low-income families claimed to have
had intercourse with scores and even hundreds of different girls. So tens
of millions of Americans were "immoral" by the standards of the received
morality.

If the practitioners of "vice" found considerable solace in the Kinsey
survey, the shock of the findings further fragmented moral attitudes in a
society that was already "half Babylonian and half Puritan," in Lerner's
phrase, further divided a religiosity that had both a "soft," tolerant side
and a "hard," condemnatory side, in John P. Diggins's. Now that their
worst suspicions had been vindicated as to how people behaved sexually
no matter how innocently they talked, media moralists and religious fundamentalists renewed their campaign against permissive laws and standards.
Civil libertarians, in turn, sprang to the defense of books, films, plays,
television programs, and, above all, magazines such as *Playboy* and later
Penthouse and the raunchier *Hustler* that depicted and exploited sexual
behavior and sexual fantasies.

Both sides—all sides—appealed to the symbol of Freedom. Sexual liberationists spoke up for the freedom to defy the majority and indulge in
deviant forms of sexual behavior in their pursuit of happiness. Moralists
pressed for censorship of sexually explicit expression, but they had to deal
with libertarians in their midst who opposed the heavy hand of the censor
and contended that family, school, and church should do the work of
combating sexual "misbehavior" and its depiction.

The conflict over erotica and its expression cut deep into the bone and
tissue of American society. Feminists, united so passionately over so many
burning issues, were divided over censorship of pornography. Some argued that the depiction of violent porn should be shorn of its First Amendment protection. Sexual degradation of women, rape, harassment, batter-
ing, sadism—the mere depiction of such misbehavior influenced men's
behavior. Others contended that "evil thoughts" did not necessarily lead
to evil action, that the problem was the depiction not of *sexual* violence but
of sexual *violence,* that damage to women could just as well be caused by
violence without sex.

The "experts," as usual, differed among themselves. A 1970 commission
found no evidence that "exposure to explicit sexual materials" played a

"significant role" in causing delinquent or criminal behavior among youth or adults, while a 1986 Reagan Administration commission found ample evidence of a causal link between violent pornography and aggressive behavior toward women.

Some feminists, conceding that thought did not always lead to action, turned to antidiscrimination laws as the vehicle for curbing the depiction of sexual violence. Antipornography feminists Andrea Dworkin and Catherine MacKinnon proposed an ordinance granting any woman a cause of action if she had been coerced into a pornographic performance and granting all women the right to bring suit against traffickers in pornography for assault or other harm alleged to be caused by pornography. Others, organized in the Feminist Anti-Censorship Taskforce (FACT), protested that the Dworkin-MacKinnon ordinance was vague in its definition of pornography, and it was largely on this and on First Amendment grounds that a federal judge invalidated an enactment of the ordinance in Indianapolis, a decision which the Supreme Court later affirmed. FACT, according to philosophy professor Rosemarie Tong, contended that the antipornography feminists had left the core question begging: "What kinds of sexually explicit acts place a woman in an inferior status? An image of rape? An image of anal intercourse? An image of the traditional heterosexual act in which a man's body presses down on and into a woman's?" What worried FACT most, according to Tong, was the refusal of the ordinance "to recognize the degree to which what we see is determined by what we are either told to see or want to see." The issue was not only content but intent and context.

Once again a policy issue had ended up—even among friends—as a sharp difference over fundamental values. Feminist antipornographers demanded to be free of masculine domination, "compulsory heterosexuality," depictions of the degradation of women; they asserted that sexual equality between men and women was integral to equal rights and legal and political equality. The feminist sexual liberationists demanded their own kind of freedom and warned, in Tong's words, that an antiporn campaign "could usher in another era of sexual suppression" and "give the moralists, the right-wingers, the conservatives a golden opportunity to limit once again human sexual exploration." Again American values were proving inadequate as guidelines to policy.

*   *   *

It has long been accepted in international affairs that nation-states are not required to observe the same standards of behavior—of mutual respect, reciprocity, understanding, honor—expected of the relationships of individuals in ordered societies. "If we had done for ourselves what we did for the state," Cavour said, "what scoundrels we would be." Niebuhr distinguished sharply between "moral man" and "immoral society." Kenneth Thompson observed that morality within the nation "can be manageable, convincing and attainable," while "the international interest is more remote, vague and ill-defined."

Religious leaders, however, have not been so willing to let nation-states evade the demands of morality and mutuality. In colonial times Quakers, Mennonites, Amish, and Shakers spread widely their teachings about peace and nonviolence. During the next century Congregationalists, Unitarians, and leaders in other Protestant denominations set up numerous "nonresistance" societies, culminating in the formation of the League of Universal Brotherhood in 1847. This organization, which after a few years boasted a membership in the tens of thousands, carried on its condemnation of all war in mass publications and at international peace congresses. In the early twentieth century the Catholic Church, preoccupied with efforts to establish itself in sometimes alien or nativist communities, had only the barest involvement in the American peace movement. While some Catholic groups embraced a tradition of social dissent and constituencies of the poor, "a patriotic inclination to celebrate American society; a fear of criticism arising from marginal social status and the general Catholic respect for authority," in Mel Piehl's words, dampened Catholic radical social efforts.

American Catholics, numbering fifty million by the 1980s, were broadening their participation in American politics, higher education, business—and peace movements. No longer did they need to prove their patriotism by uncritically embracing an aggressive foreign and military policy. While Protestant, Jewish, and other religious leaders also stepped up their peace efforts, American Catholic bishops effected an amazingly rapid transition from support of the U.S. effort in Vietnam in 1966 to condemnation in 1971 on the grounds of its "destruction of human life and moral values."

The swing of the bishops toward a strong peace stance was expedited by an earlier shift in the Vatican. Even in the face of aggressive cold war behavior by its mortal enemy, Soviet communism, the papacy called increasingly for steps to control the nuclear genies. In his historic 1963 encyclical, *Pacem in Terris*, John XXIII, recognizing the "immense suffering" that the use of modern arms would inflict on humanity, declared it "contrary to reason to hold that war is now a suitable way to restore rights which have been violated." Pressure was exerted within the American church by peace-minded groups, most notably the United States section of the international Catholic organization Pax Christi. After a faltering start, Pax Christi became well organized during the late 1970s and by 1983 had chapters in all fifty states and a powerful corps of leaders, as exemplified by Bishops Thomas J. Gumbleton of Detroit and Carroll T. Dozier of Memphis. Operating outside the institutional church but stirring Catholic consciences "from the left" were individual militants such as former nun Elizabeth McAlister and priests such as the Berrigan brothers.

In the spring of 1983, while the Reagan Administration carried on a foreign relations rhetoric that vacillated between the aggressive and the bellicose, the Catholic bishops issued their "Pastoral Letter" entitled "The Challenge of Peace: God's Promise and Our Response." The statement was at once traditional and radical, Patricia Hunt-Perry has noted—"traditional in the sense that the bishops grounded their pronouncements solidly in Catholic dogma, Biblical text, and the teachings of Catholic saints such as Augustine and Aquinas," but radical in its application of traditional doctrines to the urgency of a "whole human race" facing, in the bishops' words, a "moment of supreme crisis in its advance toward maturity."

"We are the first generation since Genesis with the power to virtually destroy God's creation," the bishops warned. "We cannot remain silent in the face of such danger." The letter assigned to Americans the "grave human, moral and political responsibilities" to see that a "conscious choice" was made to save humanity. "We must shape the climate of opinion which will make it possible for our country to express profound sorrow over the atomic bombing in 1945." The willingness to initiate nuclear war "entails a distinct, weighty moral responsibility; it involves transgressing a fragile barrier—political, psychological and moral." Striking major military or economic targets "could well involve such massive civilian casualties" as to be "morally disproportionate, even though not intentionally indiscriminate."

In general, the bishops underplayed legal, technical, and policy arguments in order to speak all the more powerfully with their collective moral voice. Indeed, the final draft eliminated earlier references in the main body of the text to such specific issues as the MX missile. But the bishops did propose that the "growing interdependence of the nations and peoples of the world, coupled with the extragovernmental presence of multinational corporations, requires new structures of cooperation." They boldly confronted one of the toughest questions—that of the "just war"—and reviewed the conditions necessary to it: just cause, declaration of war by a competent authority, comparative justice, right intention, last resort, probability of success, and proportionality between destruction inflicted and the aims to be achieved. And they expressed special concern about the

impact of the arms race—"one of the greatest curses on the human race"—
on the poor.

In the debate that followed, it was clear at least that the pastoral letter
had raised the moral tone and urgency of the nuclear issue. George Kennan called it "the most profound and searching inquiry yet conducted by
a responsible collective body into the relations of nuclear weaponry, and
indeed of modern war in general, to moral philosophy, to politics and to
the conscience of the nation state."

*   *   *

A decline in courage was the most striking feature in the West, Solzhenitsyn had said at Harvard, especially "among the ruling and intellectual
elites." America's refusal to win the Vietnam War, he added amid un-
Harvard-like hisses, was the ultimate evidence of the loss of willpower in
the West. Solzhenitsyn could hardly have been pleased by the position of
the Catholic bishops—all the more because they were religious leaders
who should have stood militantly united against Soviet communism. But
Solzhenitsyn could hardly have found the American kaleidoscope of ideas,
groups, parties, and leaders anything but baffling. The head of the European Economic Community, Jacques Delors, made a more penetrating
observation of American world policy as Reagan neared the end of his first
term. He saw an "increasingly aggressive and ideological" Administration
carrying "a bible in one hand and a revolver in the other." In truth, though,
Delors could have said this of most presidential Administrations since
World War II.

Washington's human rights policy exposed the division and confusion
about foreign policy in the American mind. In December 1948 the United
Nations General Assembly had adopted and proclaimed the Universal
Declaration of Human Rights "as a common standard of achievement for
all peoples and all nations." This elevated document laid out three sets of
fundamental rights. First, proclaiming that "all human beings are born free
and equal in dignity and rights," it set forth the historic intellectual and
political freedoms—"the right to life, liberty and the security of person"
and the "right to freedom of thought, conscience and religion." Then a
set of procedural guarantees including provisions that "no one shall be
subjected to torture or to cruel, inhuman or degrading treatment or punishment" or "be subjected to arbitrary arrest, detention or exile."

Finally, a set of basic economic and social rights: "to work, to free choice
of employment, to just and favorable conditions of work and to protection
against unemployment," the right to equal pay for equal work, "the right
to a standard of living adequate for the health and well-being of himself

and of his family," the right to free education, at least in the lower grades.

How could such a diversity of nations, with the varieties of subcultures, live up to such a wide range of specific rights which were, in turn, obligations placed on their own governments? In part merely by ignoring or evading them. In part by defining or interpreting them to suit their own political needs. And in part by establishing radically differing sets of priorities among these three major sets of basic rights in the instrument.

For Americans, individual civil and political rights emerged out of a long and precious tradition—Magna Carta, the English Petition of Right and Bill of Rights of the seventeenth century, the French Declaration of the Rights of Man of 1791, the American Bill of Rights ratified in the same year. These in essence were protections for the rights of individual citizens against the state. But it is "not enough to think in terms of two-level relationships," Vernon Van Dyke contended, "with the individual at one level and the state at another; nor is it enough if the nation is added. Considering the heterogeneity of humankind and of the population of virtually every existing state, it is also necessary to think of ethnic communities and certain other kinds of groups." Trade unions, public or semi-public corporations, cultural entities, semi-autonomous regional groups might claim rights against both the state and the individual.

The most serious potential clash among the doctrines of the Universal Declaration of Human Rights lay between the first and the third major set of rights—political freedoms such as those of thought and religion, opinion and expression, of movement within and among nations, as against social and economic freedoms such as rights to employment, decent pay, education, health, food, housing. Third World countries inescapably stressed the socioeconomic rights in the Universal Declaration over the individualist. "You know, professor," a junior minister of an African nation said to a Zimbabwean academic, "we wish imperialists could understand that the sick and hungry have no use for freedom of movement or of speech. Maybe of worship! Hunger dulls hearing and stills the tongue. Poverty and lack of roads, trains, or buses negate freedom of movement."

Russians and Americans differed even more sharply over individualistic political rights versus collective socioeconomic freedoms. When Washington accused Moscow of violating personal political rights in its treatment of dissidents, the Kremlin gleefully retaliated by accusing Washington of violating the social and economic rights of the poor in general and blacks in particular. The Carter Administration sought to deflect such ripostes by emphasizing that human rights encompassed economic and social rights as well as political and civil liberties. "We recognize that people have economic as well as political rights," Secretary of State Vance said in 1978.

Still the debate continued, and rose to new heights during the Reagan Administration as conservative ideologues found official rostrums from which to belabor Soviet repression, while Soviet propagandists found ample material for exploitation in stories in American journals and newspapers about the poor and the homeless.

At the dawn of the last decade of the second millennium A.D., as Westerners prepared to celebrate the bicentennials of the French Declaration of the Rights of Man and the American Bill of Rights, human rights as a code of international and internal behavior—especially as embodied in the UN declaration of 1948—were in practical and philosophical disarray. Rival states used the Universal Declaration to wage forensic wars with one another over the fundamental meaning of freedom. It had proved impossible for national leaders to agree on priorities and linkages among competing rights, most notably between economic-social and civil-political.

And yet the world Declaration of Rights still stood as a guide to right conduct and a symbol of global aspiration. In both domestic and international politics it was invoked, on occasion, with good effect. As cast into international instruments, human rights law, David Forsythe concluded, "is an important factor in the mobilization of concerned individuals and groups who desire more freedom, or more socio-economic justice, or both. This mobilization has occurred everywhere, even in totalitarian and authoritarian societies." And the conflict over the meaning and application of international human rights invited the tribute of hypocrisy. "The clearest evidence of the stability of our values over time," writes Michael Walzer, "is the unchanging character of the lies soldiers and statesmen tell. They lie in order to justify themselves, and so they describe for us the lineaments of justice. Wherever we find hypocrisy, we also find moral knowledge." Thus the idea of freedom and justice and human rights binds the virtuous and the less virtuous together, in hypocrisy and in hope.

CHAPTER 13

The Culture of the Workshop

O UT of the prodigious experimental workshops of America—the "enormous laboratories," the solitary one-person think tanks, the suspense-ridden observatories, the bustling engineering departments— erupted a fecundity of ideas, discoveries, and inventions during the 1960s and 1970s. Measured by Nobel Prizes, United States scientists still dominated the life sciences and physics and, to a lesser degree, chemistry. In physiology or medicine, Americans during these two decades won Nobels for discoveries about hearing, cholesterol metabolism, hormonal treatment of prostate cancer, color perception, enzymes and the growth and functioning of cells, the relation between cancer-causing viruses and genes, the origin and spread of infectious diseases, the action of hormones, the effect of restriction enzymes on genes, the CAT-scan X-ray procedure, cell immunology. In physiology and medicine, Americans, sometimes in partnership with British and continental scientists, won Nobels for seven years straight starting in 1974.

In physics, during these two decades Americans were awarded Nobel Prizes for work on the complex structure of protons and nucleons, the symmetry principle governing the interaction of nuclear particles, masers, quantum electrodynamics, the nuclear reactions involved in the production of energy in stars, superconductivity, the subatomic J/psi particle, solid-state electronics, background cosmic radiation supporting the "big bang" theory, the symmetry of subatomic particles. In chemistry, Americans won Nobel Prizes for work on the chemical reactions in photosynthesis, the synthesis of organic structures, the theory of chemical bonds holding atoms together in molecules, the reciprocal processes in interactions such as those of voltage and temperature in heat transfer, the molecular analyses of proteins and enzymes, macromolecules, the methods of diagramming the structure and function of DNA.

The Nobel committee does not grant prizes in astronomy or astrophysics, but scientists in the nation's observatories hardly needed kudos from Stockholm for incentives. Knowledge of outer space expanded immensely as more and more powerful radio telescopes were built. In 1960, quasars ("quasi-stellar radio sources") were detected at Palomar Observatory in southern California. Within a few years, astronomers were discovering that the fastest and most distant of these faint blue celestial bodies, quasar 3C-9, was speeding away from the Milky Way at almost the speed of light. In 1975, University of California observers found a new galaxy at least ten times larger than the Milky Way and around eight billion light-years away from Earth. "Black holes" were probed, including a possible one at the center of the Milky Way. During the 1960s and 1970s, the space program was bringing breathtaking information about the planets and other nearby precincts. But nothing stirred earthlings' imaginations as much as the radio waves coming in from galaxies quadrillions of miles away.

The dependence of astronomy on radio telescopes and space programs indicated the vital role of technology in scientific work. In atomic research, the 1930 cyclotron that accelerated particles to energies of a few million volts for smashing atoms was followed thirty years later by larger atom smashers at Brookhaven National Laboratory in New York and by Stanford University's two-mile, 20-billion-volt linear accelerator. Oceanography required large vessels with highly specialized equipment. The development of the atomic and hydrogen bombs had taken huge facilities and vast sums of money. The dependence of science on technology was not new in America—only its magnitude. Even while Josiah Gibbs had been working solo with meager facilities at Yale, Thomas Edison had been establishing an elaborately equipped industrial research laboratory. While Edison had enjoyed calling it his "invention factory," the German economist Werner Sombart glimpsed the new world ahead when he noted that, in the United States, Edison had made a "business" of invention. The increasing dependence of scientific research on big technology raised a number of political and intellectual problems, such as the controls implied in both corporate and governmental subsidies, excessive influence on scientific research of market forces, and discouragement of "free" scientific inquiry.

Volumes—indeed, libraries of volumes—were written about scientific discoveries and technological breakthroughs of Nobel-class stature. Was there a pattern in these developments? The growth and impact of semiconductor electronics illustrated, perhaps more dramatically than most inventions, the nature of the origin and application of scientific ideas in the twentieth century. The intellectual roots of the electronics industry went back to earlier scientific geniuses, in this case Faraday and Maxwell; the next steps were the product of fundamental, multidisciplinary academic research, which both contributed to and was greatly stimulated by the two world wars, especially the second; further development as usual turned on 90 percent perspiration, 10 percent inspiration, on the part of a large number of persons. Soon semiconductor research, like that producing other great innovations, moved far beyond the capacities of the kind of Yankee tinkerer that had pioneered American technology in earlier decades. There was no way, Ernest Braun and Stuart Macdonald wrote, in which semiconductor devices could be "tinkered with at home; no way by which a skilled craftsman could improve their performance. The mode of operation of these devices is so complex and intricate, the scale so small, the interactions so subtle, that all old-fashioned inventiveness proved of no avail."

The semiconductor breakthroughs fell upon American industry in the form of computers capable of storing and processing fantastic quantities of data and of large-scale automation, on American consumers in glittering arrays of electronic calculators, digital watches, portable tape recorders, heart pacemakers, hearing aids. An estimated 190 million integrated circuits were installed in 1980-model American cars to monitor engine efficiency and produce the increasingly elaborate dashboard displays. Entering the inner world of miniaturization was as extraordinary as exploring the universe of space. Americans developed microchips the size of a postage stamp with half a million or so transistors and associated circuitry mounted on each. These chips liberated millions of Americans from old-time chores like "figurin' " with pencil and paper; they also made bugging devices more efficient and easily concealed. Americans were moving so fast through the electronics age that the enlargement and diminution of personal freedom could hardly be calculated.

The Dicing Game of Science

Just as the rise of American capitalism had made heroes of captains of industry like Carnegie and Ford, and two world wars had created paladins like Pershing and Eisenhower, so the outpouring from the prodigious laboratories of the 1950s and 1960s produced heroes of science. Jonas E. Salk of the University of Pittsburgh Medical School, using three strains of inactivated polio, developed a vaccine that was injected into almost two million schoolchildren, with gratifying results. The frightening rise of polio cases from three or four thousand a year in the late 1930s to around 60,000 by 1952 was reversed to its levels of the 1930s. This benign curve was completed by Albert Sabin, whose widely used oral vaccine brought polio cases reported in the United States down to twenty-one in 1971. Linus Pauling, after receiving the Nobel Prize in chemistry for his research into the forces holding proteins and molecules together, became the first man to win a second unshared Nobel, the peace prize of 1962, for his leadership in the campaign against nuclear testing. James Watson achieved fame not only for his role in the discovery of the structure of DNA— suddenly "we knew that a new world had been opened"—but for writing about it in a book, *The Double Helix,* that revealed the amazing mixture of boldness and caution, planning and chance, cooperation and rank competitiveness, intensive analysis and experimental derring-do that defined the world of the top scientists.

Yet none of these scientific celebrities could compare—in scientific eminence, intellectual genius, influence on scientific thought, and impact on public attitudes toward scientists—with another American, Albert Einstein. Having fled from Nazism to the United States in 1932 and become an American citizen in 1940, the German-born scientist was proudly accepted by his adopted fellow countrymen as one of their own.

By the time of Einstein's death in 1955, aspiring young scientists knew much about his life, a kind of Horatio Alger saga, European style—how he grew up in a middle-class Jewish family in heavily Catholic Munich, learned to speak so late that his parents feared he was subnormal, received mediocre schooling, moved to Milan with his family when his father's business failed (for the second time), then struck out on his own for Zurich in order to attend the highly regarded Swiss Federal Polytechnic School. Frustrated young scientists drew solace from reading about young Einstein's ups and downs: a cheeky scholar who was rebuffed by his teachers, an iconoclast who rebutted conventional scientific wisdom, he spent years in hand-to-mouth employment until he got a low-level job in the Swiss Patent Office. While there he conducted intensive study on his own time and often on the government's.

Suddenly, from the mind of this twenty-six-year-old bureaucrat, who had neither classroom nor laboratory, neither students nor apparatus, came in 1905 a series of sensational papers. Two of these—"On the Motion of Small Particles Suspended in a Stationary Liquid According to the Molecular Kinetic Theory of Induction" and "On a Heuristic Viewpoint Concerning the Production and Transformation of Light"—exemplified not only Einstein's scientific versatility but his genius in both methodology and conceptualization. The third paper, presenting the special theory of relativity—on the mass-energy equivalence, $E = mc^2$—produced the most fundamental change in popular scientific thought about space and time in the three centuries since Newton.

The young scientist who had been denied decent teaching posts only a few years before now won a series of professorships at Zurich, at Prague, and at the newly established Kaiser Wilhelm Institute for Physics at the prestigious University of Berlin. Deeply absorbed in new concepts of relativity, Einstein in 1916 published his general theory, which challenged conventional Newtonian views of gravity. When a British solar eclipse expedition in 1919 confirmed, through photographs, the prediction that the general theory had made of the extent of starlight's gravitational deflection at the edge of the sun, the forty-year-old scientist in Berlin "awoke to find himself famous." *The Times* of London, in a leading article, opined that nearly all that had "been accepted as the axiomatic basis of physical thought" must now be swept away.

Einstein's rise to world fame coincided in 1918–19 with the collapse of the German monarchy in defeat, starvation, and revolution. The solitary scientist who had shunned politics had joined an antiwar political party that was banned in 1916, signed a petition asking the heads of state about to meet in Versailles to "make a peace that does not conceal a future war," and later worked for world intellectual cooperation under the League of Nations and enlisted in the Zionist cause. Though lampooned as a "guileless child" for supporting pacifism and internationalism, he was politically astute enough to sense the menace of Nazism and make his escape from Germany just before Hitler took power.

At the Institute for Advanced Study in Princeton, Einstein continued his search for a unified field theory, running into formidable mathematical and conceptual problems. But he did not shun political affairs in his adopted country. And in August 1939, as Europe was about to be engulfed in war once again, Einstein signed the famous letter, prepared by fellow refugee-scientist Leo Szilard, warning Roosevelt that research performed in "the course of the last four months" had made it appear possible in the near future "to set up nuclear chain reactions in a large mass of uranium, by which vast amounts of power and large quantities of new radium-like elements would be generated," and that this could lead to the construction of bombs so powerful that a single one could destroy a port and the city around it.

Later, Einstein would minimize his role in pressing for action on the atomic bomb. His participation had consisted of one act, he said—"I signed the letter to President Roosevelt." Perhaps he wanted to forget that he had done much more. In March 1940, he had sent a warning to FDR that the Germans were moving ahead on uranium research. Shortly after Pearl Harbor, he helped solve a theoretical problem relating to gaseous diffusion, and offered to help on anything else within his power. Early in the spring of 1945, as the war neared its end, he revealed his general knowledge of progress on the bomb when he confided to a reporter that if nuclear energies could be used, it would not be houses or blocks that would be destroyed in a few seconds—"it will be entire cities." And he even helped Szilard get an appointment with FDR, through the good offices of Eleanor Roosevelt, when Szilard planned to advise the President on the proper posture toward Russia should the United States make progress in developing the hydrogen bomb. The appointment was postponed until Roosevelt returned to the White House from a vacation in Warm Springs—which he never did.

During the cold war, some pundits accused Einstein of political gullibility. Others felt that he had been effective as a lifelong thinker about war and peace, freedom and oppression. A pacifist, he allowed two exceptions—the war against Nazism and the security of Israel against predatory neighbors. He was a Zionist and friend of Israel who in 1952 sensibly rejected Prime Minister David Ben-Gurion's offer of the presidency of the new nation. He was a believer in civil liberties and academic freedom who as readily and publicly supported a pacifist Heidelberg professor under nationalist attack in the interwar years as he did a Brooklyn teacher haled in 1953 before a congressional committee investigating "un-Americans." What should intellectuals do against this evil? Einstein demanded publicly.

"Frankly, I can see only the revolutionary way of non-cooperation in the sense of Gandhi's. Every intellectual who is called before one of the committees ought to refuse to testify, i.e., he must be prepared for jail and economic ruin, in short, for the sacrifice of his personal welfare in the interest of the cultural welfare of his country." Predictably, sundry newspapers attacked him for this, the *New York Times* tut-tutting him for using one evil to attack another. Einstein was disappointed by the pallid support from academics. If people were willing to testify, he said, "the intellectuals of this country deserve nothing better than the slavery which is intended for them." Einstein spoke feelingly; for years he and his secretary were under investigation by the FBI, suspected of "pro-Communist" activities.

Throughout his life Einstein's highest political commitment was the search for international understanding and world peace. As chauvinism rose to new heights during World War I, he had signed a "Manifesto to Europeans" urging all those whom Goethe had called "good Europeans" to join forces for lasting unity. Forty years later, he served as a leader in the world government movement and as chairman of the Emergency Committee of Atomic Scientists to appeal for control of nuclear arms. In April 1955, during the last week of his life, he agreed with Bertrand Russell on a manifesto that proposed a global conference of scientists to assess the peril of war. This later led to the Pugwash conferences attended by scientists from Britain, the United States, the Soviet Union, and other countries.

The scientist Einstein's supreme commitment was to a unity and coherence that transcended even global politics—the grand unification of physical theory. His work on the general theory of relativity had struck another eminent German scientist, Max Born, as "the greatest feat of human thinking about nature, the most amazing combination of philosophical penetration, physical intuition, and mathematical skill"—even more, a "great work of art." Both before and after he emigrated to the United States, Einstein labored over his unified field theory, which he viewed as the capstone of the inspired work of Maxwell, Faraday, and others. His general relativity theory, he explained to the press, reduced to one formula all laws governing space, time, and gravitation. The purpose of his continuing work was "to further this simplification, and particularly to reduce to one formula the explanation of the field of gravity and of the field of electromagnetism."

He died without achieving this supreme goal. The immense mathematical and conceptual stages still eluded him. But he died expecting that the goal would be achieved. Everything in him, as a supreme embodiment of the Western Enlightenment, cried out that there must be some ultimate harmony in the physical as well as in the moral and intellectual universe. He was convinced, he liked to say, that God would not leave things to blind chance—that the "Old One" did not "throw dice" with the world. When Einstein died, many physicists doubted the possibility of a unified theory. Thirty years later, however, his faith was being vindicated. Scientists were more hopeful than ever that, following a somewhat different path to the same goal, they were on the verge of discovering the "Grand Unified Theory." Einstein would have liked the acronym they applied to it—GUT.

*   *   *

Three decades after Einstein's death it seemed a hundredfold more likely that science would be unified than would the cultural and political thought of the world, or even of the West. In 1959 the English scientist and novelist C. P. Snow asserted in a Cambridge University lecture that Western society had become seriously fragmented, lacking even the pretense of a common culture. In particular, scientists and "literary intellectuals" had lost even the capacity to communicate with one another on the plane of serious common concerns. Soon Snow was set upon by those who insisted that there was really only one culture—the bourgeois capitalist one—or three or twenty or fifty ones, and by those who held that "culture" itself had become an ambiguous, problematic, and therefore, in Snow's sense, meaningless term. But the press and public responded to his ideas with an intensity and excitement that indicated, as Snow later noted, a deep underlying concern with intellectual and cultural fragmentation.

A few years after Snow's lecture Hans Morgenthau, in his *Science: Servant or Master?*, described an even deeper and more pervasive problem than Snow's. He found a conflict *within* the mind of man rather than between science and the mind of man—a "contrast between the achievements and promises of science and their acceptance by humanity, on the one hand," and a "malaise" that had become a "universal phenomenon encompassing humanity." This malaise stemmed from the irrelevance of institutional scholarship to the concerns of society, of people, and especially of the young who were in the process during these years, the early 1970s, of rebelling against that scholarship and its theft from them of their individual autonomy. In effect Morgenthau took Tocqueville's old insight into the intellectual gulf in America—the gap between cloudy, high-blown rhetoric and day-to-day "pragmatic" expediency—and broadened it into even more dire and far-reaching disjunctions: actions directed by utilitarian objectives rather than by effective theory, ideas measured by technological relevance and applicability rather than by a transcending grand theory, and theory governed more by "smart truth"—what is knowable—than by what is worth knowing, as measured by transcending moral principles derived from authentic human needs.

As a political theorist, Morgenthau emphasized the applicability of these gloomy findings to the physical danger resulting from scientific progress and the inability of politics to master that danger. "When science fails to protect man from the forces of nature," he wrote, "its failure can be justified by the ineluctable limits of human powers confronting those forces. But war and misery are not the result of the blind forces of nature. They are the result of purposeful human action which, in its march toward the mastery of nature, has turned against man, his freedom, and his life. This shocking paradox of man's ability to master nature and his helplessness to control the results of that mastery, his supremacy over what is inanimate and alien and his impotence in the face of man, is at the root of the contemporary revolt against science, society, and politics-as-usual."

Morgenthau was writing in the wake of almost three decades of memorable collisions between science and politics. Most of the scientists who had developed the A-bomb had wanted to avert or postpone its use, or at least have it dropped into an uninhabited area, but to no avail. They had chafed under military restrictions at Los Alamos and other scientific installations. They had heard with disbelief that army occupation forces in Japan had destroyed with welding torches and explosives five cyclotrons that the Japanese, lacking uranium, had developed chiefly for biological and medical research. Hundreds of scientists had mobilized to fight off the May-Johnson bill, which they feared would put atomic energy excessively under the control of the government in general and the military in particular, with dire implications for freedom of scientific research and experimentation. Even though a less threatening act passed, by the early 1950s many scientists outside the old leadership corps represented by Vannevar Bush and James B. Conant saw the national program for the physical sciences, in the words of science historian Daniel J. Kevles, as "dominated outside of atomic energy by the military, its dispensations concentrated geographically in the major universities, its primary energies devoted to the chief challenges of national defense and fundamental physics." This focus might be necessary for scientific progress—was it enough?

Many scientists had plunged into politics after the war, intent not only on controlling the atom but on banishing force as a means of settling disputes among nations. Although it might have appeared at first, wrote historian Alice Kimball Smith, that "the evangelical zeal with which scientists embarked on public education and lobbying was entirely out of character with the rationalist temper of their calling, yet their moral earnestness often had deep roots in backgrounds of Judaism or evangelical Protestantism." Scientists translated their moral concern into the practical tasks of speaking, testifying, raising money, and organizing the Federation of American Scientists. Even so, they were hardly prepared for the vagaries of transactional interest-group politics. Like other pressure groups, scientists wanted government support without government regulation; government wanted scientific progress at bargain rates.

In the end it was evident that "something between seduction and rape repeatedly occurred," science editor Daniel Greenberg concluded, but it was not always clear which side was the aggressor and which the victim. Depending on the times, scientists were now villains, now heroes. Sometimes they could be both. J. Robert Oppenheimer, the director of the research project at Los Alamos, became an American hero as the "father of the A-bomb." He became controversial after fighting for international control of atomic energy, wobbling on the May-Johnson bill, opposing and then accepting development of the hydrogen bomb, and disregarding official security regulations. Edward Teller, "father of the H-bomb," suspected him of being a communist. The Atomic Energy Commission in 1954, at the height of the McCarthy furor, stripped him of his security clearance. Less than a decade later, on December 2, 1963, with Teller and others in the audience, President Johnson presented Oppenheimer with the AEC's prestigious Fermi Award that Kennedy had decided to grant him. Oppenheimer in his subdued response reminded his listeners that Jefferson had spoken of the "brotherly" spirit uniting the votaries of science. "We have not, I know," Oppenheimer went on, "always given evidence of that brotherly spirit of science." This was a gentle reminder of what Greenberg described as the political fragmentation of American science.

* * *

Those who knew of Einstein's life during the opening years of the century marveled at the contrast between his daily occupations at the Swiss Patent Office and his scientific work outside it. As a "technical expert, third class, provisional, lowest salary," he spent the day examining models of household appliances and farm implements, cameras and typewriters, and various engineering devices that came in from the inventive Swiss. During his glorious "eight hours of idleness plus a whole Sunday," as he described it to a friend, he worked on abstract and advanced theoretical concepts that would revolutionize scientific thought. It is very possible, however, that the kinds of gadgets and gimmicks he examined during the day had even more influence on Western life during the century ahead than his most creative scientific theorizing.

This influence was evident not only in the immense number of mechanical devices that flooded first the Western world and then most of the globe during the twentieth century but also in the technological systems that braided societies—transportation, communications, information, medical, military. What the public tended to see and use as an array of convenient and time-saving devices were but the day-to-day manifestations of semi-autonomous entities that cut across whole cultures. Thus, something that started out as the horseless carriage, Michael Maccoby noted, became highway networks, plus a petroleum industry, plus rubber plantations, plus auto workers' unions. In earlier times factories financed by capitalists had made goods; in the most recent era laboratories with public and private money manufactured whole technological systems, such as Morton Thiokol's production of the space shuttle's booster rockets. At the start of the 1980s Bell Laboratories in its eighteen locations had an annual budget of over $1 billion and 20,000 employees, of whom 2,500 held doctorates.

During the 1980s the earlier furors over mechanization, scientific management, and automation were giving way to debate over the consequences of the information revolution. In fact, the "revolution" was a culmination of a long process stretching back to the early industrial revolution, even to Gutenberg, and embracing hundreds of developments from the invention of simple pencil erasers to the telegraph, the typewriter, the punch-card tabulating machine, word processors, computers, and the other bewildering electronic devices adorning banks, offices, factories, and, increasingly, homes. The new machines were so impressive in their capacities and versatile in their uses that once again the warning bells sounded: technology was threatening to replace human mind and feeling, information processing was no substitute for ideas, the finest computer could not capture the poetry and joy and nuances of life, the rising generation of students might even be "seriously hampered in its capacity to think through the social and ethical questions that confront us" if educators were swept into the computer cult. Even defenders of the computer granted, in J. David Bolter's words, that it would foster "a general redefinition of certain basic relationships: the relationship of science to technology, of knowledge to technical power, and, in the broadest sense, of mankind to the world of nature."

Others raised the same question about technology that Morgenthau had about science: servant or master? Granted that machines could not master anything except at the command of the human beings running them, whose interests did the new technology serve? Presumably the owners and managers of the technology. Possibly the great mass of technical people operating the machines, who tended, David F. Noble wrote, to "internalize and even consciously adopt the outlook of their patrons, an outlook translated into professional habit through such mechanisms as education, funding, reward-structures, and peer pressure." Labor? Some argued that the skilled monitoring and constant adjustments required by the new cybernetic systems were making factory jobs more interesting and remunerative for skilled labor; others noted that, for the mass of workers, making or running information systems would continue to be boring and alienating. Women? Their relationship to technology had differed sharply from men's all along, in Ruth S. Cowan's view—as evidenced even in the writing of the history of technology.

"Women menstruate, parturate, and lactate; men do not," Cowan wrote. Technologies relating to these processes had long been developed: pessaries, sanitary napkins, tampons, intrauterine devices, childbirth anesthesia, artificial nipples, bottle sterilizers, pasteurized and condensed milks. Where, Cowan asked, were the histories of these female technologies? They had yet to be written. Even more, she wrote, women had been culturally discouraged from playing a major role in general technological change. They had experienced technology and science as consumers, not producers. Hence it was not surprising that an upsurge of "antitechnology" attitudes among women during the 1970s was correlated closely with the upsurge in women's political consciousness, or that women might carry an unspoken hostility to science and technology into the political arena.

Technology as a whole had long been deeply enmeshed with politics and government, though often in complex, mysterious, and unseen ways. The design of bridges—as against the awarding of contracts for the building of bridges—would have seemed a virtually nonpolitical act, at least until the days of Robert Moses, the builder of New York highways, parks, and bridges. Moses, his biographer Robert Caro reported, built the bridges over Long Island parkways with very low clearances in order to discourage buses that would allow hordes of New York's poor—especially blacks—to invade his beloved Jones Beach. The clearances admitted middle-class people with private cars. This politically shrewd, if morally reprehensible, decision was taken without undue publicity and fuss. Many of Moses's "monumental structures of concrete and steel embody a systematic social inequality," according to Langdon Winner, "a way of engineering relationships among people that, after a time, become just another part of the landscape."

By the late 1980s the information revolution was still shrouding the play of technological politics. With their emphasis on interaction, the processes of linkage, feedback, equilibrium, cybernetics, and information systems put a premium on harmony and stability, whereas politics thrived on conflict. The massive information and other technological systems fit their operators into the internal consensus and equilibrium of the systems, thus presenting unified ranks to the often hostile outside world. But internal conflicts broke out—between employers and employees, among doctors and administrators and nurses, railroads and bus companies and air carriers, army, marine, and naval officers. And the systems were not wholly benign; some posed threats to the whole society, as in the case of arms building, environmental pollution, traffic in illegal drugs, nuclear power plants.

These conflicts and threats were catapulted into the political process, as technologists transformed themselves into pressure groups competing with rival interests. Compromises were arranged, regulations imposed or withdrawn or changed, judgments made and unmade by government. Scientists manifested a growing concern as to whether the American political process could resolve not only routine, day-to-day interest-group conflicts but the far more complex task of helping science and technology fortify, rather than threaten, core American values. If, as an MIT professor of electrical engineering feared, the American culture had "a weak value system," would it therefore be "disastrously vulnerable to technology"? If, as other scientists contended, they needed a wide measure of freedom in the early development of technologies, at what point should government step in to constrain their freedom to extend technology into such dangerous areas as genetic experimentation? If, as an MIT political scientist observed, whatever claims might be made for liberty, justice, or equality could be quickly neutralized by the answer, " 'Fine, but that's no way to run a railroad' (or steel mill, or airline, or communications system, and so on)," did such counterclaims of practical necessity eclipse the need for "moral and political reasoning"?

Faced with such bewildering intellectual and moral dilemmas, scientists, like other Americans, turned to education as the chief hope—perhaps the only one. The launching of Sputnik by the Soviet Union in 1957 had shocked Americans out of their complacent assumption of being in the scientific lead. High schools across the country intensified their science and language teaching. The National Science Foundation's budget for curriculum development jumped from half a million dollars in 1957 to ten times that two years later. Programs were expanded in "STS"—science, technology, and society—with emphasis on ideas, technology, and social institutions and on ethical values in science. Federally funded teaching materials were widely distributed as alternatives to commercial textbooks.

But these were "quickie" programs and twenty-five years later assessments of the state of science education and literacy were still bleak. "By even the most elementary standards, instruction in the sciences in most schools for most Americans is minimal," Stephen Graubard wrote. "Science is avoided—evaded—by the preponderant number of American schoolchildren. That evasion is permitted to continue in the universities." Commercially produced texts still dominated the high school classrooms. An NSF report revealed that the number of American students enrolled for graduate study in chemistry, physics, and mathematics had remained almost stationary between 1979 and 1985, while the number of foreign nationals in these programs rose by half or more.

More and more people were using modern technology, observed the chancellor of the State University of New York, while understanding it less. "Instead, we are content to be served by cadres of technicians and specialists and, thereby, to cede to them an inordinate, even ominous amount of control over our lives." He wondered whether the great mass of people, including many college graduates, were in danger of becoming what had been called "techno-peasants"—"modern-day serfs, nominally free but disenfranchised by ignorance—and fear—of prevailing technologies."

The great mass of Americans were in far greater danger of becoming "econo-peasants." Popular ignorance of economics surpassed that of science and technology. During the years when millions of Americans were becoming intimately familiar with their individual microeconomics—maintaining checking accounts, applying for mortgages, playing the market, itemizing tax returns, using desk calculators, buying foreign currency, monitoring their payroll deductions, taking out credit cards—their understanding of the macroeconomics that dominated their collective economy remained low. Even more paradoxical was the disarray in the economic theory and practice of the nation's intellectual and political leadership in the face of the refractory problems of the post-Vietnam years.

THE RICH AND THE POOR

Camp David, Friday, August 13, 1971. The limousines pulled in during the afternoon, disgorging presidential advisers. Although this summit meeting on top of the low Catoctin Mountain had been announced as a conference on defense spending, only civilians were present. Whisked away to their quarters, where they were offered food, drink, and a variety of recreations, they found themselves totally cut off from communication with the world below. The President wanted no leaks as he prepared to announce what he would describe as the "most comprehensive new economic policy" since Roosevelt's New Deal.

A participant remembered the weekend more for its atmosphere than for its decision-making. The mountaintop retreat seemed to isolate the group from the realities of economic life. "They acquired the attitudes of a group of script-writers preparing a TV special to be broadcast on Sunday evening," economic adviser Herbert Stein recalled. "The announcement—the performance—was everything." It was not viewed, he noted wryly, as part of the regular process of government. After the TV special, regular programming would be resumed. The President and Haldeman concentrated on the mechanics of the television speech. At first Nixon balked at speaking Sunday night because he feared preempting *Bonanza,* an immensely popular program, but he was advised that he had to speak before the markets opened Monday. Manfully he bumped *Bonanza.*

Nixon had inherited a booming but dangerously heated-up economy when he entered the White House two and a half years before. John Kennedy had proposed a tax cut, only to see it languish on Capitol Hill. Johnson drove it through Congress hardly three months after he took office. The biggest tax cut in American history, adopted even though the budget was running heavily into red ink, this reduction in both personal and corporate income-tax rates, along with the rising outlay for both welfare and war, helped fuel a huge expansion in both employment and the gross national product by the mid-sixties. Soon the economy showed signs of overheating, but LBJ, reluctant to change a winning game and eager to push his urban welfare programs in the face of rioting in Watts and elsewhere, fended off his economic advisers' urgings that he now ask for a tax increase. Finally, in 1967, as inflation threatened, Johnson during the height of the Vietnam effort urged a tax boost on Congress. In a classic example of institutional friction and delay, Congress failed to enact the revenue increase for another year and a half. That came too late to cool the broiling economy.

It came too late for the new President as well. Inflation was running at about 5 percent a year when Nixon took office. In accord with sound Republican doctrine, the new Administration must throttle down the social spending and the budget deficits for which they had castigated Humphrey and his fellow Democrats in the 1968 election campaign. But Nixon was wary. He still felt the scars of his defeat by Kennedy in 1960, when he had been beaten in part by the Eisenhower recession, or so he believed. Herbert Stein had encountered Nixon's ambivalence when he first met the President-elect on the day his appointment as economic adviser was announced. When his new boss asked Stein what he thought would be the nation's main economic problem, Stein answered with the conventional wisdom: inflation. To his surprise Nixon showed equal concern about unemployment.

For over two years Nixon, teetering between his two fears, tried to fine-tune the economy with a mix of monetary and budgetary policies, along with exhortation from the White House. It was hard going every inch of the way. Fine-tuning would have been difficult even for a united government. The President had to share economic policy-making with the very independent Federal Reserve Board under its imperious chairman and with the Democratic-controlled Congress. By spring 1970 both prices and unemployment were rising sharply—a remarkable combination. The federal deficit was soaring, interest rates climbed, and then the stock market took its steepest plunge since depression days. In June 1970 came the collapse of the Penn Central Railroad, called by Leonard Silk the greatest business failure in history. For some Americans that failure sounded the tocsin for the slow death of passenger railroading, one of the ineradicable and glorious memories of countless older Americans.

By 1971 the nation was beset by economic storms from abroad as well. The great edifice of Western monetary cooperation, founded during Lend-Lease days, dedicated at Bretton Woods, expanded during the era of the Marshall Plan, and buttressed by hundreds of international postwar agreements, appeared in peril. For years that edifice had stood on the firm base of the dependable, all-powerful dollar, which in turn had been stabilized by a fixed gold price. American financial dominance had been under growing threat for years as the nation spent billions abroad for foreign goods and military operations, until the mountain of foreign-held dollars had become far larger than the value of the United States gold stock. What if foreign treasury ministers began to line up at the Washington "gold window" of the financial edifice and tried to draw out more of the bullion than was now available? Britain's request, in early August 1971, for $3 billion in gold was merely the triggering device for powerful economic forces that had been building up for years, including a strong German mark and rising Japanese competition.

Now Nixon had to act, but he faced a painful dilemma. The American economy had become linked firmly with the Western and Japanese economies. He would have to move on both the domestic and the global front, in particular because ending convertibility of paper into gold and allowing the dollar to depreciate would stimulate price rises at home as the dollar price of imports mounted. Hence it would be necessary to establish mandatory price and wage controls. But if there was any man who had, year in and year out, vociferously denounced controls, it was Richard Nixon. His aversion was based in part on conventional Republican doctrine but even more on his brief working experience with price controls in the Office of Price Administration during World War II. This proved, said some, that a little experience was a dangerous thing.

But on the evening of August 15, 1971, at the culmination of the secret Camp David meeting, the President bit both bullets—indeed, several bullets. He imposed a ninety-day freeze on prices, wages, and rents, suspended the convertibility of dollars into gold, and placed a 10 percent surcharge on imports. He asked Congress to repeal the 7 percent excise tax on cars, to speed up personal income-tax exemptions, to put off welfare reform for a year, to postpone revenue-sharing programs with the states for three months, to pass a 10 percent "job development credit"—a tax credit to business for investment in new plants and equipment—that would drop to 5 percent after one year.

The President had acted. The country seemed thrilled, as it so often had been by forthright leadership after a period of doubt and disarray. Wall Street appeared to be elated, as the Dow Jones rose 32.9 points on the Monday after the presidential speech—the biggest one-day jump to that point. Three months later the President instituted Phase II, a comprehensive and mandatory system of controls. The Fed, now under the chairmanship of Arthur Burns, helpfully expanded the money supply. Then, in a series of steps and phases, the controls were gradually loosened, until June 1973, when, with food prices climbing and the Administration bleeding from Watergate, Nixon reimposed the freeze. But this time the freeze proved "a total disaster," as livestock was destroyed or kept from market and food was hoarded. Again the controls were slowly lifted and, by April 1974, eliminated.

Though economically the program had mixed results, politically Nixon's "New Economic Policy," as he called it, was a splendid success. Just as his trip to China and détente with Russia took the wind out of McGovern's peace strategy of 1972, so the President's dexterous juggling of economic policy from crisis to crisis deflated the Democrats' domestic challenge. True-blue conservatives were dismayed by the President's opportunistic interventionism. The tide was not running toward freedom, Stein concluded morosely. Thoughtful conservatives were further dismayed when Nixon tapes publicized by the Watergate inquiry shone a spotlight on Nixon as Economist-in-Chief. Late in June 1972, Haldeman had asked his boss whether he had gotten the report that London had decided to float the pound.

NIXON: That's devaluation?
HALDEMAN: Yeah. . . .
NIXON: I don't care about it. Nothing we can do about it.

Haldeman tried to arouse the President's interest by mentioning a staffer's report that the British action showed the wisdom of the President's policy. The President would not be tempted.

NIXON: Good. I think he's right. It's too complicated for me to get into.

Then Haldeman noted that Burns expected a 5 to 8 percent devaluation of the pound against the dollar.

NIXON (impatiently): Yeah. O.K. Fine.
HALDEMAN: Burns is concerned about speculation about the lira.
NIXON: I don't give a shit about the lira.

Undiscouraged, Haldeman mentioned a good reaction in the House of Representatives.

NIXON: There ain't a vote in it. . . .

Thus ended the morning's economic policy making.

*   *   *

From the resigned President, Gerald Ford inherited a festering case of what had come to be called stagflation. He faced a perplexing combination of high inflation and rising unemployment, complicated by a slowdown in economic output, a big trade deficit, and a falling stock market. Ford reacted to these conditions like the stalwart Republican he had always been, but with a public relations twist. He adopted a Madison Avenue-style slogan—Whip Inflation Now! or WIN!—and jawboned General Motors into trimming a planned price increase from almost 10 percent to 8.6. He cut government spending, sought to balance the budget, and with Congress reduced personal and corporate taxes. Harried by the Democratic-controlled Congress, outflanked on the right by Reagan Republicans, bedeviled by the aggressive efforts of the Arab-dominated Organization of Petroleum Exporting Countries to boost oil prices, Ford resorted to ad hoc, step-by-step economic policies.

He had no national constituency of his own. He could not forget that he was the first and only President chosen by one man, elevated to the vice presidency after Agnew quit under fire, elevated to the presidency after Nixon quit under fire. He chose Nelson Rockefeller as his Vice President in the hope that the former New York governor would bring support from the once-mighty presidential Republicans, but that old party was now a ghost party and Rockefeller a hate object to the resurgent Republican Right. Inundated by advice, Ford pressed his fight against the twin horsemen of inflation and unemployment, shifting back and forth without routing either. Hardly a year after entering the White House he had to launch his struggle to hold his office. Democrats attacked his tax program as regressive, his welfare programs as inadequate, his economics as thwarting growth, his military spending as excessive. And millions of Americans thought of him chiefly as the man who had pardoned Richard Nixon.

Compromised by their own failures to find a solution to the stagflation problem, congressional Democrats were vulnerable to many of the same attacks they launched against the President. Their best hope, and Ford's worst fear, was the emergence of a presidential candidate untainted by past Democratic failures. Such an outsider was Jimmy Carter. The new President pictured himself, however, much more the orderly policy maker than the passionate, "charismatic" leader. He based his "exact procedure" to some degree on his scientific and engineering background, he told Neal Peirce shortly after winding up his remarkable primary victories in 1976. He liked first to study the historical background of a problem, then "to bring together advice or ideas from as wide or divergent points of view as possible, to assimilate them personally or with a small staff," bringing in others if necessary to discuss the matter in depth. "Then I make a general decision about what should be done involving time schedules, necessity for legislation, executive acts, publicity to be focused on the issue. Then I like to assign task forces to work on different aspects of the problem," and he would remain personally involved in the whole process.

This was the operational code of a commanding, "take charge" leader, a blueprint for action—but one that Carter appeared to ignore in much of his economic policy making. The White House sent out mixed signals as to what it wanted. Advance preparation was inadequate, follow-through sporadic, lines of communication and delegation scrambled. The normal friction between the executive and legislative branches was exacerbated by exceptionally poor staff work in the White House's congressional liaison office. Above all a clear sense of priorities was lacking.

Gradually, almost imperceptibly for a while, the Carter Administration drifted to the right in economic policy. This appeared to be the result of no grand strategic reconsideration but rather, after the first year or so, of mishaps and collisions that drained the White House of a sense of resolution and consistency, even while the old populist rhetoric remained much the same. Thus the President continued to attack the oil industry and other special interests, Betty Glad noted, even while he moved toward their positions on policy. He talked about the nation's health crises, but made funding of a national health insurance plan contingent on the state of the economy and the federal budget. In his first year in office he emphasized tax reduction and raising the minimum wage; in the next three years he showed much more concern about inflation and pressed for some restriction on wage increases.

Most of this was in response to immediate, specific problems and crises. But once again "practicality" and "pragmatism" failed. By December 1980, the annual rate of inflation was at 13 percent, the prime rate had risen to 21.5 percent, and unemployment stood at 7.4 percent. Stagflation was back with a vengeance.

One by one Carter's liberal, urban constituencies began to back away from the Administration. Speaker Tip O'Neill, repeatedly bypassed and "blindsided" by the White House, proclaimed that he had not become Speaker "to dismantle programs I've fought for all my life." Hearing of proposed Social Security cuts, House Majority Whip John Brademas, a workhorse for Democratic party programs, warned that the White House would "run into a buzzsaw" if it tried to eliminate major benefits. As Carter began his third year Senator Edward Kennedy complained that the Administration's budget asked "the poor, the black, the sick, the young, the cities and the unemployed to bear a disproportionate share of the billions of dollars of reductions." Urban, black, labor, consumer, and other leaders turned more and more against the Administration during 1979 and helped project Kennedy that fall into his failed effort to wrest the 1980 nomination from the President.

* * *

White House watchers had been quick to jump on sudden and erratic shifts of policy. Nixon "clings to what is familiar until the last moment,"

Hugh Sidey of *Time* had noted. "Then, when the evidence overwhelms him or something happens in his gut, he decides to act, and nothing stands very long in his way. He abandons his philosophy, his promises, his speeches, his friends, his counselors. He marches out of one life into a new world without any apologies or glancing back." Scholars as well as journalists maintained a drumbeat of critical comments on Carter's gaps between principle and policy. Few of these critics paused to ask whether the White House during the 1970s was receiving steady and adequate intellectual nourishment from the pundits and the professors.

The answer would have been no. In the absence of that kind of nourishment, Presidents attempted a series of "practical" experiments in economic policy, many of them vague reflections of half-understood conventional economic theories.

If the Republicans had been willing to live up to their campaign oratory their path would have been well marked after they recaptured the presidency in 1968. They needed only to slash spending, balance the budget, turn key federal functions over to private enterprise, cut back heavily on regulation—in short, "get government off our backs." Philosophically, this path had been well marked not only by Herbert Spencer and William Graham Sumner in the previous century but by countless laissez-faire enthusiasts in the twentieth. The most notable of these following World War II was Friedrich August von Hayek, born in Vienna in 1899, a professor of economics at the London School of Economics and at the University of Chicago.

In 1944 Hayek had published *The Road to Serfdom,* which for a book on economics won wide attention and sales, especially in the United States. The book seemed to have special appeal in embattled Western nations whose peoples were tiring of wartime rationing, price controls, travel restrictions, endless regulations. Its message was simple: extensive governmental intervention into the economy, whether through welfare programs or nationalization or economic planning, would lead to totalitarianism, which would crush all freedoms. The next three decades proved this analysis dead wrong. All the major Western democracies had indulged intensively in peacetime intervention, with mixed economic results but with few infringements on fundamental individual rights such as freedom of speech, religion, press, assembly. On the contrary, some contended, promoting economic and social security through public programs more often protected and enlarged individual freedom.

Doctrinaire laissez-faire had become so discredited as public policy during the depression years that neither Nixon nor Ford—nor Eisenhower earlier—offered more than oratory and a few crusts of policy to the free-marketeers. This enabled the laissez-faire theorists to keep their doctrine intact by arguing that it had never really been tried.

During the depressed 1930s Keynesianism had succeeded laissez-faire as the dominant intellectual influence in Western economics. FDR had followed Keynesian policies without understanding the theory behind them, and to the extent he put federal money into public works and other spending projects he lifted the nation out of stagnation. It took World War II, however, to show what "war Keynesianism" could do to bring about a full recovery. Despite predictions of a catastrophic postwar depression, continued federal spending on welfare and war sustained a strong economy through the 1950s and 1960s. Truman and even Eisenhower were "closet Keynesians," and Kennedy by 1962 was willing to embrace the doctrine publicly. Johnson carried Keynesian spending to its practical political limit and with great success until the disastrous delay in the tax boost and other mishaps disrupted his experiment in financing both guns and butter.

It fell to Richard Nixon not only to admit but to assert proudly, "Now I am a Keynesian." While this pronouncement hardly struck Western ears with the impact of Kennedy's "I am a Berliner," it was testament to Nixon's occasional willingness to think and act boldly as well as his desire to be seen as a modern man not mired in nineteenth-century economic orthodoxy. It also fell to Nixon to embrace the still controversial doctrine at the very time when it was becoming less relevant to the specific economic problems facing the nation. The longer-run risks of Keynesianism had not escaped its more thoughtful advocates. Alvin Hansen, Keynes's leading American disciple, in calling for a bold program of public investment in 1938, had warned against overemphasis on such a program, failure to achieve "a balance in the cost-price-income structure," and choking off private investment. The hard-nosed Keynesians advising Kennedy and Johnson—Paul Samuelson, Walter Heller, Kermit Gordon, James Tobin, Arthur Okun, and others—knew that depression-style Keynesianism was not enough.

They knew, that is, Keynesianism's great flaw—its inability to deal with the raging inflations that swept Western economies during the 1970s. By the early 1980s, as the Keynesian economist Robert Lekachman granted, it was clear that the doctrine "underestimated both the inflationary potential of full employment and the impact on public expectations of continuous inflation without serious interruption for so long a period. Keynes exaggerated the competitiveness of the private sector and, in some moods, the efficacy of fiscal and monetary remedies." Non-Keynesians attacked other Keynesian assumptions—that the economy had a built-in tendency to operate with output below its potential while unemployment remained high, that enough jobs could be provided through fiscal actions of government to expand demand, that governments could estimate accurately how much spending and deficit creation would be enough to achieve employment goals.

As the Keynesians fell into some disrepute during the inflationary seventies, a new doctrine galloped to the rescue from Stage Right. It was in fact an old idea—the dominant economic doctrine of the 1920s—dressed up in mod fashion for the post-Keynesian era. This was monetarism. Associated in the United States mainly with the noted University of Chicago economist Milton Friedman, monetarism preached that regulating the supply and, if possible, the velocity of money was the way to stabilize the economy and especially to control inflation. It was a beguiling doctrine, largely because it depended mainly on a single lever of economic control, and also because the government, through the Federal Reserve Board and the Treasury Department, had far swifter and more decisive influence over the volume of money than over any other component of the economy. During the 1970s the monetarists, said Alan S. Blinder, "swept through the universities, conquered Wall Street, infiltrated the Congress, and eventually gained the upper hand at the Federal Reserve."

Since Keynesians were viewed as liberals ideologically, and monetarists as conservatives, Carter's choice of Paul Volcker as head of the Federal Reserve Board in 1979 was seen as a decisive presidential shift to the right. Volcker promptly made clear that the Board would pursue monetarist policies. There followed a classic example of Herbert Spencer's case of the murder of a beautiful theory by a brutal gang of facts. The money supply and especially money velocity fell quickly, interest rates mounted, and a short, sharp recession followed. Within three years the Fed had to abandon its monetarist experiment. The economy quickly improved, but it was far too late to save the Carter presidency.

* * *

The University of Chicago economists, popularly called the Chicago School despite their numerous internal differences, were countervailed at Harvard by a one-man school that displayed equal intellectual vigor and versatility. This school was called John Kenneth Galbraith. Canadian by birth, he had emerged from an Ontario farming community rent by social and political discord and managed to study and teach during the 1930s at a series of intellectually disputatious universities, including Berkeley, Harvard, and Cambridge. During World War II he helped run the Price Division of the Office of Price Administration, served as an editor on Henry

Luce's *Fortune,* and directed the United States Strategic Bombing Survey. After writing a scholarly book on the theory of price control, which to his considerable indignation went almost unread, he resolved never again to "place myself at the mercy of the technical economists who had the enormous power to ignore what I had written." He struck out for a broader readership, and he reached it in 1952 with his *American Capitalism.*

Equipped with a gadfly's wit, a plenitude of self-esteem, and a six-foot-eight frame, Galbraith sometimes looked like a towering farmer beating off a swarm of bees. And stinging bees there were aplenty, as critics reacted to the economist's pokes at the pieties of the day. When his lucid work on American capitalism, recognizing its modernity and productivity, argued that consolidation was a healthy force in an economy held in balance by the "countervailing power" of corporations, unions, and other forces, he was assailed from the left for ignoring the plight of the consumer and minimizing the need for vigorous antitrust enforcement. When in *The Affluent Society* (1958) Galbraith urged that the nation's enormous productive forces be shifted toward education, housing, mass transit, and other sectors that responded to people's true needs rather than artificially contrived ones, he heard from the right about his improper imposition of his own values on consumer choices and from the left about his call for a national sales tax. When in *The New Industrial State* (1967) he described the technicians who ran the top 500 corporations as the nation's de facto economic planners—and planning as much for their own status and self-esteem as for profit—he was variously assailed for overestimating the technological efficiency of the big corporation, for equating corporate or sectoral industrial planning with overall national economic planning, and again for minimizing the need for antitrust enforcement.

As the years passed and the dust settled a bit, critics had to acknowledge that, whatever the balance of Galbraith's economic truths and errors, he had brilliantly succeeded in his original determination to reach outside the profession for popular attention and, in gaining it, to force economists publicly to question conventional wisdom. Galbraith, for his part, showed a willingness, unusual for academics, to admit error and correct it. Thus in the second edition of *The New Industrial State* he conceded that a critic had properly taxed him with a failure to make clear the great difference between planning that is within the framework of and responsive to the market and planning that "replaces the market." His theory of countervailing power came to be seen as partly a reflection of the "equilibrium bias" that dominated social science thinking in the postwar years. If some of the topics he dealt with appeared to some far removed from the everyday concerns of working-class and poor people, few could doubt the abiding concern with social reform and human betterment that lay behind the merciless dissections and the mordant wit.

Into the midst of the skirmishes among rival "bourgeois" economists, intellectual cannonballs were lofted from the far left. Marxist and neo-Marxist thought in America continued to be vigorous and contentious during the heyday of the monetarists and their counterattackers. Economists of such standing in the profession as Paul Baran, Paul Sweezy, and Samuel Bowles, and publications like the *Review of Radical Political Economy* and Sweezy's *Monthly Review,* compelled American social scientists—though rarely American political leaders—to confront radical economic and political alternatives.

Marxism in the late twentieth century still to an extraordinary degree lived off the power and creativity of the master's teachings of over a century before. There was the same emphasis on the mode of production as the driving rod of economic and social change, on the class system as the foundation of political power, on the contradictions implicit in the process of capitalist accumulation, on the inevitable conflict between a compact ruling class of capitalists and a working class divided and repressed but steadily gaining in proletarian consciousness, on the coming "doom" or "twilight" or "fall" of capitalism. Criticism of Marxism had a fixed quality too: its exaggeration of the causal role of economic forces; its simplistic view of class that ignored the rich findings of sociologists and political scientists about the nuances and subtleties of class attitudes and relationships; its overemphasis on the potential solidarity of the working class; its underestimation of the resilience and resourcefulness of the capitalist "rulers."

The intellectual burden of the past that weighed most heavily on the Marxists was the haziness about alternative economic and political strategies. Just as Marx himself had been brilliant and prophetic in his analysis of capitalism but vague—perhaps deliberately so—about the process of revolutionary change that would finish it off, so the American Marxists of the 1970s and 1980s failed to match their penetrating critiques of modern capitalism with explicit analyses of possible political strategies and social transformations. To be sure, Marxists had scored one intellectual breakthrough. After decades of being mesmerized by the temptations of "nationalizing" industries and services and big administrative entities with undiscriminating zeal, they had learned the lesson that Adolf Berle had taught capitalists a half century before—technical ownership did not necessarily mean actual control. In nation after nation indiscriminate nationalization had not only failed economically but, alienating the voters, had hurt socialist regimes politically.

The failure of nationalization as a cure-all, however, left Marxists and other socialists without a weapon of change they had long depended on. Instead they were offering cloudy proposals for "democratic planning." In fact, central economic planning was perhaps the most theoretically neglected and politically underestimated doctrine available to American liberals and radicals. But the Marxists gave little intellectual aid. This was partly because they were still intoxicated by dreams of some kind of public "ownership" rather than analytically challenged by the gritty but vital processes of effective public control. Even more, it was because they faced a dilemma. On the one hand, they saw the need for central planning and coordination of monetary, budgetary, resource, environmental, and other controls. On the other hand, they feared Stalinist tendencies toward despotic and rigid centralization—tendencies they truly hated. Instead they called for "democratic" planning, which often meant worker participation in management decisions, grass-roots control of economic decision making, delegation of policy making to state, community, and even neighborhood entities. How to find the proper mix of central economic direction and local, rank-and-file democracy evaded the theoretical grasp of the Marxists, as well as of conservative, libertarian, and liberal thinkers.

Still, that grasp was firm compared to the left's intellectual grip on the question of how to achieve power. The radicals had no revolutionary plan, no street tactics, no political party strategy relevant to the peculiar American conditions of hazy ideologies, amorphous political parties, and fragmented government. Noting the leftist view that monopoly capitalism faced a continuing and intensifying state of economic crisis, Benjamin Ward wrote that "clearly there is an important immediate goal: building a movement capable of acting should a crisis opportunity emerge in the near future." But the American left had not even begun to build the kind of political movement that had reshaped politics in European democracies. More than a century after Marx, more than half a century after Lenin, it lacked an intellectual leadership that could be compared to the master political economist in London, or a political leadership comparable to the brilliant strategist of Zurich and Petrograd. This would have been of some satisfaction to the American establishments, had they been aware of it.

* * *

While these debates among economists dragged on, so did acute poverty in the United States. If the economic controversy was conducted over the heads of the poor, the poor continued to go about their ways regardless of the economists, the sociologists, and the policy-makers. Some kind of war was being conducted on behalf of the poor, but like peasants and townspeople hearing the confusing roar of battle over a distant darkling plain, many of the poor could hardly understand the marches and counter-marches of the warriors against poverty.

It was not even clear when that war had been declared—perhaps when Kennedy witnessed firsthand the poverty of West Virginia during his presidential primary campaign there, or perhaps when he praised the Social Security Act later that year for undertaking a "war on poverty," or perhaps when he repeatedly referred to poverty in his inaugural address and said, "If a free society cannot help the many who are poor, it cannot save the few who are rich." The ambivalence of those inaugural words was reflected in Kennedy's Administration. He and his brother Robert initiated numerous policies and projects for youth employment and remedial education, aid to depressed areas, accelerated public works, manpower development and training, and extension of aid to families with dependent children. But many of the programs were weakened by Congress, severely underfunded, and represented no significant redistribution of income from the rich to the poor.

Even meager programs carrying the Kennedy imprimatur, moreover, ran into vehement opposition. In the summer of 1961 the city manager of Newburgh in the Hudson Valley ordered drastic restrictions in welfare policy, including the withholding of benefits to unwed mothers if they had another illegitimate child. "It is not moral," he said, "to appropriate public funds to finance crime, illegitimacy, disease, and other social evils." Ever since the Leopold-Loeb case, he added, "criminal lawyers and all the mushy rabble of do-gooders and bleeding hearts . . . have marched under the Freudian flag toward the omnipotent state of Karl Marx."

Lyndon Johnson declared his war against poverty within a few weeks of taking office. In a few more weeks the Administration was pressing through Congress the Economic Opportunity Act, a program for a coordinated attack on the many causes of poverty—joblessness, illiteracy, poor education, meager public services. Congress authorized almost a billion dollars for an Office of Economic Opportunity, which would conduct separate programs—Job Corps, work-training, work-study, the Neighborhood Youth Corps, Volunteers in Service to America. OEO head Sargent Shriver charged into the poverty battle with energy and enthusiasm rivaling Harry Hopkins's in New Deal days. But, oversold and underfunded, the program soon ran into opposition from radical leaders like community organizer Saul Alinsky who expected too much and from conservatives like Barry Goldwater who feared too much. As controversy arose about both the poverty programs and the Vietnam War, LBJ's war against poverty flagged.

Like the Thirty Years' War of the early seventeenth century, the wars against poverty began amid great huzzahs, picked up momentum, faltered, started up all over again—and took decades. Just as some LBJ warriors against poverty concluded that JFK's efforts had been inadequate, so Richard Nixon resolved that he would do something about the "welfare mess" once and for all. Amid much fanfare he proposed a Family Assistance Plan to guarantee all families with children a minimum of $500 per adult and $300 per child every year. FAP would build a work incentive into the program by allowing a poor family to keep the first $60 per month of earned income without any reduction in government aid. The plan would help meet the needs especially of children under eighteen and of the poor in the South, where welfare payments were lower than in the West and North. A year later, urging its passage, Nixon called FAP the "most important piece of domestic legislation of the past 35 years, one of the dozen or half dozen such bills in the Nation's history."

The chief planner of Nixon's FAP was a one-man brain trust, Daniel Patrick Moynihan. A former director of the Joint Center of Urban Studies at MIT and Harvard, Moynihan had helped draft early poverty legislation under Kennedy and Johnson. He had been acutely disillusioned by the 1964 Economic Opportunity Act provision that antipoverty programs be carried out with the "maximum feasible participation" locally of the poor. The result, in his eyes, had been neighborhood conflict, racial turmoil, editorial denunciation, and a stigma attached to the whole poverty effort. Now, under Nixon, he threw himself into the battle for FAP, with the plea that this new initiative—a shift from a services strategy to an income strategy—would "almost surely define the beginning of a new era in American social policy." Soon Moynihan underwent another disillusion. After a long struggle among congressional factions, FAP was defeated by attrition, shriveled into just another disbursement to special categories of the poor. The great initiative was over before it was initiated.

Why still another failure? Blame would fall on the Vietnam War, Watergate, institutional clogs, inadequate leadership. The main reason for the lost war, it would become clear, was not only political but also intellectual—a failure of definition and concept, historical perspective, social analysis.

The poor were variously defined as the low-income, the unemployed, the "have-nots," the powerless, the proletariat, or even the *Lumpenproletariat*, described by Marx and Engels as the "social scum," that "passively rotting mass thrown off by the lowest layers of old society," far more likely to be a "bribed tool of reactionary intrigue" than to be truly proletarian. What, conceptually, was poverty—economic, social, political, material, motivational, attitudinal, or some or all of these? Where were the poor—diffused throughout the populace or fragmented in separate enclaves or occupying some discernible cultural shape of their own?

The historical record was largely ignored, even though Anglo-Americans had had six centuries of experience in dealing with such questions, going back to the English Poor Laws. "We find that throughout this period, in both England and later in the United States," Chaim Waxman wrote, "poverty has been considered a negative condition, that the poor have been perceived as 'not quite human,' and that social welfare legislation has been primarily concerned with the maintenance of public order (the order of the non-poor), rather than with the condition and care of the poor on their own account." While the New Dealers put the lives of the jobless ahead of public order, relief was to go only to the unemployables. "Work must be found for able-bodied but destitute workers," Roosevelt declared, for to "dole out relief" was to "administer a narcotic, a subtle destroyer of the human spirit." By the 1960s, the years of LBJ's war on poverty, the planners of that war spent little time analyzing the successes and failures of New Deal welfare and unemployment programs, perhaps because the Roosevelt record was so mixed. The poverty war planners had to shape their programs so hurriedly that they hardly had time to answer the question that would not disappear: who are the poor?

Were the poor, however defined, merely the people clustering around the bottom of the economic or social or prestige or self-esteem ladder, people not fundamentally different from the rest of us but suppressed by the system, cruelly stigmatized by the "haves," casually beggared by the throw of the social dice—perhaps loaded dice? Or did the poor—the persistingly poor—form a whole separate culture with its own traditions, customs, outlook, motivation, goals, social or antisocial behaviors? "Let me tell you about the very rich," said Scott Fitzgerald's narrator. "They are different from you and me." Could the same be said of the very poor? The answer to this question had critically important analytical, political, and policy implications.

To a number of American sociologists and anthropologists the poor in large American cities appeared to be locked in mutually reinforcing conditions of poor nourishment, inadequate housing, mental and physical illness, low motivation and self-esteem, limited education and skills, crime and delinquency. As a staff memorandum of the Council of Economic Advisers put it in 1963, "cultural and environmental obstacles to motivation" among the poor led to "poor health, and inadequate education, and low mobility, limiting earning potential," which in turn led to poverty, which led to poor motivation, and so on, around and around the vicious circle. Oscar Lewis's portrait of an autonomous, poverty-ridden enclave in the heart of Mexico City was one of the most graphic studies of the subculture of poverty. That subculture was not always wholly malign. It could be a world of instant gratification and delayed deprivation—social prestige built on defiance of cops and teachers, gang warfare, drug and alcohol abuse, intensive and promiscuous sex leading to high birth rates, illegitimacy, and disrupted families. "Irrational" or "immoral" behavior such as abusing teachers or fighting in the streets might be quite realistic and adaptive given the subculture's way of life and divergent value system.

For other analysts, called "situationists" or "structuralists," this was a picture of hopelessness and a counsel of despair. They described the poor as sharing the dominant hopes and values of the larger society but failing to realize them through the existing structure of opportunity. In this view, the poor turned to "deviant" or "delinquent" behavior precisely because they lacked any other means of attaining the material and psychic satisfaction propagated by the ruling culture. If money was a supreme aim, stealing might be a sensible tactic. If sex was glorified in film and glossy print, one might indulge in it without much thought of consequences nine months away.

If this analysis was correct, the solution according to situationists lay with the larger society, with the *environment* of the poor. Society must widen opportunity and thus give the poor a strong helping hand. To deal with juvenile delinquency, develop "new opportunities for the disadvantaged youth," read a staff memorandum to Attorney General Robert Kennedy in early November 1963. If poor children were doing badly in schools, improve the schools. If poor people felt uninvolved and powerless, set up a community action program for participatory democracy.

Inevitably, the divergent analyses had different policy implications. To integrate the poor into the wider culture would call for a social transformation of the poor themselves, according to the "culturalists." No, said the situationists, the overall society must be reformed to make room for all. In practice the two sides overlapped in their policy choices, but their theoretical divergence more often produced political and policy divergence as well. It also produced a great deal of intellectual confusion. Of one program Moynihan wrote, ". . . it was not social science competence that was missing in the conception and management of this program; it was intellect." The essential fact was, he wrote with emphasis, that the *government did not know what it was doing.* It had a theory. Or, rather, a set of theories. Nothing more."

This central theoretical issue—between culturalist "transformation" and structuralist "opportunity broadening"—was never resolved. Rather, the politicians spun out disparate policies and programs, some of which helped alleviate destitution but which together did not conquer poverty. The intellectual failure was all the more poignant, for it became clear after the war on poverty was fought and lost that poverty was so entrenched and intractable that both strategies were necessary. That is, the effort at regeneration must be made deep within the culture of poverty even while society as a whole broadened its opportunity structure. An effort of this magnitude, however, seemed to be beyond the intellectual as well as the institutional resources of the nation.

This made a "spearhead" strategy all the more tempting. Throughout the decades following the great depression many intellectuals as well as politicians had embraced the notion that some single solution could break through the poverty gridlock or that some special political effort by the poor themselves could hoist them out of poverty by their own bootstraps. Economic strategies such as Keynesianism and New Deal programs such as Social Security and minimum-wage legislation were expected to help the poor, and did to some degree, but they failed to break open the structure of poverty. Political action by the poor themselves brought some relief but invariably petered out.

During New Deal days the Workers' Alliance of America, with a membership estimated as high as 600,000, had appeared by 1936 to be building a strong, militant, national coalition of poor people. Members agitated, demonstrated, protested, and lobbied, but with only marginal impact on the relief and welfare policies of FDR and Harry Hopkins. After a few years the Alliance faded away amid division and frustration. In the late 1960s welfare rights groups began to band together in the National Welfare Rights Organization, which, in contrast to the mainly white Workers' Alliance, was composed largely of blacks, especially black women. Under the gifted leadership of Dr. George A. Wiley, a professor of chemistry turned civil rights activist, NWRO members staged hundreds of demonstrations, marches, and other protests against welfare restrictions. But the members divided over tactical questions, they failed to build a mass organization, and NWRO died in early 1973, a few months before Wiley's death by drowning in Chesapeake Bay. The slum organizer Saul Alinsky led blacks in Rochester and Chicago to some notable victories over rents and housing but concentrated on local efforts rather than forging a national coalition of the poor. An ambitious series of federally sponsored community action programs faltered.

It became obvious that the very condition and structure of poverty thwarted the poor in efforts toward political mobilization and activism. The poor were poor politically as well as financially, educationally, motivationally. Kenneth B. Clark looked back on the lessons of the failed community action program and reflected that "those of us who were involved in setting up the prototype of these programs" were "somewhat naive and sentimental. We did not take into account the effect of poverty and deprivation on the human personality. We did not calculate that for the poor the chief consequence of the culture of poverty is a kind of human stagnation, acceptance, defeat, which made meaningful involvement of the poor more verbal than real."

A quarter century after Lyndon Johnson launched his war against poverty, Clark's lessons seemed more pertinent than ever. To a small but significant degree, blacks—the best tests of progress—had closed the gap with whites in the percentage of high school graduates and of enrollees in college. They had held their own or caught up a bit in median family income. But the black unemployment rate had doubled. The National Urban League reported that 25 percent of black households were affected by crime; the rates of drug use, crime, and violent deaths were considerably higher among blacks than whites; and 40 percent of black children lived in homes without fathers. Thus the culture of poverty continued, and in a form that would blight lives well into the twenty-first century.

Only transforming leadership of the rarest quality—the kind that Martin Luther King, Jr., had displayed a decade before—could have combined in the late seventies the egalitarian ideals, the intellectual grasp, the educational effort, the setting of priorities, the organizational dynamics, the grass-roots mobilization, and the electoral strategy necessary to topple the structure of poverty and give the poor their share of American abundance. Such leadership was lacking in the politically and intellectually disordered wake of Vietnam and Watergate. There was no Martin Luther King for the poor.

CROSSWAYS, LAND AND SKY

During the 1970s, when the United States still loomed as the economic overlord of the Western world, European intellectuals asked barbed questions as to why this capitalist nation so steeped in affluence could not take care of its own poor. Washington had plenty of advice and even dollars for developing nations afflicted by rural and urban poverty—why could it not deal with deprivation in the Bronx and Watts and Appalachian hollows? If American leaders—even Nixon—were now posing as Keynesians, why did they not apply modernized or post-Keynesian strategies to their own economic policy making? Some pointed to the case of Sweden, which had long served as an example to Americans as an effective "middle way." By the mid-1970s Sweden was outperforming the United States in real growth per capita, employment levels, and, to some degree, even the inflation rate. To be sure, Sweden's was a more homogeneous society and a more "manageable" economy than the American, but in many respects it was even more vulnerable to outside forces.

If European critics liberally criticized American economics, however, for the most part they had unabashed admiration for American science and technology. Americans had landed on the moon, dominated the Nobel sweepstakes, flooded the world with electronic marvels and household gadgets. Above all, Europeans admired the ubiquitous American automobile, which changed its decor and contours as often as did Paris fashions. To be sure, they laughed at reports—true, as it turned out—that a California minister sermonized to ranks of cars in his drive-in church, and that a Detroit funeral home enabled mourners to drive up to a window and remain in their cars while they enjoyed a thirty-second viewing of the deceased. But even the more sophisticated critics could not escape the spell of the gleaming new American automobile. Behind the Iron Curtain too, it was a common experience for Americans returning to their parked cars to find them encircled by gaping admirers.

It was indeed the era of triumph for the American auto. Everything appeared to be coming together for the industry during the Johnson and early Nixon years. While the chart of annual new car sales in the 1960s and early 1970s was uneven, the overall trend was exuberantly upward, topping 10 million, of which only a small fraction were imports. The average price of a new car as a percentage of United States median family income had fallen steadily since the fifties. The Big Three—or at least the Big Two, GM and Ford—were thriving.

Over half a century earlier the erratic financial genius William Crapo Durant had combined Buick, Cadillac, Oldsmobile, Pontiac, and Chevrolet into the mighty General Motors Corporation, which, with the crucial help of Du Pont money, came to dominate the automobile market. Under Alfred P. Sloan, Jr., the ablest automobile industrialist of them all, General Motors modernized its financial systems and pioneered installment loans to customers, annual model changes, and a radical decentralization of operations. Sloan even applied class analysis to his products: Chevrolet, he said, was "for the hoi polloi, Pontiac for the poor but proud, Oldsmobile for the comfortable but discreet, Buick for the striving, and Cadillac for the rich." By the 1970s its buy-outs, immense capital resources, and long-range planning were paying off for GM, which steadily outpaced in sales the other domestic automakers combined.

But Ford had also prospered in the sixties and early seventies, enjoying well over 2 million new car sales a year. The company had finally shaken off the archaic hold of its founder after his grandson, Henry Ford II, took over company leadership in 1945. Young Ford quickly sacked the despised aide of the founder, Harry Bennett, made peace with the United Automobile Workers, failed dramatically with the Edsel but then triumphed with the Falcon and the Mustang. He showed a special talent for bringing into the company or promoting such high-powered executives as Ernest R. Breech, Robert S. McNamara, and Lee Iacocca.

Union labor in the auto industry shared the prosperous times. Outstripping even the steelworkers in hourly pay during the late sixties and early seventies, auto labor used its union power to gain abundant wage settlements. For years the UAW picked off GM's weaker competitors one by one to win generous agreements that the rest of the auto manufacturers were then bound to accept. When in 1970 the UAW leadership decided it was time to tackle GM first, the result was one of the most expensive strikes in American history, but once again the union won a good settlement. The auto workers conducted this strike without their widely admired leader, Walter Reuther, who was killed in a plane crash a few weeks before negotiations got underway. Two decades earlier Reuther and his brother Victor had been seriously wounded on separate occasions by shotgun blasts into their homes—a grievous portent of the assassinations of American leaders in later years.

The control that the auto industry in collaboration with union labor exercised over technology, capital investment, plant locations, wages, prices, consumer preferences made it a prime example of the kind of industrial planning Galbraith described in *The New Industrial State.* Ever since Henry the First had begun to flood the country with Model T's, automobiles had been steadily transforming American life and geography. Before World War II the automobile began to channel Americans into suburban areas that had earlier been beyond the reach of commuter trains and had converted "autocamping" into a growing roadside industry of restaurants and motels. The massive road building commissioned by the Eisenhower Administration's Interstate Highway Act of 1956 further stimulated automobile use, which in turn stimulated more road building. The spiraling of auto production and demand not only enlarged the auto network of garages, filling stations, and highway motels and restaurants but also knit together a wider array of the "Road Gang," as Helen Leavitt called it—trucking companies, the Teamsters union, automobile dealers, turnpike builders, oil importers and producers, state politicians, lobbies, legislators, highway officials.

Thus the automakers sat in the middle of a carefully spun and balanced web of group interests. But this web, in turn, lay in the middle of a pulsating and swiftly changing environment that was as chaotic as the industrial web was "rational." One-hundred-foot-wide highways speared through urban ghettos and lush farmland. Suburbia expanded faster than ever, housing subdivisions proliferated, shopping malls mushroomed, industries moved out into the hinterland. "Mini-cities" and "urban villages" sprang up. Pollution spread in rural valleys that had never known smog or factory smells. National and state parks were overwhelmed. At the same time that driving one-and-a-half-ton steel projectiles at sixty or seventy miles an hour on crowded highways became "another inalienable American right," in James Flink's words, unintended slaughter on superhighways became a daily American tragedy.

Inevitably little outside the web *was* planned. Few observers in 1956, save for those of prophetic insight like Lewis Mumford, had thought of the wider impact of spending almost $30 billion on a 41,000-mile road-building program that would devour 2 million acres of land. In particular few had analyzed its impact on *people*—people living in bypassed towns and cities, people seeking privacy and peace of mind away from the roar of traffic and the pollution of air, above all people—many of them black and Hispanic and poor—whose neighborhoods and communities had been sliced apart and pulverized by the relentless expressways.

"White roads through black bedrooms," some said, had been a prime factor in the unrest that triggered the Detroit rioting of 1967, leaving 40 dead, 2,000 injured, 5,000 homeless. The fury of the violence was a stunning surprise. Indeed, the social evils of the expansion of the auto industry and its Road Gang had been as uncalculated as the economic expansion had been analyzed, quantified, and projected. Uncalculated too was the extent to which the auto, by gulping down oil from abroad, helped transform America's relationship with a far-off region of the world.

*   *   *

In the Yom Kippur War of October 1973, Egypt suffered its third defeat at the hands of Israel since 1948. The aroused Arab world retaliated with an oil embargo against nations friendly to Israel. After abortive earlier efforts at cooperation, Saudi Arabia and the other oil-producing nations had at last formed the OPEC cartel, and now began to wield their united economic power. By March 1974, when seven Arab nations—all but Libya and Syria—lifted the embargo, the price of oil had soared from $3 to $12 a barrel.

Although Arab leaders had long threatened to use their potent economic weapon, the political leadership in Washington appeared to be unready to cope with the crisis. So did American car owners. As gasoline prices doubled and pumps ran out, people waited for hours, tempers fraying. Fights broke out as drivers tried to jump the line. The fear of running dry was greater than the experience of actually doing so; in the first quarter of 1974 gas consumption in the United States dropped only 7 percent, but Americans, long used to gasoline gushing readily and cheaply out of hoses, panicked at the very thought of being unable to jump into their cars and roar off at any time to any place for any reason.

A search for scapegoats followed, with the automakers among the first targets. Henry Ford II, whose motto in awkward personal circumstances was: "Never explain, never complain," had already been grumbling that the auto industry and the "so-called highway lobby" were being blamed for causing "a host of environmental problems—including, to name just a few, air, noise, and visual pollution, urban traffic congestion, unplanned suburban sprawl, the decay of central cities, the decline of public transportation and the segregation of minorities in urban ghettos." In the aftermath of the oil crunch, criticism escalated on all these counts. Cars were too big and were gas guzzlers. Annual style changes were simply a crafty device to raise sales through planned obsolescence. The automobile industry, once world-famous for its experimentation and innovation, had become complacent and routinized, as in its failure to shift from rear-wheel to front-wheel drive. Its concern for its customers' safety was nil. And now critics like Ralph Nader, who had briefly jolted automakers out of their complacency with *Unsafe at Any Speed,* his 1965 exposé of the "designed-in dangers" of American cars, were finding a larger and angrily receptive audience.

The capacity of the automobile industry to respond to this, the worst crisis in consumer relations it had ever faced, became a test of individual leadership in the three dominant car companies. There was no united front, despite charges from the left that the automakers formed a tight conspiracy against humankind. It was sink or swim for each company.

After World War II no large corporation had a bigger and perhaps more deserved reputation for its top leadership than General Motors. Sloan's "industrial statesmanship" was a model for such strong GM executives as William Knudsen, who became FDR's head of war production during World War II, and Charles "Engine Charlie" Wilson, later Eisenhower's Secretary of Defense. Sloan's decentralization of operations, which left major decisions in the hands of production chiefs, and his willingness to innovate had attracted innumerable bright young men to the company.

By the 1960s the rising new generation at General Motors was finding its vaunted industrial leadership to be a thing of the past. Control of the company had passed into the hands of finance officers who had had little experience in production. They played a safe game, with annual profits as their guide and god. Behind the façade of teamwork, top executives carved out private dukedoms that did silent battle with one another. Typically the finance officers were hostile to innovation, creativity, and unorthodoxy. Men had to conform in attitude, advice, and even attire—an executive wearing a brown suit one day instead of the prescribed blue or gray was sent home to change. The result, in the eyes of Young Turks who were later to write with the benefit of 20/20 hindsight, was repeated failure to innovate, to experiment boldly.

GM executives often gave speeches about the free market, private enterprise, and individual initiative, even while their dominant role in the auto industry vitiated these ideas. They denounced government for its swollen bureaucracy, waste, heavy-handed controls, even while their own organization displayed these same tendencies. Indeed, the famous Fourteenth Floor of GM's Detroit headquarters building exhibited many characteristics of the White House—crisis decision-making, jockeying for advancement, ad hoc coping, favoritism. Occasionally the Fourteenth Floor even acted like the Kremlin: on one famous occasion in the presence of a large assembly of executives, GM finance officers who had climbed the greasy pole castigated the old-line "production men" who had, they said, left the company in a shambles. It seemed a bit like new masters in the Politburo attacking past leaders to whom they had once truckled.

Restless young executives at GM often pointed to Ford as more innovative and creative, but inside GM's chief rival, Young Turks were having their own problems. The hostility of the engineering and production men at the industrial grass roots toward the bosses in the executive suites was even greater at Ford than at GM. When Ford went public with a huge stock offering in late 1955, amid huge excitement in the investment houses, the company appeared to turn its back on Henry the First's adamant opposition to control by Wall Street or "the bankers." The shift also heightened the power of the auto companies' financial officers over the production people, for now the New York men of finance could hold the Detroit men in line. Sharply budgeted and restricted, Young Turks noted that Henry the Second had inherited his grandfather's distaste for innovation. Just as the first Ford had stuck to the Model T too long, giving Chevrolet an edge it never lost, so the heir cast a dim eye on many a proposal from the engineering and production people, especially after the Edsel fiasco. Advised to diversify, he liked to say flatly, "My grandfather made cars and I make cars." Urged in the mid-1970s to build the Fiesta with a Honda engine and transmission in it, he said, "No Jap engine is going under the hood of a car with my name on it."

Few Ford executives felt more frustrated by Ford executives in general and by Henry II in particular than an up-and-coming young protégé of McNamara's named Lee Iacocca. After a meteoric rise through the ranks, Iacocca became president of Ford at the end of the euphoric sixties, which alas was the start of the dismal seventies. A tempestuous, outspoken, egotistical man, he soon came into conflict with Chairman Ford and with the finance people over change and innovation. Face-to-face confrontations followed, especially when Iacocca pressed for a strong small-car program. One of the two had to go, and it was not Ford.

For years Chrysler had been running third among the Big Three; by the late 1970s this had become a very poor third. Its sales, employment, net earnings, and common stock were all sharply down. Iacocca, freed from Ford in 1978, was summoned to the rescue. During the long months that followed, he and his crisis team put together an extraordinary combination of UAW support, the influence of Michigan black leaders in Washington, the willingness of suppliers to accept delayed payments, the cooperation of bankers and other creditors in staving off bankruptcy and putting pressure on Congress to help. Washington, moving with all deliberate slowness, at last agreed to guarantee $1.2 billion in loans, enough to keep in production the fuel-efficient, front-wheel-drive "K" car on which Iacocca had set his hopes. By mid-1982 Chrysler was beginning to show a profit again, and Iacocca was a national hero.

It had indeed been a heroic rescue operation, but some had misgivings. Tens of thousands of laid-off Chrysler workers were left unemployed, as were other thousands among its suppliers. Elinor Bachrach, who had served on the staff of Senator William Proxmire, an opponent of the bailout, said five years later that it had been "oversold." The company was saved but had the "guy on the assembly line" been substantially helped? Proxmire himself called "absolute nonsense" the claim that the bailout program had saved more jobs or factories than a Chapter Eleven reorganization. Others pointed to jobs salvaged, community stability reestablished, welfare cases avoided and hence public money saved, three-way competition extended among the Big Three. In perspective the bailout seemed to have worked for a wide array of interests except for the non-reemployed.

The rescue had once again presented American executives at their most resourceful in an emergency. A host of practical steps saved the day. At the same time it presented major institutions at their worst—a once formidable corporation in collapse, the government moving with glacial slowness, the failure of business and political leadership to anticipate crucial problems or to make institutional changes in advance. It seemed doubtful in retrospect that much had been learned, or at least changed. Amid much talk about the need for employee or union representation on the Chrysler board, the head of the auto workers' union was grudgingly admitted. This amounted to little more than a token compared with the kind of workers' participation represented by the Swedish model. Nor had this immense failure in anticipation and prevention brought about institutional changes that could help to avert recurrences of major sectoral economic breakdowns and crises. There was no agency for long-range planning that could avoid major bailouts such as those of Chrysler, Lockheed, and indeed New York City.

There remained the supreme irony—the industry that had most opposed "governmental paternalism," that had shunned government and even defied it, had seen its third most important component turn to the feds in Washington. And as the Japanese challenge intensified, the entire industry—automakers, auto unions, the whole once powerful Road Gang—had to beg Washington to adopt tariffs, quotas, and other protections against Tokyo. The Koreans, Taiwanese, and other up-and-coming industrial nations also invaded the big, tempting, high-priced American market. It was not like the old days, when Henry Ford and Al Sloan could talk with Presidents almost as equals. Automakers and workers were just another claimant. Failed economic leadership now had to depend on political leadership.

*   *   *

The Soviet embassy, Washington, Friday, October 4, 1957. The old mansion on Massachusetts Avenue had a festive air as Russians and Americans danced, sang, and laughed together. No one was enjoying the party more than William Pickering, head of the American satellite program—until the science writer of *The New York Times* burst into the room and accosted him. What was this "spootnik" that the Russians had launched into orbit? Pickering looked at him in amazement, and then, with his equally startled American colleagues, he gamely toasted the Russians. Then they rushed off to begin a crude calculation of Sputnik's orbit. American space scientists and administrators would later remember that night, wrote Clayton R. Koppes, "much as other people could recall how they felt when they heard of the deaths of presidents or the bombing of Pearl Harbor."

Indeed, Berkeley physicist Edward Teller somberly told a television audience that the United States had lost "a battle more important and greater than Pearl Harbor." Senate Majority Leader Lyndon Johnson picked up the cry, adding that "we do not have as much time as we did" after that attack. With scientists and politicians feeding the hysteria of Americans unable to absorb "the realization that Buck Rogers might prove to be a Russian peasant," President Eisenhower was prompted to reassure the nation that only its pride, not its security, had been damaged.

The surprised reactions—especially among the experts—were unwarranted. For two years the Soviets had been signaling their intentions and progress in a series of statements and press reports, and four months before Sputnik, they had announced their readiness to loft a satellite—and even advertised the frequency on which it would transmit. Some American scientists, moreover, had been urging competitiveness. In 1954 the German émigré physicist Wernher von Braun, requesting $100,000 for "a man-made satellite," which "no matter how humble (five pounds) would be a scientific achievement of tremendous impact," said that *it would be a blow to U.S. prestige if we did not do it first.*" In August 1955 the United States announced that in the eighteen-month International Geophysical Year it would put into space a series of "small, unmanned, earth-circling satellites."

But before Sputnik, speed was not the Eisenhower Administration's main consideration. The President and his advisers were concerned that the satellite work not detract from weapons research and that the nascent space program be divorced as far as possible from the military. Thus in deciding the interservice competition over whose rocket would launch the first American satellite, the Administration in fall 1955 rejected the Army's Project Orbiter, though it had the better booster and promised the earliest launch date. The Navy's proposal, with its stronger scientific, nonmilitary character, was accepted. The choice would prove fateful: Orbiter's launch date had been August 1957, Vanguard's was to be December. Sputnik left earth on October 4, 1957.

The inevitable next leg of the space race was the launching of a human being into space, and this mission was entrusted to the National Aeronautics and Space Administration, an independent civilian agency established in 1958. The first goal of NASA's Mercury program was to "shoot a man from a cannon," and the vehicle to take him up and down was a haphazardly assembled combination of an ICBM-Redstone booster and a capsule with a cramped cabin. The original seven Mercury astronauts, all of them hard-boiled test pilots, were signed to a munificent exclusive contract with *Life* magazine and aggressively promoted as "lovable freckled heroes," men who were "cheerfully facing torture, danger and perhaps death for their country." Alan B. Shepard, Jr., was chosen to man the first Mercury flight—a brief suborbital mission. But before he could be launched—a mere three weeks before—the Americans once again were trumped, as the Soviets announced that *Vostok 1* had carried cosmonaut Major Yuri A. Gagarin into orbit around the earth.

At 9:34 A.M. on May 5, 1961, as 45 million watched on television, the spacecraft *Freedom 7,* with Shepard strapped in atop the huge rocket, lifted off its pad at Cape Canaveral to "go roaring upward through blue sky toward black space"—but only toward, not into, space. He splashed down in the Atlantic fifteen minutes later, his flight an anticlimax after Gagarin. In July, *Liberty Bell 7* took Gus Grissom up and down on a longer but still suborbital ride.

For Americans, playing eternal catch-up—and not even catching up— was not the right stuff. Three weeks after Grissom, cosmonaut Gherman Titov made 17.5 orbits of the earth, on a flight lasting more than twenty- five hours. The pressure on NASA to fling a man into orbit was immense. The man whom NASA chose to fling first, a forty-year-old Korean War veteran, John Glenn, had been disappointed when Shepard was given the initial launch. But after *Vostok 1,* Glenn realized that Shepard's was no longer *the* mission. It mattered now to be the first American to orbit and, with his test pilot's cocksureness and his ambition, Glenn was ready.

Hopes rose for a December 1961 launch date, but technical procedures and run-throughs of the mission pushed the date into 1962. January 23 was finally announced to the press, but before the reporters had a chance to assemble at the now familiar dateline of Cape Canaveral, the launch was again shifted—to the twenty-seventh. Twenty minutes prior to launch, after Glenn had been in the capsule for five hours, the mission was again postponed, because of bad weather. The largely untried new Atlas rocket was purged of propellants and stored. On January 30 it was refueled, but ground support noticed a leak in a kerosene tank. Another delay; this time, until February 13. Twenty-four recovery ships and sixty aircraft manned by 18,000 personnel were recalled. More bad weather on the thirteenth, though. The forecast for Tuesday, February 20, was good, and on Monday night the ground crew began its 610-minute countdown.

Glenn was awakened at 2:20 A.M. Tuesday morning for a breakfast of steak and eggs. After a 135-minute delay while part of the booster guid- ance system was replaced and the dawn skies cleared, Glenn stepped into *Friendship 7* at 6:03. A broken bolt on the hatch and a stuck fuel valve caused further delays. One hundred million people at their television sets shared some of Glenn's tension. At T minus six and a half minutes the Bermuda tracking station experienced a power failure—further delay for repairs. Finally, at 9:47, the Atlas, with a huge tail of fire, lifted off the pad, and mission announcer John A. Powers spoke the words Americans had waited so long to hear: "Glenn reports all spacecraft systems go! Mercury Control is go!" After three orbits in just under five hours, Glenn splashed down in the Atlantic near Bermuda.

The earthbound gave Glenn a tumultuous welcome. His footprints on the deck of the recovery ship were marked with white paint. Schools and highways were renamed in his honor. Four million screaming, shoving New Yorkers jammed Broadway for a ticker-tape parade. Glenn addressed a joint session of Congress—"I still get a real hard-to-define feeling when the flag goes by"—and met with a fascinated admirer at the White House.

Ten months before Glenn's flight—and six weeks after Gagarin's—John Kennedy had taken the first step of a journey whose end he would not see: "Now it is time to take longer strides—time for a great new American enterprise—time for this nation to take a clearly leading role in space achievement, which in many ways may hold the key to our future on earth. . . . I believe that this nation should commit itself to achieving the goal, before this decade is out, of landing a man on the moon and returning him safely to the earth." The United States, he declared, had never before "made the national decisions or marshalled the national resources required for such leadership."

Congress enthusiastically acceded to the President's request. With a goal so distant in time and in place, Kennedy had dramatically lifted the Soviet-American space rivalry to a different plane: over the longer run, American economic and technological superiority would provide a crucial advantage, if indeed the Soviets dared to compete at all. And if some in the scientific community believed that $20 billion would be better spent on unmanned flights, they for the most part kept silent, knowing that $20 billion would not be forthcoming without the goal of a manned moon landing.

Before the decade was out—on July 20, 1969—a fragile lunar module hovered above the moon's rocky surface. Four hundred thousand workers, two hundred colleges and universities, many thousands of corporations had joined forces to produce this moment. As the world watched transfixed, the lander, *Eagle,* first separated from its command ship, *Columbia.* While Michael Collins waited in *Columbia,* Neil Armstrong and Edwin Aldrin looped into their own orbit around the moon's surface. Twelve minutes before landing Houston transferred control to *Eagle:* "You are go. Take it all at four minutes. Roger, you are go—you are to continue powered descent."

At 33,500 feet crisis threatened—the navigational computer was overloading near its limit. If it exceeded that limit the mission would have to be aborted. Armstrong searched the surface for a suitable landing spot, and found only rough ground which would destroy the module. As Armstrong took navigational control from the computer, Aldrin read vital figures from the control panel. The attitude control handle in Armstrong's right hand tilted the spacecraft in any direction; the thrust control handle in his left moved the craft horizontally. The computer maintained control over rate of descent.

Fuel was low, but still Armstrong rejected site after site. Finally he found his spot. A few tense moments as the craft eased down. Then he spoke: "Houston, Tranquility Base here. The Eagle has landed."

* * *

As the exploratory Mercury and Gemini had pioneered Apollo's way to the moon, so too did Apollo cut a path for the space-laboratory Skylab missions in 1973 and 1974 and the joint American-Soviet Apollo-Soyuz of 1975. Pioneer and Mariner probes surveyed Mars, Jupiter, Saturn, and Uranus. Between 1957 and 1984, nearly 14,000 objects had been launched into space and some 5,000 of them remained in earthly orbit, including telecommunications satellites of the Department of Defense, the National Weather Service, AT&T, and RCA.

On Sunday morning, April 12, 1981, four IBM computers, with a fifth as backup, kicked into gear and took over launch control. Majestically, a giant new rocket rose slowly from its platform, a truly space-age spacecraft strapped to its back. The crew could feel the swing of the vehicle and the surge of power as the booster rockets fired. The ground shook with the thrust of space shuttle *Columbia*'s main engines, running at 104 percent of their rated power. The craft accelerated as it left the earth; its engine ran more efficiently at higher altitudes, and the burning of fuel lightened the vehicle. At launch plus eleven seconds the crowd three miles below saw *Columbia* roll over in the sky onto its back and felt and heard the roar. After eight minutes the main engines had burned out, and *Columbia* achieved orbit.

After two days the engines were again turned on to slow the craft and it began its descent out of orbit. Four hundred thousand feet above the earth *Columbia* still traveled twenty-five times the speed of sound. Nothing this big had ever been brought back to earth, much less landed on an airstrip. Computers again assumed control to perform split-second navigational functions. Its speed down to four times the speed of sound, *Columbia* crossed California's northern coast and started its descent into the Mojave Desert. Across the state *Columbia*'s sonic booms drew people's attention skyward. At Edwards Air Force Base, hundreds of thousands of persons watched as the world's first reusable manned spaceship, under its pilot's control, glided in and gracefully touched down at 225 miles per hour.

Over the next five years, the American shuttle fleet flew twenty-three more missions, and NASA set an ambitious schedule of fifteen flights in 1986 alone. But as early as the second shuttle flight, technicians had noticed that the O-rings—enormous circles of rubber that helped to seal segments of the booster rocket together—had charred. Routine reports were filed, but the problem recurred on flight after flight. Both the shuttle research facility at Marshall Space Flight Center and contractor Morton Thiokol's people decided they would develop a plan to fix the O-ring seal problem themselves rather than review it with NASA management—but personnel changes and wrangling with Congress delayed action. By the end of 1985 ten flights had experienced seal failures. Rather than break the flight schedule, waivers were signed that allowed the flights to continue despite the threats to safety.

Preparations for *Challenger* mission 51-L began on a cold Monday in January 1986. Project manager Allan J. MacDonald warned his superiors that low temperatures affected the O-rings and Thiokol engineers recommended against the launch unless the temperature of the O-rings was at least fifty-three degrees Fahrenheit. But on Tuesday, January 28, at 3:10 A.M., the launch crew began pumping liquid hydrogen and liquid oxygen into the giant external tank of *Challenger*. Reports of surface temperatures were not part of the routine, so the twenty-five degrees of the left booster and the eight degrees of the right were not communicated to the launch room. The flight had already been postponed several times. Children across the country were glued to televisions for this flight of Christa McAuliffe, the first "teacher in space," part of NASA's program to loft ordinary citizens. The countdown continued and *Challenger* was launched. Tremendous pressure from the expanding gases inside the rocket booster strained against the flawed rings. Falling ice, steam, and distance obscured the puff of ominous black smoke as *Challenger* rose.

Still seconds into the ascent, *Challenger* was saved by milliseconds when the melted joint created a temporary seal. At T plus 60 seconds, as the main engines throttled up to 104 percent, rookie astronaut Mike Smith yelled, "Feel that mother go." But the rocket's vibrations had broken the temporary seal: the O-ring had failed. At T plus 73, NASA officials witnessed the explosion on their television monitors. Nine miles above the Atlantic, Mike Smith could see the flames outside his window. "Uh, Oh!" he said as the cabin broke from the rocket. It plunged 65,000 feet to the sea in two minutes and forty-five seconds. All seven astronauts died, from asphyxiation or fire or impact, as they smashed into eighty feet of water at 207 miles an hour.

*   *   *

Time and time again it had taken disasters, whether natural or man-made, to force Americans to do the kind of thinking that, had it been done in advance, might have averted or mitigated them. The deaths of seven astronauts focused the American mind. "More than the Challenger exploded in the blue sky over the Atlantic Ocean," wrote *New York Times* science correspondent John Noble Wilford. Thirty billion dollars and fourteen years after the huge shuttle effort began, "we are left full of doubts not only about the shuttles and NASA's fabled competence, but about the very fundamentals of our national space policy." At first the media concentrated on the O-rings—so simple to present graphically and ominously—and other shuttle apparatus. Gradually, as the debate widened and deepened, it was apparent that, as Joseph Trento wrote, "the destruction of *Challenger* is not a story of technological failure—it is a story of political failure," a function of policy decisions that emerged from political compromises that in turn reflected conceptual muddle.

The failure to anticipate and plan against disasters had often had its roots in complacency—over the unsinkability of the *Titanic,* the safety of hydrogen-filled dirigibles, the permanence of 1920s prosperity, the American inability to lose a war. So with the space program, and the complacency had some justification. John Kennedy had made a solid commitment to put a man on the moon—a commitment no later President could repudiate. It was his way of dramatizing his active leadership in comparison with that of Eisenhower, who, according to a Washington story, had said that unlike Queen Isabella's patronage of Christopher Columbus, he would not "hock his jewels" to send anyone to the moon. Kennedy had been attacked for grandstanding, playing politics, fighting the cold war in space. But Kennedy had his reasons: national defense, strengthening the aerospace industry, national morale. Above all for him it was a matter of national prestige—Yuri Gagarin's earth orbit was a challenge. His Vice President agreed; to be "second in space," advised LBJ, was to be "second in everything."

On this issue, as on others, Kennedy shifted later. Two months before he died he proposed before the United Nations that Russians and Americans make the moon flight together. "Let us do the big things together."

The spectacular feat of Apollo had captured the world's headlines and imagination. The moon landing became a symbol of the American will, unassailable proof of superior American technology. But Apollo's end left NASA "with a vehicle rather than a mission." What next? The boldest spirits wanted to combine a Mars landing with an earth-orbiting space station and a reusable shuttle, but the political environment was changed in the late 1960s and early 1970s. Vietnam, together with the easing of cold war tensions, made a national commitment to an adventure in space on the scale of Apollo impossible. And Apollo's very success—Apollo 11 and five subsequent moon landings—had made the public blasé even about men on the moon. The object now, in John M. Logsdon's words, "was to make access to orbit routine and relatively inexpensive, and that these objectives could be achieved within a budget substantially less than required for Apollo." But NASA, with the shuttle program it formally adopted in 1972, made a grandiose mockery of these realistic and coherent objectives. The shuttle design incorporated the "highest possible level of technology," when simpler, cheaper technology would have served the purpose as well, or better. Because the price of the shuttle was so high, the space station which it had originally been intended to service was indefinitely postponed. And in order to promote the shuttle as the only American launch vehicle, NASA reduced or deferred research and development of alternatives, thus eliminating the possibility of a balanced space program or of a fallback in the event of a shuttle failure or disaster. As Wilford wrote, "NASA mortgaged nearly everything—science, space exploration, the development of new technologies—to build the space shuttle on what was a shoestring budget, as big Government projects go."

As Congress grew more interested in the shuttle program, NASA, hungry for more funding, responded by creating still other justifications for the shuttle's existence. Like any bureaucracy, NASA had to justify its own existence, and it was also heavily cross-pressured by its contractors, for whom the agency had been in the 1960s a bottomless feedbag. NASA countered these pressures in part by encouraging the commercial use of space and space technology—the contractors would be kept busy and business would share the costs. Thus telecommunications companies developed their own satellites and NASA launched them, and the later Apollo flights and the shuttle missions conducted experiments in space manufacture. In 1984, the Reagan Administration stepped up commercial development of space. But by the time of the *Challenger* disaster, the profitability of space manufacture was still unproven. Nor had the shuttle met the expectation that it would lower the cost of space transportation: instead of a projected $260 per pound of payload, the actual price was over $4,000 per pound—and that would rise to $6,800 when shuttle flights resumed.

The Reagan Administration also accelerated the militarization of the space program. Eisenhower had set a policy followed by the next three Presidents: top priority to the open, civilian applications of the program, not to military uses. When Moscow was reported to have resumed anti-satellite tests in 1976, President Ford instructed the Defense Department to make development of space weaponry a high priority. When the Soviets in 1981 and again in 1983 offered at the United Nations serious treaty proposals for space arms control, the Reagan White House ignored them and continued to pour money—by the late 1980s billions of dollars a year—into a "Strategic Defense Initiative" whose purpose was to "counter the awesome Soviet missile threat" by developing directed-energy weapons that, shot from satellites or from earth to orbiting reflectors, would intercept Soviet missiles in flight. Scientists urged in vain that such funds be spent instead on a more realistic, multifaceted, balanced, and steady program of space research.

What, then, was space to be used for? For disinterested scientific exploration? Commercial exploitation? As a new platform for the cold war? The American space effort was a complex interweaving of scientific, military, geopolitical, and commercial influences, resulting in complex policy making and shrouded accountability and responsibility. "Because it is difficult in the pluralistic U.S. policy-making process to reach consensus on policy goals, debates about means to achieve those goals often are used as surrogates," Logsdon wrote after *Challenger*. "Substituting choices of means for choices of ends produces effective public policy only when agreement on means implies a decision on goals."

Americans followed Soviet space exploits with mortification. The Russian tortoise had got off to an early start, then the American hare had bounded far ahead with the moon landing, but by the late 1980s the hare seemed caught in a brier patch and the tortoise far ahead. A major reason was that the Soviets matched their means, their technology, to their goal of the gradual "evolution of man into space." They had, said John Glenn, now a United States senator, "a very steady, thoughtful, well-laid-out program." They used rather crude but low-cost and dependable rockets—"Big Dumb Boosters," the Americans called them—and had 90 successful launches in 91 tries in 1986, while the United States had only six successes in only nine attempts. Their cosmonauts held every endurance record in space. NASA and the Defense Department had long since rejected proposals for an American Big Dumb Booster. Lacking clear ends, stable planning, and consistent follow-through, the Americans made space decisions on the basis of what would "advance the technology," filling the policy vacuum with expensive high-tech razzle-dazzle.

By the end of the 1980s the most poignant symbol of intellectual failure in space was an object significantly not in space but rather grounded, swaddled, and isolated in an eight-story "clean room" in California. This was the Hubble Space Telescope. Lofted into the pure atmosphere far from earth's surface, the Hubble was programmed to peer almost to the edge of the universe. Its blindfold allegorized the clouded vision of key leaders of the space program.

The songwriter Neil Young in 1979:

> Out of the blue and into the black
> You pay for this but they give you that
> And once you're gone, you can't come back
> When you're out of the blue and into the black.

PART V

The Rebirth of Freedom?

CHAPTER 14

The Kaleidoscope of Thought

I N July 1979, thirty months after he entered the White House, Jimmy Carter faced a crisis of confidence. It was in part a lack of confidence in him, as people waited in gas lines, worried about energy supplies, and were squeezed by inflation rising toward an annual rate of more than 13 percent. It was even more the President's loss of confidence in himself, his leadership, his government. He suddenly postponed what was to have been his fifth speech on the energy crisis and repaired to Camp David to consult and to think.

For ten days, while the nation waited in curiosity and suspense, Carter talked with over 130 persons from virtually every major segment of society. He solicited and received blunt advice, he later reported. A southern governor told him he was not leading the nation, "just managing the government." Other admonitions: The nation was confronted with a moral and a spiritual crisis. The real issue was not energy but freedom. Some of his cabinet members were not loyal, he was told. "You don't see the people enough anymore." But most of the pleas were for stronger leadership. "Mr. President, we're in trouble. Talk to us about blood and sweat and tears." . . . "If you lead, Mr. President, we will follow." . . . "Be bold, Mr. President. We may make mistakes, but we are ready to experiment."

Carter came down from Catoctin Mountain in an apocalyptic mood. The crisis of confidence, he told the nation in an intensely hyped television address, was a crisis that "strikes at the very heart and soul and spirit of our national will. We can see this crisis in the growing doubt about the meaning of our own lives and in the loss of a unity of purpose for our Nation." People were losing faith "not only in government itself but in the ability as citizens to serve as the ultimate rulers and shapers of our democracy."

The symptoms of the crisis, Carter went on, were all around. "For the first time in the history of our country a majority of our people believe that the next 5 years will be worse than the past 5 years. Two-thirds of our people do not even vote. The productivity of American workers is actually

591

dropping, and the willingness of Americans to save for the future has fallen below that of all other people in the Western world."

What to do? Americans had turned to the federal government and found it isolated from the "mainstream of our Nation's life." People were looking for "honest answers" and "clear leadership" and not finding them. Rather they found in Washington "a system of government that seems incapable of action. . . . a Congress twisted and pulled in every direction by hundreds of well-financed and powerful special interests. . . . every extreme position defended to the last vote." The nation, he warned solemnly, was at a turning point, one path leading to "fragmentation and self-interest," the other toward common purpose, toward the restoration of "true freedom for our Nation and ourselves."

The reaction of press and people was as extraordinary as the speech. At first it was sharply positive, both in editorial columns and in the polls. Then the President, to show that he meant business, brusquely sacked several high officials whose loyalty and effectiveness he questioned. To the public, the disarray that Carter had dramatized in his address was suddenly evident in his own Administration. An aide to one of the fired officials was reminded of the story of the king who told his minister that he had been looking out of the window and perceived that his country was in trouble. "But sire," replied the minister, "that's not a window—it's a mirror." A ground swell of criticism enveloped what was now dubbed the "malaise speech" although Carter had not used the word. Confidence in the President sank further a month later when the President accepted the resignation of his old friend Andrew Young as ambassador to the United Nations after it was revealed that Young had violated an official ban against meetings with representatives of the Palestine Liberation Organization and then lied to the State Department about what he had done.

In the spirit of Winston Churchill, Carter had given one of the most candid, realistic speeches an American President had ever made. But he was no Winston Churchill. His speech was a political failure because, in contrast to Churchill's defiance, he had followed up only with the popgun of reshuffling Administration posts. It was an intellectual failure, for Carter spoke rhetorically rather than analytically about the problems, failed to define the "true freedom" and other values he celebrated, and refused to spell out specifically what he would propose to do about "paralysis and stagnation and drift." The disarray indeed appeared to be in Carter's government—and in his mind.

In essence the speech was a kind of *cri de coeur*—a heartfelt appeal for national unity, for seizing "control again of our common destiny"—but just how these rousing political war cries, however sincerely uttered, could be translated into policy and action was left unclear. The address did not hang together. While its first half was filled with grim generalities—the President warning against fragmentation, excessive individualism, against a "growing disrespect for government and for churches and for schools, the news media, and other institutions"—the second half detailed an energy program. The preacher and the engineer did not connect. Was it curious, or inevitable, that one of the most thoroughly thought-out and skillfully crafted presidential messages of recent times should reflect the central weakness of the American intellect—the Tocquevillian void between the lofty plane of abstraction and the immediate "pragmatic" action?

The ultimate paradox was the self-admitted failure of Carter and other leaders during a decade devoted to celebrating the great men of the 1770s. Reminded of the achievements of the likes of Washington and Franklin— and even more, of their conviction, their absolute dedication to their causes, their willingness literally to lay down their lives for independence, for liberty, for the Revolution—the Americans of the 1970s could be pardoned for comparing them with the LBJ of Vietnam, the Nixon of Watergate, the honest but faltering Carter, the hundreds of politicians who served as nothing more than brokers eternally calculating their self-interest in executive chambers and legislative halls.

Many Americans, however, did not need to reach back two centuries to realize the current state of "paralysis and stagnation and drift." They had grown up in the era of Eleanor and Franklin Roosevelt, of Stimson, Hughes, Willkie, and Eisenhower, of Truman and Marshall and Acheson, of administrators with the gritty idealism of Harold Ickes, David Lilienthal, Frances Perkins. Younger Americans remembered the two Kennedys and Martin Luther King, who had given up their lives, and the astronauts who had risked theirs.

In other fields too Americans glumly contrasted the current crop with the old. Who in music in the 1970s and 1980s could compare with Aaron Copland and Virgil Thomson of the 1930s and 1940s? What pundit could stand with Walter Lippmann for the sheer range and depth of his grasp of issues both philosophical and practical? Who in literature with Faulkner or Frost or Hemingway? Who with John Dewey in philosophy, Reinhold Niebuhr in theology, Hannah Arendt and Harold Lasswell in social analysis, V. O. Key in political science? Where were the newspaper publishers and editors who could rank with Henry Luce or Ralph Ingersoll for creativity and innovation? Where was the equivalent of Frank Lloyd Wright in architecture, of Martha Graham in dance, of Dave Brubeck in jazz, of Edward Steichen and Alfred Stieglitz in photography, of Alfred A. Knopf and Harry Scherman in book publishing and distribution, of Edward R. Murrow and William Shirer in radio, of Robert Hutchins in higher education, of Paul Robeson in music and drama?

HABITS OF INDIVIDUALISM

The mounting popular concern during the 1980s over the innumerable ills afflicting the republic—widespread crime, pervasive corruption, illiteracy, school dropouts and other signs of failures in education, drug and alcohol dependency, AIDS, a rash of teenage suicides—led to those time-honored resorts of perplexed Americans: legislative investigations, citizens' study groups, "blue ribbon" commissions at the national, state, and municipal levels. These investigators made numerous suggestions, most of them useful and some of them even carried out, but the more that reforms were put into effect, the more it became evident that the roots of the cultural disarray lay deeper in the body social and politic than simple, isolated remedies could reach.

Hence investigators looked closely at attitudes and behaviors shaped within the family and absorbed by children literally at their mothers' and fathers' knees. The 50 million "married couple families," as the Census Bureau identified them—about half of them "with own children under 18"—were so numerous and diverse as to make generalizations about them so general as to be commonplace and to conceal the enormous variety of learning and socialization experiences these families—especially the children—were undergoing. To many investigators it seemed more fruitful to explore the impact on attitudes of the two preeminent institutions outside the family that influenced Americans from a very early age—the church and the school.

The number of members claimed by American religious bodies in the 1980s was staggering—over 140 million, in 344,000 churches, synagogues, and other congregations, served by over 300,000 clergy of all denominations. The enrollment in Sunday schools or their equivalent numbered almost 30 million. As striking was the enormous diversity of religion in America. The National Council of Churches listed over eighty separate nationwide religious bodies claiming memberships of at least 50,000—among them the United Methodist Church with 9 million adherents, the Southern Baptist Convention (14 million), the Presbyterian Church (3.1 million), the Roman Catholic Church (52 million), and the Churches of Christ (1.6 million). Across the nation a half dozen or so Protestant "splinter" churches each numbered several million members. Memberships in non-Christian faiths were sizable; Jews, for example, were estimated to be 5.8 million strong.

Church and temple involvement by members was another matter. The percentage of Americans attending a weekly religious service wavered between 30 and 33 percent during the 1940s, rose to almost 50 percent during the late 1950s, and then leveled off to about 40 percent during the 1970s. The question of church influence over members was still another matter, and a most complex one. Asked over the years, "At the present time, do you think religion as a whole is increasing its influence on American life or losing its influence?" a cross section of Americans who answered "losing" rose to a high point of 75 percent in 1970 and then leveled off, at least for a time, to around 50 percent in the late 1970s. The ratio of church membership to population also stabilized, at around 60 percent. These overall figures concealed a degree of flux among denominations. Between the mid-1960s and the late 1980s several of the "mainline" Protestant churches lost over four million members, prompting painful self-examination on the part of church leaders.

Despite the shifting allegiances and the shallow affiliations of many, the potential influence of church and temple remained substantial. How much of that potential was realized? Of preeminent concern to investigators during the years after Vietnam and Watergate was the extent to which religious leaders not only inculcated specific everyday values of honesty, courtesy, tolerance, and the like, but, even more, offered their congregations some transcending vision of the good life and the good society and a sense of moral coherence, such as a grasp of the interrelated values of liberty, equality, and justice. Religious teachers and learners alike displayed the dichotomy Tocqueville had noticed between the flowery abstractions appealing to all and the specific belief meeting individual needs, with little connection between the two.

Many Americans, Robert Bellah and his associates noted, had lost a "language genuinely able to mediate among self, society, the natural world, and ultimate reality." They often fell back on abstractions when discussing the most important matters. "They stress 'communication' as essential to relationships without adequately considering what is to be communicated. They talk about 'relationships' but cannot point to the personal virtues and cultural norms that give relationships meaning and value." The fragmentation of American religion into an endless diversity of sects and organizations exacerbated these tendencies.

Many years earlier, Henry Thoreau, on hearing that after a tremendous effort Maine and Texas had been connected by the magnetic telegraph, had asked, What in the world did Maine and Texas have to say to each other? What did ministers and their flocks have to say to one another in the 1980s? Religious leaders and followers, Catholics and Moslems and Jews, the profusion of Protestant leaders and sects—could they communicate, whether in agreement or not, only in empty banalities and stereotypes? If so, would they drift further apart, falling back on their own internal languages, parochial ideas, and individual interests?

*   *   *

Like religion, American education was massive in scope and endlessly fragmented in structure. By the early 1990s, according to mid-1980s projections, 50 million students would be enrolled in all public schools, elementary, secondary, and college, and another 9 million in private schools at those levels. Not included in these estimates were the 10 or 20 million persons who would attend a variety of alternative, special education, vocational, and other schools. Such figures raised again the old paradox of American education. Public schools were the nation's biggest collective enterprise and at the same time its biggest experiment in socialism. For a century or so, American mothers and fathers, all the while denouncing nationalization of industry in other countries, had been putting their beloved children into the hands of government bureaucrats employed in government-controlled enterprises located on government-owned land, at the children's most impressionable and vulnerable ages.

The people's confidence in the state-run public school system had been magnificently vindicated. Mass public education had elevated the minds and skills of tens of millions of youngsters, and helped to equalize their opportunities. At the same time, this socialism, as a potential source of indoctrination in "collectivist" ideas, had been a toothless tiger. Ample criticism there had always been—of the teachers, the textbooks, the curriculum, the principals, the coaches. At the same time the teachers in general were too cautious, the classes too pedantic, the reading too tame, and above all the schools too regionalized and localized in their leadership and direction for the public school system nationally to become controversial. Private schools, moreover, afforded parents an alternative—or an escape; thus the enrollment in private secondary schools almost doubled in the decade following the Supreme Court's antisegregation decisions in *Brown* and other cases, as whites sought to evade integrated public schools.

What was happening inside the 85,000 public schools? In the wake of huge rises in spending for public schools during the post-Sputnik years, study after study supported one high school senior's answer: "Dullsville." The "recitation syndrome" continued, according to a *Harvard Educational*

Review report based on data from over 1,000 elementary and secondary classrooms. Classes, typically ranging from 30 to 35 pupils, were dominated by teacher talk, which took up over four-fifths of the time. Little used were such teaching and learning devices as give-and-take discussion, demonstration, the encouragement of informed questioning and student decision making. There was a kind of "hidden" curriculum based on authority, linear thinking, intellectual apathy, "hands-off learning." The investigators quoted Alvin Toffler: education is "not just something that happens in the head. It involves our muscles, our senses, our hormonal defenses, our total biochemistry." In American classrooms, the study concluded, rote was king.

American schools adapted to the political and community environment, Richard M. Merelman concluded, by reducing the intellectual quality of the training. This meant deemphasizing the academic competence of their teachers; setting achievement levels low enough to ensure that most students "passed"; blurring the differences between facts and values in politics; emphasizing the ritual of class participation over its quality.

Dullsville did not lack variety of course choice. Some listings of courses offered hundreds of selections and resembled university catalogues. After studying the formal curriculum, with its array of offerings from Calligraphy to Beginning French to Income Properties Management, along with the "extracurriculum" of clubs and sports, and noting the psychological and social "services curriculum" offered by some schools, three education experts wrote a book titled *The Shopping Mall High School.*

The 3,300 institutions of higher education—the 2,000 four-year and the 1,300 two-year colleges and universities, the 800,000 or more full-time and part-time teachers, the 12 million full-time or part-time students—did not escape the same accusations of intellectual disarray, moral purposelessness, lack of clear priorities, variety beyond healthy diversity. If the typical big high school could be compared to a shopping mall, big universities *were* a mall, with their long and glittering array of specialized courses, adult programs, artistic and dramatic productions, stores, banks, eateries, bigtime athletic contests, and other public and private enterprises. The missing ingredient, observed economist and former Grinnell president Howard R. Bowen, was a set of values. After decades of vigorous growth, wrote Ernest Boyer and Fred Hechinger, American higher education was confused over its goals, lacking in self-confidence, uncertain about the future.

Why? Higher education was adrift, Boyer and Hechinger said, because the nation was in some respects adrift. Universities were no longer enlisted in the fight against economic depression, the all-out effort to win a global war, the race with the Russians to the moon. Others believed that the purposelessness and disarray lay much more within higher education it-self—in the enormous amount of intellectual and curricular specialization, in the privatization of young scholars obsessed with gaining advancement through publishing rather than teaching, in the conflicts among values as well as the confusion in values. Political theorist Michael Walzer noted a fateful tendency of the "American liberal approach to moral" life in educa-tion either to relegate values to private life and thus cut them off from public discourse and education or to reduce values to quantifiable cost-benefit analysis and thus evade the harsh task of making moral choices.

*   *   *

Those who attacked religion and education for lacking clear values as guidelines and intellectual and moral coherence were not always willing or able to offer coherent critiques. It was often not clear what kinds of values they were urging—whether "modal" values, modes of conduct such as honesty, fairness, civility, courage, fidelity, honor; or those substantive, palpable goals, "core" values, such as liberty, justice, equality, community; or instrumental values, such as democratic procedures, which had some intrinsic worth but were also means of achieving broader, substantive ends. Thus in debates over civil rights there might be confusion as to whether the issue was a core value like equality, an instrumental value such as free speech or majority rule in achieving equality, or a modal value such as the orderly, fair-minded, honest, civil, and responsible conduct of the debates.

Even more critical than these ambiguities was the particular set of core values held by critics of excessive educational diversity and religious heterodoxy, many of whom supported, indeed would have given their lives for, a core value that buttressed that diversity and heterodoxy—individual freedom. "Freedom," wrote Robert Bellah and colleagues in *Habits of the Heart*, "is perhaps the most resonant, deeply held American value. In some ways, it defines the good in both personal and political life. Yet freedom turns out to mean being left alone by others, not having other people's values, ideas, or styles of life forced upon one, being free of arbitrary authority in work, family, and political life. What it is that one might do with that freedom is much more difficult for Americans to define." This, it appeared, included American intellectuals, but fortunately this did not keep them from trying. Typically they proceeded by making the case against individualism, as they found it in Reagan-era America.

That case was eloquent and powerful, if not novel. Individualism eroded or snapped the human links between persons and their families, religious leaders and groups, teachers and fellow students, neighbors and fellow workers. "The decline of church, state, and class as centers of culture in

America," Richard Merelman wrote in 1983, "has created unusually extreme individualism among Americans," leaving "the individual alone and adrift in an often alien social and political universe." They were concerned, Bellah and his associates wrote two years later, that the individualism described by Tocqueville with a mixture of admiration and anxiety "may have grown cancerous—that it may be destroying those social integuments that Tocqueville saw as moderating its more destructive potentialities, that it may be threatening the survival of freedom itself." Bellah and his colleagues were especially alarmed by the stimulus that religious sects gave to individualism, which in turn created an intellectual environment in which sects flourished.

These and other social critics of individualism granted that their case was not new—that a generation earlier Fromm and Riesman, Whyte and Marcuse, and thinkers for many centuries before them had grappled with this phenomenon. But they claimed a special urgency in the age of Reagan. Much was being made in the press of the "yuppies"—the young, upwardly mobile professionals flooding into law offices, investment firms, and corporate executive suites who were reputed to be scrambling all over one another in a mad rush for personal success, which often meant merely higher salaries rather than work that was either intellectually rewarding or socially useful. But individualism in modern-day America included much more than self-promotion, the Bellah study found—it also embraced self-protection, as in the case of Sheila Larson, a young nurse who was interviewed. "Sheilaism"—that was her term and her faith, said Sheila. "I believe in God. I'm not a religious fanatic. I can't remember the last time I went to church. My faith has carried me a long way. It's Sheilaism. Just my own little voice."

In explaining Sheilaism—"It's just try to love yourself and be gentle with yourself"—Sheila personified another trend that had caught the critical intellectual eye. This was a narcissism that took the form, Christopher Lasch had written in 1978, not of self-love or egomania but of psyches so frail as to need propping up by those in touch with them. Or narcissists might need to manipulate their appearances and feelings, often expressed as the "management of personal impressions" in a way that brought success "in political and business organizations where performance now counts for less than 'visibility,' 'momentum,' and a winning record." Thus the narcissist had become a kind of hollow man in a culture of image makers, promoters, advertisers, and passive consumers.

As the age of Reagan approached its end, much of this criticism appeared to be penetrating and sophisticated. But it failed to offer significant alternatives to the institutions under attack or to clarify alternative sets of values. These failures were marked in the discourse over individualism.

One could never know, listening to this discourse, that individualism was one of the most analyzed and debated as well as one of the most humane and spacious concepts in political and intellectual history. It had embraced the lofty principle of the dignity of man as an end in itself, as a core value; of the innate and supreme worth of the human being; and closely related values such as privacy, establishing a sphere of independence around the individual into which no unwelcome force could intrude; such as autonomy or self-direction, the right of individuals to act in response to their authentic wants and needs; such as self-development leading to the highest possible self-fulfillment of individuals, especially those with unique qualities of creativity; such as political individualism, serving as a basis for the principle of one man—one vote and an array of individual civil liberties of speech, press, and religion. And in contrast to other spacious and seminal doctrines, these tenets of individualism have existed with one another in mutual reinforcement rather than negation.

The doctrine of individualism in its various forms had engaged the intellects of a host of the greatest thinkers of the West: Luther's and Calvin's claims on and for the individual conscience; Thomas Hobbes's effort to abstract the individual mind even from the power of the state; Kant's principle that the will of every rational being underlay universal law; Bentham's dictum that each individual is to count for one and only one; Tocqueville's concept of individualism as the natural product of democracy; Durkheim's critical studies in the psychological and political *anomie* and isolation of individuals. Spongy and inflatable, the doctrine took on the intellectual and social shape of the nations in which it flourished: in France responding to the needs of socialists and revolutionaries; in Germany assuming a romantic and later a nationalist coloration; in England serving as a foundation for the emphasis on individual liberty in the writings of a series of thinkers, most notably John Stuart Mill.

And in the United States? Rarely has a spacious doctrine shriveled into a rationale for class interests as dramatically as "rugged individualism" was reduced to satisfy the promotional needs of big business in the late nineteenth century. Atomistic individualism echoed through the next century in the writings of Ayn Rand and the hyperbole of some of Ronald Reagan's speech writers; it also took on a softer edge in the oratory of Theodore Roosevelt, Woodrow Wilson, and even William Jennings Bryan, and in some thoughtful writing by Herbert Hoover. Late in the century, still largely held captive by the forces of the extreme and moderate right, the concept remained stripped of its more humane and generous dimensions.

The conversion in the United States of one of the most human and noble of Western Enlightenment doctrines into hardly more than a slogan for naked class interest and selfish privatization, combined with the atomization of religious organization and the fragmentation and trivialization of teaching and learning, lay at the heart of the intellectual disarray in the 1970s and 1980s. But that disarray was part of wider phenomena.

"In a nation that was proud of hard work, strong families, close-knit communities, and our faith in God," Jimmy Carter had said in his July 1979 "malaise speech," "too many of us now tend to worship self-indulgence and consumption. Human identity is no longer defined by what one does, but by what one owns. But we've discovered that owning things and consuming things does not satisfy our longing for meaning. We've learned that piling up material goods cannot fill the emptiness of lives which have no confidence or purpose." Increasingly, however, the longing for meaning was superficially satisfied by the huge institutions whose images and messages flashed before the eyes and pounded the ears of Americans hour after hour, day after day. These were the film, television, entertainment, and professional sports industries. How these institutions shaped American social and political thought was centrally determined by the nature of their birth, growth, structure, and strategies of influence.

KINESIS: THE SOUTHERN CALIFORNIANS

Legends sprouted about Hollywood even as the film colony was taking root. Filmmakers from the East had come here early in the century, it was said, to make better movies amid the perfect mix of air and wind and water. In fact, economics had largely shaped the rise of Hollywood from the start, as it did ever after. Some of the earliest moviemakers were fugitives from process servers dispatched by the eastern patent trust that sought to control film technology. Most were Jews, mainly from Eastern Europe, who had settled in New York and other eastern cities, had begun their rise from rags to riches in the rag business itself—clothes, gloves, furs, shoes—and then bought into penny arcades, nickelodeons, theater chains.

Above all, these men were entrepreneurs. To them California, with its cheap land and labor, its predictably good weather, and its marvelous varieties of scenery nearby that would save transportation costs, was essentially a good investment. But they were enterprisers with flamboyance, even chutzpa. When the Czar was incarcerated by the Bolsheviks, Lewis J. Selznick had wired him that while the Czar's police had mistreated him as a boy, he had no hard feelings and was prepared to offer the fallen monarch a good job in the film industry.

Hollywood itself was, increasingly, a myth. The stars and directors soon spread out from the fabled movie kingdom to Bel Air and Beverly Hills; the studios moved still farther out. Forming a great crescent around Los Angeles, from Santa Barbara through the Ojai Valley to San Bernardino, Riverside, and Palm Springs, and rejoining the Pacific at San Diego, this southeastern slope of southern California did provide film directors with desert and ocean, snow-clad mountains and city scenes, along with authentic-looking country for movies shot in the "Wild West." Economically southern California fit the movie industry like a glove, Carey McWilliams noted. Here was one industry that needed virtually no raw materials and had an enormous payroll. What could be more desirable, McWilliams asked, "than a monopolistic non-seasonal industry with 50,000,000 customers, an industry without soot or grime, without blast furnaces or dynamos, an industry whose production shows peaks but few valleys?"

Socially too the industry and the region nourished each other. Ceaseless migrations from south, west, and east had brought in thousands of potential actors, extras, and craftspeople—Mexicans and Spanish, Japanese and Chinese, drawling Texans, pious Iowans, drought-stricken Oklahomans. After the Russian Revolution, émigré White Russian aristocrats and their families and retinues had formed a colony in Hollywood. By the 1930s automobiles were a way of life in southern California, providing filmmakers with ample material and locations for wild chases, crashes, motels, eateries, general mayhem. Best of all, southern California loved the movie industry. At first the Los Angeles elite had snubbed the scruffy crowd of directors and actors who invaded Hollywood, but the 1915 success of D. W. Griffith's Civil War epic, *Birth of a Nation,* pointed the industry toward its later image of patriotism and even respectability.

The film industry blossomed in the southern California culture. In the 1920s and early 1930s Los Angeles was still an open-shop town, following years of fierce labor-industry strife that had culminated in the bombing of the anti-union Los Angeles *Times* and the disruption of the labor movement. For their labor-intensive industry the filmmakers found ample cheap manpower. There developed a symbiotic relationship between the volatile, rapidly expanding film industry and the city around it, with its rootless middle class, disorganized working class, and mainly nouveaux riches upper class. If southern Californians were heterogeneous in background, diverse in their immigrant cultures, fragmented in their social attitudes, Hollywood reflected its milieu in the themelessness and eclecticism of its productions. Films lacked intellectual and even ideological coherence except for the insipid icons of romance and violence. South Sea natives who had watched American movies, anthropologist Hortense Powdermaker noted, divided them into two types, "kiss-kiss" and "bang-bang."

Accustomed to more structured societies, visitors from abroad wrote of Hollywood flora and fauna with glee and malice. Los Angeles was the newest and strangest of all the American cities, J. B. Priestley observed, a "gaily-colored higgledy-piggledy of unending boulevards, vacant lots, oil derricks, cardboard bungalows, retired farmers, fortune-tellers, real estate dealers, film stars, false prophets, affluent pimps, women in pajamas turning on victrolas, radio men lunching on aspirin and Alka-Seltzer, Middle-Western grandmothers, Chinese grandfathers, Mexican uncles and Filipino cousins." It reminded the British author T. H. White of Elizabethan London.

It was above all the profusion of creeds, sects, and cults that gave the area its special flavor. The Krotona, Theosophy, and New Thought movements had their day. Swamis, yogis, faith healers, mind readers, spiritualists, graphologists practiced their arts. During the 1920s Aimee Semple McPherson, a resourceful showwoman, drew thousands to her Angelus Temple with her Foursquare Gospel of conversion, healing, resurrection, and redemption. After she apparently drowned in the Pacific surf and was melodramatically mourned, Aimee accomplished her own second coming by making a triumphal entrance into Los Angeles before ecstatic thousands. Press revelations that she had been trysting in a Carmel "love cottage" shook her idolaters only briefly: Aimee was like that. During the 1930s the Mighty I Am cult celebrated wealth, power, and sublimated sex. Mankind United simply promised utopia—a sixteen-hour workweek, ample pensions, and "automated" homes.

Southern California labor was as divided and turbulent as the various cults and "ham 'n' eggs" causes. The Wagner Act helped union organizers pull in large numbers of new members, but it also left the AFL and CIO in California hostile and competitive. A large "self-help" cooperative movement, with especially aggressive leadership in Los Angeles County, operated separately from the trade unions. As usual the communists stood aside from the "bourgeois" organizations; much of the New Deal and even Upton Sinclair's EPIC were "social fascism." Some remarkable women leaders helped mobilize the California left. Dorothy Healey, brought up in a socialist colony and a member of the Young Communist League at the age of fourteen, was organizing cannery workers two years later. Miranda Smith, a black militant, and Luisa Moreno, a Guatemalan, aroused working-class self-consciousness. Unionists, blacks, students, Latinos, women activists, communists, rank-and-file Democrats, coalesced in 1938 long enough to put a progressive Democrat, Culbert L. Olson, into the governorship—the first of his party to occupy the office in forty years—but the coalition was not strong enough to keep Olson in office in 1942, when he yielded the governorship to Republican Earl Warren.

One thread connected these causes, whether left or right—a flamboyant individualism that led the seekers to shop for their favorite cults and causes, quitting one for another in an endless Virginia reel. But this individualism rarely took the form of personal fulfillment and efficacy, for the faithful readily yielded their individualism to group arousals and pressures. Politically the region reflected these tendencies. California's political parties had virtually disintegrated early in the century and nothing had sprung up to take their place. Voters crossed and recrossed electoral lines, supporting their favorite in the primary of one party and casually voting for someone of quite different political view in the general election. A nominally Democratic electorate often chose Republicans for President and governor. Upton Sinclair's EPIC, Dr. Townsend's pension scheme, Robert Noble's $25-Every-Monday campaign, which was soon subverted and corrupted—these and countless lesser causes roiled California politics during the 1930s.

In this political environment Richard Nixon spent his teens. Doubtless he was far more directly influenced by his family than by the rapidly changing southern California culture. His parents and siblings believed in old-fashioned Horatio Alger industriousness and individualism, not the values of Hollywood's later plush years—the mother hardworking and moralistic, the father tightfisted, fearful of debt, ever cautious after a lifetime of drifting from job to job. Nixon did some acting, not in Hollywood but at Whittier College. He was interested enough in a business career to take a plunge in a frozen orange juice venture, which ended disastrously. He perfectly summarized, Garry Wills concluded, an older America made up of sacrifice and self-reliance. As a twelve-year-old he had told his mother that he wanted to be "an old-fashioned kind of lawyer—a lawyer who can't be bought."

*   *   *

The film industry reached its apogee during the thirties and the war years. Inside huge, walled studio lots, beneath towering sets, tens of thousands of employees worked in the projection rooms, machine shops, dressmaking rooms, scenery-making docks, planing mills, executive offices. Anyone who went to the pictures or read movie magazines knew of the Big Five: M-G-M, Warner Bros., Paramount, RKO, 20th Century–Fox; Columbia, Universal, and United Artists were the "little three." At the top were the producers, the directors, and the stars. Louis B. Mayer for a time was the highest-salaried business executive in the country. In 1941 motion-picture theaters outnumbered banks. Attendance reached an all-time high during the last year of the war.

Stung by rising criticism of their films' vulgarity and superficiality, especially during the New Deal years, the moguls boasted of the intellectual and artistic talent they had imported—notably authors F. Scott Fitzgerald, William Faulkner, Nathanael West, Bertolt Brecht, the composer Arnold Schoenberg, the conductor Leopold Stokowski. Few writers, however, boasted about working in Hollywood, except perhaps about the money they made. They saw their work reprocessed by directors, producers, other writers, and even the actors. Sometimes they saw no results at all; during a one-year contract, Faulkner worked on nine projects, only two of which were produced. Screenwriting, he complained, allowed for little individual creativity. William Saroyan stayed for a short time and left in disgust. Fitzgerald, nearing the end of his life, appeared to pose some of his own fantasies and self-delusions in his uncompleted novel, *The Last Tycoon*. West exacted a writer's revenge with his novel *The Day of the Locust*, a kaleidoscopic view of Hollywood that struck his friend Budd Schulberg as a "puke-green phantasmagoria of life in the lower depths of the house of horrors." Schulberg himself, no migrant but the son of a major producer, wrought his own revenge with *What Makes Sammy Run?*—a savage portrait of a producer clawing his way to the top.

If producers and writers often failed to engage with each other, so did actors and writers. Driving the newly introduced Clark Gable and William Faulkner through Palm Springs on a hunting expedition, Howard Hawks overheard Gable ask Faulkner who he thought were good writers. "Thomas Mann, Willa Cather, John Dos Passos, Ernest Hemingway, and myself," Faulkner answered. "Oh, do you write, Mr. Faulkner?" Gable asked. "Yeah," Faulkner said. "What do *you* do, Mr. Gable?" That was not a put-down, Hawks thought—he doubted that Gable had ever read a book or Faulkner had ever seen a movie.

Like other industries, moviemaking remained vulnerable to new technologies. The advent of sound in the 1920s had brought major changes, especially for the acting corps. The rise of television after World War II seemed for a time to spell the doom of Hollywood. Annual movie-house admissions, at 4.5 billion in the mid-1940s, stabilized at about one billion two decades later. The Hollywood producers fought television by joining it. In 1956 the Screen Actors Guild found that about 35 percent of the earnings of its members came from television programs and 25 percent from motion pictures. The industry also turned to the production of 16-millimeter home movies, educational programs, color films.

To a Hollywood nearing the height of its influence had come Ronald Reagan in 1937, and it was a declining motion-picture industry that he was to leave two decades later for television and General Electric. He brought with him a finely honed radio voice, a degree from Eureka College, and years of experience as a resourceful sportscaster. He also brought a body of ideas and notions drawn from a childhood in conservative, small-town Illinois, from an Irish-Catholic father whose long career as a salesman had been disintegrating amid alcoholism, from a mother who had musical and theatrical interests along with an abiding devotion to the Disciples of Christ, and from a deep immersion in the life of this middle-class, moralistic, temperance-preaching church. Young Reagan imbibed the dogmas of a small-town rugged individualism, tempered by an admiration for Franklin D. Roosevelt, who had inspired optimism during the depression days and helped people like his father. He held no deeply felt political beliefs; he was malleable.

In Hollywood, Reagan entered a world of illusion. At its zenith of prosperity and of power over social attitudes Hollywood was coming under increasing attack for its superficial plots, bland "message," insipid preachments of God, country, and home. Hortense Powdermaker called it the "dream factory," others the world of make-believe, the city of deceptions. Hollywood was escapism, Powdermaker wrote, escapism not into the broadening of experience and the world of the imagination, but into "saccharine sentimentality" and the stylized exaggeration of existing stereotypes, shibboleths, and fears. On the one hand, the Production Code Administration systematically cleared scripts of words like *lousy, punk, nuts, jerk,* and *damn*—except for Gable in *Gone With the Wind*—threw out all suggestions of sexual intimacy outside of marriage, lovemaking in bed, "open-mouthed or lustful kissing," prostitution, scenes of a wet baby, even doll-wetting, or of the sex organs of animals, of toilets, of the sign LADIES. Yet Hollywood continued to put out pictures with the most torrid love scenes and amoral behavior—as long as sinners were punished or redeemed by the end of the last reel. Hollywood films frowned on adultery and divorce, even while the movie magazines dealt in salacious detail with the marital goings-on of the stars, not always inaccurately.

Reagan was a performer in the dream factory. The very image of the chaste male, he had become the protégé of the Hearst columnist Louella Parsons, long feared as the maker and breaker of stars and their marriages. In her column Parsons gushed that Jane Wyman, brown eyes sparkling and voice bubbling with happiness, had told her, "Have I got a scoop for you! Ronnie and I are engaged!" The two were married at Forest Lawn, in the Wee Kirk o' th' Heather. It was the second marriage for Wyman. When Reagan and Wyman were divorced, Parsons seemed personally affronted. The couple had always stood for "so much that is right in Hollywood." She was "fighting hard" to bring them to their senses.

Make-believe of far greater import characterized Reagan's involvement in a number of organizations—the Screen Actors Guild, Americans for Democratic Action, the Music Corporation of America—despite his distrust of organized social action as against individual initiative. He voluntarily offered the FBI—the *government*—the names of SAG members suspected of following the Communist party line. Some SAG members were convinced that in granting a blanket waiver in 1952 to one of Hollywood's biggest talent agencies, MCA, that would allow it to produce television shows while continuing to represent actors—thus giving MCA an unprecedented advantage over its competitors—SAG president and MCA client Reagan had sold them out to MCA.

But if Reagan had made a deal with MCA, the agency had much the better part of it. While MCA by 1961 was producing 40 percent of all prime-time television, Reagan's own film career faltered badly. After a brief stint in a Las Vegas nightclub, he joined General Electric in 1954 as a promoter of the company and of conservatism, an easy step for a man in transition between marriages and careers. At first a liberal dubious about liberalism, later a Democrat who urged Eisenhower to run as a Democrat, still later a Democrat who supported Republican Ike, Reagan shifted steadily rightward across the political spectrum. Not only was he confirmed in his new conservatism by the GE world in which he now moved, but, in Lou Cannon's judgment, with his growing wealth he resented more and more the bite of a steeply graduated income tax. His second wife, Nancy Davis, and her conservative stepfather helped nudge him toward the right. When General Electric later let him go, evidently in part because he was *too* conservative and controversial as a spokesman for a corporation with huge government contracts, Reagan was ideologically primed to move into the political right wing—and he was available.

Hollywood continued to cope with technology. During the 1960s the major studios began to rent to television networks films made within the preceding five years and to create their own TV-film fare—not only the made-for-TV movie but the miniseries and novel-for-television. Pay television came along when Time Inc.'s Home Box Office offered cable TV viewers movies without commercials. A few years later Sony moved in with the Betamax home videocassette recorder, followed by the VHS. Despite the complaints of Jack Valenti, head of the Motion Picture Association, that the VCR was a parasitical instrument, Hollywood recouped by grossing over $1.5 billion in 1985 from selling videocassettes mainly as rental copies—which was more than it grossed from the box office. The industry also stepped up its production of blockbuster films that won huge audiences.

Whether or not the film industry was stabilizing, southern Californians appeared to have emerged from their long bewitchment by Hollywood and to have entered a period of mature growth with the creation of a larger and broader industrial base as well as a steady increase in population. Planning exuberantly for their entrance into the third millennium, southern Californians could boast of having the largest concentration of high technology in the world, the largest port in the United States, one of the leading international financial centers, and superb access to the burgeoning Pacific rim economies. The Los Angeles *Times,* once the very exemplar of stodgy, conservative journalism, had become one of the best and most aggressive newspapers in the country, and the region's universities were achieving ever greater prestige. Illusions and make-believe were declining as the region faced the economic and human costs of development.

As self-delusion slowly died, however, the region's most salient characteristic once more came to the fore—its social and political and intellectual fragmentation. Los Angeles and many of the other cities were still racially splintered. The megalopolis sprawled ever outward, engorging mountain and desert. Angelenos still insisted on their separate houses on tiny plots. Public transportation remained primitive. Few great writers comparable to Fitzgerald and West were either coming to the area or springing up from its asphalt and desert.

Above all, southern Californians continued their love affair with their cars and the freeways that slashed through city and country, linking some citizens and diking off others. By the late 1980s the road system had reached the saturation point. Congestion had spread out from central Los Angeles freeways to virtually the whole region. With five million more population expected within the next quarter century in the southern California basin, from Ventura down the coast to San Juan Capistrano and inland as far as Riverside, it was projected that even after planned freeway expansion half of all driving time would be spent stuck in traffic jams, while average rush-hour speeds for all streets and freeways would fall from 37 miles per hour to 19. Meanwhile motorists would be wasting millions of hours a year sitting on freeways.

Wasting? Drivers were not daunted. Highway police reported that motorists passed their time eating, isometric exercising, brushing and flossing teeth, singing, shaving, smooching, changing clothes, screaming to relieve tension. Said one driver to a reporter, "I think basically the car is like a movable home. You're in a private world and you can do and say and think anything you want when you're alone in that car." Not long after these benign reports there was an outburst of random shooting on the freeways. Making love inside the automobile, shooting up the other highwaymen outside, as in an old Hollywood film—perhaps the South Sea natives had understood something when they reduced things to "kiss-kiss" and "bang-bang."

SUPERSPECTATORSHIP

Even the most jaded habitués of Las Vegas looked up from their gaming tables on hearing this news. The long-anticipated title match between "Marvelous Marvin" Hagler and "Sugar Ray" Leonard would be held on April 6, 1987, in their own remote Nevada town. And it evidently would be the battle of the century, for more than 1,100 reporters from all over the world would be trekking to Vegas. Soon torrents of media publicity turned the boxing match into "Superfight." Hagler, the self-made brawler—coarse, mean, and hungry—would be pitted against Leonard, an Olympic gold medal winner, a media darling, a strategist surrounded by trainers, publicists, and groupies. And it must be Superfight because of the money involved—an anticipated purse of $25 million, the largest yet.

Only a spoilsport or two mentioned that both men were past their prime, that even at their best they were second-raters compared to such greats of the past as Jack Dempsey, Gene Tunney, Joe Louis. For boxing aficionados who remembered the epic contests in the smoky haze of Madison Square Garden, with its tens of thousands of frenzied onlookers, there was something quite depressing about this Vegas bout. Superfight would have a live audience of only a few thousand persons, those who could afford the plane fare to Vegas as well as fight tickets, many of which were reserved for celebrities or scalped far above their face value. A sports event hyped for days and weeks on national and local television was unavailable to the stations that had been ecstatically playing it up. Nor could it be seen on cable television or pay TV. The fight could be viewed only in select establishments, on closed-circuit television for sums ranging from $25 to $100. In the end the fight itself was far less of a spectacle than the media coverage of it.

Superfight was indeed a supreme achievement not of the boxing world but of the media world. It was a classic merging of television, advertisers, big money, and headline celebrities. It achieved its supreme goal—almost everyone in the country was talking about it. The fight replaced the weather as a topic of conversation, but like the lovely morning that everyone remarked on at the checkout counter or the gas station, it was here today and gone tomorrow.

Something that almost everyone in America talked about, even for half a minute, was not to be belittled in a nation so lacking in more serious topics of common concern. Countless Americans watched football who had never felt a jolting tackle, followed basketball who had never sunk a three-pointer, viewed hockey who had never shot a puck into a well-guarded cage, gazed at baseball who had never lofted a homer in the neighborhood sandlot. Perhaps that was why they spent hours in front of the tube watching—because they could never do it. And perhaps also because, having watched a game, they knew that they could enjoy instant empathy with the bus driver, the paper boy, the garage mechanic, the library assistant. "Sportswatching," Janet Podell wrote, "may well be Americans' truest expression of democratic feeling: far more people watch sports than vote in national elections."

A powerful combination of technology and personalism sustained this mass interest. Network television embraced all regions of the country, satellites girdled the globe. VCRs, now in millions of homes, enabled viewers to tape programs and watch them at any hour of the day or night. Cable challenged the preeminence of the three networks. Round-the-clock news and sports programs attracted more and more viewers, especially at times of national crises or scandals. Satellite programming and the promise of optic-fiber communications undermined traditional rationales for federal regulation, posing even greater future threats to the electronic status quo.

Yet the technology was heavily moralized, sensationalized, even fantasized, especially in athletics. Sport was elementary and moral, the bad guys against the good. The conflict was clear-cut and clearly resolvable. Sport was combat, man-to-man, gladiatorial: when Dave Winfield's six-foot-six-inch frame sped gracefully to meet an arching shot off George Brett's agile bat, there was nothing on the field except the beauty of one man's skill against another's. Sport was simple: it was "wholly intelligible to the lowest common denominators in society." Above all, sport was fantasy in a harsh, cynical world. It fed, said Richard Lipsky, "depoliticization by creating a world of meaning, a utopian refuge, within the larger technical life-world." And there was always escape into the future: "Wait till next year!" Fantasy allowed oddities too. Fans would journey to an airport to greet a conquering home team made up of numerous blacks—but would not want to live on the same block with them. Blacks were video gladiators, welcomed on the screen, not in the neighborhood.

Big sport and spectatorship required big money. In 1873, Cornell president Andrew D. White, responding to a request of his football team to travel to Michigan for a game, had proclaimed, "I will not permit thirty men to travel 400 miles merely to agitate a bag of wind." Nor would he pay thirty train fares. A century later, in January 1988, over a hundred million people watched professional football's annual championship; a minute of advertising time during that contest cost $1.3 million. This amounted to more than $30 million for the game, but even so was dwarfed by the sums television and cable contracts fetched for season telecast rights. In 1982, the National Football League received a five-year $2 billion contract from the three networks. Baseball's 1983 deal with the networks netted more than a billion over six years, and rights sales to local broadcast and cable stations brought in still more. And the 1984 Olympics, which cost $525 million to produce, was hyped as pumping $3.3 billion into southern California's economy.

Many sports fans questioned the commercialization and industrialization of their games. Large salaries contributed to cleavage between fans and the players with whom they identified; it was easier to picture oneself in a DiMaggio's shoes when his life off the playing field was not all that unlike one's own. But when star players made $2 million annually, identification was strained and resentment crept into some fans' hearts. When Boston Celtics fans were asked whether Larry Bird, the team's star forward, was worth the $2 million he was paid at the height of his career, the vast majority replied no. Yet the same majority, unwilling to lose him to another team, did not begrudge his demand or the owner's willingness to meet it.

* * *

Television long since had become one of the nation's biggest industries, taking a huge slice of the $50 billion that American businesses spent on advertising in 1986. Few TV viewers understood the impact of advertising on their programming. "The economics of television, and thus of political communication," wrote W. Russell Neuman, "is based not on the providing of programs to audiences but rather on the selling of audiences to advertisers." While producers also had to attract audiences, some complained that spontaneity was lost somewhere along the line. As a new concept was reached, tested, premarketed, polled, and analyzed before release, intuition and innovation and risk appeared to be giving way to spreadsheet analyses inside boardroom and film studio alike.

The press was not only subject to big business pressures; it was big business. Newspaper publishing had become more a business and less a journalistic calling. *The Wall Street Journal,* its circulation at 1,910,000, was not only the preeminent business newspaper; it was a major business in its own right. *USA Today,* initially designed as a working-class alternative, adopted a TV format of encapsulated news and "factoids," and was sold in vending machines that looked like television sets. *USA Today* hoped also to capture the market of young, upwardly mobile business and professional people who wanted to enjoy their news, like their food and entertainment, while on the go.

As businesses, the newspapers tended toward concentration. In 1986 ten financial and business corporations controlled the three major television and radio networks and 34 affiliated stations, 201 cable TV systems, 62 radio stations, 20 record companies, 59 magazines including *Time* and *Newsweek,* 58 newspapers including *The New York Times,* the Washington *Post, The Wall Street Journal,* and the Los Angeles *Times,* 41 book publishers, and sundry motion-picture companies. And banks accounted for 75 percent of the major stockholders of the three networks. "The American press," wrote journalist David Broder, "is a private business performing a vital public function under a specially protected constitutional status, exempt from regulation by government, immunized against many of the forms of pressure and persuasion to which other institutions are subject in our system of checks and balances." To whom, readers or stockholders, was the press corps ultimately accountable? Presumably to the readers who made everything possible. But newspaper after newspaper—some of them respected and "responsible"—had seen their customers slip away to worship electronic gods.

*   *   *

Its huge reach and alleged cannibalistic tendencies made television the cardinal concern to those worried about balance among the media. In 1974, 46 percent of those interviewed in national polls reported television as their favorite pastime. "Television expanded its audience at the expense of reading, which dropped from 21% to 14%, of movies, from 19% to 9%, and of radio, from 9% to 5%," wrote Morris Janowitz on the basis of annual reports by the Roper Organization. "Even dancing suffered; from 9% to 5%. Only playing cards held its own." Americans as a whole were watching television an average of about three hours a day by 1974; the college-educated and the affluent were watching almost as much, about two hours and a half. White-collar and blue-collar workers could not escape the intrusions of television even on the job; increasingly headquarters executives were transmitting via satellite sales information, company news, and pep talks to captive groups of employees.

Politicians eagerly seized on the changing media technology. Ready-to-print stories were transmitted by computer directly to news organs back home, and, in at least one case, messages were beamed directly to constituents with personal computers. Some congressmen produced and distributed their own cable television productions, for complete broadcast or for excerpt by news organizations. Diana Winthrop, vice president of the Washington-based midwestern radio news service GAP Communications, said of the trend, "It is irresponsible and unethical for members of Congress to present canned radio and television programs as news—and just as irresponsible for the industry to accept them."

When the networks offered original coverage they tended to concentrate more on the horse race and superficial aspects of political campaigns than on substance. Commenting on the 1976 campaign, Malcolm MacDougall observed: "I saw President Ford bump his head leaving an airplane. . . . I saw Carter playing softball in Plains, Georgia. I saw Carter kissing Amy, I saw Carter hugging Lillian. . . . I saw Ford misstate the problems of Eastern Europe—and a week of people commenting about his misstatement. I saw Ford bump his head again. . . . But in all the hours of high anxiety that I spent watching the network news, never did I hear what the candidates had to say about the campaign issues. That was not news." It was simpler to report who was leading in the New Hampshire polls than to analyze a twenty-page position paper, and more interesting too.

Was television simply the fall guy? Some media experts doubted the existence of massive video influence. They noted first of all that analysis of media influence in general was now much more sophisticated than in earlier days, when some investigators tended to equate stimulus with response. Most Americans, no matter how poorly educated, were not clean slates on which the communicators could imprint their messages. The formation of opinion was an exceedingly complex process, with "shapers" shaping themselves in anticipation of the attitudes and reactions of their targets, raising the question of just who was influencing whom. Moreover, people had grown wary of advertisers, candidates, promoters. Then too, research in the 1940s had emphasized the role of local opinion leaders—ministers, bartenders, party precinct leaders, friends with "inside information"—as brokers between the mass media and the local citizenry, while in the television age, mediation of this sort had lost its significance. Nor did it appear that TV, incapable of reducing viewers to obedient zombies, was able to make them cynics. Though a major study suggested that reliance on television news helped to foster political cynicism and distrust, television "believability" remained relatively high—especially for individual network "anchors" like Peter Jennings, Tom Brokaw, and Dan

Rather—and it could be argued that it was not the way news was reported but the news itself that produced cynicism in viewers.

And if television did have an all-pervasive influence, what political effect did it have? It was often contended that the advertisers, network owners and bosses who were also propertied capitalists, and the affluent, college-educated, upper-middle-class managers who controlled programming had produced a strong right-wing bias in television. On the other hand, the right charged that television as well as major newspapers such as *The New York Times* and the Washington *Post* slanted the news to the left. The working reporters were in fact relatively more liberal Democratic than the public as a whole.

The prime corrective to massive media influence, however, was the enormous number and variety of newspapers and journals in a nation that still liked to read. Around the beginning of the 1970s celebrated magazines folded—*The Saturday Evening Post* after almost a century and a half of continuous publication, *Look* with its circulation of seven million, the world-famous *Life*. But during the sixties and seventies other journals appeared with powerful appeals to more specialized audiences. Among these were *Psychology Today, Ms., New York*. "Underground" journals—notably the *Berkeley Barb*, the *L.A. Free Press*, modeled on New York's successful *Village Voice*, and *Rat*, published by a group of women—along with such famous environmental publications as *The Whole Earth Catalog*, did not always attain longevity but they added zest and variety to the political and social debate of the day.

All told, the media of the late 1980s were ominously bifurcated. Reaching across the nation were the huge television establishments, newspaper chains, record and cassette producers, mass-appeal comic strips. In search of the widest common denominator, no matter how synthetic, the mass media concentrated on celebrities, sports, entertainment, disasters, scandals, and the like. Appealing to the specialized interests, on the other hand, were thousands of periodicals. A kind of vacuum lay between the extremely general and the extremely particular. This vacuum had once been filled in part by hundreds of regional or local newspapers with strong editorial views, such as William Allen White's Emporia *Gazette* or the New York *Herald Tribune*, by farm and labor publications, by outspokenly partisan organs. Many of these had declined into routine publications on whose editorial pages one could find the same canned opinions as one traveled from city to city. Radio, once so promising, had become a national media tragedy, with its incessant pop music, commercials, and occasional insipid commentary.

Both nationalized and pluralized, both commercialized and trivialized, the huge communications and entertainment industries were no longer under exclusive East and West Coast control. Within a few square miles of New York City, however, were clustered the editorial offices of magazines big and small, the three networks, most of the important book publishing houses, the big art galleries, the make-or-break legitimate theaters. New York was also still the center of "serious" painting, writing, performing. How creative could these arts remain amid the pressures and temptations of mass communication, electronic commercialization, marketplace competition? Would they too become part of an ever more rapidly shifting kaleidoscope?

THE NEW YORKERS

During the 1970s writers and critics expressed a growing concern over the decline of American literature. Their worry was nothing new—every generation since the nation's founding had denigrated its current writers as compared with the "greats" of the past. But the 1970s concerns were more than generational. Critics pointed to many a morbid symptom, found many a cause, prescribed many a cure, but it was obvious to all that from the 1960s and 1970s had emerged few novelists who could compare, in universality of appeal over time and space, not only with the likes of Faulkner, Hemingway, and Frost but with black writers like Richard Wright, Ralph Ellison, and James Baldwin. Faulkner's lengthening reputation overshadowed the rising generation of southern writers, even those with the talents of a Eudora Welty or Walker Percy.

Why the alleged decline? A common explanation was the cumulative impact of the cold war and of Vietnam on American culture, especially its chilling influence on dissent. "In the past ten years," E. L. Doctorow told the graduating Sarah Lawrence class of 1983, "there has been a terrible loss of moral energy in art, in politics, in social expectations." Americans and Russians, he said, had set up an unholy alliance, each aping the other's response, creating a logic of Us or Them. "We are in thrall to our own Bomb."

Others pointed to the impact of the mass media. Saul Bellow complained of "publicity intellectuals," onetime students of literature, the social sciences, art, or drama who had left college and plunged directly into media jobs. There they had surrendered to the mass public's demand for sensation, exploiting culture for its commercial return, in effect enriching themselves rather than their culture. "The million-dollar advances and earnings," wrote Alfred Kazin, "the money-mindedness that leaves its grease stain on every discussion of a 'popular' book (and of a markedly unpopular one)—these, along with the widespread contempt for politics, the breakdown of intellectual authority that gives every sexual and ethnic faction the brief authority of anger, are not just symptoms of some profound cultural malaise—they are the malaise." Kazin pointed to the book supermarkets that gave earnest young readers no chance to discover the unexpected, the supplements that accepted "cultural comment" only if written in "snappy prose," the English departments featuring the triumph of deconstruction over some "helpless poem."

Other critics aimed at a variety of targets. Richard Kostelanetz decried the many blocks that barred the entrance of young writers, women, and other outsiders into the literary world—not only the publishers' subservience to the mass media but the bias toward established authors and the "big book," the commercial tie-ins with films, the quick shredding or dumping of books that did not take off, the decline of the creative relationship among editor, publisher, and author, growing oligopoly as conglomerates took over ancient publishing houses, the enhanced power of financial managers, the crucial influence of reviews and full-page advertisements in *The New York Times Book Review.* John W. Aldridge contended that the two currents traditionally feeding the American novel—the impulse toward "beatific transcendence" and "a hardy and altogether disenchanted pragmatism" that checked this impulse—had become disjoined, leaving the novel in a self-destructive process of demythifying itself.

As usual various literary establishments came under fire—the publishing, the academic, the old Wasp, the southern. But now a new establishment had risen that for some was the juiciest target of all—the Jewish. The "New York intellectuals," as they came to be called, were typically the sons of immigrants from the ghettos of Eastern Europe who had settled in new ghettos in Manhattan and Brooklyn and Newark. With much scrimping and saving their fathers had put them through Columbia or City College or some other city university, only to see their prodigal sons reject parents and synagogue and plunge into radical politics during depression days. They fought together and against one another in Stalinist or Trotskyist causes, were swept into World War II, gained more education perhaps on the GI Bill, then began their climb to success through teaching and writing. To their careers they brought "gutter-worldliness" and "harsh and abrasive skepticism," in Irving Howe's words.

To their careers they also brought an instinct for power—or at least a fascination with it—nurtured in their endless ideological and literary struggles. As Marxists of various hues they had railed against upper-class rule, the power elite, the literary and journalistic and academic establishments.

Some saw all human interactions as power relationships—Norman Mailer's *The Naked and the Dead* presented in 1948 a portrait of military power simplistic and exaggerated to the point of caricature. Treating power as a commodity rather than as a relationship, a physical rather than as a psychological phenomenon, these power-fixated writers rarely grasped the crucial fact that power appeared far more formidable to outsiders looking into power centers than to the wielders of power looking out.

Hence the rising New York intellectuals hardly dreamed that someday they too would be looked on as an establishment, a power elite. But that is just what happened. By the mid-1970s Kostelanetz and others were denouncing the Jewish "commercial establishment," accusing it of controlling literary careers and access points, of publishing only established and approved authors, of indulging in patronage, mutual back-scratching and the like. Kostelanetz wrote of the power and wealth, the avarice and corruption, of the "New York literary mob."

As in a novel, literature, fame, publishing, protest, and power, and the men and women who personified them, came together to do battle at a writers' gathering in the literary capital of the nation.

* * *

The Reading Room, the New York Public Library, January 12, 1986. Literary celebrities from home and abroad, delegates to the 48th Congress of International PEN, waited impatiently to file through airport-type security. Some were left outside and seething as all seats were filled. Inside the hall tempers were even shorter. Norman Mailer, president of American PEN, without consulting his board of directors, had invited Secretary of State George Shultz to address the gathering. Sixty-odd writers had already written Shultz that it was "inappropriate" for him to open the Congress because "your Administration supports governments that silence, imprison, even torture their citizens for their beliefs." It verged on the scandalous, E. L. Doctorow had written in *The New York Times,* that Mailer and his cronies had put themselves "at the feet of the most ideologically right-wing Administration this country has seen." An angry Mailer apologized to Shultz for the bad manners of the "catatonic left." Shultz then surprised the delegates with an illuminating speech.

"Freedom—that is what we are all talking about," the Secretary of State told the crowd, "and is why we are here. And the writer is at the heart of freedom. And there is no more striking image of freedom than the solitary writer—the individual of imagination, creativity and courage, imposing through language the perceptions and prescriptions that can illuminate and perhaps change the world." He acknowledged the tension between the writer and the state. "The state aims to provide social order; and the writer aims to create an imaginative order of his own." Shultz attacked the idea that "creativity forged in the crucible of totalitarianism is greater than that in politically free but culturally commercialized societies." He concluded: "Ronald Reagan and I are with you all the way."

This remark drew groans and catcalls; the following day Günter Grass pounced on him. He did not "feel comfortable traveling from Europe to New York," said the German novelist, "and the first thing I get is a lecture about freedom and literature" from the Secretary of State. He had seldom met politicians who were able to listen, Grass said. "Even if you say, 'You are right,' they say, 'No, you don't understand.' Always *they* understand better and better." Mailer took for granted the animosity toward Americans. "In the eyes of foreigners, we're righteous, we're hypocritical. We're immensely wealthy, and from a European and third-world point of view, we're filled with hideous contradictions." In an interview after the conference, Mailer appeared philosophical about the disputes that had racked the proceedings. "How can you have a literary conference without friendships and feuds being formed out of it?" But his equanimity had been sorely tested by an onslaught from indignant women delegates.

Betty Friedan, Grace Paley, and other feminists had protested the scarcity of women on the panels. Paley from the floor: "Out of 120 panelists, only 16 are women." Mailer from the chair: "Who's counting?" Novelist Erica Jong: "Why do you look at us and not see?" Mailer: "Erica Jong is the last woman in the world who can plead invisibility." Poet Cynthia Macdonald asked, "Won't we ever do the things to make this boring subject obsolete?" The session ended in a shouting match as women delegates staged a walkout.

Almost concealed in all the brawling was the serious theme of the conference, formally announced as "The Writer's Imagination and the Imagination of the State." For a time delegates struggled with this murky topic. "Our contemporary life is marked by the failure of the ruling ideologies, the bankruptcy of all the earthly delights promised or ordained by the state," Günter Grass opined. "By now we know full well how exhausted state Communism is in its self-imprisonment, even though its power persists; and capitalism struggles from crisis to crisis in a correspondingly ritualized manner." Said Israeli novelist Amos Oz, "Our title has about it a ring of romantic anarchism. Indeed, a touch of Manichaeistic kitsch." He rejected the image of "a saintly lot of writers marching fearlessly to combat" beastly bureaucracies.

As the Congress turned into a "fully clawed political organism," in

Cynthia Ozick's report of it, and meeting rooms bristled with manifestos and accusations, the real issue surfaced. It was the millennia-old dilemma of the power of the state versus the freedom of the individual writer. After Saul Bellow spoke eloquently of the American dream of democracy, the irrepressible Grass challenged the American novelist to hear the echo of his words in the South Bronx. He was not ignoring pockets of poverty, Bellow responded, "I was simply saying the philosophers of freedom of the 17th and 18th centuries provided a structure which created a society by and large free." An overflow audience at a session titled "Censorship in the U.S.A." was informed that school and library authorities in forty-six of the fifty states had recently tried to censor such works as *The Catcher in the Rye* and Anne Frank's *Diary.*

It soon became evident that the American writers knew much more about their individual liberty than they did about the politics and power of the state. John Updike benignly described his relationship to the state in terms of the vast friendly postal service culminating in his blue mailbox—"I send manuscripts away; I sometimes get praise and money in return," while some of his listeners reflected that *their* mailboxes more often contained rejection slips than checks. American speakers attacked the state as a monolithic evil, even though many of them had benefited for years from largess in the form of grants, travel money, and Fulbrights, and many also had long and successfully been urging the federal government to exercise its power to end poverty, strengthen civil rights, bolster public education, broaden the Bill of Rights. It was curious: writers who had described social and even political relationships in all their subtlety and variety, who had produced intricate, sensitive tapestries of all manner of human relationships—convoluted alliances, enmities, love affairs, rivalries, jealousies, generosities—could find for the state only the metaphor of the sledgehammer.

It remained for foreign writers, many of whom had in fact suffered at the hands of the sledgehammer state, to remind the Americans of those subtleties and complexities. A PEN committee on writers in prison told the delegates that over 400 of their peers were "detained" or missing in foreign lands. But, as Amos Oz contended, there were degrees of evil and it was the writer's particular task to make the distinctions. Present at the meeting were representatives from Nicaragua and other countries confronting the painful question that had faced Lincoln during the Civil War—to what extent could certain liberties or rights like habeas corpus be sacrificed for the sake of the victory that would protect all the Bill of Rights freedoms and indeed bring liberty to southern slaves? These delegates defended retreats and compromises on such liberties for the sake of national survival in the good old American pragmatic spirit, and for the sake of freedom as they defined it.

American writers appeared more distressed than authoritative about such complexities. More often the delegates retreated to the high moral ground, but as a refuge from hard thought rather than a place for deep analysis. Many years earlier Henry James had complained, in *The American Scene,* of the "thinness" of American life. Bellow in 1963 had sensed continually in modern literature not "the absence of a desire to be moral, but rather a pointless, overwhelming, vague, objectless moral fervor." At the PEN Congress the moral imagination as well as the understanding of many of the American writers appeared thin, vague.

Over the whole proceedings, for the foreigners at least, hovered the ghosts of the American "greats." Said a Swedish novelist, "You don't have any truly great writers." Said a German, "The strongest impact still is Faulkner." Said Amos Oz, "It's been a long time since I've read an American novel that evoked gutsy passion in me." Said South African poet Breyten Breytenbach, "There was a time when one sensed through Hemingway and Mailer the American manhood. Then, such authors as James Baldwin and Ralph Ellison explored the black experience, and Bernard Malamud and Saul Bellow gave a clear sense of growing up Jewish in America. But now, except for maybe William Styron, nothing like that is being attempted." When she drove past mobile homes in upstate New York, said South African novelist Nadine Gordimer, she wondered, "Who are these people?" She did not meet them in American fiction. To many of the writers from abroad, American novels of the past twenty years appeared to be filled with the personal, the trivial, with "tiny fictions" untouched by history and environment.

*   *   *

While the power and gore of the "literary mob" were most visible in Manhattan and in the big publishers concentrated there, fine university presses and small publishers were dispersed throughout the country. The nation's profusion of writers created their works wherever, at home or abroad, they could find a desktop for their lined yellow pads, their typewriters, or—increasingly—their word processors. Actors, on the other hand, wanted to be near Broadway or off-Broadway, although Hollywood drew its share for movies and later television. The creative people most concentrated in New York were the artists, who needed access to the city's art galleries, dealers and patrons, museums, while they lived in lofts and cold-water flats. It was in New York that there had emerged after three centuries, in John Russell's words, "an independent, self-generating and specifically American art." The formats and materials used by the "First New York School" were not new. What the artists now did with them was.

During the nineteenth century, American painters had found it necessary to study in Europe and to paint like Europeans if they were to sell in their own country. Even so, wealthy American collectors tended to buy European art. During the first part of the twentieth century, Europe was still Mecca but there and in the United States Modernism was emerging in such forms as Neo-Impressionism, Fauvism, Expressionism, Orphism, Cubism, as well as Futurism, Surrealism, and Constructivism. Spilling into America, these forms converged after World War II as Abstract Expressionism, and with this style American art came into its own.

Formidable artists gathered in New York: Arshile Gorky, Jackson Pollock, Piet Mondrian, Willem de Kooning, Mark Rothko, Barnett Newman, and many others. What a profusion of styles they created—the tension lines and stresses in a Pollock, the spatial relationships of a Mark Rothko, the touch and feel of fleshed-out cloth in a Robert Rauschenberg, Claes Oldenburg's "Giant Toothpaste Tube" that resembled a reclining woman, the serried rows of Coca-Cola bottles in a shocking Andy Warhol, for whom preformed subject matter was a condition of his art, the sensitive Helen Frankenthaler's freehand drawing with paint that, John Russell wrote, "was allowed to stain its way into the canvas rather than to sit, like a skin, on top of it," Roy Lichtenstein's dramatic "Drowning Girl" in comic-strip style complete with cartoon balloon—"I don't care! I'd rather sink—than call Brad for help!"

Serious art during the latter half of the century revealed three aspects that characterized other sets of American ideas and attitudes. It was ephemeral. It was commercial. It was eclectic. "New, Newer, Newest," wrote critic John Simon as technology combined with the rise of a literate and art-conscious public to speed the flow of new art styles. The different, the outrageous could not be produced fast enough. A style might grow to maturity and decline in a single decade while the market went on to the next fad. Something called Kinetic Art referred back to Futurism and forward to Op Art. Pop Art connected with comic books but had roots in Dadaism and the work of Marcel Duchamp earlier in the century. Minimalism now emerged as a rejection of Abstract Expressionism and was taken up by some of its practitioners. Ad Reinhardt's black paintings epitomized what was "perhaps the most difficult, embattled and controversial art ever made."

Gallery visitors gaped, politicians scoffed, buyers coughed up. A phrase, the Tyranny of the New, became current. This tyranny was aided not only by the press but by the rapid emergence of new techniques and electronic devices such as video and television that gobbled up material as fast as it could be produced and ravaged the past to satisfy its voracious appetite. High Culture and Mass Culture, once considered mutually exclusive, merged so as to become almost indistinguishable. What had been called High Culture was increasingly being supplanted by an expert culture, according to sociologist Herbert Gans, "dominated by cultural professionals: creators, critics, and especially academics."

A handful of Manhattan critics were alleged to hold immense influence over public reaction to new or newly disinterred paintings. Artists, gallery owners, collectors, and museum curators waited in trepidation for their reviews. But of course the arbiters quarreled with one another. *Time* art critic Robert Hughes derided *New York Times* art critic Hilton Kramer for being obsessed with left-wing conspiracy. "Let the New Museum put on a show called 'Art and Ideology'—stuffed with works so banal or impenetrable that their appeal as propaganda is close to zero—and he goes into his war dance about cultural Stalinism."

Hughes criticized Kramer for so deeply loathing kitsch as to blame it on camp subversion rather than on the "free-market capitalism he admires." That free market was booming in art by the 1970s. Buyers for large banks and corporations bid up the prices. Heavily promoted by the titillated media, art was becoming big business. "The change from the small, rather compact 'art world' of the 1940s to the explosive, hustling scene of today," wrote a former gallery owner, "is surely one of the most radical changes in the history of the art market." Russell called "radically wrong" a world in which "works of art which are part of our universal inheritance can be hidden in vaults until the bankers' consortium which owns them can make a sufficient return on its investment." Yesterday's canvases began to sell like old masters. In 1983, at an auction at Christie's, *Two Women* by Abstract Expressionist Willem de Kooning sold for $1.2 million, the largest sum paid to that date for a work by a living American. Surely this was market capitalism at its finest.

At the opposite end of the economic spectrum, thousands of artists, neglected by critics and well-heeled connoisseurs in the excitement over "big names," survived by moonlighting in academia or in odd, routine, often distasteful jobs. Still, many artists admitted they "never had it so good." Support from federal and state agencies and private foundations was at unprecedented levels. Small galleries proliferated. Colleges and universities built art museums and competed for prestigious shows. Rich or poor, artists were drawn increasingly into the wider political arena. Women and minority groups—especially blacks—organized to become a more visible part of the art world. The New York Art Strike of 1970, organized by the artist Robert Morris, who, protesting the Vietnam War, had canceled his own solo exhibition at the Whitney Museum, produced a series of demonstrations. To enable all artists, rich and poor, to share in the profits when their work was resold, Edward Kennedy introduced remedial legislation in the Senate.

* * *

By the mid-1960s, a kind of free-for-all had erupted as artists abandoned the idea, which had survived and even thrived under the rubric of Modernism, that the work of art—the painting in its frame, the sculpture on its pedestal, the oil on canvas, the carved stone or cast metal—deserved special and unique status as an object. For their materials, artists found and transformed—or did not transform—natural and man-made objects and even their own bodies. The traditional materials of art were turned against themselves with an irony of form or subversive allusions to the icons of art history and popular culture.

"Art today," wrote Susan Sontag, "is a new kind of instrument, an instrument for modifying consciousness and organizing new modes of sensibility." Many of these attacks on tradition, going under a panoply of labels (Performance Art, Process Art, Conceptual Art, Earthworks, Pop Art, and more), could be traced to the work of Marcel Duchamp. His "ready-mades," as he called them—exemplified by a urinal he bought from a plumbing supply warehouse and exhibited unmodified but signed—raised by means of the object itself a question about its status as art. Duchamp's influence persisted in the latter part of the century in work by the likes of Andy Warhol, Robert Morris, Vito Acconci, and many other artists, including Alice Aycock and Dennis Oppenheim, who produced mechanical works that in an electronic age seemed in some ways nostalgic.

Much of this art was an attempt to jettison the object and to bring a pure idea of idea to the foreground. But the work of art as object remained. The 1980s saw a Neo-Expressionism played off against a new Minimalism. Art in general had become a kind of "tolerated pluralism." It could include philosophy, postindustrial technologies and information processes, linguistics, mathematics, social criticism, life risking, jokes and other kinds of "narratives." Anything went—including outright appropriation of the works of other artists. On this open field, art had ample room for play, for humor and irony, for serendipity and nostalgia, and the spectacle of movements scrambling pell-mell for their fifteen minutes in the sun was itself amusing. But critic Arthur Danto noted, "When anything is allowed," the point of "doing whatever one chooses to do is lost."

No longer neatly framed by those old adversaries, High Culture and

Mass Culture, art as well as literature appeared to be changing, if not vanishing, in clouds of self-referentiality, of circular and abstruse discussions of the nature of art. The situation was mirrored in such fashionable intellectual movements as Structuralism, which attempted to do without the author in deciphering the text or object. Structuralism's child, Deconstruction, was even more radical, for here the text disappeared and only readers remained. In this scenario, the construction of relations with a text (object) was taken to be bound by self-reference. Though the progression from Structuralism to Deconstruction was not linear and practitioners disagreed heatedly among themselves, a string of high priests emerged, from Claude Lévi-Strauss to Jacques Derrida.

A third artistic-critical movement, and in some respects a product of the other two, was Postmodernism, which appeared most vividly at first in architecture and architectural writing. With its references to various pasts, Postmodernism appeared nostalgic, ironic, and playful all at the same time. In its self-consciousness it reflected the mood of America, which seemed in some sense not to be entirely serious, yet anxious and equally various.

Other arts in America also provided a mixed picture. Broadway pulled out of its sharp artistic and financial decline of the early 1970s and off-Broadway continued to play a vital role, but much of the excitement in the American theater a decade and a half later was generated by British imports and by revivals of O'Neill and Miller. The technology of music making and distribution was changing so rapidly as to make prediction impossible; even a college jazz ensemble could assemble onstage not only musicians and their instruments but a Model 2000 Pitch Reader, a Digital Delay, a TX-7 Yamaha Synthesizer, two television sets, a video recorder, and a Yamaha SPX-Bass-effects Generator. Conceivably the seventies and eighties might best be remembered for the creativity, iconoclasm, and originality of the nation's cartoonists and comic-strip creators, especially in their willingness to take on errant Presidents, from Herblock's formidable assaults on Nixon to Garry Trudeau's graphic explorations of Ronald Reagan's brain.

THE CONSERVATIVE MALL

In December 1980, a few weeks after Ronald Reagan's election to the presidency, the American Enterprise Institute—at the time the paramount conservative think tank—staged a week-long victory celebration. The leading stars of the right speechified; politicians who had before kept their distance were there working the crowd; and a politician who had not kept his distance, Ronald Reagan, his face wreathed in smiles over his black tie, paraded in while the band played "Hail to the Chief." The President-elect quickly made it clear that he would not forget his conservative friends. "I just want you to know," he told the delirious crowd, "that we'll be looking closely at your observations and proposals." Even better, key AEI staff people were already headed for the White House. "This kind of working relationship with AEI is one the next administration wants to maintain during the next four years."

A century earlier a gathering of conservatives had met with equal cheer to honor another hero of the right, Herbert Spencer. If the conservative celebrities of 1980 hardly rivaled in eminence those present at Delmonico's in 1882—not only Spencer but Carl Schurz, Andrew Carnegie, William Graham Sumner, Henry Ward Beecher—the 1980 gathering at least hosted a President-elect, while it doubtless would not even have occurred to the men of 1882 to expect Chester A. Arthur for dinner. Presidents had not been very relevant to the men at Delmonico's, whereas the new President in 1980 was of enormous importance to the crowd at the celebration. During the few weeks before his inauguration they would have time not only to celebrate but to cerebrate, to machinate—and to hope.

Fifty years of frustration going back to Hoover's repudiation made the conservative victory taste all the sweeter in these transitional days. In 1952 the American right, backing Robert "Mr. Republican" Taft, had lost to a nonpartisan general who governed as a moderate broker between congressional Democrats and Republicans. In 1960 they had lost with a promising young California conservative who had cornered Alger Hiss. Four years later they had lost with the stoutest heart of all, Barry Goldwater, against a Democrat who exploited JFK's memory and brandished promises of peace. In 1968 they had won with Nixon, who soon established price controls in Washington and, along with Rockefeller's man Kissinger, toasted the Chinese reds in Peking before he lost the whole shooting match at Watergate. Jerry Ford had been just another namby-pamby moderate Republican in the White House who had used his presidential perquisites to beat out Reagan for the 1976 GOP nomination and then had managed to lose to Carter.

But losing had not been the worst of it, at least for conservatives accustomed to putting principles before pragmatics. Almost unbearable had been the complacency and effrontery of liberalism during the long period of its intellectual and political rule. The left, they noted, simply wrote off much of the right as neurotic, paranoid, or at least extremist, operating far outside the rational consensus. Viewing the right also as politically impotent, liberals proclaimed the death of conservatism after its every defeat.

Following Goldwater's rejection, William F. Buckley, Jr., complained that liberals were holding "that the electorate had once and for all spoken on the subject, and that therefore the only realistic thing a conservative could do was to fold up his tent, and hitch-hike along with history."

Behind the complaints lay the fear that perhaps the liberal complacency was justified, perhaps liberalism did command a central fortress from which it could not be dislodged, perhaps the liberal establishment was as truly established as any state or church of old. That establishment, charged the conservative author M. Stanton Evans, "is in control. It is guiding the lives and destinies of the American people. It wields enormous, immeasurable power" by controlling popular opinion. Most mortifying of all to literate conservatives, liberals of various stripes wrote the books about conservatism that won the most respectability. Cornell political scientist Clinton Rossiter, taking a "hard look" at American conservatism, taxed it with being impotent in the realm of ideas. Harvard scholar Louis Hartz appeared to reduce conservatism to Whiggery and reaction. Columbia historian Richard Hofstadter pictured the radical right as rootless, dispossessed, paranoid, and not really conservative. Unkindest cut of all, a former editor of conservative journals, Alan Crawford, published in 1980 an exposé of the New Right as a movement, in the words of Peter Viereck, of a "lawless, rabble-rousing populism of the revolutionary Right," that threatened the authentic conservative heritage of Edmund Burke and John Adams. But now, in the same year that Crawford published his book, the ecstatic crowd was celebrating its presidential victory, and some of the celebrants were the very "extremists" that liberals and moderate conservatives had attacked.

There would be many explanations of the rise of the conservative movement from the political slough of the Goldwater and Nixon years to its triumph in the 1980s: the exhaustion of liberal ideas, energy, and agenda; the reaction to the leftist "excesses" of the 1960s; the failures of Democratic Administrations; the revived cold war in the wake of the Soviet occupation of Afghanistan and turmoil in southern Africa and Central America. But the main reason for that rise was rather remarkable in an age when change was so often attributed to the uncontrollable collision of events or the blind turnings of history. The conservative triumph stemmed to a marked degree from a considered and collective effort of rightists of various schools to build their intellectual case and to use invigorated and broadened conservative ideas as vehicles to political power. They would build not the mythical "city upon a hill" but a formidable citadel of ideas as a foundation of the conservative effort. This strategy was based on the idea that powerful ideas themselves were the most steady and dependable propellants of political action. *"Ideas Are Weapons,"* said the liberal Max Lerner. *"Ideas Have Consequences,"* wrote the conservative Richard Weaver.

But ideas as weapons must be armed and armored. Unless conservatives realized "that massive public education must precede any hope of a Presidential victory," wrote Buckley, "they will never have a President they can call their own." Journals were established or refurbished: the *National Review, The Public Interest, Commentary,* to join the long-established *Wall Street Journal* and *Reader's Digest* as purveyors of right-wing views. Think tanks were founded for incubating ideas, and foundations for incubating think tanks. Serious journals like *The Public Interest* were all the more influential for being moderate in tone and scholarly in format, with tables, charts, and footnotes. These publications drew from a remarkable array of old and new conservatives: Hayek, Friedman, L. Brent Bozell, Ralph de Toledano, George F. Gilder, James J. Kilpatrick, Clarence Manion, Frank S. Meyer, Max Rafferty, Phyllis Schlafly, William E. Simon, and others less famous but influential in diverse ways.

The avalanche of books and articles tumbling out of conservative foundations, research institutions, publishing houses, and corporate public information offices attested to the intellectual breadth of conservatism; it also dramatized its divisions. The more conservatism prospered as a creed and cause, the more the various right-wing factions advanced their competing doctrines. Their schools of thought had not changed much during the postwar years. Traditionalist conservatives, still proudly resonating to the writings of the Burkeans, preached the virtues of order, reverence, stability, moderation, gradual change, to be achieved through a harmonious balancing of the demands of hierarchy, community, privilege, and noblesse oblige. Libertarian conservatives demanded optimal individual freedom of choice in cultural, sexual, and social matters, protected especially against governmental intrusion. Free-market conservatives called for an open, competitive economy, which to them meant reductions in government, in regulation, in union power, and a drastic cutback on the environmental, affirmative-action, and other controls loaded on private enterprise from the FDR through the Carter years.

Populist conservatives, in rising numbers especially in southern and western "Sunbelt" regions, echoed the demands of the free-marketers but focused their attacks especially on the "new elites," nonelected and self-promoted—network news producers, liberal journalists, radical professors, federal bureaucrats, education administrators, left-wing writers, literary critics, and others of related breeds entrenched especially in northeastern and West Coast cities. The evangelical and fundamentalist right, embracing such groupings as the Moral Majority and Christian

Voices, overlapped the libertarians in its view of freedom and individualism as pro-market and anti-government. But the central commitment of the "new Christian right" was to family, religion, community, and old-fashioned morality, and its chief targets were moral relativism, sexual permissiveness, abortion, ERA, prohibitions on school prayer, the secular curriculum in public schools. The capacity of the Christian right to build networks, operate through local congregations, and mobilize its strength in the Republican party had been a decisive element in Reagan's 1980 victory.

These conservative groupings intertwined, overlapped, and conflicted. They formed an unstable equilibrium, much like right-wing parliamentary coalitions. Liberationists wanted free-marketers to oppose government interference in private life as vehemently as intrusion into free enterprise; populists found some of the eastern sophisticates tending toward an elitist "conservative chic"; traditionalists deplored some of the destabilizing, disruptive tendencies implied in the other conservative philosophies. Nevertheless, conservatism as a whole displayed considerable coherence. Despite much writing about "new" conservatives and "neoconservatism," the doctrinal branches of the right remained much the same over these decades. Indeed, the general terms—liberal and conservative, the right and the left—came into wider use and clearer usage during this period than in the New Deal era. When reporters referred to a "conservative" senator or "House liberals" the general public understood what they meant.

Still, the traditional differences among the doctrinal conservative groups persisted, and the left, accustomed to ferocious battles among its own warring factions, wondered whether the conservative movement could enjoy unity during its prosperity. For a time at least, the conservatives put up a relatively solid front. Journals such as Buckley's *National Review* and Irving Kristol's *The Public Interest* showed an ecumenical flair for bringing under their tents a wide variety of right-wing ideas. In particular, Buckley, who had been the scourge of liberal academics with his biting wit and carefully planned polemics, established intellectual and personal links with virtually every brand of conservative thinker; Buckley once boasted that he had had only a single resignation from the *National Review,* that of Max Eastman—and, considering the erratic career and mercurial iconoclasm of this former Marxist turned *Reader's Digest* feature writer, Buckley could readily be forgiven that exception.

A key force for conservative unity was Ronald Reagan, who emphasized the common beliefs on the right; and in any event he was not one for fine theory spinning or jesuitical hairsplitting. He displayed a winning ability to talk order and stability to the traditionalists, individual liberty to the libertarians, anti-regulation to the free-marketers, and anti-elitism to the populists. In unifying the disparate strands of conservatism, Sidney Blumenthal concluded, Reaganism "animated the intellectuals' theories with a resonant symbolism—images of idyllic small-town life, enterprising entrepreneurs whose success derived from moral character, and failure induced only by federal bureaucrats." The candidate also benefited from his skill in using anecdotage, reminiscence, misreminiscence, and jokes to glide over burdensome or hostile facts.

The most powerful source of conservative unity, however, was anticommunism. With their hostility to unregulated enterprise, to rugged individualism, to the FBI and other watchdogs against the "red network" in Washington, the communists were the perfect unifiers. Above all, anticommunism was a stimulus and attraction to the countless former communists who had deserted the "naked god" and flocked to the journals and think tanks of the right. That anticommunism would remain an enduring and dependable basis of unity appeared rather questionable, since it might depend more on communist developments abroad than on the efforts of conservative thinkers and politicians at home.

*   *   *

Liberals were in no mood to celebrate as they came to the end of their worst decade, the 1970s. During the final forlorn weeks of the Carter Administration, as they watched conservatives move into the new presidency, into a newly Republican Senate, and into the cultural and economic decision-making centers of Washington, liberals could reflect once again that nothing fails like success. Looking back over the liberal and Democratic dominance of the past five decades, they asked what had gone wrong—what had really gone wrong? The record seemed so positive. Three Republican Presidents had left virtually intact the New Deal and the Fair Deal, the New Frontier and the Great Society, almost none of their major laws repealed or key programs canceled. Who could deny that poverty had been reduced, the elderly and the young protected, the farmer subsidized, civil rights broadened, educational opportunity vastly expanded, environmental problems confronted, with considerable prosperity for all but the very poor and without confiscatory taxation or runaway federal deficits?

Three decades earlier Lionel Trilling had written that "liberalism is not only the dominant but even the sole intellectual tradition" in the United States, adding that "it is the plain fact that nowadays there are no conservative or reactionary ideas in general circulation." Now, at the start of the 1980s, everything seemed turned upside down. By the hundreds conservatives were pouring out of right-wing journals and research institutions, out of universities and corporations—liberals had not realized how large the army of the right had become. And how youthful they seemed, how self-confident, how brash, as they prepared to transform the nation. Some liberal memories reached back to the New Deal and the Kennedy years, when young people, equally brash and confident, had taken over State and Treasury, Interior and Justice, and the other federal strong points.

Already the left was challenging itself, on the eve of the touted "Reagan Revolution," to come up with fresh ideas, new proposals. But liberals were still mesmerized by their decades of success and power. Of course, they granted, there had been egregious failures, shortcomings, inadequacies, sheer blunders, follies, and idiocies. But these had been the exceptions, departures from the norm, not failings inherent in liberal programs. Obviously liberals should govern better, innovate more carefully, administer more efficiently. But cancel or drastically alter the great liberal program of the past fifty years? Never!

The deeper problem was not simply that liberals were wed to the programs they had put through—it was that they were still living off the intellectual capital of the first fifty years of the century. That capital had been ample enough in the 1950s, and even still in the early 1970s, to influence the thinking of Republican Administrations, putting Eisenhower, Nixon, Ford, and their men on the defensive even while they presided over the White House. Now everything was different. The triumphant Reaganites evinced not the slightest interest in their ideas, except as artifacts to be swept away in the conservative revolution. Liberal thinkers, out of power or access to power, out of sight as their speaking invitations dwindled, would have plenty of leisure for rethinking liberalism.

How well would they use this time? Not to arrive at some "consensus"; it was already apparent at the start of the eighties that liberalism would remain divided within itself and from the much smaller authentic American left, itself far more fractured. There was much talk of neoliberalism, the New Left, postliberalism, and so on, but once again the prefixes did not help analysis. The divisions among liberals remained much the same, only enhanced: New Deal or New Frontier "welfare" liberals who stuck with their ideas and programs and wanted only to improve, extend, and perhaps enlarge them; other liberals who, impressed or depressed by the conservative resurgence, proposed to preserve the essence of the Great Society and its predecessors but in a modified, more "fiscally responsible" form, even if this meant more federal taxation attuned to lower spending; still others who turned toward what Robert B. Reich later would call a "New Public Philosophy," which faced up to emerging industrial and technological problems and opportunities, especially on a global level, without forsaking fundamental liberal values.

Fundamental values? These were precisely what liberals were more and more abandoning, according to activists further to the left. Especially one value—equality. Liberals in general, it was charged, had so fully joined the broad American consensus behind individual rights, civil liberty, individualism, individuality, that the great competing and balancing claims of equality—at least of equality of opportunity—were being ignored. Even committed egalitarians had to grant that inequality had been far more deeply rooted than they had perceived and that the road to social justice was strewn with bogs and pitfalls. As he neared seventy, Kenneth Clark, the longtime student and preacher of racial integration and equality, confessed that he had "seriously underestimated the depth and complexity of Northern racism." Clark conceded that some major federal welfare programs might have worsened the lot of blacks by encouraging a trend toward one-parent families and helping maintain the "pathology" of ghetto life.

"But that's not God-ordained," Clark said. "I'm convinced that social engineering is no more difficult than space engineering. If a program to get us to the moon didn't work, the engineers would try another program." Why not with social engineering as well? He was bewildered, Clark said despondently, that so many liberals—old friends and students—had given up trying and had even deserted the liberal cause.

To staunch socialists further left on the spectrum, liberal weakness was no surprise. Liberal failure of commitment was one reason they were socialists. On the eve of the Reagan presidency, however, few leftists were optimistic about the future of socialism. Its leaders still showed little interest in shaking off the failed intellectual and political habits of the past. The leadership had usually had a Marxist as well as a religious orientation—a source of disunity in itself. Historically, the larger the appeal of the socialist movement, the more variegated its membership had been—militant Wobblies from the old Industrial Workers of the World, prairie populists, Wisconsin progressives, Yiddish-speaking New Yorkers, western copper miners, urban intellectuals. The socialists of the 1980s could no longer claim leaders of the quality of Eugene Debs and Norman Thomas, who had managed to transcend major divisions.

Politically socialism had long been notorious for its electoral purism and ideological sectarianism. Socialist leaders had stood aside from the New Deal, even though it brought "the greatest wave of social reform that this country had seen for many decades," in Irving Howe's view. A half century later many socialist leaders and intellectuals were still standing aside from even the most liberal of liberal initiatives and programs. Typically socialist and other left-wing movements were composed of hundreds, even thousands of local organizations focused on specific goals of their own as they responded to local needs and interests.

When the defeat in 1980 set socialists, liberals, and Democratic party strategists to considering new possibilities of a Democratic, left-wing coalition, the most perplexing problem for socialists was still the old one— whether to vote for the lesser evil between the two major parties, and thus run the risk of throwing away their vote, or to seek to build a strong third party, and thus run the risk of doing the same thing.

If a measure of rethinking about coalition strategies was taking place, the left was ignoring almost completely the question of governmental strategy when and if a liberal-labor-left party coalition took office. It had long been obvious that the fragmentation of power resulting from federalism and the checks and balances would gravely hobble a left-wing government. It was remarkable that in 1987, when politicians and professors devoted much attention to analyzing the Constitution during its bicentennial, liberal and left-wing thinkers gave so little attention to a constitutional system filled with veto traps and devices for delaying and devitalizing progressive measures and programs. How much could the left expect from a radical or socialist leadership in Washington, considering how Wilson with his Treaty of Versailles, Roosevelt in his second term, and Kennedy in his one and only term had been thwarted by political forces acting through the marvelous contrivances devised by the Framers and elaborated by their successors to balk comprehensive and forthright government action? At least, as the Reagan era dawned, leftist thinkers could settle back and plan to enjoy the spectacle of a conservative Administration being divided and frustrated by conservative constitutional arrangements largely of conservative origin.

CHAPTER 15

The Decline of Leadership

F OR Americans 1987 was to be a special year of remembrance and
perhaps of renewal. In a winter of deep cold and heavy snows New
Englanders commemorated the guerrilla struggles of the Shays rebels
during the same kind of harsh weather two hundred years earlier. Late in
May 1987 scholarly conferences in Philadelphia marked the bicentennial
of the arrival of delegates to the Constitutional Convention and the leadership of James Madison and his fellow Virginians in offering a bold new plan
for a stronger national government. In September, on the bicentenary
anniversary of the convention's close, Philadelphia burst into pomp and
pageantry as hundreds of thousands celebrated with floats and balloons
and fireworks.

The festivities barely concealed an undercurrent of concern and disillusion. The bicentennial year began amid revelations of gross failures in the
Reagan White House, of an Administration out of control as a few men
conducted their own "rogue" foreign policy with the government of Iran
and with the Contra opposition to Nicaragua's leftist Sandinista government. Reagan's erratic leadership, both foreign and domestic, compared
poorly with that of his fellow conservative Margaret Thatcher, who won
her third general election, and that of the worldly Soviet party boss,
Mikhail Gorbachev, who had launched a bold effort to modernize the
Soviet economy and democratize the political system.

At home Congress and the President gave a classic demonstration of the
workings of the checks and balances by failing to agree on or enforce
measures sharply to reduce the annual deficit and eventually tackle a national debt nearing $3 trillion. The nation continued to struggle with
economic ills whose solution appeared beyond human wit—regional decline, inner-city blight, lack of affordable housing, large sectors of entrenched poverty. Abroad Americans faced brutal competition from Japan
and other exporting nations. The United States had now become a dependent nation. Financially, wrote Felix Rohatyn, "we are being colonized."

The floundering leadership of 1987 stood in stark contrast to the bold, purposeful work of the Framers of the Constitution two centuries earlier. Even those who wondered whether the Constitution was good for another two centuries—or even two decades—freely granted that the Founding Fathers had displayed a collective intellectual leadership without peer in the Western world. Above all they had displayed during their four months in Philadelphia the capacity to stand back from the existing national government—the Articles of Confederation—and summon the institutional imagination and political audacity to fashion a whole new structure of government. Two hundred years later proposals to make even small structural changes in the constitutional system evoked emotional opposition from some members of the public and the academy—and almost complete indifference from officeholders who were struggling unsuccessfully to make the present system work.

The Framers had shown remarkable flexibility and responsiveness to the public as well, especially when it became clear that delegates to the state ratifying conventions in 1787 and 1788 would approve the new charter only if the Constitution makers guaranteed that consideration of a Bill of Rights would be one of the first duties of the new Congress. That Bill of Rights, drafted by James Madison in the summer of 1789, endorsed by Congress that fall, and ratified by the states between 1789 and 1791, became the crownpiece of the Constitution. Its enactment also meant that celebration-weary Americans would have to gird themselves for another series of bicentennial commemorations from 1989 through 1991.

New Yorkers who liked celebrations were in luck. Manhattan was where Madison had drafted the noble statement and where Congress had been sitting when it passed the proposed amendments. Indeed, New Yorkers had already held their celebration of the Bill of Rights in 1986, when they had seized on the centennial of the erection of the Statue of Liberty to stage a great weekend festivity, amid a swarm of old sailing ships in New York Harbor and a spectacular display of fireworks in the evening.

The celebration revealed a deep hunger on the part of people to return to the past, to touch and savor it. Liberty Weekend, designed to stress the great statue's welcome to immigrants, turned into a preview also of the Bill of Rights commemoration, as orators, pundits, and plain people explored the deeper meanings of freedom as the central value in American life and history. The celebrations took on a poignant aspect as speakers conjured up memories of the illustrious leaders of the past such as Thomas Jefferson and John Adams, devotees of liberty like Tom Paine and Patrick Henry. Two hundred years later, was there a single leader who could be compared with these men? What had happened to that fierce devotion to liberty?

Could Congress formulate, would the states ratify, would the people approve a *1989* Bill of Rights as bold and sweeping as that drawn up two centuries earlier?

That weekend, while President Reagan and other dignitaries paid homage to the restored and relighted Miss Liberty, a score of panelists—women's leaders, trade unionists, educators, the mayor of the city—met in a hotel on Broadway to debate the next hundred years of freedom. The future of individual liberty seemed safe in the hands of panelists who had passed in front of garish, X-rated movie houses to enter the hotel but rejected censorship of pornography, who were concerned that their children could buy rock records with sexually explicit lyrics but favored identifying the contents rather than banning them. After New York's Mayor Edward Koch complained that women had complained when his minions had placed signs in bars warning pregnant women against drinking, NOW president Eleanor Smeal asked not that the signs be taken down but rather that other signs be posted warning men against drinking and thus endangering babies while driving home.

When the question shifted from the protection of individual liberty against government to that of the advancement of freedom through government—that is, from "freedom of speech and religion" to "freedom from fear and want"—the conferees became far more divided. Elie Wiesel, a survivor of Auschwitz and head of the United States Holocaust Memorial Council, sharply posed the issue of social and collective freedom when he called on America to open its doors to anyone who wanted to enter, for economic as well as political reasons. We are all free only to the extent others are free, he said. The discussion turned to equality as inseparably linked with liberty. Could the American constitutional system not only protect liberty but broaden social freedom and deal with the nation's enduring inequalities?

Some of the conferees answered that the system worked, or at least could be made to work. However fragmented and stalemated, it could at least fend off arbitrary governmental intervention, and at the same time could be used as a positive means for expanding economic and social freedoms. Other conferees were doubtful. The system was too slow, too ponderous, too exposed to control by economic and social elites. Still others believed, though, that great leadership of the quality of Jefferson and Lincoln and FDR might make the system work. If anyone at the conference thought morosely about the state of the current leadership in both parties, no one wanted to mention the matter on a pleasant Fourth of July weekend of happy celebration.

REPUBLICANS: WAITING FOR MR. RIGHT

Few at the Liberty Weekend conference would have offered as a model leader the man who a few miles away was hailing the renovated Miss Liberty in a speech filled with his usual pieties and banalities. Even though Ronald Reagan had twice won both the governorship of California and the presidency of the United States, many in the press and academia still viewed him as merely a rigid ideologue whose hard-core conservatism was cushioned by a relaxed, easygoing manner and prettified by disarming, even self-deprecating, jokes and anecdotes. It was easy to compare his mind, as Harding's had been compared, to stellar space—a huge void filled with a few wandering clichés. Or to picture, as Garry Trudeau had in his comic strip, an intrepid explorer pushing through the tangled filaments of the President's brain in an effort to discover how—or whether—it worked.

Even after his six years in the White House spotlight, many President watchers were still misjudging Ronald Reagan. They did not see the committed political activist and strategist behind the façade. They saw the Reagan who appeared on the screen, an "aw shucks" old boy, with bobbing head, face turning and smiling, shoulders rising and falling—a showcase of ingratiating body language. They heard that long-honed voice over the radio every Saturday, easily rising and receding, alternating between mellowness and intensity, hovering at times "barely above a whisper," Roger Rosenblatt wrote, "so as to win you over by intimacy, if not by substance." They chuckled at the perfectly timed joke or anecdote or observation. Many of his stories turned out to be untrue even during his presidential years, when at least his speech writers should have been more careful, and his misstatements and tall tales were numerous enough to be collected and published in book form.

But few appeared to care when Reagan was found out, contradicted, refuted. "There he goes again," the public seemed to smile indulgently. It took a long time for President watchers to understand that Reagan was not a man of details, specifics, particulars. Theodore White had called him a man more of ideas than of intellect, but he proved to be a man less of ideas than of stances, shibboleths, stereotypes. He was a strategist rather than a tactician, a hedgehog who knew one big thing, in Herodotus' famous phrase, rather than a fox who knew many little things. What Reagan had known in the 1960s was that he must and could rid the Republican party of its liberal elements, marry the GOP to the burgeoning conservative causes and movements, fight off the far-right extremists, reunite Republicans around a clearly conservative doctrine, mobilize disaffected

Democrats and blue-collar workers behind a Reagan candidacy, denounce the Russians—and win.

In retrospect this strategy would seem obvious and even easy, but it had not so appeared at the time. The dominant image in the minds of Republican party politicians in the late 1960s and early 1970s was the crushing Goldwater defeat of 1964. Never mind the excuses—that no one could have overcome the Kennedy remembrance that year or outbid LBJ as peace leader. The practical pols knew their history—a moderate Eisenhower had won in 1952 and 1956, Nixon with his conservative, red-baiting image had lost in 1960, a "new Nixon," bleached and smoothened, had won in 1968, and any solid right-wing candidate, no matter how attractive personally, would yield centrist voters and hence presidential elections to the Democrats. It was this Goldwater syndrome that Reagan had to overcome if he was to put himself at the head of the GOP and take it to victory.

In the mid-1970s, however, many conservatives were by no means convinced that the Republican party could be their ticket to power. To them the GOP seemed irretrievably in the hands of Gerald Ford and his Vice President-select, the hated Nelson Rockefeller. Ford had been in the White House for hardly half a year when the American Conservative Union and Young Americans for Freedom jointly sponsored a conference at Washington's Mayflower Hotel to consider forming an independent party to challenge both the GOP and the Democracy. Enraptured by the vision of a new conservative party that would unite rural Southerners and northern blue-collar workers, they urged Reagan to lead the effort. He gave his answer in a banquet speech before a packed ballroom. After winning cheers for a denunciation of the Ford policies, he dampened the fire-eaters by demanding, "Is it a third party we need, or is it a new and revitalized second party . . .?"—a committedly conservative GOP.

Reagan would wait—but the movement conservatives would not let him wait. In mid-June 1975, only four months after the Mayflower conference, a group of conservative leaders, including mail-order entrepreneur Richard Viguerie, columnist Kevin Phillips, Colorado brewer Joseph Coors, several supporters of George Wallace, and a cross section of conservative organization leaders, confronted Reagan at a private dinner. Phillips led the attack, asserting that the GOP was falling apart just as the Whigs had divided and collapsed in the 1850s, that it was time for a new conservative party that could overcome both Democrats and Republicans in a three-party battle, that Reagan must make a direct bid for the Wallace backers and hence must break whatever ties he had with Republican liberals and even Republican moderates. A free-for-all followed. Some in the group told Reagan harshly that he lacked "fire in his belly" and was dawdling while Ford picked up conservative support for the approaching 1976 campaign. Viguerie, arguing that the GOP had become "unmarketable," urged the governor to unite conservatives and independents in a New Majority.

Then Reagan told them his decision—he would fight Ford for the Republican nomination; as the Republican nominee he would unite conservatives, independents, and conservative Democrats in a broad coalition; and if necessary he would propose that the Republican party change its name. In effect he would transform the GOP or, failing that, abandon it. Half persuaded, and lacking any alternative candidate of national standing (Wallace was still disabled by his gunshot wounding in 1972), the conservatives could only assent. Reagan soon demonstrated that he did have fire in his belly by taking Ford on in the 1976 presidential primaries despite pressure from many GOP leaders to wait his turn. He proved his commitment when he returned to the fray in 1980 as an unrepentant conservative and Republican, and then after winning both the nomination and the election, made clear that he would govern as a conservative, and as head of a conservative Administration.

*   *   *

The media for the most part interpreted the outcome of the 1980 presidential election as a repudiation of Carter rather than a victory for Reagan. Soaring prices, astronomical interest rates, the President's apparent scolding of the American people in his "malaise" speech, his long agonizing months of being held hostage to the hostage situation in Iran—all these and much else were cited as proof. This view of the election outcome, however, revealed the bias of some liberals, who refused to believe that any authentic, outspoken conservative could win the presidency of the United States—the Goldwater syndrome at work. In fact, Reagan won the election by persuasive appeals to the right-wing vote and to disaffected independents, full exploitation of the remarkable direct-mail and fund-raising apparatus of the Republican national party, and his skillful coalition building between GOP regulars and movement conservatives, as reflected in the choice of George Bush for running mate.

Then, to the astonishment of many, especially of Democrats who had become accustomed to their winning candidates reneging on promises of peace and reform within a year or two of coming into office, Reagan began to govern just as he had promised—as a conservative. He promptly appointed a conservative cabinet headed by Alexander Haig as Secretary of State, and ordered a freeze of federal hiring of civilian employees. Then, after recovering from a near-fatal assassination attempt, he repudiated Carter's human rights approach, crushed striking air controllers and their union, called the Russians names, and engaged in a variety of symbolic acts that left no doubt that he was a conservative who meant it.

Reagan had shrewdly recognized—or perhaps had simply sensed intuitively—that he should move ahead strongly in domestic economic policy even at the expense of dramatic initiatives abroad. Tax policy offered the best opportunity to redeem his campaign promises and publicize his departure from "discredited" New Deal policies of Carter and his Democratic predecessors. Working closely with congressional leaders, Vice President Bush, and the Republican Senate, the Administration pushed its legislative program of cutting personal income taxes across the board over thirty-three months; reducing the maximum tax on all income from 70 to 50 percent; indexing tax rates to soften the impact of graduated income taxes on rises in personal income; reducing the maximum tax on capital gains from 28 to 20 percent; liberalizing deductions for contributions to individual retirement accounts; lowering estate and gift taxes; providing business with tax breaks. The tax reductions were tied closely to a package of budget cuts that slashed toward the heart of the New Deal, Fair Deal, and Great Society domestic programs—education, health, housing, urban aid, food stamp programs, the National Endowments for the Arts and for the Humanities, and the Corporation for Public Broadcasting, and even federal subsidies for school meals—but never never never defense spending.

The Reagan Revolution was underway. The head revolutionary spurred his troops on television, in speeches to joint sessions of Congress, in huddles with key senators and representatives, in trips out into the country. Revolutionary fervor needed a doctrine, and this took the form of the supply-side theory that lowering taxes would produce prosperity by giving producers more capital for production and giving consumers more money for consumption. Savings, investment, and growth would be stimulated, the budget ultimately balanced through growth in the tax base. For all-out supply-siders, these were at the heart of a much wider program, described later by Reagan's budget chief, David Stockman, as a "whole catalogue of policy changes, ranging from natural gas deregulation, to abolition of the minimum wage, to repeal of milk marketing orders, to elimination of federal certificates of 'need' for truckers, hospitals, airlines, and anyone else desiring to commit an act of economic production. It even encompassed reform of the World Bank, and countless more." All of this was designed to overcome the stagflation of the late 1970s.

Since the House of Representatives had remained in Democratic hands in the 1980 election, it was imperative that the President bring around a large segment of the opposition. In a House vote on his crucial budget bill within four months of his inauguration, sixty-three Democrats—over a quarter of the Democracy's House membership—broke ranks to support the Administration. Many of these were from the South and West—an exciting hint of the possibilities of a future party realignment. No President since Roosevelt, *Time* opined six months after Reagan's inauguration, had "done so much of such magnitude so quickly to change the economic direction of the nation."

The euphoria was not for long. During late 1981 and 1982 the economy plunged into recession. Once again the media headlined stories of bank failures, farm closures, bankruptcies, desperate family and individual crises. The jobless rate rose to over 10 percent, the highest since the great depression of the 1930s. The hard facts threw the White House economists and their colleagues outside into disarray. The supply-siders defended themselves with the classic explanation of dogmatists who fail—their program had not been tried hard enough, or long enough, or this or that vital ingredient was missing. Stockman was now mainly concerned that future Reagan budgets would be more and more out of balance in a recession situation. Republican party leaders feared that the GOP would be tagged with another "Hoover depression."

And Reagan? The President had now fallen into a severe political and intellectual bind. He had not been able to balance the budget—politically he dared not cut Social Security and other major safety-net spendings, viscerally he not only opposed cuts in his planned military buildup but also wanted a huge boost in defense spending. And in the end he still confronted Speaker Thomas P. O'Neill's power base in the House. Doctrinally he remained absolutely rigid in the face of his failure. Time and again emergency budget meetings in the Oval Office were trivialized as the President retreated into anecdotage about timeserving bureaucrats or wasteful projects. Stockman noted that when Pete Domenici, a Republican senator friendly to the White House, confronted Reagan with the need to raise taxes, the President jotted down notes during the presentation but only in order to rebut it.

"Damn it, Pete," he said, "I'm just not going to accept this. This is just more of the same kind of talk we've heard for forty years."

It became clear during that first year that Reagan the campaign and electoral strategist was a different man from Reagan the head of government. The grand coalition builder, who had spoken from the stump in pieties and platitudes that united people, now proved himself unable to think in terms of the hard policies and priorities that linked the overall values to day-to-day governmental choices and operations. Stockman complained of Reagan's habit of castigating spending in the abstract while he shrank from the "real bullets" he would have to face politically if he took on the welfare state's gigantic entitlement programs. Few in the White House pressed their chief to make fundamental strategic choices; rather they echoed his dogmatics or lobbied for some pet solution of their own. As Ralph Nader noted in a preface to a study of "Reagan's ruling class," the people around the President showed a remarkable sameness of "attitudes, ideologies, and even styles of thinking and explaining." Not for Reagan was FDR's penchant for peopling his Administration with challenging intellectual eclectics.

But one grand asset Reagan retained—political luck. The recession came early enough for some Reaganites to blame it on the lingering effects of Carter policies, early enough too for the White House to wait it out and hope for recovery by election time. The very spending that Reagan condemned in principle while authorizing in practice, combined with such anti-inflationary developments as an oil price decline over which the White House had little control, brought a strong recovery. Although large pockets of poverty and unemployment persisted, the recovery remained vigorous enough to project Reagan toward his massive reelection triumph of 1984. It was hard enough for Walter Mondale, leading a divided, irresolute party, to take on an incumbent whose personal popularity remained high, who had managed to maintain his electoral coalition despite sporadic complaints from both movement conservatives like Viguerie and liberal and moderate Republicans in the Senate. But former Vice President Mondale, forced to share some of the blame for failed Carter economic policies, also faced a Republican Santa Claus who continued to disperse federal money to thousands of vested interests and welfare projects even while preaching economy and thrift and budget balancing. He faced a chameleon who alternated between attacking government and exploiting *his* government. It was no contest from the start.

Reagan's big reelection set the stage for a major piece of unfinished domestic business, tax reform. For some time the Administration had been tracking proposals by Republican congressman Jack Kemp, an early booster of supply-side economics, for further cuts in personal rates, and by two Democrats, Senator Bill Bradley and Congressman Richard Gephardt, for lower rates combined with a slash in deductions. The President virtually stole the issue from the Democrats during the 1984 campaign and made it his own. A few months later, in his State of the Union address to Congress, he made tax reform the central domestic initiative of his second term. "Let us move together with an historic reform of tax simplification for fairness and growth," he proclaimed, promising to seek a top rate of no more than 35 percent. Evidently having taken to heart the lessons of his first-term setbacks, Reagan showed a good deal of flexibility in bargain-

ing with congressional leaders and factions over the specifics of his tax
proposal.

Again and again the Administration measure seemed to die on Capitol
Hill, only to be resurrected by a President absolutely committed to tax
reform and ever ready to make political forays out into the country to
channel public pressure toward Congress. White House leadership was
crucial; while three-quarters of Americans in a poll favored a simplified tax
system and almost three-fifths considered the existing system unfair, they
listed the tax system fifth in importance among economic problems, behind the deficit, unemployment, interest rates, and inflation. The Administration had to fight off lobbyists who put heavy pressure on legislators. The
bill curtailed consumer interest deductions, and she had a Chrysler plant
in her district, a congresswoman said. She thought she should vote no, but
"I couldn't do it."

Reaganites were proud that they had overcome "Lame-Duck-Itis," as
they felicitously called it. Historically, however, the problem of the presidential lame duck was less the second term than the second two years in
each term, following the congressional midterm elections.

It was clear even as Reagan took command of tax policy that he must
share leadership with committee chieftains and party lieutenants in Congress, which retained its constitutional authority over revenue measures.
In foreign policy, on the other hand, the Chief Executive had held the
dominant role both under the Constitution and by custom. If many conservatives had been sorely disappointed by Reagan's compromises over taxation and domestic policies, hawkish right-wingers had been entranced by
his fulminations against communism. Rhetorically, at least, he had entered
the White House as the most bellicose peacetime President since Theodore Roosevelt. While TR had tended to strike out in all directions, however, Reagan had eyed the reds with the steely hostility of a frontiersman
targeting a band of Indians.

Reagan's anticommunist rhetoric had long been unbridled. He wrote in
a 1968 volume: "We are faced with the most evil enemy mankind has
known in his long climb from the swamp to the stars." Junior-partner
communists were just as bad: the North Vietnamese, of course controlled
by Moscow, were "hard-core, hard-nosed, vicious Communists" who were
going to "fudge, cheat and steal every chance they get." Americans should
have stayed in both Korea and Vietnam, gone all out, and won. Reagan
liked to talk about Lenin's "plan" to "take Eastern Europe," organize the
"hordes of Asia," about Lenin's "prediction" that eventually the United
States, the last bastion of capitalism, would "fall into our outstretched

hand like overripe fruit." For some hawks it was as rousing as a Hollywood scenario. Would Ronald Reagan ride to the rescue?

Many Americans were apprehensive when this fire-breather entered the White House, but experienced President watchers professed not to be worried. The reins of power, they said reassuringly, would tame the rider. It was one thing to rant outside the White House, something else to handle the perplexing everyday questions that took on all the grayish hues between black and white. Wait until he had to consult with heads of state, foreign envoys, wait until he had to read cables bristling with the endless complexities of real-life international politics. After all, hadn't Teddy Roosevelt in the White House become a conciliator, mediating the Russo-Japanese War and even winning the Nobel Peace Prize?

For a time the new President did indeed moderate his oratory. He preached peace sermons, called the nuclear threat "a terrible beast" before the West German Bundestag, told the British Parliament that nuclear weapons threatened, "if not the extinction of mankind, then surely the end of civilization as we know it." Hedrick Smith of *The New York Times* and other journalists wondered whether he was deserting his sharply ideological, anti-détente rhetoric for a more moderate, centrist foreign policy. Soon, however, the President returned to his rhetorical battles, like an old soldier pulling his saber down from over the fireplace. In a March 1983 speech to Christian evangelists in Florida, he labeled the Soviet Union an "evil empire," called totalitarian states the focus of wickedness in the modern world, and warned that America's struggle with communist Russia was a struggle between right and wrong. "Adopting a perspective very similar to John Foster Dulles in the fifties," Betty Glad wrote, "Reagan has not changed," even though technological and political change had undermined the old assumptions of a Pax Americana.

Was it perplexing that this genial, charming, worldly septuagenarian could label as diabolical the creed of a large portion of humankind, that he sounded like the Ayatollah Khomeini when the Iranian revolutionary castigated the United States as "the great Satan"? Not if one kept in mind the old actor's love for white hat–black hat scenarios, his authentic fears that the communists might stamp out the kind of individualism he had absorbed in Dixon, Illinois, or—in the view of some biographers—his displacement of earlier insecurities and embarrassments, such as his father's alcoholism, onto the treacherous world outside.

But the main reason for Reagan's bellicose rhetoric may have been much simpler. He did not really *mean it*—mean it in the sense of converting ideology into action against powerful opponents. In divorcing his foreign policy from his rhetoric he was carrying to the extreme the tendency of recent American leaders to enunciate vague and lofty values without reducing them to operating principles, policy choices, clear priorities. Reagan's 1988 summit with Gorbachev typified the President's bent for high rhetoric—now friendly, now hostile to the Kremlin—that had little relation to the skimpy policy results of the meeting.

It took anticommunist hawks a long time to recognize Reagan's separation of rhetoric and reality, in part because he gave them occasional swigs from the heady old ideological bottle, in part because Carter had moved so far toward an aggressive anti-Moscow posture after 1979 that his successor could offer no sharp break in policy even had he wished to. By the end of his first term, however, the anticommunist true believers were expressing keen disillusionment. Why did a President who attacked the "evil empire" lift the grain embargo that was destabilizing the Soviet economy? When the Polish authorities declared martial law and cracked down on the Solidarity movement, why did not Washington bring the crisis to a boil by declaring Poland in default for failure to pay interest on its debts to Western banks? Why not step up support for "freedom fighters" in Afghanistan and Angola? Why not do more for the Nicaraguan Contras despite the Boland Amendment? Why perpetuate the Democrats' abandonment of Taiwan, even if Peking was a counterweight to Moscow? In the Persian Gulf, why put America's commercial concerns about oil so far ahead of anti-Soviet militance? In Europe, why not try harder to stop the Western subsidy of an oil pipeline that would help the Soviet export economy? Could George Will's quip be true—that the Administration loved commerce more than it loathed communism?

Still, Reagan largely held the support of far-rightists even as they grumbled. His huge reelection sweep was a tribute to his continued coalition-building skills. To be sure, some in the extreme right sat on their hands, but they had no other place to go: the ballot offered no Strom Thurmond, no George Wallace, for whom they could vote in indignation. And certainly Reagan was better than Carter, better even than Nixon. The hardest test of loyalty came after the Iran-Contra revelation late in 1986. While many conservative Republican politicians recoiled in dismay, it was the movement conservatives who rallied to their leader's support.

The Iran-Contra hearings dramatized the price of stances not converted into operating policies. Bizarre initiatives, fouled-up communication, cowboy-style forays, even a little private enterprise for profit, were the colorful parts of the story. But behind it all was a lack of clear guidelines from the White House, even more a lack of knowledge in the Oval Office. The whole affair was a caricature of the incoherence and inconsistency that characterized the Reagan Administration in foreign policy. After eighteen months Alexander Haig had quit as Secretary of State in part because he could not deal with the protective cordon around Reagan, in larger part because he felt unable to "restore unity and coherence" to foreign policy. These qualities continued to elude the Reagan White House—and all the more as it moved into lame-duck status.

THE STRUCTURE OF DISARRAY

"The true Reagan Revolution never had a chance," wrote David Stockman as he reviewed his White House years. "It defied all of the overwhelming forces, interests, and impulses of American democracy. Our Madisonian government of checks and balances, three branches, two legislative houses, and infinitely splintered power is conservative, not radical. It hugs powerfully to the history behind it. It shuffles into the future one step at a time. It cannot leap into revolutions without falling flat on its face."

Stockman had come belatedly to a revelation that had struck many of his fellow practitioners years before. During the Carter presidency, several score former senators, cabinet officers, governors, mayors, women activists, as well as scholars, journalists, and lawyers, had begun meeting from month to month only a few blocks from the White House to assess the health of the American political system. The frustrations and deadlocks that most of these politicians and administrators encountered in merely trying to make the government work rivaled Stockman's more ideological disappointments. Early in 1987, even before the full import of the Iran-Contra scandals was known, this group made public its bleak diagnosis of the present condition and future prospects of the American political system.

As befitted its name—Committee on the Constitutional System—the group concentrated on structural and institutional disorders. In the bicentennial year of 1987 it found serious strains and tensions in the nation's governing processes. The committee pointed to the huge, "unsustainable deficits" that defied the good intentions of legislators and President. It pointed to foreign and national security programs, where focus and consistency were frustrated "by an institutional contest of wills between Presidents and shifting, cross-party coalitions within the Congress." It pointed to presidential-Senate conflict over treaty-making. Over forty pacts submitted to the Senate for ratification since World War II either had been rejected or had never even come to a vote. Among those not voted on were SALT II, treaties on underground nuclear tests, several human rights conventions, and a variety of trade, tax, and environmental pacts. Just as the President's threat of veto often chilled measures in Congress, so the Senate's threat of inaction or negative action could freeze the ratification process.

Other monitors found the disarray outside the constitutional system even more serious than the delay and deadlock within it. They pointed to the falling-off of voter turnout at almost all levels of government, reflecting widespread apathy toward matters political and pervasive distrust of government, which was also indicated in poll after poll. They deplored the dominance of media and personality politics, the power of interest-group politics coupled with the decline of parties, the huge and ever-rising costs of running for office, the endless campaigns that maximized problems of campaign finance while boring the public. Critics noted the hypertrophy of some organs of government in the midst of the weakness and disarray—the rise of the "imperial presidency" and of the equally imperial judiciary.

The 1987 monitors willy-nilly had joined one of the country's oldest vocations—criticizing the system. The Framers' failure in 1787 to add a Bill of Rights had left hundreds of state and local leaders suspicious of the new constitution. The most striking turnabout on the Constitution was conducted by some of the leading Framers when they had to run the government they had planned. After all their denunciations of "party spirit" and their careful engineering of a system of checks and balances designed to thwart popular majorities, Hamilton and Madison and their allies in the 1790s fashioned and captained party factions in Congress and the Administration that unified government to a degree.

During the early 1800s abolitionists attacked the Constitution for countenancing slavery and women leaders condemned it for failing to grant their sex voting and other rights. Southerners flailed it for encouraging centralizing tendencies in the national government, tendencies legitimated by the decisions of Chief Justice John Marshall and his nationalist brethren in cases striking down state interferences with national economic power. The victory of the North in the Civil War and the passage of the Reconstruction amendments consolidated national—and for several decades Republican—predominance in the constitutional system. Early in the new century, as progressives and radicals assessed the suffering and wastage caused by a virtually unregulated system of private enterprise, the Constitution came under attack as a conservative and elitist frame of government still designed to thwart the aspirations of the masses of people.

Progressives during the Theodore Roosevelt and Woodrow Wilson eras managed to democratize the Constitution. Under the Seventeenth Amendment all United States senators would be directly elected by the voters rather than by state legislatures. Many states adopted the initiative, referendum, and recall. Under their own indomitable leadership, women won the right to vote in national elections. Political parties were "purified" and "democratized" by the adoption of reform measures substituting party primaries for nominating conventions, establishing nonpartisan elections in many cities and even states, and eliminating straight-ticket voting that had encouraged less informed voters to ballot for the whole party slate with one check mark. Progressive-era democratization turned out to be a largely middle-class effort whose main result was not purifying politics but curbing the impact of party leadership and party policy on government. Since political parties were often the only "lobby" or "interest group" that low-income workers, immigrants, blacks, domestics, the jobless, the very young, and the very old possessed, the decline of party meant a major alteration in the foundations of government power.

*　　*　　*

For a century and a half the constitutional frame of the government remained intact, like some grand old pyramid towering serenely over the desert storms. It was a tribute to the wisdom of the builders of 1787 that their edifice, despite wear here and erosion there, carried on its main role of institutionalizing the checks and balances among President, two houses of Congress, and the judiciary. In a century when a number of upper houses were abolished or defanged in other Western democracies, the American Senate retained its panoply of powers. The absolute veto of House and Senate on each other remained, as did the qualified vetoes of President and Congress on each other. A Rip Van Winkle returning to Washington a century after the Capitol was built and proceeding from the White House along Pennsylvania Avenue to Capitol Hill, would have found the same several branches, separated from one another, everything quite in place, just as the Framers had wanted.

Within this structure, however, powers shifted, processes changed, with the ebb and flow of political combat. The presidency had assumed far more massive power than the Framers could have dreamed—and yet had lost control of large sections of the executive branch when regulatory commissions, the Federal Reserve Board, bureaus supported in Congress and the country by special interests, were cut off from supervision by even the most vigilant of Presidents. Even within the Executive Office itself, the President's control was not absolute, as the Iran-Contra revelations disclosed. The Senate held a veto on the rest of the government but still was subject to internal veto by a few determined filibusterers. The House of Representatives, once a relatively disciplined body under Speakers called "czars," was fragmented by party factions, committee and subcommittee chairpersons, activist staffs, and interest groups and their lobbyists.

Save in war, the Framers' fundamental strategy of government was not harshly tested until the depression years, when the public demanded that the government act. So effective was FDR's masterful combination of moral leadership, indefatigable horse trading, and delicate manipulation that the failure of the New Dealers to end unemployment and rural and urban poverty was not fully recognized. It was only after World War II, when analysts compared the limited economic success of the New Deal with the massive wartime improvement in employment, wages, public housing, nutrition, that scholars and practitioners proposed changes to strengthen the institutional linkages between President and Congress: simultaneous election of President and all legislators; a joint executive and legislative cabinet to set policy; a broadening of the impeachment power; Senate ratification of treaties by majority rather than two-thirds vote.

Two hundred years earlier the Founding Fathers had not only framed proposals far more bold and sweeping than these; they had written them into a constitution and then prevailed on suspicious but open-minded grass-roots leaders to adopt them. Politicians, scholars, and journalists largely ignored the proposals of the mid-twentieth century "re-framers" or greeted them with hostility and ridicule.

But some critics responded to would-be reformers with analysis rather than anger, challenging the reformers' basic assumption that constitutional checks and balances impeded good government. "There are two fundamental arguments for a constitutional system of separate institutions sharing powers: It helps preserve liberty and it slows the pace of political change," wrote political scientist James Q. Wilson. "Those arguments are as valid today as they were in 1787." The interplay of conflicting leaders might bring slower, more incremental progress, but it would be safer and sounder.

Was there a better way—some means of shaping a more unified, effective, and responsible government that would not open the Pandora's box of constitutional alteration? A group of political scientists, meeting in the late 1940s, had urged in effect that Americans return to the party system that the "party framers"—not only Madison and Hamilton but Jefferson, Jackson, Van Buren, and later the great Republican party leaders—had shaped in the century after the founding. Their report, "Toward a More Responsible Two-Party System," proposed some significant institutional changes: stronger national party organization in the form of a top governing council of fifty party and electoral leaders; a biennial national convention; a more representative national committee and more cohesive and disciplined House and Senate parties based on a combination of stronger leadership and democratic decision making by caucuses.

These party proposals met much the same response as had schemes for constitutional modernization: hostility, derision, inattention, along with some scholarly analysis. While the report had some impact on the thinking of journalists, it largely lay neglected both by politicians and by academics. Proposals for party change during the 1960s and 1970s took an entirely different direction: proportional representation of women, young people, and minorities in the selection of Democratic party convention delegates and other devices to "democratize" the Democracy, in the spirit of party reform.

Was it possible to have both strong parties and democratic parties? A number of state Democratic parties, such as those in Iowa, Minnesota, and Massachusetts, combined participatory, caucus-based local structures with good organization and leadership at the state level. Nationally the Republicans liberalized a bit some internal party processes and urged state parties to bring in more women, minority persons, the old and the young, and "heritage groups." The GOP also modernized its fund-raising and promotional activities, which helped bring the Republicans their stunning presidential victories of 1980 and 1984.

For some years "constitution modernizers" and "party renewers" pursued their separate paths. Each group in its own way sought to outwit the Framers—to pull together the government branches that the Constitution put asunder. The modernizers would do so by modifying the constitutional checks and balances, the renewers by building party ties that would bind President and Congress, House and Senate, despite the checks and balances. Party renewers contended that constitutional modernization, desirable though it might be, would never occur because the American people would oppose any major tampering with the sacred document. Constitution modernizers replied that strong enough party bridges could never be built over the wide constitutional chasms that separated legislators and executives.

During the 1980s the two groups bridged their own chasm to a considerable degree. Constitution modernizers recognized that they could not outwit the Framers unless they used the Framers' own strategy. If the essence of the checks and balances was to seat President, senators, and representatives in separate and rival constituencies, then the antidote was to build a nationwide two-party constituency so that the leaders of the winning party could govern with the support of their partisans across the nation. If conflict among branches of the government could be transformed into conflict between a government party and a "loyal opposition" party, the former could expect to have considerable control over policy, at least until the next presidential election.

Party renewers, for their part, came increasingly to recognize that the two major parties had become so infirm that they could never revive on their own, even to the level of strength they had enjoyed in the nineteenth century. Present-day parties needed artificial stimulation—and if institutional checks and balances had tended to fragment the parties, then knitting the government together organizationally or structurally might in turn unify the parties.

After many a summit conference, constitution and party renewers agreed on a "minimal" program: granting representatives four-year terms concurrent with the presidential, thus abolishing the "unrepresentative" midterm election; granting senators eight-year concurrent terms so that President, representatives, and senators would take office together and thus provide the basis for teamwork; permitting members of Congress to sit in the cabinet without giving up their congressional seats; replacing the two-thirds treaty requirement in the Senate with a simple majority-rule requirement in both chambers; broadening the impeachment power so that Presidents could be removed not only for malfeasance but also for losing the confidence of both parties in Congress and in the nation; strengthening national parties, especially in their opposition role; and, perhaps most important of all, establishing the foundations of party leadership unity at the grass roots by allowing voters to choose between party slates for federal offices and "vote the party ticket."

The American people as a whole were supremely uninterested in these proposals. Most leaders, having risen to office under the existing system, were reluctant to junk it. Bold thinking about radical institutional reform was as rare in the 1980s as it had been rife in the 1780s. Two hundred years later it was still hard to outthink or outperform the Framers.

* * *

As the last barrage of star bombs lighted up the Philadelphia skies in September 1987, Americans concluded months of unbridled constitution worship during that bicentennial year. It was clear that they honored the Founding Fathers in every regard—with one exception. They were in no mood to emulate the Framers' willingness to stand back from the existing constitution in 1787—the Articles of Confederation—and not only criticize but alter and in the end abolish it. During the flush times of the late 1980s Americans would only celebrate the Constitution, not criticize or even cerebrate about it.

The reason was not only Constitution worship. Americans had an instinctive feeling, buttressed by years of surviving crises, that in a pinch their ultimate safeguard lay not in constitutions and parties but in the President. It was to the White House that they had turned for reassurance, inspiration, consolation, explanation, drama. FDR's forthright actions during the Hundred Days of 1933, his later responses to the Allies' need for war aid, Truman's quick action after war broke out in Korea, Kennedy's mobilization of the whole executive branch to force Big Steel to roll back a price increase—these and countless other incidents fed the image of the President as western sheriff riding to the rescue.

Why go through the painful effort of changing the system when the law-and-order men were so easily available? But did the lawmen truly stand for law and order? Watergate, of course, revealed the opposite, but the cast of characters seemed so bizarre that defenders of the presidency could dismiss it as an aberration. Washington insiders knew of myriad other White House misadventures and cover-ups, but it remained for the Iran-Contra revelations to dramatize the extent to which the President—and hence the people—had lost control of the presidency.

The popular idea of presidential abuse of power was of a Nixon or Johnson seeking to seize control, but their reasons for power grabs may have lain more in presidential frustration than in presidential feistiness. In many cases, the White House acted because the system as a whole seemed paralyzed in the face of crisis, whether depression, Nazi aggression, civil rights violations, the "communist menace," or hostage seizures. Under such pressure the White House could become a "rogue presidency"—an unsaddled beast, unable to control itself, on the rampage through the wilderness of the American political system. Iran-Contra and all the other excesses and usurpations demonstrated that this beast might be too hard to tame, too dangerous to ride.

Hence Americans had come to rely on the judiciary both to tame the presidency and to take leadership on its own. With neither the Congress nor the President able or willing to act on civil rights, the Supreme Court had moved into the vacuum, most notably with its epochal *Brown* decision of 1954. Since that time—and even after LBJ and his Democratic Congress put through the great civil rights measures of 1964 and 1965—the Court had continued to make policy in the most sensitive areas: First Amendment liberties, women's rights, the environment, affirmative action, criminal procedure, privacy.

The resurgence of the "imperial judiciary," of "government by judiciary," of the Supreme Court as super-legislature, intensified a debate that had proceeded off and on ever since John Marshall's assertion of judicial power in 1803. During Marshall's leadership of the Court, champions of states' rights denounced its nationalizing thrust and its government by judiciary. They complained less of judicial power, and antislavery leaders complained more, with the arrival of the Taney Court and the enunciation of Dred Scott in 1857, in which the Court for the first time vetoed a major substantive act of Congress. The course of the debate over the next century demonstrated that in judicial politics as much as legislative and electoral, much depended on whose ox was gored.

The quickest flip-flop occurred during the 1930s and 1940s. As the High Court dismantled part of the New Deal in 1935 and 1936, New Dealers denounced the "nine old men" and their power, while conservatives toasted "judicial independence." Within a decade or two the right was denouncing the "Roosevelt Court" and its reach, while liberals exulted in the Court's upholding of New Deal and Fair Deal measures and their implementation—and welcomed especially its intrusion into desegregation and other civil rights areas. The stakes in this legal, political, and ideological battle became much higher as the judiciary moved into wider and wider policy fields and as claimants turned to the courts for relief because they could not win action from the legislative and executive branches.

It was clear that conservatives would have to wait for another shift of the party pendulum before they could hope for a switch in Supreme Court philosophy. Eisenhower had not been much help with his appointment of Earl Warren as chief justice—a choice the President later called his biggest mistake—but Ike after all was a moderate Republican in rightists' eyes, and hence prone to errors of this sort. With Nixon's election in 1968 and reelection in 1972, conservatives could hope for a return to judicial sanity after the excesses of Warren and his brethren. And Nixon came through with the appointments of two dependably conservative jurists in William H. Rehnquist and, above all, Warren E. Burger, whom he named chief justice in 1969 after Warren's resignation. At last the Court would be following the election returns.

But it was not all that simple. For one thing, the Burger Court harbored several holdovers from previous Administrations, including the leader of the liberal faction, William L. Brennan—another Eisenhower appointee— and Thurgood Marshall. No judge worthy of presidential appointment and Senate confirmation, moreover, was likely to tread a narrow ideological line, whatever his background. Once faced with concrete cases, the justices were constrained by constitutional heritage, judicial precedent, decisions of lower courts coming up on appeal, the exchanges in their own semiweekly conferences, the attitudes of their clerks fresh out of law school, and above all by the complexity and intractability of cases before them. Nixon's two other appointees showed the influence of office: Lewis F. Powell proved a consummate centrist, becoming in the later years of the Burger Court a crucial and unpredictable swing vote in close decisions, and Harry A. Blackmun often joined the liberals, casting the deciding vote—and writing the opinion—in *Roe* v. *Wade.*

So the Burger Court brought no judicial counterrevolution. Rather it followed a meandering middle way as it mediated among issues. Thus on school desegregation the High Court in 1973 held that the Denver school board had practiced a policy of segregation in choosing sites for school buildings and in its pupil transfer plans, but the Court reflected widespread public opposition to busing when in 1974 it rejected a broad plan to integrate the overwhelmingly black school systems of metropolitan Detroit with fifty-three overwhelmingly white suburban school districts, and in 1976 vetoed a federal district court's plan for Pasadena that barred any school from having a majority of black students. In a 1978 case, *Regents of the University of California* v. *Bakke,* the Burger Court struck down a medical school quota system that allotted a fixed number of admissions for minority applicants. Applying the Fourteenth Amendment in this first great test of "reverse discrimination," the Court held that Allan Bakke, a white applicant whose test scores were superior to those of some of the minority applicants accepted by the medical school, had been denied his right to equal protection. But while disapproving the school's "explicit racial classification" and its fixed quotas, the Court acknowledged that the State had "a legitimate and substantial interest" in ameliorating or eliminating "the disabling effects of identified discrimination." In the thorny field of discrimination against women the Court generally was protective of women's rights in specific cases but refused to adopt a rigorous test that would deem gender classification, like racial classification, as inherently suspect, unless it served an overriding State interest.

Expected to offer a consistently law-and-order interpretation of the Fourth Amendment, the High Court cautiously picked its way between upholding and vetoing state law-enforcement procedures. The Court, perhaps recognizing that for millions of American commuters their car as well as their home was now their castle, threaded an especially narrow course on searches of vehicles. "While the justices gave state police broad latitude to conduct auto searches," students of the Court wrote, "they prohibited warrantless interrogation of motorists to check driver's licenses and registrations without probable cause suggesting possible criminal activity. If the Burger Court permitted police to search the passenger compartment of a car stopped for a traffic violation and to seize evidence subsequently used to prosecute for violation of narcotics laws, it also prohibited the search of a vehicle's luggage compartment." Between the back seat and the luggage compartment lay a narrow line indeed.

In other areas the Burger Court also took a mixed position. On protection against self-incrimination, it continued the Warren Court's *Miranda* doctrine but refused to broaden it. Its ruling in *Roe* v. *Wade* was a victory for women's rights, but the Court afterward sustained denials of public funding for abortions. It protected or even enlarged free speech in some cases but narrowed it in others, as in cases of pornography or of leafleting or picketing in privately owned shopping malls.

Rejecting such eclecticism, the Republican right greeted with new hope Burger's decision to quit the Court in 1985 to head the nation's official bicentennial commission, and with even greater hope Reagan's elevation of Rehnquist to Burger's seat and his choice of two associate justices with impeccable conservative credentials. A minor consequence of conservative satisfaction was that the broad issue of the Court's power to invalidate laws on a variety of grounds—one of the most important and potentially explosive issues of American democracy—was hardly touched upon during the cerebrations of the 1987 bicentennial. Instead, oceans of ink and flights of oratory were devoted to a lesser though equally fascinating question, original intent.

This question was propelled into the forensic arena when Reagan's Attorney General, Edwin Meese III, calling for a "Jurisprudence of Original Intention," intimated that his chief would pick only judges whose applications of the Constitution would reflect the intentions of the Framers. Law school professors, historians, political scientists, and Supreme Court justices pounced on this dubious notion, proved conclusively that it was wrong historically—and then wondered whether they had won a glorious intellectual victory on a side issue. The scenario was repeated when Reagan proposed Robert H. Bork for the High Court—the Senate foes won the debate over original intent, handily vetoed Bork, but were left with a Pyrrhic victory after the President found an almost equally conservative substitute.

The central issue of judicial power was also one of intellectual leadership. In their meandering course, the Burger Court, and for a time at least the Rehnquist Court, appeared deceptively eclectic, moderate, practical. But that course concealed a lack of jurisprudential and philosophical coherence in the very heart and brain of the federal judiciary. At best the Reagan Court was marking time; at worst it was losing time, failing to develop clear and consistent operational standards related to the nation's values, storing up trouble for the future, its incoherence rivaling what the

Iran-Contra hearings revealed in the presidency, and with perhaps equally grave consequences.

In the late 1980s the structure of government remained intact, the balances in the old clock still operating, the springs and levers still in place. A Republican President and a Democratic Congress nicely checked each other; House and Senate held an absolute veto power over each other; the Supreme Court had an all but final veto over the two political branches. Inside these separated institutions lay political and intellectual conflicts that contained the seeds of enormous change and potential crisis.

REALIGNMENT?: WAITING FOR LEFTY

For a century and a half the two main parties had proceeded down the political mainstream, rolling along with the inevitability of the Mississippi. But just as storm and flood had periodically roiled the placid waters of that river of American history, so political movements and ideological tempests had disrupted the steady flow of two-party politics. And American politicians, like the people living along the riverbank, knew that the flood would come again—but they did not know when.

Social protests and political movements had risen and fallen with some regularity over time. Before the Civil War abolitionism had challenged both Democrats and Whigs and the easy accommodations they had made with slavery. In the 1890s aroused agrarians had moved into the Democratic party, even wresting the presidential nomination from the centrist Clevelandites. In the 1930s several streams of protest had coalesced as desperate farmers, urban reformers, western progressives had taken a dominant role in the Democracy. In the 1970s and 1980s conservatives of varied stripes had merged with Republican party regulars to put Ronald Reagan into office and keep him there.

These movements might appear to have erupted with the suddenness of a spring freshet and then subsided as quickly. Each protest, in fact, had sources deep within the politics and morality of its period. Outrage over slavery had aroused the consciences of men and women in both the Democratic and Whig parties, triggered third-party forays such as that of the Liberty party, cut deep divisions not only between parties and between major interests but within them, and convulsed the entire political system by the 1860s. The lightninglike capture of the Democratic party by the Bryanites in 1896 was the product of years of intense agrarian unrest, western greenback and silver movements, organizational efforts by the Farmers' Alliance leaders and rank and file, years of populist agitation, the devastatingly low farm prices and other hard times of the nineties. Fighting Bob La Follette's Progressive party of 1924 and Al Smith's presidential candidacy of 1928, followed by the farm movements of the great depression, helped pave the way for Roosevelt's presidency and for the New Deal expansion of both the political appeal and the social philosophy of the Democracy. And on the American right both economic and evangelical leaders had fought a long battle, first winning and then losing with Goldwater in 1964, flirting with George Wallace and other elements North and South hostile to civil rights, and losing once again with Reagan in the GOP nomination fight of 1976, before achieving their breakthrough in the 1980s.

Thus movement politics had collided and combined with party politics throughout American history. Like their counterparts in other countries, American social protest movements were unruly, untidy, and unpredictable in effect, but they displayed continuities and similarities in their very dynamics. The pattern was clear, even dramatic: these movements emerged out of economic stress and social tension and erupted in conflict, often violent. After a time they dominated political debate, overshadowed more traditional issues, cut across existing lines of party cleavage, polarized groups and parties. The immediate test of success was whether the movement could force one major party or both of them to embrace its cause. The test of long-run success was whether the movement left the whole party system altered and, even more, left the political landscape transformed.

The great transformations that had occurred, in the antecedents of such critical elections as those of 1860 and 1896, and the series from 1928 to 1936, have been studied in great detail by exceptionally able historians and political scientists. The main interest was usually in the rise and fall of parties, since their fate in elections could be so easily measured. But party change contained a paradox—despite all the turmoil the nation had undergone, the Democratic party had existed ever since the 1830s and the Republican party since the 1850s. These staid old parties had entered and left office like Box and Cox but had continued to move down the political mainstream, capsizing and sinking third parties in the process.

Hence on closer inspection, the critical question was not so much party realignment as party reconstitution. The most significant case of this kind of change in the twentieth century was the shift of the Democratic party under Roosevelt, Truman, Kennedy, and Johnson. Behind FDR's leadership the Democracy became much more of an urban, trade union, ethnic, and poor people's party, but—partly because of Roosevelt's need of support from internationalists of all stripes during the war years—it retained its old and solid base in the white South. Truman's bold civil rights stance, Kennedy's Catholicism and growing commitment to civil rights, and LBJ's comprehensive civil rights program accelerated the reconstitution of the party. Blacks forsook their ancient allegiance to the Republican party of Lincoln and flocked to the Democracy; white southern Democrats forsook the party of Grover Cleveland and Woodrow Wilson to move first toward third-party ventures and then toward their old partisan adversaries, the Republicans.

For Southerners, switching parties was not easy. Their leaders in particular were "in a bind with the national Democratic party," as Republican Representative Trent Lott of Mississippi noted. "If they subscribe to the national Democrat party's principles, platform, they are clearly going to alienate the overwhelming majority of the white people in Mississippi." If they stayed with the national party's base, "they wind up with blacks and labor and your more liberal, social-oriented" Democrats. "Put those groups together and they are a minority in Mississippi." So Republican party leaders were ready at the front gate to welcome the Southerners. The Goldwater-Reagan party, having ousted the liberal Rockefeller wing, was prepared to usher southern ex-Democratic leaders into the inner councils of the purified GOP. Congressional converts like South Carolina senator Strom Thurmond were soon making Republican party policy, and convert John Connally of Texas even ran for the Republican presidential nomination.

The test of this reconstitution lay in the political grass roots of the South, and here the shift was dramatic. The percentage of white Southerners identifying themselves as Republicans rose eight points between 1979 and 1984 and then jumped an astonishing ten points further the following year, a movement which public-opinion analyst Everett Carll Ladd saw as "an almost unprecedentedly rapid shift in underlying party loyalties across a large and diverse social group."

* * *

By the late 1980s the Republican party had reconstituted itself as the clearly conservative party of the nation. Ronald Reagan presided as a conservative; all the Republican presidential aspirants of 1988 endorsed his Administration and bore, in one way or another, the Reagan stamp. Reagan Republicans had conducted "half a realignment," in popular terms. They posed a challenge that the Democratic party leadership was failing to meet as the 1988 election approached.

That challenge was as much philosophical and ideological as political and electoral. The GOP's rightward tack appeared to leave a huge unoccupied space in the middle of the political spectrum. To all the Democratic presidential aspirants save Jesse Jackson this space was an enticement. How logical it appeared for Democrats to shift some of their appeal to the center while holding their traditional support on the left, and forge a moderate-centrist-liberal coalition much like the winning North-South alliance the national Democracy had maintained for decades before that strategy crumbled in the face of the black revolt. But in a battle against conservative Republicans, they could not talk centrism without being accused of the sin of "me-tooism." And me-tooism was hardly the answer to the Democratic dilemma. "If American voters are in a conservative mood," Arthur Schlesinger, Jr., wrote, "they will surely choose the real thing and not a Democratic imitation."

So what the Democrats talked was not conservatism or even centrism but pragmatism. The American Enterprise Institute political analyst William Schneider, after sitting in on a 1986 board meeting of a candidate's think tank—it happened to be Gary Hart's—noted that certain words kept coming up: *parameter, interactive, consensus, instrumental, modernize, transition, dialogue, strategic, agenda, investment, decentralize, empowering, initiative, and entrepreneur.* But the word of the day, he noted, was *pragmatic.* "Be pragmatic in all things," the group seemed to be saying. "Be not ideological." The Democrats' selection of Massachusetts Governor Michael Dukakis as their presidential nominee in 1988, and his choice in turn of Texas Senator Lloyd Bentsen as his running mate, met this test.

What did they mean by pragmatism? Whether the candidates used the term or not, it was clear they meant what was practical, realistic, sensible— *what worked.* But what was the test of workability? By what values was workability measured? Into this forbidding "ideological" land the candidates were reluctant to venture.

What politicians mean by workability is usually what promotes their immediate candidacies, rather than an ultimate cause or creed. Thus was pragmatism degraded into the most self-serving kind of doctrine, a pragmatism that would not have recognized its intellectual ancestry. Indeed, presidential candidates in the 1980s, especially the Democrats, were embracing their brand of pragmatism so enthusiastically as to make it into a doctrine, even an ideology—anathema to Charles Peirce and John Dewey.

To a degree, pragmatism was a convenient way to avoid labeling. Did it conceal an agenda? "Pragmatic," Schneider noted, had become "this season's Democratic code word of choice for market-oriented, rather than government-oriented, solutions." For most of the Democratic candidates, it seemed, pragmatism meant some form of market capitalism. Then how much of an ideological gap separated them from Reaganism? The leaders of the Democratic liberal-left answered "too little" and proposed a clearly contrasting alternative.

That alternative was a movement strategy as against a strategy of mainstream and marketplace. It was in key respects an old-fashioned idea: if social protest movements had been vital to the renewal and redirection of political parties in the past, and if the needs and aspirations of large sectors of American society remained unmet, then the Democrats must make their mightiest effort to reach out to movement leaders and rank and file. These, in some combination, were its natural and traditional constituency— women, peace groups, blacks, union labor, small farmers, ethnics, youth, the poor, and the jobless.

However familiar a political alliance this was for the Democrats, the question in the late 1980s was whether the partners—party regulars and movement activists—were ready for one another. The Democratic party leadership hardly appeared ready for bold initiatives. That leadership, indeed, had cut its structural ties with movement activists when, earlier in the 1980s, the Democrats' regular midterm policy conference had been discontinued. That midterm conference, a grand assembly of both Democratic party regulars and delegates representing women and minority groups, had been noisy, expensive, untidy, unpredictable, sometimes a bit embarrassing. But it had also linked the party establishment to creative and dynamic electoral groups; by abandoning it, the leadership cut off some of its own intellectual and political lifeblood. The presidential aspirants, focusing on their own campaigns, could not be expected to restore the connection. Several of them in fact were founders of the Democratic Leadership Council, a centrist group that made no secret of its intention to rescue the Democracy from control by "extremists" and "ideologues"— the very groups that had lost their footing at the midterm conference. Michael Dukakis, in choosing Lloyd Bentsen as his running mate and shunning liberal-left stands on tough issues like taxes, presented the moderate face of the Democratic party to the nation. In Massachusetts, however, he had won elections in part because of his skill at uniting party regulars with movement activists.

Nationwide the activists for their part had decidedly mixed desires and capacities to marry or remarry the Democratic party. The movements themselves were divided organizationally. Peace activists were morselized into tens of thousands of local groups individually or cooperatively conducting local rallies, demonstrations, and protest action. Women's groups had the same types of divisions along with a particular inhibiting factor— many women's organizations, especially the large and influential League of Women Voters, were nonpartisan and hence barred from forming organizational links with the Democrats. Blacks were overwhelmingly Democratic in their voting but proudly separate in most political endeavors. Some activists in all these movements shunned party politics as a matter of principle, on the ground that Democratic party leaders had betrayed, sold out, neglected, forgotten, or otherwise mistreated them over the years. Other movement leaders spurned any kind of conventional politics at all, preferring to put their energies into street activism.

Then there were the "young," tens of millions of them. It was calculated that by the late 1980s those born from 1946 onward, in the baby boom, would comprise around 60 percent of the electorate. But this was a demographic "cohort," not a voting bloc. Some had become the yuppies who were distinguished mainly by having no distinctive political attitudes beyond a vague and ineffectual anti-establishmentarianism. Historian Robert McElvaine, however, detected among the immense number of baby-boomers a group that was not upwardly mobile, affluent, or typically professional. "During the 1950s and '60s, the average American's inflation-adjusted income increased by 100 per cent between the ages of twenty-five and thirty-five," McElvaine noted. "For those who were twenty-five in 1973, however, their real income had risen by only 16 per cent when they reached thirty-five in 1983." Because many of these young people had lived the hard-pressed lives about which New Jersey rocker Bruce Springsteen sang, McElvaine called them the "Springsteen Coalition."

Inspired by childhood memories of King and Kennedy, disillusioned by Watergate and Vietnam and much that followed, these young persons retained both a sense of grievance and a streak of idealism that might surface in their voting in the 1990s. But would they vote? Or would they contribute more than their share to the steadily declining voter turnout of the late twentieth century? The same question could be asked of the protest movements that made up the Democratic party's natural constituency. Movements that had supplied zest and fresh blood to party politics now appeared passive, dispirited. They were part of the impasse of the system, not solvents of it.

*   *   *

If movements as well as parties were fixed in the immobility of American politics, was it likely that Americans might experience incremental, brokerage politics under transactional leadership for years to come? Or was it possible that they would enter another period of social protest, movement politics, and major party transformation and bring on a critical realignment? The answer would turn on the quality of leadership and the character of its followership.

Neither the movement nor the party leadership of the nation gave much promise in the late 1980s of moving Americans out of their political immobility. Leaders were scarce whose capacities could compare with those of the great leaders of the past—with Dr. Townsend's skill in mobilizing the elderly in the 1930s, with the kindling power of John L. Lewis or the labor statesmanship of Walter Reuther, with the intellectual and political audacity of the early leaders of the women's movement, or with the galvanizing power and charisma of King and his fellow protesters. As for the Democratic party, virtually all the candidates for President—even Jesse Jackson—exhibited great skill at working within the system. Few of these "pragmatists" hinted at a potential for transcending the system, mastering it, transforming it if necessary. To be sure, any one of the candidates might display great leadership capacities upon attaining office, as Franklin Roosevelt had done. But FDR had not had to go through the modern presidential recruitment process that tested candidates more for their ability to campaign than for their capacity to govern.

Was there no alternative, then, to politics as usual? One possible development that could "break the system wide open" was an economic catastrophe of the magnitude of the great depression, or at least of a severe recession following a stock market plunge like that of "Black Monday" in October 1987. Some liberals and Democrats were predicting such an event, some even forecast a likely time of onset, but the prospect that the nation had to wait for a catastrophe in order to take actions that might have prevented it seemed as wretched as the notion that the world would have to go through a nuclear crisis before it would take the necessary steps to forestall nuclear war.

Some kind of desperate crisis might be necessary, however, for liberal-left Democrats to employ the most ambitious and radical means of opening up the system, a mobilization of the tens of millions of Americans not participating in electoral politics. By the time of the 1984 election the number of voters, even in the presidential race, where the participation rate was much higher than for lower offices, had fallen spectacularly—to roughly half the potential electorate. Americans, who like to view their country as something of a model of democracy, had the poorest voter-turnout record of all the industrial democracies. Aside from the occasional laments of editorial writers, however, Americans did not appear unduly disturbed by this travesty of democracy.

Democrats on the left had special reasons to be concerned, for the poor, the jobless, and the ethnics were disproportionately absent from the polling place. These no-shows represented a huge array of constituencies that the Democrats were failing to tap. A strenuous effort by a national voter registration group helped persuade some states to relax the registration barriers that had kept some people from voting and to allow the use of government offices as registration places, but even in those states turnout remained low. The root difficulty was that many low-income, less educated nonvoters did not see the point of voting—for them electoral participation in America was a middle-class game which they did not care to join.

It would take rare leadership to overcome their ignorance and aliena-tion, to attract them to the polls, to enable them to vote their deepest, most authentic, and abiding needs. Aside from Jesse Jackson, who demonstrated a remarkable talent for mobilizing low-income blacks and whites in his 1988 presidential primary campaign, this kind of leadership was missing, at least on the left, in the America of the late 1980s. Such leadership could not be manufactured—it emerged out of a people's heritage, values, aspi-rations, and took its color and energy from conflict. Great leadership historically had never been possible except in conditions of ideological battle. Such conflict was not in sight in a nation whose liberal leaders, or aspirants to leadership, appeared wholly content with a politics of modera-tion, centrism, and consensus.

A REBIRTH OF LEADERSHIP?

As the 1988 presidential nominating races got underway more than a year before the first primary, it appeared unlikely that one election could break open the party and the constitutional gridlock that gripped the American political system. From the very start the presidential candidates were entangled in one of the worst leadership recruitment systems in the Western world. The presidential primary not only pitted them against fellow party leaders in endless and acrimonious combat; it forced them to mobilize personal followings that after the combat might persist as disper-sive and even destructive forces within the parties and within their Ad-ministration. It was not surprising that the governor of a large state, such as New York's Mario Cuomo, would reject this process whereas fifty-six years earlier Franklin D. Roosevelt had found it possible to perform as governor and to campaign for the presidency in the much less demanding nominating procedure of 1932. How defensible was a selection process that choked off the recruitment of some of the best and busiest leaders?

In other Western democracies the parties served not only as recruiting agencies for leaders but as training grounds for leadership. Party mentors identified, coached, and promoted promising young men and women—sometimes in actual party schools. By and large, the more doctrinal the party, the more effective its recruitment and training programs. It was only when the GOP became a more ideological party that it "engaged in an extensive program of political education for legislative candidates and their managers," John F. Bibby reported. But this effort was exceptional; in this century American parties have been too flaccid, underfinanced, and fragmented to serve as schools of leadership. Other sectors of American society, among them corporations, the military, and government agencies, taught forms of leadership, but these were specialized programs that served the purposes of the organization rather than the broader needs of the general public.

Typically, Americans were trained to be effective politicians—good brokers, manipulators, money raisers, vote winners. Since the very nature of the governmental system, with its rival branches and complex dispersion of power, put a premium on transactional leadership, American politics offered endless play to lawyers and other negotiators and mediators. The system would long ago have collapsed without their capacity to grease the machinery at the connecting points. But what if the machinery was failing anyway? Appeals for creative, transforming leadership were frequent in the 1980s but vain. Such leadership could not be summoned like spirits from the vasty deep.

* * *

When political leaders fail, Americans often turn to the next most available saviors or scapegoats—the educators. The era from Vietnam and Watergate to Iran-Contra generated even more than the usual calls for reforming or revolutionizing the nation's secondary schools and, even more, its colleges and universities. Most of the proposals, dusted off for the latest crisis, embodied the special ideological, professional, or career interests of the reformers—more cross-disciplinary studies, more emphasis on reading the classic writings of the great philosophers from Plato on, strengthening the liberal arts curriculum, and the like. There was much emphasis in the 1980s on teaching and the taught, but significantly less on the teachers. Few of the reformers appeared to comprehend that teachers were the people's first and most influential set of leaders, as role models, opinion shapers, inspirers, disciplinarians, embodiments of ongoing middle-class, ethnic, and political traditions.

If the public had recognized the central importance of teachers, perhaps proposed reforms would have focused more on these human beings. Or perhaps not, because "reforming" the human beings would have appeared far more difficult and dangerous than manipulating processes or techniques. Still, the quality of the teachers—their competence, breadth of knowledge, intellectual vigor, commitment to the classroom, and professionalism—was far more important than their specific mode of teaching, set of readings, or place in the curriculum.

This centrality of the teacher made all the more crucial and ominous a finding during the "educational crisis" of the 1980s that received little attention at the time compared with the headlines dwelling on superficialities. From a random sample of 2,500 Phi Beta Kappa members and of almost 2,000 Rhodes scholars, Howard R. Bowen and Jack H. Schuster concluded in 1985 that fewer and fewer of the nation's most intellectually promising young people were entering or planning careers in higher education. This finding had the direst implications for the quality of the best kind of teaching as leadership for the half century ahead; and, as the analysis concluded, it was also significant that "the academy, it seems, grows less and less attractive as a house of intellect, as a nurturing and stimulating environment for the gifted and creative."

This finding was widely ignored, perhaps because by implication it called for the most prodigious effort to draw the truly best and brightest of the nation's youth into teaching. The Bowen-Schuster report noted, as had so many earlier findings, that the "quality of working conditions for faculty also has deteriorated markedly over the past decade and a half; less clerical support, overcrowded facilities, outmoded instrumentation, tighter library budgets, and poorly prepared students." No improvement was expected for another decade or so. To overcome these deficiencies in public higher education would call for the kind of clear goals, dependable funding, long-range planning, firm commitment, steady policy making, and persistent follow-through that were so uncommon in American government.

What should good teachers teach? Not what to think but how to think— that is, how to think across a wide span of disciplines, values, institutions, and policies in a highly pluralistic, fragmented culture. Educators based their claim to priority ultimately on the proposition that the products of liberal arts or humanities programs, as exemplified by Rhodes scholars and Phi Betas, had shown such intellectual grasp of a variety of subjects as to equip them as political leaders to deal with the diverse and continually shifting problems they would face as leaders.

But could any group—even an educational elite—cope with the combination of political fragmentation and intellectual disarray that threatened the American future?

The intellectual disorder had manifested itself during the past half century in the loose collection of hazy ideas that passed as the American idea-system; in the flowery platitudes of candidates, whether about communism or the family or the deficit or poverty; in the once famous New York School of art that fractured into several New York schools and later into an endless succession of styles; in the hopes for a unified social science declining in the face of ever-multiplying subdisciplines and specializations; in the disintegration of the humanities into a "heap or jumble" that reminded Allan Bloom of the old Paris flea market.

* * *

A century and a half ago Tocqueville had observed that science could be divided into three parts: the most abstract and theoretical principles; general truths derived from pure theory but leading "by a straight and short road to practical results"; and methods of application and execution. On the practical matters, he noted, "Americans always display a clear, free, original, and inventive power of mind," but few concerned themselves with the theoretical and abstract. On the other hand, Tocqueville said, American orators and writers were given to speaking in the most inflated, grandiloquent style about vast topics.

The American's "ideas," Tocqueville summed up, were either extremely minute and clear or extremely general and vague: "what lies between is a void." The idea of freedom was his best example. It is the best example today of the "Tocquevillian void."

Of all the central ideas in the American experiment the concept of freedom had been the most glorious, compelling, and persistent—and also the most contrarily defined, trivialized, and debased. The Declaration of Independence of 1776 was essentially a paean to liberty, a term that has been long used as an equivalent to freedom. Eleven years later the Constitution would secure "the Blessings of Liberty to ourselves and our Posterity" and in 1791 the French Constitution, responding to the same Enlightenment values, incorporated a Declaration of Rights asserting that "men are born and live free and equal as regards their rights." Within seventy-five years "freedom" had become so evocative, and yet so hazy, as to be invoked by Union soldiers "shouting the battle cry of freedom" against slavery, by Confederate troops "shouting the battle cry of freedom" against Yankee oppression, and by a black regiment singing, "We are going out of slavery; we're bound for freedom's light." During the past century speakers and writers across the entire political spectrum, from American communists to the extreme right, have invoked the term. It was rare to hear a major speech by Reagan, or by the Democratic aspirants of 1988, that did not appeal to freedom or liberty or their equivalents. It was even rarer to hear them spell out what they meant, except in more banalities, shibboleths, and stereotypes.

Did it matter that Tocqueville's void still loomed toward the end of the twentieth century—that orators continued to "bloviate" and millions of men and women went about their minute, day-to-day decision-making with no linkage between the two? There would be no practical will to action, the philosopher Charles Frankel wrote, unless value judgments were made—and made explicit. If there was to be conversion of social theory into social action on a scale large enough to shape the whole society, a social philosophy that explored "the basic choices available" and offered "an ordered scheme of preferences for dealing with them" was indispensable.

Any one of our animating ideas was complex enough—had to be complex to be so attractive to so many different minds. Liberty was the prime example. A word that appears on our coins, on the marble walls of public monuments like the Lincoln and Jefferson memorials, in virtually every stanza of the great national anthems, had to resonate appealingly through many classes, regions, and occupations. But what did it mean, as a guide to action? Only negative liberty—freedom from arbitrary regulation by public or private power wielders? Or also positive liberty—the freedom to take purposeful steps, often in social and economic areas, to realize one's goals? Both freedoms could be left at first to the private sphere, but as society became more complex and interrelated, the two liberties increasingly impinged on each other and on the public realm. This happened most dramatically with slavery, and led to one of Lincoln's wisest reflections. "The world has never had a good definition of the word liberty," he declared in 1864, "and the American people, just now, are much in want of one. We all declare for liberty; but in using the same word we do not all mean the same thing. With some the word liberty may mean for each man to do as he pleases with himself, and the product of his labor; while with others the same word may mean for some men to do as they please with other men. . . ."

Events expanded the concept of liberty, and further complicated it. Franklin Roosevelt not only took the lead in defending the Western democratic definition of freedom against Adolf Hitler's perversion of it, but in proclaiming the Four Freedoms he nicely balanced the negative liberties of speech and religion from arbitrary public and private action against the positive liberties of national military security and personal economic security. Later, contending that "necessitous men are not free men," he said, "We have accepted, so to speak, a second Bill of Rights under which a new basis of security and prosperity can be established for all—regardless of station, race, or creed." The President then listed a set of positive economic rights that would constitute the agenda for liberal Democratic Administrations and candidacies in the years ahead.

The struggle over negative liberty—personal protection against authority—attracted some of the most impressive intellectual leadership in the history of the nation. The philosophical heritage of individual liberty, the Jeffersonian and Lincolnian defenses of this supreme value, the fervent conservative vindication of property rights, the vigilance of the American Civil Liberties Union and like-minded groups, the presence on the High Court of justices with the commitment of Louis Brandeis, Harlan Stone, Felix Frankfurter, Hugo Black, William Douglas, Earl Warren, the zeal for civil liberties on the part of appellate judges such as Learned Hand of New York—all of these had variously combined to establish the federal judiciary as, on the whole, the prime definer as well as protector of civil liberties. The enunciation by the High Court during the 1940s of the "preferred position" doctrine, holding that First Amendment freedoms deserved the highest priority in the hierarchy of constitutional protections and presuming to be unconstitutional any law that on its face limited such freedoms, further insulated individual liberty against arbitrary interference.

Still, civil libertarians could not be complacent as the Bill of Rights bicentennial neared. The judiciary's record since the founding had been uneven. And when, in 1987, the Chief Justice of the United States, along with the latest Reagan appointee, joined in a minority vote to sustain the constitutionality of a Louisiana statute requiring the teaching in public schools of the creationist theory of human origin, civil libertarians had to assess the implications for the future of appointments by a series of conservative Presidents.

*　　*　　*

"All men are created equal." If the Court had helped fill Tocqueville's void in the area of civil liberty, the same could not be said about the record of the nation's intellectual and political leadership in meeting the flat commitment that Americans of 1776 had made to the principle of equality except for slaves and women. This failure was understandable in part because the realization of economic and social equality was intellectually an even more daunting venture than the protection of individual liberty. But even the most essential preliminary questions had not been answered: What kind of equality was the issue—political, social, economic, gender, racial, or other? Guaranteed by what private or public agency, if any? Equality for whom—blacks as well as whites? Equality when? This last question was of crucial importance to low-income Americans long assured that their opportunity would come if only they waited long enough. It had taken almost a century for the nation to take the primitive step of making child labor illegal.

The intellectual confusion over equality was sharply reflected in the ancient debate between equality of condition and equality of opportunity. It was in part a false debate, for very few Americans wanted absolute or even sweeping equality of condition. But even the sides of the debate were mixed up. In part because Herbert Hoover and other enlightened conservatives had contended that inequality of condition was acceptable as long as all the "runners" had the same place at the starting line, many on the left spurned that kind of equality as brutal capitalist competitiveness.

But in fact equality of opportunity was a most radical doctrine. If the nation actually wanted persons to achieve positions for which their basic potentials of intelligence and character fitted them, then government must be more than a referee at the starting line; it must intervene at every point where existing structures of inequality barred people from realizing those potentials. If the nation wanted to open the way for people to realize their "life chance," then government or some other agency must act early in their lives to help them obtain the motivation, self-assurance, literacy, good health, decent clothes, speech habits, education, job opportunity, self-esteem that would enable them really to compete.

Neither in action nor in analysis did the government fill this Tocquevillian void. Perhaps the political leadership did not wish to, for granting true equality of opportunity would call for innovative social analysis as well as bold and comprehensive governmental action—would call indeed for a program for children's rights rivaling earlier programs for the poor, women, and minorities. Some presidential candidates in 1988 were cautiously discussing such policies as much-expanded child care and paid leaves for parents of newborns, but no Marshall Plan for children was in sight.

The vital need for a set of findings firmly seated in clear and compelling moral principles and linked in turn to explicit policy choices was met, almost miraculously it seemed, in 1984 by the 120-page first draft of the Roman Catholic bishops' "Pastoral Letter on Catholic Social Teachings and the U.S. Economy." The letter was unsparing of American leadership. The level of inequality in income and wealth in the nation was morally unacceptable. "The fulfillment of the basic needs of the poor is of the highest priority. Personal decisions, social policies and power relationships must all be evaluated by their effects on those who lack the minimum necessities of nutrition, housing, education and health care." Again and again the bishops assailed selfishness, consumerism, privilege, avarice, and other ugly characteristics of American society. Speaking from their hearts trained in compassion and their heads trained in moral reasoning, from their pastoral closeness to the needs of people and their experience with government programs, the bishops magnificently filled the gap between high moral principle and explicit economic policy.

If an air of old-fashioned morality hung over the bishops' letter, some of the solutions too sounded old-fashioned to some critics. In calling for help to the needy abroad the bishops appeared to ignore findings that a great deal of American aid, instead of helping the poor in Third World countries, had come under the control of powerful and rich elites who portioned it out among themselves. Thus the American poor to some degree were subsidizing the foreign rich. And when the bishops proposed empowering the poor, at home and abroad, critics noted that it was precisely in power, among other things, that the poor were poor; they might not know how to gain and exert power effectively any more than they were able to gain and spend money. In many other respects too, solving poverty was extraordinarily difficult. But the bishops would hardly have denied this.

In any event, few were listening, or at least acting. Three years later the richest 1 percent of American families were approaching the peak share of the nation's wealth of 36 percent attained in 1929. For the poorest 20 percent of American families, annual incomes in real dollars were one-third less than in 1972. Almost half of the new jobs created during the decade paid less than a poverty income. The stock market, however, was booming, and millions of middle-class Americans were engaged, like their government in Washington, in a spending spree.

* * *

As it turned out, the two-hundredth birthday of the Constitution in 1987 was an occasion much more for celebration than cerebration. Serious debate about the Constitution was minimal, except for one unplanned episode. Reagan's nomination of Robert Bork for the High Court provided a classic demonstration of the type of presidential-congressional struggle so carefully planned by the Framers, and provided also a Senate forum for debate over major constitutional issues such as "original intent." But those who hoped that 1988—the opening year of the Constitution's third century—might prove an occasion not only for testing Reagan conservatism at the polls but also for debate over sharply posed constitutional issues were to be disappointed on both counts. Major governmental restructuring occurred that year not in Washington but in the Soviet Union.

The electoral politics of 1988 turned out to be a disgrace to an "advanced democracy." After spending hundreds of days on the campaign road and millions of dollars before a single vote was cast, two coveys of candidates, Democratic and Republican, underwent a series of primary elections so rife with opportunism, so repetitious, and finally so anticlimactic as to bore the electorate before the main campaign even started. Two conventions full of fervid oratory but void of dramatic roll-call votes merely ratified the results of the primaries. The campaign that followed was the most scurrilous in recent American history, the most intellectually degrading since the campaign of bias against Al Smith in 1928.

A principal reason for George Bush's victory, studies indicated, was general satisfaction on the part of most voters with what the Democrats called the "credit-card economy." Most respondents in a nationwide poll during the early fall of 1988 said that they viewed themselves as better off than they had been eight years earlier, and most expected to be still better off four years hence. Few heeded warnings of future economic disarray or collapse as the trade and federal budget deficits continued to soar. Basic also to the Bush victory was a large and solid conservative constituency; 42 percent of the respondents in an August CBS News/*New York Times* poll held that the Reagan Administration's approach had not been conservative enough. Perhaps decisive in the outcome, however, was the GOP's expert manipulation of media, money, and symbols, and of the Republican candidate himself.

Long before election day, large numbers of voters were protesting the low level of the campaign. Many resolved on principle not to vote for president. An unprecedented number of newspapers refused to endorse either candidate. Voter registration campaigns floundered; after all the pronunciamentos about the biggest registration drive yet, the percentage of eligible Americans who were registered to vote by election time had dropped over two percentage points from four years before. And on election day the voter turnout—the ultimate test—fell to 50 percent, the lowest rate since the Coolidge-Davis race in 1924.

The Bush Republicans had proved that Reaganism could win without Reagan. They had failed, however, to convert presidential Republican votes into congressional or gubernatorial majorities; indeed, the Democrats gained small increases in their Senate, House, and statehouse ranks. One test for President Bush—a former chairman of the Republican National Committee—was whether he would now prove able to further modernize the GOP even while he sought to draw more Reagan Democrats into the party. Still, the Republicans had shaped a conservative, Sunbelt-based electoral strategy that worked in 1988.

And the response of the defeated? Many Democratic party leaders still failed to comprehend that for over a decade the Reagan Republican party had been conducting ideological warfare against the Democracy as the party of liberalism; that the Republicans had won this war in election after election; that the Democratic party lacked bold, creative, and innovative ideas, instead beating a timid retreat into calculation, centrism, and consensus. The Democracy would face huge tasks: to democratize and invigorate both its internal organization and the governmental system itself; to approach women, blacks, labor, peace activists, environmentalists and others less as vote pools to be tapped and more as partners in continuing social experimentation and change; to draw to the polls tens of millions who are, demographically, potential voters for the liberal-labor-left—if given inspired leadership of Rooseveltian quality.

Intellectually this would demand of the Democrats a clearheaded array of values and a grasp of priorities and relationships among values, thus filling the "Tocquevillian void" with a structure of well-formed ideas, experiments, and policies. "If you go back and read William James on pragmatism," scientist Michael Maccoby once remarked to some colleagues, "what he said was that truth would be discovered neither by the tough-minded people who live by numbers nor the tender-minded who live by ideology, but rather by people who make their ideals explicit, are willing to test them out and experiment with them constantly in the real world. That was really the essence of the American experiment." But what truth had the American experiment established? "Politics in the United States," wrote historian Alan Brinkley, "always has been afflicted with a certain conceptual barrenness. Efforts to create meaningful 'values,' to find a useful 'moral core' for our public life have competed constantly and often unsuccessfully against the belief in liberty, the commitment to personal rights unconstrained by any larger conception of a common purpose."

The volatility of the American character by the 1970s, Maccoby said, "makes the role of leadership absolutely crucial," measured by both clarity of values and the experimental attitude. Yet transformative political and intellectual leadership had been conspicuously absent in the seventies and eighties, especially on the left. Was there still a place in the American scheme for the leader who could transcend the medley of special interests, carry through great projects, and provide creative and transforming leadership to the nation? Much would depend on the propulsive force by which leadership would be projected into office. Backed by a broad and militant mandate, such leadership would have a chance. Whether such a mandate would develop in the 1990s was not clear. Believers in the pendulum theory of politics now expected a great shift toward the left, but history has been known to play tricks on people with patterns. Leadership was not in automatic supply.

Americans had no need for a hero, a spellbinder, a messiah. They needed committed men and women who could mobilize, and respond to, tens of thousands of rank-and-file leaders who in turn could activate hundreds of thousands of persons in the neighborhoods and precincts, thus creating a movement. This movement would both guide the top leaders and sustain them, just as hundreds, then thousands of black militants had rallied behind King and pressed him toward ever bolder action. Americans needed political leaders who, like Roosevelt on the left and Reagan on the right, could merge movement leadership with party and electoral organization, in order to win and hold governmental power.

Such leadership, such followership, can be founded only on intellectual and moral commitment to values and principles, to ideology in the true sense of the word. In the United States it can be founded only on the values of liberty and equality, of freedom, that Americans have been extolling for two centuries or more. Most conservatives will define freedom as individualism and libertarianism, most liberals and radicals as the Four Freedoms, as sharing and solidarity. That is a rational basis for conflict. During the next political cycle, in the wake of Reagan conservatism, it would enable a leader on the left to have a special rendezvous with destiny—as President to confront the oldest continuing challenge in America: the broadening of real equality of opportunity combined with the expansion of individual liberty.

Bob Dylan had sung in 1963:

> The line it is drawn, the curse it is cast
> The slow one now will later be fast
> As the present now will later be past
> The order is rapidly fadin'
> And the first one now will later be last
> For the times they are a-changin'

Memories of the Future:
A Personal Epilogue

THROUGH the open door of my study I can see a field of goldenrod and purple aster glowing softly in the sun of early fall, then coming to an abrupt end a quarter mile away against a dark-green line of austere, impenetrable oaks and maples. Above the trees looms the great bulk of Mount Greylock, landmark for the northern Berkshires. To the east of Greylock there is a saddle in the Hoosac Range over which Shays's rebels fled to a brief Berkshire refuge after they were cannonaded and routed in an attack on the Springfield arsenal over two centuries ago. Famous and infamous men and women have traveled through the valley beneath me—perhaps from distant Boston over the old Mohawk Trail or from the Hudson River lowlands to the west where the Dutch settled more than three centuries ago.

Henry David Thoreau first spied Greylock in 1844 when he tramped across the Hoosac Range, picking raspberries by the wayside. In the valley he packed rice and sugar into his knapsack and, with thunder rumbling at his heels, he trudged up through the open fields that then mantled Greylock. Then the wayfarer picked a path through trees that had a "scraggy and infernal look, as if contending with frost goblins." He reached the summit by dusk. In the soft green valley below, he remembered, he found "such a country as we might see in dreams, with all the delights of paradise."

From the summit Thoreau could see fifteen miles south to the town of Pittsfield. There, hardly a decade later, another young author looking north could view Greylock at its widest girth. Breaking through the clouds from the low mountains clustering around it, Greylock gave to Herman Melville the impression of a double-humped whale surfacing through ocean water. Melville's mind was on whales—he was writing *Moby-Dick.* "I have a sort of sea-feeling here in the country," he wrote. "My room seems a ship's cabin; & at nights when I wake up & hear the wind shrieking, I almost fancy there is too much sail on the house, & I had better go on the roof & rig in the chimney."

Melville lived on a farm he named Arrowhead after he had plowed up

Indian relics. During these years, the early and middle 1850s, Melville became good friends with another young writer, Nathaniel Hawthorne, who lived a few miles to the south in Lenox. The two often discussed their writing problems in Melville's hayloft, between country romps with another local literary man, Oliver Wendell Holmes. Hawthorne was still working on *The House of the Seven Gables* in his cottage called Tanglewood when Melville wrote the final pages of *Moby-Dick.*

It was another half century before the area could boast of another writer of wide renown, Edith Wharton, and some decades after that of a poet of even greater fame, Robert Frost. Looking north from my front porch, I can see the first rises of Vermont's Green Mountains enfolding Bennington, where Frost lies buried in a churchyard among the kind of woods and hills he loved. At the foot of the Green Mountains lies Williams College, where I have taught for almost fifty years and still serve and where we still sing an anthem that begins:

> O, proudly rise the monarchs of our mountain land,
> In their kingly forest robes to the sky. . . .

And concludes:

> . . . The glory and the honor of our mountain land,
> And the dwelling of the gallant and the free.

* * *

Glory, honor, gallantry—I have drawn a rather benign portrait of the Berkshires, of their natural beauty and early literary creativity. But this is also a region scarred by violence and long peopled by men going to war and—not all of them—returning. For centuries these green valleys were passages for Indian braves marauding their way into other tribal domains. To the east I can see the site of Fort Massachusetts, built in 1745 as the northwest outpost in a line of forts and stockades running back to the Connecticut River. Down the valley in front, close to the college, lies the site of Fort West Hoosac, built ten years later as defense against invading French and Indians. In 1756, during an intense attack on this fort, which the defenders repulsed, three Williamstown soldiers ventured out to search for some cows that had strayed. The men were cornered by Indians, killed, and scalped. Thus the first Williamstown casualties occurred within a few hundred yards of the slain men's homes, much as at Lexington Green less than twenty years later a Minuteman crawled across the road from the killing and died on his front stoop under his wife's eyes.

Since that day Williamstown and other Berkshire men have gone off to war in an ever-widening arc of conflict. In 1777, the third year of the Revolution, over 150 Williamstown militiamen, armed with muskets, fowling pieces, scythes, and hatchets, marched fifteen miles to Bennington to join General Stark's forces in their rout of Tories, Hessians, and Indians under General Burgoyne at the Battle of Bennington. In 1812 a few Williamstown men journeyed 200 miles or so to fight along the Canadian border. In the Civil War they entrained in large numbers to the killing grounds several hundred miles away; in the Spanish-American War they traveled a thousand miles to Florida, where some were stricken by typhoid fever and malaria; in 1917 and 1918 they sailed three thousand miles to France; in the early 1940s some flew six thousand miles across the Pacific to places like Okinawa and Iwo Jima; in the late 1960s they fought almost literally at the opposite end of the globe, in Vietnam. And—though one would certainly prefer otherwise—someday local men and women may fight tens or hundreds of thousands of miles away, in space wars.

Neither in war nor in peace has Williamstown or the rest of Berkshire County given famous generals or Presidents to the nation, though a few were schooled here. But the Berkshires have supplied hundreds of the type of second-level leaders that are most crucial to a nation's survival and progress. In 1766 Benjamin Simonds built the first tavern in Williamstown; later he took the lead in laying out the first church site, sired the first white child born in the town, and as colonel of the all-Berkshire regiment led it to Bennington. During his final years he helped clear the land and make the brick for the "Free School," shortly renamed Williams College. Or consider the twenty-two Berkshiremen who were elected in the winter of 1787 as delegates to the Massachusetts convention to ratify the new Constitution, and who took part in an historic debate that led to the addition of the Bill of Rights to the new charter.

During the next century the county contributed hundreds of educators, lawyers, ministers, businessmen, inventors who took leadership positions throughout the country. One of these was William Edward Burghardt Du Bois, born in Great Barrington in 1868. Harvard Ph.D., militant foe of Booker T. Washington's palliative tactics, author of profound studies of African and American blacks, leader of pan-African unity efforts, in 1961 he joined the Communist party, renounced his United States citizenship, and moved to Ghana, where he died two years later. There his home is a shrine. His Great Barrington birthplace at last report was a weed-choked lot with a crude wooden plaque.

Berkshire County is steeped in history, benign or not. But so is every county in the United States. I grew up in a town north of Boston, in an expanse of farm and woodland where my nearest playmates were two miles away. Yet I could walk through woods behind my house for an hour, pass by a few homes including my girlfriend's, and come onto Lexington Green, where the first Revolutionary blood was shed in April 1775. One can hardly visit any part of the United States without being struck by the richness of the local history. It simply remains to be discovered, in attics, people's memories, yellowing newspapers, artifacts, local libraries. One is struck even more by the ubiquity of group conflict in the United States—between Indians and settlers, Yanks and Rebs, blacks and whites, farmers and sheriffs, workers and bosses, outlaws and inlaws. If one could put on a map of the United States tiny X's denoting pitched battles, little else would show.

* * *

In October 1988, at the height of the presidential campaign, I was reminded of an earlier October—in 1932, when, amid the darkening red leaves on the mountainsides, Democratic nominee Franklin D. Roosevelt drove into Williamstown on the road along which the Berkshire troops had once marched to Bennington. His limousine passed Ben Simonds's old tavern and then slid through the college precincts, slackening its pace so that all could see the cheery, hat-waving governor, but it did not stop. Perhaps he had heard something about Williams students' political leanings. When the car did halt just beyond the college bounds, a frustrated throng caught up, crying, "Speech! Speech!" But FDR appeared far more interested in conversing with the politicos who crowded around his car. When an arm-waving party chieftain called for "three cheers for the next President of the United States," hearty shouts for Hoover and a few yells for Norman Thomas rose in the autumn air. Unperturbed, FDR and his party moved on.

Later Roosevelt would set a standard for the presidency, in both its creative and its dangerous aspects. What has been less appreciated is the standard set by the "second-cadre" men and women around him, in the White House, his cabinet, his brain trust, his New Deal agencies. Frances Perkins and Harold Ickes and Thomas Corcoran and later George Marshall and Leon Henderson and always of course Eleanor Roosevelt have been celebrated enough—in part because many of FDR's top people like Ickes and David Lilienthal were masterly diary-keepers—but the special greatness of these leaders lay in their capacity to draw a third cadre of leadership into the corridors of power.

It was the intellectual quality of the men and women of all three cadres that made the crucial difference. Jurists like Felix Frankfurter and Hugo Black, politicians like Corcoran and Robert La Follette, Jr., legislators like

Representatives Thomas Eliot, Mike Monroney, and Albert Gore, or personages of the stature of Perkins or Eleanor Roosevelt herself were more interested in ideas than in political promotion or maneuver. No wonder, then, the comment of John Maynard Keynes in the mid-1930s that of "all the experiments to evolve a new order, it is the experiment of young America which most attracts my own deepest sympathy," or Adlai Stevenson's observation in the mid-1950s that the "next frontier is the quality, the moral, intellectual and aesthetic standards of the free way of life."

Interviewing leaders like these, examining their lives, following the ebb and flow of their careers arouses a profound curiosity about the nature of intellectual and political leadership. Watching John Kennedy climb the greasy pole and reach the top while so young was a fascinating case study in human ambition, political skill, and audacity. As I came to know Kennedy during the 1950s, I found I was observing a politician who as a student of history and of major American politicians had had ample opportunity on Capitol Hill coolly to measure leaders at home and abroad. He had limned his own political heroes in *Profiles in Courage,* a portrayal of senators who had fought for their convictions at risk—often at fatal risk—to their political careers. Kennedy's own career, however, suggested that he would not risk election defeat in pursuit of some utopian principle.

Early in 1960 I published a study of Kennedy in which I expressed some doubt that he would show more than a profile in caution as candidate for President. The issue was intellectual and moral commitment as well as political. Though the book was generally positive toward the candidate, it did not meet the exacting standards of the Kennedy family and entourage. Jacqueline Kennedy in particular was disturbed by my portrait, which she felt made too much of the influence of his parents, his older brother Joe, and indeed his whole social background.

"You are like him in many ways," she wrote beguilingly. "You know the hard parts and the pitfalls. Can't you see that he is exceptional?

"Or is he to be just another sociological case history? Irish-Catholic, newly rich, Harvard-educated etc. — Does every man conform totally to his background? Surely there are some who contribute something of their own. . . ." She was most upset by my failure to emphasize more her husband's learning experiences. What other candidate, she asked, had in his twenties talked to Chamberlain, Baldwin, Churchill, Laski, had in his thirties known de Lattre, Nehru, Ben-Gurion, had been to Russia in Stalin's day, had had friends in the French and English parliaments? "Jack was part of all that and it influenced him enormously." She went on: "I think you underestimate him. Anyone sees he has the intelligence—magnetism and drive it takes to succeed in politics. I see, every succeeding week I am married to him, that he has what may be the single most important quality for a leader—an imperturbable self confidence and sureness of his powers."

Jacqueline Kennedy's letter was more than a wife's brief for a husband—it was a reminder to biographers that their subjects can rise far above, or, by implication, fall far below, the psychological and sociological forces that have shaped them. And if John Kennedy turned to sundry Western leaders as role models, he in turn became a model for thousands of young would-be leaders. So had Eleanor Roosevelt for countless women, and so would Robert Kennedy later for young rebels, and Martin Luther King, Jr., for blacks.

* * *

The leadership gap that afflicts us today could be rather simply explained: our leaders were shot down. Yet a nation with strong second and third cadres can survive the loss of top leaders. While some of JFK's best men left Lyndon Johnson's administration during its first year, enough remained—and enough new talent came in with LBJ—to devise and launch the sweeping domestic programs of the Great Society. So there must be a more fundamental explanation for the decline of leadership, especially among liberal Democrats.

Does our foreign policy experience give us a clue? The leadership group that had waged the battle against isolationism in the late 1930s fell victim to the cold war mentality following World War II—with considerable assistance from Stalin—and two decades later younger men and women were even more victimized by the cold war. For they were stigmatized whatever side they took on Vietnam. As the Democratic party establishment collapsed in 1968, those who stuck with the Vietnam War went down with it, while those who broke with the war became isolated in the McCarthy, Robert Kennedy, and McGovern secessions. Men and women on both sides later became university presidents or deans, foundation heads, distinguished attorneys, writers, and teachers. But what many of them in the 1970s were *not* doing was what they should have been doing when their turn came in the rise and fall of leadership generations—running the government. It is their exile, along with the withering away of the Stimson-Eisenhower-Rockefeller presidential Republican party, which helped produce the critical leadership gap of the last two decades.

And yet, the sources of our leadership failures lie deeper than electoral prudence or political assassinations, cold war attitudes, or foreign policy disasters. They lie in habits of thought long shaped in a land that has allowed ample leeway for social and political as well as economic and industrial innovation, on the part of people who like tinkering and patching up and proceeding "by guess and by God." Looking back over two hundred years, the chronicler sees the American Experiment as a series of planned or unplanned experiments—ventures in a written Constitution, a Bill of Rights, checks and balances, federalism, Jacksonian democracy; in isolationism, expansion, empire building, Wilsonian internationalism, cold war interventionism, bountiful foreign aid; in slavery, civil war butchery, emancipation, serfdom, southern white rule; in massive migration and immigration, industrial innovation and giantism, Social Darwinism, New Deal regulation, Keynesian spending, war economics, laissez-faire; in nuclear attack; in race hatred and segregation, exploitation of women and children, Prohibition, repeal, depression, joblessness, drugs, poverty; in public education, social movements, populism, desegregation, literary and artistic creativity, youth rebellion, scientific discovery, space exploration.

But the grand experiment that transcended all the others was the effort to expand both individual liberty and real equality of opportunity for all—the supreme promise of the Declaration of Independence, the campaign pledge of the Jeffersonians and Jacksonians and their successors, the subject of Tocqueville's most penetrating observations, the core of the epic struggle of the 1860s, the essence of the twentieth-century philosophical battles over the dynamic tension and interplay between liberty and equality. This experiment was called Freedom, combining as it did liberty and equality. And this doctrine of freedom was forged and promoted by liberals of all creeds, liberals in both parties and third parties, Republican liberals like Lincoln and Theodore Roosevelt, Wendell Willkie and Nelson Rockefeller, Jacob Javits and Clifford Case, Democratic liberals like Wilson and Al Smith and FDR, Eleanor Roosevelt and Barbara Jordan, Truman and LBJ, Senators Lehman and Wagner, Fulbright and Kefauver, and three leaders by the name of Kennedy.

The political and intellectual vehicle for the ideology of freedom was called liberalism. So pervasive was this doctrine in American history, so comprehensive its reach in American politics, that liberalism and liberals seemed unassailable. During the 1980s, however, Reaganites converted this mild and venerable word into a hate object. Where in the old days conservatives had attacked communism and socialism, now they were moving toward the heart of their target. At the same time, liberalism was ripe for a fall. Like some old mansion top-heavy with junk-filled attics and sagging excrescences but weak in its foundations, liberalism collapsed of overextension—its overemphasis on individualism and pluralism, its flabby appeal across the wide center of the political and intellectual spectrum that resulted in a lack of core values.

All these tendencies reflected habits of thought that foster experimentation but at the same time lead to an excessive reliance on expediency, short-run planning, opportunism, and ultimately to the erosion of the supreme values—liberty and equality—by which the experiments themselves must be tested.

* * *

I completed the writing of this volume during the bicentennial celebrations of the Constitution and the Bill of Rights. Doubtless my dismay over the quality of late-twentieth-century leadership in both parties, and especially in the Democracy, has been deepened by the inevitable contrast with the thinkers and politicians of the late eighteenth century. Historians have long studied the personal qualities of the Framers that led to that explosion of talent in Philadelphia in 1787. Some of their findings are summarized in a capsule explanation of mine I like to quote: they were well bred, well fed, well read, well led, and well wed. But the thousand or so delegates to the state ratifying conventions often lacked some or all of these advantages: many came from poor, low-status families, they had little or no formal schooling, they were cut off from the main leadership networks, and their brides rarely brought them the several thousand acres of land that could provide leisure for deep thought. How then explain the intellectual capacity of the second-cadre leadership that came to the fore in the ratification debates?

The answer, I think, lies in the transcending, even overwhelming moral and intellectual commitment that these early Americans made first to independence from Britain, then to a new constitutional order, and finally to the Bill of Rights, all within the twenty years between the early 1770s and the early 1790s. All these commitments were crucial, and each vivified the others. The leaders, national and local, had staked their hopes and their lives on a carefully thought-out balance of liberty and order. In a time of tumultuous conflict they had fought their colonial governors in America, their imperial masters in London, and then one another, for what they considered the highest purpose. And because every major step they took was informed by a powerful but incalculable moral passion as well as a calculation of grand political strategy, they spoke from the heart as well as the head.

It is this combination of moral and intellectual commitment that I find so lacking in our current politics. All political leaders in democracies are brokers, finaglers, manipulators; the question is whether they rise above this when fundamental issues reach crucial turning points. FDR transcended his foxlike maneuvering when he moved to the left in 1935 and 1936, when he tried to deal with a deadlocked political system during his second term, as he came to confront the menace of Nazism, when he sought to leave a legacy of world peace and security in postwar plans for the United Nations and in settlements with the Russians. John Kennedy made the kind of commitment of the heart as well as head that the presidency called for in his third and last year in office, setting a standard for his successors. Richard Nixon, on the other hand, struck one as merely opportunistic to the last, operational, pragmatic in the worst sense—he earned the appellation "Tricky Dick." Conservative Republicans had to wait for Reagan to make a firm, strategic commitment to rightist doctrine— a commitment hopelessly snarled in Reagan's White House.

Aside from Reagan and Jesse Jackson, presidential candidates in the 1980s seemed all of a piece—cool, calculating, prudent, carefully choosing and exploiting issues on the basis of public opinion polls and media attention. They were leading with their heads, not their hearts. A year or so after JFK became President I saw in him four Kennedys—the rhetorical radical, the policy liberal, the fiscal moderate, the institutional conservative—and I expected that the four tendencies could not live together indefinitely. Presidential candidates today seem equally fragmented—able rhetoricians, fine policy analysts, fiscally cautious, sublimely indifferent to the fact that their larger hopes and programs cannot be achieved through our splintered and often deadlocked governmental machinery. The candidates forswear ideology, not recognizing that they themselves possess ideologies of flabby liberalism or cloudy conservatism.

Moral passion informing intellectual power harnessed securely to explicit, overriding ends or values—this must be the essence of twenty-first-century leadership.

*　　*　　*

"Things fall apart; the centre cannot hold. . . ." These words of Yeats have been quoted by every generation since he wrote them in 1920, but never more than today. In the late twentieth century many Americans sense an intellectual, cultural, and political fragmentation and trivialization that pervades our public and private lives. And there has been the usual overreaction, the breast-beating about the ignorance and distorted values of the American people followed by a feverish search for scapegoats. The two leading culprits are the mass media and education. Since there is a reluctance to challenge the independence of the media, given its protected position under the Bill of Rights, the easy, all-purpose target has been the educator, whether the kindergarten teacher, the college dean, or the graduate school professor.

Once again, in the most recent "crisis of education," all the old moth-eaten solutions have been trotted out. The most popular one is that we must read the Great Books. As a former teacher of some of the "Greats," as one who believes that they should be at the heart of every liberal arts or humanistic curriculum, as one who knows that the great philosophers offer profound explorations of human nature, moral values, and political power, I balk at this cheap overselling of the classics. They are introductions to thought, not substitutes for it. They raise the enduring questions that confound humankind—they do not offer solutions necessarily relevant to our current plight.

Like Jefferson and Madison and Lincoln, like the many lesser "greats" who flowered in this country from around the second to the sixth decade of this century, we must *think* our way through our problems. This means drawing our values from the teachings of the past, arraying them in priorities based on human needs, and above all—and by far the most daunting intellectual and analytical enterprise—working out the *instrumental ends* and the *intermediate means* that enable us to apply our supreme values effectively and explicitly to everyday decisions and actions. This intellectual strategy calls for a structure of government—in essence for a team of leaders with the power to govern, an opposition party leadership with the power to oppose, full protection of procedural and substantive liberties by all branches and especially the judiciary—in short, majority rule, minority rights, and a constitutional system that fosters both.

*　　*　　*

"... The best lack all conviction, while the worst / Are full of passionate intensity," Yeats continued. It is above all the lack of moral conviction and of intellectual creativity that lies behind our present predicament, and this in turn stems largely from the decline of cutting conflict and controversy in our politics. As long as press and politicians prate about consensus and bipartisanship and centrism, both our ideas and our politics will be sterile and stalemated.

"Turning and turning in the widening gyre / The falcon cannot hear the falconer. . . ." So Yeats began his famous poem. The Berkshire hills and dales broaden out to the Taconic Range and the Green Mountains and the Alleghenies, and finally to the Appalachians and the Rockies and the great valleys in between. The mountainsides turn during the fall from dark green to brilliant red to brown and then to a blackness against the first snows. I reflect on a phenomenon that I will never fully understand—how the lushness and softness of the summer is incomprehensible as one stands in an icy field, how the rocklike soil and all-enveloping cold of winter are incomprehensible as one sits amid the gentle grass and last wildflowers of autumn.

But, I reflect, at least there is the certainty of it even as we cannot quite grasp it. And I find some consolation in the thought that coping with both the killing frosts of winter and the droughts, floods, and bugs of summer provided Americans—whether Yankee tinkerers or eminent philosophers—with the kind of stimulus, the kind of contrasting challenges that spurred their inventiveness and creativity.

I think finally of the explorers—those who made their way across the Atlantic, who penetrated the Appalachian slopes and then, under men like Lewis and Clark, pushed their way across prairie and desert and mountain chain. And I think finally of the space explorers of today, human and robotic, and of a planned space platform that will be named Freedom, and of probes called Pioneer flying past Saturn and Pluto even as these words were written and are now being read.

My hills, like the stars, endure. And in college convocations to come, I will join in singing some words that express my most fundamental commitment—singing them with a fervor that still surprises me:

> My country, 'tis of thee,
> Sweet land of liberty,
> Of thee I sing;
> Land where my fathers died,
> Land of the Pilgrims' pride,
> From ev'ry mountain side
> Let freedom ring.

The following illustrations have been reprinted with the kind permission of the institutions indicated:

Notes

━━━━━━━

1. THE CRISIS OF LEADERSHIP

p. 3 *[Flight to Chicago]*: Ed Plaut Papers (RG 31-HH), Franklin D. Roosevelt Library, Hyde Park, N.Y.; *New York Times*, July 3, 1932, pp. 1, 9; *Chicago Tribune*, July 3, 1932, pp. 1–5; *Time*, vol. 20, no. 1 (July 11, 1932), p. 10; Samuel I. Rosenman, *Working with Roosevelt* (Harper, 1952), pp. 67–77; Nathan Miller, *FDR: An Intimate History* (Doubleday, 1983), pp. 277–81; Gilbert Grosvenor, "Flying," *National Geographic*, vol. 53, no. 5 (May 1933), p. 586.

[*"I may go out by submarine"*]: quoted in *Time*, vol. 20, no. 1 (July 11, 1932), p. 10.

[*"One person in politics"*]: quoted in *New York Times*, July 2, 1932, p. 4.

4 [*"A good sailor"*]: quoted in Frank Freidel, *Franklin D. Roosevelt: The Triumph* (Little, Brown, 1956), p. 313.

[*"Put it right there"*]: quoted in *New York Times*, July 3, 1932, p. 9.

[*"It's all right, Franklin"*]: quoted in Rosenman, p. 76; see also Alfred B. Rollins, Jr., *Roosevelt and Howe* (Knopf, 1962), pp. 346–47; Kenneth S. Davis, *FDR: The New York Years, 1928–1933* (Random House, 1985), pp. 333–34.

4–5 [*At Chicago Stadium*]: *New York Times*, July 3, 1932, p. 9; *Chicago Tribune*, July 3, 1932, pp. 1–3.

5 [*Acceptance address*]: *The Public Papers and Addresses of Franklin D. Roosevelt*, Samuel I. Rosenman, comp. (Random House, 1938–50), vol. 1, pp. 647–59, quoted at pp. 648, 649, 659.

[*Roosevelt in 1932–33*]: Adolf Berle Papers, esp. containers 15–17, Franklin D. Roosevelt Library; Raymond Moley Papers, Roosevelt Library; Eleanor Roosevelt Papers, Roosevelt Library; Moley Papers, esp. boxes 1, 8, 63, Hoover Institution on War, Revolution and Peace, Stanford University, Stanford, Calif.

The Divided Legacy

6 [*"In an airplane"*]: *Chicago Tribune*, July 3, 1932, p. 1.

[*FDR's early years*]: Geoffrey C. Ward, *Before the Trumpet* (Harper, 1985); Kenneth S. Davis, *FDR: The Beckoning of Destiny, 1882–1928* (Putnam, 1971), books 1, 2; Frank Freidel, *Franklin D. Roosevelt: The Apprenticeship* (Little, Brown, 1952); Miller; Arthur M. Schlesinger, Jr., *The Crisis of the Old Order* (Houghton Mifflin, 1957), ch. 29; James MacGregor Burns, *Roosevelt: The Lion and the Fox* (Harcourt, Brace, 1956), chs. 1–2; I have used occasional phrases or passages from this earlier work in my treatment of Franklin Delano Roosevelt in the present volume.

[*"People one knows"*]: quoted in Burns, *Lion*, p. 5.

7 [*Sources of political ambition*]: Harold D. Lasswell, *Power and Personality* (Norton, 1948); Joseph A. Schlesinger, *Ambition and Politics: Political Careers in the United States* (Rand McNally, 1966); Abraham H. Maslow, *Motivation and Personality* (Harper, 1954); Stanley Renshon, *Psychological Needs and Political Behavior* (Free Press, 1974); Gordon Black, "A Theory of Political Ambition: Career Choices and the Role of Structural Incentives," *American Political Science Review*, vol. 66, no. 1 (March 1972), pp. 144–59.

[*FDR and the "nouveaux riches"*]: see Freidel, *Apprenticeship*, pp. 12–14; William D. Hassett, *Off the Record with F.D.R., 1942–1945* (Rutgers University Press, 1958), pp. 13–15, 88–89, 124–25.

7–8 [*FDR's maturation during Progressive era*]: see Davis, *Beckoning*, chs. 8–12; Daniel R. Fusfeld, *The Economic Thought of Franklin D. Roosevelt and the Economic Origins of the New Deal* (Columbia University Press, 1956), ch. 3.

8 [*Eleanor Roosevelt's early years*]: Eleanor Roosevelt, *This Is My Story* (Harper, 1937), chs. 1–4; Joseph P. Lash, *Eleanor and Franklin* (Norton, 1971), book 1; Burns, *Lion*, pp. 26–27.

[*"Honneur oblige"*]: letter of Sara Roosevelt to Eleanor and Franklin Roosevelt, October 14, 1917, in *F.D.R.: His Personal Letters*, Elliott Roosevelt, ed. (Duell, Sloan, and Pearce, 1947–50), vol. 2, pp. 274–75, quoted at p. 274.

[*"Lived like that!"*]: quoted in Lash, p. 135.

[*FDR's rising ambition*]: see Joseph Schlesinger, esp. pp. 8–10.

[*FDR as "farm-labor" legislator*]: Freidel, *Apprenticeship*, ch. 7; Burns, *Lion*, pp. 41–46.

9 [*"Listened to all his plans"*]: Eleanor Roosevelt, p. 166.

[*"Making ten servants"*]: quoted in *New York Times*, July 17, 1917, p. 3.

[*"Proud to be the husband"*]: letter, July 18, 1917, in *Personal Letters*, vol. 2, p. 349.

[*Lucy Mercer*]: Lash, pp. 220–27, quoted at p. 220.

[*"I faced myself"*]: quoted in *ibid.*, p. 220.

[*Polio*]: Frank Freidel, *Franklin D. Roosevelt: The Ordeal* (Little, Brown, 1954), ch. 6; Lash, chs. 26–27; Davis, *Beckoning*, chs. 21–22.

10 [*Eleanor's issues in the 1920s*]: see Lash, chs. 25, 27–28, 30; Elisabeth Israels Perry, "Training for Public Life: ER and Women's Political Networks in the 1920s," in Joan Hoff-Wilson and Marjorie Lightman, eds., *Without Precedent* (Indiana University Press, 1984), pp. 28–45; Maurine H. Beasley, *Eleanor Roosevelt and the Media: A Public Quest for Self-Fulfillment* (University of Illinois Press, 1987), chs. 1–2 *passim*.

[*Franklin the politician, Eleanor the agitator*]: Lash, p. 348.

[*Governor Roosevelt*]: Davis, *New York Years*, chs. 1–6, 8, *passim*; Bernard Bellush, *Franklin D. Roosevelt as Governor of New York* (Columbia University Press, 1955); Freidel, *Ordeal*, chs. 15–16; Freidel, *Triumph*.

[*Hearst and the League*]: Freidel, *Triumph*, pp. 250–54.

[*"Hasn't spoken to me!"*]: quoted in Lash, p. 347.

11 [*Schlesinger on FDR's assets*]: *Crisis*, p. 279.

[*Democratic primaries, 1932*]: Freidel, *Triumph*, chs. 17–19; Burns, *Lion*, pp. 123–34; James A. Farley, *Behind the Ballots* (Harcourt, 1938), pp. 58–112.

[*Democratic convention, 1932*]: Freidel, *Triumph*, ch. 20; Burns, *Lion*, pp. 134–38; Farley, pp. 112–54.

[*"California came here"*]: quoted in Burns, *Lion*, p. 137.

12 [*"Good old McAdoo"*]: *ibid.*

[*"The same cops"*]: Dos Passos, "Out of the Red with Roosevelt," *New Republic*, vol. 71, no. 919 (July 13, 1932), pp. 230–32, quoted at p. 232.

[*1932 campaign*]: Freidel, *Triumph*, chs. 22–24; Davis, *New York Years*, ch. 11; Burns, *Lion*, pp. 140–45; Farley, pp. 155–91; Roy V. Peel and Thomas C. Donnelly, *The 1932 Campaign: An Analysis* (Farrar & Rinehart, 1935); Herbert Hoover, *Memoirs: The Great Depression, 1929–1941* (Macmillan, 1952), chs. 19–31; Rexford G. Tugwell, *The Brains Trust* (Viking, 1968); Tugwell, *The Democratic Roosevelt* (Doubleday, 1957), ch. 12; Tugwell, *In Search of Roosevelt* (Harvard University Press, 1972), ch. 6; Schlesinger, *Crisis*, ch. 33.

[*Press on FDR*]: see *Literary Digest*, vol. 114, no. 2 (July 9, 1932), pp. 2–3; Oswald Garrison Villard, "An Open Letter to Governor Roosevelt," *Nation*, vol. 134, no. 3488 (May 11, 1932), pp. 532–33.

[New Republic *on FDR*]: "Is Roosevelt a Hero?," *New Republic*, vol. 66, no. 852 (April 1, 1931), pp. 165–66, quoted at p. 166.

[Post *on FDR*]: Freidel, *Triumph*, p. 328.

[*Mencken on FDR*]: "Where are we at?," Baltimore *Evening Sun*, July 5, 1932, reprinted in Mencken, *A Carnival of Buncombe*, Malcolm Moos, ed. (Johns Hopkins Press, 1956), pp. 256–60, esp. p. 259.

[*Lippmann on FDR*]: "Governor Roosevelt's Candidacy," New York *Herald Tribune*, January 8, 1932, reprinted in Lippmann, *Interpretations, 1931–1932*, Allan Nevins, ed. (Macmillan, 1932), pp. 259–63, quoted at p. 261.

[*Outlook on FDR*]: *Outlook*, vol. 160, no. 7 (April 1932), p. 208.

12 [*"Can't you see"*]: letter to Robert Woolley, February 25, 1932, quoted in Freidel, *Triumph*, p. 253n.

13 [*Brain trust*]: Raymond Moley, *After Seven Years* (Harper, 1939); Tugwell, *Brains Trust;* Beatrice Bishop Berle and Travis Beal Jacobs, eds., *Navigating the Rapids, 1918–1971: From the Papers of Adolf A. Berle* (Harcourt, 1973), esp. part 2; Fusfeld, ch. 15; Davis, *New York Years*, ch. 9; Bernard Sternsher, *Rexford G. Tugwell and the New Deal* (Rutgers University Press, 1964), part 2; Elliot A. Rosen, "Roosevelt and the Brains Trust: An Historiographical Overview," *Political Science Quarterly*, vol. 87, no. 4 (December 1972), pp. 531–57.
[*"Anarchy of concentrated economic power"*]: Moley, p. 24.
[*Wells on Berle*]: quoted in Schlesinger, *Crisis*, p. 400.

14 [*"Issues aren't my business"*]: quoted in Moley, p. 36.
[*Progressive Republicans*]: Alfred Lief, *Democracy's Norris* (Stackpole, 1939), ch. 16; Richard Lowitt, *George W. Norris: The Persistence of a Progressive, 1913–1933* (University of Illinois Press, 1971), pp. 549–59; Ronald L. Feinman, "The Progressive Republican Senate Bloc and the Presidential Election of 1932," *Mid-America*, vol. 59, no. 2 (April–July 1977), pp. 73–91; Harold L. Ickes, *Autobiography of a Curmudgeon* (Reynal & Hitchcock, 1943), pp. 253, 260–65.
[*Garner on staying alive*]: Bascom N. Timmons, *Garner of Texas* (Harper, 1948), p. 168.
[*Farley on active campaign*]: Farley, pp. 163–64.
[*Brain trust's desire for program*]: see Tugwell, *Brains Trust*, pp. 421–24, ch. 39; Tugwell, *In Search*, ch. 5.
[*Tugwell on FDR*]: *In Search*, p. 128.

15 [*Broun on FDR*]: quoted in Tugwell, *Brains Trust*, p. 283.
[*FDR on intellectuals and flexibility*]: see *ibid.*, pp. 286–87, 409–11, 422–24, 441–47, 467–70, 488–96.
[*Young on FDR*]: quoted in Josephine Young and Everett Needham Case, *Owen D. Young and American Enterprise* (David R. Godine, 1982), p. 601.
[*FDR-Long telephone exchange*]: quoted in Tugwell, *Brains Trust*, pp. 430–33. I have condensed, slightly rearranged, and supplied quotation marks for Tugwell's dialogue, part of a wider luncheon-table discussion that remained so vivid a recollection, wrote Tugwell, "that I am willing to stand on its accuracy" (p. 434n.).

16 [*Most dangerous man*]: *ibid.*, p. 434.
[*FDR's speaking campaign*]: *Roosevelt Public Papers*, vol. 1, ch. 24, part 2; see also Fusfeld, ch. 16.
[*"Alice-in-Wonderland" economics*]: August 20, 1932, in *Roosevelt Public Papers*, vol. 1, pp. 669–84, esp. pp. 674–75.
[*"Planned use of the land"*]: September 14, 1932, in *ibid.*, vol. 1, pp. 693–711, quoted at p. 699.
[*Freidel on Topeka address*]: *Triumph*, p. 347.
[*Commonwealth Club address*]: September 23, 1932, in *Roosevelt Public Papers*, vol. 1, pp. 742–56, quoted at pp. 743, 747, 752, 743, 750, 751–52, respectively.

17 [*Tugwell and Moley on Commonwealth Club address*]: Tugwell, *Democratic Roosevelt*, p. 246; Freidel, *Triumph*, p. 353n.; see also Tugwell, *In Search*, ch. 7.
[*"Yankee horse-trades"*]: Moley, p. 48.
[*"Weave the two together"*]: quoted in *ibid.*
[*"Reduce the cost"*]: address at Pittsburgh, Pa., October 19, 1932, in *Roosevelt Public Papers*, vol. 1, pp. 795–811, quoted at p. 808.
[*Hoover on FDR as easiest man to beat*]: entry of June 27, 1932, Henry L. Stimson Diary, quoted in Schlesinger, *Crisis*, pp. 430–31.
[*Hoover's September prediction*]: entry of September 19, 1932, Stimson Diary, quoted in Freidel, *Triumph*, p. 365.
[*Hoover's composition of own addresses*]: see Harris G. Warren, *Herbert Hoover and the Great Depression* (Oxford University Press, 1959), p. 256; Hoover, *Memoirs*, p. 234.
[*Mencken on Hoover's oratorical style*]: "The Hoover Bust," Baltimore *Evening Sun*, October 10, 1932, reprinted in Mencken, *Carnival*, pp. 260–65, esp. p. 262.
[*"Chameleon on the Scotch plaid"*]: address in Indianapolis, Ind., October 28, 1932, in *Public Papers of Herbert Hoover* (U.S. Government Printing Office, 1974–77), vol. 4, pp. 609–32, quoted at p. 619.

17 [*"In Hoover we trusted"*]: quoted in Schlesinger, *Crisis*, p. 432.
18 [*"Horsemen of Destruction"*]: address at Baltimore, Md., October 25, 1932, in *Roosevelt Public Papers*, vol. 1, pp. 831–42, quoted at p. 832.
[*Election night*]: Farley, pp. 185–89.
[*Election results*]: Svend Petersen, *A Statistical History of the American Presidential Elections* (Frederick Ungar, 1963), p. 91.
[*"I never thought particularly"*]: quoted in *Time*, vol. 20, no. 20 (November 14, 1932), p. 26.
[*Eleanor Roosevelt's reaction to election*]: quoted in Lorena Hickok, *Reluctant First Lady* (Dodd, Mead, 1962), p. 92; see also Eleanor Roosevelt, *This I Remember* (Harper, 1949), pp. 74–75.

The "Hundred Days" of Action

[*Hoover on business fears*]: Hoover, *Memoirs*, p. 269.
18–19 [*Economic conditions, fall–winter, 1932–33*]: *Time*, vol. 21, no. 11 (March 13, 1933), p. 14; Irving Bernstein, *The Lean Years: A History of the American Worker, 1920–1933* (Houghton Mifflin, 1960), pp. 319–21; Frank Freidel, *Franklin D. Roosevelt: Launching the New Deal* (Little, Brown, 1973), pp. 11–12.
19 [*Wilson on garbage dump*]: Wilson, "Hull-House in 1932: III," *New Republic*, vol. 73, no. 948 (February 1, 1933), pp. 317–22, quoted at p. 320.
[*Farm stirrings*]: John L. Shover, *Cornbelt Rebellion: The Farmers' Holiday Association* (University of Illinois Press, 1965), chs. 4–5; Schlesinger, *Crisis*, pp. 459–61; *Literary Digest*, vol. 115, no. 3 (January 21, 1933), pp. 32–33, and vol. 115, no. 5 (February 4, 1933), p. 10; Freidel, *Launching*, pp. 12, 83–85.
[*Congressional inaction*]: Burns, *Lion*, p. 146; E. P. Herring, "Second Session of the Seventy-Second Congress," *American Political Science Review*, vol. 27, no. 3 (June 1933), pp. 404–22; Laurin L. Henry, *Presidential Transitions* (Brookings Institution, 1960), ch. 23.
[*Banker on absence of solutions*]: Jackson Reynolds, quoted in Schlesinger, *Crisis*, p. 458.
[*Taylor on retrenchment*]: ibid.
[*Lippmann on business leadership*]: ibid., p. 459.
20 [*Hunger-march delegation*]: *Time*, vol. 20, no. 22 (November 28, 1932), p. 12.
[*"Fine! Fine! Fine!"*]: quoted in T. Harry Williams, *Huey Long* (Knopf, 1970), p. 619.
[*FDR-Hoover interregnum minuet*]: Herbert Feis, *1933: Characters in Crisis* (Little, Brown, 1966), chs. 3–10; Frank Freidel, "The Interregnum Struggle Between Hoover and Roosevelt," in Martin L. Fausold and George T. Mazuzan, eds., *The Hoover Presidency: A Reappraisal* (State University of New York Press, 1974), pp. 134–49; Davis, *New York Years*, chs. 12–13 passim; Tugwell, *In Search*, ch. 9; Henry, ch. 22; *Hoover Public Papers*, vol. 4, pp. 1013–88.
[*White on FDR*]: quoted in Freidel, *Launching*, p. 16.
[*Lippmann on FDR*]: ibid., p. 17.
[*"Situation is critical"*]: quoted in Ronald Steel, *Walter Lippmann and the American Century* (Little, Brown, 1980), p. 300.
21 [*Lippmann on a free hand for FDR*]: ibid.
[*"I hate all Presidents"*]: quoted in *New York Times*, February 16, 1933, p. 2; see also Freidel, *Launching*, pp. 169–74; Davis, *New York Years*, pp. 427–37.
[*Ford and Michigan banks*]: Allan Nevins and Frank Ernest Hill, *Ford: Decline and Rebirth, 1933–1962* (Scribner, 1962), pp. 11–15.
[*Bank crisis*]: Henry, pp. 343–55, Hoover quoted at p. 346; Freidel, *Launching*, ch. 11; Susan E. Kennedy, *The Banking Crisis of 1933* (University Press of Kentucky, 1973).
[*Hoover's two late calls to FDR*]: see Kennedy, pp. 148–49; Kenneth S. Davis, *FDR: The New Deal Years, 1933–1937* (Random House, 1986), p. 25.
[*"End of our string"*]: quoted in Freidel, *Launching*, p. 193.
[*"Plodding feet"*]: Robert E. Sherwood, "Inaugural Parade," in *Saturday Review of Literature*, vol. 9, no. 33 (March 4, 1933), pp. 461–62.
22 [*March 4, 1933*]: "The Talk of the Town," *New Yorker*, vol. 59 (March 7, 1983), pp. 37–38, lady in rags quoted at p. 37; Anne O'Hare McCormick, "The Nation Renews Its Faith," *New York Times Magazine*, March 19, 1933, pp. 1–2, 19; *New York Times,*

March 5, 1933, pp. 1–3; Edmund Wilson, "Inaugural Parade," *New Republic*, vol. 74, no. 955 (March 22, 1933), pp. 154–56.

22–3 [*Inaugural address*]: *Roosevelt Public Papers*, vol. 2, pp. 11–16; on the drafting of the inaugural address, see Raymond Moley, *The First New Deal* (Harcourt, 1966), ch. 7.

23 ["*Very, very solemn*"]: quoted in *New York Times*, March 5, 1933, p. 7.
[*FDR's cabinet*]: see Freidel, *Launching*, ch. 9.

24 [*FDR's diary*]: *Personal Letters*, vol. 3, pp. 333–35.
["*Nothing to be seen*"]: Tugwell, *Democratic Roosevelt*, pp. 270–71.
[*Bank holiday*]: Burns, *Lion*, p. 166; Freidel, *Launching*, pp. 214–36; Kennedy, ch. 7.
[*Freidel on FDR and banking crisis*]: *Launching*, p. 218.

25 [*Left-wing press on money changers*]: see *ibid.*, p. 219; see also "Morgan's Friends Must Go," *Nation*, vol. 136, no. 3544 (June 7, 1933), pp. 628–29.
[*Economy bill*]: Freidel, *Launching*, ch. 14; *Roosevelt Public Papers*, vol. 2, pp. 49–51, quoted at p. 50.
[*Beer!*]: William Leuchtenburg, *Franklin D. Roosevelt and the New Deal* (Harper, 1963), pp. 46–47.
[*AAA*]: Arthur M. Schlesinger, Jr., *The Coming of the New Deal* (Houghton Mifflin, 1958), chs. 4–5; Rexford G. Tugwell, *Roosevelt's Revolution: The First Year—A Personal Perspective* (Macmillan, 1977), chs. 9, 11; Sternsher, chs. 14–16; John L. Shover, "Populism in the Nineteen-Thirties: The Battle for the AAA," *Agricultural History*, vol. 39, no. 1 (January 1965), pp. 17–24; Gilbert C. Fite, "Farm Opinion and the Agricultural Adjustment Act, 1933," *Mississippi Valley Historical Review*, vol. 48, no. 4 (March 1962), pp. 656–73; Irvin May, Jr., "Marvin Jones: Agrarian and Politician," *Agricultural History*, vol. 51, no. 2 (April 1977), pp. 421–40; *Roosevelt Public Papers*, vol. 2, quoted at p. 74.
["*Foreclosing judge*"]: Schlesinger, *Coming*, pp. 43–43, Judge Charles C. Bradley quoted at p. 43.
[*CCC*]: *ibid.*, pp. 335–41; John A. Salmond, *The Civilian Conservation Corps, 1933–1942: A New Deal Case Study* (Duke University Press, 1967), ch. 1 and *passim;* press conference, March 15, 1933, in *Roosevelt Public Papers*, vol. 2, pp. 67–72, quoted at p. 67.

25–6 [*Securities supervision*]: Ralph F. de Bedts, *The New Deal's SEC: The Formative Years* (Columbia University Press, 1964), ch. 2; *Roosevelt Public Papers*, vol. 2, pp. 93–94, quoted at p. 93.

26 [*Executive order on gold hoarding*]: see *Roosevelt Public Papers*, vol. 2, pp. 111–16, quoted at pp. 111, 115.
[*TVA*]: Paul K. Conkin, "Intellectual and Political Roots," in Conkin and Erwin C. Hargrove, eds., *TVA: Fifty Years of Grass-Roots Bureaucracy* (University of Illinois Press, 1983), pp. 1–32; Gordon R. Clapp, "The Meaning of TVA," in Roscoe Martin, ed., *TVA: The First Twenty Years* (University of Alabama Press/University of Tennessee Press, 1956), pp. 1–15, esp. p. 3; Joseph C. Swidler, "Legal Foundations," in *ibid.*, pp. 16–34, esp. pp. 24–25; Schlesinger, *Coming*, ch. 19; *Roosevelt Public Papers*, vol. 2, pp. 122–23, quoted at p. 122.
[*Norris-FDR exchange*]: quoted in Lief, p. 406; see also Lowitt, pp. 567–69.
[*Mortgage act*]: Schlesinger, *Coming*, pp. 297–98.

26–7 [*Railroad legislation*]: Freidel, *Launching*, pp. 410–16.

27 [*NIRA*]: Schlesinger, *Coming*, ch. 6; Hugh S. Johnson, *The Blue Eagle from Egg tô Earth* (Doubleday, Doran, 1935), chs. 17–18; Ellis W. Hawley, *The New Deal and the Problem of Monopoly* (Princeton University Press, 1966), part 1; Kim McQuaid, "Corporate Liberalism in the American Business Community, 1920–1940," *Business History Review*, vol. 52, no. 3 (Autumn 1978), pp. 342–68, esp. pp. 354–56; James MacGregor Burns, "Congress and the Formation of Economic Policies" (doctoral dissertation; Harvard University, 1947), ch. 1; A. Cash Koeniger, "Carter Glass and the National Recovery Administration," *South Atlantic Quarterly*, vol. 74, no. 3 (Summer 1975), pp. 349–64, esp. pp. 351–53; *Roosevelt Public Papers*, vol. 2, pp. 202–4, quoted at p. 202.
[*FDR on NIRA at signing*]: *Roosevelt Public Papers*, vol. 2, pp. 246–47, quoted at p. 246.

"Discipline and Direction Under Leadership"?

[*FDR at work*]: Burns, *Lion*, pp. 264–65; Freidel, *Launching*, pp. 274–88; see also Milton Katz, "From Hoover to Roosevelt," in Katie Loucheim, *The Making of the New*

Deal: The Insiders Speak (Harvard University Press, 1983), pp. 120–29, esp. pp. 121–22; Davis, *New Deal Years*, ch. 6.

28 [*Perkins on FDR*]: Frances Perkins, *The Roosevelt I Knew* (Viking, 1946), p. 163.
[*Berle on FDR*]: Berle and Jacobs, p. 72.
["*Combine eating up grain*"]: quoted in Bernard Asbell, *The F.D.R. Memoirs* (Doubleday, 1973), p. 84.
[*Brain trust*]: see sources cited in ch. 1, first section, *supra*.
[*Frankfurter and FDR*]: see Max Freedman, annot., *Roosevelt and Frankfurter: Their Correspondence, 1928–1945* (Little, Brown, 1967), esp. chs. 2–4; Bruce A. Murphy, *The Brandeis/Frankfurter Connection* (Oxford University Press, 1982), ch. 4.

29 [*Eleanor Roosevelt as First Lady*]: Lash, ch. 35; Eleanor Roosevelt, *This I Remember*, chs. 7–9; see also Burns, *Lion*, p. 173.
[*Beard on Eleanor*]: quoted in Lash, p. 373.
[*Dewson on both Roosevelts*]: Molly Dewson Papers, Franklin D. Roosevelt Library.
[*FDR's accessibility*]: see Freidel, *Launching*, pp. 74–79; Schlesinger, *Coming*, ch. 32.
[*FDR as quarterback*]: Burns, *Lion*, p. 171.

30 [*FDR as broker*]: see Otis L. Graham, Jr., *Toward a Planned Society: From Roosevelt to Nixon* (Oxford University Press, 1976), ch. 1; Graham, "The Broker State," *Wilson Quarterly*, vol. 8, no. 5 (Winter 1984), pp. 86–97.
["*To cement our society*"]: address at Green Bay, Wisc., August 9, 1934, in *Roosevelt Public Papers*, vol. 3, pp. 370–75, quoted at p. 375; see also Moley, *Seven Years*, p. 290. The Nebraska congressman was Edward Burke.
["*The outward expression*"]: October 24, 1934, in *Public Papers*, vol. 3, pp. 435–40, quoted at p. 436.
[*Congress and the early New Deal*]: James T. Patterson, *Congressional Conservatism and the New Deal* (University of Kentucky Press, 1967), ch. 1, FDR quoted on Byrd at pp. 29–30; Burns, *Lion*, pp. 174–75; Shover, "Populism in the Nineteen-Thirties"; Koeniger; Barbara Sinclair, "Party Realignment and the Transformation of the Political Agenda: House of Representatives, 1925–1938," *American Political Science Review*, vol. 71, no. 3 (September 1977), pp. 940–53.
["*Robbing Peter to pay Paul*"]: Green Bay address, in *Public Papers*, vol. 3, p. 374.

30–1 [*Economic conditions, spring–summer 1933*]: Irving Bernstein, *A Caring Society: The New Deal Confronts the Great Depression* (Houghton Mifflin, 1985), pp. 92–93, also pp. 35–36.

31 ["*Burned down the capitol*"]: quoted in Robert Bendiner, *Just Around the Corner* (Harper, 1967), p. 35.
[*Praise from* Tribune *and* American]: see *ibid.*, p. 36.
[*Lord Roosevelt and King George*]: James E. Sargent, *Roosevelt and the Hundred Days: Struggle for the Early New Deal* (Garland Publishing, 1981), p. 214; *Personal Letters*, vol. 3, pp. 369–71; Freidel, *Launching*, pp. 278–79.
[*Families on relief*]: Bernstein, *Caring Society*, pp. 32, 34.
["*I want to talk*"]: March 12, 1933, in *Public Papers*, vol. 2, pp. 61–65, quoted at p. 61.
[*Perkins on FDR's radio delivery*]: Perkins, p. 72.
[*FDR's press conferences*]: see Graham J. White, *FDR and the Press* (University of Chicago Press, 1979), ch. 1; see also *Public Papers*, vols. 2 and 3 *passim*.

32 [*Hugh Johnson and the Blue Eagle in action*]: Johnson, chs. 19–28; Matthew Josephson, "The General," *New Yorker*, vol. 10 (August 18–September 1, 1934); Leverett S. Lyon et al., *The National Recovery Administration: An Analysis and Appraisal* (Brookings Institution, 1935), part 2; Donald R. Richberg, *The Rainbow* (Doubleday, Doran, 1936), chs. 10–11; Schlesinger, *Coming*, ch. 7; *New York Times*, September 14, 1933, pp. 1–3.
[*Ford and NRA code*]: Nevins and Hill, pp. 15–27.

33 [*Nye on NRA*]: Schlesinger, *Coming*, p. 131.
[*Tugwell on Consumers' Advisory Board*]: quoted in *ibid.*, p. 130.
[*Section 7(a)*]: Irving Bernstein, *The Turbulent Years: A History of the American Worker, 1933–1941* (Houghton Mifflin, 1969), chs. 1–3, text of 7(a) quoted at p. 34; Schlesinger, *Coming*, ch. 9; Twentieth Century Fund, *Labor and the Government* (McGraw-Hill, 1935).

33 [*Lewis on 7(a)*]: Melvyn Dubofsky and Warren Van Tine, *John L. Lewis* (Quadrangle/ New York Times Book Co., 1977), p. 184.

["*PRESIDENT WANTS YOU*"]: quoted in Burns, *Lion*, p. 216.

["*Forget about injunctions*"]: quoted in Schlesinger, *Coming*, p. 139.

["*National Run Around*"]: Burns, *Lion*, p. 193.

[*Failure and significance of NRA*]: Theda Skocpol and Kenneth Finegold, "State Capacity and Economic Intervention in the Early New Deal," *Political Science Quarterly*, vol. 97, no. 2 (Summer 1982), pp. 255-78; Schlesinger, *Coming*, ch. 10; Hawley, chs. 6-7; Berle and Jacobs, p. 102; McQuaid, pp. 355-56; Johnson, chs. 29-30; Bernard Bellush, *The Failure of the NRA* (Norton, 1975), esp. chs. 7-8.

[*FDR's private judgment on NRA*]: see Robert S. McElvaine, *The Great Depression: America 1929-1941* (Times Books, 1984), p. 162.

34 [*PWA*]: Schlesinger, *Coming*, ch. 17; Harold L. Ickes, *The Secret Diary of Harold L. Ickes* (Simon and Schuster, 1953-54), vol. 1, *passim*.

[*FERA and CWA*]: Bernstein, *Caring Society*, pp. 25-42; George McJimsey, *Harry Hopkins: Ally of the Poor and Defender of Democracy* (Harvard University Press, 1987), ch. 4; Schlesinger, *Coming*, ch. 16; Burns, *Lion*, p. 196; Robert E. Sherwood, *Roosevelt and Hopkins: An Intimate History* (Harper, 1948), ch. 3; William M. Bremer, "Along the 'American Way': The New Deal's Work Relief Programs for the Unemployed," *Journal of American History*, vol. 62, no. 3 (December 1975), pp. 636-52; Paul E. Mertz, *New Deal Policy and Southern Rural Poverty* (Louisiana State University Press, 1978), chs. 3-4; Davis, *New Deal Years*, pp. 305-14.

35 [*Sargent on FDR*]: Sargent, pp. 21-22.

["*Get somewhere*"]: quoted in Burns, *Lion*, p. 197.

[*London Conference*]: Robert Dallek, *Franklin D. Roosevelt and American Foreign Policy, 1932-1945* (Oxford University Press, 1979), pp. 39-58; Feis, chs. 12-20; Burns, *Lion*, pp. 177-78; Schlesinger, *Coming*, chs. 12-13; James R. Moore, "Sources of New Deal Economic Policy: The International Dimension," *Journal of American History*, vol. 61, no. 3 (December 1974), pp. 728-44; Freidel, *Launching*, chs. 27-28; Betty Glad, *Key Pittman: The Tragedy of a Senate Insider* (Columbia University Press, 1986), ch. 17; Davis, *New Deal Years*, ch. 5.

36 [*Tariff bill*]: Schlesinger, *Coming*, pp. 253-55.

[*Gold purchases*]: *ibid.*, ch. 14; Elmus Wicker, "Roosevelt's 1933 Monetary Experiment," *Journal of American History*, vol. 57, no. 4 (March 1971), pp. 864-79; John Morton Blum, *From the Morgenthau Diaries: Years of Crisis, 1928-1938* (Houghton Mifflin, 1959), pp. 61-75.

["*A lucky number*"]: quoted in Blum, p. 70.

[*Recognition of the Soviet Union*]: Dallek, pp. 78-81; Robert P. Browder, *The Origins of Soviet-American Diplomacy* (Princeton University Press, 1953), esp. chs. 4-6; George F. Kennan, *Russia and the West Under Lenin and Stalin* (Atlantic Monthly/Little, Brown, 1961), pp. 297-300; Loy W. Henderson, *A Question of Trust: The Origins of U.S.-Soviet Diplomatic Relations*, George W. Baer, ed. (Hoover Institution Press, 1986).

36-7 ["*Whited out*" *map*]: Lash, p. 589.

37 [*Berle on public works and NRA*]: Berle and Jacobs, p. 102.

[*Ickes and the oil industry*]: Linda J. Lear, "Harold L. Ickes and the Oil Crisis of the First Hundred Days," *Mid-America*, vol. 63, no. 1 (January 1981), pp. 3-13; *Ickes Diary*, vol. 1, pp. 10-16, 36-47 *passim*.

[*FSRC*]: C. Roger Lambert, "Want and Plenty: The Federal Surplus Relief Corporation and the AAA," *Agricultural History*, vol. 46, no. 3 (July 1972), pp. 390-400; Irvin May, Jr., "Cotton and Cattle: The FSRC and Emergency Work Relief," *ibid.*, pp. 401-13.

[*Air mail*]: Schlesinger, *Coming*, pp. 448-55; Thomas T. Spencer, "The Air Mail Controversy of 1934," *Mid-America*, vol. 62, no. 3 (October 1980), pp. 161-72.

[*1934 election*]: Schlesinger, *Coming*, pp. 503-7; Burns, *Lion*, pp. 198-203.

["*Are you better off?*"]: June 28, 1934, in *Public Papers*, vol. 3, pp. 312-18, quoted at p. 314.

[*Garner on congressional majority*]: quoted in Burns, *Lion*, p. 202.

37–8 [*Churchill on FDR*]: Churchill, "While the World Watches," *Collier's*, December 29, 1934, as quoted in Schlesinger, *Coming*, p. 23.

2. THE ARC OF CONFLICT

39 [*"We sold everything we could"*]: Jimmy Douglas, quoted in Federal Writers' Project, *These Are Our Lives* (University of North Carolina Press, 1939; reprinted by Arno Press, 1969), p. 241.
  [*NRA in Macon County*]: Arthur F. Raper, *Preface to Peasantry: A Tale of Two Black Belt Counties* (University of North Carolina Press, 1936), p. 237.
  [*"Your best tie"*]: Personal reminiscence of the author.
  [*Writer on currant pickers*]: John Macnamara, "Berry Picker," *Nation*, vol. 139, no. 3610 (September 12, 1934), pp. 302–4, quoted at p. 303.
  [*Du Pont vice president on cook*]: Robert Carpenter, quoted in Gerard Colby Zilg, *Du Pont: Behind the Nylon Curtain* (Prentice-Hall, 1974), p. 289.
  [*Indiana housewife on relief*]: quoted in Robert S. Lynd and Helen Merrell Lynd, *Middletown in Transition: A Study in Cultural Conflicts* (Harcourt, 1937), pp. 111–12.

40 [*"God damn all Roosevelts!"*]: quoted in Arthur M. Schlesinger, Jr., *The Coming of the New Deal* (Houghton Mifflin, 1958), p. 567.
  [*Garden City dust storm*]: quoted in Donald Worster, *Dust Bowl: The Southern Plains in the 1930s* (Oxford University Press, 1979), p. 17.
  [*"Eleven Cent cotton"*]: quoted in Ann M. Campbell, "Reports from Weedpatch, California: The Records of the Farm Security Administration," *Agricultural History*, vol. 48, no. 3 (July 1974), p. 402.
  [*Economic conditions, 1929–35*]: U.S. Bureau of the Census, *Historical Statistics of the United States, Colonial Times to 1970* (U.S. Government Printing Office, 1975), part 1, p. 135 (Series D 85–86) (unemployment); part 1, p. 170 (Series D 802–10) (weekly earnings); part 2, p. 610 (Series N 1–29) (construction).

Class War in America

41 [*"A nice old gentleman"*]: address delivered at Syracuse, N.Y., September 29, 1936, in *The Public Papers and Addresses of Franklin D. Roosevelt*, Samuel I. Rosenman, comp. (Random House, 1938–50), vol. 5, pp. 383–90, quoted at p. 385.
  [*FDR's conservatism in early New Deal*]: see Frank Freidel, *Franklin D. Roosevelt: The Launching of the New Deal* (Little, Brown, 1973), chs. 12–14 *passim*.

42 [*Values of American right*]: see Clinton Rossiter, *Conservatism in America* (Knopf, 1955), esp. ch. 4.
  [*Al Smith and the New Deal*]: Richard O'Connor, *The First Hurrah: A Biography of Alfred E. Smith* (Putnam, 1970), chs. 18–19; Oscar Handlin, *Al Smith and His America* (Little, Brown, 1958), ch. 8.

42–3 [*Founding of Liberty League*]: George Wolfskill, *The Revolt of the Conservatives: A History of the American Liberty League, 1934–1940* (Greenwood Press, 1962), pp. 23–25, 56–67; Frederick Rudolph, "The American Liberty League, 1934–1940," *American Historical Review*, vol. 56, no. 1 (October 1950), pp. 19–33; Zilg, pp. 283–98; Seymour Martin Lipset and Earl Raab, *The Politics of Unreason: Right-Wing Extremism in America, 1790–1970* (Harper, 1970), pp. 200–2.

43 [*Shouse-FDR meeting*]: Wolfskill, pp. 27–28, quoted at p. 27.
  [*FDR on "Commandments"*]: press conference 137, August 24, 1934, as quoted in James MacGregor Burns, *Roosevelt: The Lion and the Fox* (Harcourt, 1956), pp. 206–8, and Schlesinger, *Coming*, p. 487.
  [*Conservative attack on New Deal*]: George Wolfskill and John A. Hudson, *All but the People: Franklin D. Roosevelt and His Critics, 1933–39* (Macmillan, 1969), pp. 161–62; collection of American Liberty League pamphlets at Sawyer Library, Williams College.

43–4 [*FDR's threat to capitalists' self-esteem*]: see Burns, *Lion*, p. 240; Daniel Aaron, "Conservatism, Old and New," *American Quarterly*, vol. 6, no. 2 (Summer 1954), pp. 99–110;

Louis Hartz, "The Whig Tradition in America and Europe," *American Political Science Review*, vol. 46, no. 4 (December 1952), pp. 989–1002; Russell Kirk, *The Conservative Mind* (Henry Regnery, 1955); Rossiter, ch. 11; Robert A. Nisbet, "Conservatism and Sociology," *American Journal of Sociology*, vol. 58, no. 2 (September 1952), pp. 167–75; Richard W. Leopold, *Elihu Root and the Conservative Tradition* (Little, Brown, 1954); Louis Hartz, *The Liberal Tradition in America* (Harcourt, 1955); Peter Viereck, *Conservatism Revisited* (Scribner, 1949).

44 [*French observer on wealth and virtue*]: Burns, *Lion*, p. 240.
 [*FDR on classmate's remarks*]: quoted in *ibid.*, p. 205.
 [*FDR on "dinner-party conversations"*]: *ibid.*, pp. 205–6.
 [*Hofstadter on betrayal*]: Hofstadter, *The American Political Tradition* (Knopf, 1948), p. 330; see also Wolfskill and Hudson, ch. 6.
 [*Names for FDR*]: Wolfskill and Hudson, pp. 16–17.
 ["*The $64 question*"]: *ibid.*, p. 25.

45 ["*THE PRESIDENT'S WIFE IS SUING*"]: *ibid.*
 [*Obsession with FDR's disability*]: *ibid.*, pp. 12–15.
 [*FDR's "insanity"*]: *ibid.*, pp. 5–11.
 [*Anti-Semitism*]: *ibid.*, pp. 65–78.

45–6 [*AFL in 1920s and depression*]: Irving Bernstein, *The Lean Years: A History of the American Worker, 1920–1933* (Houghton Mifflin, 1960), pp. 83–108; see also Eugene T. Sweeney, "The A.F.L.'s Good Citizen, 1920–1940," *Labor History*, vol. 13, no. 2 (Spring 1972), pp. 200–16.

46 [*Union growth under 7(a)*]: Irving Bernstein, *The Turbulent Years: A History of the American Worker, 1933–1941* (Houghton Mifflin, 1969), chs. 2–3.
 [*San Francisco labor conflict*]: *ibid.*, pp. 252–98; Felix Riesenberg, Jr., *Golden Gate* (Knopf, 1940), ch. 23; Charles P. Larrowe, "The Great Maritime Strike of '34," *Labor History*, vol. 11, no. 4 (Fall 1970), pp. 403–51, and vol. 12, no. 1 (Winter 1971), pp. 3–37.
 [*Shape-up*]: Bernstein, *Turbulent Years*, pp. 254–56.

47 [*FDR on strike*]: quoted in *ibid.*, p. 289.
 [*Perkins's role in settlement*]: *ibid.*, pp. 288–90; George Martin, *Madam Secretary* (Houghton Mifflin, 1976), pp. 313–22; Frances Perkins, *The Roosevelt I Knew* (Viking, 1946), pp. 312–15.
 [*Minneapolis strike*]: Bernstein, *Turbulent Years*, pp. 229–52; George H. Mayer, *The Political Career of Floyd B. Olson* (University of Minnesota Press, 1951), ch. 10.

48 [*Textile strike*]: Bernstein, *Turbulent Years*, pp. 298–315.
 [*Brooks on textile strike*]: quoted in *ibid.*, p. 309.
 [*Daniels on troops*]: quoted in Schlesinger, *Coming*, p. 394.

49 ["*Destroying cities*"]: quoted in Bernstein, *Turbulent Years*, p. 313.
 [*Sharecroppers' plight*]: Erskine Caldwell, *Tenant Farmer* (Phoenix Press, 1935), quoted at p. 4; Raper.
 [*Southern Tenant Farmers' Union*]: H. L. Mitchell, *Mean Things Happening in This Land* (Allanheld, Osmun, 1979), esp. chs. 4–10; Lowell Dyson, "Southern Tenant Farmers' Union and Depression Politics," *Political Science Quarterly*, vol. 88, no. 2 (June 1973), pp. 230–52; Bernard K. Johnpoll, *Pacifist's Progress: Norman Thomas and the Decline of American Socialism* (Quadrangle, 1970), pp. 146–52; Donald H. Grubbs, *Cry from the Cotton: The Southern Tenant Farmers' Union and the New Deal* (University of North Carolina Press, 1971); Jess Gilbert and Steve Brown, "Alternative Land Reform Proposals in the 1930s: The Nashville Agrarians and the Southern Tenant Farmers' Union," *Agricultural History*, vol. 55, no. 4 (October 1981), pp. 351–69.
 [*Preacher on "this fuss"*]: quoted in Schlesinger, *Coming*, p. 377.
 [*Itinerant farm workers*]: Bernstein, *Turbulent Years*; see also Walter J. Stein, *California and the Dust Bowl Migration* (Greenwood Press, 1973), esp. ch. 8.

50 [*Bernstein on Imperial Valley dispute*]: Bernstein, *Turbulent Years*, p. 160.
 [*ACLU tour*]: *ibid.*, pp. 166–67.

51 ["*Prayer of Bitter Men*"]: quoted in Richard Lowitt and Maurine Beasley, eds., *One Third of a Nation: Lorena Hickok Reports on the Great Depression* (University of Illinois Press, 1981), p. 365.

"Lenin or Christ"—or a Path Between?

52 ["*Fight by all available means*"]: "Statutes of the Communist International Adopted at the Second Comintern Congress," August 4, 1920, in Jane Degras, ed., *The Communist International, 1919–1943: Documents* (Oxford University Press, 1956), vol. 1, quoted at p. 163.

[*Sixth World Congress on smashing capitalism*]: see Arthur M. Schlesinger, Jr., *The Politics of Upheaval* (Houghton Mifflin, 1960), p. 189.

[*Communist party, eve of 1930s*]: Harvey Klehr, *The Heyday of American Communism: The Depression Decade* (Basic Books, 1984), ch. 1, esp. p. 5.

[*Depression as potential boon to Communists*]: see Irving Howe and Lewis Coser, *The American Communist Party: A Critical History (1919–1957)* (Beacon Press, 1957), pp. 188–97.

[*Communist party membership, 1932–33*]: Klehr, pp. 91–92.

53 ["*United front from below*"]: ibid., pp. 13, 97–104; Schlesinger, *Upheaval*, pp. 197–98.

[*Browder*]: Klehr, pp. 21–23; John McCarten, "Party Linesman," *New Yorker*, vol. 14 (September 24, 1938), pp. 20–24, and (October 1, 1938), pp. 22–27; James Gilbert Ryan, "The Making of a Native Marxist: The Early Career of Earl Browder," *Review of Politics*, vol. 39, no. 3 (July 1977), pp. 332–62.

[*Browder's claims as to size of following*]: Schlesinger, *Upheaval*, p. 198.

[*Signed-up members*]: Klehr, p. 365.

[*League Against War and Fascism*]: ibid., pp. 107–12; Howe and Coser, pp. 348–55.

[*Youth Congress*]: Klehr, pp. 319–23; Earl Browder, "The American Communist Party in the Thirties," in Rita James Simon, ed., *As We Saw the Thirties* (University of Illinois Press, 1967), pp. 227–29.

[*Writers and Communist party*]: see Daniel Aaron, *Writers on the Left* (Harcourt, 1961), part 2 passim.

[*Demise of "red unions"*]: Bert Cochran, *Labor and Communism: The Conflict that Shaped American Unions* (Princeton University Press, 1977), ch. 3, esp. pp. 74–75; Jack Statchel quoted on working among AFL workers at p. 74; Klehr, chs. 7, 13; Howe and Coser, ch. 6.

[*Thomas*]: Johnpoll; W. A. Swanberg, *Norman Thomas: The Last Idealist* (Scribner, 1976).

[*Schlesinger on Thomas*]: *Upheaval*, p. 177.

53-4 [*Divisions among Socialists*]: Johnpoll, ch. 4; Swanberg, esp. ch. 9; John H. M. Laslett and Seymour Martin Lipset, eds., *Failure of a Dream?: Essays in the History of American Socialism* (Doubleday, 1974).

54 [*Attempts at Socialist-Communist union*]: Johnpoll, pp. 111–16, 140–43; Howe and Coser, pp. 325–27; Klehr, pp. 99–112; Norman Thomas, "The Thirties as a Socialist Recalls Them," in Simon, pp. 114–17.

[*Madison Square Garden meeting*]: *New York Times*, February 17, 1934, pp. 1, 3; Klehr, pp. 113–16.

[*Thomas on impossibility of united front*]: quoted in Johnpoll, p. 115; see also Peggy Lamson, *Roger Baldwin: Founder of the American Civil Liberties Union* (Houghton Mifflin, 1976), esp. ch. 14.

[*In the Archey Road*]: Finley Peter Dunne, "Proposed: A Federal Divorce Law," in Dunne, *Mr. Dooley on the Choice of Law*, Edward J. Bander, comp. (Michie Co., 1963), pp. 87–95, quoted at p. 87.

[*AFL as federation of craft and industrial workers*]: Christopher L. Tomlins, "AFL Unions in the 1930s: Their Performance in Historical Perspective," *Journal of American History*, vol. 65, no. 4 (March 1979), pp. 1021–42; see also Edwin Young, "The Split in the Labor Movement," in Milton Derber and Edwin Young, eds., *Labor and the New Deal* (University of Wisconsin Press, 1957), pp. 47–50.

55 [*Federal labor unions*]: Bernstein, *Turbulent Years*, pp. 355–60.

[*Bernstein on federal union leaders*]: ibid., p. 373; see, generally, Walter Licht and Hal Seth Barron, "Labor's Men: A Collective Biography of Union Officialdom During the New Deal Years," *Labor History*, vol. 19, no. 2 (Fall 1978), pp. 532–45.

[*Supporters of federal union leaders*]: Bernstein, *Turbulent Years*, p. 363.

[*Divisions among AFL leaders*]: see ibid., pp. 360–66 and ch. 8 passim; Maxwell C.

Raddock, *Portrait of an American Labor Leader: William L. Hutcheson* (American Institute of Social Science, 1955), ch. 14; Robert D. Leiter, *The Teamsters Union* (Bookman Associates, 1957), ch. 2; David Dubinsky and A. H. Raskin, *David Dubinsky: A Life with Labor* (Simon and Schuster, 1977), ch. 9; Matthew Josephson, *Sidney Hillman: Statesman of American Labor* (Doubleday, 1952), ch. 17.

55 [*Lewis*]: Melvyn Dubofsky and Warren Van Tine, *John L. Lewis* (Quadrangle/New York Times Book Co., 1977).

55–6 [*Debate among craft and industrial unionists, 1934–35*]: Bernstein, *Turbulent Years*, pp. 368–86; Young in Derber and Young, pp. 52–55.

56 [*1935 AFL convention*]: American Federation of Labor, *Report of Proceedings of the Fifty-fifth Annual Convention* (1935), esp. pp. 521–75, 614–65, 725–29; Bernstein, *Turbulent Years*, pp. 386–98.
[*Lewis on strong and weak unions*]: quoted in *Proceedings*, pp. 541, 542.
[*Lewis's punch*]: Bernstein, *Turbulent Years*, p. 397; *Proceedings*, p. 727.
[*Lewis-Green exchange*]: quoted in Schlesinger, *Coming*, p. 413.
[*Formation of CIO*]: Bernstein, *Turbulent Years*, pp. 397–431; Dubofsky and Van Tine, ch. 11; see also David Brody, "Labor and the Great Depression: The Interpretive Prospects," *Labor History*, vol. 13, no. 2 (Spring 1972), pp. 231–44.

56–7 [*Lewis-Green exchange of letters*]: quoted in Bernstein, *Turbulent Years*, pp. 403–4; on Green's writings in favor of industrial unionism, see *ibid.*, pp. 399–400.

57 [*Social justice in Catholic Church*]: see John F. Cronin, *Social Principles and Economic Life* (Bruce Publishing, 1959); Aaron I. Abell, *American Catholicism and Social Action: A Search for Social Justice, 1865–1950* (Hanover House, 1960); Ernst Troeltsch, *The Social Teachings of the Christian Churches*, Olive Wyon, trans. (Allen & Unwin, 1950), vol. 1.
[*Coughlin*]: David H. Bennett, *Demagogues in the Depression* (Rutgers University Press, 1969), part 1; Alan Brinkley, *Voices of Protest: Huey Long, Father Coughlin, and the Great Depression* (Knopf, 1982), chs. 4–6 and *passim;* Sheldon Marcus, *Father Coughlin: The Tumultuous Life of the Priest of the Little Flower* (Little, Brown, 1973); Charles J. Tull, *Father Coughlin and the New Deal* (Syracuse University Press, 1965).
[*"Please, God—a priest"*]: quoted in Brinkley, p. 84.

58 [*Stegner on Coughlin's voice*]: Stegner, "The Radio Priest and His Flock," in Isabel Leighton, ed., *The Aspirin Age, 1919–1941* (Simon and Schuster, 1949), p. 234.
[*Detroit in the depression*]: B. J. Widick, *Detroit: City of Race and Class Violence* (Quadrangle, 1972), ch. 3.
[*"A detriment"*]: quoted in Schlesinger, *Upheaval*, pp. 18–19.
[*"Four Horsemen"*]: *ibid.*, p. 18.
[*Coughlin on Smith*]: see Marcus, p. 64.
[*Coughlin on O'Connell*]: quoted in Bennett, p. 59.
[*Coughlin in 1934*]: Brinkley, pp. 119–20; Marcus, pp. 54–56, 61–62.
[*Coughlin in 1932 campaign*]: Brinkley, pp. 107–8; Marcus, pp. 44–48.
[*"Roosevelt or Ruin"*]: quoted in Brinkley, p. 108.
[*"Christ's Deal"*]: *ibid.*
[*Coughlin's letters to FDR*]: see Bennett, p. 38; Brinkley, p. 109.
[*Coughlin and White House*]: Tull, ch. 2; Brinkley, pp. 108–10.

59 [*Coughlin and CBS*]: Brinkley, pp. 99–101.
[*Coughlin's audience*]: *ibid.*, pp. 196–207.
[*Coughlin-FDR divergence*]: Tull, pp. 52–58; Marcus, pp. 58–70; Brinkley, pp. 124–27, 178–79, 244–46.
[*National Union for Social Justice*]: Marcus, ch. 5; Tull, ch. 3.
[*"Organized lobby"*]: quoted in Brinkley, pp. 133–34.
[*Long*]: T. Harry Williams, *Huey Long* (Knopf, 1969); Harnett T. Kane, *Louisiana Hayride: The American Rehearsal for Dictatorship, 1928–1940* (Morrow, 1941); Huey Pierce Long, *Every Man a King* (National Book Co., 1933); Brinkley, chs. 1–3 and *passim;* Huey P. Long Papers, General Correspondence, Louisiana State University Library; Glen Jeansonne, "The Apotheosis of Huey P. Long: A Critique of *Huey Long*" (typescript, n.d.); Lipset and Raab, pp. 189–99.
[*Long's use of radio*]: Williams, pp. 203, 629–30.

60 [*Long's "facts and figures"*]: Brinkley, p. 72.
[*"Come to my feast"*]: quoted in *ibid.*, pp. 71–72.

60 [*Share Our Wealth plan*]: *ibid.*, pp. 72–73, quoted at p. 72; Kane, pp. 121–24; see also Arnold Shankman, "The Five-Day Plan and the Depression," *The Historian*, vol. 43, no. 3 (May 1981), pp. 393–409. See also Sender Garlin, *The Real Huey P. Long* (Workers Library Publishers, 1935), a Communist party attack on Long.
[*"Some great minds"*]: quoted in Brinkley, p. 73.
[*Mencken on Long*]: *ibid.*
[*Brinkley on Long's plan*]: *ibid.*, p. 74.

61 [*Long's Louisiana*]: V. O. Key, Jr., *Southern Politics in State and Nation* (Knopf, 1949), ch. 8; Allan P. Sindler, *Huey Long's Louisiana: State Politics, 1920–1952* (Johns Hopkins Press, 1956), esp. ch. 1.
[*Long's hold on Louisiana politics*]: Brinkley, pp. 22–35, 67–70; Williams, pp. 712–36; see also Kane, pp. 102–15; Hodding Carter, "Huey Long: American Dictator," *American Mercury*, vol. 48, no. 304 (April 1949), pp. 435–47.
[*Long at 1932 convention*]: Williams, pp. 571–82; Long, chs. 32–33.

62 [*Long on FDR*]: quoted in Brinkley, p. 46; see also Williams, p. 6.
[*Long's opposition to Hundred Days*]: Williams, pp. 627–36; see also Michael J. Cassity, "Huey Long: Barometer of Reform in the New Deal," *South Atlantic Quarterly*, vol. 72, no. 2 (Spring 1973), pp. 255–69.
[*Long at White House*]: James A. Farley, *Behind the Ballots* (Harcourt, 1938), pp. 240–42, Long quoted at p. 242.
[*Administration action against Long*]: Williams, pp. 636–38, 689–92, 793–98, 812–13; Brinkley, pp. 79–81; Farley, *Ballots*, pp. 251–52.
[*Hoot owl and scrootch owl*]: quoted in Kane, p. 101.
[*Share Our Wealth Society*]: Williams, pp. 692–98, 700–2; Long Papers, General Correspondence, 1934–35.
[*Share Our Wealth membership*]: Williams, p. 700; see also Raymond Gram Swing, "The Menace of Huey Long: III," *Nation*, vol. 140, no. 3629 (January 23, 1935), pp. 98–100.
[*Long's communications kingdom*]: Brinkley, pp. 62, 70–71, 169; Williams, pp. 641–47; collection of radio speeches, Long Papers.

The Politics of Tumult

63 [*Condition of FDR's staff, midterm*]: Beatrice Bishop Berle and Travis Beal Jacobs, eds., *Navigating the Rapids, 1918–1971: From the Papers of Adolf A. Berle* (Harcourt, 1973), p. 102; Berle Papers, Franklin D. Roosevelt Library, Hyde Park, N.Y.; Schlesinger, *Upheaval*, p. 212; Harold L. Ickes, *The Secret Diary of Harold L. Ickes* (Simon and Schuster, 1953–54), vol. 1, p. 303; Joseph P. Lash, *Eleanor and Franklin* (Norton, 1971), pp. 435–36.

64 [*"A democracy after all"*]: quoted in Lash, p. 437; see also Molly Dewson Papers, Roosevelt Library.
[*Agriculture in first New Deal*]: Raper, pp. 243–53, Georgia tenants' conversation quoted at p. 245; Theodore Saloutos and John D. Hicks, *Agricultural Discontent in the Middle West, 1900–1939* (University of Wisconsin Press, 1959), ch. 17; Theodore Saloutos, *The American Farmer and the New Deal* (Iowa State University Press, 1982), chs. 3–7; Bernard Sternsher, *Rexford Tugwell and the New Deal* (Rutgers University Press, 1964), chs. 15–22; C. Roger Lambert, "Want and Plenty: The Federal Surplus Relief Corporation and the AAA," *Agricultural History*, vol. 46, no. 3 (July 1972), pp. 390–400; Irvin May, Jr., "Cotton and Cattle: The FSRC and Emergency Work Relief," *ibid.*, pp. 401–13.
[*Agricultural lobbying groups*]: Saloutos and Hicks, chs. 8–9; John L. Shover, *Cornbelt Rebellion: The Farmers' Holiday Association* (University of Illinois Press, 1965), chs. 9–11; Wesley McCune, *The Farm Bloc* (Doubleday, Doran, 1943); Orville Merton Kile, *The Farm Bureau Through Three Decades* (Waverly Press, 1948), esp. chs. 16–17; John A. Crampton, *The National Farmers Union: Ideology of a Pressure Group* (University of Nebraska Press, 1965); James L. Guth, "The National Cooperative Council and Farm Relief, 1929–1942," *Agricultural History*, vol. 51, no. 2 (April 1977), pp. 441–58; Robert L. Tontz, "Memberships of General Farmers' Organizations, United States, 1874–1960," *ibid.*, vol. 38, no. 3 (July 1964), pp. 143–60; Lee J. Alston and Joseph

P. Ferrie, "Resisting the Welfare State: Southern Opposition to the Farm Security Administration," *Research in Economic History* (JAI Press, 1985), Suppl. 4, pp. 83–120.

65 [*Talmadge's agricultural policies*]: see Raper, pp. 225–28.

66 [*1935 AAA "purge"*]: Sternsher, ch. 16; Saloutos, *American Farmer*, ch. 8; Richard Lowitt, "Henry A. Wallace and the 1935 Purge in the Department of Agriculture," *Agricultural History*, vol. 53, no. 3 (July 1979), pp. 607–21.

[*Townsend and Townsend Movement*]: Bennett, chs. 10–12; Abraham Holtzman, *The Townsend Movement: A Political Study* (Bookman Associates, 1963), chs. 2–3; The Committee on Old Age Security of the Twentieth Century Fund, *The Townsend Crusade* (Twentieth Century Fund, 1936); Schlesinger, *Upheaval*, ch. 3.

67 [*Parsons on the elderly*]: quoted in Holtzman, p. 20.

["*Until the whole country hears*"]: quoted in Brinkley, pp. 222–23.

["*Onward, Townsend soldiers*"]: quoted in Schlesinger, *Upheaval*, p. 34.

68 [*Time inflation of Townsend clubs*]: vol. 25, no. 2 (January 14, 1935), p. 14.

[*High on Townsend movement*]: quoted in Schlesinger, *Upheaval*, p. 34.

[*La Follette brothers*]: Donald Young, ed., *Adventure in Politics: The Memoirs of Philip La Follette* (Holt, Rinehart and Winston, 1970), esp. ch. 17; Edward N. Doan, *The La Follettes and the Wisconsin Idea* (Rinehart, 1947); Schlesinger, *Upheaval*, pp. 104–8; John E. Miller, "Philip La Follette: Rhetoric and Reality," *Historian*, vol. 45, no. 2 (February 1983), pp. 65–83.

[*FDR's endorsement of Bob La Follette*]: Burns, *Lion*, p. 201.

[*Olson*]: Mayer; Schlesinger, *Upheaval*, pp. 98–104.

[*Olson on 1940*]: quoted in Schlesinger, *Upheaval*, p. 104.

69 [*EPIC and anti-EPIC campaigns*]: Upton Sinclair, *I, Candidate for Governor and How I Got Licked* (Upton Sinclair, 1935); "The Epic of Upton Sinclair," *Nation*, vol. 139, no. 3617 (October 31, 1934), pp. 495–96; Royce D. Delmatier et al., *The Rumble of California Politics, 1848–1970* (Wiley, 1970), pp. 266–67, 272–80; Luther Whiteman and Samuel L. Lewis, "EPIC, or Politics for Use," in Dennis Hale and Jonathan Eisen, eds., *The California Dream* (Collier Books, 1968), pp. 63–71.

[*White House and Sinclair's campaign*]: Sinclair, *Candidate*, chs. 15–17, 36; Schlesinger, *Upheaval*, pp. 115–17, 119–21; Lash, pp. 386–87.

["*(1) Say nothing*"]: quoted in Lash, p. 387.

70 [*Sinclair's books on campaign*]: Sinclair, *Candidate*; Sinclair, *I, Governor of California and How I Ended Poverty* (Upton Sinclair, 1933); for Lanny Budd, see Sinclair's eleven-volume "World's End" series (Viking, 1940–53).

[*Historians' and FDR's "turn to the left"*]: see Robert S. McElvaine, *The Great Depression: America 1929–1941* (Times Books, 1984), pp. 261–63; Otis Graham, Jr., "Historians and the New Deal, 1944–1960," *Social Studies*, vol. 54 (April 1963), pp. 133–40; Sternsher, ch. 11; Barton J. Bernstein, "The New Deal: The Conservative Achievements of Liberal Reform," in Bernstein and Allen J. Matusow, eds., *Twentieth-Century America: Recent Interpretations* (Harcourt, 1972), pp. 242–64.

[*FDR's coolness to Wagner bill*]: see Joseph J. Huthmacher, *Senator Robert B. Wagner and the Rise of Urban Liberalism* (Atheneum, 1968), pp. 166–69, 189–90, 197–98.

[*1935 State of the Union address*]: January 4, 1935, in *Public Papers*, vol. 4, pp. 15–25, quoted at p. 25.

70-1 [*"Distinctly dispirited"*]: *Ickes Diary*, vol. 1, p. 306.

71 [*Chamber of Commerce conference*]: *New York Times*, May 1, 1935, pp. 1–2, Silas Strawn quoted at p. 1; *New York Times*, May 3, 1935, pp. 1, 4; Schlesinger, *Upheaval*, pp. 270–72.

72 [*Supreme Court invalidation of New Deal legislation*]: *Panama Refining Co.* v. *Ryan*, 293 U.S. 388 (1935) (hot oil provisions of NRA); *Railroad Retirement Board* v. *Alton Railroad Co.*, 295 U.S. 330 (1935); *Schechter* v. *United States*, 295 U.S. 495 (1935) (NRA); *Louisville Joint Stock Land Bank* v. *Radford*, 295 U.S. 555 (1935) (farm mortgage law); *United States* v. *Butler*, 297 U.S. 1 (1936) (AAA); *Carter* v. *Carter Coal Co.*, 298 U.S. 238 (1936) (Bituminous Coal Act); *Ashton* v. *Cameron County Water Improvement District No. 1*, 298 U.S. 513 (1936) (Municipal Bankruptcy Act).

[*Gold Clause cases*]: *Perry* v. *United States*, 294 U.S. 330 (1935); *United States* v. *Bankers Trust Co.*, 294 U.S. 240 (1935); *Norman* v. *Baltimore & Ohio R.R. Co.*, 294 U.S. 240 (1935); *Nortz* v. *United States*, 294 U.S. 317 (1935); McReynolds quoted in *Newsweek*, vol. 5, no. 8 (February 23, 1935), p. 7; John Morton Blum, *From the Morgenthau Diaries: Years of Crisis, 1928–1938* (Houghton Mifflin, 1959), pp. 130–31.

72–3 [*"Shudder at the closeness"*]: letter to Angus D. MacLean, February 21, 1935, quoted in Schlesinger, *Upheaval*, p. 260.

73 [*FDR's meeting with liberal senators*]: Max Freedman, annot., *Roosevelt and Frankfurter: Their Correspondence, 1928–1945* (Little, Brown, 1967), pp. 269–72; *Ickes Diary*, vol. 1, pp. 363–64.
[*"Eleventh hour"*]: quoted in *Ickes Diary*, vol. 1, p. 363.
[*FDR's press conference after NRA invalidation*]: May 31, 1935, in *Public Papers*, vol. 4, pp. 201–22, quoted at pp. 201, 202, 209, 221.

74 [*"Black-winged angel"*]: Schlesinger, *Upheaval*, p. 280.
[*"This is the end"*]: quoted in Philippa Strum, *Louis D. Brandeis: Justice for the People* (Harvard University Press, 1984), p. 352.
[*Brandeis and Frankfurter in FDR Administration*]: *ibid.*, pp. 380–87; Schlesinger, *Upheaval*, pp. 219–25; Bruce A. Murphy, *The Brandeis/Frankfurter Connection* (Oxford University Press, 1982), chs. 4–5; Ellis W. Hawley, *The New Deal and the Problem of Monopoly* (Princeton University Press, 1966), part 3; Rexford G. Tugwell, "Roosevelt and Frankfurter: An Essay Review," *Political Science Quarterly*, vol. 85, no. 1 (March 1970), pp. 99–114; Freedman, *passim*.

75 [*FDR's continued desire for "collectivist" control*]: see Otis L. Graham, Jr., *Toward a Planned Society: From Roosevelt to Nixon* (Oxford University Press, 1976), p. 32.
[*FDR's imperative*]: Murphy, p. 159; see also FDR memorandum to legislative leaders, June 4, 1935, in *F.D.R.: His Personal Letters*, Elliott Roosevelt, ed. (Duell, Sloan and Pearce, 1947–50), vol. 3, p. 481; and memorandum for legislative conference of August 18, 1935, in *ibid.*, pp. 502–3.
[*Congressional progressives riding high*]: see Ronald A. Mulder, "The Progressive Insurgents in the United States Senate, 1935–1936: Was There a Second New Deal?," *Mid-America*, vol. 57, no. 2 (April 1975), pp. 106–25; Freedman, pp. 269–72.
[*NLRA*]: Bernstein, *Turbulent Years*, ch. 7; Cletus E. Daniel, *The ACLU and the Wagner Act* (ILR/Cornell, 1980); R. W. Fleming, "The Significance of the Wagner Act," in Derber and Young, pp. 121–55; Huthmacher, pp. 189–98; *Public Papers*, vol. 4, quoted at p. 294.
[*Social Security*]: Roy Lubove, *The Struggle for Social Security, 1900–1935* (Harvard University Press, 1968); Schlesinger, *Coming*, ch. 18; Martin, *Madam Secretary*, ch. 26; Perkins, ch. 23; *Public Papers*, vol. 4, quoted at p. 324.
[*Banking Act*]: Hawley, pp. 309–15; Marriner S. Eccles, *Beckoning Frontiers: Public and Personal Recollections*, Sidney Hyman, ed. (Knopf, 1951), part 4, chs. 1–4.
[*"Knock-down and drag-out fight"*]: quoted in Eccles, p. 175.
[*"An eraser instead"*]: *ibid.*, p. 229.

76 [*Public Utility Holding Company Act*]: Ralph F. de Bedts, *The New Deal's SEC: The Formative Years* (Columbia University Press, 1964), ch. 5; Hawley, pp. 329–37; see also William O. Douglas Papers, esp. container 2, Library of Congress.
[*Revenue Act*]: Hawley, pp. 344–50; Schlesinger, *Upheaval*, pp. 325–34; James T. Patterson, *Congressional Conservatism and the New Deal* (University of Kentucky Press, 1967), pp. 59–69; Message to the Congress on Tax Revision, June 19, 1935, in *Public Papers*, vol. 4, pp. 270–76, quoted at p. 272.
[*WPA*]: George McJimsey, *Harry Hopkins: Ally of the Poor and Defender of Democracy* (Harvard University Press, 1987), chs. 5–8; Kenneth S. Davis, *FDR: The New Deal Years, 1933–1937* (Random House, 1986), pp. 463–71, 567–71, 621–23.

77 [*Progressive senators and bureaucracies*]: Mulder, p. 124 and *passim*.
[*Holding company bill as model*]: see Murphy, p. 165.
[*Mulder on Wheeler*]: Mulder, p. 124.
[*"Excessive centralization"*]: quoted in *ibid.*
[*Regressiveness of Social Security insurance model*]: McElvaine, pp. 256–57; Mark H. Leff, "Taxing the 'Forgotten Man': The Politics of Social Security Finance in the New Deal," *Journal of American History*, vol. 70, no. 2 (September 1983), pp. 359–81.
[*Leff on payroll tax*]: Leff, p. 379.
[*Social security and income redistribution*]: Lubove, ch. 8; James Leiby, *A History of Social Welfare and Social Work in the United States* (Columbia University Press, 1978), ch. 13.

78 [*Long's opposition to Social Security bill*]: Williams, *Long*, pp. 835–36.
   [*Long's reaction to tax message*]: ibid., pp. 836–37; Schlesinger, *Upheaval*, pp. 327–28.
   [*"Lay over, Huey"*]: quoted in Williams, p. 836.

Appeal to the People

   [*1936 State of the Union address*]: January 3, 1936, in *Public Papers*, vol. 5, pp. 8–18, quoted at pp. 13–14, 10, 14, 17, respectively; *New York Times*, January 4, 1936, pp. 1, 8.
79 [*Condition of ideological left, early 1936*]: see Johnpoll, pp. 167–70; Brinkley, pp. 190–92; Bernstein, *Turbulent Years*, pp. 404–9; Holtzman, p. 171.
   [*Democrats against FDR*]: Schlesinger, *Upheaval*, ch. 28; Patterson, pp. 250–57.
80 [*Long's plans for 1936 and 1940*]: Williams, *Long*, pp. 843–47; Kane, pp. 124–25.
   [*Long in 1935 poll*]: Farley, *Ballots*, pp. 249–50, quoted at p. 250; Brinkley, pp. 207–8.
   [*Long's assassination*]: Williams, pp. 859–76; see also Robert Penn Warren, *All the King's Men* (Harcourt, 1946), pp. 418–25.
   [*Smith and Long's legacy*]: see Bennett, ch. 9; see also Glen Jeansonne, *Gerald L. K. Smith, Minister of Hate* (Yale University Press, 1988).
   [*FDR's roll call*]: Annual Message, in *Public Papers*, vol. 5, pp. 15–16.
   [*FDR's instructions to Farley and political aides*]: see James A. Farley, *Jim Farley's Story* (McGraw-Hill, 1948), p. 59; Lester G. Seligman and Elmer E. Cornwell, Jr., eds., *New Deal Mosaic: Roosevelt Confers with His National Emergency Council, 1933–1936* (University of Oregon Books, 1965), pp. 481–501 (meeting of December 17, 1935).
81 [*FDR in polls and public esteem*]: see the results of a January 1936 *Fortune* poll, as given in Hadley Cantril and Mildred Strunk, eds., *Public Opinion, 1935–1946* (Princeton University Press, 1951), pp. 754–55 (Item 1).
   [*Economic conditions, 1936*]: *Historical Statistics*, part 1, p. 126 (Series D 1–10) and p. 235 (Series F 163–85).
   [*Poor people on the land and the New Deal*]: Mitchell, chs. 7–8; Raper, part 5; Saloutos, *American Farmer*, ch. 7; Paul E. Mertz, *New Deal Policy and Southern Rural Poverty* (Louisiana State University Press, 1978).
   [*Southern blacks and the New Deal*]: Raymond Wolters, *Negroes and the Great Depression: The Problem of Economic Recovery* (Greenwood Publishing, 1970), part 1; Harvard Sitkoff, *A New Deal for Blacks* (Oxford University Press, 1978), esp. ch. 2.
   [*Women and the New Deal*]: Susan Ware, *Holding Their Own: American Women in the 1930s* (Twayne, 1982), esp. ch. 2; Ware, *Beyond Suffrage: Women in the New Deal* (Harvard University Press, 1981); Philip S. Foner, *Women and the American Labor Movement: From World War I to the Present* (Free Press, 1980), chs. 14–17; Bernstein, *Caring Society*, pp. 290–92.
   [*"What I won't stand for"*]: O'Connor, pp. 282–84, quoted at p. 283; William E. Leuchtenburg, "Election of 1936," in Arthur M. Schlesinger, Jr., *History of American Presidential Elections, 1789–1968* (Chelsea House, 1971), vol. 3, p. 2826.
82 [*Hearst's opposition to FDR*]: see John K. Winkler, *William Randolph Hearst: A New Appraisal* (Hastings House, 1955), pp. 259–68.
   [*"You and your fellow Communists"*]: quoted in Graham J. White, *FDR and the Press* (University of Chicago Press, 1979), p. 95.
   [*"A Red New Deal"*]: quoted in Wolfskill and Hudson, p. 193.
   [*AAA decision*]: *United States* v. *Butler*, 297 U.S. 1 (1936), Stone's dissent quoted at 87; Alpheus T. Mason, *Harlan Fiske Stone: Pillar of the Law* (Viking, 1956), pp. 405–18.
   [*Minimum-wage law decision*]: *Morehead* v. *New York*, 298 U.S. 587 (1936), Stone's dissent quoted at 632; Mason, pp. 421–26.
   [*Roosevelt's coalition building*]: Schlesinger, *Upheaval*, ch. 32; Lash, pp. 439–42; Farley, *Ballots*, pp. 301–2; Dubofsky and Van Tine, pp. 248–52; FDR memorandum to Farley, July 6, 1935, in *Personal Letters*, vol. 3, p. 492; Eleanor Roosevelt memorandum to FDR and others, July 16, 1936, in *ibid.*, pp. 598–600; Bernstein, *Turbulent Years*, pp. 449–50.
83 [*"One issue"*]: quoted in Raymond Moley, *After Seven Years* (Harper, 1939), p. 342.
   [*Landon's nomination*]: Donald R. McCoy, *Landon of Kansas* (University of Nebraska Press, 1966), chs. 9–10; Leuchtenburg, pp. 2812–16.

83 [*Hoover's hopes for nomination*]: Gary Dean Best, *Herbert Hoover: The Postpresidential Years, 1933–1964* (Hoover Institution Press, 1983), vol. 1, pp. 39–65; McCoy, p. 255.
[*Landon*]: McCoy; Burns, *Lion*, p. 270.
[*1936 Democratic convention*]: Farley, *Ballots*, pp. 306–8; Schlesinger, *Upheaval*, pp. 579–85.
[*Democratic platform*]: reprinted in Schlesinger, *Elections*, vol. 3, pp. 2851–56; see also Samuel I. Rosenman, *Working with Roosevelt* (Harper, 1952), pp. 101–3.
[*FDR's acceptance address*]: June 27, 1936, in *Public Papers*, vol. 5, pp. 230–36, quoted at pp. 234, 235, 236.

84 [*Coughlin-Townsend-Smith coalition*]: Bennett, Prologue and ch. 14.
[*Lemke*]: ibid., part 2; Edward C. Blackorby, *Prairie Rebel: The Public Life of William Lemke* (University of Nebraska Press, 1963).
[*Lemke on FDR and Landon*]: quoted in Wolfskill and Hudson, p. 252.
[*Union party boast*]: see Bennett, p. 191.
[*Socialist convention and fractures*]: Swanberg, ch. 10; see, generally, Laslett and Lipset, ch. 8.

84–5 [*Communist popular front strategy*]: Klehr, chs. 9–10; Howe and Coser, pp. 327–32; Kenneth Waltzer, "The Party and the Polling Place: American Communism and an American Labor Party in the 1930s," *Radical History Review*, no. 23 (Spring 1980), pp. 104–29; Max Gordon, "The Communist Party of the Nineteen-Thirties and the New Left," *Socialist Revolution*, vol. 6, no. 1 (January–March 1976), pp. 11–48; James Weinstein, "Response to Gordon," ibid., pp. 48–59; Gordon, "Reply," ibid., pp. 59–65.

85 [*Klehr on Socialist and Communist shifts*]: Klehr, p. 194.
["*TWENTIETH-CENTURY AMERICANISM*"]: Howe and Coser, p. 333.
[*Landon's campaign*]: McCoy, chs. 11–13; Schlesinger, *Upheaval*, ch. 33 and pp. 635–38; Leuchtenburg, pp. 2816–21; Oswald Garrison Villard, "Issues and Men," *Nation*, vol. 123, no. 10 (September 5, 1936), pp. 266–67.
[*Hoover in 1936 campaign*]: Best, vol. 1, pp. 65–73; Herbert Hoover, *Addresses upon the American Road, 1933–1938* (Scribner, 1938), pp. 159–227; McCoy, pp. 279–81, 309.
[*Literary Digest polls*]: see *Literary Digest*, vol. 122, no. 18 (October 31, 1936), pp. 4–5, and no. 20 (November 14, 1936), pp. 7–8.
[*Union party campaign*]: Blackorby, pp. 222–31; Bennett, part 6; Tull, ch. 5.
["*Anti-God*"]: quoted in Bennett, p. 230.
["*Broken down Colossus*"]: ibid.
[*Church hierarchy rebuke of Coughlin*]: ibid., pp. 254–57; see also George Q. Flynn, *American Catholics & the Roosevelt Presidency, 1932–1936* (University of Kentucky Press, 1968), ch. 9.
["*As I was instrumental*"]: quoted in Bennett, p. 228.
["*If I don't deliver*"]: quoted in Tull, p. 141.
[*Coolness among Union party leaders*]: see Bennett, ch. 19; Schlesinger, *Upheaval*, pp. 626–28.

86 [*FDR's campaign*]: Farley, *Ballots*, pp. 308–27; Rosenman, pp. 107–39; Schlesinger, *Upheaval*, ch. 32 and pp. 630–35.
[*Madison Square Garden address*]: October 31, 1936, in *Public Papers*, vol. 5, pp. 566–73, quoted at pp. 568–69, 571–72, as modified by comparison with a recording of the address; *New York Times*, November 1, 1936, pp. 1, 36.

3. THE CRISIS OF MAJORITY RULE

87 [*Press on FDR's victory*]: see James MacGregor Burns, *Roosevelt: The Lion and the Fox* (Harcourt, 1956), p. 284.
[*Presidential election results, 1936*]: Robert A. Diamond, ed., *Congressional Quarterly's Guide to U.S. Elections* (Congressional Quarterly, 1975), pp. 251, 290; see also Arthur M. Schlesinger, Jr., *The Politics of Upheaval* (Houghton Mifflin, 1960), p. 642.
[*Congressional results*]: Congressional Quarterly, *Guide to U.S. Elections*, 2nd ed. (Congressional Quarterly, 1985), p. 1116.

88 [*Framers and majority rule*]: see Edwin Mims, Jr., *The Majority of the People* (Modern Age Books, 1941), esp. ch. 2; Henry Steele Commager, *Majority Rule and Minority Rights*

(Oxford University Press, 1958); James MacGregor Burns, *The Deadlock of Democracy: Four-Party Politics in America* (Prentice-Hall, 1963), ch. 1; Burns, *The Vineyard of Liberty* (Knopf, 1982), chs. 1–2.

88 [*Jefferson on majority rule*]: inaugural address, March 4, 1801, in Paul Leicester Ford, ed., *The Writings of Thomas Jefferson* (Putnam, 1892–99), vol. 8, pp. 1–6, quoted at p. 2.

89 [*McReynolds on FDR*]: Paul A. Freund, "Charles Evans Hughes as Chief Justice," *Harvard Law Review*, vol. 81, no. 1 (Autumn 1967), pp. 4–43, quoted at p. 12; see also William O. Douglas, *The Court Years, 1939–1975* (Random House, 1980), p. 13.
["*Where was Ben Cardozo?*"]: quoted in Eugene C. Gerhart, *America's Advocate: Robert H. Jackson* (Bobbs-Merrill, 1958), p. 99.

Court-Packing: The Switch in Time

[*FDR on possible defiance of Court*]: William E. Leuchtenburg, "The Origins of Franklin D. Roosevelt's 'Court-Packing' Plan," in Philip B. Kurland, ed., *The Supreme Court Review* (University of Chicago Press, 1966), pp. 347–400, quoted at p. 353; see also John Morton Blum, *From the Morgenthau Diaries: Years of Crisis, 1928–1938* (Houghton Mifflin, 1959), pp. 125–31.
["*How fortunate it is*"]: letter of February 19, 1935, in *F.D.R.: His Personal Letters*, Elliott Roosevelt, ed. (Duell, Sloan and Pearce, 1947–50), vol. 3, p. 455.
[*"Shame and humiliation"*]: quoted in Leuchtenburg, "Origins," p. 355.
[*Search for solution to Court problem*]: *ibid.*, *passim*; see also Harold L. Ickes, *The Secret Diary of Harold L. Ickes* (Simon and Schuster, 1953–54), vol. 1, pp. 494–96 and *passim*.

90 [*Labor's attack on Court*]: James C. Duram, "The Labor Union Journals and the Constitutional Issues of the New Deal: The Case for Court Restriction," *Labor History*, vol. 15, no. 2 (Spring 1974), pp. 216–30.
[*Letters to FDR from public*]: quoted in Leuchtenburg, "Origins," pp. 368, 366, respectively.
[*FDR on "marching" farmers and workers*]: *ibid.*, p. 365.
[*Long's diary on possible amendments*]: *ibid.*, p. 361.
[*FDR on Prime Minister's threat*]: *Ickes Diary*, vol. 1, pp. 467–68, 494–95.

90–1 [*FDR on difficulties of passing an amendment*]: letter to Charles C. Burlingham, February 23, 1937, in *Personal Letters*, vol. 3, pp. 661–62; letter to Felix Frankfurter, February 9, 1937, in Max Freedman, annot., *Roosevelt and Frankfurter: Their Correspondence, 1929–1945* (Little, Brown, 1967), pp. 381–82.

91 [*Norris on need for unanimous decision*]: Leuchtenburg, "Origins," p. 374.
[*Cummings on "packing the Court"*]: *ibid.*, p. 390.
[*Option of doing nothing*]: *ibid.*, p. 382; Rodney Morrison, "Franklin D. Roosevelt and the Supreme Court: An Example of the Use of Probability Theory in Political History," *History and Theory*, vol. 16, no. 2 (1977), pp. 137–46.
[*Court in 1936 election*]: Leuchtenburg, "Origins," pp. 379–80.
[*Democratic platform on Court*]: Arthur M. Schlesinger, Jr., *History of American Presidential Elections, 1789–1968* (Chelsea House, 1971), vol. 3, pp. 2854–55; see also Leuchtenburg, "Origins," pp. 378–79.
[*FDR's post-election planning*]: Leuchtenburg, "Origins," parts 5 and 6.

92 [*Corwin's proposal*]: quoted in *ibid.*, p. 389.
[*McReynolds's recommendations on retirement*]: *ibid.*, p. 391.
["*Constitution as I understand it*"]: quoted in Samuel I. Rosenman, *Working with Roosevelt* (Harper, 1952), p. 144.
[*1937 inaugural address*]: January 20, 1937, in *The Public Papers and Addresses of Franklin D. Roosevelt*, Samuel I. Rosenman, comp. (Random House, 1938–50), vol. 6, pp. 1–6, quoted at pp. 4–5; see also Rosenman, *Working*, pp. 142–44.

93 [*FDR's meeting with cabinet and congressional leaders*]: Joseph Alsop and Turner Catledge, *The 168 Days* (Doubleday, Doran, 1938), pp. 64–66; *Ickes Diary*, vol. 2, pp. 64–66.
[*Text of Court plan message*]: in *Public Papers*, vol. 6, pp. 51–59.
[*FDR at press conference*]: press conference 342, February 5, 1937, in *Public Papers*, vol. 6, pp. 35–50.
["*I cash in*"]: quoted in Burns, *Lion*, p. 294.

93 [*Reaction to plan at Court*]: ibid., pp. 294-95.
[*Thompson on plan*]: quoted in James T. Patterson, *Congressional Conservatism and the New Deal* (University of Kentucky Press, 1967), p. 87.
[*Herald Tribune on plan*]: editorial of February 6, 1937, quoted in Alfred Haines Cope and Fred Krinsky, eds., *Franklin D. Roosevelt and the Supreme Court* (D. C. Heath, 1969), p. 28; see also ibid., pp. 29-34; "Speak Frankly, Mr. President!," *Business Week*, no. 392 (March 6, 1937), p. 68.
[*Mencken on plan*]: quoted in Patterson, p. 87.
[*Hoover on plan*]: Hoover, *Memoirs: The Great Depression, 1929-1941* (Macmillan, 1952), p. 373.
[*New York bishop on plan*]: William T. Manning, quoted in *Newsweek*, vol. 9, no. 8 (February 20, 1937), p. 17.
[*"A grand fight!"*]: quoted in Burns, *Lion*, p. 298.

94 [*Congressional divisions over plan*]: Patterson, pp. 88-117.
[*Bailey on plan and "Negro vote"*]: quoted in ibid., pp. 98-99; see also *Ickes Diary*, vol. 2, p. 115.
[*"I meant it"*]: address of March 4, 1937, in *Public Papers*, vol. 6, pp. 113-21, quoted at pp. 114, 121.

95 [*Hughes's letter*]: David J. Danelski and Joseph S. Tulchin, eds., *The Autobiographical Notes of Charles Evans Hughes* (Harvard University Press, 1973), pp. 304-7 and p. 306, n. 50; Alpheus T. Mason, *Harlan Fiske Stone: Pillar of the Law* (Viking, 1956), pp. 450-53; Bruce A. Murphy, *The Brandeis/Frankfurter Connection* (Oxford University Press, 1982), pp. 179-82; Freedman, p. 396; Philippa Strum, *Louis D. Brandeis: Justice for the People* (Harvard University Press, 1984), p. 388.
[*"Smoke 'em out"*]: quoted in Burns, *Lion*, p. 303.
[*Wagner Act decisions*]: *NLRB* v. *Jones & Laughlin Steel Corp.*, 301 U.S. 1 (1937); *NLRB* v. *Freuhauf Trailer Co.*, 301 U.S. 49 (1937); *NLRB* v. *Friedman-Harry Marks Clothing Co.*, 301 U.S. 58 (1937); see also Robert L. Stern, "The Commerce Clause and the National Economy, 1933-1946," *Harvard Law Review*, vol. 59, nos. 5 and 6 (May and July, 1946), pp. 645-93, 883-947.
[*State minimum-wage decision*]: *West Coast Hotel* v. *Parrish*, 300 U.S. 391 (1937).
[*Frankfurter on Roberts's switch and Hughes's letter*]: letter of March 30, 1937, in Freedman, p. 392; see also ibid., pp. 392-95; Felix Frankfurter, "Justice Roberts and the 'Switch in Time,'" in Allen F. Westin, ed., *An Autobiography of the Supreme Court* (Macmillan, 1963), pp. 241-48.
[*Roberts's switch and 1936 election*]: John W. Chambers, "The Big Switch: Justice Roberts and the Minimum-Wage Cases," *Labor History*, vol. 10, no. 1 (Winter 1969), pp. 44-73; Michael E. Parrish, "The Hughes Court, the Great Depression, and the Historians," *Historian*, vol. 40, no. 2 (February 1978), pp. 286-308; see also Frank V. Cantwell, "Public Opinion and the Legislative Process," *American Political Science Review*, vol. 40, no. 5 (October 1946), pp. 924-35; Charles L. Black, Jr., *The People and the Court: Judicial Review in a Democracy* (Macmillan, 1960), esp. ch. 3.
[*Hughes's new stance*]: Danelski and Tulchin, pp. 311-13; Freund; Mason, pp. 455-60; Parrish.

96 [*Labor and Court reform after Wagner decisions*]: Duram, pp. 232-34.
[*"Chortling all morning"*]: press conference of April 13, 1937, in *Public Papers*, vol. 6, pp. 153-56, quoted at pp. 153, 154.
[*Court plan after switch*]: William E. Leuchtenburg, "FDR's Court-Packing Plan: A Second Life, a Second Death," *Duke Law Journal*, vol. 1985, nos. 3 and 4 (June-September 1985), pp. 673-89; *Ickes Diary*, vol. 2, pp. 161-64; Jordan A. Schwarz, *The Speculator: Bernard M. Baruch in Washington, 1917-1965* (University of North Carolina Press, 1981), p. 319.
[*Garner-FDR exchange*]: quoted in Bascom N. Timmons, *Garner of Texas* (Harper, 1948), p. 223.
[*"Organized and calculated"*]: quoted in J. Joseph Huthmacher, *Senator Robert F. Wagner and the Rise of Urban Liberalism* (Atheneum, 1968), p. 233.

97 [*Number of sit-downs, 1937*]: Irving Bernstein, *The Turbulent Years: A History of the American Worker, 1933-1941* (Houghton Mifflin, 1969), p. 500.
[*Sit-downs in practice*]: ibid., pp. 499-501; Melvyn Dubofsky and Warren Van Tine, *John*

L. Lewis (Quadrangle/New York Times Book Co., 1977), pp. 258–59; Sidney Fine, *Sit-Down: The General Motors Strike of 1937* (University of Michigan Press, 1969), pp. 121–32 and ch. 6.

97 [*"Sit down! Sit down!"*]: quoted in Bernstein, p. 501.

97–8 [*Lewis's plans for Big Steel*]: Bert Cochran, *Labor and Communism: The Conflict That Shaped American Unions* (Princeton University Press, 1977), pp. 103–5; J. Raymond Walsh, *C.I.O.: Industrial Unionism in Action* (Norton, 1937), p. 112.

98 [*Unionist's dash for toilet*]: Bernstein, p. 523.

[*Structure of auto work*]: see Nelson Lichtenstein, "Auto Worker Militancy and the Structure of Factory Life, 1937–1955," *Journal of American History*, vol. 67, no. 2 (September 1980), pp. 335–53, esp. pp. 336–40; see also Herbert Harris, "Working in the Detroit Auto Plants," in Don Congdon, ed., *The Thirties: A Time to Remember* (Simon and Schuster, 1962), pp. 477–86; Fine, pp. 54–63.

[*GM in 1937*]: Fine, ch. 2; Dubofsky and Van Tine, p. 256; Bernstein, pp. 509–19.

[*Fortune on GM*]: "General Motors," *Fortune*, vol. 18, no. 6 (December 1938), quoted at p. 41.

[*"Most critical labor conflict"*]: quoted in Bernstein, p. 525.

[*GM strike*]: ibid., pp. 519–30; Fine, chs. 5–9.

99 [*Murphy and GM strike*]: Fine, pp. 148–55 and *passim;* Bernstein, pp. 530–51; J. Woodford Howard, *Mr. Justice Murphy: A Political Biography* (Princeton University Press, 1968), pp. 123–44.

[*FDR and Perkins in GM strike*]: George Martin, *Madam Secretary: Frances Perkins* (Houghton Mifflin, 1976), pp. 400–4; Fine, ch. 10; Dubofsky and Van Tine, pp. 255–70; Bernstein, pp. 534–51; Frances Perkins, *The Roosevelt I Knew* (Viking, 1946), pp. 320–24.

[*GM's capitulation*]: quoted in Howard, p. 140; Fine, pp. 298–312; see also *General Motors Labor Policies and Procedures* (General Motors Corporation, 1937).

[*Chrysler and Ford after GM capitulation*]: Bernstein, pp. 551–54, 569–71; Howard, pp. 150–56.

[*Murray and Big Steel*]: Bernstein, pp. 441–57; see also Morris Llewellyn Cooke and Philip Murray, *Organized Labor and Production* (Harper, 1940); Daniel Nelson, "The Company Union Movement, 1900–1937: A Reexamination," *Business History Review*, vol. 56, no. 3 (Autumn 1982), pp. 335–57.

[*Kempton on Murray*]: Bernstein, p. 443.

100 [*FDR on "The President Wants"*]: ibid., p. 454.

[*SWOC membership, January 1937*]: ibid., p. 465.

[*Taylor's reassessment*]: ibid., pp. 466–70.

[*Taylor-Lewis negotiations*]: ibid., pp. 470–73; Dubofsky and Van Tine, pp. 273–77.

[*Single most important document*]: Robert R. R. Brooks, *As Steel Goes, . . .* (Yale University Press, 1959), p. 108.

[*Little Steel and unionization*]: Bernstein, pp. 473–98; Dubofsky and Van Tine, pp. 312–15.

[*Chicago Memorial Day incident*]: Donald G. Sofchalk, "The Chicago Memorial Day Incident: An Episode of Mass Action," *Labor History*, vol. 6, no. 1 (Winter 1965), pp. 3–43.

Congress-Purging: The Broken Spell

101 [*Auto industry improvement, 1933–37*]: U.S. Bureau of the Census, *Historical Statistics of the United States, Colonial Times to 1970* (U.S. Government Printing Office, 1975), part 2, p. 716 (Series Q 148–62); Bernstein, p. 503.

[*Iron and steel industry improvement, 1933–37*]: *Historical Statistics*, part 2, p. 693 (Series P 231–300); Bernstein, p. 448.

[*1937 recession and the search for a solution*]: Blum, *Morgenthau Diaries*, ch. 9; Herbert Stein, *The Fiscal Revolution in America* (University of Chicago Press, 1969), chs. 6–7; Byrd L. Jones, "Lauchlin Currie and the causes of the 1937 recession," *History of Political Economy*, vol. 12, no. 3 (1980), pp. 303–15; *Ickes Diary*, vol. 2; Donald Winch, *Economics and Policy: A Historical Study* (Walker and Co., 1969), ch. 11; Robert Lekachman, *The Age of Keynes* (Random House, 1966), ch. 5; Burns, *Lion*, ch. 16; Kenneth

D. Roose, *The Economics of Recession and Revival* (Yale University Press, 1954); Marriner S. Eccles, *Beckoning Frontiers: Public and Personal Recollections*, Sidney Hyman, ed. (Knopf, 1951), pp. 287–323; Beatrice Bishop Berle and Travis Beal Jacobs, eds., *Navigating the Rapids, 1918–1971: From the Papers of Adolf A. Berle* (Harcourt, 1973), pp. 141–77; James A. Farley, *Jim Farley's Story* (McGraw-Hill, 1948), ch. 11.

101 [*"Mob in a theater fire"*]: quoted in Blum, p. 386.
[*"Rich man's panic"*]: Berle and Jacobs, p. 142.
[*Perkins on upturn*]: see *Ickes Diary*, vol. 2, p. 212.
[*FDR's suspicions and hopes*]: ibid., p. 241.
[*Unemployment*]: *Historical Statistics*, part 1, p. 126 (Series D 1–10).
[*"Sit tight"*]: quoted in Burns, *Lion*, p. 320.
[*"Hooverish statements"*]: quoted in *Ickes Diary*, vol. 2, p. 224.
[*"We are headed"*]: quoted in Burns, *Lion*, p. 320.
[*"Ill, tired"*]: Berle and Jacobs, p. 148.
[*FDR's fears of fascism*]: Blum, p. 393.
102 [*Cabinet discussion*]: quoted in *ibid.*, pp. 391–92; see also *Ickes Diary*, vol. 2, pp. 240–43.
102–3 [*NAM platform*]: quoted in *New York Times*, December 9, 1937, p. 23.
103 [*Small businessmen, Business Advisory Council, Detroit demonstration, youth delegates*]: Burns, *Lion*, p. 326.
[*Abbott on Chicago conditions*]: letter of February 3, 1938, Dewson Papers, Franklin D. Roosevelt Library, Hyde Park, N.Y.
[*FDR on carping critics*]: press conference with editors of trade papers, April 8, 1938, in *Public Papers*, vol. 7, quoted at p. 194.
104 [*Recession in March 1938*]: see Burns, *Lion*, p. 327; Roose, ch. 3.
[*"They understand"*]: quoted in Burns, *Lion*, p. 328.
[*Temporary National Economic Committee*]: see Ellis W. Hawley, *The New Deal and the Problem of Monopoly* (Princeton University Press, 1966), pp. 404–15; Wilson P. Miscamble, "Thurman Arnold Goes to Washington: A Look at Antitrust Policy in the Later New Deal," *Business History Review*, vol. 56, no. 1 (Spring 1982), pp. 1–15.
[*Morgenthau's threat to resign*]: Blum, pp. 423–25.
[*"Discipline of democracy"*]: message of April 14, 1938, in *Public Papers*, vol. 7, pp. 221–33, quoted at p. 231.
[*"What is needed"*]: fireside chat of April 14, 1938, in *ibid.*, pp. 236–48, quoted at p. 246.
105 [*"For God's sake"*]: quoted in Burns, *Lion*, p. 339.
[*Reorganization bill*]: Richard Polenberg, *Reorganizing Roosevelt's Government: The Controversy over Executive Reorganization, 1936–1939* (Harvard University Press, 1966); Polenberg, "The Decline of the New Deal," in John Braeman et al., eds., *The New Deal: The National Level* (Ohio State University Press, 1975), pp. 250–51.
[*"Dictator bill"*]: see Polenberg, *Reorganizing*, pp. 148–49.
[*Weekend telegram blitz*]: Patterson, *Congressional Conservatism*, pp. 222–23.
[*"I have no inclination"*]: in *Public Papers*, vol. 7, pp. 179–81, quoted at p. 179.
106 [*House recommittal of bill*]: Patterson, p. 226.
[*Passage of wages-and-hours legislation*]: Burns, *Lion*, pp. 342–44; Patterson, pp. 179–82, 242–46.
[*"That's that"*]: quoted in Burns, *Lion*, p. 343.
107 [*FDR's putting off of Lawrence*]: *ibid.*, p. 349.
[*"Aggressive progressive Democrats"*]: quoted in *ibid.*
[*Rise of special-interest groups*]: see Otis L. Graham, Jr., "The Broker State," *Wilson Quarterly*, vol. 8, no. 5 (Winter 1984), pp. 86–97.
[*Lewis and FDR*]: Burns, *Lion*, pp. 350–51; Dubofsky and Van Tine, pp. 323–34; see also Mike Davis, "The Barren Marriage of American Labour and the Democratic Party," *New Left Review*, no. 124 (November–December 1980), pp. 43–84.
[*"Plague on both your houses"*]: quoted in Bernstein, p. 496.
108 [*FDR in polls, 1938*]: "Fortune Quarterly Survey: XII," *Fortune*, vol. 18, no. 1 (July 1938), p. 37; Burns, *Lion*, pp. 338–39.
109 [*Attempts at conservative coalition*]: Patterson, pp. 251–70.

109 [*FDR's June 1938 fireside chat*]: in *Public Papers*, vol. 7, pp. 391–400, quoted at pp. 395, 399.

[*Patterson on drive for realignment*]: Patterson, p. 277.

[*FDR's purge travels*]: J. B. Shannon, "Presidential Politics in the South, 1938," *Journal of Politics*, vol. 1, no. 2 (May 1939), pp. 146–70 and no. 3 (August 1939), pp. 278–300; Barkley Papers, University of Kentucky; Burns, *Lion*, pp. 361–64.

110 [*FDR's attack on George*]: in *Public Papers*, vol. 7, pp. 463–71, quoted at pp. 469–71; and Burns, *Lion*, pp. 362–63.

[*Press reaction to purge*]: see George Wolfskill and John A. Hudson, *All but the People: Franklin D. Roosevelt and His Critics, 1933–39* (Macmillan, 1969), pp. 289–90; Burns, *Lion*, p. 362.

[*Moley on White House cabal*]: Moley, "Perspective," *Newsweek*, vol. 11, no. 24 (June 13, 1938), p. 40.

[*Liberal criticism of purge*]: see T.R.B., "Washington Notes," *New Republic*, vol. 96, no. 1243 (September 28, 1938), p. 212.

[*Farley's and Garner's evasion*]: Farley's Story, p. 141; Timmons, pp. 234–37.

[*Southern Democrats' response to purge*]: Patterson, pp. 283–85, Glass quoted at p. 285; Shannon.

111 [*Purge results*]: Shannon, p. 299 (Table 2) and *passim;* Charles M. Price and Joseph Boskin, "The Roosevelt 'Purge': A Reappraisal," *Journal of Politics*, vol. 28, no. 3 (August 1966), pp. 660–70; Stuart L. Weiss, "Maury Maverick and the Liberal Bloc," *Journal of American History*, vol. 57, no. 4 (March 1971), pp. 880–95, esp. 891–95.

[*A "bust"*]: Farley, p. 144.

["*A long, long time*"]: quoted in Burns, *Lion*, p. 364.

[*Republican successes in 1938*]: Patterson, pp. 288–90; Milton Plesur, "The Republican Congressional Comeback of 1938," *Review of Politics*, vol. 24, no. 4 (October 1962), pp. 525–62, esp. pp. 544–46; Donald R. McCoy, "George S. McGill and the Agricultural Adjustment Act of 1938," *Historian*, vol. 45, no. 2 (February 1983), pp. 186–205.

[*Reasons for 1938 setbacks*]: see Plesur, pp. 544–54; Farley, pp. 149–50; Shannon, pp. 295–98; Philip F. La Follette, Elmer A. Benson, and Frank Murphy, "Why We Lost," *Nation*, vol. 147, no. 23 (December 3, 1938), pp. 586–90; Patterson, pp. 286–87.

["*Having passed the period*"]: in *Public Papers*, vol. 8, pp. 1–12, quoted at p. 7.

112 [*Jackson Day dinner speech*]: January 7, 1939, in *ibid.*, pp. 60–68, quoted at p. 63.

[*1939 appointments*]: Burns, *Lion*, p. 368; see also Patterson, pp. 298–99.

["*Not one nickel more*"]: quoted in Polenberg, "Decline," p. 261.

[*FDR's refusal to support national health program*]: Huthmacher, pp. 263–67.

["*Sick and tired*"]: quoted in John Morton Blum, *From the Morgenthau Diaries: Years of Urgency, 1938–1941* (Houghton Mifflin, 1965), pp. 41–42.

["*You undergraduates*"]: address of December 5, 1938, in *Public Papers*, vol. 7, pp. 613–21, quoted at p. 615.

[*Congressional balance of power, 1939*]: see Patterson, pp. 289–90, 322–24.

[*House Un-American Activities Committee*]: Walter Goodman, *The Committee* (Farrar, Straus and Giroux, 1968), pp. 52–58; *Ickes Diary*, vol. 2, pp. 506–7, 528–29, 546–50, 573–74.

[*Smith investigation of NLRB*]: Earl Latham, *The Communist Controversy in Washington: From the New Deal to McCarthy* (Harvard University Press, 1966), pp. 131–37; Bernstein, *Turbulent Years*, pp. 663–70.

[*Attack on FDR's appointing power*]: see A. Cash Koeniger, "The New Deal and the States: Roosevelt versus the Byrd Organization in Virginia," *Journal of American History*, vol. 68, no. 4 (March 1982), pp. 876–96.

113 [*Restriction of political activities of federal employees*]: see "Federal Workers in Politics," *New Republic*, vol. 100, no. 1289 (August 16, 1939), pp. 33–34.

[*Reductions in New Deal funds*]: Burns, *Lion*, p. 370; see also Patterson, ch. 9.

[*Eleanor Roosevelt and blacks*]: Harvard Sitkoff, *A New Deal for Blacks* (Oxford University Press, 1978), pp. 59–65, 132; Joseph P. Lash, *Eleanor and Franklin* (Norton, 1971), p. 522; Joanna Schneider Zangrando and Robert L. Zangrando, "ER and Black Rights," in Joan Hoff-Wilson and Marjorie Lightman, eds., *Without Precedent:*

The Life and Career of Eleanor Roosevelt (Indiana University Press, 1984), pp. 88–107; Nancy J. Weiss, *Farewell to the Party of Lincoln* (Princeton University Press, 1983), esp. ch. 6.

113 [*Marian Anderson and the DAR*]: Ickes Diary, vol. 2, pp. 612–16; Sitkoff, pp. 326–27; Lash, pp. 525–28.
     [*"Unique, majestic"*]: Ickes Diary, vol. 2, p. 615.

Deadlock at the Center

114 [*Why did you lose?*]: La Follette, Benson, and Murphy, "Why We Lost," La Follette, quoted at p. 586.
     [*"Price of cheese"*]: quoted in *ibid.,* p. 586.
     [*FDR as administrator*]: see Raymond Moley, *27 Masters of Politics* (Funk & Wagnalls, 1949), p. 45; Herbert A. Simon et al., *Public Administration* (Knopf, 1950), p. 168; Arthur M. Schlesinger, Jr., "Curmudgeon's Confessions," *New Republic*, vol. 129, no. 19 (December 7, 1953), pp. 14–15; Burns, *Lion*, pp. 371–75.
     [*"A wonderful person but"*]: quoted in Ickes Diary, vol. 2, p. 659.
     [*Schlesinger on FDR's fuzzy delegation*]: "Curmudgeon's Confessions," p. 15.

115 [*Executive Council and National Emergency Council*]: Otis L. Graham, Jr., "The Planning Ideal and American Reality: The 1930s," in Stanley Elkins and Eric McKitrick, eds., *The Hofstadter Aegis: A Memorial* (Knopf, 1974), p. 271; Lester G. Seligman and Elmer E. Cornwell, Jr., eds., *New Deal Mosaic: Roosevelt Confers with His National Emergency Council, 1933–1936* (University of Oregon Books, 1965).
     [*"The President needs help"*]: President's Committee on Administrative Management, *Administrative Management in the Government of the United States*, in *Senate Documents: Miscellaneous*, 75th Congress, 1st Session (U.S. Government Printing Office, 1937), Document 8, quoted at p. 19.
     [*Committee on Administrative Management*]: Graham, pp. 271–72; Polenberg, *Reorganizing*, ch. 1.
     [*"A passion for anonymity"*]: President's Committee, p. 19.

115–16 [*Effect of FDR's administrative techniques on New Deal*]: see John Braeman, "The New Deal and the 'Broker State': A Review of the Recent Scholarly Literature," *Business History Review*, vol. 46, no. 4 (Winter 1972), pp. 409–29, esp. pp. 426–27.
     [*FDR's description of three branches*]: fireside chat of March 9, 1937, in *Public Papers*, vol. 6, pp. 123–24.

116–17 [*FDR and Democratic party*]: see Burns, *Lion*, pp. 375–80; Arthur M. Schlesinger, Jr., *The Coming of the New Deal* (Houghton Mifflin, 1958), pp. 503–5; Otis L. Graham, Jr., "The Democratic Party, 1932–1945," in Arthur M. Schlesinger, Jr., *History of U.S. Political Parties* (Chelsea House, 1973), vol. 3, pp. 1939–64.

117 [*FDR's attack on George and seniority system*]: see Willmoore Kendall, *The Conservative Affirmation* (Henry Regnery, 1963), ch. 2.
     [*"Not merely about party"*]: quoted in Burns, *Deadlock*, p. 157; see also William E. Leuchtenburg, *In the Shadow of FDR: From Harry Truman to Ronald Reagan* (Cornell University Press, 1983), pp. 245–46.
     [*"Head of the Democratic party"*]: fireside chat of June 24, 1938, in *Public Papers*, vol. 7, pp. 391–400, quoted at p. 399.

118 [*FDR and Virginia*]: Koeniger, "The New Deal and the States."
     [*"Eight years in Washington"*]: quoted in Rexford G. Tugwell, *The Democratic Roosevelt* (Doubleday, 1957), p. 412.

120 [*FDR as transactional leader*]: see Braeman; Graham, "Broker State"; Burns, *Lion*, pp. 197–202.

The Fission of Ideas

120–1 [*Dewey on liberty*]: Dewey, *Liberalism and Social Action* (Putnam, 1935), p. 24.
     [*Dewey on nineteenth-century liberals*]: see *ibid.*, ch. 1 and *passim*.
     [*Dewey on means and ends of liberalism*]: *ibid.*, pp. 51, 54.
     [*Dewey and Hull-House*]: George Dykhuizen, *The Life and Mind of John Dewey* (Southern Illinois University Press, 1973), pp. 104–6.

121 [*Dewey on the experimental method*]: Dewey, "The Future of Liberalism," *Journal of Philosophy*, vol. 32, no. 9 (April 25, 1935), pp. 225–30, quoted at p. 228.
[*"Comprehensive ideas"*]: *Liberalism and Social Action*, p. 43.
[*"Coherent body of ideas"*]: "Future of Liberalism," p. 228.

122 [*Old progressives in New Deal*]: Otis L. Graham, Jr., *An Encore for Reform: The Old Progressives and the New Deal* (Oxford University Press, 1967); see also Alan Brinkley, "A Prelude," *Wilson Quarterly*, vol. 4, no. 2 (Spring 1982), pp. 51–61; John Morton Blum, *The Progressive Presidents: Roosevelt, Wilson, Roosevelt, Johnson* (Norton, 1980), ch. 3.
[*Graham's survey*]: *Encore*, pp. 166–69, quoted at p. 169.
[*"Direct reform bloodline"*]: ibid., pp. 8–9.
[*Failure of socialism*]: see sources cited in ch. 2, second section, *supra*.

122–3 [*Hartz on socialism's handicap*]: Louis Hartz, *The Liberal Tradition in America* (Harcourt, 1955), p. 228.
[*Communist party in 1930s*]: see sources cited in ch. 2, second section, *supra;* and Theodore Draper, "The Popular Front Revisited," *New York Review of Books*, vol. 32, no. 9 (May 30, 1985), pp. 44–50.
[*Communist party membership, 1938*]: Draper, p. 45.
[*Conservatism in New Deal era*]: see sources cited in ch. 2, first section, *supra*.
[*Rossiter's identification of conservative groups*]: Clinton Rossiter, *Conservatism in America* (Knopf, 1955), pp. 173–86; see also A. James Reichley, *Conservatives in an Age of Change* (Brookings Institution, 1981), ch. 1.

124 [*Individualism*]: see David Riesman, *Individualism Reconsidered and Other Essays* (Free Press, 1954), esp. part 2.
[*Dewey on "individuality"*]: quoted in Arthur A. Ekirch, *Ideologies and Utopias: The Impact of the New Deal on American Thought* (Quadrangle, 1969), p. 127.
[*"Freed intelligence"*]: *Liberalism and Social Action*, p. 50.

124–5 [*Niebuhr on "freed intelligence"*]: Niebuhr, "The Pathos of Liberalism" (review of *Liberalism and Social Action*), *Nation*, vol. 141, no. 3662 (September 11, 1935), pp. 303–4, quoted at p. 303.

125 [*"Pragmatic idealism"*]: Bernard Bailyn, *Ideological Origins of the American Revolution* (Belknap Press of Harvard University Press, 1967), p. 232.
[*"A void"*]: Alexis de Tocqueville, *Democracy in America* (Knopf, 1945), vol. 2, p. 77.
[*Softness and shapelessness of New Deal ideology*]: see Jacob Cohen, "Schlesinger and the New Deal," *Dissent*, vol. 8, no. 4 (Autumn 1961), pp. 461–72, esp. pp. 466–68; Barton J. Bernstein, "The New Deal: The Conservative Achievements of Liberal Reform," in Bernstein and Allen J. Matusow, eds., *Twentieth-Century America: Recent Interpretations* (Harcourt, 1972), pp. 242–64.

126 [*The four parties*]: Burns, *Deadlock*, esp. chs. 8–9.

126–7 [*Cohen on New Deal*]: Cohen, p. 465.

127 [*Bernstein on New Deal*]: Introduction to Bernstein in Bernstein and Matusow, p. 243, and Bernstein in ibid., pp. 259–60.
[*Conkin on New Deal*]: Paul Conkin, *The New Deal*, 2d ed. (Harlan Davidson, 1975), p. 71; see also Jerold S. Auerbach, "New Deal, Old Deal, or Raw Deal: Some Thoughts on New Left Historiography," *Journal of Southern History*, vol. 35, no. 1 (February 1969), pp. 18–30.
[*Revisionists and bank crisis*]: see Kenneth S. Davis, *FDR: The New Deal Years, 1933–1937* (Random House, 1986), pp. 49–53 and sources cited therein; Conkin, pp. 65–66, 75–76; Auerbach.

128 [*New Deal income redistribution*]: see *Historical Statistics*, part 1, p. 301 (Series G 319–36) and p. 302 (Series G 319–36 and G 337–52).

129 [*Berle on FDR*]: Berle and Jacobs, p. 149; see also Berle Papers, Personal Correspondence 1936–38, esp. container 25, Franklin D. Roosevelt Library, Hyde Park, N.Y.

130 [*Stone on taxing power*]: quoted in Perkins, p. 286.
[*FDR on Keynes and vice versa*]: FDR quoted in ibid., p. 225; Keynes's reaction in ibid., p. 226.

130–1 [*Planning in New Deal*]: see Graham, "Planning Ideal and American Reality," *passim;* Otis L. Graham, Jr., *Toward a Planned Society: From Roosevelt to Nixon* (Oxford University Press, 1976), ch. 1; Barry D. Karl, *Charles G. Merriam and the Study of Politics* (University of Chicago Press, 1974), chs. 12–13; Byrd Jones, "A Plan for Planning in the New Deal," *Social Science Quarterly,* vol. 50, no. 3 (December 1969), pp. 525–34.

131 [*Lippmann on planning*]: Lippmann, *An Inquiry into the Principles of the Good Society* (Little, Brown, 1937), *passim.*

[*FDR's hopes for further TVA-like programs*]: James MacGregor Burns, "Congress and the Formation of Economic Policies" (doctoral dissertation; Harvard University, 1947), ch. 6.

["*One of those uncommon junctures*"]: quoted in Burns, *Lion,* p. 335.

[*Sivachev on New Deal achievement*]: Sivachev, "The Rise of Statism in 1930s America: A Soviet View of the Social and Political Effects of the New Deal," *Labor History,* vol. 24, no. 4 (Fall 1983), pp. 500–25, quoted at p. 504; see also Bradford A. Lee, "The New Deal Reconsidered," *Wilson Quarterly,* vol. 4, no. 2 (Spring 1982), pp. 62–76; Cohen, pp. 471–72; William E. Leuchtenburg, "The New Deal and the Analogue of War," in John Braeman et al., eds., *Change and Continuity in Twentieth-Century America* (Ohio State University Press, 1964), pp. 81–143; Rush Welter, *Popular Education and Democratic Thought in America* (Columbia University Press, 1962), pp. 310–17.

[*Liberty and the New Deal*]: see Jerold S. Auerbach, *Labor and Liberty: The La Follette Committee and the New Deal* (Bobbs-Merrill, 1966), pp. 208–18, and sources cited therein.

["*Weakest in philosophy*"]: Alfred Kazin, *On Native Grounds* (Reynal & Hitchcock, 1942), p. 492.

[*Wells on FDR*]: quoted in *ibid.,* p. 493.

The People's Art

132 [*Short's House performance*]: quoted in *Congressional Record,* 75th Congress, 3rd Session, vol. 83, part 8, p. 9497 (June 15, 1938); see also Richard D. McKinzie, *The New Deal for Artists* (Princeton University Press, 1973), pp. 154–55.

[*Attack upon cultural programs*]: McKinzie, ch. 9; Jerre Mangione, *The Dream and the Deal: The Federal Writers' Project, 1935–1943* (Little, Brown, 1972), chs. 1, 8; Jane De Hart Mathews, *The Federal Theatre, 1935–1939: Plays, Relief and Politics* (Princeton University Press, 1967), chs. 5–6.

["*Smeared upon the walls*"]: testimony of Walter Steele, *Hearings Before a Special Committee on Un-American Activities, House of Representatives,* 75th Congress, 3rd Session (1938), vol. 1, p. 554.

["*Is he a Communist?*"]: Representative Joe Starnes of Alabama, quoted in testimony of Hallie Flanagan, *ibid.,* vol. 4, p. 2857.

133 [*Eleanor Roosevelt's support of arts programs*]: quoted in McKinzie, p. 10; see also Lash, pp. 467–68.

[*Biddle's initiative*]: McKinzie, pp. 5–10, McKinzie quoted on "social revolution" at p. 5; George Biddle, *An American Artist's Story* (Little, Brown, 1939), pp. 263–80; William F. McDonald, *Federal Relief Administration and the Arts* (Ohio State University Press, 1969), pp. 357–61.

["*Awkward embrace*"]: Joan Simpson Burns, *The Awkward Embrace: The Creative Artist and the Institution in America* (Knopf, 1975); see also McKinzie, chs. 3–5.

134 [*San Francisco murals controversy*]: McKinzie, pp. 24–26.

[*Kent's Eskimos and Puerto Ricans*]: *ibid.,* pp. 63–64.

["*The Fleet's In*"]: *ibid.,* pp. 29–30, quoted at p. 29.

[*Artistic production under public works program*]: *ibid.,* p. 27.

[*FAP*]: *ibid.,* ch. 5; McDonald, chs. 18–19; Francis V. O'Connor, ed., *Art for the Millions* (New York Graphic Society, 1973); O'Connor, ed., *The New Deal Art Projects: An Anthology of Memoirs* (Smithsonian Institution Press, 1972); New York Public Library, *FDR and the Arts: The WPA Arts Projects* (exhibition brochure, 1983); Marianne Doezma, *American Realism and the Industrial Age* (Cleveland Museum of Art/Indiana University Press, 1980), pp. 108–14; Selden Rodman, *Ben Shahn: Portrait of the Artist as an American* (Harper, 1951), ch. 3; Garnett McCoy, "Poverty, Politics and Artists, 1930–1945," *Art in America,* vol. 53, no. 4 (August–September, 1965), pp. 88–107; *Art in Public Buildings,* vol. 1: *Mural Designs, 1934–1936* (Art in Federal Buildings, Inc., 1936).

[*Output under FAP*]: McKinzie, p. 105.

135 [*Bringing people's art to the people*]: Jane De Hart Mathews, "Arts and the People: The New Deal Quest for a Cultural Democracy," *Journal of American History*, vol. 62, no. 2 (September 1975), pp. 316–39; McDonald, pp. 463–79; McKinzie, ch. 8.
[*Cahill on art*]: quoted in Mathews, "Arts and the People," p. 323.
[*New York artists' protest*]: McKinzie, p. 96.
[*Reduction of WPA rolls*]: *ibid.*, p. 97.
135–6 [*Flanagan and formation of FTP*]: Hallie Flanagan, *Arena* (Duell, Sloan and Pearce, 1940), pp. 3–47; Mathews, *Federal Theatre*, chs. 1–2; McDonald, pp. 496–533; Willson Whitman, *Bread and Circuses: A Study of the Federal Theatre* (Oxford University Press, 1937), chs. 2–3; Jay Williams, *Stage Left* (Scribner, 1974), pp. 221–22.
136 ["*A changing world*"]: quoted in Mathews, *Federal Theatre*, pp. 42–43.
[Murder in the Cathedral]: *ibid.*, pp. 74–75; Whitman, pp. 39–40; Williams, p. 223.
[Macbeth]: Mathews, *Federal Theatre*, pp. 75–76, woman quoted on Shakespeare at p. 104; Richard France, *The Theatre of Orson Welles* (Bucknell University Press, 1977), ch. 2; John Houseman, *Run-Through* (Simon and Schuster, 1972), pp. 185–205.
137 [*Gagey on Living Newspapers*]: Edmond M. Gagey, *Revolution in American Drama* (Columbia University Press, 1947), pp. 165–66; see also Williams, pp. 224–25; Flanagan, pp. 64–65, 70–73.
[Ethiopia]: Williams, pp. 225–26; Mathews, *Federal Theatre*, pp. 62–68.
[Triple-A Plowed Under]: Mathews, *Federal Theatre*, pp. 70–74; Williams, pp. 88–92.
[Injunction Granted]: Flanagan, pp. 72–73; Mathews, *Federal Theatre*, pp. 109–13; Whitman, pp. 85–86; John O'Connor and Lorraine Brown, *Free, Adult, Uncensored: The Living History of the Federal Theatre Project* (New Republic Books, 1978), pp. 76–87; Granville Vernon, review of *Injunction Granted, Commonweal*, vol. 24, no. 17 (August 21, 1936), p. 407.
[Power]: Mathews, *Federal Theatre*, pp. 113–15, Atkinson quoted at p. 114; Whitman, pp. 87–88.
[One-Third of a Nation]: Mathews, *Federal Theatre*, pp. 169–77; O'Connor and Brown, pp. 160–73; Brooks Atkinson, review of *One-Third of a Nation*, in Bernard Beckerman and Howard Siegman, eds., *On Stage: Selected Theater Reviews from The New York Times, 1920–1970* (Arno Press, 1973), p. 196.
[It Can't Happen Here]: O'Connor and Brown, pp. 58–67; Williams, pp. 228–29.
[*Regional FTP*]: Flanagan, *passim;* McDonald, ch. 22; Mathews, *Federal Theatre*, ch. 4; Whitman, pp. 73–78.
138 [*FTP's dance unit*]: O'Connor and Brown, pp. 212–23; Williams, p. 231.
["*Always dangerous*"]: quoted in Whitman, p. 172.
[*Alexander on 1930s*]: Charles C. Alexander, *Here the Country Lies: Nationalism and the Arts in Twentieth-Century America* (Indiana University Press, 1980), p. 191.
138–9 [Cradle Will Rock *controversy*]: Mathews, *Federal Theatre*, pp. 122–25; France, ch. 5; Houseman, pp. 245–49, 253–79.
139 [*FWP*]: Mangione; McDonald, chs. 26–28.
[*Publishers' letter on FWP*]: quoted in Mangione, p. 15.
[*Women as FWP state heads*]: *ibid.*, p. 88.
[*FWP writers and output*]: Ray A. Billington, "Government and the Arts: The W.P.A. Experience," *American Quarterly*, vol. 13, no. 4 (Winter 1961), p. 468; Mangione, pp. 8–9.
[*Slave narratives*]: Mangione, pp. 263–65; and see George P. Rawick, ed., *The American Slave: A Composite Autobiography* (Greenwood Press, 1972–79), 19 vols., and supplements, series 1 and 2, 22 vols.; Benjamin A. Bodkin, ed., *Lay My Burden Down: A Folk History of Slavery* (University of Chicago Press, 1945); Savannah Unit, Georgia Writers' Program, *Drums and Shadows: Survival Studies Among the Georgia Coastal Negroes* (University of Georgia Press; reprinted by Greenwood Press, 1973).
[*American Guide Series*]: Mangione, pp. 46–49.
[*Kazin on American Guides*]: Kazin, p. 486.
[*Size of Guide Series*]: Mangione, p. 352.
140 [*Aiken on Deerfield*]: Federal Writers' Project, *Massachusetts: A Guide to Its Places and People* (Houghton Mifflin, 1937), p. 223.
[*Individualism vs. collectivism controversy in Massachusetts*]: Billington, p. 475; *Massachusetts Guide*, pp. 89–109, "profound individualism" quoted at p. 90.

140 [*Controversy over Massachusetts guide*]: Mangione, pp. 216–20, *Traveler* quoted at p. 217; Billington, pp. 477–78.

[*Critics on guide*]: Mangione, pp. 351–66; Robert Cantwell, "America and the Writers' Project," *New Republic*, vol. 98, no. 1273 (April 29, 1939), pp. 323–25; Lewis Mumford, "Writers' Project," *New Republic*, vol. 92, no. 1194 (October 20, 1937), pp. 306–7; Robert Bendiner, "When Culture Came to Main Street," *Saturday Review*, vol. 50 (April 1, 1967), pp. 19–21; Daniel M. Fox, "The Achievement of the Federal Writers' Project," *American Quarterly*, vol. 13, no. 1 (Spring 1961), pp. 3–19.

[*Cantwell on guides*]: Cantwell, p. 323.

["*I'm a hog*"]: quoted in Mangione, p. 273.

140–1 [*Rockefeller at play*]: ibid., p. 362.

141 ["*A vast new literature*"]: Kazin, pp. 485–86.

["*Jus' let me get out to California*"]: John Steinbeck, *The Grapes of Wrath* (Viking, 1939), p. 112.

[*Dust bowl refugees*]: Donald Worster, *Dust Bowl: The Southern Plains in the 1930s* (Oxford University Press, 1979); Walter J. Stein, *California and the Dust Bowl Migration* (Greenwood Press, 1973); Thomas W. Pew, Jr., "Route 66: Ghost Road of the Okies," *American Heritage*, vol. 28, no. 5 (August 1977), pp. 24–33; see also Dorothea Lange and Paul S. Taylor, *An American Exodus: A Record of Human Erosion* (Reynal & Hitchcock, 1939).

["*Too nice, kinda*"]: *Grapes of Wrath*, p. 122.

[*Grapes controversy*]: see Peter Lisca, "*The Grapes of Wrath*," in Robert M. Davis, ed., *Steinbeck: A Collection of Critical Essays* (Prentice-Hall, 1972), pp. 75–101, esp. pp. 78–82; Martin S. Shockley, "The Reception of *The Grapes of Wrath* in Oklahoma," in E. W. Tedlock, Jr., and C. V. Wicker, eds., *Steinbeck and His Critics* (University of New Mexico Press, 1957), pp. 231–40.

142 ["*Quality of owning*"]: *Grapes of Wrath*, p. 206.

["*Feel like people again*"]: ibid., p. 420.

["*Use'ta be the fambly*"]: ibid., p. 606.

["*One big soul*"]: ibid., p. 33.

["*I'll be ever'where*"]: ibid., p. 572.

[*Guthrie's growing-up*]: Joe Klein, *Woody Guthrie: A Life* (Knopf, 1980), chs. 1–2; Woody Guthrie, *Bound for Glory* (E. P. Dutton, 1943); Frederick Turner, "Just What in the Hell Has Gone Wrong Here Anyhow?: Woody Guthrie and the American Dream," *American Heritage*, vol. 28, no. 6 (October 1977), pp. 34–43.

[*Twenty-three-year-old soda jerk*]: see Klein, p. 71.

["*This dusty old dust*"]: "So Long It's Been Good to Know Yuh," in Harold Leventhal and Marjorie Guthrie, eds., *The Woody Guthrie Songbook* (Grosset & Dunlap, 1976), p. 210.

[*Klein on Guthrie*]: Klein, p. 79.

142–3 [*Guthrie on his songs*]: *Bound for Glory*, p. 232.

143 ["*Living songs and dying songs*"]: quoted in *Guthrie Songbook*, p. 30.

["*We got out to the West Coast broke*"]: "Talking Dust Bowl," in ibid., p. 220.

["*Real stuff*"]: James T. Farrell, *The Young Manhood of Studs Lonigan* in Farrell, *Studs Lonigan: A Trilogy* (Modern Library, 1938), p. 107.

[*Studs in the park with Lucy*]: *Young Manhood* in ibid., pp. 110, 111, 113, 114, 115.

144 [*Farrell*]: Farrell, "My Beginnings as a Writer," in Farrell, *Reflections at Fifty and Other Essays* (Vanguard, 1954), pp. 156–63; Farrell, "How *Studs Lonigan* Was Written," in Farrell, *The League of Frightened Philistines and Other Papers* (Vanguard, 1945), pp. 82–89; Edgar M. Branch, *James T. Farrell* (University of Minnesota Press, 1963); Ann Douglas, "*Studs Lonigan* and the Failure of History in Mass Society: A Study in Claustrophobia," *American Quarterly*, vol. 29, no. 4 (Winter 1977), pp. 487–505; Alan M. Wald, *James T. Farrell: The Revolutionary Socialist Years* (New York University Press, 1978); Kazin, pp. 380–85; Farrell, *A Note on Literary Criticism* (Vanguard, 1936).

[*1919 Chicago race riot*]: Finis Farr, *Chicago: A Personal History of America's Most American City* (Arlington House, 1973), pp. 337–98; Chicago Commission on Race Relations, *The Negro in Chicago: A Study of Race Relations and a Race Riot* (University of Chicago Press, 1922), ch. 1 and *passim*.

["*Avenues of the dead*"]: *Young Manhood*, p. 74.

144 ["*Bigger took a shoe*"]: Richard Wright, *Native Son* (Harper, 1979), p. 10.
["*He had murdered*"]: ibid., p. 101.
145 ["*Never had he had the chance*"]: ibid., p. 225.
["*We must deal here*"]: ibid., p. 357.
["*Like a blind man*"]: ibid., p. 392.
["*What I killed for, I am!*"]: ibid., pp. 391–92.
[*Wright*]: Wright, *Black Boy* (Harper, 1945); Wright, in Richard Crossman, ed., *The God That Failed* (Harper Colophon, 1963), pp. 115–62; Constance Webb, *Richard Wright* (Putnam, 1968); David Ray and Robert M. Farnsworth, eds., *Richard Wright: Impressions and Perspectives* (University of Michigan Press, 1973); Keneth Kinnamon, *The Emergence of Richard Wright: A Study in Literature and Society* (University of Illinois Press, 1972).
["*Ringed by walls*"]: *Black Boy*, p. 220.
["*Tension would set in*"]: ibid., p. 65.
["*What was this?*"]: ibid., p. 218.
[*Wright's double intellectual life*]: Aaron, "Richard Wright and the Communist Party," in Ray and Farnsworth, p. 44.
["*Scattered but kindred peoples*"]: Wright in Crossman, p. 118.
[*The Group*]: Foster Hirsch, *A Method to Their Madness: The History of the Actors Studio* (Norton, 1984), chs. 4–5; Williams, chs. 4, 10, 12, and *passim;* Harold Clurman, *The Fervent Years: The Story of the Group Theatre and the Thirties* (Knopf, 1945).
145–6 ["*Blood and bones*"]: quoted in Williams, p. 63.
146 [*Odets*]: Gerald Weales, *Clifford Odets, Playwright* (Pegasus, 1971); Robert Shuman, *Clifford Odets* (Twayne, 1962); Harold Cantor, *Clifford Odets, Playwright-Poet* (Scarecrow Press, 1978).
[*Waiting for Lefty*]: in Odets, *Six Plays* (Random House, 1939); see also Weales, ch. 3; Hirsch, pp. 79–82; Williams, pp. 144–46.

4. FREEDOM UNDER SIEGE

149 [*FDR's message to Hitler*]: in *The Public Papers and Addresses of Franklin D. Roosevelt*, Samuel I. Rosenman, comp. (Random House, 1938–50), vol. 8, pp. 201–5, quoted at pp. 201, 202, 203, 204; see also Cordell Hull, *Memoirs* (Macmillan, 1948), vol. 1, p. 620.
150 [*Göring and Mussolini on FDR*]: William L. Shirer, *The Rise and Fall of the Third Reich: A History of Nazi Germany* (Simon and Schuster, 1960), p. 470.
["*Contemptible a creature*"]: quoted in Robert Dallek, *Franklin D. Roosevelt and American Foreign Policy, 1932–1945* (Oxford University Press, 1979), p. 186.
[*Pressure on Latvia*]: Shirer, pp. 470–71.
[*Hitler's response*]: April 28, 1939, in Louis L. Snyder, *Hitler's Third Reich: A Documentary History* (Nelson-Hall, 1981), pp. 311–26, quoted at pp. 317, 313, 318, 324–25, 326, respectively; Shirer, pp. 471–75, quoted on Hitler's speech at p. 471; see also Shirer, *The Nightmare Years* (Little, Brown, 1984), pp. 397–404.
151 ["*Hitler had all the better*"]: quoted in Dallek, p. 187; see also C. A. MacDonald, *The United States, Britain and Appeasement, 1936–1939* (St. Martin's Press, 1981), p. 153.
["*Sympathy with President Roosevelt*"]: quoted in James MacGregor Burns, *Roosevelt: The Lion and the Fox* (Harcourt, 1956), p. 184.

The Zigzag Road to War

152 [*FDR's pre-presidential foreign policy background*]: see Dallek, Prologue; Geoffrey C. Ward, *Before the Trumpet* (Harper, 1985).
[*FDR's criticism of Coolidge*]: quoted in Dallek, p. 17.
153 [*Isolationism*]: Wayne S. Cole, *Roosevelt and the Isolationists, 1932–45* (University of Nebraska Press, 1983), p. 9 and *passim;* Dallek; Wayne S. Cole, *Charles A. Lindbergh and the Battle Against American Intervention in World War II* (Harcourt, 1974); Cole, *America First: The Battle Against Intervention, 1940–1941* (University of Wisconsin Press, 1953); Manfred Jonas, *Isolationism in America, 1935–1941* (Cornell University Press, 1966); Sheldon Marcus, *Father Coughlin: The Tumultuous Life of the Priest of the Little Flower*

(Little, Brown, 1973), chs. 7–8 *passim;* Michele Flynn Stenehjem, *An American First: John T. Flynn and the America First Committee* (Arlington House, 1976).

153 [*Opinion polls, 1937*]: Harvey Cantril and Mildred Strunk, eds., *Public Opinion, 1935–1946* (Princeton University Press, 1951), pp. 966 (item 2), 967 (item 20); see also Jerome S. Bruner, *Mandate from the People* (Duell, Sloan and Pearce, 1944), pp. 18–20.
[*Elements in equation of world power*]: see Burns, *Lion*, p. 248.

154 [*"Groping for a door"*]: quoted in *ibid.*
[*FDR's prewar foreign policy leadership*]: *ibid.*, pp. 262–63; James MacGregor Burns, *Roosevelt: The Soldier of Freedom* (Harcourt, 1970), pp. 65–66, 119–20; Gloria J. Barron, *Leadership in Crisis: FDR and the Path to Intervention* (Kennikat Press, 1973); Mark M. Lowenthal, "Roosevelt and the Coming of War: The Search for United States Policy, 1937–1942," *Journal of Contemporary History*, vol. 16 (1981), pp. 413–40; Bruce M. Russett, *No Clear and Present Danger: A Skeptical View of the U.S. Entry into World War II* (Harper, 1972); Robert A. Divine, *Roosevelt and World War II* (Johns Hopkins Press, 1969), chs. 1–2; Divine, *The Reluctant Belligerent: American Entry into World War II* (Wiley, 1965); Richard W. Steele, "Franklin D. Roosevelt and His Foreign Policy Critics," *Political Science Quarterly*, vol. 94, no. 1 (Spring 1979), pp. 15–32; Steele, "The Great Debate: Roosevelt, the Media, and the Coming of the War, 1940–1941," *Journal of American History*, vol. 71, no. 1 (June 1984), pp. 69–92; Warren F. Kimball, ed., *Franklin D. Roosevelt and the World Crisis, 1937–1945* (D. C. Heath, 1973), part 1; Charles C. Tansill, *Back Door to War* (Henry Regnery, 1952); Arnold A. Offner, *American Appeasement: United States Foreign Policy and Germany, 1933–1938* (Belknap Press of Harvard University Press, 1969).
[*Divisions within isolationist camp*]: Cole, *Roosevelt*, pp. 6–7, quoted at p. 7.

155 [*"The blame for the danger"*]: December 28, 1933, in *Public Papers*, vol. 2, pp. 544–49, quoted at p. 546.
[*Nye committee*]: Wayne S. Cole, *Senator Gerald P. Nye and American Foreign Relations* (University of Minnesota Press, 1962), esp. chs. 5–6; Cole, *Roosevelt*, ch. 11; John E. Wiltz, *In Search of Peace: The Senate Munitions Inquiry, 1934–1936* (Louisiana State University Press, 1963); Burns, *Lion*, pp. 253–54.
[*Hull on Administration marking time*]: Cole, *Roosevelt*, p. 147.

156 [*Curtiss-Wright*]: *U.S.* v. *Curtiss-Wright Export Corp.*, 299 U.S. 304 (1936), quoted at 320; Erik M. Erikson, *The Supreme Court and the New Deal* (Rosemead Review Press, 1940), pp. 197–200; Arthur M. Schlesinger, Jr., *The Imperial Presidency* (Houghton Mifflin, 1973), pp. 100–4.
[*Neutrality legislation and FDR's foreign policy*]: see Dallek, ch. 5; Cole, *Roosevelt*, chs. 12, 15; Richard P. Traina, *American Diplomacy and the Spanish Civil War* (Indiana University Press, 1968); Robert A. Divine, *The Illusion of Neutrality* (University of Chicago Press, 1962); Burns, *Lion*, pp. 255–59; Divine, *Roosevelt*, pp. 10–14.
[*"A hat and a rabbit"*]: quoted in Dallek, p. 144.

157 [*FDR's 1937 Chicago address*]: October 5, 1937, in *Public Papers*, vol. 6, pp. 406–11, quoted at p. 408; see also Dorothy Borg, "Notes on Roosevelt's 'Quarantine' Speech," in Robert A. Divine, ed., *Causes and Consequences of World War II* (Quadrangle, 1969), pp. 47–70.
[*Response to Chicago address and FDR's response*]: Burns, *Lion*, pp. 318–19; Cole, *Roosevelt*, pp. 246–48; Dorothy Borg, *The United States and the Far Eastern Crisis of 1933–1938* (Harvard University Press, 1964), pp. 382–98, 538–39; Divine, *Reluctant Belligerent*, p. 45.
[*"A terrible thing"*]: quoted in Samuel I. Rosenman, *Working with Roosevelt* (Harper, 1952), p. 167.
[*Hitler's domestic power*]: see Edward N. Peterson, *The Limits of Hitler's Power* (Princeton University Press, 1969); Shirer, *Rise and Fall*.
[*Rhineland*]: Shirer, *Rise and Fall*, pp. 290–96, Hitler quoted at p. 293; James T. Emmerson, *The Rhineland Crisis, 7 March 1936: A Study in Multilateral Diplomacy* (Maurice Temple Smith, 1977); William L. Shirer, *The Collapse of the Third Republic: An Inquiry into the Fall of France in 1940* (Simon and Schuster, 1969), ch. 16.

158 [*Sudeten crisis*]: Shirer, *Rise and Fall*, ch. 12, Churchill quoted at p. 423; Telford Taylor, *Munich: The Price of Peace* (Doubleday, 1979); Burns, *Lion*, pp. 384–88; Shirer, *Collapse*, chs. 19–21; Larry W. Fuchser, *Neville Chamberlain and Appeasement: A Study in the Politics*

of History (Norton, 1982), chs. 6–7; Offner, pp. 245–71; Joseph Alsop and Robert Kintner, *American White Paper: The Story of American Diplomacy and the Second World War* (Simon and Schuster, 1940), ch. 2; MacDonald, chs. 6–7.

158 [*Czech dismemberment*]: Shirer, *Rise and Fall*, pp. 428–30, 437–54.

[*"Never in my life"*]: letter to Gertrude Ely, March 25, 1939, in *F.D.R.: His Personal Letters, 1928–1945*, Elliott Roosevelt, ed. (Duell, Sloan and Pearce, 1950), vol. 2, p. 872.

[*Efforts toward arms embargo repeal*]: see David L. Porter, *The Seventy-sixth Congress and World War II, 1939–1940* (University of Missouri Press, 1979), ch. 3; Betty Glad, *Key Pittman: The Tragedy of a Senate Insider* (Columbia University Press, 1986), ch. 22.

[*Pittman*]: Fred L. Israel, *Nevada's Key Pittman* (University of Nebraska Press, 1963), pp. 166–67; see also Glad, pp. 217–19 and chs. 20–24; Wayne S. Cole, "Senator Pittman and American Neutrality Policies, 1933–1940," *Mississippi Valley Historical Review*, vol. 46, no. 4 (March 1960), pp. 644–62.

[*FDR meeting with Senate leaders*]: quoted in Burns, *Lion*, pp. 392–93.

159 [*FDR on prospective Axis aggression*]: memorandum by Carlton Savage, May 19, 1939, quoted in William L. Langer and S. Everett Gleason, *The Challenge to Isolation, 1937–1940* (Harper, 1952), pp. 138–39.

[*Stalin to Churchill on Soviet turn to Germany*]: Lord Beaverbrook Papers, Cabinet Papers, House of Lords.

[*Nazi-Soviet Pact*]: Shirer, *Rise and Fall*, ch. 15, Stalin quoted at p. 540; Shirer, *Collapse*, chs. 22, 24; Vojtech Mastny, *Russia's Road to the Cold War: Diplomacy, Warfare, and the Politics of Communism, 1941–1945* (Columbia University Press, 1979), pp. 23–35; David J. Dallin, *Soviet Russia's Foreign Policy, 1939–1942*, Leon Dennen, trans. (Yale University Press, 1942), chs. 2–3; Raymond J. Strong and James S. Beddie, eds., *Nazi-Soviet Relations, 1939–1941: Documents from the Archives of the German Foreign Office* (U.S. Department of State, 1948), chs. 1–3.

[*Start of World War II*]: Nicholas Bethell, *The War Hitler Won: The Fall of Poland, September 1939* (Holt, Rinehart and Winston, 1972); Shirer, *Rise and Fall*, chs. 16–17; Shirer, *Collapse*, chs. 25–26.

160 [*"I sit in one of the dives"*]: "September 1, 1939," in *The English Auden: Poems, Essays, and Dramatic Writings, 1927–1939*, Edward Mendelson, ed. (Random House, 1977), pp. 245–47, quoted at p. 245.

[*"The end of the world"*]: quoted in Michael R. Beschloss, *Kennedy and Roosevelt: The Uneasy Alliance* (Norton, 1980), p. 190.

[*Arms embargo repeal and "cash and carry"*]: Porter, ch. 4; Divine, *Illusion*, chs. 8–9; Cole, *Roosevelt*, pp. 320–30; Burns, *Lion*, pp. 395–97; Langer and Gleason, pp. 218–35.

[*Noninterventionist mail campaign*]: Dallek, p. 200.

[*"One single hard-headed thought"*]: message to Congress, September 21, 1939, in *Public Papers*, vol. 8, pp. 512–22, quoted at p. 521.

[*"Dreadful rape"*]: FDR to Lincoln MacVeagh, letter of December 1, 1939, in *Personal Letters*, vol. 2, p. 961.

161 [*Anglo-American relations*]: see MacDonald, *passim*; Warren F. Kimball, *The Most Unsordid Act: Lend-Lease, 1939–1941* (Johns Hopkins Press, 1969); Kimball, "Lend-Lease and the Open Door: The Temptation of British Opulence, 1937–1942," *Political Science Quarterly*, vol. 86, no. 2 (June 1971), pp. 232–59; Fuchser, pp. 97–99.

[*"Much public criticism"*]: letter of February 1, 1940, in Francis L. Loewenheim et al., eds., *Roosevelt and Churchill: Their Secret Wartime Correspondence* (Saturday Review Press/E. P. Dutton, 1975), p. 93.

[*"The country as a whole"*]: quoted in Dallek, p. 211.

[*German invasion of Denmark and Norway*]: Shirer, *Rise and Fall*, ch. 20; J. L. Moulton, *The Norwegian Campaign of 1940: A Study of Warfare in Three Dimensions* (Eyre & Spottiswoode, 1960); Richard Petrow, *The Bitter Years* (Morrow, 1974), chs. 1–7.

[*"Can have no illusions"*]: April 15, 1940, in *Public Papers*, vol. 9, p. 161.

162 [*German invasion of the Netherlands, Belgium, France*]: Shirer, *Rise and Fall*, ch. 21; Shirer, *Collapse*, chs. 28–29; John Williams, *The Ides of May: The Defeat of France, May-June 1940* (Knopf, 1968).

[*"Decide the destiny"*]: quoted in Burns, *Lion*, p. 419.

162 ["*Scene has darkened swiftly*"]: in Loewenheim, pp. 94–95, quoted at p. 94.

["*Nazified Europe*"]: *ibid.*, p. 94.

[*Reynaud's appeal to FDR*]: quoted in Dallek, p. 230; see also Eleanor M. Gates, *End of the Affair: The Collapse of the Anglo-French Alliance, 1939–40* (University of California Press, 1981), Appendix D.

[*Walsh threat*]: Burns, *Lion*, pp. 421–22.

[*Opinion polls on aid*]: poll of May 23, 1940, in Cantril and Strunk, p. 973 (item 67).

163 [*Isolationist defections*]: Justus D. Doenecke, "Non-interventionism of the Left: The Keep America Out of the War Congress, 1938–41," *Journal of Contemporary History*, vol. 12, no. 2 (1977), pp. 221–36, esp. pp. 231–32.

[*FDR as Sphinx*]: see Burns, *Lion*, p. 410.

[*FDR's maneuverings to preserve options*]: *ibid.*, pp. 408–15; James A. Farley, *Jim Farley's Story* (McGraw-Hill, 1948), chs. 20–24; Bascom N. Timmons, *Garner of Texas* (Harper, 1948), chs. 15–16; Herbert S. Parmet and Marie B. Hecht, *Never Again: A President Runs for a Third Term* (Macmillan, 1968), chs. 1, 2.

163–4 [*Republican convention*]: Robert E. Burke, "The Election of 1940," in Arthur M. Schlesinger, Jr., ed., *History of American Presidential Elections, 1789–1968* (Chelsea House, 1971), vol. 4, pp. 2928–31; Steve Neal, *Dark Horse: A Biography of Wendell Willkie* (Doubleday, 1984), ch. 10; Parmet and Hecht, ch. 6; James T. Patterson, *Mr. Republican: Robert A. Taft* (Houghton Mifflin, 1972), chs. 14–15.

164 ["*Could not in these times refuse*"]: quoted in Farley, p. 251.

[*Democratic convention*]: Burns, *Lion*, pp. 426–30; Burke, pp. 2933–36; Farley, chs. 25–29; Parmet and Hecht, ch. 8.

["*Destroyer deal*"]: Philip Goodhart, *Fifty Ships That Saved the World* (Doubleday, 1965); Mark L. Chadwin, *The Hawks of World War II* (University of North Carolina Press, 1968), ch. 4; Dallek, pp. 243–48; Kimball, *Unsordid Act*, pp. 67–71; Ronald Steel, *Walter Lippmann and the American Century* (Atlantic Monthly/Little, Brown, 1980), pp. 384–86; *Public Papers*, vol. 9, pp. 376–407; Thomas A. Bailey and Paul B. Ryan, *Hitler vs. Roosevelt: The Undeclared Naval War* (Free Press, 1979), ch. 7.

["*Whole fate of the war*"]: letter of July 31, 1940, in Loewenheim, pp. 107–108, quoted at p. 107.

[*Hitler's thwarted invasion of Britain*]: see Shirer, *Rise and Fall*, ch. 22.

165 [*Selective Service*]: J. Garry Clifford and Samuel R. Spencer, Jr., *The First Peacetime Draft* (University Press of Kansas, 1986); Porter, chs. 6–7; Dallek, pp. 248–50; *Public Papers*, vol. 9, pp. 473–75.

[*Willkie campaign*]: Neal, ch. 12; Burke, pp. 2937–43; Parmet and Hecht, chs. 9–12; Muriel Rukeyser, *One Life* (Simon and Schuster, 1957), ch. 4; Donald Bruce Johnson, *The Republican Party and Wendell Willkie* (University of Illinois Press, 1960), ch. 4; Cole, *Roosevelt*, p. 396.

["*A temporary alliance*"]: Neal, pp. 158–59, quoted at p. 159.

[*FDR's campaign*]: Burns, *Lion*, pp. 442–51; Burke, pp. 2943–45; Parmet and Hecht, chs. 9–12.

["*An old campaigner*"]: in *Public Papers*, vol. 9, pp. 485–95, quoted at p. 488.

["*Ma-a-a-rtin*"]: see *ibid.*, pp. 506, 523; Rosenman, *Working*, pp. 240–41.

["*Mothers and fathers of America*"]: October 30, 1940, in *Public Papers*, vol. 9, pp. 514–24, quoted at p. 517.

["*Very ominous*"]: campaign address at Brooklyn, N.Y., November 1, 1940, in *ibid.*, vol. 9, pp. 530–39, quoted at p. 531; see also Burns, *Lion*, p. 449.

[*Election results*]: Schlesinger, vol. 4, p. 3006; Burns, *Lion*, pp. 454–55.

["*Happy I've won but*"]: quoted in James Roosevelt and Bill Libby, *My Parents: A Differing View* (Playboy Press, 1976), p. 164.

[*FDR-Willkie meeting*]: see James Roosevelt and Sidney Shalett, *Affectionately, F.D.R.: A Son's Story of a Lonely Man* (Harcourt, 1959), p. 325; Grace Tully, *F.D.R., My Boss* (Scribner, 1949), p. 58.

The War of Two Worlds

166 [*Hitler's address at Rheinmetall-Borsig*]: *New York Times*, December 11, 1940, pp. 1, 4–5, quoted at p. 4.

166 [*FDR's reply*]: fireside chat of December 29, 1940, in *Public Papers*, vol. 9, pp. 633–44, quoted at pp. 634, 639, 640, 643; Burns, *Soldier*, pp. 27–28.
167 [*Hitler on global strategy*]: quoted in Shirer, *Rise and Fall*, p. 821; see also Joachim C. Fest, *Hitler*, Richard and Clara Winston, trans. (Vintage, 1975), p. 643.
168 [*Churchill's letter to FDR*]: December 8, 1940, in Winston S. Churchill, *Their Finest Hour* (Houghton Mifflin, 1949), pp. 558–67, quoted at pp. 561, 564, 566.
["*One of the most important*"]: ibid., p. 558.
[*FDR's conception of Lend-Lease*]: quoted in Robert E. Sherwood, *Roosevelt and Hopkins: An Intimate History* (Harper, 1950), p. 224.
[*Lend-Lease*]: Kimball, *Unsordid Act;* John Morton Blum, *From the Morgenthau Diaries: Years of Urgency, 1938–1941* (Houghton Mifflin, 1965), ch. 6; William L. Langer and S. Everett Gleason, *The Undeclared War, 1940–1941* (Harper, 1953), chs. 8–9; Dallek, pp. 255–60; Cole, *Roosevelt*, ch. 28; Burns, *Soldier*, pp. 43–49; Kimball, "Lend-Lease and the Open Door"; William A. Klingaman, *1941* (Harper, 1988), ch. 3.
[*Britain's financial straits*]: Dallek, p. 255.
[*FDR's garden-hose analogy*]: press conference 702, December 17, 1940, in *Public Papers*, vol. 9, pp. 604–15, quoted at p. 607; see also Kimball, *Unsordid Act*, p. 77.
169 [*Taft on Lend-Lease*]: Patterson, *Mr. Republican*, pp. 242–44.
[*Wheeler on Lend-Lease and FDR's reply*]: quoted in Burns, *Soldier*, p. 44; and press conference 710, January 14, 1941, in *Public Papers*, vol. 9, pp. 710–12, quoted at pp. 711–12.
[Tribune *on Lend-Lease*]: quoted in Burns, *Soldier*, p. 45.
[*Coughlin on Lend-Lease*]: see Charles J. Tull, *Father Coughlin and the New Deal* (Syracuse University Press, 1965), p. 228.
[*Lindbergh's testimony*]: Cole, *Roosevelt*, pp. 416–17; Kimball, *Unsordid Act*, p. 190.
[*Smith's threat*]: Kimball, *Unsordid Act*, pp. 162–63; see also Gerald L. K. Smith, *Besieged Patriot* (Christian Nationalist Crusade, 1978).
[*Beard on Lend-Lease*]: Kimball, *Roosevelt and the World Crisis*, p. 10.
[*Pressure on FDR to convoy ships*]: Dallek, pp. 260–62; Burns, *Soldier*, pp. 89–92.
[*FDR's "undeclared naval war"*]: Bailey and Ryan; Shirer, *Rise and Fall*, pp. 878–83; H. L. Trefousse, *Germany and American Neutrality, 1939–1941* (Bookman Associates, 1951).
170 [*German invasion of the Soviet Union*]: G. Deborin, *The Second World War* (Progress Publishers, Moscow, n.d.), chs. 7–8.
[*U.S.-Japanese relations in 1930s*]: John Toland, *The Rising Sun: The Decline and Fall of the Japanese Empire, 1936–1945* (Random House, 1970), chs. 1–2; Armin Rappaport, *Henry L. Stimson and Japan, 1931–1933* (University of Chicago Press, 1963); Dorothy Borg and Shumpei Okamoto, eds., *Pearl Harbor as History: Japanese-American Relations, 1931–1941* (Columbia University Press, 1973); Howard Jaslon, "Cordell Hull, His 'Associates,' and Relations with Japan, 1933–1936," *Mid-America*, vol. 56, no. 3 (July 1974), pp. 160–74; Frederick C. Adams, "The Road to Pearl Harbor: A Reexamination of American Far Eastern Policy, July 1937–December 1938," *Journal of American History*, vol. 63, no. 1 (June 1971), pp. 73–92.
171 [*Atlantic-Pacific links*]: see Burns, *Soldier*, p. 106.
["*Knock-out fight*"]: letter of July 1, 1941, in *Personal Letters*, vol. 2, pp. 1173–74, quoted at p. 1174.
[*FDR-Churchill summit*]: Theodore A. Wilson, *The First Summit: Roosevelt and Churchill at Placentia Bay, 1941* (Houghton Mifflin, 1969); Langer and Gleason, *Undeclared War*, ch. 21.
["*Final destruction of the Nazi tyranny*"]: quoted in Wilson, p. 206.
171-2 [*Greer and Kearny incidents*]: Bailey and Ryan, chs. 12–14; Langer and Gleason, *Undeclared War*, pp. 742–60.
172 ["*Very simply and very bluntly*"]: Navy and Total Defense Day Address, October 27, 1941, in *Public Papers*, vol. 10, pp. 438–44, quoted at p. 441.
["*United States has attacked*"]: quoted in Bailey and Ryan, p. 202.
[*Approach of war in the Pacific*]: Dallek, ch. 11 *passim;* Toland, *Rising Sun*, chs. 4–5; Burns, *Soldier*, ch. 4; Shirer, *Rise and Fall*, ch. 25; Herbert Feis, *The Road to Pearl Harbor: The Coming of the War Between the United States and Japan* (Princeton University Press, 1950); Kimball, *Roosevelt and the World Crisis*, pp. 90–103; Winston S. Churchill, *The*

Grand Alliance (Houghton Mifflin, 1950), ch. 11; Christopher Thorne, *The Issue of War: States, Societies, and the Far Eastern Conflict of 1941-1945* (Oxford University Press, 1985), part 1; Thorne, *Allies of a Kind: The United States, Britain, and the War Against Japan, 1941-1945* (Oxford University Press, 1978), ch. 2; Jonathan G. Utley, *Going to War with Japan, 1937-1941* (University of Tennessee Press, 1985); Akira Iriye, *Power and Culture: The Japanese-American War* (Harvard University Press, 1981), ch. 1; Iriye, *Across the Pacific: An Inner History of American-East Asian Relations* (Harcourt, 1967), ch. 8; Kimitada Miwa, "Japanese Images of War with the United States," in Akira Iriye, ed., *Mutual Images: Essays in American-Japanese Relations* (Harvard University Press, 1975), ch. 6.

172 [*U.S. gasoline and scrap iron embargo*]: see Burns, *Soldier*, pp. 21, 107, 109-10.

173 ["*Within the hour*"]: note from Churchill to Eden, December 2, 1941, in Churchill, *Grand Alliance*, pp. 600-1, quoted at p. 601.

174 [*"Strongest fortress"*]: quoted in Gordon W. Prange, *At Dawn We Slept: The Untold Story of Pearl Harbor* (McGraw-Hill, 1981), p. 122.
["*This means war*"]: ibid., p. 475.
[*Pearl Harbor*]: ibid., chs. 61-67; Ronald H. Spector, *Eagle Against the Sun: The American War with Japan* (Free Press, 1985), pp. 1-7; Toland, *Rising Sun*, pp. 211-20; Klingaman, ch. 27.
[*Mitsuo on concentration of U.S. ships*]: Spector, p. 4.

175 [*Controversy as to foreknowledge of Pearl Harbor attack*]: see Spector, pp. 95-100; Prange, *At Dawn*, esp. ch. 81 and Appendix ("Revisionists Revisited"), pp. 839-50; Prange et al., *Pearl Harbor: The Verdict of History* (McGraw-Hill, 1986); John Toland, *Infamy: Pearl Harbor and Its Aftermath* (Doubleday, 1982); Charles A. Beard, *President Roosevelt and the Coming War, 1941: A Study in Appearances and Realities* (Yale University Press, 1948); Robert A. Theobald, *The Final Secret of Pearl Harbor: The Washington Contribution to the Japanese Attack* (Devin-Adair, 1954); Roberta Wohlstetter, *Pearl Harbor: Warning and Decision* (Stanford University Press, 1962); Telford Taylor, "Day of Infamy, Decades of Doubt," *New York Times Magazine*, April 29, 1984, pp. 107, 113, 120.
[*Washington reaction to attack*]: Toland, *Rising Sun*, pp. 216, 223-24, Knox quoted at p. 223.
[*Tokyo reaction to attack*]: ibid., pp. 227-28, song quoted at p. 228.
[*Churchill's reaction to attack*]: Churchill, *Grand Alliance*, pp. 604-8.

175-6 [*Hitler's reaction to attack*]: Shirer, *Rise and Fall*, pp. 875-76, 883-902; Fest, pp. 655-56.

176 [*FDR on Germany and Italy at war with U.S.*]: *Public Papers*, vol. 10, pp. 522-30, quoted at p. 530.
[*Hitler's declaration of war upon U.S.*]: Shirer, *Rise and Fall*, pp. 897-900; Burns, *Soldier*, pp. 67-68, 173-74; Bailey and Ryan, ch. 17; John Toland, *Adolf Hitler* (Doubleday, 1976), pp. 692-97; Robert G. L. Waite, *The Psychopathic God: Adolf Hitler* (New American Library, 1978), pp. 489-99; James V. Compton, *The Swastika and the Eagle: Hitler, the United States, and the Origins of World War II* (Houghton Mifflin, 1967), chs. 1-2, 15; Gerhard L. Weinberg, "Hitler's Image of the United States," *American Historical Review*, vol. 69, no. 4 (July 1964), pp. 1006-21.
[*Japanese attack at Philippines*]: William Manchester, *American Caesar: Douglas MacArthur, 1880-1964* (Little, Brown, 1978), ch. 5; Toland, *Rising Sun*, pp. 232-35; Spector, pp. 106-8; Louis Morton, *The Fall of the Philippines* (U.S. Department of the Army, 1953); Daniel F. Harrington, "A Careless Hope: American Air Power and Japan, 1941," *Pacific Historical Review*, vol. 48 (1979), pp. 217-38.

177 [*FDR-Churchill conference*]: Robert Beitzell, *The Uneasy Alliance: America, Britain, and Russia, 1941-1943* (Knopf, 1972), ch. 1; Richard W. Steele, *The First Offensive: Roosevelt, Marshall and the Making of American Strategy* (Indiana University Press, 1973), ch. 3; W. G. F. Jackson, *"Overlord": Normandy 1944* (Davis-Poynter, 1978), pp. 41-53; Forrest C. Pogue, *George C. Marshall: Ordeal of Hope, 1939-1942* (Viking, 1966), ch. 12; Churchill, *Grand Alliance*, chs. 14-15; see also Russell F. Weigley, *The American Way of War: A History of United States Military Strategy and Policy* (Macmillan, 1973), ch. 7.

178 [*Religious freedom in Declaration*]: Sherwood, pp. 448-49.
["*To defend life, liberty*"]: quoted in Churchill, *Grand Alliance*, p. 684.

179 [*Battle of the Coral Sea*]: Spector, pp. 158-63; Ronald Lewin, *The American Magic: Codes, Ciphers and the Defeat of Japan* (Farrar, Straus & Giroux, 1982), pp. 90-96.

179 [*Guadalcanal*]: Spector, chs. 9–10 *passim;* Toland, *Rising Sun,* part 4; Samuel B. Griffith II, *The Battle for Guadalcanal* (Lippincott, 1963); John Hersey, *Into the Valley: A Skirmish of the Marines* (Knopf, 1944); S. E. Morison, *The Struggle for Guadalcanal* (Little, Brown, 1949).
[*"Green hell"*]: Toland, *Rising Sun,* ch. 15.
[*"Loathsome crawling things"*]: Weigley, p. 276.
[*Doolittle's feat*]: Spector, pp. 153–55; Toland, *Rising Sun,* pp. 304–10; Quentin Reynolds, *The Amazing Mr. Doolittle* (Appleton-Century-Crofts, 1953), chs. 8–9.
[*Midway*]: Spector, pp. 166–78; Toland, *Rising Sun,* pp. 325–42; Gordon Prange, *Miracle at Midway* (McGraw-Hill, 1982); Lewin, pp. 96–111; Mitsuo Fuchida and Masatake Okumiya, *Midway, the Battle That Doomed Japan: The Japanese Navy's Story* (U.S. Naval Institute, 1955).
180 [*Public pressure for shift to Pacific first*]: Steele, pp. 81–92; Manchester, pp. 307–12; Burns, *Soldier,* pp. 210–11.
[*Debate over European strategy*]: see Jackson, chs. 3–4; Steele, chs. 4–8; John Grigg, *1943: The Victory That Never Was* (Hill and Wang, 1980), part 1 *passim;* Herbert Feis, *Churchill, Roosevelt, Stalin: The War They Waged and the Peace They Sought* (Princeton University Press, 1957), chs. 5–10; Joseph L. Strange, "The British Rejection of Operation SLEDGEHAMMER, An Alternative Motive," *Military Affairs,* vol. 46, no. 1 (February 1982), pp. 6–14; Pogue, chs. 12, 14–15; Beitzell, chs. 2–3. For a Soviet view of the strategic background, see Genrikh Trofimenko, *The U.S. Military Doctrine* (Progress Publishers, Moscow, 1986), pp. 1–56.
[*Eisenhower on cross-Channel attack*]: quoted in Steele, p. 79.
181 [*North Africa*]: Arthur Layton Funk, *The Politics of TORCH: The Allied Landings and the Algiers Putsch* (University Press of Kansas, 1974); William L. Langer, *Our Vichy Gamble* (Knopf, 1947); Stephen E. Ambrose, *The Supreme Commander: The War Years of General Dwight D. Eisenhower* (Doubleday, 1970), book 1, chs. 7–10; Burns, *Soldier,* ch. 9; Shirer, *Rise and Fall,* pp. 919–25; Pogue, ch. 18.
[*"Walk with the Devil"*]: quoted in Burns, *Soldier,* p. 297.
[*"The freedom of your lives"*]: *ibid.,* p. 292.
[*"I salute again"*]: November 7, 1942, in *Public Papers,* vol. 11, pp. 451–52, quoted at p. 451.

The Production of War

182 [*"Proper application of overwhelming force"*]: Churchill, *Grand Alliance,* p. 607.
[*Soldiers as production workers*]: Burns, *Soldier,* p. 470; William Manchester, *The Glory and the Dream: A Narrative History of America, 1932–1972* (Little, Brown, 1974), pp. 267–68, 280–83; Bill Mauldin, *Up Front* (Henry Holt, 1944), pp. 143–44 and *passim.*
[*Press on soldiers*]: Burns, *Soldier,* p. 470; John Morton Blum, *V Was for Victory: Politics and American Culture During World War II* (Harcourt, 1976), pp. 53–64.
[*Slow conversion to war production*]: see Richard Polenberg, *War and Society: The United States, 1941–1945* (Lippincott, 1972), pp. 10–11; see generally David Brinkley, *Washington Goes to War* (Knopf, 1988), esp. chs. 3–5.
[*FDR's production goals for 1942*]: address on the State of the Union, January 6, 1942, in *Public Papers,* vol. 11, p. 37.
[*Sample conversions*]: Manchester, *Glory and Dream,* p. 293; John R. Craf, *A Survey of the American Economy, 1940–1946* (North River Press, 1946), p. 33.
183 [*American military output*]: A. Russell Buchanan, *The United States and World War II* (Harper, 1964), vol. 1, p. 140; Manchester, *Glory and Dream,* p. 296; Alan S. Milward, *War, Economy and Society, 1939–1945* (University of California Press, 1977), pp. 69 (Table 15), 70.
[*Technology as pacing production*]: Milward, pp. 188–91; Craf, p. 41; Allan Nevins and Frank E. Hill, *Ford: Decline and Rebirth, 1933–1962* (Scribner, 1962), p. 191.
[*Wartime shipping tonnage*]: Donald M. Nelson, *Arsenal of Democracy: The Story of American War Production* (Harcourt, 1946), p. 243.
[*Rate of ship production*]: Manchester, *Glory and Dream,* p. 295.
[*Hull 440*]: Bernard Taper, "Life with Kaiser," *Nation,* vol. 155, no. 24 (December 12, 1942), pp. 644–46; Russell Bookhout, "We Build Ships," *Atlantic,* vol. 171, no.

4 (April 1943), pp. 37–42; Richard R. Lingemann, *Don't You Know There's a War On?: The American Home Front, 1941–1945* (Putnam, 1970), pp. 130–31; A. A. Hoehling, *Home Front, U.S.A.* (Crowell, 1966), pp. 51–52; Augusta Clawson, "Shipyard Diary of a Woman Welder," *Radical America*, vol. 9, nos. 4–5 (July–August 1975), pp. 134–38.

184 [*"But where is the ship?"*]: quoted in Bookhout, p. 38.

[*Labor force, workweek, wage increases*]: Buchanan, vol. 1, p. 138; Joel Seidman, *American Labor from Defense to Reconversion* (University of Chicago Press, 1953), p. 270.

[*Income redistribution*]: Geoffrey Perrett, *Days of Sadness, Years of Triumph* (Coward, McCann & Geoghegan, 1973), p. 354.

[*Consumer spending*]: Combined Production and Resources Board, *The Impact of the War on Civilian Consumption in the United Kingdom, the United States and Canada* (U.S. Government Printing Office, 1945), p. 17 (Table 11).

[*Spending on nondurables*]: *ibid.*, pp. 3, 23–25; Lingemann, pp. 241–42, 281, 295, 319; Perrett, pp. 239, 381–82.

185 [*"Rest Faster Here"*]: quoted in Lingemann, p. 241.

[*Migration in wartime*]: Francis E. Merrill, *Social Problems on the Homefront: A Study of War-time Influences* (Harper, 1948), pp. 15, 61 (Table 4).

[*Migrant children*]: Agnes E. Meyer, *Journey through Chaos* (Harcourt, 1943), pp. 152, 204–5, and *passim;* see also Merrill, ch. 3.

[*Migrant housing*]: Blair Bolles, "The Great Defense Migration," *Harper's*, vol. 183 (October 1941), p. 463; see also Meyer, p. 100; William H. Jordy, "Fiasco at Willow Run," *Nation*, vol. 156, no. 19 (May 8, 1943), pp. 655–58; Polenberg, pp. 140–42; Lingemann, pp. 82–84, 107–10.

[*Beaumont dump*]: Meyer, pp. 174–75.

[*Nelson and the WPB*]: Nelson; Eliot Janeway, *The Struggle for Survival: A Chronicle of Economic Mobilization in World War II* (Yale University Press, 1951), esp. ch. 11; Bruce Catton, *The War Lords of Washington* (Harcourt, 1948); Calvin L. Christman, "Donald Nelson and the Army: Personality as a Factor in Civil-Military Relations during World War II," *Military Affairs*, vol. 27, no. 3 (October 1973), pp. 81–83.

[*"Final authority"*]: see Perrett, p. 256.

[*"We must have down here"*]: quoted in Catton, p. 117.

[*"Replacing New Dealers"*]: quoted in Polenberg, pp. 90–91.

[*Dollar-a-year men*]: *ibid.*, p. 91.

185–6 [*Truman on dollar-a-year men*]: quoted in Catton, pp. 119, 118, respectively; see also Donald H. Riddle, *The Truman Committee: A Study in Congressional Responsibility* (Rutgers University Press, 1964), pp. 41–43, 65–66, 71–73.

186 [*Industry incentives*]: Lingemann, p. 111; Blum, p. 122.

[*"Of course it contributes to waste"*]: quoted in Meyer, p. 5.

[*Corporate profits and assets*]: Polenberg, p. 13; Perrett, p. 403.

[*"You have to let business make money"*]: quoted in Blum, p. 122.

[*Small business in the war*]: Jim F. Heath, "American War Mobilization and the Use of Small War Manufacturers, 1939–1943," *Business History Review*, vol. 46, no. 3 (August 1972), pp. 295–319; Polenberg, pp. 218–19; Lingemann, p. 65; Riddle, pp. 63–64; Blum, pp. 124–31.

[*Union membership*]: Lingemann, p. 161; Craf, pp. 181–82.

[*NWLB*]: Seidman, pp. 81–86, 272–74; Burns, *Soldier*, p. 192; *Public Papers*, vol. 11, pp. 42–48.

[*Maintenance of membership*]: see Seidman, ch. 6.

187 [*Labor's junior status in war*]: see Paul A. C. Koistinen, "Mobilizing the World War II Economy: Labor and the Industrial-Military Alliance," *Pacific Historical Review*, vol. 42 (1973), pp. 443–78.

[*Reuther's plan*]: Jean Gould and Lorena Hickok, *Walter Reuther: Labor's Rugged Individualist* (Dodd, Mead, 1972), pp. 188–95, William Knudsen on "socialism" quoted at p. 193; Irving Howe and B. J. Widick, *The UAW and Walter Reuther* (Random House, 1949), pp. 108–10; Janeway, pp. 220–25.

[*Murray on rank and file*]: quoted in Koistinen, p. 468.

[*Labor conditions*]: Meyer, *passim;* Ed Jennings, "Wildcat! The Wartime Strike Wave in Auto," *Radical America*, vol. 9, nos. 4–5 (July–August 1975), pp. 77–105.

[*"Little Steel" and inflation*]: Seidman, ch. 7; Koistinen, p. 468.

187 [*Work stoppages*]: Seidman, p. 135 (Table); Jennings, p. 89.

[*Lewis in early war years*]: Melvyn Dubofsky and Warren Van Tine, *John L. Lewis* (Quadrangle/New York Times Book Co., 1977), ch. 17.

["*When the mine workers' children cry*"]: quoted in *ibid.*, p. 419.

[*Mine workers' conflict*]: *ibid.*, ch. 18; Seidman, pp. 136–40; Burns, *Soldier*, pp. 335–37.

188 ["*Damn your coal black soul*"]: quoted in Burns, *Soldier*, p. 337.

["*Insurrection against the war*"]: quoted in Seidman, p. 144.

[*FDR on resignation and suicide*]: see Dubofsky and Van Tine, p. 424.

[*Women as percentage of war work force*]: International Labour Office, *The War and Women's Employment: The Experience of the United Kingdom and the United States* (International Labour Office, 1946), pp. 172–74.

[*Sample women's jobs*]: *ibid.*, p. 195; Lingemann, p. 152; Meyer, p. 46; Studs Terkel, "*The Good War*": *An Oral History of World War Two* (Pantheon, 1984), p. 10.

[*Numbers of women employed, 1944*]: ILO, p. 166; Susan M. Hartmann, *The Home Front and Beyond: American Women in the 1940s* (Twayne, 1982), pp. 77–78.

[*Women's wages, 1944*]: ILO, pp. 199–200, 207.

[*Women workers and unions*]: *ibid.*, pp. 237–47; Hartmann, pp. 64–69; Karen Anderson, *Wartime Women: Sex Roles, Family Relations, and the Status of Women During World War II* (Greenwood Press, 1981), pp. 55–60.

[*Rosie the Riveter*]: see Paddy Quick, "Rosie the Riveter: Myths and Realities," *Radical America*, vol. 9, nos. 4–5 (July–August 1975), pp. 115–31, esp. pp. 115–16; Maureen Honey, *Creating Rosie the Riveter: Class, Gender, and Propaganda during World War II* (University of Massachusetts Press, 1984); Sherna B. Gluck, *Rosie the Riveter Revisited: Women, the War, and Social Change* (Twayne Publishers, 1987).

[*Defense contractors' hiring policies*]: see Lingemann, p. 162.

[*Blacks as percentage of war workers, 1944*]: *ibid.*

188–9 [*Black-white wage differential*]: *ibid.*, pp. 164–65.

189 [*NAACP and CORE in the war*]: Warren D. St. James, *The National Association for the Advancement of Colored People: A Case Study in Pressure Groups* (Exposition Press, 1958), pp. 52, 54 (Table 1); August Meier and Elliott Rudwick, *CORE: A Study in the Civil Rights Movement, 1942–1968* (Oxford University Press, 1973), ch. 1; Richard M. Dalfiume, "The 'Forgotten Years' of the Negro Revolution," in Bernard Sternsher, ed., *The Negro in Depression and War: Prelude to Revolution, 1930–1945* (Quadrangle, 1969), pp. 298–316; Lee Finkle, "The Conservative Aims of Militant Rhetoric: Black Protest during World War II," *Journal of American History*, vol. 60, no. 3 (December 1973), pp. 692–713; Blum, pp. 182–99.

[*Race riots, 1943*]: Alfred M. Lee and Norman D. Humphrey, *Race Riot (Detroit, 1943)* (Octagon Books, 1968); Carey McWilliams, *North from Mexico: The Spanish-Speaking People of the United States* (Lippincott, 1949), chs. 12–13.

[*Employment of black women*]: ILO, pp. 184–85; Karen T. Anderson, "Last Hired, First Fired: Black Women Workers during World War II," *Journal of American History*, vol. 69, no. 1 (June 1982), pp. 82–97.

[*St. Louis electric company*]: Anderson, "Last Hired," p. 84.

[*Black women's jobs*]: Hartmann, p. 87; Anderson, *Wartime Women*, p. 39.

[*Japanese internment*]: Audrie Girdner and Anne Loftis, *The Great Betrayal: The Evacuation of Japanese-Americans during World War II* (Macmillan, 1969); Bill Hosokawa, *Nisei: The Quiet Americans* (Morrow, 1969), part 2 *passim;* Carey McWilliams, *Prejudice: Japanese-Americans, Symbol of Racial Intolerance* (Little, Brown, 1945); Charles Kikuchi, *The Kikuchi Diary: Chronicle from an American Concentration Camp*, John Modell, ed. (University of Illinois Press, 1973); Yoshiko Uchida, *Desert Exile: The Uprooting of a Japanese American Family* (University of Washington Press, 1982); Terkel, pp. 28–35; Michi Weglyn, *Years of Infamy* (Morrow, 1976); Thomas James, *Exile Within: The Schooling of Japanese-Americans, 1942–1945* (Harvard University Press, 1987).

["*When I first entered our room*"]: Letters of Stanley Shimabukuro, Joseph Goodman Collection, box 1, folder 1, California Historical Society, San Francisco.

190 ["*When can we go back to America?*"]: quoted in Girdner and Loftis, p. 148.

[*Political leaders and commentators and relocation*]: Morton Grodzins, *Americans Betrayed: Politics and the Japanese Evacuation* (University of Chicago Press, 1949), pp. 254–73, and *passim;* Girdner and Loftis; Weglyn, p. 72; Burns, *Soldier*, p. 216; Graham White and

John Maze, *Harold Ickes of the New Deal* (Harvard University Press, 1985), pp. 224–25; Ronald Steel, *Walter Lippmann and the American Century* (Atlantic Monthly/Little, Brown, 1980), pp. 394–95; *Korematsu* v. *U.S.*, 323 U.S. 214 (1944); Francis Biddle, *In Brief Authority* (Doubleday, 1962), ch. 13; Ted Morgan, *FDR* (Simon and Schuster, 1985), pp. 275–76.

190 [*"Politics is out"*]: quoted in Burns, *Soldier*, p. 273.

[*"When a country is at war"*]: press conference 803, February 6, 1942, in *Public Papers*, vol. 11, p. 80.

[*FDR's involvements in 1942 campaign*]: Robert E. Ficken, "Political Leadership in Wartime: Franklin D. Roosevelt and the Election of 1942," *Mid-America*, vol. 57, no. 1 (January 1975), pp. 20–37; Burns, *Soldier*, pp. 273–80; Farley, ch. 35.

191 [*"If this be treason"*]: quoted in Burns, *Soldier*, p. 279.

[*Election results, 1942*]: ibid., pp. 280–81; Polenberg, pp. 187–92.

[*Commentator on 1918 and 1942*]: Burns, *Soldier*, p. 281.

[*Congressional makeup, 1943*]: Polenberg, pp. 192–93.

[*Congressional action against New Deal agencies*]: ibid., pp. 79–86; Blum, pp. 234–40.

[*Wagner-Murray-Dingell*]: Polenberg, pp. 86–87.

[*Smith-Connally*]: Seidman, pp. 188–91.

[*"Dr. New Deal" and "Dr. Win-the-War"*]: quoted in Burns, *Soldier*, p. 423.

[*1942 tax legislation*]: Randolph E. Paul, *Taxation in the United States* (Little, Brown, 1954), pp. 294–326.

[*1943 government spending, national debt, consumer savings*]: Burns, *Soldier*, pp. 362–63, 433–34; Craf, p. 122 (Table 15); Paul, pp. 349–51.

191-2 [*Morgenthau's 1943 tax proposal and Congress's substitute*]: Paul, pp. 353–70; Blum, p. 243.

192 [*"Vicious piece of legislation"*]: quoted in Polenberg, p. 198.

[*"Tax relief bill"*]: February 22, 1944, in *Public Papers*, vol. 13, pp. 80–83, quoted at pp. 80, 82; see also Paul, pp. 371–72.

[*"Calculated and deliberate assault"*]: quoted in Burns, *Soldier*, pp. 435–36.

[*Barkley's "resignation"*]: ibid., pp. 435–37; Paul, pp. 373–75; *Public Papers*, vol. 13, pp. 85–86.

[*FDR on "Republican" Congress*]: see Polenberg, p. 199.

[*Opinion polls on war's purpose, 1942*]: Cantril and Strunk, pp. 1077–78 (item 41), 1083 (items 5–6, 8); see also Richard W. Steele, "American Popular Opinion and the War Against Germany: The Issue of Negotiated Peace, 1942," *Journal of American History*, vol. 65, no. 3 (December 1978), pp. 704–23.

193 [*Civilian participation in war effort*]: see Perrett, ch. 19, p. 394; Lingemann, ch. 2, pp. 251–52; Manchester, *Glory and Dream*, p. 303; Burns, *Soldier*, pp. 158–59; Anna W. M. Wolf and Irma S. Black, "What Happened to Younger People," in Jack Goodman, ed., *While You Were Gone: A Report on Wartime Life in the United States* (Simon and Schuster, 1946), p. 75.

[*Eighty-six-year-old Connecticut sentinel*]: Interview with Ann Hoskins, in Roy Hoopes, *Americans Remember the Home Front: An Oral Narrative* (Hawthorn Books, 1977), pp. 281–82.

[*"Private and personal concerns"*]: Polenberg, p. 137.

[*OWI*]: Allan M. Winkler, *The Politics of Propaganda: The Office of War Information, 1942–1945* (Yale University Press, 1978), chs. 1–2; Catton, pp. 186–95; Blum, pp. 21–45.

[*OWI and the military*]: Winkler, pp. 44–51.

[*OWI split between "writers" and "advertisers"*]: Blum, pp. 36–39; Polenberg, pp. 52–53.

[*"Encourage discussion"*]: MacLeish, quoted in Blum, p. 33.

[*"All levels of intelligence"*]: quoted in Polenberg, p. 53.

[*"Step right up"*]: quoted in Blum, p. 39.

[This Is War!]: quoted in Sherman H. Dyer, *Radio in Wartime* (Greenberg Publisher, 1942), p. 245.

193-4 [*Benny-Livingston routine*]: quoted in Winkler, p. 61.

194 [*Hollywood goes to war*]: Bernard F. Dick, *The Star-Spangled Screen: The American World War II Film* (University Press of Kentucky, 1985); Clayton R. Koppes and Gregory D. Black, "What to Show the World: The Office of War Information and Hollywood, 1942–1945," *Journal of American History*, vol. 64, no. 1 (June 1977), pp. 87–105; David Culbert, " 'Why We Fight': Social Engineering for a Democratic Society at War," in

K. R. M. Short, *Film & Radio Propaganda in World War II* (University of Tennessee Press, 1983), pp. 173-91; Bosley Crowther, "The Movies," in Goodman, pp. 511-32; Lingemann, pp. 168-210.

194 [*"Her spies never sleep"*]: Peter Lorre, quoted in Lingemann, p. 195.
[*"He dies for freedom"*]: Robert Taylor, quoted in *ibid.*, p. 200.
[*"STUDIOS SHELVE WAR STORIES"*]: *ibid.*, p. 206.
[*Tin Pan Alley's efforts*]: *ibid.*, pp. 210-23; Perrett, pp. 241-43.
[*War advertisements*]: Raymond Rubicam, "Advertising," in Goodman, pp. 433-34; *Life*, March 30, 1942, p. 90; *Life*, March 23, 1942, p. 111; *Life*, March 16, 1942, p. 60; see also Lingemann, pp. 291-97.
[*Coke as essential war product*]: Blum, pp. 107-8.
[*"Who's Afraid"*]: Rubicam, p. 432.
[*The GI ideology*]: Samuel Stouffer et al., *The American Soldier: Adjustment During Army Life* (Princeton University Press, 1949), vol. 1, chs. 5, 8, 9, and vol. 2, chs. 2, 3, and *passim;* Mauldin; Blum, pp. 64-70; Burns, *Soldier*, pp. 470-72; Mina Curtiss, ed., *Letters Home* (Little, Brown, 1944); Manchester, *Glory and Dream*, pp. 282-83; Ralph G. Martin, *The GI War, 1941-1945* (Little, Brown, 1967), p. 55 and *passim*.
[*"Born housewife"*]: quoted in Blum, p. 65.
195 [*"Wish to hell they were someplace else"*]: Mauldin, p. 16.
[*"Blueberry pie"*]: quoted in Blum, p. 66.
[*Soldiers' talk of creature comforts*]: *ibid.*, p. 67.
[*War photo*]: Arthur B. Tourtellot, ed., *Life's Picture History of World War II* (Simon and Schuster, 1950), p. 207.
[*". . . the slow, incessant waves"*]: Sergeant Charles E. Butler, "Lullaby," quoted in Martin, p. 240.

The Rainbow Coalition Embattled

[*FDR's trip to Casablanca*]: Burns, *Soldier*, pp. 316-17.
[*Casablanca Conference*]: Grigg, pp. 59-79; Dallek, pp. 368-72; Feis, *Churchill, Roosevelt, Stalin*, ch. 11; Winston S. Churchill, *The Hinge of Fate* (Houghton Mifflin, 1950), pp. 674-95; Burns, *Soldier*, pp. 317-24; Raymond G. O'Connor, *Diplomacy for Victory: FDR and Unconditional Surrender* (Norton, 1971); Forrest C. Pogue, *George C. Marshall: Organizer of Victory, 1943-1945* (Viking, 1973), ch. 2.
197 [*Stalin's response to Churchill's warning*]: quoted in Burns, *Soldier*, p. 327.
[*Possibility of Nazi-Soviet deal*]: see Mastny, pp. 73-85.
[*Stalin's suspicions*]: see Burns, *Soldier*, p. 373; Mastny, chs. 2-4 *passim;* Jackson, ch. 2; Feis, chs. 7-8, 15 *passim;* Churchill, *Hinge*, pp. 740-61 *passim;* Keith Sainsbury, *The Turning Point* (Oxford University Press, 1985), ch. 2; see also Mark A. Stoler, "The 'Second Front' and American Fears of Soviet Expansion, 1941-1943," *Military Affairs*, vol. 39, no. 3 (October 1975), pp. 136-41.
198 [*Quebec Conference*]: Dallek, pp. 408-21; Feis, ch. 16; Pogue, ch. 13; Winston S. Churchill, *Closing the Ring* (Houghton Mifflin, 1951), pp. 80-97; Jackson, pp. 101-8; Burns, *Soldier*, pp. 390-94.
[*FDR's trip to Cairo*]: Keith Eubank, *Summit at Teheran* (Morrow, 1985), ch. 6; Burns, *Soldier*, pp. 402-3.
[*Cairo Conference*]: Eubank, ch. 7; Churchill, *Closing*, pp. 325-41; Sainsbury, ch. 7; Barbara W. Tuchman, *Stilwell and the American Experience in China, 1911-45* (Macmillan, 1970), ch. 16; Burns, *Soldier*, pp. 403-5.
[*FDR on Stalin*]: quoted in Burns, *Soldier*, p. 407.
[*Teheran Conference*]: *ibid.*, pp. 406-14; Dallek, pp. 430-40; Eubank; Feis, chs. 25-28 *passim;* F. P. King, *The New Internationalism: Allied Policy and the European Peace, 1939-1945* (Archon Books, 1973); Sainsbury, ch. 8; Beitzell, part 5; W. Averell Harriman and Elie Abel, *Special Envoy to Churchill and Stalin, 1941-1946* (Random House, 1975), ch. 12; Mastny, pp. 122-33; Churchill, *Closing*, pp. 342-407.
[*Churchill on FDR's drifting*]: Sainsbury, p. 231.
199 [*Birthday toasts and FDR on the rainbow coalition*]: Burns, *Soldier*, p. 411.
[*Sword of Stalingrad*]: *ibid.*, p. 410.
[*General strategic background, European war*]: see Weigley, *American Way*, ch. 14.

199 [*Preparations for D-Day*]: Burns, *Soldier*, pp. 473–74; Ambrose, *Supreme Commander*, book 2, part 1; Russell F. Weigley, *Eisenhower's Lieutenants: The Campaign of France and Germany, 1944–1945* (Indiana University Press, 1981), part 1; Jackson, ch. 6; Pogue, ch. 19 *passim*.

200 [*"O.K., let's go"*]: quoted in Ambrose, *Supreme Commander*, p. 417, and see footnote. [*Normandy invasion*]: ibid., book 2, part 2; Weigley, *Lieutenants*, ch. 5; Max Hastings, *Overlord: D-Day and the Battle for Normandy* (Simon and Schuster, 1984); Shirer, *Rise and Fall*, pp. 1036–42; Jackson, ch. 8; Burns, *Soldier*, pp. 475–77.
[*Intelligence and deception at Normandy*]: see Ralph Bennett, *Ultra in the West: The Normandy Campaign, 1944–45* (Hutchinson, 1979), esp. chs. 1–3; Weigley, *Lieutenants*, pp. 53–55; Jackson, ch. 7; Stephen E. Ambrose, *Ike's Spies: Eisenhower and the Espionage Establishment* (Doubleday, 1981), chs. 6–7.
[*FDR's prayer*]: June 6, 1944, in *Public Papers*, vol. 13, pp. 152–53, quoted at p. 152.

201 [*General strategic background, Pacific war*]: see Weigley, *American Way*, ch. 13.
[*Stilwell-Chiang relations*]: Tuchman, ch. 12 and part 2 *passim*.
[*MacArthur's opposition to direct Pacific thrust*]: see Weigley, *American Way*, pp. 283–84; Spector, pp. 255–56, 276–80.

201–2 [*Pacific campaign*]: Toland, *Rising Sun*, parts 5–6 *passim*; Spector, chs. 12–14, 19–20; Thorne, *Allies of a Kind*, parts 4–5 *passim;* Samuel Eliot Morison, *History of United States Naval Operations in World War II* (Atlantic Monthly/Little, Brown, 1947–62), vols. 7–8, 12–13; Philip A. Crowl and Edmund G. Love, *Seizure of the Gilberts and Marshalls* (U.S. Department of the Army, 1955); Philip A. Crowl, *Campaign in the Marianas* (U.S. Department of the Army, 1960); M. Hamlin Cannon, *Leyte: The Return to the Philippines* (U.S. Department of the Army, 1954); Robert R. Smith, *Triumph in the Philippines* (U.S. Department of the Army, 1963); Manchester, *American Caesar*, pp. 339–55, 363–73, and ch. 7.

202 [*Popular support for Russia after Pearl Harbor*]: Ralph B. Levering, *American Opinion and the Russian Alliance, 1939–1945* (University of North Carolina Press, 1976), p. 61 (Figure 2); see also Melvin Small, "How We Learned to Love the Russians: American Media and the Soviet Union During World War II," *Historian*, vol. 36, no. 3 (May 1974), pp. 455–78.
[*Time's revised view of Stalin*]: *Time*, vol. 35, no. 1 (January 1, 1940), pp. 14–17; and *Time*, vol. 41, no. 1 (January 4, 1943), pp. 21–24.
[*Tribune on communists*]: quoted in Levering, p. 76.
[*Herald Tribune on Stalin*]: ibid., p. 89.
[*Reynolds's defense of Soviet purge*]: Reynolds, . . . *Only the Stars Are Neutral* (Random House, 1942).
[*" 'Don't say a word against Stalin' "*]: Eastman, "We Must Face the Facts About Russia," *Reader's Digest*, vol. 43, no. 255 (July 1943), pp. 1–14, quoted at p. 3.
[*Hitler's exploitation of freedom as symbol*]: Burns, *Soldier*, pp. 386–87; see also James MacGregor Burns, "The Roosevelt-Hitler Battle of Symbols," *Antioch Review*, vol. 2, no. 3 (Fall 1942), pp. 407–21; transcripts of translated Nazi broadcasts at the Franklin D. Roosevelt Library at Hyde Park, N.Y.; Z. A. B. Zeman, *Nazi Propaganda* (Oxford University Press, 1964); Alexander L. George, *Propaganda Analysis* (Row, Peterson, 1959); Paul M. A. Linebarger, *Psychological Warfare* (Infantry Journal Press, 1948); Ralph K. White, "Hitler, Roosevelt, and the Nature of War Propaganda," *Journal of Abnormal and Social Psychology*, vol. 44, no. 2 (April 1949), pp. 157–74; Ernest K. Bramsted, *Goebbels and National Socialist Propaganda* (Michigan State University Press, 1965).
[*"Essence of our struggle"*]: address to the Delegates of the International Labour Organization, November 6, 1941, in *Public Papers*, vol. 10, pp. 474–80, quoted at p. 476.

203 [*Economic bill of rights*]: see Annual Message to the Congress, January 6, 1941, in *ibid.*, vol. 9, pp. 663–72, esp. pp. 670–71.
[*"Second bill of rights"*]: Message on the State of the Union, January 11, 1944, in *ibid.*, vol. 13, pp. 32–42, quoted at p. 41, as modified by comparison with tapes of the speech.
[*FDR's vice-presidential manipulations*]: Burns, *Soldier*, pp. 503–7; Blum, *V Was for Victory*,

pp. 288–92; John Morton Blum, ed., *The Price of Vision: The Diary of Henry A. Wallace* (Houghton Mifflin, 1973), pp. 360–72; Leon Friedman, "Election of 1944," in Schlesinger, vol. 4, pp. 3023–28; James F. Byrnes, *All in One Lifetime* (Harper, 1958), ch. 13.

203 [*GOP road to nomination*]: Richard N. Smith, *Thomas E. Dewey and His Times* (Simon and Schuster, 1982), pp. 385–405; Manchester, *American Caesar*, pp. 355–63; Neal, chs. 17–18; Friedman, pp. 3017–23; Patterson, *Mr. Republican*, pp. 268–72.
[*"Sinister drama"*]: quoted in Friedman, p. 3019.

204 [*Risk to Dewey of denouncing FDR's postwar plans*]: see Richard E. Darilek, *A Loyal Opposition in Time of War: The Republican Party and the Politics of Foreign Policy from Pearl Harbor to Yalta* (Greenwood Press, 1976), ch. 7.
[*GOP rumor campaign*]: Perrett, pp. 292–93.
[*Hillman-Browder billboards*]: Manchester, *Glory and Dream*, p. 330; see also Smith, pp. 409–10.
[*FDR's Teamster address*]: September 23, 1944, in *Public Papers*, vol. 13, pp. 284–92, quoted at p. 290, as modified by comparison with tapes of the speech.
[*"Keep the record straight"*]: quoted in Smith, p. 422.
[*Dewey on FDR's "indispensability"*]: ibid., p. 424.
[*Dewey on Democratic party takeover by Hillman-Browder*]: Friedman, p. 3033.
[*"Bricker could have written it"*]: Smith, pp. 433–34, quoted at p. 433.

204–5 [*Resurgent antagonism to Russia*]: see Levering, ch. 6 and pp. 169–84.

205 [*Lippmann's reluctant vote for FDR*]: see Steel, pp. 412–14.
[*"I can't talk about my opponent"*]: campaign remarks at Bridgeport, Conn., November 4, 1944, in *Public Papers*, vol. 13, pp. 389–91, quoted at p. 391.
[*Election results, 1944*]: Schlesinger, vol. 4, p. 3096; Smith, pp. 435–36.
[*Trend toward "privatization"*]: see Polenberg, p. 137.
[*"Son of a bitch"*]: quoted in Burns, *Soldier*, p. 530.
[*FDR's arrival at Yalta*]: ibid., p. 564.

206 [*Yalta Conference*]: Diane Shaver Clemens, *Yalta* (Oxford University Press, 1970); King, ch. 10 and *passim;* Dallek, pp. 506–20; Harriman and Abel, ch. 17; James F. Byrnes, *Speaking Frankly* (Harper, 1947), ch. 2; Burns, *Soldier*, pp. 564–80; Mastny, ch. 7; Winston S. Churchill, *Triumph and Tragedy* (Houghton Mifflin, 1953), book 2, chs. 1–4; Feis, chs. 51–57; Charles E. Bohlen, *Witness to History, 1929–1969* (Norton, 1973), ch. 11; Robert A. Divine, *Second Chance: The Triumph of Internationalism in America During World War II* (Atheneum, 1967); Athan G. Theoharis, *The Yalta Myths: An Issue in U.S. Politics, 1945–1955* (University of Missouri Press, 1970); Russell D. Buhite, *Decisions at Yalta: An Appraisal of Summit Diplomacy* (Scholarly Resources, 1986); Deborin, ch. 17.
[*Battle of the Bulge*]: John Toland, *Battle: The Story of the Bulge* (Random House, 1959); John S. D. Eisenhower, *The Bitter Woods* (Putnam, 1969); Shirer, *Rise and Fall*, pp. 1089–96; Weigley, *Lieutenants*, chs. 25–29.

207 [*FDR on Polish-Americans*]: quoted in Burns, *Soldier*, p. 569.
[*Stalin on Poland*]: quoted in Harriman and Abel, p. 407.

208 [*"Pre-eminent interests"*]: quoted in ibid., p. 399.
[*Leahy-FDR exchange*]: quoted in Burns, *Soldier*, p. 572.

208–9 [*FDR's health*]: ibid., pp. 448–51, 573–74, 594–95, and sources cited therein.

5. Cold War: The Fearful Giants

210 [*FDR's address on Yalta*]: in *The Public Papers and Addresses of Franklin D. Roosevelt*, Samuel I. Rosenman, comp. (Random House, 1938–50), vol. 13, pp. 570–86, quoted at pp. 570, 586; see also James MacGregor Burns, *Roosevelt: The Soldier of Freedom* (Harcourt, 1970), pp. 581–82.

210–11 [*Deterioration of Allied relations*]: Robert Dallek, *Franklin D. Roosevelt and American Foreign Policy, 1932–1945* (Oxford University Press, 1979), pp. 521–27; Winston S. Churchill, *Triumph and Tragedy* (Houghton Mifflin, 1953), book 2, chs. 6–8; W. Averell Harriman and Elie Abel, *Special Envoy to Churchill and Stalin, 1941–1946* (Random House, 1975), ch. 18; Francis L. Loewenheim et al., eds., *Roosevelt and Churchill: Their Secret Wartime Correspondence* (Saturday Review Press/E. P. Dutton, 1975), pp. 660–709; Robert

Lovett Diary and Daily Log Sheet, July 1, 1947–Jan. 27, 1949, New-York Historical Society, New York, N.Y.

211 [*Stalin-FDR exchange over surrender talks*]: quoted in Dallek, pp. 526–27; see also Allen Dulles, *The Secret Surrender* (Harper, 1966).
[*Jefferson Day draft*]: in *Public Papers*, vol. 13, pp. 613–16, quoted at pp. 615, 616.

The Death and Life of Franklin D. Roosevelt

212 [*FDR's death and return to Hyde Park*]: Burns, *Soldier*, Epilogue; Bernard Asbell, *When F.D.R. Died* (Holt, Rinehart and Winston, 1961); Turnley Walker, *Roosevelt and the Warm Springs Story* (A. A. Wyn, 1953), ch. 7.
[*"A lonesome train"*]: Millard Lampell, "The Lonesome Train," quoted in Burns, *Soldier*, p. 604.
212-13 [*FDR's lasting influence*]: see William E. Leuchtenburg, *In the Shadow of FDR* (Cornell University Press, 1983), Preface and ch. 1.
213 [*Berlin on FDR*]: Isaiah Berlin, *Personal Impressions*, Henry Hardy, ed. (Viking, 1981), p. 31.
[*"Great men have two lives"*]: quoted in Leuchtenburg, pp. viii–ix.
214 [*Hawley on New Deal policies*]: Ellis Hawley, *The New Deal and the Problem of Monopoly* (Princeton University Press, 1966), pp. 15, 270.
[*"Fiscal drift"*]: Stein, *The Fiscal Revolution in America* (University of Chicago Press, 1969), ch. 4.
[*"Helterskelter" planning*]: entry of April 11, 1938, in Morgenthau Presidential Diaries, book 1, Franklin D. Roosevelt Library, Hyde Park, N.Y.
[*"Read it a little bit"*]: entry of April 25, 1939, in *ibid.*
[*Third New Deal*]: Barry D. Karl, *The Uneasy State* (University of Chicago Press, 1983), esp. chs. 7–8.
216 [*Dualism in FDR as war leader*]: see Burns, *Soldier*, pp. 607–9; Daniel Yergin, *Shattered Peace: The Origins of the Cold War and the National Security State* (Houghton Mifflin, 1977), ch. 2; Isaiah Berlin, *The Hedgehog and the Fox* (Simon and Schuster, 1970).
[*FDR's articulation of freedom*]: see Burns, "Battle of Symbols."
[*FDR and the military*]: Burns, *Soldier*, pp. 490–96, Stimson quoted at p. 493; see also Kent Roberts Greenfield, *American Strategy in World War II: A Reconsideration* (Johns Hopkins Press, 1963), ch. 3; William Emerson, "Franklin Roosevelt as Commander-in-Chief in World War II," *Military Affairs*, vol. 22 (1958), pp. 181–207.
216-17 [*FDR's insistence upon unconditional surrender*]: Raymond G. O'Connor, *Diplomacy for Victory: FDR and Unconditional Surrender* (Norton, 1971), esp. ch. 3; Russell F. Weigley, *The American Way of War* (Macmillan, 1973), pp. 281, 325; Gaddis Smith, *American Diplomacy During the Second World War, 1941–1945* (Wiley, 1967), ch. 3; Anne Armstrong, *Unconditional Surrender: The Impact of the Casablanca Policy upon World War II* (Rutgers University Press, 1961).
217 [*Dallek on FDR as "principal architect"*]: Dallek, p. 532.
[*FDR's refusal to share atomic secrets with Soviets*]: see *ibid.*, pp. 416–18, 470–72, 534; Barton J. Bernstein, "Roosevelt, Truman, and the Atomic Bomb: A Reinterpretation," *Political Science Quarterly*, vol. 90, no. 1 (Spring 1975), pp. 24–32.
[*De Gaulle on FDR*]: De Gaulle, *War Memoirs: Unity, 1942–1944* (Simon and Schuster, 1959), p. 270.
[*"Once-born" and "divided selves"*]: William James, *The Varieties of Religious Experience* (Longmans, Green, 1935), p. 199, as cited and interpreted in Erik H. Erikson, *Young Man Luther* (Norton, 1962), pp. 41, 117.
218 [*FDR and the Holocaust*]: David S. Wyman, *The Abandonment of the Jews: America and the Holocaust, 1941–1945* (Pantheon, 1984); Henry L. Feingold, *The Politics of Rescue: The Roosevelt Administration and the Holocaust, 1938–1945* (Rutgers University Press, 1970); Martin Gilbert, *Auschwitz and the Allies* (Holt, Rinehart and Winston, 1981); Richard Breitman and Allan M. Kraut, *American Refugee Policy and European Jewry, 1933–1945* (Indiana University Press, 1987); Martin Gilbert, *The Holocaust: The Jewish Tragedy* (Collins, 1986); Deborah E. Lipstadt, *Beyond Belief: The American Press and the Coming of the Holocaust, 1933–1945* (Free Press, 1986); Michael R. Marcus, *The Holocaust in History* (University Press of New England, 1987), ch. 8.

218 [*"Final solution"*]: Hermann Göring to Reinhard Heydrich, July 31, 1941, quoted in Gilbert, *Holocaust,* p. 176.
219 [*Berlin on Eleanor Roosevelt*]: *Personal Impressions,* p. 31.

The Long Telegram

220 [*Origins of the cold war*]: D. F. Fleming, *The Cold War and Its Origins, 1917–1960,* 2 vols. (Doubleday, 1961), esp. vol. 1, ch. 11, and vol. 2, ch. 24; Charles S. Maier, "Revisionism and the Interpretation of Cold War Origins," *Perspectives in American History,* vol. 4 (1970), pp. 313–47; John Lewis Gaddis, *The Long Peace* (Oxford University Press, 1987), esp. chs. 1–3, 8; Gaddis, "The Emerging Post-Revisionist Synthesis on the Origins of the Cold War," *Diplomatic History,* vol. 7, no. 3 (Summer 1983), pp. 171–90; Thomas G. Paterson, *On Every Front: The Making of the Cold War* (Norton, 1979); Alexander Werth, *Russia: The Post-War Years* (Taplinger, 1971), ch. 3; Barton J. Bernstein, "American Foreign Policy and the Origins of the Cold War," in Bernstein and Allen J. Matusow, eds., *Twentieth-Century America: Recent Interpretations,* 2nd ed. (Harcourt, 1972), pp. 344–94; Lloyd C. Gardiner, *Architects of Illusion: Men and Ideas in American Foreign Policy, 1941–1949* (Quadrangle, 1970), ch. 11; Gardiner, Arthur M. Schlesinger, Jr., and Hans J. Morgenthau, *The Origins of the Cold War* (Ginn and Co., 1970); Thomas T. Hammond, ed., *Witnesses to the Origins of the Cold War* (University of Washington Press, 1982); Eduard Mark, "American Policy toward Eastern Europe and the Origins of the Cold War," *Journal of American History,* vol. 68, no. 2 (September 1981), pp. 313–36; Robert J. Maddox, *The New Left and the Origins of the Cold War* (Princeton University Press, 1973); Vojtech Mastny, *Russia's Road to the Cold War, 1941–1945* (Columbia University Press, 1979); Thomas G. Paterson, *Soviet-American Confrontation: Postwar Reconstruction and the Origins of the Cold War* (Johns Hopkins University Press, 1973); Lovett Diary and Log Sheet, 1947–1949; Hugh Thomas, *Armed Truce: The Beginnings of the Cold War, 1945–46* (Atheneum, 1987), esp. pp. 541–50; Frederick L. Schuman, *The Cold War: Retrospect and Prospect* (Louisiana State University Press, 1962); John P. Diggins, *The Proud Decades: America in War and in Peace, 1941–1960* (Norton, 1988), ch. 2 *passim.*
    [*"Deep, mournful"*]: quoted in Edward Crankshaw, *Russia and the Russians* (Viking, 1948), p. 21.
    [*Crankshaw on Russian temperament*]: *ibid.,* p. 23.
221 [*Truman on German-Russian fight*]: quoted in *New York Times,* June 24, 1941, p. 7. Copy of newspaper page now displayed in Museum of the Red Army, Moscow.
    [*Polls on Soviet postwar cooperation*]: Gary J. Buckley, "American Public Opinion and the Origins of the Cold War: A Speculative Reassessment," *Mid-America,* vol. 60, no. 1 (January 1978), pp. 35–42, esp. pp. 37–38 (Table 1).
222 [*NSC-68*]: Yergin, pp. 401–4, quoted at p. 401; Gaddis, *Long Peace,* pp. 114–15; Richard A. Melanson, "The Foundations of Eisenhower's Foreign Policy: Continuity, Community, and Consensus," in Melanson and David Mayers, eds., *Reevaluating Eisenhower: American Foreign Policy in the 1950s* (University of Illinois Press, 1987), pp. 31–64, esp. pp. 36–40.
    [*"The President is dead"*]: quoted in Harry S Truman, *Memoirs: Year of Decisions* (Doubleday, 1955), p. 5.
    [*"Riding a tiger"*]: Truman, *Memoirs: Years of Trial and Hope* (Doubleday, 1956), p. 1.
222–3 [*Truman's background and character*]: Alfred Steinberg, *The Man from Missouri* (Putnam, 1962); Cabell Phillips, *The Truman Presidency* (Macmillan, 1966); Robert L. Miller, *Truman: The Rise to Power* (McGraw-Hill, 1986); Robert H. Ferrell, *Harry S. Truman and the Modern American Presidency* (Little, Brown, 1983); Bert Cochran, *Harry Truman and the Crisis Presidency* (Funk & Wagnalls, 1973); Deborah Welch Larson, *Origins of Containment: A Psychological Explanation* (Princeton University Press, 1985), ch. 3; John Lewis Gaddis, "Harry S. Truman and the Origins of Containment," in Frank J. Merli and Theodore A. Wilson, eds., *Makers of American Diplomacy: From Benjamin Franklin to Henry Kissinger* (Scribner, 1974), pp. 493–522; Paterson, *On Every Front,* ch. 5; Arnold A. Offner, "The Truman Myth Revealed: From Parochial Nationalist to Cold Warrior," paper presented at the annual meeting of the Organization of American Historians, Reno, Nev., March 1988.

223 [*FDR's divided legacy*]: see Gardner, *Architects*, pp. 307–8; see also Warren F. Kimball, ed., *Franklin D. Roosevelt and the World Crisis, 1937–1945* (D. C. Heath, 1973), part 2; Thomas, ch. 10.
[*UN organizational meeting*]: Robert A. Divine, *Second Chance: The Triumph of Internationalism in America During World War II* (Atheneum, 1967), ch. 11.
[*Truman's address to UN*]: April 25, 1945, in *Public Papers of the Presidents of the United States: Harry S Truman* (U.S. Government Printing Office, 1961–66), vol. 1, pp. 20–23, quoted at pp. 20, 21.
[*Hopkins in Moscow*]: Robert E. Sherwood, *Roosevelt and Hopkins* (Harper, 1948), ch. 35; Herbert Feis, *Between War and Peace: The Potsdam Conference* (Princeton University Press, 1960), chs. 15–18.
[*End of European war*]: John Toland, *The Last 100 Days* (Random House, 1965); Cornelius Ryan, *The Last Battle* (Simon and Schuster, 1966); William L. Shirer, *The Rise and Fall of the Third Reich: A History of Nazi Germany* (Simon and Schuster, 1960), chs. 30–31.
[*Truman and FDR's cabinet*]: see Truman to Jonathan Daniels (unsent), February 26, 1950, in Robert H. Ferrell, ed., *Off the Record: The Private Papers of Harry S. Truman* (Harper, 1980), p. 174.

224 [*Okinawa*]: Roy E. Appleman, James M. Burns, Russell A. Gugeler, and John Stevens, *Okinawa: The Last Battle* (U.S. Department of the Army, 1948); John Toland, *The Rising Sun: The Decline and Fall of the Japanese Empire, 1936–1945* (Random House, 1970), ch. 30.
[*Potsdam*]: Feis, part 4; Robert J. Donovan, *Conflict and Crisis: The Presidency of Harry S Truman, 1945–1948* (Norton, 1977), chs. 8–9; Mastny, pp. 292–304; Truman, *Decisions*, chs. 21–25; Charles E. Bohlen, *Witness to History, 1929–1969* (Norton, 1973), ch. 13; Charles L. Mee, Jr., *Meeting at Potsdam* (M. Evans & Co., 1975); Churchill, *Triumph*, book 2, chs. 19–20.
[*"Open the gates"*]: quoted in Thomas, p. 252.
[*Debate over political role of atomic bomb and its use against Japan*]: Toland, *Rising Sun*, chs. 31–32; Truman, *Decisions*, pp. 414–20; Donovan, chs. 5, 7, 10; Henry L. Stimson and McGeorge Bundy, *On Active Service in Peace and War* (Harper, 1948), chs. 22–23; Gregg Herken, *The Winning Weapon: The Atomic Bomb in the Cold War, 1945–1950* (Knopf, 1980), ch. 1 and *passim;* Gardiner, *Architects*, ch. 7; Fleming, vol. 1, pp. 296–308; Martin J. Sherwin, *A World Destroyed: The Atomic Bomb and the Grand Alliance* (Knopf, 1975), esp. part 3; Herbert Feis, *Japan Subdued: The Atomic Bomb and the End of the War in the Pacific* (Princeton University Press, 1961), parts 1, 4, and *passim;* Barton J. Bernstein, "Roosevelt, Truman, and the Atomic Bomb, 1941–1945: A Reinterpretation," *Political Science Quarterly*, vol. 90, no. 1 (Spring 1975), pp. 23–69; Maddox, ch. 3; Gar Alperovitz, *Atomic Diplomacy: Hiroshima and Potsdam* (Simon and Schuster, 1965); Yergin, pp. 115–16, 120–22, and 433–34 n. 19; Stephen Harper, *Miracle of Deliverance: The Case for the Bombing of Hiroshima and Nagasaki* (Sidgwick & Jackson, 1985).
[*Bernstein on atomic bomb legacy*]: "Roosevelt, Truman," p. 24.
[*"Most terrible weapon"*]: quoted in Stimson and Bundy, p. 635.
[*"Royal straight flush"*]: quoted in Herken, p. 17.

224–5 [*"American cards"*]: ibid.

225 [*Truman-Stalin exchange on bomb at Potsdam*]: Mastny, pp. 297–98; Bohlen, p. 237; Donovan, p. 93; Churchill, *Triumph*, pp. 669–70; see also Feis, *Potsdam*, ch. 23; Yergin, p. 121.
[*U.S. bombing of Japanese cities*]: Ronald Spector, *Eagle Against the Sun: The American War with Japan* (Free Press, 1985), pp. 487–93, 503–6; Toland, *Rising Sun*, pp. 670–77; Ronald Schaffer, *Wings of Judgment: American Bombing in World War II* (Oxford University Press, 1985), chs. 6–7; Wesley F. Craven and James L. Cate, eds., *The Army Air Forces in World War II* (University of Chicago Press, 1948–58), vol. 5, chs. 17–18, 20–21.
[*Hiroshima, Nagasaki, and surrender*]: Toland, *Rising Sun*, chs. 33–37; Craven and Cate, vol. 5, pp. 703–35; John Hersey, *Hiroshima* (Knopf, 1946); Robert J. C. Butow, *Japan's Decision to Surrender* (Stanford University Press, 1954); Barton J. Bernstein, "The Perils and Politics of Surrender: Ending the War with Japan and Avoiding the Third Atomic Bomb," *Pacific Historical Review*, vol. 46 (1977), pp. 1–27; Pacific War Research Soci-

ety, *Japan's Longest Day* (Kodansha International, 1980); Committee for the Compilation of Materials on Damage Caused by the Atomic Bombs in Hiroshima and Nagasaki, *Hiroshima and Nagasaki: The Physical, Medical, and Social Effects of the Atomic Bombings*, Eisei Ishikawa and David L. Swain, trans. (Basic Books, 1981).

226 [*"Let them"*]: quoted in Yergin, p. 121; see also Mastny, p. 298.

[*Truman on Stalin*]: quoted in Yergin, p. 119.

[*Byrnes at London Foreign Ministers' conference*]: Robert L. Messer, *The End of an Alliance: James F. Byrnes, Roosevelt, Truman, and the Origins of the Cold War* (University of North Carolina Press, 1982), ch. 7; Herken, ch. 3; Yergin, pp. 122-32; James F. Byrnes, *Speaking Frankly* (Harper, 1947), ch. 5.

[*"Here's to the atom bomb"*]: quoted in Yergin, p. 123.

227 [*American ambivalence over Soviet intentions*]: see Lynn E. Davis, *The Cold War Begins: Soviet-American Conflict over Eastern Europe* (Princeton University Press, 1974), ch. 11; Herken, ch. 2; John Lewis Gaddis, *Russia, the Soviet Union, and the United States: An Interpretive History* (Wiley, 1978), ch. 7 *passim;* Gaddis, *Long Peace*, ch. 2; Robert Dallek, *The American Style of Foreign Policy: Cultural Politics and Foreign Affairs* (Knopf, 1983), ch. 6; William Zimmerman, "Rethinking Soviet Foreign Policy: Changing American Perspectives," *International Journal*, vol. 25 (Summer 1980), pp. 548-62; see also William Welch, *American Images of Soviet Foreign Policy: An Inquiry into Recent Appraisals from the Academic Community* (Yale University Press, 1970); Thomas, book 2; Melvyn F. Leffler, "The American Conception of the National Security State and the Beginnings of the Cold War, 1945-1948," *American Historical Review*, vol. 89, no. 2 (April 1984), pp. 346-81.

[*Poll on bomb secret and UN*]: Dallek, p. 161; see also Paterson, *On Every Front*, pp. 113-29; Yergin, pp. 171-72.

[*Soviet cold war policy, sources and conflicts*]: Werth, chs. 11, 14, and *passim;* Crankshaw, ch. 5 and *passim;* Frederick C. Barghoorn, *The Soviet Image of the United States* (Harcourt, 1950); Thomas, book 1; Joseph L. Nogee and Robert H. Donaldson, *Soviet Foreign Policy Since World War II* (Pergamon Press, 1981), chs. 2-3; Marshall D. Shulman, *Stalin's Foreign Policy Reappraised* (Harvard University Press, 1963); Anatol Rapoport, *The Big Two: Soviet-American Perceptions of Foreign Policy* (Pegasus, 1971), pp. 120-26; Paterson, *On Every Front*, ch. 7; William Taubman, *Stalin's American Policy: From Entente to Detente to Cold War* (Norton, 1982), esp. chs. 5-7; Adam B. Ulam, *Expansion and Coexistence: The History of Soviet Foreign Policy, 1917-1967* (Praeger, 1968), pp. 408-55; Robert V. Daniels, *Russia: The Roots of Confrontation* (Harvard University Press, 1985), chs. 8-9; Genrikh Trofimenko, *The U.S. Military Doctrine* (Progress Publishers, Moscow, n.d.), esp. chs. 1-2.

[*"Leaving them in the lurch"*]: quoted in Daniels, p. 220.

[*"Year of Cement"*]: Yergin, p. 166.

[*Stalin's Bolshoi Theater address*]: February 9, 1946, in Walter LaFeber, ed., *The Dynamics of World Power, A Documentary History of United States Foreign Policy, 1945-1973: Eastern Europe and the Soviet Union* (Chelsea House, 1973), pp. 191-99; see also Werth, ch. 5; Yergin, pp. 166-67, 177.

[*Douglas on Stalin's speech*]: quoted in Walter Millis, ed., *The Forrestal Diaries* (Viking, 1951), p. 134.

[*Kennan's "long telegram"*]: "Telegraphic Message from Moscow to the State Department on Soviet Policies," February 22, 1946, in LaFeber, pp. 200-10, quoted at pp. 207, 208; see John Lewis Gaddis, *Strategies of Containment: A Critical Appraisal of Postwar American National Security Policy* (Oxford University Press, 1982), chs. 2-3; Rapoport, pp. 106-12; Yergin, pp. 168-71; Thomas G. Paterson, "The Search for Meaning: George F. Kennan and American Foreign Policy," in Merli and Wilson, pp. 568-76; John Lewis Gaddis, "Containment: A Reassessment," *Foreign Affairs*, vol. 55, no. 4 (July 1977), pp. 873-87; George F. Kennan, *Memoirs 1925-1950* (Atlantic Monthly/Little, Brown, 1967), ch. 11; Thomas, ch. 22.

228 [*"Complete power of disposition"*]: "Telegraphic Message" in LaFeber, quoted at p. 208.

[*"An iron curtain"*]: March 5, 1946, in *ibid.*, pp. 210-17, quoted at pp. 214, 215; see also Terry H. Anderson, *The United States, Great Britain, and the Cold War, 1944-1947* (University of Missouri Press, 1981), pp. 110-16; Fleming, vol. 1, pp. 348-57; Thomas, ch. 23.

229 [*"Call to war"*]: March 13, 1946, in LaFeber, pp. 217–21, quoted at p. 218; see also Werth, pp. 110–14.

[*"Putrid and baneful"*]: quoted in Daniels, p. 227.

[*Forrestal's anti-Sovietism*]: see Gardner, *Architects*, ch. 10; Millis, *passim.*

[*Kennan's "X" article and his concern about its influence*]: "The Sources of Soviet Conduct," *Foreign Affairs*, vol. 25, no. 4 (July 1947), pp. 566–82; Kennan, *Memoirs*, pp. 294–95, ch. 15; see also Gaddis, *Russia*, pp. 187–88.

229–30 [*Byrnes and Truman*]: Messer, chs. 8–9; Truman, *Decisions*, pp. 545–52.

230 [*1946 Congressional elections*]: Donovan, ch. 24.

[*"Greatest victory"*]: quoted in Stephen E. Ambrose, *Nixon: The Education of a Politician, 1913–1962* (Simon and Schuster, 1987), p. 141.

[*HUAC's plans for 1947*]: quoted in Richard M. Freeland, *The Truman Doctrine and the Origins of McCarthyism: Foreign Policy, Domestic Politics, and Internal Security, 1946–1948* (Knopf, 1972), p. 132.

[*"Class of '46"*]: see David M. Oshinsky, *A Conspiracy So Immense: The World of Joe McCarthy* (Free Press, 1983), p. 53; Ambrose, *Nixon*, p. 141.

[*Loyalty program*]: Athan Theoharis, *Seeds of Repression: Harry S. Truman and the Origins of McCarthyism* (Quadrangle, 1971), pp. 103–6, quoted at p. 105; Alan D. Harper, *The Politics of Loyalty: The White House and the Communist Issue, 1946–1952* (Greenwood Publishing, 1969), ch. 3; Truman, *Trial and Hope*, ch. 19; Donovan, ch. 31; Athan Theoharis, "The Escalation of the Loyalty Program," in Barton J. Bernstein, ed., *Politics and Policies of the Truman Administration* (Quadrangle, 1970), pp. 242–68; Roger S. Abbott, "The Federal Loyalty Program," in Edward E. Palmer, ed., *The Communist Problem in America* (Crowell, 1951), pp. 385–97; see, generally, Stanley I. Kutler, *The American Inquisition: Justice and Injustice in the Cold War* (Hill and Wang, 1982); Herbert Mitgang, *Dangerous Dossiers* (Donald I. Fine, 1988); Diggins, *Proud Decades*, ch. 5 *passim.*

[*"Membership in, affiliation with"*]: quoted in Abbott, p. 390.

[*Attorney General's list*]: Freeland, pp. 208–16; Palmer, Appendix.

[*Loyalty board proceedings*]: Harper, pp. 47–53, executive order quoted at p. 39; David Caute, *The Great Fear: The Anti-Communist Purge Under Truman and Eisenhower* (Simon and Schuster, 1978), pp. 269–92.

[*"The man who fears"*]: Seth W. Richardson, quoted in Richard M. Fried, *Men Against McCarthy* (Columbia University Press, 1976), p. 24.

231 [*HUAC in Hollywood, 1947*]: Walter Goodman, *The Committee: The Extraordinary Career of House Committee on Un-American Activities* (Farrar, Straus & Giroux, 1968), pp. 207–25; Victor Navasky, *Naming Names* (Viking, 1980); Larry Ceplair and Steven Englund, *The Inquisition in Hollywood: Politics in the Film Community, 1930–1960* (Anchor Press/Doubleday, 1980), esp. chs. 8, 10; Richard H. Pells, *The Liberal Mind in a Conservative Age: American Intellectuals in the 1940s and 1950s* (Harper, 1985), pp. 301–10; Gordon Kahn, *Hollywood on Trial: The Story of the 10 Who Were Indicted* (Boni & Gaer, 1948).

[*Menjou on communists*]: quoted in Roger Burlingame, *The Sixth Column* (Lippincott, 1962), p. 127.

[*Cooper on communism*]: quoted in Goodman, p. 209.

[*Hollywood and radio purge*]: Pells, p. 310; see also John Cogley, *Report on Blacklisting*, 2 vols. (Fund for the Republic, 1956).

[*Ex-communists*]: see Navasky; Herbert L. Packer, *Ex-Communist Witnesses: Four Studies in Fact Finding* (Stanford University Press, 1962).

[*Hiss case*]: Allen Weinstein, *Perjury: The Hiss-Chambers Case* (Knopf, 1978); Alistair Cooke, *Generation on Trial: U.S.A. v. Alger Hiss* (Knopf, 1950); Ambrose, *Nixon*, ch. 10; Packer, ch. 2; Goodman, ch. 8 *passim;* Leslie A. Fiedler, "Hiss, Chambers, and the Age of Innocence," in Fiedler, *The Collected Essays of Leslie Fiedler* (Stein & Day, 1971), vol. 1, pp. 3–24.

232 [*"We've been had!"*]: quoted in Weinstein, p. 15.

[*Truman on the menace of communism*]: Freeland, pp. 335–36.

[*"Red herring"*]: Weinstein, p. 15.

[*Greek crisis and Administration response*]: Freeland, ch. 2; Theoharis, *Seeds*, ch. 3; John Lewis Gaddis, "Was the Truman Doctrine a Real Turning Point?," *Foreign Affairs*, vol. 52, no. 2 (January 1974), pp. 386–402; Yergin, pp. 279–83; Truman, *Trial and Hope*, ch. 8; Joseph M. Jones, *The Fifteen Weeks (February 21-June 5, 1947)* (Viking, 1955); Michael Leigh, *Mobilizing Consent: Public Opinion and American Foreign Policy, 1937-1947* (Greenwood Press, 1976), ch. 5; Fleming, vol. 1, pp. 438-61, 465-76.

232 [*"Ripe plum"*]: Mark Ethridge, quoted in Yergin, p. 279-80.
[*Truman's address to Congress*]: "The Truman Doctrine," March 12, 1947, in LaFeber, pp. 309-13, quoted at p. 312.

233 [*Marshall's Harvard address*]: "Proposal of the Marshall Plan," June 5, 1947, in *ibid.*, pp. 320-22, quoted at pp. 320, 321.
[*Marshall Plan*]: John Gimbel, *The Origins of the Marshall Plan* (Stanford University Press, 1976); Jones; Charles L. Mee, Jr., *The Marshall Plan: The Launching of the Pax Americana* (Simon and Schuster, 1984); Freeland, ch. 4; Werth, pp. 257-81; LaFeber, pp. 322-29; Thomas G. Paterson, "The Quest for Peace and Prosperity: International Trade, Communism, and the Marshall Plan," in Bernstein, *Politics and Policies*, pp. 78-112; Michael J. Hogan, "Paths to Plenty: Marshall Planners and the Debate over European Integration, 1947-1948," *Pacific Historical Review*, vol. 53 (1984), pp. 337-66.
[*Cominform*]: see Werth, ch. 14.

234 [*White on psychological tendencies in cold war*]: see Ralph K. White, *Fearful Warriors* (Free Press, 1984), ch. 10; see also Robert Jervis, *Perception and Misperception in International Politics* (Princeton University Press, 1976); Vamik D. Volkan, *The Need to Have Enemies and Allies* (Jason Aronson Inc., 1988).
[*Lippmann on "X" article*]: Lippmann, *The Cold War: A Study in U.S. Foreign Policy* (Harper, 1947); see also Ronald Steel, *Walter Lippmann and the American Century* (Atlantic Monthly/Little, Brown, 1980), pp. 443-46; Barton J. Bernstein, "Walter Lippmann and the Early Cold War," in Thomas G. Paterson, ed., *Cold War Critics: Alternatives to American Foreign Policy in the Truman Years* (Quadrangle, 1971), pp. 18-53.
[*Wallace's Madison Square Garden address*]: September 12, 1946, in LaFeber, pp. 255-60, quoted at p. 258; Richard J. Walton, *Henry Wallace, Harry Truman, and the Cold War* (Viking, 1976), pp. 100-8; Norman D. Markowitz, *The Rise and Fall of the People's Century: Henry A. Wallace and American Liberalism, 1941-1948* (Free Press, 1973), pp. 178-82; Alonzo L. Hamby, "Henry A. Wallace, the Liberals, and Soviet-American Relations," *Review of Politics*, vol. 30, no. 2 (April 1968), pp. 153-69.

235 [*Truman's approval of Wallace's speech*]: see Walton, pp. 98-99; John Morton Blum, ed., *The Price of Vision: The Diary of Henry A. Wallace, 1942-1946* (Houghton Mifflin, 1973), pp. 612-13; Truman, *Decisions*, p. 557.
[*Washington reaction to Wallace's address*]: Walton, pp. 108-12, Vandenberg quoted at p. 111; Blum, p. 613 n. 1, and pp. 613-32; Truman, *Decisions*, pp. 557-60; Byrnes, pp. 239-43; Donovan, ch. 23.
[*"You, yourself"*]: Blum, p. 618.
[*"Pacifist one hundred per cent"*]: quoted in Walton, pp. 113-14.
[*Eleanor Roosevelt and postwar world*]: see Joseph P. Lash, *Eleanor: The Years Alone* (Norton, 1972), chs. 1-6 *passim;* Tamara K. Hareven, *Eleanor Roosevelt: An American Conscience* (Quadrangle, 1968), chs. 10-12.

235-6 [*Truman's political position, early 1948*]: see Richard S. Kirkendall, "Election of 1948," in Arthur M. Schlesinger, Jr., ed., *History of American Presidential Elections, 1789-1968* (Chelsea House, 1971), vol. 4, pp. 3100-4.

236 [*ADA*]: Clifton Brock, *Americans for Democratic Action: Its Role in National Politics* (Public Affairs Press, 1962); Mary S. McAuliffe, *Crisis on the Left: Cold War Politics and American Liberals, 1947-1954* (University of Massachusetts Press, 1978), pp. 5-10 and *passim;* Alonzo L. Hamby, "The Liberals, Truman, and FDR as Symbol and Myth," *Journal of American History*, vol. 56, no. 4 (March 1970), pp. 859-67; Norman Markowitz, "From the Popular Front to Cold War Liberalism," in Robert Griffith and Athan Theoharis, eds., *The Specter: Original Essays on the Cold War and the Origins of McCarthyism* (New Viewpoints, 1974), pp. 90-115.
[*Truman's civil rights message*]: February 2, 1948, in *Truman Public Papers*, vol. 4, pp. 121-26; see also Donald R. McCoy and Richard T. Ruetten, *Quest and Response: Minority Rights and the Truman Administration* (University Press of Kansas, 1973), ch. 6; Donovan, ch. 35; William C. Berman, *The Politics of Civil Rights in the Truman Administration* (Ohio State University Press, 1973), ch. 2 and pp. 79-85; Barton J. Bernstein,

"The Ambiguous Legacy: The Truman Administration and Civil Rights," in Bernstein, *Politics and Policies*, pp. 269–314.

236 [*Dewey's nomination*]: Richard N. Smith, *Thomas E. Dewey and His Times* (Simon and Schuster, 1982), ch. 14; Kirkendall, pp. 3113–16; James T. Patterson, *Mr. Republican: Robert A. Taft* (Houghton Mifflin, 1972), chs. 26–27.

236–7 [*Dixiecrat revolt*]: Leonard Dinnerstein, "The Progressive and States' Rights Parties of 1948," in Arthur M. Schlesinger, Jr., ed., *History of U.S. Political Parties* (Chelsea House, 1973), vol. 4, pp. 3314–19, 3324–28; V. O. Key, Jr., *Southern Politics in State and Nation* (Knopf, 1949), pp. 329–44; Numan V. Bartley, *The Rise of Massive Resistance: Race and Politics in the South During the 1950's* (Louisiana State University Press, 1969), pp. 28–37; McCoy and Ruetten, ch. 7; Truman, *Trial and Hope*, pp. 179–87.

237 [*Progressive convention*]: Curtis D. MacDougall, *Gideon's Army* (Marzani & Munsell, 1965), vol. 2, chs. 22–25; Irving Howe and Lewis Coser, *The American Communist Party: A Critical History (1919–1957)* (Beacon Press, 1957), pp. 469–77; David A. Shannon, *The Decline of American Communism: A History of the Communist Party Since 1945* (Harper, 1959), pp. 164–75.

[*Democratic civil rights plank*]: see Schlesinger, *Elections*, vol. 4, p. 3154; see also Kirkendall, pp. 3117–18; Truman, *Trial and Hope*, pp. 181–83.

[*1948 campaign*]: Donovan, chs. 41–43; Smith, ch. 15; Kirkendall, pp. 3123–45; Dinnerstein, pp. 3321–27; MacDougall, vol. 3; Walton, chs. 5–9 *passim;* Berman, ch. 3 *passim;* Markowitz, *Rise and Fall*, ch. 8; Truman, *Trial and Hope*, ch. 15; Susan M. Hartmann, *Truman and the 80th Congress* (University of Missouri Press, 1971), ch. 8; Robert A. Divine, "The Cold War and the Election of 1948," *Journal of American History*, vol. 59, no. 1 (June 1972), pp. 90–110; Harvard Sitkoff, "Harry Truman and the Election of 1948: The Coming of Age of Civil Rights in American Politics," *Journal of Southern History*, vol. 37, no. 4 (November 1971), pp. 597–616; Allen Yarnell, *Democrats and Progressives: The 1948 Presidential Election as a Test of Postwar Liberalism* (University of California Press, 1974); Irwin Ross, *The Loneliest Campaign: The Truman Victory of 1948* (New American Library, 1968); Oral History of Henry Wallace, Columbia University, pp. 21–72.

[*Truman's reaction to poll of fifty experts*]: quoted in Phillips, pp. 243–44.

[*Dewey on overconfidence*]: Donovan, p. 437.

["*Very barbarous*"]: Wallace Oral History, p. 72.

238 [*Election results*]: Schlesinger, *Elections*, vol. 4, p. 3211.

["*A brave man*"]: Kirkendall, p. 3099.

The Spiral of Fear

[*Polling in 1948*]: Angus Campbell and Robert L. Kahn, *The People Elect a President* (Survey Research Center, University of Michigan, 1952); Schlesinger, *Elections*, vol. 4, pp. 3192–97; Frederick Mosteller et al., *The Pre-election Polls of 1948: Report to the Committee on Analysis of Pre-election Polls and Forecasts* (Social Science Research Council, 1949); Bernard R. Berelson et al., *Voting: A Study of Opinion Formation in a Presidential Campaign* (University of Chicago Press, 1954).

[*1948 as "maintaining election"*]: see Walter Dean Burnham, *Critical Elections and the Mainsprings of American Politics* (Norton, 1970); James Sundquist, *Dynamics of the Party System: Alignment and Realignment of Political Parties in the United States* (Brookings Institution, 1973), chs. 11–12; Kirkendall, p. 3144.

239–40 [*Soviet atomic bomb*]: "Announcement by President Truman," September 23, 1949, in LaFeber, pp. 406–7; see also Herken, chs. 14–15; Yergin, ch. 5 *passim;* Robert J. Donovan, *Tumultuous Years: The Presidency of Harry S Truman, 1949–1953* (Norton, 1982), ch. 9; "Reactions of 150,000,000," *Newsweek*, vol. 34, no. 14 (October 3, 1949), pp. 25–26.

240 [*Germany in the cold war*]: Bruce Kuklick, *American Policy and the Division of Germany: The Clash with Russia over Reparations* (Cornell University Press, 1972); W. Phillips Davison, *The Berlin Blockade: A Study in Cold War Politics* (Princeton University Press, 1958); Lucius D. Clay, *Decision in Germany* (Doubleday, 1950), chs. 19–20 and *passim;* Avi Shlaim, *The United States and the Berlin Blockade, 1948–1949: A Study in Crisis Decision-Making* (University of California Press, 1983); Yergin, ch. 14.

240 [*Chinese revolution and the U.S.*]: U.S. Department of State, *United States Relations with China* (U.S. Government Printing Office, 1949); Tang Tsou, *America's Failure in China, 1941–1950* (University of Chicago Press, 1963); H. Bradford Westerfield, *Foreign Policy and Party Politics: Pearl Harbor to Korea* (Yale University Press, 1955), chs. 12, 16; Lewis M. Purifoy, *Harry Truman's China Policy: McCarthyism and the Diplomacy of Hysteria, 1947–1951* (New Viewpoints, 1976); Donovan, *Tumultuous Years*, chs. 6–7; John K. Fairbank, *The United States and China*, 4th ed. (Harvard University Press, 1983); Russell D. Buhite, *Soviet-American Relations in Asia, 1945–1954* (University of Oklahoma Press, 1981), chs. 1–3; Kenneth S. Chern, *Dilemma in China: America's Policy Debate, 1945* (Archon Books, 1980); Okabe Tatsumi, "The Cold War and China," in Yonosuke Nagai and Akira Iriye, eds., *The Origins of the Cold War in Asia* (Columbia University Press/University of Tokyo Press, 1977), pp. 224–51.

[*Korean War*]: Joseph C. Goulden, *Korea: The Untold Story of the War* (Times Books, 1982); David Rees, *Korea: The Limited War* (St. Martin's Press, 1964); Ronald J. Caridi, *The Korean War and American Politics: The Republican Party as a Case Study* (University of Pennsylvania Press, 1968); Bevin Alexander, *Korea: The First War We Lost* (Hippocrene, 1986); Donovan, *Tumultuous Years*, ch. 8 and parts 3–4 *passim;* Truman, *Trial and Hope*, chs. 22–28 *passim;* David J. Dallin, *Soviet Foreign Policy After Stalin* (Lippincott, 1961), pp. 60–69; Glenn D. Paige, *The Korean Decision* (Free Press, 1968); Buhite, ch. 5; Allen Guttmann, ed., *Korea: Cold War and Limited War*, 2nd ed. (D. C. Heath, 1972); Charles M. Dobbs, *The Unwanted Symbol: American Foreign Policy, the Cold War, and Korea, 1945–1950* (Kent State University Press, 1981); Allen S. Whiting, *China Crosses the Yalu* (Macmillan, 1960); Strobe Talbott, ed. and trans., *Khrushchev Remembers* (Little, Brown, 1970–74), vol. 1, ch. 11; Dean Acheson, *The Korean War* (Norton, 1971); Gaddis, *Strategies*, ch. 4; John Lewis Gaddis, "Korea in American Politics, Strategy, and Diplomacy, 1945–50," in Nagai and Iriye, pp. 277–98; Robert M. Slusser, "Soviet Far Eastern Policy, 1945–50: Stalin's Goals in Korea," in *ibid.*, pp. 123–46; Robert R. Simmons, *The Strained Alliance: Peking, Pyongyang, Moscow and the Politics of the Korean War* (Free Press, 1975); James I. Matray, "Truman's Plan for Victory: National Self-Determination and the Thirty-eighth Parallel Decision in Korea," *Journal of American History*, vol. 66, no. 2 (September 1979), pp. 314–33; Daniels, pp. 239–41; Taubman, pp. 201–2, 211–22; Shulman, chs. 6–7; William Manchester, *American Caesar: Douglas MacArthur, 1880–1964* (Little, Brown, 1978), chs. 9–10.

[*"Administrative dividing line"*]: Acheson, quoted in Manchester, p. 539.

240-1 [*Acheson on U.S. defense perimeter*]: quoted in Goulden, p. 30; see also Dobbs, pp. 180–81; Gaddis, *Long Peace*, ch. 4.

242 [*Ulam on Soviet blunder in Korea*]: Adam B. Ulam, "Washington, Moscow, and the Korean War," in Guttmann, pp. 258–85, quoted at p. 277.

243 [*Smith Act*]: quoted in Howe and Coser, p. 418.

[*Smith Act trial of communist leaders*]: *ibid.*, pp. 481–82; Shannon, pp. 198–200; Packer, pp. 11–13.

[*"Government . . . on trial"*]: William Z. Foster, quoted in Shannon, p. 198.

[*"Sufficient danger"*]: Judge Harold R. Medina, quoted in *ibid.*, p. 200.

[*China-Korea links*]: see Purifoy, chs. 8–9.

[*China Lobby*]: Ross Y. Koen, *The China Lobby in American Politics* (Octagon Books, 1974), esp. ch. 2; Stanley D. Bachrack, *The Committee of One Million: "China Lobby" Politics, 1953–1971* (Columbia University Press, 1976), esp. part 1.

[*Taft on communism in China*]: quoted in Fried, p. 4; and E. J. Kahn, Jr., *The China Hands: America's Foreign Service Officers and What Befell Them* (Viking, 1975), p. 2.

[*Acheson as target*]: see Westerfield, pp. 327–29.

[*"Whined" and "whimpered" and "slobbered"*]: quoted in William Manchester, *The Glory and the Dream: A Narrative History of America, 1932–1972* (Little, Brown, 1974), p. 492.

244 [*Acheson and Hiss*]: Weinstein, pp. 505–6, Acheson quoted at p. 505.

[*Butler on Acheson*]: quoted in Eric F. Goldman, *The Crucial Decade: America, 1945–1955* (Knopf, 1956), p. 125.

[*McCarthy*]: Richard H. Rovere, *Senator Joe McCarthy* (Harcourt, 1959); Oshinsky; Fried; Thomas C. Reeves, *The Life and Times of Joe McCarthy* (Stein & Day, 1982); Edwin R. Bayley, *Joe McCarthy and the Press* (University of Wisconsin Press, 1981); Daniel Bell, ed., *The New American Right* (Criterion Books, 1955); Earl Latham, ed., *The Meaning of McCarthyism,* 2nd ed. (D. C. Heath, 1973); Michael P. Rogin, *The Intellectuals and McCarthy: The Radical Specter* (MIT Press, 1967); Robert Griffith, *The Politics of Fear: McCarthy and the Senate* (University Press of Kentucky, 1970); Donald F. Crosby, *God, Church, and Flag: Senator Joseph R. McCarthy and the Catholic Church, 1950-1957* (University of North Carolina Press, 1978); Joseph R. McCarthy, *McCarthyism: The Fight for America* (Devin-Adair, 1952; reprinted by Arno Press, 1977).

244 [*"Multiple untruth"*]: see Rovere, pp. 109-10.
[*Wheeling*]: Reeves, pp. 222-33, McCarthy quoted at p. 224; Oshinsky, pp. 107-12; Bayley, ch. 1.

245 [*McCarthy's Senate performance*]: Reeves, pp. 236-42, quoted at p. 239; and Oshinsky, pp. 112-14, quoted at p. 112.
[*"Perfectly reckless"*]: quoted in Patterson, *Mr. Republican,* p. 446.
[*Tydings committee*]: Reeves, pp. 249-314, conclusion quoted at p. 304; Rovere, pp. 145-59.
[*"Keep talking"*]: quoted in Patterson, p. 446.
[*"Declaration of Conscience"*]: Oshinsky, pp. 163-65; Fried, p. 83.
[*McCarthy in 1950 campaign*]: Reeves, ch. 14, reporter quoted at p. 346; Fried, ch. 4.

246 [*Buckley on McCarthyism*]: quoted in Rovere, p. 22.
[*McCarthy and the press*]: Bayley, esp. ch. 3, Reedy quoted at p. 68; see also James A. Wechsler, *The Age of Suspicion* (Random House, 1953); Oshinsky, ch. 12.
[*Courting of Eisenhower*]: Herbert S. Parmet, *Eisenhower and the American Crusades* (Macmillan, 1972), chs. 9-10; Stephen E. Ambrose, *Eisenhower: Soldier, General of the Army, President-Elect, 1890-1952* (Simon and Schuster, 1983), ch. 25; Dwight D. Eisenhower, *The White House Years: Mandate for Change, 1953-1956* (Doubleday, 1963), ch. 1.

247 [*"Completely foreign field"*]: quoted in Barton J. Bernstein, "Election of 1952," in Schlesinger, *Elections,* vol. 4, p. 3225.
[*GOP nomination battle*]: Ambrose, *Soldier,* ch. 26; Eisenhower, ch. 2; Patterson, part 6; Parmet, chs. 12-14; Bernstein, "Election," pp. 3224-34.
[*GOP as two parties*]: see James MacGregor Burns, *The Deadlock of Democracy: Four-Party Politics in America* (Prentice-Hall, 1963), esp. ch. 8.

248 [*"Path to defeat"*]: quoted in Bernstein, "Election," p. 3230.
[*"Why do they hate me so?"*]: quoted in Patterson, p. 547.
[*Morningside Heights statement*]: quoted in Parmet, p. 130; see also *ibid.,* pp. 128-30; Patterson, pp. 572-78; Eisenhower, p. 64.
[*"Surrender at Morningside Heights"*]: quoted in Bernstein, "Election," p. 3242.

249 [*Courtship of Stevenson*]: Kenneth S. Davis, *A Prophet in His Own Country: The Triumphs and Defeats of Adlai E. Stevenson* (Doubleday, 1957), ch. 24; John Bartlow Martin, *Adlai Stevenson of Illinois* (Doubleday, 1976), pp. 513-78; Walter Johnson, *How We Drafted Adlai Stevenson* (Knopf, 1955); Truman, *Trial and Hope,* pp. 491-96.
[*"Could not," not "would not"*]: quoted in Davis, p. 394.
[*Stevenson's convention welcome*]: July 21, 1952, in Walter Johnson, ed., *The Papers of Adlai E. Stevenson* (Little, Brown, 1972-79), vol. 4, pp. 11-14, quoted at p. 12; author's personal observations, July 21, 1952, Chicago.
[*Democratic convention*]: Davis, pp. 397-409; Martin, pp. 578-604; Bernstein, "Election," pp. 3236-40; Johnson, *Papers,* vol. 4, ch. 1.
[*Eisenhower in Indiana*]: Parmet, pp. 127-28, Jenner quoted on Marshall at p. 127; Ambrose, *Soldier,* pp. 552-53.

249-50 [*Eisenhower in Wisconsin*]: Reeves, pp. 436-40, praise of Marshall quoted at p. 437; Ambrose, *Soldier,* pp. 563-67.

250 [*Nixon's second crisis*]: Richard M. Nixon, *Six Crises* (Doubleday, 1962), ch. 2; Parmet, pp. 134-41; Fawn M. Brodie, *Richard Nixon: The Shaping of His Character* (Norton, 1981), ch. 19; Smith, *Dewey,* pp. 599-603; Garry Wills, *Nixon Agonistes: The Crisis of the Self-Made Man* (Houghton Mifflin, 1970), pp. 91-114; Eisenhower, pp. 65-69.
[*"My boy"*]: quoted in Nixon, p. 123.
[*Stevenson on Taft winning nominee*]: Johnson, *Papers,* vol. 4, p. 90.
[*Stevenson on Eisenhower's backbone*]: Ambrose, *Soldier,* p. 567.
[*"Two Republican" parties*]: see Johnson, *Papers,* vol. 4, pp. 66-68.
[*Civil rights and the South in 1952 campaign*]: Schlesinger, *Elections,* vol. 4, pp. 3280-81; Bernstein, "Election," pp. 3247, 3251-52; Eisenhower, pp. 55, 69-71; Donald S.

Strong, "The Presidential Election in the South, 1952," *Journal of Politics*, vol. 17, no. 1 (August 1955), pp. 343–89; Johnson, *Papers*, vol. 4, pp. 47–48, 54–60, 89, 151–53, 157; Robert F. Burk, *The Eisenhower Administration and Black Civil Rights* (University of Tennessee Press, 1984), ch. 1 *passim*.

250 [*"Go to Korea"*]: Parmet, pp. 142–43, Eisenhower quoted at p. 143.

251 [*1952 election results*]: Schlesinger, *Elections*, vol. 4, p. 3337; see also Bernstein, "Election," pp. 3264–65; Strong.

[*Stevenson on his loss*]: Johnson, *Papers*, vol. 4, p. 188.

The Price of Suspicion

[*Army-McCarthy hearings*]: U.S. Senate, Committee on Government Operations, Special Subcommittee on Investigations, *Charges and Countercharges Involving: Secretary of the Army Robert T. Stevens . . .*, 83rd Congress, 2nd Session (U.S. Government Printing Office, 1954); Oshinsky, chs. 27–31; Reeves, chs. 21–22; Michael W. Straight, *Trial by Television* (Beacon Press, 1954); Fred I. Greenstein, *The Hidden-Hand Presidency: Eisenhower as Leader* (Basic Books, 1982), pp. 198–212.

[*Oshinsky on hearings*]: Oshinsky, p. 416.

252 [*"Largest single group"*]: quoted in *ibid.*, p. 319.

[*"Got his Ph.D."*]: quoted in Brodie, p. 290.

[*"The dark days of the Hiss case"*]: quoted in *ibid.*, p. 284.

[*Nixon on Stevenson and Hiss*]: quoted in Johnson, *Papers*, vol. 4, p. 392.

[*McCarthy on Stevenson*]: quoted in Reeves, p. 445.

[*"Get into the gutter"*]: quoted in Oshinsky, p. 260.

[*"Trouble-maker"*]: see entry of April 1, 1953, in Robert H. Ferrell, ed., *The Eisenhower Diaries* (Norton, 1981), pp. 233–34.

[*McCarthy's depredations, early Eisenhower Administration*]: see Reeves, ch. 18; Parmet, ch. 26; see also Griffith, *Politics of Fear*, ch. 6.

[*McCarthy and Dirksen on Bohlen*]: quoted in Parmet, p. 246; see also Athan G. Theoharis, *The Yalta Myths: An Issue in U.S. Politics, 1945–1955* (University of Missouri Press, 1970), ch. 9 and *passim*.

253 [*"No more Bohlens"*]: quoted in Stephen E. Ambrose, *Eisenhower: The President* (Simon and Schuster, 1984), p. 60.

[*Stalin's death and the succession*]: Svetlana Alliluyeva, *Twenty Letters to a Friend*, Priscilla Johnson McMillan, trans. (Harper, 1967), pp. 5–14; *Khrushchev Remembers*, vol. 1, pp. 306–41; Dallin, pp. 117–34; Daniels, pp. 246–50; Eisenhower, *Mandate*, pp. 143–45.

[*Dulles*]: Townsend Hoopes, *The Devil and John Foster Dulles* (Atlantic Monthly/Little, Brown, 1973); Ronald W. Pruessen, *John Foster Dulles: The Road to Power* (Free Press, 1982); John R. Beal, *John Foster Dulles, 1888–1959* (Harper, 1959); Herbert S. Parmet, "Power and Reality: John Foster Dulles and Political Diplomacy," in Merli and Wilson, pp. 589–619; Ambrose, *President*, pp. 20–22; Gaddis, *Strategies*, pp. 136–45; *Khrushchev Remembers*, vol. 2, pp. 362–64.

253-4 [*Smith on Dulles*]: Gaddis Smith, "The Shadow of John Foster Dulles" (review of Hoopes), *Foreign Affairs*, vol. 52, no. 2 (January 1974), pp. 403–8, quoted at p. 406.

254 [*Eisenhower's inaugural address*]: January 20, 1953, in *Public Papers of the Presidents of the United States: Dwight D. Eisenhower* (U.S. Government Printing Office, 1958–61), vol. 1, pp. 1–8, quoted at pp. 1, 2.

[*Dulles on communism*]: January 15, 1953, in LaFeber, pp. 464–68, quoted at p. 466.

[*Dulles's hard line vs. Eisenhower's soft*]: see Seyom Brown, *The Faces of Power: Constancy and Change in United States Foreign Policy from Truman to Reagan* (Columbia University Press, 1983), chs. 7–8; Robert A. Divine, *Eisenhower and the Cold War* (Oxford University Press, 1981), pp. 19–23 and *passim*; Ambrose, *President, passim*; Hoopes, *passim*; Charles C. Alexander, *Holding the Line: The Eisenhower Era, 1952–1961* (Indiana University Press, 1975), pp. 64–66; Gaddis, *Strategies*, ch. 5 *passim*; Richard M. Saunders, "Military Force in the Foreign Policy of the Eisenhower Administration," *Political Science Quarterly*, vol. 100, no. 1 (Spring 1985), pp. 97–116.

[*"United States of Europe"*]: see Ambrose, *President*, pp. 49–50, 120.

[*Eisenhower, Dulles and "book burning"*]: see *ibid.*, pp. 81–83; Reeves, pp. 477–96 *passim*.

255 [*Iran*]: Ambrose, *President*, pp. 109–12; Kermit Roosevelt, *Countercoup: The Struggle for the Control of Iran* (McGraw-Hill, 1979); Sepehr Zabih, *The Mossadegh Era: Roots of the Iranian Revolution* (Lake View Press, 1982); Dallin, pp. 203–17; Anthony Eden, *Full Circle* (Houghton Mifflin, 1960), ch. 9; Stephen E. Ambrose, *Ike's Spies: Eisenhower and the Defense Establishment* (Doubleday, 1981), chs. 14–15.
[*Eden on Eisenhower's "obsession"*]: quoted in Eden, p. 235.
[*Lebanon*]: Ambrose, *President*, pp. 462–75 *passim;* Fahim I. Qubain, *Crisis in Lebanon* (Middle East Institute, 1961); Leila M. T. Meo, *Lebanon, Improbable Nation: A Study in Political Development* (Indiana University Press, 1965); Hoopes, ch. 27.
[*"Five times he said no"*]: Ambrose, *President*, p. 229; see also Gaddis, *Long Peace,* ch. 6.
[*"Bland leading the bland"*]: quoted in Melanson in Melanson and Mayers, p. 47.
[*Eisenhower revisionism*]: see Murray Kempton, "The Underestimation of Dwight D. Eisenhower," *Esquire*, vol. 68, no. 3 (September 1967), pp. 108–9, 156; Vincent P. De Santis, "Eisenhower Revisionism," *Review of Politics*, vol. 38, no. 2 (April 1976), pp. 190–207; Richard H. Rovere, "Eisenhower Revisited—A Political Genius? A Brilliant Man?," in Bernstein and Matusow, pp. 436–54; Greenstein; Ambrose, *President*, chs. 1, 27; Mary S. McAuliffe, "Eisenhower, The President," *Journal of American History*, vol. 68, no. 3 (December 1981), pp. 625–32; Divine, *Eisenhower*, pp. 6–7; Wills, pp. 115–38; Melanson and Mayers, *passim.*
[*New Look*]: Ambrose, *President*, pp. 171–73, 224–26; Melanson in Melanson and Mayers, pp. 49–54; Gaddis, *Long Peace*, pp. 123–24, 140–45; Ambrose, *Ike's Spies*, pp. 275–76.
256 [*Operation Alert*]: Ambrose, *President*, pp. 256–57; Peter Lyon, *Eisenhower: Portrait of the Hero* (Little, Brown, 1974), p. 655.
[*Eisenhower's address to editors*]: "The Chance for Peace," April 16, 1953, in *Eisenhower Public Papers*, vol. 1, pp. 179–88, quoted at pp. 185, 186, 182, respectively; see also Ambrose, *President*, pp. 94–96.
[*"Atoms for peace"*]: December 8, 1953, in *Eisenhower Public Papers*, vol. 1, pp. 813–22; Ambrose, *President*, pp. 147–51.
256–7 [*Bikini atoll test*]: Robert A. Divine, *Blowing in the Wind: The Nuclear Test Ban Debate, 1954–1960* (Oxford University Press, 1978), ch. 1.
257 [*Geneva summit*]: Ambrose, *President*, ch. 11; Hoopes, ch. 18; Dallin, pp. 279–83; Eisenhower, *Mandate*, ch. 21; *Khrushchev Remembers*, vol. 1, ch. 13.
[*"Complete blueprint"*]: "Statement on Disarmament," July 21, 1955, in *Eisenhower Public Papers*, vol. 3, pp. 713–16, quoted at p. 715.
[*Stevenson's proposal of test suspension*]: Divine, *Blowing on the Wind*, pp. 86–87, Nixon quoted at p. 87.
[*Dulles and Aswan*]: Hoopes, chs. 20–21.
[*Suez*]: Hoopes, chs. 22–24; Ambrose, *President*, chs. 14–15 *passim;* Dwight D. Eisenhower, *The White House Years: Waging Peace, 1956–1961* (Doubleday, 1965), ch. 3 *passim;* Herman Finer, *Dulles Over Suez: The Theory and Practice of His Diplomacy* (Quadrangle, 1964); Eden, book 3.
258 [*Gomulka's warning*]: quoted in Ambrose, *President*, p. 354; see also Dallin, pp. 358–64; Konrad Syrop, *Spring in October: The Story of the Polish Revolution, 1956* (Praeger, 1957).
[*Hungary*]: Paul E. Zinner, *Revolution in Hungary* (Columbia University Press, 1962); Melvin J. Lasky, ed., *The Hungarian Revolution: A White Book* (Praeger, 1957); Ambrose, *President*, ch. 15.
[*"Liberation was a sham"*]: Ambrose, *President*, p. 355.
[*Welch-McCarthy clash*]: Oshinsky, ch. 31, quoted at pp. 462, 463, 464.
[*McCarthy's "condemnation"*]: Reeves, ch. 23; Rovere, pp. 222–31.
[*Eisenhower's hidden hand against McCarthy*]: see Greenstein, ch. 5; see also Sherman Adams, *Firsthand Report: The Story of the Eisenhower Administration* (Harper, 1961), ch. 8; Oshinsky, pp. 258–60, 387–88, and ch. 23.
[*"Purely negative act"*]: Ambrose, *President*, p. 620.
[*Communist Control Act*]: see McAuliffe, *Crisis on the Left*, ch. 9.
259 [*Sputnik*]: Walter A. McDougall, . . . *The Heavens and the Earth: A Political History of the Space Age* (Basic Books, 1985), pp. 131–34, chs. 6–7; James R. Killian, Jr., *Sputnik, Scientists, and Eisenhower* (MIT Press, 1977), Introduction and chs. 1–2; Dallin, pp.

453–54; Eisenhower, *Waging*, ch. 8 *passim;* Tom Wolfe, *The Right Stuff* (Farrar, Straus & Giroux, 1979), pp. 69–74.

259 [*"Distinct surprise"*]: quoted in Brown, p. 114.

[*Vanguard failure*]: McDougall, p. 154; Constance M. Green and Milton Lomask, *Vanguard: A History* (NASA, 1970), pp. 204–12.

[*Gaither report*]: Ambrose, *President*, pp. 433–35; Morton H. Halperin, "The Gaither Committee and the Policy Process," *World Politics*, vol. 13, no. 3 (April 1961), pp. 360–84; Samuel P. Huntington, *The Common Defense: Strategic Programs in National Politics* (Columbia University Press, 1961), pp. 106–13; Brown, ch. 10; Eisenhower, *Waging*, pp. 219–23.

[*Eisenhower on U.S. as "scared"*]: quoted in Ambrose, *President*, p. 451.

[*Eisenhower's knowledge of U.S. strategic superiority*]: Ambrose, *Ike's Spies*, pp. 275–78; Robert A. Strong, "Eisenhower and Arms Control," in Melanson and Mayers, pp. 255–56.

[*Khrushchev*]: Dallin, pp. 218–19; *Khrushchev Remembers*, vols. 1, 2; Edward Crankshaw, *Khrushchev* (Viking, 1966); Roy A. Medvedev and Zhores A. Medvedev, *Khrushchev: The Years in Power*, Andrew R. Durkin, trans. (Columbia University Press, 1976).

260 [*Khrushchev's attack upon Molotov*]: Dallin, pp. 227–35, Dallin quoted at p. 230.

[*Khrushchev's Twentieth Party Congress address*]: Khrushchev, "The Crimes of the Stalin Era," text reprinted in *The New Leader*, sect. 2, July 16, 1956, S7–S65; see also Dallin, pp. 322–27.

[*Khrushchev in America*]: *Khrushchev in America* (Crosscurrents Press, 1960); "Great Encounter, Part Two," *Newsweek*, vol. 54, no. 13 (September 28, 1959), pp. 33–46; Ambrose, *President*, pp. 541–44; Eisenhower, *Waging*, pp. 405–14, 432–49; *Khrushchev Remembers*, vol. 2, ch. 16.

[*Khrushchev on his being denied Disneyland*]: quoted in *Khrushchev in America*, pp. 112–13.

[*U-2*]: David Wise and Thomas B. Ross, *The U-2 Affair* (Random House, 1962); Michael R. Beschloss, *Mayday: Eisenhower, Khrushchev and the U-2 Affair* (Harper, 1986); Ambrose, *President*, pp. 571–77; Eisenhower, *Waging*, pp. 543–52; M. S. Venkataramani, "The U-2 Crisis: An Inquiry into Its Antecedents," in Venkataramani, *Undercurrents in American Foreign Relations: Four Studies* (Asia Publishing House, 1965), pp. 157–208; Carl A. Linden, *Khrushchev and the Soviet Leadership, 1957–1964* (Johns Hopkins Press, 1966), ch. 6.

261 [*Khrushchev on having "parts of the plane" and the pilot*]: quoted in Ambrose, *President*, p. 574.

262 [*Reston on Washington*]: *New York Times*, May 9, 1960, p. 1.

[*Paris summit*]: Beschloss, ch. 11; Wise and Ross, ch. 10; Ambrose, *President*, pp. 577–79; Eisenhower, *Waging*, pp. 553–59; *Khrushchev Remembers*, vol. 2, ch. 18; Jack M. Schick, *The Berlin Crisis, 1958–1962* (University of Pennsylvania Press, 1971), pp. 111–33; Harold Macmillan, *Pointing the Way, 1959–1961* (Macmillan, 1972), ch. 7.

[*Ambrose on summit*]: Ambrose, *President*, p. 579.

[*Eisenhower's Farewell Address*]: January 17, 1961, in *Eisenhower Public Papers*, vol. 8, pp. 1035–40, quoted at p. 1038.

262–3 [*"Kept the peace" . . . "didn't just happen"*]: quoted in Beschloss, p. 388.

263 [*"Stalemate"*]: ibid.

6. The Imperium of Freedom

264 [*Soviet and American military power*]: John M. Collins, *U.S.-Soviet Military Balance: Concepts and Capabilities, 1960–1980* (McGraw-Hill, 1980), pp. 25–38, Collins quoted on "bombers could burst through" at p. 36; Genrikh Trofimenko, *The U.S. Military Doctrine* (Progress Publishers, Moscow, 1986).

[*American economic power*]: U.S. Bureau of the Census, *Historical Statistics of the United States, Colonial Times to 1970* (U.S. Government Printing Office, 1971), part 2, p. 948 (Series W 1–11) and part 1, p. 224 (Series F 1–5); Gertrude Deutsch, ed., *The Economic Almanac 1962* (National Industrial Conference Board, 1962), pp. 498, 500; U.S. Library of Congress, Legislative Reference Service, *Trends in Economic Growth: A Comparison of the Western Powers and the Soviet Bloc* (U.S. Government Printing Office, 1955), pp. 1–5 and *passim*.

264 [*"Expansive time"*]: David F. Noble, *Forces of Production: A Social History of Industrial Automation* (Knopf, 1984), p. 3; see also, generally, David M. Potter, *People of Plenty: Economic Abundance and the American Character* (University of Chicago Press, 1954).

265 [*American treaty commitments*]: see Roland A. Paul, *American Military Commitments Abroad* (Rutgers University Press, 1973), pp. 14-15.
[*European attacks on America*]: see Andre Visson, *As Others See Us* (Doubleday, 1948); Wolfgang Wagner, "The Europeans' Image of America," in Karl Kaiser and Hans-Peter Schwarz, eds., *America and Western Europe: Problems and Prospects* (Lexington Books, 1978), pp. 19-32; Richard Mayne, *Postwar: The Dawn of Today's Europe* (Schocken Books, 1983), pp. 111-17; Sidney Alexander, "The European Image of America," *American Scholar*, vol. 21, no. 1 (Winter 1951-52), pp. 49-55.
[*Lerner on Europe and America*]: Max Lerner, *America as a Civilization* (Simon and Schuster, 1957), p. 930.
[*European admiration and support of America*]: Henry Lee Munson, *European Beliefs Regarding the United States* (Common Council for American Unity, 1949), pp. 16, 22, 49, and passim.
[*Soviet responses and fears*]: see J. M. Mackintosh, *Strategy and Tactics of Soviet Foreign Policy* (Oxford University Press, 1963); Joseph L. Nogee and Robert H. Donaldson, *Soviet Foreign Policy Since World War II* (Pergamon Press, 1981), chs. 2, 4; William Zimmerman, *Soviet Perspectives on International Relations, 1956-1967* (Princeton University Press, 1969); Charles Gati, "The Stalinist Legacy in Soviet Foreign Policy," in Stephen F. Cohen et al., eds., *The Soviet Union Since Stalin* (Indiana University Press, 1980), pp. 279-301; David J. Dallin, *Soviet Foreign Policy After Stalin* (Lippincott, 1961).
[*Aviation Day and the "bomber gap"*]: see Allen Dulles, *The Craft of Intelligence* (Harper, 1963), pp. 149, 162-63; Nogee and Donaldson, p. 109; Arnold L. Horelick and Myron Rush, *Strategic Power and Soviet Foreign Policy* (University of Chicago Press, 1966), pp. 17-18, 27-30, 66; Lincoln P. Bloomfield et al., *Khrushchev and the Arms Race: Soviet Interests in Arms Control and Disarmament, 1954-1964* (MIT Press, 1966), ch. 2 passim.

The Technology of Freedom

266 [*Per capita and national income*]: Potter, pp. 81-84.

267 [*American intolerance in 1950s*]: see Charles C. Alexander, *Holding the Line: The Eisenhower Era, 1952-1961* (Indiana University Press, 1975), pp. 121-22.
[*"Entered a period"*]: quoted in James Gilbert, *Another Chance: Postwar America, 1945-1968* (Temple University Press, 1981), p. 186.
[*Mergers and acquisitions, 1950s*]: Harold G. Vatter, *The U.S. Economy in the 1950s: An Economic History* (Norton, 1963), pp. 205-6, Schumpeter quoted at p. 206; survival rate of large firms given at *ibid.;* see also John Kenneth Galbraith, *The Affluent Society*, 2nd ed. (Houghton Mifflin, 1969), ch. 8; Robert Sobel, *The Age of Giant Corporations: A Microeconomic History of American Business, 1914-1970* (Greenwood Press, 1972), ch. 8; Willard F. Mueller, "Concentration in Manufacturing," in Edwin Mansfield, ed., *Monopoly Power and Economic Performance: Problems of the Modern Economy* (Norton, 1978), pp. 69-73.
[*World War II and technological advances*]: Noble, ch. 1 passim, pp. 334-35; Ralph Sanders, "Three-Dimensional Warfare: World War II," in Melvin Kranzberg and Carroll W. Pursell, Jr., eds., *Technology in Western Civilization: Technology in the Twentieth Century* (Oxford University Press, 1967), pp. 561-78.
[*Federal share of research and development, late 1950s*]: W. David Lewis, "Industrial Research and Development," in Kranzberg and Pursell, p. 632; see also Donald J. Mrozek, "The Truman Administration and the Enlistment of the Aviation Industry in Postwar Defense," *Business History Review*, vol. 48, no. 1 (Spring 1974), pp. 73-94.

267-8 [*Rosenberg on technological change and systematized knowledge*]: Rosenberg, *Technology and American Economic Growth* (Harper, 1972), p. 117.

268 [*Air speed records*]: Gene Gurney, *A Chronology of World Aviation* (Franklin Watts, 1965), pp. 139, 144, 171, 192, 207; Roger E. Bilstein, *Flight in America, 1900-1983: From the Wrights to the Astronauts* (Johns Hopkins University Press, 1984), p. 183; Patrick

Harper, ed., *The Timetable of Technology* (Hearst Books, 1982), p. 154; Thomas M. Smith, "The Development of Aviation," in Kranzberg and Pursell, pp. 158–59; Tom Wolfe, *The Right Stuff* (Farrar, Straus & Giroux, 1979), esp. ch. 3.

268 [Nautilus]: Richard G. Hewlett and Francis Duncan, *Nuclear Navy, 1946–1962* (University of Chicago Press, 1974), esp. chs. 6–7.

[*Machine tool industry growth, postwar*]: Noble, pp. 8–9.

[*Federal share of R&D, electrical equipment industry, mid-1960s*]: ibid., p. 8.

[*Technological advances in agriculture*]: Gilbert C. Fite, *American Farmers: The New Minority* (Indiana University Press, 1981), pp. 110–15; Wayne D. Rasmussen, "Scientific Agriculture," in Kranzberg and Pursell, pp. 337–53; Reynold M. Wik, "Mechanization of the American Farm," in *ibid.*, pp. 353–68; Rosenberg, *Technology and Growth*, pp. 127–46; Zvi Griliches, "Research Costs and Social Returns: Hybrid Corn and Related Innovations," in Nathan Rosenberg, ed., *The Economics of Technological Change* (Penguin, 1971), pp. 182–202; Griliches, "Hybrid Corn and the Economics of Innovation," in *ibid.*, pp. 211–28.

[*Decline of farm labor force*]: Rosenberg, *Technology and Growth*, p. 130; see also Fite, p. 115.

[*Increase of per-acre corn yield*]: Rasmussen, p. 343.

[*Return on hybrid corn research*]: Griliches, "Research Costs," p. 183.

268–9 [*Agribusiness*]: Fite, ch. 7 and pp. 194–97.

269 ["*Enormous Laboratory*"]: Lerner, p. 216.

[*Gibbs*]: Lynde Phelps Wheeler, *Josiah Willard Gibbs: The History of a Great Mind* (Yale University Press, 1951); Muriel Rukeyser, *Willard Gibbs* (Doubleday, Doran, 1942); J. G. Crowther, *Famous American Men of Science* (Norton, 1937), pp. 227–98.

[*Marx on science as social activity*]: Marx, *Capital: A Critique of Political Economy*, Samuel Moore and Edward Aveling, trans. (Charles H. Kerr & Co., 1906–9), vol. 1, esp. ch. 15; see also Nathan Rosenberg, "Karl Marx on the economic role of science," in Rosenberg, *Perspectives on Technology* (Cambridge University Press, 1976), ch. 7; M. M. Bober, *Karl Marx's Interpretation of History*, 2nd. ed. (Harvard University Press, 1968), esp. chs. 1, 8, and pp. 363–76.

[*Corporate R&D and American science*]: George H. Daniels, *Science in American Society: A Social History* (Knopf, 1971), esp. ch. 14; Sobel, ch. 9; John Jewkes, David Sawers, and Richard Stillerman, *The Sources of Invention* (Macmillan, 1958), esp. chs. 2, 6–7; Jack Raymond, *Power at the Pentagon* (Harper, 1964), chs. 8–9; William H. Whyte, Jr., *The Organization Man* (Simon and Schuster, 1956), part 5; Jacob Schmookler, "Technological Progress and the Modern Corporation," in Edward S. Mason, ed., *The Corporation in Modern Society* (Harvard University Press, 1960), ch. 8; Jay M. Gould, *The Technical Elite* (Augustus M. Kelley, 1968), ch. 7; David C. Mowery, "Firm Structure, Government Policy, and the Organization of Industrial Research: Great Britain and the United States, 1900–1950," *Business History Review*, vol. 58, no. 4 (Winter 1984), pp. 504–31.

270 ["*Underlying principle*"]: Jewkes et al., p. 238.

[*Oppenheimer's classification as security risk*]: United States Atomic Energy Commission, *In the Matter of J. Robert Oppenheimer, Transcript of Hearing Before Personnel Security Board, April 12–May 6, 1954* (United States Government Printing Office, 1954); Philip M. Stern, *The Oppenheimer Case: Security on Trial* (Harper, 1969).

[*Conant on subsidies*]: Lerner, p. 218.

[*Gibbs on Yale payroll*]: see Wheeler, pp. 57–59, 90–93, quoted at p. 91.

271 [*Taylor and scientific management*]: Frederick W. Taylor, *The Principles of Scientific Management* (Harper, 1929); Taylor, *Shop Management* (Harper, 1911); Daniel Nelson, *Frederick W. Taylor and the Rise of Scientific Management* (University of Wisconsin Press, 1980); Samuel Haber, *Efficiency and Uplift: Scientific Management in the Progressive Era, 1890–1920* (University of Chicago Press, 1964); David F. Noble, *America by Design: Science, Technology, and the Rise of Corporate Capitalism* (Knopf, 1977), pp. 264–77.

[*Watertown strike*]: Noble, *America by Design*, p. 272; Nelson, pp. 164–66; see also U.S. Ordnance Department, *Report of the Chief of Ordnance to the Secretary of War: 1913* (U.S. Government Printing Office, 1913), pp. 12–15 and Appendix 1.

["*Train of gearwheels*"]: quoted in Daniels, p. 309.

271 [*"Human engineering"*]: Loren Baritz, *The Servants of Power: A History of the Use of Social Science in American Industry* (1960; reprinted by Greenwood Press, 1974), chs. 8–10 and sources cited therein.
[*"Problem of human relations"*]: quoted in Baritz, p. 190.
[*Union heads on "human relations" approach*]: ibid., p. 183.

271–2 [*Spot welder on his job*]: "J.D.," quoted in Robert H. Guest, "The Rationalization of Management," in Kranzberg and Pursell, pp. 56–59.

272 [*Automation*]: John Diebold, *Automation: Its Impact on Business and Labor* (National Planning Association, May 1959); James R. Bright, "The Development of Automation," in Kranzberg and Pursell, pp. 635–55; Noble, *Forces*, ch. 4 and *passim;* Ben B. Seligman, *Most Notorious Victory: Man in an Age of Automation* (Free Press, 1966); Simon Marcson, ed., *Automation, Alienation and Anomie* (Harper, 1970), esp. parts 2–3.
[*Automatic equipment sales, late 1950s*]: Diebold, p. 22.
[*Automation at Ford*]: ibid., pp. 9–10, observer on "whoosh" quoted at p. 9; Bright, pp. 651–53; Allan Nevins and Frank Ernest Hill, *Ford: Decline and Rebirth, 1933–1962* (Scribner, 1962), pp. 354–57, 364–66.
[*"Magical key of creation"*]: quoted in Diebold, p. 2.

273 [*Carey on automation*]: ibid., p. 35.
[*Fortune's "automatic factory"*]: "The Automatic Factory" and E. W. Leaver and J. J. Brown, "Machines without Men," *Fortune*, vol. 34, no. 5 (November 1946), pp. 160–65, 192–204.
[*Reuther on automation*]: Reuther, "The Impact of Automation," in Reuther, *Selected Papers*, Henry M. Christman, ed. (Macmillan, 1961), pp. 67–100, quoted at p. 76.
[*"Everybody's slice"*]: Diebold, p. 43.
[*Automation and auto worker militancy*]: see Nelson Lichtenstein, "Auto Worker Militancy and the Structure of Factory Life, 1937–1955," *Journal of American History*, vol. 67, no. 2 (September 1980), pp. 335–53; William A. Faunce, "Automation in the Automobile Industry: Some Consequences For In-Plant Social Structure," in Marcson, pp. 169–81.

274 [*Butler on man and machine*]: Butler, *Erewhon, or Over the Range* (A. C. Fifield, 1917), pp. 246, 268.
[*Bell on work and the machine*]: Bell, *Work and Its Discontents* (Beacon Press, 1956), p. 56.
[*Mumford on machine as part of system of power*]: see Mumford, *Technics and Civilization* (Harcourt, 1934), pp. 41–45, 273, 324, and *passim.*
[*Mumford on two technologies*]: Mumford, "Authoritarian and Democratic Technics," *Technology and Culture*, vol. 5, no. 1 (Winter 1964), pp. 1–8, quoted at p. 2.
[*Wiener*]: Norbert Wiener, *The Human Use of Human Beings: Cybernetics and Society* (Houghton Mifflin, 1950); Wiener, *Cybernetics, or Control and Communication in the Animal and the Machine* (Wiley, 1948).

275 [*Alienation and* anomie]: see Emile Durkheim, *The Division of Labor in Society*, George Simpson, trans. (1933; Free Press, 1960); Erich Fromm, *The Sane Society* (Holt, Rinehart and Winston, 1955), ch. 5 and *passim;* Karl Mannheim, *Man and Society in an Age of Reconstruction*, Edward Shils, trans. (Kegan Paul, Trench, Trubner & Co., 1940); Wilbert E. Moore, *Industrial Relations and the Social Order* (Macmillan, 1951), esp. chs. 9–10; Robert Blauner, *Alienation and Freedom: The Factory Worker and His Industry* (University of Chicago Press, 1964), esp. chs. 2, 5; Seligman, *Notorious Victory;* William A. Faunce, "Automation and the Division of Labor," in Marcson, pp. 79–96; Faunce, "Industrialization and Alienation," in *ibid.*, pp. 400–16; Melvin Seeman, "On the Meaning of Alienation," in *ibid.*, pp. 381–94.
[*"Fortune, Chance, Luck"*]: Merton, *Social Theory and Social Structure: Toward the Codification of Theory and Research* (Free Press, 1949), p. 138.
[*Seeman on* anomie]: Seeman, pp. 388–89.

275–6 [*Marcuse on values and labor*]: quoted in Douglas Kellner, *Herbert Marcuse and the Crisis of Marxism* (University of California Press, 1984), p. 140; see also *ibid.*, esp. chs. 6, 10; Marcuse, "Aggressiveness in Advanced Industrial Society," in Marcuse, *Negations: Essays in Critical Theory*, Jeremy J. Shapiro, trans. (Beacon Press, 1968), pp. 248–68; Marcuse, *Eros and Civilization: A Philosophical Inquiry into Freud* (Beacon Press, 1955); H. Stuart Hughes, *The Sea Change: The Migration of Social Thought, 1930–1965* (Harper, 1975), pp. 170–88.

The Language of Freedom

276 [*"Children of freedom"*]: quoted in Adam B. Ulam, *The Rivals: America and Russia Since World War II* (Viking, 1971), p. 157.

[*"Dynamic center"*]: quoted in John P. Mallan, "Luce's Hot-and-Cold War," *New Republic*, vol. 129, no. 9 (September 28, 1953), p. 12.

[*"Founding purpose"*]: Luce, "National Purpose and Cold War," in John K. Jessup, ed., *The Ideas of Henry Luce* (Atheneum, 1969), pp. 131–33, quoted at pp. 131–32.

[*"Elementary truth"*]: quoted in Richard H. Pells, *The Liberal Mind in a Conservative Age: American Intellectuals in the 1940s and 1950s* (Harper, 1985), pp. 124–25.

277 [*"An American Century"*]: Luce, "The American Century," in Jessup, pp. 105–20, quoted at p. 117.

[*"Egotistic corruption"*]: quoted in *ibid.*, p. 16.

[*Luce as Cecil Rhodes of journalism*]: *ibid.*, p. 15.

[*Century of the common man*]: Wallace, "The Price of Free World Victory," in John M. Blum, *The Price of Vision: The Diary of Henry A. Wallace, 1942–1946* (Houghton Mifflin, 1973), pp. 635–40, esp. p. 638.

[*1949 Conference for World Peace*]: Pells, pp. 123–24; Irving Howe, "The Culture Conference," *Partisan Review*, vol. 16, no. 5 (May 1949), pp. 505–11; Joseph P. Lash, "Weekend at the Waldorf," *New Republic*, vol. 120, no. 16 (April 18, 1949), pp. 10–14.

[*Congress for Cultural Freedom*]: Sidney Hook, "The Berlin Congress for Cultural Freedom," *Partisan Review*, vol. 17, no. 7 (September–October 1950), pp. 715–22; Alexander Bloom, *Prodigal Sons: The New York Intellectuals & Their World* (Oxford University Press, 1986), pp. 259–73; Christopher Lasch, "The Cultural Cold War: A Short History of the Congress for Cultural Freedom," in Barton J. Bernstein, ed., *Towards a New Past: Dissenting Essays in American History* (Pantheon, 1968), pp. 322–59; Mary S. McAuliffe, *Crisis on the Left: Cold War Politics and American Liberals, 1947–1954* (University of Massachusetts Press, 1978), pp. 115–29; *New York Times*, April 27, 1966, p. 28; Pells, pp. 128–30.

[*"Opium of the intellectuals"*]: Raymond Aron, *The Opium of the Intellectuals*, Terence Kilmartin, trans. (Norton, 1962).

[*"End of ideology"*]: Bell, *The End of Ideology: On the Exhaustion of Political Ideas in the Fifties*, rev. ed. (Free Press, 1962); see also Edward Shils, "Ideology and Civility: On the Politics of the Individual," *Sewanee Review*, vol. 66, no. 3 (July–September 1958), pp. 450–80; Arthur M. Schlesinger, Jr., "Liberalism in America: A Note for Europeans," in Schlesinger, *The Politics of Hope* (Houghton Mifflin, 1963), ch. 6; James Nuechterlein, "Arthur M. Schlesinger, Jr., and the Discontents of Postwar Liberalism," *Review of Politics*, vol. 39, no. 1 (January 1977), pp. 3–40; Stephen J. Whitfield, "The 1950's: The Era of No Hard Feelings," *South Atlantic Quarterly*, vol. 74, no. 3 (Summer 1975), pp. 289–307, esp. pp. 297–98; Bernard Sternsher, "Liberalism in the Fifties: The Travail of Redefinition," *Antioch Review*, vol. 22, no. 3 (Fall 1962), pp. 315–31; McAuliffe; Pells, esp. ch. 3; John P. Diggins, *The Proud Decades: America in War and in Peace, 1941–1960* (Norton, 1988), ch. 7 *passim*.

277–8 [*Shils on intellectuals*]: Shils, p. 456.

278 [*Pells on intellectuals*]: Pells, p. 181.

[*Shils on social critics and Enlightenment ideals*]: Shils, p. 455.

279 [*Lerner on the new middle classes*]: Lerner, p. 490.

[*Fromm*]: Fromm, *Escape from Freedom* (Rinehart, 1941); Fromm, *Sane Society;* Fromm, *The Revolution of Hope: Toward a Humanized Technology* (Harper, 1968); Fromm, *May Man Prevail?: An Enquiry into the Facts and Fictions of Foreign Policy* (Anchor, 1961); see also John H. Schaar, *Escape from Authority: The Perspectives of Erich Fromm* (Basic Books, 1961), esp. chs. 3–4.

279–80 [*Riesman*]: Riesman, with Reuel Denney and Nathan Glazer, *The Lonely Crowd: A Study of the Changing American Character* (Yale University Press, 1950); Riesman, *Individualism Reconsidered and Other Essays* (Free Press, 1954); see also Seymour Martin Lipset and Leo Lowenthal, eds., *Culture and Social Character: The Work of David Riesman Reviewed* (Free Press, 1954).

280 [*Whyte*]: Whyte, *Organization Man;* see also Robert Lekachman, "Organization Men: The Erosion of Individuality," *Commentary,* vol. 23, no. 3 (March 1957), pp. 270–76.

281 [*Marcuse*]: Marcuse, *One Dimensional Man: Studies in the Ideology of Advanced Industrial Society* (Beacon Press, 1964); Marcuse, *Eros and Civilization;* Marcuse, "Aggressiveness"; Marcuse, *Soviet Marxism: A Critical Analysis* (Columbia University Press, 1958); see also Kellner; Jerzy J. Wiatr, "Herbert Marcuse: Philosopher of a Lost Radicalism," *Science & Society,* vol. 34 (1970), pp. 319–30.
[*Technological advances in newspaper production*]: Frank Luther Mott, *American Journalism: A History, 1690–1960* (Macmillan, 1962), pp. 807–9, *Editor & Publisher* quoted at pp. 807–8.

282 [*Press consolidation*]: *ibid.,* pp. 813–17.
["*Outside the pale*"]: Lerner, p. 762.
[*Press and cold war*]: James Aronson, *The Press and the Cold War* (Beacon Press, 1970); Bernard C. Cohen, *The Press and Foreign Policy* (Princeton University Press, 1963), pp. 36–39 and *passim;* Douglass Cater, *The Fourth Branch of Government* (Houghton Mifflin, 1959); see also Michael Schudson, *Discovering the News: A Social History of American Newspapers* (Basic Books, 1978), ch. 5; Potter, esp. ch. 8.

282–3 [*Protestant on press*]: quoted in Aronson, p. 36.

283 [*MacDougall on press*]: *ibid.,* p. 37.
[*Polls on inevitability of war, 1945, 1948*]: *ibid.*
[*Lippmann and Marshall Plan*]: see Joseph M. Jones, *The Fifteen Weeks (February 21–June 5, 1947)* (Viking, 1955), pp. 226–32.
[*Cater on press as fourth branch*]: see Cater, pp. 2–3, 7–8, 67–74, and *passim.*
[PM]: Roy Hoopes, *Ralph Ingersoll* (Atheneum, 1985), chs. 9–14; Stephen Becker, *Marshall Field III* (Simon and Schuster, 1964), ch. 6 and pp. 398–402; Mott, pp. 771–75; Carey McWilliams, "The Continuing Tradition of Reform Journalism," in John M. Harrison and Harry H. Stein, eds., *Muckraking: Past, Present and Future* (Pennsylvania State University Press, 1973), p. 124; Louis Kronenberger, *No Whippings, No Gold Watches: The Saga of a Writer and His Jobs* (Atlantic Monthly/Little, Brown, 1970), ch. 5.
[*FDR on* PM]: quoted in Becker, p. 209.

284 [Time *circulation growth, 1950s*]: Dan Golenpaul Associates, *Information Please Almanac 1952* (Macmillan, 1951), p. 143; Dan Golenpaul Associates, *Information Please Almanac 1962* (Simon and Schuster, 1961), p. 310.
[*Mass-circulation magazines' circulations*]: Dan Golenpaul Associates, *Information Please Almanac 1957* (Macmillan, 1956), p. 318.
[Life *advertising revenues*]: Robert T. Elson, *The World of Time Inc.: The Intimate History of a Publishing Enterprise, 1941–1960* (Atheneum, 1973), p. 404.
[*Assets of Time Inc.*]: *ibid.,* p. 459.
[*Luce's management of his enterprises*]: Elson, *Time Inc.: 1941–1960;* Elson, *Time Inc.: The Intimate History of a Publishing Enterprise, 1923–1941* (Atheneum, 1968); T. S. Matthews, *Name and Address* (Simon and Schuster, 1960), pp. 215–74; Hoopes, chs. 5–8 *passim;* Kronenberger, ch. 4; Joan Simpson Burns, *The Awkward Embrace: The Creative Artist and the Institution in America* (Knopf, 1975), pp. 142–50; David Cort, "Once Upon a Time Inc.: Mr. Luce's Fact Machine," *Nation,* vol. 182, no. 7 (February 18, 1956), pp. 134–37; John Kobler, *Luce: His Time, Life, and Fortune* (Doubleday, 1968).
[*Luce on editorial convictions*]: Elson, *Time Inc.: 1941–1960,* pp. 74–75.
[*Luce in politics*]: see *ibid.,* chs. 7, 20, 23, and *passim;* Mallan, pp. 12–15; W. A. Swanberg, *Luce and His Empire* (Scribner, 1972), pp. 176–79, 219–22, 268–73, and *passim.*
[*Kobler on Luce and "top performers"*]: quoted in Joan Burns, *Awkward Embrace,* p. 142.
[*Luce and White*]: see Theodore H. White, *In Search of History: A Personal Adventure* (Harper, 1978), pp. 126–30, 205–13, 246–49.

284–5 [*Development of commercial television*]: Erik Barnouw, *A History of Broadcasting in the United States* (Oxford University Press, 1966–70), vol. 2, pp. 293–95 and *passim,* and vol. 3, chs. 1–2; James L. Baughman, "Television in the 'Golden Age': An Entrepreneurial Experiment," *Historian,* vol. 47, no. 2 (February, 1985), pp. 175–95; Leo Bogart, *The Age of Television: A Study of Viewing Habits and the Impact of Television on American Life* (Frederick Ungar, 1956); James L. Baughman, "The National Purpose and the Newest Medium: Liberal Critics of Television, 1958–1960," *Mid-America,* vol. 64, no. 2

(April–July 1982), pp. 41–55; William Y. Elliott, ed., *Television's Impact on American Culture* (Michigan State University Press, 1956).

285   [*Radio in the 1950s*]: J. Fred MacDonald, *Don't Touch That Dial* (Nelson-Hall, 1979), pp. 85–90; Arnold Passman, *The Deejays* (Macmillan, 1971).

285–6   [*Democratic and Republican parties, 1950s*]: Gary W. Reichard, "Divisions and Dissent: Democrats and Foreign Policy, 1952–1956," *Political Science Quarterly*, vol. 93, no. 1 (Spring 1978), pp. 51–72; Reichard, *The Reaffirmation of Republicanism: Eisenhower and the Eighty-third Congress* (University of Tennessee Press, 1975); Herbert S. Parmet, *The Democrats: The Years After FDR* (Macmillan, 1976), part 2; Samuel Lubell, *Revolt of the Moderates* (Harper, 1956); Norman A. Graebner, *The New Isolationism: A Study in Politics and Foreign Policy Since 1950* (Ronald Press, 1956); Ralph M. Goldman, *Search for Consensus: The Story of the Democratic Party* (Temple University Press, 1979), pp. 196–207; James MacGregor Burns, *The Deadlock of Democracy: Four-Party Politics in America* (Prentice-Hall, 1963), part 3; James L. Sundquist, *Politics and Policy: The Eisenhower, Kennedy, and Johnson Years* (Brookings Institution, 1968), part 2, esp. ch. 9.

286   [*Divine on containment in 1948 campaign*]: Divine, "The Cold War and the Election of 1948," *Journal of American History*, vol. 59, no. 1 (June 1972), pp. 90–110, quoted at p. 110.
[*Newspaper support of Wallace, 1948*]: see Aronson, p. 47.
[*Election results, 1956*]: Arthur M. Schlesinger, Jr., ed., *History of American Presidential Elections, 1789–1968* (Chelsea House, 1971), vol. 4, p. 3445.

287   [*Democratic Advisory Committee*]: Parmet, pp. 151–61; John Bartlow Martin, *Adlai Stevenson and the World* (Doubleday, 1977), pp. 395–402; Sundquist, pp. 405–15; Goldman, pp. 202–4; Burns, *Deadlock*, pp. 254–55.
["*Strong, searching*"]: quoted in Martin, p. 395.
[*1956 campaign*]: Malcolm Moos, "Election of 1956," in Schlesinger, *Elections*, vol. 4, pp. 3341–54; Martin, ch. 2; Reichard, "Divisions," pp. 65–69; Walter Johnson, ed., *The Papers of Adlai E. Stevenson: Toward a New America, 1955–1957* (Little, Brown, 1976); Dwight D. Eisenhower, *The White House Years: Waging Peace, 1956–1961* (Doubleday, 1965), ch. 1; Kenneth S. Davis, *A Prophet in His Own Country: The Triumphs and Defeats of Adlai E. Stevenson* (Doubleday, 1957), chs. 28–29; Robert A. Divine, *Foreign Policy and U.S. Presidential Elections, 1952–1960* (New Viewpoints, 1974), chs. 3–4.

287–8   [*Eleanor Roosevelt, mid-1950s*]: Eleanor Roosevelt, *On My Own* (Harper, 1958), chs. 10–22; Joseph P. Lash, *Eleanor: The Years Alone* (Norton, 1972), chs. 11–13; Tamara K. Hareven, *Eleanor Roosevelt: An American Conscience* (Quadrangle, 1968), pp. 210–14.

Dilemmas of Freedom

288   [*Hofstadter on the intellectual*]: quoted in James MacGregor Burns, *Leadership* (Harper, 1978), p. 141.

289   ["*Physicists have known sin*"]: quoted in Whitfield, p. 292.
[*Lippmann in the postwar world*]: Lippmann, *The Cold War: A Study in U.S. Foreign Policy* (Harper, 1947); Lippmann, *Essays in the Public Philosophy* (Atlantic Monthly/Little, Brown, 1955); Ronald Steel, *Walter Lippmann and the American Century* (Atlantic Monthly/Little, Brown, 1980), chs. 32–41 *passim;* Anwar Hussain Syed, *Walter Lippmann's Philosophy of International Politics* (University of Pennsylvania Press, 1963), 340–44 *and passim;* Barton J. Bernstein, "Walter Lippmann and the Early Cold War," in Thomas G. Paterson, ed., *Cold War Critics: Alternatives to American Foreign Policy in the Truman Years* (Quadrangle, 1971), pp. 18–53; Kenneth W. Thompson, *Political Realism and the Crisis of World Politics: An American Approach to Foreign Policy* (Princeton University Press, 1960), pp. 38–50.
[*Lippmann on popular rule*]: *The Public Philosophy*, pp. 14, 61.

289–90   [*MacLeish on Lippmann and Lippmann's reply*]: MacLeish, "The Alternative," *Yale Review*, vol. 44, no. 4 (June 1955), pp. 481–96, esp. p. 487; Lippmann, "A Rejoinder," *ibid.*, pp. 497–500.

290   [*Kennan's continued opposition to "legalistic-moralistic" approach*]: see Kennan, "Morality and Foreign Policy," *Foreign Affairs*, vol. 64, no. 2 (Winter 1985–86), pp. 205–18; Kennan, *Memoirs*, 2 vols. (Atlantic Monthly/Little, Brown, 1967–72); Kennan, *American Diplomacy, 1900–1950* (University of Chicago Press, 1951); Kennan, *Realities of*

American Foreign Policy (Norton, 1966); Kennan, *Soviet-American Relations, 1917–1920,* 2 vols. (Princeton University Press, 1956–58); Kennan, *Russia and the West Under Lenin and Stalin* (Little, Brown, 1961).

290 [*Pitfalls of "realism"*]: see Christopher Lasch, " 'Realism' as a Critique of American Diplomacy," in Lasch, *The World of Nations: Reflections on American History, Politics & Culture* (Knopf, 1973), pp. 205–15; Robert C. Good, "The National Interest and Political Realism: Niebuhr's 'Debate' with Morgenthau and Kennan," *Journal of Politics,* vol. 22, no. 4 (November 1960), pp. 597–619; Thompson, *Political Realism,* pp. 50–61; Dean Acheson, "The Illusion of Disengagement," *Foreign Affairs,* vol. 36, no. 3 (April 1958), pp. 371–82; John W. Coffey, "George Kennan and the Ambiguities of Realism," *South Atlantic Quarterly,* vol. 73, no. 2 (Spring 1974), pp. 184–98.

291 [*Morgenthau*]: Morgenthau, *Scientific Man vs. Power Politics* (University of Chicago Press, 1946); Morgenthau, *Politics Among Nations: The Struggle for Power and Peace* (Knopf, 1948); Morgenthau, *In Defense of the National Interest: A Critical Examination of American Foreign Policy* (Knopf, 1951); Morgenthau, *The Impasse of American Foreign Policy* (University of Chicago Press, 1962); George Eckstein, "Hans Morgenthau: A Personal Memoir," *Social Research,* vol. 48, no. 4 (Winter 1981), pp. 641–52; *ibid.,* vol. 48, no. 4 (Winter 1981), *passim;* Robert W. Tucker, "Professor Morgenthau's Theory of Political 'Realism,' " *American Political Science Review,* vol. 46, no. 1 (March 1952), pp. 214–24; Stanley Hoffmann, "Realism and Its Discontents," *Atlantic,* vol. 256, no. 5 (November 1985), pp. 131–36; Kenneth W. Thompson, "Moral Reasoning in American Thought on War and Peace," *Review of Politics,* vol. 39, no. 3 (July 1977), pp. 386–99, esp. pp. 391–94; see also Thompson, *Morality and Foreign Policy* (Louisiana State University Press, 1980).
[*"Lust for power"*]: Morgenthau, *Scientific Man,* p. 9.
[*"We must sin"*]: *ibid.,* p. 201; see also Kenneth W. Thompson, *Moralism and Morality in Politics and Diplomacy* (University Press of America, 1985), pp. 93–107.
[*Morgenthau on public opinion*]: Morgenthau, "What Is Wrong with Our Foreign Policy," in *Impasse,* pp. 68–94, quoted at p. 74.

292 [*Niebuhr*]: Niebuhr, *Moral Man and Immoral Society: A Study in Ethics and Politics* (Scribner, 1932); Niebuhr, *The Irony of American History* (Scribner, 1952); Niebuhr, *Christian Realism and Political Problems* (Scribner, 1953); Niebuhr, *The Structure of Nations and Empires* (Scribner, 1959); Richard W. Fox, *Reinhold Niebuhr* (Pantheon, 1985); Fox, "Reinhold Niebuhr and the Emergence of the Liberal Realist Faith, 1930–1945," *Review of Politics,* vol. 38, no. 2 (April 1976), pp. 244–65; Donald B. Meyer, *The Protestant Search for Political Realism, 1919–1941* (University of California Press, 1960), esp. chs. 13–14; Charles Frankel, *The Case for Modern Man* (Harper, 1955), ch. 6; Good; Arthur M. Schlesinger, Jr., "Reinhold Niebuhr's Role in American Political Thought and Life," in Schlesinger, *Politics of Hope,* pp. 97–125; Morton White, "Of Moral Predicaments" (review of Niebuhr, *Irony*), *New Republic,* vol. 126, no. 18 (May 5, 1952), pp. 18–19.

293 [*"Companionship in a common purpose"*]: quoted in Fox, "Niebuhr and Emergence," p. 260.
[*"Play hardball"*]: quoted in William E. Leuchtenburg, "Preacher of Paradox" (review of Fox, *Niebuhr*), *Atlantic,* vol. 257, no. 1 (January 1986), p. 94.
[*"Father of us all"*]: quoted in Fox, "Niebuhr and Emergence," p. 245.
[*"Spiritual father"*]: *ibid.*
[*"Atheists for Niebuhr"*]: Thompson, "Moral Reasoning," p. 387.
[*"Dizziness of freedom"*]: quoted in Frankel, p. 88.
[*"Narcosis of the soul"*]: *ibid.,* p. 89.
[*"Instant Niebuhrian"*]: Harvey Cox, "In the Pulpit and on the Barricades" (review of Fox, *Niebuhr*), *New York Times Book Review,* January 5, 1986, pp. 1, 24–25, quoted at p. 24.

294 [*"Russia, the Atom and the West"*]: Kennan, *Russia, the Atom and the West* (Harper, 1958); see also Kennan, *Memoirs,* vol. 2, ch. 10.
[*De Gaulle on Lippmann*]: quoted in Steel, p. 495.
[*American products in Europe*]: see Edward A. McCreary, *The Americanization of Europe: The Impact of Americans and American Business on the Uncommon Market* (Doubleday, 1964), pp. 13–15, 89–90.

295 [*American corporations in Europe*]: see *ibid.*, ch. 4; Mayne, pp. 112–17.
["*49th State*"]: British shipowner, quoted in Visson, p. 68.
["*Americans are not served*"]: *ibid.*
[*American product failures in Europe*]: McCreary, p. 91; see also *ibid.*, pp. 128–35; Mayne, pp. 114–15.
[*European view of America's "imperialism," "dollar noose," and "shabby money-lending"*]: Visson, pp. 13, 75, 115, and *passim;* Bruce Hutchinson, *Canada's Lonely Neighbor* (Longmans, Green, 1954), p. 11 and *passim;* "Why Is US Prestige Declining?," *New Republic*, vol. 131, no. 8 (August 23, 1954), p. 8; Jean Rikhoff Hills, "The British Press on 'The Yanks,' " *ibid.*, pp. 9–12; Franz M. Joseph, ed., *As Others See Us: The United States through Foreign Eyes* (Princeton University Press, 1959).
["*Spiritual standardization*"]: quoted in Visson, p. 161.
["*Coco-colonization*"]: Mayne, p. 115.
[*Koestler on American ubiquity*]: quoted in Wilson P. Dizard, *The Strategy of Truth: The Story of the U.S. Information Service* (Public Affairs Press, 1961), p. 10.

296 [*USIA*]: Dizard; Thomas C. Sorenson, *The Word War: The Story of American Propaganda* (Harper, 1968); Thomas C. Reeves, *The Life and Times of Joe McCarthy* (Stein & Day, 1982), pp. 476–91 *passim;* Robert E. Elder, *The Information Machine: The United States Information Agency and American Foreign Policy* (Syracuse University Press, 1968).
["*McCarthyism . . . is a tragedy*"]: Hutchinson, p. 26.
["*France was a land*"]: quoted in Dizard, p. 20.
[*Ford Foundation international programs*]: Dwight Macdonald, *The Ford Foundation: The Men and the Millions* (Reynal & Co., 1956), p. 60 and *passim;* Edward H. Berman, *The Influence of the Carnegie, Ford, and Rockefeller Foundations on American Foreign Policy: The Ideology of Philanthropy* (State University of New York Press, 1983).
[*Ford support of Congress for Cultural Freedom*]: Berman, pp. 143–45, "combat tyranny" quoted at p. 144.

297 [*Lewis in France*]: Thelma M. Smith and Ward L. Miner, *Transatlantic Migrations: The Contemporary American Novel in France* (Duke University Press, 1955), p. 17.
["*Greatest literary development*"]: quoted in *ibid.*, pp. 20–21; see also Henri Peyre, "American Literature Through French Eyes," *Virginia Quarterly Review*, vol. 23, no. 3 (Summer 1947), pp. 421–38.

298 [*Gide on American literature*]: Smith and Miner, p. 21.
[*French appreciation of Hemingway*]: see *ibid.*, ch. 8 and *passim;* Roger Asselineau, "French Reactions to Hemingway's Works Between the Two World Wars," in Asselineau, ed., *The Literary Reputation of Hemingway in Europe* (New York University Press, 1965), pp. 39–72; Peyre, p. 435.
[*Maurois on Hemingway's subjects*]: Maurois, "Ernest Hemingway," in Carlos Baker, ed., *Hemingway and His Critics: An International Anthology* (Hill and Wang, 1961), p. 38.
[*Sales of French-language* Bell Tolls]: Smith and Miner, p. 30.
[*French appreciation of Faulkner*]: see *ibid.*, ch. 9.
["*Magical, fantastic*"]: quoted in *ibid.*, pp. 129–30.
[*Sartre on Faulkner and de Beauvoir*]: *ibid.*, pp. 62–63.
[*Faulkner as "universal writer"*]: see *ibid.*, p. 141.
[*German on cadging American books*]: Hans Magnus Enzenberger, "Mann, Kafka and the Katzenjammer Kids," *New York Times Book Review*, November 11, 1985, pp. 1, 37–39, quoted at p. 37.
["*Thoughtful and barbaric*"]: quoted in Mayne, p. 109.

299 [*Hemingway's politics*]: see Scott Donaldson, *By Force of Will: The Life and Art of Ernest Hemingway* (Viking, 1977), ch. 5; John Killinger, *Hemingway and the Dead Gods: A Study in Existentialism* (University of Kentucky Press, 1960), esp. ch. 5; Carlos Baker, *Hemingway: The Writer as Artist* (Princeton University Press, 1963), pp. 197–202, ch. 10 and *passim;* Ray B. West, Jr., "Ernest Hemingway: The Failure of Sensibility," *Sewanee Review*, vol. 53 (1945), pp. 120–35; Lionel Trilling, "Hemingway and His Critics," in Baker, *Hemingway and His Critics*, pp. 61–70.
["*You believe in Life*"]: Hemingway, *For Whom the Bell Tolls* (Scribner, 1940), p. 305.
["*Presentness of the past*"]: Hyatt H. Waggoner, "William Harrison Faulkner," in John A. Garraty, ed., *Encyclopedia of American Biography* (Harper, 1974), pp. 343–45, quoted at p. 344.

299 [*Faulkner in two American traditions*]: *ibid.*, p. 344.

[*Faulkner and public and private values*]: Faulkner, "Speech of Acceptance upon the Award of the Nobel Prize for Literature," in *The Faulkner Reader* (Random House, 1954), pp. 3–4; Hyatt H. Waggoner, *William Faulkner: From Jefferson to the World* (University of Kentucky Press, 1959), esp. chs. 11–12; R. W. B. Lewis, "William Faulkner: The Hero in the New World," in Robert Penn Warren, ed., *Faulkner: A Collection of Critical Essays* (Prentice-Hall, 1966), pp. 204–18; Edmund Wilson, "William Faulkner's Reply to the Civil-Rights Program," in *ibid.*, pp. 219–25; Vincent F. Hopper, "Faulkner's Paradise Lost," *Virginia Quarterly Review*, vol. 23, no. 3 (Summer 1947), pp. 405–20; see also Joseph Blotner, *Faulkner*, 2 vols. (Random House, 1974). [*"Moving from a terror"*]: quoted in Hopper, p. 420.

300 [*"We prate of freedom"*]: quoted in George W. Nitchie, *Human Values in the Poetry of Robert Frost: A Study of a Poet's Convictions* (Duke University Press, 1960), pp. 88–89.

[*"Keep off each other"*]: "Build Soil—A Political Pastoral," in Robert Frost, *Complete Poems* (Holt, Rinehart and Winston, 1963), pp. 421–30, quoted at p. 429.

[*"Freedom I'd like to give"*]: quoted in Lawrance R. Thompson, *Fire and Ice: The Art and Thought of Robert Frost* (Henry Holt, 1942), p. 216; see also *ibid.*, pp. 177–232 *passim*; Nitchie; Malcolm Cowley, "Frost: A Dissenting Opinion" and "The Case Against Mr. Frost: II," *New Republic*, vol. 111, no. 11 (September 11, 1944), pp. 312–13, and no. 12 (September 18, 1944), pp. 345–47; William H. Pritchard, *Frost: A Literary Life Reconsidered* (Oxford University Press, 1984).

[*Hicks on Frost*]: Hicks, "The World of Robert Frost," *New Republic*, vol. 65, no. 835 (December 3, 1930), pp. 77–78, quoted at p. 78.

[*"Wise primitive"*]: Mailer, "The White Negro: Superficial Reflections on the Hipster," in Mailer, *Advertisements for Myself* (Putnam, 1959), pp. 337–58, quoted at p. 343.

[*Miller*]: Arthur Miller, *Timebends: A Life* (Grove Press, 1987); Leonard Moss, *Arthur Miller* (Twayne, 1967); Robert A. Martin, ed., *The Theatre Essays of Arthur Miller* (Viking, 1978); Benjamin Nelson, *Arthur Miller: Portrait of a Playwright* (David McKay, 1970); Richard Corrigan, ed., *Arthur Miller* (Prentice-Hall, 1969).

[*"Right dramatic form"*]: Miller, "The Family in Modern Drama," in Martin, pp. 69–85, quoted at p. 85.

301 [*"I always said"*]: Miller, "Introduction to the *Collected Plays*," in *ibid.*, pp. 113–70, quoted at p. 141; see also Richard T. Brucher, "Willy Loman and *The Soul of a New Machine*: Technology and the Common Man," *Journal of American Studies*, vol. 17, no. 3 (December 1983), pp. 325–36.

[*Europeans on America's commitment to freedom*]: see Wagner in Kaiser and Schwarz, pp. 19–32, esp. pp. 24–25; see also Jean-Paul Sartre, "Individualism and Conformism in the United States," in Sartre, *Literary and Philosophical Essays*, Annette Michelson, trans. (Criterion Books, 1955), pp. 97–106.

[*Shaw on Americans*]: quoted in Wagner, p. 25.

[*Khrushchev's meeting with American labor leaders*]: "Free Labor Meets Khrushchev," in Reuther, *Papers*, pp. 299–315, quoted at pp. 312, 313; *Khrushchev in America* (Crosscurrents Press, 1960), pp. 124–40; see also Herbert Mitgang, *Freedom to See: The Khrushchev Broadcast and Its Meaning for America* (Fund for the Republic, April 1958); Alexander Rapoport, "The Russian Broadcasts of the Voice of America," *Russian Review*, vol. 16, no. 3 (July 1957), pp. 3–14; Alexander Anikst, "American Books and Soviet Readers," *New World Review*, vol. 4, no. 3 (March 1956), pp. 18–20; Melville J. Ruggles, "American Books in Soviet Publishing," *Slavic Review*, vol. 20 (1961), pp. 419–35.

7. THE FREE AND THE UNFREE

303 [*Lives of the poor*]: see Robert L. Heilbroner, *The Great Ascent: The Struggle for Economic Development in Our Time* (Harper, 1963), chs. 2–3; see also Aidan W. Southall and Peter C. W. Gutkind, *Townsmen in the Making: Kampala and Its Suburbs* (East African Institute of Social Research, 1957).

[*Untouchable children in lime pits*]: Margaret Bourke-White, *Halfway to Freedom: A Report on the New India* (Simon and Schuster, 1949), ch. 14.

304 [*Division of world GNP*]: P. N. Rothenstein-Rodan, "International Aid for Under-

developed Countries," *Review of Economics and Statistics*, vol. 43, no. 2 (May 1961), p. 118 (Table 1-A).

304 [*GNP per capita*]: *ibid.*, p. 118 (Table 1-B); see also *ibid.*, p. 126 (Table 2-C); Paul G. Hoffman, *World Without Want* (Harper, 1962), pp. 38–39 (Table 1).

[*Population growth and its causes*]: J. O. Hertzler, *The Crisis in World Population* (University of Nebraska Press, 1956), pp. 20–21 (Table 1), p. 22 (Figure 1), p. 23 (Table 2).

[*Nationalism, war, and decolonization*]: Peter Worsley, *The Third World*, 2nd ed. (University of Chicago Press, 1970), chs. 2–3; T. O. Lloyd, *The British Empire, 1558–1983* (Oxford University Press, 1984), pp. 276–92, 312–20; Milton Osborne, *Region of Revolt: Focus on Southeast Asia* (Penguin, 1970), ch. 5; Tony Smith, "Introduction," in Tony Smith, ed., *The End of the European Empire: Decolonization After World War II* (D. C. Heath, 1975), pp. vii–xxiii; Rudolf von Albertini, "The Impact of the Two World Wars on the Decline of Colonialism," in *ibid.*, pp. 3–19; William R. Louis, *Imperialism at Bay: The United States and the Decolonization of the British Empire, 1941–1945* (Oxford University Press, 1978).

[*Worsley on sense of common fate*]: Worsley, p. 84.

["*O masters, lords*"]: "The Man with the Hoe," in Markham, *The Man with the Hoe and Other Poems* (Doubleday, Page, 1913), pp. 15–18, quoted at pp. 17, 18.

305 [*Imperviousness of Indian villages*]: see Kusum Nair, *Blossoms in the Dust: The Human Element in Indian Development* (Gerald Duckworth, 1961).

[*Forms of nationalist revolt and postcolonial government*]: see Worsley, chs. 3–5.

The Boston Irish

306 [*Numbers of Irish immigrants into Boston, late 1840s–1850s*]: Oscar Handlin, *Boston's Immigrants, 1790–1865: A Study in Acculturation* (Harvard University Press, 1941), p. 229 (Table 5).

[*Irish famine*]: Thomas Gallagher, *Paddy's Lament, Ireland 1846–1847: Prelude to Hatred* (Harcourt, 1982), ch. 1 and *passim;* Cecil Woodham-Smith, *The Great Hunger: Ireland, 1845–9* (Hamish Hamilton, 1962); R. Dudley Edwards and T. Desmond Williams, eds., *The Great Famine: Studies in Irish History, 1845–52* (Browne and Nolan, 1956).

[*Famine deaths and emigration*]: see William P. MacArthur, "Medical History of the Famine," in Edwards and Williams, pp. 308–12; William V. Shannon, *The American Irish* (Macmillan, 1966), p. 1; Oliver MacDonagh, "Irish Emigration to the United States of America and the British Colonies during the Famine," in Edwards and Williams, pp. 317–88, esp. p. 388 (Appendix 1).

[*Ireland under British rule*]: J. C. Beckett, *The Making of Modern Ireland, 1603–1923* (Knopf, 1966); T. W. Freeman, *Pre-Famine Ireland: A Study in Historical Geography* (Manchester University Press, 1957); Thomas A. Emmet, *Ireland Under English Rule, or A Plea for the Plaintiff*, 2 vols. (Knickerbocker Press, 1903); Lawrence J. McCaffrey, *The Irish Question, 1800–1922* (University of Kentucky Press, 1968); Edward M. Levine, *The Irish and Irish Politicians: A Study of Cultural and Social Alienation* (University of Notre Dame Press, 1966), ch. 2; Kevin B. Nowlan, "The Political Background," in Edwards and Williams, ch. 3; Shannon, ch. 1.

["*Always went forth*"]: quoted in Shannon, p. 9.

307 [*Irish in Boston*]: Handlin; Levine, ch. 3; Donald B. Cole, *Immigrant City: Lawrence, Massachusetts, 1845–1921* (University of North Carolina Press, 1963), esp. ch. 3; Shannon, ch. 11, also ch. 2; see also Gallagher, ch. 23; Woodham-Smith, ch. 12.

[*Irish in sports*]: Carl Wittke, *The Irish in America* (Louisiana State University Press, 1956), ch. 24; Shannon, pp. 95–102.

[*Irish in politics*]: Levine, esp. chs. 4–5; Arthur Mann, *Yankee Reformers in the Urban Age* (Belknap Press of Harvard University Press, 1954), ch. 2; Handlin, ch. 5; Shannon, chs. 4–5; Edgar Litt, *Beyond Pluralism: Ethnic Politics in America* (Scott, Foresman, 1970), ch. 8; see also Wittke, ch. 10; Nathan Glazer and Daniel Patrick Moynihan, *Beyond the Melting Pot: The Negroes, Puerto Ricans, Jews, Italians and Irish of New York City* (MIT Press, 1963), pp. 217–87.

308 [*Irish economic progress*]: Stephan Thernstrom, *The Other Bostonians: Poverty and Progress in an American Metropolis, 1880–1970* (Harvard University Press, 1973), esp. pp. 130–44, 160–75; Handlin, esp. ch. 3; Cole, chs. 3–4, 7, and *passim;* Wittke, chs. 3–5, 7, 21;

Marjorie R. Fallows, *Irish Americans: Identity and Assimilation* (Prentice-Hall, 1979), chs. 4–5; H. M. Gitelman, "The Waltham System and the Coming of the Irish," *Labor History*, vol. 8, no. 3 (Fall 1967), pp. 227–53; Stephen Birmingham, *Real Lace: America's Irish Rich* (Harper, 1973); Shannon, ch. 6.

308 [*"None need apply"*]: quoted in Handlin, p. 67.

[*Irish in* Puck]: John J. Appel, "From Shanties to Lace Curtain: The Irish Image in *Puck, 1876–1910*," *Comparative Studies in Society and History*, vol. 13 (1971), pp. 365–75, quoted at p. 367; see also Shannon, ch. 9.

[*Continued social exclusion of Irish*]: see Helen Howe, *The Gentle Americans, 1864–1960: Biography of a Breed* (Harper, 1965), pp. 97–99; Cleveland Amory, *The Proper Bostonians* (E. P. Dutton, 1947), esp. ch. 15; Birmingham; Rose Fitzgerald Kennedy, *Times to Remember* (Doubleday, 1974), pp. 49–52; Richard J. Whalen, *The Founding Father: The Story of Joseph P. Kennedy* (New American Library, 1964), pp. 24–27, 34, 59, 401–2, 417–18; David E. Koskoff, *Joseph P. Kennedy: A Life and Times* (Prentice-Hall, 1974), pp. 18–19, 378–80.

309 [*Limits of Irish liberalism*]: see Levine, chs. 4–6; Mann, ch. 2; Glazer and Moynihan, pp. 229–34, 264–74; Litt, ch. 8; Fallows, ch. 8.

[*Two Patrick Kennedys*]: Tim Pat Coogan, "Sure, and It's County Kennedy Now," *New York Times Magazine*, June 23, 1963, pp. 7–9, 32–36; Koskoff, chs. 1–2; Whalen, ch. 1; see also the genealogical tables in James MacGregor Burns, *Edward Kennedy and the Camelot Legacy* (Norton, 1976), pp. 344–46.

[*Honey Fitz*]: Doris Kearns Goodwin, *The Fitzgeralds and the Kennedys* (Simon and Schuster, 1987), book 1; John Henry Cutler, *"Honey Fitz": Three Steps to the White House* (Bobbs-Merrill, 1962); Kennedy, chs. 2–5; Francis Russell, *The Great Interlude: Neglected Events and Persons from the First World War to the Depression* (McGraw-Hill, 1964), pp. 162–90.

310 [*Joe Kennedy*]: Whalen; Koskoff; Goodwin, book 2 *passim;* Michael R. Beschloss, *Kennedy and Roosevelt: The Uneasy Alliance* (Norton, 1980); Birmingham, ch. 16; Matthew Josephson, *The Money Lords: The Great Finance Capitalists, 1925–1950* (Weybright and Talley, 1972), pp. 176–87.

[*John Kennedy and Catholicism*]: see Garry Wills, *The Kennedy Imprisonment: A Meditation on Power* (Atlantic Monthly/Little, Brown, 1982), p. 61; Lawrence H. Fuchs, *John F. Kennedy and American Catholicism* (Meredith Press, 1967); James MacGregor Burns, *John Kennedy: A Political Profile* (Harcourt, 1960), ch. 13; Donald F. Crosby, *God, Church, and Flag: Senator Joseph R. McCarthy and the Catholic Church, 1950–1957* (University of North Carolina Press, 1978), p. 35; Arthur M. Schlesinger, Jr., *A Thousand Days: John F. Kennedy in the White House* (Houghton Mifflin, 1965), pp. 107–8; see also Goodwin, p. 635.

[*Kennedy and liberalism*]: see Schlesinger, pp. 9–19; Burns, *Profile*, pp. 73–81, 132–36, 264–68; Crosby, pp. 106–7; Herbert S. Parmet, *Jack: The Struggles of John F. Kennedy* (Dial Press, 1980), pp. 175–82, 188–89, 461–62, and ch. 26; David Burner and Thomas R. West, *The Torch Is Passed: The Kennedy Brothers and American Liberalism* (Atheneum, 1984), ch. 3 *passim*.

[*Schlesinger on Kennedy's detachment*]: Schlesinger, p. 108; see also Goodwin, pp. 752–55.

[*Kennedy's womanizing*]: see Joan Blair and Clay Blair, Jr., *The Search For J.F.K.* (Berkley, 1976), *passim;* Wills, chs. 1–2.

311 [*Curley*]: Joseph F. Dineen, *The Purple Shamrock: The Hon. James Michael Curley of Boston* (Norton, 1949); James Michael Curley, *I'd Do It Again* (Prentice-Hall, 1957); Russell, pp. 191–212; Shannon, ch. 12.

[*Kennedy's first congressional campaign*]: Parmet, ch. 10; Whalen, ch. 22; Blair and Blair, part 4; Goodwin, pp. 705–21; Koskoff, pp. 405–9; Burns, *Profile*, ch. 4; Kennedy, pp. 306–20.

[*The two Joseph Russos*]: Koskoff, p. 407; Cutler, p. 308; independent anonymous source.

[*Kennedy in the House*]: Blair and Blair, chs. 41–43; Parmet, chs. 11–12; Burns, *Profile*, ch. 5; Goodwin, ch. 40.

312 [*"Felt like a worm there"*]: Interview with Senator John F. Kennedy, 1959.

[*Kennedy's Senate campaign*]: Parmet, ch. 13; Burns, *Profile*, ch. 6; Goodwin, pp. 755–68; Kennedy, pp. 320–27; Crosby, pp. 108–11; Whalen, ch. 23; Koskoff, pp. 413–17.

312 [*Kennedy's distance from other Democrats*]: see Parmet, p. 254.
[*Joe Kennedy and the* Post]: Koskoff, pp. 415-16; Whalen, pp. 429-31; Parmet, pp. 242-43.
313 [*Kennedy and McCarthyism*]: Burns, *Profile*, ch. 8; Crosby, pp. 108-13, 205-16; Parmet, pp. 243-52, 300-11.

The Southern Poor

[*Macon County, 1930s*]: Charles S. Johnson, *Shadow of the Plantation* (University of Chicago Press, 1934; reprinted 1979), p. 100.
314 [*FDR on the South*]: message to the Conference on Economic Conditions of the South, July 4, 1938, in *The Public Papers and Addresses of Franklin D. Roosevelt*, Samuel I. Rosenman, comp. (Random House, 1938-50), vol. 7, pp. 421-22, quoted at p. 421.
[*Proportion of American poor black families in South*]: Alan Batchelder, "Poverty: The Special Case of the Negro," in Louis A. Ferman, Joyce L. Kornbluh, and Alan Haber, eds., *Poverty in America* (University of Michigan Press, 1965), p. 114.
[*Plessy v. Ferguson*]: 163 U.S. 537 (1896).
[*Black poverty and class structure in South*]: see John Dollard, *Caste and Class in a Southern Town*, 3rd ed. (Doubleday Anchor, 1957), ch. 5 and *passim;* Morton Rubin, *Plantation County* (University of North Carolina Press, 1951), pp. 123-32 and *passim;* Nathan Hare, "Recent Trends in the Occupational Mobility of Negroes, 1930-1960: An Intracohort Analysis," *Social Forces*, vol. 44, no. 2 (December 1965), pp. 166-73; Batchelder in Ferman et al., pp. 112-19; Tom Kahn, "The Economics of Equality," in *ibid.*, pp. 153-72; Vivian W. Henderson, *The Economic Status of Negroes: In the Nation and in the South* (Southern Regional Council, 1963); Charles S. Johnson, *Growing Up in the Black Belt: Negro Youth in the Rural South* (1941; Schocken Books, 1967); Johnson, *Shadow;* Robert Coles, *Children of Crisis* (Little, Brown, 1967-78), vol. 2, chs. 4, 7; V. O. Key, Jr., *Southern Politics in State and Nation* (Knopf, 1949), esp. part 5; Truman M. Pierce et al., *White and Negro Schools in the South: An Analysis of Biracial Education* (Prentice-Hall, 1955); see also Neil R. Peirce, *The Deep South States of America* (Norton, 1974); Jack Bass and Walter DeVries, *The Transformation of Southern Politics: Social Change and Political Consequence Since 1945* (Basic Books, 1976).
[*Peonage*]: Pete Daniel, *The Shadow of Slavery: Peonage in the South, 1901-1969* (University of Illinois Press, 1972), p. 188 and *passim.*
[*Rowan in the South*]: Rowan, *South of Freedom* (Knopf, 1952).
["*Momma, momma*"]: *ibid.*, p. 40.
315 [*Black migration from Southeast, 1950s*]: Selz C. Mayo and C. Horace Hamilton, "The Rural Negro Population of the South in Transition," *Phylon*, vol. 24, no. 2 (July 1963), p. 165.
[*Decline in proportion of American blacks in Southeast, 1940-60*]: *ibid.*, p. 161.
[*Decline in black farm population*]: *ibid.* (Table 1).
[*Migrant workers*]: Dale Wright, *They Harvest Despair: The Migrant Farm Worker* (Beacon Press, 1965); Truman Moore, *The Slaves We Rent* (Random House, 1965); Michael Harrington, *The Other America: Poverty in the United States* (Macmillan, 1962), pp. 48-56; Coles, vol. 2, chs. 3, 8.
[*Black migration within South and economic opportunities*]: Mayo and Hamilton, pp. 162, 166-71.
[*Black women as household or service laborers*]: *ibid.*, p. 168 (Table 5).
316 [*Appalachia*]: Harry M. Caudill, *Night Comes to the Cumberlands: A Biography of a Depressed Area* (Atlantic Monthly/Little, Brown, 1963), esp. parts 5-7; William J. Page, Jr., and Earl E. Huyck, "Appalachia: Realities of Deprivation," in Ben B. Seligman, ed., *Poverty as a Public Issue* (Free Press, 1965), pp. 152-76; Laurel Shackelford and Bill Weinberg, *Our Appalachia* (Hill and Wang, 1977); Roul Tunley, "The Strange Case of West Virginia," *Saturday Evening Post*, vol. 232, no. 32 (February 6, 1960), pp. 19-21, 64-66; William H. Turner, "Blacks in Appalachian America: Reflections on Biracial Education and Unionism," *Phylon*, vol. 44, no. 3 (1983), pp. 198-208.
["*Low income, high unemployment*"]: Page and Huyck, p. 153.
["*Fire every damn Nigger*"]: Interview with Milburn (Big Bud) Jackson, in Shackelford and Weinberg, pp. 300-3, quoted at p. 302.

316 [*Harlan County*]: see John W. Hevener, *Which Side Are You On?: The Harlan County Coal Miners, 1931–39* (University of Illinois Press, 1978); G. C. Jones, *Growing Up Hard in Harlan County* (University Press of Kentucky, 1985).
[*TVA*]: David E. Lilienthal, *TVA: Democracy on the March* (Harper, 1953); Frank E. Smith, *Land Between the Lakes* (University Press of Kentucky, 1971); Gordon R. Clapp, *The TVA: An Approach to the Development of a Region* (University of Chicago Press, 1955); Caudill, pp. 318–24.

317 [*Texas*]: Robert A. Caro, *The Years of Lyndon Johnson: The Path to Power* (Knopf, 1982), esp. ch. 1; T. R. Fehrenbach, *Lone Star: A History of Texas and the Texans* (Macmillan, 1968); George N. Green, *The Establishment in Texas Politics: The Primitive Years, 1938–1957* (Greenwood Press, 1979); Neil R. Peirce, *The Megastates of America* (Norton, 1972), pp. 495–563; Key, ch. 12.

317–18 [*Johnson, birth to Senate*]: Caro; Alfred Steinberg, *Sam Houston's Boy* (Macmillan, 1968), chs. 1–27; Doris Kearns, *Lyndon Johnson and the American Dream* (Harper, 1976), chs. 1–3; Ronnie Dugger, *The Politician: The Life and Times of Lyndon Johnson, The Drive For Power, from the Frontier to the Master of the Senate* (Norton, 1982), parts 1–10; Merle Miller, *Lyndon: An Oral Biography* (Putnam, 1980), ch. 1; Sam Houston Johnson, *My Brother Lyndon* (Cowles Book Co., 1970), chs. 2–4; Seth S. McKay, *W. Lee O'Daniel and Texas Politics, 1938–1942* (Texas Tech Press, 1944), ch. 6; Monroe Billington, "Lyndon B. Johnson and the Blacks: The Early Years," *Journal of Negro History*, vol. 42, no. 1 (January 1977), pp. 26–42; T. Harry Williams, "Huey, Lyndon, and Southern Radicalism," *Journal of American History*, vol. 40, no. 2 (September 1973), pp. 267–93.

318 [*"Endless chains"*]: Megastates, p. 509.
[*Jones*]: Bascom N. Timmons, *Jesse H. Jones: The Man and the Statesman* (Henry Holt, 1956); Jesse H. Jones and Edward Angly, *Fifty Billion Dollars: My Thirteen Years with the RFC* (Macmillan, 1951).

319 [*Texas oilmen*]: Carl Coke Rister, *Oil! Titan of the Southwest* (University of Oklahoma Press, 1949); Richard O'Connor, *The Oil Barons: Men of Greed and Grandeur* (Little, Brown, 1971); Ed Kilman and Theon Wright, *Hugh Roy Cullen: A Story of American Opportunity* (Prentice-Hall, 1954); Harry Hurt III, *Texas Rich: The Hunt Dynasty from the Early Oil Days through the Silver Crash* (Norton, 1981); John Bainbridge, *The Super-Americans* (Doubleday, 1961).
[*Johnson's 1948 Senate campaign*]: Steinberg, chs. 28–29, "Landslide Lyndon" quoted at p. 276; Dugger, chs. 52–58.
[*Johnson in the Senate*]: Rowland Evans and Robert Novak, *Lyndon B. Johnson: The Exercise of Power* (New American Library, 1966), chs. 3–10; William S. White, *The Professional: Lyndon B. Johnson* (Houghton Mifflin, 1964), chs. 10–11; Kearns, *Johnson*, chs. 4–5 and pp. 379–84; Steinberg, *Johnson*, chs. 30–54; Miller, ch. 2; Alfred Steinberg, *Sam Rayburn* (Hawthorn Books, 1975), ch. 26; Dugger, part 12; William S. White, *Citadel: The Story of the U.S. Senate* (Houghton Mifflin, 1968), pp. 88–89, 101–5, 201–2, 209–10, and *passim*.
[*Kearns on Johnson's election as party whip*]: Kearns, *Johnson*, p. 102.

321 [*FDR and civil rights*]: Harvard Sitkoff, *A New Deal for Blacks: The Emergence of Civil Rights as a National Issue* (Oxford University Press, 1978); Raymond Wolters, *Negroes and the Great Depression: The Problem of Economic Recovery* (Greenwood Publishing, 1970); John B. Kirby, "The Roosevelt Administration and Blacks: An Ambivalent Legacy," in Barton J. Bernstein and Allen J. Matusow, eds., *Twentieth-Century America: Recent Interpretations*, 2nd ed. (Harcourt, 1972), pp. 265–88.
[*Truman and civil rights*]: Donald R. McCoy and Richard T. Ruetten, *Quest and Response: Minority Rights and the Truman Administration* (University Press of Kansas, 1973), chs. 9, 13, and *passim*; Barton J. Bernstein, "The Ambiguous Legacy: The Truman Administration and Civil Rights," in Bernstein, ed., *Politics and Policies of the Truman Administration* (Quadrangle, 1970), pp. 269–314.
[*Sundquist on the filibuster*]: Sundquist, *Politics and Policy: The Eisenhower, Kennedy, and Johnson Years* (Brookings Institution, 1968), p. 222.
[*Brown*]: 347 U.S. 483 (1954); see also Richard Kluger, *Simple Justice: The History of Brown v. Board of Education and Black America's Struggle for Equality* (Knopf, 1976); Daniel M. Berman, *It Is So Ordered: The Supreme Court Rules on School Desegregation* (Norton, 1966); Numan V. Bartley, *The Rise of Massive Resistance: Race and Politics in*

the South During the 1950's (Louisiana State University Press, 1969), chs. 4–5; Robert F. Burk, *The Eisenhower Administration and Black Civil Rights* (University of Tennessee Press, 1984), ch. 7.

322 [*1950 Court decisions*]: *Sweatt* v. *Painter,* 339 U.S. 629 (1950); *McLaurin* v. *Oklahoma State Regents,* 339 U.S. 637 (1950).

["*If I failed to produce*"]: quoted in Kearns, *Johnson,* pp. 147–48; see also Billington.

[*Civil Rights Act of 1957*]: Burk, ch. 10; Steven F. Lawson, *Black Ballots: Voting Rights in the South, 1944–1969* (Columbia University Press, 1976), chs. 6–7; Sundquist, pp. 222–38; J. W. Anderson, *Eisenhower, Brownell and the Congress: The Tangled Origins of the Civil Rights Bill of 1956–1957* (Inter-University Case Program/University of Alabama Press, 1964); Kearns, *Johnson,* pp. 146–52; Evans and Novak, ch. 7; Dwight D. Eisenhower, *The White House Years: Waging Peace, 1956–1961* (Doubleday, 1965), pp. 154–62; Carl Solberg, *Hubert Humphrey* (Norton, 1984), pp. 179–80.

[*Black registration, 1959, in Alabama*]: Sundquist, pp. 244–45; see also Burk, ch. 11; Lawson, pp. 203–20; Foster Rhea Dulles, *The Civil Rights Commission: 1957–1965* (Michigan State University Press, 1968).

[*Little Rock*]: Eisenhower, pp. 162–76; Burk, ch. 9; Tony Freyer, *The Little Rock Crisis: A Constitutional Interpretation* (Greenwood Press, 1984); Sherman Adams, *Firsthand Report: The Story of the Eisenhower Administration* (Harper, 1961), ch. 16; Bartley, ch. 14 and *passim;* see also John Bartlow Martin, *The Deep South Says "Never"* (Ballantine, 1957); James J. Kilpatrick, *The Southern Case for School Segregation* (Crowell-Collier Press, 1962).

323 [*Struggle over strengthening the act*]: see Lawson, pp. 222–49; Sundquist, pp. 238–50; Daniel M. Berman, *A Bill Becomes a Law: Congress Enacts Civil Rights Legislation,* 2nd ed. (Macmillan, 1966); see also Burk, ch. 11.

["*Very little faith*"]: quoted in Sundquist, p. 243.

[*Kennedy and civil rights*]: Carl M. Brauer, *John F. Kennedy and the Second Reconstruction* (Columbia University Press, 1977), pp. 11–29; Theodore C. Sorensen, *Kennedy* (Harper, 1965), pp. 470–72; Burns, *Profile,* pp. 200–6; Parmet, *Jack,* pp. 408–14.

324 ["*Shaped primarily*"]: quoted in Parmet, *Jack,* p. 409.

[*Campaign for Democratic nomination*]: ibid., chs. 24–27, 29; Theodore C. Sorensen, "Election of 1960," in Arthur M. Schlesinger, Jr., *History of American Presidential Elections, 1789–1968* (Chelsea House, 1971), vol. 4, pp. 3450–54, 3456–61; Sorensen, *Kennedy,* chs. 4–5; Schlesinger, *Thousand Days,* chs. 1–2; Solberg, ch. 20; Evans and Novak, chs. 11–13; Whalen, pp. 443–56; Theodore H. White, *The Making of the President 1960* (Atheneum, 1961), chs. 2, 4–6; Walt Anderson, *Campaigns: Cases in Political Conflict* (Goodyear Publishing, 1970), ch. 10.

["*Dear Jack*"]: quoted in Parmet, *Jack,* p. 439.

["*All of us*"]: ibid., p. 508.

325 [*Johnson's selection as running mate*]: Schlesinger, *Thousand Days,* pp. 39–57; Herbert S. Parmet, *JFK: The Presidency of John F. Kennedy* (Dial Press, 1983), pp. 21–30; Sorensen, *Kennedy,* pp. 162–66; Burner and West, pp. 85–88; Miller, pp. 254–60.

["*Little shit-ass*"]: quoted in Arthur M. Schlesinger, Jr., *Robert Kennedy and His Times* (Houghton Mifflin, 1978), p. 210.

["*Evil threat*"]: quoted in Parmet, *JFK,* p. 34.

[*Truman and Roosevelt defections*]: Joseph P. Lash, *Eleanor: The Years Alone* (Norton, 1972), pp. 292–97; Marie B. Hecht, *Beyond the Presidency: The Residues of Power* (Macmillan, 1976), pp. 144–45; *New York Times,* July 3, 1960, pp. 1, 18–19, Truman quoted on "prearranged affair" at p. 1.

325–6 [*Kennedy-Roosevelt reconciliation*]: Lash, pp. 297–99, Kennedy quoted at p. 297; Parmet, *JFK,* pp. 35–36.

326 [*Nixon's nomination*]: Stephen E. Ambrose, *Nixon: The Education of a Politician, 1913–1962* (Simon and Schuster, 1987), ch. 24; Sorensen, "Election," pp. 3454–56, 3461–69; White, chs. 3, 7.

[*1960 campaign*]: Sorensen, "Election," pp. 3461–69; Sorensen, *Kennedy,* chs. 7–8; Ambrose, *Nixon,* chs. 25–26; Schlesinger, *Thousand Days,* ch. 3; Schlesinger, *Robert Kennedy,* pp. 211–21; Parmet, *JFK,* ch. 2; Burk, ch. 12; Eisenhower, ch. 25; White, part 2; Richard M. Nixon, *Six Crises* (Doubleday, 1962), pp. 293–426; Fawn M. Brodie, *Richard Nixon: The Shaping of His Character* (Norton, 1981), pp. 410–34; Evans and

Novak, ch. 14; Brauer, ch. 2; Robert A. Divine, *Foreign Policy and U.S. Presidential Elections, 1952–1960* (New Viewpoints, 1974), pp. 183–287; Eric F. Goldman, "The 1947 Kennedy-Nixon 'Tube City' Debate," *Saturday Review*, vol. 4, no. 2 (October 16, 1976), pp. 12–13.

326 [*Kennedy on separation of church and state*]: quoted in Sorensen, *Kennedy*, p. 190; see also Fuchs, pp. 179–82.

[*1960 election results*]: Schlesinger, *Elections*, vol. 4, p. 3562; see also Bernard Cosman, "Presidential Republicanism in the South, 1960," *Journal of Politics*, vol. 24, no. 2 (May 1962), pp. 303–22.

The Invisible Latins

[*Kennedy's inaugural address*]: January 20, 1961, in *Public Papers of the Presidents of the United States: John F. Kennedy* (U.S. Government Printing Office, 1962–64), vol. 1, pp. 1–3.

328 [*Kennedy on Alliance for Progress*]: March 13, 1961, in *ibid.*, vol. 1, pp. 170–75, quoted at pp. 172, 175.

["*Heard such words*"]: quoted in Schlesinger, *Thousand Days*, p. 205.

[*Coolidge's intervention in Nicaragua*]: L. Ethan Ellis, *Republican Foreign Policy, 1921–1933* (Rutgers University Press, 1968), pp. 252–61; Harold N. Denny, *Dollars for Bullets: The Story of American Rule in Nicaragua* (1929; reprinted by Greenwood Press, 1980); Gregorio Selser, *Sandino* (Monthly Review Press, 1981); William Kamman, *A Search for Stability: United States Diplomacy Toward Nicaragua, 1925–1933* (University of Notre Dame Press, 1968).

[*Hoover and Stimson in Latin America*]: Bryce Wood, *The Making of the Good Neighbor Policy* (Columbia University Press, 1961), pp. 123–28, 131–35; Donald M. Dozer, *Are We Good Neighbors?: Three Decades of Inter-American Relations, 1930–1960* (University of Florida Press, 1959), pp. 9–16; Ellis, ch. 8.

[*FDR and the Good Neighbor*]: Wood; Dozer, chs. 1–4; Irwin F. Gellman, *Roosevelt and Batista: Good Neighbor Diplomacy in Cuba, 1933–1945* (University of New Mexico Press, 1973).

[*Latin America in the American consciousness*]: see D. H. Radler, *El Gringo: The Yankee Image in Latin America* (Chilton Co., 1962), p. 3 and *passim*.

329 [*Figures of Latin poverty*]: Samuel Shapiro, *Invisible Latin America* (Beacon Press, 1963), p. 3 and chs. 1–7 *passim;* see also Tad Szulc, *The Winds of Revolution: Latin America Today—and Tomorrow* (Praeger, 1963), ch. 2; Robert J. Alexander, *Today's Latin America* (Anchor Books, 1962), pp. 57–83; Nathan L. Whetten, *Guatemala: The Land and the People* (Yale University Press, 1961), parts 2–3.

["*Culture of poverty*"]: Oscar Lewis, "The Culture of Poverty," in Arthur I. Blaustein and Roger R. Woock, eds., *Man Against Poverty: World War III* (Vintage, 1968), pp. 260–74, esp. pp. 264–68; see also Lewis, *Five Families: Mexican Case Studies in the Culture of Poverty* (Basic Books, 1959); Lewis, *The Children of Sanchez: Autobiography of a Mexican Family* (Random House, 1961); Lewis, *La Vida: A Puerto Rican Family in the Culture of Poverty—San Juan and New York* (Random House, 1966).

[*Mexican oil dispute*]: see Wood, chs. 8–9; Robert F. Smith, *The United States and Revolutionary Nationalism in Mexico, 1916–1932* (University of Chicago Press, 1972); Harlow S. Person, *Mexican Oil: Symbol of Recent Trends in International Relations* (Harper, 1942); Ellis, pp. 229–52.

329–30 [*Forms of government in Latin America*]: Shapiro, pp. 18–24, quoted at p. 23.

330 [*Cuban revolt against Spain*]: Hugh Thomas, *Cuba: The Pursuit of Freedom* (Harper, 1971), book 3; David F. Trask, *The War with Spain in 1898* (Macmillan, 1981); Philip S. Foner, *The Spanish-Cuban-American War and the Birth of American Imperialism, 1895–1902*, 2 vols. (Monthly Review Press, 1972).

[*U.S. intervention in Cuba*]: Thomas, books 4–8, 10 *passim;* Henry Wriston, "A Historical Perspective," in John Plank, ed., *Cuba and the United States: Long-Range Perspectives* (Brookings Institution, 1967), pp. 1–30; Robert F. Smith, *The United States and Cuba: Business and Diplomacy, 1917–1960* (Bookman Associates, 1960), esp. chs. 10–11;

Wood, chs. 2-3; Gellman; William Appleman Williams, "The Influence of the United States on the Development of Modern Cuba," in Robert F. Smith, ed., *Background to Revolution: The Development of Modern Cuba* (Knopf, 1966), pp. 187-94.

330 [*"Cheating, mañana lot"*]: quoted in Wriston, p. 13.

[*Figures of U.S. companies' control of Cuban economy*]: Shapiro, p. 75.

[*U.S. investment as one-third Cuban GNP*]: ibid.

330-1 [*Cuban sugar-mill workers and the jobless*]: see Thomas, p. 1109.

331 [*Castro's revolution*]: ibid., book 8 passim; Robert F. Smith, "Castro's Revolution: Domestic Sources and Consequences," in Plank, pp. 45-68; Herbert L. Matthews, *The Cuban Story* (George Braziller, 1961); Warren Miller, *90 Miles from Home: The Face of Cuba Today* (Little, Brown, 1961); Tad Szulc, *Fidel* (Morrow, 1986), parts 1-3.

[*U.S.-Cuban relations after revolution*]: Thomas, chs. 98-102 passim; Richard E. Welch, Jr., *Response to Revolution: The United States and the Cuban Revolution, 1959-1961* (University of North Carolina Press, 1985); Philip W. Bonsal, *Cuba, Castro, and the United States* (University of Pittsburgh Press, 1971); see also F. Parkinson, *Latin America, the Cold War, & the World Powers, 1945-1973* (Sage Publications, 1974), ch. 5.

[*Plans for CIA-backed invasion*]: Peter Wyden, *Bay of Pigs: The Untold Story* (Jonathan Cape, 1979), chs. 1-2 passim; Brodie, ch. 27; Stephen E. Ambrose, *Eisenhower: The President* (Simon and Schuster, 1984), pp. 504-7, 556-57, 582-84, 608-10.

[*The "Guatemala model"*]: see Lucien S. Vandenbroucke, "Anatomy of a Failure: The Decision to Land at the Bay of Pigs," *Political Science Quarterly*, vol. 99, no. 3 (Fall 1984), pp. 471-91, esp. pp. 474-75; Richard H. Immerman, *The CIA in Guatemala: The Foreign Policy of Intervention* (University of Texas Press, 1982), esp. pp. 188-97; Trumbull Higgins, *The Perfect Failure: Kennedy, Eisenhower, and the CIA at the Bay of Pigs* (Norton, 1987), esp. ch. 1.

[*Kennedy on Castro*]: Kennedy, *The Strategy of Peace*, Allan Nevins, ed. (Harper, 1960), pp. 132, 133.

[*Nixon on eliminating "cancer"*]: Nixon, pp. 352-53.

[*"Kennedy Asks Aid"*]: *New York Times*, October 21, 1960, p. 1; see also Nixon, pp. 353-54.

[*Nixon on Kennedy's proposals*]: *New York Times*, October 22, 1960, p. 8; see also Nixon, pp. 354-57.

[*JFK's "middle way"*]: see Wyden, pp. 92, 99-101, 149-52, and chs. 3-4 passim; see also Schlesinger, *Thousand Days*, ch. 10 passim; Sorensen, *Kennedy*, pp. 294-98.

[*Advisers' group-think*]: Vandenbroucke; Wyden, pp. 314-16.

332 [*Bay of Pigs invasion*]: Wyden, chs. 5-7; Haynes B. Johnson, *The Bay of Pigs: Brigade 2506* (Norton, 1964); Higgins, esp. ch. 8; Thomas, ch. 106; Parmet, *JFK*, ch. 7; Parkinson, ch. 6; Schlesinger, *Thousand Days*, ch. 11; John Bartlow Martin, *Adlai Stevenson and the World* (Doubleday, 1977), pp. 622-36; Beatrice Bishop Berle and Travis Beal Jacobs, eds., *Navigating the Rapids, 1918-1971: From the Papers of Adolf A. Berle* (Harcourt, 1973), pp. 740-43; Wills, *Kennedy Imprisonment*, chs. 18-19; Szulc, *Fidel*, pp. 532-61.

[*"An old saying"*]: quoted in Wyden, p. 305.

[*"All my life"*]: quoted in Sorensen, *Kennedy*, p. 309.

[*Paris and Vienna summits, Berlin crisis and war fears, summer 1961*]: Schlesinger, *Thousand Days*, chs. 14-15; Parmet, *JFK*, pp. 183-202; Jack M. Schick, *The Berlin Crisis, 1958-1962* (University of Pennsylvania Press, 1971), chs. 5-6; Jean E. Smith, *The Defense of Berlin* (Johns Hopkins Press, 1963), chs. 11-12 passim; Robert M. Slusser, *The Berlin Crisis of 1961* (Johns Hopkins University Press, 1973); Ralph G. Martin, *A Hero for Our Time: An Intimate Story of the Kennedy Years* (Macmillan, 1983), ch. 18; Charles de Gaulle, *Memoirs of Hope: Renewal and Endeavor*, Terence Kilmartin, trans. (Simon and Schuster, 1971), pp. 254-60; Strobe Talbott, ed. and trans., *Khrushchev Remembers* (Little, Brown, 1970-74), vol. 2, pp. 487-509; Bruce Miroff, *Pragmatic Illusions: The Presidential Politics of John F. Kennedy* (David McKay, 1976), pp. 64-82; Alexander L. George and Richard Smoke, *Deterrence in American Foreign Policy: Theory and Practice* (Columbia University Press, 1977), ch. 14; Montague Kern et al., *The Kennedy Crises: The Press, the Presidency, and Foreign Policy* (University of North Carolina Press, 1983), part 3; "Gun

Thy Neighbor?," *Time*, vol. 78, no. 7 (August 18, 1961), p. 58; "The Sheltered Life," *Time*, vol. 78, no. 16 (October 20, 1961), pp. 21-25.

332 [*"Shake her hand first"*]: quoted in Parmet, *JFK*, p. 187.

333 [*"Missile gap"*]: see George and Smoke, pp. 449-59; Arnold L. Horelick and Myron Rush, *Strategic Power and Soviet Foreign Policy* (University of Chicago Press, 1966), chs. 8-9 *passim;* Roy E. Licklider, "The Missile Gap Controversy," *Political Science Quarterly*, vol. 85, no. 4 (December 1970), pp. 600-15; see also Ambrose, *Eisenhower*, pp. 312-14, 561-63.

[*Kennedy-McNamara discussions*]: Parmet, *JFK*, p. 196.

[*Kennedy's address*]: July 25, 1961, in *Kennedy Public Papers*, vol. 1, pp. 533-50; Parmet, *JFK*, p. 197.

[*Truman on address*]: quoted in Parmet, *JFK*, p. 198.

[*Roosevelt on civilian defense and negotiations*]: *ibid.;* Lash, p. 319.

[*Berlin Wall*]: Schick, pp. 172-73; Smith, *Defense*, ch. 13; George and Smoke, pp. 437-42; Schlesinger, *Thousand Days*, pp. 394-97.

[*Cuban missile crisis*]: David Detzer, *The Brink: The Missile Crisis, 1962* (Crowell, 1979); Elie Abel, *The Missile Crisis* (Lippincott, 1966); Abram Chayes, *The Cuban Missile Crisis* (Oxford University Press, 1974); Herbert S. Dinnerstein, *The Making of a Missile Crisis: October 1962* (Johns Hopkins University Press, 1976); Robert F. Kennedy, *Thirteen Days: A Memoir of the Cuban Missile Crisis* (Norton, 1969); Parmet, *JFK*, ch. 12; Martin, *Stevenson*, pp. 719-48; Sorensen, *Kennedy*, ch. 24; Thomas, chs. 107-10; *Khruskchev Remembers*, vol. 1, ch. 20, and vol. 2, pp. 509-14; Schlesinger, *Robert Kennedy*, ch. 22; Szulc, *Fidel*, pp. 562-92; Parkinson, ch. 8; Jerome H. Kahan and Anne K. Long, "The Cuban Missile Crisis: A Study of Its Strategic Context," *Political Science Quarterly*, vol. 87, no. 4 (December 1973), pp. 564-90; Roberta Wohlstetter, "Cuba and Pearl Harbor: Hindsight and Foresight," *Foreign Affairs*, vol. 43, no. 4 (July 1965), pp. 691-707; George and Smoke, ch. 15; Andrés Suárez, *Cuba: Castroism and Communism, 1959-1966*, Joel Carmichael and Ernest Halperin, trans. (MIT Press, 1967), ch. 7; Carl A. Linden, *Khrushchev and the Soviet Leadership, 1957-1964* (Johns Hopkins Press, 1966), ch. 8; Kern et al., part 4; Wills, chs. 21-22; Miroff, pp. 82-100; Raymond L. Garthoff, *Reflections on the Cuban Missile Crisis* (Brookings Institution, 1987); J. Anthony Lukas, "Class Reunion: Kennedy's Men Relive the Cuban Missile Crisis," *New York Times Magazine*, August 30, 1987, pp. 22-27, 51, 58-61, esp. pp. 58, 61.

334 [*"Bullfight critics"*]: quoted in Parmet, *JFK*, p. 286.

335 [*Robert Kennedy on lessons learned*]: *Thirteen Days*, pp. 124, 126.

The Revolutionary Asians

[*"To those new states"*]: *Kennedy Public Papers*, vol. 1, p. 1.

[*"Lenin or any of the Soviet"*]: Charles Bohlen, quoted in Parmet, *JFK*, p. 191.

335-6 [*Khrushchev on Kennedy*]: *Khrushchev Remembers*, vol. 2, p. 495.

336 [*U.S. and Cuba after missile crisis*]: see Schlesinger, *Robert Kennedy*, ch. 23; Warren Hinckle and William C. Turner, *The Fish Is Red: The Story of the Secret War Against Castro* (Harper, 1981); K. S. Karol, *Guerrillas in Power: The Course of the Cuban Revolution*, Arnold Pomerans, ed. (Hill and Wang, 1970), pp. 270-87.

[*Debray*]: Debray, *Revolution in the Revolution?: Armed Struggle and Political Struggle in Latin America*, Bobbye Ortiz, trans. (Monthly Review Press, 1967); see also Hartmut Ramm, *The Marxism of Regis Debray: Between Lenin and Guevara* (Regents Press of Kansas, 1978), esp. ch. 4; Leo Huberman and Paul M. Sweezy, eds., *Regis Debray and the Latin American Revolution* (Monthly Review Press, 1968).

[*Guevara*]: Daniel James, *Ché Guevara* (Stein & Day, 1969); Luis J. González and Gustavo A. Sánchez Salazar, *The Great Rebel: Che Guevara in Bolivia*, Helen R. Lane, trans. (Grove Press, 1969); Ernesto "Che" Guevara, "La Guerra de Guerrillas," in Franklin M. Osanka, ed., *Modern Guerrilla Warfare* (Free Press of Glencoe, 1962), pp. 336-75; see also Parkinson, pp. 215-18; Karol, ch. 4.

[*Alliance for Progress*]: see Jerome Levinson and Juan de Onís, *The Alliance That Lost Its Way: A Critical Report on the Alliance for Progress* (Quadrangle, 1970); Department of Economic Affairs, Pan American Union, *The Alliance for Progress and Latin-American Development Prospects: A Five-Year Review, 1961-1965* (Johns Hopkins Press, 1967);

Szulc, *Winds of Revolution*, ch. 6; Rader, ch. 9; Miroff, pp. 110–42; Schlesinger, *Thousand Days*, ch. 8; Abraham F. Lowenthal, " 'Liberal,' 'Radical,' and 'Bureaucratic' Perspectives on U.S. Latin American Policy: The Alliance for Progress in Retrospect," in Julio Cotler and Richard R. Fagen, eds., *Latin America and the United States: The Changing Political Realities* (Stanford University Press, 1974), pp. 212–35; Heraclio Bonilla, "Commentary on Lowenthal," in *ibid.*, pp. 236–37.

337 [*Stevenson's missile crisis proposal*]: see Martin, *Stevenson and the World*, pp. 723–24.

[*American Revolution in Asia*]: Richard B. Morris, *The Emerging Nations and the American Revolution* (Harper, 1970), pp. 199–205, Nagasaki report quoted at p. 200, Sun Yat-sen at p. 202, Mao at pp. 204, 205.

337-8 [*1942 poll on locations of China and India*]: Gary R. Hess, *America Encounters India, 1941–1947* (Johns Hopkins Press, 1971), p. 2.

338 [*Churchill on limited application of Atlantic Charter*]: *ibid.*, pp. 28–29.

[*FDR and India during World War II*]: *ibid.;* Christopher Thorne, *Allies of a Kind: The United States, Britain, and the War Against Japan, 1941–1945* (Oxford University Press, 1978), chs. 8, 14, 21, 28; see also, generally, Louis.

["*Dear Friend*"]: quoted in Hess, pp. 68–69.

["*Restore to India*"]: cable of July 25, 1942, quoted in *ibid.*, p. 76.

["*1,100,000,000 potential enemies*"]: quoted in *ibid.*, p. 155.

[*Postwar Indian criticism of U.S.*]: see *ibid.*, pp. 163–72 *passim.*

339 [*Gandhi's "congratulatory" telegram*]: quoted in *ibid.*, p. 155.

[*Roosevelt's voyage to India*]: Eleanor Roosevelt, *India and the Awakening East* (Harper, 1953); Lash, pp. 195–205.

[*Indian conditions*]: see Nair; Bourke-White; Ronald Segal, *The Anguish of India* (Stein & Day, 1965); Chester Bowles, *Ambassador's Report* (Harper, 1954); Amlam Datta, "India," in Adamantios A. Pepelasis et al., *Economic Development: Analysis and Case Studies* (Harper, 1961), ch. 13; Donald K. Faris, *To Plow with Hope* (Harper, 1958), esp. part 1.

[*Senator Kennedy's anticolonial speeches*]: see Schlesinger, *Thousand Days*, pp. 507–8; Parmet, *Jack*, pp. 399–408; Burns, *Profile*, pp. 193–200.

[*Representative Kennedy's tour of Asia*]: Parmet, *Jack*, pp. 226–28; Schlesinger, *Thousand Days*, p. 522; see also W. W. Rostow, *The Diffusion of Power: An Essay in Recent History* (Macmillan, 1972), p. 106.

["*Key area*"]: Schlesinger, *Thousand Days*, p. 522.

[*Foreign aid to India*]: P. J. Eldridge, *The Politics of Foreign Aid in India* (Schocken, 1970), *passim;* see also Segal, ch. 4; Rostow, ch. 20.

340 [*India and the Soviet Union*]: see Eldridge, ch. 4 and *passim;* Bowles, chs. 15–16; Arthur Stein, *India and the Soviet Union: The Nehru Era* (University of Chicago Press, 1969); Robert H. Donaldson, *Soviet Policy towards India: Ideology and Strategy* (Harvard University Press, 1974), chs. 3–5; see also Robert Trumbull, *As I See India* (William Sloane Associates, 1956), ch. 17.

[*Indian polls on U.S. and Soviet prestige*]: see Eldridge, pp. 98–111 *passim.*

[*Chinese-Indian border conflict*]: Neville Maxwell, *India's China War* (Pantheon, 1970); John Kenneth Galbraith, *Ambassador's Journal: A Personal Account of the Kennedy Years* (Houghton Mifflin, 1969), chs. 19–22.

[*Nehru in the U.S., 1961*]: Schlesinger, *Thousand Days*, pp. 523–26, Kennedy quoted at p. 526; Galbraith, pp. 245–51; India Information Services, *The Prime Minister Comes to America* (Information Service of India, n.d.).

[*Jackie Kennedy in India and Pakistan*]: Galbraith, pp. 305–33 *passim;* Schlesinger, *Thousand Days*, pp. 530–31; Sorensen, *Kennedy*, p. 383.

341 [*Budding revolution in Southeast Asia*]: see Osborne, esp. chs. 3–4; Erich H. Jacoby, *Agrarian Unrest in Southeast Asia* (Columbia University Press, 1949); Frank N. Trager, ed., *Marxism in Southeast Asia: A Study of Four Countries* (Stanford University Press, 1959); Virginia Thompson and Richard Adloff, *The Left Wing in Southeast Asia* (William Sloane Associates, 1950).

[*Ho and the American Declaration of Independence*]: see Marvin E. Gettleman et al., eds., *Vietnam and America: A Documentary History* (Grove Press, 1985), pp. 39–42; Morris, p. 220; Stanley Karnow, *Vietnam* (Viking, 1983), pp. 135–36; see also Jean Lacouture, *Ho Chi Minh*, Peter Wiles, trans. (Random House, 1968), ch. 14; David V. J. Bell and

Allen E. Goodman, "Vietnam and the American Revolution," *Yale Review*, vol. 61, no. 1 (October 1971), pp. 26–34.

341 [*Roosevelt and Indochina*]: Gary R. Hess, "Franklin Roosevelt and Indochina," *Journal of American History*, vol. 59, no. 2 (September 1972), pp. 353–68; Walter LaFeber, "Roosevelt, Churchill, and Indochina, 1942–45," *American Historical Review*, vol. 80, no. 5 (December 1975), pp. 1277–95; Thorne, chs. 7, 13, 20, 27.
[*"Cheerful fecklessness"*]: quoted in Hess, "Roosevelt and Indochina," p. 356.

342 [*U.S. and Indochina, Truman and Eisenhower Administrations*]: George McT. Kahin, *Intervention: How America Became Involved in Vietnam* (Knopf, 1986), chs. 1–4; Karnow, chs. 4–6; Townsend Hoopes, *The Devil and John Foster Dulles* (Atlantic Monthly/Little, Brown, 1973), chs. 15–16; Leslie H. Gelb and Richard K. Betts, *The Irony of Vietnam: The System Worked* (Brookings Institution, 1979), pp. 36–68; F. M. Kail, *What Washington Said: Administration Rhetoric and the Vietnam War, 1949–1969* (Harper, 1973), *passim*; Ronald H. Spector, *Advice and Support: The Early Years of the United States Army in Vietnam, 1941–1960* (Free Press, 1985), parts 2–3; Jeanette P. Nichols, "United States Aid to South and Southeast Asia, 1950–1960," *Pacific Historical Review*, vol. 32, no. 2 (1963), pp. 171–84.
[*President Kennedy and Indochina*]: Kahin, chs. 5–6; Karnow, chs. 7–8; Gelb and Betts, ch. 3; Schlesinger, *Thousand Days*, chs. 13, 20; Kail, *passim*; David Halberstam, *The Best and the Brightest* (Random House, 1972), chs. 1–16; William J. Rust, *Kennedy in Vietnam* (Scribner, 1985); Richard J. Walton, *Cold War and Counterrevolution: The Foreign Policy of John F. Kennedy* (Viking, 1972), ch. 10; Kern et al., parts 2, 5; Maxwell D. Taylor, *Swords and Plowshares* (Norton, 1972), chs. 17–18, 23; Ralph L. Stavins, "Kennedy's Private War," *New York Review of Books*, vol. 17, no. 1 (July 22, 1971), pp. 20–32; Roger Hilsman, *To Move a Nation* (Doubleday, 1967), part 9.

343 [*"There are limits"*]: quoted in Schlesinger, *Robert Kennedy*, p. 705.
[*Kennedy on danger of escalation*]: see Kahin, p. 138.
[*Kennedy and Diem coup*]: Rust, chs. 6–10; Kahin, ch. 6; Schlesinger, *Thousand Days*, pp. 981–98; Karnow, ch. 8.
[*"Thwart a change"*]: quoted in Karnow, p. 295.

344 [*Kennedy Administration assumptions about Third World aspirations*]: see Robert A. Pakenham, *Liberal America and the Third World* (Princeton University Press, 1973), esp. pp. 59–85 and chs. 3–4.
[*Bowles on Kennedy Administration*]: Bowles, *Promises to Keep: My Years in Public Life, 1941–1969* (Harper, 1971), pp. 435–36, quoted at p. 435; see also Bowles, "Reminiscences," Oval History Project, Columbia University (1963), pp. 841, 846.

8. STRIDING TOWARD FREEDOM

347 [*"That institutional arrangement"*]: Schumpeter, *Capitalism, Socialism, and Democracy* (Harper, 1942), p. 269.

348 [*Erikson on Gandhi and his followers*]: see Erik H. Erikson, *Gandhi's Truth: On the Origins of Militant Nonviolence* (Norton, 1969), p. 408; see also Richard H. Solomon, *Mao's Revolution and the Chinese Political Culture* (University of California Press, 1971).

Onward, Christian Soldiers

[*Martin Luther King, Jr., other leaders, and the civil rights struggle*]: Primary correspondence (1955–68), esp. box 1, King Library and Archives, Martin Luther King, Jr., Center, Atlanta.
[*Parks*]: Howell Raines, *My Soul Is Rested: Movement Days in the Deep South Remembered* (Putnam, 1977), pp. 40–42, 44; David L. Lewis, *King* (Praeger, 1970), pp. 47–48; George R. Metcalf, *Black Profiles* (McGraw-Hill, 1968), pp. 255–64.
[*"Time had just come"*]: Parks radio interview with Sidney Roger, 1956 (Pacifica Radio Archive, Los Angeles); Raines, p. 44.

349 [*Highlander*]: Aldon D. Morris, *The Origins of the Civil Rights Movement: Black Communities Organizing for Change* (Free Press, 1984), pp. 139–57; Frank Adams and Myles Horton, *Unearthing Seeds of Fire: The Idea of Highlander* (John F. Blair, 1975).
[*"A unified society"*]: quoted in Adams and Horton, p. 122.

349 [*Montgomery boycott*]: Martin Luther King, Jr., *Stride Toward Freedom: The Montgomery Story* (Harper, 1958); Lewis, ch. 3; Stephen B. Oates, *Let the Trumpet Sound: The Life of Martin Luther King, Jr.* (Harper, 1982), pp. 64-107; Morris, pp. 40-63; Raines, book 1, ch. 1.

[*"Beat this thing"*]: Raines, p. 44.

[*"Gift of laughing people"*]: King, *Stride*, p. 74.

[*King*]: David J. Garrow, *Bearing the Cross: Martin Luther King, Jr., and the Southern Christian Leadership Conference* (Morrow, 1986); Oates; Lewis; Hanes Walton, Jr., *The Political Philosophy of Martin Luther King, Jr.* (Greenwood Publishing, 1971); August Meier, "The Conservative Militant," in C. Eric Lincoln, ed., *Martin Luther King, Jr.* (Hill and Wang, 1970), pp. 144-56; Sidney M. Willhelm, "Martin Luther King, Jr., and the Black Experience in America," *Journal of Black Studies*, vol. 10, no. 1 (September 1979), pp. 3-19.

350 [*"Old Testament patriarch"*]: Oates, p. 8.

[*"Real father"*]: quoted in *ibid.*, p. 12.

[*King's studies*]: see *ibid.*, pp. 17-41; David J. Garrow, "The Intellectual Development of Martin Luther King, Jr.: Influences and Commentaries," *Union Seminary Quarterly Review*, vol. 40 (January 1986), pp. 5-20; John J. Ansbro, *Martin Luther King, Jr.: The Making of a Mind* (Orbis Books, 1982).

351 [*King's address at mass meeting*]: King, *Stride*, pp. 61-63, quoted at p. 63; see also Oates, pp. 69-72.

[*"Military precision"*]: quoted in King, *Stride*, p. 77.

[*"My feet is tired"*]: quoted in Oates, pp. 76-77.

351-2 [*King and nonviolence*]: *ibid.*, pp. 23, 30-33, 77-79; Lewis, ch. 4 *passim;* Ansbro, esp. chs. 4, 7; Walton, esp. ch. 4; Warren E. Steinkraus, "Martin Luther King's Personalism and Nonviolence," *Journal of the History of Ideas*, vol. 34, no. 1 (January–March 1973), pp. 97-111.

352 [*Till*]: Oates, p. 62.

353 [*White southern ideology*]: see W. F. Cash, *The Mind of the South* (Knopf, 1941); I. A. Newby, *Jim Crow's Defense: Anti-Negro Thought in America, 1900-1930* (Louisiana State University Press, 1965); Lawrence J. Friedman, "The Search for Docility: Racial Thought in the White South, 1861-1917," *Phylon*, vol. 31, no. 3 (Fall 1970), pp. 313-23; Neil R. McMillen, *The Citizens' Council: Organized Resistance to the Second Reconstruction, 1954-1964* (University of Illinois Press, 1971), part 3 *passim*; James G. Cook, *The Segregationists* (Appleton-Century-Crofts, 1962); Julia K. Blackwelder, "Southern White Fundamentalists and the Civil Rights Movement," *Phylon*, vol. 40, no. 4 (Winter 1979), pp. 334-41; David C. Colby, "White Violence and the Civil Rights Movement," in Laurence H. Moreland et al., eds., *Blacks in Southern Politics* (Praeger, 1987), pp. 31-48; Charles W. Chesnutt, *The Marrow of Tradition* (1901; reprinted by Arno Press, 1969); James W. Silver, *Mississippi: The Closed Society* (Harcourt, 1964); John Hope Franklin and Isidore Starr, eds., *The Negro in Twentieth Century America* (Vintage, 1967), pp. 34-38; Reese Cleghorn, "The Segs," in Harold Hayes, ed., *Smiling Through the Apocalypse: Esquire's History of the Sixties* (McCall Publishing, 1969), pp. 651-68; Bertram W. Doyle, *The Etiquette of Race Relations in the South: A Study in Social Control* (1937; reprinted by Kennikat Press, 1968).

[*"Other South"*]: Carl N. Degler, *The Other South: Southern Dissenters in the Nineteenth Century* (Harper, 1974); William Peters, *The Southern Temper* (Doubleday, 1959), esp. chs. 7, 10.

[*"I'm a Jew"*]: quoted in Peters, p. 126.

[*Golden's plan*]: *ibid.*, pp. 125-26.

[*"Great period of Southern dissent"*]: Degler, p. 371.

[*"Kill him!"*]: Peters, p. 117.

[*Racist stereotypes*]: see Cook, *Segregationists*, pp. 15, 17, 18, 51, 59, 213, 223, and *passim*.

[*Racism, anti-Semitism, anticommunism*]: see McMillen, ch. 10; Cook, *Segregationists*, chs. 4, 7, and pp. 293-303.

[*Blacks in southern textbooks*]: Melton McLaurin, "Images of Negroes in Deep South Public School State History Texts," *Phylon*, vol. 32, no. 3 (Fall 1971), pp. 237-46, "bright rows" quoted at p. 239; see also Franklin and Starr, pp. 45-52.

354 [*Citizens' Councils*]: McMillen; Cook, *Segregationists*, ch. 2; Samuel DuBois Cook, "Politi-

cal Movements and Organizations," in Avery Leiserson, ed., *The American South in the 1960's* (Praeger, 1964), pp. 130–53, esp. pp. 133–44; see also David M. Chalmers, *Hooded Americanism: The First Century of the Ku Klux Klan, 1865–1965* (Doubleday, 1965), esp. chs. 46–48; Wyn Craig Wade, *The Fiery Cross: The Ku Klux Klan in America* (Simon and Schuster, 1987), chs. 10–12.

354 [*Councils' platform*]: quoted in Cook, *Segregationists*, p. 51.
   [*Southern politics*]: V. O. Key, Jr., *Southern Politics in State and Nation* (Knopf, 1949); Numan V. Bartley, *The Rise of Massive Resistance: Race and Politics in the South During the 1950's* (Louisiana State University Press, 1969); Bartley and Hugh D. Graham, *Southern Politics and the Second Reconstruction* (Johns Hopkins University Press, 1975), esp. ch. 3; Cook, "Political Movements"; Donald R. Matthews and James W. Prothro, *Negroes and the New Southern Politics* (Harcourt, 1966); Earl Black, "Southern Governors and Political Change: Campaign Stances on Racial Segregation and Economic Development, 1950–1969," *Journal of Politics*, vol. 33 (1971), pp. 708–19; McMillen, esp. ch. 14; Cash, *passim*; Cook, *Segregationists*, esp. ch. 8; Silver, chs. 1–3; Robert Sherrill, *Gothic Politics in the Deep South: Stars of the New Confederacy* (Grossman, 1968).
   [*Key on southern politics*]: Key, p. 4.

355 [*"Employing the powerful weapons"*]: Cook, "Political Movements," p. 136.
   [*Ashmore on restrictive legislation*]: ibid., p. 133.
   [*Black churches*]: Morris, pp. 4–12; Benjamin E. Mays and Joseph W. Nicholson, *The Negro's Church* (1933; reprinted by Negro Universities Press, 1969), ch. 17 and *passim*; Charles V. Hamilton, *The Black Preacher in America* (Morrow, 1972); James H. Cone, *Black Theology and Black Power* (Seabury Press, 1969), ch. 4; William H. Pipes, *Say Amen, Brother!: Old-Time Negro Preaching, A Study in American Frustration* (1951; reprinted by Negro Universities Press, 1970).
   [*Frazier on Negro church*]: quoted in Morris, p. 60.
   [*"Common church culture"*]: ibid., p. 11.

356 [*Formation of SCLC and its strategic floundering*]: Garrow, *Bearing*, ch. 2; Oates, pp. 122–24, 129–30, 144–46, 156–58; Morris, chs. 4–5; Harvard Sitkoff, *The Struggle for Black Equality, 1954–1980* (Hill and Wang, 1981), pp. 64–66; Louis E. Lomax, *The Negro Revolt* (Harper, 1962), pp. 92–96.
   [*"Unite community leaders"*]: Morris, p. 46.
   [*"Rare talent"*]: Lerone Bennett, quoted in ibid., p. 94.
   [*CORE*]: August Meier and Elliott Rudwick, *CORE: A Study in the Civil Rights Movement, 1942–1968* (Oxford University Press, 1973), part 1; Morris, pp. 128–38.
   [*Lunch-counter sit-ins*]: Howard Zinn, *SNCC: The New Abolitionists* (Beacon Press, 1964), ch. 2; Clayborne Carson, *In Struggle: SNCC and the Black Awakening of the 1960s* (Harvard University Press, 1981), ch. 1; Morris, ch. 9; Raines, book 1, ch. 2 *passim*; Meier and Rudwick, ch. 4; Miles Wolff, *Lunch at the 5 & 10: The Greensboro Sit-Ins* (Stein & Day, 1970); William H. Chafe, *Civilities and Civil Rights: Greensboro, North Carolina, and the Black Struggle for Freedom* (Oxford University Press, 1980), ch. 3.
   [*"I'm sorry"*]: quoted in Raines, p. 76.

357 [*"Instilled within each other"*]: Franklin McCain, quoted in ibid., p. 75.
   [*"Like a fever"*]: quoted in Carson, p. 12.
   [*"Time to move"*]: quoted in Morris, p. 201.
   [*Baker*]: Morris, pp. 102–4; Zinn, pp. 32–33; Ellen Cantarow and Susan Gushee O'Malley, "Ella Baker: Organizing for Civil Rights," in Cantarow et al., *Moving the Mountain: Women Working for Social Change* (Feminist Press/McGraw-Hill, 1980), pp. 52–93; Mary King, *Freedom Song* (Morrow, 1987), pp. 42–43.
   [*Baker and SCLC*]: see Morris, pp. 103–4, 112–15; Cantarow and O'Malley, p. 84; Garrow, *Bearing*, pp. 120–21, 131, 141.

358 [*Formation of SNCC*]: Morris, pp. 215–21; Carson, ch. 2; James Forman, *The Making of Black Revolutionaries* (Macmillan, 1972), ch. 29; Raines, book 1, ch. 2 *passim*, and book 1, ch. 5; Zinn, pp. 33–36; Oates, pp. 154–55.
   [*"Direct their own affairs"*]: Baker interview with Clayborne Carson, New York, May 5, 1972.
   [*"Foundation of our purpose"*]: SNCC founding statement, in Judith C. Albert and Stewart E. Albert, eds., *The Sixties Papers: Documents of a Rebellious Decade* (Praeger, 1984), quoted at p. 113.

358 [*"He is the movement"*]: Ella Baker, "Developing Community Leadership," in Gerda Lerner, ed., *Black Women in White America* (Pantheon, 1972), quoted at p. 351.
[*"We are all leaders"*]: quoted in Morris, p. 231.

359 [An American Dilemma]: Myrdal, *An American Dilemma: The Negro Problem and Modern Democracy* ("Twentieth Anniversary Edition": Harper, 1962), quoted at p. 1023.

360 [*King on Bay of Pigs*]: quoted in Oates, p. 173.
[*King-Kennedy meeting*]: ibid., p. 172; see also Harris Wofford, *Of Kennedys and Kings: Making Sense of the Sixties* (Farrar, Straus & Giroux, 1980), pp. 128-29.
[*The Kennedy White House and the civil rights movement*]: Burke Marshall Papers, esp. boxes 17-19, John F. Kennedy Library.
[*"Or the Devil himself"*]: quoted in Carl M. Brauer, *John F. Kennedy and the Second Reconstruction* (Columbia University Press, 1977), p. 48.
[*"Terrible ambivalence"*]: Schlesinger, *A Thousand Days: John F. Kennedy in the White House* (Houghton Mifflin, 1965), p. 930; see also Brauer, ch. 3; James L. Sundquist, *Politics and Policy: The Eisenhower, Kennedy, and Johnson Years* (Brookings Institution, 1968), pp. 256-59; John Hart, "Kennedy, Congress and Civil Rights," *Journal of American Studies*, vol. 13, no. 1 (April 1979), pp. 165-78; Steven F. Lawson, *Black Ballots: Voting Rights in the South, 1944-1969* (Columbia University Press, 1976), ch. 9; Wofford, ch. 5; Bruce Miroff, *Pragmatic Illusions: The Presidential Politics of John F. Kennedy* (David McKay, 1976), ch. 6 passim; Victor S. Navasky, *Kennedy Justice* (Atheneum, 1971), pp. 96-99.

Marching as to War

361 [*1961 Freedom Rides*]: Zinn, ch. 3; Carson, ch. 3; Raines, book 1, ch. 3; Morris, pp. 231-36; James Peck, *Freedom Ride* (Simon and Schuster, 1962), chs. 8-9; Forman, ch. 18; Brauer, pp. 98-111; James Farmer, *Lay Bare the Heart: An Autobiography of the Civil Rights Movement* (Arbor House, 1985), chs. 17-18; Arthur M. Schlesinger, Jr., *Robert Kennedy and His Times* (Houghton Mifflin, 1978), pp. 294-300; Wofford, pp. 151-58; Meier and Rudwick, ch. 5; Oates, pp. 174-78.
[*"Movement on wheels"*]: Raines, p. 110.
[*"As we entered"*]: Peck, p. 128.
[*FBI informant on beatings*]: Gary Thomas Rowe, Jr., quoted in Schlesinger, *Robert Kennedy*, p. 295.

362 [*"Stop them"*]: quoted in Wofford, p. 153.
[*"Have been cooling off"*]: quoted in Farmer, p. 206.

363 [*"All on probation"*]: ibid., p. 207.
[*King-Kennedy exchange*]: quoted in Schlesinger, *Robert Kennedy*, pp. 299-300.

364 [*Albany*]: Carson, ch. 5; Garrow, *Bearing*, ch. 4; Morris, pp. 239-50; Oates, pp. 188-201; Brauer, pp. 168-79; Zinn, ch. 7; Forman, ch. 33.
[*"Just speak for us"*]: William G. Anderson, quoted in Oates, p. 189.
[*Sherrod on the singing*]: quoted in Forman, p. 247; see also Bernice Johnson Reagon, "Songs of the Civil Rights Movement, 1955-1965: A Study in Culture History" (doctoral dissertation; Howard University, 1975), chs. 2, 3, 5; Reagon, "In Our Hands: Thoughts on Black Music," *Sing Out!*, vol. 24, no. 6 (January-February 1976), pp. 1 ff.
[*Brauer on "Pritchett's jails"*]: Brauer, p. 177.

365 [*Meredith*]: Metcalf, pp. 219-54; Brauer, ch. 7; Schlesinger, *Robert Kennedy*, pp. 317-27; Navasky, ch. 4 passim.
[*"Nobody handpicked me"*]: quoted in Schlesinger, *Robert Kennedy*, p. 317.
[*Barnett on "that boy"*]: ibid., p. 319.

366 [*"Sense of Southern history"*]: Edwin Guthman, quoted in ibid., p. 325; see also Brauer, p. 204.
[*"Republic had been trapped"*]: Schlesinger, *Robert Kennedy*, p. 326.
[*"Breaking out"*]: quoted in ibid., p. 327.
[*Black disagreements over goals and strategy*]: see Carson, ch. 3 passim; Garrow, *Bearing*, pp. 216-30 passim; Forman, ch. 31; Martin Luther King, Jr., *Why We Can't Wait* (Harper, 1964), chs. 2, 8 passim; Lomax, ch. 12.

367 [*The "magic city"*]: see King, *Why We Can't Wait*, pp. 37–43; Morris, pp. 257–58; Silver, *passim*.

[*Birmingham campaign*]: King, *Why We Can't Wait;* Garrow, *Bearing*, pp. 231–64; Oates, pp. 209–43; Morris, pp. 250–74; Raines, book 1, ch. 1, part 1; Forman, ch. 40.

367–8 [*"Letter from Birmingham Jail"*]: in King, *Why We Can't Wait*, ch. 5, quoted at pp. 82, 83, 87, 91; see also Wesley T. Mott, "The Rhetoric of Martin Luther King, Jr.: *Letter from Birmingham Jail,"* *Phylon*, vol. 36, no. 4 (Winter 1975), pp. 411–21.

368 [*The movement and the media*]: see Garrow, *Bearing*, pp. 247–50; Catherine A. Barnes, *Journey from Jim Crow: The Desegregation of Southern Transit* (Columbia University Press, 1983), p. 203; Mary King, esp. ch. 6.

[*"Fan the flames"*]: quoted in Lois L. Duke, "Cultural Redefinition of News: Racial Issues in South Carolina, 1954–1984" (doctoral dissertation; University of South Carolina, 1979), p. 175.

[*"Doesn't live down here"*]: quoted in Garrow, *Bearing*, p. 257.

369 [*Kennedy on photo of dog attack*]: quoted in Brauer, p. 238.

[*"Above all, it is wrong"*]: Special Message to the Congress on Civil Rights, February 28, 1963, in *Public Papers of the Presidents of the United States: John F. Kennedy* (U.S. Government Printing Office, 1962–64), vol. 3, pp. 221–30, quoted at p. 222; see also Brauer, pp. 211–29; Theodore C. Sorensen, *Kennedy* (Harper, 1965), pp. 493–96; Oates, p. 214.

[*King on Kennedy proposals*]: quoted in Brauer, p. 228.

[*Robert Kennedy's meeting with blacks*]: Schlesinger, *Robert Kennedy*, pp. 330–35, Smith quoted at p. 332, Horne at p. 333, Kennedy at p. 334, Schlesinger at p. 335; Brauer, pp. 242–45.

370 [*Tuscaloosa confrontation*]: Brauer, pp. 252–59; Marshall Frady, *Wallace* (New American Library, 1975), pp. 148–70; Schlesinger, *Robert Kennedy*, pp. 337–42; see also Robert J. Norrell, *Reaping the Whirlwind: The Civil Rights Movement in Tuskegee* (Knopf, 1985), chs. 9–10.

[*"Draw the line"*]: quoted in Jody Carlson, *George C. Wallace and the Politics of Powerlessness* (Transaction Books, 1981), p. 24.

[*"Segregation now!"*]: quoted in Frady, p. 142.

[*"Out-nigguhed"*]: quoted in Carlson, p. 22.

[*"Negro baby born"*]: in *Kennedy Public Papers*, vol. 3, pp. 468–71, quoted at pp. 468, 469.

370–1 [*Kennedy's proposals and their reception*]: June 19, 1963, in *ibid.*, vol. 3, pp. 483–94; Sorensen, pp. 496–504; Oates, pp. 243–45; Sundquist, pp. 259–65; Brauer, pp. 245–52, 259–64, and ch. 10 *passim;* see also Steven F. Lawson, " 'I Got It from *The New York Times*': Lyndon Johnson and the Kennedy Civil Rights Program," *Journal of Negro History*, vol. 67, no. 2 (Summer 1982), pp. 159–72.

371 [*March on Washington*]: *New York Times*, August 29, 1963, pp. 1, 16–21; Oates, pp. 246–47, 256–64; Garrow, *Bearing*, pp. 265–86 *passim;* Schlesinger, *Robert Kennedy*, pp. 349–52; Carson, ch. 7; Brauer, pp. 272–73, 290–93; Forman, ch. 43.

[*"May seem ill-timed"*]: quoted in Schlesinger, *Robert Kennedy*, p. 350.

[*Lewis's speech at March*]: Carson, pp. 91–95, quoted at p. 95.

371–2 [*King's speech at March*]: Oates, pp. 261–62, quoted at p. 262.

372 [*Post-March meeting with Kennedy*]: Garrow, *Bearing*, p. 285.

[*Wilkins on Kennedy*]: quoted in Oates, p. 262.

[*Moody*]: Moody, *Coming of Age in Mississippi* (Dial, 1968), p. 275.

[*"Fuck that dream"*]: quoted in Schlesinger, *Robert Kennedy*, p. 351.

[*Evers shooting and Kennedy*]: *New York Times*, June 13, 1963, pp. 1, 12–13; *ibid.*, June 21, 1963, p. 14; Metcalf, pp. 195–218; Schlesinger, *Robert Kennedy*, pp. 344–45.

[*Arrests in South*]: see Theodore H. White, *The Making of the President: 1964* (Atheneum, 1965), p. 171.

[*Birmingham church bombing*]: *New York Times*, September 16, 1963, pp. 1, 26; Oates, pp. 267–69.

372–3 [*Dallas 1963*]: William Manchester, *The Death of a President* (Harper, 1967), pp. 34–51 *passim;* Herbert S. Parmet, *JFK: The Presidency of John F. Kennedy* (Dial, 1983), pp. 340, 344–45.

373 [*WANTED FOR TREASON*]: quoted in Parmet, p. 340.

[*Kennedy in Texas*]: *ibid.*, pp. 341–46; Manchester, book 1 *passim*.

373 ["*That'll add interest*"]: quoted in Parmet, p. 341.
["*You know the French author*"]: Moynihan papers, Nixon Administration Papers, Subject File II, excerpt from interview, December 5, 1963, uncatalogued folder.
374 ["*Caught in cross currents*"]: quoted in James MacGregor Burns, *John Kennedy: A Political Profile* (Harcourt, 1960), p. 155.
375 ["*Historic crossroad*"]: Mark Stern, "Black Interest Group Pressure on the Executive: John F. Kennedy as Politician," paper prepared for delivery at the 1987 Annual Meeting of the American Political Science Association, King quoted at p. 51.
[*Baker's principle*]: quoted in Mary King, p. 456 (italics added).

We Shall Overcome

[*The Johnson White House and the civil rights struggle*]: Burke Marshall Papers, esp. boxes 17-19, John F. Kennedy Library.
["*Talked long enough*"]: in *The Public Papers of the Presidents of the United States: Lyndon B. Johnson* (U.S. Government Printing Office, 1965-70), vol. 1, part 1, pp. 8-10, quoted at p. 9. On the ambivalence of LBJ over civil rights legislation when Vice President in 1963, as contrasted with his presidential leadership, see telephone conversation between LBJ and Theodore Sorensen, Edison Dictaphone recording, June 3, 1963, Lyndon B. Johnson Library.
376 ["*Resort to arson*"]: quoted in Charles Whalen and Barbara Whalen, *The Longest Debate: A Legislative History of the 1964 Civil Rights Act* (Seven Locks Press, 1985), p. 90.
["*Nefarious bill*"]: ibid., p. 91.
[*Smith and "sex" amendment*]: ibid., pp. 115-17; Carl M. Brauer, "Women Activists, Southern Conservatives, and the Prohibition of Sex Discrimination in Title VII of the 1964 Civil Rights Act," *Journal of Southern History*, vol. 49, no. 1 (February 1983), pp. 37-56.
[*House passage of civil rights bill*]: Whalen and Whalen, p. 121; Sundquist, p. 266 and p. 266 n. 144; see also Joe R. Feagin, "Civil Rights Voting by Southern Congressmen," *Journal of Politics*, vol. 34, no. 2 (May 1972), pp. 484-99.
[*Senate filibuster*]: Whalen and Whalen, chs. 5-7; Sundquist, pp. 267-69.
["*To the last ditch*"]: Russell, quoted in Whalen and Whalen, p. 142.
[*Thurmond's filibuster record*]: ibid., p. 143.
377 ["*Billion dollar blackjack*"]: ibid., p. 145.
[*Russell on lobbyists*]: quoted in Sundquist, p. 268.
[*Length of Senate debate*]: see ibid., p. 267 n. 146.
["*Bill can't pass*"]: quoted in Whalen and Whalen, p. 148.
[*Aide on LBJ and Dirksen*]: quoted in Sundquist, p. 268.
377-8 [*Senate approval of cloture and bill*]: ibid., pp. 269-70; Whalen and Whalen, pp. 199-200; see also Rowland Evans and Robert Novak, *Lyndon B. Johnson: The Exercise of Power* (New American Library, 1966), pp. 76-80.
["*More abiding commitment*"]: in *Johnson Public Papers*, vol. 1, part 2, pp. 842-44, quoted at p. 843.
[*Provisions of civil rights bill*]: see Whalen and Whalen, pp. 239-42 (Appendix).
378-9 [*Hamer on Ruleville meeting*]: Hamer, *To Praise Our Bridges* (KIPCO, 1967), p. 12.
379 [*Hamer*]: Hamer; Raines, pp. 249-55; Zinn, pp. 93-96; Susan Kling, "Fannie Lou Hamer: Baptism by Fire," in Pam McAllister, ed., *Reweaving the Web of Life: Feminism and Nonviolence* (New Society, 1982), pp. 106-11; Mary King, pp. 140-44.
["*Just listenin' at 'em*"]: quoted in Raines, p. 249.
[*Hamer on literacy test*]: ibid., p. 250.
["*Too yellow*"]: Hamer, p. 12.
[*Reprisals against Hamer*]: ibid., p. 13; Zinn, p. 94; Raines, pp. 250-51.
[*Mississippi voter registration drive*]: Carson, chs. 4, 8, 9; Zinn, chs. 4-6; Forman, chs. 30, 34, 36, 38, 48; Sally Belfrage, *Freedom Summer* (Viking, 1965); Mary A. Rothschild, *A Case of Black and White: Northern Volunteers and the Southern Freedom Summers, 1964-1965* (Greenwood Press, 1982); Meier and Rudwick, *CORE*, ch. 9; Emily Stoper, "The Student Nonviolent Coordinating Committee: Rise and Fall of a Redemptive Organization," *Journal of Black Studies*, vol. 8, no. 1 (September 1977), pp. 13-34; Bob Moses, "Mississippi: 1961-1962," *Liberation*, vol. 14, no. 9 (January 1970), pp. 7-17; Canta-

row and O'Malley, pp. 86–88; Seth Cagin and Philip Dray, *We Are Not Afraid* (Macmillan, 1988).

379 [*Baker's mediation at Highlander*]: Carson, pp. 41–42.
380 [*"Born in prison"*]: quoted in Zinn, p. 80.
    [*Hamer on jail beatings*]: Raines, pp. 253–54, quoted at p. 253; Hamer, p. 14.
    [*Casting of "freedom ballots"*]: Zinn, pp. 98–101; Carson, pp. 97–98; Forman, pp. 354–56.
    [*MFDP*]: Carson, pp. 108–9, 117; Belfrage, ch. 12; Hanes Walton, Jr., *Black Political Parties* (Free Press, 1972), pp. 80–95.
381 [*"Extraordinary inner sense"*]: Belfrage, p. 201.
    [*MFDP at Democratic convention*]: Forman, pp. 384–97; Carson, pp. 123–28; Mary King, pp. 343–52; Belfrage, pp. 236–46; Walton, pp. 95–103; White, pp. 277–82; Sitkoff, pp. 179–85; Evans and Novak, pp. 451–56.
    [*"Popcorn and seaweed"*]: Belfrage, p. 240.
    [*"Woesome time"*]: quoted in Raines, p. 252.
    [*"I question America"*]: "The Life of Fannie Lou Hamer," Pacifica radio program (Pacifica Radio Archive, Los Angeles).
381–2 [*"Come all this way"*]: quoted in Forman, p. 395.
382 [*1964 election*]: White, *passim;* John Bartlow Martin, "Election of 1964," in Arthur M. Schlesinger, Jr., *History of American Presidential Elections, 1789–1968* (Chelsea House, 1971), vol. 4, pp. 3565–94; *ibid.*, p. 3702; Eric Goldman, *The Tragedy of Lyndon Johnson* (Knopf, 1969), chs. 8–10; Evans and Novak, chs. 20–21; Robert D. Novak, *The Agony of the G.O.P., 1964* (Macmillan, 1965); John H. Kessel, *The Goldwater Coalition: Republican Strategies in 1964* (Bobbs-Merrill, 1968); Richard H. Rovere, *The Goldwater Caper* (Harcourt, 1965); Samuel A. Kirkpatrick, "Issue Orientation and Voter Choice in 1964," *Social Science Quarterly,* vol. 49, no. 1 (June 1968), pp. 87–102.
    [*Southern black voting, 1964*]: James C. Harvey, *Black Civil Rights During the Johnson Administration* (University and College Press of Mississippi, 1973), p. 27 (Table 1).
    [*Selma and Voting Rights Act*]: David J. Garrow, *Protest at Selma: Martin Luther King, Jr., and the Voting Rights Act of 1965* (Yale University Press, 1978); Charles E. Fager, *Selma 1965: The March That Changed the South* (Scribner, 1974); Garrow, *Bearing,* ch. 7; Sundquist, pp. 271–75; Raines, book 1, ch. 4, part 2; Wofford, ch. 6; Lawson, pp. 307–22; Carson, pp. 157–62; Mary King, pp. 216–28; Oates, pp. 325–65 *passim,* 369–72.
383 [*"Put on their walking shoes"*]: quoted in Garrow, *Bearing,* p. 403.
    [*"Turning point"*]: "The American Promise," March 15, 1965, in *Johnson Public Papers,* vol. 2, part 1, pp. 281–87, quoted at p. 281.
    [*"Mudcaked pilgrims"*]: Fager, p. 158.
384 [*"How long?"*]: quoted in *ibid.,* p. 162.
    [*Murder of Viola Liuzzo*]: *ibid.,* pp. 163–64; Garrow, *Protest,* pp. 117–18; Wade, pp. 347–54.
    [*"They came in darkness"*]: August 6, 1965, in *Johnson Public Papers,* vol. 2, part 2, pp. 840–43, quoted at p. 840.
    [*Conflict within SNCC*]: Carson, part 2 *passim;* Forman, chs. 62–63; Mary King, chs. 12–13 *passim.*
385 [*Black migration, 1960–70*]: Thomas L. Blair, *Retreat from the Ghetto: The End of a Dream?* (Hill and Wang, 1977), p. 228; see also John D. Reid, "Black Urbanization of the South," *Phylon,* vol. 35, no. 3 (Fall 1974), pp. 259–67; Hollis R. Lynch, ed., *The Black Urban Condition: A Documentary History, 1866–1971* (Crowell, 1973), pp. 439–40 (Appendix D).
    [*Black proportion of urban populations by 1960*]: Kenneth B. Clark, *Dark Ghetto: Dilemmas of Social Power* (Harper, 1965), pp. 24 (Tables 2 and 2A), p. 25 (Table 3).
    [*Cost of being black and of discrimination*]: Paul M. Siegel, "On the Cost of Being a Negro," in John F. Kain, ed., *Race and Poverty: The Economics of Discrimination* (Prentice-Hall, 1969), pp. 60–67, quoted at p. 67; and Council of Economic Advisers, "The Economic Cost of Discrimination" (1965), in *ibid.,* pp. 58–59.
    [*Clark's Harlem*]: Clark, quoted on his family's movements at p. xv; see also U.S.

Commission on Civil Rights, *A Time to Listen . . . A Time to Act: Voices from the Ghettoes of the Nation's Cities* (U.S. Government Printing Office, 1967); Paul Jacobs, *Prelude to Riot: A View of Urban America from the Bottom* (Random House, 1967); Daniel R. Fusfeld and Timothy Bates, *The Political Economy of the Urban Ghetto* (Southern Illinois University Press, 1984); Robert Coles, "Like It Is in the Alley," in David R. Goldfield and James B. Lane, eds., *The Enduring Ghetto* (Lippincott, 1973), pp. 104–15; James Baldwin, "Fifth Avenue Uptown," in *ibid.*, pp. 116–24.

385 ["*Anguished cry*"]: Clark, p. xx.
[*Street talk*]: quoted in *ibid.*, pp. 6, 16, 1, 4, respectively.

385–6 [*Malcolm X and the Black Muslims*]: Malcolm X and Alex Haley, *The Autobiography of Malcolm X* (Grove Press, 1965); George Breitman, ed., *Malcolm X Speaks* (Grove Press, 1965); Eugene V. Wolfenstein, *The Victims of Democracy: Malcolm X and the Black Revolution* (University of California Press, 1981); Louis E. Lomax, *When the Word Is Given . . .* (Greenwood Press, 1963); Peter Goldman, *The Death and Life of Malcolm X* (Harper, 1973); C. Eric Lincoln, *The Black Muslims in America*, rev. ed. (Beacon Press, 1973); Blair, ch. 2; Oates, pp. 251–53; Hank Flick, "Malcolm X: The Destroyer and Creator of Myths," *Journal of Black Studies*, vol. 12, no. 2 (December 1981), pp. 166–81; Peter Schrag, "The New Black Myths," *Harper's*, vol. 238, no. 1428 (May 1969), pp. 37–42; Lawrence L. Tyler, "The Protestant Ethic Among the Black Muslims," *Phylon*, vol. 27, no. 1 (Spring 1966), pp. 5–14; Raymond Rodgers and Jimmie N. Rodgers, "The Evolution of the Attitude of Malcolm X toward Whites," *ibid.*, vol. 44, no. 1 (Spring 1983), pp. 108–15; Peter Goldman, "Malcolm X," in John A. Garraty, ed., *Encyclopedia of American Biography* (Harper, 1974), pp. 723–24; Clifton E. Marsh, *From Black Muslims to Muslims: The Transition from Separatism to Islam, 1930–1980* (Scarecrow Press, 1984); Elijah Muhammad, *Message to the Black Man in America* (Muhammad Mosque of Islam No. 2, 1965).

386 [*From "civil rights" to "human rights"*]: "The Ballot or the Bullet," April 3, 1964, in *Malcolm X Speaks*, pp. 23–44, quoted at p. 34.
["*By ballots or by bullets*"]: "With Mrs. Fannie Lou Hamer," December 20, 1964, in *Malcolm X Speaks*, p. 111; see also "Ballot or Bullet" in *ibid.*
["*By any means necessary*"]: see Wolfenstein, pp. 8–9, 324–25; Goldman in Garraty, p. 724.
[*Carmichael*]: Carson, pp. 162–63; Donald J. McCormack, "Stokely Carmichael and Pan-Africanism: Back to Black Power," *Journal of Politics*, vol. 35, no. 2 (May 1973), pp. 386–409; "Stokely Carmichael," in Charles Moritz, ed., *Current Biography Yearbook 1970* (H. W. Wilson Co., 1971), pp. 66–69.
[*Lowndes County Freedom Organization*]: Stokely Carmichael and Charles V. Hamilton, *Black Power: The Politics of Liberation in America* (Vintage, 1967), ch. 5; Carson, pp. 162–66; Walton, ch. 4; "Lowndes County Freedom Organization Voting Pamphlet," in Paul Jacobs and Saul Landau, *The New Radicals* (Random House, 1966), pp. 143–44.
["*Comes out fighting*"]: John Hulett, quoted in Carson, p. 166.
[*SNCC May 1966 meeting*]: *ibid.*, pp. 191–206; Forman, ch. 54.
[*Meredith march*]: Garrow, *Bearing*, pp. 473–89; Oates, pp. 395–405; Martin Luther King, Jr., *Where Do We Go from Here: Chaos or Community?* (Harper, 1967), pp. 23–32; Carson, pp. 207–11; Paul Good, "The Meredith March," *New South*, vol. 21, no. 3 (Summer 1966), pp. 2–16; Steven F. Lawson, *In Pursuit of Power: Southern Blacks and Electoral Politics, 1965–1982* (Columbia University Press, 1985), pp. 49–63.

387 ["*Highlight the need*"]: quoted in Lawson, *In Pursuit*, p. 52.
["*Ain't going to jail no more*"]: quoted in Oates, p. 400.
[*King-Carmichael exchange*]: *Where Do We Go*, pp. 30–32, quoted at pp. 30–31.

388 [*Assassination of Malcolm X*]: Alex Haley, "Epilogue," in Malcolm X and Haley, pp. 422–52; Marsh, p. 89.
[*Black Power and divisions within movement*]: Carson, chs. 14–15; Forman, chs. 47, 55; Blair, ch. 3; Carmichael and Hamilton, esp. ch. 2; Garrow, *Bearing*, ch. 9 *passim*; Walton, pp. 114–28; King, *Where Do We Go*, ch. 2 and *passim*; Meier and Rudwick, *CORE*, ch. 12 and Epilogue; Rhoda L. Blumberg, *Civil Rights: The 1960s Freedom Struggle* (Twayne, 1984), ch. 8; Julius Lester, *Look Out, Whitey! Black Power's Gon' Get*

Your Mama! (Dial, 1968); Charles V. Hamilton, "An Advocate of Black Power Defines It," in August Meier and Elliott Rudwick, eds., *Black Protest in the Sixties* (Quadrangle, 1970), pp. 154–68; Ansbro, pp. 211–24; Bruce Miroff, "Presidential Leverage over Social Movements: The Johnson White House and Civil Rights," *Journal of Politics*, vol. 43, no. 1 (February 1981), pp. 2–23; Joel D. Aberbach and Jack L. Walker, "The Meanings of Black Power: A Comparison of White and Black Interpretations of a Political Slogan," *American Political Science Review*, vol. 64, no. 2 (June 1970), pp. 367–88; Irwin Klibaner, "The Travail of Southern Radicals: The Southern Conference Educational Fund, 1946–1976," *Journal of Southern History*, vol. 49, no. 2 (May 1983), pp. 195–201; Chafe, ch. 7; Bayard Rustin, "'Black Power' and Coalition Politics," *Commentary*, vol. 42, no. 3 (September 1966), pp. 35–40; David Danzig, "In Defense of 'Black Power,'" *ibid.*, pp. 41–46.

388 [*King's shift leftward*]: see Oates, pp. 365–68, 418–26, 431–43; Lewis, ch. 10 *passim*; see also Ansbro, ch. 7; King, *Where Do We Go*.
[*"Reconstruction of the entire society"*]: quoted in Oates, p. 442.
[*CORE approval and NAACP rejection of Black Power*]: Meier and Rudwick, *CORE*, p. 414; *New York Times*, July 5, 1966, pp. 1, 22; *ibid.*, July 6, 1966, pp. 1, 14; *ibid.*, July 10, 1966, p. 53.

9. The World Turned Upside Down

389 [*Medicare*]: Theodore R. Marmor, *The Politics of Medicare* (Aldine, 1973), esp. ch. 4; Eric F. Goldman, *The Tragedy of Lyndon Johnson* (Knopf, 1969), pp. 284–96; Lyndon B. Johnson, *The Vantage Point: Perspectives on the Presidency, 1963–1969* (Holt, Rinehart and Winston, 1971), pp. 212–20.
[*Omnibus Housing bill and creation of HUD*]: John Nicholson et al., eds., *Housing a Nation* (Congressional Quarterly Service, 1966), pp. 60–86; Robert Taggart III, *Low-Income Housing: A Critique of Federal Aid* (Johns Hopkins Press, 1970), ch. 5; John B. Willmann, *The Department of Housing and Urban Development* (Praeger, 1967), ch. 2.
[*National Foundation for the Arts and the Humanities*]: Stephen Miller, *Excellence and Equity: The National Endowment for the Humanities* (University Press of Kentucky, 1984), ch. 1; Michael M. Mooney, *The Ministry of Culture* (Wyndham Books, 1980), pp. 46–49.
[*Water Quality bill and 1965 Clean Air Act*]: J. Clarence Davies III, *The Politics of Pollution* (Pegasus, 1970), pp. 38–44, 49–54; Charles O. Jones, *Clean Air: The Policies and Politics of Pollution Control* (University of Pittsburgh Press, 1975), pp. 62–66; Rachel Carson, *Silent Spring* (Houghton Mifflin, 1962); Frank Graham, Jr., *Since Silent Spring* (Houghton Mifflin, 1970), esp. part 1.
[*School aid program*]: Hugh Davis Graham, *The Uncertain Triumph: Federal Education Policy in the Kennedy and Johnson Years* (University of North Carolina Press, 1984), ch. 3 *passim*; Vaughn D. Bornet, *The Presidency of Lyndon B. Johnson* (University Press of Kansas, 1983), pp. 222–24; Goldman, pp. 296–308; Johnson, pp. 206–12; *New York Times*, April 12, 1965, pp. 1, 22.

390 [*Great Society and LBJ's presidential style generally*]: see Doris Kearns, *Lyndon Johnson and the American Dream* (Harper, 1976), chs. 7–8; Rowland Evans and Robert Novak, *Lyndon B. Johnson: The Exercise of Power* (New American Library, 1966), chs. 17, 19, 22; Bornet, chs. 1–2, 10; Harry McPherson, *A Political Education* (Atlantic Monthly/Little, Brown, 1972), pp. 248–333 *passim*; Goldman, esp. chs. 2, 4–5, 12, and pp. 164–67; Jack Valenti, *A Very Human President* (Norton, 1975); Hugh Sidey, *A Very Personal Presidency: Lyndon Johnson in the White House* (Atheneum, 1968); Frank Cormier, *LBJ: The Way He Was* (Doubleday, 1977); David Halberstam, *The Best and the Brightest* (Random House, 1972), esp. ch. 20.
[*Peace Corps*]: Gerald T. Rice, *The Bold Experiment: JFK's Peace Corps* (University of Notre Dame Press, 1985); Robert G. Carey, *The Peace Corps* (Praeger, 1970); David Hapgood and Meridan Bennett, *Agents of Change: A Close Look at the Peace Corps* (Little, Brown, 1968); Marshall Windmiller, *The Peace Corps and Pax Americana* (Public Affairs Press, 1970).
[*U.S. personnel in Vietnam at Kennedy's death*]: Johnson, p. 42.

390–1 [*American deaths in Vietnam, 1963*]: George McT. Kahin and John W. Lewis, *The United States in Vietnam* (Dial, 1967), p. 188 (Table 4).

People of This Generation

391 [*Scientists and the bomb*]: Paul Boyer, *By the Bomb's Early Light: American Thought and Culture at the Dawn of the Atomic Age* (Pantheon, 1985), part 3; Morton Grodzins and Eugene Rabinowitch, eds., *The Atomic Age: Scientists in World and National Affairs* (Basic Books, 1963); Alice Kimball Smith, *A Peril and a Hope: The Scientists' Movement in America, 1945–47* (University of Chicago Press, 1965); Joseph Rotblat, *Scientists, the Arms Race and Disarmament* (Taylor & Francis, 1982); Linus Pauling, *No More War!* (Dodd, Mead, 1958); Lawrence S. Wittner, *Rebels Against War: The American Peace Movement, 1933–1983* (Temple University Press, 1984), pp. 143–50, 165–69, 175–78, 188–90, 199–201.

["*Bridge the gap*"]: Wittner, p. 251.

[*CNVA*]: ibid., pp. 246–50, 252–53, 261–62; see also Thomas B. Morgan, "Doom and Passion Along Rt. 45," in Harold Hayes, ed., *Smiling Through the Apocalypse: Esquire's History of the Sixties* (McCall Publishing, 1970), pp. 548–60.

[*Voyage of the* Phoenix]: Earle Reynolds, *Forbidden Voyage* (David McKay, 1961); Albert Bigelow, *The Voyage of the Golden Rule: An Experiment with Truth* (Doubleday, 1959); Wittner, pp. 247–50; Barbara Deming, *Revolution & Equilibrium* (Grossman, 1971), pp. 124–35.

["*Gigantic flash bulb*"]: Reynolds, p. 61.

[*Omaha Action*]: Wittner, p. 262; Wilmer J. Young, "Visible Witness," in A. Paul Hare and Herbert H. Blumberg, eds., *Nonviolent Direct Action, American Cases: Social-Psychological Analyses* (Corpus Books, 1968), pp. 158–70.

[*New London action*]: Deming, pp. 23–37; Wittner, pp. 261–62.

[*March to Moscow*]: Deming, pp. 51–72, Lyttle quoted at p. 69; Jules Rabin, "How We Went," in Lillian Schlissel, ed., *Conscience in America: A Documentary History of Conscientious Objection in America, 1757–1967* (E. P. Dutton, 1968), pp. 376–83.

392 [*Women Strike for Peace*]: *New York Times*, November 2, 1961, p. 5; Wittner, p. 277; Amy Swerdlow, "Ladies' Day at the Capitol: Women Strike for Peace Versus HUAC," *Feminist Studies*, vol. 8, no. 3 (Fall 1982), pp. 493–520; Walter Goodman, *The Committee* (Farrar, Straus & Giroux, 1968), pp. 437–42.

[*SANE*]: Wittner, pp. 242–46, 251–52, 257–61, 280; Robert A. Divine, *Blowing on the Wind: The Nuclear Test Ban Debate, 1954–1960* (Oxford University Press, 1978), pp. 165–69; Deming, pp. 38–50.

[*1963 limited test ban*]: Harold K. Jacobson and Eric Stein, *Diplomats, Scientists, and Politicians: The United States and the Nuclear Test Ban Negotiations* (University of Michigan Press, 1966); Glenn T. Seaborg, *Kennedy, Khrushchev and the Test Ban* (University of California Press, 1981); Arthur M. Schlesinger, Jr., *A Thousand Days: John F. Kennedy in the White House* (Houghton Mifflin, 1965), ch. 17 and pp. 893–915 *passim*; Wittner, pp. 279–81; see also Divine.

[*SDS origins and Port Huron conference*]: James Miller, *"Democracy is in the Streets": From Port Huron to the Siege of Chicago* (Simon and Schuster, 1987), chs. 1–6; Kirkpatrick Sale, *SDS* (Random House, 1973), chs. 2–4 and pp. 673–93; Todd Gitlin, *The Sixties: Years of Hope, Days of Rage* (Bantam, 1987), ch. 5.

["*Bones*," "*widgets*," and "*gizmos*"]: quoted in Sale, p. 49.

393 [*Port Huron Statement*]: in Paul Jacobs and Saul Landau, *The New Radicals* (Random House, 1966), pp. 150–62, quoted at pp. 150, 152–53, 155; see also Miller, chs. 5, 8; Wini Breines, *The Great Refusal: Community and Organization in the New Left, 1962–68* (Praeger, 1982), esp. ch. 4; G. David Garson, "The Ideology of the New Student Left," in Julian Foster and Durward Long, eds., *Protest! Student Activism in America* (Morrow, 1970), pp. 184–201; David Westby and Richard Braungart, "Activists and the History of the Future," in *ibid.*, pp. 158–83; Irwin Unger, *The Movement: A History of the New American Left, 1959–1972* (Dodd, Mead, 1974), pp. 52–56.

[*Breines on SDS goals*]: Breines, p. 57.

[*Freedom struggle and New Left*]: see Sara Evans, *Personal Politics: The Roots of Women's Liberation in the Civil Rights Movement and the New Left* (Knopf, 1979); Clayborne Carson, *In Struggle: SNCC and the Black Awakening of the Sixties* (Harvard University Press, 1981), pp. 53–55 and ch. 12 *passim*; Mitchell Cohen and Dennis Hale, eds., *The New Student*

Left (Beacon Press, 1966), pp. 50–109; see also Mario Savio, "An End to History," in Hal Draper, *Berkeley: The New Student Revolt* (Grove Press, 1965), pp. 179–82.

394 [*"No Honor"*]: Goodman, *Growing Up Absurd: Problems of Youth in the Organized System* (Random House, 1960), p. 12; see also Richard Flacks, "Who Protests: The Social Bases of the Student Movement," in Foster and Long, pp. 134–57; Steven Warnecke, "American Student Politics," *Yale Review*, vol. 60, no. 2 (December 1970), pp. 185–98; Kenneth Keniston, *The Uncommitted: Alienated Youth in American Society* (Harcourt, 1965); Keniston, *Young Radicals: Notes on Committed Youth* (Harcourt, 1968); Paul Cowan, *The Making of an Un-American: A Dialogue with Experience* (Viking, 1970); Unger, pp. 25–42.

[*The Beats*]: Gitlin, *Sixties*, pp. 45–54; Lawrence Lipton, *The Holy Barbarians* (Julian Messner, 1959), part 4 and *passim;* Bruce Cook, *The Beat Generation* (Scribner, 1971); Daniel Wolf and Edwin Fancher, eds., *The Village Voice Reader* (Doubleday, 1962); Jack Newfield, *A Prophetic Minority* (New American Library, 1966), ch. 2.

[*"Rise of the cheerful robot"*]: Mills, "The Politics of Responsibility," in Carl Oglesby, ed., *The New Left Reader* (Grove Press, 1969), pp. 23–31, quoted at p. 26; see also Mills, "Letter to the New Left," *New Left Review*, no. 5 (September–October 1960), pp. 18–23; Miller, ch. 4; Ronald Berman, *America in the Sixties: An Intellectual History* (Free Press, 1968), pp. 110–18.

[*Free Speech Movement*]: Draper; Editors of *California Monthly*, "Chronology of Events: Three Months of Crisis," in Seymour Martin Lipset and Sheldon S. Wolin, eds., *The Berkeley Student Revolt: Facts and Interpretations* (Anchor/Doubleday, 1965), pp. 99–199; Lipset and Wolin *passim;* Sale, pp. 162–69; *Daily Californian* (University of California, Berkeley), October 1, 1984; Breines, pp. 23–31, 46–47; Berman, pp. 156–64; Bettina Aptheker talk at University of California, Berkeley, October 2, 1984.

395 [*"Take all of us!"*]: Draper, p. 39.

[*Aptheker's speech*]: Stewart Burns interview with Aptheker, February 18, 1986.

[*Berkeley students at HUAC hearings, 1960*]: Goodman, *The Committee*, pp. 429–34; Unger, pp. 45–47; see also Max Heirich and Sam Kaplan, "Yesterday's Discord," in Lipset and Wolin, pp. 10–35.

[*"Had to convince people"*]: Savio talk at University of California, Berkeley, October 2, 1984.

396 [*"We students parted ranks"*]: Aptheker talk at University of California, Berkeley, October 2, 1984.

[*The multiversity*]: see Lipset and Wolin, part 2; Wolin and John H. Schaar, "The Abuses of the Multiversity," in *ibid.*, pp. 350–63; Clark Kerr, *The Uses of the University* (Harvard University Press, 1963); Berman, pp. 145–56; Michael W. Miles, *The Radical Probe: The Logic of Student Rebellion* (Atheneum, 1971), ch. 3; Immanuel Wallerstein and Paul Starr, eds., *The University Crisis Reader* (Random House, 1971), vol. 1, chs. 2–3, 7.

[*"Ill-housed"*]: Wolin and Schaar, p. 360.

397 [*Kerr on university president*]: Kerr, "Selections from *The Uses of the University*," in Lipset and Wolin, pp. 38–60, quoted at p. 38; see also Kerr, "Reply to Wolin and Schaar," in *ibid.*, pp. 364–66; Kerr, "Presidential Discontent," in David C. Nichols, ed., *Perspectives on Campus Tensions* (American Council on Education, 1970), pp. 137–62.

[*"Delicate balance"*]: Rudolph, *The American College and University: A History* (Knopf, 1962), p. 423.

[*"Southern struggle"*]: in Jacobs and Landau, p. 150.

[*Watts*]: Jerry Cohen, *Burn, Baby, Burn!: The Los Angeles Riot, August 1965* (E. P. Dutton, 1966); Robert E. Conot, *Rivers of Blood, Years of Darkness* (Bantam, 1967); Paul Jacobs, *Prelude to Riot: A View of Urban America from the Bottom* (Random House, 1966); William Manchester, *The Glory and the Dream* (Little, Brown, 1974), pp. 1062–65; Stephen B. Oates, *Let the Trumpet Sound: The Life of Martin Luther King, Jr.* (Harper, 1982), pp. 377–78.

398 [*"Burning their city"*]: Robert Richardson, quoted in Manchester, p. 1064.

[*"How can you say you won . . . ?"*]: quoted in Oates, p. 377.

[*Muhammad on need for "complete separation"*]: in John H. Bracey, Jr., et al., eds., *Black*

Nationalism in America (Bobbs-Merrill, 1970), pp. 404–7, quoted at pp. 404, 405; see also C. Eric Lincoln, *The Black Muslims in America* (Beacon Press, 1961), pp. 84–97 and *passim.*

399 [*National Conference on Black Power*]: *New York Times*, July 21, 1967, pp. 1, 34; *ibid.*, July 22, 1967, pp. 1, 10–11; *ibid.*, July 24, 1967, pp. 1, 16; Thomas L. Blair, *Retreat to the Ghetto: The End of a Dream?* (Hill and Wang, 1977), p. 202.

[*Black Panther party*]: Gene Marine, *The Black Panthers* (New American Library, 1969); Huey P. Newton, *Revolutionary Suicide* (Harcourt, 1973); Eldridge Cleaver, *Soul on Ice* (McGraw-Hill, 1968); Bobby Seale, *A Lonely Rage* (Times Books, 1978); Blair, pp. 86–103 *passim;* Don A. Schanche, *The Panther Paradox: A Liberal's Dilemma* (David McKay, 1970); Paul Chevigny, *Cops and Rebels: A Study of Provocation* (Pantheon, 1972); James Forman, *The Making of Black Revolutionaries* (Macmillan, 1972), ch. 64.

[*Seale on arming blacks*]: quoted in Blair, p. 92.

[*Fragmentation of movement groups along political spectrum*]: see Blair, pp. 81–83; Carson, pp. 144–45, 189, 191.

[*"Thrust of Black Power"*]: Blair, p. 82.

[*Black culture*]: see *ibid.*, ch. 5 *passim;* Lee Rainwater, ed., *Soul* (Transaction Books, 1970); Al Calloway, "An Introduction to Soul," in Hayes, pp. 708–12; Ulf Hannerz, "The Significance of Soul," in August Meier, ed., *The Transformation of Activism* (Aldine, 1970), pp. 155–78; Adrian Dove, "Soul Story," in August Meier and Elliott Rudwick, eds., *Black Protest in the Sixties* (Quadrangle, 1970), pp. 243–51; Peter Schrag, "The New Black Myths," *Harper's*, vol. 238, no. 1428 (May 1969), pp. 37–42.

[*Black theology*]: see Charles V. Hamilton, *The Black Preacher in America* (Morrow, 1972), esp. ch. 5; James H. Cone and Gayraud S. Wilmore, eds., *Black Theology: A Documentary History, 1966–1979* (Orbis Books, 1979); James H. Cone, *Black Theology and Black Power* (Seabury Press, 1969); Blair, pp. 128–33.

[*Growth in number of black Roman Catholics*]: Blair, p. 133.

400 [*"Gonna knock the hell"*]: quoted in Oates, p. 397.

[*"We Shall Overrun"*]: *ibid.*

[*King in Chicago*]: David J. Garrow, *Bearing the Cross: Martin Luther King, Jr., and the Southern Christian Leadership Conference* (Morrow, 1986), chs. 8–9 *passim;* Oates, pp. 365–69, 387–95, 405–19; David L. Lewis, *King* (Praeger, 1970), ch. 11; Bill Gleason, *Daley of Chicago* (Simon and Schuster, 1970), chs. 4–5; see also CORE (Chicago Chapter), 1956–64, boxes 1 and 2, Chicago Historical Society.

[*"Unable to deliver"*]: quoted in Oates, p. 406; see also August Meier and Elliott Rudwick, "Negro Protest and Urban Unrest," *Social Science Quarterly*, vol. 49, no. 3 (December 1968), pp. 438–43.

[*"Never seen anything like it"*]: quoted in Oates, p. 413.

401 [*"We want freedom"*]: in Bracey et al., p. 404.

[*"Full and complete freedom"*]: *ibid.*

[*"Power to determine"*]: in *ibid.*, pp. 526–29, quoted at p. 526.

[*Black opposition to Vietnam*]: Henry E. Darby and Margaret N. Rowley, "King on Vietnam and Beyond," *Phylon*, vol. 47, no. 1 (March 1986), pp. 43–50; Garrow, esp. ch. 10 *passim;* Oates, pp. 373–76, 431–44; Lewis, pp. 307–12, 355–71 *passim;* Carson, pp. 183–89; Forman, pp. 444–47; Michael Ferber and Staughton Lynd, *The Resistance* (Beacon Press, 1971), pp. 29–33; Adam Fairclough, "Martin Luther King, Jr., and the War in Vietnam," *Phylon*, vol. 45, no. 1 (1984), pp. 19–39.

[*"We must combine"*]: quoted in Oates, p. 431.

Rolling Thunder

[*"If I left the woman"*]: quoted in Kearns, pp. 251–53; see also F. M. Kail, *What Washington Said: Administration Rhetoric and the Vietnam War, 1949–1969* (Harper, 1973), pp. 97–103 and *passim;* Goldman, chs. 14–15, 18 and *passim;* Philip Geyelin, *Lyndon B. Johnson and the World* (Praeger, 1966), chs. 1, 5–6; Halberstam, esp. ch. 20; James Deakin, "The Dark Side of L.B.J.," in Hayes, pp. 506–22; Joseph Kraft, *Profiles in Power: A Washington Insight* (New American Library, 1966), ch. 2.

402 [*Morgenthau's warning*]: see McPherson, pp. 389–90; see also Hans J. Morgenthau, "We Are Deluding Ourselves in Viet-Nam," in Marcus G. Raskin and Bernard B. Fall, eds., *The Viet-Nam Reader* (Random House, 1965), pp. 37–45.

403 [*Tonkin*]: George C. Herring, *America's Longest War: The United States and Vietnam, 1950–1975*, 2nd ed. (Temple University Press, 1986), pp. 118–23; George McT. Kahin, *Intervention: How America Became Involved in Vietnam* (Knopf, 1986), pp. 219–26; Joseph C. Goulden, *Truth Is the First Casualty: The Gulf of Tonkin Affair—Illusion and Reality* (Rand McNally, 1969); Kathleen J. Turner, *Lyndon Johnson's Dual War: Vietnam and the Press* (University of Chicago Press, 1985), pp. 81–85; Anthony Austin, *The President's War* (Lippincott, 1971); Sandy Vogelgesang, *The Long Dark Night of the Soul: The American Intellectual Left and the Vietnam War* (Harper, 1974), pp. 53–55; Stanley Karnow, *Vietnam* (Viking, 1983), pp. 365–76.

[*Pleiku*]: Herring, pp. 128–29; Halberstam, pp. 520–26; Karnow, pp. 411–15.

[*Johnson's men*]: Halberstam; Kraft; Richard J. Barnet, "The Men Who Made the War," in Ralph Stavins et al., *Washington Plans an Aggressive War* (Random House, 1971), pp. 199–252; Roger Hilsman, *To Move a Nation: The Politics of Foreign Policy in the Administration of John F. Kennedy* (Doubleday, 1967), ch. 4; Henry L. Trewhitt, *McNamara: His Ordeal in the Pentagon* (Harper, 1971); Warren I. Cohen, *Dean Rusk* (Cooper Square Publishers, 1980); John B. Henry II and William Espinosa, "The Tragedy of Dean Rusk," *Foreign Policy*, no. 8 (Fall 1972), pp. 166–89.

404 [*Dominican intervention*]: Theodore Draper, *The Dominican Revolt: A Case Study in American Policy* (Commentary, 1968); Abraham F. Lowenthal, *The Dominican Intervention* (Harvard University Press, 1972); Evans and Novak, ch. 23; Turner, pp. 135–37; Geyelin, ch. 10.

405 [*Mao's advice*]: see Karnow, p. 329.

[*Lin Piao's article*]: see John J. Duiker, *The Communist Road to Power in Vietnam* (Westview Press, 1981), p. 245; Karnow, p. 453.

[*Vietnam, China, Soviet Union*]: Duiker, *passim;* Donald S. Zagoria, *Vietnam Triangle: Moscow, Peking, Hanoi* (Pegasus, 1967); Daniel S. Papp, *Vietnam: The View from Moscow, Peking, Washington* (McFarland & Co., 1981); Jon M. Van Dyke, *North Vietnam's Strategy for Survival* (Pacific Books, 1972), pp. 217–28; King C. Chen, *Vietnam and China, 1938–1954* (Princeton University Press, 1969); Jean Lacouture, *Ho Chi Minh*, Peter Wiles, trans. (Random House, 1968), ch. 13; Frances FitzGerald, *Fire in the Lake: The Vietnamese and the Americans in Vietnam* (Atlantic Monthly/Little, Brown, 1972), ch. 2 *passim;* Adam B. Ulam, *The Rivals: America and Russia Since World War II* (Viking, 1971), ch. 11 *passim;* Victor C. Funnell, "Vietnam and the Sino-Soviet Conflict, 1965–1976" and "Documents: Vietnam and the Sino-Soviet Conflict," *Studies in Comparative Communism*, vol. 11, nos. 1–2 (Spring–Summer, 1978), pp. 142–99.

[*Rolling Thunder*]: Herring, pp. 129–30, 146–47, 149–50; see also Kahin, chs. 10–11; James C. Thompson, *Rolling Thunder: Understanding Policy and Program Failure* (University of North Carolina Press, 1980); Turner, pp. 114–18.

[*McNamara on civilian casualties*]: Herring, p. 147.

405-6 [*Divisions within Administration*]: see Herring, pp. 137–43; Larry Berman, *Planning a Tragedy: The Americanization of the War in Vietnam* (Norton, 1982); Halberstam, *Best and Brightest*, chs. 24–26 *passim;* Henry F. Graff, *The Tuesday Cabinet: Deliberation and Decision on War and Peace under Lyndon B. Johnson* (Prentice-Hall, 1970), ch. 1; George W. Ball, *The Past Has Another Pattern* (Norton, 1982), pp. 380–403; Geyelin, pp. 213–35, 291–302; Leslie H. Gelb and Richard K. Betts, *The Irony of Vietnam: The System Worked* (Brookings Institution, 1979), pp. 116–43 *passim;* Harvey A. DeWeerd, "Strategic Decision-Making in Vietnam, 1965–1968," *Yale Review*, vol. 67, no. 4 (June 1978), pp. 481–92.

406 [*North Vietnam's defense and mobilization against U.S. bombing and escalation*]: see Herring, pp. 147–49, "ant labor" quoted at p. 148; Karnow, pp. 454–59; see also Van Dyke, *passim;* Duiker, pp. 240–46; Wilfred G. Burchett, *Vietnam North* (International Publishers, 1966).

["*Most sophisticated war*"]: quoted in Herring, p. 151.

["*To locate an ever elusive enemy*"]: *ibid.;* see also William A. Buckingham, Jr., *Operation Ranch Hand: The Air Force and Herbicides in Southeast Asia: 1961–1971* (Office of Air Force History, 1982); William Heseltine, "The Automated Air War," *New Republic*, vol. 165, no. 16 (October 16, 1971), pp. 15–17; Paul F. Cecil, *Herbicidal Warfare: The RANCH HAND Project in Vietnam* (Praeger, 1986).

406 [*"I have no army"*]: quoted in FitzGerald, p. 169; see also *ibid.*, esp. ch. 4; Duiker; Douglas Pike, *Viet Cong: The Organization and Techniques of the National Liberation Front of South Vietnam* (MIT Press, 1966); Van Dyke; Paul Berman, *Revolutionary Organization: Institution-Building Within the People's Liberation Armed Forces* (Lexington Books, 1974); Vo Nguyen Giap, *People's War, People's Army* (Praeger, 1962); Susan Sheehan, "The Enemy," *New Yorker*, vol. 42, no. 29 (September 10, 1966), pp. 62–100; George A. Carver, Jr., "The Faceless Viet Cong," *Foreign Affairs*, vol. 44, no. 3 (April 1966), pp. 347–72; David Hunt, "Villagers at War: The National Liberation Front in My Tho Province, 1965–1967," *Radical America*, vol. 8, nos. 1–2 (January–April 1974), pp. 3–181; Cincinnatus, *Self-Destruction: The Disintegration and Decay of the United States Army During the Vietnam Era* (Norton, 1981), Appendix D.

[*"Key to the vast, secret torrents"*]: FitzGerald, p. 169.

407 [*Washington protest, April 1965*]: *New York Times*, April 18, 1965, pp. 1, 3; Sale, ch. 11; Miller, pp. 226–34; Todd Gitlin, *The Whole World Is Watching: Mass Media in the Making & Unmaking of the New Left* (University of California Press, 1980), pp. 46–60; Gitlin, *Sixties*, pp. 177–87; Nancy Zaroulis and Gerald Sullivan, *Who Spoke Up?: American Protest Against the War in Vietnam, 1963–1975* (Doubleday, 1984), pp. 38–42.

[*Potter's speech*]: quoted in Sale, p. 189.

[*King's break with Johnson*]: Oates, pp. 373–76.

[*Lippmann's break with Johnson*]: Ronald Steel, *Walter Lippmann and the American Century* (Atlantic Monthly/Little, Brown, 1980), pp. 571–72, quoted at p. 572.

[*Teach-ins*]: Louis Menashe and Ronald Radoshe, eds., *Teach-Ins, U.S.A.* (Praeger, 1967); Zaroulis and Sullivan, pp. 37–38, 43; Vogelgesang, pp. 70–74.

[*March on New York induction center*]: Zaroulis and Sullivan, pp. 51, 53–54, sign quoted at p. 51; *New York Times*, July 30, 1965, p. 2; Ferber and Lynd, pp. 21–22; on the draft and resistance, see also Michael Useem, *Conscription, Protest, and Social Conflict: The Life and Death of a Resistance Movement* (Wiley, 1973); Alice Lynd, ed., *We Won't Go: Personal Accounts of War Objectors* (Beacon Press, 1968); Wallerstein and Starr, vol. 1, ch. 6; *Handbook for Conscientious Objectors*, Arlo Tatum, ed., 8th ed. (Central Committee for Conscientious Objectors, 1966); Jessica Mitford, *The Trial of Dr. Spock* (Knopf, 1969); Lawrence M. Baskir and William A. Strauss, *Chance and Circumstance: The Draft, the War, and the Vietnam Generation* (Knopf, 1978); Ferber and Lynd.

408 [*"Assembly of Unrepresented People"*]: *New York Times*, August 9, 1965, p. 4; *ibid.*, August 10, 1965, p. 3; Zaroulis and Sullivan, pp. 51–53.

[*Antiwar self-immolations*]: see Zaroulis and Sullivan, pp. 1–5, "Burn yourselves" quoted at p. 4.

[*Miller's burning of draft card*]: *ibid.*, pp. 56–57; Ferber and Lynd, pp. 22–27.

[*Fall 1965 international days of protest*]: *New York Times*, October 16, 1965, pp. 1–2; *ibid.*, October 17, 1965, pp. 1, 42–44; Zaroulis and Sullivan, pp. 56–57.

[*Strategic and organizational debate within the movement*]: see Sale, chs. 12–16 *passim*; Miller, pp. 234–59; Breines, ch. 5; Gitlin, *Whole World*, esp. ch. 4; Gitlin, *Sixties*, pp. 188–92, 225–30.

408–9 [*Old Left and New*]: Milton Cantor, *The Divided Left: American Radicalism, 1900–1975* (Hill and Wang, 1978), ch. 10 *passim*; Mills, "Letter to the New Left"; Ronald Berman, *America in the Sixties*, chs. 5–6 *passim*; Breines, pp. 13–17; James Weinstein, "The Left, Old and New," *Socialist Revolution*, vol. 2, no. 4 (July–August 1972), pp. 7–60; Newfield, ch. 8; David Caute, *The Year of the Barricades: A Journey Through 1968* (Harper, 1988), pp. 33–38, 40–43; see also Bogdan Denitch, "The New Left and the New Working Class," in J. David Colfax and Jack L. Roach, eds., *Radical Sociology* (Basic Books, 1971), pp. 341–52.

409 [*"Criminal, sinister country"*]: quoted in Vogelgesang, p. 73.

[*"Alienated intellectuals"*]: *ibid.*, p. 91.

[*April 1967 New York demonstration*]: *New York Times*, April 16, 1967, pp. 1–3; Zaroulis and Sullivan, pp. 110–14; Ferber and Lynd, ch. 5; Lynd, *We Won't Go*, pp. 220–25; Paul Goodman, "We Won't Go," *New York Review of Books*, vol. 8, no. 9 (May 18, 1967), pp. 17–20.

[*From protest to resistance*]: Zaroulis and Sullivan, pp. 86, 94–96, 104–7; Gitlin, *Sixties*, ch. 10 *passim;* Durward Long, "Wisconsin: Changing Styles of Administrative Response," in Foster and Long, pp. 246–70; see also Sale, part 3; Ferber and Lynd, ch. 4 and *passim;* Wallerstein and Starr, vol. 2, ch. 6.

409 [*Pentagon march*]: *New York Times,* October 21, 1967, pp. 1, 8; *ibid.,* October 22, 1967, pp. 1, 58–59; *ibid.,* October 23, 1967, pp. 1, 32–33; Norman Mailer, *The Armies of the Night: History as a Novel, the Novel as History* (New American Library, 1968); Zaroulis and Sullivan, pp. 135–42; David Dellinger, "Gandhi and Guerrilla—The Protest at the Pentagon," in Dellinger, *Revolutionary Nonviolence* (Bobbs-Merrill, 1970), pp. 285–92; Vogelgesang, pp. 130–33; "The Pentagon Demonstration," in Hare and Blumberg, pp. 241–70; Sale, pp. 383–86; Ferber and Lynd, pp. 135–40.

[*"Creative synthesis"*]: Dellinger, "Gandhi and Guerrilla," p. 287.

[*"Witches, warlocks"*]: quoted in Sale, p. 384.

[*"Anarchists of the deed"*]: Gitlin, *Sixties,* p. 223.

410 [*"Join us"*]: quoted in David Dellinger, *More Power Than We Know: The People's Movement Toward Democracy* (Anchor Books, 1975), p. 126.

[*"Burn a draft card!"*]: quoted in Zaroulis and Sullivan, p. 139.

[*U.S. troops in Vietnam, 1967*]: see Karnow, p. 512.

[*Divisions within Administration and LBJ*]: Kearns, ch. 11; Karnow, ch. 13 *passim;* Turner, ch. 7 *passim;* Johnson, pp. 366–78; Townsend Hoopes, *The Limits of Intervention* (David McKay, 1969), chs. 3–6; Gelb and Betts, pp. 156–70; Graff, ch. 3; Herring, pp. 175–83; DeWeerd.

[*"Bomb, bomb, bomb"*]: quoted in Herring, p. 178.

[*"Spit in China's face"*]: quoted in Karnow, p. 504.

[*"Can't hunker down"*]: quoted in Herring, p. 179.

[*Ebbing of revolutionary zeal*]: quoted in Duiker, p. 262.

410–11 [*Preparations for Tet*]: Don Oberdorfer, *Tet!* (Doubleday, 1971), ch. 2; Duiker, pp. 263–65; Herring, pp. 187–88.

411 [*Tet and its effects upon American opinion*]: Oberdorfer; Karnow, pp. 523–44; FitzGerald, ch. 15; Herring, pp. 186–92, 200–3; Turner, pp. 217–23; Duiker, pp. 265–71, 273–76; Gitlin, *Sixties,* pp. 298–301; Robert Pisor, *The End of the Line: The Siege of Khe Sanh* (Norton, 1982); Peter Braestrup, *Big Story,* 2 vols. (Westview Press, 1977); John B. Henry II, "February, 1968," *Foreign Policy,* no. 4 (Fall 1974), pp. 3–33; Herbert Y. Schandler, *The Unmaking of a President: Lyndon Johnson and Vietnam* (Princeton University Press, 1977), ch. 4; see also Harry G. Summers, Jr., *On Strategy* (Presidio Press, 1982), ch. 1.

[*"What the hell is going on?"*]: quoted in Herring, p. 191; see also Oberdorfer, pp. 246–50.

[*"It seems now more certain"*]: quoted in Oberdorfer, p. 251.

[*"American people know the facts"*]: quoted in Turner, pp. 221–22.

[*Debate over post-Tet strategy*]: Herring, pp. 192–206 *passim;* Oberdorfer, pp. 257–77 and ch. 8; Hoopes, chs. 8–10; Karnow, pp. 549–57; Johnson, pp. 383–415 *passim;* DeWeerd; Schandler, chs. 5–13 *passim.*

412 [*Conclusion of the Wise Men*]: Oberdorfer, pp. 308–15; Hoopes, pp. 214–18; Ball, pp. 407–9; Schandler, ch. 14; Walter Isaacson and Evan Thomas, *The Wise Men* (Simon and Schuster, 1986), ch. 23.

[*"Growing with such acuteness"*]: quoted in Hoopes, p. 216.

[*"Establishment bastards"*]: quoted in Herring, p. 206.

[*"President is confronted"*]: Lippmann, "This Draft Is Difficult to Justify," *Washington Post,* March 24, 1968, p. B3.

[*LBJ in polls, post-Tet*]: Herring, pp. 201–2.

[*McCarthy campaign and New Hampshire primary*]: David S. Broder, "Election of 1968," in Arthur M. Schlesinger, Jr., ed., *History of American Presidential Elections* (Chelsea House, 1971), vol. 4, pp. 3716–18; Theodore H. White, *The Making of the President 1968* (Atheneum, 1969), ch. 3 *passim;* Lewis Chester et al., *An American Melodrama: The Presidential Campaign of 1968* (Viking, 1969), ch. 3; Vogelgesang, pp. 142–46; Sidney Hyman, *Youth in Politics: Expectations and Realities* (Basic Books, 1972), pp. 97–133; David Halberstam, "McCarthy and the Divided Left," *Harper's,* vol. 236, no. 1414 (March 1968), pp. 32–44; Gitlin, *Sixties,* pp. 294–97.

[*Kennedy's dilemma and entry into race*]: Arthur M. Schlesinger, Jr., *Robert Kennedy and His*

Times (Houghton Mifflin, 1978), chs. 37–38; David Halberstam, *The Unfinished Odyssey of Robert Kennedy* (Random House, 1968), ch. 1; Broder, pp. 3718–19; Kearns, pp. 338–39; Chester et al., pp. 105–26.

412 [*Poll on public support for bombing*]: John Mueller, *War, Presidents and Public Opinion* (Wiley, 1973), p. 72 (Table 4.3).

413 [*LBJ's withdrawal*]: in *Public Papers of the Presidents of the United States: Lyndon B. Johnson* (U.S. Government Printing Office, 1965–70), vol. 5, part 1, pp. 469–76, quoted at p. 476; see also "The President's News Conference of March 31, 1968," in *ibid.*, pp. 476–82; Johnson, ch. 18; Turner, pp. 233–48; Herring, pp. 207–9; Kearns, ch. 12 *passim;* Schlesinger, *Kennedy,* pp. 868–69; McPherson, pp. 430–35; Lady Bird Johnson, *A White House Diary* (Holt, Rinehart and Winston, 1970), pp. 642–47; Schandler, ch. 15; Gitlin, *Sixties,* p. 304.

[*"Rioting blacks, demonstrating students"*]: quoted in Kearns, p. 343.

[*King's assassination and rioting*]: Manchester, pp. 1128–29; Oates, pp. 483–98; Lewis, pp. 383–92; *Newsweek,* vol. 71, no. 16 (April 15, 1968), pp. 31–34; *ibid.,* vol. 71, no. 17 (April 22, 1968), pp. 24–26; Schlesinger, *Kennedy,* pp. 874–75; Garry Wills, "Martin Luther King Is *Still* on the Case," in Hayes, pp. 731–50.

[*Columbia rising*]: Jerry L. Avorn et al., *Up Against the Ivy Wall: A History of the Columbia Crisis* (Atheneum, 1969); Fact-Finding Commission on Columbia Disturbances, *Crisis at Columbia* (Vintage, 1968); Joanne Grant, *Confrontation on Campus: The Columbia Pattern for the New Protest* (Signet, 1969); Daniel Bell, "Columbia and the New Left," in Bell and Irving Kristol, eds., *Confrontation: The Student Rebellion and the Universities* (Basic Books, 1969), pp. 67–107; Michael A. Baker et al., *Police on Campus: The Mass Police Action at Columbia University, Spring, 1968* (New York Civil Liberties Union, 1969).

[*"Go all the way"*]: Avorn et al., p. 61.

414 [*"Violence going to stop?"*]: quoted in Schlesinger, *Kennedy,* p. 874.

[*"Year of the barricades"*]: Caute, "free art, free theatre," quoted at p. 71.

[*Kennedy campaign*]: Schlesinger, *Kennedy,* chs. 39–41; Halberstam, *Odyssey,* chs. 2, 4–6; White, pp. 166–79; Chester et al., pp. 127–79 *passim* and 297–349 *passim;* Carl Solberg, *Hubert Humphrey* (Norton, 1984), chs. 28–30.

[*"Sad rather than cold"*]: quoted in Schlesinger, *Kennedy,* p. 756.

[*The poor "are hidden"*]: quoted in Halberstam, *Odyssey,* p. 94.

[*Liberal McCarthyites' anger at Kennedy*]: see Schlesinger, *Kennedy,* pp. 859–61, 896–99.

[*"Personalization of the presidency"*]: quoted in *ibid.,* p. 893.

[*Kennedy's assassination*]: Chester et al., pp. 349–62; Schlesinger, *Kennedy,* pp. 907–16; see also Gitlin, *Sixties,* pp. 310–11; Miller, pp. 287–88, 292–94.

[*Broder on shock of assassination*]: Broder, p. 3725.

[*Chicago convention*]: *ibid.,* pp. 3731–39; White, ch. 9; Chester et al., ch. 10; Daniel Walker, *Rights in Conflict* (E. P. Dutton, 1968); Donald Myrus, ed., *Law & Disorder: The Chicago Convention and Its Aftermath* (Donald Myrus and Burton Joseph, 1968); David Farber, *Chicago '68* (University of Chicago Press, 1988); Zaroulis and Sullivan, pp. 175–201; Gitlin, *Sixties,* ch. 14; Miller, pp. 295–306; Sale, pp. 472–77; Norman Mailer, *Miami and the Siege of Chicago* (World Publishing, 1968), part 2; Caute, chs. 15–16; Solberg, ch. 31; Dellinger, *Revolutionary Nonviolence,* part 5.

415 [*Ribicoff on "Gestapo tactics"*]: quoted in Broder, p. 3739.

[*Nixon's nomination*]: *ibid.,* pp. 3709–15, 3725–31; White, chs. 2, 5, 8; Chester et al., chs. 5, 9; Richard Nixon, *Memoirs* (Grosset & Dunlap, 1978), pp. 297–316; Mailer, *Miami,* part 1.

[*Presidential campaign, fall 1968*]: Broder, pp. 3739–50; White, part 3; Chester et al., chs. 11–12; Marshall Frady, "The American Independent Party," in Arthur M. Schlesinger, Jr., ed., *History of U.S. Political Parties* (Chelsea House, 1973), vol. 4, pp. 3429–44; Jody Carlson, *George C. Wallace and the Politics of Powerlessness* (Transaction Books, 1981), chs. 1–2, 7–9; Solberg, chs. 32–34; Nixon, pp. 316–35; George Christian, *The President Steps Down* (Macmillan, 1970); Philip E. Converse et al., "Continuity and Change in American Politics: Parties and Issues in the 1968 Election," *American Political Science Review,* vol. 63, no. 4 (December 1969), pp. 1083–1105; Benjamin I. Page and Richard A. Brody, "Policy Voting and the Electoral Process: The Vietnam War Issue," *ibid.,* vol. 66, no. 3 (September 1972), pp. 979–95.

[*"Irate buffalo"*]: Frady, p. 3441.

416 ["*Master of ambiguity*"]: Page and Brody, p. 987.
["*Alternated between protestations*"]: *ibid.*, p. 989.
["*Dime's worth of difference*"]: quoted in Carlson, p. 131.
["*Ask my Attorney General*"]: quoted in Page and Brody, p. 992.
[*Election results*]: Schlesinger, *Elections*, vol. 4, p. 3865; and Broder, pp. 3707, 3750–52; see also Page and Brody; Richard W. Boyd, "Popular Control of Public Policy: A Normal Vote Analysis of the 1968 Election," *American Political Science Review*, vol. 66, no. 2 (June 1972), pp. 429–49.
[*Broder on 1968 election*]: Broder, p. 3705.

Into the Quicksand

[*Inaugural protest*]: *New York Times*, January 20, 1969, "militant—but for the most part genial," quoted at p. 21; *ibid.*, January 21, 1969, p. 24; see also Gitlin, *Whole World*, p. 214.
417 [*Lippmann on "new Nixon"*]: quoted in Steel, p. 589; see also Jonathan Schell, *The Time of Illusion* (Knopf, 1976), p. 20.
[*White on Nixon*]: White, *Making 1968*, p. 143.
[*Nixon's election night promises*]: quoted in Schell, p. 17.
[*Nixon's Vietnam strategy*]: Richard M. Nixon, "Asia After Viet Nam," *Foreign Affairs*, vol. 46, no. 1 (October 1967), pp. 111–25; Henry A. Kissinger, "The Viet Nam Negotiations," *Foreign Affairs*, vol. 47, no. 2 (January 1969), pp. 211–34; Nixon, *Memoirs*, pp. 347–51; Tad Szulc, *The Illusion of Peace: Foreign Policy in the Nixon Years* (Viking, 1978), pp. 23–31; Seymour M. Hersh, *The Price of Power: Kissinger in the Nixon White House* (Summit, 1983), ch. 4; Roger Morris, *Uncertain Greatness: Henry Kissinger and American Foreign Policy* (Harper, 1977), pp. 149–54; Herring, pp. 221–26; Gelb and Betts, pp. 348–50, 354–58.
["*We will not make*"]: quoted in Herring, p. 221.
["*Seek the opportunity*"]: Address to the Nation on Vietnam, May 14, 1969, in *Public Papers of the Presidents of the United States: Richard Nixon* (U.S. Government Printing Office, 1971–75), vol. 1, pp. 369–75, quoted at p. 371.
418 ["*War for peace*"]: quoted in Herring, p. 223.
["*Not going to end up*"]: quoted in H. R. Haldeman and Joseph DiMona, *The Ends of Power* (Times Books, 1978), p. 81.
["*Madman Theory, Bob*"]: *ibid.*, p. 83.
[*Peak level of American troops*]: see Richard Dean Burns and Milton Leitenberg, *The Wars in Vietnam, Cambodia and Laos, 1945–1982: A Bibliographic Guide* (ABC-Clio Information Services, 1984), p. 144 (Table 4).
[*Secret Cambodian bombing*]: see William Shawcross, *Sideshow: Kissinger, Nixon and the Destruction of Cambodia* (Simon and Schuster, 1979), ch. 1; Hersh, ch. 5; Szulc, pp. 36–39, 52–61; Karnow, pp. 589–92; Schell, pp. 32–38; U.S. House of Representatives, Committee on the Judiciary, *Impeachment of Richard M. Nixon, President of the United States: Report*, 93rd Congress, 2nd Session (U.S. Government Printing Office, 1974), pp. 217–19; Henry Kissinger, *White House Years* (Little, Brown, 1979), pp. 239–54.
419 ["*Only by revolutionary violence*"]: Giap, "The South Vietnamese People Will Win," in Russell Stetler, ed., *The Military Art of People's War: Selected Writings of General Vo Nguyen Giap* (Monthly Review Press, 1970), pp. 185–225, quoted at p. 213.
[*Nixon's "Vietnamization"*]: FitzGerald, pp. 404–14; Gelb and Betts, pp. 349–50; Herring, pp. 229–32; Kissinger, *White House Years*, pp. 271–77.
[*American attitudes toward the South Vietnamese*]: see FitzGerald, chs. 10–14, 16–17 *passim*.
420 [*Numbers of South Vietnamese troops, late 1969*]: Herring, p. 231.
[*Demoralization and decay among American troops*]: David Cortright, *Soldiers in Revolt: The American Military Today* (Anchor Press/Doubleday, 1975), chs. 1–2; Richard Boyle, *The Flower of the Dragon: The Breakdown of the U.S. Army in Vietnam* (Ramparts Press, 1972); Herring, pp. 243–44; John Helmer, *Bringing the War Home: The American Soldier in Vietnam and After* (Free Press, 1974); Baskir and Strauss, ch. 4; Cincinnatus; Edward Shils, "A Profile of the Military Deserter," *Armed Forces and Society*, vol. 3, no. 3 (May

1977), pp. 427-31; Alfred W. McCoy, *The Politics of Heroin in Southeast Asia* (Harper, 1972), pp. 181-85 and ch. 5 *passim;* Col. Robert D. Heinl, Jr., "The Collapse of the Armed Forces," in Marvin E. Gettleman et al., eds., *Vietnam and America: A Documented History* (Grove Press, 1985), pp. 322-31.

420 [*My Lai*]: Seymour M. Hersh, *My Lai 4: A Report on the Massacre and Its Aftermath* (Random House, 1970); U.S. Department of the Army, *The My Lai Massacre and Its Cover-up* (Free Press, 1976); Seymour Hersh, *Cover-up: The Army's Secret Investigation of the Massacre at My Lai 4* (Random House, 1972); Boyle, pp. 127-43.
[*Service people against the war*]: Cortright, part 1 *passim;* Matthew Rinaldi, "The Olive-Drab Rebels: Military Organizing During the Vietnam Era," *Radical America*, vol. 8, no. 3 (May-June 1974), pp. 17-52.
[*Draft offenders*]: Baskir and Strauss, p. 5 (Figure 1) and 69 (Figure 4); see also *ibid.*, ch. 3; G. David Curry, *Sunshine Patriots: Punishment and the Vietnam Offender* (University of Notre Dame Press, 1985); Willard Gaylin, *In the Service of Their Country: War Resisters in Prison* (Viking, 1970).
[*Exiles*]: Baskir and Strauss, p. 169 (Figure 7) and ch. 5; Renée G. Kasinsky, *Refugees from Militarism: Draft-Age Americans in Canada* (Transaction Books, 1976).

421 [*Women Against Daddy Warbucks*]: New York Times, July 3, 1969, pp. 1, 5; *ibid.*, July 4, 1969, pp. 1-2; Ferber and Lynd, pp. 202, 210-11; Women Against Daddy Warbucks, "Our Statement," in Robin Morgan, ed., *Sisterhood Is Powerful* (Vintage, 1970), p. 530.
[*Baltimore draft office action*]: New York Times, October 28, 1967, p. 5; Zaroulis and Sullivan, p. 230; Ferber and Lynd, pp. 201-2.
[*Catonsville Nine*]: New York Times, May 18, 1968, p. 36; Ferber and Lynd, ch. 14 *passim;* Zaroulis and Sullivan, pp. 229-37 *passim;* see also William Van Etten Casey and Philip Nobile, eds., *The Berrigans* (Praeger, 1971); Jack Nelson and Ronald J. Ostrow, *The FBI and the Berrigans: The Making of a Conspiracy* (Coward, McCann & Geoghegan, 1972).
["*Some property has no right*"]: quoted in New York Times, May 18, 1968, p. 36.
[*SDS internal quarrels*]: Sale, chs. 22-23; Breines, ch. 6; Gitlin, *Whole World*, ch. 6; Gitlin, *Sixties*, pp. 377-91; Miller, pp. 284-85, 311-13.
["*Vanguarditis*"]: Carl Oglesby, "Notes on a Decade Ready for the Dustbin," *Liberation*, August-September 1969, p. 6.
["*A weapon*"]: Miller, p. 285.
[*SDS Chicago convention*]: Sale, pp. 557-79; Karin Ashley et al., "You Don't Need a Weatherman to Know Which Way the Wind Blows," in Harold Jacobs, ed., *Weatherman* (Ramparts Press, 1970), pp. 51-90; Andrew Kopkind, "The Real SDS Stands Up," in *ibid.*, pp. 15-28; Zaroulis and Sullivan, pp. 251-55.
["*A peculiar mix*"]: Sale, p. 562.

422 [*Flacks on disintegration of the New Left*]: Flacks, *Youth and Social Change* (Markham, 1971), p. 101.
["*Go for broke*"]: Nixon, *Memoirs*, p. 393.
["*Once the summer was over*"]: ibid.
[*Administration deadline threats and plans for major offensive*]: see Hersh, *Price*, ch. 10 *passim;* Szulc, pp. 149-56; Morris, pp. 163-68; Nixon, *Memoirs*, pp. 393-96, 405-7 *passim;* Kissinger, *White House Years*, pp. 284-86, 303-4.
[*Moratorium day*]: New York Times, October 16, 1969, pp. 1, 18-22; *Time*, vol. 94, no. 17 (October 24, 1969), pp. 16-20; Zaroulis and Sullivan, pp. 264-73; Schell, pp. 52-55; Nixon, *Memoirs*, pp. 400-3.

423 ["*Flame of life*"]: quoted in New York Times, October 16, 1969, p. 19.
["*This is my son*"]: quoted in *Newsweek*, vol. 74, no. 17 (October 27, 1969), p. 32.
[*Nixon's address*]: November 3, 1969, in *Nixon Public Papers*, vol. 1, pp. 901-9, quoted at pp. 908, 909; see also Schell, pp. 62-66; Nixon, *Memoirs*, pp. 407-11.
[*November 1969 demonstrations*]: New York Times, November 14, 1969, pp. 1, 20-21; *ibid.*, November 15, 1969, pp. 1, 26-27; *ibid.*, November 16, 1969, pp. 1, 60-61; Zaroulis and Sullivan, pp. 276-300 *passim;* *Time*, vol. 94, no. 21 (November 21, 1969), pp. 23-26.

424 [*Lon Nol coup*]: see Shawcross, ch. 8; Hersh, *Price*, ch. 15; Kissinger, *White House Years*, pp. 457-65; Norodom Sihanouk and Wilfred Burchett, *My War with the CIA* (Pantheon, 1973).
[*North Vietnamese Cambodian "sanctuaries"*]: Shawcross, ch. 1 *passim*, pp. 64-72; Duiker,

pp. 283–84; see also Roger M. Smith, *Cambodia's Foreign Policy* (Cornell University Press, 1965).

424 [*Invasion of Cambodia*]: Shawcross, ch. 9, pp. 150–51, 171–75; Herring, pp. 234–37; Karnow, pp. 606–10; Szulc, pp. 244–49, 252–75, 279–84; Nixon, *Memoirs*, pp. 448–51; Duiker, pp. 285–88; Hugh Sidey, "Anybody See *Patton?*" in Lloyd C. Gardner, *The Great Nixon Turnaround* (New Viewpoints, 1973), pp. 183–86; Kissinger, *White House Years*, pp. 467–75, 483–509, 517–20; Hersh, *Price*, ch. 16.
[*"If, when the chips are down"*]: April 30, 1970, in *Nixon Public Papers*, vol. 2, pp. 405–10, quoted at p. 409; see also Shawcross, pp. 146–49; Schell, pp. 89–95.

424–5 [*Protests against invasion*]: New York Times, May 2, 1970, pp. 1, 9; *ibid.*, May 5, 1970, pp. 1, 17–18; *Time*, vol. 95, no. 19 (May 11, 1970), pp. 19–25; *ibid.*, vol. 95, no. 20 (May 18, 1970), pp. 6–15; Zaroulis and Sullivan, pp. 318–31; Sale, pp. 635–42; Shawcross, pp. 152–53; Kissinger, *White House Years*, pp. 509–17; U.S. President's Commission on Campus Unrest, *Report* (Arno Press, 1970), pp. 233–465; James A. Michener, *Kent State: What Happened and Why* (Random House, 1971); I. F. Stone, *The Killings at Kent State: How Murder Went Unpunished* (New York Review, 1971); Nixon, *Memoirs*, pp. 456–59.

425 [*"You see these bums"*]: quoted in *New York Times*, May 2, 1970, p. 1; see also Nixon, *Memoirs*, pp. 453–56.
[*Veterans' occupation of Statue of Liberty*]: New York Times, December 27, 1971, pp. 1, 21; *ibid.*, December 29, 1971, p. 32; see also John Kerry and Vietnam Veterans Against the War, *The New Soldier*, David Thorne and George Butler, eds. (Macmillan, 1971); Zaroulis and Sullivan, pp. 354–58; Vietnam Veterans Against the War, *The Winter Soldier Investigation* (Beacon Press, 1972).
[*Pentagon Papers publication*]: New York Times, June 13, 1971, pp. 1, 35–40; *The Pentagon Papers: The Defense Department History of United States Decisionmaking on Vietnam*, 4 vols. and index vol. (Senator Gravel, ed.: Beacon Press, 1971–72); Neil Sheehan et al., *The Pentagon Papers: As Published by the New York Times* (Bantam, 1971); George McT. Kahin, "The Pentagon Papers: A Critical Evaluation," *American Political Science Review*, vol. 69, no. 2 (June 1975), pp. 675–84; H. Bradford Westerfield, "What Use Are Three Versions of the Pentagon Papers?," *ibid.*, pp. 685–96; Stewart Burns interview with Randy Kehler, August 1976; Peter Schrag, *Test of Loyalty: Daniel Ellsberg and the Rituals of Secret Government* (Simon and Schuster, 1974), pp. 35–37, 45–65, 80–100; Hersh, *Price*, pp. 325–32; Schell, pp. 151–54; David Halberstam, *The Powers That Be* (Knopf, 1979), ch. 22 *passim;* Harrison E. Salisbury, *Without Fear or Favor:* The New York Times *and Its Times* (Times Books, 1980).
[*Ellsberg*]: Stewart Burns interviews with Daniel Ellsberg, October 29, 1976, December 16, 1977, October 5, 1978; Ellsberg talk in Santa Rita county jail, Pleasanton, Calif., June 26, 1983; Robert Ellsberg, "On Daniel Ellsberg: Remembering the Pentagon Papers," *1976 Peace Calendar* (War Resisters League); Daniel Ellsberg, *Papers on the War* (Simon and Schuster, 1972); Schrag, pp. 24–54 *passim.*

426 [*"Concept of enemy doesn't exist"*]: Janaki Tschannerl, quoted in Daniel Ellsberg talk at Isla Vista, Calif., May 13, 1975.
[*"Guilt-ridden, fanatic extremists"*]: "An Interview with Daniel Ellsberg," *WIN*, November 1, 1972, quoted at p. 7.
[*"Lots of people around the world"*]: transcribed in *Liberation & Revolution: Gandhi's Challenge*, Report of the Thirteenth Triennial Conference of the War Resisters' International (War Resisters' International, 1969), p. 107.
[*"Our best, our very best"*]: J. Anthony Lukas, "After the Pentagon Papers: A Month in the Life of Daniel Ellsberg," *New York Times Magazine*, December 12, 1971, pp. 29, 95, 98–106, quoted at p. 106.
[*Supreme Court decision on Pentagon Papers*]: New York Times Co. v. U.S., 403 U.S. 713 (1970); see also Schrag, pp. 92–100.
[*Nixon's war on Ellsberg*]: J. Anthony Lukas, *Nightmare: The Underside of the Nixon Years* (Viking, 1976), ch. 4 *passim;* Hersh, *Price*, ch. 28; Schrag, pp. 100–24 and *passim;* Schell, pp. 161–68; Nixon, *Memoirs*, pp. 511–15; Jim Hougan, *Secret Agenda: Watergate, Deep Throat and the CIA* (Random House, 1984), ch. 3; *Nixon Impeachment: Report*, pp. 36, 157–70.
[*"Tailor-made issue"*]: quoted in *Nixon Impeachment: Report*, p. 158.

Songs of the Sixties

426 [*Woodstock*]: Cook, *Beat Generation*, pp. 230–39, quoted at p. 230; Robert S. Spitz, *Barefoot in Babylon: The Creation of the Woodstock Music Festival, 1969* (Viking, 1979), pp. 389–486; Andrew Kopkind, "Woodstock Nation," in Jonathan Eisen, ed., *The Age of Rock: Sights and Sounds of the American Cultural Revolution* (Random House, 1969–70), vol. 2, pp. 312–18.

427 [Life *on Woodstock*]: "The Big Woodstock Rock Trip," *Life*, vol. 67, no. 9 (August 29, 1969), pp. 14B–23, quoted at p. 14B.
[*Roots of rock 'n' roll*]: Ed Ward, "The Fifties and Before," in Ward, Geoffrey Stokes, Ken Tucker, *Rock of Ages* (Rolling Stone Press/Prentice-Hall, 1986), pp. 17–248; Carl Belz, *The Story of Rock* (Oxford University Press, 1969), chs. 2–3; Howard Junker, "The Fifties," in Eisen, vol. 2, pp. 98–104; Charlie Gillett, *The Sound of the City: The Rise of Rock and Roll* (Outerbridge and Dienstfrey, 1970), ch. 1; Nik Cohn, *Rock from the Beginning* (Stein & Day, 1969), chs. 1, 4.
[*Black originals and white covers*]: Arnold Shaw, *The Rockin' '50s* (Hawthorn, 1974), ch. 14; on racism in music, see Steve Chapple and Reebee Garofalo, *Rock 'n' Roll Is Here to Pay: The History and Politics of the Music Industry* (Nelson-Hall, 1977), ch. 7.
["*Little men with cigars*"]: quoted in Jerry Hopkins, *The Rock Story* (Signet, 1970), p. 24; on the rock industry, see Michael Lydon, "Rock for Sale," in Eisen, vol. 2, pp. 51–62; Chapple and Garofalo, ch. 2 and *passim*.

427–8 ["*Stem the tide*"]: A. M. Meerio, quoted in Hopkins, p. 31.
428 [*Boston Catholic leaders and San Antonio city council*]: *ibid.*
["*I need it*"]: "Honey Love," quoted in *ibid.*, p. 18, words and music by Clyde McPhatter and J. Gerald, copyright 1954, Progressive Music Publishing Co., Inc.
["*Wop-bop-a-loo-bop*"]: "Tutti Frutti," recorded by Little Richard, words and music by Richard Penniman, D. LaBostrie, and Joe Lubin, Venice Music, Inc., Specialty Records.
["*Shared with adults*"]: Cohn, p. 15.
["*Something in common*"]: Janet Podell, ed., *Rock Music in America* (H. W. Wilson Co., 1987), p. 5.
["*Culturally alienated*"]: Jeff Greenfield, "They Changed Rock, Which Changed Culture, Which Changed Us," *New York Times Magazine*, February 16, 1975, pp. 12–13, 37–46, quoted at p. 38.
[*Folk music*]: R. Serge Denisoff, *Great Day Coming: Folk Music and the American Left* (University of Illinois Press, 1971); Denisoff and Richard A. Peterson, eds., *The Sounds of Social Change: Studies in Popular Culture* (Rand McNally College Publishing Co., 1972), *passim;* Wayne Hampton, *Guerrilla Minstrels: John Lennon, Joe Hill, Woody Guthrie, and Bob Dylan* (University of Tennessee Press, 1986).
[*Dylan*]: Wilfrid Howard Mellers, *A Darker Shade of Pale: A Backdrop to Bob Dylan* (Oxford University Press, 1985); Robert Shelton, *No Direction Home: The Life and Music of Bob Dylan* (Morrow, 1986); Lawrence Goldman, "Bobby Dylan—Folk-Rock Hero," in Eisen, vol. 1, pp. 208–13; Ellen Willis, "The Sound of Bob Dylan," *Commentary*, vol. 44, no. 5 (November 1967), pp. 71–78; Hampton, ch. 6; Cohn, ch. 17.
["*Hungry, restless*"]: Goldman, p. 211.
["*Greatest holiest*"]: quoted in Hampton, pp. 152–53.
["*Blowing in the Wind*"]: quoted in Willis, p. 73, initially recorded by Peter, Paul and Mary, words and music by Bob Dylan, copyright 1962, M. Witmark and Sons, Warner Brothers Records.

429 ["*Established topical song*"]: *ibid.*, p. 73.
["*Musical great white hope*"]: Denisoff, *Great Day Coming*, p. 181.
[*Dylan at Newport, 1965*]: Shelton, pp. 301–4, "Play folk music!" quoted at p. 302; Hampton, pp. 176–78; Paul Wolfe, "Dylan's Sellout of the Left," in Denisoff and Peterson, pp. 147–150.
["*If Whitman were alive*"]: quoted in Willis, p. 77.
[*Release of forty-eight Dylan originals*]: Hopkins, p. 83.
[*The Beatles*]: Hunter Davies, *The Beatles*, rev. ed. (McGraw-Hill, 1978); Wilfrid Howard Mellers, *Twilight of the Gods: The Music of the Beatles* (Schirmer Books, 1973);

Geoffrey Stokes, *The Beatles* (Times Books, 1980); Jon Wiener, *Come Together: John Lennon in His Time* (Random House, 1984); Hopkins, ch. 15; Ned Rorem, "The Music of the Beatles," *New York Review of Books*, vol. 10, no. 1 (January 18, 1968), pp. 23–27.

429 [*"Most persistent noises"*]: *Newsweek*, quoted in Hopkins, p. 70.

430 [*"Not even for kings and queens!"*]: *ibid.*

[*"You really do believe"*]: quoted in Davies, p. 198.

[*"Mainstream of mass culture"*]: Willis, p. 76.

[*"Twentieth century working-class songs"*]: Hopkins, p. 79; on the Rolling Stones, see David Dalton, *The Rolling Stones: The First Twenty Years* (Knopf, 1981); Stanley Booth, *The True Adventures of the Rolling Stones* (Vintage, 1985); Hopkins, pp. 79–80.

[*"Asked for their pants"*]: Hopkins, p. 79.

[*Reagan's pop music appreciation*]: see Fred Bruning, "The Reagans and the Beach Boys," *Maclean's*, vol. 96, no. 18 (May 2, 1983), p. 13.

[*San Francisco rock*]: Hopkins, ch. 7; Belz, pp. 197–208; Cohn, ch. 12; Lar Tusb, "West Coast Then . . . and Now," in Eisen, vol. 2, pp. 251–56.

[*"LSD experience without the LSD"*]: Hopkins, p. 92.

[*"1-2-3 What are we fightin' for"*]: "I-Feel-Like-I'm-Fixin'-to-Die Rag," quoted in *ibid.*, pp. 97–98, recorded by Joe McDonald, words and lyrics by Joe McDonald, copyright 1965, Alkatraz Music Co.

431 [*Counterculture and New Left*]: Gitlin, *Sixties*, esp. ch. 8; Hampton, chs. 1–3, 6–7; Denisoff and Peterson, ch. 3; William L. O'Neill, *Coming Apart* (Quadrangle Books, 1971), esp. ch. 8.

[*"Rock and Roll, Rock culture"*]: Smucker, "The Politics of Rock: Movement vs. Groovement," in Eisen, vol. 2, pp. 83–91, quoted at p. 88.

[*"Getting stoned"*]: quoted in O'Neill, p. 244.

[*"Open a new space"*]: Gitlin, *Sixties*, p. 202.

[*O'Neill on countercultural materialism*]: O'Neill, p. 264.

[*Record sales, 1968*]: Hopkins, p. 121.

[*"Try to dig it"*]: quoted in *ibid.*, p. 123.

[*"Hey people now"*]: quoted in Gitlin, *Sixties*, p. 204.

[*SUPERZAP THEM*]: quoted in *Time*, vol. 90, no. 1 (July 7, 1967), p. 20.

[*"Cultural and spiritual revolution"*]: Robert A. Rosenstone, " 'The Times They Are A-Changin': The Music of Protest," *Annals of the American Academy of Political and Social Science*, vol. 382 (March 1969), p. 142.

[*"We want the world"*]: quoted in Hopkins, p. 100.

[*"Sex starts with me"*]: quoted in O'Neill, p. 243.

432 [*"Idea of leadership"*]: quoted in Hampton, p. 20.

[*Kopkind on countercultural sea*]: Kopkind, "Woodstock Nation," p. 318.

[*"Founded on privilege"*]: Gitlin, *Sixties*, p. 212.

[*Smucker at Woodstock*]: Smucker, quoted at pp. 85, 87, 88, 89, 90; see also Kopkind; Jon Wiener, "Woodstock Revisited," in Eisen, vol. 2, pp. 170–72.

[*"Sing 'Solidarity Forever' "*]: quoted in Denisoff, *Great Day Coming*, p. 193.

10. LIBERTY, EQUALITY, SISTERHOOD

433 [*Eleanor Roosevelt's last years*]: Joseph P. Lash, *Eleanor: The Years Alone* (Norton, 1972), ch. 15; Tamara K. Hareven, *Eleanor Roosevelt: An American Conscience* (1968; reprinted by Da Capo Press, 1975), ch. 13; Maurine H. Beasley, *Eleanor Roosevelt and the Media: A Public Quest for Self-Fulfillment* (University of Illinois Press, 1987), pp. 182–85.

[*"Save 6,000 lives"*]: quoted in Lash, p. 304.

[*Roosevelt and women's issues*]: see Elisabeth Israels Perry, "Training for Public Life: ER and Women's Political Networks in the 1920s," in Joan Hoff-Wilson and Marjorie Lightman, eds., *Without Precedent: The Life and Career of Eleanor Roosevelt* (Indiana University Press, 1984), pp. 28–45; Susan Ware, "ER and Democratic Politics: Women in the Postsuffrage Era," in *ibid.*, pp. 46–60; Lois Scharf, "ER and Feminism," in *ibid.*, pp. 226–53; Hareven, pp. 24–32, 63–68, 135–36, 233–34, 278, and *passim*.

434 [*"Most Admired Woman"*]: Lash, p. 302.

[*President's commission report*]: U.S. President's Commission on the Status of Women,

Report: American Women (U.S. Government Printing Office, 1963); see also Margaret Mead and Frances Bagley Kaplan, eds., *American Women: The Report of the President's Commission on the Status of Women and Other Publications of the Commission* (Scribner, 1965); Scharf, pp. 247–49; Cynthia E. Harrison, "A 'New Frontier' for Women: The Public Policy of the Kennedy Administration," *Journal of American History*, vol. 67, no. 3 (December 1980), pp. 630–46; Judith Hole and Ellen Levine, *Rebirth of Feminism* (Quadrangle, 1971), pp. 18–24.

434 [*"Problem that has no name"*]: Betty Friedan, *The Feminine Mystique* (Norton, 1963), p. 15.

434–6 [*Marion Hudson's diary*]: "Diary of a Student-Mother-Housewife-Worker," in Rosalyn Baxandall et al., eds., *America's Working Women* (Vintage, 1976), pp. 336–40, quoted at pp. 336–38.

Breaking Through the Silken Curtain

436 [*Friedan's writings for popular magazines*]: see Sara Evans, *Personal Politics: The Roots of Women's Liberation in the Civil Rights Movement and the New Left* (Knopf, 1979), p. 3.
[*Maslow*]: Maslow, "Dominance, Personality, and Social Behavior in Women," *Journal of Social Psychology*, vol. 10, no. 1 (February 1939), pp. 3–39; Maslow, *Motivation and Personality* (Harper, 1954); Friedan, *Feminine Mystique*, pp. 316–26.
[*Kinsey*]: Kinsey et al., *Sexual Behavior in the Human Female* (W. B. Saunders, 1953); Friedan, *Feminine Mystique*, esp. ch. 11 and pp. 327–29.
[*"Progress to equal participation"*]: Friedan, *Feminine Mystique*, p. 329.
[*"Scientific religion"*]: ibid., p. 125.
[*"Our culture does not permit"*]: ibid., p. 77.

437 [*"Conceived out of wedlock"*]: Donald A. Robinson, "Two Movements in Pursuit of Equal Opportunity," *Signs*, vol. 4, no. 3 (Spring 1979), pp. 413–33, quoted at p. 423; see also Carl M. Brauer, "Women Activists, Southern Conservatives, and the Prohibition of Sex Discrimination in Title VII of the 1964 Civil Rights Act," *Journal of Southern History*, vol. 49, no. 1 (February 1983), pp. 37–56; Martha Griffiths, "Women and Legislation," in Mary Lou Thompson, ed., *Voices of the New Feminism* (Beacon Press, 1970), pp. 112–14.
[*Weak enforcement of antidiscrimination law*]: Robinson, pp. 420–26 passim; Jo Freeman, *The Politics of Women's Liberation: A Case Study of an Emerging Social Movement and Its Relation to the Policy Process* (David McKay, 1975), pp. 178–83; Jane De Hart Mathews, "The New Feminism and the Dynamics of Social Change," in Linda K. Kerber and Mathews, eds., *Women's America: Refocusing the Past* (Oxford University Press, 1982), p. 408; Betty Friedan, *It Changed My Life: Writings on the Women's Movement* (Random House, 1976), pp. 78–80; Joan Abramson, *Old Boys, New Women: The Politics of Sex Discrimination* (Praeger, 1979), ch. 5; Pauli Murray and Mary Eastwood, "Jane Crow and the Law: Sex Discrimination and Title VII," in Anne Koedt et al., eds., *Radical Feminism* (Quadrangle/New York Times Book Co., 1973), pp. 165–77.
[*June 1966 conference and formation of NOW*]: Hole and Levine, pp. 81–86; Friedan, *It Changed My Life*, pp. 75–86.
[*"Seething underground"*]: Betty Friedan, "Up From the Kitchen Floor," *New York Times Magazine*, March 4, 1973, pp. 8–9, 28–35, 37, quoted at p. 28.
[*"Talked down to us"*]: Friedan, *It Changed My Life*, p. 83.
[*Organization and structure of NOW*]: Maren Lockwood Carden, *The New Feminist Movement* (Russell Sage, 1974), chs. 8–9 passim; Freeman, ch. 3; Friedan, *It Changed My Life*, pp. 95–96; Joyce Gelb and Marian Lief Palley, *Women and Public Policies* (Princeton University Press, 1982), chs. 2–3 passim.
[*"We, men and women"*]: "NOW Statement of Purpose," in Friedan, *It Changed My Life*, pp. 87–91, quoted at pp. 87, 88, 90.

438 [*"To hand over"*]: ibid., p. 95.
[*Conflict among women leaders during Kennedy Administration*]: Cynthia E. Harrison, *On Account of Sex: The Politics of Women's Issues, 1945–1968* (page proofs: University of California Press, 1988), parts 2–3 passim; see also Leila J. Rupp and Verta Taylor,

Survival in the Doldrums: The American Women's Rights Movement, 1945 to the 1960's (Oxford University Press, 1987).

438 [*"Specific bills"*]: Esther Peterson, quoted in Harrison, *On Account of Sex*, p. 116.
[*"Special emphasis"*]: William H. Chafe, *The American Woman: Her Changing Social, Economic, and Political Roles, 1920–1970* (Oxford University Press, 1972), p. 127.

438–9 [*Policy differences within NOW*]: Freeman, pp. 80–83; Hole and Levine, pp. 87–92, 95; Friedan, *It Changed My Life*, pp. 104–6.

439 [*WEAL*]: Freeman, pp. 81, 152–54; Gayle Graham Yates, *What Women Want: The Ideas of the Movement* (Harvard University Press, 1975), pp. 46–48; Hole and Levine, pp. 95–98; Karen O'Connor, *Women's Organizations' Use of the Courts* (Lexington Books, 1980), pp. 96–98 (Table 5–1), 105–8; Gelb and Palley, chs. 2–3 *passim.*
[*Executive order on federal contracts*]: Freeman, pp. 75–76, 191–96; Friedan, "The First Year: President's Report to NOW," in *It Changed My Life*, pp. 97–99; see also Abramson, ch. 4; Bernice Sandler, "A Little Help from Our Government: WEAL and Contract Compliance," in Alice S. Rossi and Ann Calderwood, eds., *Academic Women on the Move* (Russell Sage, 1973), pp. 439–62.
[*NOW suit on want ads*]: Hole and Levine, pp. 40–44, 86–87; Freeman, pp. 76–79; Friedan, *It Changed My Life*, pp. 94–95; see also O'Connor, pp. 96–98 (Table 5–1), 103–5.
[*NOW, AT&T and flight attendants*]: Freeman, pp. 76–77, 188–90; Friedan, *It Changed My Life*, pp. 92–95.
[*Women's legislation, 92nd Congress*]: Freeman, pp. 184, 202–5, 209–29; see also Gelb and Palley; Anne E. Costan, "Representing Women: From Social Movement to Interest Group," *Western Political Quarterly*, vol. 34, no. 1 (March 1981), pp. 100–13; George P. Sape and Thomas J. Hart, "Title VII Reconsidered: The Equal Employment Opportunity Act of 1972," *George Washington Law Review*, vol. 40 (July 1972), pp. 824–89.
[*ECOA*]: Gelb and Palley, ch. 4.
[*NWPC*]: Freeman, pp. 160–62; Gelb and Palley, pp. 26–31 *passim;* Yates, pp. 48–50; Friedan, *It Changed My Life*, pp. 165–83.
[*Black women's employment gains*]: Allen L. Sorkin, "Education, Occupation, and Income of Nonwhite Women," *Journal of Negro Education*, vol. 41 (1972), pp. 343–51; Lynn Y. Weiner, *From Working Girl to Working Mother: The Female Labor Force in the United States, 1820–1980* (University of North Carolina Press, 1985), pp. 89, 96.

440 [*"Virginia Slims" poll*]: Freeman, p. 38.
[*Black women and white women's organizations*]: see Carden, pp. 28–30; Freeman, pp. 37–42; Cellestine Ware, *Woman Power: The Movement for Women's Liberation* (Tower Publications, 1970), ch. 2.
[*Women's Strike for Equality*]: *New York Times*, August 27, 1970, pp. 1, 30; Freeman, pp. 84–85; Hole and Levine, pp. 92–93; Friedan, *It Changed My Life*, pp. 137–54.
[*"How powerful"*]: Friedan, *It Changed My Life*, p. 141.
[*"Your own thing"*]: see Freeman, p. 84.

441 [*"Not a bedroom war"*]: "Strike Day: August 26, 1970," in Friedan, *It Changed My Life*, pp. 152–54, quoted at p. 153.
[*Women in the 1950s*]: Friedan, *Feminine Mystique;* Evans, pp. 3–15 *passim;* Chafe, *American Woman*, ch. 9; Maxine L. Margolis, *Mothers and Such: Views of American Women and Why They Changed* (University of California Press, 1984), pp. 166–76, 218–25; Sheila M. Rothman, *Woman's Proper Place: A History of Changing Ideals and Practices, 1870 to the Present* (Basic Books, 1978), pp. 224–31; Wiener, pp. 89–96 *passim;* Helena Znaniecki Lopata, *Occupation: Housewife* (Oxford University Press, 1971); Susan M. Hartmann, *The Home Front and Beyond: American Women in the 1940s* (Twayne, 1982); Judy Syfers, "Why I Want a Wife," in Koedt et al., pp. 60–62; Alan L. Sorkin, "On the Occupational Status of Women, 1870–1970," *American Journal of Economics and Sociology*, vol. 32, no. 3 (July 1973), pp. 235–43; Nancy Walker, "Humor and Gender Roles: The 'Funny' Feminism of the Post-World War II Suburbs," *American Quarterly*, vol. 37, no. 1 (Spring 1985), pp. 98–113; Joann Vanek, "Time Spent in Housework," in Nancy F. Cott and Elizabeth H. Pleck, eds., *A Heritage of Her Own: Toward a New Social History of American Women* (Simon and Schuster, 1979), pp. 499–506.
[*"Busy Wife's Achievements"*]: *Life*, vol. 41, no. 26 (December 24, 1956), p. 41.

441 [*"Ready for a padded cell"*]: quoted in Friedan, *Feminine Mystique*, p. 28.
[*"All hell would break"*]: Jan Schakowsky, quoted in Evans, pp. 227-28.
[*Civil rights movement, New Left, and women's movement*]: Evans; Gunnar Myrdal, *An American Dilemma: The Negro Problem and Modern Democracy* (Harper, 1962), Appendix 5 ("A Parallel to the Negro Problem"); Mathews, "New Feminism," pp. 410-12; Hole and Levine, pp. 109-14; Carden, pp. 26, 59-63; Mary King, *Freedom Song* (Morrow, 1987), esp. ch. 12; Todd Gitlin, *The Sixties: Years of Hope, Days of Rage* (Bantam, 1987), ch. 16; Shirley N. Weber, "Black Power in the 1960s: A Study of Its Impact on Women's Liberation," *Journal of Black Studies*, vol. 11, no. 4 (June 1981), pp. 483-97; Gail Paradise Kelly, "Women's Liberation and the Cultural Revolution," *Radical America*, vol. 4, no. 2 (February 1970), pp. 19-25; Marlene Dixon, "On Women's Liberation," *ibid.*, pp. 26-34; Myra Marx Ferree and Beth B. Hess, *Controversy and Coalition: The New Feminist Movement* (Twayne, 1985), pp. 31-35, 45-48, 59-62; Barbara Burris et al., "The Fourth World Manifesto," in Koedt et al., pp. 322-57; Marge Piercy, "The Grand Coolie Damn," in Robin Morgan, ed., *Sisterhood Is Powerful* (Random House, 1970), pp. 421-38; Roxanne Dunbar, "Female Liberation as the Basis for Social Revolution," in *ibid.*, pp. 477-92; Robin Morgan, "Goodbye to All That," in Betty Roszak and Theodore Roszak, eds., *Masculine/Feminine: Readings in Sexual Mythology and the Liberation of Women* (Harper Colophon, 1969), pp. 241-50; Mary Aickin Rothschild, "White Women Volunteers in the Freedom Summers: Their Life and Work in a Movement for Social Change," *Feminist Studies*, vol. 5, no. 3 (Fall 1979), pp. 466-95.

442 [*"Widespread and deep rooted"*]: "Women in the Movement," November 1964, reprinted in Evans, pp. 233-35, quoted at p. 234; see also Mary King, pp. 443-55 *passim*.
[*"Only position for women"*]: Evans, p. 87.
[*"Generated feminist echoes"*]: *ibid.*, p. 88; see also Mary King, pp. 451-52.
[*Women at SDS "rethinking conference"*]: Evans, pp. 156-69 *passim*.
[*"Sex-caste system"*]: Casey Hayden and Mary King, "Sex and Caste," November 18, 1965, reprinted in *ibid.*, pp. 235-38, quoted at p. 237.
[*"Shit-workers" and "free movement 'chicks'"*]: Sue Munaker, Evelyn Goldfield, and Naomi Weisstein, quoted in Kirkpatrick Sale, *SDS* (Random House, 1973), p. 526.
[*"Liberation Workshop"*]: Evans, pp. 187-92.
[*"Colonial relationship"*]: "Liberation of Women," reprinted in *ibid.*, pp. 240-42, quoted at pp. 240, 241.

443 [*"Constant hubbub"*]: quoted in *ibid.*, p. 192.

The Liberation of Women

[*Women at NCNP*]: Evans, pp. 195-99; Freeman, pp. 59-60; Hole and Levine, pp. 112-14.
[*Formation of first women's liberation groups*]: Evans, pp. 199-211; Freeman, pp. 56-62; Hole and Levine, pp. 114-22 *passim*; Carden, pp. 63-65.
[*Washington counter-demonstration*]: Hole and Levine, pp. 117-19, Kathie Amatniek quoted at p. 118; Carden, p. 61; *New York Times*, January 16, 1968, p. 3.

444 [*Redstockings*]: "Redstockings Manifesto," in Morgan, *Sisterhood*, pp. 533-36; Yates, pp. 94-95, 100-1; Hole and Levine, pp. 136-42.
[*Atkinson's break with NOW*]: Atkinson, "Resignation from N.O.W.," in Atkinson, *Amazon Odyssey* (Links Books, 1974), pp. 9-11, quoted at p. 10; Freeman, pp. 81-82; Hole and Levine, p. 90.
[*The Feminists*]: "The Feminists: A Political Organization to Annihilate Sex Roles," in Koedt et al., pp. 368-78; The Feminists, "Women: Do You Know the Facts About Marriage?," in Morgan, *Sisterhood*, pp. 536-37; Hole and Levine, pp. 142-47; Atkinson.
[*Ease of starting women's groups*]: see Evans, p. 211.
[*Radical feminist ideology*]: see Simone de Beauvoir, *The Second Sex*, H. M. Parshley, trans. (Knopf, 1952); Koedt et al., part 3; Marlene Dixon, "The Rise of Women's Liberation," in Roszak and Roszak, pp. 186-201; Hole and Levine, chs. 3-4; Yates, ch. 3 *passim*; Carden, ch. 4; Mathews, pp. 413-15.
[*"Primary class system"*]: Barbara Mehrhof, quoted in Yates, p. 93.

444 [*Redstockings Manifesto on male supremacy*]: Morgan, *Sisterhood,* quoted at p. 534.

444-5 [*Millett*]: Millett, *Sexual Politics* (Doubleday, 1970), quoted at p. 363; see also Yates, pp. 79-84.

445 [*Firestone*]: Firestone, *The Dialectic of Sex: The Case for Feminist Revolution* (Morrow, 1970); see also Yates, pp. 84-87.

[*Consciousness-raising*]: Pamela Allen, *Free Space: A Perspective on the Small Group in Women's Liberation* (Times Change Press, 1970); Claudia Dreifus, *Women's Fate: Raps from a Feminist Consciousness-Raising Group* (Bantam, 1973); Vivian Gornick, "Consciousness," in Gornick, *Essays in Feminism* (Harper, 1978), pp. 47-68; Carol Williams Payne, "Consciousness Raising: A Dead End?," in Koedt et al., pp. 282-84; Ronnie Lichtman, "Consciousness Raising—1970," in Gerda Lerner, ed., *The Female Experience* (Bobbs-Merrill, 1977), pp. 456-58; Freeman, pp. 116-19; Yates, pp. 103-6; Carden, pp. 33-37; Mathews, pp. 412-13.

[*"Overview of our potential"*]: Allen, pp. 6-7.

[*Miss America protest*]: Robin Morgan, "Women Disrupt the Miss America Pageant," in Morgan, *Going Too Far: The Personal Chronicle of a Feminist* (Vintage, 1978), pp. 62-67, quoted on "Mindless Sex Object Image," "Murder mascot," "commercial shill-game," and " 'ideal' symbol," at p. 64; *New York Times,* September 8, 1968, p. 81; "No More Miss America!," in Morgan, *Sisterhood,* pp. 521-24.

446 [*"Instruments of torture"*]: quoted in Ann Popkin, "The Personal Is Political: The Women's Liberation Movement," in Dick Cluster, ed., *They Should Have Served That Cup of Coffee: Seven Radicals Remember the 60s* (South End Press, 1979), p. 190.

[*WITCH*]: Morgan, *Going Too Far,* pp. 71-81; Hole and Levine, pp. 126-30; Morgan, *Sisterhood,* pp. 538-53, 556; "The WITCH Manifesto," in Roszak and Roszak, pp. 259-61.

[*"Pit their ancient magic"*]: Robin Morgan, "WITCH Hexes Wall Street," in Morgan, *Going Too Far,* pp. 75-77, quoted at p. 75.

[*Feminists and the media*]: Ferree and Hess, pp. 74-78; Hole and Levine, pp. 247-70; Freeman, pp. 111-14, 148-50; see also Matilda Butler and William Paisley, *Women and the Mass Media: Sourcebook for Research and Action* (Human Sciences Press, 1980).

[*"Grand press blitz"*]: Freeman, p. 148.

[*"A political statement"*]: Morgan, "Miss America Pageant," p. 63.

[*"Ghetto" of women's page*]: ibid., p. 63.

[*Newsweek accord*]: *New York Times,* August 27, 1970, p. 30; Hole and Levine, pp. 258-60.

447 [Ladies' Home Journal *sit-in*]: Hole and Levine, pp. 255-58; *Ladies' Home Journal,* August 1970; *Newsweek,* vol. 75, no. 13 (March 30, 1970), p. 61; *ibid.,* vol. 76, no. 5 (August 3, 1970), p. 44.

[*Feminist publications*]: see Hole and Levine, pp. 270-76; Carden, pp. 65, 69-70, 144-45, 211-17; Freeman, pp. 110-11; Ferree and Hess, pp. 72-74.

[*Women's studies*]: Florence Howe and Carol Ahlum, "Women's Studies and Social Change," in Rossi and Calderwood, pp. 393-423; Gloria Bowles and Renate Duelli Klein, eds., *Theories of Women's Studies* (Routledge & Kegan Paul, 1983); Ellen Carol DuBois et al., *Feminist Scholarship: Kindling in the Groves of Academe* (University of Illinois Press, 1985); Freeman, pp. 166-69; Hole and Levine, pp. 326-28; Kathleen O'Connor Blumhagen and Walter D. Johnson, eds., *Women's Studies: An Interdisciplinary Collection* (Greenwood Press, 1978).

[*Women's health movement*]: Boston Women's Health Book Collective, *Our Bodies, Ourselves* (Simon and Schuster, 1973); Ellen Frankfort, *Vaginal Politics* (Quadrangle/New York Times Book Co., 1972); Gena Corea, *The Hidden Malpractice: How American Medicine Treats Women as Patients and Professionals* (Morrow, 1977); Margolis, pp. 247-51; Hole and Levine, pp. 358-62; Ferree and Hess, pp. 96-98; Dorothy Rosenthal Mandelbaum, "Women in Medicine," *Signs,* vol. 4, no. 1 (Autumn 1978), pp. 136-45; see also Miriam Galper and Carolyn Kott Washburne, "A Woman's Self-Help Program in Action," *Social Policy,* vol. 6, no. 5 (March-April 1976), pp. 46-52.

[*Abortion*]: Rosalind Pollack Petchesky, *Abortion and Woman's Choice: The State, Sexuality, and Reproductive Freedom* (Longman, 1984); Beverly Wildung Harrison, *Our Right to Choose: Toward a New Ethic of Abortion* (Beacon Press, 1983); Kristin Luker, *Abortion and the Politics of Motherhood* (University of California Press, 1984), esp. chs. 3,

5, 7–9; Hole and Levine, ch. 7; Yates, pp. 110–12; Lucinda Cisler, "Abortion Law Repeal (sort of): A Warning to Women," in Koedt et al., pp. 151–64; see also Linda Gordon, *Woman's Body, Woman's Right: A Social History of Birth Control in America* (Grossman, 1976).

447–8 [*"Talk about women's rights"*]: quoted in Luker, p. 97.
  448 [Roe *v.* Wade]: 410 U.S. 113 (1973); see also Luker, pp. 125–27; Janet Benshoof, "The Legacy of Roe v. Wade," in Jay L. Garfield and Patricia Hennessey, eds., *Abortion: Moral and Legal Perspectives* (University of Massachusetts Press, 1984), pp. 35–44; Hyman Rodman et al., *The Abortion Question* (Columbia University Press, 1987), pp. 183–90; James C. Mohr, *Abortion in America: The Origins and Evolution of National Policy, 1800–1900* (Oxford University Press, 1978), pp. 250–57.
    [*Abortion backlash*]: Luker, chs. 6–9 *passim;* Andrew H. Merton, *Enemies of Choice: The Right-to-Life Movement and Its Threat to Abortion* (Beacon Press, 1981); Petchesky, chs. 7–8; Benshoof; Andrea Dworkin, *Right-Wing Women* (Coward-McCann, 1983), ch. 3 *passim;* Ferree and Hess, pp. 130–39.
    [*Luker on backlash's meaning*]: Luker, pp. 193–94, quoted at p. 193.

  449 [*Rape*]: Susan Brownmiller, *Against Our Will: Men, Women and Rape* (Simon and Schuster, 1975); Andra Medea and Kathleen Thompson, *Against Rape* (Farrar, Straus & Giroux, 1974); Susan Griffin, "Rape: The All-American Crime," *Ramparts,* vol. 10, no. 3 (September 1971), pp. 26–35; Griffin, *Rape: The Power of Consciousness* (Harper, 1979); New York Radical Feminists, *Rape: The First Sourcebook for Women,* Noreen Connell and Cassandra Wilson, eds. (New American Library, 1974); Diane E. H. Russell, *The Politics of Rape: The Victim's Perspective* (Stein & Day, 1984); Rosemarie Tong, *Women, Sex, and the Law* (Rowman & Allenheld, 1984), ch. 4; Margolis, pp. 252–59.
    [*"All the hatred"*]: Medea and Thompson, p. 11.
    [*"Masculine ideology"*]: see Brownmiller, pp. 12, 14, 396.
    [*Feminist mobilization against rape*]: Jane Benson, "Take Back the Night" (unpublished manuscript, 1983); *Our Bodies, Ourselves,* ch. 8; New York Radical Feminists; Susan Pascalé et al., "Self-Defense for Women," in Morgan, *Sisterhood,* pp. 469–77; Medea and Thompson, pp. 125–30, 144–51; Carol V. Horos, *Rape* (Dell/Banbury, 1981).
    [*"Speakable crime"*]: Brownmiller, p. 396.
    [*Pornography*]: Laura Lederer, ed., *Take Back the Night: Women on Pornography* (Morrow, 1980); Ferree and Hess, pp. 105–7; *The Report of the Commission on Obscenity and Pornography* (Bantam, 1970); Susan Griffin, *Pornography and Silence: Culture's Revenge Against Nature* (Harper, 1981); Alan Soble, *Pornography: Marxism, Feminism, and the Future of Sexuality* (Yale University Press, 1986); Ray C. Rist, ed., *The Pornography Controversy: Changing Standards in American Life* (Transaction Books, 1975); Tong, ch. 1; Brownmiller, pp. 392–96.

  450 [*Lesbianism*]: Sidney Abbott and Barbara Love, *Sappho Was a Right-On Woman: A Liberated View of Lesbianism* (Stein & Day, 1972); Abbott and Love, "Is Women's Liberation a Lesbian Plot?," in Vivian Gornick and Barbara K. Moran, eds., *Women in Sexist Society: Studies in Power and Powerlessness* (Basic Books, 1971), pp. 436–51; Jill Johnston, *Lesbian Nation: The Feminist Solution* (Simon and Schuster, 1973); Estelle B. Freedman et al., eds., *The Lesbian Issue: Essays from SIGNS* (University of Chicago Press, 1985); Freeman, pp. 134–42; Anne Koedt, "Lesbianism and Feminism," in Koedt et al., pp. 246–58; Radicalesbians, "The Woman Identified Woman," in *ibid.,* pp. 240–45; Yates, pp. 108–10.
    [*"What is a lesbian?"*]: Radicalesbians, p. 240.
    [*"Carried the women's movement"*]: quoted in Abbott and Love, *Sappho,* p. 146.
    [*Police raid on gay bar*]: see *ibid.,* pp. 159–60.
    [*"Doubly outcast"*]: Abbott and Love, "Lesbian Plot," p. 443.
    [*"Economic independence"*]: Abbott and Love, *Sappho,* p. 136.
    [*"Lavender menace"*]: quoted in *ibid.,* p. 110.
    [*Congress to Unite Women, 1970*]: *ibid.,* pp. 113–16.
    [*New York NOW president and lavender armbands*]: *ibid.,* pp. 121–22; see also Friedan, *It Changed My Life,* pp. 158–59.

450–1 [*1971 NOW resolution on lesbians*]: quoted in Freeman, p. 99; see also Abbott and Love, *Sappho,* pp. 125–34.

451 ["*Primary cornerstone of male supremacy*"]: Nancy Myron and Charlotte Bunch, eds., *Lesbianism and the Women's Movement* (Diana Press, 1975), p. 10.

["*Vanguardism*"]: Freeman, p. 138; see also Koedt, "Lesbianism and Feminism."

[*Black feminism*]: Frances M. Beal, "Double Jeopardy: To Be Black and Female," in Morgan, *Sisterhood*, pp. 340-53; Firestone, ch. 5; Phyllis Marynick Palmer, "White Women/Black Women: The Dualism of Female Identity and Experience in the United States," *Feminist Studies*, vol. 9, no. 1 (Spring 1983), pp. 151-70; Pauli Murray, "The Liberation of Black Women," in Thompson, pp. 87-102; Angela Davis, *Women, Race & Class* (Random House, 1981); Cellestine Ware, "Black Feminism," in Koedt et al., pp. 81-84; Kay Lindsey, "The Black Woman as Woman," in Toni Cade, ed., *The Black Woman* (New American Library, 1970), pp. 85-89; Toni Cade, "On the Issue of Roles," in *ibid.*, pp. 101-10; Gloria I. Joseph and Jill Lewis, *Common Differences: Conflicts in Black and White Feminist Perspectives* (Anchor Press, 1981); Audre Lorde, *Sister Outsider: Essays and Speeches* (Crossing Press, 1984); Ware, *Woman Power*, ch. 2; Bell Hooks, *Ain't I a Woman: Black Women and Feminism* (South End Press, 1981).

["*Organize around those things*"]: "Black Feminism: A New Mandate," *Ms.*, vol. 2, no. 11 (May 1974), pp. 97-100, quoted at p. 97.

[*National Black Feminist Organization*]: *ibid.*; Freeman, pp. 156-57; Joseph and Lewis, pp. 33-34.

["*We were married*"]: "Black Feminism: A New Mandate," p. 98.

["*Male-dominated media image*"]: "Statement of Purpose," *ibid.*, p. 99.

["*Committed to working*"]: Combahee River Collective, "A Black Feminist Statement," in Cherríe Moraga and Gloria Anzaldúa, eds., *This Bridge Called My Back: Writings By Radical Women of Color* (Persephone Press, 1981), pp. 210-18, quoted at p. 217.

452 [*Latina feminism*]: "Women of 'La Raza' Unite!," in Angela G. Dorenkamp et al., eds., *Images of Women in American Popular Culture* (Harcourt, 1985), pp. 430-32; Mirta Vidal, *Chicanas Speak Out: Women—New Voice of La Raza* (Pathfinder Press, 1971); Sylvia Alicia Gonzales, "The Chicana Perspective: A Design for Self-Awareness," in Arnulfo D. Trejo, ed., *The Chicanos: As We See Ourselves* (University of Arizona Press, 1979), pp. 81-99; Morgan, *Sisterhood*, pp. 376-84; Gilberto López y Rivas, *The Chicanos: Life and Struggles of the Mexican Minority in the United States*, López y Rivas and Elizabeth Martínez, eds. and trans. (Monthly Review Press, 1973), pp. 168-74.

[*National Women's Conference*]: Lindsy Van Gelder, "Four Days That Changed the World," *Ms.*, vol. 6, no. 9 (March 1978), pp. 52-57, 86-93; U.S. National Commission on the Observance of International Women's Year, *The Spirit of Houston: The First National Women's Conference* (U.S. Government Printing Office, 1978); Alice S. Rossi, *Feminists in Politics: A Panel Analysis of the First National Women's Conference* (Academic Press, 1982).

["*My name is Susan B. Anthony*"]: quoted in Van Gelder, p. 90.

[*Minority resolution*]: *Spirit of Houston*, pp. 155-60.

["*Simultaneity of oppressions*"]: Barbara Smith, "Introduction," in Smith, ed., *Home Girls: A Black Feminist Anthology* (Kitchen Table: Women of Color Press, 1983), p. xxxiii; see also Bernice Johnson Reagon, "Coalition Politics: Turning the Century," in *ibid.*, pp. 356-68.

453 ["*Change means growth*"]: Audre Lorde, "Age, Race, Class, and Sex: Women Redefining Difference," in Lorde, pp. 114-23, quoted at p. 123.

The Personal Is Political

[*Analysis of women's movement*]: see Freeman, pp. 1-70 and ch. 7 *passim*, and sources cited therein; see also Ferree and Hess, pp. 1-27 and ch. 8.

[*Rise in percentage of women in work force, 1947-68*]: Freeman, p. 30; see also Chafe, esp. pp. 218-25, 234-37.

[*Freeman on occupational rewards*]: Freeman, p. 31.

454 ["*Hot-house plants*"]: Alice S. Rossi, quoted in *ibid.*, p. 27.

["*Rage of Women*"]: *ibid.*, p. 27, n. 40.

[*Varieties of feminist ideology*]: see Alison Jaggar, "Political Philosophies of Women's Liberation," in Mary Vetterling-Braggin et al., eds., *Feminism and Philosophy* (Rowman and Littlefield, 1977), pp. 5-21; see also Jaggar and Paula Rothenberg Struhl, eds.,

Feminist Frameworks: Alternative Theoretical Accounts of the Relations Between Women and Men (McGraw-Hill, 1978); Ferree and Hess, pp. 41–43; Yates.

454 [*Black and Maoist origins of consciousness-raising*]: see Yates, p. 103.

455 [*Growth and organizational difficulties of NOW*]: Freeman, pp. 86–97; Carden, ch. 9 *passim.*
[*Anti-leadership ethic and its difficulties*]: see Joreen, "The Tyranny of Structurelessness," in Koedt et al., pp. 285–99; Carden, ch. 7 and pp. 128–32; Freeman, pp. 119–29, 142–46; Hole and Levine, pp. 157–61; Galper and Washburne.
[*"Possession of the self"*]: Vivian Gornick, "Feminist Writers," in Gornick, *Essays*, pp. 164–70, quoted at p. 169.
[*"So many of our struggles"*]: Leah Fritz, *Dreamers and Dealers: An Intimate Appraisal of the Women's Movement* (Beacon Press, 1980), pp. 16–17.
[*"Tyranny of structurelessness"*]: Joreen, "Tyranny."

456 [*"Euphoric period"*]: "Editorial: Notes from the Third Year," December 1971, in Koedt et al., p. 300.
[*Feminist "stars"*]: see Cardin, pp. 89–90; Freeman, pp. 120–21; Joreen, pp. 292–93; Claudia Dreifus, "The Selling of a Feminist," in Koedt et al., pp. 358–61; see also Todd Gitlin, *The Whole World Is Watching: Mass Media in the Making & Unmaking of the New Left* (University of California Press, 1980), ch. 5.
[*"Sending double signals"*]: Millett, *Flying* (Knopf, 1974), p. 92.
[*Millett's career in* Time]: see *Time*, vol. 96, no. 9 (August 31, 1970); and "Women's Lib: A Second Look," *Time*, vol. 96, no. 24 (December 14, 1970), p. 50; see also Abbott and Love, *Sappho*, pp. 119–25; Millett, *Flying.*

457 [*Feminists and labor and professional organizations*]: Hole and Levine, pp. 98–107, 338–55, 362–71; Philip S. Foner, *Women and the American Labor Movement: From World War I to the Present* (Free Press, 1979–80), vol. 2, chs. 24–27; Kay Klotzburger, "Political Action by Academic Women," in Rossi and Calderwood, pp. 359–91; Anne M. Briscoe, "Phenomenon of the Seventies: The Women's Caucuses," *Signs*, vol. 4, no. 1 (Autumn 1978), pp. 152–58.

457-8 [*Feminists and religion*]: Mary Daly, *The Church and the Second Sex* (Harper, 1968); Daly, *Beyond God the Father: Toward a Philosophy of Women's Liberation* (Beacon Press, 1973); Matilda Joslyn Gage, *Woman, Church & State* (1893; reprinted by Persephone Press, 1980); Yates, pp. 65–73, 140–41; Hole and Levine, ch. 11 *passim.*

458 [*"Their hierarchical status"*]: quoted in Freeman, p. 163.
[*Women and the 1972 Democratic convention*]: Byron E. Shafer, *Quiet Revolution: The Struggle for the Democratic Party and the Shaping of Post-Reform Politics* (Russell Sage, 1983), chs. 6–7, 17 *passim;* Denis G. Sullivan et al., *Explorations in Convention Decision Making: The Democratic Party in the 1970s* (W. H. Freeman, 1976); Theodore H. White, *The Making of the President 1972* (Atheneum, 1973), chs. 3, 7; Wilma E. McGrath and John W. Soule, "Rocking the Cradle or Rocking the Boat: Women at the 1972 Democratic National Convention," *Social Science Quarterly*, vol. 55, no. 1 (June 1974), pp. 141–50; see also Kristi Andersen, "Working Women and Political Participation, 1952–1972," *American Journal of Political Science*, vol. 19, no. 3 (August 1975), pp. 439–53.
[*Black delegates at 1968 and 1972 Democratic conventions*]: Steven F. Lawson, *In Pursuit of Power: Southern Blacks and Electoral Politics, 1965–1982* (Columbia University Press, 1985), pp. 195–96.
[*Feminist disappointments at convention*]: see Shirley Chisholm, *The Good Fight* (Harper, 1973), pp. 128–31.
[*ERA*]: Janet K. Boles, *The Politics of the Equal Rights Amendment: Conflict and the Decision Process* (Longman, 1979); Boles, "Building Support for the Equal Rights Amendment," in James David Barber and Barbara Kellerman, eds., *Women Leaders in American Politics* (Prentice-Hall, 1986), pp. 37–41; Hole and Levine, pp. 54–77; Ferree and Hess, pp. 125–30; Equal Rights Amendment Project of the California Commission on the Status of Women, ed., *Impact ERA: Limitations and Possibilities* (Les Femmes Publishing, 1976); Yates, pp. 52–58; Mathews, "New Feminism," pp. 416–19; Sylvia Ann Hewlett, *A Lesser Life: The Myth of Women's Liberation in America* (Morrow, 1986), ch. 9; Foner, vol. 2, pp. 482–87; Lisa Cronin Wohl, "White Gloves and Combat Boots: The Fight for ERA," *Civil Liberties Review*, vol. 1, no. 4 (Fall 1974), pp. 77–86; Wohl, "Phyllis Schlafly: 'The Sweetheart of the Silent Majority,'" *Ms.*, vol. 2, no. 9 (March 1974), pp. 54–57, 85–89; Sarah Slavin, ed., "The Equal Rights Amendment: The

Politics and Processes of Ratification of the 27th Amendment to the U.S. Constitution," *Women & Politics*, vol. 2, nos. 1–2 (Spring–Summer 1982); see also Donald G. Mathews and Jane De Hart Mathews, "Gender and the U.S. Constitution," paper delivered at the annual meeting of the American Historical Association, Washington, D.C., December 28, 1987.

459 [*"Now forced women!"*]: quoted in Mathews, "New Feminism," p. 418; see also Rebecca E. Klatch, *Women of the New Right* (Temple University Press, 1987).
[*Achievements of women's movement*]: Mathews, "New Feminism," pp. 419–21; Ferree and Hess, chs. 7–8; Hole and Levine, pp. 397–400; Margolis, esp. Epilogue; Carden, pp. 158–71; O'Connor; Gelb and Palley, esp. ch. 8; Judith M. Bardwick, *In Transition: How Feminism, Sexual Liberation, and the Search for Self-Fulfillment Have Altered Our Lives* (Holt, Rinehart and Winston, 1979); Hewlett.

460 [*1972 campaign*]: White, chs. 8–13; Ripon Society and Clifford W. Brown, Jr., *Jaws of Victory* (Little, Brown, 1974), part 1 *passim;* Edward W. Knappman et al., eds., *Campaign 72: Press Opinion from New Hampshire to November* (Facts on File, 1973), part 3; Irwin Unger, *The Movement: A History of the American New Left, 1952–1972* (Dodd, Mead, 1975), pp. 199–202.
[*1972 election results*]: White, pp. 342–43, 372–73 (Appendix A).

460–1 [*Women in 1972 election*]: Andersen, "Working Women."

461 [*King's studies*]: see David J. Garrow, "The Intellectual Development of Martin Luther King, Jr.: Influences and Commentaries," *Union Seminary Quarterly Review*, vol. 40 (January 1986), pp. 5–20.

462 [*Evaluations of sixties movements*]: see Charles Perrow, "The Sixties Observed," in Mayer N. Zald and John D. McCarthy, eds., *The Dynamics of Social Movements: Resource Mobilization, Social Control, and Tactics* (Winthrop Publishers, 1979), pp. 192–211; Roberta Ash, *Social Movements in America* (Markham, 1972), ch. 9; Mathews, "New Feminism," pp. 398–412; Donald Von Eschen et al., "The Disintegration of the Negro Non-violent Movement," *Journal of Peace Research*, vol. 6 (1969), pp. 215–34; Anthony Oberschall, "The Decline of the 1960s Social Movements," in Louis Kriesburg, ed., *Research in Social Movements, Conflict and Change* (JAI Press, 1978), pp. 257–89; Aldon D. Morris, *The Origins of the Civil Rights Movement: Black Communities Organizing for Change* (Free Press, 1984), chs. 1, 11, and *passim;* Clayborne Carson, *In Struggle: SNCC and the Black Awakening of the 1960s* (Harvard University Press, 1981), ch. 18 and *passim;* Frances Fox Piven and Richard A. Cloward, *Poor People's Movements: Why They Succeed, How They Fail* (Pantheon, 1977), ch. 4; Chafe, part 3 *passim;* Jo Freeman, "Women and Public Policy: An Overview," in Ellen Boneparth, ed., *Women, Power and Policy* (Pergamon, 1982), pp. 47–67; Wini Breines, *The Great Refusal: Community and Organization in the New Left, 1962–1968* (Praeger, 1982); Gitlin, *Whole World;* Gitlin, *Sixties*, ch. 19; Arthur Schweitzer, *The Age of Charisma* (Nelson-Hall, 1984), pp. 210–21; August Meier and Elliott Rudwick, "Negro Protest and Urban Unrest," *Social Science Quarterly*, vol. 49, no. 3 (December 1968), pp. 438–43.

11. PRIME TIME: PEKING AND MOSCOW

465 [*Davis on Nixon*]: Davis, "Richard Milhous Nixon," in John A. Garraty, ed., *Encyclopedia of American Biography* (Harper, 1974), pp. 811–15, quoted at p. 812; on Nixon and his character, see also Stephen E. Ambrose, *Nixon: The Education of a Politician, 1913–1962* (Simon and Schuster, 1987), esp. chs. 1–7; Garry Wills, *Nixon Agonistes: The Crisis of the Self-Made Man* (Houghton Mifflin, 1970); Fawn M. Brodie, *Richard Nixon: The Shaping of His Character* (Norton, 1981); Eli S. Chesen, *President Nixon's Psychiatric Profile* (Peter H. Wyden, 1973); David Abrahamsen, *Nixon vs. Nixon: An Emotional Tragedy* (Farrar, Straus & Giroux, 1977); Bruce Mazlish, *In Search of Nixon: A Psychohistorical Inquiry* (Basic Books, 1972); Lloyd Etheredge, "Hardball Politics: A Model," *Political Psychology*, vol. 1, no. 1 (Spring 1979), pp. 3–26; Mauricio Mazon, "Young Richard Nixon: A Study in Political Precocity," *Historian*, vol. 41, no. 1 (November 1978), pp. 21–40.
[*"What'll I wear today?"*]: Washington *Post*, February 15, 1956, p. 14.

466 [*Barber on Nixon*]: James D. Barber, *The Presidential Character: Predicting Performance in the White House* (Prentice-Hall, 1972), part 5.

466 [*Mazlish on Nixon*]: Mazlish, p. 74.

[*Wills on Nixon*]: Wills, p. 406.

[*Nixon's domestic policy*]: Herbert Stein, *Presidential Economics: The Making of Economic Policy from Roosevelt to Reagan and Beyond* (Simon and Schuster, 1984), ch. 5; A. James Reichley, *Conservatives in an Age of Change: The Nixon and Ford Administrations* (Brookings Institution, 1981), pp. 68–78, chs. 7–11; Theodore H. White, *Breach of Faith: The Fall of Richard Nixon* (Atheneum, 1975), p. 139; Rowland Evans, Jr., and Robert D. Novak, *Nixon in the White House: The Frustration of Power* (Random House, 1971), chs. 6–8.

[*1971 State of the Union*]: January 22, 1971, in *Public Papers of the Presidents of the United States: Richard Nixon* (U.S. Government Printing Office, 1971–75), vol. 3, pp. 50–58, quoted at p. 52.

467 [*Burns on Nixon's quick decisions*]: Reichley, p. 138.

[*Dispute over welfare reform*]: *ibid.*, pp. 130–43, Ehrlichman quoted at p. 139.

["*A coherent vision*"]: First Annual Report to Congress on United States Foreign Policy for the 1970's, February 18, 1970, in *Nixon Public Papers*, vol. 2, pp. 116–90, quoted at p. 124.

467–8 [*Nixon's foreign policy advisers and apparatus*]: Seymour M. Hersh, *The Price of Power: Kissinger in the Nixon White House* (Summit, 1983), chs. 1–3; Henry Kissinger, *White House Years* (Little, Brown, 1979), ch. 2 *passim;* Reichley, pp. 64–68; Marvin Kalb and Bernard Kalb, *Kissinger* (Little, Brown, 1974), ch. 5; Roger Morris, *Uncertain Greatness: Henry Kissinger and American Foreign Policy* (Harper, 1977), pp. 78–93.

Finding China

468 [*Nixon as anticommunist*]: Brodie, chs. 13–17; Mazlish, pp. 81–87; Richard M. Nixon, *Six Crises* (Doubleday, 1962), sect. 1 and *passim;* Nixon, *Memoirs* (Grosset & Dunlap, 1978), pp. 343–44; Earl Mazo, *Richard Nixon: A Political and Personal Portrait* (Harper, 1959).

["*What do the Chinese Communists want?*"]: quoted in Kalb and Kalb, p. 218.

468–9 [*Nixon's changing line on China*]: Nixon, "Asia After Viet Nam," *Foreign Affairs*, vol. 46, no. 1 (October 1967), pp. 111–23, quoted at pp. 121, 123, 121, respectively.

469 [*Nixon's attempt to visit mainland China*]: William Safire, *Before the Fall: An Inside View of the Pre-Watergate White House* (Doubleday, 1975), p. 366.

[*Start of rapprochement between the U.S. and China*]: Warren I. Cohen, *America's Response to China: An Interpretative History of Sino-American Relations* (Wiley, 1971), pp. 239–42; John King Fairbank, *The United States and China*, 4th ed. (Harvard University Press, 1979), pp. 457–58; Hersh, ch. 26, pp. 363–71; Kissinger, *White House Years*, chs. 6, 18; Nixon, *Memoirs*, pp. 545–52; Seymour Topping, *Journey Between Two Chinas* (Harper, 1972), ch. 27; Kwan Ha Yim, ed., *China and the U.S.: 1964–72* (Facts on File, 1975), pp. 215–23; John W. Garver, *China's Decision for Rapprochement with the United States, 1968–1971* (Westview Press, 1982); Michael Schaller, *The United States and China in the Twentieth Century* (Oxford University Press, 1979), pp. 163–71; Frank van der Linden, *Nixon's Quest for Peace* (Robert B. Luce, 1972), pp. 139–43; Michael I. Handel, *The Diplomacy of Surprise: Hitler, Nixon, Sadat* (Center for International Affairs, Harvard University, 1981), ch. 4.

["*Curious ambivalence*"]: Fairbank, *United States and China*, p. 314.

469–70 [*U.S.-China historical background*]: *ibid.*, chs. 12–13 and *passim;* Fairbank, *China: The People's Middle Kingdom and the U.S.A.* (Belknap Press of Harvard University Press, 1967), esp. chs. 8, 10; Akira Iriye, "The United States in Chinese Foreign Policy," in William J. Barnds, ed., *China and America: The Search for a New Relationship* (New York University Press, 1977), pp. 13–37; Michael H. Hunt, *The Making of a Special Relationship: The United States and China to 1914* (Columbia University Press, 1983); Michael Oksenberg and Robert B. Oxnam, eds., *Dragon and Eagle: United States-Chinese Relations* (Basic Books, 1973); A. T. Steele, *The American People and China* (McGraw-Hill, 1966).

470 ["*When we step in here*"]: quoted in Barbara W. Tuchman, *Stilwell and the American Experience in China, 1911–45* (Macmillan, 1971), p. 39.

[*The American memory*"]: Bloodworth, *The Messiah and the Mandarins: Mao Tsetung and the Ironies of Power* (Atheneum, 1982), p. 266; see also Oksenberg and Oxnam, part 2.

470 [*"When the moment comes"*]: quoted in Handel, p. 176.
471 [*Washington's ignorance in approaching China*]: see Kissinger, *White House Years*, pp. 164, 167, 685–88.
[*"Take the glow off"*]: Kissinger, *White House Years*, p. 711.
[*"An intricate minuet"*]: ibid., p. 187; see also Hersh, p. 351.
[*Plans for Kissinger's trip*]: Kissinger, *White House Years*, pp. 718–40; Hersh, pp. 372–73.
[*Kissinger's trip to Peking*]: Kissinger, *White House Years*, pp. 738–55; Schaller, pp. 170–72; Nixon, *Memoirs*, pp. 553–54; Hersh, ch. 27.
[*"Toward the heavens"*]: Kissinger, *White House Years*, p. 742.
472 [*Chou*]: Dick Wilson, *Zhou Enlai* (Viking, 1984).
[*Chou's trip to Hanoi*]: Hersh, p. 375.
[*Nixon's announcement*]: July 15, 1971, in *Nixon Public Papers*, vol. 3, pp. 819–20, quoted at p. 820.
[*Preparations for Nixon trip*]: Kissinger, *White House Years*, pp. 774–84, 1049–53; Schaller, pp. 173–74; Hersh, pp. 489–93; Nixon, *Memoirs*, pp. 554–59.
473 [*"Great opportunity"*]: Kissinger, *White House Years*, p. 1050.
[*Nixon's arrival*]: Nixon, *Memoirs*, pp. 559–60; Schaller, p. 174; Kissinger, *White House Years*, pp. 1053–56; see also Townsend Hoopes, *The Devil and John Foster Dulles* (Atlantic Monthly/Little, Brown, 1973), p. 222.
[*Nixon in China*]: Kissinger, *White House Years*, ch. 24; Hersh, ch. 35; Nixon, *Memoirs*, pp. 560–80; *Newsweek*, vol. 79, no. 10 (March 6, 1972), pp. 14–29.
[*"A great wall"*]: exchange with reporters at the Great Wall of China, February 24, 1972, in *Nixon Public Papers*, vol. 4, pp. 370–72, quoted at p. 370.
[*Nixon-Mao exchange*]: quoted in Nixon, *Memoirs*, pp. 561–62.
474 [*Shanghai Communiqué*]: reprinted in Kissinger, *White House Years*, pp. 1490–92, n. 3, quoted at pp. 1491, 1492; see also ibid., pp. 1085–86; Gene T. Hsiao, "The Legal Status of Taiwan in the Normalization of Sino-American Relations," in Hsiao and Michael Witunski, eds., *Sino-American Normalization and Its Policy Implications* (Praeger, 1983), ch. 2, esp. pp. 41–57.
[*Reactions to China initiative*]: Kissinger, *White House Years*, pp. 1091–94, Reagan quoted at p. 1093.
474–5 [*Kissinger's request to the press*]: Hersh, pp. 499–500, quoted at p. 500.
475 [*"Week that changed the world"*]: quoted in Nixon, *Memoirs*, p. 580.
[*"Transformed the structure"*]: Kissinger, *White House Years*, p. 580.
[*Chinese internal conflict*]: Garver, ch. 4; Raymond L. Garthoff, *Détente and Confrontation: American-Soviet Relations from Nixon to Reagan* (Brookings Institution, 1985), pp. 235–36.
475–6 [*North Vietnamese offensive and preparations for Moscow summit*]: Kissinger, *White House Years*, chs. 25–27; George C. Herring, *America's Longest War: The United States and Vietnam, 1950–1975* (Wiley, 1979), pp. 239–42; Nixon, *Memoirs*, pp. 586–608; Stanley Karnow, *Vietnam* (Viking, 1983), pp. 639–47; Hersh, ch. 36; Georgi A. Arbatov and Willem Oltmans, eds., *The Soviet Viewpoint* (Dodd, Mead, 1981), pp. 61–64.
476 [*Kissinger-Dobrynin exchange*]: Kissinger, *White House Years*, p. 1117.
[*Moscow summit*]: ibid., ch. 28; Nixon, *Memoirs*, pp. 609–21; Safire, pp. 440–59; Garthoff, ch. 9; Hersh, ch. 37.
476–7 [*Kissinger on mood aboard Air Force One*]: Kissinger, *White House Years*, p. 1202.
477 [*"One of the great diplomatic coups"*]: quoted in Nixon, *Memoirs*, p. 609.
[*"If we leave all the decisions"*]: quoted in ibid., p. 610.
478 [*"Hid the appalling realities"*]: Weisberger, *Cold War, Cold Peace: The United States and Russia Since 1945* (American Heritage Publishing, 1984), p. 268.
[*"Reciprocity, mutual accommodations"*]: quoted in Garthoff, p. 290.
478–9 [*"A First Step"*]: quoted in Hersh, p. 530.
479 [*SALT ratification vote*]: *New York Times*, August 4, 1972, pp. 1–2.

Peace Without Peace

[*"Peace is at hand"*]: quoted in Kissinger, *White House Years*, p. 1399; see also Nikolai V. Sivachev and Nikolai N. Yakovlev, *Russia and the United States*, Olga Adler Titelbaum, trans. (University of Chicago Press, 1979), pp. 252–55.

479 [*Nixon's post-election melancholy*]: Nixon, *Memoirs*, p. 717.

[*Demand for staff resignations*]: Kissinger, *White House Years*, pp. 1406–7.

["*Eastertide*" *offensive and U.S. retaliation*]: Hersh, pp. 503–8, Nixon quoted on the weather and the Air Force at p. 506; Karnow, pp. 639–43; Herring, pp. 240–43.

480 [*Giap's strategy*]: see William J. Duiker, *The Communist Road to Power in Vietnam* (Westview Press, 1981), pp. 227, 292.

[*Haig's trip to Saigon*]: Kissinger, *White House Years*, pp. 1338–39; Nixon, *Memoirs*, pp. 689–91; Arnold R. Isaacs, *Without Honor: Defeat in Vietnam and Cambodia* (Johns Hopkins University Press, 1983), p. 35.

481 ["*I sympathized*"]: Nixon, *Memoirs*, p. 690.

["*Personally with you*"]: quoted in *ibid.*, p. 690.

[*Kissinger's negotiations in Paris*]: Allan E. Goodman, *The Lost Peace: America's Search for a Negotiated Settlement of the Vietnam War* (Hoover Institution Press, 1978), pp. 125–52; Kissinger, *White House Years*, chs. 31–33; Nixon, *Memoirs*, pp. 687–701; Hersh, ch. 38; Herring, pp. 244–46.

482 ["*Finest compromise*"]: Kissinger, *White House Years*, p. 1358.

[*Kissinger's report to Nixon*]: *ibid.*, pp. 1360–62; Nixon, *Memoirs*, pp. 691–93.

[*Kissinger's trip to Saigon*]: Herring, p. 245; Kissinger, *White House Years*, pp. 1367–91; Hersh, pp. 593–603.

[*Nixon's misgivings about agreement*]: see Nixon, *Memoirs*, pp. 701–7; Hersh, ch. 39 *passim*.

482–3 [*Post-election negotiations*]: Kissinger, *White House Years*, pp. 1410–46; Nixon, *Memoirs*, pp. 717–33; Goodman, pp. 152–60; Hersh, pp. 610–23.

483 ["*Up and down*"]: quoted in Nixon, *Memoirs*, p. 735.

["*Bunch of shits*"]: *ibid.*, p. 733.

[*Renewed bombing*]: Goodman, pp. 160–61; Hersh, pp. 616–28; Kissinger, *White House Years*, pp. 1444–57; Nixon, *Memoirs*, pp. 733–41.

["*This is your chance*"]: quoted in Nixon, *Memoirs*, p. 734.

484 ["*War by tantrum*"]: James Reston, quoted in *ibid.*, p. 738.

["*Sorry Christmas present*"]: quoted in Herring, p. 249.

[*Newspaper headlines*]: quoted in Kissinger, *White House Years*, p. 1453.

[*Pope on "blessed" Vietnam*]: quoted in Karnow, p. 653.

[*Resumption of negotiations*]: Herring, pp. 249–50; Goodman, pp. 162–64; Kissinger, *White House Years*, pp. 1457–70; Nixon, *Memoirs*, pp. 741–51 *passim;* Hersh, pp. 631–35; see also Gareth Porter, *A Peace Denied: The United States, Vietnam, and the Paris Agreement* (Indiana University Press, 1975), ch. 5; Maynard Parker, "Vietnam: The War That Won't End," *Foreign Affairs*, vol. 53, no. 2 (January 1975), pp. 352–74.

["*Respond with full force*"]: letter of Nixon to Thieu, January 5, 1973, in Nguyen Tien Hung and Jerrold L. Schechter, *The Palace File* (Harper, 1986), pp. 143–44, quoted at p. 144.

["*All that I can*"]: quoted in Herring, p. 250.

["*The chance today*"]: in *Nixon Public Papers*, vol. 5, pp. 12–15, quoted at pp. 13–14.

["*Just to show*"]: quoted in Nixon, *Memoirs*, p. 752.

485 ["*On the other hand*"]: *ibid.*, p. 753.

[*Preliminaries to Summit II*]: Henry Kissinger, *Years of Upheaval* (Little, Brown, 1982), pp. 228–86; Garthoff, pp. 319–30.

[*Summit II*]: Kissinger, *Years of Upheaval*, pp. 286–301; Nixon, *Memoirs*, pp. 876–87; Garthoff, pp. 330–44.

["*Act in such a manner*"]: quoted in Garthoff, p. 334; see also *ibid.*, pp. 334–44; Kissinger, *Years of Upheaval*, pp. 274–86.

486 [*Nixon's suspicions of Brezhnev's motives*]: Nixon, *Memoirs*, pp. 880–81.

["*Landmark*" *step*]: quoted in Garthoff, p. 335.

["*Bland set of principles*"]: Kissinger, *White House Years*, p. 1152.

[*Summit conflict over Middle East*]: Kissinger, *Years of Upheaval*, pp. 297–99; Nixon, *Memoirs*, pp. 884–86; Garthoff, pp. 364–65.

487 [*Middle East crisis*]: Kissinger, *Years of Upheaval*, chs. 11–12; Garthoff, ch. 12; Alan Dowty, *Middle East Crisis: U.S. Decision-Making in 1958, 1970, and 1973* (University of California Press, 1984), part 3; John G. Stoessinger, *Henry Kissinger: The Anguish of Power* (Norton, 1976), pp. 175–95.

["*Appropriate steps unilaterally*"]: quoted in Garthoff, p. 377.

487 [*"Strangelove Day"*]: *ibid.*, p. 378.
[*"In no event"*]: *ibid.*, p. 380.
[*Garthoff on Kissinger's motives*]: *ibid.*, p. 384.
[*"Soviets subsided"*]: Kissinger, *Years of Upheaval*, p. 980.

488 [*NATO and détente*]: see *ibid.*, chs. 5, 16 *passim*; Kissinger, *White House Years*, pp. 1273–75.
[*Doubts concerning détente*]: Garthoff, ch. 12 *passim*; Kissinger, *Years of Upheaval*, ch. 22 *passim*.
[*Vladivostok summit*]: Gerald R. Ford, *A Time To Heal* (Harper, 1979), pp. 213–19; Garthoff, pp. 443–50; Thomas W. Wolfe, *The SALT Experience* (Ballinger, 1979), ch. 9.

488–9 [*Helsinki agreements*]: Garthoff, pp. 473–79; Ford, pp. 298–306 *passim*.

489 [*Schlesinger firing*]: Ford, pp. 320–24; Reichley, pp. 348–51; Garthoff, pp. 441–42.
[*Fall of South Vietnam*]: Isaacs, ch. 13; Karnow, pp. 659–70; Herring, pp. 252–63; Alan Dawson, *55 Days: The Fall of South Vietnam* (Prentice-Hall, 1977); see also Frances FitzGerald, *Fire in the Lake: The Vietnamese and the Americans in Vietnam* (Atlantic Monthly/Little, Brown, 1972), esp. ch. 17.
[*Farmer and bullock*]: story related to author.

Foreign Policy: The Faltering Experiments

491 [*"A new leadership"*]: press conference of A. A. Gromyko, *Pravda*, April 1, 1977, as quoted in Garthoff, p. 809.
[*"Ruling circles"*]: "On the Present Policy of the U.S. Government," *Pravda*, June 17, 1978, as quoted in *ibid.*, p. 604.
[*"Explicit value and means calculations"*]: Gabriel A. Almond, *The American People and Foreign Policy* (Harcourt, 1950), pp. 66–85, quoted at p. 69; see also Frank L. Klingberg, "The Historical Alternation of Moods in American Foreign Policy," *World Politics*, vol. 4, no. 4 (January 1952), pp. 239–73.

492 [*"Fortress America"*]: Henry A. Kissinger, *The Necessity for Choice: Prospects of American Foreign Policy* (Harper, 1961), p. 1.
[*"In a revolutionary period"*]: *ibid.*, pp. 355–56.

493 [*Kissinger on "middle way"*]: *ibid.*, ch. 8.

493–4 [*Alternative strategies*]: James MacGregor Burns, "A Way Out in Vietnam," *Harper's*, vol. 233, no. 1394 (August 1966), pp. 34–35; see also Anthony Eden, "Toward Peace in Indochina, Twelve Steps to a Long-range Settlement," *ibid.*, pp. 36–43. See, generally, Joseph W. and Stewart Alsop Papers, General Correspondence, esp. containers 69–77, Library of Congress.

494 [*"No true Nixon"*]: Kissinger, *Years of Upheaval*, pp. 73–74.
[*Stevenson on Nixon*]: John Bartlow Martin, *Adlai Stevenson and the World* (Doubleday, 1977), p. 547.

495 [*"Early presidents deliberately selected"*]: Schlesinger, *The Cycles of American History* (Houghton Mifflin, 1986), pp. 296–97; see also Abraham D. Sofaer, *War, Foreign Affairs and Constitutional Power: The Origins* (Ballinger, 1976).
[*Media and foreign policy*]: see Montague Kern, Patricia W. Levering, and Ralph B. Levering, *The Kennedy Crises: The Press, the Presidency, and Foreign Policy* (University of North Carolina Press, 1983); David L. Paletz and Robert M. Entman, *Media Power Politics* (Free Press, 1981), ch. 13.
[*"Caused severe damage"*]: in *The Public Papers and Addresses of Franklin D. Roosevelt*, Samuel I. Rosenman, comp. (Random House, 1938–50), vol. 10, pp. 514–16, quoted at p. 514.
[*"Hell of a beating"*]: quoted in Tuchman, p. 300.

496 [*"Appearances contributed to reality"*]: John Kennedy, quoted in Robert Dallek, *The American Style of Foreign Policy* (Knopf, 1983), p. 230.
[*Johnson's fear of appearing "soft"*]: see Doris Kearns, *Lyndon Johnson and the American Dream* (Harper, 1976), pp. 258–59, 269.
[*"Pitiful, helpless giant"*]: Address to the Nation on the Situation in Southeast Asia, April 30, 1970, in *Nixon Public Papers*, vol. 2, pp. 405–10, quoted at p. 409.
[*Gaddis on the perception of power*]: John Lewis Gaddis, *Strategies of Containment* (Oxford

University Press, 1982), p. 277; see also James Chace and Caleb Carr, *America Invulnerable: The Quest for Absolute Security from 1812 to Star Wars* (Summit, 1988).

12. VICE AND VIRTUE

497 [*"Guerrilla war to end"*]: Max Frankel, "A Divided Nation Lost Its Way," *New York Times*, January 28, 1973, sect. 4, p. 2.

498 [*"Full, free, and absolute"*]: Proclamation 4311, Granting Pardon to Richard Nixon, in *Public Papers of the Presidents of the United States: Gerald R. Ford* (U.S. Government Printing Office, 1975–79), vol. 1, pp. 103–4, quoted at p. 104; see also Gerald R. Ford, *A Time to Heal* (Harper, 1979), pp. 157–71, 196–99; Robert Sam Anson, *Exile: The Unquiet Oblivion of Richard M. Nixon* (Simon and Schuster, 1984), chs. 3–4.

[*"Our people would again"*]: in Ford Public Papers, vol. 1, pp. 101–3, quoted at p. 102.

[*Suspicions of Ford-Nixon deal*]: Hersh, "The Pardon," *Atlantic*, vol. 252, no. 2 (August 1983), pp. 55–78; J. Anthony Lukas, *Nightmare: The Underside of the Nixon Years* (Viking, 1976), p. 545.

[*Nixon's alleged call to Ford*]: Hersh, p. 76.

[*"No deal, period"*]: October 17, 1974, in Ford Public Papers, vol. 1, pp. 338–71, quoted at p. 363; see also Ford, *Time to Heal*, pp. 196–99.

[*"The greatest good"*]: in Ford Public Papers, vol. 1, p. 102.

499 [*Enemies list*]: Lukas, pp. 12–13.

[*Huston Plan*]: memoranda reprinted in Steve Weissman, ed., *Big Brother and the Holding Company* (Ramparts Press, 1974), pp. 321–32; Frank J. Donner, *The Age of Surveillance* (Knopf, 1980), pp. 261–68; Lukas, pp. 32–37; Steve Weissman, "Tom Huston's Plan," in Weissman, pp. 45–60; Richard Gid Powers, *Secrecy and Power: The Life of J. Edgar Hoover* (Free Press, 1987), pp. 448–58.

[*"Flag-waving"*]: quoted in Lukas, p. 11.

500 [*"Going to change now"*]: Gerald Gold, ed., *The White House Transcripts* (Bantam, 1974), p. 63.

Watergate: A Morality Tale

[*At the Beverly Hills Hotel*]: Jeb Stuart Magruder, *An American Life: One Man's Road to Watergate* (Atheneum, 1974), pp. 211–15; see also Lukas, ch. 7.

[*Magruder-Liddy exchange*]: quoted in Magruder, p. 211.

[*"We were the government"*]: ibid., p. 214.

[*Magruder*]: ibid., chs. 1–8; Lukas, pp. 7–8.

501 [*"State of permanent crisis"*]: Magruder, p. 72.

[*Cover-up*]: Lukas, chs. 8–9; Magruder, chs. 11–12; John W. Dean III, *Blind Ambition* (Simon and Schuster, 1976), chs. 4–6; Thomas Powers, *The Man Who Kept the Secrets: Richard Helms & the CIA* (Knopf, 1979), pp. 258–67.

[*"This dirty work"*]: Dean, p. 123.

[*Kalmbach's fund-raising*]: ibid., pp. 123–24, 139–40; Lukas, pp. 250–55.

[*Post investigations*]: Bernstein and Woodward, *All the President's Men* (Simon and Schuster, 1974), quoted at p. 142; see also Barry Sussman, *The Great Cover-Up: Nixon and the Scandal of Watergate* (Crowell, 1974), part 4.

[*McCord's admission*]: Lukas, pp. 302–6; John J. Sirica, *To Set the Record Straight* (Norton, 1979), ch. 5.

502 [*"Come a long road"*]: White House Transcripts, p. 91.

[*"Certain domino situation"*]: ibid., p. 119.

[*"Get a million dollars"*]: ibid., pp. 146–47.

[*"No doubt about the seriousness"*]: ibid., p. 134.

[*"Fall on his sword"*]: Dean, pp. 194, 195.

503 [*Ervin committee*]: Sam J. Ervin, Jr., *The Whole Truth: The Watergate Conspiracy* (Random House, 1980); Sam Dash, *Chief Counsel* (Random House, 1976); Dean, ch. 10; Magruder, pp. 304–7; Gerald Gold, ed., *The Watergate Hearings: Break-In and Cover-Up* (Viking, 1973); Gladys Engel Lang and Kurt Lang, *The Battle for Public Opinion: The President, the Press, and the Polls During Watergate* (Columbia University Press, 1983), ch. 5; Mary McCarthy, *The Mask of State: Watergate Portraits* (Harcourt, 1974).

503 [*"Public posture"*]: quoted in Lukas, p. 278.
[*Dean's testimony*]: *Watergate Hearings*, pp. 266–363, quoted at pp. 266, 302, 307–8, 353–54.

504 [*"Make it fourteen"*]: quoted in McCarthy, p. 37.
[*Other charges against Nixon*]: see Lukas, ch. 10; Bob Woodward and Carl Bernstein, *The Final Days* (Simon and Schuster, 1976), pp. 23–24.

504–5 [*Agnew*]: Richard M. Cohen and Jules Witcover, *A Heartbeat Away: The Investigation and Resignation of Spiro T. Agnew* (Viking, 1974); Lukas, ch. 12.

505 [*Struggle over tapes*]: Sirica, chs. 7–14; Lukas, chs. 11, 13–14 *passim;* Leon Jaworski, *The Right and the Power* (Reader's Digest Press/Gulf Publishing, 1976); James Doyle, *Not Above the Law* (Morrow, 1977); Richard Ben-Veniste and George Frampton, Jr., *Stonewall* (Simon and Schuster, 1977).
[*"Immediate settlement"*]: quoted in Lukas, p. 495.
[U.S. *v.* Nixon]: 418 U.S. 683 (1974), quoted at pp. 712, 713; see also Leon Friedman, ed., *United States v. Nixon: The President before the Supreme Court* (Chelsea House, 1974).

506 [*"The President exploded"*]: Lukas, p. 518; see also John Osborne, "Judgment Days," *New Republic*, vol. 171, nos. 6 & 7 (August 10 & 17, 1974), pp. 9–11.
[*Judiciary Committee*]: Lukas, ch. 15, pp. 522–35; Frank Mankiewicz, *U.S. v. Richard Nixon: The Final Crisis* (Quadrangle/New York Times Book Co., 1975), pp. 183–237; Lang and Lang, ch. 7; Jimmy Breslin, *How the Good Guys Finally Won* (Viking, 1975).
[*"Make no mistake"*]: quoted in Lukas, p. 522.
[*Committee polarization*]: *ibid.*, pp. 496–97.

507 [*"Fair and impartial"*]: quoted in *ibid.*, p. 508.
[*"Right in the gut"*]: *ibid.*, p. 509.
[*"Earlier today we heard"*]: *ibid.*, pp. 530–31.
[*"For years we Republicans"*]: *ibid.*, p. 531.
[*Committee votes on impeachment*]: articles of impeachment reprinted in Mankiewicz, pp. 257–63, quoted at p. 257; roll calls given in *ibid.*, pp. 259, 261–62.

508 [*June 23, 1972, tapes*]: *Time*, vol. 104, no. 8 (August 19, 1974), pp. 18–19.
[*"He had lied to me"*]: quoted in Lukas, p. 549.
[*"The painful conclusion"*]: quoted in Woodward and Bernstein, *Final Days*, p. 379.
[*Final days*]: *ibid.*, pp. 403–56; *Time*, vol. 104, no. 8 (August 19, 1974), pp. 13B–22; Lukas, pp. 558–69; Henry Kissinger, *Years of Upheaval* (Little, Brown, 1982), pp. 1198–1214; see also Fawn M. Brodie, *Richard Nixon: The Shaping of His Character* (Norton, 1981), chs. 1, 34.
[*"We've asked Barry"*]: Woodward and Bernstein, *Final Days*, pp. 413–17, quoted at pp. 415–16.

509 [*"As we look to the future"*]: in *Public Papers of the Presidents of the United States: Richard Nixon* (U.S. Government Printing Office, 1971–75), vol. 6, pp. 626–29, quoted at pp. 627, 628.
[*"Has a great heart"*]: in *ibid.*, pp. 630–32, quoted at pp. 630, 631, 632.

510 [*Mind of Watergate*]: see Brodie, chs. 1, 34, and *passim;* Leo Rangell, *The Mind of Watergate: An Exploration of the Compromise of Integrity* (Norton, 1980); Douglas Muzzio, *Watergate Games: Strategies, Choices, Outcomes* (New York University Press, 1982); and sources cited for the introduction of ch. 11 *supra.*
[*"Covered up a little operation"*]: quoted in Brodie, pp. 18–19.
[*"A little bit of Richard Nixon"*]: *ibid.*, p. 18.
[*"Swelling of the presidency"*]: Cronin, "The Swelling of the Presidency," in Paul J. Halpern, ed., *Why Watergate?* (Palisades Publishers, 1975), pp. 92–102, quoted at pp. 92–93, 94.
[*"Mass of intrigue"*]: George E. Reedy, *The Twilight of the Presidency* (New American Library, 1970), p. xiv.
[*"No one forced me"*]: Magruder, p. 317.

510–11 [*Watergate, public opinion, the press*]: Lang and Lang; David L. Paletz and Robert M. Entman, *Media Power Politics* (Free Press, 1981), pp. 158–66; Mankiewicz, pp. 81–141; John C. Spear, *Presidents and the Press: The Nixon Legacy* (MIT Press, 1984), ch. 7.

511 [*"More morally reprehensible"*]: quoted in "Watergate Trails Kopechne Death in a National Poll," *New York Times*, August 4, 1973, p. 10.
[*Newspaper endorsements, 1972 campaign*]: Lang and Lang, p. 28.

511 [*Berman on "presidential imperialism"*]: Berman, *The New American Presidency* (Little, Brown, 1986), p. 292; see also Arthur M. Schlesinger, Jr., *The Imperial Presidency* (Houghton Mifflin, 1973), ch. 8 and *passim;* Samuel Hendel, "Separation of Powers Revisited in Light of 'Watergate,' " *Western Political Quarterly*, vol. 27, no. 4 (December 1974), pp. 575–88.

512 [*"A certain self-righteousness"*]: Magruder, pp. 229–30.
[*"Capable of looking at us"*]: Elizabeth Drew, *Washington Journal: The Events of 1973–1974* (Random House, 1975), p. 392; see also Robert G. Meadow, "Information and Maturation in Children's Evaluation of Government Leadership During Watergate," *Western Political Quarterly*, vol. 35, no. 4 (December 1982), pp. 539–53.
[*"Look, Nixon's no dope"*]: quoted in Brodie, p. 18.

Crime and Punishment

[*"Instinct to overreact"*]: Magruder, p. 317.
512-13 [*Magruder on his teachers*]: *ibid.*, pp. 22, 25–26, 27–30, 306–7, 309, quoted on Schuman at p. 22, on "two wrongs" at p. 306; author's personal correspondence with Magruder.

513 [*Fates of Watergate participants*]: Donald P. Doane, "How Time Has Treated the Watergate Crew," *U.S. News & World Report*, vol. 92, no. 23 (June 14, 1982), pp. 51–53; see also John W. Dean III, *Lost Honor* (Stanford Press, 1982), Epilogue.
[*Nixon after resignation*]: Anson; Doane, p. 51; *Newsweek*, vol. 107, no. 20 (May 19, 1986), pp. 26–34; *ibid.*, vol. 106, no. 18 (October 28, 1985), p. 45; see also Rangell, chs. 5–6.
[*"Not going to spend my time"*]: quoted in Anson, p. 264.

514 [*Rise in white-collar crime*]: W. H. Webster, "Examination of FBI Theory and Methodology Regarding White-Collar Crime Investigation and Prevention," *American Criminal Law Review*, vol. 17, no. 3 (Winter 1980), pp. 275–86.
[*Difficulties in defining white-collar crime*]: see Gilbert Geis, ed., *White-Collar Criminal: The Offender in Business and the Professions* (Atherton, 1968), esp. parts 1, 6.
[*"Intuitively satisfying"*]: Gilbert Geis and Ezra Stotland, eds., *White-Collar Crime: Theory and Research* (Sage Publications, 1980), quoted at p. 11.
[*"Illegal acts committed"*]: Donn B. Parker, "Computer-Related White-Collar Crime," in *ibid.*, pp. 199–220, quoted at p. 199.
514-15 [*Corporate crime*]: John C. Coffee, Jr., " 'No Soul to Damn: No Body to Kick': An Unscandalized Inquiry into the Problem of Corporate Punishment," *Michigan Law Review*, vol. 79 (January 1981), pp. 386–459; W. Allen Spurgeon and Terence P. Fagan, "Criminal Liability for Life-Endangering Corporate Conduct," *Journal of Criminal Law and Criminology*, vol. 72, no. 2 (1981), pp. 400–33; Geis, part 2; Geis and Stotland, esp. chs. 3–7; Harold C. Barnett, "Corporate Capitalism, Corporate Crime," *Crime & Delinquency*, vol. 27, no. 1 (January 1981), pp. 4–23.

515 [*Computer-related crime*]: Parker, quoted at p. 219; see also M. E. Baldigo, "Computer Abuse—Past Is Prologue," *Internal Auditor*, vol. 37, no. 2 (April 1980), pp. 90–95.
[*"Did you ever expect"*]: Edward, First Baron Thurlow, quoted in Coffee, p. 386 and 386 n. 1.
[*Pinto trial*]: Spurgeon and Fagan, pp. 417–18, 426; *New York Times*, March 14, 1980, pp. 1, D12.
[*Firestone recall*]: Spurgeon and Fagan, pp. 403 n. 11, 416 n. 76.

516 [*Concern with street over white-collar crime*]: Laura Shill Schrager and James F. Short, Jr., "How Serious a Crime? Perceptions of Organizational and Common Crimes," in Geis and Stotland, pp. 14–31.
[*Rise in offenses, 1960–83*]: Edmund F. McGarrell and Timothy J. Flanagan, eds., *Sourcebook of Criminal Justice Statistics—1984* (U.S. Government Printing Office, 1985), p. 380 (Table 3.81).
[*Polls on crime*]: *ibid.*, pp. 170–79 (Tables 2.3–2.9); see also John E. Conklin, *The Impact of Crime* (Macmillan, 1975), ch. 2.
[*"Liberals first denied"*]: Wilson, *Thinking About Crime*, rev. ed. (Vintage, 1985), p. 14.
517 [*Baby boom and crime rise*]: Samuel Walker, *Popular Justice: A History of American Criminal Justice* (Oxford University Press, 1980), pp. 205, 228.

517 [*Capitalist structures and crime*]: Barnett; see also Jeffrey H. Reiman and Sue Headlee, "Marxism and Criminal Justice Policy," *Crime & Delinquency*, vol. 27, no. 1 (January 1981), pp. 24–47.
[*Criminal cases filed and criminal trials completed in federal courts*]: Richard A. Posner, *The Federal Courts: Crisis and Reform* (Harvard University Press, 1985), pp. 61 (Table 3.1), 64 (Table 3.2), 68 (Table 3.3); see also *Sourcebook 1984*, sects. 4–5.
[*Federal civil filings*]: Posner, pp. 61 (Table 3.1), 64 (Table 3.2).

518 [*"Isolable, incidental features"*]: Lloyd L. Weinreb, *Denial of Justice: Criminal Process in the United States* (Free Press, 1977), p. ix.
[*"Revolution in criminal procedure"*]: ibid., p. viii.
[*Criminal justice analyses*]: see Wilson, ch. 3, quoted on "reasonable cost" at p. 49.
[*"Assumptions about human nature"*]: ibid., p. 145.

519 [*Critical legal studies*]: Roberto M. Unger, *The Critical Legal Studies Movement* (Harvard University Press, 1986); Unger, *Law in Modern Society: Toward a Criticism of Social Theory* (Free Press, 1976); Mark Kelman, *A Guide to Critical Legal Studies* (Harvard University Press, 1987).
[*Weinreb on plea bargaining*]: Weinreb, p. 86; see also Milton Heumann, *Plea Bargaining* (University of Chicago Press, 1978).
[*"Might control his subordinates"*]: Walker, p. 216.

520 [*Attica*]: Tom Wicker, *A Time to Die* (Quadrangle/New York Times Book Co., 1975); Herman Badillo and Milton Haynes, *A Bill of No Rights: Attica and the American Prison System* (Outerbridge & Lazard, 1972); New York State Special Commission on Attica, *Attica* (Praeger, 1972).
[*"Negative–negative!"*]: quoted in Wicker, p. 276.
[*"What makes a man free?"*]: Phillips, "What Makes a Man Free?," in Celes Tisdale, ed., *Betcha Ain't: Poems from Attica* (Broadside Press, 1974), p. 38.

Carter: The Arc of Morality

521 [*Carter*]: Betty Glad, *Jimmy Carter: In Search of the Great White House* (Norton, 1980); James Wooten, *Dasher* (Summit, 1978); Jimmy Carter, *A Government as Good as Its People* (Simon and Schuster, 1977); William Lee Miller, *Yankee from Georgia: The Emergence of Jimmy Carter* (Times Books, 1978); James MacGregor Burns, *The Power to Lead: The Crisis of the American Presidency* (Simon and Schuster, 1984), ch. 1, from which I have borrowed or paraphrased.
[*"Not extraordinary governor"*]: Glad, p. 187.
[*"Idealist without illusions"*]: quoted in Burns, *Power to Lead*, p. 25.

522 [*Inaugural walk*]: Glad, p. 409.
[*Massachusetts town meeting*]: ibid., p. 411.
[*Carter and human rights*]: Jimmy Carter, *Keeping Faith* (Bantam, 1982), pp. 141–51; Zbigniew Brzezinski, *Power and Principle: Memoirs of the National Security Adviser, 1977–1981* (Farrar, Straus & Giroux, 1983), pp. 122–29; Raymond L. Garthoff, *Détente and Confrontation: American-Soviet Relations from Nixon to Reagan* (Brookings Institution, 1985), chs. 17–18 passim; Seyom Brown, *The Faces of Power* (Columbia University Press, 1983), chs. 27–28; Gaddis Smith, *Morality, Reason, and Power: American Diplomacy in the Carter Years* (Hill and Wang, 1986), pp. 49–55; Subject File, Human Rights, boxes HU-1 through HU-18, Jimmy Carter Library.
[*"Gained the trust"*]: Carter, *Keeping Faith*, pp. 141–42, quoted at p. 142.
[*"Demonstration of American idealism"*]: ibid., p. 143.
[*"The first nation"*]: quoted in ibid., p. 144.
[*"Craving, and now demanding"*]: January 20, 1977, in *Public Papers of the Presidents of the United States: Jimmy Carter* (U.S. Government Printing Office, 1977–82), vol. 1, part 1, pp. 1–4, quoted at pp. 2–3.
[*"Principled yet pragmatic"*]: Cyrus R. Vance, *Hard Choices: Critical Years in America's Foreign Policy* (Simon and Schuster, 1983), p. 44.

523 [*"Accepted international standards"*]: quoted in Garthoff, p. 569.
[*Administration attention to Soviet human rights violations*]: Smith, pp. 67–68; Garthoff, pp. 568–74; see also Brzezinski, pp. 155–56.

523 [*Vance's trip to Moscow*]: Vance, pp. 53-56; Garthoff, p. 573.
[*"Defense of freedom"*]: quoted in Garthoff, p. 610.
524 [*Carter and Latin America*]: Smith, pp. 109-10, quoted at p. 110.
[*Canal negotiations*]: Carter, *Keeping Faith*, pp. 152-85; Smith, pp. 110-15; Vance, ch. 8; Brzezinski, pp. 134-39; J. Michael Hogan, *The Panama Canal in Domestic Politics: Domestic Advocacy and the Evolution of Policy* (Southern Illinois University Press, 1986), pp. 83-131.
[*"We bought it"*]: quoted in Smith, p. 112.
[*"Cooperative effort"*]: quoted in Carter, *Keeping Faith*, p. 155.
525 [*"Plus one President"*]: *ibid.*, p. 184.
[*"Jews who had survived"*]: *ibid.*, p. 274; see also Carter, *The Blood of Abraham: Insights into the Middle East* (Houghton Mifflin, 1985), esp. pp. 31-36.
[*Carter and search for Middle East peace*]: Carter, *Keeping Faith*, pp. 273-429; Vance, chs. 9-11; Smith, pp. 157-68; Brown, ch. 29; Brzezinski, pp. 83-122, 234-88; William B. Quandt, *Camp David: Peacemaking and Politics* (Brookings Institution, 1986); Eric Silver, *Begin: The Haunted Prophet* (Random House, 1984), chs. 19-20.
[*"Had to postpone"*]: quoted in Carter, *Keeping Faith*, p. 313.
[*"To go all out"*]: quoted in *ibid.*, p. 316.
526 [*"We are privileged"*]: September 18, 1978, in *Carter Public Papers*, vol. 2, part 2, pp. 1533-37, quoted at p. 1537.
[*"Act of desperation"*]: Carter, *Keeping Faith*, p. 416.
[*"Out of the negotiating business!"*]: quoted in *ibid.*, p. 426.
527 [*The Yemens*]: Garthoff, pp. 653-60; Smith, pp. 172-74; Robin Bidwell, *The Two Yemens* (Longman/Westview Press, 1983), pp. 262-337.
[*"Demonstrate our concern"*]: quoted in Smith, p. 174.
528 [*Smith on American response*]: *ibid.*
[*"Excessive Soviet buildup"*]: address at Wake Forest University, March 17, 1978, in *Carter Public Papers*, vol. 2, part 1, pp. 529-35, quoted at p. 533; see also Garthoff, pp. 593-95.
[*Vance's request for review*]: Brzezinski, pp. 319-20, Vance quoted on "differing views" at p. 319; Vance, pp. 99-102; Garthoff, pp. 600-1.
[*Annapolis speech*]: in *Carter Public Papers*, vol. 2, part 1, pp. 1052-57.
[*Press reaction*]: Garthoff, p. 603.
[*Soviet view*]: *ibid.*, pp. 604-5.
[*"Any further delay"*]: quoted in David Detzer, *The Brink: Cuban Missile Crisis, 1962* (Crowell, 1979), p. 234.
[*"Visceral anti-Sovietism"*]: Vance, p. 394.
[*Brzezinski on Vance*]: Brzezinski, p. 43.
528-9 [*Brzezinski's trip to China*]: *ibid.*, pp. 202-19; Smith, pp. 88-89; Garthoff, pp. 701-10.
529 [*Deng in U.S.*]: Garthoff, pp. 718-26; Brzezinski, pp. 405-11; Carter, *Keeping Faith*, pp. 202-11; Smith, pp. 92-94; *Time*, vol. 113, no. 7 (February 12, 1979), pp. 10-16.
[*Vienna summit*]: Garthoff, pp. 728-40; Carter, *Keeping Faith*, pp. 239-61; Brzezinski, pp. 340-44; Smith, pp. 208-11.
[*Afghanistan and SALT*]: Garthoff, chs. 26-27 *passim;* Carter, *Keeping Faith*, pp. 264-65; Brown, ch. 32; Vance, ch. 18; Smith, ch. 9; Glad, pp. 460-62.
[*Most profound disappointment*]: Carter, *Keeping Faith*, p. 265.
529-30 [*Camp David consultations*]: Carter, *Keeping Faith*, pp. 114-20; *Newsweek*, vol. 94, no. 4 (July 23, 1979), pp. 20-26; Glad, pp. 444-47.
530 [*"Rekindle our sense"*]: July 15, 1979, in *Carter Public Papers*, vol. 3, part 2, pp. 1235-41, quoted at p. 1240.
[*"Not leading the country"*]: quoted in Joseph A. Califano, "Getting Fired by Jimmy Carter," Washington *Post*, May 24, 1981, pp. C1, C5, quoted at p. C5.
[*Carter on 60 Minutes*]: "Carter: Toll of a Clockwork Presidency," Washington *Post*, October 27, 1980, pp. A1, A4, quoted at p. A4.
[*Kennedy campaign*]: Jack W. Germond and Jules Witcover, *Blue Smoke and Mirrors* (Viking, 1981), chs. 3-4, 7, 9; Glad, ch. 24 *passim;* Burns, *Power to Lead*, pp. 80-89.
[*"Umpteen billions"*]: quoted in Burns, *Power to Lead*, p. 84.
[*Hostage seizure*]: Smith, ch. 8; Brown, ch. 30; Vance, chs. 17, 19; Glad, pp. 458-60.
531 [*"Many forces at play"*]: "Hamilton Jordan: Looking back," Washington *Post*, Decem-

ber 2, 1980, p. A19; see also Hamilton Jordan, *Crisis: The Last Year of the Carter Presidency* (Putnam, 1982), pp. 378–81.

531 [*"Any sense of political strategy"*]: Hargrove, review of Glad, *Jimmy Carter*, in *American Political Science Review*, vol. 75, no. 2 (June 1981), pp. 493–95, quoted at p. 494.
[*Gulf between pronouncements and policies*]: Samuel P. Huntington, "Renewed Hostility," in Joseph S. Nye, Jr., ed., *The Making of America's Soviet Policy* (Yale University Press, 1984), pp. 265–89, esp. p. 275; Burns, *Power to Lead*, pp. 29–30; John Steuart and Steve Lietman, "Carter's Unkept '76 Promises—A Time Bomb?," *New York Times*, September 7, 1980, sect. 4, p. 19.

Gun and Bible

532 [*"Destructive and irresponsible freedom"*]: Solzhenitsyn, *A World Split Apart*, Irina I. Alberti, trans. (Harper, 1978), pp. 21, 37.
[*"On hands and knees"*]: quoted in Arthur M. Schlesinger, Jr., *The Cycles of American History* (Houghton Mifflin, 1986), p. 113.
[*"Object of our existence"*]: *ibid.*
[*"Affirming the values"*]: quoted in Samuel P. Huntington, *American Politics: The Promise of Disharmony* (Belknap Press of Harvard University Press, 1981), p. 2.
[*"Have we not"*]: quoted in Schlesinger, p. 111.
[*Approaches to vice and virtue*]: John Patrick Diggins, *The Lost Soul of American Politics* (Basic Books, 1984); J. G. A. Pocock, *The Machiavellian Moment: Florentine Political Thought and the Atlantic Republican Tradition* (Princeton University Press, 1975), esp. chs. 14–15; John F. Kasson, *Civilizing the Machine: Technology and Republican Values in America, 1776–1900* (Grossman, 1976); John Witherspoon, *Lectures on Moral Philosophy*, Varnum L. Collins, ed. (Princeton University Press, 1912); Garry Wills, *Explaining America: The Federalist* (Doubleday, 1981), esp. ch. 22; James MacGregor Burns, *The Vineyard of Liberty* (Knopf, 1982), pp. 58–63.

533 [*Lerner on 1950s mores*]: Lerner, *America as a Civilization* (Simon and Schuster, 1957), p. 673.

533–4 [*Sexual studies*]: Alfred C. Kinsey et al., *Sexual Behavior in the Human Male* (W. B. Saunders, 1948), pp. 499, 550–51, 623, 670; Kinsey et al., *Sexual Behavior in the Human Female* (W. B. Saunders, 1953), pp. 142, 286, 453, 505; Charles H. Whiteley and Winifred M. Whiteley, *Sex & Morals* (Basic Books, 1967); Michael G. Schofield, *The Sexual Behaviour of Young People* (Little, Brown, 1965); Lerner, pp. 679–87.

534 [*"Half Babylonian"*]: Lerner, p. 686.
[*"Soft"* and *"hard"*]: Diggins, p. 335.
[*Campaign against sexual permissiveness*]: Robert B. Fowler, *A New Engagement: Evangelical Political Thought, 1966–1976* (William B. Eerdmans Publishing, 1982), ch. 10; Louis A. Zurcher, Jr., and R. George Kirkpatrick, *Citizens for Decency: Antipornography Crusades as Status Defense* (University of Texas Press, 1976); Robert C. Liebman and Robert Wuthnow, eds., *The New Christian Right* (Aldine, 1983), esp. chs. 7–8, 10.

534–5 [*Commissions on pornography*]: U.S. Commission on Obscenity and Pornography, *Report* (U.S. Government Printing Office, 1970), quoted at p. 27; Attorney General's Commission on Pornography, *Final Report* (Department of Justice, 1986).

535 [*Dworkin-MacKinnon ordinance*]: Rosemarie Tong, "Women, Pornography and the Law," *Williams Alumni Review*, vol. 79, no. 1 (Fall 1986), pp. 3–11; Indianapolis *Star*, November 20, 1984, pp. 1, 6; *Freedom to Read Foundation News*, vol. 13, no. 1 (1986); *Hudnut* v. *American Booksellers Association*, Supreme Court affirming lower court's judgment, February 24, 1986 (no. 85-1090); interview with John Swan; see also Catharine A. MacKinnon, *Feminism Unmodified: Discourses on Life and Law* (Harvard University Press, 1987).
[*Tong on FACT*]: Tong, p. 8.
[*"Usher in another era"*]: *ibid.*, p. 9.

536 [*"What scoundrels we would be"*]: quoted in Kenneth Thompson, *Moralism and Morality in Politics and Diplomacy* (University Press of America, 1985), p. 8.
[*"Moral man"* and *"immoral society"*]: Niebuhr, *Moral Man and Immoral Society: A Study in Ethics and Politics* (Scribner, 1941).
[*"Can be manageable"*]: Thompson, p. 55.

536 [*Peace and nonviolence in early America*]: Peter Brock, *Pacifism in the United States from the Colonial Era to the First World War* (Princeton University Press, 1968).

[*"Patriotic inclination"*]: Piehl, *Breaking Bread: The Catholic Worker and the Origin of Catholic Radicalism in America* (Temple University Press, 1982), p. 54; see also Sydney E. Ahlstrom, *A Religious History of the American People* (Yale University Press, 1972), pp. 330–42, 527–68.

[*Catholic Church and peace movement*]: Eric O. Hanson, *The Catholic Church in World Politics* (Princeton University Press, 1987), pp. 281–322; George Weigel, *Tranquillitas Ordinis* (Oxford University Press, 1987); Jim Castelli, *The Bishops and the Bomb: Waging Peace in a Nuclear Age* (Doubleday, 1983); James E. Dougherty, *The Bishops and Nuclear Weapons* (Archon Books, 1984); William A. Au, *The Cross, the Flag, and the Bomb: American Catholics Debate War and Peace, 1960–1983* (Greenwood Press, 1985); *Never Again War!* (Office of Public Information, United Nations, 1965); Patricia Hunt-Perry, "Peace, Politics and Theology: The Institutional Catholic Church Enters the Peace Movement in the United States," presented at the annual meeting of the International Society of Political Psychology, St. Catherine's College, Oxford University, 1983.

[*Catholic switch on Vietnam*]: quoted in Hunt-Perry, p. 36.

[*"Contrary to reason"*]: reprinted in *Never Again War!*, pp. 81–126, quoted at p. 112.

537 [*"The Challenge of Peace"*]: reprinted in *Origins*, vol. 13, no. 1 (May 19, 1983), pp. 1–32, quoted at pp. 1, 30, 2, 27, 15, 18, 25, respectively.

[*"Traditional in the sense"*]: Hunt-Perry, p. 21.

[*Issue of "just war"*]: see "Challenge of Peace," pp. 9–12; Michael Walzer, *Just and Unjust Wars* (Basic Books, 1977); Terry Nardin, *Law, Morality, and the Relations of States* (Princeton University Press, 1983), esp. ch. 11; Alan Donagan, *The Theory of Morality* (University of Chicago Press, 1977), esp. chs. 1, 3.

538 [*"Most profound and searching"*]: Kennan, "The Bishops' Letter," *New York Times*, May 1, 1983, sect. 4, p. 21; see also Kennan, *The Nuclear Delusion: Soviet-American Relations in the Nuclear Age* (Pantheon, 1982).

[*"Ruling and intellectual elites"*]: Solzhenitsyn, *World Split Apart*, p. 11.

[*"Increasingly aggressive"*]: quoted in Schlesinger, p. 57.

[*Universal Declaration of Human Rights*]: reprinted in *Never Again War!*, pp. 127–34.

539 [*"Not enough to think"*]: Van Dyke, "The Individual, the State, and Ethnic Communities in Political Theory," in Donald P. Kommers and Gilburt D. Loescher, eds., *Human Rights and American Foreign Policy* (University of Notre Dame Press, 1979), pp. 36–62, quoted at p. 36.

[*"You know, professor"*]: Eddison J. M. Zvobgo, "A Third World View," in *ibid.*, pp. 90–106, junior professor quoted at p. 97.

[*Vance on economic and political rights*]: quoted in David P. Forsythe, *Human Rights and World Politics* (University of Nebraska Press, 1983), p. 95.

540 [*"Factor in the mobilization"*]: *ibid.*, p. 87.

[*"Evidence of the stability"*]: Walzer, p. 19.

13. THE CULTURE OF THE WORKSHOP

541 [*"Enormous laboratories"*]: Max Lerner, *America as a Civilization* (Simon and Schuster, 1957), p. 209.

[*American Nobel Prize recipients*]: Bernard Schlessinger and June H. Schlessinger, eds., *The Who's Who of Nobel Prize Winners* (Oryx Press, 1986).

541–2 [*Advances in astronomy*]: Martin Harwit, *Cosmic Discovery: The Search, Scope, and Heritage of Astronomy* (Basic Books, 1981); Patrick Moore, *The Story of Astronomy* (MacDonald and Jane's, 1978); Otto Struve and Velta Zebergs, *Astronomy of the 20th Century* (Macmillan, 1962).

542 [*Advances in atomic research*]: Alex Keller, *The Infancy of Atomic Physics: Hercules in His Cradle* (Clarendon Press, 1983); *Physics Through the 1990's: Nuclear Physics* (National Academy Press, 1986).

[*"Invention factory"*]: Matthew Josephson, "Thomas Alva Edison," in John A. Garraty, ed., *Encyclopedia of American Biography* (Harper, 1974), pp. 321–23, Edison quoted at p. 322.

[*"Business" of invention*]: quoted in *ibid.*, p. 322.

542–3 [*Development, applications, and implications of semiconductors*]: Ernest Braun and Stuart Macdonald, *Revolution in Miniature*, 2nd ed. (Cambridge University Press, 1982), quoted at p. 6; T. R. Reid, *The Chip* (Simon and Schuster, 1984).

543 [*Integrated circuits in autos*]: Braun and Macdonald, p. 202.

The Dicing Game of Science

[*Salk and Sabin*]: John R. Paul, *A History of Poliomyelitis* (Yale University Press, 1971), chs. 39, 41, and p. 439 (Figs. 58–59); Richard B. Morris et al., eds., *Encyclopedia of American History*, 6th ed. (Harper, 1982), p. 814.

544 [*Discovery of DNA*]: James Watson, *The Double Helix: A Personal Account of the Discovery of the Structure of DNA* (Atheneum, 1968); Horace Freeland Judson, *The Eighth Day of Creation: Makers of the Revolution in Biology* (Simon and Schuster, 1979), esp. part 1.

["*New world*"]: quoted in Judson, p. 581.

[*Einstein*]: Ronald W. Clark, *Einstein* (World Publishing, 1971); Jamie Sayen, *Einstein in America: The Scientist's Conscience in the Age of Hitler and Hiroshima* (Crown, 1985); Abraham Pais, *"Subtle is the Lord . . .": The Science and the Life of Albert Einstein* (Clarendon Press, 1982); Otto Nathan and Heinz Norden, eds., *Einstein on Peace* (Schocken, 1968).

[*Einstein's pathbreaking papers*]: "On the Motion of Small Particles," reprinted in Einstein, *Investigations on the Theory of the Brownian Movement*, A. D. Cowper, trans. (London, 1926); "On a Heuristic Viewpoint," in *Annalen der Physik*, ser. 4, vol. 17, pp. 132–48; "On the Electrodynamics of Moving Bodies" (special theory), in H. A. Lorentz et al., *The Principle of Relativity*, W. Perrett and G. B. Jeffery, trans. (Dover, 1952), pp. 35–65; "The Foundation of the General Theory of Relativity," in *ibid.*, pp. 109–64; see also Clark, chs. 4–5, 8–10 *passim*; Pais, parts 3–4 *passim*; Max Born, *Einstein's Theory of Relativity*, Henry L. Brose, trans. (Methuen, 1924); Albert Einstein, *Relativity: The Special and the General Theory*, Robert B. Lawson, trans. (Crown, 1961); Gerald Tauber, ed., *Albert Einstein's Theory of General Relativity* (Crown, 1979), esp. part 2.

545 ["*Awoke to find himself famous*"]: Clark, p. 237; see also *ibid.*, pp. 227–33; Pais, pp. 303–12; Tauber, part 3.

["*Axiomatic basis*"]: "The Fabric of the Universe," London *Times*, November 7, 1919, p. 13.

["*Peace that does not conceal*"]: quoted in Clark, p. 219.

[*Einstein and League of Nations*]: Clark, ch. 13 *passim*; Nathan and Norden, ch. 3.

[*Einstein and Zionism, interwar*]: Clark, ch. 14 *passim*.

["*Guileless child*"]: quoted in Clark, p. 145.

[*Einstein and the Nazis*]: Clark, chs. 15–17 *passim*; Nathan and Norden, chs. 6–7.

[*Einstein's letter to FDR*]: Clark, pp. 550–58, quoted at p. 556.

["*I signed the letter*"]: quoted in *ibid.*, p. 554.

[*Einstein and the making of the atomic bomb*]: *ibid.*, ch. 20 *passim*; Sayen, pp. 117–23, 147–48, 171; Nathan and Norden, ch. 9; see also Richard Rhodes, *The Making of the Atomic Bomb* (Simon and Schuster, 1986).

["*Entire cities*"]: quoted in Clark, p. 582.

546 [*Szilard appointment*]: *ibid.*, pp. 581–83.

[*Einstein's refusal of Israeli presidency*]: Clark, pp. 617–19; Nathan and Norden, pp. 571–74.

[*Defense of Heidelberg professor*]: Clark, p. 597.

["*Revolutionary way of non-cooperation*"]: *New York Times*, June 12, 1953, pp. 1, 9, quoted at p. 9; see also Clark, pp. 597–99; Sayen, pp. 267–79; Nathan and Norden, ch. 16.

[*Times criticism of Einstein*]: *New York Times*, June 13, 1953, p. 14.

["*Intellectuals of this country*"]: *ibid.*, June 12, 1953, p. 9.

["*Manifesto to Europeans*"]: Clark, pp. 180–82; Nathan and Norden, pp. 3–8.

[*Einstein and world government movement*]: Clark, pp. 587–91; Nathan and Norden, esp. ch. 13.

[*Russell manifesto*]: Clark, pp. 624–27; Nathan and Norden, ch. 18.

546–7 [*Einstein's search for grand unified theory*]: Clark, pp. 405–9, 612–14; Pais, esp. ch. 17; see also Barry Parker, *Einstein's Dream: The Search for a Unified Theory of the Universe* (Plenum Press, 1986); Tauber, part 7.

547 [*Born on general relativity*]: quoted in Clark, p. 200.
[*"Further this simplification"*]: *ibid.*, p. 407.
[*"Old One" did not "throw dice"*]: *ibid.*, p. 340.
[*Snow on intellectual fragmentation*]: Snow, *The Two Cultures and the Scientific Revolution* (Cambridge University Press, 1959); Snow, *The Two Cultures and a Second Look* (Cambridge University Press, 1964), esp. pp. 53–100.

548 [*"Achievements and promises"*]: Morgenthau, *Science: Servant or Master?* (New American Library, 1972), p. 4; see also Farrington Daniels and Thomas M. Smith, eds., *The Challenge of Our Times: Contemporary Trends in Science and Human Affairs as Seen by Twenty Professors at the University of Wisconsin* (Burgess Publishing, 1953); George H. Daniels, *Science in American Society* (Knopf, 1971); Gerald James Holton, *The Advancement of Science, and Its Burdens: The Jefferson Lectures and Other Essays* (Cambridge University Press, 1986).
[*"When science fails"*]: Morgenthau, pp. 46–47.
[*Collisions between science and politics*]: Daniel S. Greenberg, *The Politics of Pure Science* (New American Library, 1967); Vannevar Bush, *Pieces of the Action* (Morrow, 1970); C. P. Snow, *Science and Government* (Harvard University Press, 1961); Jerome B. Wiesner, *Where Science and Politics Meet* (McGraw-Hill, 1965); Rae Goodell, *The Visible Scientists* (Little, Brown, 1977); Hilary Rose and Steven Rose, *Science and Society* (Penguin, 1969).
[*Army destruction of Japanese cyclotrons*]: Greenberg, p. 118.

549 [*"Dominated outside of atomic energy"*]: Kevles, *The Physicists: The History of a Scientific Community in Modern America* (Knopf, 1978), p. 365.
[*"Evangelical zeal"*]: Alice Kimball Smith, *A Peril and a Hope: The Scientists' Movement in America, 1945–47* (University of Chicago Press, 1965), p. 529.
[*"Seduction and rape"*]: Greenberg, p. 125.
[*Oppenheimer*]: Kevles, pp. 380–82, 391, Oppenheimer quoted at p. 391; U.S. Atomic Energy Commission, *In the Matter of J. Robert Oppenheimer* (U.S. Government Printing Office, 1954); Philip M. Stern and Harold P. Green, *The Oppenheimer Case: Security on Trial* (Harper, 1969).

550 [*Einstein as patent clerk*]: Clark, pp. 45–51, "eight hours of idleness" quoted at p. 51; Pais, pp. 46–47.
[*Maccoby on growth of technological systems*]: "Some Issues of Technology: A Symposium," *Daedalus*, vol. 109, no. 1 (Winter 1980), pp. 3–24, esp. p. 15.
[*Bell Laboratories*]: N. Bruce Hannay and Robert E. McGinn, "The Anatomy of Modern Technology," *ibid.*, p. 40; see also Braun and Macdonald, ch. 4 *passim;* Jeremy Bernstein, *Three Degrees Above Zero: Bell Labs in the Information Age* (Scribner, 1984).
[*Information revolution*]: see James R. Beniger, *The Control Revolution* (Harvard University Press, 1986).

551 [*"Seriously hampered"*]: James Fallows, "Terminal Paranoia" (review of Theodore Roszak, *The Cult of Information: The Folklore of Computers and the True Art of Thinking* [Pantheon, 1986]), *New Republic*, vol. 195, nos. 2–3 (July 14–21, 1986), pp. 30–32, Roszak quoted at p. 30.
[*"A general redefinition"*]: Bolter, *Turing's Man: Western Culture in the Computer Age* (University of North Carolina Press, 1984), p. 9.
[*"Internalize and even consciously adopt"*]: Noble, *Forces of Production: A Social History of Industrial Automation* (Knopf, 1984), p. 43; see also *ibid.*, *passim;* Larry Hirschhorn, *Beyond Mechanization: Work and Technology in a Postindustrial Age* (MIT Press, 1984), ch. 7 and *passim.*
[*Ignored history of women's technologies*]: Cowan, "From Virginia Dare to Virginia Slims: Women and Technology in American Life," *Technology and Culture* (University of Chicago Press), vol. 20, no. 1 (January 1979), quoted at p. 51.
[*Antitechnology attitudes among women in the 1970s*]: *ibid.*, pp. 61–63.

552 [*Moses's parkway bridges*]: Langdon Winner, "Do Artifacts have Politics?," *Daedalus,*

vol. 109, no. 1 (Winter 1980), pp. 121–36, esp. pp. 123–24; Robert A. Caro, *The Power Broker: Robert Moses and the Fall of New York* (Knopf, 1974), pp. 318–19, 546, 951–58.

552 [*"A weak value system"*]: Joseph Weizenbaum, quoted in "Some Issues of Technology," p. 3; see also *ibid.*, p. 14.

553 [*"No way to run a railroad"*]: Winner, p. 133.
[*Post-Sputnik rush*]: Philip W. Jackson, "The Reform of Science Education: A Cautionary Tale," *Daedalus*, vol. 112, no. 2 (Spring 1983), pp. 143–66, esp. pp. 147–48.
[*Graubard on science education*]: Graubard, "Nothing to Fear, Much to Do," *ibid.*, pp. 231–48, quoted at p. 233.
[*Commercial textbooks*]: Jackson, p. 150.
[*Graduate enrollment*]: Theodore P. Perros, "U.S. Heads Down the Road to Scientific Dotage," *New York Times*, December 8, 1986, p. A26.
[*"Content to be served"*]: Kenneth Prewitt, "Scientific Illiteracy and Democratic Theory," *Daedalus*, vol. 112, no. 2 (Spring 1983), pp. 49–64, Clifton R. Wharton quoted at p. 53; see also Manfred Stanley, *The Technological Conscience: Survival and Dignity in an Age of Expertise* (Free Press, 1978).

The Rich and the Poor

554 [*Camp David conference*]: Herbert Stein, *Presidential Economics: The Making of Economic Policy from Roosevelt to Reagan and Beyond* (Simon and Schuster, 1984), pp. 176–80; Leonard Silk, *Economics in the Real World* (Simon and Schuster, 1984), pp. 37–41; Richard Nixon, *Memoirs* (Grosset & Dunlap, 1978), pp. 518–20.
[*"Comprehensive new economic policy"*]: Address to the Nation Outlining a New Economic Policy: "The Challenge of Peace," August 15, 1971, in *Public Papers of the Presidents of the United States: Richard Nixon* (U.S. Government Printing Office, 1971–75), vol. 3, pp. 886–90, quoted at p. 890.
[*Stein on Camp David conference*]: Stein, pp. 176–77.
[*Johnson's economic policies*]: *ibid.*, ch. 4; Hobart Rowen, *The Free Enterprisers: Kennedy, Johnson, and the Business Establishment* (Putnam, 1964), chs. 3, 13; James L. Sundquist, *Politics and Policy: The Eisenhower, Kennedy, and Johnson Years* (Brookings Institution, 1968), chs. 2–4, 11 *passim*.

555 [*Stein on Nixon's ambivalence*]: see Stein, p. 135.
[*Nixon's economic policies*]: A. James Reichley, *Conservatives in an Age of Change: The Nixon and Ford Administrations* (Brookings Institution, 1981), chs. 3–5, 7–8, 10–11 *passim*; Leonard Silk, *Nixonomics: How the Dismal Science of Free Enterprise Became the Black Art of Controls* (Praeger, 1972); Stein, ch. 5; Rowland Evans, Jr., and Robert D. Novak, *Nixon in the White House* (Random House, 1971), ch. 7.
[*Penn Central collapse*]: Silk, *Economics*, p. 36; Robert Sobel, *The Fallen Colossus* (Weybright and Talley, 1977); Stephen Salsbury, *No Way to Run a Railroad* (McGraw-Hill, 1982).

555–6 [*Economic storms from abroad and Nixon's reaction*]: Silk, *Nixonomics*, chs. 9–12; Silk, *Economics*, ch. 4 *passim*; Stein, pp. 163–68.

556 [*"New Economic Policy" and reactions*]: Nixon *Public Papers*, vol. 3, pp. 886–90, quoted at p. 886; see also Silk, *Nixonomics*, chs. 6–7; Stein, pp. 179–87; *Time*, vol. 98, no. 9 (August 30, 1971), pp. 4–18; *New York Times*, August 16, 1971, pp. 1, 14–15; *ibid.*, August 17, 1971, p. 1.
[*"Total disaster"*]: Stein, p. 186.

557 [*Stein on Nixon's economic policies*]: *ibid.*, p. 207.
[*"That's devaluation?"*]: quoted in Silk, *Economics*, pp. 45–46.

557–8 [*Ford's economic policies*]: Reichley, chs. 14–15, 17–18 *passim*; Stein, pp. 209–16; Silk, *Economics*, ch. 6; John Osborne, *White House Watch: The Ford Years* (New Republic Books, 1977), pp. 67–76, 204–9, 229–35.

558 [*Carter on his "exact procedure"*]: quoted in Laurence E. Lynn, Jr., and David DeF. Whitman, *The President as Policymaker: Jimmy Carter and Welfare Reform* (Temple University Press, 1981), p. 262.

559 [*Carter's drift to the right in economic policies*]: Betty Glad, *Jimmy Carter: In Search of the Great White House* (Norton, 1980), pp. 426–27; Stein, pp. 216–33; Silk, *Economics*, chs.

10–11; William Greider, *Secrets of the Temple: How the Federal Reserve Runs the Country* (Simon and Schuster, 1988), part 1 *passim.*

559 [*Economy in December 1980*]: *Time*, vol. 117, no. 3 (January 19, 1981), pp. 62, 63.
[*Democratic congressional opposition to Carter*]: quoted in Glad, p. 427.
[*"Clings to what"*]: quoted in *Time*, vol. 98, no. 9 (August 30, 1971), p. 5.

560 [*Hayek*]: Friedrich August von Hayek, *Road to Serfdom* (University of Chicago Press, 1944); see also Silk, *Economics*, ch. 8.

561 [*New Deal Keynesian economics*]: Alvin Harvey Hansen, *Full Recovery or Stagnation?* (Norton, 1938); Stein, ch. 2.
[*Truman, Eisenhower, JFK, LBJ as Keynesians*]: see Stein, chs. 3, 4.
[*"Now I am a Keynesian"*]: quoted in *ibid.*, p. 135.
[*Hansen on Keynesianism*]: Hansen, pp. 327–28.
[*Lekachman on Keynesianism*]: Lekachman, "A Keynes for All Seasons," *New Republic*, vol. 188, no. 24 (June 20, 1983), pp. 21–25, quoted at p. 24.

561–2 [*Attacks on Keynesian assumptions*]: Stein, pp. 46–53; see also Henry Hazlitt, *The Critics of Keynesian Economics* (Van Nostrand, 1960).

562 [*Monetarism*]: Milton Friedman and Anna Schwartz, *A Monetary History of the United States, 1867–1960* (Princeton University Press, 1963); Milton Friedman, *The Optimum Quantity of Money and Other Essays* (Aldine, 1969); Lester C. Thurow, *Dangerous Currents: The State of Economics* (Random House, 1983), ch. 3 *passim;* William Breit and Roger L. Ransom, *The Academic Scribblers: American Economists in Collision* (Holt, Rinehart and Winston, 1971), chs. 13–14.
[*"Swept through the universities"*]: Alan S. Blinder, "Keynesians Regain Some Courage," *New York Times*, February 12, 1984, sect. 3, p. 3.
[*Volcker as Fed head*]: Greider, *passim;* Stein, pp. 229–32; John T. Woolley, *Monetary Politics: The Federal Reserve and the Politics of Monetary Policy* (Cambridge University Press, 1984), pp. 103–5; Donald F. Kettl, *Leadership at the Fed* (Yale University Press, 1986), pp. 175–78, 183–84, 191–92); Ralph C. Bryant, *Controlling Money: The Federal Reserve and Its Critics* (Brookings Institution, 1983).
[*Galbraith*]: John Kenneth Galbraith, *A Life in Our Times* (Houghton Mifflin, 1981); Charles H. Hession, *John Kenneth Galbraith & His Critics* (New American Library, 1972).

563 [*"Place myself at the mercy"*]: quoted in Hession, p. 25.
[*American Capitalism*]: Galbraith, *American Capitalism: The Concept of Countervailing Power* (Houghton Mifflin, 1952); see also Hession, chs. 2–3.
[*Affluent Society*]: Galbraith, *The Affluent Society* (Houghton Mifflin, 1958); see also Hession, chs. 4–5; David T. Bazelon, *The Paper Economy* (Vintage, 1965).
[*New Industrial State*]: Galbraith, *The New Industrial State* (Houghton Mifflin, 1967); Hession, ch. 6; Irving Kristol, "Professor Galbraith's 'New Industrial State,' " *Fortune*, vol. 76, no. 1 (July 1967), pp. 90–91, 194–95; Robert L. Heilbroner, "Capitalism Without Tears," *New York Review of Books*, vol. 8, no. 12 (June 29, 1967), pp. 16–19.
[*Two types of planning*]: Galbraith, *The New Industrial State*, 2nd ed. (Houghton Mifflin, 1971), p. xx.

564 [*American Marxism and the economic dilemma*]: Paul A. Baran and Paul M. Sweezy, *Monopoly Capital: An Essay on the American Economic and Social Order* (Monthly Review Press, 1966); Baran, *The Political Economy of Growth* (Monthly Review Press, 1957); Sweezy, *Post-Revolutionary Society* (Monthly Review Press, 1980); Benjamin Ward, *The Ideal Worlds of Economics* (Basic Books, 1979), book 2.

565 [*"Important immediate goal"*]: Ward, p. 305.

566 [*Kennedy on Social Security Act*]: quoted in James T. Patterson, *America's Struggle Against Poverty, 1900–1980* (Harvard University Press, 1981), p. 126.
[*"If a free society"*]: January 20, 1961, in *Public Papers of the Presidents of the United States: John F. Kennedy* (U.S. Government Printing Office, 1962–64), vol. 1, pp. 1–3, quoted at p. 1.
[*Kennedy's war on poverty*]: Patterson, ch. 8 *passim;* Sundquist, *Politics and Policy*, chs. 2–4, 11 *passim;* Daniel Knapp and Kenneth Polk, *Scouting the War on Poverty: Social Reform Politics in the Kennedy Administration* (Heath Lexington Books, 1971).
[*"It is not moral"*]: Joseph Mitchell, quoted in Patterson, pp. 107–8.
[*Johnson's war on poverty*]: Sar A. Levitan, *The Great Society's Poor Law: A New Approach to Poverty* (Johns Hopkins Press, 1969); Patterson, chs. 8–10 *passim;* Sundquist, *Politics*

and Policy, chs. 2–4, 11 *passim;* James L. Sundquist, ed., *On Fighting Poverty: Perspectives from Experience* (Basic Books, 1969); see also William J. Wilson, *The Truly Disadvantaged: The Inner City, the Underclass, and Public Policy* (University of Chicago Press, 1987).

567 [*Nixon's war on poverty*]: Vincent J. Burke and Vee Burke, *Nixon's Good Deed: Welfare Reform* (Columbia University Press, 1974); Patterson, chs. 11–12 *passim;* Reichley, ch. 7; Daniel Patrick Moynihan, *The Politics of Guaranteed Income: The Nixon Administration and the Family Assistance Plan* (Random House, 1973); Moynihan Papers, Nixon Administration Files, Subject File II, boxes 1, 6, 7, 10, Library of Congress.

[*"Most important piece"*]: August 28, 1970, in *Nixon Public Papers,* vol. 2, pp. 690–91, quoted at p. 690.

[*Moynihan*]: Douglas Schoen, *Pat: A Biography of Daniel Patrick Moynihan* (Harper, 1979); Daniel Patrick Moynihan, *Maximum Feasible Misunderstanding: Community Action in the War on Poverty* (Free Press, 1969).

[*"Maximum feasible participation"*]: quoted in Moynihan, *Misunderstanding,* p. xvi.

[*"Almost surely define"*]: text of Moynihan address in Moynihan Papers, n.d., quoted at p. 10.

[*Defining poverty*]: Chaim I. Waxman, *The Stigma of Poverty: A Critique of Poverty Theories and Policies,* 2nd ed. (Pergamon, 1983), esp. chs. 1–2; Patterson, chs. 6–7; Daniel Patrick Moynihan, ed., *On Understanding Poverty: Perspectives from the Social Sciences* (Basic Books, 1969); Charles A. Valentine, *Culture and Poverty: Critique and Counter-Proposals* (University of Chicago Press, 1968); Burton A. Weisbrod, ed., *The Economics of Poverty: An American Paradox* (Prentice-Hall, 1965); Moynihan, *Misunderstanding,* ch. 8 and *passim.*

[*"Social scum"*]: Karl Marx and Friedrich Engels, *Manifesto of the Communist Party,* Samuel Moore, trans. (International Publishers, 1948), p. 20.

568 [*Waxman on poverty*]: Waxman, p. 75.

[*"Work must be found"*]: annual message to the Congress, January 4, 1935, in *The Public Papers and Addresses of Franklin D. Roosevelt,* Samuel I. Rosenman, comp. (Random House, 1938–50), vol. 4, pp. 15–25, quoted at pp. 20, 19, respectively.

[*"The very rich"*]: Fitzgerald, "The Rich Boy," in Arthur Mizener, ed., *The Fitzgerald Reader* (Scribner, 1963), pp. 239–75, quoted at p. 239.

[*"Cultural and environmental obstacles"*]: quoted in Moynihan, *Misunderstanding,* p. 79.

569 [*Poverty in Mexico City*]: Oscar Lewis, *Children of Sanchez: Autobiography of a Mexican Family* (Random House, 1961).

[*"New opportunities for disadvantaged youth"*]: quoted in Moynihan, *Misunderstanding,* p. 71.

[*"Not social science competence"*]: ibid., pp. 169, 170.

570 [*Workers' Alliance*]: Frances Fox Piven and Richard A. Cloward, *Poor People's Movements: Why They Succeed, How They Fail* (Pantheon, 1977), pp. 72–76, 85–92.

[*NWRO*]: ibid., ch. 5.

[*Alinsky*]: Saul D. Alinsky, *Rules for Radicals: A Practical Primer for Realistic Radicals* (Random House, 1971); Robert Bailey, Jr., *Radicals in Urban Politics: The Alinsky Approach* (University of Chicago Press, 1974); Patrick Anderson, "Making Trouble Is Alinsky's Business," in Harold L. Sheppard, ed., *Poverty and Wealth in America* (Quadrangle, 1970), pp. 247–62.

[*Community action*]: Moynihan, *Misunderstanding, passim;* Sundquist, *Fighting Poverty,* chs. 4–5; Patterson, pp. 138–41, 145–52; Frances Fox Piven and Richard A. Cloward, *Regulating the Poor: The Functions of Public Welfare* (Pantheon, 1971), ch. 10; Gary Delgado, *Organizing the Movement: The Roots and Growth of ACORN* (Temple University Press, 1986).

571 [*"Somewhat naive and sentimental"*]: quoted in Waxman, p. 107.

[*Black progress and setbacks*]: Richard Bernstein, "King's Dream," *New York Times,* January 17, 1988, sect. 4, p. 1.

Crossways, Land and Sky

[*Sweden as "middle way"*]: Marquis Childs, *Sweden, The Middle Way,* rev. ed. (Yale University Press, 1947); Philip Arestis, "Post Keynesian Economic Policies: The Case of Sweden," *Journal of Economic Issues*, vol. 20, no. 3 (September 1986), pp. 709-23, esp. p. 719.

572 [*Drive-in church*]: "The Automobile Age," *Wilson Quarterly*, vol. 10, no. 5 (Winter 1986), pp. 64-79, esp. p. 77.
[*Auto industry in 1960s and early 1970s*]: Lawrence J. White, *The Automobile Industry since 1945* (Harvard University Press, 1971).
[*Annual new car sales*]: David L. Lewis, "The Industry," *Wilson Quarterly*, vol. 10, no. 5 (Winter 1986), pp. 47-63, esp. p. 60.
[*New car price as percentage of family income*]: ibid.
[*Formation and rise of General Motors*]: Ed Cray, *Chrome Colossus: General Motors and Its Times* (McGraw-Hill, 1980), chs. 1-10; Alfred P. Sloan, Jr., *Adventures of a White-Collar Man* (Doubleday, 1970); Bernard A. Weisberger, *The Dream Maker: William C. Durant, Founder of General Motors* (Little, Brown, 1979).
["*Pontiac for the poor*"]: quoted in Lewis, pp. 51-52.

572-3 [*Fall and rise of Ford*]: Allan Nevins and Frank Ernest Hill, *Ford: Decline and Rebirth, 1945-1963* (Scribner, 1963); David Halberstam, *The Reckoning* (Morrow, 1986), ch. 5, parts 4, 6 *passim*; Charles E. Sorenson and Samuel T. Williamson, *My Forty Years with Ford* (Norton, 1956), esp. ch. 20; Lee Iacocca and William Novak, *Iacocca* (Bantam, 1984), chs. 3-8; Robert Lacey, *Ford: The Men and the Machine* (Little, Brown, 1986), chs. 15-29 *passim*.

573 [*Auto labor*]: Victor G. Reuther, *The Brothers Reuther and the Story of the UAW* (Houghton Mifflin, 1976); William Serrin, *The Company and the Union* (Knopf, 1973), esp. ch. 4.
[*1970 strike*]: Serrin.
[*Assassination attempts on Reuthers*]: Reuther, pp. 276-91 *passim*.
[*Effects of the automobile on American life*]: James J. Flink, *The Car Culture* (MIT Press, 1975); Helen Leavitt, *Superhighway, Superhoax* (Ballantine, 1970); John C. Esposito, *Vanishing Air: The Ralph Nader Study Group Report on Pollution* (Grossman, 1970); Richard O. Davies, *The Age of Asphalt: The Automobile, the Freeway, and the Condition of Metropolitan America* (Lippincott, 1975); Warren J. Belasco, *Americans on the Road: From Autocamp to Motel, 1910-1945* (MIT Press, 1979); "Automobile Age."
[*Interstate Highway Act*]: Flink, pp. 190, 213-15; Leavitt, pp. 26-50.
["*Road Gang*"]: see Leavitt, pp. 111-55, esp. p. 152.

574 ["*Another inalienable American right*"]: Flink, p. 219.
["*White roads through black bedrooms*"]: quoted in "Automobile Age," p. 76.
[*The rise of OPEC and the oil crisis*]: Dankwart A. Rustow, *Oil and Turmoil: America Faces OPEC and the Middle East* (Norton, 1982), esp. chs. 3-5; Flink, pp. 226-31; Halberstam, ch. 27; Henry Kissinger, *Years of Upheaval* (Little, Brown, 1982), chs. 19-20; Raymond Vernon, ed., *The Oil Crisis* (Norton, 1976).

575 ["*Never explain, never complain*"]: quoted in Halberstam, p. 202.
["*A host of environmental problems*"]: quoted in Emma Rothschild, *Paradise Lost: The Decline of the Auto-Industrial Age* (Random House, 1973), p. 18.
[*Nader*]: Nader, *Unsafe at Any Speed: The Designed-in Dangers of the American Automobile* (Grossman, 1965); see also Halberstam, ch. 30.

575-6 [*GM's leadership failure in 1960s*]: Cray, esp. Introduction and pp. 430-31; J. Patrick Wright, *On a Clear Day You Can See General Motors: John Z. De Lorean's Look Inside the Automotive Giant* (Wright Enterprises, 1979).

576 [*GM executive's brown suit*]: Wright, p. 33.
[*Conflicts between engineering and accounting at Ford*]: Halberstam, chs. 11-13, 20-21 *passim*.
["*My grandfather made cars*"]: quoted in Halberstam, p. 479.

577 ["*No Jap engine*"]: ibid., p. 535.
[*Ford and Iacocca*]: ibid., pp. 470-80, chs. 32-33; Iacocca, chs. 9-12; Lacey, chs. 35-36 *passim*.
[*Chrysler crisis*]: Robert B. Reich and John D. Donahue, *New Deals: The Chrysler Revival and the American System* (Times Books, 1985); Iacocca, chs. 14-24.
[*Bachrach on Chrysler bailout*]: Reich and Donahue, p. 265.
["*Absolute nonsense*"]: ibid.

578 [*Swedish model for long-range development*]: Arestis.
[*Challenge to American auto from abroad*]: Halberstam, chs. 49-54 *passim*; Cray, ch. 19;

Reich and Donahue, chs. 6–7; Tetsuo Sakiya, *Honda Motor: The Men, the Management, the Machines* (Kodansha International, 1982), ch. 1; Douglas H. Ginsburg and William J. Abernathy, eds., *Government, Technology, and the Future of the Automobile* (McGraw-Hill, 1980), ch. 5; Iacocca, ch. 27.

578 [*At the Soviet embassy*]: Clayton R. Koppes, *JPL and the American Space Program: A History of the Jet Propulsion Laboratory* (Yale University Press, 1982), pp. 82–83, quoted at p. 83.

[*"Battle more important"*]: quoted in *ibid.*, p. 84.

579 [*"Do not have as much time"*]: *ibid.*

[*"Buck Rogers might prove"*]: Erlend A. Kennan and Edmund H. Harvey, Jr., *Mission to the Moon: A Critical Examination of NASA and the Space Program* (Morrow, 1969), p. 58.

[*Eisenhower's assurance*]: in *Public Papers of the Presidents of the United States: Dwight D. Eisenhower* (U.S. Government Printing Office, 1958–61), vol. 5, pp. 789–99.

[*Soviet signals*]: Kennan and Harvey, p. 62.

[*"No matter how humble"*]: quoted in Walter A. McDougall, . . . *The Heavens and the Earth: A Political History of the Space Age* (Basic Books, 1985), p. 119.

[*1955 U.S. satellite announcement*]: quoted in Loyd S. Swenson, Jr., James M. Grimwood, and Charles C. Alexander, *This New Ocean: A History of Project Mercury* (NASA, 1966), p. 28.

[*Satellite decision*]: McDougall, pp. 112–24; Constance McLaughlin Green and Milton Lomask, *Vanguard* (NASA, 1970), ch. 3; Hugo Young, Bryan Silcock, and Peter Dunn, *Journey to Tranquility* (Doubleday, 1970), pp. 41–45; Koppes, pp. 79–80.

[*Origins of NASA*]: McDougall, ch. 7; Swenson et al., ch. 4; Koppes, pp. 94–102; Young et al., pp. 62–66.

[*Project Mercury*]: Swenson et al., *passim*; Young et al., pp. 158–60.

[*"Shoot a man"*]: McDougall, p. 243.

[*Mercury astronauts*]: Swenson et al., pp. 159–65, chs. 7–8; Young et al., ch. 8; Tom Wolfe, *The Right Stuff* (Farrar, Straus & Giroux, 1979); M. Scott Carpenter et al., *We Seven* (Simon and Schuster, 1962).

[*"Lovable freckled heroes"*]: Young et al., p. 140.

580 [Vostok 1]: *ibid.*, pp. 83–85; Swenson et al., pp. 332–35.

[Freedom 7]: Swenson et al., pp. 341–65, quoted at p. 342; *Time*, vol. 77, no. 20 (May 12, 1961), pp. 52–58.

[Liberty Bell 7]: Swenson et al., pp. 365–77; Wolfe, pp. 277–96.

[*Titov's flight*]: Swenson et al., pp. 377–79.

580–1 [*Glenn's flight and return*]: *ibid.*, ch. 8; Wolfe, ch. 12; *Time*, vol. 79, no. 9 (March 2, 1962), pp. 11–18; *ibid.*, vol. 79, no. 10 (March 9, 1962), pp. 22–23.

581 [*"All spacecraft systems go!"*]: quoted in Swenson et al., p. 426.

[*"Real hard-to-define feeling"*]: quoted in *Time*, vol. 79, no. 10 (March 9, 1962), p. 22.

[*"Now it is the time"*]: Special Message to the Congress on Urgent National Needs, May 25, 1961, in *Kennedy Public Papers*, vol. 1, pp. 396–406, quoted at pp. 403, 404, 403, respectively.

[*Congressional reaction to Kennedy challenge*]: Young et al., p. 92; McDougall, pp. 361–62, 373–76, 392–97; *New York Times*, May 26, 1961, pp. 1, 13.

[*July 20, 1969*]: Young et al., ch. 13; *Time*, vol. 94, no. 4 (July 25, 1969), pp. 10–19; Charles R. Pellegrino and Joshua Stoff, *Chariots for Apollo: The Making of the Lunar Module* (Atheneum, 1985), chs. 43–52.

[*"You are go"*]: quoted in Young et al., p. 269.

582 [*"The Eagle has landed"*]: *ibid.*, p. 272.

[*Objects in space*]: J. E. S. Fawcett, *Outer Space: New Challenges to Law and Policy* (Clarendon Press, 1984), p. 116.

[*Space shuttle* Columbia's *launch*]: Joseph J. Trento, *Prescription for Disaster* (Crown, 1987), pp. 187–93; *Time*, vol. 117, no. 17 (April 27, 1981), pp. 16–23.

583 [*Early hints of O-ring problems*]: Trento, pp. 205, 259–61, 276, 281.

[Challenger mission 51-L]: *ibid.*, pp. 249–50, 280–92; *Newsweek*, vol. 107, no. 6 (February 10, 1986), pp. 26–42.

[*"Feel that mother go"*]: quoted in Trento, p. 290.

[*"Uh, Oh!"*]: *ibid.*

584 [*"More than the Challenger exploded"*]: Wilford, "After the Challenger: America's Future

in Space," *New York Times Magazine*, March 16, 1986, pp. 38–39, 93, 102–6, quoted at p. 38.

584 [*"Story of political failure"*]: Trento, Acknowledgments; see also U.S. Presidential Commission on the Space Shuttle Challenger Accident, *Report to the President*, 5 vols. (1986).

[*"Hock his jewels"*]: quoted in Young et al., p. 72.

[*Reasons for Kennedy's moon decision*]: McDougall, ch. 15; Young et al., ch. 5; Kennan and Harvey, pp. 74–83; John M. Logsdon, *The Decision to Go to the Moon: Project Apollo and the National Interest* (MIT Press, 1970).

[*"Second in everything"*]: quoted in McDougall, p. 320.

[*"Do the big things together"*]: *ibid.*, pp. 394–95, quoted at p. 395.

[*"Vehicle rather than a mission"*]: Trento, p. 105.

584–5 [*Post-Apollo planning and shuttle decision*]: McDougall, pp. 420–23; Trento, pp. 88–94, ch. 5; John M. Logsdon, "The Shuttle Program: A Policy Failure?," *Science*, vol. 232 (May 30, 1986), pp. 1099–1105; Gregg Easterbrook, "Big Dumb Rockets," *Newsweek*, vol. 110, no. 7 (August 17, 1987), pp. 50–54; see also Logsdon, *Decision*, ch. 6.

585 [*"Make access to orbit routine"*]: John M. Logsdon, "After Challenger Does the U.S. Have a Future in Space?," *American Politics*, vol. 1, no. 7 (August 1986), pp. 6–9, quoted at p. 7.

[*"Highest possible level"*]: quoted in Easterbrook, p. 52.

[*"Mortgaged nearly everything"*]: John Noble Wilford, "At NASA, All That's Up Is the Shuttle Columbia," *New York Times*, November 1, 1981, sect. 4, p. 9.

[*Space commercialization*]: Pamela E. Mack, "Government and Enterprise: Commercialization and Privatization in the U.S. Space Program," paper prepared for delivery at the annual meeting of the American Historical Association, Washington, D.C., December 1987; Nathan C. Goldman, *Space Commerce: Free Enterprise on the High Frontier* (Ballinger, 1985); David Osborne, "Business in Space," *Atlantic*, vol. 255, no. 5 (May 1985), pp. 45–58.

[*Projected and actual costs of payload per pound*]: Easterbrook, pp. 54–55.

[*Space militarization*]: Paul B. Stares, *The Militarization of Space: U.S. Policy, 1945–1984* (Cornell University Press, 1985), pp. 178–79, 225–35, and *passim;* Stares, *Space and National Security* (Brookings Institution, 1987); Zbigniew Brzezinski et al., eds., *Promise or Peril: The Strategic Defense Initiative* (Ethics and Public Policy Center, 1986); *Daedalus*, vol. 114, nos. 2–3 (Spring–Summer 1985); Jonathan B. Stein, *From H-Bomb to Star Wars: The Politics of Strategic Decision Making* (Lexington Books, 1984), chs. 8–9.

586 [*"Awesome Soviet missile threat"*]: Address to the Nation on Defense and National Security, March 23, 1983, in *Public Papers of the Presidents of the United States: Ronald Reagan* (U.S. Government Printing Office, 1982–   ), vol. 3, part 1, pp. 437–43, quoted at p. 442.

[*Logsdon on ends and means*]: Logsdon, "Space Shuttle Program," p. 1105.

[*Soviet space progress*]: Larry Martz, "America Grounded," *Newsweek*, vol. 110, no. 7 (August 17, 1987), pp. 37, 40–41; Nicholas Johnson quoted on "evolution of man into space" at p. 37, Glenn quoted at p. 37; Easterbrook, pp. 46, 60; see also William H. Schauer, *The Politics of Space: A Comparison of the Soviet and American Space Programs* (Holmes & Meier, 1976); Roald Sagdeev, "Soviet Space Science," *Physics Today*, vol. 41, no. 5 (May 1988), pp. 30–38; Louis J. Lanzerotti and Jeffrey D. Rosendhal, "Policy Challenges Facing the US Space Research Program," *ibid.*, pp. 78–83.

[*"Advance the technology"*]: quoted in Easterbrook, p. 52.

586–7 [*Hubble telescope*]: *Newsweek*, vol. 110, no. 7 (August 17, 1987), pp. 52–53.

587 [*"Out of the blue"*]: Young, "Hey Hey, My My," quoted in McDougall, p. 450. Copyright 1979, Silver Fiddle Music.

14. The Kaleidoscope of Thought

591 [*Carter's retreat*]: *Newsweek*, vol. 94, no. 3 (July 16, 1979), pp. 19–21; *ibid.*, vol. 24, no. 4 (July 23, 1979), pp. 21–26; Jimmy Carter, *Keeping Faith* (Bantam, 1982), pp. 114–20; Godfrey Hodgson, *All Things to All Men: The False Promise of the Modern American Presidency* (Simon and Schuster, 1980), pp. 162–63 and *passim;* Betty Glad, *Jimmy Carter: In Search of the Great White House* (Norton, 1980), pp. 444–46.

591 [*Advice to Carter*]: Energy and National Goals, July 15, 1979, in *Public Papers of the Presidents of the United States: Jimmy Carter* (U.S. Government Printing Office, 1977–82), vol. 3, part 2, pp. 1235–41, quoted at p. 1236.
[*Carter's address*]: *ibid.;* see also Jeffrey K. Tulis, *The Rhetorical Presidency* (Princeton University Press, 1987), pp. 3, 136, 141.

592 [*Carter's firings and public response*]: *Newsweek*, vol. 94, no. 5 (July 30, 1979), pp. 22–28, anecdote of the king told at p. 27.

Habits of Individualism

594 [*Census family statistics*]: U.S. Bureau of the Census, *Statistical Abstract of the United States: 1987* (U.S. Government Printing Office, 1986), p. 45 (Table 61).
[*Numbers of religious bodies and membership*]: *ibid.*, pp. 51–52 (Table 74); Leo Rosten, ed., *Religions in America* (Simon and Schuster, 1963), esp. pp. 220–48, 318–24.

595 [*Church attendance, 1940s–1970s*]: Hadley Cantril, ed., *Public Opinion 1935–1946* (Princeton University Press, 1951), pp. 699–701 (early polling data may be only approximations); Theodore Caplow et al., *All Faithful People: Change and Continuity in Middletown's Religion* (University of Minnesota Press, 1983), p. 27.
[*Polls on religious influence*]: Gallup Opinion Index Question quoted in Caplow et al., p. 28.
[*Ratio of church membership to population*]: *ibid.*, pp. 28–29.
[*Declining membership of "mainline" Protestant churches*]: *Newsweek*, vol. 108, no. 25 (December 22, 1986), pp. 54–56.
["*Language genuinely able*"]: Robert N. Bellah et al., *Habits of the Heart: Individualism and Commitment in American Life* (University of California Press, 1985), p. 237; see also Bellah, *The Broken Covenant: American Civil Religion in Time of Trial* (Seabury Press, 1975).

595–6 [*Thoreau on telegraph between Maine and Texas*]: Thoreau, *A Week on the Concord and Merrimack Rivers; Walden; The Maine Woods; Cape Cod*, Robert F. Sayre, ed. (Library of America, 1985), p. 364.

596 [*Projected enrollments early 1990s*]: *Statistical Abstract*, p. 117 (Table 189).
[*Enrollment in private secondary schools after* Brown]: Jeffrey A. Raffel, *The Politics of School Desegregation: The Metropolitan Remedy in Delaware* (Temple University Press, 1980), pp. 175–88, esp. pp. 178–80.
[*Public education in modern America*]: Robert B. Everhart, ed., *The Public School Monopoly: A Critical Analysis of Education and the State in American Society* (Ballinger Publishing, 1982), part 3; Benjamin D. Stickney and Laurence R. Marcus, *The Great Education Debate: Washington and the Schools* (Charles C Thomas, 1984), chs. 1, 5, and *passim*.

596–7 [*Typical public school classroom*]: Kenneth A. Sirotnik, "What You See Is What You Get—Consistency, Persistency, and Mediocrity in Classrooms," *Harvard Educational Review*, vol. 53, no. 1 (February 1983), pp. 16–31.

597 [*Toffler on learning*]: quoted in *ibid.*, p. 29.
[*Merelman on education*]: Merelman, *Making Something of Ourselves* (University of California Press, 1984), pp. 195–99.
[*Schools as supermarkets*]: Arthur G. Powell, Eleanor Farrar, and David K. Cohen, *The Shopping Mall High School: Winners and Losers in the Educational Marketplace* (Houghton Mifflin, 1985), esp. ch. 1.
[*Higher education in modern America*]: Ernest L. Boyer and Fred M. Hechinger, *Higher Learning in the Nation's Service* (Carnegie Foundation for the Advancement of Teaching, 1981); Barry M. Richman and Richard N. Farmer, *Leadership, Goals, and Power in Higher Education* (Jossey-Bass, 1974); Derek Bok, *Beyond the Ivory Tower: Social Responsibilities of the Modern University* (Harvard University Press, 1982).
[*Institutions, teachers, students in higher education*]: *Statistical Abstract*, p. 138 (Table 233).
[*Bowen on missing ingredient*]: Bowen, *The State of the Nation and the Agenda for Higher Education* (Jossey-Bass, 1982), pp. 76–78; see also Philip E. Jacob, *Changing Values in College: An Exploratory Study of the Impact of College Teaching* (Harper, 1957); Richard L. Morrill, *Teaching Values in College: Facilitating Development of Ethical, Moral, and Value Awareness in Students* (Jossey-Bass, 1980).
[*Boyer and Hechinger on higher education*]: Boyer and Hechinger, esp. p. 3.

598 [*"American liberal approach"*]: Walzer, "Teaching Morality," *New Republic*, vol. 178, no. 23 (June 10, 1978), pp. 12–14, quoted at p. 13; see also Roger L. Shinn, "Education in Values: Acculturation and Exploration," in Douglas Sloan, ed., *Education and Values* (Teachers College Press, 1980), pp. 111–22.

[*Debates over values*]: James MacGregor Burns, *Leadership* (Harper, 1978), pp. 74–75; see also Milton Rokeach, *Beliefs, Attitudes, and Values: A Theory of Organization and Change* (Jossey-Bass, 1969); Burns, *Uncommon Sense* (Harper, 1972), ch. 6.

[*"The most resonant"*]: Bellah et al., *Habits*, p. 23.

598–9 [*"Decline of church"*]: Merelman, pp. 1–2.

599 [*"May have grown cancerous"*]: Bellah et al., *Habits*, p. viii.

[*Yuppies*]: "The Year of the Yuppie," *Newsweek*, vol. 104, no. 28 (December 31, 1984), pp. 14–20; "Life of a Yuppie Takes a Psychic Toll," *U.S. News & World Report*, vol. 98, no. 16 (April 29, 1985), pp. 73–74; "That Word," *New Yorker*, vol. 61, no. 10 (April 29, 1985), pp. 30–31.

[*Sheila*]: Bellah et al., *Habits*, pp. 220–21, quoted at p. 221.

[*"Management of personal impressions"*]: Christopher Lasch, *The Culture of Narcissism: American Life in an Age of Diminishing Expectations* (Norton, 1978), p. 44; see also Lasch, *The Minimal Self: Psychic Survival in Troubled Times* (Norton, 1984).

600 [*Individualism*]: Crawford B. Macpherson, *The Political Theory of Possessive Individualism: Hobbes to Locke* (Oxford University Press, 1962); A. D. Lindsay, "Individualism," in Edwin R. A. Seligman, ed., *Encyclopedia of the Social Sciences* (Macmillan, 1930–34), vol. 7, pp. 674–80; Steven Lukes, *Individualism* (Basil Blackwell, 1973); Isaiah Berlin, "Two Concepts of Liberty," in Berlin, *Four Essays on Liberty* (Oxford University Press, 1969), pp. 118–72; Karl R. Popper, *The Open Society and Its Enemies* (Princeton University Press, 1950); Bellah et al., *Habits*, esp. chs. 2, 6.

601 [*"Nation that was proud"*]: *Carter Public Papers*, vol. 3, part 2, p. 1237.

Kinesis: The Southern Californians

[*Hollywood's beginnings*]: Carey McWilliams, *Southern California: An Island on the Land* (Peregrine Smith, 1979), ch. 16; Lary Linden May, "Reforming Leisure: The Birth of Mass Culture and the Motion Picture Industry, 1896–1920" (doctoral dissertation; University of California, Los Angeles, 1977); Robert Sklar, *Movie-Made America: A Social History of the American Movies* (Random House, 1975), chs. 2–3; W. H. Hutchinson, *California: The Golden Shore by the Sundown Sea* (Star Publishing, 1980), pp. 247–54; see also Hortense Powdermaker, *Hollywood, the Dream Factory* (Little, Brown, 1950), chs. 1, 15.

[*Selznick's wire to the Czar*]: Walton Bean, *California: An Interpretive History*, 2nd ed. (McGraw-Hill, 1973), p. 384.

602 [*"Monopolistic non-seasonal industry"*]: McWilliams, *Southern California*, pp. 339–40, quoted at p. 340.

[*Southern California's migrants*]: McWilliams, *Southern California*, chs. 3, 5, 7–9, 15 *passim;* see also Robert F. Heizer and Alan F. Almquist, *The Other Californians* (University of California Press, 1971).

[*Birth of a Nation*]: McWilliams, *Southern California*, pp. 332–33; Michael Paul Rogin, *Ronald Reagan, the Movie, and Other Episodes in Political Demonology* (University of California Press, 1987), pp. 190–235; Sklar, ch. 4; Charles Higham, *The Art of the American Film, 1900–1971* (Doubleday, 1973), pp. 10–12.

[*Labor strife in Los Angeles*]: Andrew F. Rolle, *California* (Crowell, 1964), ch. 31.

602–3 [*"Kiss-kiss" and "bang-bang"*]: Powdermaker, p. 14.

603 [*Priestley on Los Angeles*]: quoted in McWilliams, *Southern California*, p. 328; see also Robert Kirsch, "The Cultural Scene," in Carey McWilliams, ed., *The California Revolution* (Grossman, 1968), p. 205.

[*Esoteric religions in southern California*]: Carey McWilliams, "California: Mecca of the Miraculous," in Dennis Hale and Jonathan Eisen, eds., *The California Dream* (Collier Books, 1968), pp. 279–92; Michael Davie, *California: The Vanishing Dream* (Dodd, Mead, 1972), ch. 8; McWilliams, *Southern California*, ch. 13; Lately Thomas, *Storming Heaven* (Morrow, 1970).

603–4 [*Left-wing California politics*]: Dorothy Healey, "Tradition's Chains Have Bound Us" (1982), Oral History, Research Library, University of California at Los Angeles; Carey McWilliams, "The Economics of Extremism," in Hale and Eisen, pp. 83–95.

604 [*Olson*]: Robert E. Burke, *Olson's New Deal for California* (University of California Press, 1953), esp. chs. 3, 15.
[*California political culture*]: Luther Whiteman and Samuel L. Lewis, "EPIC, or Politics for Use," in Hale and Eisen, pp. 63–71; McWilliams, *Southern California*, ch. 14; Gladwin Hill, "California Politics," in McWilliams, *California Revolution*, pp. 172–84; Davie, chs. 6–7; James Q. Wilson, "The Political Culture of Southern California," in Hale and Eisen, pp. 215–33.
[*Young Nixon*]: Fawn M. Brodie, *Richard Nixon: The Shaping of His Character* (Norton, 1981), chs. 2–8; Garry Wills, *Nixon Agonistes: The Crisis of the Self-Made Man* (Houghton Mifflin, 1970), pp. 150–86; Davie, pp. 88–90.
[*Wills on Nixon*]: Wills, *Nixon Agonistes*, p. 184.
["*Old-fashioned kind of lawyer*"]: quoted in Bruce Mazlish, *In Search of Nixon* (Basic Books, 1972), p. 28.
[*Hollywood in 1930s and 1940s*]: Otto Friedrich, *City of Nets: A Portrait of Hollywood in the 1940's* (Harper, 1986); Higham, parts 2–3 *passim;* Tino Balio, ed., *The American Film Industry*, rev. ed. (University of Wisconsin Press, 1985), part 3; Charles Higham and Joel Greenberg, *Hollywood in the Forties* (Tantivy Press, 1968); Larry Ceplair and Steven Englund, *The Inquisition in Hollywood: Politics in the Film Community, 1930–1960* (University of California Press, 1983).

605 [*Writers in Hollywood*]: Walter Goodman, "Why Some Novelists Cast Hollywood as the Heavy," *New York Times*, August 17, 1986, sect. 2, pp. 19–20; Friedrich, pp. 228–46, esp. pp. 237–40; Harry M. Geduld, ed., *Authors on Film* (Indiana University Press, 1972), esp. parts 3–4; Morris Beja, *Film and Literature* (Longman, 1979), part 1.
["*Puke-green phantasmagoria*"]: quoted in Goodman, "Why Some Novelists," p. 20.
[*Gable-Faulkner exchange*]: quoted in Friedrich, p. 240.
[*Hollywood and television*]: Tino Balio, "Retrenchment, Reappraisal, and Reorganization, 1948–," in Balio, pp. 422–38; David J. Londoner, "The Changing Economics of Entertainment," in *ibid.,* pp. 603–30; Andrew Dowdy, *The Films of the Fifties: The American State of Mind* (Morrow, 1973), ch. 1 *passim;* Douglas Gomery, "Brian's Song: Television, Hollywood, and the Evolution of the Movie Made for Television," in John E. O'Connor, ed., *American History/American Television* (Frederick Ungar, 1983), ch. 9.
[*Movie admissions*]: Douglas Gomery, "Hollywood's Business," *Wilson Quarterly*, vol. 10, no. 3 (Summer 1986), p. 53.

606 [*Reagan's youth*]: Ronald Reagan and Richard G. Hubler, *Where's the Rest of Me? The Autobiography of Ronald Reagan* (Karz Publishers, 1981), chs. 1–4; Anne Edwards, *Early Reagan: The Rise to Power* (Morrow, 1987), chs. 2–7; Garry Wills, *Reagan's America: Innocents at Home* (Doubleday, 1987), parts 1–3.
[*Reagan in Hollywood*]: Reagan and Hubler, pp. 71–243; Edwards, chs. 8–21; Wills, *Reagan's America*, part 4; Rogin, ch. 1.
[*Powdermaker on Hollywood escapism*]: Powdermaker, pp. 12–14, quoted at pp. 12–13.
[*Production Code Administration and censorship*]: Powdermaker, ch. 3 *passim;* see also Richard S. Randall, *Censorship of the Movies: The Social and Political Control of a Mass Medium* (University of Wisconsin Press, 1968).

607 ["*A scoop for you!*"]: quoted in Wills, *Reagan's America*, p. 159.
["*So much that is right*"]: *ibid.,* p. 161.
[*Reagan, SAG, and MCA*]: *ibid.,* chs. 23–29, esp. pp. 249–50, 272–74; Edwards, chs. 14–17, 21 *passim;* Reagan and Hubler, pp. 222–30, 275–88.
[*Reagan's movement across political spectrum*]: Wills, *Reagan's America*, esp. pp. 257–58, 283–84; Robert Dallek, *Ronald Reagan: The Politics of Symbolism* (Harvard University Press, 1984), pp. 23–28; Lou Cannon, *Reagan* (Putnam, 1982), chs. 7–8 *passim.*
[*Cannon on income tax and Reagan's new conservatism*]: Cannon, p. 91.

607–8 [*Hollywood in the 1960s–1980s*]: Gomery, pp. 56–57; Robin Wood, *Hollywood from Vietnam to Reagan* (Columbia University Press, 1986); Balio, "Retrenchment."

608 [*Development of southern California*]: Charles Lockwood and Christopher B. Leinberger,

"Los Angeles Comes of Age," *Atlantic*, vol. 261, no. 1 (January 1988), pp. 31–56; B. Marchand, *The Emergence of Los Angeles: Population and Housing in the City of Dreams, 1940–1970* (Pion Limited, 1986); McWilliams, *California Revolution;* Davie, chs. 3–4.

608 [*The auto in southern California*]: Los Angeles *Times*, April 19, 1987, part 1, pp. 1, 20–22, and part 6, pp. 1, 6; Richard G. Lillard, "Revolution by Internal Combustion," in McWilliams, *California Revolution*, pp. 84–99; Samuel E. Wood, "The Freeway Revolt and What It Means," in *ibid.*, pp. 100–9; *New York Times*, August 21, 1987, p. A8; Davie, pp. 53–62.

609 [*"A movable home"*]: quoted in Los Angeles *Times*, April 19, 1987, part 6, p. 6.

Superspectatorship

[*Hagler-Leonard*]: *Sports Illustrated*, vol. 66, no. 13 (March 30, 1987), pp. 58–78; *ibid.*, vol. 66, no. 16 (April 13, 1987), pp. 18–25; *New York Times*, April 6, 1987, pp. C1, C6.

610 [*Sportswatching*]: *Statistical Abstract*, p. 216 (Table 375); see also Allen Guttmann, *Sports Spectators* (Columbia University Press, 1986), *passim;* Dick Schaap, "Sports and Television: The Perfect Marriage," in Marvin Barrett, ed., *The Politics of Broadcasting* (Crowell, 1973), pp. 197–202.

[*Podell on sportswatching*]: Podell, "Preface," in Podell, ed., *Sports in America* (H. W. Wilson Co., 1986), pp. 5–6, quoted at p. 5.

[*"Wholly intelligible"*]: Larry Gerlach, "Telecommunications and Sports," in Podell, pp. 66–74, quoted at p. 73.

[*Lipsky on sports*]: Lipsky, *How We Play the Game: Why Sports Dominate American Life* (Beacon Press, 1981), p. 63.

611 [*"Agitate a bag of wind"*]: quoted in Gerlach, p. 72.

[*Advertising rate for 1988 football championship*]: *New York Times*, January 25, 1988, p. C7.

[*Football and baseball TV contracts*]: Robert Kilborn, Jr., "Trying to Limit Out-of-the-Ballpark Salaries in Professional Sports," in Podell, pp. 74–77, esp. p. 75.

[*1984 Olympics' economic impact*]: Roger Rosenblatt, "Why We Play These Games," in *ibid.*, pp. 135–43, esp. p. 135.

[*Bird's worth*]: Kilborn, p. 76.

[*TV advertising*]: W. Russell Neuman, *The Paradox of Mass Politics* (Harvard University Press, 1986), p. 145; see Todd Gitlin, "Car Commercials and *Miami Vice*: 'We Build Excitement,' " in Gitlin, ed., *Watching Television* (Pantheon, 1986), pp. 136–61; *Statistical Abstract*, pp. 538 (Table 926), 539 (Tables 928–30).

[*"Economics of television"*]: Neuman, p. 135.

612 [Wall Street Journal *circulation*]: James MacGregor Burns, J. W. Peltason, and Thomas E. Cronin, *Government By the People*, 13th ed. (Prentice-Hall, 1987), p. 244 (table).

[*USA Today*]: Peter Prichard, *The Making of McPaper: The Inside Story of USA Today* (Andrews, McMeel & Parker, 1987).

[*Media concentration*]: Michael Parenti, *Inventing Reality: The Politics of the Mass Media* (St. Martin's Press, 1986), pp. 27–32, esp. p. 27; see also Ben H. Bagdikian, *The Media Monopoly* (Beacon Press, 1983).

[*Broder on the press*]: Broder, *Behind the Front Page: A Candid Look at How the News Is Made* (Simon and Schuster, 1987), p. 12.

[*Television watching*]: Morris Janowitz, *The Last Half-Century: Societal Change and Politics in America* (University of Chicago Press, 1978), pp. 337–38, quoted at p. 337; *Statistical Abstract*, p. 531 (Table 907); see also Benjamin Stein, "This Is Not Your Life: Television as the Third Parent," *Public Opinion*, vol. 9, no. 4 (November–December 1986), pp. 41–42; Joshua Meyrowitz, "The 19-Inch Neighborhood," *Newsweek*, vol. 106, no. 4 (July 22, 1985), p. 8.

[*TV in the workplace*]: *Newsweek*, vol. 111, no. 1 (January 4, 1988), pp. 34–35.

613 [*Politicians and the electronic media*]: Edwin Diamond and Stephen Bates, *The Spot: The Rise of Political Advertising on Television* (MIT Press, 1984); Kathleen Hall Jamieson, *Packaging the Presidency* (Oxford University Press, 1984); Austin Ranney, *Channels of Power: The Impact of Television on American Politics* (Basic Books, 1983); Ronald Berkman

and Laura W. Kitch, *Politics in the Media Age* (McGraw-Hill, 1986); Timothy E. Cook, "Marketing the Members: Evolving Media Strategies in the House of Representatives," unpublished typescript, presented at the Midwest Political Science Association, Chicago, April 18–20, 1985; Neil Postman, *Amusing Ourselves to Death: Public Discourse in the Age of Show Business* (Viking, 1985), ch. 9; Broder, *passim;* Keith Blume, *The Presidential Election Show* (Bergin & Garvey, 1985); Anne Haskell, "Congress Exploits the New Media," *Proceedings* (Institute of Politics, John F. Kennedy School of Government, 1981–82), pp. 56–59.

613   [*"It is irresponsible"*]: quoted in Haskell, p. 58.

[*"I saw President Ford bump his head"*]: quoted in Parenti, p. 15.

[*TV and opinion formation*]: Janowitz, ch. 9 *passim;* Ronald E. Frank and Marshall G. Greenbury, *The Public's Use of Television* (Sage Publications, 1980); Joshua Meyrowitz, *No Sense of Place: The Impact of Electronic Media on Social Behavior* (Oxford University Press, 1985); Paul F. Lazarsfeld, Bernard Berelson, and Hazel Gaudet, *The People's Choice*, 2nd ed. (Columbia University Press, 1948), ch. 16 and *passim;* Elihu Katz and Paul F. Lazarsfeld, *Personal Influence: The Part Played by People in the Flow of Mass Communications* (Free Press, 1955).

[*TV and political cynicism*]: Michael J. Robinson, "Public Affairs Television and the Growth of Political Malaise: The Case of 'The Selling of the Pentagon,' " *American Political Science Review*, vol. 70, no. 2 (June 1976), pp. 409–32; Burns, Peltason, and Cronin, p. 247 (table).

614   [*Political bias in the media*]: Burns, Peltason, and Cronin, pp. 253–55 and sources cited therein; Michael J. Robinson, "Just How Liberal Is the News? 1980 Revisited," *Public Opinion*, vol. 6, no. 1 (February–March 1983), pp. 55–60; Nick Thimmesch, ed., *A Liberal Media Elite?* (American Enterprise Institute for Public Policy Research, 1985); Sally Bedell Smith, "Conservatism Finds Its TV Voice," *New York Times*, May 19, 1985, sect. 2, p. 32; Parenti, ch. 6 and *passim;* Broder, ch. 9; Ranney, ch. 2; Peter Stoler, *The War Against the Press: Politics, Pressure and Intimidation in the 80s* (Dodd, Mead, 1986), chs. 8, 12 and *passim.*

[*Decline of mass-circulation magazines*]: Loudon Wainwright, *The Great American Magazine: An Inside History of* Life (Knopf, 1986), esp. chs. 15, 20; James K. Glassman, "One Life to Live" (review of Wainwright), *New Republic*, vol. 196, no. 6 (February 9, 1987), pp. 36–40; Otto Friedrich, *Decline and Fall* (Harper, 1970), ch. 23.

[*Specialized and alternative periodicals*]: Abe Peck, *Uncovering the Sixties: The Life and Times of the Underground Press* (Pantheon, 1985); Robert K. Glessing, *The Underground Press in America* (Indiana University Press, 1970); David Owen, "The Fifth Estate," *Atlantic*, vol. 256, no. 1 (July 1985), pp. 80–85; see also Theodore Peterson, *Magazines in the Twentieth Century* (University of Illinois Press, 1964), ch. 13.

[*Decline of independent local newspapers*]: see Philip Weiss, "Invasion of the Gannettoids," *New Republic*, vol. 196, no. 5 (February 2, 1987), pp. 18–22.

The New Yorkers

615   [*State of black literature*]: see Nathan A. Scott, Jr., "Black Literature," in Daniel Hoffman, ed., *Harvard Guide to Contemporary American Writing* (Belknap Press of Harvard University Press, 1979), ch. 7; C. W. E. Bigsby, *The Second Black Renaissance: Essays in Black Literature* (Greenwood Press, 1980); Herbert Hill, ed., *Anger, and Beyond: The Negro Writer in the United States* (Harper, 1966); Mari Evans, ed., *Black Women Writers (1950–1980): A Critical Evaluation* (Anchor Press/Doubleday, 1984).

[*State of southern literature*]: see Lewis P. Simpson, "Southern Fiction," in Hoffman, ch. 4; Louis D. Rubin, Jr., et al., eds., *The History of Southern Literature* (Louisiana State University Press, 1985), parts 3–4; Rubin and Robert D. Jacobs, eds., *Southern Renascence: The Literature of the Modern South* (Johns Hopkins Press, 1953); Richard Gray, *The Literature of Memory: Modern Writers of the American South* (Johns Hopkins University Press, 1977).

[*"Terrible loss of moral energy"*]: Doctorow, "It's a Cold War Out There, Class of '83," *Nation*, vol. 237, no. 1 (July 2, 1983), pp. 6–7, quoted at pp. 6, 7; see also Doctorow, "Living in the House of Fiction," *ibid.*, vol. 226, no. 15 (April 22, 1978), pp. 459–60, 462.

615 [*Bellow on "publicity intellectuals"*]: Mark Christhilf, "Saul Bellow and the American Intellectual Community," *Modern Age*, vol. 28, no. 1 (Winter 1984), pp. 55–67, esp. pp. 59–61.

615–16 [*"Million-dollar advances"*]: Kazin, "American Writing Now," *New Republic*, vol. 183, no. 16 (October 18, 1980), pp. 27–30, quoted at p. 28.

616 [*Kostelanetz on the literary marketplace*]: Kostelanetz, *The End of Intelligent Writing: Literary Politics in America* (Sheed & Ward, 1974), *passim;* see also Joan Simpson Burns, *The Awkward Embrace: The Creative Artist and the Institution in America* (Knopf, 1975), esp. ch. 22; Ted Solotaroff, "The Literary-Industrial Complex," *New Republic*, vol. 196, no. 23 (June 8, 1987), pp. 28–45.

[*Aldridge on the modern novel*]: Aldridge, "The State of the Novel," *Commentary*, vol. 64, no. 4 (October 1977), pp. 44–52, esp. pp. 45–47, quoted at p. 46; see also Warner Berthoff, "The Novel in a Time of Troubles," in Berthoff, *Fictions and Events* (E. P. Dutton, 1971), pp. 102–17; Philip Roth, "Writing American Fiction" (1960), in Roth, *Reading Myself and Others* (Farrar, Straus & Giroux, 1975), pp. 117–35; Janet Groth, "Fiction vs. anti-fiction revisited," *Commonweal*, vol. 106, no. 9 (May 11, 1979), pp. 269–71; Joseph Epstein, "A Conspiracy of Silence," *Harper's*, vol. 255, no. 1530 (November 1977), pp. 77–92.

[*New York intellectuals*]: Alan M. Wald, *The New York Intellectuals: The Rise and Decline of the Anti-Stalinist Left from the 1930s to the 1980s* (University of North Carolina Press, 1987); Alexander Bloom, *Prodigal Sons: The New York Intellectuals and Their World* (Oxford University Press, 1986); Bernard Rosenberg and Ernest Goldstein, eds., *Creators and Disturbers: Reminiscences by Jewish Intellectuals of New York* (Columbia University Press, 1982); Kostelanetz; James B. Gilbert, *Writers and Partisans: A History of Literary Radicalism in America* (Wiley, 1968); Irving Howe, "The New York Intellectuals," in Howe, *Decline of the New* (Harcourt, 1970), pp. 211–68; Richard H. King, "Up from Radicalism," *American Jewish History*, vol. 75, no. 1 (September 1985), pp. 61–85.

[*"Gutter-worldliness"*]: Frank Kermode, "A Herd of Independent Minds" (review of Bloom), *New York Times Book Review*, April 27, 1986, pp. 12–13, Howe quoted at p. 12.

617 [*Kostelanetz on "literary mob"*]: Kostelanetz, p. 75 and part 1 *passim.*

[*PEN Congress*]: Rhoda Koenig, "At Play in the Fields of the Word," *New York*, vol. 19, no. 5 (February 3, 1986), pp. 40–47; Edward Rothstein, "Lead Me Not into PEN Station," *New Republic*, vol. 194, no. 8 (February 24, 1986), pp. 20–23; "A Rampancy of Writers," *Time*, vol. 127, no. 2 (January 13, 1986), p. 22; "Independent States of Mind," *ibid.*, vol. 127, no. 4 (January 27, 1986), pp. 74–77; "Mightier Than the Sword," *Newsweek*, vol. 107, no. 4 (January 27, 1986), pp. 60–61; see also William H. Gass, "East vs. West in Lithuania: Rising Tempers at a Writers' Meeting," *New York Times Book Review*, February 2, 1986, pp. 3, 29, 31.

[*"Your Administration"*]: text of letter in *Nation*, vol. 242, no. 4 (February 1, 1986), p. 117; see also Maria Margaronis and Elizabeth Pochoda, "Bad Manners & Bad Faith," *ibid.*, pp. 116–19; Koenig, pp. 40–41; "Independent States," pp. 74–75; Walter Goodman, "Shultz Faces Critics in Speech Opening 48th PEN Assembly," *New York Times*, January 13, 1986, pp. 1, C11.

[*"Most ideologically right-wing"*]: Doctorow, "Why Invite Shultz?," *New York Times*, January 11, 1986, p. 23.

[*"Catatonic left"*]: quoted in "Mightier Than the Sword," p. 60.

[*Shultz's address*]: excerpts in *New York Times*, January 19, 1986, sect. 4, p. 6.

618 [*"With you all the way"*]: quoted in Koenig, p. 41.

[*"First thing I get"*]: quoted in *New York Times*, January 14, 1986, p. C12.

[*"Even if you say"*]: quoted in Koenig, p. 42.

[*"In the eyes of foreigners"*]: quoted in Walter Goodman, "Norman Mailer Offers a PEN Post-mortem," *New York Times*, January 27, 1986, p. C24.

[*Mailer on Congress "friendships and feuds"*]: ibid.

[*Women's protest*]: Paley quoted in Koenig, p. 47; Mailer and Jong in "Independent States," p. 77; Macdonald in "Mightier Than the Sword," p. 61; Edwin McDowell, "Women at PEN Caucus Demand a Greater Role," *New York Times*, January 17, 1986, p. C26; McDowell, "PEN Congress Ends with a Protest," *ibid.*, January 18, 1986, p. 11.

618 [*"Failure of the ruling ideologies"*]: excerpts from remarks in *New York Times*, January 19, 1986, sect. 4, p. 6.

[*"Ring of romantic anarchism"*]: quoted in "Independent States," p. 77; see also Amos Oz, "A Writer's Guide," *New Republic*, vol. 194, no. 8 (February 24, 1986), p. 28.

618–19 [*"Fully clawed"*]: Ozick, "Literature Lost," *New York Times*, January 22, 1986, p. A23; see also Ozick, "Innovation and Redemption: What Literature Means," in Ozick, *Art & Ardor* (Knopf, 1983), pp. 238–48.

619 [*Bellow-Grass debate*]: Bellow quoted in "Independent States," p. 77; Koenig, pp. 44–45; see also Leon Wieseltier, "A Fable," *New Republic*, vol. 194, no. 8 (February 24, 1986), pp. 26–29; Günter Grass, "The Artist's Freedom of Opinion in Our Society," in Grass, *On Writing and Politics, 1967–1983*, Ralph Manheim, trans. (Harcourt, 1985), pp. 127–36.

[*"Censorship in the U.S.A."*]: "Mightier Than the Sword," p. 61; *New York Times*, January 16, 1986, p. C17; see also Eli M. Oboler, ed., *Censorship and Education* (H. W. Wilson Co., 1981).

[*Updike on postal service*]: quoted in "Independent States," p. 75; see also Updike, "One Writer's Testimony," *National Review*, vol. 30, no. 21 (May 26, 1978), p. 641.

620 [*James on "thinness" of American life*]: James, *The American Scene* (Scribner, 1946), pp. 44, 54, and *passim*; see also James, *Hawthorne* (Harper, 1880), pp. 41–43.

[*"Absence of a desire"*]: Bellow, "The Writer as Moralist," *Atlantic*, vol. 211, no. 3 (March 1963), pp. 58–62, quoted at p. 62; see also Bellow, "Where Do We Go from Here: The Future of Fiction," in Irving Mallow, ed., *Saul Bellow and the Critics* (New York University Press, 1967), pp. 211–20; Bellow, "The Nobel Lecture," *American Scholar*, vol. 46, no. 3 (1977), pp. 316–25; Bellow, "Literature in the Age of Technology," in *Technology and the Frontiers of Knowledge* (Doubleday, 1975), pp. 3–22.

[*Foreign authors on contemporary American writing*]: quoted in "Where's the New Faulkner?," *U.S. News & World Report*, vol. 100, no. 3 (January 27, 1986), p. 65; see also Aleksandr Mulyarchik, "The New American Literature," *World Press Review*, vol. 30, no. 4 (April 1983), p. 51; Edward Hoagland, "Americans Exclude the Globe," *New York Times*, January 11, 1986, p. 23.

621 [*"Independent, self-generating"*]: John Russell, *The Meanings of Modern Art* (Harper, 1981), p. 291.

[*Late-nineteenth- and early-twentieth-century American art*]: ibid., pp. 291–96; Meyer Schapiro, *Modern Art: 19th and 20th Centuries* (George Braziller, 1982), pp. 135–78; Arthur Frank Wertheim, *The New York Little Renaissance: Iconoclasm, Modernism, and Nationalism in American Culture, 1908–1917* (New York University Press, 1976); Peter Selz, *Art in Our Times: A Pictorial History, 1890–1980* (Harry N. Abrams, 1981), chs. 1–3 *passim*; Peter Conrad, *The Art of the City: Views and Versions of New York* (Oxford University Press, 1984).

[*Abstract Expressionism*]: Harry F. Gaugh, "Reappraising the New York School," in Sam Hunter, ed., *An American Renaissance: Painting and Sculpture since 1940* (Abbeville Press, 1986), pp. 27–61; Charles Harrison, "Abstract Expressionism," in Nikos Stangos, ed., *Concepts of Modern Art*, 2nd ed. (Harper, 1981), pp. 169–211; Maurice Tuchman, ed., *New York School: The First Generation* (New York Graphic Society, 1972); Irving Sandler, *The Triumph of American Painting: A History of Abstract Expressionism* (Praeger, 1970); Russell, pp. 302–27 *passim*; see also Leo Steinberg, *Other Criteria: Confrontations with Twentieth-Century Art* (Oxford University Press, 1972), chs. 10, 11.

[*Russell on Frankenthaler*]: Russell, p. 357.

[*"Drowning Girl"*]: reproduced in *ibid.*, p. 348.

[*"New, Newer, Newest"*]: John Simon, "New, Newer, Newest," *New York Times*, September 21, 1969, sect. 2, pp. 1, 7; see also Burns, *Awkward Embrace*, ch. 13 *passim*.

[*"Most difficult, embattled"*]: Suzi Gablik, "Minimalism," in Stangos, pp. 244–55, quoted at p. 248; see also Hal Foster, "The Crux of Minimalism," in Howard Singerman, ed., *Individuals: A Selected History of Contemporary Art, 1945–1986* (Abbeville Press, 1986), pp. 162–83.

622 [*Merging of High and Mass Culture*]: Herbert J. Gans, "American Popular Culture and High Culture in a Changing Class Structure," in Judith H. Balfe and Margaret Jane Wyszomirski, eds., *Art, Ideology, and Politics* (Praeger, 1985), pp. 40–57, quoted at p. 49; Dwight Macdonald, "A Theory of Mass Culture," in Bernard Rosenberg and

David M. White, eds., *Mass Culture: The Popular Arts in America* (Free Press, 1957), pp. 59-73; Clement Greenberg, "Avant-Garde and Kitsch," in Greenberg, *The Collected Essays and Criticism*, John O'Brian, ed. (University of Chicago Press, 1986), vol. 1, pp. 5-22; "Culture and the Present Moment: A Round-Table Discussion," *Commentary*, vol. 58, no. 6 (December 1974), pp. 31-50; Susan Sontag, "Notes on 'Camp,' " in Sontag, *Against Interpretation and Other Essays* (Farrar, Straus & Giroux, 1966), pp. 275-92.

622 [*Hughes on Kramer*]: Robert Hughes, "Kramer vs. Kramer" (review of Hilton Kramer, *The Revenge of the Philistines: Art and Culture 1972-1984* [Free Press, 1985]), *New Republic*, vol. 194, no. 15 (April 14, 1986), pp. 28-33, quoted at p. 32.

[*"Free-market capitalism"*]: *ibid.*, p. 32; see also Kramer, "Postmodern: Art and Culture in the 1980s," in Kramer, pp. 1-11.

[*Free market in art*]: John Bernard Myers, "The Art Biz," *New York Review of Books*, vol. 30, no. 15 (October 13, 1983), pp. 32-34, quoted at p. 32; see also Steven W. Naifeh, *Culture Making: Money, Success, and the New York Art World* (Princeton University Undergraduate Studies in History: 2, 1976); Harold Rosenberg, *Art on the Edge: Creators and Situations* (Macmillan, 1975), ch. 26; Laura de Coppet and Alan Jones, *The Art Dealers* (Clarkson N. Potter, 1984).

[*"Radically wrong"*]: Russell, p. 381.

[*"Two Women" sale*]: Myers, p. 32.

[*Artists and politics*]: Corinne Robins, *The Pluralistic Era: American Art, 1968-1981* (Harper, 1984), ch. 3; Balfe and Wyszomirski; Hilton Kramer, "Turning Back the Clock: Art and Politics in 1984," in Kramer, pp. 386-94; Paul Von Blum, *The Art of Social Conscience* (Universe Books, 1976), ch. 9.

622-3 [*New York Art Strike*]: Robins, pp. 2-3, 39.

623 [*Kennedy's proposed legislation for the resale of art*]: see "U.S. Bill on Artists' Rights Is Debated," *New York Times*, November 19, 1986, p. C33; see also Franklin Feldman, "Reflections on Art and the Law: Old Concepts, New Values," *Proceedings of the American Philosophical Society*, vol. 131, no. 2 (June 1987), pp. 141-47.

[*Sontag on "art today"*]: Susan Sontag, "One Culture and the New Sensibility," in Sontag, pp. 293-304, quoted at p. 296.

[*Attacks on tradition, 1960s-1980s*]: Gregory Battcock and Robert Nickas, eds., *The Art of Performance* (E. P. Dutton, 1984); Robert Smith, "Conceptual Art," in Stangos, pp. 256-70; Edward Lucie-Smith, "Pop Art," in *ibid.*, pp. 225-38; Lucy Lippard et al., *Pop Art* (Oxford University Press, 1966); Carla Gottlieb, *Beyond Modern Art* (E. P. Dutton, 1976); Robins, esp. chs. 2, 4, 8; Robert C. Morgan, "Beyond Formalism: Language Models, Conceptual Art, and Environmental Art," in Hunter, pp. 147-75; *Machineworks: Vito Acconci, Alice Aycock, Dennis Oppenheim*, catalogue (Institute of Contemporary Art, University of Pennsylvania, 1981); Moira Roth, ed., *The Amazing Decade: Women and Performance Art, 1970-1980* (Astro Artz, 1983); see also Arthur C. Danto, *The Transfiguration of the Commonplace: A Philosophy of Art* (Harvard University Press, 1981).

[*Influence of Duchamp*]: John Tancock, "The Influence of Marcel Duchamp," in Anne d'Harnoncourt and Kynaston McShine, eds., *Marcel Duchamp* (Museum of Modern Art, 1973), pp. 159-78; Rosenberg, ch. 1; Calvin Tomkins, *The World of Marcel Duchamp, 1887-* (Time Inc., 1966), chs. 7-8.

[*Neo-Expressionism*]: *1985 Whitney Biennial Exhibition*, catalogue (Whitney Museum of Modern Art, 1985); Arthur C. Danto, "Julian Schnabel," in Danto, *The State of the Art* (Prentice-Hall, 1987), pp. 43-47; Howard N. Fox, *Avant-Garde in the Eighties*, catalogue (Los Angeles County Museum of Art, 1987); Kim Levin, "Appropriating the Past: Neo-Expressionism, Neo-Primitivism, and the Revival of Abstraction," in Hunter, pp. 215-53; John Russell, "American Art Gains New Energies," *New York Times*, August 19, 1984, sect. 2, pp. 1, 18; Kramer, pp. 366-86.

[*Postindustrial technologies and art*]: John G. Hanhardt, ed., *Video Culture* (Visual Studies Workshop Press, 1986); Cynthia Goodman, *Digital Visions: Computers and Art* (Harry N. Abrams, 1987); see also J. David Bolter, *Turing's Man: Western Culture in the Computer Age* (University of North Carolina Press, 1984).

[*"When anything is allowed"*]: Danto, "Approaching the End of Art," in Danto, *State of the Art*, pp. 202-18, quoted at p. 204.

624 [*Structuralism and Deconstruction*]: see Jonathan D. Culler, *The Pursuit of Signs: Semiotics, Literature, Deconstruction* (Cornell University Press, 1981); Culler, *On Deconstruction: Theory and Criticism After Structuralism* (Cornell University Press, 1982); Vincent B. Leitch, *Deconstructive Criticism: An Advanced Introduction* (Columbia University Press, 1983).

[*Postmodernism*]: Charles Newman, "The Post-Modern Aura: The Act of Fiction in an Age of Inflation," *Salmagundi*, nos. 63–64 (Spring–Summer 1984), pp. 3–199; Jean-François Lyotard, *The Postmodern Condition: A Report on Knowledge*, Geoff Bennington and Brian Massumi, trans. (University of Minnesota Press, 1984); Hal Foster, ed., *The Anti-Aesthetic: Essays on Postmodern Culture* (Bay Press, 1983); Kramer, "Postmodern"; Heinrich Klotz, ed., *Postmodern Visions* (Abbeville Press, 1985); Charles Jencks, *The Language of Post-Modern Architecture*, 4th ed. (Rizzoli, 1984).

[*Broadway in the 1970s–1980s*]: Barbara Gelb, "O'Neill's 'Iceman' Sprang from the Ashes of His Youth," *New York Times*, September 29, 1985, sect. 2, pp. 1, 4; Mel Gussow, "Arthur Miller: Stirred by Memory," *ibid.*, February 1, 1987, sect. 2, pp. 1, 30; D. J. R. Bruckner, "Playwrights Rediscover the Uses of Politics," *ibid.*, September 22, 1985, sect. 2, p. 3.

[*Advances in the technology of music*]: Irwin Shainman, "Those Golden Sounds of Yesteryear Have Gone High-Tech," *Berkshire Eagle*, December 27, 1986, p. B4.

The Conservative Mall

[*AEI celebration*]: Sidney Blumenthal, *The Rise of the Counter-Establishment: From Conservative Ideology to Political Power* (Times Books, 1986), pp. 32–34, quoted at pp. 32, 33.

625 [*Dinner at Delmonico's*]: James MacGregor Burns, *The Workshop of Democracy* (Knopf, 1985), pp. 161–62, and sources cited therein.

[*Fifty-year conservative eclipse*]: see Arthur M. Schlesinger, Jr., *The Cycles of American History* (Houghton Mifflin, 1986), ch. 2; Michael W. Miles, *The Odyssey of the American Right* (Oxford University Press, 1980).

626 ["*Hitch-hike along*"]: quoted in Jonathan Martin Kolkey, *The New Right, 1960–1968: With Epilogue, 1969–1980* (University Press of America, 1983), p. 248.

[*Liberal establishment*]: quoted in Blumenthal, p. 4.

[*Rossiter on conservatism*]: Rossiter, *Conservatism in America* (Knopf, 1955), pp. 224–35 and *passim*.

[*Hartz on conservatism*]: Hartz, *The Liberal Tradition in America: An Interpretation of American Political Thought Since the Revolution* (Harcourt, 1955).

[*Hofstadter on conservatism*]: Richard Hofstadter, *The Paranoid Style in American Politics and Other Essays* (Knopf, 1965), chs. 3, 4.

[*Crawford's exposé of the New Right*]: Crawford, *Thunder on the Right* (Pantheon, 1980), Viereck quoted on "rabble-rousing populism" on jacket.

[*Explanations for rise of conservative movement*]: George H. Nash, *The Conservative Intellectual Movement in America Since 1945* (Basic Books, 1976), chs. 9–11; Blumenthal, ch 12 and *passim*; Crawford, pp. 30–41; Kolkey, esp. chs. 13–15; Peter Steinfels, *The Neo Conservatives* (Simon and Schuster, 1979), ch. 2 and *passim*.

627 [*Ideas as weapons*]: Max Lerner, *Ideas Are Weapons: The History and Uses of Ideas* (Viking, 1939); Richard M. Weaver, *Ideas Have Consequences* (University of Chicago Press, 1948).

["*Massive public education*"]: quoted in Kolkey, p. 250.

[*Conservative journals*]: Crawford, pp. 30–32, 181–207; Steinfels, pp. 4–12.

[*Conservative factions*]: see Blumenthal, ch. 13 *passim*; Miles, esp. part 3; Steinfels; Kolkey, ch. 1 and pp. 334–39; Crawford; Richard Striner, "Can Conservatism Survive Laissez Faire?," *American Politics* (December 1986), pp. 19–21; George F. Will, "The Soul of Conservatism," *Newsweek*, vol. 106, no. 20 (November 11, 1985), p. 92; Will, *Statecraft As Soulcraft: What Government Does* (Simon and Schuster, 1983).

627-8 [*New Christian right*]: Robert C. Liebman and Robert Wuthnow, eds., *The New Christian Right: Mobilization and Legitimation* (Aldine, 1983); George Marsden, ed., *Evangelicalism and Modern America* (William B. Eerdmans Publishing, 1984); James D. Hunter, *Evangelicalism: The Coming Generation* (University of Chicago Press, 1987); A. James Reichley, *Religion in American Public Life* (Brookings Institution, 1985), pp. 311–31.

628 [*Buckley and Eastman*]: John Patrick Diggins, *Up from Communism: Conservative Odysseys in American Intellectual History* (Harper, 1975), p. 346.
[*Reagan and the conservative movement*]: Blumenthal, ch. 9; Robert Dallek, *Ronald Reagan: The Politics of Symbolism* (Harvard University Press, 1984), ch. 2.

629 [*Blumenthal on Reaganism*]: Blumenthal, p. 241.
[*Liberalism's successes*]: see John E. Schwarz, *America's Hidden Success: A Reassessment of Twenty Years of Public Policy* (Norton, 1983); see also Walter R. Mead, *Mortal Splendor: The American Empire in Transition* (Houghton Mifflin, 1987).
[*Trilling on liberalism*]: quoted in *Wall Street Journal*, April 15, 1986, p. 64.

630 [*"New Public Philosophy"*]: Robert B. Reich, "Toward a New Public Philosophy," *Atlantic*, vol. 255, no. 5 (May 1985), pp. 68–79; see also Reich, "An Industrial Policy of the Right," *The Public Interest*, vol. 73 (Fall 1983), pp. 3–17; Reich, *Tales of a New America* (Times Books, 1987); commencement address of Senator Gary Hart at Talladega College, Talladega, Ala., May 19, 1985.

631 [*"Seriously underestimated"*]: quoted in Walter Goodman, "Dr. Kenneth B. Clark: Bewilderment Replaces 'Wishful Thinking' on Race," *New York Times*, December 27, 1984, p. A14.
[*"Not God-ordained"*]: ibid.
[*"Greatest wave of social reform"*]: Irving Howe, *Socialism and America* (Harcourt, 1985), p. 84.

632 [*Possibilities of socialist-liberal coalition*]: see *ibid.*, pp. 147–75; see also Samuel P. Huntington, "The Visions of the Democratic Party," *The Public Interest*, vol. 79 (Spring 1985), pp. 63–78.

15. THE DECLINE OF LEADERSHIP

633 [*Gorbachev's leadership*]: Robert C. Tucker, *Political Culture and Leadership in Soviet Russia: From Lenin to Gorbachev* (Norton, 1988); Michael Mandelbaum and Strobe Talbott, *Reagan and Gorbachev* (Vintage, 1987); Jerry Hough, *Russia and the West: Gorbachev and the Politics of Reform* (Simon and Schuster, 1988); Mikhail Gorbachev, *Perestroika: New Thinking for Our Country and the World* (Harper, 1987).
[*"Being colonized"*]: Rohatyn, "On the Brink," *New York Review of Books*, vol. 34, no. 10 (June 11, 1987), pp. 3–6, quoted at p. 3.

634 [*Reactions to proposals to amend the Constitution*]: see Richard Lacayo, "Is It Broke? Should We Fix It?," *Time*, vol. 130, no. 1 (July 6, 1987), pp. 54–55; Arthur M. Schlesinger, Jr., "Leave the Constitution Alone," in Donald L. Robinson, ed., *Reforming American Government: The Bicentennial Papers of the Committee on the Constitutional System* (Westview Press, 1985), pp. 50–54; Hendrik Hertzberg, "Let's Get Representative," *New Republic*, vol. 196, no. 26 (June 29, 1987), pp. 15–18; "Move Over, James Madison," *ibid.*, pp. 19–21.
[*Liberty Weekend*]: *Time*, vol. 128, no. 2 (July 14, 1986), pp. 10–20.

635 [*Liberty Weekend conference*]: Richard D. Heffner, ed., "Summary of Proceedings," New York Marriott Marquis, July 5–6, 1986; Walter Goodman, "Liberty Panel Ponders Wherefores of Freedom," *New York Times*, July 7, 1986, p. B4.

Republicans: Waiting for Mr. Right

636 [*Harding's mind*]: James MacGregor Burns, *The Workshop of Democracy* (Knopf, 1985), p. 471.
[*Trudeau on Reagan*]: G. B. Trudeau, *In Search of Reagan's Brain* (Henry Holt, 1981).
[*"Barely above a whisper"*]: quoted in Paul D. Erickson, *Reagan Speaks: The Making of an American Myth* (New York University Press, 1985), p. 14.
[*Reagan's misstatements*]: Mark Green and Gail MacColl, eds., *There He Goes Again: Ronald Reagan's Reign of Error* (Pantheon, 1983).
[*White on Reagan*]: White, *America in Search of Itself: The Making of the President, 1956–1980* (Harper, 1982), p. 419.

637 [*GOP in 1960s and 1970s*]: Jonathan Martin Kolkey, *The New Right, 1960–1968: With Epilogue, 1969–1980* (University Press of America, 1983); Kevin P. Phillips, *The Emerging Republican Majority* (Anchor, 1970); John F. Bibby, "Party Renewal in the National

Republican Party," in Gerald M. Pomper, ed., *Party Renewal in America: Theory and Practice* (Praeger, 1981), pp. 102–15; Alan Crawford, *Thunder on the Right* (Pantheon, 1980).

637 [*Mayflower conference*]: Frank van der Linden, *The Real Reagan* (Morrow, 1981), pp. 111–12, Reagan quoted at p. 112.

[*Reagan's meeting with conservative leaders*]: ibid., pp. 112–16, quoted at pp. 115, 116.

638 [*1980 election*]: Elizabeth Drew, *Portrait of an Election: The 1980 Presidential Campaign* (Simon and Schuster, 1981); Jack W. Germond and Jules Witcover, *Blue Smoke and Mirrors* (Viking, 1981); Marlene Michels Pomper, ed., *The Election of 1980: Reports and Interpretations* (Chatham House, 1981); Hamilton Jordan, *Crisis: The Last Year of the Carter Administration* (Putnam, 1982); Walter J. Stone and Alan I. Abramowitz, "Winning May Not Be Everything, But It's More than We Thought: Presidential Party Activists in 1980," *American Political Science Review*, vol. 77 (1983), pp. 945–56.

639 [*Tax and budget cuts*]: David A. Stockman, *The Triumph of Politics: How the Reagan Revolution Failed* (Harper, 1986), chs. 3–6; Robert Dallek, *Ronald Reagan: The Politics of Symbolism* (Harvard University Press, 1984), pp. 65–72; Paul Craig Roberts, *The Supply-Side Revolution* (Harvard University Press, 1984), chs. 4–5; Isabel Sawhill and John L. Palmer, eds., *The Reagan Experiment* (Urban Institute Press, 1982), part 1; Laurence I. Barrett, *Gambling with History: Ronald Reagan in the White House* (Doubleday, 1983), chs. 8–9; Martin Anderson, *Revolution* (Harcourt, 1988), esp. chs. 11–12.

[*Supply-side economics*]: Stockman, pp. 39–42, 64–66, quoted at p. 40; Roberts, chs. 1–3 passim; Robert Lekachman, *Reaganomics: Greed Is Not Enough* (Pantheon, 1982); Anderson, ch. 13.

639–40 [*House vote on budget*]: New York Times, May 8, 1981, pp. A1, A18.

640 ["*So much of such magnitude*"]: Time, vol. 118, no. 6 (August 10, 1981), p. 12.

[*Recession*]: Dallek, ch. 4 passim.

[*Reagan's rigidity in recession*]: Stockman, chs. 11–12; Dallek, ch. 4; Roberts, chs. 7–8.

["*Damn it, Pete*"]: quoted in Stockman, p. 351.

["*Real bullets*"]: ibid., p. 354.

641 ["*Attitudes, ideologies*"]: Ralph Nader, "Introduction," in Ronald Brownstein and Nina Easton, *Reagan's Ruling Class* (Pantheon, 1983), pp. xv–xxvi, quoted at p. xvi.

[*1984 election*]: Ellis Sandoz and Cecil V. Crabb, eds., *Election '84: Landslide Without a Mandate?* (Mentor, 1985); Gerald Pomper et al., *The Election of 1984: Reports and Interpretations* (Chatham House, 1985); William A. Henry III, *Visions of America: How We Saw the 1984 Election* (Atlantic Monthly Press, 1985); Jack W. Germond and Jules Witcover, *Wake Us When It's Over* (Macmillan, 1985); Elizabeth Drew, *Campaign Journal: The Political Events of 1983–1984* (Macmillan, 1985).

[*Tax reform*]: Joseph A. Pechman, ed., *Tax Reform and the U.S. Economy* (Brookings Institution, 1987); Eugene Steuerle, "The New Tax Law," in Phillip Cagan, ed., *Deficits, Taxes, and Economic Adjustments* (American Enterprise Institute, 1987), pp. 275–303; New York Times, September 26, 1986, pp. A1, D17; Eric D. Adelstein, "Reagan and the New Possibilities of Presidential Power," unpublished thesis, Williams College, Williamstown, Mass., May 1987, pp. 89–138.

["*Let us move together*"]: "Transcript of President's State of Union Address," *New York Times*, February 7, 1985, p. B8.

642 [*Poll on tax simplification and tax system*]: Everett Carll Ladd, "Tax Attitudes," *Public Opinion*, vol. 8, no. 1 (February–March 1985), pp. 8–10; and ibid., pp. 19–27.

["*Couldn't do it*"]: Lynn Martin, quoted in New York Times, September 26, 1986, p. D17.

[*Reagan and foreign policy*]: Dallek, part 3; Barrett, chs. 13–17; Strobe Talbott, *The Russians and Reagan* (Vintage, 1984); Betty Glad, "Black and White Thinking: Ronald Reagan's Approach to Foreign Policy," paper prepared for presentation at the 50th Anniversary Program of the Institute for Psychoanalysis, n.d.; William D. Anderson and Sterling J. Kernek, "How 'Realistic' Is Reagan's Diplomacy?," *Political Science Quarterly*, vol. 100, no. 3 (Fall 1985), pp. 389–409; Jeff McMahan, *Reagan and the World: Imperial Policy in the New Cold War* (Monthly Review Press, 1985); Kenneth A. Oye et al., eds, *Eagle Defiant: United States Foreign Policy in the 1980s* (Little, Brown, 1983); some passages have been drawn from my earlier work, *The Power to Lead: The Crisis of the American Presidency* (Simon and Schuster, 1984), esp. pp. 64–66.

[*Reagan on communism and communists*]: quoted in Burns, *Power to Lead*, p. 64.

643 [*"Terrible beast"*]: June 9, 1982, in *Public Papers of the Presidents of the United States: Ronald Reagan* (U.S. Government Printing Office, 1982–   ), vol. 2, part 1, pp. 754–59, quoted at p. 757.

[*"Extinction of mankind"*]: June 8, 1982, in *ibid.*, vol. 2, part 1, pp. 742–48, quoted at p. 743.

[*Smith on Reagan*]: Smith, "Events Force a Clearer Outline of Foreign Policy," *New York Times*, May 20, 1982, p. A28.

[*Reagan's address to evangelists*]: March 8, 1983, in *Reagan Public Papers*, vol. 3, part 1, pp. 359–64, quoted on "evil empire" at p. 364.

[*Glad on Reagan*]: quoted in Burns, *Power to Lead*, p. 65.

644 [*Reagan-Gorbachev summit, 1988*]: Fred Barnes, "In the Evil Empire," *New Republic*, vol. 198, no. 25 (June 20, 1988), pp. 8–9.

[*Conservative criticisms of Reagan*]: Norman Podhoretz, "The Reagan Road to Détente," *Foreign Affairs*, vol. 63, no. 3 (1985), pp. 447–64, Will's quip at p. 459; William F. Buckley, Jr., "The Blandification of Ronald Reagan," *National Review*, vol. 36, no. 6 (April 6, 1984), p. 62.

[*Iran-Contra*]: *Report of the Congressional Committees Investigating the Iran-Contra Affair* (U.S. Government Printing Office, 1987); President's Special Review Board, *Report* (U.S. Government Printing Office, 1987); see also Leslie Cockburn, *Out of Control* (Atlantic Monthly Press, 1987); Theodore Draper, "An Autopsy," *New York Review of Books*, vol. 34, no. 20 (December 17, 1987), pp. 67–77.

645 [*"Restore unity"*]: Alexander M. Haig, Jr., *Caveat: Realism, Reagan, and Foreign Policy* (Macmillan, 1984), p. 312.

The Structure of Disarray

[*"The true Reagan Revolution"*]: Stockman, p. 9.

[*Committee on the Constitutional System diagnosis*]: Committee on the Constitutional System (co-chairs Nancy Landon Kassebaum, C. Douglas Dillon, Lloyd N. Cutler), *A Bicentennial Analysis of the American Political Structure: Report and Recommendations* (January 1987), quoted on "institutional contest of wills" at p. 3; see Kassebaum, "Statement on Campaign Finance," in Robinson, pp. 30–32; Dillon, "The Challenge of Modern Governance," in *ibid.*, pp. 24–29; Cutler, "To Form a Government," *Foreign Affairs*, vol. 59, no. 1 (1980), pp. 126–43.

646 [*Framers' Constitution and parties*]: Richard Hofstadter, *The Idea of a Party System* (University of California Press, 1969), esp. ch. 2; Roy F. Nichols, *The Invention of the American Political Parties* (Macmillan, 1967); John F. Hoadley, *Origins of American Political Parties, 1789–1803* (University Press of Kentucky, 1986).

[*Marshall's nationalist decisions*]: see McCulloch v. Maryland, 4 Wheaton 315 (1819); Gibbons v. Ogden, 9 Wheaton 1 (1824).

648 [*Proposals for constitutional reform*]: "Bicentennial Analysis," pp. 8–18; James L. Sundquist, *Constitutional Reform and Effective Government* (Brookings Institution, 1986); Charles M. Hardin, *Presidential Power and Accountability: Toward a New Constitution* (University of Chicago Press, 1974); Robinson, *passim*; Stephen Horn, *The Cabinet and Congress* (Columbia University Press, 1960); Thomas K. Finletter, *Can Representative Government Do the Job?* (Reynal & Hitchcock, 1945).

[*"Two fundamental arguments"*]: Wilson, "Does the Separation of Powers Still Work?," *The Public Interest*, no. 86 (Winter 1987), pp. 36–52, quoted at p. 49.

[*Scholars on party renewal*]: Committee on Political Parties, American Political Science Association, "Toward a More Responsible Two-Party System," *American Political Science Review*, vol. 44, no. 3 (September 1950), supplement; Austin Ranney, "Toward a More Responsible Two-Party System: A Commentary," *American Political Science Review*, vol. 45, no. 2 (June 1951), pp. 488–99; William J. Crotty, "The Philosophies of Party Reform," in Pomper, *Party Renewal*, pp. 31–50.

649 [*Critical reactions to scholars' report*]: Evron M. Kirkpatrick, "Toward a More Responsible Two-Party System: Political Science, Policy Science, or Pseudo-Science?," *American Political Science Review*, vol. 65, no. 4 (December 1971), pp. 965–90; T. William Goodman, "How Much Political Party Centralization Do We Want?," *Journal of Politics*, vol. 13, no. 4 (November 1951), pp. 536–61; Murray S. Stedman, Jr., and Herbert Sonth-

off, "Party Responsibility—A Critical Inquiry," *Western Political Quarterly,* vol. 4, no. 3 (September 1951), pp. 454–68; Gerald M. Pomper, "Toward a More Responsible Two-Party System? What, Again?," *Journal of Politics,* vol. 33 (1971), pp. 916–40; see also David S. Broder, *The Party's Over: The Failure of Politics in America* (Harper, 1972), ch. 10 and pp. 244–47.

649 [*Party reform and renewal, 1960s–1970s*]: see Nelson W. Polsby, *Consequences of Party Reform* (Oxford University Press, 1983); Pomper, *Party Renewal, passim;* Austin Ranney, "The Political Parties: Reform and Decline," in Anthony King, ed., *The New American Political System* (American Enterprise Institute for Public Policy Research, 1978), pp. 213–47; Ranney, "Changing the Rules of the Nominating Game," in James David Barber, ed., *Choosing the President* (Prentice-Hall, 1974), pp. 71–93; Xandra Kayden and Eddie Mahe, Jr., *The Party Goes On: The Persistence of the Two-Party System in the United States* (Basic Books, 1985), ch. 3; see also *Party Line,* an occasional publication of the Committee on Party Renewal.

651 [*Judicial review*]: Jesse H. Choper, *Judicial Review and the National Political Process: A Functional Reconsideration of the Role of the Supreme Court* (University of Chicago Press, 1980); Raoul Berger, *Government by Judiciary: The Transformation of the Fourteenth Amendment* (Harvard University Press, 1977); see also Gary J. Jacobsohn, *The Supreme Court and the Decline of Constitutional Aspiration* (Rowman & Littlefield, 1986).

652 [*Eisenhower on his Warren appointment*]: Bernard Schwartz, *Super Chief: Earl Warren and His Supreme Court* (New York University Press, 1983), p. 173.
[*Burger Court*]: Vincent Blasi, ed., *The Burger Court: The Counter-Revolution That Wasn't* (Yale University Press, 1983); Herman Schwartz, ed., *The Burger Years: Rights and Wrongs in the Supreme Court, 1969–1986* (Viking, 1987); Richard Y. Funston, *Constitutional Counter-Revolution?* (Schenkman Publishing, 1977), ch. 9 and *passim.*

653 [*Court and Denver schools*]: *Keyes* v. *School District No. 1, Denver, Colorado,* 413 U.S. 189 (1973).
[*Detroit integration plan*]: *Milliken* v. *Bradley,* 418 U.S. 717 (1974); see also Alfred H. Kelly, Winfred A. Harbison, and Herman Belz, *The American Constitution: Its Origins and Development,* 6th ed. (Norton, 1983), pp. 710–11.
[*Pasadena desegregation plan*]: *Pasadena City Board of Education* v. *Spangler,* 427 U.S. 424 (1976).
[Bakke]: 438 U.S. 265 (1978), quoted at 319, 307, respectively; see also Kelly, Harbison, and Belz, pp. 711–15; Paul Brest, "Race Discrimination," in Blasi, pp. 124–31; Timothy J. O'Neill, *Bakke & the Politics of Equality* (Wesleyan University Press, 1985); Laurence H. Tribe, *Constitutional Choices* (Harvard University Press, 1985), ch. 14.
[*Women's discrimination and the Burger Court*]: Kelly, Harbison, and Belz, pp. 715–18; Ruth Bader Ginsburg, "The Burger Court's Grappling with Sex Discrimination," in Blasi, pp. 132–57.
[*Burger Court and the Fourth Amendment*]: Kelly, Harbison, and Belz, pp. 645–48, 718–21; Funston, ch. 4; Yale Kamisar, "The Warren Court (Was It Really So Defense-Minded?), the Burger Court (Is It Really So Prosecution-Oriented?), and Police Investigatory Practices," in Blasi, pp. 62–91; Schwartz, *Burger Years,* part 4.
["*Justices gave state police*"]: Kelly, Harbison, and Belz, p. 719.

654 ["*Jurisprudence of Original Intention*"]: Meese address before the American Bar Association, July 9, 1985, Washington, D.C. (Department of Justice, 1985); "Excerpts of Brennan's Speech on Constitution," *New York Times,* October 13, 1985, p. 36; "Excerpts from Stevens's Rebuttal of Meese," *ibid.,* October 26, 1985, p. 11; see also *ibid.,* October 17, 1985, p. B10.
[*Bork*]: Ronald Dworkin, "The Bork Nomination," *New York Review of Books,* vol. 34, no. 13 (August 13, 1987), pp. 3–10; Dworkin, "From Bork to Kennedy," *ibid.,* vol. 34, no. 20 (December 17, 1987), pp. 36–42.

Realignment?: Waiting for Lefty

655 [*Realignment and realigning eras*]: V. O. Key, Jr., "A Theory of Critical Elections," *Journal of Politics,* vol. 17, no. 1 (February 1955), pp. 3–18; Walter Dean Burnham, *Critical Elections and the Mainsprings of American Politics* (Norton, 1970); James L. Sundquist, *Dynamics of the Party System: Alignment and Realignment of Political Parties in the United*

States (Brookings Institution, 1973); Bruce A. Campbell and Richard J. Trilling, eds., *Realignment in American Politics: Toward a Theory* (University of Texas Press, 1980); Kristi Andersen, *The Creation of a Democratic Majority, 1928-1936* (University of Chicago Press, 1979); Stanley Kelley, Jr., "Democracy and the New Deal Party System," *Working Paper 10: Democratic Values* (Project on the Federal Social Role/National Conference on Social Welfare, 1986); Dale Baum, *The Civil War Party System: The Case of Massachusetts, 1848-1876* (University of North Carolina Press, 1984).

655 [*A 1980s realignment?*]: Nelson W. Polsby, "Did the 1984 Election Signal Major Party Realignment?," *Key Reporter*, vol. 50, no. 3 (Spring 1985), pp. 1-4; Walter Dean Burnham, "The 1984 Elections and the Future of American Politics," in Sandoz and Crabb, pp. 204-60; Kevin P. Phillips, "A G.O.P. Majority?," *New York Times*, April 19, 1984, p. A19; Jerome M. Clubb, William H. Flanigan, and Nancy H. Zingale, *Partisan Realignment: Voters, Parties, and Government in American History* (Sage Publications, 1980), pp. 273-98; Paul R. Abramson, John H. Aldrich, and David W. Rohde, *Change and Continuity in the 1984 Elections* (Congressional Quarterly Press, 1986), ch. 11; Martin P. Wattenberg, "The Hollow Realignment: Partisan Change in a Candidate-Centered Era," *Public Opinion Quarterly*, vol. 51, no. 1 (Spring 1987), pp. 58-74; Robert S. McElvaine, *The End of the Conservative Era: Liberalism After Reagan* (uncorrected proofs: Arbor House, 1987), ch. 1; *Public Opinion*, vol. 8, no. 5 (October-November 1985), pp. 8-17, 21-40.

657 [*"In a bind"*]: Alexander P. Lamis, "Mississippi," in Robert P. Steed, Laurence W. Moreland, and Tod A. Baker, eds., *The 1984 Presidential Election in the South: Patterns of Southern Party Politics* (Praeger, 1986), pp. 45-73, Lott quoted at p. 50.
[*Realignment in the South*]: Alexander P. Lamis, *The Two-Party South* (Oxford University Press, 1984); Harold W. Stanley, "The 1984 Presidential Election in the South: Race and Realignment," in Steed, Moreland and Baker, *1984 Presidential Election*, pp. 303-35; Robert P. Steed, Laurence W. Moreland, and Tod A. Baker, eds., *Party Politics in the South* (Praeger, 1980), part 2.
[*White southern Republican identification*]: Everett Carll Ladd, "Alignment and Realignment: Where Are All the Voters Going?," *The Ladd Report #3* (Norton, 1986), p. 8.

658 [*Democrats and liberals, late 1980s*]: Randall Rothenberg, *The Neoliberals: Creating the New American Politics* (Simon and Schuster, 1984); Robert Kuttner, *The Life of the Party: Democratic Prospects in 1988 and Beyond* (Viking, 1987), chs. 1, 5, and *passim*; Robert Lekachman, *Visions and Nightmares: America After Reagan* (Macmillan, 1987), ch. 6; McElvaine, esp. ch. 2; William Schneider, "The Democrats in '88," *Atlantic*, vol. 259, no. 4 (April 1987), pp. 37-59; see also Henry Fairlie, "Jackson's Moment: What Jesse Can Teach the Democrats," *New Republic*, vol. 190, no. 8 (February 27, 1984), pp. 11-14; Lucius J. Barker, "Black Americans and the Politics of Inclusion: The Significance of Jesse Jackson's Presidential Campaigns," paper prepared for presentation at the American Politics Workshop, Nankai University, China, November 19, 1988.
[*"If American voters"*]: Arthur M. Schlesinger, Jr., "For Democrats, Me-Too Reaganism Will Spell Disaster," *New York Times*, July 6, 1986, sect. 4, p. 13.
[*"Pragmatic in all things"*]: Schneider, p. 38.
[*"Democratic code word"*]: ibid., p. 37.

659 [*Democratic midterm conferences*]: Leon D. Epstein, *Political Parties in the American Mold* (University of Wisconsin Press, 1986), pp. 213-14; *New York Times*, June 26, 1985, p. B8.
[*Democratic Leadership Council*]: see Schneider, pp. 44, 46; Kuttner, pp. 28-29, 203-4.

660 [*The young in the 1980s*]: McElvaine, ch. 8; Crocker Coulson, "Lost Generation: The Politics of Youth," *New Republic*, vol. 195, no. 22 (December 1, 1986), pp. 21-22.
[*McElvaine on baby-boomers*]: McElvaine, p. 210.
[*"Springsteen Coalition"*]: ibid., pp. 215-16, 228-31, quoted at p. 216.

661 [*"Black Monday"*]: *Newsweek*, vol. 110, no. 18 (November 2, 1987), pp. 14-53.
[*Voter alienation*]: Walter Dean Burnham, "The Turnout Problem," in A. James Reichley, ed., *Elections American Style* (Brookings Institution, 1987), pp. 97-133; Abramson, Aldrich, and Rohde, ch. 4 *passim*; Martin P. Wattenberg, *The Decline of American Political Parties, 1952-1980* (Harvard University Press, 1984); Curtis B. Gans, "The Empty Ballot Box: Reflections on Nonvoters in America," *Public Opinion*, vol. 1, no. 4 (Sep-

tember–October 1978), pp. 54–57; Frances Fox Piven and Richard A. Cloward, *Why Americans Don't Vote* (Pantheon, 1988), esp. chs. 4, 7, Appendix A.

661 [*1984 voting percentage*]: Thomas E. Cronin, "The Presidential Election of 1984," in Sandoz and Crabb, pp. 30–31.

661–2 [*Movements, nonvoters, and their transforming potential*]: Richard A. Cloward and Frances Fox Piven, "Toward a Class-Based Realignment of American Politics: A Movement Strategy," *Social Policy*, vol. 13, no. 3 (Winter 1983), pp. 3–14; press report, Human Service Employees Registration & Voter Education Campaign, New York, N.Y., June 15, 1987.

A Rebirth of Leadership?

662 [*Cuomo's decision*]: *New York Times*, February 20, 1987, pp. 1, B5; *ibid.*, February 21, 1981, pp. 1, 6–7.

663 [*"Extensive program of political education"*]: Bibby, p. 110.
[*Transactional and transforming leadership*]: see James MacGregor Burns, *Leadership* (Harper, 1978).
[*Demands for education reform*]: National Commission on Excellence in Education, *A Nation at Risk: The Imperative for Educational Reform* (U.S. Government Printing Office, 1983); Allan Bloom, *The Closing of the American Mind* (Simon and Schuster, 1987); William J. Johnston, ed., *Education on Trial: Strategies for the Future* (ICS Press, 1985); Beatrice Gross and Ronald Gross, eds., *The Great School Debate: Which Way for American Education?* (Touchstone, 1985); and sources cited in ch. 14, *supra*, in section titled "Habits of Individualism."

664 [*Phi Beta Kappa and Rhodes scholar survey*]: Bowen and Schuster, "The Changing Career Interests of the Nation's Intellectual Elite," *The Key Reporter*, vol. 51, no. 1 (Autumn 1985), pp. 1–4; see also Bowen and Schuster, *American Professors: A National Resource Imperiled* (Oxford University Press, 1986); Russell Jacoby, *The Last Intellectuals: American Culture in the Age of Academe* (Basic Books, 1987).
[*"Less and less attractive"*]: Bowen and Schuster, "Changing Career Interests," p. 3.
[*"Working conditions for faculty"*]: *ibid.*, p. 4.

665 [*"Heap or jumble"*]: Bloom, p. 371.
[*"Straight and short road"*]: Alexis de Tocqueville, *Democracy in America* (Knopf, 1945), vol. 2, pp. 41, 42.
[*"What lies between"*]: *ibid.*, vol. 2, p. 77.
[*"Men are born"*]: quoted in James MacGregor Burns, *Uncommon Sense* (Harper, 1972), p. 98. In this section I have borrowed concepts and phraseology from *ibid.*, ch. 6.
[*"Battle cry of freedom"*]: Irwin Silber, ed., *Songs of the Civil War* (Columbia University Press, 1960), pp. 17–20, 26.

666 [*"Basic choices available"*]: Frankel, "The Relation of Theory to Practice: Some Standard Views," in Herman D. Stein, ed., *Social Theory and Social Invention* (Press of Case Western Reserve University, 1968), pp. 3–21, quoted at p. 20.
[*Lincoln on liberty*]: quoted in *The Public Papers and Addresses of Franklin D. Roosevelt*, Samuel I. Rosenman, comp. (Random House, 1938–50), vol. 9, p. 484.
[*"Second Bill of Rights"*]: Message to the Congress on the State of the Union, January 11, 1944, in *ibid.*, vol. 13, pp. 32–44, quoted at p. 41.

667 [*Judiciary and civil liberties*]: M. Glenn Abernathy, *Civil Liberties Under the Constitution*, 2nd ed. (Dodd, Mead, 1972); Zechariah Chaffee, Jr., *Free Speech in the United States* (Harvard University Press, 1941); Schwartz, *Burger Years*, part 2; Kelly, Harbison, and Belz, pp. 722–27.
[*Court and Louisiana creationism statute*]: *Edwards, Governor of Louisiana* v. *Auillard*, 482 U.S. (1987).

668 [*"Pastoral Letter"*]: excerpts in *New York Times*, November 12, 1984, p. B10; see also Victor Ferkiss, "The Bishops' Letter and the Future," in R. Bruce Douglass, ed., *The Deeper Meaning of Economic Life* (Georgetown University Press, 1986), pp. 139–55; John Langan, "The American Context of the U.S. Bishops' Pastoral Letter on the Economy," in *ibid.*, pp. 1–19.

669 [*American distribution of wealth*]: Jim Hightower, "Where Greed, Unofficially Blessed by Reagan, Has Led," *New York Times*, June 21, 1987, sect. 4, p. 25; see also Frank Levy,

Dollars and Dreams: The Changing American Income Distribution (Russell Sage Foundation/
Basic Books, 1987).

670 [*Early fall 1988 poll on sense of economic well-being*]: Everett C. Ladd, *The Ladd 1988
Election Update,* vol. 3 (October 1988), p. 5.
[*August 1988 poll on Reagan Administration's conservatism*]: ibid.
[*Voter turnout, 1988 election*]: *New York Times,* November 10, 1988, p. B7 (table).

671 [*Maccoby on James*]: "A Symposium: Some Issues of Technology," *Daedalus,* vol. 19,
no. 1 (Winter 1980), pp. 3–24, quoted at p. 21.
[*"Politics in the United States"*]: Brinkley, "What Hart's Fall Says About America," *New
York Times,* May 21, 1987, p. A31.
[*"Makes the role of leadership"*]: "Some Issues of Technology," p. 21.
[*Pendulum theory of politics*]: McElvaine, pp. 4–10 and *passim;* Arthur M. Schlesinger, Jr.,
The Cycles of American History (Houghton Mifflin, 1986), esp. ch. 2.

672 [*"The line it is drawn"*]: "The times they are a-changin'," recorded by Bob Dylan,
words and music by Bob Dylan, copyright 1963, Columbia Records.

Memories of the Future: A Personal Epilogue

673 [*"Memories of the Future"*]: the name of a *pulquería* I saw as a boy on the outskirts of
Mexico City.
[*Williamstown and the Berkshires*]: Robert R. R. Brooks, ed., *Williamstown: The First Two
Hundred Years, 1753–1953, and Twenty Years Later, 1953–1973,* 2nd ed. (Williamstown
Historical Commission, 1974); Arthur Latham Perry, *Origins in Williamstown,* 3rd ed.
(privately printed, 1904); Bliss Perry, *Colonel Benjamin Simonds, 1726–1807* (privately
printed, 1944); Theodore M. Hammett, "The Revolutionary Ideology in Its Social
Context: Berkshire County, Massachusetts, 1725–1785" (doctoral dissertation: Bran-
deis University, 1976).
[*Thoreau in the Berkshires*]: Thoreau, *A Week on the Concord and Merrimack Rivers,* Carl F.
Hovde et al., eds. (Princeton University Press, 1980), pp. 180–90, quoted at pp. 184,
188.
[*"A sort of sea-feeling"*]: letter to Evert Duyckinck, December 13, 1850, in Jay Leyda,
ed., *The Melville Log* (Harcourt, 1951), p. 401.

676 [*Roosevelt in Williamstown*]: Brooks, pp. 352–54, party chieftain quoted at p. 353.

677 [*"To evolve a new order"*]: *New York Times,* June 10, 1934, sect. 4, pp. 1, 6, quoted at
p. 6.
[*"Next frontier"*]: Stevenson, "Liberalism," address at Los Angeles, May 31, 1956, in
Stevenson, *The New America,* Seymour E. Harris et al., eds. (Harper, 1957), pp. 256–
61, quoted at p. 260.
[*My views of JFK, 1960*]: James MacGregor Burns, *John Kennedy: A Political Profile*
(Harcourt, 1960).
[*Jacqueline Kennedy on her husband*]: letter of Jacqueline Kennedy (in Hyannisport) to
the author, n.d. [late 1959].

681 [*"Things fall apart"*]: Yeats, "The Second Coming," in *The Collected Poems of W. B. Yeats*
(Macmillan, 1959), pp. 184–85.

Acknowledgments

In this final volume of my trilogy in American political and intellectual history I have continued to stress the role of leadership—but of the second and third cadres of leadership, and not merely of a few notables at the top. This emphasis has centrally influenced my treatment of American presidents. I have given much attention to FDR and his four successors—Truman, Eisenhower, Kennedy in his third year in office, and Lyndon Johnson during his first two years in the White House—because these men in their diverse ways markedly influenced the course of history. I have played down the influence of LBJ in his last three years and of his four successors—Nixon, Ford, Carter, and Reagan during most of his two terms—because they appear to me as far more the victims than the makers of events.

Victims of events—but those events were not impersonal happenings like an ice age but the work of other men and women. The last three decades have brought extraordinary leadership from second-cadre figures such as Martin Luther King, Jr., and Robert F. Kennedy, as well as from third-cadre rank-and-file activists who influenced them. I regret that even three substantial volumes cannot do justice to all the leaders of causes and movements who variously stimulate, sustain, challenge, and obstruct presidents. And if, on the other hand, second-cadre officials in the White House fail their president, as happened most direly in the Nixon and Reagan administrations, presidents are brought down by events for which they must take responsibility.

This volume, even more than the first two, is the product of a collective effort. Two collaborators had indispensable roles. Stewart Burns, deeply immersed in the peace and environmental struggles of recent decades, served as chief co-author with me of Part III (chapters 8–10), critiqued major portions of the manuscript, and directly influenced the coverage of ideas and events elsewhere in the work. Milton Djuric shared much of the burden of research, cast a critical eye on successive drafts of the manuscript, and made important contributions in the realms of both ideas and facts, demonstrating throughout creativity and versatility, whether in conceptualizing, in drafting, in critiquing, or in editing.

Historians Alan Brinkley and David Burner reviewed the entire manuscript and made numerous suggestions for its improvement, as did two longtime friends and colleagues at Williams, historians Russell H. Bostert and Robert C. L. Scott. Physicist David A. Park, astronomer-physicist Jay M. Pasachoff, and musician and music critic Irwin Shainman counseled me expertly in their respective spheres of scholarship. I thank these critics for the time and thought they so generously gave to the manuscript. Others at Williams who gave invaluable help were Kurt Tauber and Rosemarie Tong, and two students, Nicholas King and David F. Wagner. My friends in the Faculty Secretarial Office were as cheerfully efficient as ever.

Deborah Burns, author, editor, and illustrator, provided the admirable endpapers for this volume as she did for the first two. My longtime friend and editor Ashbel Green supplied the solid and consistent counsel necessary for such a long-term writing project, while Melvin Rosenthal, also at Knopf, provided his special kind of meticulous editing. Jeffrey Trout thoroughly critiqued the manuscript on the basis of both his historical and his legal knowledge. Wendy Severinghaus reviewed the early chapters. Maurice Greenbaum continued to contribute in significant ways. My fellow author Joan Simpson Burns offered useful advice and criticism. Gisela Knight compiled the painstakingly comprehensive index.

I wish to thank the archivists and librarians at institutions where I conducted research: Baker Library of the Graduate School of Business Administration at Harvard; the Columbia University Oral History Program; Franklin D. Roosevelt Library; Jimmy Carter Library; John Fitzgerald Kennedy Library; House of Lords Records Office, London; Language Laboratory of the University of California at Berkeley; Library of Congress, Manuscripts Division; Louisiana State University Library; Lyndon Baines Johnson Library; the Martin Luther King, Jr., Library and Archives; the New-York Historical Society; the New York Public Library; Research Library, University of California at Los Angeles; the Stanford University libraries; University of Kentucky Library; University of Oklahoma Western History Collections; and the Williams College Library, whose staff was invariably helpful and resourceful.

I conducted research and writing also at Bellagio under the Rockefeller Foundation; the Hoover Institution on War, Revolution, and Peace; and the University of California at Los Angeles. I should state here, as I have done in a number of places in this work, that I have borrowed from earlier writings of mine in an effort to make some of my imperishable prose still more imperishable.

Any errors or deficiencies are solely my responsibility, and I would appreciate being informed of them at Williams College, Williamstown, MA 01267. I wish to thank those who sent in corrections for the second volume, *The Workshop of Democracy*. Those corrections are: (p. 189) the number of Populist newspapers was nearer several hundred than 100; (p. 218) General George Custer chased Crazy Horse's warriors for about six weeks, not six months; (p. 231) Tom Watson's position at the 1896 Populist convention should be identified as anti-fusionist; (p. 234) Dingell should be Dingley; (ch. 5) the Colored Farmers' National Alliance should be mentioned as an important black organization that was parallel in its work and activities to the National Farmers' Alliance, which in the South refused to admit black farmers to membership.

J.M.B.

Index

823

ABOUT THE AUTHOR

James MacGregor Burns is one of America's most prominent scholars and biographers. Born in Melrose, Massachusetts, he received his B.A. from Williams College in 1939, and his M.A. and Ph.D. degrees from Harvard University. He has been a member of the Political Science Department at Williams since 1941, and a professor of political science since 1953. Among his books are *Roosevelt: The Lion and the Fox* (1956), *John Kennedy: A Political Profile* (1960), *The Deadlock of Democracy* (1963), *Roosevelt: The Soldier of Freedom* (1970), which was awarded both the Pulitzer Prize and the National Book Award, *Leadership* (1978), *The Vineyard of Liberty* (1982), and *The Workshop of Democracy* (1985). He served as co-chairman of Project 87, an interdisciplinary study of the American Constitution during the Bicentennial Era. Currently he is Senior Fellow at the Center for Humanities and Social Sciences, Williams College. Also available from Vintage are *The Vineyard of Liberty* and *The Workshop of Democracy*.